HISTORY

OF A FREE NATION

HISTORY
OF A FREE NATION

Henry W. Bragdon

Samuel P. McCutchen

Donald A. Ritchie

GLENCOE
McGraw-Hill

New York, New York   Columbus, Ohio   Mission Hills, California   Peoria, Illinois

Authors

★★★

Henry W. Bragdon was for many years a much-admired teacher at the Phillips Exeter Academy in Exeter, New Hampshire, winding up his career there as Cowles Professor in the Humanities Emeritus. In addition to his work on this textbook, he is the author of a biography of President Woodrow Wilson entitled *Woodrow Wilson: The Academic Years,* which was nominated for a National Book Award. Bragdon has also served as president of the New England History Teachers' Association, chief examiner in Social Studies for the College Entrance Examination Board, and lecturer at Harvard College.

Samuel P. McCutchen spent a long career as teacher of high school social studies and as a teacher of social studies teachers. He was professor of education at New York University. On the high school level, he taught at Fayette (Mississippi) High School and was chairperson of the social studies department of the John Burroughs School, St. Louis, Missouri. McCutchen also served as president of the National Council for the Social Studies.

Donald A. Ritchie is Associate Historian of the United States Senate Historical Office. Dr. Ritchie received his doctorate in American history from the University of Maryland after service in the U.S. Marine Corps. He has taught American history at various levels, from high school to the university. He edits the Historical Series of the Senate Foreign Relations Committee and is the author of several books, including *Press Gallery: Congress and the Washington Correspondents,* which received the Organization of American Historians' Richard W. Leopold Prize. Dr. Ritchie has served as president of the Oral History Association and as a council member of the American Historical Association.

Glencoe/McGraw-Hill

A Division of The **McGraw·Hill** Companies

Printed in the United States of America

Send all inquiries to:

Glencoe/McGraw-Hill
8787 Orion Place
Columbus, OH 43240

ISBN 0-02-821383-1 (Student Edition)
ISBN 0-02-821384-X (Teacher's Wraparound Edition)

8 9 10 11 12 027/043 09 08 07 06 05

Academic Consultants

★★★

Delbert A. Jurden, M.A.
Instructor of History
Johnson County
 Community College
Overland Park, Kansas

Keith Ian Polakoff, Ph.D.
Assistant Vice President
 for Adademic Affairs and
 Dean of Graduate Studies
California State University,
 Long Beach
Long Beach, California

Sarah Witham Bednarz, M.A.T.
Visiting Assistant Professor
Department of Geography
Texas A&M University
College Station, Texas

Yolanda Elaine Childers
Reviewer/Consultant
Austin Community College
Austin, Texas

John F. Waukechon, M.A.
Member, American Indian Resource
 and Education Coalition
Austin, Texas

K. Austin Kerr, Ph.D.
Professor of History
The Ohio State University
Columbus, Ohio

Teacher Reviewers

★★★

Mary C. Burkett
Social Studies Teacher
Jackson City Schools
Jackson, Mississippi

Rose Marie Floyd
Social Studies Teacher
Jefferson Davis High School
Montgomery, Alabama

George W. Henry, Jr.
Teacher, Chair History
 Department
St. Mark's School
Salt Lake City, Utah

Marjorie B. Hollowell
Chair, Social Studies Department
John A. Holmes High School
Edenton, North Carolina

Michael L. Manson, Ed.D.
Teacher of Social Studies (retired)
Townsend Harris High School
New York City, New York

Simmie G. Plummer
History Teacher
Valley High School
Albuquerque, New Mexico

Irene Ramnarine
Secondary Social Studies
 Resource Teacher
Brevard County
 School District
Melbourne, Florida

James M. Wolfe
History Teacher
Suitland University High School
Forestville, Maryland

Contents

Features

Cultural Kaleidoscope

Features

CONNECTIONS History AND CONNECTIONS

Features

American Literary Heritage

Features

Life of the Times

Features

★★★★ AMERICAN PORTRAITS

Black Heritage USA 15c

Features

★ ★

Social Studies Skills

Critical Thinking Skills

Interpreting Primary Sources

Map and Graph Skills

Study and Writing Skills

Features

★ ★

Maps, Graphs, Charts, and Tables

Maps

Charts, Graphs, and Tables

Themes in American History

★ ★

*I*MAGINE a United States without computers, telephones, or automobiles, where women and most minorities cannot vote, a place where 8 of 10 people work on farms, and higher education is a privilege reserved for the fortunate few.

That we live today in a totally different country—yet one that is indeed still the United States—is no accident. What connects past generations and our own is an unbroken chain of events that shapes our lives. Every event in our personal lives has contributed to who we are today. So too have events throughout our nation's history created the American people of the 1990s. Like individual threads in a cloth, events by themselves may lack substance and seem insignificant. Seen together as part of the whole, however, events gain clarity and form.

To help make sense of countless events in history, historians use themes to organize events into meaningful patterns. Themes are recurrent threads, surfacing within an assortment of events, making up the substance of history's fabric—a rich design emblazoned with brilliant colors on the cloth of time.

American Democracy

Abraham Lincoln perhaps explained the meaning of democracy best when he called it "government of the people, by the people, for the people." Democracy at its best, according to many of our nation's leaders, is "among" the people, as exhibited by this "stump-speaking" politician of the mid-1800s, an era of frontier democracy championed by Andrew Jackson.

▲ *Stump Speaking* by George Caleb Bingham, 1853–1854

Civil Rights and Liberties

The foundation of democracy is the right of every person to take part in government and to voice one's views on issues. Not all people in our nation's past have had this basic right. This lithograph illustrates when all African American men were granted suffrage in 1870 with the passage of the Fifteenth Amendment. Preservation of such civil rights and liberties for all citizens is how we guarantee that "we the people" control the government.

◄ MISSOURI'S COMMEMORATION OF THE FIFTEENTH AMENDMENT

Economic Development

The Preamble to the Constitution sets out the purposes of American government, one of which is to "promote the general welfare." Framers of the Constitution recognized that one of government's purposes must be to provide a climate in which citizens can better themselves economically. With few government restrictions, the nation's economy was built on the hard work of farmers and agricultural business.

► *CLASSIC LANDSCAPE*
by Charles Sheeler, 1931

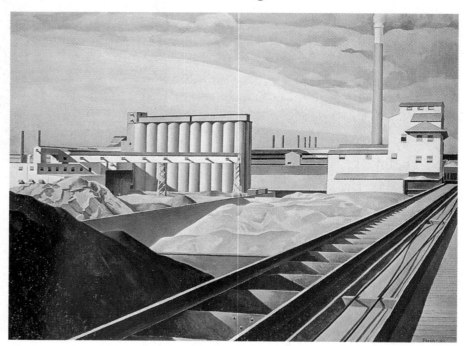

Geography and Environment

The United States succeeded in part because of its rich natural resources and its vast open spaces. But in most regions of the nation, the natural landscape was transformed to accommodate ambitions that hard work could make dreams come true. The steel plow and the railroad helped Americans settle the West, but the unblemished environment of the Native American gave way to the demands of expansion.

◄ *MERCED RIVER, YOSEMITE*
by Albert Bierstadt, 1861

Conflict and Cooperation

It has been said that democracy is a poor form of government, but that no better form has been invented. President George Washington established the principle of placing the good of the nation above individual or sectional grievances in 1794, when he led troops against Pennsylvania farmers protesting a tax on whiskey. The conflict over, Washington pardoned the convicted leaders in the spirit of cooperation.

▶ *WASHINGTON RECEIVING THE WESTERN ARMY AT FORT CUMBERLAND, MARYLAND* by Frederick Kemmelmeyer, c. 1795

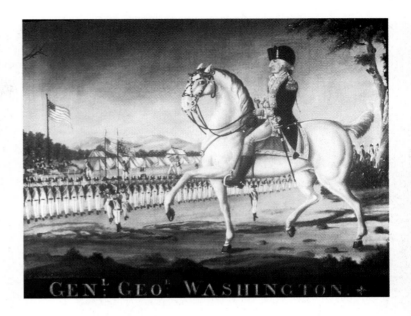

Influence of Technology

Americans have always been quick to embrace innovations—the country was settled and built by people who gave up old ways and sought new. Americans' lives are profoundly influenced by technology, the use of science and machines. Perhaps no machine has so shaped modern life as the automobile.

◀ FORD AUTOMOBILE, EARLY 1900s

The Individual and Family Life

Americans have a strong tradition of individual freedom sheltered by the protective core of the family unit. Families during the 1950s moved to suburban areas outside the central city to provide themselves with more living space and protection from the perceived dangers of the city. Our earliest experiences of freedom, which were limited by the rights of other individuals, come from interactions within our homes.

◀ Young suburban
family of the 1950s

Humanities and Religion

Some of the earliest European settlers came to America for religious freedom. But a number of these groups turned around and promptly denied others the right to think for themselves and to question the teachings of their ministers. Anne Hutchinson and Roger Williams, among others, believed in their own ability to interpret religious teachings and founded settlements in Rhode Island where genuine religious freedom was practiced.

▶ ANNE HUTCHINSON PREACHING IN HER BOSTON HOME, from a painting by Howard Pyle

Cultural Diversity

American is not a pure nationality but a peculiar mosaic of ideals and ideas. People from around the world for generations have sung of this "land of the Pilgrims' pride, land where our fathers died" even though their ancestors arrived on these shores long after such events transpired. The public schools were the method by which those seeking a new future were transformed into Americans. These immigrant children in New York in the 1890s pledged allegiance to a flag under which none had been born but which was justly theirs in every way.

◀ Students saluting the flag in New York City's Mott Street Industrial School, photographed by Jacob Riis, 1889

U.S. Role in World Affairs

A nation composed of peoples from around the world—buying and selling goods around the world, with economic and military might felt across continents, displaying a form of government emulated in all four corners of the globe—cannot but play a leading role in world affairs. The American people have carried on a long tradition as champions of democracy.

▶ President Clinton addressing Jordan's parliament, 1994

Geography in History

★ ★

*G*EOGRAPHY—the study of Earth's surface and the processes that shape it, the relationship between people and their environments, and people and place connections—is an integral part of the web of history.

Indeed, all history happens somewhere. It is the task of geography to supply answers about where a place is, what it is like, how the people live there, how people from different places interact with one another, and how one place on Earth is like others on Earth.

The geography of a region not only includes its physical landscape, natural resources, and climate but also the people who have settled there and their distinctive way of life. The history of the American people—the countless events that make up who we are—is notably influenced by the interplay of our nation's geographic features.

Like historians, geographers use themes to help organize their study of geography into purposeful patterns. Organizing information by themes helps make sense of the vast amount of information we have learned about the myriad of distinctive places that make up the United States.

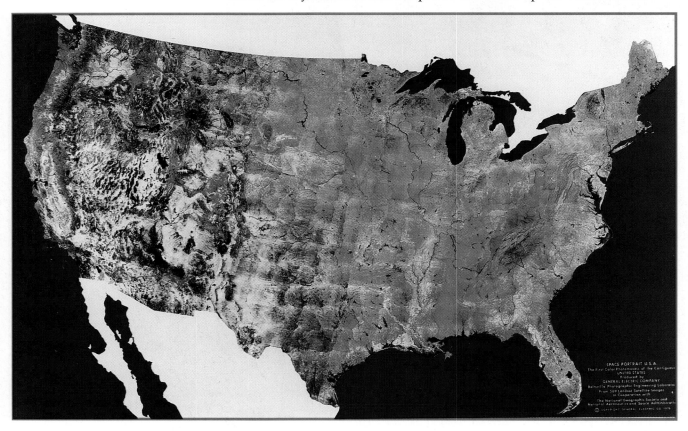

Location

A place's position on the earth's surface—its location—constitutes one of the five themes of geography. Location can be either absolute (one particular spot of ground) or relative (position as compared to some other place). *Location* answers the question "Where is that and why is its location significant?"

▶ The Southeast, by virtue of its location on the Atlantic Coast, was one of the first parts of North America settled by Europeans. Colonial Williamsburg recreates daily life as it unfolded in the Southeast three centuries ago.

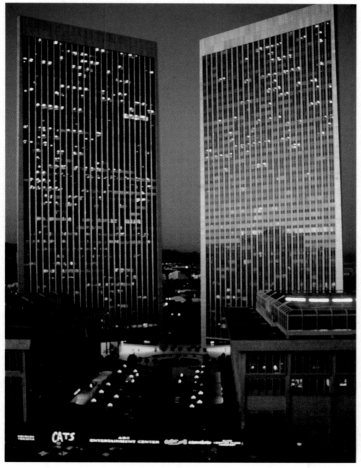

◀ Los Angeles, California, one of the most densely populated urban areas in the United States, is located atop a network of active fault lines. Its Southwest location is a mixed blessing for Los Angeles—the city enjoys a Mediterranean climate, but it lives with the knowledge that earthquakes can strike at any time.

Place

A place's physical and human characteristics tell what is special about it and what makes it different from all others. Landforms, climate, and culture combine to make up the particular flavor of a particular place. *Place* answers the question "What is that place like?"

► Settlement of the Great Plains coincided with the development of machines for plowing, planting, and harvesting on a grand scale; the combination made the Midwest a supplier of meat and grain to the world.

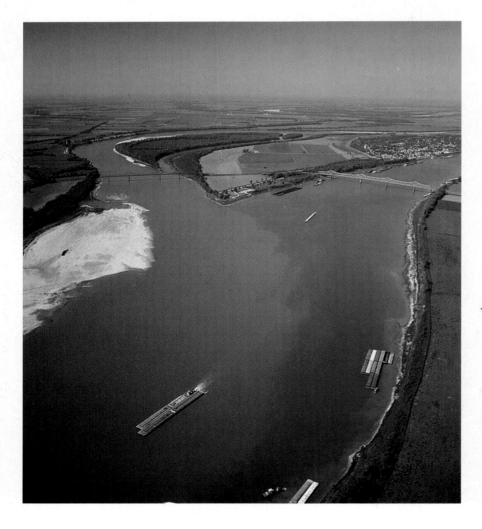

◄ Rivers have had a tremendous impact on American history and life. The confluence of the Mississippi (left) and Ohio (right) rivers south of Cairo, Illinois, in the heart of the Midwest, imparts a special quality to land that is quite different from that found in the desert Southwest. Water is of paramount importance to both places—in the Midwest for its abundance, in the Southwest for its lack.

Human/Environment Interaction

The theme of human/environmental interaction describes how people use, affect, and are affected by their surroundings. Through such interaction, people change the environment in which they live. *Human/environment interaction* answers the question "How does the interaction of people within an environment affect their way of life?"

▶ Warm climate, abundant rainfall, and rich soil combined to make large parts of the Southeast ideally suited for the cultivation of cotton. The use of slave labor for this industry set the stage for a confrontation between North and South that became this nation's bloodiest war.

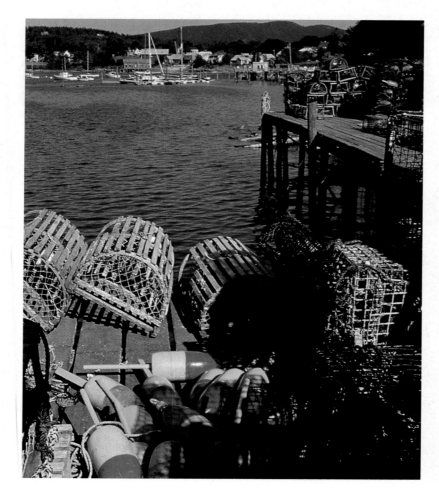

◀ Fishing boats ply the coastal waters of the Northeast in search of such delicacies as lobster. The nutrient-rich waters of the Atlantic drew people to the sea. Yet centuries of fishing have reduced the ocean's bounty.

Movement

People interacting across the globe exemplifies interdependence, the need humans have to utilize skills and resources from around the earth. People travel, communicate, and trade goods, ideas, and information. *Movement* answers the question "How do the people in this place interact with peoples in other places?"

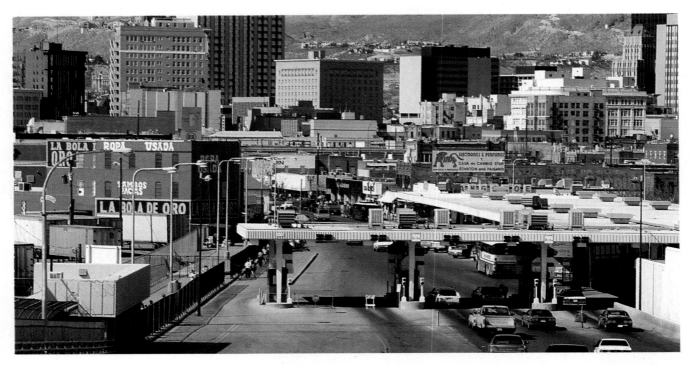

▲ Southwesterners who live along the border between the United States and Mexico can experience dramatic changes in culture and lifestyle by simply walking a few feet from one country to another. The movement of people between countries has political, social, and economic implications.

◄ Lewis and Clark, guided by the Shoshone woman Sacajawea, were the vanguard for wave after wave of Americans seeking land and adventure in the West.

Regions

Regions is the ultimate theme of geography. Regions—how areas form and change—display unity through their characteristics, some physical, some human. The study of regions allows geographers to answer the question "How is this place like other places on the earth?"

◄ The Northeast, like other coastal regions around the world, used its natural advantages to become a center of fishing, shipping, and trade. Yankee clipper ships were the fastest merchant vessels in the world; in 1854 the *Flying Cloud* set a record of 89 days, 8 hours, between Boston and San Francisco.

► New England is known not only for its brilliant foliage but also for its charming countryside of small villages inhabited by descendants of early settlers whose motto was, "Use it up, wear it out, make it do."

UNIT ONE
A NEW WORLD
PREHISTORY TO 1776

★★

CHAPTER
1
The World in Transition
Prehistory–1500s

CHAPTER
2
The Age of Exploration
1000–1682

CHAPTER
3
Colonial America
1578–1776

▼ Arrowhead,
HAND-CHIPPED
STONE

History AND ART

Prehistoric Drawing
Baja California, Mexico

Native Americans came to the Western Hemisphere
thousands of years ago. Artists have provided a
glimpse of their way of life through cave and rock
paintings.

2

Setting the Scene

The Americas were inhabited by a rich variety of cultures. Almost 500 years ago, however, other peoples—Europeans, filled with dreams of adventure and wealth, and enslaved Africans—set foot in what to them was a New World.

Themes

- Geography and the Environment
- The Individual and Family Life
- Humanities and Religion
- Cultural Diversity

Key Events

- First Americans cross the Bering Strait
- Hopewells build mounds in the Ohio River valley
- Height of Maya culture
- Norse seafarers land at Newfoundland
- Voyages of Columbus
- Spanish conquer Aztec and Incan empires
- Spanish bring enslaved Africans to America
- Founding of New France
- Founding of English colonies

Major Issues

- The environment influences the development of Native American cultures and European colonies in the Americas.
- The search for wealth and a direct route to Asia prompts European exploration and settlement.
- Interaction among Native Americans, European colonists, and African Americans leads to the creation of a new American society.

▼ **JAPANESE MILITARY EQUIPMENT**

▲ **SIR WALTER RALEIGH**

◄ **ASTROLABE, ITALY 1500s**

Portfolio Project

Prepare a short report on a Native American culture in the United States today. Describe its peoples' occupations, living standards, and social life as well as traditional crafts, legends, and beliefs.

Global Perspectives

★★★★★★★ ★★

The World

	Prehistory		500 B.C.
Asia and Oceania		▼ **660 B.C.** *Jimmu becomes first emperor of Japan*	
Europe	**c. 4000 B.C.** *Civilizations develop in Asia and Africa*		**509 B.C.** *Romans set up a republic*
Africa	**c. 1,750,000 B.C.** *First groups of people appear in Africa*		**200s B.C.** *Axum emerges as a trading power*
South America			
North and Central America	**c. 35,000–20,000 B.C.** *First migrants from Asia cross the Bering Strait*		

The United States

Pacific and Northwest		**c.1500 B.C.** *People learn metalworking techniques*	
Southeast			
Midwest		◄ **200 B.C.–A.D. 400** *Hopewell culture reaches its zenith*	
Southwest			
Atlantic Northeast	Prehistory		500 B.C.

Linking Across TIME

Native Americans have left an indelible mark on American life. Perhaps the most obvious sign of our country's Native American heritage is the hundreds of place names that dot the map. Some of these names offer a vivid physical description of the place. Chattanooga, for example, means "rock rising to a point," while Nantucket means "the faraway place." Other names indicate what went on at the place. Milwaukee was the "gathering place by the river" and Kalamazoo was the "boiling pot."

1400 A.D.

1368 *Ming Dynasty begins rule of China*

▶ **1400s** *Explorers set out, and Age of Exploration begins*

▼ **1400s** *Inca and Aztec empires flourish*

1492 *Columbus lands in the Americas*

1578 *Sir Francis Drake explores the California coast*

1607 *First permanent English settlement is formed at Jamestown*

◀ **1050–1200** *Great Pueblo period*

1620 *Pilgrims found Plymouth*

1400 A.D.

1700 A.D.

1684 *LaSalle establishes Fort St. Louis*

1700 A.D.

CHAPTER 1

★★★

The World in Transition
Prehistory–1500s

▶ INCAN KNIFE, 1100s

Setting the Scene

Focus

The first immigrants came to North America long before written history. They arrived by walking across a broad grassy "land bridge" where the Bering Strait now separates Siberia and Alaska. These Native Americans developed unique cultures in North and South America. Then a series of events in Europe, Asia, and Africa opened the way to European voyages of discovery and exploration across the Atlantic. From these ventures, the United States was born.

Concepts to Understand

★ Why diverse cultures among Native Americans came into being
★ How economic change developed from trade with East Asia

Read to Discover . . .

★ who were the major native North American groups.
★ what circumstances in Europe, Asia, and Africa led to voyages of exploration.

Journal Notes

How do the accomplishments and ideas of a culture reflect values? Note important details about various cultures in your journal as you read the chapter.

	CULTURAL			
	● **c. 1150 B.C.** *Olmec civilization begins in Mexico*	● **200 B.C.** *Hopewell culture begins to build burial mounds*	● **900** *Mayan civilization begins to decline*	

1000 B.C.	**500 B.C.**	**A.D. 500**

	POLITICAL			
	● **1000 B.C.** *People inhabit present-day Peru and Ecuador*	● **507 B.C.** *Athenians establish democracy*	● **618** *Tang Dynasty is founded in China*	

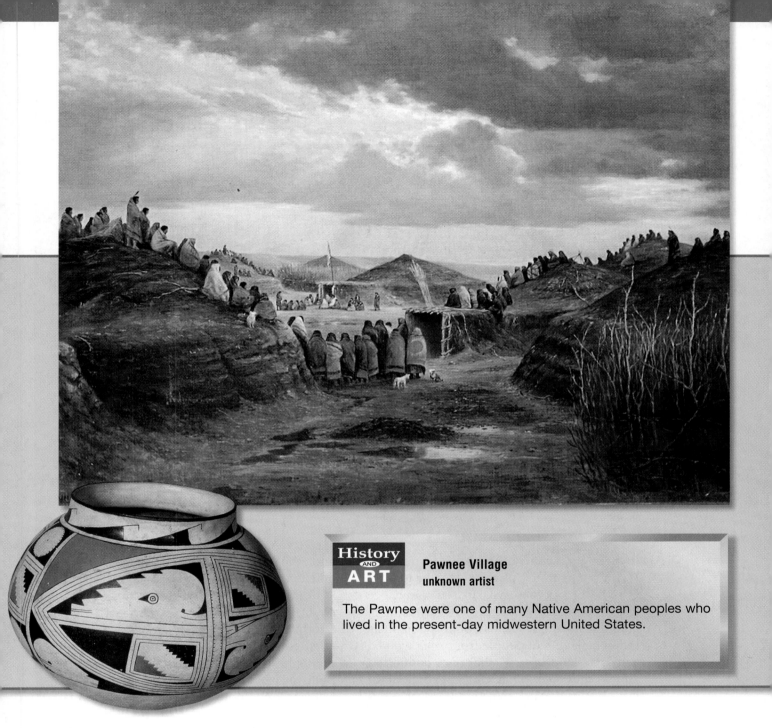

Pawnee Village
unknown artist

The Pawnee were one of many Native American peoples who lived in the present-day midwestern United States.

▲ SOUTHWESTERN POTTERY

- **1085** *Anasazi build pueblos, oldest standing buildings in North America*

- **1300** *Cahokia is largest North American community*

- **1500** *Aztec and Incan empires are at their height*

| 1000 | 1250 | 1500 |

- **1210** *Genghis Khan controls a vast empire*

- **1433** *Ming rulers in China stop outside trade*

- **1500** *European expeditions reach Venezuela and Brazil*

★★

The First Americans

Setting the Scene

Section Focus

The first people to come to the Americas are called Native Americans. Over time they formed many rich and diverse cultures. Some cultures became elaborate empires, while others remained simple in organization.

Objectives

After studying this section, you should be able to

★ explain the origins and paths of settlement of the first immigrants to the Americas.

★ compare the cultures in Mexico and South America to those in North America.

Key Terms

maize, pueblos, confederation

◀ PAINTED CLAY IMAGE

Twenty thousand years ago, much of the water in today's oceans was frozen. Huge ice sheets covered much of present-day Canada and the northern United States. Scientists today believe that people from Asia walked across a "land bridge" that once connected Alaska and Asia. They did not come all at once but in waves often hundreds or thousands of years apart. Most were groups of several families, following great herds of game animals. As groups reached North America, they moved south along the coasts and mountain valleys. Migrations continued until about 12,000 years ago when rising seawater destroyed the land bridge.

The first Americans gathered wild plants and hunted large animals—mammoths, giant sloths, and beavers. Their spear points have been found with the bones of many animals now extinct in America: mastodons, tapirs, and giant bison. In addition to these and other large animals, people hunted deer, antelope, and elks.

Groups of the earliest Americans moved south slowly until they reached the tip of South America. Over time these people adapted to their "New World" environments and became the peoples known today as Native Americans.

For many thousands of years, humans lived in bands of hunter-gatherers, adapting to the land or moving on. Some groups felt so close to their land that they came to believe that they had always been there.

■ Empires in America

Over time some hunters took up different ways of living. In South America groups moved onto the dry seacoast of Peru and Ecuador. By harvesting the rich oceans and farming the river valleys, they developed a more complicated culture. By about 1000 B.C., they and the mountain peoples above them began to draw on the abundance of both the jungles and sea. From the jungles they got dyes and medicine. Skillful farming of the mountainsides provided potatoes, peanuts, squash, and beans. Fine engineers designed and built great cities—some of which were larger than those of Europe at the time—with canals, pyramids, temples, and markets. Their way of life became more complex, with bureaucrats and taxes, and city-states and empires that rose and fell. Because these people had no written language, however, precise knowledge of this history is uncertain.

The Inca

The last of the great empires in the Andes was the Inca. The Inca were a mountain culture who, about 100 years before Columbus, controlled a 3,000-mile stretch of South America from its northern coast to the middle of Chile. The empire was linked through its 10,000-mile-long road system. Woven suspension bridges crossed canyons and rivers. Terraced hillside farms with complicated irrigation systems produced abundant food. The Incan government provided for orphans, the aged, and the sick.

To the north, in the area called Mesoamerica—parts of the modern nations of Mexico, Guatemala, and Honduras—similar developments occurred. About the time the fishing people of Peru began to settle down, the gathering people in the central valley of Mexico were cultivating a large-seeded grass, **maize**, the forerunner of corn.

The Olmec

Along the Gulf of Mexico coast, a group called the Olmec developed a much more complex society with large villages, temple complexes, and pyramids. The Olmec were the first Mesoamerican people to use large masses of stone, sculpting it into large monuments. Their civilization strongly influenced their neighbors.

Visualizing History

▲ **EARLY PEOPLES** People had spread throughout the Western Hemisphere and had developed cultures in keeping with the different terrains and climates in which they had settled. ***How did the first people come to the Americas?***

Hiawatha
c. 1570

The character in the poem "The Song of Hiawatha" is not based on the life of the actual Native American leader. The real Hiawatha, a Mohawk, enjoyed a reputation as a magician and a prophet.

Dedicated to ending violence and warfare, Hiawatha devoted his final years to creating a union from among hostile Native American nations. About 1570, he brought together the Mohawk, Onondaga, Oneida, Cayuga, and Seneca into the League of the Five Nations, also known as the Iroquois Confederacy. One remarkable aspect of the league was its ruling council in which each nation had a single vote. This early form of "government based on the consent of the governed" influenced the course of early American democracy. The United States began as a confederacy of states much like the Iroquois Confederacy.

The Maya

Farther south the Maya were building ever larger pyramids and villages. Their trade networks spread along the coasts. Corn, cocoa, cotton, tomatoes, beans, and squash were traded both north and south. Mayan seeds and cloth were traded for the pottery and precious stones of the South Americans. Both peoples became skilled at metalwork and pottery. No doubt ideas also moved back and forth from group to group.

As people increased their food supply, societies became more and more complex. Small groups grew into city-states and small countries. Market and trade centers sprang up. The Maya developed a vast group of city-states that competed with one another in battle and in building grand public works. Then about A.D. 1000, the Maya changed and scattered over their area. The Maya and their trade routes continued but on a smaller scale.

Throughout this era the Maya were fascinated with mathematics. They invented the concept of zero. They developed complicated calendars linked to the study of the stars. Their temple-pyramids reflect an understanding of the earth's relation to the sun.

The Aztec

Many other equally advanced groups rose in Mesoamerica. The last group were the Aztec. In about 1325 they settled on islands in the middle of Lake Texcoco and built their city, Tenochtitlán, the site of modern Mexico City. Tenochtitlán was connected to the mainland by causeways. By the late 1400s, it had gold-adorned temples, floating gardens, and an enormous market. Its population of 100,000 was far larger than that of any city in Europe at the time.

■ Cultures North of Mexico

The people living north of Mexico traded with the natives of Mexico. By 400 B.C., maize had been introduced into what would become the southwestern United States and the fertile Mississippi Valley. From these two areas, knowledge of maize cultivation spread.

North of Mexico, the population was only one-tenth that of Mexico and the Incan empire. The way of life was also much different. Most people lived in small villages and bands.

Southwestern Communities

About the time of the fall of the classic Maya and the rise of cultures in Mexico, people in the present-day southwestern United States began to form larger groups with more complex village structures. Several groups began to build large, close-knit villages in the area where present-day Utah, Colorado, Arizona, and New Mexico come together. These people, called Anasazi, built large, multistory apartment-like buildings of adobe and cut stone with connecting causeways and elaborate ceremonial rooms. Early Spanish explorers called these houses **pueblos**, the Spanish word for "villages."

To the south in Arizona, the Hohokam were building large villages with elaborate irrigation canals, ball-playing courts, and temple mounds. Their trade goods and decorations show close contact with northern Mexico. Other groups in the area also built large villages and developed trade.

Then, in A.D. 1300, all this changed. Perhaps a severe drought and climate change took place. The Hohokam vanished; other groups scattered and moved closer to established water. The Anasazi moved to the springs on the Hopi mesas and the Rio Grande. Other groups moved to similar places. Their descendants remain as the Pueblo people of New Mexico and Arizona.

The Moundbuilders

Another area that showed a great growth in population was the Mississippi Valley. Around A.D. 900, people along the Mississippi River flourished as farmers and traders. They built great temple mounds of earth similar to those in Mexico. Settlements along the river grew into large towns. Cahokia (near present-day St. Louis) had a population of perhaps 10,000 people, with hundreds of temple mounds.

An earlier group of moundbuilders, the Hopewell culture, grew up in the Ohio River valley about 200 B.C. and lasted about 700 years. The Hopewell people farmed their rich land and traded across the Midwest for copper and shells. They built huge mounds of earth as both ceremonial centers and burial sites. Some of the Hopewells' elaborate and enormous mounds—as high as 30 feet—are in the shapes of snakes, turtles, and other animals. Inside the burial mounds, archaeologists have found pearl beads, woven cloth, copper ornaments, and striking objects of stone and mica.

On the Great Plains, the last of the hunter-gatherers still hunted the enormous herds of buffalo, which were all that remained of the mighty herds their ancestors had followed from Asia. With the arrival of the Spanish and their horses, these people would also undergo a tremendous change. With horses to ride, the buffalo hunters would become a powerful force on the plains.

In other parts of the country, other groups also flourished: the rich fishing cultures of the Pacific Northwest, the seed gatherers of California, and the farmers of the Southeast.

Visualizing History

▼ EARLY DWELLINGS Housing styles of Native Americans were as varied as their cultures. The Cliff Palace, Mesa Verde, is one of the grandest of all cliff dwellings. It was the hub of a Colorado chiefdom nearly 1,000 years ago. *What are pueblos?*

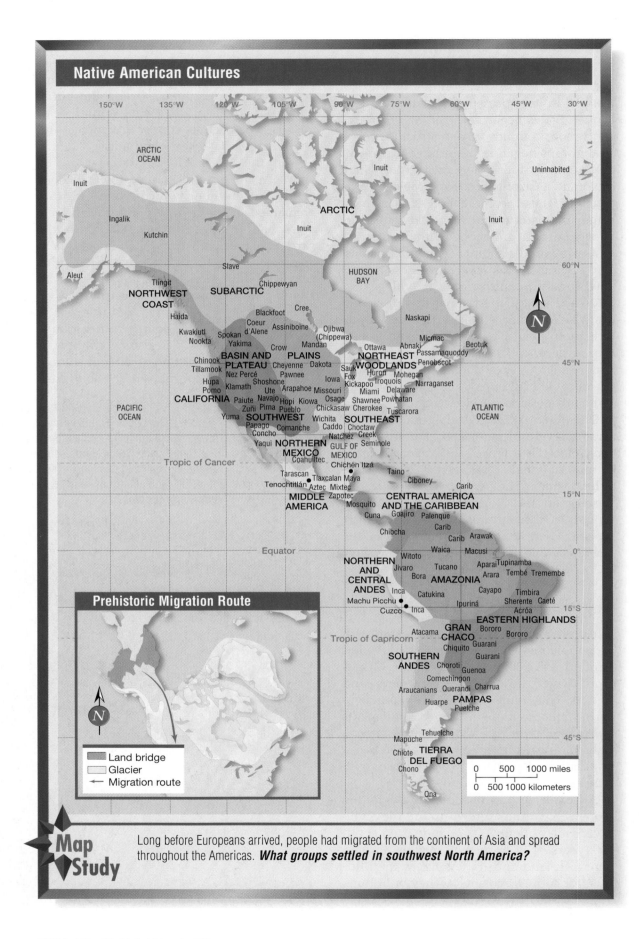

Native American Cultures

Long before Europeans arrived, people had migrated from the continent of Asia and spread throughout the Americas. **What groups settled in southwest North America?**

Prehistoric Migration Route

Land bridge
Glacier
← Migration route

Map Study

The Iroquois

The Iroquois, an alliance of farming people, dominated the Northeast in the 1500s and 1600s. They were made up of Mohawk, Seneca, Oneida, Onondaga, and Cayuga nations. Large groups of several families shared a "long house" of poles and bark. A large village might have 50 or more long houses and 300 to 400 people. Their league was a representative **confederation**, or government made up of independent units, probably formed about 1580. It was founded by two of the culture's heroes, Dekanawida and Hiawatha. The female leaders of each clan chose their chief, who would attend league councils. The confederation worked to maintain peace between the various tribes.

The Five Civilized Tribes

In the southeastern United States, the Creek, Cherokee, Choctaw, Seminole, and Chickasaw formed another confederation, which they called the Five Civilized Tribes. This group later devised a written language and a dictionary. They practiced a loose-knit form of democracy.

Just as the people of Europe and Asia were aware of each other, so groups within the Americas knew about each other and shared similar ideas. For example, despite their diversity, the Native American people felt a close relationship to the land and their environment. They felt that all things, themselves included, were part of a universal spirit.

A Clash of Values

In the 1400s Native Americans and Europeans were unaware of each other. Native Americans continued to develop their ways of life isolated from other peoples of the world. Similarly, the people of other continents were unaware of America. Then a chain of events began, moving the peoples of Europe, Asia, and Africa toward interdependence. European nations initiated the ventures that led to the colonization of America. By the late 1400s the world stood on the brink of enormous changes.

The Native American way of life was one that the Europeans who arrived seeking wealth were unable to understand. The Europeans' values seemed strange to the Native Americans as well. For example, during the conquest of Peru, an Incan citizen asked a European, "What do you do with gold? Do you eat it?" Reportedly, during the conquest of Mexico, Cortés told the ambassador to the Aztec ruler Moctezuma, "We have an illness only gold will cure."

These two different viewpoints and the conviction that there was only one valid outlook would lead to misunderstandings for centuries to come.

▲ TOTEM BY TLINGIT-TSMISYAN CARVER

Section 1 ★ Review

Checking for Understanding

1. **Identify** Olmec, Hopewell, Iroquois League, Mesoamerica.

2. **Define** maize, pueblos, confederation.

3. **Summarize** the process by which the Americas were first settled.

4. **Discuss** three elements of Aztec and Incan cultures.

Critical Thinking

5. **Evaluating Causes**   Why would towns and complex societies tend to grow up among farmers, rather than among hunter-gatherers?

Prehistory and Archaeology

Collectors of Native American relics buy and sell arrowheads, spear points, and bits of pottery and jewelry for prices ranging from 50 cents for common arrowheads to hundreds of thousands of dollars for rare ancient specimens. Native Americans and archaeologists object to this practice. They claim that "pothunters" destroy America's historic legacy and that an isolated artifact can add little to the understanding of prehistoric cultures.

Some native people also object to the work of archaeologists, claiming that sacred sites are destroyed. Archaeologists defend their work.

They say their digs aid historical understanding. As they excavate they observe and note details about the placement of each object. Their observations, combined with scientific techniques of dating and classification, can tell much about a particular culture. Archaeologists

ARCHAEOLOGISTS AT WORK

can show how people got their food, whether they built permanent homes, what they used to make tools, and whether they traded with others. Theories can then be developed about a culture's ideas and beliefs. This helps to preserve the prehistoric culture, even though the artifacts have been removed from their original sites.

Making the Science Connection

1. What can archaeologists learn about a particular culture from excavating a prehistoric site?

2. Why do archaeologists object to "pothunters"?

Linking Past and Present

3. What are some artifacts of our own culture?

★★★★★★★★★★★★★★★★★★★★★★★★★★★★★★

The New Europe

Setting the Scene

Section Focus

During the Middle Ages, the western part of the old Roman Empire recovered from decline and developed a new civilization rooted in Christianity. Powerful monarchs emerged in several countries, and contacts with the Middle East and East Asia stimulated trade, learning, and national rivalries.

Objectives

After studying this section, you should be able to

★ describe how European society changed from medieval times.

★ explain the significance of the Renaissance and the Reformation.

Key Terms

feudalism, manor, serf, charter, parliament, Renaissance, classical, humanism, dynasty

◀ Cross of Lothar, c. 1000

The collapse of the Roman Empire was nearly complete by A.D. 550. With the collapse of the western Roman empire's government, western Europe entered the Middle Ages. During this period, from about A.D. 500 to 1500, **feudalism**—a system in which powerful lords gave land to nobles in return for pledges of loyalty—replaced centralized government. The Roman Catholic Church, the western branch of Christianity, became a powerful force in Europe.

◼ The Middle Ages

During the Middle Ages—A.D. 500 to 1500—most of European society was organized by the manorial system. The majority of the people of Europe were peasants who worked on farmlands that belonged to a **manor**, or large estate, held by a noble.

Peasants lived in a village on the manor. Most were **serfs**, who were "bound to the soil"; that is, they were considered part of the property. A manor also included woods; common fields and pastures; a church; and shops for weavers, blacksmiths, and others who made the manor nearly self-sufficient.

In this period, the Church was the center of life in western Europe. Catholic clergy not only performed religious ceremonies but also helped govern the small feudal manors and the larger emerging kingdoms.

In 1095 Pope Urban II, head of the Roman Catholic Church, called for a "holy war" against the Seljuk (sehl•JOOK) Turks, a Muslim people who held the Christian shrines in Palestine. The Church began a series of wars called Crusades to recapture the Holy Land, including Jerusalem. Over the next 200 years, Crusaders went to war in the Holy Land. By 1291, however, the Muslims had driven out the Crusaders.

THE CRUSADES Beginning in the 1000s, western European forces carried out a series of religious wars to win Palestine from Muslim rule. *What effect did the Crusades have on trade?*

▲ ILLUMINATED MANUSCRIPT, illustrated and hand-written document

Although the Crusades were a failure, their effects upon western Europe were enormous. They helped bring western Europe out of isolation and into contact with other parts of the world. Trade for Eastern luxury goods started a series of events that completely changed Europe's economic, political, and social life.

When cities began to serve as trade centers, new job opportunities developed. The manorial system began to break down as competition enabled some serfs to demand higher wages and benefits to stay on the manor. Eventually, many could afford to buy their own land. Others began to pay rent for land with money rather than labor or produce. Farming for profit increased agricultural production, and better living conditions enabled the population to grow.

Because of their access to trade routes, towns along the Mediterranean Sea—in Italy, southern France, and Spain—grew first. As early as 1200, Venice and Genoa were strong city-states with busy shipyards.

Cities in northern Europe also emerged as centers for trade, shipping, and profitable craft industries such as weaving. Those with access to the sea would eventually rival the growth of Italian cities.

■ The Late Middle Ages

The rise of commerce brought prosperity to much of western and central Europe. The use of money and the need for credit turned some merchants into bankers. They lent money to finance new business and provided credit for shipments of goods. Well-to-do bankers, merchants, and master craftsworkers made up a new part of the social system—the middle class—which stood between the nobility at the top of the social system and the peasants at the bottom.

The Decline of Feudalism

The middle class supported the king—who represented stable government—against the feudal nobility, who disrupted trade by conducting local wars. As towns grew in population and wealth, some townspeople were able to buy a **charter** from the local lord and win the right to control their own affairs. In England, townspeople and knights gained a voice in government, sending representatives to meetings of a **parliament**, or assembly.

The Renaissance

The power of the towns helped weaken the feudal system and strengthen national governments. Townspeople used their financial power to win rights and favors from ambitious monarchs. In return they supplied funds for ships or soldiers. Powerful bankers dealt on almost equal terms with European rulers who needed to borrow money. Prosperity, optimism, and an emphasis on human potential set the mood for far-reaching social and cultural changes in the 1400s and 1500s. This period is known as the **Renaissance**, a French word for the "rebirth" of interest in the culture and learning of ancient Greece and Rome. The meaning of the Renaissance, however, went far beyond this definition. Even today, people marvel at the accomplishments of Renaissance artists and scholars.

The Renaissance began about 1350 in the city-states of northern Italy. Wealthy families bought books and paintings, hired architects to design buildings, and supported painters and sculptors. These wealthy patrons were especially interested in **classical** culture—the arts, literature, and knowledge of ancient Greece and Rome. This interest in the classics came to be called **humanism**.

While the Middle Ages had emphasized the human inner or spiritual nature and the need for self-discipline, the Renaissance awakened human creativity and demanded an outward expression of talent. Renaissance writers, artists, and thinkers were brimming with new ideas. Writers tried new styles, writing in everyday language instead of scholarly Latin. Painters developed new techniques and tried to portray people realistically. Humanism took on a broader meaning, including an appreciation for all aspects of human life.

The Renaissance in Italy reached its height in the late 1400s. Three of the most famous of the many Italian artists working at that time were Raphael, Michelangelo, and Leonardo da Vinci. Around 1500, Renaissance ideas spread northward into France, the Holy Roman Empire, the Netherlands, and England.

The new craft of printing with movable type, invented about 1440 by a German, Johannes Gutenberg, helped spread ideas. Because more people could afford books, they were exposed to new thoughts.

▼ *REAPING AND SHEARING IN JULY* Miniature from Très Riches Heures, by Jean duc de Berry, c. 1413 During feudal times, power was based on the ownership of land. The land was divided into manors, or farming communities. ***Does the artist view feudalism in a favorable light?***

▲ NEW MARKETS By the 1400s trade had created markets in Europe where Eastern goods sold for great profit. *How did this trade bring a Renaissance to northern Italy?*

End of Religious Unity

For most Europeans in the Middle Ages, the Roman Catholic Church was the center of life and the most stable and unifying influence. But by the late 1400s, Europe was in the early stages of a religious upheaval.

What would later be known as the Protestant Reformation began simply with demands for reforms in the Roman Catholic Church. Among the leading early reformers were John Wycliffe in England and John Huss in Bohemia, part of the Holy Roman Empire. These early reformers criticized the Church's wealth and the luxurious lifestyles of some clergy. They also printed Bibles in the language of the common people rather than the official Latin. The Church feared widespread rebellion against its leadership. Soon arguments broke out between Church supporters and reformers.

In the early 1500s, Martin Luther, a Catholic and a professor in a German university, challenged several Church practices. Luther believed that salvation was achieved by faith, not by good works. In 1521, when he was called before Emperor Charles V to answer charges brought against him by Church authorities, Luther declared:

" *Unless I be convinced by Scripture and reason, I neither can nor dare retract anything, for my conscience is a captive to God's word, and it is neither safe nor right to go against conscience.* "

This stand marked Luther's separation from the Catholic Church. The first Protestant faith, Lutheranism, was born. Soon other Protestant sects developed and grew in Scandinavia, parts of modern Germany, the Netherlands, and England. In other parts of Europe, particularly Spain and the Holy Roman Empire, Catholic rulers became the Church's defenders.

■ Emerging Nations

During most of the Middle Ages, Europe was splintered into many small states. Ruled by princes and other lords, these small states were part of the feudal system. This system rested on ties of protection and obligation between landowning nobles and those who lived on their lands.

During the late Middle Ages, strong monarchs began to replace feudalism in western Europe. Rulers brought unity to their countries and gained authority over the powerful nobles.

In England it took 30 years of bloody civil war from 1455 to 1485 to unify the kingdom. Hundreds of English nobles died in the fighting. The winning Lancastrian leader, Henry Tudor, came to the throne in 1485 as King Henry VII. He married Elizabeth of York, the daughter of one of his defeated rivals, unifying the kingdom. Henry VII's ruling house, or **dynasty**, produced several outstanding rulers.

The monarchs of France, too, gradually consolidated their power and territory. As the French fought the English in the Hundred Years' War from 1337 to 1453, French rulers won the confidence of the people. France's victory in the war, aided by the heroism of Joan of Arc, increased the people's feeling of patriotism and unity.

A different motivation brought political unity to Spain. In about A.D. 711, Muslims, or Moors, from North Africa conquered most of the Iberian peninsula—Spain and Portugal—and established a sophisticated culture. Christian rulers, led by the kingdom of Castile, tried continuously to drive the Moors out of Spain. By the mid-1400s, the Muslims held only the territory around Granada on the southeast coast.

In 1469 Christian unity in Spain was aided by the marriage of the heirs to the largest kingdoms: Isabella of Castile and Leon, and Ferdinand of Aragon. "The Catholic monarchs" believed that Christianity would unify the country. In 1492 they ordered all Jews to leave Spain. In the same year, their armies took Granada from the Moors.

Once part of Spain, Portugal won its independence in the twelfth century. By the late 1300s the country was unified under King John I. In the late 1400s, the Holy Roman Empire, which included parts of the modern nations of Germany, Austria, and Italy as well as Poland and Russia, would lack the unified direction to participate in exploration and discovery with the western European kingdoms:

Spain, Portugal, France, and England. All four had seaports on the Atlantic Ocean— soon to become a great avenue of trade and exploration.

Europeans, once isolated and bound by a rigid feudal system, were developing a spirit of curiosity and adventure. Unified monarchies and national rivalry led to competition for trade with Asia. The search for an all-water route to East Asia encouraged explorers to cross unknown oceans and seek new lands.

▲ ARMED KNIGHT, 1300s

Section 2 ★ Review

Checking for Understanding

1. **Identify** Martin Luther, Henry Tudor, Moors, Isabella of Castile and Leon, Ferdinand of Aragon.

2. **Define** feudalism, manor, serf, charter, parliament, Renaissance, classical, humanism, dynasty.

3. **Discuss** the political changes in Europe in the late 1400s.

4. **Explain** the broad meaning of the term *Renaissance* as it applies to the art, science, and culture of the period.

Critical Thinking

5. **Analyzing Cause and Effect**   Why did the growth of towns and a middle class of bankers and merchants lessen the influence of feudal lords?

★★★

Medieval Asia and Africa

Setting the Scene

Section Focus

Europeans' desire for trade provided a compelling reason for contact with the East. Trade between Asia and Africa, however, had transpired for centuries. The rise of Islam was a major influence on contacts between Europe, Asia, and Africa.

Objectives

After studying this section, you should be able to

★ explain the impact of Islam.

★ describe the extent and importance of the Mongol Empire.

★ identify some of the trading kingdoms of Africa.

Key Terms

samurai, shogun

◀ MIDDLE EASTERN METAL HELMET

*S*ince ancient times, trade had linked the different peoples and cultures of the "Old World"—Europe, Asia, and Africa. Both the Greeks and Romans had established profitable routes of trade with Asia and Africa. Seeking slaves and luxuries such as silks, spices, and precious stones, traders also carried ideas and information over great distances.

With the fall of the Roman Empire, Europe's participation in foreign trade had declined. Roads and bridges fell into disrepair, and robbers preyed on travelers because there was no government to keep order. While most people in Europe lived in the country, isolated into small villages, trade between Asia and Africa continued. African merchants, for example, traded iron, skins, and ebony for goods from the Red Sea region. They also conducted trade throughout the Indian Ocean area.

■ Spread of Muslim Ideals

The most important influence in medieval Asia and Africa—with consequences for Europe as well—was the rise of the religion of Islam in the 600s. Inspired by the teachings of the prophet Muhammad, the prophet's followers spread Islam quickly from the Arabian Peninsula through the Middle East to Asia and North Africa into Spain and the Mediterranean region. About 682 an Arab general, Achbar Ben Nafi Al-Fahri, and his warriors had reached the Atlantic in North Africa. Achbar expressed his zeal for Islam:

“ *Did not these waters present an insuperable barrier, I would carry the faith and the law of the faithful to countries reaching from the rising of the sun to the setting thereof!* ”

▲ INNOVATIONS Islamic doctors' discoveries helped develop European medicine in the 1100s. *Where did Arabic numbers originate?*

The original Islamic empire led by Arabs was soon divided. Rival groups of Muslims—the name for followers of Islam—organized and took control over different areas in Asia, Africa, and parts of Europe. In some places—for example, Spain—they met fierce resistance and eventually lost power.

By the late 1400s, the rapidly growing empire of the Ottoman Turks was the leading Muslim power. From their base in Asia Minor—modern Turkey—the Ottomans had taken over Greece and much of the Balkan Peninsula.

Contact Between Muslims and Christians

As Islam spread, Muslims and Christians came into direct conflict. Knights from Christian Europe fought to recapture lands that the Muslims occupied in Spain and Sicily. In 1095, at the urging of the Pope, the knights' main goal became control of Palestine and its Christian shrines.

In the long run, the Crusades into the Holy Land, which was sacred to both Christians and Muslims, influenced trade and learning. From Middle Eastern and Islamic cultures, the returning knights and soldiers brought back new foods and products—spices, sugar, silk, cotton, dyes, perfumes, and fruits such as peaches and melons. Increased trade enriched the Italian city-states.

Contact also brought new ideas. Arab scholars had made advances in medicine, astronomy, mathematics, and other sciences. From the Arabs, Europeans learned algebra and the system of Arabic numerals, which the Arabs had learned in India. In Spain the Muslims introduced the Arabian horse as well as oranges and lemons.

Expansion into India

One of the early areas of Muslim expansion was India. Beginning in A.D. 712, groups of Muslims from Persia (Iran) and Afghanistan occupied parts of northern India. The beliefs of the Muslim people clashed with the ancient Hindu traditions of India. While some Indians converted to Islam, conflict led to divisions within the country.

In the late 1400s, a weak Muslim kingdom was in power in northern India. The rest of the country was divided among many small states and kingdoms controlled by princes and rajas, most of whom were Hindu. Early in the 1500s, another group of

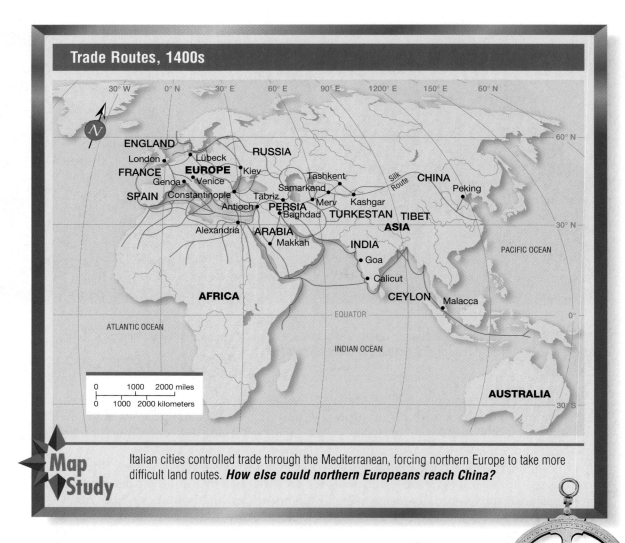

Trade Routes, 1400s

Map Study Italian cities controlled trade through the Mediterranean, forcing northern Europe to take more difficult land routes. *How else could northern Europeans reach China?*

▶ ASTROLABE

Muslims established the powerful Mogul Empire, which would unite and rule India for several hundred years.

■ Empires of the East

In the early 1200s, the ancient empire of China was conquered by the invading "Golden Horde" of Mongols from central Asia. Under the strong leadership of Genghis Khan, the Mongol army of fierce, swift riders also swept westward across central Asia, through Russia, terrorizing the Slavic people of Poland, Hungary, and Austria. For nearly 200 years, the Mongols ruled an enormous empire, including China, central Asia, Russia, and the Middle East.

China

Although the Chinese considered the Mongols "barbarians," China prospered under their rule. Overland travel was safe while the Mongols controlled the huge central Eurasian plain. East-west trade was revived, along with cultural exchanges among China, Europe, and Muslim Asia. European traders, travelers, and missionaries were welcome in China. They returned not only with silks and spices but also with important inventions such as the compass, printing, and gunpowder.

European traders also brought back exciting descriptions of the wonders they had seen in Asia. Marco Polo was a young merchant from Venice who traveled to the court of Kublai Khan in 1275. His description of the luxury of the "Great Khan's" palace stirred the imaginations of his readers in Europe:

> *Inside, the walls and halls and chambers are all covered with gold and silver and decorated with pictures of dragons and birds and horsemen and various breeds of beasts and scenes of battle. . . . The hall is so vast that a meal might be served there for more than 6,000 men.*

In the late 1400s, when the spirit of the Renaissance was transforming Europe, the mood in China was to preserve tradition. Following the death of the Great Khan in 1294, the Chinese overthrew their Mongol rulers. The rulers of the new Ming Dynasty wanted to restore their traditional Chinese heritage. New ideas were discouraged, and students studied only the ancient, classic books. At first the Ming rulers encouraged trade, sending expeditions around the Indian Ocean and to the coast of east Africa. Then in 1433 the Ming rulers cut China's contacts with the outside world. China would remain relatively isolated for centuries.

Japan

Like medieval Europe, Japan had a feudal society, based on the bonds between landowning nobles and the knights who served them. **Samurai**, the warriors of feudal Japan, lived by a strict code of honor. Since the 1100s, the country had been led by **shoguns**, military dictators who had far more power than the emperor.

Japan's island location had helped protect it from conquest during Mongol rule in China. When Kublai Khan's navy tried to invade Japan in 1281, a typhoon destroyed the fleet. Fighting off the Mongols, however, weakened the shoguns' government. In the late 1400s, local lords, backed by their private armies of samurai, were almost constantly at war. Nonetheless, towns and trade prospered in medieval Japan.

Life of the Times

Golden Age of Mali

A firsthand account of life in Mali was given by the Arab geographer ibn-Battutu. Traveling through Mali in the fourteenth century, he marveled at the law, order, and racial tolerance of the African kingdom.

"The Negroes possess some admirable qualities. They are seldom unjust and have a greater abhorrence of injustice than any other people. Their Sultan shows no mercy to any one guilty of the least act of it. There is complete security in their country. Neither traveler nor inhabitant in it has anything to fear from robbers or men of violence. They do not confiscate the property of any white man who dies in their country, even if it be uncounted wealth. On the contrary, they give it into the charge of some trustworthy person among the whites, until the rightful heir takes possession of it."

▶ **CARVED RITUAL STOOL**

▲ **ANTELOPE FIGURINE**

▲ BENIN IVORY MASK, SIXTEENTH CENTURY

■ African Trading Kingdoms

From ancient times, trade linked areas of the continent of Africa with other cultures. While Egypt and parts of North Africa traded with others around the Mediterranean, North African merchants also followed caravan trails south across the Sahara to exchange precious salt for gold and slaves.

Early African Civilizations

The earliest African civilizations developed east of the Sahara. Egypt dominated the region for more than 2,000 years. Kushites from the southern Nile then became an independent kingdom. During the time of the Roman Empire, another powerful state, Axum, expanded to challenge the Kushite rule. Axum made Christianity the official religion of the kingdom in A.D. 330. When Islam spread across northern Africa in the 600s, Axum lost much of its coastal territory. Its rulers set up the Christian kingdom of Ethiopia. While Ethiopian rulers attempted to spread Christianity throughout Africa, civil war and Muslim expansion weakened the nation.

Islamic Expansion

Between A.D. 500 and 1500, three wealthy trading kingdoms—Ghana, Mali, and Songhai—developed one after the other in the western Sudan, the grasslands south of the Sahara. The Muslim conquest of North Africa greatly increased trade, and Muslim culture spread to the area.

In the 1300s the trading city of Timbuktu in Mali became a center of Islamic culture, with a university and a great mosque. In 1468 the Songhai people rebelled and captured Timbuktu. Askia Mohammed, a general and devout Muslim, ruled Songhai between 1493 and 1528.

East Africa, on the other hand, looked eastward, trading with Arabia, Persia, India, and China. Wealthy city-states such as Kilwa were centers for gold, ivory, cinnamon, palm oil, and slaves. Swahili, an African-based language mixed with Arabic words, was widely used in trade.

Civil wars brought internal disorder to Bantu nations in central and southern Africa. The resulting loss of power left little defense against Europeans who arrived in the 1500s.

Section 3 ★ Review

Checking for Understanding

1. **Identify** Muslims, Ottomans, Crusades, Marco Polo, Axum, Swahili.

2. **Define** samurai, shogun.

3. **Analyze** the way in which the spread of Islam affected Europe, Asia, and Africa.

4. **Discuss** the importance of the Mongol Empire.

Critical Thinking

5. **Predicting Outcomes**   How might interest in exploration have increased as a result of the Crusades?

Study and Writing Skills

Using Literature as a Historical Source

Literature is imaginative or creative writing in all its forms. It can be poetry or prose, fiction or nonfiction. Some of what we now consider literature actually began in oral form—the legends, histories, and stories told and retold before written language developed.

Each culture's literature is unique. Through its literature, a culture reveals the values it holds important, as well as its beliefs and customs. Each unit of this textbook presents a piece of literature selected to help you better understand the people and period you are studying.

▲ IBIBIO CARVED WOOD MASK

The reading that follows is a creation legend from the Ibibio people of Nigeria. As you read this selection, observe how the characters' actions reveal the beliefs of the ancient Ibibio.

Years ago the sun, the moon, and the water lived on the earth together. The sun often visited the house where water lived and they would sit talking for hours. But the water never came to visit the sun.

One day the sun asked, "Why don't you and your family ever visit my house? My wife and I would be pleased to welcome you."

The water answered, "I'm sorry I have not visited you, but your house is small. I was afraid that if I and my people came to see you, we would drive you and your wife away."

"We are going to build a larger home," replied the sun. "Then will you come to visit us?"

The sun seemed so sad that the water promised to visit when the new house was complete.

The sun and his wife, the moon, set to work, and with the help of their friends, built a magnificent home.

"Come and visit us now," urged the sun.

The water was still doubtful, but the sun begged so hard that the water decided to enter. Through the door into the house he flowed, bringing with him hundreds of fish, some water rats, and even a few water snakes.

When the water was knee-deep, he asked the sun, "Do you still want us to come in?"

"Yes," cried the foolish sun.

The water continued to stream in, and the sun and the moon climbed onto the roof to stay dry.

"Do you still want my people and me to come into your home?" asked the water once more.

The sun did not want to go back on his word, so he replied, "Yes, let them all come in."

Soon the water reached the very top of the roof. The sun and moon were forced into the sky, where they have lived ever since.

Practicing the Skill

1. What is the theme of the literature selection?

2. Do the events help you understand the historical setting, circumstance, or specific culture? Explain.

3. What have you learned from this work about a particular period or culture?

4. For further practice in using literature as a historical source, read the excerpts on pages 30 and 31 of this book, and answer the suggested questions for each selection.

★★

Europeans Seek the East

Setting the Scene

Section Focus

By the last decades of the fifteenth century, technological and economic changes in Europe made long sea voyages possible. The prime goal of these ventures was a sea route from Europe to Asia. Encouraged by their rulers, Portuguese sea captains were the first to find this route.

Objectives

After studying this section, you should be able to

★ explain the changes in commerce and in technology that enabled Europeans to sponsor long ocean voyages.

★ state the importance of the Portuguese discovery of a sea route to Asia.

Key Terms

joint-stock company, stock, capital, compass, astrolabe, quadrant, carrack, caravel, scurvy

◀ BINOCULARS AND COMPASS

he Renaissance spirit of curiosity and adventure that swept over Europe helped launch the bold voyages of the Age of Exploration. Many other motivations sent travelers across unknown oceans: Europeans wanted luxury goods from Asia, as well as the spices—pepper, nutmeg, cinnamon, cloves—that preserved foods and made them taste better. European merchants hoped to break the monopoly that Arab traders and Venetian merchants had on the overland routes to Asia. European monarchs hoped to enrich and strengthen their countries—and themselves. The Roman Catholic Church sent missionaries to bring Christianity to millions of new souls.

While six countries on the Atlantic coast—Portugal, Spain, France, the Netherlands, Sweden, and England—would eventually undertake voyages of discovery, the pioneer in these ventures was Portugal.

■ A Revolution in Commerce

Italian city-states had proven that great profit awaited those willing to take risks to trade with the distant East. They had a monopoly on trade through the Mediterranean, but northern European merchants and bankers would soon sponsor voyages.

Financing Exploration

The great expense of ocean voyages made new ways of raising finances necessary. In England, France, and the Netherlands, the **joint-stock company** became a useful form for raising money. The company sold shares, called **stock,** to investors, thus providing money or **capital** for its venture. Each shareowner then received a portion of the venture's profits—or losses.

▲ FLORINS, ITALIAN COINS

▲ *THE MONEYCHANGER AND HIS WIFE* by Quentin Metys, 1514 Increased trade demanded changes in the organization and operation of commercial activities. *What do you think is happening in this painting?*

The joint-stock company let small investors, who could not afford to outfit an entire ship, take part in overseas commercial ventures by buying shares of stock. It also enabled wealthy people to spread their risks by investing in several joint-stock companies at the same time. A joint-stock company might have hundreds of shareholders, thus creating enough wealth to support long expeditions or found colonies.

New Technology

No matter how well financed, long voyages could not have succeeded without better technology. With sailors ready to strike out in new directions, advances in shipbuilding and navigation were important. For thousands of years, Mediterranean ship captains had tried to sail within sight of land, guided mainly by written descriptions of coasts and harbors.

By the fifteenth century, captains were using precise maps for both the Mediterranean and the Atlantic coasts of Europe and North Africa. In addition, Arab sailors taught Europeans how to use several improved navigational instruments. The **compass**, which was invented in China, reliably showed the direction of magnetic north—even at night or in cloudy weather. The **astrolabe** and the **quadrant** measured the positions of the sun and stars, allowing the navigator to determine distance north and south from a given point.

Ships built to new designs were faster and more seaworthy. The **carrack**, for example, had several masts and a rudder. Smaller but easier to handle was the Portuguese **caravel**, a double-rigged ship with both square and triangular sails. On Christopher Columbus's first voyage, the flagship *Santa Maria* was a carrack; the *Niña* and the *Pinta* were caravels.

■ Pioneering Portuguese

Portugal was the first European country to search for a sea route to Asia. This small nation had a long Atlantic coast with good ports and a rich seafaring tradition.

Prince Henry's Expeditions

The groundwork for Portugal's accomplishments was laid in the early 1400s by Prince Henry, an individual who neither sailed to other lands nor explored any new areas. Yet his efforts kindled the fires of exploration.

Through exploration, Henry wanted to bring Portugal more trade and power and to spread Christianity. In his mind, the key to reaching these goals lay in the open seas. Henry's first step was to bring together mapmakers, astronomers, and shipbuilders from throughout the Mediterranean world to study and plan voyages of exploration. These experts pooled their talents to uncover knowledge about the seas and to extend the art of navigation.

Drawing on this collected expertise, Prince Henry sent expeditions beyond the safety of the Mediterranean. One of Henry's plans was to have his ships sail around Africa and find a path to India and the Spice Islands. Such a route might lead to Prester John, the legendary Christian monarch said to rule a rich, powerful kingdom. The new route also might reveal the source of the gold dust and other precious goods the Moors brought to Mediterranean ports. Portuguese ships traveled southward along the African coast. As expeditions returned, Henry's mapmakers corrected and improved their sailing charts.

Bit by bit, expedition after expedition, the Portuguese inched their way down the coast of Africa. For people at that time, these were fearsome voyages. Europeans were convinced that great dangers awaited in the open ocean: a Sea of Darkness, sea monsters, oceans that boiled at the equator. A big obstacle was exploring new areas where geographical knowledge stopped and myth took over. Said one Portuguese sailor about reaching these limits:

> **Beyond this there is no race of men or place of inhabitants. Nor is the land less sandy than the deserts of Libya, where there is no water, no tree, no green herb. And the sea is so shallow that a whole league from land is only a fathom deep, while the currents are so terrible that no ship, having once passed the Cape, will ever be able to return.**

There were, in fact, some dangerous currents and treacherously shallow waters along the African coast. By the time Prince Henry—known as "the Navigator"—died in 1460, his ships had reached just beyond Cape Verde, the westernmost tip of Africa.

The Slave Trade

By this time, the Portuguese had well-established trade patterns with African merchants for gold, ivory, pepper, palm oil, and slaves. Soon they added profitable trading posts on the West African coast and built sugar plantations.

Slavery and the slave trade were not new in the region. Using war captives as slaves had long been a practice in North Africa and

History AND ART

▼ HENRY THE NAVIGATOR Shown in this detail of the painting, *Panel of the Infanta*, is Prince Henry. **What role did Portugal play in navigation?**

in other parts of the world as well. The first African slaves were taken to Portugal as servants in 1441. Probably 1,000 Africans were taken to Portugal over the next 5 years. But by the 1490s, the growth and profits of the African sugar plantations had increased the demand for local slave labor. To meet the new demand, slave traders turned to kidnapping and "slave raids" in the African interior.

Rounding the Tip of Africa

In 1487 and 1488 a Portuguese expedition led by Bartholomeu Dias was caught in a storm that blew the ships off course near the southern tip of Africa. As the skies cleared, Dias realized from the position of the sun that they had rounded the tip of Africa without knowing it. The Portuguese ruler, King John II, named the area the "Cape of Good Hope" because it seemed to promise the existence of a new sea route to India.

Crossing the Indian Ocean

Ten years later another Portuguese expedition set sail, headed by Vasco da Gama. After almost a year's travel, they rounded the Cape of Good Hope and sailed up the eastern coast of Africa past the rich Muslim city-states of Kilwa and Malindi. With an Arab pilot, the expedition crossed the Indian Ocean to Calicut on the coast of India.

The voyage home took another year and was much more difficult. Many sailors died of **scurvy**, a sickness caused by a lack of vitamin C. Da Gama finally returned home to Portugal in September 1499. It is said that the profits on his cargo of cinnamon, cloves, nutmeg, ginger, and pepper covered the cost of his expedition 60 times over.

▶ CARAVEL

Growing Rivalry

The trade rivalry among Italian city-states had been intense. Now Portugal's sea venture could cost the Italian cities their monopoly on trade. When news of da Gama's voyage reached Venice, the effect was dramatic. A writer reported:

> 66 ... if this voyage should continue, the King of Portugal could call himself the King of Money, because all would convene to that country to obtain spices, and the money would accumulate greatly in Portugal. ... this news was held by the learned to be the worst news which the Venetian Republic could have had. ... 99

Da Gama's ships had traveled 24,000 miles. The sea route that he opened challenged the other European nations to make their own explorations. In the following four centuries, western Europe's quest for wealth and empire would affect the lives of people on every continent.

Section 4 ★ Review

Checking for Understanding

1. **Identify** Prince Henry "the Navigator," Bartholomeu Dias, Vasco da Gama.

2. **Define** joint-stock company, stock, capital, compass, astrolabe, quadrant, carrack, caravel, scurvy.

3. **Enumerate** the reasons the Europeans undertook voyages of discovery.

4. **Describe** the effects on other nations of the Portuguese discovery of a sea route around Africa to Asia.

Critical Thinking

5. **Making Deductions** Why would wealthy investors want to buy a small share in several overseas voyages rather than a large share in one?

Among the Native American groups with the richest oral literary traditions are the Iroquois and Navajo. During the 1500s a prophet named Dekanawida (DEK•uhn•uh•WEE• duh) appeared among the Iroquois and urged them to lay down their weapons and join hands in the spirit of friendship and peace. His influence led to the formation of the Iroquois Confederation of the Five Nations. The Navajo expressed themselves in songlike chants and legends that provide a window on their ideals and beliefs.

The Constitution of the Five Nations (excerpts)

I am Dekanawida and with the Five Nations confederate lords I plant the Tree of the Great Peace. I name the tree the Tree of the Great Long Leaves. Under the shade of this Tree of the Great Peace we spread the soft white feathery down of the globe thistle as seats for you . . . and your cousin lords.

We place . . . at the top of the Tree of the Long Leaves an eagle who is able to see afar. If he sees in the distance any evil approaching or any danger threatening he will at once warn the people of the confederacy. . . .

All lords of the Five Nations Confederacy must be honest in all things. . . . It shall be a serious wrong for anyone to lead a lord into trivial affairs, for the people must ever hold their lords high in estimation out of respect to their honorable positions. . . .

We now do crown you with the sacred emblem of the deer's antlers, the emblem of your lordship. You shall now become a mentor of the people of the Five Nations. The thickness of your skin shall be seven spans—which is to say that you shall be proof against anger, offensive actions and criticism. Your heart shall be filled with peace and good will and your mind filled with a yearning for the welfare of the people of the confederacy. With endless patience you shall carry out your duty and your firmness shall be tempered with tenderness for your people. Neither anger nor fury shall find lodgement in your mind and all your words and actions shall be marked with calm deliberation. . . .

▲ **Iroquois notched staff**

Navajo Song of the Rain Chant

Far as man can see,
Comes the rain,
Comes the rain with me.

From the Rain-Mount,
Rain-Mount far away,
Comes the rain,
Comes the rain with me.

O'er the corn,
O'er the corn, the tall corn,
Comes the rain,
Comes the rain with me.

'Mid the lightnings,
'Mid the lightning zigzag,
'Mid the lightning flashing
Comes the rain,
Comes the rain with me.

'Mid the swallows,
'Mid the swallows blue
Chirping glad together,
Comes the rain,
Comes the rain with me.

Through the pollen,
Through the pollen blest,
All in pollen hidden,
Comes the rain,
Comes the rain with me.

Far as man can see,
Comes the rain,
Comes the rain with me.

▲ NAVAJO RUG

Interpreting Literature

1. In the Iroquois Constitution, what is the function of the eagle that sits atop the Tree of the Long Leaves?

2. How does the Rain Chant reflect Navajo beliefs about nature?

Analyzing Culture

3. In what ways are the qualities desired for Iroquois leaders similar to or different from those desired for today's leaders in the United States government?

Using Vocabulary

Classify each of the terms listed below into one of the following categories: Political Structures and Systems, Economic Activity and Systems, Inventions and Technology, Religion and Culture.

astrolabe	humanism
capital	joint-stock company
caravel	manor
carrack	parliament
charter	pueblos
classical	quadrant
compass	Renaissance
confederation	samurai
dynasty	serfs
feudal system	shoguns

Reviewing Facts

1. **Discuss** the major changes in the political and social structure of Europe in the late 1400s.

2. **Describe** the characteristics of the Renaissance.

3. **Identify** advanced cultures of Africa and Asia and the importance of their trade with Europe.

4. **Report** on the effects of religious conflicts during the Middle Ages.

5. **Compare** the cultures of Mesoamerican and North American native peoples.

6. **List** the motives of the nations interested in voyages of discovery.

7. **Summarize** the development of the middle class and its role in the voyages of exploration.

8. **Enumerate** the achievements of the Portuguese voyages of discovery.

Understanding Concepts

Diverse Cultures

1. Compare the differences and similarities between each of the following sets of cultures: medieval European and medieval Japanese culture; the West African trading kingdoms and the Aztec empire.

2. Both European Renaissance scholars and Ming Dynasty rulers restored interest in ancient classic works of their cultures. How did their motives differ?

Economic Change

3. How did the middle class gain economic power comparable to that of feudal landowners?

4. What new form of investment made more voyages of exploration possible? In what ways did these new forms affect economic opportunity in general?

Critical Thinking

1. **Classifying Causes** What factors facilitated the change from feudalism to nationalism? Label each cause political, economic, or religious.

2. **Analyzing Motivation** What forces and events motivated voyages of exploration?

3. **Understanding Global Events** How did the spread of Islam contribute to the growth of nationalism? To the Renaissance? To the interest in exploration?

4. **Analyzing Artifacts** Examine the picture of the Renaissance shield on this page and answer the questions that follow.

   a. How many men and how many women are portrayed on the shield?

   b. What seems to be the attitude of the people in the picture?

   c. What conclusions can you draw about the artist's feelings toward the Renaissance? Explain your answer.

▶ RENAISSANCE SHIELD

Writing About History

Narration

Imagine you are captain of one of Vasco da Gama's ships. Write a few days' entries in the ship's log book, relating the day's events and challenges and detailing the crew's reactions. You may need to conduct research at your school or local library for authentic details, but imaginary details are also acceptable.

Cooperative Learning

Working in a group of four, make a set of four parallel time lines covering the years 600 to 1500. Indicate major events and developments in China, among the Native Americans in present-day Mexico, among the Europeans in present-day Italy, and among major Arab Muslim groups. Each member should research the history of one culture and show the major events on that culture's time line.

Social Studies Skills

Reading a Travel Route Map

A map can convey travel route information more accurately and efficiently than verbal description alone. To maximize the information gained from a travel route map, follow these steps:

- Read the map legend. The legend is the map-maker's means of drawing attention to key data.
- Study the map scale to gain perspective on the distance traveled.
- Look at the physical features portrayed on the map. Can you make inferences about the difficulty of the travel?
- Evaluate the travel routes. Do some cities on the map serve as hubs where several travel routes intersect?

Practicing the Skill

Use the map of the African trading kingdoms to answer the following questions.

1. What map scale is used?
2. What physical features are shown on the map?
3. What city is the easternmost trade partner? The westernmost trade partner?
4. What two cities show the largest number of intersecting trade routes?
5. Other than the information on trade routes, what key historic information is supplied by the map?

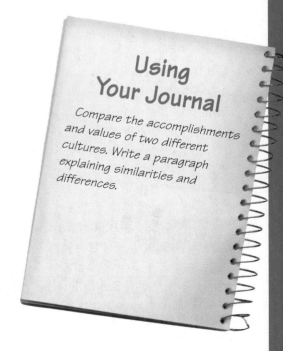

Using Your Journal

Compare the accomplishments and values of two different cultures. Write a paragraph explaining similarities and differences.

CHAPTER 2

★★

The Age of Exploration
1000–1682

Setting the Scene

▶ EXPLORER'S LOG BOOK

Focus

The first Europeans to visit North America were Norse seafarers who reached Newfoundland about 1000. Interest in exploration and settlement of the Americas, however, did not truly begin until the first voyage of Christopher Columbus in 1492. Thereafter, until the early 1600s, various nations—Spain, Portugal, France, England, and the Netherlands—sent explorers to the Americas.

Concepts to Understand

★ How European nations sought wealth through voyages of discovery and exploration to the New World

★ How European values and beliefs differed from those of the Native American population

Read to Discover . . .

★ why European nations wanted to explore the Americas.

★ how the Spanish and French treated Native Americans.

Journal Notes

Did European explorers usually find what they were looking for? Note the aims of various expeditions and their degree of success in your journal as you read the chapter.

CULTURAL	● **1050** *European traders bring technology from East Asia*	● **1400** *Incan and Aztec empires flourish*	● **1469** *Lorenzo de' Medici rules Florence*
	1000	**1400**	**1450**
POLITICAL	● **1000** *Norse seafarers establish settlements in Iceland, Greenland, and Newfoundland*	● **1400s** *Age of Exploration begins*	● **1492** *First voyage of Christopher Columbus begins*

History AND ART

Cabot's Departure, 1497
by Ernest Board, 1906

English merchants persuaded their king to send John Cabot, an Italian navigator, to Asia by a northwest route. This painting, completed more than 400 years after the event, communicates a feeling of solemn pageantry.

◀ VIKING HELMET

1540 *Ignatius of Loyola founds the Society of Jesus, or Jesuits*

1556 *Ordinary of the Mass is first book printed in the Americas*

1593 *John White publishes detailed drawings of Native Americans*

1500	1550	1600

1539 *Hernando de Soto explores North America*

1570 *Iroquois form League of Five Nations*

1608 *Samuel de Champlain founds Quebec*

★★

Voyages of Columbus

Setting the Scene

Section Focus

In their eagerness to find easier routes for trade in Asia, some Europeans had a new idea: instead of sailing south and east around Africa, they could sail west. The idea led to discoveries that brought drastic change to those who lived on the continents that lay between Europe and Asia.

Objectives

After studying this section, you should be able to

★ compare the purposes and results of the four voyages of Columbus.

★ discuss the purpose and results of Magellan's expedition.

Key Terms

saga, line of demarcation, isthmus, strait

◀ CUBICAL SUNDIAL

The first Europeans to arrive in the Americas were Norse seafarers from Scandinavia. Between A.D. 800 and 1100, the Norse established settlements in Iceland, Greenland, and present-day Newfoundland, which they called Vinland. The Norse settlements in Vinland were unsuccessful because of conflicts with Native Americans and lack of support from home. The Vinland settlements soon disappeared—forgotten except in Norse **sagas**, or long, heroic stories.

Not until the voyage of Christopher Columbus in 1492 did European exploration of the Americas begin in earnest. After Europeans learned that Columbus had sailed to continents not yet known to them, Spain, Portugal, France, the Netherlands, and England sent expeditions to the New World. They pursued a passage to Asia through or around the giant landmass. In time these nations all established colonies in the Americas.

■ Columbus's First Venture

Christopher Columbus was born in Genoa, Italy, in 1451. His early interest in navigation led him to Lisbon, Portugal, in 1477. There, Portuguese explorations of the Atlantic coast of Africa brought him new knowledge of geography and cartography.

Preparing for the Expedition

Columbus studied the atlas of the ancient Greek geographer, Ptolemy, who had greatly underestimated the size of the earth. In 1477, Columbus was one of the first to read the newly printed "Travels" of Marco Polo. On the basis of this information, Columbus shrank Ptolemy's calculations. He figured the distance between Japan and the Canary Islands, off the northwestern coast of Africa, at only 2,400 miles. His calculations resulted in an obsession to undertake a voyage to Asia by sailing west.

For years Columbus sought financial backing. Having no success with the kings of Portugal, France, and England, he spent six years trying to persuade Ferdinand and Isabella of Spain that his scheme would bring them wealth, empire, and converts to Catholicism. Finally, Isabella and Ferdinand provided Columbus with three ships, the *Niña*, the *Pinta*, and the *Santa Maria*.

Voyage Into the Unknown

Columbus left Spain in August 1492 with about 90 sailors. He sailed south to the Canary Islands, where he repaired his ships and took on fresh supplies. Columbus then charted his course westward, noting ". . . nothing to the north, nothing to the south."

By early October the fleet had already gone farther than Columbus had thought would be necessary to reach Japan. The sailors were frightened and wanted to turn back. On October 9 the crew "heard birds passing all night long" and believed they were close to land. On October 11 Columbus wrote in his log:

66 *The crew of the Pinta spotted some . . . reeds and some other plants; they also saw what looked like a small board or plank. A stick was recovered that looks man-made, perhaps carved with an iron tool. . . . but even these few [things] made the crew breathe easier; in fact the men have even become cheerful.* 99

In the early morning of October 12, 1492, the lookout aboard the *Pinta* saw white cliffs glistening in the moonlight. At dawn, Columbus went ashore onto a small island in the Bahamas (San Salvador) and claimed it for Spain. Believing he had reached the East Indies off the coast of Asia, he called the native people Indians.

▶ **CHRISTOPHER COLUMBUS**

Visualizing History

▲ **VOYAGES OF COLUMBUS** An Italian sailor and mapmaker, Christopher Columbus believed that Asia could be reached by sailing directly west from Europe. *Why do you think Columbus did not realize that he had reached a new world?*

Marvels of a New World

In April 1493, Columbus returned triumphantly to the Spanish court. The king and queen gave him the titles "Admiral of the Ocean Sea" and "Viceroy and Governor of the Indies." All were fascinated by both the copper-skinned people Columbus brought back and his reports of lands where every bird, tree, and flower was new to Europeans. Isabella and Ferdinand were most interested in the reports of gold and in trade.

Columbus made three more voyages across the Atlantic. Despite his achievements, Columbus died in 1506 a broken, frustrated dreamer, unaware that he had reached new continents in the Western Hemisphere.

■ Spain and Portugal Divide the World

Accounts of Columbus's travels soon set off a flurry of exploration, particularly by Spain and Portugal. Seafaring explorers considered the lands reached by Columbus to be a barrier between Europe and Asia, and they sought to find a way around them. They clearly were uncertain how to deal with this world.

Treaty of Tordesillas

Columbus's exploration put Spain and Portugal in direct competition for trade and empire-building. In 1493, because of potential conflict, Pope Alexander VI convinced the two Catholic nations to divide any new overseas trading interests between them. A **line of demarcation**, a north-south line drawn on a map through the Atlantic Ocean by the pope, gave Spain all the non-Christian lands to the west of the line and Portugal all those to the east. In 1494 Spain and Portugal resolved their differences "for the sake of peace and concord" in the Treaty of Tordesillas (TAWR•duh•SEE•yuhs). The treaty established the demarcation line at about 48° west longitude and extended it around the earth to secure Portuguese claims in Asia.

In 1500 a fleet of Portuguese ships under the command of Pedro Álvares Cabral (PAY•droh AHL•vuh•REHZ kuh•BRAHL) set out for India by going east around the coast of Africa. Swinging west to get favorable winds, Cabral's expedition was blown off course and unintentionally reached present-day Brazil. Because a part of Brazil's coastline lay to the east of the line set by the treaty, Portugal claimed it.

America Is Named

In 1499 another Portuguese expedition, with an Italian-born navigator and merchant, Amerigo Vespucci (vay•SPOO•chee), sailed along the coast of South America. Vespucci concluded that this land was a vast new continent. In 1504 Vespucci's sensational account was published, and he erroneously received credit for reaching the mainland of this land before Columbus. German mapmakers named the New World "America," and the name stuck.

A Vast New Ocean Revealed

On expeditions into what is now Panama, Vasco Núñez de Balboa (VAHS•koh NOO•nyayth day bal•BOH•uh) learned from the native people of "great waters" to the west. Balboa led an expedition to find this body of water, guided by the Indians who knew trails through the difficult countryside.

They did indeed reach a huge body of water, which Balboa claimed for Spain. Having climbed a peak alone to see the water first, Balboa in 1513 became the first European to see the eastern coast of the Pacific Ocean. It now appeared that the lands Columbus had reached were separated from Asia by this seemingly endless ocean.

▲ **AMERIGO VESPUCCI**

Voyages of Exploration

Verrazano explored the Atlantic Coast from Cape Fear, North Carolina, to perhaps as far as Newfoundland, and viewed Narragansett Bay and the Hudson River.

John Cabot suggested that the time of a voyage across the Atlantic could be shortened by sailing at a more northerly latitude than did Columbus. He reasoned that the earth's greatest circumference is at the equator, and sailing north or south of the equator would cut the distance.

On his first voyage, Columbus landed in the present-day Bahama Islands and also explored Cuba and Hispaniola, the island now occupied by the Dominican Republic and Haiti.

GREENLAND
SCANDINAVIA
ICELAND
NETHERLANDS
ENGLAND EUROPE
LABRADOR
FRANCE
NEWFOUNDLAND
PORTUGAL SPAIN
NORTH AMERICA
30° N
15° N
ATLANTIC OCEAN
Gulf of Mexico
1 (1492)
AFRICA
0°
Caribbean Sea
2 (1493)
4 (1502)
EQUATOR
3 (1498)
PACIFIC OCEAN
15° S
ATLANTIC   OCEAN
SOUTH AMERICA
BRAZIL
60° S
30° W
75° W 60° 45° W 45° S 30° W 15° W 0°

Norse (about 1000)
Spanish
Christopher Columbus (1492-1502)
Amerigo Vespucci (1499)
Portuguese
Pedro Cabral (1500)
English
John Cabot (1497)
Martin Frobisher (1576)
French
Giovanni da Verrazano (1524)
Jacques Cartier (1534)
Dutch
Henry Hudson (1609)

NORTH AMERICA
EUROPE
ATLANTIC OCEAN
ASIA
PACIFIC OCEAN
DRAKE (1577-1580)
AFRICA
EQUATOR
SOUTH AMERICA
INDIAN OCEAN
MAGELLAN (1519-1522)
DRAKE (1577-1580)
AUSTRALIA
MAGELLAN (1519-1522)
PACIFIC OCEAN
ANTARCTICA

Map Study Several European explorers visited the Caribbean area and the coast of the Americas following Columbus's voyages. These explorers were in the service of different countries. *Who claimed for the Portuguese the land that is present-day Brazil?*

■ Magellan's Voyage

Balboa's expedition did, however, revive hope of sailing west to reach Asia. Since only a strip of land, or **isthmus**, separated the oceans at Panama, it was thought that perhaps there was a **strait**, or narrow waterway, connecting the two bodies of water. Portuguese navigator Ferdinand Magellan believed he could find such a passage.

Magellan's Plan

Magellan hoped to sail around the world to the Spice Islands, a center for the valuable spice trade located in what is now Indonesia. Out of favor in the Portuguese court, Magellan approached King Charles I of Spain with his plan. A Spanish missionary to America, Bartolemé de Las Casas, described this meeting:

❝ *Magellan brought with him a well-painted globe, and thereon traced the course he proposed to take . . . he intended to follow the coast . . . until he found the strait [passage to the other ocean].* ❞

Difficult Passage

The Spanish king agreed to finance Magellan, and in 1519 Magellan set sail with 5 ships. By October 1520, Magellan had reached the strait that now bears his name at the southern tip of South America.

The strait, with its fierce winds and strong tides, was so difficult to navigate that it took over a month for the expedition to pass through. Because the ocean on the other side seemed so calm, Magellan called it the Pacific, meaning "peaceful." During the voyage across the Pacific that followed, the sailors suffered extreme hardships, and many died. Magellan met his own death in April 1521 as the result of a local war in the Philippines. Only one of his ships, carrying 18 survivors, finally reached Spain in 1522. These survivors and their ship were the first to circumnavigate the world.

▲ FERDINAND MAGELLAN

Section 1 ★ Review

Checking for Understanding

1. **Identify** Pedro Álvares Cabral, Amerigo Vespucci.

2. **Define** saga, line of demarcation, isthmus, strait.

3. **Name** the first Europeans to establish settlements in North America, and describe their experience.

4. **Evaluate** Columbus's achievements.

Critical Thinking

5. **Analyzing Solutions** The Panama Canal was built at great cost. On the map on page 39, examine the route Magellan opened and explain why building the canal was important.

CONNECTIONS History AND GEOGRAPHY CONNECTIONS

▲ MAP OF THE WORLD, C. 1502

"'Twas a Small World," Columbus Thought

Around the sixth century B.C., the Greek philosopher Thales proposed the idea that the earth was a disc floating in water. Shortly after, Pythagoras advanced a different idea, that the earth was a sphere. Several centuries later Aristotle tested this idea by observing the circular shadow of the earth on the moon during eclipses.

The size of the earth was more difficult to determine than its shape. Greek geographer Eratosthenes, however, almost correctly calculated the circumference of the earth at about 25,000 miles by measuring the angles of the sun's rays at separated points. This figure was known by Columbus, but he chose to use the calculations made by a number of later scholars who underestimated the size of the earth by nearly one-half. Mapmakers compounded the errors by showing Europe, Asia, and Africa much larger than they actually are and by showing the Atlantic Ocean as a narrow gulf.

Columbus made four voyages in all. He explored the coasts of Venezuela and Central America. He returned from his last voyage in 1504. He died two years later, still convinced he had found an accurate route to Asia. After all, he had found it just where he had calculated it to be.

Magellan's voyage was a great achievement. By circumnavigating, or sailing completely around the world, Magellan proved that the earth is indeed round. The voyage opened the Pacific Ocean to European ships. It also proved that Columbus had not landed in Asia but in the Americas.

Making the Geography Connection

1. What contributions did early Greeks make to geography?

2. Why did Columbus think he had reached Asia?

Linking Past and Present

3. Compare the level of technology Columbus used with that used by modern astronauts.

★★★★★★★★★★★★★★★★★★★★★★★★★★★★★★★

Spain in America

Setting the Scene

Section Focus

Europeans had not found a new trade route to Asia, but they soon began to look upon the Americas as a source of wealth. Explorers heard stories of fabulously rich cities in the interior. Among the most vigorous in searching for treasure in the Americas were Spanish explorers. Their activities, along with those of the Christian missionaries, changed the world of the native peoples of the Americas.

Objectives

After studying this section, you should be able to

★ describe the Spanish exploration and conquest of the South and Central American mainlands.

★ discuss life in the Spanish colonies.

Key Terms

conquistador, *peninsulares*, creole, mestizo, mulatto, *encomienda*, viceroy, presidio

◀ COMPASS, 1500S

*I*n the 25 years after Columbus's first voyage, Spaniards carved out small outposts through the West Indies—on Cuba, Jamaica, Puerto Rico, and Hispaniola. Generally they were not interested in creating permanent settlements in the Americas. Instead, they flocked to the islands in search of land and precious metals. The peoples of these islands suffered greatly, however, because of Spanish ambition.

■ The Conquistadors

The many **conquistadors** (kohn•KEES•tuh•dohrs)—Spanish conquerors who made their way to the Caribbean islands in the early 1500s—were eager to find great wealth, especially gold and silver. They did not hesitate to use harsh means to obtain this end. The natives of the Caribbean, many of whom were enslaved and put to work washing for gold or raising crops, were virtually exterminated in less than 20 years. Most succumbed to such European diseases as smallpox and measles, from which they had no immunity. By 1520 the Spanish were importing Africans as slaves to replace the Native American populations.

The Spaniards did not confine themselves to the Caribbean islands for very long. Fantastic stories from the mainland soon sent bold Spanish adventurers into the interior of Mexico, Central America, and South America.

Cortés and Moctezuma

Among the most successful of these conquistadors was Hernán Cortés (kawr•TEHZ). In 1519 Cortés led an expedition from Cuba to the eastern shore of Mexico. Although Cortés's army numbered only 600, the Spaniards had luck—and sophisticated weapons—on their side. The Spanish also had horses, which the Indians had never seen, that they used in cavalry charges.

Cortés gained invaluable help from Malinche, an enslaved native who quickly learned Spanish. She may have told Cortés of Quetzalcoatl (keht•SAHL•KWAHT•uhl), the legendary god who had promised to return as a fair-skinned man.

When Cortés landed on the Mexican coast, reports of "floating mountains bearing fair-skinned gods" were sent to Moctezuma, the Aztec emperor. Moctezuma believed that Cortés might indeed be Quetzalcoatl, and he sent the Spaniards dazzling gifts.

As Cortés marched inland toward the Aztec capital of Tenochtitlán (tay•NAWCH•teet•LAHN), subjects of the Aztec allied with him, hoping to free themselves from Aztec rule. At first Moctezuma reluctantly welcomed the Spaniards and lodged them in Tenochtitlán. Cortés wrote:

66 *The city itself is as big as Seville or Córdoba. . . . [it] has many squares where . . . markets are held continuously. . . . There are . . . many temples. . . . Amongst these temples there is one . . . whose great size and magnificence no human tongue could describe.* 99

To insure their safety, the Spaniards took Moctezuma captive. They also looted the city of gold and silver. Eight months later, when Moctezuma was killed by a stone thrown by one of his subjects, the Aztec rose up against the Spanish. Many Spaniards were killed during a retreat.

In 1521 Cortés returned to the Aztec capital, having amassed huge numbers of allies among the native peoples. He cut off supplies to Tenochtitlán and, after a long siege, destroyed this city whose magnificence had so impressed him. Mexico City was built on its ruins, and the area's rich silver mines soon produced vast wealth.

Destruction of the Incan Empire

The conquest of Mexico encouraged other conquistadors to seek their fortune in the Americas. One such conquistador was Francisco Pizarro, an illiterate soldier who had been stirred by rumors of fabulously rich cities on the Pacific coast of South America.

In 1531 Pizarro set sail from Panama with an army of only 180 soldiers. His destination was the Incan empire in present-day Peru. After an exhausting journey, the Spaniards reached the city of Cajamarca (KAH•huh•MAHR•kuh). The Incan empire had been badly weakened by a civil war from which the new emperor Atahualpa (AH•tah•WAHL•pah) had emerged victorious. The Spaniards greeted him with swords and guns, taking him captive. In an effort to save his life, Atahualpa gave the Spaniards a room filled with gold objects and other treasures. Despite the ransom, the Spanish later executed Atahualpa. Within a short time many Spanish settlers had immigrated to Peru, where they mined silver and gold.

Visualizing History ▲ FALL OF THE AZTEC EMPIRE Cortés, with only a small army, marched on the Aztec capital of Tenochtitlán in 1519 and eventually destroyed this magnificent city. *What new city was built on its site?*

Junípero Serra
1713–1784

Most Spanish conquests in the New World were marked by a terrible slaughter of the local people. In contrast, a gentle priest established Spanish control in California by setting up a string of missions to care for and convert the Native Americans.

Born on an island off the Spanish coast, Junípero Serra became a Franciscan priest and professor of philosophy. Because he wanted to work as a missionary among Native Americans, in 1749 he left Spain to travel to Mexico.

At the age of 55, he was sent to take control of Upper California. He established a mission at San Diego, and later founded several missions stretching up the California coast to San Francisco. Taking as his motto "Always go forward and never turn back," Junípero Serra traveled by foot from mission to mission, making sure that Native Americans were not abused.

Elusive Fountain of Youth

Other Spanish conquistadors explored areas to the north. Juan Ponce de León, the governor of Puerto Rico, was one of the first to head to northern lands. De León had heard native tales of a wondrous fountain whose water would restore youth. In 1513 he set sail in search of this magical fountain. When the Spaniards reached land near what is now the city of St. Augustine, they named the area Florida for the blooming wild flowers and fragrant plants. De León never found the mythical "Fountain of Youth," but he claimed the land for Spain.

After 1542 the Spanish worked to consolidate their empire in the Americas. Because the northern lands appeared so inhospitable, the Spanish considered these borderlands unsuitable for colonization.

■ Colonial Life

The people of Spain's American colonies formed a structured society, where position was determined predominately by birth. At the top were *peninsulares*—high government and church officials who had been born in Spain. Below the *peninsulares* were **creoles**—those born in the Spanish colonies of Spanish parents. **Mestizos** (meh•STEE•zohs), those born of Native American and Spanish parents, made up the next level of colonial society. At the lowest levels of society were Native Americans, African slaves, and **mulattoes**—people of Spanish and African or Native American and African ancestry.

Land and Agriculture

Through the *encomienda* system, the Spanish monarch rewarded conquistadors and others with vast tracts of land and the right to demand both taxes and labor from the Native Americans who lived there. The *encomenderos* were supposed to protect the Native Americans, teach them Catholicism, and pay them for their labor. In reality, the Spanish colonists often treated the natives cruelly, overworking them and using their forced labor to gain vast personal wealth.

The mingling of Spanish and Native American cultures produced a new kind of society in the Spanish colonies. Spanish became the language of the colonies, though many Native Americans continued to speak their original languages. The Spanish introduced European crops, such as wheat, alfalfa, oranges, and figs, as well as horses, cattle, and firearms.

Likewise, products from the Americas made significant changes in Europe when the Spaniards returned with plants such as potatoes, tomatoes, and corn. For example, the potato decreased Europeans' reliance on flour—to the extent that towns and cities whose economies centered around mills declined.

Colonial Administration and Religious Missions

Spain's system for governing its huge colonial empire included the appointment of **viceroys**—Spanish nobles appointed by the monarch to look after the interests of the crown. The Spanish monarch also set up a special court in Mexico City known as the *audiencia*. The purpose of the court was to oversee the viceroys and control the behavior of the conquistadors. It also was supposed to provide a forum for justice to the native peoples.

The Spaniards established missions in their colonies to help convince Native Americans to become loyal Spanish subjects and Catholics. Some priests sought to protect the natives from the conquistadors. Father Bartolomé de Las Casas insisted that, like all humans, Native Americans were children of God and therefore should be protected by the Church and the king.

Beginning in 1769 Father Junípero Serra began a chain of missions in California, the northern part of Spain's empire. A road called The Royal Highway, or *El Camino Real* (EHL kah•MEE•noh ray•AHL), linked

Visualizing History

▲ SPAIN IN THE AMERICAS By the middle of the 1500s, Spain had established the base of a colonial empire in the Americas. Spain's empire was first settled by soldiers, adventurers, and missionaries. *What was the* encomienda *system?*

these missions. **Presidios,** or forts, were generally built nearby to protect the missions. Native peoples were brought to the missions to be fed, clothed, taught European methods of agriculture, and to attend religious instruction and services.

Section 2 ★ Review

Checking for Understanding

1. **Identify** Hernán Cortés, Francisco Pizarro, Junípero Serra, *El Camino Real.*

2. **Define** conquistador, *peninsulares,* creole, mestizo, mulatto, *encomienda,* viceroy, presidio.

3. **Discuss** the effects of Spanish colonization on the peoples of the West Indies.

4. **Summarize** the Spanish exploration and conquest of the American mainland.

Critical Thinking

5. **Verifying Predictions** Spanish explorers introduced horses to Native Americans. Predict how the lives of the Plains peoples in North America might have been significantly altered by having horses.

Study and Writing Skills

Asking Effective Questions

Effective questions are questions that serve a specific purpose and provide desired information. Asking effective questions involves a three-step process. If you ask questions without having a carefully planned strategy for doing so, much time can be wasted and confusion may result. Effective questions help you "get to the point" and allow you to better understand any given topic.

The three steps involved in developing effective questions are:

a. **Determine** what information you need to know.

b. **Decide** what materials or people you should consult.

c. **Consider** what questions you should ask.

For a report on the conquistadors, for example, important questions include: Who were the conquistadors? What were they doing in Spain before they came to America? How were they funded? What were their specific goals?

Having determined what it is you need to understand, the sources of information, and the topics that could be covered, you are prepared to ask questions as you read and absorb materials during your study of American history. By following these guidelines, the questions you ask will be effective ones.

▲ **PONCE DE LEÓN**

▲ **CONQUISTADORS IN AMERICA**

Practicing the Skill

For further practice in asking effective questions, apply the three steps to preparing a research report on one of the following:

a. Spanish conquistadors

b. the exploration of Amerigo Vespucci

c. Spanish missions in the Americas

d. life in Tenochtitlán

e. Ponce de León

★★★★★★★★★★★★★★★★★★★★★★★★★

New Ventures

Setting the Scene

Section Focus

Like the Spanish, the English, French, and Dutch sought a water route through the New World. In this search they explored the northern regions of the continent. Unlike the Spanish, though, they did not quickly establish colonies. For the first century or so, these nations' activities in the New World were neither as far-reaching nor as forceful as those of Spain.

Objectives

After studying this section, you should be able to

★ describe early English exploration of North America.

★ discuss French and Dutch colonization in North America.

Key Terms

northwest passage, Spanish Armada, mercantilism

◀ FRENCH HELMET

*A*lthough the English participated in early voyages of exploration, they failed to establish permanent colonies in America until the early 1600s. Poor finances, religious conflict, the colonization of Ireland, and the threat of war with Spain overshadowed English interest in the Americas.

In 1497 King Henry VII of England authorized John Cabot "to sayle to all partes, countreys, and seas, of the East, of the West, and of the North" and to discover new lands unknown to Christians. English merchants hoped that Cabot would discover a route to Asia. Cabot explored the shores of present-day Nova Scotia, Newfoundland, and Labrador. Like Columbus, Cabot believed he had found Asia. But when a second expedition found only the barren coasts of Labrador and Greenland, English interest in westward exploration and settlement waned.

■ Rivalry Between England and Spain

By the 1570s, however, Queen Elizabeth I had become increasingly anxious about Spain's growing global power. Wishing to challenge Spain's influence in the Americas—but fearing to do so openly—she secretly financed voyages by Martin Frobisher, whose purpose was to search for a **northwest passage** through North America to Asia. Frobisher explored the Atlantic coast of what is now Canada, but he too failed to find a route to the East.

On the High Seas

Elizabeth also gave her unofficial approval to piracy against Spanish ships and settlements. Daring English sea captains, such as Francis Drake, cruised the shores of Spanish America, capturing treasure ships, looting towns, and inflicting heavy damage to the Spanish. Because Spain was still the strongest power in Europe, however, the English did not attempt colonization in America or take any open action against the Spanish.

Defeat of the Spanish Armada

The eventual challenge to open conflict came from Spain rather than England. In 1588, seeking revenge for English attacks on Spanish ships and colonies, King Philip II of Spain dispatched a huge fleet of ships, known as the **Spanish Armada**, to sail against the English fleet. The "invincible armada" included 130 ships and 27,000 troops.

Although the English fleet was greatly outnumbered, their ships were faster and far easier to handle than the slow, heavy Spanish galleons. The English ships attacked the Spanish vessels one by one. Before a Spanish galleon could get close enough for its soldiers to board an English warship, it was pounded by artillery. The result was devastating to the Spanish fleet. The badly damaged armada was forced up the English Channel and into the North Sea. A fierce storm off the coast of Scotland further crippled the Spanish fleet. Only 60 to 70 ships returned to Spain. In a single battle, Spain had lost most of its naval forces. The way was now cleared for English colonization in the Americas.

Mercantilism

The age of exploration and colonization brought sweeping changes to European society and culture. Beginning in the 1600s, many European nations, including England, followed a theory of national economic policy called **mercantilism.** This theory held that a state's power depended on its wealth. Accordingly, the aim of every nation was to become as wealthy as possible.

Colonies played an important role in the mercantilist system. They were the sources of raw materials and provided markets for manufactured goods from the parent country. The goal of the colonies was to make the parent country self-sufficient. Mercantilism

▲ **Queen Elizabeth I**

helped England amass enormous national wealth that it used to build a colonial empire. Some other nations, however, found it more difficult to establish colonies.

■ French Presence in America

In 1524 the French king, Francis I, had sent Italian sea captain Giovanni da Verrazano to search for a northwest passage. Verrazano sailed the Atlantic coast from Newfoundland south to North Carolina. In 1534 Jacques Cartier made the first of three voyages to northern North America, searching for the elusive passage. Although he explored the St. Lawrence River as far as what is now Montreal, he also failed to find the passage. While French fishers sometimes visited North American waters, it was not until the early 1600s that the French made a serious attempt to establish a colony. In 1608 Samuel de Champlain founded Quebec on the banks of the St. Lawrence River. Few French settlers, however, were attracted to this northern outpost. In 1609 Champlain joined the Algonquian and Huron peoples in a raid against the Iroquois confederacy. Champlain described the hostilities:

French Fur Traders

In the early 1700s, the most stylish Europeans wore hats and other garments fashioned from felt

◀ **FUR TRADER**

cloth. Beaver furs from North America produced the highest quality and most durable felt. Pelts supplied by French fur traders were therefore highly prized. To keep the supply of furs constant, French traders maintained a close relationship with Native Americans who trapped the beaver.

The French government, hoping to keep the lucrative fur trade from the English, encouraged traders and settlers to live with the Algonquin. Many traders and missionaries moved into Algonquin villages.

As a result, the Algonquin changed the French colonists in America. Frenchmen married Algonquin women and raised their children as Algonquin. Other French settlers adopted Algonquin ways. In 1749 a Swedish traveler observed:

▲ **FRENCH MAP OF NORTH AMERICA, 1550**

"The French in Canada in many respects follow the customs of the Indians, with whom they have constant relations. They use the tobacco pipes, shoes, gaiters [leg coverings], and girdles [loincloths] of the Indians. They follow the Indian way of waging war exactly and have adopted many other Indian fashions."

> 66 *When I saw them getting ready to shoot their arrows at us, I leveled my arquebuse [gun] . . . and aimed straight at one of the three chiefs. The shot brought down two and wounded another. . . . The Iroquois were greatly astonished and frightened to see two of their men killed so quickly . . . they abandoned the field and fled into the depth of the forest.* 99

As a result of this battle, the formidable Iroquois warriors became sworn enemies of the French.

Exploration of the Mississippi

The French were generally confined to present-day Canada until the late 1600s. In 1673 Louis Joliet, an American-born fur trader, and the Jesuit priest Jacques Marquette embarked on a search for a river known to native Americans as the "big river"—the Mississippi. They canoed from St. Ignace on the northern tip of Lake Michigan to the Mississippi along inland waterways and followed it as far as the Arkansas River. In 1682 Robert de La Salle followed the Mississippi to its delta and claimed the vast lands drained by it for France. He named the region Louisiana.

Fur Trappers and Priests

The colonies established by France in North America formed a long string of outposts, extending from the Gulf of Mexico to Canada. French interests were directed largely toward the development of the fur trade. Beaver skins sent to France and made into hats were a particularly profitable item.

European Exploration of the New World

La Salle became the first European to trace the Mississippi River to its mouth on the Gulf of Mexico, claiming the Mississippi River valley for France.

In 1540 Coronado led an army overland from Mexico into the present-day United States. The forces reached Arizona, New Mexico, Texas, and Oklahoma but returned without finding any treasure.

Pizarro's conquest of the Inca strengthened Spain's role in South America and shaped the future of the continent.

← Spanish explorations
← French explorations

0   500   1,000 miles
0 500 1,000 kilometers

Map Study

European explorers searched endlessly for wealth and adventure in the Americas. Coronado traveled through the American southwest in search of mythical cities. He found no gold, but he introduced Native Americans to horses. *How far north did his expedition explore?*

Except with the Iroquois, the French generally had better relations with Native Americans than did the Spanish. French trappers and traders known as *coureurs de bois*—"runners of the woods"—did not threaten to take over Native American lands. They lived among the Native Americans, learned their ways, spoke their languages, and often married among them.

French missionaries, who were known to Native American peoples as "black robes," journeyed into the North American wilderness to convert Native Americans to Catholicism. Not accompanied by armies as

the Spanish missionaries were, the French Jesuits often suffered torture and death. In spite of their troubles, most of the Jesuits did not despair. One French priest wrote in the mid-1600s:

“ *Do not imagine that the . . . loss of many Christians can bring to nought the mystery of the cross of Jesus Christ. . . . We shall die; we shall be captured, burned, butchered: be it so. Those who die in their beds do not always die the best death.* ”

Disinterest in the Colonies

The French government had difficulty recruiting colonists for its North American settlements for several reasons. First of all, these colonies were not as valuable as French possessions in the West Indies—the islands of Guadeloupe, Martinique, and Saint Domingue, which all produced rich sugar crops. Second, most French rulers were more interested in extending their rule over European territory than in settling North America. In addition, the French missed an opportunity to gain an energetic group of settlers when they forbade French Protestants, known as Huguenots, to settle in America. Persecuted in France, many Huguenots would have gladly emigrated to America.

■ The Dutch in America

The Netherlands, which had won its independence from Spain in the late 1500s, was also interested in expansion. This small country had few natural resources and limited farmland. The key to survival, then, was to increase trade and commerce.

The period of the 1600s was the golden age of the Netherlands. Dutch ships were efficient, carrying more cargo and smaller crews than other ships, and the Dutch enjoyed a high standard of living.

Like the French, the Dutch were late in setting up colonies in North America. They were, however, making great strides in other parts of the world. The first Dutch expedition to the Far East returned in 1599. Three years later Dutch companies expanded trade with Asia. In 1619 Dutch traders set up headquarters in present-day Indonesia. Soon, the Dutch controlled island trade in sugar, spices, coffee, and tea.

They controlled the East Indies; set up the only trading post in Japan; maintained many West African slave ports; established a colony in Cape Town, South Africa; and had holdings in the Caribbean islands.

New Amsterdam

Dutch ventures on the North American continent were not nearly so impressive. In 1609 the Dutch East India Company funded an expedition by an English navigator, Henry Hudson. He reached New York Harbor and sailed up the river, which today bears his name, as far as present-day Albany, New York. The Dutch soon set up trading posts on Manhattan Island, which they named New Amsterdam, and along the Hudson River. A profitable fur trade was established with the Native Americans.

To attract settlers, the Dutch West Indies Company promised to give huge tracts of land along the Hudson and Delaware rivers to proprietors if at least 50 people could be hired and kept on the land. Few settlers, however, were interested. Although the Dutch colony was small, it contained a remarkable ethnic mix. One visitor reported that he had heard "eighteen different languages" being spoken in New Amsterdam in the mid-1600s. Because of poor leadership and weak government, though, the Dutch colony easily fell to the growing colonial influence of England in 1664.

Section 3 ★ Review

Checking for Understanding

1. **Identify** John Cabot, Jacques Cartier, Samuel de Champlain, Robert de La Salle, Henry Hudson.
2. **Define** northwest passage, Spanish Armada, mercantilism.
3. **Summarize** English voyages of exploration in North America.

4. **Contrast** patterns of French settlement with colonization patterns of other European nations.

Critical Thinking

5. **Citing Evidence** What evidence can you find of the importance of the Catholic faith to the French?

Using Vocabulary

Match each word or phrase with the correct definition below.

a. saga   e. strait

b. creole   f. *peninsulares*

c. *encomienda*   g. mestizo

d. armada   h. northwest passage

1. people born in the Spanish colonies of Spanish parents

2. people with Native American and Spanish parents

3. a fleet of ships

4. system of awarding conquistadors land and the right to collect taxes and labor

5. fabled water route through North America to the Pacific

6. long narrative

7. in the Spanish colonies, high officials born in Spain

8. a narrow body of water between two landmasses

Reviewing Facts

1. **Identify** the first Europeans to attempt to settle North America.

2. **Summarize** Spanish exploration, exploitation, and colonization in America.

3. **Describe** the class system in the Spanish colonies.

4. **Discuss** French exploration and settlement patterns in North America.

Understanding Concepts

Discovery and Exploration

1. What explorations were undertaken in search of something that was never found?

2. What discoveries were made when searching for something else?

Values and Beliefs

3. What role did religion play in the colonization of the Americas?

4. How did the religious values of the French rulers interfere with their efforts to attract French colonists to North America?

Critical Thinking

1. **Analyzing Motivation** Compare the motives of the early European explorers with those who explore areas such as outer space and the ocean floor today.

2. **Comparing Effects** Compare the effects of French and Spanish settlers on Native American peoples.

3. **Analyzing Art** Spanish priest Bartolomé de Las Casas devoted most of his life to speaking out for Native American peoples and condemning the brutality of Spanish troops in the Americas.

   a. Do you think this is a realistic portrait of Las Casas?

   b. Do you think the artist has captured the dignity of his subject? Explain.

▲ BARTOLOMÉ DE LAS CASAS

Writing About History

Argumentation

Imagine you are a friend of Columbus's. He is frustrated by his failure to persuade the monarchs of Europe to fund a voyage to find a water route around the world to Asia and has asked you to write a persuasive letter to King Ferdinand and Queen Isabella of Spain. Begin by describing the hardships of the land route to Asia, then present your solution.

Cooperative Learning

Work in a group of five to map the routes of Columbus, Magellan, Cabral, Cabot, and La Salle. Each member should research one explorer, then trace the route of that explorer on a single map large enough to display in the classroom or elsewhere in the school. Each member of the group should write a short paragraph on the explorer, describing his motivations, exploits, and significance.

Social Studies Skills

Using a Gazetteer

What if you wanted to find Cuba on a map, but you had no idea where it was located? To find out, you could look up *Cuba* in a gazetteer, a dictionary of geographical names.

A gazetteer lists geographical place-names in alphabetical order. Gazetteers differ somewhat, but most entries include a description, relative location, and exact location with map coordinates—latitude and longitude. The coordinates for Cuba are 22°N/79°W. To find this exact location on a map, simply find the correct latitudinal and longitudinal lines and follow them until they intersect.

Practicing the Skill

Study the gazetteer entries in the next column, then answer the questions that follow:

1. Which of the locations are found in the United States? Which are outside the United States?

2. What is the exact location of the Columbia River?

3. If Cuzco, the Incan capital in Peru, had been listed in the gazetteer, where would it have been placed?

4. Choose four geographic locations from the maps on pages 39 and 50, and write gazetteer entries for each of them, including latitude and longitude coordinates where possible.

5. Choose two cities that are in your home state and write complete gazetteer entries for them.

Columbia River river flowing through southwest Canada and northwestern United States into the Pacific Ocean (46°15′N/124°W)

Concord village northeast of Boston, Massachusetts; site of first battle of the American Revolution in 1775 (42°N/71°W)

Connecticut state in the northeastern United States (41°45′N/73°15′W)

Cuba country in the West Indies, North America (22°N/79°W)

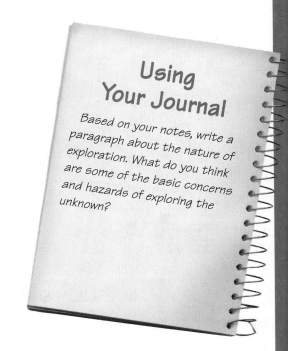

Using Your Journal

Based on your notes, write a paragraph about the nature of exploration. What do you think are some of the basic concerns and hazards of exploring the unknown?

CHAPTER 3

★★

Colonial America
1578–1776

▶ DOCTOR'S SADDLEBAG

Setting the Scene

Focus

The British entered the race for colonial empire in the Americas in the early 1600s. Although their early efforts were not as dramatic as those of the Spanish, the British colonies became the most populous American settlements within a century of colonization. The British used their colonies as a source of raw materials and a market for manufactured goods. In time, a distinctly new American society emerged. This in turn led to tensions and strained relations between the colonies and Great Britain.

Concepts to Understand

★ How migration from Europe shaped the character of colonial society
★ What political, social, and religious values and beliefs the colonists brought to America

Read to Discover . . .

★ what contributed to the growth and success of the Middle Colonies, New England, and the Southern Colonies.
★ in what ways Americans differed from the British by 1750.

Journal Notes

In what ways did religious groups exert their influence? Note details about it in your journal as you read the chapter.

CULTURAL	•**1598** *Spanish establish missions in present-day New Mexico*	•**1647** *Massachusetts establishes elementary schools*	•**1654** *First Jewish colonists arrive in New Amsterdam from Brazil*
	1570	**1610**	**1650**
POLITICAL	•**1607** *English found Jamestown*	•**1630** *Massachusetts Bay becomes a haven for Puritan dissenters*	•**1660** *Navigation Acts passed*

▼ COLONIAL GRINDSTONE

History AND ART

Hooker and Company Journeying through the Wilderness from Plymouth to Hartford in 1636 by Frederic Edwin Church, 1846

Many of Church's paintings show nature in repose. Like other artists aligned with the Hudson River School, Church focused on scenes of nature untouched by settlement.

- **1690** New England Primer, *first elementary textbook, published*

- **1741** *Height of "Great Awakening" religious revival*

- **1774** *Mozart writes Mass in F Major*

| 1690 | 1730 | 1770 |

- **1701** *French establish Fort Detroit*

- **1733** *Georgia, last British colony in North America, founded*

- **1772** *Americans set up committees of correspondence*

★★

The Southern Colonies

Setting the Scene

Section Focus

In the 1500s England's response to Spanish enterprise in America was nothing more creative than piracy of Spanish sea trade. By 1600, however, England had a naval power in the Atlantic, adequate finances for colonization, and a surplus population willing to take risks for religious, political, or economic reasons.

▲ WOOD PLANE, 1600S

Objectives

After studying this section, you should be able to
★ explain the effect of the environment on Virginia's settlement and lifestyle.
★ describe the economic conditions that influenced the development of the Southern Colonies.

Key Terms

indentured servant, proprietor, subsistence farming, naval stores

As early as 1578, Sir Humphrey Gilbert and Sir Walter Raleigh, his half brother, tried to plant a permanent English colony in North America. But on Gilbert's voyage back to England, his ships were lost at sea. In 1587 Raleigh sent 91 men, 17 women, and 9 children to settle on Roanoke Island near the coast of what is now North Carolina. He named the land "Virginia" in honor of the "Virgin Queen," Elizabeth I. This effort to build a colony failed because Spanish control of the Atlantic delayed Raleigh's efforts to resupply the settlement until after England defeated the Spanish Armada in 1588.

When English ships returned to Roanoke, they found none of the settlers. The only clue was a word carved on a tree—*CROATOAN*, the name of a Native American group and of a nearby island. The fate of the "Lost Colony" remains a mystery.

■ Jamestown, 1607

In 1606 King James I created the Virginia Company from two separate groups of merchants who had petitioned for permission to found colonies. Two divisions, the Virginia Company of London and the Virginia Company of Plymouth, were granted exclusive settlement rights in North America. The London group's charter permitted the planting of a colony in Virginia, where, it was believed, precious metals abounded.

The Struggle to Survive

In 1606 the London Company sent out 3 ships. After being driven back by Native Americans on the first attempted landing in Virginia, they sought a more secure place for a settlement on a peninsula 60 miles up the James River. There, in the spring of 1607, they founded Jamestown.

The long ocean voyage, an outbreak of disease in the swampy and unhealthy settlement site, attacks, and starvation worked against the colonists. Captain John Smith led the colony through some of its most trying times. Mixing friendship, force, bluff, and bargaining, he saved the starving colony by trading beads, knives, pots, and fish hooks for corn, vegetables, turkeys, and venison from Native Americans.

Some of Jamestown's difficulties resulted from the London Company's poor management. Houses and buildings were the immediate need for the colonists, but the company had sent only four carpenters. Jamestown was a business venture for the London Company, expected to make a profit for its shareholders. For this reason the company supplied jewelers and goldsmiths and "gentlemen" who wanted to look for gold—not carpenters to build houses or farmers to raise crops for survival.

The tragic result was that most of the 500 colonists who came in the first few years died. George Percy, one of the survivors, wrote of the sufferings at Jamestown:

66 *Our men were destroyed with cruell diseases as Swellings, Flixes, Burning Fevers, and by warres, and some departed suddenly, but for the most part they died of mere famine. There were never Englishmen left in a forreigne Countrey in such miserie. . . .* 99

Effective leadership might have spared Jamestown these hardships. As it was, John Smith, injured in a gunpowder explosion, had returned to England in 1609, and not until 1611 did the company supply a new governor.

The End of the London Company

Mismanagement eventually cost the London Company its charter. By 1616 the investment made by company shareholders had brought no real profits. The company's reform program of 1618 expanded land sales, extended English law and rights to

Settlement of the Colonies, 1587–1760

Map Study

England's American colonies were founded along the Atlantic coast from present-day Maine to Georgia. *How did rivers and natural harbors influence settlement?*

colonists, and allowed settlers to elect a representative assembly. Soon after, new recruits, including various craftspeople, arrived in Virginia. Even an additional 4,000 settlers did not end Virginia's troubles, however. Poor treatment of nearby Native Americans resulted in an attack that cost 350 lives. A royal investigation found that the badly governed settlers were dying faster

★★

Bride Ships

The first colonists of the London Company in 1607 to inhabit Jamestown were men. Women did not arrive until several years later. The population remained heavily male for nearly two decades. A ratio of 15 men to 1 woman was the norm.

The London Company decided that "The Plantacion can never flourish till families be planted and the respect of wives and Children fix the people on the Soyle." In 1619 the members of the first legislative assembly agreed: "In a newe plantation it is not knowen whether man or women be more necessary." To solve the problem of the shortage of women, the London Company sent the first "bride ship" to America. Its passengers included nearly 100 "young, handsome, and honestly educated maids" suitable for marriage.

Cost of transport for these maidens was paid by the London Company. The average payment for a bride by a Virginia colonist was 120 pounds of tobacco, or about $20.

After a few instances in which a woman became engaged to two men at the same time, the London Company stopped sending bride ships. Instead, a type of travel brochure was written boasting of the advantages of living in the Americas.

 ► **BRIDE SHIP ARRIVING AT JAMESTOWN**

★★

than they could be replaced. King James I dissolved the company and took control of the colony in 1624.

■ Growth of Virginia

From the native peoples, the settlers learned to grow corn, beans, squash, and tobacco. Despite the fact that King James I loathed tobacco, its use soon spread in England. As a result, tobacco became a profitable cash crop for Virginia. The native Virginia tobacco was of poor quality compared with that from the Spanish Caribbean islands, but in 1612 John Rolfe secured and planted some West Indies tobacco seeds. After this change, Virginia's tobacco exports grew rapidly. In 1640 almost 1.5 million pounds of tobacco entered the port of London.

Meeting the Demand for Labor

Tobacco, a labor-intensive crop, produced a great demand for colonists and farmers. Thousands of settlers streamed into Virginia, lured by the promise of free, abundant farmland. This source of labor was not enough, however.

To provide a work force, homeless children from the streets of London were sent to serve as apprentices to tradespeople in the colony. Convicts, farmers who had lost their lands, and the poor also came to share this opportunity.

A source of workers for wealthy settlers and tobacco farmers were the **indentured servants.** Indentured servants worked from four to seven years to pay off their passage across the Atlantic. After the period of indenture was completed, they were free to start their own farms.

The Introduction of Slave Labor

In 1619 a Dutch warship brought 20 enslaved Africans to Jamestown. Virginians, desiring an additional source of labor for their tobacco fields, purchased them. At first Africans were treated somewhat like indentured servants, many earning their freedom by several years of work. Slavery was first recognized in Virginia law in 1661. The following year, Virginia law declared that the status of a newborn child depended on the status of the mother. Slavery became a permanent, inherited condition. From 1600 to 1850, Europeans brought 15 million enslaved West Africans to the Americas.

■ Governing Virginia

In the 1660s an oversupply of tobacco pushed down its price. Only the very largest plantations were able to remain profitable. Many former indentured servants, now free, had to rent farmland or move west to

Economy of the Colonies

Cattle and grain
Tobacco
Rice and indigo
Fishing and whaling
Lumber and timber
Shipbuilding
Naval stores
Ironworks
Fur trapping

Colonial Trade Routes

Overseas trade routes
Coastal trade routes

Manufactured goods
Tobacco, fur, indigo, naval stores
Rice, fish, meat
Sugar, molasses, fruit wood
Flour, fish, meat, lumber
Sugar, molasses
Wine, fruit
Rum, iron bars
Slaves, gold

NORTH AMERICA
Boston
New York
Philadelphia
Charles Town
THE AMERICAN COLONIES
SOUTH AMERICA
ENGLAND
FRANCE
EUROPE
SPAIN
AFRICA
ATLANTIC OCEAN

Map Study The American colonies carried on trade among themselves and with distant ports across the Atlantic. *Make a list of the items that the colonies imported and those they exported.*

AMERICAN PORTRAITS

Margaret Brent
1601–1671

Born a Roman Catholic at a time when England was denying Catholics many civil rights, Margaret Brent moved to Maryland in 1638. She quickly became one of the largest landowners, and, according to colonial records, was the first woman to own land in her own name.

Brave and forceful, Brent helped put down a rebellion from neighboring Virginia, and she took charge of paying Maryland's troops. Refusing to be confined to the restricted life of most colonial women, she later served as attorney for Lord Baltimore, Maryland's proprietor.

Brent came into conflict with the colonial government when she appeared before the assembly and demanded the right to vote. After the governor denied her claim, she moved to a large plantation in Virginia. There, the woman some call "America's first feminist" lived the rest of her life.

---

the interior, where they were exposed to attack. These depressed economic conditions produced bands of homeless people who wandered through the colony. In June 1676, Nathaniel Bacon brought together many people who were angry with the government of Virginia. In September Bacon's force burned Jamestown; Bacon died of dysentery, however, in October. Leaderless, the rebellion lost its momentum.

Changes in Labor

Wealthy planters began to rely less upon indentured servants and more upon enslaved people. Unlike indentured servants, enslaved persons could be denied their freedom permanently and could be punished without appeal to the courts. Because they were black, identification was easy and escape difficult. African slavery expanded rapidly in Virginia after 1670.

The Growth of Self-Government

In the beginning Virginia had been ruled by a council and an appointed governor. In 1619, however, the London Company gave the settlers a voice in the government by permitting the first representative assembly in America, the House of Burgesses. These burgesses and a council appointed by the governor together made the laws. When King James I took control from the London Company, making Virginia a royal colony, he appointed the governor but allowed the House of Burgesses to continue.

Over the years the House of Burgesses gained more power. It assumed control over taxes that paid the governor's and other officials' salaries—the "power of the purse."

■ Other Southern Colonies

Proprietors colonized Maryland, the Carolinas, and Georgia. Like Virginia, these colonies built their economies on crops suited to the land.

Maryland

In 1632 King Charles I gave his friend George Calvert, Lord Baltimore, a grant of 10 million acres north of Virginia. Calvert became **proprietor** of the Maryland colony, meaning that he had authority over its government. By 1634 his son, Cecil Calvert, sent the first 200 settlers there. The Calverts intended Maryland to be a refuge for Catholics. Soon, however, more Protestants than Catholics were arriving. To protect Catholics from persecution, Cecil offered religious freedom to all Christian settlers. Later the legislative assembly of Maryland affirmed this freedom by the Toleration Act of 1649, the first of its kind in America.

Like Virginia, Maryland grew tobacco. Because of extensive farming, its towns were few and small. Baltimore, the chief city, had only 7,000 inhabitants by 1765.

The Carolinas

Profits from tobacco in Virginia and Maryland lured others to areas farther south along the Atlantic coast. In 1663 eight nobles received a grant to settle Carolina. From the start, northern Carolina was an area for **subsistence farming** where farmers grew only enough to live on. As northern Carolina grew, its principal exports became **naval stores**—tar, pitch, and turpentine—products of its pine forests that are used in shipbuilding.

Southern Carolina offered a better harbor than in the north and attracted more settlers. The first English colonists came from the West Indies island of Barbados to found the only major city in the South, Charles Town—present-day Charleston—in 1669. Some of these settlers had used slave labor on their sugar plantations in the Caribbean. With the thorough knowledge of rice-growing that the enslaved Africans brought, these settlers built plantations. Eliza Lucas, a settler from the West Indies, introduced the growing of indigo, a plant that produced a blue dye. By 1746 indigo had become an important cash crop.

Anthony Cooper, one of the proprietors, persuaded John Locke, an English political philosopher, to write a framework of government for South Carolina. The result was The Fundamental Constitutions of Carolina, providing for a legislature of wealthy nobles chosen by landholders. The proprietors surrendered control in 1729, and the king made both Carolinas royal colonies.

Georgia

Georgia, named after King George II, was the last of the 13 English colonies. Its proprietor, James Oglethorpe, a wealthy philanthropist and soldier, wanted Georgia to be both a refuge for debtors and a military outpost against the Spaniards in Florida. The first settlement, founded in 1733, was Savannah.

At first, Oglethorpe governed with strict controls, forbidding slavery and rum and controlling land sales. These restrictions limited Georgia's growth. In the 1740s the trustees who controlled Georgia lifted the restrictions against slavery and rum. They also let the colonists elect an assembly, but Georgia failed to prosper until after control was returned to the king in 1752.

Section 1 ★ Review

Checking for Understanding

1. **Define** indentured servant, proprietor, subsistence farming, naval stores.

2. **Compare** the organizations that established and governed the Southern Colonies with those that governed European nations.

3. **Explain** the factors that created hardships and initially limited the success of the Virginia colonies.

4. **Relate** the economic activity and conditions that prevailed in early Virginia to the development of the class system and slavery.

Critical Thinking

5. **Evaluating Social Changes** Planters prospered by growing tobacco. Today we know tobacco is an unhealthy substance. If tobacco were discovered today, do you think our government would permit its sale? Explain.

Stock Exchanges

The age of exploration brought sweeping changes to European society and to culture. Overseas trade and colonial ventures stimulated the European economy and helped it develop and grow. Business practices and banking practices soon became more sophisticated in order to facilitate profit from the flourishing world trade.

Launching an overseas trading venture was a major financial undertaking. Merchants in the sixteenth century reduced the risks of ocean trade by forming trading companies. Governments of western European states controlled the trade of their merchants and provided company charters that included the rights of stock ownership. Shares of stock allow the buyer a certain part of the future profits and assets of the company selling the stock. The person buying stock, therefore, becomes part owner of a company.

The early trading companies eventually led to the establishment of joint-stock companies such as the Dutch United East India Company, formed in the early 1600s. In order to sell large blocks of shares to investors, this company created a stock exchange in Amsterdam. The money raised became a permanent fund the company could draw money from when it initiated trading ventures.

In 1650 the English adopted the Dutch method of creating a permanent fund to finance trading enterprises. Before 1773, however, when English investors wanted to buy or sell shares of stock, they had to locate a broker to carry out their transactions. Then the London brokers founded the first English stock

▲ COUNTING HOUSE

exchange. The first stock exchanges in the United States were organized in Philadelphia in 1791 and in New York City a year later.

Not all the trading companies made money. England's Virginia Company was a costly failure, as were other European companies. By 1700, however, joint-stock companies had proved that free enterprise could raise the capital necessary for costly ventures, regardless of the risk.

Making the Economics Connection

1. Why did merchants form joint-stock companies?
2. What advantage did the Dutch United East India Company have over English companies in 1690?

Linking Past And Present

3. What is a stock exchange? Do you consider buying stock today a form of investment or savings? Explain.

★★★★★★★★★★★★★★★★★★★★★★★★

New England

Setting the Scene

Section Focus

The Virginia Company of Plymouth sent Captain John Smith to explore the region north of Virginia, which he named "New England." When New England was settled, it was by accident rather than design by people seeking a religious haven, not investors seeking a fortune.

Objectives

After studying this section, you should be able to

★ explain the relationship of church and state in the New England colonies.

★ list three reasons why self-government developed in New England.

Key Terms

dissenter, congregation, commonwealth, constitution

▲ WILLIAM BRADFORD'S BIBLE

The Church of England—the Anglican Church—broke away from the Catholic Church in 1534. Some Anglicans, called Puritans, believed that the Church of England had not done enough to "purify" itself of all symbols of Catholic worship. Most Puritans wanted to reform the Church of England. One group, called Separatists, believed that it was better to separate themselves entirely and to form their own church. Because the Anglican Church was the official state church, Separatists, like all other religious **dissenters,** or protesters, faced persecution, jail, and even death.

In 1607 a group of Separatists, soon to be known as Pilgrims, left England to escape persecution. They settled in Holland (known today as the Netherlands), where, despite the freedom to worship as they pleased, they were dissatisfied. Their children grew up speaking a different language and learning new customs. Where might they maintain their language, customs, and form of worship? America beckoned.

■ On to Plymouth

In 1619 the Pilgrims secured a grant of land in Virginia from the London Company. After much preparation, in September 1620, 73 men and boys and 29 women and girls set sail on the *Mayflower* from Plymouth, England. Violent storms blew the ship off course. In November the ship landed far to the north of Virginia on the Massachusetts coast. Because they had no charter for an area outside the control of the London Company, the Pilgrims drew up the Mayflower Compact. It was a simple document that expressed their feelings that a government derives its just powers from the people who are governed.

The First Year's Hardships

In the bleak, cold, snowy New England winter, the Pilgrims, like the Virginia colonists, had their "starving time." By spring almost half of them had died. Even the few survivors might have starved if it had not been for Squanto of the Pawtuxet people, who taught them about their new environment. William Bradford, one of the colonists, wrote that Squanto "directed them how to set their corn, where to take fish, and to procure other commodities" and that he was also their pilot "to bring them to unknown places for their profit, and never left them until he died."

The First Thanksgiving

The Pilgrims' deep sense of religious purpose and determination to endure hardships sustained the colony. In 1621 the survivors elected Bradford governor, a post that he would hold for more than 30 years. In the spring they planted crops. A good harvest in the autumn and the arrival of more provisions on the ship *Fortune* inspired a day of thanksgiving to God.

More Settlers Arrive

Additional settlers from England built a cluster of small villages near Plymouth, but the colony never became very large. It elected its own officials and ran its own affairs until 1691, when it became part of the larger Massachusetts Bay Colony.

■ Puritan Massachusetts

In 1625 when Charles I became king of England, he decided to rule without Parliament and to suppress Puritanism. When Puritan ministers were deprived of their pulpits, the dissenters turned their thoughts

Visualizing History

▲ SIGNING THE MAYFLOWER COMPACT Pilgrims on board the *Mayflower* signed a compact, or agreement, to obey the officers elected and the laws passed. All those who signed received the right to share in the government. *What was the intent of the Compact?*

▲ *PILGRIMS GOING TO CHURCH* by George H. Boughton, 1867 Religion was important in Pilgrim life. ***What evidence shown in this picture suggests that the settlers did not yet feel safe?***

to America. Several prominent Puritans bought a trading company, changed its name to the Massachusetts Bay Company, and secured a charter directly from the king. Twelve members signed an agreement at Cambridge in 1629.

This marked the beginning of the great Puritan migrations to New England to build a Christian society they believed would be a lighthouse for all the world. The first governor of Massachusetts, John Winthrop, made their intentions clear:

> **❝** *We shall be as a city upon a hill. The eyes of all people are upon us.* **❞**

In 1630, 17 ships with about 1,000 Puritan settlers sailed for Massachusetts. During the next 10 years, 20,000 settlers followed. Boston, the leading town, and surrounding settlements such as Dorchester, Roxbury, Watertown, and Charlestown, flourished.

Congregationalists

When they left England, the Puritans thought of themselves as members of the Anglican Church. As they settled Massachusetts, they organized their churches under ministers elected by each **congregation,** or a body of church members. The ministers set about reforming religious ceremonies, while the congregation became the final authority on church decisions. Compared to the Anglican clergy, the New England minister had limited authority. He was to teach, preach, pray, and administer; but the congregation held power over membership and church discipline. In the colonies, the Puritans became known as Congregationalists.

From Trading Company to Commonwealth

The Massachusetts Bay charter, unlike those of other colonies, did not specify the location of the company's headquarters or where its shareholders' meetings would be held. Taking advantage of this loophole, the shareholders voted to move the company from England to Massachusetts. Governor John Winthrop carried the charter across the Atlantic Ocean, where shareholders would have more freedom from the king's control. Winthrop transformed the Massachusetts Bay Company from a trading company into a **commonwealth**, a self-governing political unit, the first of its kind in America.

In the beginning, the few shareholders of the Massachusetts Bay Company, called "freemen," held all the power in the colony. Under Governor Winthrop, these shareholders made up the General Court, or the lawmaking body. Soon, however, more

The American Colonies, 1607–1776

Colony and date of settlement	Founders	Type of government
NEW ENGLAND		
Plymouth Colony 1620	Pilgrims	Charter, 1620–1686; Part of Massachusetts, 1691–1776
New Hampshire 1623	Puritans, Proprietors	Proprietary, 1629–1679; Royal, 1679–1776
Massachusetts Colony 1630	Puritans	Charter, 1629–1686; Royal, 1691–1776
Rhode Island 1636	Roger Williams	Charter, 1644–1776
Connecticut 1636	Thomas Hooker	Charter, 1662–1776
MIDDLE COLONIES		
New York (New Netherland) 1626	Dutch West India Company	Dutch charter, 1626–1664; Proprietary, 1664–1685; Royal, 1685-1776
New Jersey (as part of New Netherland 1626	Dutch West India Company	Dutch charter, 1626–1664; Proprietary, 1664–1702; Royal, 1702-1776
Delaware (New Sweden) 1638	Swedish West India Company	Swedish charter, 1638–1655; Dutch charter, 1655–1664; Proprietary, 1664–1776
Pennsylvania 1682	William Penn	Proprietary, 1681–1776
SOUTHERN COLONIES		
Virginia 1607	London Company	Charter, 1606–1624; Royal, 1624–1776
Maryland 1634	George Calvert (Lord Baltimore)	Proprietary, 1632–1691; Royal, 1691–1715; Proprietary, 1715–1776
North Carolina 1650	Proprietors	Proprietary, 1663–1729; Royal, 1729–1776
South Carolina 1670	Proprietors	Proprietary, 1663–1729; Royal, 1729–1776
Georgia 1733	James Oglethorpe	Proprietary, 1732–1752; Royal, 1752–1776

Chart Study

Most of the 13 colonies (Plymouth became part of Massachusetts) were founded under charters issued to investing companies. By 1752, however, 8 colonies had come under the direct control of the monarch. *How many colonies that were once controlled by proprietors became royal colonies?*

than 100 colonists demanded to be admitted to the company as freemen. Under pressure, Governor Winthrop consented to the demands of the freemen.

A law passed in 1631 gave all Puritan men who were church members admission to the General Court as freemen. When the population grew too large to operate the government in this way, the Massachusetts Bay Company made a change. The company allowed the freemen in each town to elect two representatives to the General Court. What began as a directors' meeting of a trading company ended up as a colonial legislature with power to make law.

■ Dissent and Division

The Puritans who came to Massachusetts to worship as they pleased had no intention of granting this freedom to others. They drove out Baptists, Quakers, and others who disagreed with them. Others simply left to find more fertile land. Those who left founded other colonies in New England.

Rhode Island

Roger Williams arrived in the Massachusetts Bay Colony in 1631. According to William Bradford, Williams was "a man godly and zealous but very unsettled in judgment." When Williams became pastor of a church in Salem, he began to raise embarrassing issues. He preached that the church and government should remain separate because involvement in political affairs would corrupt the church. He also asserted that the colonists had no right to settle on the land unless the land was purchased from the Native American people. Finally, he challenged the right of Puritan rulers to compel people to take part in religious services. Because Williams's views threatened basic Puritan ideas, Winthrop and the General Court banished him from the colony.

▲ ANNE HUTCHINSON

Facing deportation to England, Williams fled south and spent the winter with friendly Wampanoags. In 1636 he started the colony of Rhode Island on land purchased from the Native Americans. The new colony, chartered in 1644, welcomed Jews as well as all Christians and guaranteed their religious freedom. In Rhode Island church and state were completely separate, a principle that was to become an important part of America's political heritage.

New Settlements

Not long after Williams departed, Massachusetts faced a similar challenge. Anne Hutchinson began to openly challenge Puritan ministers and their interpretations of the Bible. When her teachings attracted a growing band of disciples, authorities brought her to trial. Ordered to leave the colony, she went to Rhode Island to begin a new settlement later called Portsmouth.

In 1637 the Reverend John Wheelwright, one of the few ministers Anne Hutchinson admired, was also expelled from Massachusetts for criticizing Puritan teaching. He and his followers settled in New Hampshire. Following the example of the Mayflower Compact, they created and signed the Exeter Compact and set up a civil government. In 1679 New Hampshire obtained a charter from King Charles II. Other pioneer settlers pushed farther north into Maine, which remained part of Massachusetts until 1820.

In 1636 settlers who wanted richer farmland and more freedom followed Thomas Hooker, a Puritan minister, to the fertile valley of the Connecticut River. Hartford and a series of other "river towns" sprang up along the river. Later, these communities annexed New Haven and other towns to form the colony of Connecticut. In 1639 the colony adopted the Fundamental Orders of Connecticut, the first written **constitution**, or plan of government, in America. It provided for a representative government similar to the one in Massachusetts, except that voting for representatives and government was not limited to church members.

Section 2 ★ Review

Checking for Understanding

1. **Identify** Mayflower Compact, Squanto, Roger Williams, Anne Hutchinson, Exeter Compact.

2. **Define** dissenter, congregation, commonwealth, constitution.

3. **Explain** the objectives of the Puritans and Pilgrims in settling the Massachusetts Bay Colony.

4. **Discuss** the relationship of church and state in New England.

Critical Thinking

5. **Analyzing Motives** Most New England colonies were settled by people escaping religious persecution. Which of these groups sought true religious freedom? How did they differ from the others?

Interpreting Primary Sources

▲ PURITANS SUBJECTING WRONGDOERS TO PUBLIC RIDICULE

Women in the Colonies

Historians have used documents, such as the following from the records of the Suffolk County Court in Massachusetts, to uncover information about colonial women. Read the excerpts below and answer the questions.

Order abt Hitt (8 July, 1674)

In Answer to the request of Anne Hitt widdow . . . that Shee might have Liberty to dispose of & put to Sale some part of [her husband's] Estate for the paiment of debts & Legacies & maintenance of herselfe & Children: The Court Orders & Empowres the saide Anne Hitt (with the consent & advice) of those that are Sureties for her true Administracion upon the saide Estate) to dispose of & put to Sale the house & ground at Charlestown valued in the Inventory at £:170. Shee rendring an Account of Sd Sale unto the Court of this County.

Walsebee's discharge (28 April, 1674)

The wife of David Walsebee of Brantery being presented for her Idleness and sottish carriage [drunken behavior]. *upon hearing of the case The Court judge there is noe ground for the presentment & soe discharge her.*

Examining the Primary Source

1. List examples in the colonial documents of alphabetical, spelling, and capitalization changes that have appeared in the English language since these documents were written.

2. What freedom was originally denied Anne Hitt that resulted in the court order?

Critical Thinking

3. **Drawing Conclusions** What does the charge against the wife of David Walsebee indicate about the manners expected of women?

68

★★★

The Middle Colonies

Setting the Scene

Section Focus

From 1640 to 1660 a bitter struggle for power between the king and Parliament postponed further colonization in America. Parliament overthrew King Charles I in 1649 and established a commonwealth under Puritan Oliver Cromwell. When the monarchy was restored in 1660, the new king, Charles II, revived English interest in starting new colonies. He rewarded some of his supporters by granting them proprietorships. These became the Middle Colonies.

Objectives

After studying this section, you should be able to

★ describe the role of proprietors in the development of the Middle Colonies.

★ give reasons for Pennsylvania's rapid growth.

Key Term

patroon

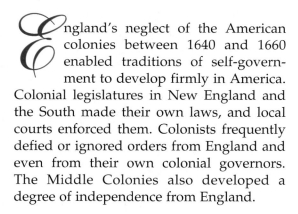

▶ PINE TREE SHILLING, 1652

*E*ngland's neglect of the American colonies between 1640 and 1660 enabled traditions of self-government to develop firmly in America. Colonial legislatures in New England and the South made their own laws, and local courts enforced them. Colonists frequently defied or ignored orders from England and even from their own colonial governors. The Middle Colonies also developed a degree of independence from England.

New York

In 1664 King Charles II granted his brother James, the Duke of York, the land west and south of New England, from the Connecticut River to the Delaware River. He did this even though the territory had already been settled by the Dutch. For years the English had viewed the Dutch colony as a threat because of its trade, its expanding settlements, and its location as a wedge between New England to the north and Virginia to the south. Consequently, in 1664 the Duke of York sent a fleet of four English warships to capture the settlement of New Amsterdam. Peter Stuyvesant (STY•vuh•sant), the Dutch governor of New Netherland, tried to defend the colony. But he lacked the support of his own colonists and was forced to surrender New Netherland without a struggle. The Duke of York did not hesitate to change the colony's name to New York.

Colonial Government

Governors appointed by the Duke of York ruled New York until 1683, when the Duke agreed to demands for an elected representative assembly. Two years later, however, the Duke of York became King James II,

Visualizing History

▲ **CLAIMS FOR THE NETHERLANDS** While the Spaniards searched for gold and the French searched for furs, Dutch leaders wanted new lands for trade centers. ***What factors limited the growth of New York?***

making New York a royal colony. He dissolved the assembly and returned full power to the governor.

When the English overthrew James II in the Glorious Revolution of 1688, Jacob Leisler, a German trader, led a rebellion in New York. He established a government with an elected assembly that lasted until 1690, when a new British royal governor arrived. The new governor captured Leisler and put him on trial. Leisler was convicted and the governor had him hanged. The governor, however, permitted the colony to continue to elect an assembly.

Limited Growth

Several factors delayed New York's rapid growth. Few settlers came because large landowners, called **patroons,** still held much of the land along the Hudson River. The French in Canada prevented expansion to the north, and the Iroquois Confederacy blocked expansion westward. New York City's magnificent harbor made it a natural trade center, but for many years the small population of the colony did not supply enough goods for export.

A Diverse Population

New York's varied population included Dutch, Swedes, Native Americans, Africans, Jews, some English and French settlers, and people of many other nationalities. But Dutch customs remained strong, and the Dutch Calvinist churches endured. The city, as it appeared in 1679, was described by a Dutch traveler, Jasper Dankers:

> *[The fort] has only one gate, and that is on the land side, opening upon a broad plain or street, called the Broadway or Beaver-way. Over this gate are the arms of the Duke of York. . . . We went on up the hill, along open roads and a little woods, through the first village, called Breukelen [Brooklyn]. . . .*

■ New Jersey

Shortly after the Duke of York received his grant of land in 1664, he started giving out parts of it to his friends. He gave New

Jersey to John Lord Berkeley and Sir George Carteret. Finding it sparsely inhabited, these proprietors offered religious freedom and large land grants.

In 1674 Berkeley sold his proprietary rights in western New Jersey to members of a religious group called the Society of Friends, or Quakers, who were seeking escape from persecution. In 1682 Carteret's heirs sold eastern New Jersey to another Quaker group. The English government created the royal colony of New Jersey by combining the two parts, placing it under the authority of New York's governor in 1702.

Penn's Colonies

William Penn started the most successful colony in America. The son of a British admiral, Penn won the favor of both King Charles II and King James II. To his father's dismay, however, Penn had joined the Quakers when he was a student at

Oxford. Quakers were considered religious radicals in England because they believed that paid clergy were unnecessary and that every person could know God's will through his or her own "inner light." They were detested in England and persecuted as anarchists in America.

Pennsylvania

Neither his father's anger nor jail could make Penn give up his views, and King Charles II remained his friend. Penn wanted to start a colony in America that would serve as a refuge for persecuted Quakers. After his father's death, Penn took advantage of a debt that Charles II owed Admiral Penn, asking the king for land in America. In 1681 Charles II made Penn the proprietor of a vast area west of the Delaware named "Penn's Woods," or Pennsylvania.

Arriving in Pennsylvania in 1682, Penn worked out a plan for a "city of brotherly love," Philadelphia. His agents advertised

▲ WILLIAM PENN

▲ *WILLIAM PENN'S TREATY WITH THE INDIANS* by Edward Hicks, 1830–1840 Although the overall English policy toward Native Americans was harsh, some settlers did treat the Native Americans favorably. *What details in the painting give you clues about the Native Americans' relationship with William Penn?*

▲ PHILADELPHIA William Penn founded Philadelphia on the west banks of the Delaware River not far from the Atlantic coast. The city grew quickly and by the middle of the 1700s was the largest city in the American colonies. *What was the first major task in a new settlement?*

for settlers from Europe. Their promises of religious freedom and tolerance attracted many other groups besides the Quakers, especially Germans.

Because Penn believed in equality, he drew up a "Frame of Government" that provided for an elected council and an assembly. Pennsylvania gave the right to vote to a large number of colonists. Penn also insisted that Native Americans be paid for their land.

These measures meant rapid growth for the colony. By the time Penn left for England in 1684, there were 7,000 colonists. When he returned in 1699, Philadelphia rivaled Boston and New York City as both a commercial and cultural center. Thousands of prosperous farms dotted the countryside.

A boundary dispute with Maryland to the south led to the hiring of two surveyors, Mason and Dixon, to draw borders between the two colonies. This border became known as the Mason-Dixon Line.

Delaware

In 1682 William Penn bought the three counties south of Pennsylvania along the Atlantic Coast from the Duke of York. These "lower counties," known as Delaware, had first been settled by the Dutch, then the Swedes, before the English captured them in 1664. Although Delaware was not part of Penn's grant from the king, he allowed the lower counties to elect their own assembly.

Section 3 ★ Review

Checking for Understanding

1. **Identify** Quakers, Duke of York, William Penn, Mason and Dixon.

2. **Define** patroon.

3. **Discuss** the role of proprietors in the political and economic development of the Middle Colonies. Compare how they pursued their personal goals.

4. **Explain** the conditions, in England and in the Middle Colonies, that supported the development of self-government in the Middle Colonies.

Critical Thinking

5. **Supporting an Opinion** Argue for or against this statement: In the Middle Colonies, democracy developed more because of its economic advantages than because of ideology.

★★★

People of the Colonies

Setting the Scene

Focus

By the mid-1700s, colonial society differed from Britain in many ways. A diversity of peoples and new economic opportunities helped to produce a society uniquely American. The history of social development in America is a story of progress for many. It is blemished by the enslavement of Africans and the eviction of Native Americans from their lands.

Objectives

After studying this section, you should be able to

★ describe social class and the role of women, indentured servants, and African Americans.

★ discuss the relationship between English colonists and Native Americans.

★ explain why religious toleration and freedom developed during the colonial period.

Key Term

gentry

◀ CHILDREN'S DOLLS

By European standards the society of Elizabethan England was remarkably mobile. An apprentice might become rich and marry his daughter to a noble. In turn, a noble's younger son, who inherited no property, might become an apprentice or hire himself out as a soldier. Like England, the colonies' social structure had many classes, but from the start it was more democratic.

■ Colonial Social Classes

In each of the 13 colonies there was an upper class. In New England, merchants, shipowners, and the clergy composed this class. In the South and along the Hudson River in New York, great landowners imitated the country **gentry**, or upper class, of England. Early colonial laws permitted only upper-class men to wear silver buttons and upper-class women and girls to wear silk dresses. Social rank was indicated on marriage certificates and even on tombstones.

Near the bottom of society were indentured servants, bound by contract to work in the colonies in return for their passage to America. When the contract expired, the servant was free to work for wages. Because labor was scarce, wages in the colonies were 2 or 3 times those in England. Indentured servants could move up in society. For example, in the 1660s, 13 of 28 members of the Virginia House of Burgesses had come to the colony as indentured servants.

Life in the Colonies

For most people, life in colonial America was better than it had been in Europe. Still, many died within the first year because of hardships encountered during the ocean voyage. Frontier settlements faced conflict

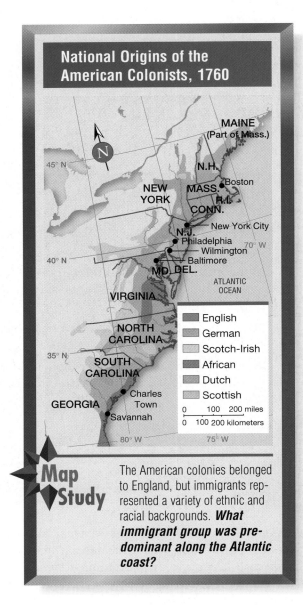

National Origins of the American Colonists, 1760

MAINE
(Part of Mass.)

45° N

N.H.

NEW
YORK

MASS.
Boston

CONN.

R.I.

New York City

N.J.

Philadelphia

70° W

Wilmington

40° N

Baltimore

MD. DEL.

ATLANTIC
OCEAN

VIRGINIA

NORTH
CAROLINA

35° N

SOUTH
CAROLINA

GEORGIA

Charles
Town

Savannah

80° W   75° W

English
German
Scotch-Irish
African
Dutch
Scottish

0   100   200 miles
0 100 200 kilometers

Map Study

The American colonies belonged to England, but immigrants represented a variety of ethnic and racial backgrounds. *What immigrant group was predominant along the Atlantic coast?*

per woman in New England—and the long period of colonial history—1607 to 1776—meant that most of these were born in the colonies. From about the time of the founding of Pennsylvania in 1681, people of different nationalities and religions—Scots, Irish Catholics, French Huguenots, Spanish Jews, and German Protestants—arrived in increasing numbers. Together with the Dutch in New York, these accounted for nearly one-third of the colonists.

Beginning in Virginia in 1619, the first enslaved Africans were brought by the Dutch from the West Indies. Africans, both enslaved and free, made up about 20 percent of the total population. The proportion of African Americans was highest in the Southern Colonies because slave labor proved profitable on rice and tobacco plantations. In South Carolina three out of four people were enslaved Africans.

■ Women in the Colonies

English colonial population grew rapidly because proportionately there were more women than in the Spanish and French colonies. The only respectable option for women at that time was thought to be marriage. As in all European societies of the time, women were denied higher education. Women generally married in their early twenties and had five or six children. Their principal task was rearing children, although most women died during the child-bearing years.

The second occupation for most women was farming. A farm could not carry on without the skills of women in making cloth, garments, candles, soap, and breadstuffs. A visitor to the North Carolina-Virginia border region in 1710 gave this description of a frontierswoman:

with Native Americans, starvation due to crop failures, disastrous fires, and epidemics of smallpox, dysentery, malaria, diphtheria, and yellow fever.

By the 1700s conditions had improved, although epidemics continued to make life uncertain. There was widespread prosperity—a product of cheap land, a ready market for colonial exports, and hard work. Idleness was generally regarded as a sin like drunkenness or gluttony.

The Colonies' Varied Population

By 1775 people of English origin accounted for just under half the population. The high birthrate—an average of seven births

“ *. . . [S]he is a very civil woman and shows nothing of ruggedness or Immodesty in her carriage, yett she will carry a gunn in the woods and kill deer, turkeys, etc., shoot down wild cattle, catch and tye hoggs. . . .* ”

In the South plantation wives helped direct the workforce. When seafaring New England husbands left their wives, sometimes for years at a time, women were successful as merchants or storekeepers. Widespread home manufacturing allowed women to learn trades. Some women were printers, publishers, druggists, and doctors.

■ Slavery in the Colonies

At first it was not clear that enslaved Africans were to be treated differently from white indentured servants. Gradually legal distinctions were adopted. Indentured servants retained the rights of English people and the protection of the law. Africans were protected by no law or tradition. The South gave marriages between enslaved persons no legality, and children could be sold away from their mothers. Enslaved persons could own no property and had little legal protection against irresponsible or cruel owners.

Slavery and the Southern Plantation System

Slave labor was adopted for the southern plantations, where the work was done in fields and easily overseen. The profits of large plantations made slavery seem necessary to the South's prosperity. Southern colonial laws declared Africans to be enslaved for life. It was illegal to teach Africans to read for fear that learning would spoil them for physical labor.

There were, in the South, slaveholders who disapproved of slavery but hesitated to act on their feelings because free blacks faced serious discrimination. In addition, whites feared them as possible leaders of slave insurrections. Most southern colonies passed laws that made it difficult to give enslaved people their freedom.

Slavery in the North

In the North, slavery was less profitable and enslaved people less numerous. New England not only allowed, but required, people who were enslaved to marry; they could acquire property and testify in court. An owner might punish a slave, but an owner who killed a slave could be charged with murder. A growing number of people argued that slavery was a moral wrong.

In Pennsylvania, Quakers and Mennonites, a German religious sect, denounced slavery. The number of free African Americans increased. In Jaffrey, New Hampshire, Amos Fortune bought other African Americans out of slavery and left money for the town school. But the northern colonies did not permit equality to free African Americans. Custom usually kept them in menial positions, and the laws denied them the right to vote or hold office.

■ Native Americans

The first meetings between English settlers and Native Americans gave little evidence of the eventual destruction of the Native Americans' ways of life. A few colonial leaders, notably Roger Williams and William Penn, tried to treat them fairly, and

Visualizing History

▲ THE SLAVE TRADE Trade that furnished Africans to American markets was a horrible example of inhumanity. It has been estimated that about 30 percent of the enslaved Africans died crossing the Atlantic. *How were Africans treated in the northern colonies?*

some Protestant ministers regarded the native people principally as souls to be brought to knowledge of Christ.

Who Owns the Land?

The expansion of colonial farms became the principal cause of numerous conflicts. The colonists reasoned that since Native Americans did not have settled dwellings, but were on the move like "the foxes and wild beasts . . . so it is lawful now to take a land which none useth; and make use of it."

Some of the conflicts resulted from misunderstandings each culture had of the other's values. Europeans viewed land ownership as essential to progress.

Individual native peoples did not own land, but jointly shared territory with all the members of the group. In general, Native Americans adapted their lifestyles to suit the physical surroundings. Native Americans viewed the land as a resource to be used and left unchanged. Native Americans who sold or by treaty gave up lands did so without any authority, since no chief could dispose of land.

Visualizing History ▼ COLONIAL POLITICS A twentieth-century artist provided this view of a political discussion in colonial America. *What options did colonial women have for careers?*

Colonists justified wars against Native Americans in many ways. Some Puritan ministers even claimed that Native Americans were children of the devil, so they could be killed in good conscience.

Weapons of Conquest

Individually, a colonist may not have been a match for a brave who had learned the art of war in struggles over territory, but because of sheer numbers and weapons the whites were destined to win. They also had grim allies in diseases such as smallpox. European diseases sometimes wiped out whole Native American communities that had not developed immunities. Of the estimated 120,000 Native Americans who had lived in the area occupied by the 13 colonies, perhaps only 20,000 survived. Most native nations, too small to resist, simply disappeared as social units. The Iroquois Confederacy was the only group that had the ability to protect its members from destruction.

■ The Colonial Mind

Although many came to America to worship as they pleased, they were not ready to grant others the same privilege. In New England and the Southern Colonies, a single official church was "established"—that is, supported by taxes. Massachusetts Puritans believed that religious toleration was a weakness inspired by the devil. Anyone who advocated it would suffer the consequences. While they expelled many like Roger Williams, they hanged Quakers on Boston Common. Virginia, on the other hand, expelled ministers from Massachusetts.

The Great Awakening

In the 1740s the colonies experienced a religious revival called the Great Awakening. Some Puritan ministers in Massachusetts, concerned over declining religious fervor in their communities, began to preach sermons that warned of the impending dangers of hell. They were influenced by Jonathan Edwards, one of America's greatest colonial Christian theologians. As ministers took sides favoring or opposing the revivalists, new churches sprang up. The diversity of churches helped to make religious toleration even more essential. Other products of the revival were new colleges such as Princeton, Brown, Rutgers, and Dartmouth.

By the late 1700s, open religious persecution in the colonies was largely a thing of the past, although not all religious groups were equal before the law. Visitors from other countries were especially struck by the freedom granted Jews, who still suffered severe persecution in most European countries.

Education in the Colonies

History AND ART

The Puritans believed that citizens should learn enough English to read the Bible and understand the laws. The Massachusetts General School Act of 1647 stated two principles of education that remain today: local communities have a duty to set up schools, and this duty is enforced by law.

In the Middle Colonies, schooling was not as universal as in New England, but it was widespread. In the Southern Colonies, formal education was generally limited to children of large landowners and professionals. Even where schools were desired, the widely separated plantations and farms of the South made them impractical.

By modern standards schools in the colonies were primitive. There were few books, and instruction was given only two or three months a year. Most girls received little formal education. Two-thirds of the women whose names appear on Massachusetts legal documents in the early 1700s could not write their signatures. Despite these shortcomings, no other region of equal size in the world had such a high proportion of the population that could read and write.

▲ THE MASON CHILDREN: DAVID, JOANNA, AND ABIGAIL unknown artist, c. 1670 Usually a person's place in colonial society was obvious from his or her appearance and dress. **What can you conclude about the children's family from this painting?**

Religion was the principal force behind most institutions of higher learning in the colonies. The earliest colleges—Harvard, William and Mary, and Yale—were founded to train young men for the ministry.

The Influence of the Enlightenment

By the middle of the eighteenth century, the college curriculum began to change, as interest in science and a demand for practical subjects arose. When King's College—later Columbia—opened in New York City in 1754, it announced that studies would include not only the traditional Latin, Greek, and Hebrew, but also:

“ *Surveying and Navigation, Geography, History, Husbandry, Commerce, Government, the Knowledge of All Nature in the Heavens above us and in the Air, Water, and Earth Around us. . . .* ”

▲ FREEDOM OF THE PRESS John Peter Zenger, publisher of the *New York Weekly Journal*, was arrested and imprisoned for criticizing the governor of New York, and copies of the newspaper were burned in Wall Street. Andrew Hamilton, Zenger's lawyer, argued that the publisher had the right to speak and write the truth and to oppose arbitrary power. **What was the result of the trial?**

This interest in science originated in Europe, where it was known as the Enlightenment. English philosopher John Locke produced works that were widely read in America. In *An Essay Concerning Human Understanding*, Locke maintained that people could best gain knowledge of the universe by observing and by experimenting. This knowledge would guide them in developing a reasonable society. In the second of two *Treatises on Government*, Locke taught that people were born with certain natural rights to life, liberty, and property; that people formed governments to protect these rights; and that a government interfering with these might rightfully be overthrown. Many readily accepted the idea that government was the agent of the people, not their ruler.

The Press in America

In addition to schools and colleges, newspapers, almanacs, and books helped raise the level of public information. Because paper and type were expensive and the reading public in America small, most books came from Britain. But by 1750 there were 25 or 30 American newspapers, mostly 4 pages long, printed weekly. Printed on tough rag paper, these newspapers were passed from hand to hand at the local inn until often half the men in a village had read a single copy. European travelers in the colonies were amazed to find that political discussions in public inns were joined intelligently by everybody from the college educated to stable help.

The Zenger Case

Colonial editors occasionally criticized British laws or officials. In 1735 John Peter Zenger of the *New York Weekly Journal* accused the royal governor of corruption. As a result, copies of the paper were publicly burned by the sheriff, and Zenger was brought to trial on a charge of libel. His lawyer, Andrew Hamilton, argued that the editor was not guilty since the charges were true and since free speech was a basic right of English people. As a result, Zenger was acquitted. At the time the case attracted little attention, but today it is regarded as a landmark in the development of free press in America.

■ New Directions

By 1776 America was well on its way to establishing economic independence. Thirty percent of the ships in the British merchant marine were American, and most of these sailed from New England ports.

The Economy

New Englanders carried on a share of the African slave trade. They were the first to hunt whales in the Antarctic; in 1774, 360 whaling ships sailed from the island of Nantucket alone. While New England was a formidable competitor in trade, no colony offered much competition to the British in manufacturing. The American colonists usually obtained manufactured goods from Britain.

To pay for fine European goods such as clothing, books, wine, and cutlery, the colonies had to trade staples that Europeans needed or to pay in gold or silver. Trade with the West Indies netted Spanish dollars, the common colonial currency. Later the new nation, the United States, would adopt the dollar instead of the British pound as its monetary unit. Gradually the colonies developed a culture distinctly different from that of Europe.

Stirrings of Independence

The degree of power exercised by British officials varied from colony to colony, but it was limited everywhere. In all colonies the voters elected their own legislature, and in charter colonies, their governor as well. In proprietary colonies the governor was appointed by the proprietor or by his heirs; in royal or crown colonies the governor was chosen by the king. The governor of a proprietary or crown colony had wide powers, such as a veto over the legislature and control of land grants.

Government at the town and county levels was run entirely by the colonists themselves. In New England, the important local unit was the township. Decisions were made at the town meeting, which most heads of families had a right to attend. The town meeting was the most direct form of democracy in the colonies. In the Southern and Middle colonies, local government was usually less democratic but, nevertheless, entirely independent of British control.

None of the colonies was so democratic as to allow full political rights to all men or to any women. Active citizenship and the right to vote and hold office were limited to adult white males owning property, who usually had to be members of the established church. In spite of these limitations, a higher proportion of people were involved in government in the British colonies than anywhere in the European world. This wide participation gave Americans training that was valuable when the colonies later became independent.

Section 4 ★ Review

Checking for Understanding

1. **Identify** the Iroquois Confederacy, the Great Awakening, John Locke.

2. **Define** gentry.

3. **Describe** the position of indentured servants, women, and African Americans in the colonies.

4. **Give** reasons for the development of religious freedom and toleration in the British colonies.

Critical Thinking

5. **Evaluating Causes** Most colonists were common people, rather than titled aristocracy. What became the new basis for class structure, and how did it lead to class mobility?

Using Vocabulary

Use all the terms below in one of four sentences or paragraphs, each about one of the following: the class hierarchy in the colonies, the religious groups who colonized New England, government in the colonies, major exports.

congregation	indentured servants
commonwealth	naval stores
constitution	patroons
dissenters	proprietor
gentry	subsistence farming

Reviewing Facts

1. **Describe** the role of religion in settling the American colonies.
2. **Summarize** the growth of self-government in the colonies.
3. **Explain** the role economics played in the settlement of the colonies.
4. **Detail** the government in three types of colonies.
5. **Analyze** why slavery became more prevalent in the South than in New England.

Understanding Concepts

Migration

1. The colonists who left England to settle in America endured formidable hardships. List three reasons why different groups of colonists migrated to America in the face of these risks and hardships. How do their motives compare to the reasons people migrate today?

Values and Beliefs

2. What values and beliefs were instrumental in establishing democratic institutions in the American colonies?

Critical Thinking

1. **Proposing Solutions** Imagine you are appointed to resolve disputes between Native Americans and colonists who want farmland. Propose a fair plan for expansion. Remember that Native Americans did not own land.
2. **Analyzing Fine Art** Analyze the two paintings on this page and answer the questions that follow.
   a. What details in the paintings give you clues about the people's occupations?
   b. What can you tell about town life by looking at these paintings?

Writing About History

Description

Imagine you are an author who traveled in the first supply ship to reach Jamestown the year after it was settled. Write a description, to be published in Britain, of the condition of the colony when you arrived.

Cooperative Learning

Working in a group with four members, study slavery around the world and throughout history. Assign each member one or more cultures or geographic areas to study. Report your findings and conduct a discussion comparing and contrasting slavery in other cultures with slavery of African Americans in the colonies.

Social Studies Skills

Reading a Thematic Map

No doubt you have seen and studied maps in textbooks, magazines, atlases, even on television weather or news reports. Although there is almost no limit to the kinds of information that maps can show, most maps, depending on the type of information they present, fit into one of two broad categories. Maps that show general information such as countries, cities, rivers, and other features are called general reference maps. A second category of maps is thematic maps. These maps depict or emphasize more specific information than general reference maps. Often the information is on a single topic. The map below is a thematic map because it depicts information about a particular topic—land holdings in New England during the 1600s and early 1700s.

Practicing the Skill

Use the map and what you have read in the chapter to answer the following questions.

1. Based on the title, what can you learn from the map?

2. In what year was the Rhode Island Grant bestowed?

3. What grants of land were made in 1629?

4. **Drawing Conclusions** The map shows that there were many grants of land made during the 1600s and early 1700s. What do you think the British Crown was trying to accomplish by making these land grants?

New England Land Grants, 1609–1732

80°W 75°W 70°W

Duke of York Grant, 1664

Gorges Grant, 1639

St. Lawrence R.

Plymouth Grant, 1630

LAKE HURON
45°N

LAKE ONTARIO

Connecticut R.

Mason Grant, 1629

Massachusetts Grant, 1629

Plymouth Grant, 1630

LAKE ERIE

Duke of York Grant, 1664

Connecticut Grant, 1662

Rhode Island Grant, 1663

ATLANTIC OCEAN

40°N

0   100   200 miles
0   100   200 kilometers

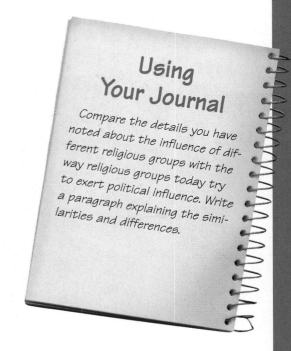

Using Your Journal

Compare the details you have noted about the influence of different religious groups with the way religious groups today try to exert political influence. Write a paragraph explaining the similarities and differences.

Cultural Kaleidoscope

Native American Life

SPORTS AND GAMES

From the earliest recorded history, people have taken part in play and games. Athletic competition has served as a way for individuals to interact with others and to display skills and physical ability as well as provide an expression for the love of competition. The first people of the Americas invented and enjoyed games of competition that tested skill and bravery.

▼
The game of Arrows was a popular competition. One by one, each contestant would shoot arrows into the air trying to put the largest number in the air before the first struck the ground. There were other competitions in marksmanship with bow and arrow.

◄
California peoples' game tray with acorn dice, eighteenth century

Lacrosse is an authentic Native American sport and the oldest game in North America. Some Canadian groups called the game bagataway, and the Seneca knew it as otada-jish-qua-age. The Mandan game of Tchungkee (above) was another of the many forms of lacrosse.

Lacrosse is a popular sport in many schools today.

◀ CEREMONIAL BOW

Jim Thorpe won both the pentathlon and decathlon medals at the 1912 Olympics. Thorpe of the Sac and Fox was a superb athlete who was an All-American football player, an outfielder for the New York Giants, and an important figure in the emergence of professional football. Sportswriters selected Thorpe the best football player of the first half of the twentieth century.

Chapter 1

The World in Transition

The first Americans traveled across a land bridge that once connected Siberia and Alaska and spread throughout North and South America. The Olmec, Maya, Aztec, and Incan civilizations developed highly organized and sophisticated societies. The monuments of the Anasazi and the Hopewell people attest to their level of cultural sophistication.

Across the Atlantic Ocean, a new Europe was emerging as strong monarchs unified their territories. A wealthy middle class developed from the increase in commerce and growth of cities. A rebirth of interest in the classical heritage of Greece and Rome brought a profound cultural awakening known as the Renaissance. Religious leaders called for the reform of the Roman Catholic Church, which led to the Reformation.

In Asia and Africa, Muslim empires expanded their territories. Ancient trade routes continued to flourish. Ming China, however, turned inward, halting trade to shield its people from outside influences.

Many factors caused Europeans to turn outward. Improved technology gave navigators the compass; the astrolabe; and faster, more seaworthy ships. Bankers, merchants, and joint-stock companies provided the money to finance expeditions. In search of spices and luxury goods, explorers braved the uncharted seas to find an all-water route from Europe to Asia. Portuguese sailors rounded the tip of Africa to reach India.

Chapter 2

The Age of Exploration

Not until the voyages of Christopher Columbus in the 1490s were Europeans aware that the Americas existed. Spain and Portugal were competing for

◀ **SIR WALTER RALEIGH**

▼ **RECONSTRUCTION OF JAMESTOWN SETTLEMENT**

▲ HUSKING BEE, 1700S

exclusive rights for trade. The pope drew a line of demarcation between Portuguese and Spanish interests that extended around the earth. Meanwhile, Portugal prospered because it controlled the eastern route to the Indies. In 1519 Spain sent Ferdinand Magellan to find a westerly route to Asia. His expedition was the first to circumnavigate the world.

Commerce led to empire building. The Spaniards wanted to acquire wealth and to spread Christianity in the Americas. In 1521 Hernán Cortés conquered the Aztecs and shipped huge amounts of Aztec gold to Spain. His success encouraged other conquistadors such as Francisco Pizarro, who conquered the Incan empire, to seek their fortunes in the Americas. In the process, the Spaniards claimed vast territories that eventually formed a great colonial empire.

France, England, and the Netherlands searched for a northwest passage to Asia during the 1500s and 1600s. As a result, the French established permanent colonies along the St. Lawrence River and developed a lucrative fur trade. By 1682 French explorers had claimed the Mississippi River basin. The Dutch settled in the rich Hudson River valley.

Chapter 3

Colonial America

In 1607 the English founded Jamestown in Virginia—their first permanent settlement in the Americas. Despite many hardships the colonists survived, and their success lured new settlers to Virginia. In time, the colonists formed a representative government body, the House of Burgesses. The first enslaved Africans were brought to Jamestown in 1619.

The Pilgrim and Puritan settlers in New England wanted freedom from religious persecution. Upon arrival in North America in 1620, the Pilgrims signed the Mayflower Compact and established the Plymouth colony in present-day Massachusetts. However, religious differences soon forced some of them to move on and found settlements in Rhode Island and Connecticut.

Other colonies were created when the king granted huge tracts of land to proprietors. These proprietorships included the Southern Colonies of Maryland, the Carolinas, and Georgia, and the Middle Colonies of New York, New Jersey, Pennsylvania, and Delaware.

New England, Middle, and Southern colonies developed differently. Diverse economies were built on crops or enterprises suited to regional climates. England largely left the colonies to govern themselves. Religious diversity eventually made religious toleration necessary. With a thriving export and trade economy, many people moved up in class.

Women could not vote, but they were full partners in running farms and sometimes businesses. Enslaved persons became property with no legal protection in the South. Native Americans suffered from battles with colonists over land and from epidemics of European diseases. At first, churches provided most schools and colleges, but later public education began to emerge, especially in New England.

Understanding Unit Themes

1. **Geography and the Environment**   How did the location of Asian centers of trade relative to Europe lead to colonies in the Americas?

2. **The Individual and Family Life**   Compare the lives and obligations of medieval serfs and colonial indentured servants.

3. **Humanities and Religion**   What roles did religion play in motivating voyages of exploration and in colonizing America?

4. **Cultural Diversity**   What role did cultural diversity play in the colonization of North and South America?

UNIT TWO
CREATING A NATION
1650–1789

★★

CHAPTER **4**	CHAPTER **5**	CHAPTER **6**
The Road to Revolution 1650–1775	War for Independence 1775–1783	A More Perfect Union 1775–1789

▲ COLONIAL HORNBOOK, SEVENTEENTH CENTURY

▲ SWORDS AND SABERS

History AND ART

George Washington Before Yorktown, 1781
by Rembrandt Peale, 1824

Rembrandt Peale was one of 17 children, many of whom became artists. Peale was only 17 when he painted his first portrait of Washington in 1795.

Setting the Scene

Harsh measures passed by Parliament in an effort to control the American colonies were met with outrage and hostile countermeasures. Gradually united, the colonists rebelled against their parent country. Their independence secured, Americans created for themselves a remarkable new form of democratic government.

Themes

- American Democracy
- Civil Rights and Liberties
- Economic Development
- Conflict and Cooperation

Key Events

- French and Indian War
- Fall of Quebec
- Treaty of Paris, 1763
- Stamp Act
- Boston Tea Party
- Battles of Lexington and Concord
- Declaration of Independence
- Battle of Saratoga
- British defeat at Yorktown
- Treaty of Paris, 1783
- Ratification of the Constitution

Major Issues

- British defeat of the French in North America prompts Parliament to attempt tightening commercial and political control of the 13 English colonies.
- Patriot determinism, military skill, and French aid enable the colonies to win independence from Britain.
- Key compromises lead to the formation of a strong and democratic central government.

▲ **AMERICAN BATTLE FLAG**

◄ **MOLLY PITCHER**

Portfolio Project

Compare the events of the American Revolution to the circumstances of a political or social upheaval that has taken place elsewhere in the world. Outline the major developments in both and identify some of the causes and effects.

Global Perspectives

★★

The World

	1650	1700
Asia and Oceania	**1644** *Ming Dynasty of China collapses*	
Europe		
Africa	▶ **1652** *Cape Town is founded at Cape of Good Hope*	**1660** *Several small kingdoms are established on the upper Niger*
South America		**1693** *Gold rush begins in Brazil*
North and Central America	**1650** *Spanish introduction of horses to the Plains alters Native Americans' lives*	

The United States

Pacific and Northwest		**1697** *Jesuit missionaries enter California*
Southeast		
Midwest		
Southwest		▲ **1689** *Spaniards establish missions in Texas*
Atlantic Northeast	▲ **1673** *Jacques Marquette and Louis Joliet explore the Upper Mississippi River for France*	
	1650	1700

Linking Across TIME

The English, the first Europeans to settle the eastern seaboard, gave our country its language. The adoption of Native American words and the contributions of successive waves of immigrants have created a truly *American* form of English. However, people in isolated areas of Chesapeake Bay, Maryland, and the Outer Banks in North Carolina still speak in a similar fashion to the first English settlers. For example, they pronounce *s* and the soft *c* as *z*, and the long *i* as *oi*. So cider, a popular drink in the region, is pronounced *zoider*.

1750   **1770** *Captain James Cook discovers Australia*   **1800**

1727 *Robert Walpole becomes Britain's first prime minister*   ▼ **1769** *James Watt perfects the steam engine*   **1789** *Revolution breaks out in France*

1789 *Alexander Mackenzie reaches Arctic Ocean*

1778 *Captain James Cook discovers Hawaiian Islands*

1718 *French found city of New Orleans*

▲ **1754** *French and Indian War begins*   ▲ **1776** *Declaration of Independence signed*

1750   **1800**

CHAPTER 4

★★★

The Road to Revolution
1650–1775

▶ **BEDFORD FLAG**

Setting the Scene

Focus

Through hard work, the colonists created a prosperous economy based on agriculture and trade, and they learned to govern themselves. In settling this new land, colonists also developed a sense that they were taking part in the birth of a new society, different from Europe, where men and women were able to better themselves. Once their need for British protection ended, the road to independence was not far behind.

Concepts to Understand

★ How Parliament sought to tighten political control over the colonies

★ Why colonists resorted to political protest against British policies

Read to Discover . . .

★ the causes and results of the French and Indian War.

★ the events that led the colonists to armed resistance to British control over the colonies.

Journal Notes

Put yourself in the role of a colonial merchant with a product to export. As you read the chapter, keep notes on your position on the issues.

CULTURAL

● **1763** *Benjamin Franklin perfects the harmonica*

● **1767** Letters from a Farmer in Pennsylvania *published by John Dickinson*

| 1760 | 1765 |

● **1763** *French and Indian War ends*

● **1765** *Stamp Act passed*
● **1767** *Townshend Acts passed*

POLITICAL

am forry to be obliged to acquaint my readers that as the Stamp Act is feared to be obligatory upon us after the *first of November* ensuing (The Fatal To-morrow), The publifher of this paper, unable to bear the Burthen, has thought it expedient to ftop awhile, in order to

deliberate, whether any methods can be found to elude the chains forged for us, and efcape the infupportable flavery, which it is hoped, from the laft reprefentation now made againft that act, may be effected. Mean while I muft earneftly Requeft every individual of my Subfcribers, many of whom have been long be-

hind Hand, that they would immediately difcharge their refpective Arrears, that I may be able, not only to fupport myfelf during the Interval, but be better prepared to proceed again with this Paper whenever an opening for that purpofe appears, which I hope will be foon.
WILLIAM BRADFORD.

▲ COLONIAL NEWSPAPER ATTACKING STAMP ACT

History AND ART

Patrick Henry Before the Virginia House of Burgesses
by Peter F. Rothermel, 1851

Best known for his historical works, Rothermel also turned out paintings based on religious and literary themes. This work illustrates Rothermel's technique of combining sharp details with shadowy forms in a single painting.

• **1774** *Shakers settle in Watervliet, New York*

• **1775** *Quakers establish first antislavery society in the United States*

1770

1775

• **1770** *Boston Massacre takes place*
• **1773** *Colonists dump tea into Boston Harbor*

• **1775** *Revolutionary War begins*

★★

Struggle for Empire

▲ CARTOON PROMOTING COLONIAL UNITY

While allowing the colonies to run local affairs with little interference, Great Britain attempted to control their foreign trade. From the British point of view, the colonies existed to supply raw materials and to provide markets for British goods.

■ New Policies

Beginning in 1651, Parliament passed a series of laws known as Trade and Navigation Acts. The Navigation Act of 1651 stated that all goods shipped between England and the colonies had to be carried in ships built either in England or in the colonies. Then in 1660 Parliament listed, or enumerated, specific colonial products that could be shipped only to Britain. These **enumerated commodities** included tobacco, cotton, indigo, and sugar.

Another measure required American ships returning from Europe to make a "broken voyage," stopping at an English port to pay a **duty,** or tax, on the goods they had purchased. As a result, the colonies received less for some of their exports and paid more for some of their imports than if they had been permitted to trade freely.

Colonial Response

A number of other laws were designed to help special groups. For example, the Molasses Act of 1733 helped the owners of sugar plantations in the British West Indies by putting a heavy tax on the importation of sugar and molasses. Development of colonial industry was slowed by the Woolen Act of 1699, which forbade the colonies to export woolen goods; the Hat Act of 1732, which made it illegal for hatmakers to sell their goods outside the colonies; and the

Iron Act of 1750, which restricted the manufacture of iron.

Often, these restrictions were the result of pressure on Parliament by British manufacturers who wanted to kill colonial competition. Benjamin Franklin's reaction was typical of the Americans' views:

> 66 *A colonist cannot make a button, a horse shoe, nor a hobnail but some sooty ironmonger or respectable buttonmaker of Britain shall bawl . . . that his honor's worship is . . . injured, cheated and robbed by the rascally Americans.* 99

Salutary Neglect

During the early colonial years, Parliament opted for a policy of **salutary neglect,** or non-interference, which allowed the colonists to do what they wished. One reason for the policy was distance—it was simply too difficult to control a situation 3,000 miles away. Another reason was that few revenue officers bothered to go to America; instead they appointed deputies, who were often lax in their duties. Soon colonists began to evade British laws, and smuggling became an accepted practice.

■ The French and Indian War

The Anglo-French contest for North America had two phases. The wars fought between 1689 and 1713 were known in the colonies as King William's War (1689–1697) and Queen Anne's War (1702–1713). At the close of this first phase, Great Britain gained Nova Scotia, Newfoundland, and Hudson's Bay Territory. The second phase, from 1742 to 1763, included the wars known in the colonies as King George's War (1742–1748) and the French and Indian War (1754–1763). In Europe they were called the War of the Austrian Succession and the Seven Years' War.

Visualizing History

▲ FRANKLIN IN LONDON Benjamin Franklin journeyed to London to present the colonists' views on taxation to the Lords of the Privy Council. *Why was it difficult for the British government to enforce laws strictly in the colonies?*

★★★

Colonial Dance

The long work week of most colonists was often filled with physically draining labor. The few moments spent on leisure activities generally centered around quiet activities such as reading or card games. Spectator sports for men—horse racing and turkey shoots—were also popular. Dancing, too, was a popular pastime.

From rural farms to urban mansions, dance in colonial America was a common recreation. While some clergy members condemned dancing as evil, others recommended it as healthy exercise. "Dancing masters"—teachers—opened schools in com-munities and were often employed by wealthy families to demonstrate the latest steps.

Taverns were often the site of impromptu dances. Couples performed line dances such as the reel to the accompaniment of a fiddler. The reel soon gave way to a more daring dance called the cotillion, a dance imported from the courts of France. In this forerunner of modern square dancing, four couples formed a group and moved to the directions of a "caller."

▲ DANCING THE MINUET

★★★

The Albany Plan

In 1754 delegates from seven northern colonies met with representatives of the Iroquois nations in Albany, New York. The stated purpose was to persuade the Iroquois to ally with the British against the French. But many delegates hoped to create a union of the colonies. Benjamin Franklin presented the Albany Plan of Union, a proposal that the colonies form a council with the power to levy taxes, raise troops, and regulate trade.

Although Franklin's plan was adopted by the delegates, it was rejected by both the colonial and British governments who feared loss of power. The lack of cooperation seriously handicapped the war effort. Americans seldom consented to fight outside their own colonies, and colonies ignored taxes imposed by Britain for their own defense. Nor would they tax themselves.

War Begins

The final struggle between England and France for control of North America began in the Ohio Valley. The French drove out English fur traders and in 1754 built Fort Duquesne (doo•KAYN) at the point where the Monongahela (muh•NAHN•guh•HEE•luh) and Allegheny rivers meet to form the Ohio River. The fort, located in territory claimed by both Virginia and Pennsylvania, was a threat to the safety of these colonies.

Facing this threat, the colonists sent a force of Virginia **militia**—a group of civilians trained as soldiers to fight in emergencies—to attack the fort. Under the command of an inexperienced 22-year-old major from Virginia named George Washington, the militia advanced on the fort and ambushed a French scouting party. The French later captured Washington's entire force but released them. War had begun even though there had been no formal declaration.

In the summer of 1755, British General Edward Braddock led 1,450 British and colonial soldiers in another attack on Fort Duquesne. Once more, the British forces were driven back.

Native American Support Shifts

Braddock's defeat caused many Native Americans to switch their support from the British to the French. The French were winning the war, and French fur traders, who mixed peacefully with the Native Americans, seemed less a threat to their way of life than did the land-hungry English settlers.

William Pitt

Disasters continued after Great Britain and France formally declared war in 1756. British generals were no match for French commander Louis Montcalm. British expeditions that tried to control the St. Lawrence River failed.

The tide shifted, however, when William Pitt became Britain's minister of war in 1758. By giving aid to France's enemies in Europe, Pitt forced France to split its forces. Pitt also sent talented, young officers to lead the campaigns in North America. By the end of 1758, Louisburg and Fort Duquesne were in British hands; and in June 1759, a British army of 9,000 was encamped on the St. Lawrence River a few miles below Quebec.

British commander James Wolfe had tried in vain to find a weak spot in the French defenses at Quebec. Finally, Wolfe proposed to have his troops land at night and scale a wooded cliff located under the guns of the fortress. Wolfe had observed Canadian women washing clothes in the river and hanging them to dry on the cliffs above. He realized that there had to be a pathway up the cliffs to the fortress! Wolfe suspected that the French would not have a strong guard at a point considered safe from attack.

Quebec Falls

Wolfe's soldiers climbed the cliffs and overpowered the few guards. Before daybreak 4,500 soldiers were prepared for battle on the fields at the top of the cliffs known as the Plains of Abraham. Commander Montcalm quickly gathered his forces to meet them. In the battle that followed, the French were forced to surrender.

■ Treaty of Paris, 1763

Great Britain won its war with France—in America, Europe, and Asia. Under the terms of the Treaty of Paris of 1763, Great Britain obtained all of Canada it did not already control and all the land east of the Mississippi River. From Spain, France's ally, Great Britain gained Florida. To repay Spain for its losses and to avoid losing it to Great Britain, France transferred the Louisiana Territory to Spain. North America was now

Land Claims in North America

English
French
Spanish
Russian
Unexplored

0   300   600 miles
0   600 kilometers

Map Study

In 1754 Great Britain, France, Spain, and Russia all claimed land in North America. *Which two countries controlled the most land on the continent?*

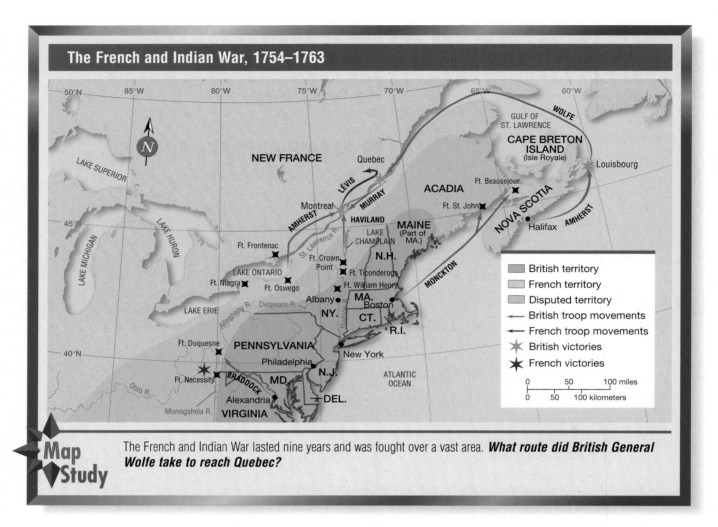

The French and Indian War, 1754–1763

Map Study

The French and Indian War lasted nine years and was fought over a vast area. *What route did British General Wolfe take to reach Quebec?*

divided between Great Britain and Spain with the Mississippi River forming the boundary.

For the French, defeat was bitter. France was left with no land on the continent of North America. After 150 years of coloniza-tion, the enterprise and heroism of French pioneers, missionaries, and soldiers were halted. There was only one small crumb of comfort—the 13 colonies might revolt. A French leader likened them to a "ripe fruit," ready to drop off the branch.

Section 1 ★ Review

Checking for Understanding

1. **Identify** Albany Plan of Union, George Washington, Treaty of Paris.

2. **Define** enumerated commodity, duty, salutary neglect, militia.

3. **State** two ways in which the interests of the British and the colonists differed.

4. **Explain** why control of the Ohio Valley was important.

Critical Thinking

5. **Recognizing Stereotypes** In a war, the two sides are usually categorized as good and bad or the right side and the wrong side. In the French and Indian War, the British and the American colonists who fought for them are usually portrayed as the right side, while the French and their Native American allies are portrayed as the wrong side. Discuss how this results in stereotyping.

Native American and European Land Values

Struggles between white settlers and Native Americans continued intermittently from the time Europeans first came to the Americas until the end of the 1800s. A major underlying cause of these struggles was conflict over land. Native Americans were quick to understand European desire for their own territory, but colonists seemed unable—or unwilling—to understand how deeply the Native Americans valued the land. Chief Pontiac, of the Ottawa people, speaking to Englishman Alexander Henry, explained: *"These lakes, these woods, and mountains were left us by our ancestors. They are our inheritances, and we will part with them to no one. . . . you ought to know that He, the Great Spirit and Master of Life, has provided food for us in these spacious lakes and on the woody mountains. . . ."*

Englishman George Thomas, when negotiating the price paid to the Iroquois for lands in New York, stated a very different view: *"It is very true, that the lands are of late become more valuable, but what raises their value? Is it not entirely owing to the industry and labor used by the white people, in their cultivation and improvement? Had not they come amongst you, these lands would have been of no use to you . . . and the value of land is no more than it is worth in money."*

The steady expansion of colonial settlements transformed the Native American way of life. Few among the colonists were willing to treat the Native Americans as equals or acknowledge their rights to the land. In 1635 the Pequot people of southern New England rose up against the colonists and were defeated. A combined force of settlers from Plymouth, Massachusetts, and Connecticut followed and attacked the Pequots who fled.

▲ NATIVE AMERICAN VILLAGE

Increasingly feeling the pressure of colonial expansion, five Native American peoples formed an alliance in 1675. Under the alliance's leader Metacomet, called King Philip by the Puritans, the Native Americans were also defeated. Native Americans continued to raid frontier villages, however, and their bitterness against the English grew.

Making the Geography Connection

1. What was the value of the land to Native Americans?

2. How did the colonists' idea of land value differ from the Native Americans' view?

Linking Past and Present

3. How does Thomas's view compare with the current practice of valuing land?

★★★★★★★★★★★★★★★★★★★★★★★★★★★★★★★★★★★★★

Control and Protest

Setting the Scene

Section Focus

Although the colonists did not realize it at the time, the French and Indian War changed their relationship with Britain forever. Freed from danger of French attack, Americans no longer needed British protection.

DONT TREAD ON ME

▲ **WARNING TO THE BRITISH**

Objectives

After studying this section, you should be able to

★ list and explain British attempts to tighten control over the colonies.

★ identify the ways in which the colonies resisted British control.

Key Terms

land speculator, writ of assistance, specie, direct tax, boycott, nonimportation agreement, redcoat

After the French and Indian War, Britain turned its attention to America. Victory had brought Britain vast new territories—and new problems. The British government first had to cope with the huge debt left by the war. Then it needed to decide what to do with the recently acquired western territory beyond the Appalachian and Allegheny mountains.

■ Proclamation of 1763

In 1763 Pontiac's Rebellion broke out in the West. Pontiac, chief of the Ottawa people, had foreseen that Britain's defeat of France meant a hard fate for his people. The French had traded with the Native Americans and lived among them. By contrast, the ever-advancing settlers of the British colonies threatened to wipe them out. Pontiac welded several Native American peoples into a fighting force and formed a confederacy in the Ohio Valley. Pontiac's forces captured a chain of British forts northwest of the Ohio River but failed to drive the settlers back across the Appalachian Mountains.

During Pontiac's Rebellion, the British government issued the Proclamation of 1763, which ended all settlement west of the Appalachian Mountains. The government also maintained thousands of troops along the frontier—as much to protect the Native Americans from the settlers as the settlers from the native peoples.

Although Americans at first accepted the Proclamation of 1763, they soon resented it. Colonists protested that the Proclamation deprived them of land they had a right to settle and interfered with charter rights of colonies whose grants extended "from sea to sea." Perhaps the biggest outcry came from **land speculators**—people who purchased land to resell it for profit. They claimed American interests were being sacrificed to fill the pockets of the British fur traders who wished to leave the Native Americans undisturbed.

■ Stricter Enforcement

The selection of George Grenville as Britain's minister of finance in 1763 signaled a change in policy. Grenville was an energetic administrator who believed that laws should be strictly enforced. He was said to be the first minister in a generation who read dispatches from American revenue collectors and was aware of the extent of smuggling in the colonies. In addition, Grenville noted that the revenue service in the 13 colonies was costing the British government 4 times as much as it collected.

Grenville required customs officers to go to their posts in America rather than stay in England and hire deputies as before. These officers were armed with **writs of assistance**—general search warrants allowing them to seek smuggled goods without swearing out a particular warrant for every building they entered. Grenville also mandated that colonists accused of smuggling be tried in admiralty courts, where the accused was denied the right of trial by jury and the judges pocketed a percentage of the fines they imposed.

■ New Taxes

Between 1764 and 1767, Parliament levied new taxes that shifted part of the burden of the war debt to the colonies. With the acquisition of Canada and other territories after the war, the size of the British Empire had more than doubled, and the problems of governing it grew more complicated and expensive. The war left the British government with a national debt more than twice what it was in 1754, and the people of Britain objected strongly to paying any more in taxes. They felt it was

The Proclamation of 1763

- ■ 13 Colonies
- ■ Other British territory
- ■ Spanish territory
- — Proclamation Line of 1763

0   200 miles
0   200 kilometers

Map Study The Proclamation of 1763 forbade colonists from settling west of an imaginary line along the crest of the Appalachian Mountains. *Why did the British goverment want to halt westward movement?*

only fair that the colonists pay a part of the cost of defending and administering the empire.

The Sugar Act

Grenville also persuaded Parliament to levy duties on colonial imports, the most important of these being the Sugar Act of

1764. Although this law cut the rates of the Molasses Act of 1733, the British government had always winked at evasions of the Molasses Act of 1733. The troubling thing about the Sugar Act was that the British intended to enforce it. Colonial merchants realized that strict enforcement would wipe out the profits of the trade with the Spanish and French West Indies that brought much-needed **specie**—gold and silver coins—into the colonies. In that same year, Parliament forbade colonial governments to issue paper money. Caught in a two-way squeeze of lower profits and scarcity of hard currency, many merchants faced bankruptcy.

Visualizing History

▲ **PONTIAC IN COUNCIL** Pontiac's forces, which included members from many different Native American nations, captured most of the British outposts west of Fort Niagara. *How did the British change their settlement policy?*

The Stamp Act

In 1765 Parliament passed another revenue law called the Stamp Act. This law differed from previous tax measures because it was a **direct tax**—a tax paid directly to the government rather than being included in the price of goods. It required that stamps be placed on many kinds of articles and documents, including wills, playing cards, newspapers, dice, almanacs, and licenses. Duties ranged from 1 cent on newspapers to $10 for college diplomas, and payment had to be made in specie.

Protest

While Grenville's previous tax laws had affected those engaged in foreign trade, namely New England merchants and shippers, the Stamp Act affected colonists everywhere. It especially offended the most powerful and articulate groups in the colonies: lawyers, newspaper editors, and ministers. On the day the Stamp Act was to go into effect, men and women wore mourning clothes and church bells tolled all the way from Portsmouth, New Hampshire, to Savannah, Georgia.

Colonists backed their protests with a **boycott**—a refusal to buy British goods. Men and women made solemn promises to wear homespun clothing instead of British woolens. Colonial merchants signed **nonimportation agreements,** promising not to buy British goods until Parliament repealed the unpopular law. Soon imports from Britain dropped, and British merchants, saying that they were faced with "utter ruin," besieged Parliament with petitions against the Stamp Act. Under such pressure, Parliament backed down and repealed the law in 1766.

The Townshend Acts

The next year Parliament tried to raise revenue through the Townshend (TOWN• zehnd) Acts, which placed import duties on tea, paper, glass, and paint. The British could not effectively collect these taxes either, and all the Townshend duties were repeated in 1770, except the tax on tea, which was retained to assert the principle of Parliament's authority.

Threats to Colonial Self-Government

Grenville's new customs collectors and admiralty judges were followed by 10,000 British soldiers. These troops were sent, it was said, to protect the Americans. But to protect them from whom? The French had been defeated, and the Native Americans were at peace. Colonists noted that the British soldiers, called **redcoats** because of the color of their uniforms, were not stationed in frontier posts, but in towns such as Boston and New York where there was no more danger from Native Americans than in London. But the presence of the redcoats served other purposes—to strengthen the hand of colonial governors and to frighten colonial legislatures into line.

▲ COLONIAL RESPONSE Patrick Henry attacked the Stamp Act in a speech given before the Virginia legislature. *What did the colonists mean by "no taxation without representation"?*

It was also clear that the British wanted to free royal officials from colonial control. For this reason, the British government shifted customs cases to the admiralty courts and ruled that royal judges and governors were to be paid out of customs revenues that British revenue officers collected. Now colonial legislatures could no longer check the power of royal governors by holding up their salaries.

Disobedience to British Laws

The efforts of the British government to tighten control met such swift and determined resistance that it surprised even the Americans themselves. The resistance took a variety of forms, including disobedience to British laws, protests, increased cooperation among the 13 colonies, boycotts, and violence.

The Americans, long accustomed to evading British revenue laws, did not hesitate to disobey new ones. In spite of a much stronger British customs service, smuggling went on much as usual. The long coast of America prevented revenue officers from inspecting all incoming ships, especially when the local inhabitants were constantly trying to thwart them.

In 1765 Parliament passed the Quartering Act directing the colonies to provide barracks and supplies for the thousands of British troops ordered to America. The New York and Massachusetts legislatures regarded the act as concealed taxation and flatly refused to provide funds. Most of the other colonies found other ways to disobey the law.

After 1765 many colonists crossed the Appalachian Mountains and began to establish settlements in the western lands. Led by Daniel Boone and others, settlers spilled into western New York, Kentucky, and Tennessee, staking their land claims on Native American land. Although this westward movement met the colonists' need for expansion, it violated the Proclamation of 1763.

The Question of Representation

One of the first public colonial protests took place in Virginia in May 1765 when the House of Burgesses met to consider the Stamp Act. Patrick Henry introduced the Virginia Resolutions protesting Parliament's action. Henry claimed that, since Americans elected no members to the British Parliament, they could not be taxed by that body. The House of Burgesses had "the only exclusive right and power to lay taxes" upon Virginians. This bold stand by the largest of the colonies encouraged the other colonies to follow suit, and the principle of "no taxation without representation" was accepted as a basic right.

Virtual Representation

To most people in Britain the argument against "taxation without representation" was faulty. The colonies were represented under the principle of "virtual" representation. It did not matter that Americans did not elect members to the House of Commons, the only branch of the government that could tax. Many other citizens were not directly represented either. It did not matter where these citizens lived or even if they had the right to vote because the House of Commons was pledged to represent every person in Britain and the empire. Americans had little regard for the idea of virtual representation, largely because, since the time of the earliest settlements, the people had always had direct representation—electing colonial assembly members to represent their interests.

The Stamp Act Congress

Resistance to the Stamp Act brought about the first real cooperation among the 13 colonies. A committee of the Massachusetts legislature sent letters to leaders of the other colonial legislatures urging them to send delegates to a convention to decide on a common policy toward the British government. As a result, the Stamp Act Congress met in New York in October 1765. Nine colonial legislatures were represented, and the colonies that did not participate sent messages of support.

The delegates drew up resolutions and organized a boycott of British-made goods. In 1768 the Massachusetts legislature issued a Circular Letter calling on all the other colonial legislatures to join in protest against the measure.

John Dickinson helped promote colonial unity in his *Letters from a Farmer in Pennsylvania* published in 1767 and 1768. Dickinson argued that the people of the American colonies, "separated from the rest of the world, and firmly held together by the same rights, interests, and dangers," created "one political body of which each colony is a member."

▶ JOHN DICKINSON

Section 2 ★ Review

Checking for Understanding

1. **Identify** Pontiac, Proclamation of 1763, Stamp Act, Townshend Acts, Stamp Act Congress.

2. **Define** land speculator, writ of assistance, specie, direct tax, boycott, nonimportation agreement, redcoat.

3. **Explain** why Great Britain ended salutary neglect of the colonies after 1763.

4. **State** the primary reason American colonists opposed direct taxes.

Critical Thinking

5. **Understanding Cause and Effect** Compose a series of American newspaper headlines that describe British actions (causes) and American reactions (effects) between 1763 and 1770.

Interpreting Primary Sources

The Stamp Act Crisis

During the decade between the passage of the Stamp Act in 1765 and the outbreak of the Revolution, colonial resistance to Parliament took several forms. Colonial legislatures issued many resolutions and petitions to the Crown criticizing their perceived loss of some rights and "taxation without representation." Early colonial successes, though—notably the repeal of the Stamp Act—came from boycotts and other acts of defiance by ordinary citizens.

Open protest against unjust rulers and laws had long been an accepted part of English political life. In the colonies, efforts to bring about political change through protest were aided by weak British control. Although colonial officials had the authority to suppress "disturbances of the peace," they frequently did not have the means to do so. In rural areas, police power consisted only of a county sheriff and, sometimes, a deputy. In towns, the sheriff might have had a night watch, but this was seldom effective. In New York, for example, the night watch was described as a "parcel of idle, drinking, vigilant snorers who never quelled any nocturnal tumult in their lives."

The hated Stamp Act placed a tax on every type of legal document, newspapers, almanacs—even playing cards and dice. A stamp on the paper testified that the tax had been paid. Money raised from the sale of stamps was to be used to help pay for British soldiers stationed in the colonies. The measure created a great protest because it was Parliament's first attempt to tax the colonists directly. Previously, each colony had been assessed a portion of the revenue needed, and the assemblies raised the money by whatever means they chose.

Colonists reacted swiftly. Radical groups formed, riots broke out, and delegates from most of the colonies declared at a Stamp Act Congress that Parliament had no legal right to tax the colonists.

▲ BURNING STAMPS TO PROTEST THE STAMP ACT

The illustration on this page depicts the unrest that convinced stamp agents throughout the colonies to resign their posts. Images such as this also served to justify violent action.

Examining the Primary Source

1. Describe the mood of the crowd. What details in the picture help you determine this?

2. Would publicity of such a protest reinforce or strengthen colonial resistance? Explain.

Critical Thinking

3. **Demonstrating Reasoned Judgment** What circumstances today might justify using intimidation tactics to protest unjust laws? Explain.

★★★★★★★★★★★★★★★★★★★★★★★★★★★★★★★★★★★

The Breach Widens

Setting the Scene

Section Focus

The period between 1770 and 1773 marked a slowdown in the struggle between the colonies and Great Britain. This respite ended when Parliament granted a monopoly on the sale of tea in the colonies to the East India Company. After that every British action triggered an American response—the Boston Tea Party, the Intolerable Acts, and the First Continental Congress. Even as late as the winter of 1775, many colonists hoped for a reconciliation with Britain.

Objectives

After studying this section, you should be able to

★ list the Intolerable Acts and describe how the colonists responded to them.

★ describe the events that led to war between Great Britain and the American colonies.

Key Terms

effigy, monopoly

▶ PAUL REVERE'S RIDE

*R*esistance to taxation caused a new spirit of cooperation and a rising spirit of patriotism. In a speech to the Stamp Act Congress, Christopher Gadsden of South Carolina declared, "There ought to be no New England Man, no New Yorker, known on the continent, but all of us Americans."

■ Boycotts and Violence

Although most colonial leaders who opposed efforts of the British Parliament to tax Americans were from the wealthy planter and merchant classes, they were supported and aided by many others. Among those who fueled the resistance were shopkeepers, clerks, and laborers. These colonists were the driving force behind two vital resistance groups—the Sons and Daughters of Liberty.

Sons of Liberty

The Sons of Liberty carried out organized resistance by keeping watch on shopkeepers suspected of selling British goods. They publicly denounced or threatened those they caught. When the Sons of Liberty learned that Andrew Oliver was going to be appointed Distributor of Stamps for Boston, they hung his **effigy**, or likeness, on the Liberty Tree and stoned it. Then they looted his house and coerced him to refuse the job.

American and British opposition to the Stamp Act forced Parliament to repeal it. In an effort to save face, Parliament passed the Declaratory Act, which affirmed its rights as the supreme legislator of the British empire.

Parliament was following the principle of this law when it passed the Townshend Acts in 1767, but the colonists argued that any

▲ MERCY OTIS
WARREN

 Visualizing History

▲ REVOLUTIONARY ACTIONS Some Americans used force against British sympathizers. Mercy Otis Warren of the Daughters of Liberty was a witty and skillful propagandist for the American cause. *In what other way did the Sons and Daughters of Liberty help the resistance?*

law designed to raise revenue from them without their consent was a violation of their liberties.

Daughters of Liberty

Colonial women organized the Daughters of Liberty to boycott British goods. The Daughters of Liberty gave up imported clothes, made tea out of local herbs, and produced homespun cloth. One of the most influential of the Daughters was Mercy Otis Warren, who published pamphlets supporting the resistance—although she had to use a man's name to be published.

The Boston Massacre

In the same year that Parliament repealed the Townshend duties, the first clash between Americans and British troops took place. On the night of March 5, 1770, a crowd of 50 or 60 men and boys gathered to taunt British soldiers outside the Boston Customs House. When the crowd threw sticks and snowballs at the redcoats, the soldiers

panicked and opened fire, killing five men. News of the event, which became known as the "Boston Massacre," spread throughout the colonies. It soon became a symbol of British force and tyranny.

An Uneasy Calm

From 1770 to 1773 a lull quieted the controversy between Great Britain and the 13 colonies. Having won relief from some taxes, the Americans allowed the British to collect others. Imports of British goods rose—from $8 million in 1768 to $21 million in 1771.

The calm was interrupted periodically by acts of violence. In 1771 a British customs schooner that had taken a smugglers' ship into custody was attacked at night. When another British revenue boat, the *Gaspée*, ran aground off Rhode Island, "persons unknown" attacked and burned it.

Meanwhile, leaders of the American resistance were busy forming a variety of organizations to translate popular discontent into action. The most effective of these were the committees of correspondence. Keeping in contact with each other, these committees helped keep the resistance movement going.

The Boston Tea Party

The period of calm between the colonies and Britain came to an end with the Boston Tea Party. This dramatic event started a chain reaction that led to war and broke the ties between Great Britain and the colonies.

Monopoly

By 1773 the British East India Company was experiencing severe financial problems. Facing bankruptcy, the company appealed to Parliament for assistance. Parliament quickly voted to grant it a **monopoly,** or sole control of the trade, for tea in America.

Announcement of the plan produced an outcry in America. Colonists objected to the tea monopoly because they suspected its real purpose was to bribe them into acknowledging Parliament's right to tax the colonies.

Opposition

Opposition groups mobilized to prevent the sale of the East India tea. Ships arriving in the Atlantic ports were unable to sell a pound of tea. At New York and Philadelphia the tea ships were forced to turn back.

In Boston, however, Governor Hutchinson ordered that no ship could leave the harbor without unloading its tea. Colonists led by Sam Adams were just as determined that no tea would come ashore. For days, crowds milled in the street and attended rallies discussing what action to take. Then on December 16, about 8,000 people attended a meeting where they learned that Hutchinson would not back down. On a signal from Sam Adams, a group of colonists, disguised as Mohawks, rushed to the wharf. Before a cheering crowd, they boarded the tea ships and heaved 342 chests of tea into the harbor.

The Intolerable Acts

Benjamin Franklin called the Boston Tea Party "an act of violent injustice." Some Boston merchants were willing to start a collection to pay for the damage.

Crispus Attucks
1723(?)–1770

★★★★★★★★ AMERICAN PORTRAITS

Little is known about the life of Crispus Attucks before the evening of March 5, 1770. Attucks may well have been a runaway slave in Boston, where he probably worked on the docks; but for one brief moment that night, Attucks stood at the forefront of American resistance to British rule.

After Attucks finished his dinner in an inn, he joined a nearby crowd that had formed on King Street. Young boys were taunting a group of British soldiers, hurling snowballs and sticks. Tensions grew between the soldiers and the unruly mob. A soldier's musket suddenly fired, and Attucks fell to the ground and died instantly.

Four others were also killed, and several were wounded in what has become known as the Boston Massacre. Attucks became a martyr to the patriot cause—an African American who gave his life in the name of liberty.

▲ THE BOSTON MASSACRE Bitter feelings erupted in bloodshed on March 5, 1770 in Boston, when British soldiers fired into a crowd, killing five. *What happened when news of the Boston Massacre spread?*

▲ SAM ADAMS

The Coercive Acts

To the British government, however, the Boston Tea Party was an act of lawlessness that deserved swift and severe punishment. In March 1774, Parliament passed a series of laws known as the Coercive Acts. One of the acts closed the port of Boston until payment was made for the tea. Another act stipulated that British officials accused of a crime were to be tried in English rather than American courts. Still another provided that British troops could be quartered in any town in Massachusetts—even in private homes. Finally, the Massachusetts charter was amended to greatly reduce the colony's right of self-government. Colonists considered the provisions of the Coercive Acts so harsh that they called them the "Intolerable Acts."

The Quebec Act

Passed at the same time, and considered by the colonists as one of the Intolerable Acts, was the Quebec Act, which extended the Canadian province of Quebec south to the Ohio River. It also allowed French Canadians use of their own legal system, which did not provide for trial by jury, and which recognized the legality of the Roman Catholic Church. Americans saw the Quebec Act as the first step toward doing away with jury trials and Protestantism in the 13 colonies. They also believed the boundary changes were made to keep American settlers out of western lands forever.

The Intolerable Acts revealed that the British government intended to show the colonists who had authority.

■ The First Continental Congress

When Parliament passed the Coercive Acts, British leaders expected that the other colonies would agree that Massachusetts deserved punishment. William Pitt had warned, however, that the acts would give the colonies a new reason to unite.

▲ KING GEORGE III

▲ *DEATH OF GENERAL WARREN AT THE BATTLE OF BUNKER HILL* by JOHN TRUMBULL, 1786 The bright red uniforms, the stormy sky, and the heroic scene reflect the patriotic temper of the times. ***Why was the battle symbolic for the colonists?***

Declaration of Rights and Grievances

Pitt proved to be right. The acts convinced many Americans that the leaders of Britain were conspiring to take away their liberties. In response, the 56 delegates to the First Continental Congress met in Philadelphia in September 1774.

The Congress petitioned the king for relief from the Intolerable Acts and vowed to stop trade with Britain until the acts were repealed. A Declaration of Rights and Grievances denounced every revenue-raising or power-limiting step taken by Britain since 1763 as a violation of colonial charters and the rights of colonists as British citizens.

"The Association"

Congress tried to enforce its boycott by setting up "in every county, city, and town" an organization known as "The Association." The Association exerted a surprising degree of control over Americans, telling them what they should eat, drink, and wear, as well as how they should behave in public. The Association did its work effectively; imports of British goods into New York, for example, dropped from more than $2 million in 1774 to $6,000 in 1775.

■ The Final Break

Meanwhile, every colony was organizing. In New England, "minutemen" assembled to drill on village greens, while town officials collected ammunition, uniforms, and food. In the Southern Colonies, planters undertook to recruit and equip companies of soldiers at their own expense. It appeared that the dispute between Great Britain and the colonies would be settled only by force.

Lexington and Concord

Fighting between the Americans and the British broke out near Boston, which had been occupied in 1774 by a British army under General Thomas Gage. Early on April 19, 1775, 700 British soldiers were secretly sent to destroy the military supplies colonists had collected at Concord, 21 miles from Boston. Learning of the soldiers' destination, the Boston Sons of Liberty sent Paul Revere and William Dawes to alert the minutemen in the towns and villages along the way. When the British reached the town of Lexington, about 70 armed minutemen awaited them. The colonists were ordered to drop their weapons and disperse. Then someone fired a shot. A spontaneous skirmish ensued, and the colonists fled. Eight colonists were killed, and ten were wounded; only one British soldier was wounded. The British pushed on to Concord and burned what little gunpowder the colonists had not used for themselves.

By the time the British began their march toward Boston, the countryside was swarming with minutemen, who fired at the redcoats from behind trees, buildings, and stone walls. Only a brigade sent out from Boston saved the British troops from complete annihilation. About 250 British and 100 Americans were killed or wounded at Concord.

The Colonists Mobilize

News of Lexington and Concord, carried by riders on horseback, electrified the colonies. The Massachusetts Committee of Public Safety called for an army of 30,000 men "to defend our wives and children from the butchering hands of an inhuman soldiery." Groups of militia from all over New England marched toward Boston. General Gage found himself besieged.

Battle of Bunker Hill

On June 17, 1775, the British discovered that American troops occupied Breed's Hill, a peninsula overlooking the city of Boston from the north. The American army could easily have been trapped from behind, but the British commander decided to make a frontal attack uphill. Because the range of a musket was scarcely more than 50 yards, the Americans were ordered to hold their fire until they could see the "whites of their enemies' eyes."

The Americans turned back two British attacks but finally ran out of ammunition. The Battle of Bunker Hill, as it came to be called, was a moral victory for the Americans because their untrained militia had stood up to professional troops. The British, whose casualties in the battle were more than 40 percent, made no further attempt to attack.

Second Continental Congress

On May 10, 1775, a Second Continental Congress met in Philadelphia. The Congress assumed the powers of a central government and took steps to conduct the war that had, in fact, begun at Lexington. The Congress voted to ask the colonies for supplies and troops.

For commander in chief, Congress chose George Washington. It valued his experience and ability, but the fact that he was a Virginian was also important because it would keep the Southern and Middle colonies from thinking of the conflict as New England's war. Although it would be more than a year until independence was declared, the American Revolution had begun.

Section 3 ★ Review

Checking for Understanding

1. **Identify** Declaratory Act, Boston Massacre, Boston Tea Party, Intolerable (Coercive) Acts, Lexington and Concord, Breed's Hill, Second Continental Congress.

2. **Define** effigy, monopoly.

3. **Compare** the British reason for giving the East India Company a monopoly on tea with the colonists' reasons for opposing it.

4. **Explain** the purpose and significance of the two Continental Congresses.

Critical Thinking

5. **Supporting an Opinion** Some historians place the cause of the Revolution on the series of tax laws passed after 1763. Others believe that the cause was a growing national consciousness of Americans. Point out the strengths of each theory.

The American Crisis, Number 1 (excerpt)

▲ **THOMAS PAINE** *Common Sense* was important in swaying the colonists toward the idea of separation from Great Britain.

The call to arms during the Revolution was heard not only on fields of battle but off, echoed by the leading writers of the day. Some of the most inspiring words that rang out against British tyranny were those of Thomas Paine. As you read this excerpt, notice the language Paine uses to rally support for the American cause.

These are the times that try men's souls. The summer soldier and the sunshine patriot will in this crisis, shrink from the service of his country; but he that stands it now deserves the love and thanks of man and woman. Tyranny, like hell, is not easily conquered; yet we have this consolation with us, that the harder the conflict, the more glorious the triumph. What we obtain too cheap, we esteem too lightly; 'tis dearness only that gives everything its value. Heaven knows how to put a proper price upon its goods; and it would be strange indeed, if so celestial an article as FREEDOM should not be highly rated. Britain, with an army to enforce her tyranny, has declared that she has a right (not only to tax) but "to bind us in all cases whatsoever," and if being bound in that manner, is not slavery, then is there not such a thing as slavery upon earth. Even the expression is impious, for so unlimited a power can belong only to God. . . .

I have as little superstition in me as any man living, but my secret opinion has ever been, and still is, that God Almighty will not give up a people to military destruction, or leave them unsupportedly to perish, who have so earnestly and so repeatedly sought to avoid the calamities of war, by every decent method which wisdom could invent. Neither have I so much of the infidel in me, as to suppose that he has relinquished the government of the world, and given us up to the care of devils; and as I do not, I cannot see on what grounds the king of Britain can look up to heaven for help against us: a common murderer, a highwayman, or a housebreaker, has as good a pretense as he. . . .

Not a place upon earth might be so happy as America. Her situation is remote from all the wrangling world, and she has nothing to do but to trade with them. A man can distinguish himself between temper and principle, and I am as confident, as I am that God governs the world, that America will never be happy

▲ **WASHINGTON CROSSING THE DELAWARE**
by Emanuel Gottlieb Leutze, 1851

till she gets clear of foreign domination. Wars, without ceasing, will break out till that period arrives, and the continent must in the end be conqueror; for though the flame of liberty may sometimes cease to shine, the coal can never expire. . . .

. . . Let it be told to the future world that in the depth of winter, when nothing but hope and virtue could survive, that the city and the country, alarmed at one common danger, came forth to meet and to repulse it. Say not that thousands are gone, turn out your tens of thousands; throw not the burden of the day upon Providence, but *"show your faith by your works,"* that God may bless you. . . .

▶ **TITLE PAGE OF COMMON SENSE**

Interpreting Literature

1. What does Paine mean by the phrase "the summer soldier and the sunshine patriot"?

2. What does Paine believe must be accomplished before America can be happy?

Identifying Viewpoints

3. Point to several sentences that give evidence of Paine's views about the British cause and the American cause.

Using Vocabulary

Using the words below, write an editorial for the *Boston Gazette* that might have appeared the day after the battle at Lexington.

salutary neglect	direct tax
duty	boycott
writ of assistance	redcoat

Reviewing Facts

1. **Describe** the British strategy and execution of the battle fought against the French at Quebec.

2. **State** how the series of laws passed by Parliament after 1763 differed from those passed before 1763.

3. **Explain** how the Proclamation of 1763 affected the colonists and tell why they were angry over it.

4. **Identify** the incidents that became turning points in the relationship between the colonies and Britain.

5. **List** the acts of Parliament between 1763 and 1774 that colonists considered direct taxes.

6. **List** the organizations that came into being in the colonies to protest British tax laws and describe the ways in which the colonists defied those laws.

Understanding Concepts

Political Control

1. When the colonists refused to pay the taxes imposed by Parliament, the crown took measures to force obedience. List these measures and tell what effect they had on British-American relations.

Political Protest

2. Describe three forms of political protest used by the colonists.

3. Protest documents helped unite Americans against the British crown. Cite two of these documents, along with the names of their authors and a summary of their contents.

Critical Thinking

1. **Identifying Alternatives** Historians argue whether any war is inevitable. How could war between Britain and the American colonies have been avoided?

2. **Interpreting Illustrations** Examine closely the picture of the painting *A View of the Town of Concord, 1775,* (below) attributed to Ralph Earl. In the background, the British are destroying barrels of gunpowder and throwing them into the river. What was the objective of the British march on Concord, and did it meet its objective?

Writing About History

Definition

Write a letter from Benjamin Franklin to Parliament following passage of the Coercive Acts. In the letter, attempt to explain the reasons for the Boston Tea Party and the colonial position on taxation.

Cooperative Learning

Your group will write a play in three acts about the incidents leading to the American Revolution. Your play should have British and American characters. Each act should have one scene that takes place in Britain and one that follows it in America. Use these time periods in writing the acts: Act I, 1763–1767; Act II, 1767–1773; Act III, 1773–1776.

Social Studies Skills

Reading Military Maps

Military maps, besides giving you a visual representation of an event, can provide helpful information that sometimes the text does not include. For example, a map might show what kind of terrain is involved. You could tell if the soldiers had to march over hills or through rivers. A military map could also show which ports had to be protected, how much area the soldiers covered, and what their advances and retreats were.

Practicing the Skill

To help you read military maps, follow these guidelines.

- Look at the title to determine the subject.
- Find the legend. It will include symbols to help you find routes and battle sites.
- Study the mileage chart to get an idea of how much land they covered. For example, in this map, you can see that it is about 21 miles from Boston to Concord. Remember that Paul Revere and the other riders were covering this distance on horseback.
- If the map is *topographical*, or shows land features, consider what the soldiers had to deal with in marching and fighting battles.

Study the map and then answer the questions that follow.

1. Who took over for Paul Revere when he was captured?

Lexington and Concord

- ← Paul Revere's route
- ← William Dawes' route
- ← Samuel Prescott's route
- ← Route of British troops to Concord
- ★ Battles

2. Why did Paul Revere and William Dawes take different routes?
3. **Making Inferences** Considering what you've read about trade between England and the colonies, why would it be important for the colonists to control Boston and its harbor?

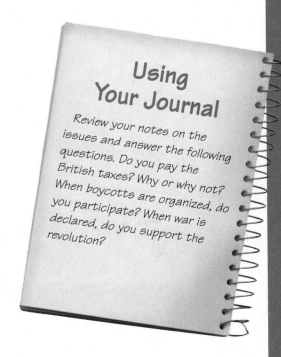

Using Your Journal

Review your notes on the issues and answer the following questions. Do you pay the British taxes? Why or why not? When boycotts are organized, do you participate? When war is declared, do you support the revolution?

CHAPTER 5

★★★

War for Independence
1775–1783

Setting the Scene

◀ EAGLE AND
CROSSED FLAGS

Focus

Even after the first skirmishes, the colonists still hoped to reconcile with the British crown. Events during the winter of 1775–1776, however, moved them toward separation. The writings of Thomas Paine, the king's inflexible attitude, and Britain's use of German mercenaries all led the Second Continental Congress to issue a Declaration of Independence on July 4, 1776. Under George Washington's leadership, the new United States fought its war for independence over six long years.

Concepts to Understand

★ Why revolution against Great Britain seemed the only option left for the colonies
★ How colonists believed their civil rights and liberties could be secured and protected

Read to Discover . . .

★ what factors caused the American Revolution.
★ why the Americans were able to win the war.

Journal Notes

What contributions did women, African Americans, and Native Americans make to the American Revolution? Note details in your journal as you read the chapter.

CULTURAL

● **1776** *Thomas Paine writes* Common Sense

● **1778** *William Brown publishes first American book about medicines*

| 1775 | 1778 |

POLITICAL

● **1776** *Declaration of Independence is signed*
● **1777** *Continental Army victorious at Saratoga*

● **1778** *George Rogers Clark's forces capture Kaskaskia*

◀ REVOLUTIONARY WAR DRUM

• **1783** *Noah Webster publishes first spelling book*

• **1784** *American Methodist Church formed in Baltimore, Maryland*

1781	1784

• **1781** *Cornwallis surrenders at Yorktown*
• **1783** *Treaty of Paris signed*

• **1784** *Congress drafts land ordinance*

★★★

Foundations of Freedom

Setting the Scene

Section Focus

Delegates to the Second Continental Congress faced a difficult decision—whether to separate from or to seek reconciliation with Great Britain. The delegates would weigh carefully any official action announcing independence, since they would be committing treason against the British crown.

Objectives

After studying this section, you should be able to

★ list the arguments for American independence.

★ explain the purposes and principles of the Declaration of Independence.

Key Terms

treason, mercenary, Patriot, Loyalist, artillery, grievance, preamble, social contract, right of self-determination

▲ BETSY ROSS FLAG

After the bloodshed in Massachusetts, colonial leaders such as Patrick Henry of Virginia appealed for separation from Great Britain. Most colonists, however, were not ready for independence, and neither was the Second Continental Congress that convened in Philadelphia in May 1775.

■ Moving Toward Independence

Most of the members of the Continental Congress wanted the colonies to remain part of the British Empire but rule themselves through their own legislatures. In a petition that tried to appease the king, the delegates blamed all their troubles on his ministers.

Charge of Treason

King George III refused to read the conciliatory petition from the Continental Congress and denounced the "diverse wicked and desperate persons" leading the rebels. He called on loyal subjects to charge the American leaders with **treason,** or attempting to overthrow the government, and to punish them according to British law.

The king then took direct action. In October 1775, a British naval force burned the defenseless port of Falmouth, Maine. In December, George III declared the American colonies entirely outside his protection and placed all their ports under blockade by the British fleet. Unable to raise sufficient troops in Great Britain because the war was unpopular, the king hired **mercenaries,** or paid soldiers, from the rulers of small German states. They were generally known as "Hessians," because a large number were supplied by the

Prince of Hesse. By 1776 it was becoming obvious that compromise between the colonies and Britain was impossible. Yet the American Congress held back, unwilling to declare the final separation.

Thomas Paine and *Common Sense*

At this critical moment, *Common Sense* was published. It was written in January 1776 by Thomas Paine, who had recently arrived in America from England. Paine attacked the strongest bond tying America to Britain—loyalty to the king. He assaulted monarchy in general and George III in particular, discrediting hereditary kingship as superstition.

Paine pointed to the advantages Americans might gain if they were free of British commercial restrictions and of Britain's quarrels with its European neighbors. He appealed to the Americans' belief that they were a chosen people, pioneers of liberty.

Common Sense divided Americans into either **Patriots**, those who favored separation, or **Loyalists**, those who supported the British government. The early successes of American Patriots supported Paine's arguments. In Virginia they expelled the royal governor and the soldiers defending him; in North Carolina the militia repulsed an attempted landing of redcoats; in South Carolina a British attack on Charleston was driven back.

The greatest American success occurred in the New England region. When George Washington arrived to take charge of the Continental Army near Boston, he had almost no **artillery**, or large guns to use against British forces. During the winter rebels seized more than 50 cannons from Fort Ticonderoga. Weighing 2 to 6 tons apiece, they were lashed to sledges and dragged by oxen 200 miles over snowy trails and frozen rivers to Dorchester Heights overlooking Boston. During the night of March 4, 1776, about 2,000 militiamen positioned groups of these cannons. In the morning this threat greeted General William Howe. He was left with no choice but to abandon the city.

 Visualizing History ▲ SYMBOLS OF FREEDOM "Raising the Liberty Pole" symbolizes the idea of freedom that was growing in the American colonies. *On what European philosophy were the ideas expressed in the Declaration of Independence based?*

Visualizing ⒽHistory

▲ COLONIAL REACTION Colonists pull down the statue of King George III in New York on July 9, 1776. *On what grounds could the colonists argue that English subjects had the right to overthrow a king?*

Arguments for Independence

Colonists made strong arguments for independence from their need for military supplies and for reopening foreign trade. The Americans lacked guns, gunpowder, ammunition, uniforms, tents, and medical supplies. The cutoff of trade with the British Empire caused acute distress among American shippers and merchants, who had to find new markets. However, commercial treaties with other nations could be written only by an independent nation—not by rebellious colonies.

Members of the Continental Congress hoped for aid from France. Since 1763 the French had desired revenge on Great Britain for the terrible defeat they suffered in the Seven Years' War. As early as November 1775, a French agent had secretly conferred with members of the Congress. Within a few months the French government had started to smuggle arms to the Americans. France, nevertheless, refused to enter into a formal alliance or sign a commercial treaty until the Americans declared independence.

The Colonies Declare Independence

Beginning with North Carolina in April 1776, the colonies advised their delegates in Congress to vote for independence. On June 7, Richard Henry Lee of Virginia introduced a brief "Resolution of Independence." The delegates debated for nearly a month while the moderates in Congress made a last stand for reconciliation. On July 2, 1776, the Continental Congress adopted Lee's resolution "that these united colonies are, and of right ought to be free and independent states." The official Declaration of Independence was agreed upon by Congress on July 4. Its purpose was to justify the revolution, to state that the colonies were independent, and to express the new nation's principles.

The Declaration of Independence

The Declaration of Independence (see pages 122–125) was principally the work of Thomas Jefferson, a young Virginian who had been an inconspicuous member of Congress. A poor public speaker and shy by nature, Jefferson was known as an able writer. When Congress appointed a committee to draw up a public statement justifying independence, he was asked to write the first draft of the Declaration.

Writing the Declaration

Since time was limited, Jefferson drew upon several sources—a declaration of **grievances,** or complaints, he had written earlier; the new Virginia Bill of Rights; Lee's resolution; and writings by European political philosophers. Jefferson was influenced by the ideas of "natural rights" and government by social contract written by the English philosopher John Locke. Jefferson gave the idea of natural rights its most eloquent expression in the Declaration.

Jefferson submitted his draft to Benjamin Franklin, who made a few changes before sending it to Congress. There, additional changes were made before its acceptance.

Preamble

The Declaration has four main parts: the **preamble**, or introduction, which states why the Continental Congress chose to explain their separation from Britain formally and publicly; a declaration of rights, which describes the general theories of government upon which the American Revolution was founded; a long list of grievances against George III; and finally, the formal resolution of independence. The declaration of rights sets forth a philosophy of human rights that has influenced generations.

Declaration of Rights

After a statement in the preamble that the Americans were publishing the Declaration out of "a decent respect to the opinions of mankind," Jefferson wrote this famous sentence, the basis for all that follows:

> **We hold these truths to be self-evident, that all men are created equal, that they are endowed by their Creator with certain unalienable Rights, that among these are Life, Liberty, and the pursuit of Happiness.**

Jefferson did not mean that everyone has the same abilities or the same circumstances. True equality of condition for men and women was not a subject for consideration by even the most enlightened leaders. The self-evident truths to which Jefferson referred were that rights are God-given or "natural," not subject to the whim of a monarch or even an elected government.

The next lines of the Declaration set forth the idea of government by social contract:

> **That to secure these rights, Governments are instituted among Men, deriving their just powers from the consent of the governed, That whenever any Form of Government becomes destructive of these ends, it is the Right of the People to alter or to abolish it. . . .**

Like Locke, Jefferson suggested that the purpose of government is to secure natural rights. Locke had argued that in a "state of nature" people were all free, equal, and independent. They gave up their complete freedom in order to join a community for their own safety and comfort. Jefferson agreed that the origin of government was a **social contract** in which people granted power to the rulers in exchange for protection of their rights. Jefferson insisted that the only rightful aim of government is to protect the individual, and that government is the agent of the people.

If a just government rests on popular consent, the document continues, the people may refuse their consent to an unjust government, may "alter or abolish it," and may set up another government. This passage, then, justified revolution. In the twentieth century it has sometimes been called the **right of self-determination**, meaning the right of people to be free from foreign rule.

Next the Declaration charges that the British government had attempted to put Americans under the king's power. An early version of the document blamed Parliament, but this was altered to read "the present King of Great Britain." This change increased the document's effectiveness because revolt against a tyrannical monarch was more powerful than was a revolt against Parliament.

List of Grievances

The largest section of the Declaration is a list of grievances against George III. Jefferson heaped wrong upon wrong. Note his use of repetition: "He has refused. . . . He has forbidden. . . . He has utterly neglected. . . . He has obstructed. . . . He has plundered. . . ." These charges were not entirely fair. George III did not begin the quarrel with the colonies, nor did he play an important role in shaping policy toward America until 1774. From that point on, however, the king resisted conciliation.

Formal Declaration of Independence

The Declaration of Independence closes by maintaining that the American colonies did everything possible to preserve peace but were spurned by Great Britain. In their mind, there was no other choice for them but to declare the colonies "Free and Independent States." To defend this action, the Americans pledged their lives, their fortunes, and their honor.

■ Influence of the Declaration

The Declaration of Independence became one of the world's most important political documents. In it Americans made a commitment, as Lincoln later stated in the Gettysburg Address, "to the proposition that all men are created equal." The Declaration has been a lever for change—toward equal rights, equal opportunities, and equal voice in government. At different times in our history, it has operated toward ending slavery, giving women the right to vote, enlarging job opportunities, and extending opportunities for education. With his genius for simple and eloquent prose, Jefferson managed to plant the ideals of equality and self-government in the American tradition.

The Declaration demanded independence from Britain on the basis of the natural, inborn rights of all persons. Thus, the Declaration acquired worldwide significance. When the Spanish-American colonies revolted in the early nineteenth century, several drew up declarations based on the United States' model. In the twentieth century, Jawaharlal Nehru, the first prime minister of India, called the Declaration of Independence a "landmark in human freedom."

Section 1 ★ Review

Checking for Understanding

1. **Identify** Hessians, Thomas Paine, General William Howe, Richard Henry Lee.
2. **Define** treason, mercenary, Patriot, Loyalist, artillery, grievance, preamble, social contract, right of self-determination.
3. **Name** three reasons for separating from Great Britain as described in *Common Sense*.

4. Cite the four main sections of the Declaration of Independence and tell what each contains.

Critical Thinking

5. **Making Value Judgments** Explain why unalienable rights were so important that the colonists were willing to fight a war to preserve them.

The Revolutionary Pulpit

The origins of the American Revolution can be traced to changes and developments from the early 1700s. Ideas of self-government were transplanted to the American colonies, and these ideas took root and thrived. The colonial economy, though still sustaining itself through its economic ties with England, was flourishing. Colonial cities were bustling with activity and developing into powerful centers of commerce and trade.

Changes could also be seen in colonial culture. Public schools and institutions of higher learning were on the increase. Colonists set up libraries, and creative thinkers made enduring contributions to knowledge.

Among the most influential thinkers were religious leaders. Their efforts led to a rekindling of religious faith, known as the Great Awakening, which reached its peak around 1740. In New England the fiery sermons of Jonathan Edwards spread the ideas of religious revival. Preacher George Whitefield took the message of revivalism to countless communities.

"If the Americans shall be taught to believe Resistance to be lawful . . . it will not be long before . . . [they] publicly appear in Arms," remarked an English citizen in 1774. His fears were well-founded. The Revolutionary War effort drew powerful support from Congregational, Presbyterian, and other Christian churches, whose clergy had no official ties with England. Boston minister Samuel West interpreted the New Testament discussion on submitting to civil authority as applying only to those leaders who "punish the wicked and encourage the good." Those who do not, he continued, "forfeit their authority to govern the people."

In contrast, the Episcopal Church in America had strong ties with the Church of England. Episcopal clergy, who were ordained in England, saw opposition to British rule as a danger to all authority. Their support of the Crown drew widespread acceptance among the colonial aristocracy, particularly in the Southern colonies.

◀ GEORGE WHITEFIELD PREACHING

Making the Religion Connection

1. How did the strength of their ties with England affect the support or opposition of American clergy to the Revolution?

2. In what ways did Jonathan Edwards and George Whitefield influence Americans?

Linking Past and Present

3. Describe a current political issue on which American clergy are divided.

The Declaration of Independence

    elegates at the Second Continental Congress faced an enormous task. The war against Great Britain had begun, but to many colonists the purpose for fighting was unclear. As sentiment increased for a complete break with Britain, Congress decided to act. A committee was appointed to prepare a document that declared the 13 colonies free and independent from Britain. More important, the committee needed to explain why separation was the only fitting solution to long-standing disputes with Parliament and the British Crown. Thomas Jefferson was assigned to prepare a working draft of this document, which was then revised. It was officially adopted on July 4, 1776. More than any other action of the Congress, the Declaration of Independence served to make the American colonists one people.

★★★

The printed text of the document shows the spelling and punctuation of the parchment original. To aid in comprehension, selected words and their definitions appear in the side margin, along with other explanatory notes.

impel *force*

endowed *provided*

People create governments to ensure that their natural rights are protected.

If a government does not serve its purpose, the people have a right to abolish it. Then the people have the right and duty to create a new government that will safeguard their security.

Despotism *unlimited power*

In Congress, July 4, 1776. The unanimous Declaration of the thirteen united States of America,

Preamble

When in the Course of human events, it becomes necessary for one people to dissolve the political bands which have connected them with another, and to assume among the powers of the earth, the separate and equal station to which the Laws of Nature and Nature's God entitle them, a decent respect to the opinions of mankind requires that they should declare the causes which impel them to the separation.—

Declaration of Natural Rights

We hold these truths to be self-evident, that all men are created equal, that they are endowed by their Creator with certain unalienable Rights, that among these are Life, Liberty, and the pursuit of Happiness.—

That to secure these rights, Governments are instituted among Men, deriving their just powers from the consent of the governed,—

That whenever any Form of Government becomes destructive of these ends, it is the Right of the People to alter or to abolish it, and to institute new Government, laying its foundation on such principles and organizing its powers in such form, as to them shall seem most likely to effect their Safety and Happiness. Prudence, indeed, will dictate that Governments long established should not be changed for light and transient causes; and accordingly all experience hath shewn, that mankind are more disposed to suffer, while evils are sufferable, than to right themselves by abolishing the forms to which they are accustomed. But when a long train of abuses and usurpations, pursuing invariably the same Object evinces a design to reduce them under absolute Despotism, it is their right, it is their duty, to throw off such Government, and to provide new Guards for their future security.—

★★★★★★ ▲ *DECLARATION OF INDEPENDENCE IN CONGRESS* by John Trumbull, 1824 ★★★★★★★★★★★★★★★★★★★★★★★★★★★★★★

List of Grievances

Such has been the patient sufferance of these Colonies; and such is now the necessity which constrains them to alter their former Systems of Government. The history of the present King of Great Britain is a history of repeated injuries and usurpations, all having in direct object the establishment of an absolute Tyranny over these States. To prove this, let Facts be submitted to a candid world.—

usurpations
unjust uses of power

He has refused his Assent to Laws, the most wholesome and necessary for the public good.—

He has forbidden his Governors to pass Laws of immediate and pressing importance, unless suspended in their operation till his Assent should be obtained; and when so suspended, he has utterly neglected to attend to them.—

Each paragraph lists alleged injustices of George III.

He has refused to pass other Laws for the accommodation of large districts of people, unless those people would relinquish the right of Representation in the Legislature, a right inestimable to them and formidable to tyrants only.—

relinquish *give up*
inestimable *priceless*

He has called together legislative bodies at places unusual, uncomfortable, and distant from the depository of their public Records, for the sole purpose of fatiguing them into compliance with his measures.—

He has dissolved Representative Houses repeatedly, for opposing with manly firmness his invasions on the rights of the people.—

He has refused for a long time, after such dissolutions, to cause others to be elected; whereby the Legislative powers, incapable of Annihilation, have returned to the People at large for their exercise; the State remaining in the meantime exposed to all the dangers of invasion from without, and convulsions within.—

Annihilation *destruction*

convulsions
violent disturbances

He has endeavoured to prevent the population of these States; for

The Declaration of Independence **123**

Naturalization of Foreigners
process by which foreign-born persons become citizens

tenure *term*

Refers to the British troops sent to the colonies after the French and Indian War.

Refers to the 1766 Declaratory Act.

quartering *lodging*

Refers to the 1774 Quebec Act.

render *make*

abdicated *given up*

perfidy *violation of trust*

insurrections *rebellions*

Petitioned for Redress
asked formally for a correction of wrongs

that purpose obstructing the Laws for Naturalization of Foreigners; refusing to pass others to encourage their migrations hither, and raising the conditions of new Appropriations of Lands.—

He has obstructed the Administration of Justice, by refusing his Assent to Laws for establishing Judiciary powers.—

He has made Judges dependent on his Will alone, for the tenure of their offices, and the amount and payment of their salaries.—

He has erected a multitude of New Offices, and sent hither swarms of Officers to harass our people, and eat out their substance.—

He has kept among us, in times of peace, Standing Armies without the Consent of our legislatures.—

He has affected to render the Military independent of and superior to the Civil power.—

He has combined with others to subject us to a jurisdiction foreign to our constitution, and unacknowledged by our laws; giving his Assent to their Acts of pretended Legislation:—

For quartering large bodies of troops among us:—

For protecting them, by a mock Trial, from punishment for any Murders which they should commit on the Inhabitants of these States:—

For cutting off our Trade with all parts of the world:—

For imposing Taxes on us without our Consent:—

For depriving us in many cases, of the benefits of Trial by Jury:—

For transporting us beyond Seas to be tried for pretended offences:—

For abolishing the free System of English Laws in a neighbouring Province, establishing therein an Arbitrary government, and enlarging its Boundaries so as to render it at once an example and fit instrument for introducing the same absolute rule into these Colonies:—

For taking away our Charters, abolishing our most valuable Laws, and altering fundamentally the Forms of our Governments:—

For suspending our own Legislatures, and declaring themselves invested with power to legislate for us in all cases whatsoever.—

He has abdicated Government here, by declaring us out of his Protection and waging War against us.—

He has plundered our seas, ravaged our Coasts, burnt our towns, and destroyed the Lives of our people.—

He is at this time transporting large Armies of foreign Mercenaries to compleat the works of death, desolation and tyranny, already begun with circumstances of Cruelty & perfidy scarcely paralleled in the most barbarous ages, and totally unworthy the Head of a civilized nation.—

He has constrained our fellow Citizens taken Captive on the high Seas to bear Arms against their Country, to become the executioners of their friends and Brethren, or to fall themselves by their Hands.—

He has excited domestic insurrections amongst us, and has endeavoured to bring on the inhabitants of our frontiers, the merciless Indian Savages, whose known rule of warfare, is an undistinguished destruction of all ages, sexes and conditions.

In every stage of these Oppressions We have Petitioned for Redress in the most humble terms: Our repeated Petitions have been answered only by repeated injury. A Prince, whose character is thus marked by every act which may define a Tyrant, is unfit to be the ruler of a free people.

Nor have We been wanting in attentions to our British brethren. We have warned them from time to time of attempts by their legislature to extend an unwarrantable jurisdiction over us. We have reminded them of the circumstances of our emigration and settlement here. We have appealed to their native justice and magnanimity, and we have conjured them by the ties of our common kindred to disavow these usurpations, which would inevitably interrupt our connections and correspondence. They too have been deaf to the voice of justice and of consanguinity. We must, therefore, acquiesce in the necessity, which denounces our Separation, and hold them, as we hold the rest of mankind, Enemies in War, in Peace Friends.—

Resolution of Independence by the United States

We, therefore, the Representatives of the united States of America, in General Congress, Assembled, appealing to the Supreme Judge of the world for the rectitude of our intentions, do, in the Name, and by Authority of the good People of these Colonies, solemnly publish and declare, That these United Colonies are, and of Right ought to be Free and Independent States; that they are Absolved from all Allegiance to the British Crown, and that all political connection between them and the State of Great Britain, is and ought to be totally dissolved; and that as Free and Independent States, they have full Power to levy War, conclude Peace, contract Alliances, establish Commerce, and to do all other Acts and Things which Independent States may of right do.—

And for the support of this Declaration, with a firm reliance on the protection of divine Providence, we mutually pledge to each other our Lives, our Fortunes and our sacred Honour.

unwarrantable jurisdiction *unjustified authority*

consanguinity *originating from the same ancestor*

rectitude *rightness*

The signers, as representatives of the American people, declared the colonies independent from Great Britain. Most members signed the document on August 2, 1776.

John Hancock
    President from
    Massachusetts

Georgia
Button Gwinnett
Lyman Hall
George Walton

North Carolina
William Hooper
Joseph Hewes
John Penn

South Carolina
Edward Rutledge
Thomas Heyward, Jr.
Thomas Lynch, Jr.
Arthur Middleton

Maryland
Samuel Chase
William Paca
Thomas Stone
Charles Carroll
    of Carrollton

Virginia
George Wythe
Richard Henry Lee
Thomas Jefferson
Benjamin Harrison
Thomas Nelson Jr.
Francis Lightfoot Lee
Carter Braxton

Pennsylvania
Robert Morris
Benjamin Rush
Benjamin Franklin
John Morton
George Clymer
James Smith
George Taylor
James Wilson
George Ross

Delaware
Caesar Rodney
George Read
Thomas McKean

New York
William Floyd
Philip Livingston
Francis Lewis
Lewis Morris

New Jersey
Richard Stockton
John Witherspoon
Francis Hopkinson
John Hart
Abraham Clark

New Hampshire
Josiah Bartlett
William Whipple
Matthew Thornton

Massachusetts
Samuel Adams
John Adams
Robert Treat Paine
Elbridge Gerry

Rhode Island
Stephen Hopkins
William Ellery

Connecticut
Samuel Huntington
William Williams
Oliver Wolcott
Roger Sherman

★★

Fighting for Independence

Setting the Scene

Section Focus

Having announced their separation from Britain, the Americans faced a draining military struggle to maintain independence. The British would not willingly surrender so large a part of their colonial empire to a band of rebels. During the early stages of the war, it was all Washington could do to prevent the capture of his entire army.

Objectives

After studying this section, you should be able to

★ list two reasons why the American victories at Trenton and Princeton were important.

★ compare the difficulties faced by the Americans and the British in the Revolutionary War.

Key Term

Continental

◄ CONTINENTAL MONEY

arly in 1776 Parliament authorized an army of 55,000, including 30,000 German mercenaries. In August 1776, perhaps the largest single military force ever sent from Europe to America appeared off the coast of New York City—more than 400 transports bearing 32,000 troops, guarded by 30 warships, under the command of Sir William Howe.

With his brother, Admiral Richard Howe, he addressed a conciliatory letter to "George Washington, Esq.," offering to pardon the rebels if they laid down their arms, restored the local governments that existed before 1775, and accepted royal governors and councils. Washington adamantly refused to consider proposals that offered nothing but pardons.

After Washington's refusal, the British war machine moved into action. Easily defeating an ill-trained militia of 20,000

under Washington's command, the British took New York City and held it until the war ended seven years later.

■ British Army Invades America

The British forces followed Washington's army up the Hudson River and, when he crossed to New Jersey, pursued him southward to the Delaware River. Through desertions, deaths, and captures, the American army was now reduced to 5,000, and the Continental Congress was forced to flee from Philadelphia to Baltimore.

Trenton

When all seemed lost, Washington planned a bold move. On the evening of December 25, the first issue of *The Crisis* by

Thomas Paine was read to the troops ("These are the times that try men's souls. . . ."). Hoping to win at least one battle before his troops' terms were up, Washington ferried his soldiers back across the Delaware River in a freezing winter wind.

Nine miles away lay Trenton, held by 1,300 Hessians under the command of Colonel Johann Gottlieb Rall, who regarded the Americans as "country clowns." Rall had taken few precautions against attack. Washington guessed correctly that these German troops would celebrate Christmas by getting thoroughly drunk and took a chance on surprising them the morning after. He attacked at dawn on December 26, killing or capturing more than 1,000 Hessians in only 45 minutes.

Rall, gravely wounded, was carried back to his headquarters. As doctors cut away his clothes to treat his wounds, they found an unopened note from a Loyalist who had tried to warn him the night before that Washington was coming. Had the colonel read this note, he might have ambushed Washington and changed the course of history.

Princeton

When General Howe heard of the defeat at Trenton, he sent General Charles Cornwallis from New York with 8,000 soldiers to capture Washington's force. Washington, whose troops now numbered only 1,500, pretended to be trapped, then slipped away and surprised a British force at Princeton on January 3, 1777. He then moved his army into the highlands of New Jersey out of Cornwallis's reach.

These victories saved the American cause. Philadelphia celebrated when the captured Hessians were paraded through the streets. Because of his earlier failures, Washington had been in danger of being removed from command. Now Congress gave him more power, and new enlistees joined his army as it moved to winter quarters at Morristown, New Jersey.

Visualizing History

▲ VICTORY AT TRENTON With morale sinking among his troops, Washington launched a surprise attack on Christmas night. Crossing the Delaware River into New Jersey, his army captured the British garrison at Trenton and then defeated a second British force at Princeton on January 3, 1777. **Why were the victories at Trenton and Princeton important to the American cause?**

AMERICAN PORTRAITS

Haym Salomon
1740(?)–1785

Forced to flee from his native Poland after championing the cause of Polish freedom, Haym Salomon went first to England and then to America. Arriving in New York in 1772, he soon joined the Patriot struggle.

A Jewish businessman of remarkable ability, Salomon acquired wealth, all of which he risked during the American Revolution. Twice arrested as a spy, Salomon was condemned to death for plotting to burn British ships at anchor outside New York City. He escaped by bribing his jailer and fled to Philadelphia. There he opened a prosperous private banking business and donated thousands of dollars for military supplies and government salaries. He also worked with Robert Morris to secure loans for the war effort. As a result of his devotion to America—and business problems after the war—Salomon died penniless.

■ Financial Problems

Victory was sweet, but harder tests of Patriot endurance lay ahead. Raising a volunteer army for short-term duty was difficult enough; keeping troops in service was nearly impossible. Although some 300,000 persons eventually took up arms as Patriots, Washington could never count on more than 20,000 under his command at any point. Most soldiers served during the winter months, then returned home for the spring planting, and many refused to fight outside their own home areas. Throughout the war Washington begged for more troops, but Congress was powerless to do anything more than pass these requests along to the states.

Paying for the war was equally difficult. Lacking the power to tax, Congress issued **Continentals**, or paper money to be used as currency instead of British coins. These Continentals, which had nothing to support their value, soon became nearly worthless, forcing many American merchants and farmers to sell goods to the British. Fortunately, Robert Morris, a Pennsylvania merchant and banker, personally pledged large amounts of money for the war effort.

A member of the Continental Congress, Morris was elected superintendent of finance in 1781, a position that earned him the title "financier of the American Revolution." Largely through his efforts, sufficient funds were raised to move Washington's army from New York to the final campaign at Yorktown.

■ American Advantages

The Americans faced financial problems and a larger, better-equipped army. However, the American army also held several advantages.

Washington Commands Respect

Washington's leadership was undoubtedly America's greatest asset, even though he lost more battles than he won. He may have been mistaken in training his army on strictly European lines. He sometimes annoyed his troops by his stiff manner and a tendency to talk as though all were lost. Yet no one on the American side did more to win the war.

While British commanders often returned to England for the winter, Washington remained at his post. He saw his home at Mount Vernon only once during the war, and then only for a few hours. He alone commanded sufficient respect to keep the frail Continental Army from dissolving. As one former soldier later told his grandchildren, "He was a fine man, General Washington—he was everything a man should be."

The British People and the War

Great Britain's military strength should have been sufficient to defeat the rebels. The British government had hard cash to pay its troops and to buy food from Loyalist farmers. The disciplined army, well-trained officers, and a strong navy kept supplies flowing. But the British faced several major hurdles. First, the war was unpopular in Britain. General Thomas Gage, who was relieved of his command in 1775, observed:

> 66 *They [colonists] give out that they expect peace on their own terms through the inability of Britain to contend with them; and it is no wonder that such reports gain credit with the people, when letters from England and English newspapers give so much encouragement to rebellion.* 99

Britain's Military Strength Divided

In addition, Britain's sprawling colonial empire, threatened by other European powers, demanded that troops be stationed around the globe. While American soldiers defended their homes, the British, thousands of miles from home, fought for a cause that many did not understand or even support. Finally, in order to win, the British had to gain control of a vast American territory. This task was especially difficult because the Americans' hit-and-run tactics frustrated British generals, and Washington established an effective spy system that brought information from behind British lines at critical times.

Despite these problems, British generals believed they could defeat the poorly equipped Americans. Lieutenant General John Burgoyne devised a plan to divide and conquer the rebels. Neither he nor the Americans could foresee that this effort would backfire, resulting in America's obtaining the key ingredient for its success—French aid.

▲ GENERAL GEORGE WASHINGTON AMONG HIS TROOPS

Section 2 ★ Review

Checking for Understanding

1. **Identify** Trenton, Princeton, General Cornwallis, Robert Morris, General Thomas Gage.

2. **Define** Continental.

3. **List** the American and British advantages at the beginning of the war. Which side do you think had the better chance of winning?

Critical Thinking

4. **Analyzing Ideas** It has been said that George Washington was America's greatest asset in winning the Revolution. Analyze this thesis using the battles at Trenton and Princeton. Use Washington's personal commitment to duty and his leadership qualities to support your argument.

★★★★★★★★★★★★★★★★★★★★★★★★★★★★★★★★

The War Deepens

Setting the Scene

Section Focus

The American Revolution divided opinion both in America and in Europe. Although European rulers hoped that Britain would be humbled and the balance of power restored, they were concerned that their open support for a revolution might encourage rebellion in their own colonies or even at home.

◀ **BENJAMIN FRANKLIN**

Objectives

After studying this section, you should be able to

★ list two reasons why France supported the American Revolution.

★ describe the roles of women, African Americans, and Native Americans in the war.

Key Term

envoy

The first efforts to secure French assistance came as early as 1776 when Silas Deane was sent to Paris. Deane was successful in securing secret aid, but after the Declaration of Independence, the United States desired open support. Benjamin Franklin became the principal American **envoy** [EHN•voy], or delegated representative, to France. Perhaps no foreign diplomat in history was as popular as Franklin in Paris. However, France would not provide funds for the American struggle unless there was some hope of success.

■ British Strategy

Although an American attempt to conquer Canada in 1776 had failed, it forced the British to divert to Canada troops that might have been better used in New York and New Jersey. In 1777 General John Burgoyne planned a great three-pronged attack that would divide the colonies along the line of Lake Champlain and the Hudson Valley. According to the plan, while General Howe moved up the Hudson River from New York City, Burgoyne's army would move south from Montreal. A force under British officer Barry St. Leger would invade by way of Lake Ontario and the Mohawk River. The three armies would meet near Albany.

Because the British war office failed to keep in touch with him, Howe's army never participated in the plan. Hoping to catch Washington, Howe led an expedition from New York to Philadelphia, the capital. He captured Philadelphia in September, overcoming Washington at the Battle of Brandywine and inflicting a further defeat on the Americans at Germantown, Pennsylvania, in October. This time Congress fled to York, Pennsylvania.

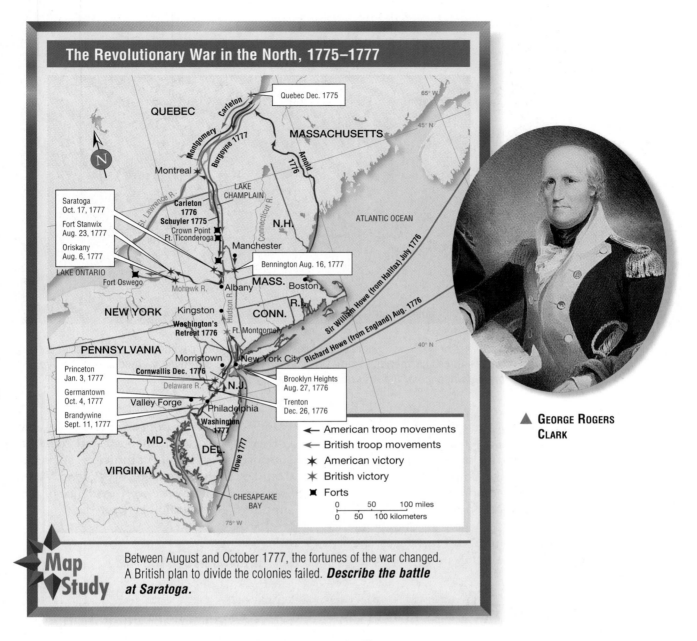

The Revolutionary War in the North, 1775–1777

Quebec Dec. 1775

QUEBEC

MASSACHUSETTS

Montreal

LAKE CHAMPLAIN

Saratoga
Oct. 17, 1777

Fort Stanwix
Aug. 23, 1777

Oriskany
Aug. 6, 1777

Carleton
1776
Schuyler 1775
Crown Point
Ft. Ticonderoga

N.H.

ATLANTIC OCEAN

Manchester

LAKE ONTARIO

Fort Oswego

Bennington Aug. 16, 1777

Mohawk R.

Albany

MASS.

Boston

Sir William Howe (from Halifax) July 1776

NEW YORK

Kingston

CONN.

R.I.

Washington's
Retreat 1776

Ft. Montgomery

Richard Howe (from England) Aug. 1776

PENNSYLVANIA

Morristown

New York City

Princeton
Jan. 3, 1777

Cornwallis Dec. 1776

Germantown
Oct. 4, 1777

Delaware R.

N.J.

Brooklyn Heights
Aug. 27, 1776

Brandywine
Sept. 11, 1777

Valley Forge

Philadelphia

Trenton
Dec. 26, 1776

Washington
1777

MD.

DEL.

Howe 1777

VIRGINIA

CHESAPEAKE
BAY

← American troop movements
← British troop movements
★ American victory
✷ British victory
⚔ Forts

0   50   100 miles
0 50 100 kilometers

▲ **GEORGE ROGERS CLARK**

Map Study Between August and October 1777, the fortunes of the war changed. A British plan to divide the colonies failed. ***Describe the battle at Saratoga.***

Meanwhile, Burgoyne's force of 8,000 troops, unaware that Howe's army would not meet them, started south toward Albany. They easily recaptured Fort Ticonderoga in midsummer.

After such an effortless victory, however, Burgoyne faced one obstacle after another. A force of 1,000 Americans felled trees across the only road to Albany, so that Burgoyne's army could move no more than 1 mile a day.

To further delay Burgoyne's plan, St. Leger's advance from Lake Ontario was slowed by his own troops' bloody ambush of Americans at Oriskany, New York. The stage was set for a dramatic American victory.

■ Saratoga

In spite of his difficulties near Philadelphia, Washington sent some of his best troops to General Horatio Gates, commanding officer for the northern campaigns. Meanwhile, with their homes threatened by the British advance and Burgoyne's Native American allies, New York and New England militia began to gather at Bemis Heights. Eventually, Burgoyne was surrounded by a force nearly twice as large as his own. He was unable to get food, to retreat to Ticonderoga, or to advance on Albany. His force surrendered at Saratoga in October 1777.

▲ BATTLE OF SARATOGA Short of supplies, Burgoyne's forces withdrew to Saratoga where Gates's forces surrounded them. On October 17, 1777, Burgoyne surrendered. *What was the significance of the American victory at Saratoga?*

The victory at Saratoga proved crucial. British ministers offered to grant the Americans generous rights of self-government within the British Empire. Fearing that the offer might be accepted, France signed two treaties with the Continental Congress. The first recognized American independence and granted commercial privileges; the second offered an alliance on favorable terms.

Valley Forge

Before French aid reached America, Washington's army had to endure the unusually harsh winter of 1777 and 1778 encamped at Valley Forge, Pennsylvania. Many of the soldiers lacked food, shoes, and coats. Huddled together in small huts, they wrapped themselves in blankets. By spring nearly one-fourth of the original 10,000 soldiers had died. Others had deserted.

The Prussian Baron Friedrich W.A. von Steuben and the French Marquis de Lafayette joined Washington at Valley Forge, bringing discipline and encouragement. By spring, the tattered army began to regain morale as new provisions arrived from France. Several European nations joined with France to lend financial and military support. Individual volunteers such as Count Casimir Pulaski of Poland, von Steuben, and Lafayette were evidence of the support the Revolution generated.

Difficult Choices

When the Declaration of Independence called the United States "one people," it expressed a hope rather than a fact. Only about one-third of the American people actively supported the war. Another third were indifferent to the Patriot cause. The rest supported the British.

Americans Choose Sides

The American Revolution was a civil war as well as a war against Great Britain. Loyalists, sometimes called Tories, refused to abandon allegiance to the king, and many joined the British army. The struggle between the Patriots and the Loyalists was as bitter as the struggle between the rebels and the British. Patriots thought of the Loyalists as traitors to the American cause.

African Americans

From the beginning of the war, at Lexington, Concord, and Bunker Hill, African American soldiers fought for the American cause. Slaveholders were afraid to give guns to African Americans, however, whether enslaved or free.

In November 1775, orders went out to discharge all African American soldiers in the Continental Army and not to permit others to enlist. Soon after, the royal governor of Virginia promised to free any enslaved person who joined the British army. Many slaves were reportedly crossing into the British lines. As a result, the Continental Congress reversed its policy and allowed free African Americans to reenlist.

Jehu Grant, a slave in Rhode Island, joined the American army fearing that his Loyalist master planned to send him to work on a British ship. Jehu Grant served for 10 months and later achieved freedom.

Other slaves who were recruited into the army either won freedom from the start or at the end of their military service.

Native Americans

Some groups of Native Americans remained neutral, but many joined the British. They knew the Americans opposed the Proclamation of 1763, which reserved the land west of the Appalachian Mountains for Native Americans. British agents encouraged the Native Americans to attack settlements on the frontier. They provided weapons and ammunition to Cherokee to raid the Virginia, Georgia, and Carolina frontiers. These actions diverted many state militia from fighting against British troops. The British stirred up similar trouble throughout the Northwest.

In New York four nations of the Iroquois Confederation supported the British. General Washington sent troops against the Iroquois and broke their confederation. Many

Life of the Times

Yankee Peddler

Farm families during the Revolution had difficulty producing all the materials required for food, shelter, and clothing. Peddlers—traveling hawkers of dry goods—canvased the countryside with pack horses and wagons laden with merchandise. Such Yankee vendors dated from early colonial times and were a prominent fixture in rural America for generations.

Wherever crowds assembled, a peddler selling wares was usually present. In between times the peddler traveled house to house and was a welcome visitor. His inventory varied, of course, but goods ranged from such notions as pins, combs, buttons, and ribbon to necessities such as clocks, tinware, drugs, shoes, spices, cloth, even books. The peddler brought news and gossip, gave advice, and sometimes even treated the sick. Due to customary shortages of currency and coin, barter for goods was the usual practice. Some successful peddlers eventually established themselves in a general store. For others the appeal of the road was simply too great to resist.

▲ YANKEE PEDDLER DISPLAYING GOODS

Visualizing History ▲ WOMEN AND RIGHTS Abigail Adams was a crusader for women's rights, demonstrating the careful thought of educated women of this period. *To what group did the new state bill of rights reserve the full privileges of citizenship?*

Native Americans—including almost all of the Mohawk—moved permanently to Canada.

Women

Many women actively served the American cause. Women often served as secret agents supplying information about British positions and plans. They raised money to equip troops. They ran farms and businesses while their husbands were away at war. John Adams's family would have gone bankrupt had not Abigail Adams capably managed their family farm in Braintree, Massachusetts.

During the war it was common for women to accompany the troops—both American and British—serving as cooks, medics, laundresses, and guides. Sarah Osburn went with her husband's regiment from West Point to Yorktown, washing, mending, and cooking for the soldiers.

A few women fought in the ranks, the most famous being Mary Ludwig Hays, better known as Molly Pitcher. Carrying water to the gunners during the battle of Monmouth, New Jersey, in 1778, she saw her husband fall and took his place at the cannon. For her services she later received a pension of $50 a year. Deborah Sampson disguised herself as a man and enlisted in a Massachusetts regiment. She fought in many battles and was seriously wounded. Sampson was honorably discharged from the army and returned home to marry and raise a family.

Women who supported the Revolution expected to gain from its ideals of democracy and equality. However, the American Revolution did very little to change the political rights of women. Although new state bills of rights declared that all people are equal, they reserved full privileges of citizenship for white males.

▶ DEBORAH SAMPSON

Section 3 ★ Review

Checking for Understanding

1. **Identify** Silas Deane, John Burgoyne, Saratoga, Horatio Gates, Baron Friedrich W.A. von Steuben, Count Casimir Pulaski, Marquis de Lafayette, Tories, Molly Pitcher, Abigail Adams.

2. **Define** envoy.

3. **Cite** both military and diplomatic reasons why the victory at Saratoga was crucial to the American cause.

4. **Explain** the decisions facing African Americans and Native Americans during the Revolutionary War.

Critical Thinking

5. **Analyzing Beliefs** The Revolution has been described as a civil war as well as a rebellion against Great Britain. Analyze this theory based on the conflict between Loyalists and Patriots. Consider each group's political beliefs.

Critical Thinking Skills

Identifying Alternatives

In order to make an informed decision, you must identify the alternatives or the possible options in each situation. Almost any decision you make has alternatives, even if the choices are unpleasant.

Use the following steps to identify and evaluate alternatives:

- **State** the problem or decision to be made.
- **List** all the possible options you can think of.
- **Gather** information to evaluate the alternatives. Map out both positive and negative consequences of each alternative.

Revolutionary leader and public official Samuel Adams early on took a firm position for independence. In 1765 he was elected to the Massachusetts House of Representatives, where he was linked with the colonists arousing public feeling against British measures. As one of the main spokespersons for this position, Adams agitated against the Stamp Act, the Townshend duties, and other measures imposed by Parliament.

Adams wrote many articles alerting Americans of Parliament's actions and helped organize the committees of correspondence in New England.

In 1772 Adams wrote *A List of Infringements and Violations of Rights,* detailing what he considered to be the wrongs committed by Great Britain against the colonists. Adams wrote to convince other colonists of his position:

> "We cannot help thinking, that an enumeration [list] of some of the most open infringements of our rights [by Great Britain], will by every candid person be judged sufficient to justify whatever measures have been already taken, or may be thought proper to be taken, in order to obtain a redress of the grievances under which we labour. . . ."

▲ **SAMUEL ADAMS**

Practicing the Skill

1. What is the topic Adams is discussing?

2. What position does Adams advocate?

3. Identify at least two alternative viewpoints to Adams's position.

4. Following Adams's advice might lead to war with Great Britain. What are some possible consequences of the alternative positions you listed in question 3 above?

5. In August 1776, King George III sent 32,000 troops to the colonies, along with a letter offering pardon for any rebels who laid down their arms. How else could King George III have responded to the Declaration of Independence? In other words, identify Great Britain's alternatives.

★★★★★★★★★★★★★★★★★★★★★★★

The War Ends

Section Focus

Britain hoped to prevent the rebels from securing arms from France and other nations. Yet the rebels held on by avoiding direct confrontation and capture. The rebellion had broken out in the north, but the conclusion would be played out in the south at Yorktown, Virginia.

Objectives

After studying this section, you should be able to

★ identify the problems that the British and Americans faced in continuing the war effort.

★ explain the military strategy that defeated Lord Cornwallis.

Key Term

traitor

◄ COLONIAL SOLDIER

*I*n 1778 the British evacuated Philadelphia and marched across New Jersey toward New York. At Monmouth, Washington attacked General Henry Clinton's baggage train. A mistaken order and perhaps treachery prevented an American victory, but Clinton was not able to take advantage of American blunders. While New York City remained in British hands, Washington kept an eye on the enemy from his camp in nearby White Plains.

■ The Final Years

Unable to capture Washington's army or to put down the rebellion in the north, the British turned their main military efforts to the south. For three years, beginning in 1778, the redcoats marched through Georgia, the Carolinas, and Virginia, never suffering major defeat.

Spain Enters the War

The British were not as successful in the southwest. General Bernardo de Galvez, the governor of Spanish Louisiana, helped Americans ship supplies up the Mississippi River. When Spain officially entered the war in 1779, Galvez's troops defeated the British at Baton Rouge, Natchez, and Pensacola. These battles forced the British to divert troops from their campaigns along the Atlantic coast.

Poor Morale and a Traitor

The American cause suffered a year of gloom in 1780. When 6,000 French troops landed at Newport, Rhode Island, a British fleet promptly blockaded them. The Continental Army had not been paid for a month and was on the verge of mutiny. Civilians suffered from high prices as a result of the flood of paper money that had been printed. American morale received its most severe blow when a major general turned **traitor**— one who commits treason.

Benedict Arnold, a brilliant military leader, had won several battles for the American cause. In 1780 he attempted to turn over to the British the American fort at West Point. Arnold tried to deliver a secret message to the head of British secret service, but three American militiamen intercepted his notes. Washington was given the evidence in Arnold's own writing.

The British were having their troubles, too. Ireland had rebelled, and pro-American riots erupted in London. The British armies could not keep their conquests in the south because they could not win the loyalty of the inhabitants. The British were also harassed by guerrilla fighters under the leadership of Francis Marion, "the Swamp Fox." Sometimes commanding as few as 30 men, Marion repeatedly surprised and defeated small British forces.

Beginning of the End

Believing that Georgia and South Carolina were secure, Lord Cornwallis, the British commander of forces in the south, moved

The Revolutionary War in the South, 1778–1781

- ← American and allied troop movements
- ← British troop movements
- ✳ American victory
- ✳ British victory

Guilford Courthouse March 15, 1781
Kings Mountain Oct. 7, 1780
Cowpens Jan. 17, 1781

Yorktown Oct.19, 1781

Charleston May 12, 1780
Camden Aug.16, 1780

Savannah Dec. 29, 1778

Map Study After Cornwallis moved his troops to Yorktown, Virginia, he was trapped by the French and Americans. *Trace and describe the routes taken by the colonial forces under Washington and de Grasse and British troops under Cornwallis.*

toward North Carolina. At Kings Mountain on October 7, 1780, rebels ambushed an army of 1,100 Loyalists. After this victory Daniel Morgan and General Nathaniel Greene defeated part of a British force under Cornwallis at Cowpens in January, but were forced to retreat at Guilford Courthouse in March 1781.

The most serious setbacks for the British in 1780 and 1781 were naval defeats at the hands of the French, causing them to lose command of the Atlantic. This made possible the capture of the principal British force in the south under Lord Cornwallis, who had moved out of North Carolina to what he believed to be the safety of Yorktown, Virginia.

General Washington learned that a French fleet under Admiral de Grasse was heading for the Chesapeake Bay. At the urging of General Jean Baptiste Rochambeau (ROH•SHAM•BOH), commander of the French troops in America, Washington agreed to a remarkable combined operation against the British. Washington sped south with a large force. The French fleet blocked the entrance to Chesapeake Bay, beating back a British fleet sent to relieve Cornwallis. Meanwhile,

a French army sailed from Rhode Island to Virginia. Additional forces under Anthony Wayne and Lafayette converged on Yorktown. Besieged on land and hemmed in by sea, Cornwallis was forced to surrender on October 19, 1781.

The Treaty of Paris, 1783

The Treaty of Paris in 1783 acknowledged American independence and granted the new nation land from the Atlantic Ocean to the Mississippi River. Although several provisions of the treaty led to later disputes, it was a great diplomatic victory. The United States gained an area four times the size of France and nearly ten times that of the British Isles.

■ Influence of the American Revolution

When British troops marched out of Yorktown to lay down their arms, American bands played a march called "The World Turn'd Upside Down." Perhaps it had. The American victory gave new hope to the oppressed in Europe and endangered the old system of monarchy and aristocracy.

The American Revolution was one of the causes of the French Revolution. The large sums of money France poured into the American Revolution brought its government to the verge of bankruptcy. When the king's ministers proposed new loans or taxes to balance the budget in 1778, French people raised the familiar cry of "no taxation without representation" and forced King Louis XVI to call representatives of the people together in a body known as the Estates-General. The American example of rebellion against a tyrant inspired French revolutionaries.

The British defeat in the Revolutionary War discredited George III and put an end to his attempt to buy control of Parliament. However, in a letter the king wrote in 1782, he refused any blame for the loss of the colonies:

Visualizing History

▲ BATTLE OF COWPENS Daniel Morgan and Nathaniel Greene led American forces at the battle of Cowpens in January 1781. *What was the result of this battle?*

▼ THE MARQUIS DE LAFAYETTE

History AND ART

▲ *SURRENDER OF LORD CORNWALLIS AT YORKTOWN* by John Trumbull, 1824 Surrounded by American and French forces, General Charles Cornwallis was forced to surrender. Although other skirmishes followed, the victory at Yorktown assured America's independence. **Why did Britain offer generous peace terms?**

❝ *I cannot conclude without mentioning how sensibly I feel the dismemberment of America from this empire, and that I should be miserable indeed if I did not feel that no blame on that account can be laid at my door. . . .* ❞

After the defeat at Yorktown, Parliament voted Lord North, George III's prime minister, out of office and took steps to ensure that no king could ever again corrupt and control its members as George III had done. Thus, the American Revolution helped to make the British monarch a figurehead. It also persuaded the British to allow their remaining colonies more self-government. Ralph Waldo Emerson did not exaggerate when he wrote in the "Concord Hymn" that the shot fired by the minutemen on April 19, 1775, was "heard 'round the world."

Section 4 ★ Review

Checking for Understanding

1. **Identify** Benedict Arnold, Francis Marion, Yorktown, General Clinton, Lord Cornwallis, Treaty of Paris.
2. **Define** traitor.
3. **List** three problems that the Americans and the British each faced toward the end of the war.
4. **Detail** the French-American operation that brought about the end of the war.

Critical Thinking

5. **Analyzing Results** A military band played "The World Turn'd Upside Down" when British troops marched out of Yorktown to surrender. Analyze and explain how the world had been turned upside down by the United States's victory in the Revolution and how the course of British and American history was changed.

Using Vocabulary

Each of the following terms pertains to the Declaration of Independence. Use these terms to explain the four parts of the Declaration.

grievance	right of self-
social contract	determination
preamble	

Reviewing Facts

1. **Compare** the plan the British devised to win the war in 1777 with that of the Americans and French in 1780, noting similarities and differences in the two plans.

2. **Describe** the guerrilla tactics used by General Francis Marion and the effect of these methods on the British army.

3. **List** three important military leaders on each side of the conflict, and tell how each influenced the war's outcome.

4. **Explain** the many significant contributions and achievements made by women to the war effort.

5. **Tell** how the participation of African American soldiers in the war enhanced the American cause.

Understanding Concepts

Revolution

1. The American Revolution has been described as the most conservative revolution in history. After looking up the definition of *conservative*, prove or refute the above statement based on what Americans wanted to "conserve," as stated in the Declaration of Independence, and how successful they were in their endeavor.

Civil Rights and Liberties

2. Jefferson turned to natural rights and the contract theory of government when he was writing the Declaration of Independence. Explain why he used these particular concepts.

Critical Thinking

1. **Linking Past and Present** Detail the relationship you see between the theory of government as outlined in the Declaration of Independence and political changes that have occurred in Eastern Europe in recent years.

2. **Understanding Cause and Effect** Analyze the effects of a long and indecisive war on citizen morale and war support. Describe the factors that produce positive effects and negative effects.

3. **Analyzing Artifacts** Study the artifact below and answer the questions that follow.

   a. What is the artifact?

   b. What is its purpose?

   c. How might a modern recruitment poster differ in appearance from this poster?

Writing About History

Narration

Imagine that you are George Washington, Commander in Chief of the Continental Army. Keep a diary of your thoughts and experiences during the awful winter at Valley Forge, 1777–1778. Include items from your expense ledger and accounts of how the

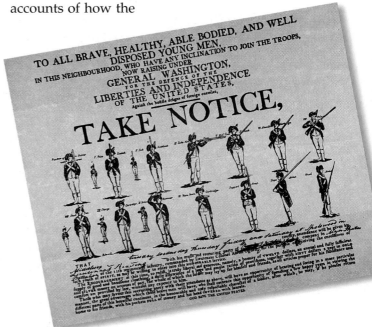

men reacted to the cold, the scarcity of food and clothing, the lack of pay, and the failure of Congress to provide even basic necessities for fighting the war.

Cooperative Learning

You and a partner will take sides in the Revolutionary cause. Decide which one will assume the Loyalist position and which the Patriot position. Adopt an appropriate name for the characters you portray and choose a role that includes personal information such as your occupation, your family, and your community. Write a series of letters to your partner in which you convey your feelings before, during, and after the war. Include your reactions to such events as the Stamp Act, the Boston Massacre, the Boston Tea Party, the Declaration of Independence, the various campaigns and battles of the war, and the Treaty of Paris.

Date your letters so that they follow each event that you discuss. Remember that your personal circumstances and your age will change over the course of the 20 years in which these events took place. In reacting to the events, explain how each relates to the position you took as a Patriot or a Loyalist. Write a final letter that concludes by telling what happened to you and your family at the end of the war. When you finish, present several letters to the class as if it were a script of a play.

Social Studies Skills

Interpreting a Table

Study the table on this page. On a separate sheet of paper, answer the questions that follow.
1. What is the title of the table?
2. How is the table organized?
3. Read the following statements. Write a *T* on your paper if the statement is true based on the information in the table. Write an *F* if the statement is false based on the information. Write an *X* if the validity of the statement cannot be determined from the information.
   a. More than 10,000 Americans died in service.
   b. Fewer than 20,000 Americans were captured.

c. Deaths due to naval engagements outnumber deaths from militia engagements.
d. More American troops than British troops were killed during the Revolution.

American Casualties in the Revolution

	Militia	Naval	Total
Killed in action	5,992	832	6,824
Died as prisoners	—	—	8,500
Total American deaths in service 15,324			
Wounded	7,988	457	8,445
Captured	15,427	2,725	18,152
Missing	1,426	—	1,426
Deserted	99	1	100

Source: Howard H. Peckham. *The Toll of Independence.* Chicago: University of Chicago Press, 1974.

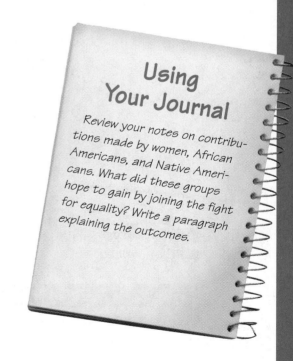

Using Your Journal

Review your notes on contributions made by women, African Americans, and Native Americans. What did these groups hope to gain by joining the fight for equality? Write a paragraph explaining the outcomes.

CHAPTER 6

★★★

A More Perfect Union
1775–1789

▼ FARMERS PLOWING

Setting the Scene

Focus

Americans successfully met the challenge of establishing state governments and a national government under the Articles of Confederation. It soon became apparent, however, that weaknesses of this new national government might break it apart. During this period of experiment and uncertainty, farsighted American political leaders laid the foundations of a free and democratic government embodied in a new constitution.

Concepts to Understand

★ How political control was allocated within the government under the Articles of Confederation

★ Why a strong central authority was needed to keep the republic intact

Read to Discover . . .

★ why people considered the government under the Articles of Confederation weak.

★ what important compromises made the Constitution possible.

Journal Notes

As you read, note in your journal ways in which Americans continued to be divided following the Revolution.

CULTURAL	●**1775** *Smallpox epidemic strikes colonies*	●**1780** *The first Universalist Church in the nation built in Gloucester, Massachusetts*
	1775	**1779**
POLITICAL	●**1776** *New Hampshire adopts the first written state constitution*	●**1781** *Articles of Confederation ratified*

◀ COIN, 1787

The Signing of the Constitution
by Howard Chandler Christy

The delegates sign the final draft of the Constitution in Independence Hall. Despite mixed feelings regarding some aspects of the Constitution, most of those present were hopeful about the future.

● **1784** Empress of China *sails from New York to Canton, China*

● **1787** The Contrast *is first successful stage comedy in New York City*
● **1789** *University of North Carolina founded*

1783

1787

● **1785** *Land Ordinance passed*

● **1787** *Constitutional Convention held in Philadelphia*
● **1788** *Constitution is ratified*

★★★

Government in Transition

Section Focus

As the Revolution progressed, some Americans recognized the need for unity, as well as the need to maintain law. While soldiers fought for freedom, their leaders struggled to create a government to replace British authority. The result was a unique blend of British political heritage and the American experience.

Objectives

After studying this section, you should be able to

★ describe the governments that resulted from state constitutions.

★ list the strengths and weaknesses of the Articles of Confederation.

Key Terms

bicameral, veto, emancipation, disestablished, ratify, public land, unicameral

◀ **SLAVE SHACKLES, 1700S**

A s the fighting spread from Massachusetts in 1775, royal governors throughout the colonies watched their authority collapse. At first a few tried to organize Loyalist resistance, but eventually all royal governors abandoned their offices and fled. In May 1776, Congress urged the colonies to replace their colonial charters with new constitutions.

■ New State Governments

Most state constitutions established state governments similar to the colonial governments they replaced. All states except Pennsylvania and Georgia created **bicameral,** or two-house, legislatures. Members of each house represented geographic districts and, in nearly all the states, were directly elected by the voters.

Major changes were made in the executive branch, however. Many Americans had come to distrust strong executive power. So most state governors were elected to one-year terms by their legislatures and had no power to **veto,** or reject, bills passed.

Citizenship Restrictions

For the most part, citizenship was restricted to white male property owners. Neither women nor African Americans could vote in most states.

Although the Revolution did not win full equality for all Americans, it did move American society in that direction. Because it was difficult to claim that "all men are created equal" in a society where some people were enslaved, many Americans began to question the institution of slavery. Some states passed laws to prohibit the importation of more slaves, and by 1804 every state north of Maryland had provided for the **emancipation**, or freeing, of African American slaves.

Religious Freedom

As the Southern colonies gained independence, the Church of England was **disestablished**—that is, no longer supported by taxation. In Virginia a bill for religious freedom written by Jefferson proclaimed that:

> ❝ . . . [N]o man shall be compelled to frequent or support any religious worship, place or ministry . . . nor shall otherwise suffer on account of his religious opinions or belief, but that all men shall be free to profess, and by argument to maintain, their opinion in matters of religion. ❞

In New England, however, the descendants of the Puritans continued tax support of the Congregational Church and allowed only Protestants to vote. In addition, Roman Catholics could not hold office in five states, and Jews were barred from office in nine.

Although states discriminated against their residents on the basis of race, sex, religion, and economic standing, most state constitutions included bills of rights spelling out the "unalienable rights" that government must recognize and protect. State bills of rights guaranteed trial by jury and freedom of the press.

■ The Articles of Confederation

While the individual states were drafting their constitutions, Congress developed a plan to unite the states and establish its own legal authority. In 1777 Congress completed the document, called the Articles of Confederation, and proposed that it go into effect only after every state had approved it.

Claims on the West

Not until 1781, however, did all the states **ratify**, or agree to, the Articles of Confederation. The main reason for delay was that several states claimed large tracts of western land. Based mainly on colonial charters that had granted land "from sea to sea,"

 ▲ RELIGION, CHURCHES, AND THE COLONIES Churches played a central role in the lives of most early Americans. Virginia's Old Bruton Church is shown in this nineteenth century painting by New York artist A. Wordsworth Thompson. *What was the established church in Virginia before independence?*

Western Land Claims of the Original States

95° W 90° W 85° W 80° W 75° W 70° W

50° N

LAKE OF THE WOODS

LAKE SUPERIOR

BRITISH NORTH AMERICA

VT., 1791 (Claimed by N.Y., Mass., and N.H.)

MAINE (Part of Mass.)

45° N

Mississippi R.

LAKE MICHIGAN

LAKE HURON

LAKE ONTARIO

N.H.

43°43' N

LAKE ERIE

NEW YORK

MASS.

CONN. R.I.

Massachusetts, 1785

42°2' N

Connecticut, 1786

PENNSYLVANIA

N.J.

41° N

Connecticut, 1800

40° N

Ohio R.

MD.

DEL.

ATLANTIC OCEAN

VIRGINIA

LOUISIANA (Ceded to France by Spain, 1800)

36°30' N

NORTH CAROLINA

North Carolina, 1790

35° N South Carolina, 1787

SOUTH CAROLINA

Georgia, 1802

GEORGIA

32°28' N

Ceded by Spain, 1795
Ceded by Georgia, 1802

31° N

30° N

SPANISH FLORIDA

— Boundary of land ceded by New York, 1782
— Boundary of land ceded by Virginia, 1784
▨ State of Franklin
▨ Thirteen original states after land cessions

0   100   200 miles
0 100 200 kilometers

Map Study States without western land claims feared that states with western lands would expand to become so rich and powerful that they would dominate any central government. Therefore, states without western lands refused to agree to a central government until the other states surrendered their land claims. *Which state had the largest land claims in the West?*

these claims often overlapped, causing confusion and conflict. In addition, the six states without western land claims argued that the West should become **public land**, or land belonging to the national government. Maryland refused to ratify the Articles until this demand was met. Virginia, which had huge claims—the present-day

states of Kentucky, West Virginia, Ohio, Indiana, Illinois, Michigan, and Wisconsin—also refused to cooperate. Finally, in 1781, with Lord Cornwallis and the British army moving toward Virginia, the state agreed to give up its land claims. Maryland ratified the Articles, and at last the rebelling states were united.

Fear of Centralized Power

Most members of the Continental Congress were quite wary of a strong central government. They took Benjamin Franklin's Albany Plan of Union as their guide and created what John Dickinson, the main author of the Articles, called a "firm league of friendship" among the states. Governing authority was placed in a **unicameral**, or one-house, Congress in which each state had one vote. Congress could wage war and make treaties. It could raise an army and navy, borrow money, establish a postal system, and manage Native American affairs.

National Government Ineffective

Despite these features, the national government under the Articles proved too weak to operate effectively. There was no executive branch to carry out laws, and no federal courts to interpret them. Executive power was divided among several congressional committees. Two important functions were denied to Congress—the power to tax and the power to regulate commerce.

Unable to collect taxes, Congress had to depend on the generosity of the states for its income. Between 1781 and 1789, however, the states gave Congress only about one-sixth of the funds it requested. Without

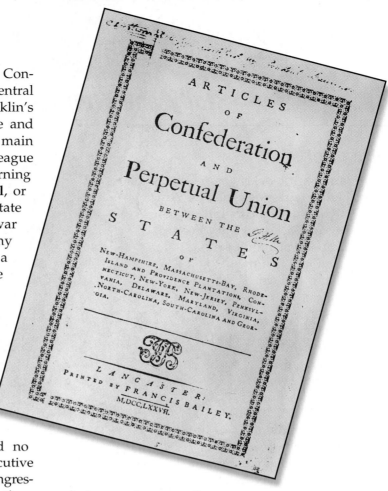

▲ **COVER OF ARTICLES OF CONFEDERATION**

money or real power over the states, the Confederation Congress commanded so little respect that its members often did not bother to attend sessions. In 1783 it was difficult even to convene enough members to ratify the treaty ending the Revolutionary War.

Section 1 ★ Review

Checking for Understanding

1. **Identify** Articles of Confederation, Confederation Congress.

2. **Define** bicameral, veto, emancipation, disestablished, ratify, public land, unicameral.

3. **Explain** why the newly formed states made major changes in their executive branches.

4. **Describe** the positive and negative features of the Articles of Confederation.

Critical Thinking

5. **Expressing Viewpoints** Imagine that you live in the new United States after the Revolution. Based on your own sex, race, and religion, tell to what extent the Revolution has brought about equality for you.

Study and Writing Skills

Taking Notes

A committee of delegates to the Second Continental Congress designed the Articles of Confederation. The committee members had heard Richard Henry Lee's original proposal of a confederation. No doubt, while they were listening to Lee, delegates dashed down notes about the plan and their opinions about it.

Experts agree that one of the best ways to remember something is to write it down. Taking notes—writing down information in an orderly and brief form—not only helps you remember, but it also makes your studying easier.

▲ Lap desk invented by Thomas Jefferson

There are several styles of note taking, but all clarify and put information in a logical order. When taking notes, it will help to keep in mind these guidelines:

- **Identify** the subject and write it at the top of the page. In your text, for example, look at the chapter title, section title, or subsection headings.

- **Select** specific information for your notes. For example, anything your teacher writes on the chalkboard or shows you from a transparency should be included. If your teacher emphasizes a point or spends a considerable amount of time on a given topic, this is also a clue to its importance.

- **Paraphrase** the information. That is, put the information in your own words rather than trying to take it down word for word. That will make you think about what the author or speaker meant.

In order to save time, you might want to develop different strategies. One way is to create a personal "shorthand." For example, eliminate vowels from words: "develop" becomes "dvlp," "government" changes to "gov." Use symbols, arrows, or rough drawings: "+" for "and." Practice your shorthand in all of your classes.

- **Write** legible and neat notes so that you will be able to understand them when you read them again.

Practicing the Skill

Review the guidelines for taking notes. Then read Section 2, entitled "The Confederation." After you have carefully analyzed the section, follow the guidelines and create shorthand notes for the subsection entitled "Settling the West," which begins on page 151.

★★★★★★★★★★★★★★★★★★★★★★★★★★★★★★★★

The Confederation

Setting the Scene

Section Focus

The United States, under the Articles of Confederation, was an unstable nation. America expanded westward, but it continued to have problems with other nations. There was constant bickering among the states, and many groups in society were discontented.

◀ FARMER HARROWING FIELDS

Objectives

After studying this section, you should be able to

★ discuss the problems between the United States and other nations.

★ explain the process of settling the West.

★ identify the domestic problems of the new nation.

Key Terms

right of deposit, tribute, seceding, depression, currency

One of the blessings of independence predicted by Thomas Paine in *Common Sense* was that America would at last be free of European rivalries. Even before the Treaty of Paris was ratified, the Confederation Congress resolved that "the true interest of these states requires that they should be as little as possible entangled in the politics and controversies of European nations." Yet total isolation from Europe was impossible.

The prosperity of the United States depended, as before the Revolution, on trade with European nations and their colonies. Satisfactory trading arrangements required that the United States make commercial treaties with those nations. There also were problems with the Spanish in Florida and New Orleans to the south, and with the British in the north. These problems, too, could be settled only through diplomatic efforts.

■ Foreign Relations

Predictably, the United States did not enjoy good relations with Great Britain. The British agreed to receive John Adams as minister from the United States, even though he had been a prominent rebel during the war. They refused, however, to send a minister to the United States, explaining that they did not know whether to send 1 or 13—a representative for each individual state.

Treaty Violations

Neither country carried out the terms of the Treaty of Paris. The United States had agreed that British creditors could recover prewar debts by suing in American courts, and that Congress would ask the states to cease persecution of Loyalists. But when British merchants sued in state courts, unfriendly judges and juries usually sided

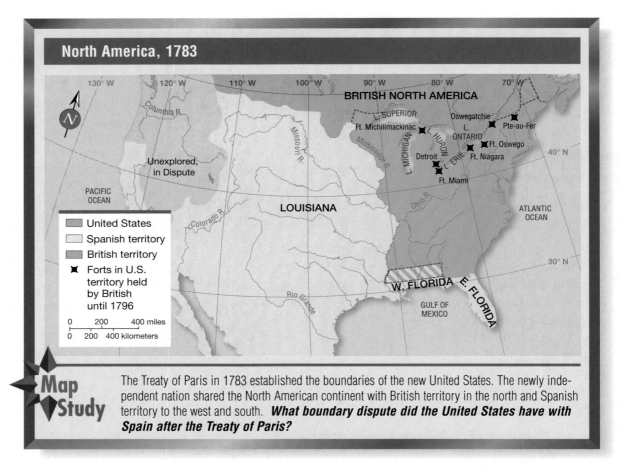

North America, 1783

United States
Spanish territory
British territory
Forts in U.S. territory held by British until 1796

0   200   400 miles
0   200   400 kilometers

Map Study

The Treaty of Paris in 1783 established the boundaries of the new United States. The newly independent nation shared the North American continent with British territory in the north and Spanish territory to the west and south. *What boundary dispute did the United States have with Spain after the Treaty of Paris?*

with American debtors. The states also ignored Congress and continued to treat Loyalists harshly. The British government used these treaty violations as an excuse to remain in northern forts they had agreed to abandon. These posts were the centers of a million-dollar annual fur trade that Great Britain was determined to keep.

American Trade Suffers

Tobacco and naval stores no longer enjoyed a preferred position in British markets. American ships were banned from the British West Indies, and they were allowed to enter English ports only with the products of their home states. When the United States tried to negotiate, Britain showed little desire to grant economic privileges.

Trouble With Spain

The Spanish were unhappy about the vast western lands the United States acquired in the Treaty of Paris, fearing that future expansion would threaten the Spanish empire in America. Spain insisted that the southern boundary of the United States was not the border described in the Treaty of Paris, but a line nearly 100 miles to the north. To protect its claims, Spain formed alliances with the Cherokee, Creek, and Chickasaw nations and incited them against American settlers in the disputed territory.

By controlling the mouth of the Mississippi River, Spain also was able to threaten western trade. Bulky goods from the West—lumber, grain, and deerskins—could not be easily carried over the mountains to the East, but had to float down the Ohio and Mississippi rivers on rafts and flatboats. Westerners wanted the **right of deposit** at New Orleans—that is, permission to put goods ashore for transfer to ocean-going ships without paying duties. When Spain refused this request, westerners asked Congress for a treaty with Spain that would grant free navigation along the Mississippi River. Although a treaty was proposed, it did not address western interests.

Strained Relations with France

During the Revolutionary War, French loans helped the Americans. Now rising debt interest on loans created serious problems in France. Hoping to stave off bankruptcy, the government introduced reforms and universal land taxes. The French were also disappointed that few commercial opportunities resulted from American independence.

The Barbary Pirates

The most humiliating foreign relations problem for the nation was its treatment by the Barbary Pirates. Four North African states—Morocco, Tunis, Tripoli, and Algiers—made a practice of capturing the ships and crews of nations who refused to pay them an annual **tribute**, a payment to sail in their waters. No longer protected by the British fleet and treasury, American ships were subject to attack.

■ Settling the West

Until the end of the 1800s, "the West" was not a specific geographic region of the United States. Instead, it was a term for the next area of settlement, as pioneers invaded the territory of Native Americans and moved them off the land. During the Confederation period, the West lay just beyond the Appalachian Mountains. Between 1780 and 1790 the western population grew from 2,000 to 100,000.

Congress was powerless to meet these westerners' needs. It could not dislodge the British from their forts in the North or persuade Spain to grant the right of deposit in the South. Without money, Congress could neither purchase Native American land nor provide troops to protect settlers.

Westerners had other grievances with the national government as well. Many resented that eastern speculators held large tracts of western land.

▲ *DANIEL BOONE ESCORTING SETTLERS THROUGH THE CUMBERLAND GAP* by George Caleb Bingham, 1851–2 In many of his works, George Caleb Bingham depicts life along the Missouri and Mississippi rivers. ***Who was living on the land settled by these pioneers?***

Talk of Secession

In 1784, after making a journey to the West, George Washington reported that the region was hanging to the Confederation by a thread. In present-day Tennessee, settlers created a government called the State of Franklin. Unable to obtain statehood from Congress, some Tennessee leaders considered **seceding**, or withdrawing, from the Union. Settlers in the Kentucky territory also talked of secession. The Confederation Congress responded with two laws that established a precedent for the future growth of the nation.

The Land Ordinance of 1785

Determined not to repeat the problems in Kentucky and Tennessee—and also to raise money—Congress passed the Land Ordinance of 1785. This law provided a more orderly method for settling public land north of the Ohio River. The land would be surveyed and divided into townships six miles square. Every township was to contain 36 sections of one square mile, 640 acres, each. The land would sell for $1 per acre. To attract land speculators, the law required that buyers take at least one whole section. Speculators could divide their sections into smaller rectangular tracts and sell them to settlers at a profit.

The Northwest Ordinance of 1787

To provide for a strong government, Congress passed the Northwest Ordinance of 1787. The region bounded by the Ohio River, the Great Lakes, and the Mississippi River was to be divided into not fewer than three territories nor more than five. Whenever 5,000 adult male citizens settled in a territory, they could set up a territorial government modeled on a British royal colony. The settlers would elect a territorial legislature. The national government

Life of the Times

★★

Home Remedies

In an age before germs and proper sanitation were understood, home remedies for illness became an everyday, and perhaps necessary, part of pioneer life. While some folk remedies, such as herbal teas, might have had positive effects, other cures could make the patient worse. Consider these examples.

For venomous snakebite, a part of the reptile that inflicted the wound was placed on top of the incision. This, it was thought, would draw out the poison.

Mumps were treated by rubbing the ill person's spine with garlic. One cure for measles was to make a warm broth of water and sheep dung. The patient sipped the broth until recovery.

Indigestion was a common problem. A mixture of cayenne pepper and alcohol applied to the stomach supposedly spelled relief.

Worms in children could be treated by boiling sage in milk, turning it to whey with vinegar or alum, then having the child drink it. If the worms did not harden in the stomach, the child would live.

Some of the best cures were learned from the Native Americans, who used native plants in pastes and teas.

★★★★★★★★★★★★★★★★★★★★★★★★★

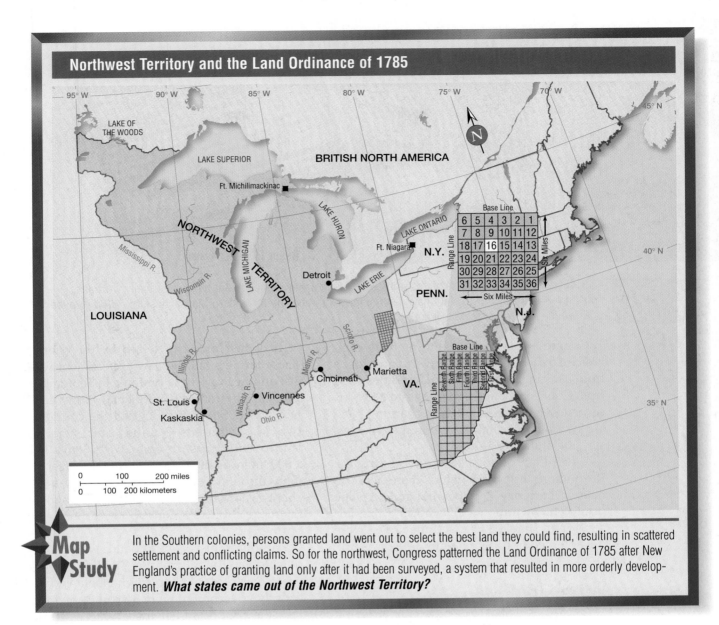

Northwest Territory and the Land Ordinance of 1785

LAKE OF THE WOODS

LAKE SUPERIOR

BRITISH NORTH AMERICA

Ft. Michilimackinac

NORTHWEST TERRITORY

LAKE HURON

LAKE MICHIGAN

LAKE ONTARIO

Ft. Niagara

N.Y.

Detroit

LAKE ERIE

PENN.

N.J.

LOUISIANA

Mississippi R.

Wisconsin R.

Illinois R.

Miami R.

Scioto R.

Wabash R.

Ohio R.

Cincinnati

Marietta

Vincennes

VA.

St. Louis

Kaskaskia

Base Line

6	5	4	3	2	1
7	8	9	10	11	12
18	17	16	15	14	13
19	20	21	22	23	24
30	29	28	27	26	25
31	32	33	34	35	36

Range Line

Six Miles

Six Miles

Base Line

Range Line

Seventh Range · Sixth Range · Fifth Range · Fourth Range · Third Range · Second Range · First Range

0   100   200 miles
0   100   200 kilometers

Map Study

In the Southern colonies, persons granted land went out to select the best land they could find, resulting in scattered settlement and conflicting claims. So for the northwest, Congress patterned the Land Ordinance of 1785 after New England's practice of granting land only after it had been surveyed, a system that resulted in more orderly development. ***What states came out of the Northwest Territory?***

appointed and paid judges and a territorial governor.

The Northwest Ordinance provided a democratic model for national expansion. When the population of a territory reached 60,000, its people could organize a new state and apply for admission to the Union as the equal of the other states.

The Northwest Ordinance also extended into the territories personal rights guaranteed in the constitutions of the original 13 states, such as freedom of religion, speech, and assembly. Perhaps more important, it prohibited slavery north of the Ohio River, an act that had a lasting effect on the political geography of the United States.

■ State Disputes

While the Confederation Congress was providing for stability in the West, the eastern states engaged in disputes with one another. These difficulties resulted from suspicion and rivalry, from the postwar **depression**—or economic slowdown—and from the weak central government.

Boundary and Tax Disputes

Conflicts erupted as states engaged in boundary disputes. Parts of present-day Vermont were claimed by other states. A serious conflict between Connecticut and Pennsylvania almost resulted in war.

▲ RHODE ISLAND CURRENCY

▲ SHAYS'S REBELLION Some states printed so much paper money that it became virtually worthless. Jacobb Shattucks and Daniel Shays led the farmers' rebellion in western Massachusetts. *What grievances did these rebelling farmers have?*

Congress was powerless to regulate commerce, so each state passed laws taxing goods from its neighbors. New York taxed firewood from Connecticut and cabbage from New Jersey. New Jersey retaliated by charging New York for a harbor lighthouse on the New Jersey side of the Hudson River.

When the Continentals issued during the Revolution lost their value, there was no national **currency**, or paper money. Each state printed its own money. The notes' value differed from state to state, and they often were not accepted outside the states issuing them.

Shays's Rebellion

In Massachusetts the economic situation became explosive. Unable to pay their debts, farmers in western Massachusetts were jailed or had their property seized by the courts. These farmers felt the new government was just another variety of tyranny. In September 1786, led by former Continental Army captain Daniel Shays, they closed the courts in two Massachusetts counties and stopped land confiscations. In early 1787, Shays led 1,000 men against the Springfield arsenal. Only through donations from wealthy merchants was Massachusetts able to raise a militia force strong enough to meet Shays at Springfield.

Although his rag-tag band was easily defeated by the militia, the rebellion caused great alarm, and people who believed in orderly government were fearful. It seemed that the prophecies of those who said the United States could not form an effective system of government were coming true.

Section 2 ★ Review

Checking For Understanding

1. **Identify** John Adams, Cherokee, New Orleans, Barbary Pirates.

2. **Define** right of deposit, tribute, secede, depression, currency.

3. **Describe** the difficulty between the United States and Spain over right of deposit at New Orleans.

4. **Specify** the reasons for Shays's Rebellion and show how it led to the Constitutional Convention.

Critical Thinking

5. **Contrasting Ideas** This period saw the beginnings of a "sectional" awareness within the new United States. Contrast the economic interests in various areas of the country at this time.

★★★

Toward a New Constitution

Section Focus

Some Americans became convinced that the Articles of Confederation were an inadequate framework for government. At a convention to address this problem, a new constitution was drawn up. Acceptance of the new government by the public, however, was not assured.

Objectives

After studying this section, you should be able to

★ explain the arguments for and against the new constitution.

★ explain how the Constitution corrected the weaknesses of the Confederation government.

Key Terms

federalism, amendment

◀ **CELEBRATING THE CONSTITUTION**

*A*fter the war, George Washington had retired to Mount Vernon, his Virginia estate on the Potomac River. But concern about the nation's problems moved him to action once again. In 1785 he invited representatives of Virginia and Maryland to Mount Vernon to discuss their differences. The meeting's success inspired Maryland and Virginia to invite all states to meet at Annapolis, Maryland, to discuss common problems.

When the Annapolis Convention met in September 1786, delegates from only five states were present, so they could do little. Included in this group, however, was Alexander Hamilton of New York, an outspoken supporter of a strong national government. Hamilton persuaded the delegates to propose another convention. Its purpose would be to regulate commerce and to propose measures making the national government more effective. Congress responded by

calling a meeting of the states in Philadelphia, "for the sole and express purpose of revising the Articles of Confederation."

■ The Philadelphia Convention

The date set for the Philadelphia Convention was May 14, 1787, but it was May 24 before enough delegates arrived to do business. Eventually 12 of the 13 states were represented. Only Rhode Island was not represented.

Assembling the Delegates

The 55 delegates at the convention included many of the most able political leaders in the United States. Most were lawyers or judges; 21 had college degrees, a high

The young Virginia lawyer first came to public attention in 1774 as a political thinker and writer when he penned a pamphlet in defense of colonial rights. Jefferson acquired his lifelong love of books on science, philosophy, and literature from his childhood teachers and as a student at William and Mary College.

Jefferson's effectiveness as a writer went far beyond his literary style. His writings reflected careful reading and study. Jefferson loved ideas—as well as book collecting. His enormous library later became the basis of the Library of Congress. As minister to France from 1785 to 1789, he shipped nearly 200 volumes to his good friend James Madison. These books—mostly works on political theory—had a profound impact on Madison's thinking about a new government for the United States.

Thomas Jefferson
1743–1826

number in a time when few people had any formal education. Nearly all the delegates had practical experience in government. Most had helped write their state constitutions. More than half had sat in the Continental Congress and so had seen for themselves the unhappy consequences of a weak central government.

Franklin, the oldest delegate at 81, was in poor health and did not attend regularly. Washington was elected to preside over the proceedings, so, like Franklin, his participation in the discussions was limited. But they were the best-known Americans of their time and their presence gave the convention great prestige.

The Virginia Plan

James Madison, a 36-year-old Virginian, was the first delegate to arrive at the convention, and he was the most prepared. He came to Philadelphia with a draft of a completely new framework of government. Virginia governor Edmund Randolph immediately presented Madison's proposal, known as the Virginia Plan. This document became the basis for discussion in the convention; it is the foundation for the Constitution of the United States.

■ Conflicting Plans

Almost all delegates at the convention agreed that the Articles were hopelessly weak, but there were two serious conflicts that proved difficult to resolve. Differences developed between large states and small states over representation in Congress and between northern and southern states over economic issues and the institution of slavery.

Representation

The dispute between large and small states nearly broke up the convention. The large states demanded that each state be represented by population in the bicameral Congress Madison had proposed. By what possible right, they asked, should Delaware's 59,000 inhabitants have equality with Virginia's 692,000? The small states insisted that they would never give up the equal power they enjoyed under the Articles of Confederation to be swallowed up by the large states. William Paterson of New Jersey presented an alternative proposal, known as the New Jersey Plan, which would have merely strengthened the Articles of Confederation.

Disagreement also arose over the structure of the new government. Large-state delegates generally favored Madison's plan for a national government with separate executive, legislative, and judicial branches and with the states subordinate to the national government. Most small-state delegates supported the New Jersey Plan, which continued the Confederation and left the states supreme.

For two weeks, bitter debate raged over these differences. There seemed no middle ground between the large and the small states. Washington wrote a friend that he had lost all hope for the convention and regretted having anything to do with it. Franklin proposed that each session be opened with prayer, to ask divine guidance in finding an acceptable compromise.

The deadlock was broken when the delegates took a day off to celebrate the Fourth of July. During the recess, a committee worked out what became known as the "Great Compromise." According to this agreement, state representation in the lower house of Congress would be based on population; in the upper house each state would have an equal vote. The delegates' ability to resolve this dispute increased their confidence in compromise as the key to a successful convention. For this reason, the Constitution that emerged from Philadelphia has been called a "bundle of compromises." Compromise can be found in nearly every section of the document.

Economic Interests

A dispute arose between the commercial interests of the North and the plantation interests of the South. Southerners wanted to count slaves to determine representation to Congress but not for direct taxation. The North wanted to count slaves for taxation but not for representation. A "three-fifths compromise" established that five slaves would be equal to three free persons for both representation and taxation.

South Carolina and Georgia, afraid that a strong national government might act against slavery, insisted that the Constitution forbid interference with the slave trade. The delegates agreed that for 20 years the national government would not prevent the importation of slaves nor charge an import duty of more than ten dollars a head.

Compromises Yield a New Government

These compromises allowed the delegates to complete their two essential tasks: to give the national government more power and to provide a framework for a workable government. The delegates granted to the central government the powers it had needed most under the Articles of Confederation. The new government could levy and collect taxes, provided such taxes were "uniform throughout the United States." It could regulate commerce with foreign nations and between the states. Thus it could write and enforce commercial treaties that would increase foreign trade, and it could keep trade among the states free of barriers. It could also coin money and regulate its value, so there could be a national standard of money instead of state currencies with differing values.

Visualizing History

▲ JAMES MADISON As one of the delegates from Virginia, James Madison participated in the lengthy, often heated debates that created a foundation of government for the United States. *What other contributions did Madison make to the Constitution?*

The Executive Branch

Although the greatest disputes at the convention were over the structure and powers of the legislative branch, the delegates also disagreed about the executive branch. Everyone at the convention agreed on the need for an executive branch to operate the government, but some delegates favored a group executive, so that no one individual could become too powerful. The executive committees of the Confederation Congress had not worked out well, and Hamilton's proposal for a single executive chosen by Congress for life was too reminiscent of monarchy. In the final weeks of the convention, two more compromises were achieved. A single executive would serve a four-year term. This person would be chosen not directly by the people but indirectly by special electors named by the legislature of each state.

The Judicial Branch

As the long hot summer drew to a close, the exhausted delegates merely roughed out the framework of the judicial branch. In so doing, they created only a Supreme Court and empowered the new government to create "such inferior Courts as the Congress may from time to time ordain and establish."

Their work concluded, the delegates reviewed their efforts. No one was completely happy with the final plan, but most agreed it was a vast improvement on the Articles. Madison recorded the reaction of Benjamin Franklin:

 Doctor Franklin, looking toward the President's chair, at the back of which a rising sun happened to be painted . . . "I have," said he, "often and often in the course of the Session . . . looked at that [sun] behind the President without being able to tell whether it was rising or setting; but now, at length I have the happiness to know it is a rising and not a setting Sun. 99

■ The Ratification Struggle

On September 17, 1787, after four months of work, the delegates to the Constitutional Convention gathered one last time to sign their work. Of the 55 who had come to Philadelphia that spring, 42 were still on hand, and all but 3 agreed to sign the

 ▲ INDEPENDENCE HALL George Washington sat at this platform desk in Philadelphia's Independence Hall to preside over the Constitutional Convention. *Why was Washington's presence so important?*

The Ninth *PILLAR* erected !

"The Ratification of the Conventions of nine States, shall be sufficient for the establishment of this Constitution, between the States so ratifying the same." *Art. vii.*

INCIPIENT MAGNI PROCEDERE MENSES.

If it is not up it will rise.

The Attraction must be irresistible

▲ SUPPORT FOR RATIFICATION A 1788 cartoon celebrates Virginia and New York's becoming the tenth and eleventh states to ratify the Constitution. *When approval of only nine states was needed, why was the approval of Virginia and New York so important?*

document. Then the delegates adjourned to a nearby tavern for a farewell dinner before beginning their journeys home to campaign for ratification.

The Framers of the Constitution anticipated that ratification would be difficult. Rhode Island, which had boycotted the convention, certainly would not approve. So it seemed foolish to insist on the unanimous approval required to amend the Articles. Instead, the Constitution provided that "the ratification of nine States shall be sufficient for the establishment of this Constitution."

The Constitution Opposed

To get even nine states to ratify the Constitution was no small task. Some states objected to surrendering their power and independence to the national government. Mercy Otis Warren, an influential political writer, observed:

> ❝ *Not one legislature in the United States had any idea when they sent delegates to the convention at Philadelphia that it would destroy their state governments and offer them a consolidated system instead.* ❞

Nor were supporters of states' rights pleased that the new Constitution bypassed state governments in the ratification process.

Ratification was to be decided by special conventions to be called in each state, a process implementing the idea expressed in the Declaration of Independence that governments "derive their just powers from the consent of the governed."

Even among the "governed," however, opposition was strong. Debtors and paper-money advocates were opposed to any plan forcing full payment of debts and restoring sound currency. There was certainly suspicion of a powerful central government. Why revolt from Great Britain, people asked, simply to fall under a new kind of tyranny? Popular leaders such as John Hancock, Samuel Adams, and Patrick Henry opposed it.

Support Organized

Those who favored the new plan of government called themselves "Federalists." They took this name to emphasize that the Constitution was based on the principle of **federalism**, a system in which power is divided between a central government and regional governments, and to remind Americans that the states would retain many of their powers. Of course, those who opposed the Constitution were "Federalists" too, because the league of states created by the Articles also was based on federalism. The real issue was whether the national government or the state governments would be supreme. By taking the name "Federalists," however, the supporters of the Constitution caused their opponents to be tagged with the negative label "Anti-Federalists."

Although the two sides were almost equally divided, several factors worked against the Anti-Federalists. Their campaign was a negative one. They attacked almost everything about the Constitution and complained that it failed to protect basic liberties such as freedom of speech and religion. But the Anti-Federalists had nothing to offer in its place.

The Federalists, on the other hand, presented a definite program to meet the difficulties facing the nation. They promised that if the Constitution were ratified, **amendments**, or additions and changes, would be made to provide a Bill of Rights to protect the people.

The Federalists

The Federalists also made better use of communications. They were supported by most of the nation's newspapers. They presented their case more convincingly in sermons, pamphlets, and debates in state conventions.

The Federalists' campaign for ratification produced one of the finest pieces of political writing in the history of the world, *The Federalist*—a collection of 85 essays written by Hamilton, Madison, and John Jay. Originally published as newspaper articles in the *New York Journal*, the essays explained in detail the importance of the Constitution to the success of the nation.

The Constitution Is Ratified

The Federalists succeeded in getting the Constitution ratified not merely because they were good speakers and writers, but because they were politically shrewd. In the states where strong opposition existed, the Federalists were able to outmaneuver their opponents.

In Pennsylvania, the Federalists called the election for the state's ratifying convention before the Anti-Federalists had an opportunity to organize. In Massachusetts, the Federalists used influential Anti-Federalist leader John Hancock to gain support for the Constitution. They suggested that if the Constitution were ratified, Hancock could be the first President of the United States.

In New York, two-thirds of the State Convention were Anti-Federalists. But the persuasiveness of John Jay and the news that 10 states had already ratified the Constitution convinced enough Anti-Federalists to change sides so that New York became the "eleventh pillar" of the new federal roof.

The vote in several key states was extremely close: in the Massachusetts ratifying convention, 187 voted in favor of the Constitution, 168 voted in opposition to it; in Virginia the vote was 89 to 79; and in New York 30 to 27. By July 1788, however, all the states except Rhode Island and North Carolina had ratified, and preparations were made to launch the new government without them.

Section 3 ★ Review

Checking for Understanding

1. **Identify** Philadelphia Convention, Virginia Plan, New Jersey Plan, Federalists, Anti-Federalists.

2. **Define** federalism, amendment.

3. **Describe** the key compromises that were made in the Constitution concerning representation, slavery, and the executive branch.

4. **Distinguish** between the positions of the Federalists and the Anti-Federalists.

Critical Thinking

5. **Making Inferences**   Why would it have been considered significant when people such as John Hancock, Samuel Adams, and Patrick Henry opposed the new Constitution?

CONNECTIONS

CONNECTIONS

Astronomy and the Constitution

Like most delegates to the Constitutional Convention, James Madison was greatly influenced by the ideas of the European Enlightenment. Madison recognized the Enlightenment idea of the need for careful investigation of accepted principles and authorities, whether in politics, religion, or science. Madison also endorsed the theory that the universe was an orderly machine that worked according to natural laws. Like other Enlightenment thinkers, Madison also believed that there were "natural laws" that governed human behavior. These natural laws operated much like the laws that governed the physical universe.

Madison was much impressed by an intricate working model of the solar system, an orrery (AWR•uh•ree), built in 1767 by Philadelphia astronomer David Rittenhouse. Rittenhouse was one of the prominent leaders in American science. He built the first observatory in the colonies and constructed a telescope that may have been the first made in the colonies. After the American Revolution, Rittenhouse served as treasurer of Pennsylvania and director of the United States Mint. Rittenhouse used the orrery to illustrate the theories of Isaac Newton. Newton believed that the solar system was held in place by a balance between centrifugal force and the power of gravity. Centrifugal force is the force that tends to move an object outward from a center of rotation.

Just as the solar system was stabilized by equal but opposing forces, Madison reasoned, so might a stable government result from a

▼ RITTENHOUSE'S ORRERY

balance of political powers. Thus Madison found in the theories of Isaac Newton support for federalism—a strong national government balanced by the power of the states.

Making the Science Connection

1. What was Rittenhouse's orrery supposed to demonstrate?
2. How did Newtonian theory influence Madison?

Linking Past and Present

3. What other examples of balances in power are there in national government today?

161

Using Vocabulary

Each of the following terms has a meaning that relates to government. Find the definition of each word and then write a sentence in which you give an example of its meaning.

bicameral   veto
federalism   amendments
ratify

Reviewing Facts

1. **Describe** the problems faced by the United States under the Articles of Confederation.

2. **List** reasons why England and Spain refused to negotiate trade treaties with the United States after the Revolution.

3. **Explain** why right of deposit at New Orleans was essential to western farmers.

4. **State** the main purposes for passage of the Land Ordinance of 1785 and the Northwest Ordinance of 1787.

5. **Explain** why the delegates' backgrounds at the Constitutional Convention were helpful.

6. **Identify** the disagreements that divided the delegates at the Constitutional Convention.

7. **Detail** why *The Federalist* helped win public support for the new Constitution.

Understanding Concepts

Political Control

1. How were the political values of the newly independent states reflected in the form of government created under the Articles?

2. Show how the changes made by the Framers of the Constitution preserved those same values.

Authority

3. The states gave their legislatures a great deal of power after the war. Explain the view of authority that prompted them to do so.

4. Propose possible reasons why a distrust of strong central authority after the Revolutionary War gradually gave way to its acceptance at the Constitutional Convention.

Critical Thinking

1. **Analyzing Ideas** Explain why phrases such as "government by supplication" and "a shadow without substance" so well described the Confederation government.

2. **Formulating Alternatives** If Tennessee settlers had seceded from the Union and Shays's Rebellion had succeeded, what immediate effects do you think they would have had on Americans?

3. **Analyzing Illustrations** Study the illustration on the tobacco trade on this page and answer the questions that follow.

   a. What two groups are shown in the painting?

   b. What are each of the two groups doing?

   c. Does the artist give the work a central focus?

   d. What clues in the painting suggest a particular period of time or era? Explain.

▲ **TRANSPORTING TOBACCO**

Writing About History

Cause and Effect

Imagine that you are an observer at the Constitutional Convention listening to the delegates argue about how to set up a legislative branch. Record their various proposals and the effect each proposal would have.

Cooperative Learning

In order for people to operate effectively in a free society, individuals must give up some personal freedoms and agree to live by rules that operate in the best interests of all citizens. Imagine that you are part of a group that is being sent to the moon in order to establish a colony there. Together, write a constitution by which you agree to be governed while you are living on the moon. Decide which portions of the United States Constitution will work for your new situation and the changes that will need to be made to serve the best interests of your group.

Social Studies Skills

Organizing in a Table

A table presents information in a visually appealing, easy-to-use format. Tables organize data into a series of columns and rows, so they are especially useful tools when comparing information. The table's title supplies the subject under study. Headings over the columns tell the category of information listed in each column. Read each row in the table from left to right.

Practicing the Skill

Use this table and your knowledge from the chapter to answer the questions.

1. What information is found in this table?

2. How is color used to organize the table?

3. What determines the order in which the states are listed in the table? Explain one other criterion that could have been used to order the states.

4. How much time passed between the first state's ratification and the last?

5. Which state had the closest vote?

6. How was Rhode Island's voting pattern consistent with its position on the Constitutional Convention?

Ratification of the Constitution

State	Date	Vote
Delaware	Dec. 7, 1787	30-0
Pennsylvania	Dec. 12, 1787	46-23
New Jersey	Dec. 18, 1787	38-0
Georgia	Jan. 2, 1788	26-0
Connecticut	Jan. 9, 1788	128-40
Massachusetts	Feb. 6, 1788	187-168
Maryland	Apr. 28, 1788	63-11
South Carolina	May 23, 1788	149-73
New Hampshire	June 21, 1788	57-47
Virginia	June 25, 1788	89-79
New York	July 26, 1788	30-27
North Carolina	Nov. 21, 1789	194-77
Rhode Island	May 29, 1790	34-32

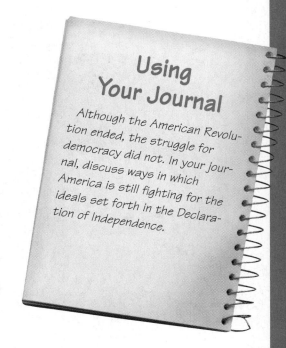

Using Your Journal

Although the American Revolution ended, the struggle for democracy did not. In your journal, discuss ways in which America is still fighting for the ideals set forth in the Declaration of Independence.

Cultural Kaleidoscope

Colonial Life

In The Kitchen

When Europeans first settled in America, they found no great treasures of gold or rare spices. From Native American peoples, however, they did gain something more vital for survival—plentiful foods and methods of cultivation. For early colonists, Indian corn, or maize, was the main food staple. Gradually, the colonists came to appreciate other native foods.

▶
Children performed chores to help prepare the day's meals. In many colonial households, children had no place at the table. They stood to eat and were not allowed to speak.

◀
New England farmers in the mid-1700s often grew apples, pears, peaches, and plums in orchards. They learned from Native Americans methods of grinding corn and recipes for cooking it.

During the summer, maize was eaten green, but colonists usually allowed it to ripen and then ground it into cornmeal. Sometimes it was hulled and eaten whole as hominy.

Cooking in the early 1700s was done over an open fire, and utensils for cooking necessarily had long handles. Metal was usually reserved for cooking tools. Utensils that today are made of metal, ceramic, or plastic, were made of wood.

Table, cutting board, and bowl

UNIT TWO DIGEST

Chapter 4

The Road to Revolution

The road from colonies to nation began with Parliament's attempt to control the colonies' foreign trade. Most of these laws, however, were not enforced. Parliament's concern was part of a larger issue, the struggle between Britain and France over control of North America. In the French and Indian War, Britain emerged victorious and, with the Treaty of Paris in 1763, France was eliminated as a contender for power in North America.

Britain's victory brought it a host of new problems, among them a huge war debt and a question of how to administer their newly acquired territory. Parliament levied new taxes that shifted part of the financial burden onto the colonies and passed the Proclamation of 1763, which forbade all settlement west of the Appalachians. The colonists protested, and as tensions grew, so did the means of protest. In their challenge to British authority, the colonies discovered a sense of unity and patriotism.

King George III refused to compromise, arguing that the colonies must "submit or triumph." The colonists responded by calling the First Continental Congress and organizing volunteer armies. Soon fighting broke out between Massachusetts "minutemen" and British troops at Concord. Although it would be another year before the colonies formally declared their independence, the American Revolution had begun.

Chapter 5

War for Independence

Most colonists wanted to remain part of the British empire as long as they could govern themselves through their own legislatures. The British government, though, was inflexible and wanted to punish the rebels.

In January 1776, Thomas Paine published the persuasive and widely read pamphlet *Common Sense*. In it, Paine argued for separation from Britain and appealed to the Americans' belief that they were a select people.

Beginning in April 1776, the colonies advised their delegates in Congress to vote for independence. The Declaration of Independence formally notified the world on July 4 that the colonies were indeed independent.

Announcing their independence was not as challenging as maintaining it. Britain, unwilling to surrender its large territory in North America, dispatched a large military force to America. George Washington's early victories at Trenton and Princeton helped save the American cause. Nevertheless, the Americans faced a long struggle with a volunteer army and insufficient funds to pay for the war. The struggle was eased when France allied itself with the American cause following a major victory over British forces at Saratoga.

Many women courageously served the American war effort, in some cases fighting in the ranks. African Americans and Native Americans also served in the Revolutionary War. In 1780, British General Cornwallis surrendered at Yorktown, Virginia, marking the last significant battle of the war. The colonies were, at last, independent.

Chapter 6

A More Perfect Union

With independence, the colonies needed new state constitutions to replace colonial charters. Most adopted a bicameral, or two-house, legislature and restricted the

executive branch. The right to vote, however, was restricted to white males who were property owners. Some of the states also began to question the institution of slavery.

Meanwhile, Congress developed a plan to unite them. Known as the Articles of Confederation, this document placed governing authority in Congress, in which each state had one vote.

Under the Articles, the national government was weak. Domestically, it was unable to collect taxes, enforce the laws, or interpret them. It also faced difficulties dealing with settling the West, although Congress passed two important documents—the Land Ordinance of 1785 and the Northwest Ordinance of 1787. In addition, the government had difficulty mediating disputes between the states over boundaries, commerce, and currency. Internationally, the new nation experienced difficulties with Britain, Spain, France, and the Barbary States.

Because of these problems, it became apparent that a new framework for government was needed. Before political anarchy and financial irresponsibility destroyed the ideals for which Americans had fought, a bold group of leaders met and drafted a new plan of government over the summer of 1787. States put aside jealousies and compromised on the crucial issues of representation and slavery and created a powerful two-house Congress, a strong

chief executive, and a national judicial system. Most delegates believed that the new Constitution was a vast improvement over the Articles.

Some states were cautious about surrendering their power. Finally, though, supporters of the Constitution, the Federalists, emerged victorious. The new government was set to be launched in 1789.

Understanding Unit Themes

1. **American Democracy** How did the new state constitutions strive for democratic ideals?

2. **Civil Rights and Liberties** What civil rights were denied colonists by British laws and actions before the Revolutionary War?

3. **Economic Development** How did Great Britain's view of the American colonies before the Revolution and its view of the new United States after the war affect trade relations between the two nations?

4. **Conflict and Cooperation** How did the conflicting interests of the British and Americans lead to the Revolutionary War?

The Constitution Today

The entire system of federal government in the United States rests on a single document: the Constitution. It has served as the "supreme law of the land" for more than 200 years, making it the oldest written constitution in the world. Institutions that we take for granted—the Congress, the President, the Supreme Court—were created by the Constitution. Major governmental decisions that are made every day depend upon constitutional authority.

The authors of the Constitution created a strong central government. Article I, Section 8, which has been called the "heart of the Constitution," gave the new Congress various powers not possessed by the Confederation Congress, including the authority to levy taxes and regulate interstate commerce. The power to levy taxes enabled Congress to finance the federal government.

Through its authority over interstate commerce, Congress has enacted laws ranging from prohibitions against racial discrimination to regulations on consumer credit.

The "elastic clause" that appears in Article I, Section 8, says that Congress shall make all laws "necessary and proper" for putting into effect its enumerated powers. Determining what laws are necessary and proper has provided for ongoing debate and controversy over the years, beginning with the debate over the National Bank in 1790.

The Constitution reinforced the idea that the states were to remain sovereign in some matters. Through their authority in common law and criminal law, the state governments were left in control of local affairs. Their separate identities were protected, and their authority in matters not specifically given to the national government was limited only by the rights of the people within each state. The Tenth Amendment assured this basic protection of each state's sovereignty.

Another assurance of state and popular sovereignty is provided by the amending process. Because the Constitution and the states both derive their authority from the people, provisions for changing the Constitution depend upon the will of the people. This careful arrangement has resulted in only 27 amendments. The first 10 were added almost immediately—in 1791—as a Bill of Rights to protect against national government encroachments on individual freedom.

Division of Powers

EXCLUSIVE POWERS GRANTED TO THE FEDERAL GOVERNMENT	CONCURRENT POWERS SHARED BY THE FEDERAL AND STATE GOVERNMENTS	RESERVED POWERS SET ASIDE FOR THE STATES
• Regulate interstate and foreign commerce • Establish an army and navy • Declare war • Coin money • Establish postal system • Establish federal courts • Set standards for weights and measures • Regulate patents and copyrights • Admit new states • Establish laws of citizenship • Pass laws needed to carry out its powers	• Enforce the laws • Borrow money • Lay and collect taxes • Establish courts • Charter banks • Provide for the general welfare	• Regulate intrastate commerce • Conduct elections • Determine voting requirements • Establish local governments • Provide for public safety • Tenth Amendment reserves to the state governments all powers not granted to the federal government or prohibited by the Constitution

Chart Study

When the Constitution was written, the states reserved certain powers. The Constitution gave certain powers and rights to the national government. ***Who retains all other rights?***

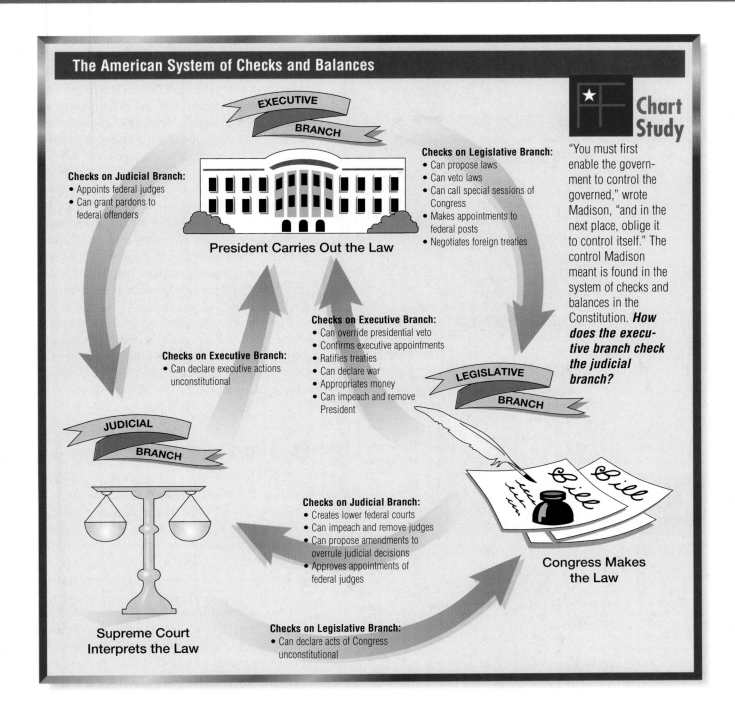

The American System of Checks and Balances

EXECUTIVE BRANCH

President Carries Out the Law

Checks on Judicial Branch:
- Appoints federal judges
- Can grant pardons to federal offenders

Checks on Legislative Branch:
- Can propose laws
- Can veto laws
- Can call special sessions of Congress
- Makes appointments to federal posts
- Negotiates foreign treaties

Checks on Executive Branch:
- Can override presidential veto
- Confirms executive appointments
- Ratifies treaties
- Can declare war
- Appropriates money
- Can impeach and remove President

Checks on Executive Branch:
- Can declare executive actions unconstitutional

JUDICIAL BRANCH

LEGISLATIVE BRANCH

Checks on Judicial Branch:
- Creates lower federal courts
- Can impeach and remove judges
- Can propose amendments to overrule judicial decisions
- Approves appointments of federal judges

Congress Makes the Law

Supreme Court Interprets the Law

Checks on Legislative Branch:
- Can declare acts of Congress unconstitutional

"You must first enable the government to control the governed," wrote Madison, "and in the next place, oblige it to control itself." The control Madison meant is found in the system of checks and balances in the Constitution. ***How does the executive branch check the judicial branch?***

Congress

The Constitution provided different legislative powers for the Senate and House. The Senate approves treaties and presidential appointments and tries all **impeachment** cases of government officials formally accused of wrongdoing in office; the House originates all revenue bills, and has the power to impeach members of the executive and judicial branches. Legislation must pass both Houses before it can be sent to the President to be signed into law.

Most of the enumerated powers of Congress leave little room for interpretation. When the constitutional authority of Congress seems to conflict with the authority of the President, it is often because of a deliberate effort by the Constitutional Convention to limit the power of government. The framers of the Constitution chose to divide government powers among three separate

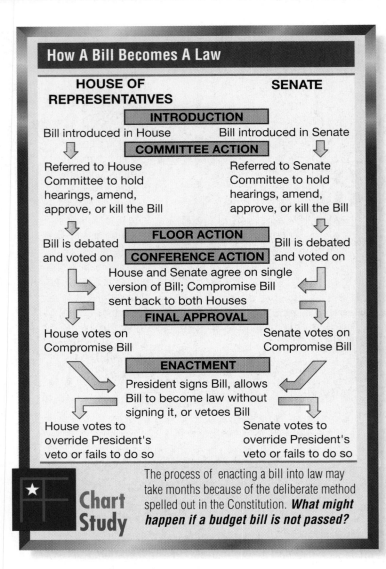

How A Bill Becomes A Law

HOUSE OF REPRESENTATIVES	SENATE

INTRODUCTION

Bill introduced in House · Bill introduced in Senate

COMMITTEE ACTION

Referred to House Committee to hold hearings, amend, approve, or kill the Bill

Referred to Senate Committee to hold hearings, amend, approve, or kill the Bill

FLOOR ACTION

Bill is debated and voted on · Bill is debated and voted on

CONFERENCE ACTION

House and Senate agree on single version of Bill; Compromise Bill sent back to both Houses

FINAL APPROVAL

House votes on Compromise Bill · Senate votes on Compromise Bill

ENACTMENT

President signs Bill, allows Bill to become law without signing it, or vetoes Bill

House votes to override President's veto or fails to do so

Senate votes to override President's veto or fails to do so

Chart Study The process of enacting a bill into law may take months because of the deliberate method spelled out in the Constitution. *What might happen if a budget bill is not passed?*

branches. This separation of powers is one of the most distinctive features of the Constitution.

Duties

The federal government is separated into legislative, executive, and judicial branches. These branches, described in the first three articles of the Constitution, are each given separate authority. Under this **separation of powers**, each branch exercises a check on the powers of the other two.

The Constitution describes the duties of the three branches, but it does not detail how those duties are to be carried out. To handle the heavy volume of legislation efficiently, both houses of Congress, from the very beginning, divided into committees.

These smaller units do most of the work of both houses. Each committee deals with particular problems, such as labor, banking, agriculture, foreign affairs, and armed services. Some committees are permanent, or standing committees, while others are temporary, formed to deal with a specific issue.

Legislation

Legislation begins with written proposals called bills. Any member of Congress may introduce a bill on any subject. Long before going to the full membership of each house for a vote, however, the bill must pass through the committee with responsibility for the subject in question.

The Constitution provided for a deliberate and sometimes slow method of passing legislation. One factor is the requirement that the legislation passed by both houses be exactly the same.

■ The Presidency

The Constitution gives the President extensive powers. Four of the most important are as follows: the command of the country's military forces; the power to conduct foreign affairs; the power to appoint the cabinet and other executive officers, as well as all federal judges; and the legislative veto power.

The Constitution did not foresee the development of political parties, one source of additional presidential power. As head of one of the two major political parties, the President can exert pressure for legislation and can give or withhold support for a senator's or representative's reelection.

Presidential power increases during crises involving actual or perceived danger from abroad. It is affected by the tendency of Congress to yield much of its power to the President for the duration of the crisis.

The President, who has access to a vast military and foreign service network, can control information that Congress receives. In addition, Congress, working as a whole or through committees, is inherently less capable of exercising decisive action quickly.

In domestic policy the Constitution clearly gives "the power of the purse" to Congress. Over time, the President has come to dominate many processes of allocating the government's money. The creation of the Bureau of the Budget in 1921 (now the Office of Management and Budget), whose director was appointed by the President, heralded the transfer of major budgetary power out of the hands of Congress.

■ The Courts

The judiciary is only briefly described in the Constitution. Article III provides that there shall be "one Supreme Court" and such lower courts as Congress may establish.

The Court System

The first Congress passed the Judiciary Act of 1789. This law set up the federal court system, the basics of which are still in place today. The federal judiciary may be envisioned as a three-tiered pyramid, with many district courts at the bottom, a smaller number of circuit courts in the middle, and one Supreme Court at the top.

Cases from a district court may be appealed, or taken for review, to the circuit court for the area in which the district court is located. Cases may be appealed to the Supreme Court, which currently consists of nine members: eight associate justices and one Chief Justice. Because the cases that reach them are so complex, the justices must decline to rule upon all but a small fraction of the cases they are asked to hear.

The main purpose of the federal judiciary is to provide a forum for disputes involving federal laws. The most important power of the federal courts, that of **judicial review**, is not stated in the Constitution. This is the power of the Court to decide whether a given law, federal or state, conflicts with the Constitution. If so, the law can be declared unconstitutional and ceases to have effect. This acts as a form of veto power over laws. If the Supreme Court rules a law unconstitutional, the Congress or the states may initiate an amendment to the Constitution.

The Court cannot rule on just any law, but only on those that come before it. In this sense its role is passive; it cannot take the initiative to correct problems that the justices see or hear about, but must wait for others to file lawsuits. The Court also must rely on the President to enforce its rulings.

Unlike Congress and the President, federal judges do not have to face reelection. The Constitution provides that they shall hold office "during good behavior"—which generally means for life or until they choose to resign—and that their salaries may not be reduced. The Framers wanted to protect federal judges from political pressures so they could rule fairly and wisely, without fear of popular hostility. A federal judge can be removed through the difficult process of impeachment by Congress.

■ A Living Document

When the Constitution reached its bicentennial year in 1989, it inspired interest in the significance of the document. Two broadly different views emerged. Some people saw the limitations and problems that the federal government faced and suggested a new constitutional convention to restructure the government to meet today's difficult challenges. Others emphasized the remarkable enduring quality of the Constitution and its basic principles that remain important today.

It is likely that if changes are to be made in basic principles of government, they will come by amendment or interpretation. Amendment, however, has historically been approached with caution. The founders wanted the Constitution to be safe from the passions of the public and political schemes.

The Constitution's adaptability to new circumstances has made it a lasting framework of government. It has permitted, perhaps even encouraged, debate over the proper role of each branch of government, or of government itself. Through the first two centuries of federal government, the Constitution has served to moderate change in government. It has also ably guarded those freedoms that we the people have entrusted it to preserve.

The Constitution of the United States

*The Constitution of the United States
is truly a remarkable document. It was one of the
first written constitutions in modern history. The Framers
wanted to devise a plan for a strong central government that would
unify the country, as well as preserve the ideals of the Declaration of
Independence. The document they wrote created a representative legislature, the
office of president, a system of courts, and a process for adding amendments. For over
200 years, the flexibility and strength of the Constitution has guided the nation's
political leaders. The document has become a symbol of pride and a force for
national unity. For easier study of the Constitution, those passages that have
been set aside or changed by the adoption of amendments are printed in blue.
Also included are explanatory notes that will help clarify the
meaning of each article and section.*

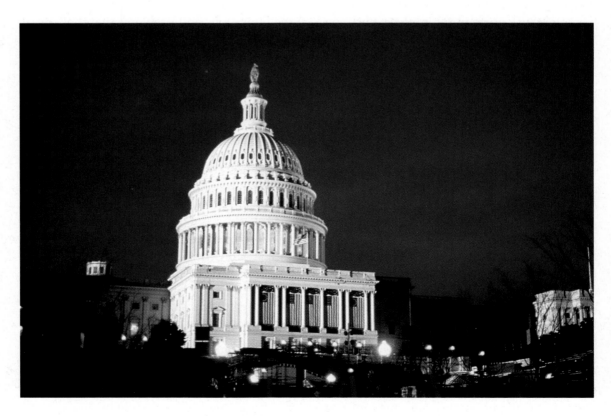

▲ THE CAPITOL, WASHINGTON, D.C.

Preamble

We, the people of the United States, in Order to form a more perfect Union, establish Justice, insure domestic Tranquility, provide for the common defence, promote the general Welfare, and secure the Blessings of Liberty to ourselves and our Posterity, do ordain and establish this Constitution for the United States of America.

The Preamble introduces the Constitution and sets forth the general purposes for which the government was established. The preamble also declares that the power of the government comes from the people.

The printed text of the document shows the spelling and punctuation of the parchment original.

Article I

Section 1

All legislative Powers herein granted shall be vested in a Congress of the United States, which shall consist of a Senate and House of Representatives.

Section 2

1. The House of Representatives shall be composed of Members chosen every second Year by the People of the several States, and the Electors in each State shall have the Qualifications requisite for Electors of the most numerous Branch of the State Legislature.

2. No Person shall be a Representative who shall not have attained to the Age of twenty-five Years, and been seven Years a Citizen of the United States, and who shall not, when elected, be an Inhabitant of that State in which he shall be chosen.

3. Representatives and direct Taxes shall be apportioned among the several states which may be included within this Union, according to the respective Numbers, which shall be determined by adding to the whole Number of free Persons, including those bound to Service for a Term of Years, and excluding Indians not taxed, three-fifths of all other Persons. The actual Enumeration shall be made within three Years after the first Meeting of the Congress of the United States, and within every subsequent Term of ten Years, in such Manner as they shall by Law direct. The Number of Representatives shall not exceed one for every thirty Thousand, but each state shall have at Least one Representative; and until such enumeration shall be made, the State of New Hampshire shall be entitled to chuse three; Massachusetts eight, Rhode Island and Providence Plantations one, Connecticut five, New York six, New Jersey four, Pennsylvania eight, Delaware one, Maryland six, Virginia ten; North Carolina five, South Carolina five, and Georgia three.

4. When vacancies happen in the Representation from any State, the Executive Authority thereof shall issue Writs of Election to fill such Vacancies.

5. The House of Representatives shall chuse their Speaker and other Officers; and shall have the sole Power of Impeachment.

Article I. The Legislative Branch

Section 1. Congress

The power to make laws is given to a Congress made up of two chambers to represent different interests: the Senate to represent the states; the House to be more responsive to the people's will.

Section 2. House of Representatives

1. Election and Term of Office

"Electors" means voters. Every two years the voters choose new Congress members to serve in the House of Representatives. The Constitution states that each state may specify who can vote. But the 15th, 19th, 24th, and 26th Amendments have established guidelines that all states must follow regarding the right to vote.

2. Qualifications

Representatives must be 25 years old, citizens of the United States for 7 years, and residents of the state they represent.

3. Division of Representatives Among the States

The number of representatives from each state is based on the size of the state's population. Each state is divided into congressional districts, with each district required to be equal in population. Each state is entitled to at least one representative. The number of representatives in the House was set at 435 in 1929. Since then, there has been a reapportionment of seats based on population shifts rather than on addition of seats.

Only three-fifths of a state's slave population was to be counted in determining the number of representatives elected by the state. Native Americans were not counted at all.

The "enumeration" referred to is the census, the population count taken every 10 years since 1790.

4. Vacancies

Vacancies in the House are filled through special elections called by the state's governor.

5. Officers

The speaker is the leader of the majority party in the House and is responsible for choosing the heads of various House committees. "Impeachment" means indictment, or bringing charges against an official.

Section 3. The Senate
1. Number of Members, Terms of Office, and Voting Procedure
Originally, senators were chosen by the state legislators of their own states. The 17th Amendment changed this, so that senators are now elected directly by the people. There are 100 senators, 2 from each state.

2. Staggered Elections; Vacancies
One-third of the Senate is elected every two years. The terms of the first Senate's membership was staggered: one group served two years, one four, and one six. All senators now serve a six-year term.

The 17th Amendment changed the method of filling vacancies in the Senate.

3. Qualifications
Qualifications for the Senate are more restrictive than those for the House. Senators must be at least 30 years old and they must have been citizens of the United States for at least 9 years. The Framers of the Constitution made the Senate a more elite body in order to produce a further check on the powers of the House of Representatives.

4. President of the Senate
The Vice President's only duty listed in the Constitution is to preside over the Senate. The only real power the Vice President has is to cast the deciding vote when there is a tie. However, modern Presidents have given their Vice Presidents new responsibilities.

5. Other Officers
The Senate selects its other officers, including a presiding officer (president pro tempore) who serves when the Vice President is absent or has become President of the United States.

6. Trial of Impeachments
When trying a case of impeachment brought by the House, the Senate convenes as a court. The Chief Justice of the Supreme Court acts as the presiding judge, and the Senate acts as the jury. A two-thirds vote of the members present is necessary to convict officials under impeachment charges.

7. Penalty for Conviction
If the Senate convicts an official, it may only remove the official from office and prevent that person from holding another federal position. However, the convicted official may still be tried for the same offense in a regular court of law.

Section 4. Elections and Meetings
1. Holding Elections
In 1842 Congress required members of the House to be elected from districts in states having more than one Representative rather than at large. In 1845 it set the first Tuesday after the first Monday in November as the day for selecting presidential electors.

2. Meetings
The 20th Amendment, ratified in 1933, has changed the date of the opening of the regular session of Congress to January 3.

Section 3
1. The Senate of the United States shall be composed of two Senators from each State, chosen by the Legislature thereof; for six Years; and each Senator shall have one Vote.

2. Immediately after they shall be assembled in Consequence of the first Election, they shall be divided as equally as may be into three Classes. The Seats of the Senators of the first Class shall be vacated at the Expiration of the second Year, of the second Class at the Expiration of the fourth Year, and of the third Class at the Expiration of the sixth Year, so that one-third may be chosen every second Year; and if Vacancies happen by Resignations, or otherwise, during the Recess of the Legislature of any State, the Executive thereof may make temporary Appointments until the next Meeting of the Legislature, which shall then fill such Vacancies.

3. No person shall be a Senator who shall not have attained the Age of thirty Years, and been nine Years a Citizen of the United States, and who shall not, when elected, be an Inhabitant of that State in which he shall be chosen.

4. The Vice President of the United States shall be President of the Senate, but shall have no vote, unless they be equally divided.

5. The Senate shall chuse their Officers, and also a President pro tempore, in the absence of the Vice-President or when he shall exercise the Office of the President of the United States.

6. The Senate shall have the sole Power to try all impeachments. When sitting for that purpose they shall be on Oath or Affirmation. When the President of the United States is tried, the Chief Justice shall preside: And no person shall be convicted without the Concurrence of two-thirds of the Members present.

7. Judgment in Cases of Impeachment shall not extend further than to removal from Office, and disqualification to hold and enjoy any Office of Honor, Trust or Profit under the United States: but the Party convicted shall nevertheless be liable and subject to Indictment, Trial, Judgment and Punishment, according to Law.

Section 4

1. The Times, Places, and Manner of holding Elections for Senators and Representatives, shall be prescribed in each state by the Legislature thereof; but the Congress may at any time by Law make or alter such Regulations, except as to the Places of Chusing Senators.

2. The Congress shall assemble at least once in every Year, and such Meeting shall be on the first Monday in December, unless they shall by Law appoint a different Day.

Visualizing History

▲ THE WILL OF THE PEOPLE The idea of representative democracy works well when the legislature is responsive to the citizens. **Which chamber was not originally elected by the people?**

Section 5

1. Each House shall be the Judge of the Elections, Returns and Qualifications of its own Members, and a Majority of each shall constitute a Quorum to do Business; but a smaller Number may adjourn from day to day, and may be authorized to compel the Attendance of absent Members, in such Manner, and under such Penalties as each House may provide.

2. Each House may determine the Rules of its Proceedings, punish its Members for disorderly Behaviour, and, with the Concurrence of two-thirds, expel a Member.

3. Each House shall keep a Journal of its Proceedings, and from time to time publish the same, excepting such Parts as may in their Judgment require Secrecy; and the Yeas and Nays of the Members of either House on any question shall, at the desire of one-fifth of those Present, be entered on the Journal.

4. Neither House during the Session of Congress, shall, without the Consent of the other, adjourn for more than three days, nor to any other Place than that in which the two Houses shall be sitting.

Section 6

1. The Senators and Representatives shall receive a Compensation for their Services, to be ascertained by Law, and paid out of the Treasury of the United States. They shall in all Cases, except Treason, Felony and Breach of the Peace be privileged from Arrest during their attendance at the Session of their respective Houses, and in

Section 5. Organization and Rules of Procedure

1. Organization

Until 1969 Congress acted as the sole judge of qualifications of its own members. In that year, the Supreme Court ruled that Congress could not legally exclude victorious candidates who met all the requirements listed in Article I, Section 2.

A "quorum" is the minimum number of members that must be present for the House or Senate to conduct sessions. For a regular House session, a quorum consists of the majority of the House, or 218 of the 435 members.

2. Rules

Each house sets its own rules, can punish its members for disorderly behavior, and can expel a member by a two-thirds vote.

3. Journals

In addition to the journals, a complete official record of everything said on the floor, as well as the roll call votes on all bills or issues, is available in the *Congressional Record*, published daily by the Government Printing Office.

4. Adjournment

Neither house may adjourn for more than three days or move to another location without the approval of the other house.

Section 6. Privileges and Restrictions

1. Pay and Privileges

To strengthen the federal government, the Founders set congressional salaries to be paid by the United States Treasury rather than by members' respective states. Originally, members were paid $6 per day. Salaries for Senators and Representatives are $129,500.

The "immunity" privilege means members cannot be sued or be prosecuted for anything they say in Congress. They cannot be arrested while Congress is in session, except for treason, major crimes, or breaking the peace.

2. Restrictions

"Emoluments" means salaries. The purpose of this clause is to prevent members of Congress from passing laws that would benefit them personally. It also prevents the President from promising them jobs in other branches of the federal government.

Section 7. Passing Laws

1. Revenue Bills

"Revenue" is income raised by the government. The chief source of government revenue is taxes. All tax laws must originate in the House of Representatives. This insures that the branch of Congress which is elected by the people every two years has the major role in determining taxes. This clause does not prevent the Senate from amending tax bills.

2. How Bills Become Laws

A bill may become a law only by passing both houses of Congress and by being signed by the President. If the President disapproves, or vetoes, the bill, it is returned to the house where it originated, along with a written statement of the President's objections. If two-thirds of each house approves the bill after the President has vetoed it, it becomes law. In voting to override a President's veto, the votes of all members of Congress must be recorded in the journals or official records. If the President does not sign or veto a bill within 10 days (excluding Sundays), it becomes law. However, if Congress has adjourned during this 10-day period, the bill does not become law. This is known as a "pocket veto."

going to and returning from the same; and for any Speech or Debate in either House, they shall not be questioned in any other place.

2. No Senator or Representative shall, during the Time for which he was elected, be appointed to any civil Office under the Authority of the United States, which shall have been created, or the Emoluments whereof shall have been encreased, during such time; and no Person holding any Office under the United States, shall be a Member of either House during his continuance in Office.

Section 7

1. All Bills for raising Revenue shall originate in the House of Representatives; but the Senate may propose or concur with Amendments as on other bills.

2. Every Bill which shall have passed the House of Representatives and the Senate, shall, before it become a Law, be presented to the President of the United States; If he approve he shall sign it, but if not he shall return it, with his Objections, to that House in which it shall have originated, who shall enter the Objections at large on their Journal, and proceed to reconsider it. If after such Reconsideration two-thirds of that House shall agree to pass the bill, it shall be sent, together with the objections, to the other House, by which it shall likewise be reconsidered, and if approved by two-thirds of that House, it shall become a Law. But in all such Cases the Votes of both Houses shall be determined by Yeas and Nays, and the Names of the Persons voting for and against the Bill shall be entered on the Journal of each House respectively. If any Bill shall not be returned by the President within ten Days (Sundays excepted) after it shall have been presented to him, the Same shall be a Law, in like Manner as if he had signed it, unless the Congress by their Adjournment prevent its Return, in which Case it shall not be a Law.

▲ **PREAMBLE OF THE CONSTITUTION**

Visualizing History

▲ THE WORK OF CONGRESS Although some of the work of the legislature is done on the floor of Congress, most of it is done outside the chambers by committees. Each member of Congress has a staff of legislative assistants and other aides who research issues, draft bills, and organize the member's office. *How does a resolution differ from a bill?*

3. Every Order, Resolution, or Vote to which the Concurrence of the Senate and House of Representatives may be necessary (except on a question of Adjournment) shall be presented to the President of the United States; and before the Same shall take Effect, shall be approved by him, or, being disapproved by him, shall be repassed by two-thirds of the Senate and House of Representatives, according to the Rules and Limitations prescribed in the case of a Bill.

Section 8
The Congress shall have the Power
1. To lay and collect Taxes, Duties, Imposts and Excises, to pay the Debts and provide for the common Defence and general Welfare of the United States; but all Duties, Imposts and Excises shall be uniform throughout the United States;
2. To borrow money on the credit of the United States;
3. To regulate Commerce with foreign Nations, and among the several States, and with the Indian Tribes;
4. To establish an uniform Rule of Naturalization, and uniform Laws on the subject of Bankruptcies throughout the United States.
5. To coin Money, regulate the Value thereof, and of foreign Coin, and fix the Standard of Weights and Measures;
6. To provide for the Punishment of counterfeiting the Securities and current Coin of the United States;

3. Presidential Approval or Veto
The Framers included this paragraph to prevent Congress from passing joint resolutions instead of bills to avoid the possibility of a presidential veto. A bill is a draft of a proposed law, whereas a resolution is the legislature's formal expression of opinion or intent on a matter.

Section 8. Powers Granted to Congress
1. Revenue
This clause gives Congress the power to raise and spend revenue. Taxes must be levied at the same rate throughout the nation.
2. Borrowing
The federal government borrows money by issuing bonds.
3. Commerce
The exact meaning of "commerce" has caused controversy. The trend has been to expand its meaning and, consequently, the extent of Congress's powers.
4. Naturalization and Bankruptcy
"Naturalization" refers to the procedure by which a citizen of a foreign nation becomes a citizen of the United States.
5. Currency
Control over money is an exclusive federal power; the states are forbidden to issue currency.
6. Counterfeiting
"Counterfeiting" means illegally imitating or forging.

7. Post Office
In 1970 the United States Postal Service replaced the Post Office Department.

8. Copyrights and Patents
Under this provision, Congress has passed copyright and patent laws.

9. Courts
This provision allows Congress to establish a federal court system.

10. Piracy
Congress has the power to protect American ships on the high seas.

11. Declare War
While the Constitution gives Congress the right to declare war, the United States has sent troops into combat without a congressional declaration.

12. Army
This provision reveals the Framers' fears of a standing army.

13. Navy
This clause allows Congress to establish a navy.

14. Rules for Armed Forces
Congress may pass regulations that deal with military discipline.

15. Militia
The "militia" is now called the National Guard. It is organized by the states.

16. National Guard
Even though the National Guard is organized by the states, Congress has the authority to pass rules for governing its behavior.

17. Nation's Capital
This clause grants Congress the right to make laws for Washington, D.C.

18. Elastic Clause
This is the so-called "elastic clause" of the Constitution and one of its most important provisions. The "necessary and proper" laws must be related to one of the 17 enumerated powers.

Section 9. Powers Denied to the Federal Government.

1. Slave Trade
This paragraph contains the compromise the Framers reached regarding regulation of the slave trade in exchange for Congress's exclusive control over interstate commerce.

2. Habeas Corpus
Habeas corpus is a Latin term meaning "you may have the body." A writ of habeas corpus issued by a judge requires a law official to bring a prisoner to court and show cause for holding the prisoner. The writ may be suspended only during wartime.

3. Bills of Attainder
A "bill of attainder" is a bill that punishes a person without a jury trial. An "ex post facto" law is one that makes an act a crime after the act has been committed.

7. To establish Post Offices and post Roads;

8. To promote the Progress of Science and useful Arts, by securing for limited Times to Authors and Inventors the exclusive Right to their respective Writings and Discoveries;

9. To constitute Tribunals inferior to the Supreme Court;

10. To define and punish Piracies and Felonies committed on the high Seas, and Offenses against the Law of Nations.

11. To declare War, grant Letters of Marque and Reprisal, and make Rules concerning Captures on Land and Water;

12. To raise and support Armies, but no Appropriation of Money to that Use shall be for a longer Term than two Years;

13. To provide and maintain a Navy;

14. To make Rules for the Government and Regulation of the land and naval forces;

15. To provide for calling forth the Militia to execute the Laws of the Union, suppress Insurrections, and repel Invasions;

16. To provide for organizing, arming, and disciplining, the Militia, and for governing such Part of them as may be employed in the Service of the United States, reserving to the States respectively, the Appointment of the Officers, and the Authority of training the Militia according to the discipline prescribed by Congress;

17. To exercise exclusive Legislation in all Cases whatsoever, over such District (not exceeding ten Miles square) as may, by Cession of particular States, and the acceptance of Congress, become the Seat of Government of the United States, and to exercise like Authority over all Places purchased by the Consent of the Legislature of the State in which the Same shall be, for the Erection of Forts, Magazines, Arsenals, dock-Yards, and other needful Buildings;—And

18. To make all Laws which shall be necessary and proper for carrying into Execution the foregoing Powers, and all other Powers vested by this Constitution in the Government of the United States, or in any Department or Officer thereof.

Section 9

1. The Migration or Importation of such Persons as any of the States now existing shall think proper to admit, shall not be prohibited by the Congress prior to the Year one thousand eight hundred and eight, but a tax or duty may be imposed on such importation, not exceeding ten dollars for each Person.

2. The privilege of the Writ of Habeas Corpus shall not be suspended, unless when in Cases of Rebellion or Invasion the public Safety may require it.

3. No Bill of Attainder or ex post facto Law shall be passed.

▲ INAUGURATION OF THE PRESIDENT The inauguration is held on January 20 following a presidential election. Generally held on the steps of the Capitol, the ceremony centers on swearing into office the new President. *What does Article II, Section 1, Clause 5 describe?*

4. No capitation, or other direct, Tax shall be laid unless in Proportion to the Census or Enumeration herein before directed to be taken.

5. No Tax or Duty shall be laid on Articles exported from any State.

6. No Preference shall be given by any Regulation of Commerce or Revenue to the Ports of one State over those of another: nor shall Vessels bound to, or from, one State, be obliged to enter, clear, or pay Duties in another.

7. No Money shall be drawn from the Treasury, but in Consequence of Appropriations made by Law; and a regular Statement and Account of the Receipts and Expenditures of all public Money shall be published from time to time.

8. No Title of Nobility shall be granted by the United States:—And no Person holding any Office of Profit or Trust under them, shall, without the Consent of the Congress, accept of any present, Emolument, Office, or Title, of any kind whatever, from any King, Prince, or foreign State.

4. Direct Taxes
The 16th Amendment allowed Congress to pass an income tax.

5. Tax on Exports
Congress may not tax goods that move from one state to another.

6. Uniformity of Treatment
This prohibition prevents Congress from favoring one state or region over another in the regulation of trade.

7. Appropriation Law
This clause protects against the misuse of funds. All of the President's expenditures must be made with the permission of Congress.

8. Titles of Nobility
This clause prevents the development of a nobility in the United States.

Section 10
1. No State shall enter into any Treaty, Alliance, or Confederation; grant Letters of Marque and Reprisal; coin Money; emit Bills of Credit; make any Thing but gold and silver Coin a Tender in Payment of Debts; pass any Bill of Attainder; ex post facto Law, or Law impairing the Obligation of Contracts, or grant any Title of Nobility.

Section 10. Powers Denied to the States
1. Limitations on Power
The states are prohibited from conducting foreign affairs, carrying on a war, or controlling interstate and foreign commerce. States are also not allowed to pass laws that the federal government is prohibited from passing, such as enacting ex post facto laws or bills of attainder. These restrictions on the states were designed, in part, to prevent an overlapping in functions and authority with the federal government that could create conflict and chaos.

The Constitution of the United States **179**

2. Export and Import Taxes

This clause prevents states from levying duties on exports and imports. If states were permitted to tax imports and exports they could use their taxing power in a way that weakens or destroys Congress's power to control interstate and foreign commerce.

3. Duties, Armed Forces, War

This clause prohibits states from maintaining an army or navy and from going to war, except in cases where a state is directly attacked. It also forbids states from collecting fees from foreign vessels or from making treaties with other nations. All of these powers are reserved for the federal government.

Article II. The Executive Branch

Section 1. President and Vice President
1. Term of Office

The President is given power to enforce the laws passed by Congress. Both the President and the Vice President serve four-year terms. The 22nd Amendment limits the number of terms the President may serve to two.

2. Election

The Philadelphia Convention had trouble deciding how the President was to be chosen. The system finally agreed upon was indirect election by "electors" chosen for that purpose. The President and Vice President are not directly elected. Instead, the President and Vice President are elected by presidential electors from each state who form the electoral college. Each state has the number of presidential electors equal to the total number of its senators and representatives. State legislatures determine how the electors are chosen. Originally, the state legislatures chose the electors, but today they are nominated by political parties and elected by the voters. No senator, representative, or any other federal officeholder can serve as an elector.

2. No State shall, without the Consent of the Congress, lay any Imposts or Duties on Imports or Exports, except what may be absolutely necessary for executing its inspection Laws: and the net Produce of all Duties and Imposts, laid by any State on Imports and Exports, shall be for the Use of the Treasury of the United States; and all such Laws shall be subject to the Revision and Controul of the Congress.

3. No State shall, without the Consent of Congress, lay any duty on Tonnage, keep Troops, or Ships of War in time of Peace, enter into any Agreement or Compact with another State, or with a foreign Power, or engage in War, unless actually invaded, or in such imminent Danger as will not admit of delay.

Article II

Section 1

1. The executive Power shall be vested in a President of the United States of America. He shall hold his Office during the Term of four years, and together with the Vice-President chosen for the same Term, be elected, as follows:

2. Each State shall appoint, in such Manner as the Legislature thereof may direct, a Number of Electors, equal to the whole Number of Senators and Representatives to which the State may be entitled in the Congress: but no Senator or Representative, or Person holding an Office of Trust or Profit under the United States, shall be appointed an Elector.

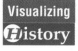

▲ STATE OF THE UNION Presidents use the annual State of the Union Address to outline yearly goals. *In which sections of the Constitution are the President's powers and duties defined?*

3. The Electors shall meet in their respective States, and vote by Ballot for two Persons, of whom one at least shall not be an Inhabitant of the same State with themselves. And they shall make a List of all the Persons voted for and of the Number of Votes for each; which List they shall sign and certify, and transmit sealed to the Seat of the Government of the United States, directed to the President of the Senate. The President of the Senate shall, in the Presence of the Senate and House of Representatives, open all the Certificates, and the Votes shall then be counted. The Person having the greatest Number of Votes shall be the President, if such Number be a Majority of the whole Number of Electors appointed; and if there be more than one who have such Majority, and have an equal Number of Votes, then the House of Representatives shall immediately chuse by Ballot one of them for President; and if no Person have a Majority, then from the five highest on the List the said House shall in like Manner chuse the President. But in chusing the President, the Votes shall be taken by States, the Representation from each State having one Vote; a quorum for this Purpose shall consist of a Member or Members from two-thirds of the States, and a Majority of all the States shall be necessary to a Choice. In every Case, after the Choice of the President, the Person having the greatest Number of Votes of the Electors shall be the Vice-President. But if there should remain two or more who have equal votes, the Senate shall chuse from them by Ballot the Vice President.

4. The Congress may determine the Time of chusing the Electors, and the Day on which they shall give their Votes; which Day shall be the same throughout the United States.

5. No person except a natural born Citizen, or a Citizen of the United States, at the time of the Adoption of this Constitution, shall be eligible to the Office of President; neither shall any Person be eligible to that Office who shall not have attained to the Age of thirty-five years, and been fourteen Years a Resident within the United States.

6. In Case of the Removal of the President from Office, or of his Death, Resignation, or Inability to discharge the Powers and Duties of the said Office, the same shall devolve on the Vice-President, and the Congress may by Law provide for the Case of Removal, Death, Resignation or Inability, both of the President and Vice-President, declaring what Officer shall then act as President, and such Officer shall act accordingly, until the disability be removed, or a President shall be elected.

7. The President shall, at stated Times, receive for his Services a Compensation, which shall neither be encreased nor diminished during the Period for which he shall have been elected, and he shall not receive within that Period any other Emolument from the United States, or any of them.

8. Before he enter on the execution of his office, he shall take the following Oath or Affirmation "I do solemnly swear (or affirm) that I will faithfully execute the Office of President of the United States, and will to the best of my Ability, preserve, protect and defend the Constitution of the United States.

3. Former Method of Election

This clause describes the original method of electing the President and Vice President. According to this method, each elector voted for two candidates. The candidate with the most votes (as long as it was a majority) became President. The candidate with the second highest number of votes became Vice President. In the election of 1800, the two top candidates received the same number of votes, making it necessary for the House of Representatives to decide the election. To prevent such a situation from recurring, the 12th Amendment was added in 1804.

4. Date of Elections

Congress selects the date when the presidential electors are chosen and when they vote for President and Vice President. All electors must vote on the same day. The first Tuesday after the first Monday in November has been set as the date for presidential elections. Electors cast their votes on the Monday after the second Wednesday in December.

5. Qualifications

The President must be a citizen of the United States by birth, at least 35 years old, and a resident of the United States for 14 years. See Amendment 22.

6. Vacancies

If the President dies, resigns, is removed from office by impeachment, or is unable to carry out the duties of the office, the Vice President becomes President. (Amendment 25 deals with presidential disability.) If both the President and Vice President are unable to serve, Congress has the power to declare by law who acts as President. Congress set the line of succession in the Presidential Succession Act of 1947.

7. Salary

Originally, the President's salary was $25,000 per year. The President's current salary of $200,000 plus a $50,000 taxable expense account per year was enacted in 1969. The President also receives numerous fringe benefits including a $120,000 non-taxable allowance for travel and entertainment, and living accommodations in two residences—the White House and Camp David. However, the President cannot receive any other income from the United States Government or state governments while in office.

8. Oath of Office

The oath of office is generally administered by the chief justice, but can be administered by any official authorized to administer oaths. All Presidents-elect except Washington have been sworn into office by the chief justice. Only Vice Presidents John Tyler, Calvin Coolidge, and Lyndon Johnson in succeeding to the office have been sworn in by someone else.

▲ THE PRESIDENT'S POWER As commander in chief of the United States armed forces, the President is the people's check on the power of the military. *What limits are placed on the President's power to make treaties?*

Section 2. Powers of the President

1. Military, Cabinet, Pardons

Mention of "the principal officer in each of the executive departments" is the only suggestion of the President's Cabinet to be found in the Constitution. The Cabinet is a purely advisory body, and its power depends on the President. Each Cabinet member is appointed by the President and must be confirmed by the Senate. This clause also makes the President, a civilian, the head of the armed services. This established the principle of civilian control of the military.

2. Treaties and Appointments

The President is the chief architect of American foreign policy. He or she is responsible for the conduct of foreign relations, or dealings with other countries. All treaties, however, require approval of two-thirds of the senators present. Most federal positions today are filled under the rules and regulations of the civil service system. Most presidential appointees serve at the pleasure of the President. Removal of an official by the President is not subject to congressional approval. But the power can be restricted by conditions set in creating the office.

3. Vacancies in Offices

The President can temporarily appoint officials to fill vacancies when the Senate is not in session.

Section 2

1. The President shall be Commander in Chief of the Army and Navy of the United States, and of the Militia of the several States, when called into the actual Service of the United States; he may require the Opinion, in writing, of the principal Officer in each of the executive Departments, upon any subject relating to the Duties of their respective Offices, and he shall have Power to Grant Reprieves and Pardons for Offences against the United States, except in Cases of Impeachment.

2. He shall have Power, by and with the Advice and Consent of the Senate, to make Treaties, provided two-thirds of the Senators present concur; and he shall nominate, and by and with the Advice and Consent of the Senate, shall appoint Ambassadors, other public Ministers and Consuls, Judges of the supreme Court, and all other Officers of the United States, whose Appointments are not herein otherwise provided for, and which shall be established by Law. But the Congress may by Law vest the Appointment of such inferior Officers, as they think proper, in the President alone, in the Courts of Law, or in the Heads of Departments.

3. The President shall have Power to fill up all Vacancies that may happen during the Recess of the Senate, by granting Commissions which shall expire at the End of their next Session.

Section 3

He shall from time to time give to Congress Information of the State of the Union, and recommend to their Consideration such Measures as he shall judge necessary and expedient; he may, on extraordinary occasions, convene both Houses, or either of them, and in Case of Disagreement between them, with respect to the Time of Adjournment, he may adjourn them to such Time as he shall think proper; he shall receive Ambassadors and other public Ministers; he shall take Care that the Laws be faithfully executed, and shall Commission all the Officers of the United States.

Section 4

The President, Vice-President and all civil Officers of the United States, shall be removed from Office on Impeachment for, and Conviction of, Treason, Bribery, or other high Crimes and Misdemeanors.

Article III

Section 1

The Judicial Power of the United States, shall be vested in one supreme Court, and in such inferior Courts as the Congress may from time to time ordain and establish. The judges, both of the supreme and inferior Courts, shall hold their Offices during good Behaviour, and shall, at stated Times, receive for their Services, a Compensation, which shall not be diminished during their Continuance in Office.

Section 3. Duties of the President

Under this provision the President delivers annual State-of-the-Union messages. On occasion, Presidents have called Congress into special session to consider particular problems.

The President's duty to receive foreign diplomats also includes the power to ask a foreign country to withdraw its diplomatic officials from this country. This is called "breaking diplomatic relations" and often carries with it the implied threat of more drastic action, even war. The President likewise has the power of deciding whether or not to recognize foreign governments.

Section 4. Impeachment

This section states the reasons for which the President and Vice President may be impeached and removed from office. (See annotations of Article I, Section 3, Clauses 6 and 7.)

Article III. The Judicial Branch

Section 1. Federal Courts

The term *judicial* refers to courts. The Constitution set up only the Supreme Court but provided for the establishment of other federal courts. There are presently nine justices on the Supreme Court. Congress has created a system of federal district courts and courts of appeals, which review certain district court cases. Judges of these courts serve during "good behavior," which means that they usually serve for life or until they choose to retire.

▲ **THE SUPREME COURT** Supreme Court proceedings are held in this room. The Constitution established the jurisdiction of the federal courts by defining the kinds of cases these courts may hear. *What is statute law?*

Visualizing
History

▲ **Justices of the Supreme Court** Because we have judicial review, the Supreme Court is the official interpreter of the Constitution and has the final say in deciding what the Constitution means. ***What is the term of office for a Supreme Court Justice?***

Section 2. Jurisdiction

1. General Jurisdiction

Use of the words *in law and equity* reflects the fact that American courts took over two kinds of traditional law from Great Britain. The basic law was the "common law," which was based on over five centuries of judicial decisions. "Equity" was a special branch of British law developed to handle cases where common law did not apply.

Federal courts deal mostly with "statute law," or laws passed by Congress, treaties, and cases involving the Constitution itself. "Admiralty and maritime jurisdiction" covers all sorts of cases involving ships and shipping on the high seas and on rivers, canals, and lakes.

2. The Supreme Court

When a court has "original jurisdiction" over certain kinds of cases, it means that the court has the authority to be the first court to hear a case. A court with "appellate jurisdiction" hears cases that have been appealed from lower courts. Most Supreme Court cases are heard on appeal from lower courts.

3. Jury Trials

Except in cases of impeachment, anyone accused of a crime has the right to a trial by jury. The trial must be held in the state where the crime was committed. Jury trial guarantees were strengthened in the 6th, 7th, 8th, and 9th Amendments.

Section 2

1. The judicial Power shall extend to all Cases, in Law and Equity, arising under this Constitution, the Laws of the United States, and treaties made, or which shall be made, under their Authority; to all Cases affecting ambassadors, other public ministers and consuls; to all cases of admiralty and maritime Jurisdiction; to Controversies to which the United States shall be a party; to Controversies between two or more states; between a State and Citizens of another State; between Citizens of different States; between Citizens of the same State claiming Lands under Grants of different States, and between a State, or the Citizens thereof, and foreign States, Citizens or Subjects.

2. In all Cases affecting Ambassadors, other public Ministers and Consuls, and those in which a State shall be Party, the supreme Court shall have original Jurisdiction. In all the other Cases before mentioned, the supreme Court shall have appellate Jurisdiction, both as to Law and Fact, with such Exceptions, and under such Regulations as the Congress shall make.

3. The trial of all Crimes, except in Cases of Impeachment, shall be by Jury; and such Trial shall be held in the State where the said Crimes shall have been committed; but when not committed within any State, the Trial shall be at such Place or Places as the Congress may by Law have directed.

Section 3

1. Treason against the United States, shall consist only in levying War against them, or in adhering to their Enemies, giving them Aid and Comfort. No Person shall be convicted of Treason unless on the Testimony of two Witnesses to the same overt Act, or on Confession in open Court.

2. The Congress shall have power to declare the Punishment of Treason, but no Attainder of Treason shall work Corruption of Blood, or Forfeiture except during the Life of the Person attainted.

Article IV

Section 1

Full Faith and Credit shall be given in each State to the public Acts, Records, and judicial Proceedings of every other State. And the Congress may by general Laws prescribe the Manner in which such Acts, Records, and Proceedings shall be proved, and the Effect thereof.

Section 2

1. The Citizens of each State shall be entitled to all Privileges and Immunities of Citizens in the several States.

2. A Person charged in any State with Treason, Felony, or other Crime, who shall flee from Justice, and be found in another State, shall on demand of the executive Authority of the State from which he fled, be delivered up, to be removed to the State having Jurisdiction of the crime.

3. No Person held to Service of Labour in one State, under the Laws thereof, escaping into another, shall, in Consequence of any Law or Regulation therein, be discharged from such Service or Labour, but shall be delivered up on Claim of the Party to whom such Service or Labour may be due.

Section 3

1. New States may be admitted by the Congress into this Union; but no new State shall be formed or erected within the Jurisdiction of any other State; nor any State be formed by the Junction of two or more States, or parts of States, without the Consent of the Legislatures of the States concerned as well as of the Congress.

2. The Congress shall have Power to dispose of and make all needful Rules and Regulations respecting the Territory of other Property belonging to the United States; and nothing in this Constitution shall be so construed as to Prejudice any Claims of the United States, or of any particular State.

Section 4

The United States shall guarantee to every State in this Union a Republican Form of Government, and shall protect each of them against Invasion; and on Application of the Legislature, or of the Executive (when the Legislature cannot be convened) against domestic Violence.

Section 3. Treason

1. Definition

Knowing that the charge of treason often had been used by monarchs to get rid of people who opposed them, the Framers of the Constitution defined treason carefully, requiring that at least two witnesses be present to testify in court that a treasonable act was committed.

2. Punishment

Congress is given the power to determine the punishment for treason. The children of a person convicted of treason may not be punished nor may the convicted person's property be taken away from the children. Convictions for treason have been relatively rare in the nation's history.

Article IV. Relations Among the States

Section 1. Official Acts

This provision insures that each state recognizes the laws, court decisions, and records of all other states. For example, a marriage license or corporation charter issued by one state must be accepted in other states.

Section 2. Mutual Duties of States

1. Privileges

The "privileges and immunities," or rights of citizens, guarantee each state's citizens equal treatment in all states.

2. Extradition

"Extradition" means that a person convicted of a crime or a person accused of a crime must be returned to the state where the crime was committed. Thus, a person cannot flee to another state hoping to escape the law.

3. Fugitive-Slave Clause

Formerly this clause meant that slaves could not become free persons by escaping to free states.

Section 3. New States and Territories

1. New States

Congress has the power to admit new states. It also determines the basic guidelines for applying for statehood. One state, Maine, was created within the original boundaries of another state (Massachusetts) with the consent of Congress and the state.

2. Territories

Congress has power over federal land. But neither in this clause nor anywhere else in the Constitution is the federal government explicitly empowered to acquire new territory.

Section 4. Federal Protection for States

This section allows the federal government to send troops into a state to guarantee law and order. The President may send in troops even without the consent of the state government involved.

Article V. The Amending Process

There are now 27 Amendments to the Constitution. The Framers of the Constitution deliberately made it difficult to amend or change the Constitution. Two methods of proposing and ratifying amendments are provided for. A two-thirds majority is needed in Congress to propose an amendment, and at least three-fourths of the states (38 states) must accept the amendment before it can become law. No amendment has yet been proposed by a national convention called by the states, though in the 1980s a convention to propose an amendment requiring a balanced budget had been approved by 32 states.

Article VI. National Supremacy

1. Public Debts and Treaties

This section promised that all debts the colonies had incurred during the Revolution and under the Articles of Confederation would be honored by the new United States government.

2. The Supreme Law

The "supremacy clause" recognized the Constitution and federal laws as supreme when in conflict with those of the states. It was largely based on this clause that Chief Justice John Marshall wrote his historic decision in *McCulloch v. Maryland*. The 14th Amendment reinforced the supremacy of federal law over state laws.

3. Oaths of Office

This clause also declares that no religious test shall be required as a qualification for holding public office. This principle is also asserted in the First Amendment, which forbids Congress to set up an established church or to interfere with the religious freedom of Americans.

Article VII. Ratification of the Constitution

Unlike the Articles of Confederation, which required approval of all thirteen states for adoption, the Constitution required approval of only nine of thirteen states. Thirty-nine of the 55 delegates at the Constitutional Convention signed the Constitution. The Constitution went into effect in June 1788.

Article V

The Congress, whenever two-thirds of both Houses shall deem it necessary, shall propose Amendments to this Constitution, or, on the Application of the Legislatures of two-thirds of the several States, shall call a Convention for proposing Amendments, which, in either Case, shall be valid to all Intents and Purposes, as part of this Constitution, when ratified by the Legislatures of three-fourths of the several States, or by Conventions in three-fourths thereof, as the one or the other Mode of Ratification may be proposed by the Congress; Provided that no Amendment which may be made prior to the Year One thousand eight hundred and eight shall in any Manner affect the first and fourth clauses in the Ninth Section of the first Article; and that no State, without its Consent, shall be deprived of its equal Suffrage in the Senate.

Article VI

1. All Debts contracted and Engagements entered into, before the Adoption of this Constitution, shall be as valid against the United States under this Constitution as under the Confederation.

2. This Constitution, and the Laws of the United States which shall be made in Pursuance thereof; and all Treaties made, or which shall be made, under the Authority of the United States, shall be the supreme Law of the Land; and the Judges in every State shall be bound thereby, any Thing in the Constitution or Laws of any State to the Contrary notwithstanding.

3. The Senators and Representatives before mentioned, and the Members of the several State Legislatures, and all executive and judicial Officers, both of the United States and of the several States, shall be bound by Oath or Affirmation, to support this Constitution; but no religious Test shall ever be required as a Qualification to any Office or public Trust under the United States.

Article VII

The Ratification of the Conventions of nine States shall be sufficient for the Establishment of this Constitution between the States so ratifying the same.

Done in Convention, by the Unanimous Consent of the States present, the Seventeenth Day of September, in the Year of our Lord one thousand seven hundred and Eighty-seven, and of the Independence of the United States of America the Twelfth. In Witness whereof We have hereunto subscribed our Names.

Signers

George Washington, **President and Deputy from Virginia**

New Hampshire
John Langdon
Nicholas Gilman

Massachusetts
Nathaniel Gorham
Rufus King

Connecticut
William Samuel Johnson
Roger Sherman

New York
Alexander Hamilton

New Jersey
William Livingston
David Brearley
William Paterson
Jonathan Dayton

Pennsylvania
Benjamin Franklin
Thomas Mifflin
Robert Morris
George Clymer
Thomas FitzSimons
Jared Ingersoll
James Wilson
Gouverneur Morris

Delaware
George Read
Gunning Bedford, Jr.
John Dickinson
Richard Bassett
Jacob Broom

Maryland
James McHenry
Daniel of St. Thomas Jenifer
Daniel Carroll

Virginia
John Blair
James Madison, Jr.

North Carolina
William Blount
Richard Dobbs Spaight
Hugh Williamson

South Carolina
John Rutledge
Charles Cotesworth Pinckney
Charles Pinckney
Pierce Butler

Georgia
William Few
Abraham Baldwin

Attest: William Jackson,
Secretary

Amendment I

Congress shall make no law respecting an establishment of religion, or prohibiting the free exercise thereof; or abridging the freedom of speech, or of the press; or the right of the people peaceably to assemble, and to petition the Government for a redress of grievances.

Amendment II

A well-regulated Militia, being necessary to the security of a free State, the right of the people to keep and bear Arms, shall not be infringed.

Amendment III

No soldier shall, in time of peace be quartered in any house, without the consent of the Owner, nor in time of war, but in a manner to be prescribed by law.

Amendment IV

The right of the people to be secure in their persons, houses, papers, and effects, against unreasonable searches and seizures, shall not be violated, and no Warrants shall issue, but upon probable cause, supported by Oath or affirmation, and particularly describing the place to be searched, and the persons or things to be seized.

Amendment 1.
Freedom of Religion, Speech, Press, and Assembly (1791)

The 1st Amendment protects the civil liberties of individuals in the United States. The 1st Amendment freedoms are not absolute, however. They are limited by the rights of other individuals.

Amendment 2.
Right to Bear Arms (1791)

The purpose of this amendment is to guarantee states the right to keep a militia.

Amendment 3.
Quartering Troops (1791)

This amendment is based on the principle that people have a right to privacy in their own homes. It also reflects the colonists' grievances against the British government before the Revolution. Britain had angered Americans by quartering (housing) troops in private homes.

Amendment 4.
Searches and Seizures (1791)

Like the 3rd Amendment, the 4th amendment reflects the colonists' desire to protect their privacy. Britain had used writs of assistance (general search warrants) to seek out smuggled goods. Americans wanted to make sure that such searches and seizures would be conducted only when a judge felt that there was "reasonable cause" to conduct them. The Supreme Court has ruled that evidence seized illegally without a search warrant may not be used in court.

Amendment 5.
Rights of Accused Persons (1791)

To bring a "presentment" or "indictment" means to formally charge a person with committing a crime. It is the function of a grand jury to see whether there is enough evidence to bring the accused person to trial. A person may not be tried more than once for the same crime (double jeopardy).

Members of the armed services are subject to military law. They may be tried in a court martial. In times of war or a natural disaster, civilians may also be put under martial law.

The 5th Amendment also guarantees that persons may not be forced in any criminal case to be a witness against themselves. That is, accused persons may refuse to answer questions on the ground that the answers might tend to incriminate them.

Amendment 6.
Right to Speedy, Fair Trial (1791)

The requirement of a "speedy" trial insures that an accused person will not be held in jail for a lengthy period as a means of punishing the accused without a trial. A "fair" trial means that the trial must be open to the public and that a jury must hear witnesses and evidence on both sides before deciding the guilt or innocence of a person charged with a crime. This amendment also provides that legal counsel must be provided to a defendant. In 1963, the Supreme Court ruled, in *Gideon* v. *Wainwright*, that if a defendant cannot afford a lawyer, the government must provide one to defend the accused person.

Amendment V

No person shall be held to answer for a capital, or otherwise infamous crime, unless on a presentment or indictment of a Grand Jury, except in cases arising in the land or naval forces, or in the Militia, when in actual service in time of War or public danger; nor shall any person be subject for the same offence to be twice put in jeopardy of life or limb; nor shall be compelled in any criminal case to be a witness against himself, nor be deprived of life, liberty, or property, without due process of law; nor shall private property be taken for public use, without just compensation.

Amendment VI

In all criminal prosecutions, the accused shall enjoy the right to a speedy and public trial, by an impartial jury of the State and district wherein the crime shall have been committed, which district shall have been previously ascertained by law, and to be informed of the nature and cause of the accusation; to be confronted with the witnesses against him; to have compulsory process for obtaining witnesses in his favor, and to have the Assistance of Counsel for his defence.

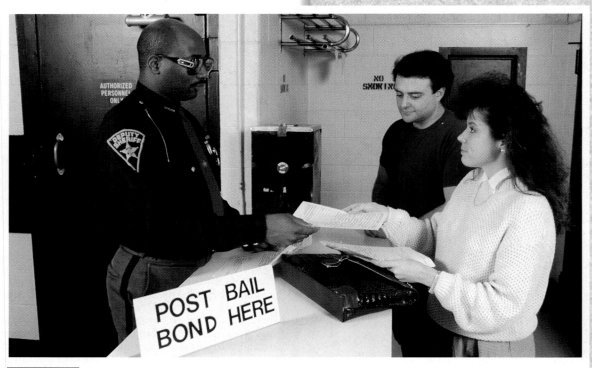

Visualizing History

▲ RIGHTS OF THE ACCUSED Several amendments protect the rights of the accused. While awaiting trial, a defendant may be released by posting bail, a procedure regulated by the Eighth Amendment. *Which amendment guarantees the right to a speedy and fair trial?*

Amendment VII

In suits at common law, where the value in controversy shall exceed twenty dollars, the right of trial by jury shall be preserved, and no fact tried by a jury, shall be otherwise reexamined in any Courts of the United States, than according to the rules of common law.

Amendment VIII

Excessive bail shall not be required, nor excessive fines imposed, nor cruel and unusual punishments inflicted.

Amendment IX

The enumeration in the Constitution, of certain rights, shall not be construed to deny or disparage others retained by the people.

Amendment X

The powers not delegated to the United States by the Constitution, nor prohibited by it to the States, are reserved to the States respectively, or to the people.

Amendment XI

The Judicial power of the United States shall not be construed to extend to any suit in law or equity, commenced or prosecuted against one of the United States by Citizens of another State, or by Citizens or Subjects of any Foreign State.

Amendment XII

The Electors shall meet in their respective States and vote by ballot for President and Vice-President, one of whom, at least, shall not be an inhabitant of the same State with themselves; they shall name in their ballots the person voted for as President, and in distinct ballots the person voted for as Vice-President, and they shall make distinct lists of all persons voted for as President, and of all persons voted for as Vice-President, and of the number of votes for each, which lists they shall sign and certify, and transmit sealed to the seat of the government of the United States, directed to the President of the Senate;—The President of the Senate shall, in the presence of the Senate and House of Representatives, open all the certificates and the votes shall then be counted;—The person having the greatest number of votes for President, shall be the President, if such number be a majority of the whole number of Electors appointed; and if no person have such majority, then from the persons having the highest numbers not exceeding three on the list of those voted for as President, the House of Representatives shall choose immediately, by ballot, the President. But

Amendment 7.
Civil Suits (1791)

"Common law" means the law established by previous court decisions. In civil cases where one person sues another for more than $20, a jury trial is provided for. But customarily, federal courts do not hear civil cases unless they involve a good deal more money.

Amendment 8.
Bail and Punishment (1791)

"Bail" is money that an accused person provides to the court as a guarantee that he or she will be present for a trial. This amendment insures that neither bail nor punishment for a crime shall be unreasonably severe.

Amendment 9.
Powers Reserved to the People (1791)

This amendment provides that the people's rights are not limited to those mentioned in the Constitution.

Amendment 10.
Powers Reserved to the States (1791)

This amendment protects the states and the people from an all-powerful federal government. It provides that the states or the people retain all powers except those denied them or those specifically granted to the federal government. This "reserved powers" provision is a check on the "necessary and proper" power of the federal government provided in the "elastic clause" in Article I, Section 8, Clause 18.

Amendment 11.
Suits Against States (1795)

This amendment provides that a lawsuit brought by a citizen of the United States or a foreign nation against a state must be tried in a state court, not in a federal court. This amendment was passed after the Supreme Court ruled that a federal court could try a lawsuit brought by citizens of South Carolina against a citizen of Georgia. This case, *Chisholm* v. *Georgia*, decided in 1793, was protected by many Americans, who insisted states would lose authority if they could be sued in federal courts.

Amendment 12.
Election of President and Vice President (1804)

This amendment changes the procedure for electing the President and Vice President as outlined in Article II, Section 1, Clause 3.

To prevent the recurrence of the election of 1800 whereby a candidate running for Vice President (Aaron Burr) could tie a candidate running for President (Thomas Jefferson) and thus force the election into the House of Representatives, the Twelfth Amendment specifies that the electors are to cast separate ballots for each office. The votes for each office are counted and listed separately. The results are signed, sealed, and sent to the president of the senate. At a joint session of Congress, the votes are counted. The candidate who receives the most votes, providing it is a majority, is elected President. Other changes include: (1) a reduction from five to the three highest candidates receiving votes among whom the House is to choose if no candidate receives a majority of the electoral votes, and (2) provision for the Senate to choose the Vice President from the two highest candidates if neither has received a majority of the electoral votes.

The Twelfth Amendment does place one restriction on electors. It prohibits electors from voting for two candidates (President and Vice President) from their home state.

Amendment 13.
Abolition of Slavery (1865)

This amendment was the final act in ending slavery in the United States. It also prohibits the binding of a person to perform a personal service due to debt. In addition to imprisonment for crime, the Supreme Court has held that the draft is not a violation of the amendment.

This amendment is the first adopted to be divided into sections. It is also the first to contain specifically a provision granting Congress power to enforce it by appropriate legislation.

Amendment 14.
Rights of Citizens (1868)

The clauses of this amendment were intended 1) to penalize southern states that refused to grant African Americans the vote, 2) to keep former Confederate leaders from serving in government, 3) to forbid payment of the Confederacy's debt by the federal government, and 4) to insure payment of the war debts owed the federal government.

Section 1. Citizenship Defined By granting citizenship to all persons born in the United States, this amendment granted citizenship to former slaves. The amendment also guaranteed "due process of law." By the 1950s, Supreme Court rulings used the due process clause to protect civil liberties. The last part of Section 1 establishes the doctrine that all citizens are entitled to equal protection of the laws. In 1954 the Supreme Court ruled, in *Brown* v. *Board of Education* of Topeka, that segregation in public schools was unconstitutional because it denied equal protection.

Section 2. Representation in Congress This section reduced the number of members a state had in the House of Representatives if it denied its citizens the right to vote. This section

in choosing the President, the votes shall be taken by states, the representation from each state having one vote; a quorum for this purpose shall consist of a member or members from two-thirds of the states, and a majority of all the states shall be necessary to a choice. And if the House of Representatives shall not choose a President whenever the right of choice shall devolve upon them, before the fourth day of March next following, then the Vice-President shall act as President, as in the case of the death or other constitutional disability of the President.—The person having the greatest number of votes as Vice-President, shall be the Vice-President, if such number be a majority of the whole number of Electors appointed, and if no person have a majority, then from the two highest numbers on the list, the Senate shall choose the Vice-President; a quorum for the purpose shall consist of two-thirds of the whole number of Senators, and a majority of the whole number shall be necessary to a choice. But no person constitutionally ineligible to the office of President shall be eligible to that of Vice-President of the United States.

Amendment XIII

Section 1
Neither slavery nor involuntary servitude, except as a punishment for crime whereof the party shall have been duly convicted, shall exist within the United States, or any place subject to their jurisdiction.

Section 2
Congress shall have power to enforce this article by appropriate legislation.

Amendment XIV

Section 1
All persons born or naturalized in the United States, and subject to the jurisdiction thereof, are citizens of the United States and of the State wherein they reside. No State shall make or enforce any law which shall abridge the privileges or immunities of citizens of the United States; nor shall any State deprive any person of life, liberty, or property, without due process of law, nor deny to any person within its jurisdiction the equal protection of the laws.

Section 2
Representatives shall be apportioned among the several States according to their respective numbers, counting the whole number of persons in each State, excluding Indians not taxed. But when the right to vote at any election for the choice of electors for President and Vice-President of the United States, Representatives in Congress, the Executive and Judicial officers of a

▲ POLITICAL PARTIES The Constitution did not provide for the existence of political parties, which today play a major role in the election of the President and Vice President. *What restrictions does the Twelfth Amendment place on electors?*

State, or the members of the Legislature thereof, is denied to any of the male inhabitants of such State, being twenty-one years of age, and citizens of the United States, or in any way abridged, except for participation in rebellion, or other crime, the basis of representation therein shall be reduced in the proportion which the number of such male citizens shall bear to the whole number of male citizens twenty-one years of age in such State.

Section 3

No person shall be a Senator or Representative in Congress, or elector of President and Vice-President, or hold any office, civil or military, under the United States, or under any State, who, having previously taken an oath, as a member of Congress, or as an officer of the United States, or as a member of any State legislature, or as an executive or judicial officer of any State, to support the Constitution of the United States, shall have engaged in insurrection or rebellion against the same, or given aid or comfort to the enemies thereof. But Congress may by a vote of two-thirds of each House, remove such disability.

was not implemented, however. Later civil rights laws and the 24th Amendment guaranteed the vote to African Americans.

Section 3. Penalty for Engaging in Insurrection The leaders of the Confederacy were barred from state or federal offices unless Congress agreed to revoke this ban. By the end of Reconstruction all but a few Confederate leaders were allowed to return to public life.

Section 4. Public Debt The public debt incurred by the federal government during the Civil War was valid and could not be questioned by the South. However, the debts of the Confederacy were declared to be illegal. And former slave owners could not collect compensation for the loss of their slaves.

Section 5. Enforcement Congress was empowered to pass civil rights bills to guarantee the provisions of the amendment.

Amendment 15.
The Right to Vote (1870)
Section 1. Suffrage for African Americans The 15th Amendment replaced Section 2 of the 14th Amendment in guaranteeing African Americans the right to vote, that is, the right of African Americans to vote was not to be left to the states. Yet, despite this prohibition, African Americans were denied the right to vote by many states by such means as poll taxes, literacy tests, and white primaries.
Section 2. Enforcement Congress was given the power to enforce this amendment. During the 1950s and 1960s, it passed successively stronger laws to end racial discrimination in voting rights.

Amendment 16.
Income Tax (1913)
The origins of this amendment went back to 1895, when the Supreme Court declared a federal income tax unconstitutional. To overcome this Supreme Court decision, this amendment authorized an income tax that was levied on a direct basis.

Amendment 17.
Direct Election of Senators (1913)

Section 1. Method of Election The right to elect senators was given directly to the people of each state. It replaced Article I, Section 3, Clause 1, which empowered state legislatures to elect senators. This amendment was designed not only to make the choice of senators more democratic but also to cut down on corruption and to improve state government.

Section 2. Vacancies A state must order an election to fill a senate vacancy. A state may empower its governor to appoint a person to fill a Senate seat if a vacancy occurs until an election can be held.

Section 4
The validity of the public debt of the United States incurred for payment of pensions and bounties for service, authorized by law, including debts in suppressing insurrections or rebellion, shall not be questioned. But neither the United States nor any State shall assume or pay any debt or obligation incurred in aid of insurrection or rebellion against the United States, or any claim for the loss or emancipation of any slave; but all such debts, obligations and claims shall be held illegal and void.

Section 5
The Congress shall have power to enforce, by appropriate legislation, the provisions of this article.

Amendment XV

Section 1
The right of citizens of the United States to vote shall not be denied or abridged by the United States or by any State on account of race, color, or previous condition of servitude.

Section 2
The Congress shall have power to enforce this article by appropriate legislation.

Amendment XVI
The Congress shall have power to lay and collect taxes on incomes, from whatever source derived, without apportionment among several States, and without regard to any census or enumeration.

Amendment XVII

Section 1
The Senate of the United States shall be composed of two Senators from each State, elected by the people thereof, for six years; and each Senator shall have one vote. The electors in each state shall have the qualifications requisite for electors of the most numerous branch of the state legislatures.

Section 2
When vacancies happen in the representation of any State in the Senate, the executive authority of such State shall issue writs of election to fill such vacancies: *Provided*, that the legislature of any State may empower the executive thereof to make temporary appointments until the people fill the vacancies by election as the legislature may direct.

Section 3

This amendment shall not be so construed as to affect the election or term of any Senator chosen before it becomes valid as part of the Constitution.

Amendment XVIII

Section 1

After one year from ratification of this article the manufacture, sale, or transportation of intoxicating liquors within, the importation thereof into, or the exportation thereof from the United States and all territory subject to the jurisdiction thereof for beverage purposes is hereby prohibited.

Section 2

The Congress and the several states shall have concurrent power to enforce this article by appropriate legislation.

Section 3

This article shall be inoperative unless it shall have been ratified as an amendment to the Constitution by the legislatures of the several States, as provided in the Constitution, within seven years from the date of the submission hereof to the states of the Congress.

Amendment XIX

Section 1

The right of citizens of the United States to vote shall not be denied or abridged by the United States or by any state on account of sex.

Section 2

Congress shall have power to enforce this article by appropriate legislation.

Amendment XX

Section 1

The terms of the President and Vice President shall end at noon on the 20th day of January, and the terms of the Senators and Representatives at noon on the 3rd day of January, of the years in which such terms would have ended if this article had not been ratified; and the terms of their successors shall then begin.

Section 3. Time in Effect This amendment was not to affect any senate election or temporary appointment until it was in effect.

Amendment 18.
Prohibition of Alcoholic Beverages (1919)

This amendment prohibited the production, sale, or transportation of alcoholic beverages in the United States. Prohibition proved to be difficult to enforce, especially in states with large urban populations. This amendment was later repealed by the 21st Amendment.

Amendment 19.
Women's Suffrage (1920)

This amendment, extending the vote to all qualified women in federal and state elections, was a landmark victory for the women's suffrage movement, which had worked to achieve this goal for many years. The women's movement had earlier gained full voting rights for women in four western states in the late nineteenth century.

Amendment 20.
"Lame-Duck" Amendment (1933)
Section 1. New Dates of Terms This amendment had two major purposes: 1) to shorten the time between the President's and Vice President's election and inauguration, and 2) to end "lame-duck" sessions of Congress.

When the Constitution first went into effect, transportation and communication were slow and uncertain. It often took many months after the election in November for the President and Vice President to travel to Washington, D.C., and prepare for their inauguration on March 4. This amendment ended this long wait for a new administration by fixing January 20 as inauguration day.

Section 2. Meeting Time of Congress
"Lame-duck" sessions occurred every two years, after the November congressional election. That is, the Congress that held its session in December of an election year was not the newly elected Congress but the old Congress that had been elected two years earlier. This Congress continued to serve for several more months, usually until March of the next year. Often many of its members had failed to be re-elected and were called "lame-ducks." The 20th Amendment abolished this lame-duck session, and provided that the new Congress hold its first session soon after the November election, on January 3.

Section 3. Succession of President and Vice President
This amendment provides that if the President-elect dies before taking office, the Vice President-elect becomes President. In the cases described, Congress will decide on a temporary President.

Section 4. Filling Presidential Vacancy
If a presidential candidate dies while an election is being decided in the House, Congress may pass legislation to deal with the situation. Congress has similar power if this occurs when the Senate is deciding a vice-presidential election.

Section 5. Beginning the New Dates
Sections 1 and 2 affected the Congress elected in 1934 and President Roosevelt, elected in 1936.

Section 6. Time Limit on Ratification
The period for ratification by the states was limited to seven years.

Amendment 21.
Repeal of Prohibition Amendment (1933)
This amendment nullified the 18th Amendment. It is the only amendment ever passed to overturn an earlier amendment. It remained unlawful to transport alcoholic beverages into states that forbade their use. It is the only amendment ratified by special state conventions instead of state legislatures.

Section 2
The Congress shall assemble at least once in every year, and such meeting shall begin at noon on the 3rd day of January, unless they shall by law appoint a different day.

Section 3
If, at the time fixed for the beginning of the term of the President, the President elect shall have died, the Vice President elect shall become President. If a President shall not have been chosen before the time fixed for the beginning of his term, or if the President elect shall have failed to qualify, then the Vice President elect shall act as President until a President shall have qualified; and the Congress may by law provide for the case wherein neither a President elect nor a Vice President elect shall have qualified, declaring who shall then act as President, or the manner in which one who is to act shall be selected, and such person shall act accordingly until a President or Vice President shall have qualified.

Section 4
The Congress may by law provide for the case of the death of any of the persons from whom the House of Representatives may choose a President whenever the right of choice shall have devolved upon them, and for the case of the death of any of the persons from whom the Senate may choose a Vice President whenever the right of choice shall have devolved upon them.

Section 5
Sections 1 and 2 shall take effect on the 15th day of October following the ratification of this article.

Section 6
This article shall be inoperative unless it shall have been ratified as an amendment to the Constitution by the legislatures of three-fourths of the several States within seven years from the date of its submission.

Amendment XXI

Section 1
The eighteenth article of amendment to the Constitution of the United States is hereby repealed.

Section 2
The transportation or importation into any State, Territory, or possession of the United States for delivery or use therein of intoxicating liquors, in violation of the laws thereof, is hereby prohibited.

Section 3
This article shall be inoperative unless it shall have been ratified as an amendment to the Constitution by conventions in the several States, as provided in the Constitution, within seven years from the date of the submission hereof to the States by the Congress.

Amendment XXII

Section 1

No person shall be elected to the office of the President more than twice, and no person who had held the office of President, or acted as President, for more than two years of a term to which some other person was elected President shall be elected to the office of the President more than once.

But this Article shall not apply to any person holding the office of President when this Article was proposed by the Congress, and shall not prevent any person who may be holding the office of President, or acting as President, during the term within which this Article becomes operative from holding the office of President or acting as President during the remainder of such term.

Section 2

This article shall be inoperative unless it shall have been ratified as an amendment to the Constitution by the legislatures of three-fourths of the several States within seven years from the date of its submission to the States by the Congress.

Amendment XXIII

Section 1

The District constituting the seat of Government of the United States shall appoint in such manner as the Congress may direct:

A number of electors of President and Vice President equal to the whole number of Senators and Representatives in Congress to which the District would be entitled if it were a State, but in no event more than the least populous State; they shall be in addition to those appointed by the States, but they shall be considered, for the purposes of the election of President and Vice President, to be electors appointed by a State; and they shall meet in the District and perform such duties as provided by the twelfth article of amendment.

Section 2

The Congress shall have power to enforce this article by appropriate legislation.

Amendment 22.
Limit on Presidential Terms (1951)

This amendment wrote into the Constitution a custom started by Washington, Jefferson, and Madison, whereby Presidents limited themselves to two terms in office. Although both Ulysses S. Grant and Theodore Roosevelt sought third terms, the two-term precedent was not broken until Franklin D. Roosevelt was elected to a third term in 1940 and then a fourth term in 1944. The passage of the 22nd amendment insures that no President is to be considered indispensable. It also provides that anyone who succeeds to the presidency and serves for more than two years of the term may not be elected more than one more time.

Amendment 23.
Presidential Electors for the District of Columbia (1961)

This amendment granted people living in the District of Columbia the right to vote in presidential elections. The District casts three electoral votes. The people of Washington, D.C., still are without representation in Congress.

Amendment 24.
Abolition of the Poll Tax (1964)

A "poll tax" was a fee that persons were required to pay in order to vote in a number of Southern states. This amendment ended poll taxes as a requirement to vote in any presidential or congressional election. In 1966 the Supreme Court voided poll taxes in state elections as well.

Amendment 25.
Presidential Disability and Succession (1967)

Section 1. Replacing the President The Vice President becomes President if the President dies, resigns, or is removed from office.

Section 2. Replacing the Vice President The President is to appoint a new Vice President in case of a vacancy in that office, with the approval of the Congress.

The 25th Amendment is unusually precise and explicit because it was intended to solve a serious constitutional problem. Sixteen times in American history, before passage of this amendment, the office of Vice President was vacant, but fortunately in none of these cases did the President die or resign.

This amendment was used in 1973, when Vice President Spiro Agnew resigned from office after being charged with accepting bribes. President Nixon then appointed Gerald R. Ford as Vice President in accordance with the provisions of the 25th Amendment. A year later, President Richard Nixon resigned during the Watergate scandal, and Ford became President. President Ford then had to fill the Vice Presidency, which he had left vacant upon assuming the Presidency. He named Nelson A. Rockefeller as Vice President. Thus both the presidency and vice-presidency were held by men who had not been elected to their offices.

Section 3 Replacing the President With Consent If the President informs Congress, in writing, that he or she cannot carry out the duties of the office of President, the Vice President becomes Acting President.

Amendment XXIV

Section 1

The right of citizens of the United States to vote in any primary or other election for President or Vice President, for electors for President or Vice President, or for Senator or Representative in Congress, shall not be denied or abridged by the United States or any State by reason of failure to pay any poll tax or other tax.

Section 2

The Congress shall have power to enforce this article by appropriate legislation.

Amendment XXV

Section 1

In case of the removal of the President from office or his death or resignation, the Vice President shall become President.

Section 2

Whenever there is a vacancy in the office of the Vice President, the President shall nominate a Vice President who shall take the office upon confirmation by a majority vote of both houses of Congress.

Section 3

Whenever the President transmits to the President pro tempore of the Senate and the Speaker of the House of Representatives his written declaration that he is unable to discharge the powers and duties of his office, and until he transmits to them a written declaration to the contrary, such powers and duties shall be discharged by the Vice President as Acting President.

Section 4

Whenever the Vice President and a majority of either the principal officers of the executive departments or of such other body as Congress may by law provide, transmit to the President pro tempore of the Senate and the Speaker of the House of Representatives their written declaration that the President is unable to discharge the powers and duties of his office, the Vice President shall immediately assume the power and duties of the office of Acting President.

Thereafter, when the President transmits to the President pro tempore of the Senate and the Speaker of the House of Representatives his written declaration that no inability exists, he shall resume the powers and duties of his office unless the Vice President and a majority of either the principal officers of the executive departments or of such other body as Congress may by law provide, transmit within four days to the President pro tempore of the Senate and the Speaker of the House of Representatives their written declaration that the President is unable to discharge the powers and duties of his office. Thereupon Congress shall decide the issue, assembling within forty-eight hours for that purpose if not in session. If the Congress within twenty-one days after receipt of the latter written declaration, or, if Congress is not in session, within twenty-one days after Congress is required to assemble, determines by two-thirds vote of both houses that the President is unable to discharge the powers and duties of his office, the Vice President shall continue to discharge the same as Acting President; otherwise, the President shall resume the power and duties of his office.

Amendment XXVI

Section 1
The right of citizens of the United States, who are eighteen years of age or older, to vote shall not be denied or abridged by the United States or by any State on account of age.

Section 2
The Congress shall have power to enforce this article by appropriate legislation.

Amendment XXVII
No law, varying the compensation for the services of Senators and Representatives, shall take effect, until an election of Representatives shall have intervened.

Section 4 Replacing the President Without Consent If the President is unable to carry out the duties of the office but is unable or unwilling to so notify Congress, the Cabinet and the Vice President are to inform Congress of this fact. The Vice President then becomes Acting President. The procedure by which the President may regain the office if he or she recovers is also spelled out in this amendment.

Amendment 26.
Eighteen-Year-Old Vote (1971)
This amendment made 18-year-olds eligible to vote in all federal, state, and local elections. Until then, the minimum age had been 21 in most states.

Amendment 27.
Restraint on Congressional Salaries (1992)
Any increase in the salaries of members of Congress will take effect in the subsequent session of Congress.

Visualizing History

▲ VOTING RIGHTS The Twenty-sixth Amendment, ratified in 1971, extended the right and the responsibility of voting. *In what way did the amendment change voting eligibility?*

UNIT THREE
LAUNCHING THE REPUBLIC
1789–1824

★★★

CHAPTER
7
The Federalist Era
1789–1800

CHAPTER
8
Age of Jefferson
1800–1815

CHAPTER
9
Nationalism and Change
1816–1824

▲ CHEROKEE BEADED
SHOULDER BAG

 History AND ART   *Liberty in the Form of the Goddess of Youth*
based on an engraving by Edward Savage, 1796

The hope and sense of adventure that most
Americans felt at the launching of their new nation
are expressed in this illustration.

198

Setting the Scene

The American people faced an uncertain future, but the new government put finances in order, witnessed the birth of political parties, improved its transportation system, and more than doubled its territory. By 1824 the United States had been transformed into a strong, independent nation.

Themes

- American Democracy
- Geography and Environment
- Conflict and Cooperation
- United States Role in World Affairs

Key Events

- Washington's Inauguration
- Bill of Rights ratified
- Whiskey Rebellion
- Treaty of Greenville
- "Revolution of 1800"
- *Marbury* v. *Madison*
- Louisiana Purchase
- Lewis and Clark Expedition
- War of 1812
- Battle of New Orleans
- Acquisition of Florida
- The Monroe Doctrine

▲ PRO-WASHINGTON POLITICAL BUTTONS

▲ POCKET WATCH, EARLY 1800S

Major Issues

- The plan for a strong central government, as set forth in the Constitution, becomes a reality.
- Disagreements within Congress and Washington's cabinet result in the formation of political parties.
- Backed by the Supreme Court, the power and authority of the national government grow at the expense of the states.

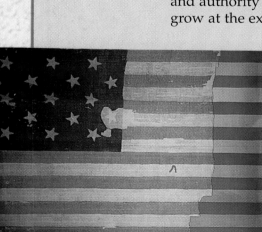

◀ FLAG FLOWN AT FORT McHENRY

Portfolio Project

Prepare a report on 1 of the 10 states admitted to the Union between 1791 and 1821. Describe its admission to statehood and details of the first legislature, governor, and state capital.

Global Perspectives

★★★★★★ ★★

The World

	1790	1805
Asia and Oceania		
Europe		**1800** Napoleon Bonaparte becomes ruler of France
Africa		◀ **1799** Rosetta Stone found in Egypt
South America		
North and Central America	▶ **1791** Toussaint-L'Ouverture leads slave revolt in Saint-Domingue (Haiti)	

The United States

	1790	1805
Pacific and Northwest		
Southeast		
Midwest		▶ **1804** Lewis and Clark explore the Louisiana Territory
Southwest	▲ **1793** Eli Whitney, with backing of Catherine Greene, invents the cotton gin	
Atlantic Northeast	**1790** First copyright law passes	

| 1790 | 1805 |

Linking Across TIME

Henry Wadsworth Longfellow's poem "Evangeline" tells of the British expulsion of French settlers from Acadia—present-day Nova Scotia and Prince Edward Island—in 1755. Most of these settlers migrated to Louisiana, where they became known as Cajuns—a slurring of the word *Acadians*. Today, Cajuns continue to exhibit their French heritage through their Creole language (a French dialect), their special cuisine, and their *joie de vivre* (zestful enjoyment of life).

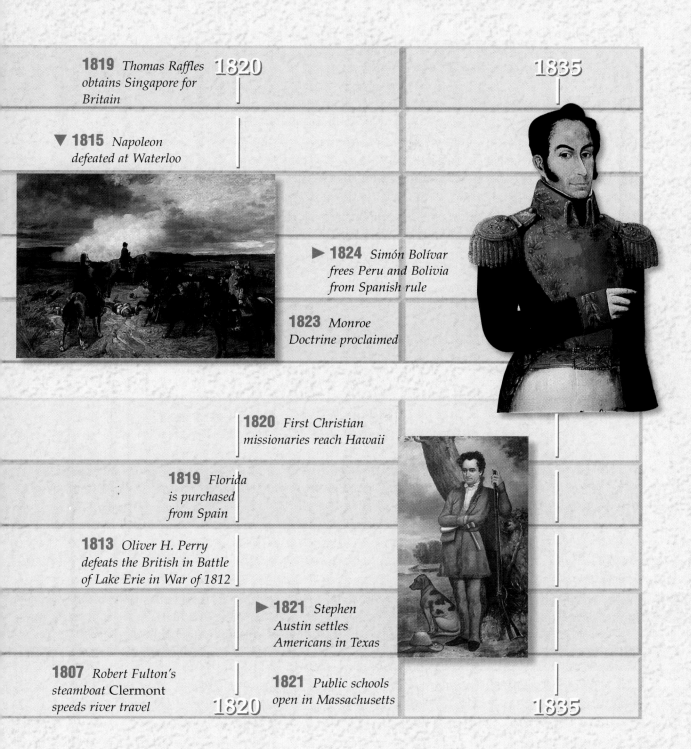

1820   **1835**

1819 *Thomas Raffles obtains Singapore for Britain*

▼ **1815** *Napoleon defeated at Waterloo*

► **1824** *Simón Bolívar frees Peru and Bolivia from Spanish rule*

1823 *Monroe Doctrine proclaimed*

1820 *First Christian missionaries reach Hawaii*

1819 *Florida is purchased from Spain*

1813 *Oliver H. Perry defeats the British in Battle of Lake Erie in War of 1812*

► **1821** *Stephen Austin settles Americans in Texas*

1807 *Robert Fulton's steamboat Clermont speeds river travel*

1821 *Public schools open in Massachusetts*

1820   **1835**

CHAPTER 7

★★

The Federalist Era
1789–1800

▲ HOOKED RUG, 1790S

Setting the Scene

Focus

With the ratification of the Constitution and national elections, a new government was in place by the spring of 1789. One of the most urgent problems it faced was the poor financial condition of the country. Largely through the efforts of Alexander Hamilton and Federalist leaders, sound policies were implemented. Controversy developed over Hamilton's program, however, resulting in the formation of political parties.

Concepts to Understand

★ How George Washington's strong leadership brought stability to the new government

★ How political values shaped the formation of political parties

Read to Discover . . .

★ some of the major issues that Washington faced as President.

★ how foreign affairs contributed to the growth of American political parties.

Journal Notes

What were the personal characteristics and beliefs of the country's early leaders? Note details about them in your journal as you read the chapter.

CULTURAL

• **1789** *Church of England becomes the Protestant Episcopal Church*

• **1790** *Samuel Slater builds first cotton mill*

• **1791** *Washington, D.C., is surveyed*

1785   1789

• **1787** *Northwest Ordinance passes*

POLITICAL

• **1789** *George Washington is inaugurated*

• **1791** *Bank of the United States is chartered*

Congress OF THE United States
begun and held at the City of New York, on
Wednesday the Fourth of March, one thousand seven hundred and eighty nine.

History AND ART

The Washington Family
by Edward Savage, c. 1798

When Washington took the oath of office on April 30, 1789, the machinery of government did not exist. There were no federal laws, no federal courts, and no federal law-enforcement officials.

◀ **BILL OF RIGHTS**

- **1794** *Connecticut inventor Eli Whitney patents cotton gin*

- **1799** American Review and Literary Journal *published; first quarterly literary review*

1793

1797

- **1794** *Whiskey Rebellion breaks out*
- **1795** *Northwest Territory opens for settlement*

- **1797** *John Adams is inaugurated*
- **1798** *Undeclared naval war with France rages*

★★

Organizing the Government

Setting the Scene

Section Focus

With the ratification of the Constitution in 1788, a new framework of government was in place. The obvious choice as leader of the new government was the hero of the Revolution, George Washington. Although he was reluctant to take the job, his reputation and stature were critical to the nation's success.

Objectives

After studying this section, you should be able to

★ list the precedents set by Washington as first President.

★ describe the first Congress under the Constitution.

Key Terms

cabinet, quorum

◀ BIBLE USED FOR WASHINGTON'S OATH OF OFFICE

*G*eorge Washington accepted the presidency reluctantly. On the day he left for his inauguration, he wrote in his diary:

❝ *About ten o'clock I bade adieu to Mt. Vernon, to private life, and to domestic felicity, and with a mind oppressed with more anxious and painful sensations than I care to express, set out for New York.* ❞

At almost every town and village on the way from Virginia to the nation's temporary capital, Washington was met by welcoming speeches, cheering crowds, and troops of cavalry. When he reached New York on April 23, 1789, he was rowed across the Hudson River on a barge built especially for the occasion. Most of New York's 33,000 residents lined the wharves and cheered as the

barge neared shore. Seven days later, Washington took the oath of office and gave the first Inaugural Address.

After the inauguration ceremony concluded, the festivities began with the ringing of church bells and the firing of cannons. Throughout the land there was public rejoicing for the man many believed to be the United States's greatest national asset.

■ Washington as President

Washington's background was as plantation manager and soldier. Because he lacked experience in government and had only limited knowledge of political theory and history, he felt he was unprepared to be the chief executive. Although Washington doubted his own qualifications, many

Americans regarded him with admiration bordering on awe. As early in his career as his first military victories at Trenton and Princeton, a Philadelphia newspaper wrote of Washington: "If there are any spots in his character they are like the spots on the sun, only discernible through a telescope." Such hero worship had its value to the new government. As a visible symbol of unity and power, Washington provided a focus for loyalty to the nation.

Washington's Qualifications

Washington was far more than a national symbol or figurehead. He knew the United States as well as any person alive, having traveled in every state except Georgia and having met or exchanged letters with most of the nation's prominent leaders. From the time he took charge of the Continental Army in 1775, he worked, as he said, to "discourage all local attachments" and to substitute "the greater name of American."

Organizing the New Government

Even with Washington in office and Congress in session, the Constitution was still little more than a paper plan. It would be months before the government could be functioning effectively. Laws had to be passed to establish executive departments such as the Treasury and the Post Office. A federal court system was needed to fill the gap left by the Framers of the Constitution.

Once federal offices were established, hundreds of people had to be found who were willing to give up their current jobs to serve as judges, tax collectors, and postmasters. Here, Washington's wide range of acquaintances and his reputation were invaluable in helping him find competent government officials.

Washington himself proved to be a first-rate administrator. On important matters, he sought the advice of his department heads, establishing what became known as the **cabinet**, a group of advisers to the President that continues to serve the same function today.

▲ PRESIDENTIAL SEAL

▲ THE FIRST CABINET Washington's original cabinet included Henry Knox, Thomas Jefferson, Edmund Randolph, and Alexander Hamilton. Washington held no regular meetings with these officers but did rely on their expert opinions. Hamilton became the most influential because the Treasury post gave him a strong position in proposing legislation. Washington claimed to have no particular political expertise. *What other qualifications did he bring to the presidency?*

Setting Precedents

Creating a cabinet was only one of several precedents set by Washington in areas where the Constitution was silent or unclear. He determined that the Senate's approval power over presidential appointments did not extend to their removal from office. He took control of foreign affairs, limiting the Senate's role of advice and consent to ratifying or rejecting treaties only after they were made.

Although he headed the executive branch, Washington assumed leadership in legislative affairs as well. In written messages to Congress and indirectly through reports prepared by Secretary of the Treasury Alexander Hamilton, Washington urged passage of laws he believed were in the public interest. With such encouragement Congress almost invariably followed his lead. Later Presidents would follow suit and become what some have called "chief legislator."

■ The First Congress

When the Confederation came to an end in 1788, it left behind 70 unpaid clerks, a military of 672 soldiers, and millions of dollars in debts. Before it disbanded, the Confederation Congress had arranged for the new government to be elected in November 1788 and start work on March 4, 1789. When March arrived, however, fewer than one-third of the senators and one-fourth of the representatives had reached New York. "The people will forget the new government before it is born," lamented a senator from Massachusetts. Not until April did each house of Congress have a **quorum**, or a majority of its members present in order to conduct business.

The Senate

The Senate was a small body consisting of two members from each state elected by their state legislature. The Framers of the Constitution had expected the Senate to serve as an advisory body to the President.

With this in mind, Washington came to the Senate in August 1789 with a treaty with the Creek people and asked for the senators' advice as well as their consent to the treaty. Because some senators felt uncomfortable discussing the treaty in the presence of the President, they instead referred it to a committee for study. Washington then left the Senate, departing, wrote Senator William Maclay, "with a discontented air." Although he returned later to watch the Senate debate, amend, and ratify the treaty, it was the last time that any President formally sought the advice of the Senate.

The Senate was a quiet and formal body. Its members dressed in powdered wigs, lace, and velvet. For its first five years, the Senate conducted its business in private. Not until 1794 was a gallery built for the public and the press.

The House of Representatives

The House of Representatives was more informal. Elected by the people, the House welcomed the public and the press from the beginning. Debate was loud, and members often wore their hats inside the chamber. The House took the lead in legislative matters, especially in dealing with the nation's troubled finances and in providing a Bill of Rights.

Executive Departments

After debates that lasted through the summer of 1789, Congress established three executive departments: a Department of State to take charge of foreign affairs, a Department of the Treasury to handle the nation's finances, and a Department of War to manage the military. Congress also created the position of Attorney General to handle the government's legal matters. None of these offices was specifically called for in the Constitution.

Creation of the Judiciary

Congress then turned its attention to the judicial branch and passed the Judiciary Act of 1789, setting up the Supreme Court and

History AND ART

▲ THE INSPECTION OF THE FIRST U.S. COINS by John W. Dunsmore, 1914 The half disme [dime] was the first coin struck by the United States government in July 1792. **What cabinet department was created to handle the government's legal matters?**

lower federal courts as called for by the Constitution. President Washington quickly named the first Supreme Court justices, deliberately choosing three from Northern and three from Southern states.

The Bill of Rights

Although a majority in both the Senate and the House had supported ratification of the Constitution, the Anti-Federalist minority insisted that Congress quickly provide the Bill of Rights promised during the ratification campaign. In his Inaugural Address, Washington also urged that careful attention be given to such demands. Finally in September 1789, after much debate, Congress proposed 12 amendments. Of these, 10 were ratified by the states and added to the Constitution in 1791.

▶ MEMORIAL TANKARD

Section 1 ★ Review

Checking for Understanding

1. **Identify** Department of State, Judiciary Act of 1789.

2. **Define** cabinet, quorum.

3. **List** the characteristics that made George Washington the ideal choice to become the first President of the United States.

4. **Describe** the precedents set by Washington that are still practiced by Presidents today.

Critical Thinking

5. **Evaluating Performance** Given his lack of experience in government and politics, explain why Washington was able to head a new framework of government.

Solving National Problems

Setting the Scene

Section Focus

The United States needed money to pay its war debts and to finance national growth. Raising these funds was the huge but vital task of Secretary of the Treasury Alexander Hamilton. His plans would bring financial stability to the new government. The plans also rekindled debate over the amount of power exercised by the national government.

Objectives

After studying this section, you should be able to

★ discuss Hamilton's financial program for the United States and the opposition to it.

★ describe the problems settlers faced during western expansion.

Key Terms

tariff, protective tariff, revenue tariff, bond, excise tax, enumerated power, implied power, suffrage

◀ **UNITED STATES GOLD QUARTER EAGLE, 1796**

*I*f the United States were to survive, the new government had to be able to pay its way. All members in both houses of Congress agreed that as soon as possible the federal government should begin to collect **tariffs,** or taxes on imports.

A tariff law was not passed, though, until July 1789 because some sections of the nation wanted a **protective tariff**—a high tax on imports to protect their products from foreign competition—while they opposed protection for goods produced in other sections. For example, the South wanted a high tariff on imported hemp, which was used in making rope, to protect its own hemp crop. New England opposed this because it would cost more to rig ships. New England, in turn, wanted a high tariff to protect its rum distilleries, while the South preferred to import rum directly from Jamaica.

The tariff of 1789 represented a compromise between the South and New England. Representatives to Congress from both sections of the country dropped their demands for protection and agreed to a **revenue tariff**, a low tax on imports designed to provide income for the government rather than protection for private business. Although there were a few exceptions, tariffs on imports averaged between 5 percent and 8 percent.

■ Hamilton's Program

Most of the money raised by the tariff was needed to pay off the $54 million national debt. The United States owed $12 million to France and the Netherlands for loans made during and after the Revolutionary War. The Continental Congress also had borrowed more than $40 million from individual Americans by selling them **bonds,** or certificates that promised repayment with interest. In addition, the government felt responsible for paying soldiers and army suppliers as the Continental Congress had promised. Finally, the individual states owed money totaling $25 million.

A Strong Federal Hand

In the debate over federal finances, the dominant figure was 33-year-old Alexander Hamilton. An aide to General Washington during the American Revolution, Hamilton had now been chosen by Washington to be secretary of the treasury. A poor man who married into a wealthy family, Hamilton believed in a strong government that favored prosperous merchants and large landowners. He had grown to distrust small farmers and laborers and expressed this view in writing:

> All communities divide themselves into the few and the many. The first are the rich and well-born, the other the mass of the people. . . . The people are turbulent and changing; they seldom judge or determine right.

When Congress asked Hamilton to prepare a financial plan, his proposals reflected his attitudes about wealth, power, and government. In a two-part *Report on the Public Credit* and a *Report on Manufactures,* he convinced Congress to pass a series of laws in 1790 and 1791. His recommendations, however, produced conflict and controversy.

Hamilton believed it was vital to the nation that the government have enough income to operate, pay the interest on the national debt, and gradually reduce the debt itself. So, in addition to the tariff, Hamilton proposed an **excise tax** on American whiskey. An excise tax is a tax paid by the manufacturer of a product and passed on to those who buy the product. In 1791 Congress approved Hamilton's proposal by enacting an excise tax on whiskey.

Paying Debts in Full

In dealing with the national debt, Hamilton proposed that foreign creditors be paid at once. As long as the United States owed money to other nations, he argued, it could not be truly independent. Congress responded by repaying France and the Netherlands by 1796.

Hamilton believed that the domestic debt also should be paid in full, even though the value of the bonds issued by the Continental Congress had fallen in value to as little as 20 cents on the dollar. Hamilton argued that in paying these bonds in full, the United States would tell its citizens and the world that its promises were good. After much debate, Congress passed the Funding Bill in 1790.

Hamilton also proposed that the federal government pay the states' debts. The states had fought for the entire nation, he argued, so the cost of their help during the Revolution should be assumed by the national government. Hamilton believed that federal

Visualizing History

▲ **ALEXANDER HAMILTON** Educated at King's College, Alexander Hamilton served Washington during the Revolutionary War and married into a rich and powerful New York family. Hamilton later served as Washington's secretary of the treasury. *What did he propose to make the nation wealthier?*

▲ THE FIRST BANK The Bank of the United States was built on Third Street in Philadelphia. *On what grounds did Madison oppose the Bank?*

payment of state debts would give the states a strong commitment to the success of the central government. Congress agreed and in 1790 passed the Assumption Act.

The National Bank

A key element of Hamilton's proposals was that the federal government establish a national bank modeled on the Bank of England. The bank would be a place for the federal government to deposit its tax receipts, as well as a place where tax revenues and private deposits could be used for large loans to government and to businesses.

Most important, the proposed bank would issue paper money backed by gold and silver in the bank's vaults. The public could have confidence in this currency because it could be exchanged for coins on demand.

Hamilton believed that the federal government should encourage development of American industries. He contended that industrial growth would make the country wealthier, because manufacturing often yielded higher profits than agriculture. Industrial growth would also encourage the immigration of skilled laborers. He proposed protective tariffs and government aid to new or expanding businesses. Although Congress did not act on this part of Hamilton's program, later events would prove that his vision was a clear one.

On the whole, Hamilton's program had immediate success in restoring the credit of the United States. By 1792, for example, bonds that had sold at a discount just four years earlier were selling for 120 percent to 125 percent of face value.

There was another, more personal, motive behind Hamilton's proposals. Because he believed in government by the wealthy and distrusted common people, his plans were intended to enlist the "rich and well-born" to support the federal government. He hoped to make such people personally interested in its survival. Although most of his proposals were enacted by Congress, the debate over many of them became bitter and divisive.

■ Opposition to Hamilton's Program

Despite its merits, Alexander Hamilton's program encountered a great deal of opposition. Much of the opposition was led by Thomas Jefferson, Washington's secretary of state. These tensions between Hamilton and Jefferson involved a personal struggle for power in Washington's cabinet. In addition, their conflict also reflected larger differences in the vision each man had for the nation's future.

The self-made Hamilton called democracy "poison" and characterized the general public as selfish, unreasonable, and violent. He believed that a powerful central government was necessary to keep law and order. Also, he wanted to reduce the power of the states.

Thomas Jefferson

Jefferson, born to wealth and social position, believed that if people were given the opportunity, they would be decent and reasonable. A defender of liberty, Jefferson believed in a minimum of government and favored power at the local level. Because Jefferson could not block Hamilton in the executive branch, the conflict was played out in Congress, where Jefferson's ally, James Madison, represented Virginia.

James Madison

Led by Madison, Hamilton's critics attacked the Funding Bill as unfair to the original purchasers of the bonds issued by the Continental Congress—"the warworn soldiers" and their "widows and orphans," one anti-Hamilton newspaper called them.

Life of the Times

Frontier Weddings

Weddings were major social events on the frontier. Often a justice of the peace would hear the couple's vows. This union was followed with festivities orchestrated by neighbors and friends that lasted for days.

The party began at the bride's home when her father placed a jug of whiskey on his doorstep. Male guests positioned themselves one mile from the house, then raced to seize the jug. The winner carried the jug to the groom, who took the first drink. Next, the groom and his party traveled to the bride's home for a daylong party. Around 9 o'clock in the evening, the female guests carried the bride to a bed in her parents' cabin. Later the male guests brought the groom to the bed. Guests would continue their party outside the cabin, often looking in on the newlyweds.

The next morning the couple led a procession of the guests to the cabin of the groom's parents. Another daylong party, or "infare," followed. On the third day the new couple moved into their own cabin. In the evening a "shivaree," or housewarming, took place. Guests surrounded the cabin armed with noise-making devices. On a designated signal, the woods erupted in a din of noise. The newlyweds opened their home for yet another party that generally ended near dawn. This party marked the end of the wedding celebration.

▼ WEDDING PARTY IN KENTUCKY

As time had passed, the original holders of these bonds, facing hard times and fearing that they would never be paid, had sold their bonds to speculators at a discount. Madison was outraged that New England merchants who had paid as little as $10 for a $100 bond now would receive full value. In addition, because federal funds would pay these speculators, tax money from the South would end up in the pockets of New Englanders.

Settling the Dispute

Madison's objection to the Assumption Bill was based on similar sectional concerns. Most of the Southern states had already paid their debts in full and did not want their taxes used to pay the debts of the Northern states. This major dispute was settled only when Hamilton, Madison, and Jefferson struck a deal. Southerners in Congress would vote for Hamilton's Assumption Bill. In return, the nation's capital would move from New York to Philadelphia for a period of 10 years and then to a new federal city on the Potomac River between Maryland and Virginia.

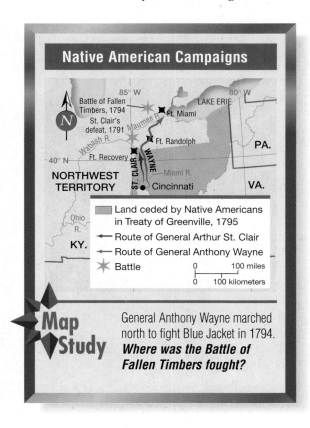

Native American Campaigns

Land ceded by Native Americans in Treaty of Greenville, 1795

← Route of General Arthur St. Clair

← Route of General Anthony Wayne

✳ Battle

0   100 miles

0   100 kilometers

Map Study

General Anthony Wayne marched north to fight Blue Jacket in 1794. *Where was the Battle of Fallen Timbers fought?*

A Question of Power

When Congress debated the bill to establish a national bank, Madison attacked it on constitutional grounds. Congress had no power to establish a bank, he argued, because it was not among the **enumerated powers**, or powers mentioned specifically, in the Constitution. Nor was it an **implied power**, a power that, while not directly stated in the Constitution, is suggested and does allow Congress to exercise its stated powers. If the federal government established a national bank, he feared there would be no limits to federal power.

Despite Madison's arguments, Congress passed the Bank Bill by an almost two-to-one majority. Washington hesitated to act, however, realizing that whether he signed this controversial bill or vetoed it, he would be setting an important precedent. Instead, he asked Attorney General Edmund Randolph and Secretary of State Jefferson, both fellow Virginians, for written opinions on the constitutionality of a national bank. Each opposed it using the same argument as Madison—that it was an overextension of federal power.

Washington passed Jefferson's and Randolph's opinions on to Hamilton. Working day and night, Hamilton composed a reply that convinced President Washington he should sign the Bank Bill. In a classic statement of implied powers, Hamilton argued that because the bank's functions were among the powers given Congress, the Constitution gave Congress the right to choose any legal means to carry out those functions. In 1791 the Bank of the United States was established.

■ Problems in the West

In addition to its financial problems, the new government faced continuing concerns about the western territories. The most immediate cause for alarm was relations with Native American nations. Armed to defend their lands, encouraged by the British and Spanish, and unimpressed by the federal government, Native Americans battled settlers over frontier land. Thousands of people were killed. Washington hoped to improve relations, but the bloodshed had to stop.

South of the Ohio River, treaties were signed with the Cherokee in 1791 and the Chickamauga in 1794—and the Creek asked the federal government for protection from the settlers. Once relations in the southern regions had been stabilized, the bluegrass meadows of Kentucky and the rich bottomlands along the rivers of Tennessee began to draw more settlers. Population increases enabled Kentucky to gain admission to the Union in 1792 and Tennessee to do so in 1796.

St. Clair Defeated

After a military expedition into the Northwest Territory was badly beaten by the Miami Confederation, led by Little Turtle, Washington ordered the governor of the territory,

General Arthur St. Clair, to the area with the largest force the West had ever seen—2,300 regular troops plus several companies of militia. As St. Clair moved north from Cincinnati, desertion and disease reduced his army to 1,400. Underestimating his enemy and rejecting the pleas of his weakened troops, St. Clair continued into Native American territory. In November 1791, near the present-day Ohio-Indiana border, he was attacked. Only 500 of his command survived one of the worst defeats in American military history.

Blue Jacket Defeated

The Native Americans demanded that all settlers north of the Ohio River leave the territory. Washington turned to General

The Westward Movement, 1790–1820

▲ ON THE ROAD WEST

Settled by 1790
Settled by 1820
Boundaries as of 1820

Map Study

Westward settlement was rapid in the years between 1790 and 1820. Within eight years of the Treaty of Greenville that opened the territory to settlement, Ohio was admitted to the Union. *What river was the avenue to the West?*

Anthony Wayne, who had distinguished himself in the Revolutionary War. In August 1794, his force defeated 800 Native Americans under Shawnee Chief Blue Jacket at the Battle of Fallen Timbers. Wayne pursued his foes all the way to Fort Miami, near present-day Toledo, Ohio, a British fur post that had been supplying weapons to the Native Americans. In the Treaty of Greenville (1795), the Native Americans agreed to surrender most of the present-day state of Ohio. As a result, settlers flocked to the new land, and in 1803 Ohio was admitted to the Union.

The Whiskey Rebellion

While settlers and Native Americans fought, another uprising was occurring in the West. In the days before canals and railroads, Westerners did not sell their grain east of the Appalachian Mountains because wagon transportation was costly. Since a wagonload of whiskey was worth much more than a wagonload of grain, Western farmers distilled their grain into whiskey before they transported it to market. Whiskey also served as currency in the West, where gold and silver coins were scarce.

Westerners believed that Hamilton's excise tax on whiskey, first levied in 1791, was aimed directly at them. There may have been some truth to this claim. Hamilton viewed the excise tax not only as a source of revenue for the national government but also as a way to get the West to recognize federal authority.

Antitax sentiment was especially strong in western Pennsylvania, where citizens refused to pay the tax, attacked revenue officers, and burned the barns of neighbors who told authorities where stills were located. Known as the Whiskey Rebellion, this revolt was as much a challenge to law and order as Shays's Rebellion had been eight years before. The outcome of the Whiskey Rebellion under the new government, however, was very different. The Massachusetts militia had suppressed Shays without help from the nearly bankrupt Confederation government.

When the governor of Pennsylvania hesitated to take action against the Whiskey Rebellion, the federal government stepped in and crushed it. President Washington, with Hamilton at his side, personally led 12,000 militia into western Pennsylvania. Some rebellion leaders were seized and taken to Philadelphia for trial. Two were found guilty of treason, but Washington pardoned both of them. The new government had shown its strength, he felt. Now it could afford to be merciful.

The rapid settlement of the West had a profound effect on politics. Reflecting the spirit of the frontier, the new Western states extended **suffrage**, or voting rights. Because land was so plentiful in the West, the constitutions of Kentucky and Tennessee required no property qualifications for voting. All white males over 21 years of age had the franchise. The argument for extending suffrage was that any man who helped clear the land and fight Native Americans had a right to a say in the government. Like Jefferson, Westerners tended to believe in common people.

Section 2 ★ Review

Checking for Understanding

1. **Identify** Fallen Timbers, Whiskey Rebellion.
2. **Define** tariff, protective tariff, revenue tariff, bond, excise tax, enumerated power, implied power, suffrage.
3. **Describe** why protective tariffs created sectional disagreements.
4. **Explain** the purpose and function of the national bank.

Critical Thinking

5. **Predicting Outcomes** Predict why Hamilton's and Jefferson's differing views might eventually lead to the formation of political parties.

Critical Thinking Skills

Distinguishing Between Fact and Value Judgment

A fact is a statement that can be proved by evidence. This evidence can be empirical (something you can actually see or feel) or a reliable written account as in a book or document. In contrast, a value judgment is a statement that includes a person's opinions based on one's values or feelings.

At one time or another, everyone is faced with the need to make a decision based on facts and value judgments. The following guidelines will help you in distinguishing between these two kinds of statements:

a. When reading or listening to any statement, keep in mind the definitions of fact and value judgment. Could the statement be supported with evidence?

b. Which statements are you being asked to accept as fact without evidence?

▲ CONGRESS HALL, PHILADELPHIA

Read the following statements and note how the guidelines have been applied.

1. Hamilton said in 1790 that a central bank of the United States would be "an institution of primary importance to the prosperous administration of the finances." Could this statement have been supported with evidence?

   (*No. This is a value judgment. The statement reflected Hamilton's belief that a central bank would be of primary importance, yet there was no evidence or proof to support it.*)

2. Hamilton stated that the bank and its branches would provide places where the government could deposit money obtained through taxes.

   (*This is a fact. If created, the bank would provide such places.*)

3. Madison, however, argued that the federal government had no right to establish a central bank because it was not among the enumerated powers of Congress found in the Constitution.

   (*This is a fact. Such authority was not among the powers of Congress. Evidence, therefore, supported it.*)

4. Madison stated that if the federal government were allowed to set up a central bank, there would be no limits to the power of the federal government. What evidence did Madison have to support this statement?

   (*None. He was personally against too much governmental control over the states and was, therefore, suspicious of federal power.*)

Practicing the Skill

For practice in this skill, find two examples of both factual statements and value judgments or opinions of the authors in Section 1 of this chapter.

★★★

Foreign Affairs Under Washington

Setting the Scene

Section Focus

Although an ocean away from Europe, the United States could not hope to exist in isolation, and the nation had to forge a response to overseas pressures. Treaties improved relations, but the end of Washington's presidency found the United States facing renewed problems with other nations.

Objectives

After studying this section, you should be able to

★ describe the effects of the French Revolution on the United States.

★ explain the importance of the Jay and Pinckney treaties.

Key Term

privateer

◀ GLASSWARE HONORING PRESIDENT WASHINGTON

Shortly after Washington was inaugurated in 1789, the French Revolution began. Americans sympathized with the French revolutionaries because they were demanding the same rights that Americans had won a few years earlier. The French "Declaration of the Rights of Man and the Citizen" proclaimed that all "men are born and remain free and equal in rights," and declared the rights of "liberty, property, security and resistance to oppression." The French revolutionaries readily acknowledged their debt to the United States in the expression and defense of these rights.

In this country, popular enthusiasm for France became almost a madness. Americans sang French revolutionary songs such as the "Marseillaise," erected "liberty poles" and wore "liberty caps," and even took to calling each other Citizen and Citizeness instead of Mr. and Mrs. In New York, King Street was renamed Liberty Street, and in Boston, Royal Exchange Alley became Equality Lane.

Cheers for France were often joined with damnation of Britain. Not only was the memory of the American Revolution still strong, but there was resentment because of the British refusal to give up the fur posts and to stop arming the Native Americans of the Northwest.

■ America's European Problems

When France and Great Britain went to war in 1793, the French expected American aid. According to treaties signed in 1778 between France and the American revolutionaries, France would have been justified in asking for American military assistance.

They did not go that far, but they hoped to recruit American volunteers for the French army and navy and to use American ports as bases to attack British merchant ships.

France's expectations placed the United States in a difficult position. Three-fourths of America's trade was with Britain, and tariff duties on British products provided the bulk of federal revenues. Because the British fleet controlled the seas, war would have ended foreign trade and meant bankruptcy for the new government.

Proclamation of Neutrality

When the war began, Washington called a cabinet meeting to discuss whether he should issue a declaration of neutrality. All cabinet members supported neutrality, even though Jefferson did so reluctantly. Jefferson, who had served as American minister to France and greatly respected the French people, believed that a formal declaration of neutrality would help Britain, and so he cautioned Washington against it. Hamilton, who despised the democracy of the French Revolution, argued that Britain was more to

be feared than France, and he urged Washington to announce America's neutrality. Again, Hamilton's arguments prevailed, and in April 1793, Washington issued a Proclamation of Neutrality. The President declared that the United States would be "friendly and impartial." He warned that Americans who helped either side would be denied the protection of the government and would be subject to punishment.

A Visit from the French Minister

The arrival of a new French minister, Citizen Edmond Genet (zhuh•NAY), put Washington's neutrality proclamation to the test. Genet traveled to the capital at Philadelphia. Along the way he was invited to so many pro-French celebrations that his journey became a triumphant procession. He arranged to place American crews on French **privateers**, or armed private ships, and offered George Rogers Clark a commission in the French army. Arriving confidently in Philadelphia, Genet demanded that the United States advance him money to pay his new recruits.

Visualizing
History

▲ STORMING THE BASTILLE The French Revolution of 1789, in which the French people overthrew their king to establish a republic, found most Americans sympathetic to a cause that seemed much like their own. As the French Revolution became more radical, however, American opinion divided sharply. *What action did the United States government take when war began between France and Britain?*

THE ARCH STREET FERRY by William Birch This engraving shows a busy trade center in Philadelphia. *How did Britain threaten American trade?*

The French minister's efforts to involve the United States in war were soon thwarted. Washington received him with icy politeness. Hamilton used all his influence against Genet. Even Jefferson flatly refused Genet's demands and came to dislike him intensely. Finally, an outraged Washington demanded that France recall the diplomat. Genet, however, begged to remain in the United States, because changes in France's government caused him to fear for his life. Washington granted the request, and Genet remained in America.

British Provocation

Great Britain also tested American foreign policy. When the British realized that the new federal government was more powerful than its predecessor, they at last consented to send a minister to the United States. Once war began in Europe, however, they issued a series of orders forbidding neutral ships to trade with the French West Indies, to carry French West Indian produce,

or to carry any weapons or food to France. These restrictions fell most heavily on the United States, which had the largest neutral merchant marine. British warships seized hundreds of American vessels and confiscated their cargoes, a clear violation of the rights of a neutral nation under international law.

In the spring of 1794, these provocations, coupled with news of British support for Native Americans in the Northwest Territory, pushed Congress to the brink of war. Hamilton urged Washington to make one last effort to come to a peaceful solution to the disputes by sending John Jay, Chief Justice of the Supreme Court, as a special envoy to Great Britain.

■ Treaties with Britain and Spain

The British were willing to sign a treaty. A war with the United States would only make it harder to carry on the war with France, and the United States was Britain's best market. Jay got rather poor treaty terms, however, partly because Alexander Hamilton committed a serious mistake: he let the British know Jay's instructions.

Treaty with Britain

The Jay Treaty was completed late in 1794. The British promised once again to evacuate their forts in American territory if the United States let them keep the fur trade with the Native Americans. American ships were allowed into ports in the British Isles on the same terms as British ships in American ports. The treaty permitted the United States a very limited trade with the British West Indies but none with Canadian ports. On the whole, it seemed that the British gave fewer concessions than they received. There was no promise that the violation of American neutral rights at sea would cease. Nor was there any assurance that British agents would stop giving weapons to Native Americans.

When the news of the Jay Treaty became known, there was a tremendous outcry against it. Jay's effigy was hanged in city squares. Hamilton, speaking in support of the treaty in New York City, was stoned by a mob. Despite the public's outrage, the Senate narrowly ratified the treaty by a two-thirds vote, 20 to 10. Dissatisfied with the treaty and dismayed by public reaction, Washington reluctantly signed it. Resistance continued in the House, where opponents of the treaty refused to vote funds necessary to put it into effect. Because a growing fear that the alternative to an unsatisfactory treaty was war with Britain, a 50-to-49 vote to release the funds resulted.

Treaty with Spain

When the treaty's terms became public, Spain's government suspected that a secret agreement had been made providing British support for an American attack on Spanish New Orleans and Florida. Thomas Pinckney was sent to Spain to try to settle long-standing differences between the two nations. In 1795 the Pinckney Treaty granted the United States all the concessions it had been seeking

since the end of the Revolutionary War—free navigation of the Mississippi River, the right of deposit at New Orleans, and acknowledgment of the United States's southern boundary at the 31st parallel and western boundary at the Mississippi.

■ Washington Steps Down

Washington had wanted to retire after his first term as President, saying he would rather dig ditches than continue. He agreed to serve a second term only after leaders, including both Jefferson and Hamilton, urged him to do so. In 1792, as in 1789, he received no opposition in the electoral college. Washington, however, enjoyed his second term even less than his first.

Jefferson Resigns from the Cabinet

Forced to choose in the bitter conflict between Jefferson and Hamilton, Washington continued to favor Hamilton. When Jefferson resigned from the cabinet in 1793, Washington was harshly attacked by Jefferson's supporters. By the end of his second term, Washington had become more and more sensitive to criticism. He confessed that he wished to

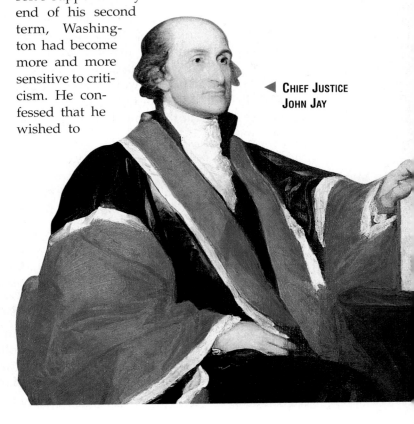

◀ CHIEF JUSTICE JOHN JAY

escape these attacks made "in such exaggerated and indecent terms as could scarce be applied to a Nero, a notorious defaulter, or even a common pickpocket."

Farewell Address

The last major act of Washington's presidency was his Farewell Address, which was published in the *American Daily Advertiser* on September 17, 1796. This address was Washington's explanation for not seeking a third term as President. Even more important, he gave the young republic his best advice on the conduct of politics and foreign affairs.

Upon returning to his beloved Mount Vernon, Washington had every reason to feel proud of his administration's achievements. Most of the difficulties of the Confederation had been overcome, and the credit of the United States was as solid as any European nation's.

The suppression of the Whiskey Rebellion had demonstrated the power of the new government. The major demands of the West had been fulfilled. In the difficult situation presented by war between France and Britain, Washington had steered a course that kept the United States prosperous and at peace.

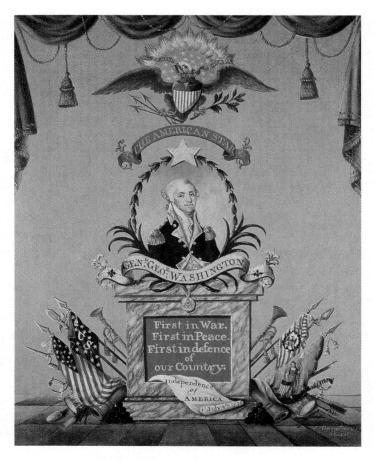

Visualizing History ▲ GEORGE WASHINGTON'S FAREWELL Washington, feeling that the government had been safely launched, refused nomination for a third term. The poster (above) and the painting (right) celebrate Washington's success in office. *What issues did he address in his Farewell Address?*

Section 3 ★ Review

Checking for Understanding

1. **Identify** Declaration of the Rights of Man and the Citizen, Proclamation of Neutrality, Citizen Edmond Genet, Jay Treaty, Pinckney Treaty, Farewell Address.

2. **Define** privateer.

3. **Describe** the activities of Citizen Genet that caused President Washington to demand his recall.

4. **Show** how Great Britain's actions against the United States nearly resulted in war.

Critical Thinking

5. **Supporting Positions** Washington warned of political divisions at home and entanglements abroad. Cite three events in American history that prove his warnings were not heeded.

Planning Washington, D.C.

By using inspiration, imagination, and his skill in geometry, engineer Pierre Charles L'Enfant created the design for a national capital unlike any other. When L'Enfant, who fought in the Revolution, heard that Congress was planning a new national capital, he quickly offered his services. President Washington hired L'Enfant, and the President himself negotiated purchase from the farmers who owned the land where the capital was to rise.

Although L'Enfant's design was soon modified, his basic plan allowed a spacious, modern city to develop. He envisioned a rationally laid-out metropolis that would embody the new nation's republican ideals, with wide boulevards connecting the branches of government, national monuments, parks, and entry gates.

L'Enfant began by choosing the spots for the Capitol and President's house. The Congress building became the central point in a square grid of streets occupying the terrain between the Potomac and Anacostia rivers. The grid was slashed by avenues that radiated from the capitol hill like spokes on a wheel. These avenues provided a direct route to different parts of the city. At strategic spots, L'Enfant's unique blend of topography and geometric symmetry called for circular intersections to join three or more avenues.

▲ WASHINGTON AND L'ENFANT AT CAPITOL SITE, 1791

◀ THE CAPITOL, 1824

Making the Science Connection

1. What geometric forms did L'Enfant use in planning the design of Washington, D.C.?

2. What are the advantages of locating a capital in a planned city? What might be some disadvantages?

Linking Past and Present

3. What kinds of geometric shapes are used in the design of modern government buildings?

★★★

President John Adams

Setting the Scene

Section Focus

It was inevitable that a nation of people holding different political philosophies would establish political parties. Foreign affairs provided further reasons for partisan politics. Led by a new President, the government would soon have to deal with problems on foreign soil as well as suspected treason at home.

Objectives

After studying this section, you should be able to

★ explain why political parties arose in the United States.

★ describe the problems John Adams encountered as President.

Key Terms

nonpartisan, nullification

◀ FROM A CARTOON ABOUT THE XYZ AFFAIR

The origins of America's two-party political system are found in the conflicts within Washington's cabinet and in congressional debates over Hamilton's financial program. Shortly after Washington took office, it became clear that Hamilton had the President's ear on almost every government matter. To counter Hamilton's strong influence, Madison and Jefferson began to gather support for their views both inside the government and outside.

■ Formation of Parties

Washington's first administration was **nonpartisan**—that is, there were no permanent divisions based on politics or causes. Differences arose over specific issues, which were hotly debated, but harmony returned after a cause triumphed or lost. Jefferson's resignation from Washington's cabinet, however, signaled a formal split in the ranks of the nation's political leadership.

The Republicans

After resigning, Jefferson openly allied with Madison, who was already opposing the Washington administration in Congress, to form what they called the "Republican" interest. They chose this name to suggest that they were defending freedom and self-government from the antidemocratic influence of Hamilton.

The Federalists

Hamilton's supporters took the name "Federalists," the label used by supporters of the Constitution during the ratification campaign. This maneuver was intended to imply that the Republicans were anti-Federalists and that they did not support the Constitution.

The Federalists included people who stood to profit from Hamilton's financial program—creditors, merchants, and bondholders. Federalists gained support from wage earners in the shipping industry and from residents of states that benefited when the federal government assumed state debts. Reflecting Hamilton's distrust of the people, the Federalists hoped to put the direction of government into the hands of the "rich, well-born, and able." The Republicans' strength was among Southern planters, subsistence farmers of the backcountry, and "mechanics" such as carpenters, shoemakers, and masons. Republican leaders advocated limiting the power of the central government.

Election of 1796

As the presidential election of 1796 drew near, both sides planned strategy. Under Madison's leadership, the Republicans tried to gain public support by opposing the unpopular Jay Treaty. Washington gave the Federalists an election advantage by delaying his retirement announcement. The Republicans were unwilling to offer any candidate to oppose a national hero.

When Washington withdrew two months before the election, the Federalists selected Vice President John Adams to run. The Republicans countered with a candidate of equal national reputation and sectional strength—Thomas Jefferson. In selecting its candidate for Vice President, each party tried to achieve geographic balance between its candidates. The Federalists chose Thomas Pinckney of South Carolina, who was currently popular because of his successful treaty negotiations with Spain. The Republicans balanced Jefferson, the Virginian, with Aaron Burr of New York.

Because the Framers of the Constitution had not anticipated political parties, the nation's first partisan presidential election was a confusing contest. The Constitution provided that the candidate with the highest number of votes in the electoral college would become President and the runner-up, Vice President. Therefore, some New England Federalist electors left Pinckney off their ballots in order to make sure that Adams would get the highest vote. The result was that Adams, a Federalist, was elected President with 71 electoral votes, while Jefferson, a Republican, became Vice President with 68.

■ Adams in Office

John Adams had spent most of his life in public service. An early leader of the revolutionary movement in Massachusetts, he was a prominent member of the First and Second Continental Congresses. During the war, he served as envoy to France and Holland and was a representative at the Treaty of Paris. He later became the nation's first minister to Great Britain. Under Washington, he served two terms as Vice President. In each office, he served with distinction.

Visualizing History ▲ ADAMS IN OFFICE John Adams's influence in the Constitutional Convention helped to produce the strong office of the President. *As President, Adams faced opposition from what political party?*

Benjamin Banneker
1731–1806

Born into a free family in Maryland, Benjamin Banneker was largely self-educated. When his father died, Banneker sold the family farm and devoted the rest of his life to mathematics and natural science.

Banneker's skill in mathematics prompted Thomas Jefferson to secure him a job surveying the land for the new national capital at Washington, D.C. Legend has it that when the French architect Pierre L'Enfant quit the project and took his detailed maps with him, Banneker reproduced L'Enfant's plans from memory.

Later, Banneker wrote and published a most successful almanac. His picture on the cover proclaimed it as the work of an African American. Banneker's efforts and his achievements brought attention to racial injustice in a land not yet willing to grant him rights of citizenship.

Tension with France

When Adams took office, he inherited the dispute with France. French disappointment over Washington's Neutrality Proclamation turned to hostility after the Jay Treaty. During the election of 1796, the French minister to the United States actively campaigned against Adams. When Charles C. Pinckney was sent as minister to France in 1796, he was ordered out of the country. Meanwhile, the French navy started to prey on American shipping.

Adams was anxious to make peace. Immediately after taking office, he sent envoys to Paris to negotiate a treaty. When the Americans arrived, they were approached by three representatives of Charles Maurice de Talleyrand, the French minister of foreign affairs. The agents demanded that a bribe be paid to Talleyrand.

An Undeclared War

Unwilling to pay the bribe, the Americans broke off negotiations. Because their reports labeled Talleyrand's agents as X, Y, and Z, this situation came to be known as the XYZ Affair, and it produced an outburst of popular anger against France. Adams was cheered in Congress when he declared that he would never send another minister without France assuring its respect to "the representative of a great, free, powerful, and independent nation." The slogan of the day became: "Millions for defense, but not one cent for tribute." Congress created a Department of the Navy in May 1798, and soon warships and privateers were waging an undeclared naval war with France.

War fever suited Federalist party leaders. The national emergency strengthened the federal government, made the Federalists popular, and discredited the pro-French Republicans. If war continued, Federalists expected to win reelection in 1800, but President Adams refused to let election politicking dominate American foreign policy. When Talleyrand changed his mind and decided to receive American diplomats, Adams opposed others in his party and sent an American minister to France. Federalist senators were furious, but they could not long oppose an effort to make peace. By the end of Adams's presidency, peace with France had been restored.

Adams's action in making peace against the wishes of most of his party was a courageous act. Proud of his nonpartisan action, Adams wrote that on his gravestone he wanted written "Here lies John Adams who took upon himself the responsibility of the peace with France in the year 1800."

Partisan Legislation

Many Federalists were convinced that prominent Republicans were actively in league with France. So in 1798, in the midst of war fever, the Federalist majority in Congress pushed through three laws designed to hurt the Republican party—a Naturalization Act, an Alien Act, and a Sedition Act.

Many French and Irish refugees had recently come to America. Because they were anti-British, most supported the Republican party. The Naturalization Act tried to weaken this Republican strength by extending the residency requirement for citizenship from 5 to 14 years. The Alien Act required all immigrants to register with the federal government and allowed the President to deport without trial any alien whom he considered "dangerous." The Sedition Act attempted to muzzle the Republican press by making it a crime to speak or publish anything false or malicious against the federal government or any of its officers.

Instead of weakening the Republican party, these laws gave Republicans the issues that broadened their support. Republicans were horrified by these attacks on freedom of speech and press. In 1798 and 1799, the Republican legislatures of both Kentucky and Virginia passed resolutions denouncing

Visualizing History

▲ **HOT-TEMPERED REPRESENTATIVES** In *Congressional Pugilists*, 1798, Roger Griswold, wielding a cane, fights with Matthew Lyon, the most notable victim of the Sedition Act of 1798. *What was the aim of the Sedition Act?*

the Sedition Act as unconstitutional. The Kentucky Resolutions presented the theory of **nullification**. According to this theory, the Constitution was an agreement among the states to establish a central government. If an act of the government exceeded the powers granted by the Constitution, a state had the right to refuse to obey.

The nullification theory was denounced by other state legislatures as threatening to the Union. If a state could nullify any federal law it considered unconstitutional, the power of the federal government would cease.

Section 4 ★ Review

Checking for Understanding

1. **Identify** XYZ Affair, Naturalization Act, Alien and Sedition acts, Kentucky and Virginia resolutions.

2. **Define** nonpartisan, nullification.

3. **List** the main differences between the Republicans and the Federalists.

4. **Describe** the effects of the XYZ Affair.

Critical Thinking

5. **Evaluating Ideas** List what you consider to be the strengths and weaknesses of having political parties. Use your list to write an opinion statement of 3 to 4 sentences explaining why you favor or oppose having political parties.

Understanding Vocabulary

For each term below, write a sentence explaining why it had either a unifying effect or a divisive effect on the new government.

cabinet

protective tariff

revenue tariff

excise tax

enumerated powers

implied powers

nonpartisan

nullification

Reviewing Facts

1. **List** the actions taken during Washington's presidency that reflected the Federalist principle of strong central government authority.

2. **Outline** the causes that gradually led to the development of political parties.

3. **Identify** the economic problems facing the nation in 1789, and tell how Hamilton's financial program addressed those problems.

4. **State** the causes, their effects, and the final outcomes of the problems that the United States faced with France and Britain between 1789 and 1800.

5. **Show** how the actions of George Washington and improved foreign relations opened up the West for settlement.

Understanding Concepts

Leadership

1. **Characterize** the leadership style that George Washington exercised as President.

2. **Describe** the kind of leadership the Federalists provided in relation to the kind provided in the Confederation government.

Political Values

3. **Describe** the political values that motivated President Washington.

4. **Explain** the ideals of the Republicans under Thomas Jefferson, and compare them with Federalist principles.

Critical Thinking

1. **Drawing Conclusions** Washington was the first of several generals who later became President. Why do people think that a good general will make a good President?

2. **Analyzing Illustrations** Study the illustration below and answer these questions.

   a. What do you think the two individuals are doing?

   b. What tools are they using?

   c. What feeling about their work do the individuals' physical stances and expressions convey?

Writing About History

Classification and Division

Read an encyclopedia article about the life of George Washington. Then, divide the many facts about Washington's life into several different periods or categories. Write a report on George Washington's life and be prepared to explain why you have classified Washington's life into the categories you have chosen.

▲ AMERICAN SURVEYORS, NINETEENTH CENTURY

CHAPTER 7 ★ REVIEW

Cooperative Learning

You and four class members will portray a banker and the following persons asking for a loan: 1) a New England manufacturer wanting to build a furniture factory, 2) a Western farmer wanting to buy 100 acres of land, 3) a Southern plantation owner wanting to acquire more land and enslaved persons, 4) a land speculator wanting to buy a million acres of land in the West. Each team member should portray a different person. After interviews are finished, decide together whether and why each of the loans should be granted or denied.

Social Studies Skills

Recognizing Historical Reasoning When historians write about history, they often use certain words to connect the facts to other words that help the reader understand their meaning. These clue words point out the deductions they have made.

The chart that follows lists four kinds of historical reasoning. By learning to recognize these four methods, you can better determine for yourself whether or not a historian has supported his or her argument adequately.

Kinds of Historical Reasoning

KIND	CLUE WORDS
Cause and Effect	led to, brought on, resulted in
Example: *The ratification of the Constitution in 1788 resulted in a new framework for government.*	
Analogies	like, as, similar to, different from
Example: *Westerners tended, like Jefferson, to believe in common people.*	
Generalizations	some, most, all, few
Example: *Most people were opposed to the Jay Treaty.*	
Proof	for example, this statement shows
Example: *Washington made it clear that he wanted to retire after his first term. For example, he pointed out that he would rather dig ditches than continue.*	

Practicing the Skill

After studying the chapter and the kinds of historical reasoning shown in the chart, answer the following questions concerning the story told about the Federalist Era by this text's authors.

1. What statements in Section 1 give *proof* to Washington's leadership skills?

2. How is *cause and effect* used in Section 2 to explain how settlement north of the Ohio River caused conflict with Native Americans?

3. Read the following statement Thomas Jefferson made in regard to his differences with Hamilton.

   "Every difference of opinion is not a difference in principle. We have called by different names brethren of the same principle. We are all Republicans, we are all Federalists."

   What kind of reasoning do you think Jefferson was using to make his point? Explain your answer.

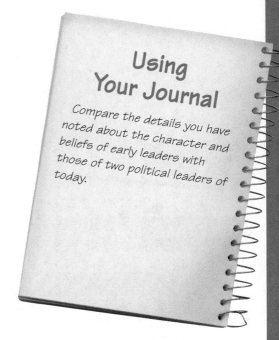

Using Your Journal

Compare the details you have noted about the character and beliefs of early leaders with those of two political leaders of today.

CHAPTER 8

★★

Age of Jefferson
1800–1815

▶ THE SECOND U.S.
FLAG, 1795–1818

Setting the Scene

Focus

Between 1800 and 1815, the United States experienced rapid expansion as well as the challenge of war. The Louisiana Territory doubled the size of the nation, creating remarkable new opportunities, and Americans looked to the future confidently. However, when war between France and Great Britain was renewed, the United States found its peace and neutrality threatened. By 1812 the United States and Great Britain had once more plunged into war.

Concepts to Understand

★ How geographic expansion changed the social and economic character of the United States

★ How expansion, economic change, and conflict unified Americans and helped them form a national identity

Read to Discover . . .

★ the opportunities that resulted from the Louisiana Purchase.

★ the factors that caused the War of 1812.

Journal Notes

How did the Republican views held by Jefferson differ from the Federalist views held by Washington and Adams? Note the differences as you read the chapter.

CULTURAL

● **1801** *"Second Great Awakening" religious revival in the West begins*

● **1807** *Inventor Robert Fulton perfects the steamboat* Clermont

| 1800 | 1805 |

POLITICAL

● **1801** *Jefferson is inaugurated President*
● **1803** *Louisiana Purchase completed*

● **1807** *The* Chesapeake *is attacked*
● **1809** *Embargo Act is repealed*

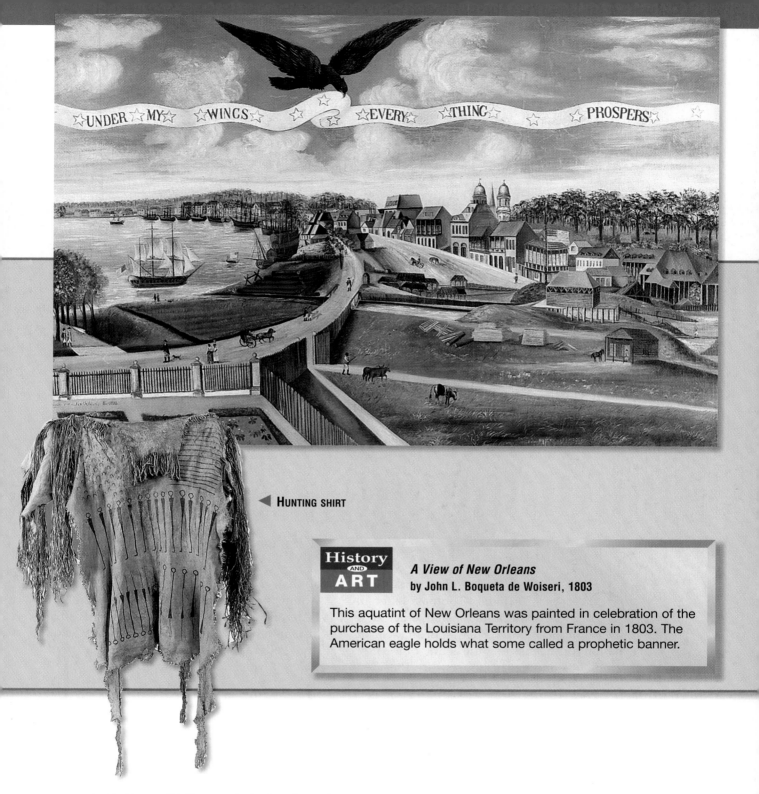

UNDER MY WINGS EVERY THING PROSPERS

◀ HUNTING SHIRT

History AND ART

A View of New Orleans
by John L. Boqueta de Woiseri, 1803

This aquatint of New Orleans was painted in celebration of the purchase of the Louisiana Territory from France in 1803. The American eagle holds what some called a prophetic banner.

• **1810** *Boston Philharmonic Society formed*
• **1813** *Francis Scott Key writes "The Star-Spangled Banner"*

• **1815** North American Review *is published*

1810

• **1812** *War with Great Britain begins*

1815

• **1815** *Treaty of Ghent ratified*

★★

The Changing Political Scene

Setting the Scene

Section Focus

The election of 1800 marked a turning point for the United States. For the first time, the Federalist party was not in power. The growing democratic spirit of the nation found its expression in the Republican party. Jefferson's primary task was to unite the nation and prove that he would represent all Americans. Partly for this reason, Jefferson left intact many Federalist programs.

Objectives

After studying this section, you should be able to

★ explain Thomas Jefferson's views on government.

★ compare similarities and differences between Jefferson's administration and those of Washington and Adams.

★ discuss the significance of judicial review.

Key Terms

laissez-faire, judicial review, writ of mandamus

◀ THOMAS JEFFERSON

s Vice President under John Adams, Thomas Jefferson became the active leader of the Republican party. He was in an ideal situation for the task—at the center of the government—and yet his job as Vice President carried with it very few official duties.

■ The Election of 1800

As the presidential election of 1800 approached, the Federalists selected John Adams and Charles Pinckney as their candidates; the Republicans, Jefferson and Aaron Burr. During the campaign, Jefferson and his followers concentrated their fire on the Sedition Act and heavier taxes brought on by the undeclared war with France. The Federalists countered by predicting that Jefferson would cancel the public debt and

abolish the navy. Republicans pictured Adams as a tyrant who wanted to be king. Federalists portrayed Jefferson as a drunkard, an atheist, and a French agent. A leading Federalist newspaper, *The Hartford Courant*, voiced the opinion that

❝ *Mr. Jefferson has long felt a spirit of deadly hostility against the Federal Constitution. . . . If he should be elected President, the Constitution will inevitably fall. . . . The result will be dreadful to the people of the United States.* ❞

Jefferson Defeats Adams

Realizing that lack of support in all the states north of Pennsylvania had cost them the election in 1796, the Republicans worked hard in 1800 to gain the backing of laborers and immigrants in northeastern cities. The vote was so close that the voters in New York state would determine which candidate would win. Aaron Burr's organization was so effective in getting out the vote in New York City that the Republicans carried every district in the city. That victory gave them the state and, with it, the national election.

The election results posed a new question: the Republicans had won, but *which* Republican candidate became President? There was no doubt that the party had intended Jefferson as President and Burr as Vice President. But unlike today's election practices, candidates in 1800 were not designated as the candidate for President or the candidate for Vice President. Because every Republican elector had two votes and voted separately for both Jefferson and Burr, each candidate received 73 electoral votes. Where there is no majority, the Constitution stipulates that the House of Representatives selects the President. Some Federalists schemed to deny Jefferson the presidency and elect Burr—and came close to doing so. The House was so evenly divided that it took 6 days and 36 ballots. The deadlock was broken after a group of Federalists led by Hamilton supported Jefferson because they considered him better suited for the job and abler than Burr.

Transfer of Political Control

Although the Federalists were unhappy at losing the presidency, they accepted their loss and surrendered control of the federal government. This marked the first time in modern history that the political control of a country had been transferred through a democratic election. Despite animosity between Federalists and Republicans, the party system was beginning to work for the nation. The political parties that Washington had feared and warned against had developed national organizations that selected competent candidates for public office, maintained communications between federal officials and their constituents, and dealt effectively with factional and sectional differences.

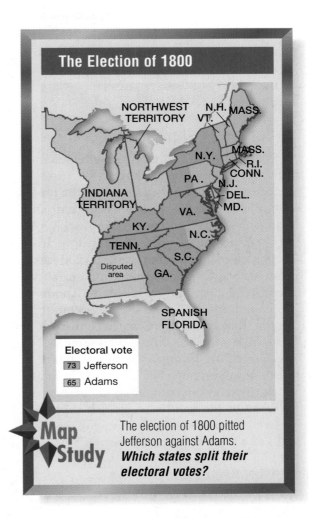

The Election of 1800

Electoral vote
73 Jefferson
65 Adams

Map Study

The election of 1800 pitted Jefferson against Adams. *Which states split their electoral votes?*

■ Jefferson the Individual

If the Washington, D.C., of 1801—with its muddy streets and half-finished buildings—was an odd sort of national capital, the first President inaugurated there was in many ways an odd sort of man to be the founder of a political party and head of state. Thomas Jefferson hated crowds, avoided making speeches, and was too thin-skinned to enjoy rough-and-tumble politics.

Jefferson's Accomplishments

Jefferson's interest in agriculture led him to import hundreds of foreign plants into this country and to send hundreds of American plants abroad. One of the finest architects of his day, Jefferson designed his own home, Monticello, and was the chief architect of the Virginia Capitol and a complex of buildings for the University of Virginia. His many inventions included an improved plow, a swivel chair, and a folding carriage top. A lover of literature, he collected a library that eventually became the nucleus of the Library of Congress.

Jefferson in Washington, D.C.

In appearance and manner, Jefferson had little of Washington's dignity. He tried to reduce the ceremony surrounding the presidency because he felt Washington and Adams had acted too much like British royalty. For example, instead of riding in a coach, Jefferson chose to walk the 200 yards from his boardinghouse to his inauguration. He also sent written messages to Congress instead of appearing in person, beginning a custom that lasted more than a century. Visitors from other countries were amazed to see him riding through the dusty streets of Washington on horseback, dressed in faded corduroy overalls with a bag of clover seed in front of the saddle. A British diplomat described Jefferson as having the appearance of a "tall, large-boned farmer."

■ Jefferson and Government

Jefferson brought both a political and a philosophical change to the presidency. He believed the people were the source of a government's power, an idea he expressed in his Inaugural Address. Pleading for national harmony after the bitter election, Jefferson said:

❝ *Let us restore to social intercourse that harmony and affection without which liberty and even life itself are but dreary things. . . . We are all Republicans, we are all Federalists.* ❞

By this he meant that despite their distrust of democracy, Federalists recognized the principle that problems are finally settled by the will of the people, and that despite their distrust of centralized power, the Republicans did not propose to destroy the federal government.

Visualizing History

▲ JEFFERSON'S ACCOMPLISHMENTS In addition to being an inventor and a scientist, Thomas Jefferson helped design the University of Virginia. Jefferson brought a new outlook to the presidency as well. *Why did the new President focus on the theme of unity in his Inaugural Address?*

Visualizing History

▲ THE NATION'S CAPITAL Washington, D.C., at the time of Jefferson's presidency, did not resemble the capital city familiar to citizens today. *How did Jefferson attempt to quiet the fears of his opponents?*

Laissez-faire

Jefferson described what he thought were the principles of "wise and frugal government." In contrast to Hamilton's idea that the government should actively promote banking, commerce, and industry, Jefferson advocated a "hands-off" policy called **laissez-faire,** meaning generally, "let people do as they choose." A government should not control the way people do business or farm but should keep its role to restraining people from injuring each other and allowing them to be "free to regulate their own pursuits."

Quieting Fears

Jefferson's views on democracy and individual freedom quieted the fears of the Federalists. He called for "the preservation of the General Government in its whole constitutional vigor," which surely did not suggest his earlier theory of nullification. He also spoke of "the honest payment of our debts." This came as a great relief to owners of federal bonds who feared that Jefferson would prevent repayment to the bondholders.

■ Jefferson the Leader

Jefferson liked to speak of his election in 1800 as a "revolution." Perhaps in the sense that leaders who distrusted democracy were replaced by those who believed in it, it was a mild revolution.

Congressional Leadership

Before he became President, Jefferson had argued that the executive branch held too much power. In his Inaugural Address, he hinted that he would allow Congress to guide policy. As President, Jefferson made gestures toward giving Congress more control over day-to-day affairs of government. However, he had to provide strong leadership or watch his party divide into factions.

For this reason Jefferson used his position as party leader to influence legislation. By working with Republican leaders in Congress and by giving his supporters key positions, Jefferson became just as much chief legislator as Washington had been.

The Judiciary

The congressional elections of 1800 gave the Republicans solid majorities in both the House and Senate, enabling them to repeal Federalist legislation they disliked. The only change they attempted to make, however, was to cut the power of the federal judiciary and remove some federal judges.

Republicans feared the judiciary for three reasons. One was that federal judges, holding their positions "during good behavior," or for life, were beyond the people's control. Another was that federal courts had declared several state laws unconstitutional, thereby strengthening the power of the federal government while reducing that of the states. Finally, Federalists had "packed" the judiciary. The number of federal judges was increased by the Judiciary Act of 1801, and Adams had filled many positions with members of his party. These judges were known as "midnight judges" because Adams supposedly signed appointments until midnight of his last day in office.

One of the first acts of Congress after Jefferson took office was to repeal the Judiciary Act. After doing away with the "midnight judges" by abolishing their offices, the Republicans tried to remove other Federalist judges by impeachment.

In 1804 a Federalist district judge from New Hampshire, John Pickering, was impeached by the House and convicted by the Senate for actions that indicated he was unfit to serve. The House then impeached Associate Justice Samuel Chase of the Supreme Court for biased conduct. He had attacked democracy in general and Jefferson in particular while addressing a Baltimore jury. The Senate, however, refused to convict Chase because it was not convinced that he had been proved guilty of "treason, bribery, or other high crimes and misdemeanors." (See Article II, Section 4 of the Constitution.)

The failure to remove Chase reduced the use of impeachment in the future to serious wrongdoing. Only once more, in the case of President Andrew Johnson in 1868, was it used as a political weapon.

■ Judicial Review

Shortly before leaving office, President Adams appointed John Marshall Chief Justice of the United States. Marshall was a Federalist and detested his cousin, Thomas Jefferson. In *Marbury* v. *Madison* (1803), Marshall greatly strengthened the power of the federal judiciary. In his decision he claimed that the federal courts had the power of **judicial review** over acts of Congress—that is, the power to decide whether laws passed by Congress were constitutional.

Marbury v. Madison

When James Madison took over as Jefferson's secretary of state, he found on his desk the commissions of several justices of the peace for the new District of Columbia. President Adams had signed the commissions,

Life of the Times

Telling Time

Whether rich or poor, urban or rural, Americans measured their activity primarily in days, months, and seasons—not in hours or minutes.

Most families in the early 1800s could afford neither clocks nor watches. Although accurate clocks existed, the few timepieces within a community often told different times. People used the position of the sun during the various seasons to estimate time during the day and to determine when they slept and rose from bed. Church bells tolled to announce worship services and town meetings, not the hour of the day.

The routine of daily life moved at a different pace without standardized time. Nature, for example, arranged a farmer's schedule. Farm families planted, cultivated, and harvested their crops according to the cycle of the seasons. Weather patterns influenced when families could set out for town or market—by wagon, over dirt roads—or when visitors were likely to arrive. A storm could easily upset plans by turning the roads to mud.

▼ Box clock, c. 1815

but they had not been delivered. Jefferson instructed Madison to withhold the commissions. One of the appointees, William Marbury, petitioned the Supreme Court for a **writ of mandamus**—a court order requiring specific action—instructing Madison to give him his commission.

The Supreme Court was faced with a difficult decision. If it ruled that Marbury was entitled to be a judge and issued a writ, Jefferson and Madison could simply ignore it, diminishing the power and prestige of the Court. If the Court did not issue a writ, the Republicans would win by default. Marshall came up with a brilliant solution.

Acknowledging that Marbury had a legal right to his commission, Marshall argued that the Supreme Court could not issue the writ because the Constitution specifically listed the cases in which the Court had *original* jurisdiction. The writ of mandamus was not among them. In attempting to extend the Court's original jurisdiction to issue writs, the Judiciary Act of 1789 violated the Constitution, so the law was void.

Marshall said that the Constitution was the supreme law of the land. It could not be changed at the whim of the legislative branch. In this way Marshall had sidestepped his political dilemma. He gave the Republicans the result they sought by not issuing the writ. He even limited the original jurisdiction of the Court. Far more important, he laid down the cornerstone of the Court's power, judicial review—the authority to interpret the Constitution—which gives the judicial branch a "check of the legislative branch" in the system of checks and balances.

▲ JOHN MARSHALL

A New Term

Aside from this setback, Jefferson viewed his first term as a success. War had broken out in Europe, but its first effect in the United States was to increase foreign trade. Taxes had been reduced, and the income of the federal government from tariffs was sufficient to pay everyday expenses and reduce the national debt. Nearly everything that had happened during President Jefferson's first term added to the popularity of the Republican party, and Jefferson's reelection was assured. Running against Charles Pinckney of South Carolina, Jefferson received 162 of 176 electoral votes. The prospects for continuing what he had started looked good, but Jefferson's second term was to be far less successful than his first.

Section 1 ★ Review

Checking for Understanding

1. **Identify** Charles Pinckney, Aaron Burr, John Marshall, *Marbury* v. *Madison*.

2. **Define** laissez-faire, judicial review, writ of mandamus.

3. **State** the main points of Jefferson's political philosophy.

4. **Name** three important accomplishments of Jefferson during his first term in office.

Critical Thinking

5. **Analyzing Issues**   How did Marshall go beyond the issues of his case to establish the power of the Supreme Court for all time?

Interpreting Primary Sources

Female Equality

In the early 1800s, some American women began to challenge the accepted notion of female inferiority to men. They began to demand a greater role in public life. They also worked for better opportunities in education and in the workplace for women. An organized movement for woman's rights—with a substantial number of supporters—did not begin until the Seneca Falls Convention in 1848, however.

The following letter shows a young woman trying to make sense of the contradictory doctrines of female subordination and sexual equality. Eliza Southgate wrote to a male cousin in 1801:

▲ **Mother and daughter, 1790s**

But every human being who has contemplated human nature on a large scale will certainly justify me when I declare that the inequality of privilege between the sexes is very sensibly felt by us females, and in no instance is it greater than in the liberty of choosing a partner in marriage; true, we have the liberty of refusing those we don't like, but not of selecting those we do. This is undoubtedly as it should be. . . .

I never was of opinion that the pursuits of the sexes ought to be the same; on the contrary, I believe it would be destructive to happiness, there would a degree of rivalry exist[;] each should have a separate sphere of action—in such a case there could be no clashing unless one or the other should leap their respective bounds. Yet to cultivate the qualities with which we are endowed can never be called infringing the prerogatives of man. . . .

The cultivation of the power we possess, I have ever thought a privilege (or I may say duty) that belonged to the human species, and not man's exclusive prerogative. Far from destroying the harmony that ought to subsist, it would fix it on a foundation that would not totter at every jar. Women would be under the same degree of subordination that they now are; enlighten and expand their minds, and they would perceive the necessity of such a regulation to preserve the order and happiness of society. . . .

Examining the Primary Source

1. What does Southgate suggest is a prime example of the inequality of privilege between the sexes?

2. What disadvantage does Southgate see to men and women following the same pursuits?

Critical Thinking

3. Do you agree or disagree with Southgate's assertion that competition between men and women creates unhappiness in male-female relationships? Explain your answer.

★★

Looking Westward

Setting the Scene

Section Focus

The Louisiana Purchase was a notable achievement of the Jefferson administration. Committed to interpreting the Constitution in its strictest sense, Jefferson doubted that he possessed the power to make the purchase. On the other hand, the opportunity to gain the land west of the Mississippi River might never come again.

Objectives

After studying this section, you should be able to

★ explain the significance of the Louisiana Purchase.

★ identify the reasons why unrest between Native Americans and the American government was increasing.

Key Term

expedition

◄ THE LOUISIANA PURCHASE TREATY

he news that Spain had ceded Louisiana, including New Orleans, to France in 1800 was of great concern to the United States. The French were now ruled by Napoleon Bonaparte, whose conquests kept Europe in turmoil for many years. Napoleon increased France's power in Europe and planned to create a new French empire in North America.

■ The Louisiana Purchase

Jefferson was alarmed at the prospect of New Orleans being in French hands. The city was a major trade center for the United States, especially as a market for Western goods. Jefferson feared that the French might close New Orleans to American trade, thus blocking the development of the American West. He authorized Robert Livingston, United States minister stationed in Paris, to offer France $10 million for New Orleans and West Florida and sent James Monroe as a special envoy to Paris to negotiate the purchase.

Trouble in Saint Domingue

It is unlikely that American dollars would have moved Napoleon if his plans for a French empire had not suffered a great defeat in the most valuable of France's American colonies, Saint Domingue (Haiti). During the 1700s, its exports of sugar, indigo, coffee, and cotton were almost equal in value to the combined exports of the 13 colonies. In 1791 its enslaved people rebelled. Under the leadership of Pierre Toussaint-L'Ouverture (TOO•SAN LOO•vuhr•TYUR), "the black Napoleon," Haitian blacks attempted to make their island an independent state.

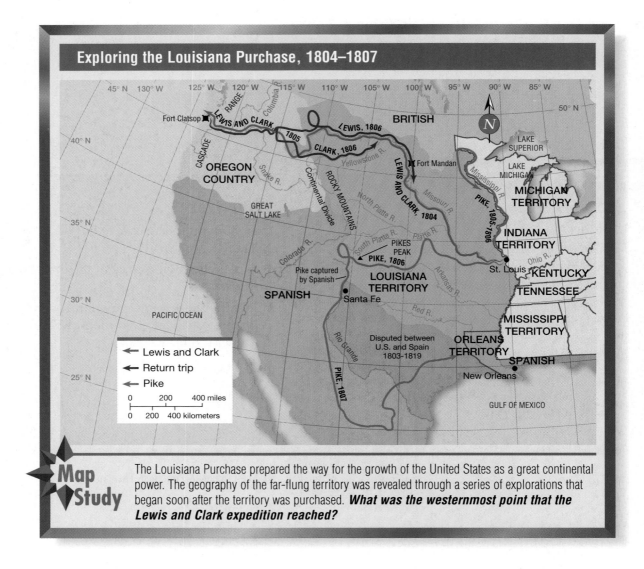

Exploring the Louisiana Purchase, 1804–1807

Map Study

The Louisiana Purchase prepared the way for the growth of the United States as a great continental power. The geography of the far-flung territory was revealed through a series of explorations that began soon after the territory was purchased. *What was the westernmost point that the Lewis and Clark expedition reached?*

In 1801 Napoleon sent soldiers to put down the Haitian revolt. Toussaint-L'Ouverture organized such effective resistance that the French expedition failed, although he himself was captured. When the French lost almost all their troops to battle and yellow fever, Napoleon was forced to abandon his American ambitions.

French Offer to Sell Louisiana Territory

Meanwhile, Livingston had been urging the French to sell New Orleans. In April 1803, Talleyrand, the French foreign minister, asked Livingston how much the United States would pay for the entire Louisiana Territory. Livingston, who had been joined by James Monroe, took only a few days to negotiate an agreement by which the United States was to pay about $15 million for the territory—about 4 cents an acre.

Jefferson was torn between a desire to extend the nation's boundaries and concern over whether the government could legally acquire foreign territory. Finally, Jefferson decided to ask the Senate to ratify the treaty and the Senate gave its consent, despite opposition from New England Federalists. Although this action did not follow Jefferson's belief in strict construction of the Constitution, he justified the acquisition on the grounds that it was part of the President's implied powers to protect the nation. The Louisiana Purchase doubled the size of the United States and opened the way for westward expansion by removing the threat of French interference.

■ Lewis and Clark

Very little was known about the area west of the Mississippi, and it excited Jefferson's curiosity. He sent an **expedition,** a journey with a specific purpose, led by two officers in the United States Army—Meriwether Lewis and William Clark—up the Missouri River to explore the new territory. The expedition was the first scientific project to receive federal funds, and Jefferson himself drew up their instructions. He told Lewis and Clark to find the sources of the Missouri River, to try to find a usable route across the Rocky Mountains to the Pacific Ocean, and to observe the customs of the Native Americans they met. They were also instructed to note carefully the features of the land, the weather, and the plants and animals they saw.

The expedition left St. Louis in May 1804. It returned over two years later with its mission accomplished, having surmounted hardships that ranged from "ticks and musquiters" to near starvation and floods.

Among the members of the expedition was York, an enslaved person. York's skills in hunting and fishing made him a valuable member of the expedition. He was particularly successful in making friends with the Native Americans they met along the way. Sacajawea (SA•kuh•juh•WEE•uh), a Shoshone woman, and her French-Canadian husband later joined the party as interpreters and guides. Her role was important because Lewis and Clark wanted to build peaceful relations with the Native Americans living in the newly acquired territory.

The Lewis and Clark expedition added immensely to the knowledge of the huge area that had been purchased. It also helped the United States lay claim to the northern region between the Rocky Mountains and the Pacific Ocean known as Oregon. Within a few years, fur traders based in St. Louis were traveling to and settling in the Rockies, and by 1812 there were about 70,000 people living in the southern section of the Louisiana Territory.

▼ COMMEMORATIVE STAMP

▲ EXPLORING THE NEW LANDS After the Louisiana Territory became part of the United States, Jefferson authorized an army expedition to the territory. Sacajawea accompanied Lewis and Clark on the trip westward, acting as guide and interpreter. *Why was the expedition important?*

▲ AARON BURR

■ Burr's Conspiracies

The Louisiana Purchase troubled die-hard Federalists in the Northeast. They feared that westward expansion would weaken New England's power in national affairs and would subordinate its commercial interests to the agricultural interests of the South and West.

Burr and Hamilton

A group of Federalists drafted a plan to take New England out of the Union and form a northern confederacy. The plotters realized that, if the confederacy were to last, it had to include New York as well as New England. They found an ally in Aaron Burr, who was willing to desert the Republican party and run for governor of New York on the Federalist ticket in 1804.

The plan went awry, however, when Burr was soundly defeated. Alexander Hamilton, who had worked to prevent Burr's election to the presidency in 1800, campaigned against him.

When Hamilton continued after the election to criticize his integrity, Burr challenged Hamilton to a duel. Hamilton accepted the challenge.

On a July morning in 1804, Hamilton, Burr, their assistants, and a physician rowed across the Hudson River to a rock shelf at the foot of the Palisades. At the signal Burr fired a bullet into Hamilton's body. Hamilton died the next day.

Western Conspiracy

When a New York coroner's jury indicted Burr for murder, he escaped from New York but not from his troubles. He headed west and took part in arranging a conspiracy. Sometimes Burr talked of secession of the western territories, sometimes of the conquest of Mexico—with himself as emperor. Whatever Burr's final goal, he collected arms, bought flatboats on the Ohio River, and floated down toward New Orleans with between 80 and 100 followers. His movements became so widely known, however, that the federal government had time to prepare for anything he might do. When President Jefferson ordered his arrest, Burr fled to Spanish Florida.

Burr was captured in 1807 and taken to Richmond, Virginia, to stand trial for treason. At the trial, Chief Justice Marshall, following the Constitution's provisions regarding the rights of a person accused of treason, insisted that the prosecution produce two witnesses to an "overt act" on Burr's part. Because there were no trustworthy witnesses against him, Burr was acquitted and went into exile.

■ Conflict with Native Americans

During both Jefferson's and James Madison's administrations, settlers, hunters, and land speculators pressured the Native Americans hard. Jefferson, himself, favored moving Native Americans who lived east of the Mississippi River to unoccupied lands in the Louisiana Territory. He insisted that the Chickasaw and Cherokee nations give up their lands in Alabama and Georgia and move to present-day Arkansas.

North of the Ohio River, the Treaty of Greenville had not satisfied the pioneers' desire for land. By persuasion, force, and fraud, Native Americans were forced to give up more and more land. In spite of treaty promises that were to last "as long as the sun shall climb the heavens or the waters shall run in the streams," white settlers persisted in moving into Native American land. William Henry Harrison, governor of the Indiana Territory, has been described as "the most talented American at depriving the Native Americans of their ancestral lands." In the 15 treaties he negotiated, Native Americans gave up nearly all of present-day Indiana and Illinois.

During these difficult times, a remarkable leader named Tecumseh (tuh•KUHM•suh) became chief of the Shawnee. He wanted to unite all the peoples of the Mississippi Valley into a great federation to protect themselves against the white intruders. Tecumseh went to Harrison and urged that the United States give up some recently "purchased" territory on the grounds that the chiefs who signed the treaty had no authority to do so. Harrison replied that only the President of the United States could answer such a request. Tecumseh answered:

Visualizing History

▲ TECUMSEH Shawnee chief Tecumseh was a bold and imaginative leader along the frontiers of the northwest. *What did Tecumseh hope to achieve by establishing a confederation?*

66 *Well, as the great chief is to decide the matter, I hope the Great Spirit will put sense enough into his head to induce him to give up this land. It is true, he is so far off he will not be injured by the war; he may sit still in his town and drink his wine, while you and I will have to fight it out.* 99

The prediction came true. In 1811 Harrison launched a war against Tecumseh's followers, knowing that the great leader had journeyed south to persuade Native American communities to join the confederation. Harrison became a national hero after leading American troops in battle at Tippecanoe near present-day West Lafayette, Indiana. Tecumseh's death in 1813 destroyed the dream of a Native American confederation. Afterward, several Native American nations made peace with Harrison.

Section 2 ★ Review

Checking for Understanding

1. **Identify** Louisiana Purchase, Lewis and Clark, York, Sacajawea, Tecumseh.

2. **Define** expedition.

3. **State** why New Orleans was a city important to the nation.

4. **Specify** Jefferson's reasons for making the Louisiana Purchase.

Critical Thinking

5. **Predicting Outcomes** Aaron Burr was tried for treason but was acquitted. How did his acquittal affect future treason charges?

American Literary Heritage

The Prairie (excerpts)

When he had placed his guests in front of the dying man, Hard-Heart . . . [a young Pawnee chief and Natty Bumppo's adopted son] leaned a little forward and demanded: "Does my father hear the words of his son?"

. . . "Let the wise chief have no cares for his journey," continued Hard-Heart with an earnest solicitude that led him to forget, for the moment, that others were waiting to address his adopted parent; "a hundred . . . [Pawnee] shall clear his path from briars."

"Pawnee, I die as I have lived, a Christian man," resumed the trapper with a force of voice that had the same startling effect upon his hearers as is produced by the trumpet when its blast rises suddenly and freely on the air after its obstructed sounds have been heard struggling in the distance: "as I came into life so will I leave it. Horses and arms are not needed to stand in the presence of the Great Spirit of my people. He knows my color, and according to my gifts will he judge my deeds. . . ."

Middleton [an army officer whose life Natty Bumppo has saved] took one of the meager hands of the trapper, and, struggling to command his voice, he succeeded in announcing his presence. . . .

[Bumppo said,] "Will you do a favor to an old and dying man?"

"Name it," said Middleton; "it shall be done."

"It is a far journey to send such trifles," resumed the old man, who spoke at short intervals, as strength and breath permitted; "a far and weary journey is the same; but kindnesses and friendships are things not to be forgotten. There is a settlement among the Otsego hills—"

"I know the place," interrupted

▲ BEADED BUCKSKIN LEGGING MOCCASINS

▲ JAMES FENIMORE COOPER

Romanticism, a movement that emphasized imagination and inner feelings, won adherents among many writers of the era.

One of the most celebrated was James Fenimore Cooper. Cooper left a legacy of five novels whose central character, Natty Bumppo, is a trapper forced increasingly westward by the encroachment of civilization on his beloved frontier. In the following excerpt, Natty Bumppo, surrounded by the Pawnee who have become his family, is near death.

Middleton, observing that he spoke with increasing difficulty; "proceed to tell me what you would have done."

"Take this rifle and pouch and horn, and send them to the person whose name is graven on the plates of the stock—a trader cut the letters with his knife—for it is long that I have intended to send him such a token of my love."

"It shall be so. Is there more that you could wish?"

"Little else have I to bestow. My traps I give to my Indian son; for honestly and kindly has he kept his faith. Let him stand before me." . . .

"Pawnee," continued the old man, always changing his language to suit the person he addressed, and not infrequently according to the ideas he expressed, "it is a custom of my people for the father to leave his blessing with the son before he shuts his eyes forever. This blessing I give to you; take it, for the prayers of a Christian man will never make the path of a just warrior to the blessed prairies either longer or more tangled. May the God of a white man look on your deeds with friendly eyes, and may you never commit an act that shall cause him to darken his face. I know not whether we shall ever meet again. There are many traditions concerning the place of Good Spirits. It is not for one like me, old and experienced though I am, to set up my opinions against a nation's. You believe in the blessed prairies, and I have faith in the sayings of my fathers. If both are true, our parting will be final; but if it should prove that the same meaning is hid under different words, we shall yet stand together. . . ."

▲ FUR TRADERS

Interpreting Literature

1. What requests does Natty Bumppo make of his friend Middleton?

2. Describe the trapper's feelings about Pawnee customs and traditions.

3. What support can you find for the view that Natty Bumppo is a product of the prairie?

Determining Relevance

4. What symbolism can be witnessed in Natty Bumppo's death?

★★★★★★★★★★★★★★★★★★★★★★★★★★★★

Foreign Affairs

Setting the Scene

Section Focus

Thomas Jefferson had entered the presidency committed to Washington's policy of neutrality. Yet, the United States and Europe were dependent upon each other. When Britain and France each tried to manipulate trade with the United States as a weapon against the other, the United States sought ways to fight back.

Objectives

After studying this section, you should be able to

★ identify the problems that the United States faced in its attempt to remain neutral in the conflict between Great Britain and France.

★ identify three ways the United States tried to maintain its freedom of the seas.

★ explain the reasons for the increasing demand for war.

Key Terms

piracy, impressment

◀ **AMERICAN SAILORS**

*J*efferson hoped that "nature and a wide ocean" would keep the United States entirely isolated from European rivalries. "Peace," he wrote to an English friend, "is our passion."

■ Barbary Coast Piracy

The first threat to peace came not from one of the great powers of Europe, but from Tripoli (part of present-day Libya), a small country on the north coast of Africa. **Piracy**, or preying on ships at sea, was a principal business of Tripoli and the other Barbary Coast states of Morocco, Algiers, and Tunis. The ships of countries that did not pay tribute to the Barbary States were likely to be captured and their sailors enslaved.

Between 1789 and 1801, the United States paid over $2 million in tribute.

Despite his desire for peace, Jefferson was determined that the United States would not be robbed by the Barbary pirates. Consequently, he carried on a four-year war with Tripoli. The American navy eventually had 14 ships stationed in the Mediterranean Sea.

In 1805 the ruler of Tripoli made peace after receiving a ransom of $60,000 for captured American sailors. For a time, this discouraged the other Barbary Coast states from asking for additional tribute. Still, in 1807 after President Jefferson withdrew the American navy, attacks started again. The piracy ended in 1815 when an American fleet of ships under Stephen Decatur, joined by warships of European nations, put an end to the practice.

Britain and France

Most of Jefferson's second term, coinciding with war in Europe, was spent trying to maintain American neutrality. In 1803 Great Britain and France had once again gone to war.

Neutrality

The United States was an important source of supply to both sides. Each side tried to limit what it saw as aid to the enemy and, in doing so, violated American freedom of the seas. Napoleon issued the Berlin and Milan decrees, which forbade any country under French control to import British goods or to allow British ships to enter its harbors. Neutral ships bringing British goods, stopping at British ports, or even submitting to search by British naval vessels were to be seized.

Great Britain answered the Napoleonic decrees with the Orders in Council. British traders feared that the United States would take over the trade with Europe forbidden to the British by Napoleon and replace Britain as the greatest trading nation in the world. Therefore, the Orders in Council of 1807 forbade neutral ships to trade with Europe unless they stopped in Britain first.

Impressment

Even more distressing than the attempt to cut off the United States trade was the British practice of taking sailors from American ships. For centuries Britain had secured sailors by a legalized form of kidnapping known as **impressment**. Sailors were impressed in port and taken off merchant ships at sea. British sailors frequently deserted and signed on with American vessels, where the conditions and pay were better. Sometimes a British warship calling in an American port found it difficult to sail away because so many of the crew had deserted. To combat this problem, Britain claimed the right to stop American ships, search for former British subjects, and force them back into service.

Visualizing History

▲ IMPRESSMENT Americans resented the British method of recruiting for their navy by impressment. *How did public opinion change after the British ship* Leopard *attacked the American frigate* Chesapeake*?*

Visualizing History

▲ THE APPROACH OF WAR The United States was not well prepared for war. The British Royal Navy, with frigates like the 38-gun *Shannon*, vastly outnumbered the United States Navy. *How did the Embargo Act affect the United States?*

In June 1807, a United States warship, the *Chesapeake*, was leaving the United States for the Mediterranean Sea when it was stopped by a British naval vessel, the *Leopard*. The commander of the *Leopard* demanded that he be allowed to search the *Chesapeake* for British deserters. When he was refused, the British ship fired 3 broadsides at the *Chesapeake*, killing 3 and wounding 18. After the *Chesapeake* surrendered, the British boarded the ship and carried off 4 sailors.

The attack on the *Chesapeake* aroused great anger, and American newspapers clamored for war. Jefferson, however, delayed calling Congress into session until tempers had had time to cool. Although the President did not intend to let these actions by the British go unanswered, he sought a course of action other than war.

The Embargo Act

Jefferson reasoned that both Britain and France were so dependent upon American goods that if the United States cut off trade with them, they would stop violating the nation's neutral rights. With the President's urging, Congress passed the Embargo Act in December 1807, forbidding United States ships to sail for any foreign ports.

The Embargo Act caused some suffering in Britain, hurt France very little, but was almost disastrous for the United States. Wheat, cotton, and tobacco piled up on wharves. Thousands of sailors were put out of work. Ships rotted at the docks. Exports fell from $198 million in 1807 to $22 million in 1808. Imports fell from $138 million to $55 million.

The law was bitterly resisted. Merchant ships made secret runs to European ports. Smuggling between the northeastern states and Canada flourished. To stop violations of the embargo, Jefferson stationed militia along the Canadian border and permitted officials to search for smuggled goods without proper warrants. Ironically, President Jefferson was accused of using his great power at the expense of the Bill of Rights, which he himself had championed years before as a check against tyranny.

Drifting Into War

After two terms, Jefferson was glad to retire to Monticello. He used his influence to secure the nomination of his close friend and secretary of state, James Madison. In the election of 1808, Madison easily defeated the Federalist candidate, Charles Pinckney.

Economic Warfare

Before Jefferson left office in March 1809, Congress repealed the Embargo Act and replaced it with the Non-Intercourse Act, which banned trade with ports under British or French control but allowed trade with the rest of the world. Although less harmful to American trade than the Embargo Act, the Non-Intercourse Act was no more successful in forcing France and Britain to respect the rights of the United States.

In May 1810, Congress tried another tactic by passing Macon's Bill No. 2, which stated that, if either France or Britain agreed to respect neutral rights, the United States would cut off trade with the other nation. In August Napoleon responded with offers to remove his decrees. Not even waiting for the actual repeal of the French decrees, Madison cut off trade with Great Britain, effective March 2, 1811. Napoleon revealed how insincere his offer had been when the French navy continued to seize American ships.

▶ **DOCK AT PORTLAND, MAINE**

The War Hawks

Although neither Britain nor the United States really wanted war, their actions steered them in that direction. In May 1811, an American ship attacked a British warship. Americans saw it as revenge for the British attack on the *Chesapeake*.

Some young members of Congress, most of them Republicans from the West and the South, called for war. Hunger for land heightened this war fever. Westerners were eager to take Canada, while Southerners wanted Spanish Florida.

Alone, the war hawks did not have enough votes in Congress to pass a declaration of war. More Americans became angry over seizure of American sailors and ships, and pressure to fight increased. Finally, Congress decided that the United States must accept the risks of war rather than be pushed around.

Section 3 ★ Review

Checking for Understanding

1. **Identify** Tripoli, Stephen Decatur, Berlin and Milan decrees, *Chesapeake, Leopard*, Embargo Act, Non-Intercourse Act, Macon's Bill No. 2.

2. **Define** piracy, impressment.

3. **Describe** the conflicts with the Barbary pirates that inhibited American trade in North Africa.

4. **Explain** how the Berlin and Milan decrees and the Orders in Council interfered with American neutrality.

Critical Thinking

5. **Analyzing Events** There were a number of opposing influences leading to the War of 1812. Explain the sectional interests to be served by war with England.

★★★★★★★★★★★★★★★★★★★★★★★★★★★★★★★★★

The War of 1812

Setting the Scene

Section Focus

President Madison listed a number of grievances against Great Britain in his war message, including impressment, blockades, inciting Native American uprisings, and rejecting diplomatic efforts. Yet the war was not a popular one, especially in New England. The fighting ended in 1814 with the Treaty of Ghent, but it did not settle the issues that had caused the war.

Objectives

After studying this section, you should be able to

★ describe the major campaigns of the War of 1812.

★ summarize the results of the War of 1812 and the Treaty of Ghent.

Key Term

frigate

▶ AMERICAN MILITIA COAT, 1812

The British government repealed the Orders in Council on June 23, 1812. British harvests had been poor, and the British desperately needed grain from the United States. British manufacturers had bombarded Parliament with pleas that they faced utter ruin unless trade with the United States was reestablished. The repeal came too late, however. The United States had declared war four days earlier. Declaring war against Great Britain did not suggest an alliance with France. A proposal to include France in the declaration was defeated in the Senate by a vote of 18 to 14.

■ The War in Canada

General Andrew Jackson expressed a popular opinion when he predicted that the conquest of Canada by the United States would be a "mere military promenade." There were several reasons why an attack northward was feasible. Canada was sparsely populated, and French Canadians were lukewarm toward their British rulers. The narrow strip of settlement along the St. Lawrence River and north of Lake Ontario was close to the United States and open to attack. Montreal, the strategic center of Canada, was only 30 miles from New York state.

Lack of Preparation

The conquest of Canada stalled, however, because the military forces of the United States were unprepared. The regular army, numbering about 6,000 soldiers, was scattered throughout the frontier posts. The top commanders, veterans of the Revolution, were too old for warfare. There was no single commanding general and no overall strategy.

To compensate for the small size of the army, Madison called on the states to furnish militia. Some New England governors refused to supply any troops because they were opposed to "Mr. Madison's War." Members of New York's militia refused to cross the Niagara River into Canada because they had enlisted only to defend their state from invasion.

Failures and Successes

The lack of preparation was evident when small but ably led Canadian forces took Detroit and two forts on Lake Michigan. An American attack across the Niagara River was turned back.

In 1813 matters improved at the western end of the war zone. Commodore Oliver Hazard Perry, having constructed a small fleet, won a brilliant victory over a British squadron and established American control of Lake Erie. Perry's victory made possible an invasion of Canada by way of Detroit. Kentucky volunteers under William Henry Harrison advanced into Canada and defeated a British army at the Battle of the Thames, about 60 miles northeast of Detroit. In the East, however, attempted invasions of Canada from Sackett Harbor and Lake Champlain failed.

During 1812 and 1813, the British, preoccupied with the war against France, had put little effort into the war against the United States. But when Napoleon was defeated and forced into exile in 1814, the British were free to strike hard at the United States. In late summer an army of more than 14,000 British veterans advanced southward from Montreal to invade New York. Blocking its way was an American army stationed at Plattsburg on Lake Champlain. Although outnumbered nearly 3 to 1, American forces drove back the attacks, and the British retreated to Montreal. The northern border of the United States was safe.

■ The British Offensive

In 1814 the British sent two other expeditions into the United States—one to attack Washington, D.C., and Baltimore, the other to take New Orleans.

Washington, D.C., and Baltimore

In August British transports landed an army of about 4,000 soldiers at Chesapeake Bay. It marched into the capital and very nearly captured the President. To retaliate

★★★★★★★★★★★
AMERICAN PORTRAITS

Dolley Madison
1768–1849

Born in North Carolina, Dolley Payne grew up in Virginia until, at age 15, she moved with her parents to Philadelphia. There she married John Todd, Jr. Dolley Todd gave birth to two children, but in the yellow-fever epidemic in 1793, she lost one of her children and her husband.

The following year Dolley Todd married James Madison. When James became secretary of state, Dolley served as unofficial first lady, entertaining White House guests of widower Thomas Jefferson. As official first lady from 1809 to 1817, Dolley was known for her elaborate parties—including the first inaugural ball. She also displayed remarkable bravery during the War of 1812. Packing up Gilbert Stuart's famous painting of George Washington and White House belongings, she conveyed them safely out of town before the British burned the White House in 1814.

against the burning of public buildings in York (now Toronto) in 1813, the British burned the public buildings of Washington, destroying the Capitol and the White House.

From Washington the British proceeded to Baltimore but were turned back by the forces guarding the city. During the bombardment of Fort McHenry in Baltimore harbor, Francis Scott Key wrote "The Star-Spangled Banner."

New Orleans

Unable to crack the defenses at Baltimore, the British army joined forces with the expedition attempting to capture New Orleans. The British, now almost 10,000 strong, reached the mouth of the Mississippi River in December 1814. Awaiting them were 4,500 Americans under the command of Andrew Jackson of Tennessee. His army consisted of regular soldiers and militia, with a few pirates recruited for their ability to handle artillery. Jackson also called upon the free African Americans of New Orleans to volunteer for service, promising them the same wages as the white soldiers. Two all-African American battalions contributed to the American victory at New Orleans.

When the final British attack came on January 8, 1815, American forces were sheltered behind a barricade of cotton bales. The British, advancing in the open, were no match for Jackson's well-protected soldiers. More than 2,000 soldiers were killed or wounded before the British surrendered. However, the Battle of New Orleans, the greatest American victory of the war, was a useless slaughter. News traveled slowly in those days, and it was learned only after the battle that a peace treaty had been signed in Europe two weeks earlier.

Visualizing History ▲ WAR ON THE SEAS On August 19, 1812, the United States frigate *Constitution* decisively defeated the British warship *Guerriere*. **Why was it surprising that American ships were victorious in many early battles?**

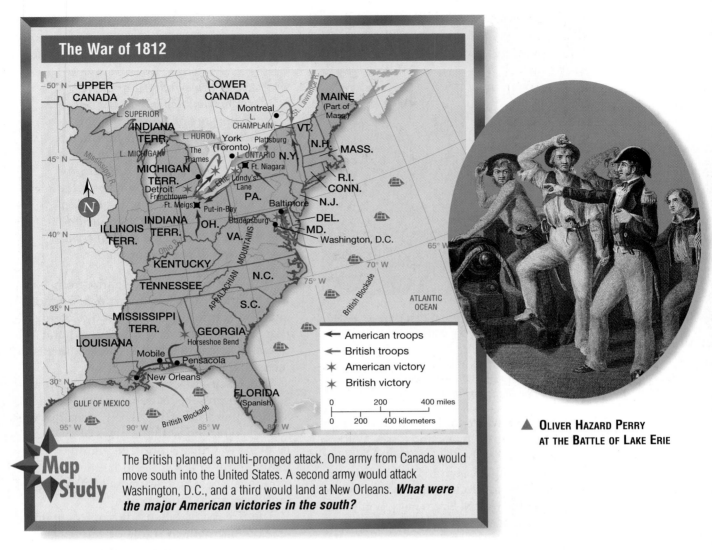

The War of 1812

MAP LEGEND:
→ American troops
← British troops
✳ American victory
✳ British victory

0   200   400 miles
0   200   400 kilometers

Map Study

The British planned a multi-pronged attack. One army from Canada would move south into the United States. A second army would attack Washington, D.C., and a third would land at New Orleans. *What were the major American victories in the south?*

▲ OLIVER HAZARD PERRY AT THE BATTLE OF LAKE ERIE

■ The War at Sea

At the beginning of the war, the small navy of the United States appeared to be no match for the British fleet. Only four small ships plus a few small gunboats for coastal defense had been built during the administrations of Jefferson and Madison. During John Adams's term in office, however, half a dozen excellent **frigates**—medium-sized warships—had been built. These frigates had more firepower than any European ships of the same size and were speedy enough to escape from larger warships.

When war broke out, the frigates put to sea and within a few months had won a series of victories in battles with British vessels. The victories had little effect on Britain, however, since its navy outnumbered that of the United States at least 20 to 1. Still, Britain had ruled the sea so long that even a few defeats by the United States came as a shock to British leaders. After yet another loss, a British newspaper lamented:

❝ *Can this be true? Will the English people read this unmoved? Any man who foretold such disasters this day last year would have been treated as a madman or a traitor. . . [U.S. frigates] leave their ports when they choose and return when it suits their convenience.* ❞

In addition to the frigates, the United States sent more than 500 privateers to sea. They captured more than 1,300 British vessels, some within sight of Britain.

▲ JACKSON AT NEW ORLEANS American forces under Andrew Jackson resoundingly defeated the British troops at the Battle of New Orleans, fought on January 8, 1815. *What effect did the battle have on the treaty that ended the war?*

As the war went on, however, American victories at sea grew fewer and fewer. With its superior numbers, the British fleet blockaded the entire Atlantic coast from Boston to Savannah. United States trade with other countries ceased, and the United States navy, bottled up in port, could not repeat its early successes.

■ The War's End

As the war dragged on, opposition grew, especially in New England, where people balked at buying United States bonds issued to cover the cost of the war. Public meetings were held to protest the conflict. Above all, they foresaw that the war would be damaging, even ruinous to their economies:

❝ *About three-fourths of our townsmen depend on the sea for the means of subsistence for themselves and their families. By the recent declaration of war more than one-half of that proportion is liable to fall into the hands of the enemy. . . . We feel therefore most strongly incumbent. . . . to seek a speedy termination of the present war.* ❞

In December 1814, delegates from New England met in secret at Hartford, Connecticut. The Hartford Convention did not insist that New England leave the Union, but it did demand seven constitutional amendments to increase the region's political power.

The Hartford Convention sent commissioners to present its demands to President Madison and Congress. Their arrival in the capital coincided with the news of the victory at New Orleans and the signing of the treaty ending the war. Amidst the great celebrations, the commissioners had no choice but to return to their homes.

The Treaty of Ghent did not contain a word about neutral rights or impressment. Not a square mile of territory changed hands. The warring nations simply agreed to stop fighting, to restore the old boundaries, and to put other problems off for future settlement. Signed on Christmas Eve, 1814, the treaty was unanimously ratified by the Senate in February 1815.

Section 4 ★ Review

Checking for Understanding

1. **Identify** Andrew Jackson, Mr. Madison's War, Oliver Perry, Francis Scott Key, Battle of New Orleans, Hartford Convention, Treaty of Ghent.

2. **Define** frigate.

3. **Explain** why American troops failed to capture Canada.

4. **State** why the battle of New Orleans was a useless slaughter.

Critical Thinking

5. **Comparing Actions** The United States entered the war in Vietnam and left it without winning or losing. Compare the War of 1812 and the Vietnam War.

Exploring the Louisiana Purchase

Even before the Louisiana Purchase was considered, President Thomas Jefferson was interested in exploring the lands west of the United States. Meriwether Lewis, Jefferson's private secretary, shared that dream. After the Louisiana Territory became part of the United States, Jefferson made plans to send an exploration party to the territory. He selected Lewis to lead the expedition.

William Clark, the brother of Revolutionary War hero George Rogers Clark, was chosen to be second in command. William Clark had resigned from the army but reenlisted in order to go on the expedition.

than 7,600 miles to the Pacific. They returned with maps and information that helped make possible the great western migration during the mid-1800s.

William Clark constructed 60 maps—some eight feet in length—depicting the expedition's route. Although the expedition carried various surveying and measuring instruments, Clark seems to have relied primarily on the compass and his own estimates of distances in making his maps. It is likely that Clark took a series of back sightings to render his maps. For example, after reaching an easily identifiable landmark such as a bend in a stream, Clark would turn and take a compass reading back to his previous point of sighting. Clark could then plot each shift in the route on the map.

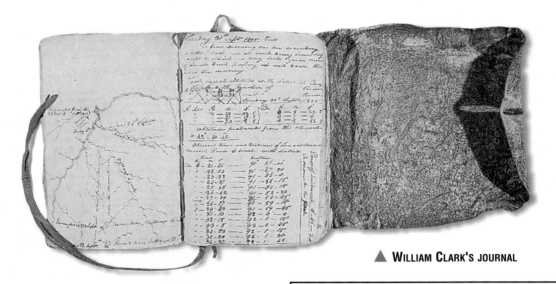

▲ WILLIAM CLARK'S JOURNAL

What lay in the vast Louisiana Territory? How far was it to the Pacific Ocean? Certainly, the members of the Lewis and Clark expedition had little idea of what distances and difficulties they would face on their trek. Starting from St. Louis, the expedition traveled northward up the Missouri River into present-day North Dakota. Eventually, it crossed the Rocky Mountains and sailed on the Columbia River to the Pacific Ocean. The members had traveled more

Making the Geography Connection

1. What do you think was the major obstacle facing Lewis and Clark?

2. Would you classify Clark's method of mapmaking as scientific? Explain.

Linking Past and Present

3. How might an unknown region of the earth be mapped today?

Using Vocabulary

Use the vocabulary words to create a newspaper article on the main events of the War of 1812.

laissez-faire	writ of mandamus
judicial review	piracy
impressment	frigate

Reviewing Facts

1. **Compare** the views of Thomas Jefferson and Alexander Hamilton on the role of government and society.

2. **Explain** why *Marbury* v. *Madison* was a great victory for Federalists and the judiciary.

3. **Indicate** how Jefferson planned to use some of the territory gained within the Louisiana Purchase to relocate Native Americans.

4. **Discuss** the factors that influenced Jefferson's decision to purchase Louisiana.

5. **Describe** the military accomplishments of Andrew Jackson between 1813 and 1815.

6. **State** where the Republicans wanted Native Americans to move and the measures Jefferson and Madison took to force that move.

Understanding Concepts

National Identity

1. In his Inaugural Address, Jefferson reminded Americans, "We are all Republicans, we are all Federalists." Explain how that statement was meant to create a national identity.

2. Show how the Treaty of Ghent enhanced the nation's identity even though the United States gained none of its goals in fighting the war.

Geographic Expansion

3. When Jefferson doubled the size of the United States through the Louisiana Purchase, many people believed it was God's will that the United States should extend from sea to sea. Explain why Americans held this belief.

4. American expansion also occurred through the cession of Native American lands. How did William Henry Harrison handle the conflict with the Native Americans?

Critical Thinking

1. **Making Judgments** Imagine that you are walking along a Washington street and see President Jefferson dressed in faded corduroy overalls. How would you feel about Jefferson running the country today? On what criteria have you based your judgment?

2. **Comparing Policy** Describe ways Jefferson was like Washington.

3. **Cause and Effect** What effects did the Louisiana Purchase have on the United States politically and economically?

4. **Analyzing Results** Explain why neither side won or lost under the terms of the Treaty of Ghent.

5. **Analyzing Illustrations** Study the illustration on impressment below and answer the questions.

   a. Who are the central figures in the picture?

   b. What is happening?

   c. Does the artist express a point of view in this illustration? Explain.

▲ **IMPRESSMENT OF AMERICAN SAILORS**

CHAPTER 8 ★ REVIEW

Writing About History

Narration

Although they were political enemies in office, Thomas Jefferson, a Republican, and John Adams, a Federalist, later became friends. They kept up a correspondence until they died. Select a partner and write a series of letters that Adams and Jefferson might have written to each other on the state of the nation after 1808—about the War of 1812, Native American affairs, and the settlement of the West.

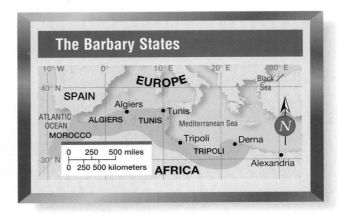

The Barbary States

Cooperative Learning

Organize a group within your classroom to simulate a discussion among Bill Clinton, John Adams, and Thomas Jefferson. Possible discussion topics might include the budget deficit, the situation in the Middle East, civil rights, and any other foreign or domestic issues you think relevant. Present the group discussion to your class.

Social Studies Skills

Describing Exact and Relative Location

Geographers use lines of latitude and longitude to locate places on Earth's surface. The degrees at which the latitude and longitude lines meet are the exact location of that place. For example, to describe the exact location of a city, geographers would first find on the map the line of latitude nearest to the city. Then they would follow this line until it intersects the nearest line of longitude. The latitude and longitude coordinates together provide the city's exact location. On the map of the Barbary States, the exact location of Tripoli is 32° N, 13° E.

Besides exact location, places also have relative location. Relative location is indicated by using the cardinal directions—north, south, east, and west—as well as the intermediate directions—northeast, southeast, northwest, and southwest—to describe the location of one place in relation to another. For example, Tripoli is located west of the city of Derna and southeast of Algiers. The use of latitude and longitude can also be helpful in determining the relative location of one place to another.

Practicing the Skill

Study the map and then answer the questions.

1. What body of water borders the Barbary States to the north?

2. What is the exact location of Tunis?

3. In which direction would a traveler go from Tunis to reach Tripoli?

4. In between approximately which lines of longitude do the Barbary States fall?

5. Use a map of the world to describe the relative location of Tripoli to these cities: Moscow, Russia; Johannesburg, South Africa; and Bombay, India.

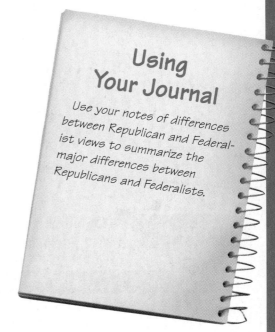

Using Your Journal

Use your notes of differences between Republican and Federalist views to summarize the major differences between Republicans and Federalists.

CHAPTER 9

★★

Nationalism and Change
1816–1824

► QUILT, SUNBURST
PATTERN

Setting the Scene

Focus

During the peacetime that followed the War of 1812, a powerful spirit of nationalism swept through American life. Nationalism was reflected in many ways. It included the push for internal improvements, better economic ties among sections of the country, and a strengthening of the central government. Many Federalist ideals were implemented in spite of the disappearance of the Federalist party. This new sense of American pride also resulted in a more forceful foreign policy.

Concepts to Understand

★ How a feeling of national community emerged during the presidency of James Monroe

★ How foreign policy helped shape the United States as an emerging world power

Read to Discover . . .

★ the forces that helped unite the United States after the War of 1812.

★ what circumstances prompted the Monroe Doctrine.

Journal Notes

What impact did the nationalistic legislation, court decisions, and internal improvements of this era have on state governments? Note examples in your journal as you read the chapter.

CULTURAL

● **1816** *African Methodist Episcopal Church organized*

● **1819** *University of Virginia founded*

● **1820** *United States missionaries travel to Hawaii*

| 1816 | 1818 | 1820 |

POLITICAL

● **1816** *Second Bank of the United States chartered*

● **1818** *National Road reaches Wheeling*

● **1821** *Moses Austin receives land grant in Texas*

130

TO

WHEELING

to

Frostburgh

10

◀ **NATIONAL ROAD MILE MARKER**

History AND ART

Fourth of July Celebration in Center Square, Philadelphia
by John Lewis Krimmel, 1819

Celebrations on the Fourth of July show that the Fourth had become a national tradition less than 50 years after the nation gained its independence.

• **1823** "Twas the Night Before Christmas" *published*

• **1825** *Robert Owen founds New Harmony, Indiana*

• **1828** *American Peace Society forms*

| 1822 | 1824 | 1826 |

• **1823** *Monroe Doctrine proclaimed*

• **1824** Gibbons *v.* Ogden

• **1826** *Pan-American Conference held*

★★

The Era of Good Feelings

Section Focus

After the War of 1812, United States economic growth continued to be limited by geography. Because long-range commercial activity was difficult, most Americans traded close to home. As industry grew in Northern cities, manufacturers wanted to expand their markets and enjoy conditions that encouraged growth. Rural Americans also desired prosperity. New government legislation was directed toward meeting these goals.

Objectives

After studying this section, you should be able to
★ list events that showed a spirit of nationalism.
★ explain how the Supreme Court increased the national government's power.

Key Terms

nationalism, internal improvement

▶ CANDLE MOLD

Nationalism is a feeling of intense loyalty and devotion to one's country. It is a spirit that unifies into one nation diverse groups who share a geographic area. Nationalism can be demonstrated by people's actions; illustrated by such symbols as a flag; and expressed in a nation's art, literature, and music.

■ Nationalistic Legislation

In the United States, the spirit of nationalism declined after the Revolution but was revived by the War of 1812. The conduct of the war revealed the dangers of disunion, and the war's outcome increased national pride and self-confidence. Albert Gallatin, one of the United States commissioners at the peace conference in Ghent, recognized the revival of nationalism in a letter written shortly after the war's end:

❝ *The war had renewed & reinstated the National feelings & character, which the Revolution had given, & which were daily lessened. The people . . . are more American: they feel & act more as a Nation, and I hope that the permanency of the Union is thereby better secured.* ❞

In 1816 James Monroe, a Virginia Republican, was elected President over New York Federalist Rufus King. On a national goodwill tour, the new President promoted a spirit of unity everywhere he went. His warm reception by cheering crowds in Boston caused a local Federalist newspaper to proclaim that an "Era of Good Feelings" had begun. By 1820 the Federalists, discredited by their antiwar position during the War of 1812, had vanished from national politics, and President Monroe was reelected without opposition.

Postwar nationalism was revealed in legislation as well as in politics. The War of 1812 had clearly demonstrated that Jefferson's ideal of a central government with strictly limited functions could not meet the needs of a nation in crisis. After the war, a Republican Congress passed a series of laws that sounded as though they had been written by Federalists.

The "American System"

Henry Clay of Kentucky and John C. Calhoun of South Carolina proposed an ambitious program that Clay called the "American System," based on protection and **internal improvements**—roads, canals, and other transportation needs. They advocated a protective tariff for manufacturers, an improved market for farmers, and better transportation for agricultural and industrial goods. Transportation improvements would be financed with money raised by the tariff. Both leaders wanted to reinstate the national bank to create a national currency and encourage economic growth. They hoped that this nationalistic program would bring prosperity to all sections of the country and, to the nation, economic independence from the rest of the world.

Establishment of a National Currency

Republicans traditionally had opposed the idea of a national bank. They blocked the recharter of the first Bank of the United States in 1811 and substituted nothing in its place. The results were disastrous because the notes of the Bank of the United States already had become the national currency. Without a currency and lacking sufficient gold and silver for coins, the country had only the notes of state-chartered banks, which had little or no value beyond the localities where they were issued. Without a national bank, the federal government also had a difficult time borrowing money during the War of 1812.

Because of the nation's financial problems, the Republicans changed their minds and supported creation of a new national bank. In 1816 Congress passed a bill to establish a second Bank of the United States. Like its predecessor, the second Bank of the United States could issue notes to be used as national currency and could act in a number of ways to control state banks.

Trade Protection

During the War of 1812, Americans had difficulty obtaining British products and thus encouraged the growth of American

Henry Clay
1777–1852

AMERICAN PORTRAITS

Virginia-born and raised, Henry Clay moved to Kentucky, a state that kept him in Congress—and in the forefront of national politics—for nearly 50 years.

A fierce political rivalry soon developed between Clay and another Westerner, Andrew Jackson of Tennessee. The two first clashed in 1819 when Clay blasted Jackson's Florida invasion. The election of 1824 made them bitter enemies. Ignoring instructions from Kentucky to back Jackson for President, Clay supported John Quincy Adams, who appointed Clay secretary of state. Jackson's revenge came when he defeated Clay in the presidential election of 1832. Clay sought the presidency three more times before retiring. In 1849, however, he returned to Congress and put together a compromise between North and South that helped delay the Civil War.

industry. But once the war was over, Britain dumped goods in the United States at such low prices that they threatened to put American companies out of business. Protecting American industry meant that consumers would pay more for imported products, but to business leaders and nationalists alike this price seemed a fair exchange for economic independence.

Congress responded with the Tariff of 1816. Unlike earlier revenue tariffs, which had provided income for the federal government, this tariff was designed to protect American manufacturers by placing high taxes on imports.

■ Supreme Court Nationalism

Nationalism also was demonstrated in a series of Supreme Court decisions by Chief Justice John Marshall. Marshall was appointed in 1801 as one of the last acts of President John Adams, a Federalist. By 1815 the majority of the justices had been appointed by Republican Presidents, but Marshall still dominated the Court. He was a brilliant debater and possessed such strong convictions, friendliness, and persuasiveness that, according to one historian, he "molded his fellow judges like putty." During his 34 years as Chief Justice, Marshall was in the minority on only one case dealing with a constitutional issue. Between 1819 and 1824, Marshall ruled in three important Court cases that established the dominance of the nation over the states and that shaped the future of American government.

"Necessary and Proper" Powers

McCulloch v. *Maryland* (1819) involved an attempt by Maryland to tax the Baltimore branch of the newly created second Bank of the United States. The case answered basic questions about the federal government's power and its relationship with the states.

The national bank was constitutional, Marshall said, even though the Constitution did not specifically give Congress the power to create one. He repeated Alexander Hamilton's 25-year-old argument that the federal government was not limited to the powers listed in the Constitution. Marshall observed that the Constitution specifically permitted Congress to issue money, borrow money, and

Visualizing History

▲ **GROWING CITIES** The serenity of small town America made a striking contrast with the hustle of the expanding factory system in New England and the Northeast. *Why did manufacturing interests favor a protective tariff?*

The Marshall Court and the National Interest

Case and Year	Issue and Decision
Marbury v. *Madison* (1803)	Declared an act of Congress unconstitutional. Court given power of judicial review and power to declare congressional and state legislation unconstitutional.
Fletcher v. *Peck* (Yazoo land fraud case, 1810)	Declared sanctity of contracts. Gave Supreme Court right to overturn state laws that ran counter to specific provisions of Constitution.
Martin v. *Hunter's Lessee* (1816)	Gave Supreme Court right to reverse decisions of state courts.
Trustees of Dartmouth College v. *Woodward* (1819)	Reaffirmed sanctity of contracts. Protected banks and corporations with state charters from meddling by state legislators.
Sturges v. *Crowninshield* (1819)	Tested constitutionality of state bankruptcy laws. Court determined that in absence of federal regulation, states were free to legislate.
McCulloch v. *Maryland* (1819)	Challenged constitutionality of Bank of the United States. Court said "implied powers" enabled Congress to enact any legislation within letter and spirit of Constitution.
Cohens v. *Virginia* (1821)	Tested constitutionality of Judiciary Act of 1789. Court said states gave up some sovereignty in ratifying Constitution so state courts must accept federal jurisdiction.
Gibbons v. *Ogden* (1824)	Invalidated a state monopoly. Court gave Congress right to regulate interstate commerce, a decision of great importance for national development.

Source: *The Guide to American Law,* vol. 7 (1984).

Chart Study

Chief Justice John Marshall dominated the Supreme Court until his death in 1835. The Marshall Court handed down a series of decisions that increased federal power over state governments. **What was significant about the Martin decision?**

collect taxes. He noted that the national bank would assist in exercising these enumerated powers. Therefore, he concluded, the federal government could choose any method that was "necessary and proper" to exercise the powers the Constitution had given it.

Marshall noted that the people, acting collectively, had created the federal government. Thus it was a truly "national" government, not created by the states or subordinate to them. Therefore, he reasoned, no state had the power to tax the national bank, a legal creation of the federal government.

Contracts and Property Rights

The second important decision of the Marshall Court during this period was *Dartmouth College* v. *Woodward* (1819). This case was one of several in which the Court handed down decisions protecting contracts and property rights from state power. Dartmouth College was a private school chartered in 1769 by King George III. In 1815 the New Hampshire state legislature passed a law to change the charter, allowing Dartmouth to become a state college. But Dartmouth officials did not want to give up their private school, and they refused to turn over college records and funds to the state. When New Hampshire courts upheld the legislature, Dartmouth appealed to the Supreme Court. In writing the Court's decision, Marshall noted that "the state legislatures were forbidden 'to pass any law impairing the obligation of contracts,' that is, of contracts respecting property." A college charter is a contract, he said, and a state has no right to interfere with it. Thus, the state's attempt to seize this private college was unconstitutional.

▲ COMMERCE As transportation grew, questions over state and federal rights grew. The case of *Gibbons* v. *Ogden* concerned an attempt by New York to grant a monopoly over steamboat traffic on the Hudson River. *How did the Court rule in this case?*

Interstate Commerce

Gibbons v. *Ogden* (1824) involved a company that operated steamboats in New York. The company had been given a monopoly over steamboat traffic in New York waters. The company took it upon itself to extend its monopoly to include traffic across the Hudson River between New York and New Jersey.

Marshall declared this monopoly was unconstitutional. In his decision, Marshall stated that in allowing the extension, the state legislature had overstepped its power, according to the Constitution, which gave the federal government control over interstate commerce.

In writing the Court's decision, Marshall defined interstate commerce in a way that went far beyond the mere exchange of trade goods between states. By ruling, in effect, that anything crossing state boundaries comes under federal control, Marshall provided the federal government with the constitutional basis for many of the broad and sweeping powers it exercises today.

In these cases and others, Marshall's nationalism strengthened the power of the federal government at the expense of the states. Although he was attacked for his decisions by defenders of states' rights, Marshall's views made the Constitution flexible enough to meet the nation's changing needs.

Section 1 ★ Review

Checking for Understanding

1. **Identify** Era of Good Feelings, American System, Tariff of 1816, John Marshall, *McCulloch* v. *Maryland*, *Gibbons* v. *Ogden*.

2. **Define** nationalism, internal improvement.

3. **Compare** the powers of the second Bank of the United States with the powers of the first Bank.

4. **List** two ways in which the Republicans adopted a Federalist point of view of government after 1812.

Critical Thinking

5. **Determining Relevance** Explain how John Marshall's ruling in *McCulloch* v. *Maryland* was an example of "the end justifies the means."

★★

Tying the Nation Together

Setting the Scene

Section Focus

The United States had a need for better transportation. The number of states had nearly doubled by 1820, and many new states were west of the Appalachians. Yet there was no easy way to move products long distances. As a transportation network began to crisscross the country, it stimulated movement of people and products and helped build a stronger nation.

Objectives

After studying this section, you should be able to

★ explain the advantages and disadvantages of each type of transportation improvement.

★ discuss the ways that internal improvements changed the nation.

Key Terms

turnpike, toll, lock

◀ **FIRST UNITED STATES GENERAL ISSUE POSTAGE STAMPS**

The War of 1812 made the need for a better transportation system clear. It had been extremely difficult to move armies, cannons, and supplies from one place to another. Indeed, American plans to invade and annex Canada during the war had failed, in part because America lacked good roads. Now, in peacetime, the only way to move products long distances overland was in wagons on roads that weather made impassable much of the year. With the steamboat in its infancy, travel on the Mississippi River was still one-way. Goods could be floated downriver on flatboats or keelboats, but very little could be powered upstream. Some Americans, especially in the West, felt it was the federal government's responsibility to improve transportation. One such Westerner was Henry Clay.

Not all of Clay's fellow Republicans were ready to support federal financing of internal improvements. In 1816 Representative John C. Calhoun of South Carolina proposed a "Bonus Bill" to build roads and canals with the $1.5 million fee paid by the Bank of the United States for its charter. The bill passed, but President Madison vetoed it, arguing that to spend money improving transportation was an unconstitutional extension of federal power.

■ Transportation by Road

A vital east-west road was already underway when Madison vetoed the Bonus Bill. In 1806 Congress funded the National Road from the sale of Western lands, and construction started from the Potomac River at Cumberland, Maryland, in 1811. By 1818 the road reached Wheeling, Virginia (in present-day West Virginia), spanning the Ohio River on the longest suspension bridge in the world—an engineering marvel. The bridge was 1,010 feet long and hung from towers rising 153 feet above the river.

The National Road went west to Vandalia, Illinois, cutting a path 80 feet wide through the wilderness. The center 30 feet were "paved" with crushed stone, and the road crossed streams and rivers on stone bridges. Great Conestoga wagons drawn by oxen or teams of 4, 6, or 8 horses moved westward along this route.

State Road-Building Projects

In general, states or private businesses undertook improvements in transportation. State-chartered private companies constructed hundreds of miles of **turnpikes,** roads that were barricaded at intervals by poles that stopped travelers until they paid a **toll,** or fee. However, turnpikes were profitable only on main routes, such as between Albany and Lake Erie, or in populated areas where traffic was heavy. In the West, highways usually were constructed by the states themselves, at times with the aid of federal funds.

The Ordeal of Overland Travel

Although by 1840 the country was crisscrossed with roads, they did not provide satisfactory transportation. Except in the East, few were surfaced or spanned by adequate bridges. When the routes passed through woods, foot-high stumps remained in the roadbed. Spring rains turned roads to mud and mired wagons up to their axles. In swampy places, "corduroy"—logs laid sideways across the roadbed—hurt horses' legs and jolted wagons to pieces.

David Stevenson described a journey by stagecoach along a typical route of the time in his book *Sketch of the Civil Engineering* of *North America,* published in 1838:

" *Sometimes our way lay for miles through extensive marshes, which we crossed by corduroy-roads. . . . At others the coach stuck fast in mud, from which it could be extricated only by the combined efforts of the coachman and passengers; and at one place we traveled . . . through a forest flooded with water, which stood to a height of several feet. . . . The distance of the route from Pittsburgh to Erie is 128 miles, which was accomplished in forty-six hours . . . although the conveyance by which I traveled carried the mail, and stopped only for breakfast, dinner, and tea, but there was considerable delay by the coach being once upset and several times 'mired.'* "

Such difficult travel was necessary for families moving west with their belongings and for farmers herding cattle and hogs to market. But bulky goods, such as farm crops or manufactured products, could not be quickly or profitably moved long distances by land. The price of products was out of reach for many people because merchants passed shipping costs on to consumers. Far more important to commerce, therefore, were America's inland waterways.

▼ **CONESTOGA WAGON**

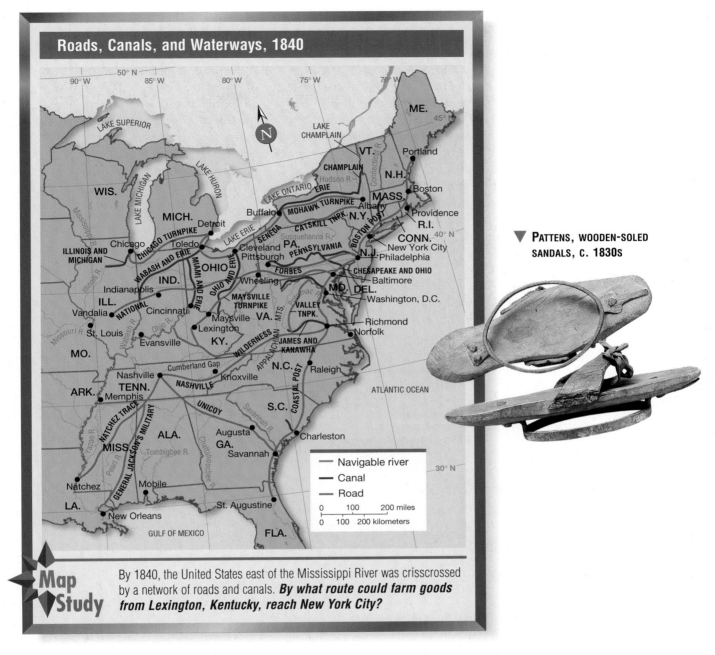

Roads, Canals, and Waterways, 1840

LAKE SUPERIOR

LAKE MICHIGAN

LAKE HURON

WIS.

MICH.

Detroit

Chicago

Toledo

ILLINOIS AND MICHIGAN

CHICAGO TURNPIKE

WABASH AND ERIE

IND.

Indianapolis

ILL.

NATIONAL

Vandalia

MO.

St. Louis

Evansville

Cincinnati

OHIO

MIAMI AND ERIE

OHIO AND ERIE

Cleveland

Pittsburgh

PA.

PENNSYLVANIA

Wheeling

FORBES

MAYSVILLE TURNPIKE

Maysville

Lexington

VA.

WILDERNESS

KY.

LAKE ONTARIO

ERIE

Buffalo

MOHAWK TURNPIKE

CATSKILL TNPK.

SENECA

Susquehanna R.

ME.

LAKE CHAMPLAIN

VT.

CHAMPLAIN

N.H.

Portland

Hudson R.

Connecticut R.

Albany

MASS.

Boston

N.Y.

BOSTON POST

Providence

R.I.

New York City

CONN.

Philadelphia

N.J.

CHESAPEAKE AND OHIO

Baltimore

MD.

DEL.

Washington, D.C.

Potomac R.

VALLEY TNPK.

Richmond

Norfolk

JAMES AND KANAWHA

APPALACHIAN MTS.

N.C.

COASTAL POST

Raleigh

ATLANTIC OCEAN

Missouri R.

Wabash R.

Ohio R.

Cumberland Gap

Nashville

NASHVILLE

Knoxville

UNICOY

TENN.

Memphis

ARK.

NATCHEZ TRACE

GENERAL JACKSON'S MILITARY

Yazoo R.

Pearl R.

MISS.

Natchez

LA.

New Orleans

Mobile

Tombigbee R.

Chattahoochee R.

ALA.

Augusta

GA.

Savannah

Savannah R.

S.C.

Charleston

FLA.

St. Augustine

GULF OF MEXICO

Navigable river
Canal
Road

0   100   200 miles
0   100   200 kilometers

50° N
90° W   85° W   80° W   75° W   70° W
45° N
40° N
30° N

N

▼ **PATTENS, WOODEN-SOLED SANDALS, C. 1830S**

Map Study

By 1840, the United States east of the Mississippi River was crisscrossed by a network of roads and canals. **By what route could farm goods from Lexington, Kentucky, reach New York City?**

■ Transportation by Water

Rivers had long been the primary means of moving commercial goods, but travel was one-way—flatboats and rafts floated only downstream. Trips against the current were slow and difficult. Although steamboats were built before 1800, they initially did not attract much attention. In 1807, however, Robert Fulton's steamboat, the *Clermont,* made its first voyages on the Hudson River, chugging the 150 miles from New York City to upstream Albany in an amazing 32 hours. By demonstrating the practicality of two-way river travel, Fulton launched the steamboat era.

The Growth of Steamboat Travel

In 1811 the first steamboat in Western waters steamed down the Ohio and Mississippi rivers from Pittsburgh to New Orleans and then returned upriver as far as Louisville. Steamboats proved their ability to carry passengers and goods quickly and efficiently, and by 1850 nearly 800 of them regularly traveled the Mississippi and its tributaries. Flat-bottomed steamboats were developed to navigate rivers less than three feet deep.

The benefits of steamboat travel were great, but risks were high. The average life of a river steamboat was three to six years—not surprising considering the dangers presented by snags, ice, bursting boilers, collisions, fires, and sandbars. About one-third of the steamboats built before 1850 were lost in accidents. In 1839 Michael Chevalier, a French traveler in America, noted that his Mississippi steamboat trip posed more dangers than his Atlantic crossing:

> *There have been many accidents by fire in the steamers, and many persons have perished in this way. . . . The Brandywine was burnt near Memphis, in 1832, and every soul on board, to the number of 110, was lost.*

> *The Americans show a singular indifference in regard to fire . . . they smoke without the least concern in the midst of half-open cotton bales . . . they ship gunpowder with no more precaution than if it were so much maize or salt pork. . . . it matters little, if they move at a rapid rate, and are navigated at little expense.* 99

The Erie Canal

For moving heavy goods, the thousands of miles of canals built during the first part of the nineteenth century were far more efficient than even the best roads. On a good road, it took 4 horses to haul a 1.5-ton load; 2 horses or mules could pull a canal boat with a load of 50 tons. Before 1815 a number of short canals had been built, most of them

History AND ART

▲ *ON THE RIVER* by George Catlin Steamboats and canal boats speeded the movement of people and the transportation of goods. *How did New York City benefit from the Erie Canal?*

bypassing rapids and falls in rivers or linking natural waterways. The canal-building craze did not really begin, however, until completion of the Erie Canal in 1825.

Begun by New York state in 1817, the Erie Canal was 40 feet wide, 4 feet deep, and 363 miles long—running from Albany on the Hudson River to Buffalo on Lake Erie. The canal lowered the cost of moving a ton of goods from almost 20 cents per mile to less than 2 cents and reduced travel time from 20 days to 6. It quickly made New York City the greatest port in America and brought instant prosperity to rural areas upstate.

The success of the Erie Canal encouraged other states to invest in canals. Pennsylvania built a canal system across the Appalachian Mountains, linking Pittsburgh with the East and allowing Philadelphia to challenge New York as the nation's major port. Ohio went deeply into debt to build 500 miles of canals connecting the Ohio River and Lake Erie. Indiana's canal-building program nearly bankrupted the state.

Canal Construction

In an era before dynamite, concrete, and steel, building canals took astonishing physical effort by countless workers. By 1840 more than 3,000 miles of canals had been dug by workers using shovels and scoops pulled by horses and oxen. **Locks**—enclosures with gates at each end to raise or lower the water level—were constructed as canals crossed hills and valleys. The stone for these locks had to be cut and set completely by hand.

Construction workers labored on the canals from dawn to dusk for wages that averaged less than $1 a day. Many farmers earned extra income by working on nearby canal projects. But farmers were not available during the growing season, and frequently the population was too small to supply enough workers. So construction depended on thousands of Irish immigrants who moved from project to project as canal building spread. Canals also created opportunities for new businesses to supply food, shelter, and other necessities to workers—and later to travelers on the canals. In rural areas, towns sprang up along canals, especially at locks, which were typical stopping points for boats. Soon, however, an even quicker means of transportation was developing.

■ Transportation by Rail

Railroads proved the most practical of all internal improvements. They were faster than roads and were passable in almost all weather. They did not freeze in winter or dry up in summer like canals and rivers; nor were they limited by topography.

Early trains were nearly as unsafe as steamboats. Engineers operated locomotives at top speed down hills and around curves, giving passengers the nineteenth-century equivalent of a roller-coaster ride. Sparks from belching smokestacks ignited wooden railroad cars, haystacks, and buildings along the track. To save money, only a single set of tracks was laid to carry trains in both directions, so collisions were frequent. Experienced travelers rode in the middle cars.

Despite their dangers, railroads excited Americans. In his book *Walden,* Henry David Thoreau captured this spirit:

> 66 *When I hear the iron horse make the hills echo with his snort like thunder, shaking the earth with his feet and breathing fire and smoke from his nostrils . . . it seems as if the earth had got a race now worthy to inhabit it.* 99

Nevertheless, railroads were slow to take hold, mainly because of opposition from state governments, which had heavy investments in roads and canals. New York, for example, attempted to protect the Erie Canal by prohibiting trains from carrying freight. By 1840 the number of miles

▲ **POLICE ALARM RATTLE, EARLY 1800s**

▲ EXPANSION Settlements grew in rural areas, partly because of improved means of transportation. **Why was railway travel practical?**

The Accessibility of Information

Transportation changed America in other ways as well. Information joined the flow of products as mail became deliverable throughout the nation. In 1825 Congress established home delivery of letters and in 1847 created the first national postage stamps. With the mail came newspapers, which brought national issues to the attention of the most remote rural communities. Improved transportation also brought circuit-riding preachers more frequently. No longer did isolated areas wait months for formal religious services, marriage ceremonies, or baptisms.

An American Culture

As technology and the accessibility of information changed the way people worked and lived, American artists and writers were beginning to explore American topics and developing styles that reflected American scenes. Beginning in the 1820s, a group of realistic landscape painters, called the Hudson River School, focused on scenes of the Hudson River valley and the Adirondack and Catskill mountains.

Other artists worked in other forms. Among the most popular were printmakers Nathaniel Currier and James Merritt Ives, whose works celebrated holidays, sporting events, and American rural life.

American writers were turning away from European influences and writing about contemporary America. Writers such as James Fenimore Cooper and Washington Irving reveal the spirit of the expanding American frontier and of the possibilities for improvement and change. Cooper produced one of the first truly American heroes, Natty Bumppo, in his *Leatherstocking Tales.* Bumppo was a frontier scout who was constantly in conflict; he was drawn to life in the wilderness as well as life among American settlers. Irving's romantic tales explored the legends of New York. His stories "The Legend of Sleepy Hollow" and "Rip Van Winkle" are adaptations of folktales with American characters and locales.

of track laid equaled the number of miles of canals that had been dug. But not until the second half of the century would railroads dominate the nation's transportation system.

■ Transportation and Daily Life

Roads, canals, steamboats, and railroads had created a truly national economy in the United States by the mid-1800s. People could now buy goods produced in distant places. Rural Americans could have glass windows in their homes and hang curtains sewn from cloth manufactured in the mills of New England. Citizens of Illinois could enjoy the same foods, fashions, and household furnishings as residents of Vermont.

▲ CONNECTING ONE PLACE TO ANOTHER Although it provided a bumpy trip for travelers, the safety coach averaged the trek from Washington, D.C., to Baltimore in about 5 hours. *How did improved transportation affect relations between the West and the Northeast?*

Women in the Labor Force

For women, the effects of the transportation revolution were mixed. The constant need to make household necessities once required the help of the whole family. The availability of manufactured goods, however, changed the division of labor. Household work required less time and became the sole responsibility of women. It also became less valued than labor that produced income, and many women moved into paid employment outside the home.

An important result of the transportation system was that it forged a link between the Northeast and the old Northwest Territory. The natural geographic connection of the West was with the South by way of the Mississippi River. But the best market for Western farm products was the populous industrial Northeast. Food prices fell in the Northeast, while farm production more than doubled. By 1840 more Western farm products were being shipped on the Erie Canal than down the Mississippi River. Building roads, canals, and railroads created a strong economic tie between the West and the Northeast that later would have important consequences for the nation.

Section 2 ★ Review

Checking for Understanding

1. **Identify** Bonus Bill, National Road, Robert Fulton, Erie Canal.

2. **Define** turnpike, toll, lock.

3. **Describe** the environmental problems that were involved in building early roads and canals.

4. **Explain** the effect the transportation revolution had on women.

Critical Thinking

5. **Linking Past and Present** Roads, canals, and railroads were early transportation links between East and West. What major links tie different sections of the country together today?

▲ VIEW OF LOCKPORT, NEW YORK

Canal Locks

Get up there mule, here comes a lock
We'll make Rome 'fore 6 o'clock
And back we'll go to our home dock
Right back home to Buffalo.

The "lock" in the verse of this early nineteenth-century song was one of 83 along the Erie Canal. Locks are chambers, with gates at each end, that raise and lower ships to compensate for elevation changes along a waterway.

A ship traveling downstream enters a lock and remains there while a gate is closed behind it, creating a watertight chamber. Water is slowly released through the downstream gate to lower the water level in the lock. The downstream gate is then opened, and the ship continues on its way at a lower elevation. To raise a ship, water is added to the lock through the upstream gate.

In places where elevation changes are great, such as at a waterfall, locks are combined in a sort of water staircase. Ships pass from one lock to another, each lock like a step on the staircase.

Among the earliest canals in the United States were the Great Lakes canals begun in the 1700s. The first locks between Lakes Huron and Superior were constructed in 1798.

Locks remain important even today on the Ohio and Mississippi rivers. Many locks from times past can be found still standing in towns, forests, and fields—remnants of the nineteenth century.

Making the Technology Connection

1. What do canal locks do?

2. What materials and technologies common today were not available for building or operating nineteenth-century locks?

Linking Past and Present

3. What canals are important in world commerce today?

★★

Monroe and Foreign Affairs

Setting the Scene

Section Focus

Nationalism also affected the young nation's foreign affairs. Americans approved as Spain's colonies in Latin America gained independence. At the same time, the United States worked to establish peace along its borders and to expand them where possible. Out of these events came a policy that for the next 150 years guided America's attitude toward affairs in the Western Hemisphere.

Objectives

After studying this section, you should be able to

★ describe America's problems with Britain and Spain and how they were settled.

★ explain the foreign policy principles established by the Monroe Doctrine.

Key Term

ultimatum

◀ **JAMES MONROE**

United States foreign affairs after the War of 1812 were dominated by John Quincy Adams, Monroe's secretary of state until he became President himself in 1825. Few Americans could match his qualifications. He had spent 18 years abroad in diplomatic service as the United States minister to the Netherlands, Portugal, Russia, and Great Britain. Furthermore, as the son of a former Federalist President and a native New Englander, his appointment to the cabinet was in the spirit of national unity sought by President Monroe.

■ Disputes and Diplomacy

Although peace with Great Britain had been achieved in 1815, bitter feelings remained. The Treaty of Ghent was widely regarded as a mere truce because it had not resolved the differences between the two nations. "That man must be blind to the indications of the future," declared Henry Clay in 1816, "who cannot see that we are destined to have war after war with Great Britain." Disputes over fishing rights at the mouth of the St. Lawrence River led to violence between Canadians and New Englanders. Britain and the United States competed for naval supremacy on the Great Lakes. From Maine to Oregon the boundary between the United States and Canada was unsettled, and in several places it was disputed.

Tensions with Britain Ease

There were strong reasons for improving relations with Great Britain. Chief among these was trade. Britain remained a buyer of American raw materials and America a market for British manufactured goods. Realizing that neither country had anything to gain by continued hostilities, Britain made attempts to smooth out relations. Between 1815 and 1817, Great Britain and the United States worked out several of their disputes peacefully.

The Rush-Bagot Agreement

As minister to England, John Quincy Adams used Great Britain's desire for better relations with the United States to negotiate the Rush-Bagot Agreement of 1817, the first mutual naval disarmament in history. The United States and Britain agreed to remove all warships from the Great Lakes except for a few small vessels to control smuggling. This precedent later encouraged the United States and Canada to demilitarize their entire 3,000-mile border, creating what continues to be the longest unfortified international boundary in the world.

The Rush-Bagot Agreement also set the stage for the Convention of 1818, which specified where American ships could fish in Canadian waters and set the northern boundary of the Louisiana Purchase along the forty-ninth parallel from the Lake of the Woods in Minnesota to the Rocky Mountains. Beyond the Rockies, the treaty provided "joint occupation" of the disputed Oregon territory for 10 years. Each country would be free to carry on fur trade and settle the region without interference from the other.

Florida Border Dispute

Spanish Florida remained a source of friction. Spain insisted that Florida's western boundary was the Mississippi River, while the United States claimed that it was the Perdido River 200 miles farther east. During the War of 1812, the United States resolved the controversy by simply seizing the disputed territory.

Because Spain was an ally of Great Britain in the War of 1812, Florida became a base of British and Native American operations against the United States. After the war, it remained a refuge for Seminoles and Creeks, who continued to battle Georgia settlers. In 1818 Andrew Jackson, commanding the Tennessee militia, pursued a Seminole force into Florida, where he seized Spanish settlements at Pensacola and St. Marks.

The Adams-Onís Treaty

The Spanish government demanded that the United States pay for the "outrage." But Adams defended Jackson and argued that true blame lay in Spain's failure to keep order in Florida. He convinced Monroe to issue Spain an **ultimatum,** a demand that would have serious consequences if ignored, likely a resort to force: either govern Florida effectively or surrender it to the United States.

Occupied with problems throughout its Latin American empire, Spain ceded Florida to the United States in the Adams-Onís Treaty of 1819. In return the United States agreed to reimburse American citizens who had claims against Spain. The treaty also set the western boundary of the Louisiana Purchase: it ran from the Gulf of Mexico northwest to the Oregon Territory and then west to the Pacific. The United States gave up a weak claim to Texas, while Spain gave up a much stronger claim to Oregon.

■ The Monroe Doctrine

The most significant accomplishment of Secretary of State Adams was the Monroe Doctrine of 1823. This famous statement of foreign policy had a complex background that involved events in Latin America, in Europe, and on the Pacific coast of North America.

Between 1814 and 1824, Spain's Latin American colonies declared independence. Armies led by Simón Bolívar (see•MOHN buh•LEE•VAHR) and José de San Martín (hoh• SAY day SAHN mahr•TEEN) exceeded even the Patriots' heroics in the American Revolution and captured the attention of the American people.

Threat from Europe

After defeating Napoleon at Waterloo in 1815, the victorious monarchies of Europe—Russia, Austria, Prussia, and Britain—formed

Life of the Times

Seminole Survival

In order to avoid defeat by Andrew Jackson in 1818 and 1819, many Seminoles of the Southeast fled deep into the swamps of the Florida Everglades. Isolated from the world, the Seminoles had to adapt to a new environment.

Seminole houses called *chickees* were made from the palmetto trees that flourished in the swamp. The floor of the house was raised off the ground on poles to keep it dry. Open walls and thatched roofs kept the dwelling cool.

The Seminoles' birchbark canoes were replaced by sleek dugouts. These were made by throwing embers from a fire along the center of prepared logs and then scraping out the charred wood. The walls of the dugouts were thin, sometimes no more than one inch thick. Using streams as trails, the pilots stood on platforms at the rear of the dugouts. From this vantage point, they used long poles to push the vessels through the swamps. The hunters who rode in the dugout could spear fish, which provided the Seminoles with a rich supply of food. Seminoles continue to live in the Everglades today.

► SEMINOLE LEADER TUKO-SEE-MATHLA

▲ PRESENT-DAY SEMINOLES

---

the Quadruple Alliance to suppress the democratic ideas of the French Revolution. Klemens von Metternich (MEHT•uhr•nihk), prime minister of Austria, branded democracy "the disease which must be cured, the volcano which must be extinguished, the gangrene which must be burned out with the hot iron." The Quadruple Alliance, with France or a new member replacing Britain, helped defeat revolutions in Italy and Spain.

The success of the Quadruple Alliance caused some European leaders to talk of taking similar action in the Americas. Although there was little chance that they could carry out such action, rumors of it caused concern in the United States and Great Britain. Both the British and the Americans were enjoying a profitable trade with Latin American nations. If the Quadruple Alliance returned the region to Spain, restrictions would reappear and this trade would be lost. The British government looked for a way to discourage moves to restore Spanish rule in Latin America.

British Initiative

In August 1823, the British foreign minister suggested to the United States minister in London that the two nations issue a joint statement about the independence of Latin America. The statement would say that the United States and Britain opposed intervention in Latin America by any power and that neither nation would acquire any part of Latin America for itself—a surprising proposal from an old enemy. The American minister informed President Monroe.

The British proposal was an attractive and timely one. The Monroe administration was wrestling with a number of foreign-policy concerns. Russia already claimed Alaska and was making aggressive moves on the

States act on its own. The nationalism of John Quincy Adams prevailed.

Statement of American Resolve

For what would become a landmark of American foreign policy, the Monroe Doctrine was presented in an undramatic way. It appeared in two widely separated passages in President Monroe's annual message to Congress on December 2, 1823. The Monroe Doctrine provided both a warning and a reassurance to European countries regarding their conduct in the Western Hemisphere (see Appendix).

If the nations of the Quadruple Alliance ever seriously contemplated intervention in the Americas, it was the British navy, not Monroe's warning, that made them back down. In 1824 the Russians, already in possession of more land than they could effectively govern, agreed to withdraw from Oregon.

The significance of the Monroe Doctrine is in later events. Its bold warnings gained meaning only when the United States became a major sea power—a development that took nearly a century. Nor did the Monroe Doctrine restrict the nationalism, expansion, and intervention of the United States itself over the next 150 years.

Visualizing History ▲ THE MONROE DOCTRINE President Monroe consulted his cabinet before issuing the Monroe Doctrine. *What warning did the Doctrine contain?*

Pacific coast. In 1821 the Russian czar announced that his empire extended south into Oregon, a claim that conflicted with American and British claims there.

Should the United States allow Russia to expand its holdings in the Western Hemisphere? How should the United States meet the threat of intervention in Latin America—accept the British offer of cooperation or act alone? President Monroe discussed these questions with his cabinet and consulted Jefferson and Madison, who favored a joint statement with Great Britain. But Secretary of State Adams argued that it would look as though the United States were following "in the wake of the British man-of-war." He urged that the United

Section 3 ★ Review

Checking for Understanding

1. **Identify** John Quincy Adams, Rush-Bagot Agreement, Adams-Onís Treaty, Simón Bolívar, José de San Martín, Quadruple Alliance, Monroe Doctrine.

2. **Define** ultimatum.

3. **List** the disputes that the United States had with Britain and Spain.

4. **Describe** the chain of events that formed the background to the Monroe Doctrine.

Critical Thinking

5. **Applying Principles** Argue how United States government involvement in Central American affairs could be interpreted as violating the principles of the Monroe Doctrine.

Map and Graph Skills

Drawing Conclusions from Maps

Your best friend comes back from a hiking trip to Colorado. Taking out a map, she describes a dangerous situation she survived near the top of Pikes Peak. After talking about all the factors that could have created the situation and looking closely at the map, you conclude that she must have lost the trail at about 10,000 feet.

Drawing conclusions is a process of making decisions through analysis of available information. To draw a conclusion, you make a series of inferences, or deductions based on facts or circumstances. Inferences act as clues that help in making decisions or judgments. In this situation you reached a conclusion based on your knowledge of Pikes Peak and experience reading a map.

The following guidelines will help you draw conclusions from maps:

a. **Analyze** the map for bodies of water. How might they be used in the future? Are they strategic for trade or defense?

b. **Study** the landscape. Is it mountainous or flat? Is the land suitable for farming?

c. **Study** the boundaries. Do physical boundaries match natural boundaries? Are there any border disputes?

d. **Examine** other map data. Examine routes, resources, labels, etc.

Examine the historical map of Florida on this page. Following the guidelines, you can draw a conclusion as to why Florida was acquired by the United States in 1819:

a. Bodies of water—all locations along these waterways would provide ports for trade and strategic locations for defense.

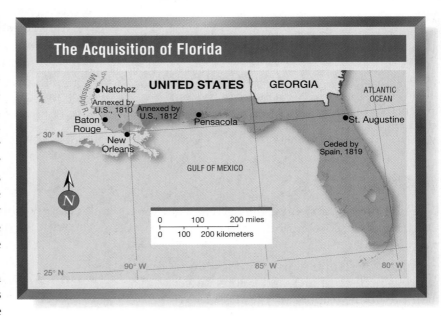

The Acquisition of Florida

b. Landscape—Florida is a peninsula, and most land lies near coasts; land would be too wet for farming.

c. The borders are clearly defined, except for the New Orleans area. Spain, England, France, and the United States all had interests in this area.

d. Data primarily deal with border disputes—land in three different areas between the Mississippi River and the eastern coast of Florida was annexed or ceded.

You conclude that the need to expand to its natural borders, obtain good ports, and gain a strategic position for defense made the acquisition of Florida appealing for the United States.

Practicing the Skill

Apply these same guidelines to the map of roads, canals, and rivers in 1840 in this chapter, and draw conclusions as to why the states of New York, Ohio, and Indiana had the most mileage of canals.

Using Vocabulary

Write a paragraph describing the awakening of American nationalism from 1812 to 1823 using the following terms:

internal improvement
protective tariff
turnpike

Era of Good Feelings
American System
Monroe Doctrine

Reviewing Facts

1. **Describe** how establishing the second Bank of the United States contributed to the spirit of nationalism.

2. **Compare** the Republicans' attitudes on internal improvements, banking, and federal power with their previous positions on these issues.

3. **Explain** how the federal judiciary strengthened nationalism in key decisions between 1819 and 1824.

4. **Cite** Madison's reason for vetoing the Bonus Bill.

5. **Summarize** the changes that resulted from internal improvements in transportation.

6. **List** transportation improvements of the era and the advantages and disadvantages of each.

Understanding Concepts

National Community

1. How did the United States begin to change from local communities to a more national community in the Era of Good Feelings?

World Power

2. What perception of United States power resulted from the Monroe Doctrine?

Critical Thinking

1. **Understanding Cause and Effect** How did the transportation revolution bring about a communications revolution in the West?

2. **Interpreting Illustrations** Study the illustration of the city of New York during the early-to-mid-1800s on this page and answer the questions that follow.

   a. Do you think this artist's portrayal of New York would make a good illustration for a travel poster designed to attract tourists to the city? Why or why not?

   b. Do you think the illustration is an accurate portrayal of the city? Explain.

Writing About History

Comparison

Compare the advantages of each of the following means of transportation during the early 1800s: roads, rivers, canals, railroads.

Cooperative Learning

Imagine that you work for a local newspaper in Cincinnati, Ohio, in 1823. Like most newspapers even today, your news staff holds daily meetings to discuss which news items to print in the upcoming edition. Discuss with other members of your staff what international, national, and local topics should be included in tomorrow's newspaper. Also determine on what you will base your decision to include certain articles.

Social Studies Skills

Interpreting Historical Maps

Historical maps might resemble modern maps in style and content, but they show a geography of the past. Because they show the past, they can confuse or disorient you unless you study them carefully. The following guidelines will help you interpret a historical map:

- Read the map title and any information contained in legends, keys, or captions. It is essential to know precisely what time period the map portrays.

- Pay close attention to the use of color, pattern, line, or text since this will help you distinguish various pieces of information.

- Compare the historical map to a modern map of the same region and look for differences. Place names may have changed, borders may have shifted, and roads and towns disappeared. The physical landscape may be different. Often these changes are important in explaining historical developments.

Practicing the Skill

Study the map of Latin America on this page and answer the questions.

1. Why was the year 1825 selected as the time to show the political situation occurring in Latin America?

2. Independence movements in Latin America had been taking place for approximately how many years?

3. Describe some of the changes you see when comparing this map to a modern map of Latin America. What do the changes suggest about independence movements in Latin America after 1825?

Latin America, 1825

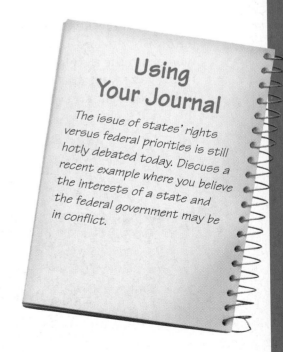

Using Your Journal

The issue of states' rights versus federal priorities is still hotly debated today. Discuss a recent example where you believe the interests of a state and the federal government may be in conflict.

Cultural Kaleidoscope

The Early Republic

Transportation

The Louisiana Purchase and victory in the War of 1812 sent a clear message to the world: Americans were going to control their own destinies. An ever-growing freedom of mobility infused Americans in the period from 1789 to 1824. People moved westward in a variety of ways. Many traveled on foot and horseback, their possessions piled in handcarts or wagons. Still others traveled via America's waterways on the nation's natural rivers and lakes as well as on the network of artificial waterways that followed construction of the Erie Canal.

▲
Trade began to increase rapidly with the development of bigger and quicker merchant ships. Clipper ships made the voyage from New York City to San Francisco around the tip of South America in 3 to 4 months—about twice as fast as the overland journey.

◄
The canoe, which was developed from the seagoing vessels of the Carib people and played an important part in the exploration of North America, was still an important means of travel.

From its opening in 1818, the National Road was heavily traveled by stagecoaches, Conestoga wagons, and other vehicles, besides droves of cattle, sheep, and hogs. Pennsylvania Dutch wagon drivers preferred handling a team from the left, which provided better visibility when the vehicle kept to the right. This may have been the start of the custom of vehicles driving on the right side of the road in later years.

While stagecoaches might make 6 miles per hour, steamboats reached upwards of 12 miles per hour—and the engines were just as fresh and energetic as ever after hundreds of miles.

A typical toll fee for a rider on horseback traveling 10 miles on an early turnpike was $6\frac{1}{2}$ cents. A carriage with 2 horses was assessed 25 cents.

Chapter 7

The Federalist Era

The people elected George Washington, the hero of the Revolution, to lead the new nation. Washington set several precedents as the first President, such as creating a cabinet, directing foreign affairs, and serving as "chief legislator."

Washington also tackled the nation's war debts. He delegated much of the nation's financial policy to Alexander Hamilton, his secretary of the treasury. On the whole, Hamilton's program restored the credit of the United States, although it met with bitter opposition from people who believed the federal government should not wield such power.

The defeat of the Miami Confederation and the Treaty of Greenville pushed Native Americans out of Ohio and opened the way for settlement in the Northwest. Washington also snuffed out the Whiskey Rebellion.

At the outbreak of the Anglo-French War, Washington issued the Proclamation of Neutrality, which stated that the nation would be "friendly and impartial" toward both warring parties. However, it was still necessary to negotiate the Jay Treaty in order to escape a war with England and the Pinckney Treaty to resolve a border dispute with Spain.

John Adams, who succeeded Washington as the nation's leader, faced a difficult term in office. Adams's tenure was marked by the XYZ Affair, an undeclared war with France, and anti-Republican legislation that ultimately hurt Adams's Federalist party.

Chapter 8

Age of Jefferson

Republican Thomas Jefferson brought a political and philosophical change to the presidency in 1800. The thrust of his beliefs was that the people were the source of a government's power. Once in office, however, Jefferson found that he had to provide strong leadership to prevent his party from dividing into factions.

During Jefferson's first term, much of the earlier Federalist legislation remained in effect. In addition, foreign trade was increased, taxes and the national debt were reduced, and the principle of judicial review was established. Jefferson's accomplishments led to an easy victory for a second term.

A major event during Jefferson's presidency was the Louisiana Purchase. The new territory doubled the size of the United States by extending its boundaries west of the Mississippi. Not all people supported the purchase of Louisiana, however. In particular, Federalists in the Northeast feared that it would ultimately weaken New England's power in national affairs.

During Jefferson's presidency, he tried to remain neutral in foreign affairs despite the threat of foreign attacks on American ships. In response to British policies, Congress passed the Embargo Act, which sanctioned an economic boycott that was later repealed.

Under James Madison, Jefferson's successor, the United States became embroiled in an unpopular war with Britain, which finally ended in 1814 with the Treaty of Ghent.

Chapter 9

Nationalism and Change

The period following the War of 1812 was marked by a spirit of nationalism. Internal improvements were encouraged, a new national bank stimulated the economy, and tariffs protected American manufacturers from foreign goods. Nationalism was also demonstrated in a series of Supreme Court decisions that strengthened the power of the federal government at the expense of the states. The early 1800s were also marked by a transportation revolution on America's inland waterways while highway and railroad development were in their infancy. Fulton's steamboat turned rivers into two-way routes.

This, along with the building of thousands of miles of canals, dramatically lowered the time and cost required to ship goods from place to place.

Transportation improvements helped unite Americans and increased the spread of information and the changes to the geographic landscape of the country.

The United States was also looking after its foreign affairs. Relations improved with Britain following the Rush-Bagot Agreement and with Spain following the Adams-Onís Treaty. The Monroe Doctrine proclaimed that the Western Hemisphere was closed to further European colonization. Although insignificant when it was issued, it has had lasting importance in American foreign policy.

Understanding Unit Themes

1. **American Democracy**   What beliefs held by Jefferson furthered the spirit of democracy?

2. **Geography and Environment**   As settlers poured into the country's expanded Western lands, what effects did they have on the American environment?

3. **Conflict and Cooperation**   Why did some issues threaten to disrupt the spirit of American nationalism and unity?

4. **United States Role in World Affairs**   Explain George Washington's rationale for recommending noninvolvement in Europe.

UNIT FOUR
TOWARD A DEMOCRACY
1820–1854

★★★

◀ JACKSON CAMPAIGN BOX

History AND ART

The County Election
by George Caleb Bingham, 1852

While many artists of the mid-1800s made the frontier appear romantic and picturesque, George Caleb Bingham painted it realistically. As a result, his pictures show the frontier as a way of life.

Setting the Scene

The years between 1820 and 1854 were a time of national optimism and the growth of democracy. At the same time, the nation's economy grew. Confident of their future, Americans experimented with social reform movements aimed at bettering society.

Themes

- American Democracy
- Economic Development
- Humanities and Religion
- Conflict and Cooperation

Key Events

- Missouri Compromise
- Founding of New Harmony
- Tariff of Abominations
- Maysville Road veto
- *The Liberator* published
- Native American Removal
- Nullification Crisis
- Bank Recharter Bill veto
- American Anti-Slavery Society
- Panic of 1837
- Seneca Falls Convention

Major Issues

- Distinct sections—North, South, and West—cooperate and compete for economic development.
- Jacksonian democracy results in increased power of the President and popular participation in political life.
- Religious motivation and democratic ideals spark the abolitionist movement and other efforts for social reform.

▲ CEDAR AND DEERSKIN DRUM

▲ CORN HUSK DOLL

◀ IDENTIFICATION TAGS

Portfolio Project

Use the library to locate sources about one of the important individuals, events, or developments discussed in this unit. Organize information about these sources to create an efficient reference guide for someone interested in writing an in-depth study of the subject.

Global Perspectives

The World

	1820		1830	
Asia and Oceania				
Europe			◄ **1830** *July Revolution in France*	
Africa				**1835** *Boer farmers start the "Great Trek"*
South America	**1821** *Peru becomes independent of Spain*		**1830** *Venezuela and Ecuador become nations*	
North and Central America		**1826** *Pan-Americanism gets under way at Panama Congress*		

The United States

	1820		1830	
Pacific and Northwest	**1821** *California becomes a Mexican province*			
Southeast				
Midwest	**1820** *Missouri Compromise creates a balance between slave and free states*			
Southwest			▲ **1827** *Mission era ends with expulsion of all Franciscans from present-day New Mexico and Arizona*	
Atlantic Northeast			**1826** *Educational lyceum movement begins in Massachusetts*	

The Spanish were the first European settlers in North America. The Spanish town St. Augustine in Florida was North America's first permanent settlement established by Europeans. Today, the vast majority of Hispanic Americans do not come from Spain, but from Latin America and the Caribbean. According to the 1990 census, more than 22 million people of Hispanic origin reside in the United States. This total includes 13.5 million Mexican Americans, 2.7 million Puerto Rican Americans, and 1 million Cuban Americans.

► **1839** *Britain and China battle in First Opium War*

1840   **1850**

▼ **1837** *Victoria becomes Queen of Great Britain*

1847 *Liberia becomes an independent republic*

1845 *Peruvian President Ramón Castilla becomes one of the first mestizos to hold high public office*

1840 *Act of Union unites Upper and Lower Canada*

► **1838** *Cherokee endure the "Trail of Tears"*

1845 *Texas annexed*

1839 *Charles Goodyear makes first vulcanized rubber*

1840   **1850**

CHAPTER 10

★★★

Sectionalism
1820–1842

▼ COLLECTION OF WRITINGS
BY WOMEN WORKERS

Setting the Scene

Focus

At the same time that national spirit and pride were evident throughout the country, a strong sectional rivalry was also developing. Each region—the North, South, and West— wanted to further its own economic and political interests. Issues such as land policy, the tariff, and internal improvements were favored or opposed by different regions. The question of extending slavery, however, became the issue that proved the most difficult to resolve.

Concepts to Understand

★ Why early labor movements challenged the free enterprise system
★ How economic and cultural change brought about by the Industrial Revolution led to the creation of the factory system

Read to Discover . . .

★ how the Industrial Revolution affected the textile industry.
★ how each section viewed the major issues faced by the nation.

Journal Notes

How did different regions respond to the idea of protective tariffs? Note details about how they responded in your journal as you read the chapter.

CULTURAL

• **1790** *Samuel Slater builds first cotton mill at Pawtucket, Rhode Island*
• **1800** *Library of Congress founded*

• **1816** *African Colonization Society formed*

1790	1805

POLITICAL

• **1791** *Bill of Rights ratified*
• **1800** *Nation's capital moved from Philadelphia to Washington, D.C.*

• **1819** *Slavery prohibited in Missouri*

Where Cotton Is King
by Konstantin Rodko, 1908

This work depicts a style of art called "folk art," a term almost interchangeable with "primitive art" or "naive art." One art scholar defines folk art as "the expression of the common people, made by them and intended for their use and enjoyment."

◀ **FACTORY WORKER**

• **1825** *Erie Canal completed*

• **1839** *Edgar Allan Poe publishes first book*

1820

1835

• **1820** *Missouri Compromise reached*
• **1824** *House decides presidential election*

• **1837** *Financial panic sweeps nation*

★★

Growth in the North

Setting the Scene

Section Focus

The late eighteenth and early nineteenth centuries brought developments that would forever change life in all regions of the United States. With newly developed machines, goods could be produced more quickly and efficiently than ever before. With the growth of industry, however, came new problems.

Objectives

After studying this section, you should be able to

★ discuss the impact of the Industrial Revolution on American life.

★ examine the formation of trade societies.

★ explain why early attempts at unionization in the United States failed.

Key Terms

textile, emigration, closed shop, mechanics' lien law

◀ **SAMUEL SLATER**

*I*n the thousands of years between the building of the first pyramids in 2650 B.C. and the construction of log cabins in the eighteenth century, there was not much change with regard to building tools or sources of power. Then came the Industrial Revolution—a revolution that would change ways of life more in the next 200 years than they had changed in the previous 4,500 years.

■ The Industrial Revolution

The Industrial Revolution consisted of several basic developments: in industry there were shifts from simple tools to complex machines; from natural sources of power, such as draft animals and falling water, to artificial sources, such as the steam engine and the electric motor; and from regional to nationwide distribution of products. Jobs

became more specialized, so that many workers concentrated on particular, narrow tasks rather than on creating an entire product. In addition, new inventions made transportation and communication faster and more efficient.

From Britain to America

The Industrial Revolution began in Great Britain. Between 1730 and 1800, new mechanical methods of spinning and weaving cotton cloth transformed Britain's clothing industry. These machines operated so efficiently that cotton cloth, formerly a luxury, became the cheapest **textile,** or woven fabric, in the world.

Initially, manufacturing was a British monopoly; many of the machines that characterized the Industrial Revolution were developed by British inventors. Furthermore, British laws forbade the export of this machinery, as well as the **emigration**—the leaving of one's country permanently for another country—of skilled workers. Many Americans believed it was time to start producing their own goods. As Thomas Jefferson wrote in 1816:

" *. . . to be independent for the comforts of life we must fabricate them ourselves. . . . [S]hall we make our own comforts or go without them at the will of a foreign nation?* "

The new technology finally reached America in 1789 with the arrival of Samuel Slater. While a young man in Britain, Slater apprenticed in a textile factory, where he memorized every detail of the finest textile machinery. Soon after arriving on American soil, he formed a partnership with two other men in Providence, Rhode Island, and began to duplicate British textile machinery from memory. In 1790 America's first textile mill, built on the banks of the Seekonk River, opened its doors for business. The Industrial Revolution had come to America.

New England and the Middle Atlantic States

The embargo against England in 1812 had given the cotton-textile industry a chance to develop in the United States. This industry, which soon became more prosperous than the North's lucrative trade, was centered in New England for a number of reasons. The region boasted many swift-flowing streams, an abundant source of waterpower. New England's shippers were seeking additional enterprises in which to invest their profits. Also, after the 1820s, European immigration to the region provided a large labor force. By 1840, 800 cotton mills and 500 woolen mills in New England employed nearly 50,000 workers. Shipping continued to thrive, and many small factories were turning out such products as shoes, clocks, carriages, and paper.

Manufacturing also took hold in the Middle Atlantic states—Pennsylvania, New Jersey, and New York. Although there were textile mills in this region, too, the area was better known for its coal and iron ore resources. Improved roads and expansion of the nation's railway systems opened

Visualizing History

▲ SLATER'S MILL Technology from the Industrial Revolution was used by Samuel Slater in a mill he built at Pawtucket, Rhode Island, in 1790. *How was Slater's textile mill powered?*

▲ RISE OF AMERICAN FACTORIES As the Industrial Revolution spread, factories sprang up in many cities and towns in New England. *What types of products did these new factories produce?*

Western markets, and increased the demand for machinery. It was discovered that coal could be used in the manufacture of iron, which was used to make machines. The coal-fields of Pennsylvania turned the area into a great center for the iron industry and for the manufacture of machinery. Pittsburgh, located near plentiful deposits of coal and iron ore, became a center for these industries.

■ Early Effects

The Industrial Revolution transformed the Northeast from a region where families lived and worked together at farming, crafts, and home-based businesses to one in which people lived mostly in cities and earned their livings by working for others in industry. Factories that required a large labor force and nearby sources of power sprang up in existing cities, such as New York and Philadelphia. Such new cities as Lowell and Lawrence in Massachusetts were built along the falls and rapids of New England's rivers. As the cities grew, so did the demand for better transportation to carry raw materials to the factories and finished products to markets. Improved transportation brought food into the cities to feed the thousands of factory workers.

Industrialization created two new classes of people—the industrial capitalists who built and owned the factories and the industrial laborers who worked in them. These new owners and workers performed distinctly different functions. The differences even extended to their dress, and these differences became symbols that are still understood today: in political cartoons, a top hat and frock coat designate a capitalist; a cap and overalls, a factory worker.

Much of the profit from the Northeast's manufacturing and shipping went back into business, but a great deal of money was also invested all over the country. Banks loaned money to speculators in the West, to companies building Mississippi River steamboats, and to Alabama cotton producers. Thus, even though the regions of the nation developed in different ways, the whole country began to be tied together by a web of credit.

The Labor Movement

As machines replaced hand tools, jobs for skilled craftsworkers became scarcer, and many such workers were reduced to performing unskilled labor. Before industrialization, there had been enjoyment in skilled work and pride in good handicraft. Now, though, tending machines proved monotonous, and workers could take little pride in the completed product.

The First Labor Unions

In an effort to improve working conditions, workers organized into labor unions. In the United States, the first labor unions were formed by skilled craftspeople, such as carpenters, shoemakers, and printers. By 1830 most of the major crafts had "trade societies" in all the major Northeastern cities. The trade societies worked to improve the lives of their members by demanding higher wages, shorter hours, and the **closed shop**—a place of employment open only to union members.

In some cities, different crafts joined together to form citywide federations. In 1835 the Philadelphia trade societies called a citywide strike to force employers to grant members a 10-hour workday. In addition, city trade societies from several cities formed a National Trades Union, which claimed 300,000 members.

Unskilled factory workers were less successful in forming unions. Strikes could be easily broken by employers who simply hired recent immigrants to fill vacant factory positions. Incentive to organize was low, too, among textile workers, many of whom were young women from poor farms. To these hardworking young women, $3 a week was good pay and a 12- or 13-hour workday not unusual. Some factory owners even provided these women with educational opportunities, comfortable quarters, and chaperones.

▲ *MORNING BELL* by Winslow Homer, 1866 After the Civil War, Winslow Homer often painted scenes of everyday life. Homer's painting *Morning Bell* depicts young women carrying their lunches going off to work in a New England textile mill. ***About how many hours per day did laborers such as these young women work?***

AMERICAN PORTRAITS

Elizabeth Ann Seton
1774-1821

Elizabeth Ann Seton was 31 years old when she converted from the Episcopal Church to Roman Catholicism. Newly widowed with five young children, she drew strength from her new faith and determined to see that her children would receive a Catholic education.

Seton opened a free Catholic elementary school—the first such school in the United States—in Baltimore, Maryland, in 1809. She not only provided the children of newly arrived immigrants with schooling, but she also fed them lunch! Seton later founded the American Sisters of Charity, one of the earliest American religious societies.

Elizabeth Ann Seton guided the Sisters into aiding the sick, founding orphanages, and bringing new converts to the Roman Catholic faith. In 1975, "Mother Seton" became the first native-born American to be declared a Roman Catholic saint.

Female Workers Unionize

As competition for jobs in the textile mills increased, however, conditions worsened, and some of the female workers decided to organize. This led to the first women's strike, which occurred in 1824 among the weavers of Pawtucket, Rhode Island. In 1833 a union for female factory workers appeared in Lynn, Massachusetts, followed shortly by a "Factory Girls' Association" open to all female workers.

Often these early labor unions were ineffective. As Harriet Hanson Robinson wrote of an 1836 textile strike in Lowell, where she had worked as a child:

> *It is hardly necessary to say that so far as results were concerned this strike did no good. . . . [T]hough the authorities did not accede to their demands, the majority returned to their work, and the corporation went on cutting down the wages.*

Nonetheless, such unions represented the first attempts at large-scale organization of women workers in the United States.

■ Demands of Labor

The unions stood behind many demands for reform. No groups were more interested in the founding of public schools than the trade societies, whose members wanted to eliminate competition from children in the labor market. Unions also led the movement to abolish imprisonment for being unable to pay one's debts. In the 1830s, an estimated 75,000 people were thrown into jail for unpaid debts each year, often for trifling amounts. Another labor demand was for **mechanics' lien** (LEEN) **laws,** which would require that the wages owed to workers be the first payments a bankrupt employer would have to make.

Labor and Politics

In order to obtain their goals, laborers began to enter politics. In 1829 the Workingmen's party put up candidates for local offices in New York City and won a surprising 6,000 out of 20,000 votes. This party and others like it did not last long, for they were torn apart by infighting between radicals and moderates and between representatives of different unions. Professional politicians lured many workers into the major parties by including some of labor's demands in their platforms. The Democrats were especially successful in encouraging workers to support Andrew Jackson. In 1840 Martin Van Buren revealed his debt to the labor vote by establishing a 10-hour workday for federal government workers.

Legal Opposition

The early trade societies faced severe legal difficulties. In 1806 a Pennsylvania court ruled against a strike by Philadelphia's shoemakers' union—the Federal Society of Journeymen Cordwainers—stating that workers organizing to force employers to raise wages constituted criminal conspiracy, punishable by fines or imprisonment. This ruling became a precedent followed in other states.

In 1835 employers prosecuted another group of shoemakers, this time in Geneva, New York. In finding the workers guilty of conspiracy because their trade society demanded that they be paid at least $1 to make a pair of shoes, the court said:

> **Competition is the life of trade. If the defendants cannot make coarse boots for less than one dollar per pair, let them refuse to do so: but let them not directly or indirectly undertake to say that others shall not do the same work for less price.**

Limited Gains

The legal right of trade societies to carry on collective action against employers was finally recognized in 1842 in the case of *Commonwealth* v. *Hunt*. The Massachusetts Supreme Court held that an attempt by a trade society to improve the lot of its members through organized pressure, such as a strike or a boycott, might be legal if the methods employed were peaceful. This rather cautious tolerance of trade societies had force only in Massachusetts, however, and employers were still able to use the courts to break many strikes.

In any event, the decision came too late to help most of the early unions. The Panic of 1837 had already caused the collapse of many trade unions. Unemployment was so widespread that in order to avoid starvation, workers accepted whatever wages were offered. It would be nearly a generation before labor again tried to organize on a large scale.

The labor movement did secure some permanent gains, however. Labor was a major force in promoting public schools and in making it easier for settlers to acquire public lands. Several states passed laws limiting the workday to 10 hours. In 1840 President Van Buren declared a 10-hour day for work done for the federal government. Some states also limited child labor. Many states passed mechanics' lien laws, and imprisonment for debt was almost universally abandoned.

Section 1 ★ Review

Checking for Understanding

1. **Identify** Samuel Slater, National Trades Union, Factory Girls' Association, *Commonwealth* v. *Hunt*.

2. **Define** textile, emigration, closed shop, mechanics' lien law.

3. **Describe** the effects of the Industrial Revolution on the economy and lifestyles of the Northeast.

4. **Explain** the conditions that led workers to form trade societies.

Critical Thinking

5. **Analyzing Viewpoints**   United States law prohibits "industrial espionage," or theft of technology between firms, and the export of certain technologies to foreign countries. Give your opinion of such laws and of Slater's conduct.

Growth in the South and West

Setting the Scene

Section Focus

During this time of industry, ingenuity, and migration, Americans quickly adapted to the changing times. They altered production methods to take advantage of new technology and redefined the westward-moving frontier. In doing so they influenced American life and society for years to come.

Objectives

After studying this section, you should be able to

★ explain how industrialization contributed to wider acceptance of slavery in Southern states.

★ describe the importance of cotton to the South.

★ identify reasons for the rapid growth experienced by the Northwest.

Key Term

cotton gin

◀ COTTON GIN

The effects of the Industrial Revolution were felt in the South even earlier than they were felt in the Northeast. As British cotton mills produced cheaper goods for a worldwide market, they demanded more and more raw cotton. Much of this cotton came from the Southern states. To produce more cotton, Southern planters needed a technological advancement.

■ Plantation Slavery

Before the Industrial Revolution, some Southern planters profited greatly from their use of enslaved people—especially owners of large rice fields and tobacco plantations. Most other planters, however, made little profit from slave labor. Keeping enslaved persons fed and clothed was costly. To prevent them from attempting to run away from the cruel and harsh working conditions, slaveholders had to supervise their workforce continually.

With Eli Whitney's invention of the cotton gin in 1793, however, slave labor was made profitable throughout the South. The **cotton gin,** a machine that cleaned the seeds from the cotton fibers, made it possible to process cotton much more quickly, cheaply, and efficiently than by hand. Now, rather than cleaning 1 pound of cotton per day, a worker could clean 50. If the cotton gin were operated with waterpower, this total was increased to 1,000 pounds a day.

Cotton production proved to be ideally suited to the use of enslaved labor. The planting, hoeing, picking, and ginning all required manual labor, and enslaved persons provided a fairly cheap source. Furthermore, most of the field work was done in groups and could thus be easily supervised. Because the growing and harvesting of cotton continued throughout much of the year in the Deep South, there were no long periods of idleness. Thus, slave labor suddenly became profitable for cotton growers. Between the invention of the cotton gin and the beginning of the Civil War, the number of enslaved persons in the United States more than quintupled, even though enslaved Africans could not be legally imported after 1808, when the slave trade was ended.

■ Cotton Is King

"Cotton is king" was a common Southern phrase that accurately reflected the importance of cotton to the South's economy. Because the South had few factories, cotton continued to be sent out of the region for manufacture. Cotton was the greatest export, especially to Britain, the center of world textile production.

Class Structure

The profound influence of cotton on the South was reflected in the class structure of Southern society. At the top were a few wealthy planters, who enslaved 50 to 200 or more people and cultivated the best land. Below these rich owners was a larger class of less wealthy planters who owned medium-sized farms and usually had fewer than 20 enslaved persons. Then there were the owners of small farms, who made up a large majority of Southern farmers and owned either a few enslaved

▲ ELI WHITNEY

Visualizing History

▲ THE PLANTATION SYSTEM The invention of the cotton gin by Eli Whitney helped make cotton the most important Southern agricultural product. Bountiful cotton harvests, particularly in the newer growing regions of Alabama and Mississippi, were the basis of the South's increasing prosperity. The cultivation of cotton, however, required intensive hand labor. *What tasks in cotton production did enslaved people perform?*

▲ THE WILDERNESS TRAIL The journey across the mountains into the Ohio Valley on roads such as the Wilderness Trail was difficult and often took several weeks. *What was the greatest lure for settlers to the Northwest?*

persons or none at all. Many cotton farmers also raised crops and meat for their own needs and some cash crops, as a way to combat low cotton prices.

Near the bottom of the social scale was a class of impoverished white people, about 1 percent of the white population. They were usually illiterate and did not have regular employment, obtaining food by hunting, raising a few hogs or cows, and farming the exhausted soils for which cotton growers had no use. Seen as lowest on this cotton-created scale were the African Americans. All but a few were enslaved, and nearly all performed heavy labor or menial tasks.

Cotton Production Moves West

To keep up with the demand for raw cotton, cotton plantations sprang up to the west, in the fertile "black belt" (so called for its rich, black soil) of Mississippi and Alabama,

and in the rich bottomlands along the Mississippi River and its tributaries. This westward movement of the cotton crop contributed to the population growth that led to statehood for Mississippi in 1817, for Alabama in 1819, and for Arkansas in 1836.

The rapid movement of cotton production was not just the result of increasing demand. It also came from the movement of plantation owners, who depleted the soil by planting one cotton crop after another in the same location. When the fertility of the soil was exhausted, the planters had to find new land. It was cheaper to migrate than to restore the soil's fertility.

Slavery and the Founding of Liberia

Many Southerners, including Thomas Jefferson, George Washington, and Patrick Henry, publicly condemned slavery. In 1787 many Southerners even supported passage of the Northwest Ordinance, which prohibited slavery north of the Ohio River. This same group advocated the abolition of the slave trade at the earliest date allowed by the Constitution.

Few Southern planters were as enthusiastic about freeing their enslaved workers. Many Southerners feared that if too many African Americans were freed in the South, it would create social and cultural problems. In addition, most did not believe that freed African Americans should have equality with whites. As a result, in 1817 slaveholders in Virginia, Maryland, and Kentucky formed the American Colonization Society, whose purpose was to send freed slaves to Africa, from which continent their ancestors had been forcibly transported.

Members of the society encouraged free African Americans to emigrate. In 1819 Congress appropriated $100,000 to support the project, and in 1822 the society founded the republic of Liberia—"land of freedom"—on the west coast of Africa as a haven for American ex-slaves. However, the society lacked the necessary funds to relocate more than a few thousand people. More important, most African Americans felt that America, not Africa, was their home. One group wrote:

> *This is our home, and this is our country. Beneath its sod lies the bones of our fathers: for it, some of them fought, bled, and died. Here we were born, and here we will die.*

■ Settlement of the Northwest

Because of the hostilities between settlers and Native Americans, settlement of the Northwest had been tentative until the end of the War of 1812. That war resulted in the breakup of Tecumseh's league and put an end to British support of the northern nations. After the defeat of the Sauk (SAWK) leader, Chief Black Hawk, in 1832, the Native Americans were driven west of the Mississippi.

Perhaps the greatest lure of the Northwest was vast, rich, unsettled land. Available land was cheap. Many settlers "squatted" on whatever unoccupied acres they could find. The settlers poured in. From the South came independent farmers and impoverished whites anxious to acquire land and to move to the new frontier. From the Northeast came farmers lured by tales of the fertility of the land. Eventually, Europe supplied a third stream of immigrants, often arriving in New York or Philadelphia and traveling west by the Erie Canal or the Ohio River to the nation's frontier.

■ Growth of Towns

Farmers alone did not develop the West. They needed sawmills for lumber and flour mills for grain, barges and wagons to carry produce to market, merchants to buy it, and storekeepers to provide the goods they could not make themselves. These suppliers gathered in towns where cargo was transferred, such as Cincinnati (where three tributaries flow into the Ohio River) and Louisville (at the falls of the Ohio River).

Life of the Times

Moving West

Rich soil and cheap land drew farmers to the Northwest like a magnet. Between 1800 and 1840, thousands of settlers poured into the region. They came from all sections of the United States—cotton planters from the South, cattle and sheep farmers from New England, grain farmers from Virginia. All were looking for new economic opportunities.

Conestoga wagons, developed by Pennsylvania's German Americans during the colonial era, carried all the family's possessions on their journey west. These sturdy wagons, pulled by yoked oxen, had canvas tops.

Once the pioneers arrived, their survival depended upon the long-handled axe and rifle. With the axe the farmer not only cleared trees from the land but fashioned the wood from those trees into cabins and crude furniture.

A good rifle was essential for people moving West. It was used for defense from enemies—human and otherwise—and for providing game for food. Until the 1840s, the weapon

most settlers chose was the "Kentucky Rifle." With its long barrel, small bore, and accurate sights, a skilled pioneer could split a sapling at 200 yards.

▲ GROWTH OF CITIES Cincinnati, the "Queen City of the West," had become a major transportation and manufacturing center by the 1840s. *What was the major form of commercial travel on the Ohio River during this period?*

Thus, manufacturing began to develop in these cities. At one time Cincinnati's showpiece was a combined flour and textile mill run by steam. This stone and brick mill reached an amazing nine stories high. The West's largest manufacturing center, however, was Pittsburgh. Located at the site where the Allegheny and Monongahela rivers flow into the Ohio River, Pittsburgh had access to the area's mineral resources. Here were glass factories, which in 1815 produced glassware worth $235,000. The entire region derived benefits from Pittsburgh's ironworks.

In Western towns, people could often make more money in manufacturing than they could on the farms. Such skilled workers as masons and wheelwrights were so scarce that they commanded high wages. Manufacturers could charge high prices because of the increasing demand for their articles and because of the cost of transporting products across or around the Appalachians. Western towns offered such prospects of wealth that selling lots in future cities of the West became a standard way for speculators to make money.

Section 2 ★ Review

Checking for Understanding

1. **Identify** Eli Whitney, Northwest Ordinance, American Colonization Society, Liberia.

2. **Define** cotton gin.

3. **Explain** the importance of cotton to the South and its effect on the region's way of life.

4. **Summarize** the reasons for the rapid growth of the Northwest and Western cities.

Critical Thinking

5. **Examining Causes**   In what way did industry and the plantation system encourage settlement in the Northwest?

▲ **COTTON PICKERS BY ETHEL MAGAFAN**

Songs of Slavery

Enslaved African Americans used music to help endure long, tedious hours of forced labor and to relax when they were released from chores. Although slaveholders forbade enslaved Africans from playing horns or drums, for fear that these could be used to send messages about planned rebellions, they were permitted to sing.

One kind of African American music that developed in the early 1800s was the spiritual. Sung in a lively style with strong rhythms and rich harmonies, the spirituals usually express themes of redemption from sin and from slavery and of a better life waiting in the future. Well-known spirituals include "Jacob's Ladder" and "Many a Thousand Gone."

The repertoire of songs African Americans sang was much more extensive than the slaveholders knew. It was not uncommon for African Americans to slip out of their quarters at night for secret meetings. In these secret gatherings, they poked fun at the slaveholders by telling folktales and singing songs such as "They Give Us the Husk."

They Give Us the Husk
We raise the wheat,
They give us the corn;
We bake the bread,
They give us the crust;
We sift the meal,
They give us the husk;
We peel the meat,
They give us the skin;
And that's the way
They take us in.

Making the Music Connection

1. Identify the "we" and "they" in this song.

2. What response might enslaved persons make to the idea that the slaveholders cared for them? Why do you think this is the case?

Linking Past and Present

3. How might workers today protest unfair treatment?

★★

Rivalry and Compromise

Setting the Scene

Section Focus

The issue of the expansion of slavery was only one factor that threatened the nation's unity. Despite these threats, leaders of the United States struggled to cooperate, and "compromise" became part of the national vocabulary.

Objectives

After studying this section, you should be able to

★ identify four areas of sectional conflict.

★ explain how the Missouri Compromise temporarily maintained a balance between slave states and free states.

★ explain how John Quincy Adams won the 1824 presidential election.

Key Term

favorite son

◀ PREPARING FOR MARKET

Given the physical differences between the regions of the United States—the harsh and unforgiving land of certain areas of the Northeast; the warm, fertile Southern region; and the forests and mountains of the West—it is not surprising that Americans in these regions had different concerns and reacted differently to important issues. How to apportion public lands, how to protect American products, how to improve life in the United States, and what to do about slavery were questions whose resolutions would affect each region differently.

■ Points of Conflict

Political leaders were the ones who assumed the task of finding compromises to smooth over the sectional differences that threatened the Union. One of the issues they tackled was public land policy. Should land be offered to settlers at a low price or a high one? Should land be opened for settlement rapidly or slowly? Should squatters, who had occupied lands before they were opened for sale, have any rights to the lands they farmed?

Each region of the nation had different answers to these questions. Western frontier farmers naturally favored cheap land, rapid settlement, and "squatters' rights." Eastern manufacturers, on the other hand, opposed such policies for fear the West would draw off their labor supply. Eastern farmers believed that cheap Western lands would result in unfair competition.

Southerners were divided on this issue. Plantation owners wanted lands opened for sale but opposed "squatters' rights" because the squatters might claim the best lands.

Protective Tariffs

Another caustic issue was protective tariffs. Should there be high tariffs to protect United States industries? Should tariffs be kept low to allow foreign goods to come into the country cheaply? Northeastern manufacturers and laborers naturally favored protective tariffs to ensure that their factories could compete successfully with foreign manufacturers. As Southerners came to realize that their region would not become a manufacturing center, they became opposed to the system of protection. High tariffs caused them to pay more for imported manufactured goods.

Surprisingly, the Northwest, a farming region, was the section most completely in favor of protection. This was because they thought that the growth of industrial cities would increase the market for farm products. In addition, Westerners believed that protection might encourage manufacturing west of the Appalachians; revenue from the tariffs could then be used for building needed roads and canals.

Money was at the core of arguments over internal improvements. Should the federal government spend money to build roads and canals or at least help states and private companies to build them? The West was overwhelmingly in favor of using federal money for such purposes because it needed roads and canals to get its goods to market. The South, with a fine river system for transportation, was opposed. The Northeast generally favored internal improvements, partly because tariffs would be required to pay for them.

The Issue of Slavery

Among all the issues, the extension of slavery into territories seemed to raise the most feverish emotion. Should the territories be closed to slavery following the precedent set in the Northwest Ordinance? Because cotton production demanded the movement of plantations onto new lands and the plantation system depended on slave labor, Southerners insisted that they be allowed to take their enslaved workers with them anywhere but into the free states.

In the Northern and Western states, which were not economically dependent on the slave system, there was an increasing conviction that slavery was a moral wrong. While conceding that Southern states had a right to maintain slavery where it already existed, Northerners protested it should not be allowed to be extended to the territories. To Southerners, this meant that no new slave states could be formed, and the political power of the South would decrease.

▼ Iron Ladles

Visualizing History

▲ The Tariff Question   Generally, Northeastern manufacturers and laborers favored protective tariffs while Southerners did not. *Why did the people of the Northwest support tariffs?*

Missouri Compromise Line (36°30´N)

MISSOURI

PACIFIC OCEAN

ATLANTIC OCEAN

Free states
Free territories
Slave states
Slave territories
Non-United States territory

0   200   400 miles
0 200 400 kilometers

Map Study

The Missouri Compromise was an attempt to resolve the question of slavery in the western territories. *What boundary did the 36°30´ parallel form?*

The Missouri Compromise

The question of the expansion of slavery became politically controversial in 1819 when Missouri applied for admission to the Union as a slave state. As soon as the bill reached the floor of Congress, Representative James Tallmadge of New York proposed an amendment that would gradually abolish slavery in Missouri and forbid future importation of slaves into the state. His amendment stated, in part:

> *. . . That the further introduction of slavery or involuntary servitude be prohibited . . . and that all children of slaves, born within the said state . . . shall be free. . . .*

Reaching a Compromise

The Tallmadge Amendment would gradually end slavery in an area where it already existed. A new twist to the debate was introduced when Maine petitioned to be separated from Massachusetts and admitted to the Union as a free state. At this time slave and nonslave states were evenly represented in the Senate, although the North's population gave it a majority in the House of Representatives. If Missouri alone were admitted, the slave states would enjoy an important advantage in the Senate. However, if Maine were admitted as a free state at the same time, the balance would remain unchanged.

As a compromise, Missouri and Maine were admitted together. In the unsettled portions of the Louisiana Purchase, slavery would be forbidden north of the parallel 36° 30', a line running west from the southern boundary of Missouri.

The Spread of Slavery

This solution gave Southerners their immediate goal—the admission of Missouri as a slave state. The area closed to the future expansion of slavery was still far greater than the area potentially open to slaveholders. The South allowed the North this advantage partly because of a widely held belief that the prairie region west of the Mississippi River was unfit for human settlement. When Southerners realized that this region was not "a great American desert," they began to demand changes in the provisions of the Missouri Compromise.

The Election of 1824

The four candidates who ran for President in 1824 were **favorite sons**—candidates supported by the political leaders from their own state and region. Two of the candidates, Henry Clay of Kentucky and Andrew Jackson of Tennessee, were from the West. John Quincy Adams of Massachusetts received his strongest support from New England, while William Crawford of Georgia represented the South. John C. Calhoun of South Carolina withdrew from the race early and ran for the vice presidency, which he easily won.

Only one-fourth of the electorate bothered to vote. When the results were tallied,

Jackson had received a plurality of the popular vote, but he did not have a majority in the electoral college. Here he led with 99 votes, followed by Adams with 84. Crawford and Clay were far in the rear with 41 and 37, respectively.

The House Votes

In such situations, the Twelfth Amendment to the Constitution provides that the President is to be chosen by the House of Representatives, each state having one vote. The state delegations are to select the President from the three candidates with the highest number of electoral votes.

Clay was eliminated because he had placed fourth. Crawford was President Monroe's favorite, but illness took him out of the running. The choice was between Jackson and Adams. As speaker of the house, Clay was in a position to swing the election either way. Not wanting to aid the fortunes of a rival Westerner, he threw his support to Adams. Adams easily won on the first ballot,

▲ JOHN CALHOUN

which was taken February 9, 1825. Clay was even able to convince his own Kentucky delegation—under clear instructions from the state legislature to support Jackson—to

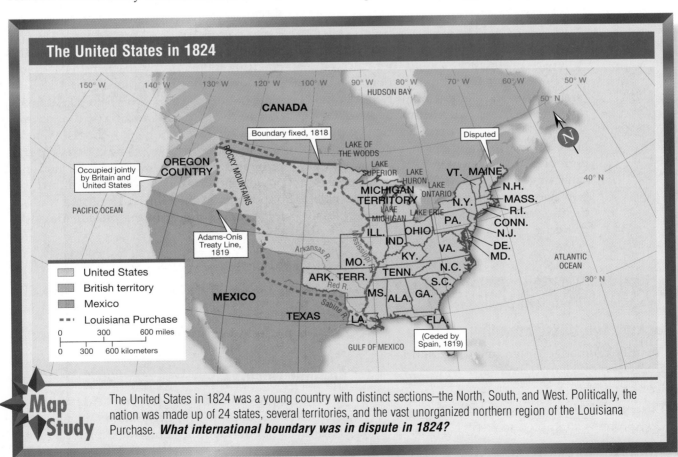

The United States in 1824

Map Study

The United States in 1824 was a young country with distinct sections—the North, South, and West. Politically, the nation was made up of 24 states, several territories, and the vast unorganized northern region of the Louisiana Purchase. *What international boundary was in dispute in 1824?*

switch their vote. The tally was 13 states for Adams against only 7 for Jackson and 4 for Crawford.

Charges of a "Corrupt Bargain"

The new President named Clay his secretary of state, a position then considered to be an important stepping-stone to the presidency. An anonymous letter to the newspapers charged that Clay was given the job as the result of a "corrupt bargain." The story claimed that Adams had promised to make Clay secretary of state in return for his leverage over key votes in the House of Representatives. Adams, a devoutly religious man, protested his innocence, as did Clay. Their denials, however, failed to remove suspicion. For the next three years, critics of the Adams administration repeated the cry of the "bargain and corruption" that had betrayed the will of the people.

■ Adams in the White House

Jackson supporters were determined that Adams's presidency should not succeed, and throughout his administration the differences among Jeffersonian Republicans deepened. Those who supported Adams and Clay became known as National Republicans. They generally favored a strong role for federal government in funding roads and canals and other national projects. In opposition were the Jacksonians, soon to call themselves Democrats, who favored a less powerful government.

 Visualizing History ▲ JOHN QUINCY ADAMS By the time of his election in 1824, John Quincy Adams was already an established figure in American political life. *Why was Adams's presidency not a successful one?*

Although Adams could have strengthened his following by discharging Jackson supporters from federal jobs, he refused to play politics on his own behalf. Adams's own code of ethics also prevented him from answering his opponents' criticisms publicly. Because of this, his ambitious federal programs received little support, and his power as President was neutralized by opponents in the House. The stage was set for Adams's defeat in the presidential election of 1828.

Section 3 ★ Review

Checking for Understanding

1. **Identify** Tallmadge Amendment, Missouri Compromise, Henry Clay.
2. **Define** favorite son.
3. **Describe** the sectional conflict the Missouri Compromise attempted to resolve.

4. **Explain** why Adams was accused of a "corrupt bargain" with Henry Clay.

Critical Thinking

5. **Predicting Outcomes** Do you think Adams would have become President had sectional conflicts not divided the country? Explain.

Study and Writing Skills

Using Reference Works in Research

Standard reference works are general encyclopedias, biographical dictionaries, periodical guides, books of quotations, atlases, and almanacs. These are found in the reference section of the library.

General encyclopedias are sets of books that contain relatively short articles on many subjects. Because encyclopedia reading levels and the amount of detail in content coverage vary, check several to see which is the most appropriate for you.

Biographical dictionaries offer condensed biographies of famous individuals. They are useful when you need more information than an encyclopedia provides, but less than a full biography or autobiography.

Periodical guides help you find articles in magazines and newspapers. Articles are indexed by subject or by the author's last name. Under a subject heading the entry will contain the title of the article; author name(s); and the title of the publication, date, and page number(s). Periodical guides are especially helpful when you need to have current information.

Books of quotations contain statements by individuals. Quotations may be arranged by the author's last name or by subject. Make it a habit to use quotations to support your main ideas and "add color" to your writing.

Atlases contain maps and charts, and *almanacs* contain statistics. Each also includes additional data that may give supporting evidence for your report. If the report is to contain illustrations, atlases and almanacs may provide ideas or suggestions.

A term paper has been assigned, and you decide to research the presidency of John Quincy Adams. For a report on John Quincy Adams, follow these steps:

- **Check** several encyclopedias to see which one has the appropriate reading level and best coverage of Adams.
- **Locate** and read about Adams in a biographical dictionary. Does the material add to what was in the encyclopedia?
- **Look up** "Adams, John Q." in a periodical guide under "Subjects." With the assistance of a librarian, obtain the periodicals listed.
- **Locate** books of quotations, and scan the index for quotes by Adams. Read them and decide if any could be used in your report.
- **Check** atlases and almanacs on United States history or United States Presidents for illustrations or maps pertaining to Adams's administration.

Practicing the Skill

For further practice, make a list of the titles of all the reference works in your school library that you could use to complete a report on Samuel Slater and the early American textile industry.

Using Vocabulary

Use each vocabulary word in a sentence about the Industrial Revolution or its effect on sectional conflict.

closed shop   favorite sons
cotton gin   mechanics' lien law
emigration   textile

Reviewing Facts

1. **Compare** the effects of the Industrial Revolution on different sections.

2. **Describe** the conditions that organized workers tried to change and what limited their success.

3. **List** four issues on which the sections had major differences.

4. **Identify** factors that led to the rapid development of the Northwest.

5. **Explain** why "Cotton [was] King" in the South.

6. **Name** the plan that temporarily resolved sectional conflict over slavery.

7. **State** why the Tallmadge Amendment angered Southerners.

8. **Summarize** the events that brought John Q. Adams to the presidency.

Understanding Concepts

Free Enterprise

1. What were some of the abuses of the free enterprise system that factory workers experienced? In what way did the government and citizens address these abuses?

Economic and Cultural Change

2. What factors caused a shift from small-scale production by independent workers to large-scale production in factories owned by a few capitalists?

Critical Thinking

1. **Making Comparisons** Compare the capitalist factory system and the plantation system with the class structures they created and related human rights issues.

2. **Analyzing Art** Study the illustration on this page and answer the questions that follow.

   a. What kind of work are the individuals doing?

   b. Do you think this is a realistic portrayal? Explain.

▼ WORKING AT HOME

Writing About History

Description

Imagine it is 1800. You have moved to the city to work in a factory or textile mill. Write a letter to your family on the farm, describing something they have not seen, such as a spinning frame, a factory, a tenement, or the city.

Cooperative Learning

Working in a group of three, research the current status of NAFTA and GATT. Examine the arguments that put these policies into effect and point out any criticisms. Choose a spokesperson to share your findings with other groups.

Social Studies Skills

Analyzing Tabular Data

Analyzing involves breaking information into smaller pieces so that it can be examined more easily. Information presented in tables, or tabular data, can often help you analyze information because tables summarize a large amount of information in a small space. Tabular data is presented in rows and columns to make it easy to read.

Practicing the Skill

Use the tables on this page and your understanding of Chapter 10 content to answer the two questions that follow.

1. How did Adams succeed in winning the presidency in 1824?

2. How could Clay have received more popular votes but fewer electoral votes than Crawford?

3. Why did the industrial labor force grow more rapidly between 1800 and 1830 than did slave labor?

4. How many laborers worked on farms by 1810? How many laborers performed industrial work by 1820?

Growth of the Labor Force (In Thousands)				
Year	Free	Slave	Farm	Industrial
1800	1,370	530	1,400	1
1810	1,590	740	1,950	15
1820	2,185	950	2,470	17
1830	3,020	1,180	2,965	75

Election of 1824			
Candidate	Electoral Vote	Popular Vote	House Vote
Jackson	99	153,544	7
Adams	84	108,740	13
Crawford	41	46,618	4
Clay	37	47,136	—

Using Your Journal

Controversy still exists over tariffs and other legislation to protect American industry from foreign competition. In a paragraph, discuss how such measures affect American consumers and workers.

CHAPTER 11

★★★

Age of Jackson
1828–1842

► **CHEROKEE LEADER BLACK COAT**

Setting the Scene

Focus

Andrew Jackson's victory in the election of 1828 marked the beginning of a new era. His election symbolized the growth of popular democracy, and Jackson himself became a symbol for the age. Although a Westerner, he fought sectionalism by insisting upon the supremacy of federal laws over the states. He also fought economic injustice and social inequality. Jackson's political movement resulted in the formation of the Democratic party and also an opposition party, the Whigs.

Concepts to Understand

★ How political change in state voting laws advanced democracy

★ How economic policy shaped controversies over the tariff and the national banking system

Read to Discover . . .

★ in what ways Andrew Jackson was a symbol of his times.

★ how Jackson's nationalism was shown during the nullification crisis and his war on the national bank.

Journal Notes

What kind of campaigns did political parties wage against presidential candidates of the opposing party? Jot down the information in your journal.

CULTURAL

● **1828** Cherokee Phoenix, *first news-paper in a Native American language, published*

● **1830** *Church of Jesus Christ of Latter-day Saints (Mormons) organized in New York*

1825 | **1830**

POLITICAL

● **1825** *Democratic Republican and National Republican parties emerge*
● **1828** *Andrew Jackson elected*

● **1830** *Webster debates Hayne*
● **1832** *South Carolina adopts Nullification Ordinance*

◄ PORCELAIN DOLL

History AND ART

Stump Speaking
by George Caleb Bingham, 1854–1855

Bingham's series of election paintings expresses faith in the democratic process. For nearly five years, the artist devoted his talent to illustrating the human aspect of the political process.

● **1837** *Nathaniel Hawthorne publishes Twice-Told Tales*

● **1842** American Agriculturalist *first published*

1835

1840

● **1836** *Bank of the United States charter expires*
● **1837** *Worldwide economic depression strikes*

● **1840** *Whigs nominate Harrison*

★★

Growth of Democracy

Setting the Scene

Section Focus

Although sectional rivalries overshadowed the national spirit and proved divisive during John Quincy Adams's presidency, a powerful force was rising that would influence American politics more than sectionalism or nationalism. The spirit of democracy soon would significantly influence voters, election rules, and government decisions. The presidency of Andrew Jackson would give this spirit momentum and would itself be carried along by democracy's swelling tide.

Objectives

After studying this section, you should be able to

★ describe campaign methods used by both political parties in the election of 1828.

★ summarize the life and political career of Andrew Jackson.

Key Term

mudslinging

▶ ANDREW JACKSON'S DUELING PISTOLS

*W*ell before the presidential election of 1828, it was clear that President John Quincy Adams and challenger Andrew Jackson would be the only candidates. Without much help from the President, Adams's supporters had built a loosely organized following, primarily in the Northeast. They tended to represent established property interests and favored nationalist legislation. Jackson's supporters, on the other hand, included farmers of the South and West, skilled workers, and owners of small businesses. Like the Republican party of Jefferson's time, Jacksonians favored limiting federal power. The Adams supporters called themselves National Republicans in order to emphasize the President's commitment to a national program. Jacksonians took the name Democratic Republicans, or simply Democrats, to stress their ties to the common people.

■ The Election of 1828

The United States in the 1820s was undergoing rapid change. Conflicting sectional interests and a shifting population made political forecasts difficult. In this environment both political parties decided not to risk the presidential election of 1828 by taking a strong position on any issue. Instead, they focused on comparisons of the candidates' personal traits.

A Mudslinging Campaign

The electioneering soon turned to **mudslinging**, making malicious, often untrue, charges against an opponent. The National Republicans portrayed Jackson as a barbarian who "misspelled every fourth word," a Julius Caesar who would destroy American liberties, and a "butcher" who had murdered a number of people. The Democrats revived the "bargain and corruption" smear from the 1824 election. They went on to charge that Adams had allowed the federal civil service to become scandalously dishonest and had wasted the people's money on "gaming tables"—actually a billiard table and a chess set bought with Adams's own money for the White House. Adams's backers went so far as to accuse Jackson of adultery based on a technicality concerning his wife's divorce from a former husband years earlier. Rachel Jackson suffered terribly from this attack and died shortly after the election—a tragedy for which Jackson never forgave the slanderers.

While both parties were equally adept at misrepresentation, the Democrats found an advantage in their candidate's humble beginnings. Democratic newspapers began to call Andrew Jackson "the candidate of the people."

"The Candidate of the People" Wins

The election of 1828 was a decisive victory for Jackson—178 electoral votes to 83. Adams was strong only in New England. Jackson swept nearly every Southern and Western state and carried Pennsylvania and New York.

Although the campaign was a national disgrace, the election was one of the most significant in American history. For the first time, a candidate from the region west of the Appalachians was elected President. The rapid growth of the Western states was swinging the political center of gravity away from the Eastern seaboard. The results also showed the developing political split between the nation's sections.

New Voters

Three times as many people voted for President in 1828 as had in 1824. This was partly because many states had lowered or eliminated property ownership as a voting qualification and also because twice as many eligible voters participated. Many reasons have been given for the elimination of property ownership as a qualification for voting in the early 1800s, including the ideals of the Declaration of Independence and the social equality of frontier life. In addition, as cities and towns grew, the percentage of working people who did not own property increased. These people paid taxes and had an interest in the political affairs of their communities. By the 1820s Pennsylvania, Massachusetts, and New York recognized this interest and substituted the payment of taxes for property ownership as a basis for voting rights. By 1852 the last state, Virginia, had given the franchise to all adult white males.

Andrew Jackson's victory in 1828 was partly the result of his party's appeal to the new voters. Jackson's supporters believed that he represented the "common man." All former Presidents had enjoyed the advantages of inherited wealth or education or both. Jackson, orphaned at 14, had made his way entirely on his own. He became the symbol of the growing power of democracy.

 ▲ KING ANDREW His supporters viewed Jackson as a strong President who represented the common people. Critics denounced him as a would-be tyrant. They called him "King Andrew the First," and he is shown in this cartoon trampling on the Constitution and ruling by veto. *What was significant about the election of 1828?*

Getting Out the Vote

The election of Andrew Jackson in 1828 signaled a new era in politics. Property-holding qualifications for voting had been gradually abolished by the states, which extended the franchise to most adult white males. With this increase in voters, political party organizations and candidates soon learned to make appeals tailored for mass audiences.

Candidates and political parties participated in every kind of community gathering. Political rallies featuring parades, flags, speeches, and free-flowing liquor became hallmarks of electioneering.

The potential for vote fraud was everywhere. The polls might be open for several days, which made it easier for enterprising voters to cast more than one ballot. None of the states used a secret ballot. Rather, parties printed their own ballots, or "tickets" with the names of candidates. Voters going to the polls might be harassed by high-pressure ballot hawkers from rival parties into accepting their ticket.

State nominating conventions also encouraged participation in elections. Convention proceedings were reported in the local press, which aroused citizens to work for their party's choices.

★★

▶ **ANDREW JACKSON ON HORSEBACK**

Andrew Jackson was such a controversial figure that it is difficult to find the truth between the slander of his enemies and the praise of his admirers. According to James Parton, his first important biographer, the evidence could be interpreted to show Jackson as either a patriot or a traitor:

❝ *He was one of the greatest of generals and wholly ignorant of the art of war. A writer, brilliant, elegant, eloquent, without being able to compose a correct sentence or spell words of four syllables. . . . A democratic autocrat. An urbane savage. An atrocious saint.* ❞

■ A Symbol of His Times

Born in a log cabin on the North Carolina frontier, Jackson rose to the highest office—visible evidence of the American success story. In his time Jackson became almost a mythical figure. George Bancroft, a New Englander and an ardent Democrat, wrote:

❝ *Behold, then, the unlettered man of the West, the nursling of the wilds, the farmer of the Hermitage, little versed in books, unconnected by science with the tradition of the past, raised by the will of the people to the highest pinnacle of honor, to the central post of republican freedom, to the station where all the nations of the earth would watch his actions—where his words would vibrate through the civilized world, and his spirit be the moving-star to guide the nations.* ❞

Jackson's Early Career

Jackson was elected Tennessee's first representative to Congress before the age of 30. In the War of 1812, he had been one of the few generals who could get ill-trained militia to stand up to the British redcoats. His most obvious trait was his force of will, a characteristic that became evident when someone tried to defy him.

Jackson's early life was notable for violent personal quarrels. He took part in five duels, once killing a man. From that encounter, a bullet that lodged next to his heart remained with him for the rest of his life, surgeons believing it too dangerous to risk removing. As Jackson grew older, his temper and actions became milder.

The Inauguration

As the time for Jackson's inauguration approached, his supporters poured into Washington, D.C. Men slept five or six in a room; when no more beds were available, they spent the night on sofas, billiard tables, and floors. John Quincy Adams left the city rather than attend the ceremony that Jackson's detractors thought could mean the end of the republic. A typical reaction was that of Daniel Webster, senator from Massachusetts:

> **Nobody knows what he will do when he does come. . . . My fear is stronger than my hope.**

Jackson followed Jefferson's precedent of walking to the inaugural ceremony. His hands shook as he read a rather cautious and colorless Inaugural Address. What happened later, however, seemed to justify those who had gloomily predicted that Jackson's election would mean the reign of "King Mob." From the Capitol, he rode on horseback to the White House surrounded by a cheering crowd. There, a reception had been prepared only for invited guests and officials. There were no means, however, to prevent the crowd from pushing in. Chairs and china were broken; several people fainted. The crowd pressing around Jackson was so great that he had to be helped to escape through a back window.

"A Gentleman and a Soldier"

By the time Jackson reached the White House, he had become a person of dignity and courtesy. A visiting Englishwoman at his inauguration said he looked like "a gentleman and a soldier."

Jackson surely did not have the training or education that Thomas Jefferson or John Quincy Adams had. In addition, his political opinions were sometimes vague and continually changing. Yet when questions came to him for decision, he showed quick and firm judgment.

Like Washington, he often sought advice from several sources, and as President, he had a group of personal friends, called by his enemies the "kitchen cabinet," who advised him on all major decisions. "The character of his mind," wrote his friend Senator Thomas H. Benton of Missouri, "was that of judgment, with a rapid and almost intuitive perception, followed by instant and decisive action."

Entering office at age 62, Jackson was tortured by several physical agonies. He suffered from headaches, digestive disorders, coughing spells, and old wounds. His wife Rachel's death before the inauguration in 1829 added bereavement and loneliness. Still, his inner toughness enabled him to perform the duties of the office with a firm and steady hand.

Section 1 ★ Review

Checking for Understanding

1. **Identify** National Republicans, Democratic Republicans.
2. **Define** mudslinging.
3. **Describe** the central focus of the 1828 election.
4. **Explain** why the campaigning parties chose not to take positions on the issues.

Critical Thinking

5. **Analyzing Results** How might changes during the Industrial Revolution have become factors in the extension of voting privileges?

Interpreting Primary Sources

▲ PIGEON'S EGG HEAD GOING TO AND RETURNING FROM WASHINGTON BY GEORGE CATLIN, 1832

The Light

A self-taught artist, George Catlin (1796–1872) devoted his life to documenting the history and culture of Native Americans through the art of painting. Catlin moved westward from Pennsylvania in 1830 and became the first painter to shape the national image of the proud Plains peoples. During the mid-1830s, Catlin spent several summers among various Native American peoples. He saw and recorded with his brush the earthen lodge villages of the Pawnee, the scalp dance of the Sioux, and the practices of Blackfoot medicine men. He was so accurate and detailed in his paintings that descendants of those he immortalized easily recognized their ancestors.

By 1840 Catlin had made almost 500 portraits and sketches. He established Catlin's Indian Gallery, a traveling exhibition of paintings, costumes, and artifacts that toured major cities in Great Britain and France as well as the United States. During the 1850s Catlin traveled to South America and to the Pacific coast of North America and recorded the appearances, surroundings, and ways of life of the Native Americans of these regions. Many of the paintings Catlin produced can be viewed in the Smithsonian Institution in Washington, D.C., and in the American Museum of Natural History in New York.

The two-pose painting shown here is of Wi-jun-jon, or Pigeon's Egg Head—also known as The Light—the son of an Assiniboin chief, whom Catlin painted in 1832. The Assiniboin lived on the northern Plains and were distant relatives of the Dakota Sioux. Wi-jun-jon was part of a delegation of Plains peoples who, in 1831, traveled to Washington, D.C., where they met with President Jackson.

Catlin shows Wi-jun-jon resplendent in Native American dress upon his arrival in Washington and ridiculous in a colonel's uniform (a gift from the President) on his way back to his people. The Assiniboin barely recognized Wi-jun-jon when he arrived and dismissed his stories of the life he had seen in Washington as preposterous lies. Once respected by his people, The Light lost his credibility while in the white man's land.

Examining the Primary Source

1. Compare the clothing, accessories, and posture in each pose.

2. Identify and explain the significance of the scenery that The Light faces in each pose.

Critical Thinking

3. **Identifying Central Issues** What point does the artist make by showing back-to-back poses?

★★

Jacksonian Democracy

Setting the Scene

Section Focus

While Jackson's name is used to describe this period of American history, American democracy in these years had much broader sources than the character of the President. Jacksonian democracy is also defined by the political optimism of his time. It was a period of celebration for the rights of the "common man."

Objectives

After studying this section, you should be able to

★ list three democratic changes that developed during this period.

★ describe attitudes toward Native Americans and African Americans during this period.

Key Terms

spoils system, pocket veto

◀ BLACK HAWK, SAC AND FOX LEADER

During the administration of Andrew Jackson, the United States was a nation of change, a nation on the move—socially and economically as well as politically. American society was viewed as a society of opportunity. Americans felt that, given a chance, they could make a better life for themselves. This was the era of the common people, and Andrew Jackson appealed to the American people because he stood for values that many regarded with favor.

■ The People's Government

Before Jackson's time, voters expected public officials to use their own best judgment. Now they came to believe that officials should act according to the demands of the people. To make government respond more directly to popular will, state and local governments began to fill some positions such as judges, constables, and public surveyors by election rather than appointment. The terms of office were also shortened so that popular opinion had a more direct effect on the actions of elected officials.

The Spoils System

As new voters made demands on government, they learned the power of political organization. National issues became as much topics of conversation as local issues had always been. As national parties built stronger state and local ties, they began to rely upon a growing number of professional or career politicians. These changes helped to initiate the **spoils system,** the practice of appointing people to government positions on the basis of party loyalty and party service. This was not an entirely new development, but Jackson was the first to oust large numbers of government employees in order to appoint his followers to office. He argued that there should be rotation in office—a point he emphasized in his first State of the Union message:

" *The duties of all public officers are . . . so plain and simple that men of intelligence may readily qualify themselves for their performance; and I cannot but believe that more is lost by the long continuance of men in office than is generally to be gained by their experience.* "

Some believed that the spoils system set a poor precedent. A contemporary observer not unfriendly to Jackson noted that "office-seeking and office-getting was becoming a regular business, where impudence [boldness] triumphed over worth." Jackson amplified presidential power by using the veto more than all previous Presidents. He was also one of the first Presidents to use the **pocket veto**, killing a bill by taking no action on it and waiting for Congress to adjourn.

Removal of Native Americans, 1820–1840

Lands ceded by Native Americans
Native American reservations
← Cherokee Trail of Tears
← Migration route

0   100   200 miles
0   100 200 kilometers

Map Study The federal government relocated Native Americans living in the United States to reservations in Indian Territory. *Identify the peoples that were removed according to the map.*

Sequoya
1760(?)–1843

Although he was the son of a white trader, Sequoya was raised among his mother's Cherokee people. He never learned English, but he was fascinated by the "talking leaves" of books.

Sequoya was convinced that reading and writing gave whites power. After being disabled by an accident, he dedicated himself to creating written symbols for the Cherokee language. At first, Sequoya tried to create simple pictures to represent Cherokee words, but later he developed 86 symbols to represent all syllables in Cherokee speech. He then had his six-year-old daughter demonstrate his system of reading and writing to Cherokee leaders.

Following their approval of his system, thousands of the Cherokee learned how to read and write. Sequoya even published a Cherokee newspaper and translated parts of the Bible into Cherokee.

Some Gains for Women

Jacksonian democracy did not offer women suffrage, but women did make some gains. Emma Willard, Catharine Beecher, and Mary Lyon established female academies promoting education among women. During the 1830s some states passed the first women's property acts, guaranteeing women the right to control property.

■ Minorities

Whereas women made some strides under Jackson's presidency, Native Americans and African Americans did not. Jacksonian democracy had nothing to offer these two oppressed minorities.

Removal

Most Americans believed that the area between the Missouri River and the Rocky Mountains, "the Great American Desert," would provide a permanent Native American reservation. Jackson and, later, President Van Buren spoke of protecting the Native Americans from fraud and of how humane the government's removal policy was, but the policy as carried out was cruel.

The Cherokee

In Georgia the Cherokee had developed a lifestyle that included schools, mills, and turnpikes. In the 1820s, under pressure from the state to give up their lands, they wrote a constitution, hired lawyers, and sued in the Supreme Court. Chief Justice John Marshall upheld the rights of the Cherokee against Georgia. However, Jackson refused to carry out the decision that ordered Georgia to return Cherokee lands. "Marshall has made his opinion," he reportedly said, "now let him enforce it."

When the Cherokee resisted the government's "generous" offer of lands farther west, Jackson sent in the army. Forced to move from their homes to what is now Arkansas and Oklahoma, an estimated 4,000 died of starvation, disease, or exposure on the march that the Cherokee called the "Trail of Tears."

Mistreatment Continues

Another tragedy took place in Illinois. The Sac and Fox people were forced to move to Iowa, where the Sioux and the settlers harassed them. In 1832 Black Hawk, the leader of the Sac and Fox, moved them back into Illinois to recover their lands. When

▲ THE TRAIL OF TEARS Native Americans who were forced from their land traveled west in the 1830s. *Why did the Cherokee call the forced march from their land the "Trail of Tears"?*

farmers in Illinois panicked, the state militia massacred Black Hawk's entire group.

By 1840 the government had moved the few Native Americans still living east of the Mississippi to reservations, except for the Seminoles of Florida. After years of fighting, Osceola, their chief, was captured and later died in prison. Some Seminoles settled deep in the Everglades.

Although most citizens supported Jackson's Native American removals, a few leaders, like Henry Clay, said that Jackson's attitude stained the nation's honor. Religious denominations, especially Methodists and Quakers, also denounced the harsh treatment of Native Americans, but these voices were a small minority.

"The Great Silence"

In the 1830s the cotton culture in the South had firmly established the institution of slavery, and criticism of the system became increasingly unwise. Those who spoke out against slavery risked physical harm. In the North, African Americans were free, but they were generally second-class citizens.

The debates of the 1820s leading to the Missouri Compromise had shown the slavery issue to be so explosive that a policy called "the great silence" began, and discussion of slavery as a national issue faded. Antislavery literature was often barred from the mails. From 1836 to 1844, antislavery petitions to Congress were ignored.

Section 2 ★ Review

Checking for Understanding

1. **Identify** John Marshall, the Trail of Tears, Black Hawk, Osceola.

2. **Define** spoils system, pocket veto.

3. **Summarize** the political changes that took place in the United States during the Jacksonian period.

4. **Compare** the fates of African Americans and Native Americans during this era.

Critical Thinking

5. **Evaluating Leadership** In what way did the Jackson administration violate the constitutional system of checks and balances?

★★

Political Controversies

Setting the Scene

Section Focus

Although Andrew Jackson was the people's President, Americans in 1828 had diverse interests. Westerners believed that Jackson would favor internal improvements and curb the power of the Bank of the United States while inflating the currency. Southern Democrats began to oppose high tariffs and national spending on internal improvements. The Northeastern wing of the party was split on the tariff issue but strongly opposed inflationary money policies. It was a setting ripe for conflict that would test Jackson's leadership.

Objectives

After studying this section, you should be able to

★ identify the various sectional interests of the nation in this period.

★ explain how the tariff and nullification issue developed into a crisis.

Key Terms

nullification, compact

▶ **ANTI-JACKSON IMAGE**

Both supporters and opponents were interested in President Jackson's position on such matters as internal improvements, the question of tariffs, and banking. In his first term of office, Jackson made bold decisions on these issues—sometimes delighting, sometimes dismaying, members of his own Democratic party.

Jackson surprised the West with his answer to the issue of federally financed roads. Congress had passed a bill promising to pay for half the cost of extending the Cumberland Road inside the state of Kentucky. This legislation, known as the Maysville Road Bill, was vetoed by Jackson. He said that the Constitution did not grant the federal government power to spend money on local transportation—the road was to be

entirely inside one state. In his veto message he explained that grants of federal money

> " ... [h]ave always been professedly under the control of the general principle that the works which might be thus aided should be 'of a general, not local; national, not state,' character. A disregard of that distinction would of necessity lead to the subversion of the federal system. "

While Westerners were dismayed at Jackson's decision, the veto pleased Southerners, who opposed federal support of internal improvements. The veto demonstrated that although Jackson was a strong nationalist, he also believed in a strict interpretation of the Constitution. The fact that the proposed extension was to be inside the home state of Henry Clay, Jackson's chief political adversary, probably influenced his strict interpretation of the Constitution.

■ Sectional Issues

The Northeast and the West were divided over federal land policy. Senator Samuel A. Foot of Connecticut represented Eastern manufacturers who were worried about losing their labor supply. In 1830 he proposed a limit on Western land sales to discourage people from moving west. Senator Thomas Hart Benton of Missouri angrily attacked Foot for promoting the interests of the Northeast at the expense of the West. Senator Robert Y. Hayne of South Carolina supported Benton. In several days of debate, senators from both the South and the Northeast attempted to win the support of Western politicians. With Vice President Calhoun of

South Carolina presiding, Hayne and Daniel Webster of Massachusetts eventually engaged in a full-scale discussion of many of the issues.

Webster and Calhoun

Webster's political career followed a course exactly opposite Calhoun's. Calhoun had been a War Hawk during the War of 1812. Webster had opposed the war, even to the extent of considering **nullification**, or making null and void federal laws calling for raising troops. When Calhoun supported nationalist legislation after the war, Webster supported the Northeast. By 1830, however, the two had reversed positions. To preserve his political future in South Carolina, Calhoun changed his views. South Carolina was suffering from low cotton prices and a depressed economy. Calhoun could no longer support high tariffs because the people of his home state believed that high tariffs were a cause of their local economic

▲ STATES' RIGHTS OR UNION During the Webster-Hayne debate in the Senate, Daniel Webster argued that the Union was a national government of all people in all states, and if it passed laws that infringed on the rights of the states, the Supreme Court would declare the laws unconstitutional. *What was Robert Hayne's major argument?*

problems. Opposing the tariff, Calhoun became a states' rights advocate, while Webster's support for a protective tariff made him favor a strong federal government.

In a "Second Reply to Hayne," Webster pointed out that nullification could only mean the end of the Union. Webster said the Union was not a creature of the states: it was the people's government, forged for their own welfare and meant to endure.

The greatness of Webster's speech lay in his use of American patriotism to support the idea of a Constitution flexible enough to meet the needs of a growing country. His audience was not so much the Senate as the people at large.

Thousands of copies of the speech were published. Schoolchildren memorized the closing paragraph with the famous final words: "Liberty and Union, now and forever, one and inseparable!"

The antitariff forces rallied around Calhoun's ideas published anonymously in a work called *The South Carolina Exposition.* Calhoun denounced the Tariff of 1828, claiming that it made the South a servant of Northern industrialists. In brief, Calhoun's argument was that the federal government was created by a **compact**, or contract among the states. Each state gave up only such powers as were expressly granted in the Constitution. If the federal government passed laws that infringed on the remaining state powers, each individual state, not the Supreme Court, had the right to decide whether or not that federal law was constitutional. A state could declare the law null and void within its own borders. Behind this doctrine of nullification lurked the threat to secede from the Union.

The Tariff of 1828

The protective tariff of 1816 was not costly enough to satisfy American manufacturers. In response to their demands, duties on imported manufactures and on some raw materials were raised twice more—in 1824 and 1828. These laws aroused increasing resentment in the South, especially in South Carolina where the cotton economy was depressed. Increased cotton production on rich lands farther west had reduced cotton

Visualizing History ▲ PEGGY EATON President Jackson viewed the refusal of cabinet members and spouses to meet socially with Peggy Eaton as a plot to discredit him politically. *What caused Jackson's final break with John Calhoun?*

prices. Instead of blaming local causes, South Carolinians attributed their ills to the tariff.

When news of the Tariff of 1828, often called the "Tariff of Abominations," reached Charleston, people were indignant. Flags were hung at half-mast; college students threatened to buy no Northern goods; and there was talk of leaving the Union. South Carolina, however, held back from acting against the tariff because John C. Calhoun, the state's leading politician, was Andrew Jackson's running mate for Vice President. Calhoun's influence in a new administration might bring about tariff reduction.

The Nullification Crisis

Which side would Jackson take in the argument over nullification? Southerners hoped that the President, a slaveholder and planter himself, would support their interests. The nullifiers tried to get Jackson to show his hand at a dinner celebrating Jefferson's birthday on April 13, 1830. Controlling the committee in charge of the banquet, they printed on the menu 24 toasts, many of them expressing sentiments against the tariff and for nullification. When Jackson's turn came to make a toast, the Old Warrior asked everyone to rise, looked straight at Calhoun, and echoed Webster when he stated, "Our Federal Union: it must be preserved." Calhoun, pale and trembling, responded, "Our Union, next to our liberty, the most dear."

Jackson and Calhoun

The break between Jackson and Calhoun was personal as well as political. Major John Eaton, Jackson's secretary of war, had married a young woman who was not socially accepted by Mrs. Calhoun and the other cabinet members' wives. Of the cabinet members, only Martin Van Buren was pleasant to Peggy Eaton. Jackson, remembering his own wife's suffering from slander, stopped meeting with most of his cabinet advisers. Jackson's final break with Calhoun came when he discovered that, years earlier, Calhoun had wanted to have "Old Hickory" censured for mistreatment of the Seminoles in Florida. From this point on, Van Buren became Jackson's choice to succeed him in office.

The Tariff of 1832

In 1832 Congress passed a new tariff law. The rates, while lower than those of 1828, were still high. South Carolina called a special convention that passed an Ordinance of Nullification declaring that the tariff was "null, void, and no law." The ordinance threatened secession, and the state began to arm and drill a volunteer military force.

In response, Jackson issued a "Proclamation to the People of South Carolina" pointing out that nullification meant disunion and disunion meant treason. Privately, he warned Senator Hayne that if there was bloodshed he would hang the first nullificationist he could get his hands on from the first tree he could find. Hayne resigned from the Senate to become governor of South Carolina, and Calhoun resigned the vice presidency to lead the fight in the Senate.

Compromise Tariff

Compromise settled the crisis. Jackson asked Congress to pass a Force Bill to give him the powers necessary to suppress disunion in South Carolina. While Congress debated the measure, Henry Clay introduced a compromise tariff bill. It provided for gradual scaling down of duties. The Tariff of 1833, supported by both Webster and Calhoun, and the Force Bill were passed the same day. Thus Congress removed South Carolina's grievance about the tariff and at the same time denied its right to nullify a law.

Jackson agreed to the compromise, yet he felt it was probably a mistake to give in at all. "The nullifiers in the South intend to blow up a storm on the slave question next," he wrote a friend. "This ought to be met." The next step, predicted Jackson, would be an attempt to form a Southern confederacy bounded on the north by the Potomac River.

Section 3 ★ Review

Checking for Understanding

1. **Identify** Daniel Webster, John C. Calhoun, Ordinance of Nullification.

2. **Define** nullification, compact.

3. **Describe** the differing sectional interests during Jackson's presidency.

4. **Summarize** the crisis over the tariff and nullification and its resolution.

Critical Thinking

5. **Inferring Values**   At a celebration, President Andrew Jackson and Vice President John Calhoun exchanged toasts to the Union. Although they used similar words, they planted themselves firmly on opposing sides of a sensitive issue. In your own words, restate the implied messages these two leaders were giving to one another.

★★

The Bank and the Whigs

Setting the Scene

Section Focus

The fight over the second Bank of the United States divided the nation. This issue caused panic and depression. Opposition to Jackson resulted in the formation of the Whig party. After electing two Presidents, the Whig party split over slavery in the 1850s.

Objectives

After studying this section, you should be able to

★ explain the role that the Bank of the United States played in political debate and in the election of 1832.

★ list three factors that helped cause the Panic of 1837.

Key Term

platform

▲ GOLD QUARTER EAGLES, C. 1834

At the time the question of nullification was dividing the nation, Jackson was also engaged in a dramatic struggle with the Bank of the United States. Chartered in 1816, the "B.U.S.," as it was nicknamed, was a useful institution. Like the original Bank of the United States, it performed much of the financial business of the country and controlled the supply of currency.

■ Popular Distrust of Banks

Despite its importance, the Bank had many enemies. Opposition came from smaller banks chartered by state legislatures, because the B.U.S. was a powerful competitor and because it prevented state banks from lending too freely. Another group, mostly farmers, were against all banks. They believed the only honest currency was "hard money"—silver and gold. Farmers respected real wealth—corn, hogs, grain, cotton, tobacco—and resented paying tribute to those who controlled paper wealth, such as mortgages and banknotes.

The Bank also suffered because of a rising feeling against monopolies. Although 80 percent of the Bank of the United States was owned by private individuals, it enjoyed a monopoly of all government business. State legislatures granted somewhat similar privileges to state banks and also made monopoly grants to companies running toll bridges, steamship lines, and turnpikes. Feeling against this sort of privilege was strong in the Northeast among small businesses and workers, who believed that monopolistic charters created an unfair advantage. Such people said monopolistic charters made certain people wealthy and kept others from acquiring property.

Jackson versus the Bank

Jackson, like most Westerners, was a hard-money man who distrusted all banks and all paper money. While the President believed that high finance was dangerous, he also remembered that the Bank had opposed his candidacy in 1828 and had refused jobs and loans to his supporters.

A Campaign Issue

For the first three years of his presidency, Jackson took no action against the Bank. The President's inaction may have encouraged Bank president Nicholas Biddle's supporters to use the difference of opinion on the Bank issue to challenge Jackson in the election of 1832.

The National Republicans fired the first shot in the Bank war when they made the Bank the main issue of the election. Henry Clay, the likely presidential challenger, introduced a bill to give the Bank a new charter even though the old one would not run out until 1836. Clay hoped to embarrass Jackson by forcing him either to sign a bill he disliked or to veto it. He did not believe Jackson could defend a veto in the presidential campaign.

Jackson Vetoes the Bill

When Congress passed the Recharter Bill, Jackson remarked, "The Bank, Mr. Van Buren, is trying to kill me; but I will kill it." His veto message to Congress showed little

GENERAL JACKSON SLAYING THE MANY HEADED MONSTER.

Visualizing History ▲ JACKSON VS. THE BANK One of Jackson's biggest political battles was fought over the Bank of the United States. The Bank issue provided a rich source for cartoonists. *Why did many Americans distrust the Bank?*

knowledge of banking but great understanding of why many people disliked the B.U.S. Jackson wrote that the Bank favored the few against the many; it made "the rich richer and the potent more powerful." He called it un-American because more than one-fourth of its stock had been purchased by foreigners. Finally, he said it was an overextension of federal power because the Constitution nowhere explicitly granted the government the right to establish a central bank.

Election of 1832

The Bank issue did determine the presidential election, but not in the way Henry Clay had anticipated. The National Republicans accused Jackson of "appealing to the worst passions of the uninformed part of the people and endeavoring to stir up the poor against the rich." They produced arguments to show the value of the Bank to the nation's finances, but the Bank issue backfired. When the returns were counted, they showed that Jackson had won an overwhelming victory. He received 687,000 popular votes to Clay's 530,000 and carried the electoral college 219 to 49.

Jackson Destroys the Bank

Jackson took his reelection as a directive from the people to destroy the power of the Bank at once, even though its charter ran until 1836. Although the law required funds of the federal government to be deposited in the Bank, Jackson resolved to remove them. This required an order from the secretary of the treasury. Two secretaries resigned rather than sign the order. Finally, a third secretary agreed, and the government gradually began to withdraw deposits from the vaults of the B.U.S. New funds from taxation and land sales were placed in strong state banks that National Republicans scornfully called "pet banks."

The removal of the deposits caused a great outcry among Jackson's opponents. Nicholas Biddle claimed that removal of the deposits forced him to call in the B.U.S.'s loans and stop lending. Biddle's policy created such a scarcity of credit that hundreds

▲ NICHOLAS BIDDLE

of businesspeople were driven into bankruptcy and scores of banks failed. Factories closed down and workers were laid off. Since Jackson had vetoed the Bank Bill, businesspeople sent petitions urging him to save the country from depression. The President replied, "Go to Nicholas Biddle!" Eventually, Democrats shifted the blame to Biddle, arguing that if one man at the head of a private institution could drive the country into depression, then Jackson was right in saying the Bank had too much power.

Finally Biddle surrendered. The B.U.S. reversed its policies and began to extend easy credit to state banks. With money once again plentiful, the administration threw millions of acres of public land on the market. The resulting land boom sparked a time of reckless investment. Congress stimulated the boom by issuing $30 million in surplus funds to the states, triggering a host of internal improvement schemes in turnpikes, canals, and railroads.

A Change in Policy

The free spending, speculation, and resulting inflation worried Jackson's hard-money supporters. Jackson decided to halt the trend by issuing the Specie Circular, ordering that all payments for public lands be made in silver or gold. This drastic reversal of policy virtually stopped land sales, eliminated easy credit, and set the stage for a severe panic and depression in 1837.

■ The Election of 1836

As the election of 1836 approached, Jackson used his control of the Democratic party to pick his successor. His choice was Martin Van Buren, the Vice President, a New York politician whose reputation for craftiness had earned him the nickname "the Fox of Kinderhook."

The Whigs were so divided they could not agree on any single candidate. Instead, they nominated three favorite sons, or leading politicians from different states, hoping to divide the electoral college vote. The Whig candidates were William Henry Harrison of Ohio, Daniel Webster of Massachusetts, and Hugh Lawson White of Tennessee. If the three candidates could prevent Van Buren from getting a majority, the election would be thrown into the House of Representatives, which was controlled by the Whigs. Jackson's continuing popularity and the nation's perceived prosperity were enough to give the Democrats the election. Van Buren won 170 electoral votes against a combined total of 124 votes for all his opponents, although his edge in the popular vote was small.

■ The Panic of 1837

Van Buren had hardly taken office when the country was hit by the Panic of 1837 and one of the most severe depressions in American history. Jackson's Specie Circular had sent the economy into a tailspin, but like most depressions that of 1837 had several causes. One factor was a withdrawal of British investments. British gold and silver deposits in American banks had supported American economic growth in the 1830s. In 1837 Great Britain suffered from hard times, and British investors became more cautious.

A Deepening Depression

As British and American investors in state banks withdrew deposits, banks failed. There was no Bank of the United States to restore confidence in the banking system. People hoarded their gold and silver, merchandise went unsold, crops found no markets, and businesses closed. Thousands of farmers lost their farms through mortgage foreclosures. Unemployment soared among Eastern factory workers, and work on canals and railroads nearly ceased. As the depression deepened, workers fought over the meager relief that city governments provided.

Today, faced with such a crisis, the people would demand action by the federal government, and the federal government would respond with legislation. In the 1830s, however, a depression was regarded as an act of nature like a drought or a hurricane. Instead of recognizing that both state

Visualizing History ▲ **MARTIN VAN BUREN** Jackson used his influence to have Vice President Martin Van Buren nominated for President in 1836. *What economic woes struck the nation soon after Van Buren took office?*

▲ **GENERAL WILLIAM HENRY HARRISON**

▲ THE LOG CABIN CAMPAIGN The 1840 election campaign was full of slogans, banners, rallies, and parades. *What was the Whigs' campaign plan?*

and federal governments had helped to cause the depression, laissez-faire philosophers said it was not the function of the government to do much about the problem.

Van Buren's Term of Office

In his Inaugural Address, Van Buren emphasized the laissez-faire policy when he said that "all communities are apt to look to government for too much." His one great legislative effort was to try to get the federal government entirely out of banking. He shared Jackson's disapproval of a great central bank like the B.U.S. but recognized that depositing federal funds in pet banks had also failed.

Van Buren proposed an Independent Treasury System, under which the federal government would collect its taxes in specie to be stored in vaults throughout the country. Federal expenditures would be paid in specie, making federal credit literally as good as gold. This would discourage inflated bank notes because state banks would have to keep a sufficient reserve to allow their depositors and those holding their notes to do business with the government. The Independent Treasury Act successfully passed in 1840.

■ The "Log Cabin" Campaign of 1840

The Whigs eagerly looked forward to the election of 1840, even though they were so divided on major issues that they did not even try to write a **platform,** or statement of beliefs. Their campaign plan was simple: nominate a military hero and attack Van Buren. For their presidential candidate they passed over known leaders of the party and chose General William Henry Harrison, whose principal attraction was that he had fought Native Americans at the Battle of Tippecanoe in 1811.

Democrats jeered that all Harrison was fit for was to sit in front of a log cabin, drink hard cider, and draw a pension. The Whigs adopted the very methods the Jacksonians had used against Adams in 1828. Harrison—born to wealth and social position—was pictured as a simple frontiersman, while Van Buren—born in humble circumstances—was portrayed as a champagne-drinking aristocrat with cologne-scented whiskers. John Tyler, a former Democrat who had left the party in protest over Jackson's policy against nullification, was selected as Harrison's running mate. The Whigs' campaign slogan became "Tippecanoe and Tyler too." The result of this campaign was a decisive victory for Harrison—234 electoral votes to 60—although the popular vote was quite close.

The election of 1840 was the first to illustrate a recurring principle of American politics: during a depression, the party in power is likely to be punished at the polls. Twelve years before, when Jackson had defeated Adams, a little more than 50 percent of the eligible voters had gone to the polls. In 1840 nearly 80 percent of those eligible voted—in some states almost 90 percent. The high turnout revealed that the party organizations had penetrated every county, village, and city precinct. Parties had set up machinery for informing the electorate and had ensured that voters came to the polling places.

■ Tyler and Whigs Split

The elderly Harrison was expected to be a figurehead while Clay and Webster ran the party. Clay, now in the Senate, had worked out a legislative program designed to appeal to as many different interests as possible. However, only a month after Harrison's inauguration the President died of pneumonia.

John Tyler of Virginia became the first Vice President to become President by the death of the incumbent. Having been placed on the Whig ticket simply to attract Southern support, Tyler was opposed to most of the Clay and Webster programs. They were nationalists; the new President was a believer in states' rights. Nevertheless, he did sign the first of several bills in Clay's program. The Tariff of 1842 pleased Eastern manufacturers by raising the rates to about what they had been ten years earlier. The Pre-emption Act of 1841 satisfied the Western demand that "squatters" on public lands have first right to buy the lands they had settled. Tyler, however, vetoed a bill establishing another national bank and vetoed a second bill that was drawn up to meet his objections. In disgust at the President's actions, all the Whigs except Daniel Webster resigned from the cabinet, and Clay resigned from the Senate. Divided, without a program or leadership, the Whigs lost heavily in the congressional elections of 1842, and John Tyler became a President without a party.

▲ THE LOG CABIN SONG BOOK

Section 4 ★ Review

Checking for Understanding

1. **Identify** Specie Circular, Whigs, Martin Van Buren, John Tyler.
2. **Define** platform.
3. **Describe** the role the Bank of the United States played in the election of 1832.
4. **List** factors that led to the panic and depression of 1837.

Critical Thinking

5. **Evaluating Political Systems** Several Vice Presidents, starting with John Tyler, have succeeded to the presidency during another's term. In effect, they have been chosen by the presidential candidate, not by the voters. Suggest another method by which the Vice President might be chosen.

CONNECTIONS CONNECTIONS

Banks and the Money Supply

In the 1800s a bank served three functions in the community: it provided a secure place to deposit gold and silver coins; it loaned its deposits to individuals and local businesses; and it issued paper notes to borrowers—the value on each banknote representing a like amount of coins in its vault. These notes then circulated in the economy as money.

In theory, a bank's loans could not exceed its deposits. However, the interest on loans was profit, and by issuing more notes banks could loan many times the specie in their vaults. If enough people who held a bank's notes wanted hard cash, however, all its assets would be paid out and its depositors' funds would be lost.

The second Bank of the United States sought to regulate the nation's economy by controlling banknotes. By purchasing huge amounts of notes and redeeming them at the issuing banks, the B.U.S. could exhaust the assets of unsound banks and force them to close. Even this crude central banking system ended when the B.U.S. lost its charter. Not until the Federal Reserve System was created in 1913 was banking brought under effective control.

This system, which is still in effect today, was created by the Federal Reserve Act of 1913. The act divided the United States into 12 banking districts, each with a Federal Reserve bank. All national banks—those chartered by the federal government—are required to become members. Banks chartered by the states may also join if they choose to do so. Each member bank has to deposit a certain amount of money in the district Federal Reserve bank. This reserve requirement helps protect people's deposits.

Federal Reserve banks do not do business with individuals but are bankers' banks. They serve as clearinghouses for checks, make loans to member banks, and provide a more flexible currency. The Federal Reserve Board is appointed by the President. The board has the power to set interest rates on loans that the district

▲ BANKNOTE ISSUED IN 1840

banks make to member banks. This power gives the Board control over the credit supply. If the Board lowers rates, that makes loans easier to obtain. This increases the money supply and stimulates the economy. If the Federal Reserve Board raises rates, that tightens the supply and slows economic growth.

Making the Economics Connection

1. How did banks get the paper money they printed into the nation's money supply?

Linking Past and Present

2. What clues on today's paper money show that the government is involved in banking?

Using Vocabulary

Use the following terms to write a short essay about presidential leadership style.

platform   pocket veto
spoils system

Reviewing Facts

1. **Compare** the campaigns of 1828 and 1840.

2. **Identify** the important democratic changes that developed during the Jackson era.

3. **Identify** the groups that did not benefit from democracy under Jackson and explain why.

4. **List** examples of Jackson's authoritative style and extension of presidential power.

5. **State** the reasons Jackson and others objected to the second Bank of the United States.

6. **Describe** the Panic of 1837 and its causes.

7. **Summarize** the rise and fall of the Whigs.

▲ SEMINOLE LEADER OSCEOLA

Understanding Concepts

Political Change

1. What political and democratic changes helped bring about Andrew Jackson's election victory in 1828?

2. In what ways was the presidential election of 1840 significant?

Economic Policy

3. How did the tariff and nullification issue develop into a crisis?

4. What changes, both in the United States as well as in other countries, contributed to the Panic of 1837?

Critical Thinking

1. **Linking Past and Present** Political parties often choose vice-presidential candidates for the reasons the Whigs selected Tyler: to attract voters with views different from those of the presidential candidate. Review news accounts of the 1992 presidential election. Do you think the Republicans should have chosen Robert Dole as George Bush's running mate instead of Dan Quayle? Explain your answer.

2. **Analyzing Executive Performance** How did Andrew Jackson's conduct as President reflect the growing spirit of democracy? Cite specific examples.

3. **Evaluating Policy** Argue for or against the spoils system.

4. **Comparing Institutions** Compare the Bank of the United States with the Independent Treasury System created to replace it. What were the advantages of each?

5. **Analyzing Art** When the Seminoles were told to give up their land and move west, Osceola refused. He led a series of guerrilla raids against federal troops. Osceola was captured after being invited to peace talks and died in prison. What qualities and attributes does the artist portray in this painting of Osceola?

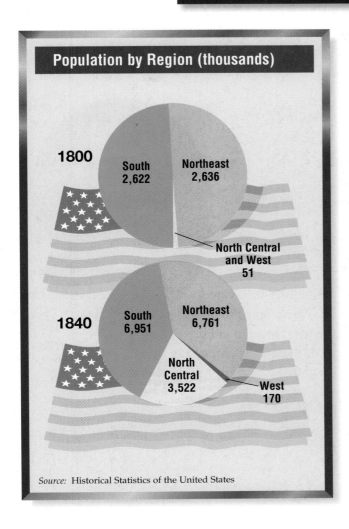

Population by Region (thousands)

1800

South
2,622

Northeast
2,636

North Central
and West
51

1840

South
6,951

Northeast
6,761

North
Central
3,522

West
170

Source: Historical Statistics of the United States

Social Studies Skills

Reading a Circle Graph

One way to present numerical information is to use a circle graph. Circle graphs make it easy both to compare parts of a whole and to compare changes in the relationships of the parts. For example, the two circle graphs on this page compare population by region in the United States for 1800 and 1840.

Practicing the Skill

Use the circle graphs and information from the chapter to answer the following questions.

1. In the circle graph for 1800, which region has the largest population?

2. Which region decreased the most in percentage of the total population between 1800 and 1840?

3. In terms of numbers of people, how did the population of the Northeast change between 1800 and 1840?

4. The text notes that in the 1820s "conflicting sectional interests and a shifting population made political forecasts difficult." According to the circle graphs, how was the population shifting? What effect might a shift in the population have on sectional interests?

Writing About History

Cause and Effect

Imagine you are a financial reporter. Write an article explaining to your readers the chain of causes and effects that led to the Panic of 1837. Prepare before you begin writing by organizing your ideas.

Cooperative Learning

Working in pairs, research the history of the government's and settlers' dealings with Black Hawk's nation. Imagine it is 1832 and Black Hawk has returned with his followers to reclaim lands that farmers now hold. You and your partner have been appointed by Jackson to recommend a solution. Agree on a fair plan and present it to your class.

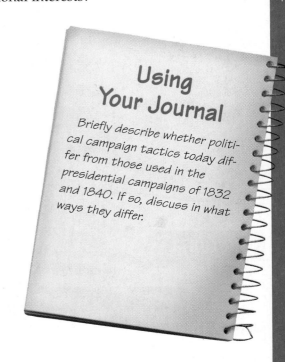

Using Your Journal

Briefly describe whether political campaign tactics today differ from those used in the presidential campaigns of 1832 and 1840. If so, discuss in what ways they differ.

CHAPTER 12

★★★

The Spirit of Reform
1820–1854

Setting the Scene

Focus

American reformers during the first half of the nineteenth century worked selflessly to create a more perfect society. Many reformers were religiously motivated, while others traced their reform spirit to ideas in the Declaration of Independence. In either case, the noble goal of achieving a just American society would serve as a model for the rest of the world.

▲ NATHANIEL HAWTHORNE

Journal Notes

As you read the chapter, make notes about the types of reform that occurred during the first half of the nineteenth century.

Concepts to Understand

★ Why social reform movements were so widespread during this period

★ How new values and beliefs influenced educators, artists, and writers

Read to Discover . . .

★ the factors that motivated a wide variety of reform movements.

★ how the spirit of reform affected the status of prisoners, women, and African Americans.

CULTURAL

• **1825** *Robert Owen organizes utopian community at New Harmony, Indiana*

• **1833** *National temperance movement founded*

1820	1830

POLITICAL

• **1825** *John Quincy Adams inaugurated as sixth U.S. President*

• **1830** *Maysville Road Bill is vetoed*
• **1832** *Black Hawk War fought*
• **1837** *Panic strikes the economy*

The Sermon
by Julius Gari Melchers, 1886

Melchers often portrayed villagers in scenes of everyday life. Many of his works stressed religion and worship.

◀ JOHN J. AUDUBON PAINTING

• **1846** *Smithsonian Institution founded*

• **1852** *Harriet Beecher Stowe's* Uncle Tom's Cabin *published*

1840	1850

• **1846** *United States and Mexico go to war*

• **1850** *Compromise of 1850 reached*

★★★

Advances in Education

Setting the Scene

Section Focus

Americans began examining their society on the basis of ideas in the Declaration of Independence. During the early 1800s, many Americans in search of a better, more democratic world formed organizations to persuade others to their way of thinking. Perhaps never before or since the Jacksonian period have Americans shown such optimistic faith in improving the quality of life.

Objectives

After studying this section, you should be able to

★ identify improvements and reforms that were made at various levels of education during the 1800s.

★ discuss the obstacles to establishing public schools.

Key Term

lyceum

THE AMERICAN SPELLING BOOK: CONTAINING, An easy standard of Pronunciation. Being the FIRST PART of a Grammatical Institute OF THE English Language. In THREE PARTS. By NOAH WEBSTER, Jun'r. Esquire. The eleventh Edition. HARTFORD: PRINTED BY HUDSON AND GOODWIN.

◀ **WEBSTER'S SPELLING BOOK**

Although the idea of universal education had a long history, dating back as far as the Massachusetts General School Act of 1647, public school systems had not developed adequately. As late as 1834, 250,000 of the 400,000 children in Pennsylvania did not attend school. In the 1830s and 1840s, however, there was a tremendous increase in the number of tax-supported schools.

■ Need for Education

As more people gained the right to vote, the need for education grew. Nonwhites, women, and white men without property had all been denied the vote in the early days of the Republic. In the 1820s and 1830s, however, most states amended their laws,

extending the vote to white men who did not own land. In addition, it became necessary to educate the increasing number of immigrants who came to the United States in the mid-1800s. Thus, the increase in the number of eligible voters became a compelling reason for free public education. Democracy demanded an informed, educated electorate, a goal not easy to achieve.

Horace Mann, president of the Massachusetts Senate, pressed for public education and signed a bill in 1837 creating a state board of education in Massachusetts. He served as secretary of the state board of education for 12 years. During that time he doubled teachers' salaries, opened 50 new high schools, grouped students by grades, and established schools for teacher training called "normal schools." Massachusetts quickly became the model for all other Northern states.

Resistance to Public Education

The establishment of public schools was not achieved without a fight. Communities that declared themselves in favor of public schools were often unwilling to tax their citizens to raise the necessary money. Lutherans, Roman Catholics, and other religious groups ran private schools of their own. Many of these people wondered why they should pay taxes to support public schools. Many people without children were also opposed.

Educating African Americans presented even more difficult problems. It was illegal in the South, and in the Northern states, people wavered on the need to provide education for African Americans. Although there were 15,000 African Americans in New York City in 1828, there were only 2 schools for them; in Philadelphia, there were only 3 schools for 20,000 students.

Efforts to educate African Americans sometimes met with violence. Prudence Crandall's white students withdrew when she admitted one African American girl to her Connecticut school in 1831. When her school filled with African American girls from all over the Northeast, the school was vandalized. Food had to be brought in secretly to the students. Connecticut then made it illegal to educate "a person of color" from out of state, which led to Crandall's arrest and conviction. The verdict, however, was reversed. When Crandall reopened the school, it was again attacked, and she was forced to give up her efforts there.

Others, especially in the West, saw no reason why children should learn more than the "three Rs." As an Indiana newspaper put it:

> ❝ . . . Give them a little spelling, a little ciphering, and a little handwriting, with a liberal sprinkling of the rod, and they'll have more than their fathers had before them. Did Tippecanoe Harrison graduate from a seminary? Did Old Hickory Jackson know any Latin or Greek?. . . ❞

▲ *THE COUNTRY SCHOOL* by Winslow Homer By the mid-1800s, public elementary schools were being established in many states, and public high schools were also growing in number. Horace Mann was one of the leaders in educational reform. **Why did some groups resist Mann's ideas about public education?**

U.S. Student Enrollment, 1840–1860

	1840	1850	1860
Total population (in millions)	17.1	23.2	31.4
Total students: primary, secondary, and higher education (in millions)	2.0	3.6	5.5
Students as percent of total population	11.7	15.5	17.5
Total white population, ages 5–19 (in millions)	5.3	7.2	9.5
Students as percent of total white population, ages 5–19	37.7	50.0	57.8

Source: Lawrence A. Cremin, *American Education: The National Experience, 1783–1876* (1980).

Chart Study

The number of students enrolled in school more than doubled between 1840 and 1860. ***In which 10-year period covered in the table did enrollments increase the fastest?***

Special Needs Education

There was even less public support for education for children with special needs. Reformers who worked for this cause went to great lengths to give these children an equal opportunity for a better life. Reverend Thomas Gallaudet traveled to Europe to learn how to help people with impaired hearing. In 1817 he opened a school in Hartford, Connecticut, that became a model in education for the hearing impaired.

Samuel Gridley Howe, head of the New England Asylum for the Blind, taught the unsighted to read by pasting string on cards to make raised letters. His prize student was Laura Bridgman, a girl who entered the school at age eight and learned to read, write, and sew. She became the first sight- and hearing-impaired person to be successfully educated.

▲ LAURA BRIDGMAN

Teachers and Education

Often teachers were untrained young men or women. Since teachers were paid salaries of only $155 a year for men and as little as one-third of that for women, schools could not attract skilled professionals. Classroom instruction was characterized by memorization and harsh discipline.

Fortunately, the spirit of reform was strong enough to influence lawmakers. By 1850 most free states provided tuition-free elementary education. Free high schools had replaced many private academies.

An American Language

Despite a popular mistrust of "book learning," Noah Webster's *American Spelling Book* became a bestseller after it was first published in 1783. By 1837 sales had reached 15 million copies.

Webster was dedicated to "a uniformity and purity of language." He was eager not simply to preserve the language for its own sake; he saw it as a way to promote national spirit. His spelling book contained a preface encouraging Americans to respect their own literature. Webster also wrote the famous dictionaries that bore his name.

William McGuffey, a cleric and college president, had similar ideas. In 1836 he introduced the first of six McGuffey's Readers. Filled with moral instructions and patriotic sayings, these literature anthologies influenced schoolchildren for generations.

Higher Education

Interest in training teachers helped the cause of higher education for women. One argument for training women as teachers was that it was more economical because women teachers could be paid less than men. Although many men feared that higher education for women would disrupt home life, feminist leaders such as Emma Willard, Catharine Beecher, and Mary Lyon argued that chemistry could be used in cooking and math in household finance.

Oberlin College in Ohio, the first coeducational school, saw its first female student graduate in 1841. Oberlin and Bowdoin College in Maine were the first institutions to allow African Americans to attend as students. Because African American men and women were generally barred from educational opportunities, there were fewer than 15 African American college students in the United States before 1840. Aside from one African American college, Lincoln University, which opened in Pennsylvania in 1854, there was little progress in education for African Americans until the years after the Civil War.

Other Adult Education

While opportunities for formal higher education were limited for most people, there was a move toward adult education for the common person. Libraries began to take hold as free public institutions. The first was established in Peterboro, New Hampshire, in 1833.

Even more popular was the **lyceum** (ly•SEE•uhm) movement begun in 1826. A lyceum was a voluntary organization designed to promote "the improvement of its members in useful knowledge." Supporting their organization with small membership fees, the group used the money they collected to purchase books, scientific equipment, and specimens for study.

▶ PAGE FROM *McGUFFEY'S READER*

Section 1 ★ Review

Checking for Understanding

1. **Identify** Noah Webster, William McGuffey, Horace Mann.

2. **Define** lyceum.

3. **Summarize** the progress in public education, including the problems facing those who wanted to educate African American children.

4. **List** the groups that objected to public education and the reasons for their objections.

Critical Thinking

5. **Analyzing Causes** In what ways did the *McGuffey's Reader* and Webster's dictionaries and spelling book play a part in keeping American English uniform?

Critical Thinking Skills

Making Comparisons

Imagine that your younger brother cannot decide between joining the debate team or playing intramural baseball. He has limited free time, so he asks you to help him compare the two. You tell him that you cannot because that is "like comparing apples and oranges." Your friend hears the conversation and comes in to tell you that you indeed can compare the debate team to baseball.

▲ EARLY AMERICAN SCHOOL

To compare means to examine in order to identify similarities and differences. You can compare any two things. To get an accurate comparison, however, you must note at least one similarity and one difference.

Making comparisons does not involve analysis or evaluation. There are no judgments being made, and no conclusions being drawn.

In the example you just read, there are obvious differences between debating and baseball. Yet, you can identify at least two similarities. Both are group activities, and both are competitive in the nature in which points are scored. This means that a comparison is possible.

No matter what you are comparing, there are questions that can be asked that help in making effective comparisons. They are:

- What is it that I want to compare?
- What do they have in common that I can compare?

- On which common area do I want to concentrate?
- What similarities are there in this common area? What differences are there in this common area?

Note that these questions can be applied in a variety of ways. For practice, apply these questions in making a comparison between public and private schools in the 1800s.

In addition, this method can be applied to other movements or institutions in your study of history.

Practicing the Skill

For further practice in making comparisons, read Section 2 entitled "Struggle for Rights" and apply the above questions in making a comparison between the woman's rights movement and the antislavery movement.

★★★★★★★★★★★★★★★★★★★★★★★★★★★★★★★★★★★★

Struggle for Rights

Setting the Scene

Section Focus

Numerous reforms were advocated during the Jacksonian period. There were organizations to do away with flogging in the navy, drinking alcohol, and eating meat. The great reform movements of the 1830s and 1840s could boast of solid achievement, especially in state legislation dealing with such problems as prisons, the mentally ill, child labor, liquor, and public schools.

Objectives

After studying this section, you should be able to

★ list reform movements of the 1800s and discuss their achievements.

★ explain the ways in which women were treated as second-class citizens.

★ discuss the efforts made to end slavery.

Key Terms

abolitionist, Underground Railroad

◄ SOJOURNER TRUTH

Calling for action on such issues as care for the mentally ill, woman's rights, and abolition of slavery, reformers appealed to their state legislatures and the federal government with little success. The persistent message of the reformers eventually awakened the United States to many of the needs of more than one-half of the population.

■ Prison Reform

As Emerson had suggested, there was a wealth of opportunity for reform; one had only to turn a critical eye to the world and make a choice.

Prisons began to experiment with ways to reform criminals. Unfortunately, the results were more severe punishments. For example, in Pennsylvania criminals were put in solitary confinement day and night to allow convicts to meditate on their crimes and, thus, reform. At Auburn, New York, treatment was less severe. There group labor in absolute silence was allowed. Instead of public hangings—commonplace before the 1830s—reformers sought more humane private executions.

Obviously, much reform remained to be done. When Dorothea Dix began visiting prisons in 1841, she found that mentally ill persons were still treated as criminals. In her report to the Massachusetts legislature, she wrote:

> ❝ *I proceed, gentlemen, briefly to call your attention to the present state of insane persons confined within this commonwealth, in cages, closets, cellars, stalls, pens! Chained, naked, beaten with rods, and lashed into obedience. . . .* ❞

The Language of Etiquette

In the early 1800s a strict code of behavior governed relationships between unmarried men and women. Public displays of affection of any sort were prohibited. Modesty required that words referring to body parts were never spoken in mixed company.

In 1839 the English novelist Frederick Marryat toured the United States. His journals provide a glimpse of the obsession with modesty that pervaded American social etiquette. While visiting Niagara Falls, a female companion of Mr. Marryat's fell and grazed her leg. The novelist asked if she had "hurt her leg." Much to his astonishment, she was deeply offended by his question. She later explained that the word "leg" was not used in mixed company. Rather, the novelist should have asked if she had "hurt her limb."

If Mr. Marryat was not fully convinced of the lengths to which Americans would take this social modesty, a trip to a girls school a few months later probably persuaded him. In the parlor of the school stood a grand piano with four "limbs." Much to his surprise, each piano leg had been covered with a frilly trouser!

▼ YOUNG COUPLE, MID-1800S

Dix's findings led Massachusetts to pass a law establishing asylums where mental illness could be treated as a disease rather than as a crime. Dix traveled throughout the United States visiting more than 800 jails and almshouses, or homes for the poor. Largely as a result of her influence, 20 more states founded insane asylums.

Later she traveled to other countries, helping to promote better treatment of the mentally ill in European nations. Through her influence and friendship with a Japanese diplomat, the first insane asylums in Japan were built.

■ Woman's Rights Movement

Even though the Declaration of Independence promised equality for all, the promise rang hollow for women. Women had actually lost ground in their political equality since colonial times.

Status of Women

While certain women had the right to vote under colonial charters, that privilege was revoked after the colonies declared their independence. Despite the fact that by 1850 nearly all white males could vote, women were still denied an active part in politics.

Women were perceived as "second-class citizens" in other ways, too. According to the English common law that formed the basis of American law, "husband and wife are one and that one is the husband." Similarly, a woman had no legal right to manage the affairs of her own children, and only in the state of Ohio was a woman given the right to make a will.

As factories opened in the Northeast, many new jobs for women were created. As in teaching, women received considerably less pay than men did, and when they took it home, the money became their husbands'. Women also felt social pressures directed against those who took these jobs.

▲ LUCRETIA MOTT

Almost all institutions of higher education and most professional careers were closed to women. It took Elizabeth Blackwell years to be allowed to take medical courses. When she finally completed her training to become the country's first female physician, sexist prejudice nearly kept her from practicing.

Even in the reform movements themselves, women were often forced to defer to men. It was considered improper, for example, for a woman to address a mixed audience. When nine women went as United States delegates to the World Antislavery Convention, they were greeted with cries of "Turn out the women!" from American clerics. The women, Lucretia Mott and Elizabeth Cady Stanton among them, refused to leave and, as a compromise, were seated behind a curtain and allowed only to listen.

Seneca Falls Convention

Frustrated by the limits on their actions, female reformers began a campaign for their own rights. In 1848 Mott and Stanton organized the Seneca Falls Convention. This gathering of female reformers drew up a "Declaration of Sentiments and Resolutions" that echoed the words of the Declaration of Independence:

❝ *We hold these truths to be self-evident: that all men and women are created equal; that they are endowed by their Creator with certain inalienable rights; that among these are life, liberty, and the pursuit of happiness. . . .* ❞

Stanton shocked many of the women when she proposed a resolution that they devote themselves to gaining the right to vote. Frederick Douglass, an African American antislavery reformer, seconded the resolution and gave a speech in support. The resolution narrowly passed.

Most politicians were either indifferent or hostile to the issue of woman's rights. During this time women gained neither the right to vote nor admission to professions; most colleges continued to exclude them. They did, however, gain relief from some of their worst legal handicaps. For example, many states passed laws permitting women to retain and manage their own property.

Visualizing History ▲ ELIZABETH BLACKWELL Elizabeth Blackwell was a noted physician, educator, and writer. *What examples of prejudice did Blackwell face?*

■ Antislavery Crusade

A glaring violation of democratic principles in the United States was African American slavery. How could the nation claim to be "the land of the free" when human beings were bought and sold like common property? The question had become increasingly acute by 1840. By then most Latin American countries had abolished slavery, and Great Britain had banned the practice. It is not surprising, then, that the upsurge of democratic feeling in the Jacksonian period made antislavery the dominant reform effort.

Abolitionists

The organized movement to abolish slavery began among religious groups. As early as 1776, the Quakers—in both the South and the North—agreed not to enslave people. In Virginia in 1789 the Baptists recommended "every legal measure to extirpate this horrid evil from the land." The abolition movement at first made many converts in the South. Benjamin Lundy, a native of New Jersey, spent most of his active career organizing antislavery societies in Southern communities. James G. Birney, an Alabama lawyer and cotton planter, freed his slaves and attempted to get others to do the same.

The voices of **abolitionists,** or those persons in favor of doing away with slavery, grew stronger. On January 1, 1831, the first edition of *The Liberator,* a Boston antislavery newspaper, was published. Editor William Lloyd Garrison wrote in a strong, unrelenting tone:

▶ FREDERICK DOUGLASS

Visualizing History

▲ MOVING TOWARD FREEDOM Before the Civil War, thousands of enslaved people fled hundreds of miles and endangered their lives to reach the first station on the Underground Railroad. Frederick Douglass (inset) published *The North Star* and spoke on behalf of the emancipation of women as well as of enslaved people. ***Who were the abolitionists?***

> _I will be as harsh as truth, and as uncompromising as justice. On this subject, I do not wish to think, or speak, or write, with moderation. . . . I am in earnest. I will not equivocate. I will not excuse. I will not retreat a single inch. AND I WILL BE HEARD._

Garrison denounced both Northerners who refused to be shocked by slavery and Southerners who held enslaved people. He demanded immediate freedom for enslaved African Americans without compensation for the slaveholders. Garrison and his followers made no attempt to win their way by political action. They were willing to divide the Union to rid the free states of the shame of being tied to the slave states.

A group who proposed to abolish slavery by the use of the ballot box founded the Liberty party. It nominated James G. Birney for the presidency in 1840 and 1844, but Birney received only a few thousand votes.

The Underground Railroad

Another leader who favored political action was Frederick Douglass, self-educated and formerly enslaved, who edited an abolitionist newspaper, _The North Star._ The title was meant to remind people of the **Underground Railroad.** This secret abolitionist organization, which had hiding places, or stations, throughout the Northern states and even into Canada, brought enslaved people out of the South and thus ensured their freedom. Moving at night, the agents of the Underground Railroad had only Polaris, the fixed star in the northern skies, to guide them. They not only took care of African Americans after they had come North, but they risked their lives to go into the slave states and lead enslaved others to freedom.

One of the most successful agents was Harriet Tubman, the "Black Moses," who herself had been born into slavery. After escaping, she returned to the South many times, liberating more than 300 enslaved people. Tubman avoided arrest, despite a reward of $40,000 offered for her capture.

Visualizing History

▲ THE ANTISLAVERY MOVEMENT Sarah and Angelina Grimké played a major role in the antislavery crusade of the 1800s. _**How did some Southerners combat the spread of abolitionist literature?**_

Southern Reaction to Abolition

The first edition of _The Liberator_ coincided with a slave insurrection in Virginia in 1831. That revolt was led by Nat Turner, an African American preacher and enslaved person who believed himself divinely inspired to lead his people from bondage. Turner's rebellion was quelled, but only after about 60 white persons had been killed. The revolt spread panic throughout the South. The belief that Turner had been inspired by abolitionist propaganda effectively ended the antislavery movement in the South. From that time on, Southerners who favored abolition usually remained silent or moved north.

Among Southern abolitionists who fled to the North were sisters Sarah and Angelina Grimké (GRIHM•kee). As daughters of a slaveholder in South Carolina, they had learned through firsthand experience to abhor slavery. They moved to Philadelphia, became Quakers, and were among the first women to speak out for both abolition and woman's rights.

One of the few Southerners who did not leave was Cassius Marcellus Clay, a distant relative of Henry Clay, who edited abolitionist newspapers in Kentucky. As a Southerner who held unpopular beliefs, Clay carried

AMERICAN PORTRAITS

Amelia Bloomer
1818–1894

A single episode in Amelia Bloomer's life so catapulted her to fame that today few remember she was a leading reformer. Publisher of *The Lily*, her own newspaper, Bloomer called for just marriage laws, temperance, and woman's suffrage.

It was, however, the clothing she first wore in 1851 that made Amelia Bloomer a household name. Seeking a more practical style than the hoopskirt, she donned a short skirt over loose pants gathered at the ankles. She did not invent the fashion, but her insistence on wearing it—despite ridicule—led to the outfit's becoming known as "bloomers." Large crowds came to hear her lecture. The novelty of seeing a woman wearing pants accounted for much of her popularity. She finally concluded that her bloomers distracted attention from her reform efforts, and she returned to more traditional garb.

two pistols and a bowie knife. He even fortified his office with two cannons and a keg of gunpowder set to go off. When he was absent one day, however, a mob seized his presses and sent them across the Ohio River to Cincinnati.

Southern hostility to abolition grew stronger. The South demanded the suppression of abolitionist material as a condition for remaining in the Union. Southern postal workers refused to deliver abolitionist newspapers. In 1835 a bill to bar abolitionist literature from the mails passed the United States Senate but eventually was abandoned. In 1836, under Southern pressure, the House of Representatives passed a "gag rule" providing that all abolitionist petitions should be shelved without debate.

Despite the excitement it aroused, the antislavery movement affected politics very little at first. The Missouri Compromise had supposedly averted civil war by fixing the boundary between slave and free territory. No prominent politician, however, proposed endangering the Union by attacking slavery where it was protected by law.

▲ **WOMAN IN BLOOMERS**

Section 2 ★ Review

Checking for Understanding

1. Identify Dorothea Dix, Seneca Falls Declaration, Frederick Douglass, William Lloyd Garrison, Harriet Tubman.

2. Define abolitionist, Underground Railroad.

3. Discuss the reform movements of the 1800s and their achievements.

4. Describe the contributions of three key individuals to the antislavery movement.

Critical Thinking

5. Making Decisions Imagine that you are a Northern male teacher who has strong feelings against slavery. Would you join the abolitionists? Why or why not?

▲ COMMUNITY OF NEW HARMONY, INDIANA

The Scientists of New Harmony

The short-lived economic community that Robert Owen founded at New Harmony, Indiana, in 1825 was an exciting place. Although isolated, it boasted an excellent library, school, musical societies, art collections, even a public lecture series. This environment attracted some of the finest scientific minds of the day. Primarily naturalists, these scientists collected and classified specimens, and wrote on biological and geological subjects.

A key supporter of Owen's community was geologist William Maclure. In 1817 Maclure had produced a detailed United States geological map, the first of its scope. A member of New Harmony until its failure in 1827, he had hoped to put into practice new European teaching methods. Another New Harmony geologist, Gerard Troost, a native of Holland, acquired an impressive mineral collection.

Entomologist Thomas Say settled at New Harmony permanently and published a descriptive work on insects, the third volume of *American Entomology.* Say later edited books on shells and birds.

Making the Science Connection

1. Why were scientists like Maclure, Troost, and Say attracted to life at New Harmony?

2. What scientific interests did the New Harmony naturalists pursue?

Linking Past and Present

3. What is the interest of naturalists today?

★★★

Social and Cultural Change

Setting the Scene

Section Focus

The Pilgrims had come to the New World with a vision of a different life. The years that followed were filled with the work of carving out an existence in a new land. Americans wanted to prove that their country was truly independent of Europe. They wanted to create a distinct civilization rivaling that of the Old World. They were concerned not only with rights but with the quality and flavor of life in the United States.

◀ RIP VAN WINKLE

Objectives

After studying this section, you should be able to

★ identify the prominent artists, writers, and scientists of the 1800s and their important contributions.

★ explain the goals of nineteenth-century religious movements.

★ discuss the temperance movement.

Key Term

socialism

---

*A*mericans themselves had a sense of inferiority. People could not write poetry without "a legendary past nor a poetic present," remarked one young scholar. "Large mountains, extensive prairies, tall cataracts, long rivers [and] millions of dirty acres" did not seem suitable subjects for literature. James Fenimore Cooper set the scene of his first novel, *Precaution* (1820), in England and tried to attract readers by promoting himself as "a prominent Englishman." In 1820 the Reverend Sydney Smith, writing in a British magazine, sneered at the low cultural level of Americans and their lack of artistic and scientific achievement.

The second quarter of the nineteenth century saw many advances by American scientists and an outpouring of books by American writers that are still read on both sides of the Atlantic.

■ Writers and the American Scene

Editors such as Garrison, Clay, and Douglass used their talents to directly influence social reform. American writers had different motivations—to reform America's attitude toward itself.

Washington Irving invented a literary past out of the history of the Hudson River valley, once an area of Dutch settlement. With this material he created characters such as Rip Van Winkle. As a result of reading James Fenimore Cooper's novels, generations of children—not only here but in France and Great Britain—gloried in the drama of Native Americans and pioneers on the New York frontier. In his novels and short stories, Nathaniel Hawthorne mined the Puritan history of his native New England. In *Moby*

Dick, Herman Melville used his experience as a sailor to write a fascinating account of whaling that was also an allegorical drama of the human struggle itself.

American poets, too, began to use American subjects. Henry Wadsworth Longfellow immortalized the Native American hero Hiawatha. John Greenleaf Whittier in "Snow-Bound" described winter on a New England farm. William Cullen Bryant in "To a Waterfowl" drew a haunting picture of sunset over a lonely marsh. Edgar Allan Poe wrote of the terrors that lurk in the world of imagination and dreams.

Many American writers took an active part in reform movements. Whittier and Longfellow joined the crusade against slavery, as did poet James Russell Lowell and poet and novelist Lydia Maria Child. Henry David Thoreau himself spent a night in jail rather than pay taxes to support the Mexican War.

■ Scientific Advances

Men and women in the United States also won fame in the field of science. As a child Maria Mitchell taught herself astronomy while checking navigational instruments

Visualizing History ▲ AMERICAN LITERATURE James Fenimore Cooper's series of books about the frontier, the *Leatherstocking Tales,* included *The Last of the Mohicans* (1826) and *The Deerslayer* (1841). ***How did Cooper's new series differ from his first novel,*** Precaution?

Visualizing History ▲ MARIA MITCHELL Maria Mitchell taught herself astronomy and made a name for herself by discovering a comet in 1847. ***What advances did the physicians Long and Morton make to the field of medicine?***

for whaling captains. She discovered a new comet, several groups of distant stars, and wrote important studies of Jupiter and Saturn. Mitchell was the first woman elected to several learned societies. Joseph Henry, the inventor of the electromagnetic motor, headed the Smithsonian Institution, established in 1846. Research there laid the basis for the accurate prediction of weather.

Matthew Maury, an officer of the United States Navy, developed tables predicting winds and ocean tides at different seasons and gave directions for the shortest travel time. These tables helped reduce the average sailing time from New York to San Francisco by 47 days. His findings aided worldwide navigation so greatly that 13 foreign nations honored him. Known as the founder of the science of oceanography, Maury also made a systematic study of the ocean bottom and selected the route for the first transatlantic cable.

▲ *AMONG THE SIERRA NEVADA MOUNTAINS* by Albert Bierstadt, 1868 Albert Bierstadt's most popular works deal with the frontier, reflecting both Americans' pride in their country's natural beauty and their love of nature. ***Why did painters, including Samuel F. B. Morse, seek to excel in their art?***

An important advance in medicine is credited to two physicians from the United States. Working independently, Dr. Crawford W. Long of Georgia in 1842 and Dr. W. T. G. Morton of Boston in 1846 were the first physicians to use ether as an anesthetic during surgery.

■ The Arts

American painters and sculptors were eager to produce works as great as those of Europe. The artists of the time set a standard that served to inspire later artists.

Artists

Samuel F. B. Morse, the inventor of the telegraph, began his career as a painter who wanted to "rival the genius of a Raphael, a Michelangelo, a Titian," in order to refute the charge that the United States "has produced no men of genius." American art, however, did not develop quickly. American artists had little opportunity for the skilled training available abroad, and European styles were still the standard by which art was judged.

American artists did best when, like the writers, they turned their attention to the American scene. George Caleb Bingham painted the life he had seen on the Missouri frontier as a boy. A group of landscape painters in the East was known as the Hudson River School. Their romantic paintings of the Catskill Mountains and Hudson River are highly prized.

Architects

Early nineteenth-century American architects continued to use classical models developed in the Renaissance. In New England, Charles Bulfinch, influenced by English models, developed a distinctive "Federal" style of architecture that can be seen in the Massachusetts State House, the largest building in America at the time it was designed. Bulfinch later worked for 14 years in Washington, D.C., and helped to complete the design of the Capitol. His influence can be seen in architecture in the Northeast.

The type of architecture that most appealed to the American taste, however, was the style known as "Greek Revival." Based on classical Greek and Roman forms, it was used both in domestic architecture and in public and private buildings, the most famous of which is Virginia's State Capitol.

■ Social Experiments

From Europe came a new idea—**socialism.** Socialists believed that the means of production should be owned by society, not by private individuals. They believed that business competition and individual ownership of property caused poverty and inequality. Socialists proposed to substitute cooperation for competition and common ownership for individual ownership. Early followers of the idea wanted to start small, voluntary communities where their ideas could be put into practice.

Most of these experiments took place in the United States where land was easy to acquire. A famous English socialist, Robert Owen, started a cooperative venture at New Harmony, Indiana. Charles Fourier, a Frenchman, proposed to organize society into "phalanxes" of just 1,620 people living in villages called "phalansteries." His converts included Horace Greeley, editor of the *New York Tribune,* the most widely read newspaper in the United States.

The goal of the Brook Farm community in Massachusetts, founded by George Ripley, was to free its members for intellectual activity by running a self-sufficient farm. Members became disillusioned, however, because of the time, energy, and hard work required by farm labor. Nathaniel Hawthorne was persuaded to live at Brook Farm for a time. He, too, found it difficult to write—his primary aim—because of the hard work. He wrote to his fiancée:

❝ *It is my opinion . . . that a man's soul may be buried under a dungheap, or in a furrow of the field, just as well as under a pile of money. . . .* **❞**

The Brook Farm community ultimately collapsed after a large fire left the group greatly in debt.

■ Religious Movements

A great ferment in religious thought occurred in the first half of the nineteenth century. During this period a number of new religious denominations and religious bodies arose, including some that practiced communal living. Among these were the Church of Jesus Christ of Latter-day Saints and the Shakers.

Religious Communal Groups

Religious groups, having an additional basis for unity, were successful in community living. One rapidly growing religious body was the Church of Jesus Christ of Latter-day Saints, or the Mormon Church. This church was founded in 1830 by a New Englander, Joseph Smith, who believed he had been called to restore the Christian church to its original form. Smith wrote the *Book of Mormon* from golden plates that he said an angel had led him to discover. Mormonism enjoyed rapid growth and established a distinctive pattern of communal living at Kirtland, Ohio. Persecution drove the Mormons west to Utah.

The Shakers were founded by Mother Ann Lee in 1772 as an offshoot of the Quakers. Supporting themselves by small industries in orderly communities that were isolated from the rest of the world, the Shakers reached their peak in the mid-1800s with some 6,000 members. They did not marry or have children; the society survived by making converts. Few Shakers are left, but their handiwork—especially Shaker furniture, with its clean lines—is highly valued by collectors today.

The Oneida Community in central New York state was another group that aspired to found a successful utopian society. Practicing a form of Christian socialism, members supported themselves by manufacturing steel game traps and silver plate. The group prospered for some 30 years but then broke up.

Visualizing
History

▲ REVIVAL MEETINGS The first half of the nineteenth century saw a great variety of religious movements in the United States. Throughout the country, the immense growth of Protestant denominations was marked by great revival meetings. *In what other ways did the Protestant faith spread?*

Other Religious Activity

The creed for the Unitarian Church was formulated in New England in 1819 by Reverend William Ellery Channing. Breaking away from the Congregational Church, Unitarians rejected the doctrine of the Trinity, preferring the concept of the oneness of Deity. The Unitarians also believed that human beings were by nature good, not evil.

Unitarians were attracted to Transcendentalism, an American movement that emphasized the relationship between human beings and nature as well as the importance of the individual conscience. Writers such as Margaret Fuller, Ralph Waldo Emerson, and Henry David Thoreau were among the leading Transcendentalist thinkers. Through her life and writings, Fuller advocated rights for women. In his

poems and essays, Emerson urged people to trust themselves, to listen to the inner voice of conscience, and to break the bonds of prejudice. In *Walden* (1854) Thoreau extolled a life of thoughtful solitude.

Protestantism experienced a renewal, a "Second Great Awakening." Throughout the country, beginning in New England and spreading westward, growth of Protestant denominations was marked by great revival meetings, the building of thousands of new churches, and the founding of scores of colleges and universities.

In cities a similar stirring of religious activity arose in the Catholic churches. In Boston and New York, for example, the Roman Catholic Church provided not only places of worship for Catholic European immigrants, but also schools, orphanages, and charitable organizations.

The Temperance Movement

While some religious groups attempted to revise their philosophies or create alternative societies, others put their energies into changing what they felt undermined the quality of life. This was how many groups, especially Baptists and Methodists, viewed liquor. The temperance movement, which began in the United States and spread to England, attempted to ban the use of alcohol.

Most of the movement's leaders were clergy interested in doing away with social evils, poverty, and crime that were often brought on by heavy drinking. Like many other reform groups, temperance groups founded a national organization, the United States Temperance Union, in 1833. Heavy drinkers were persuaded to "take the pledge" to give up alcohol. Temperance propaganda even included a "Cold Water Army" of children with uniforms and marching songs.

In addition to trying to persuade people not to drink, temperance societies demanded laws to put an end to the sale of liquor. They were able to convince many politicians of the justice of their cause. Abraham Lincoln, for example, favored prohibition by state action, arguing that just as the American Revolution freed people from the tyranny of Britain, so would prohibition free people from the tyranny of alcohol. In 1851 Maine passed the first state prohibition law,

an example followed by about a dozen states. Other states passed "local option" laws, which allowed towns and villages to prohibit the sale of liquor.

The achievements of the 1830s and 1840s had beneficial and long-lasting results. The years of reform helped establish the spirit of free thinking in the American character.

▲ THE TRANSCENDENTALISTS Margaret Fuller was a leader in the Transcendentalist movement. *What ideas did Transcendentalists express?*

Section 3 ★ Review

Checking for Understanding

1. **Identify** Hudson River School, Maria Mitchell, Charles Bulfinch, Greek Revival, Brook Farm community, Transcendentalism, Second Great Awakening.

2. **Define** socialism.

3. **List** the prominent American artists and writers of the 1800s.

4. **Describe** the temperance movement in the 1800s.

Critical Thinking

5. **Analyzing Reform** The reform movements of the 1800s were initiated to extend rights and freedom of choice. What movement was an exception? What laws exist today that have similar goals to those of this movement?

Walden (excerpt)

I went to the woods because I wished to live deliberately, to front only the essential facts of life, and see if I could not learn what it had to teach, and not, when I came to die, discover that I had not lived. I did not wish to live what was not life, living is so dear; nor did I wish to practice resignation, unless it was quite necessary. I wanted to live deep and suck out all the marrow of life, to live so sturdily and Spartan-like as to put to rout all that was not life, to cut a broad swath and shave close, to drive life into a corner, and reduce it to its lowest terms, and, if it proved to be mean, why then to get the whole and genuine meanness of it, and publish its meanness to the world; or if it were sublime, to know it by experience, and be able to give a true account of it in my next excursion. For most men, it appears to me, are in a strange uncertainty about it, whether it is of the devil or of God, and have *somewhat hastily* concluded that it is the chief end of man here to "glorify God and enjoy him forever."

Still we live meanly, like ants. . . . Our life is frittered away by detail. An honest man has hardly need to count more than his ten fingers, or in extreme cases he may add his ten toes, and lump the rest. Simplicity, simplicity, simplicity! I say, let your affairs be as two or three, and not a hundred or a thousand; instead of a million count half a dozen, and keep your accounts on your thumb-nail. In the midst of this chopping sea of civilized life, such are the clouds and storms and quicksands and thousand-and-one items to be allowed for, that a man has to live, if he would not founder and go to the bottom and not make his port at all, by dead reckoning, and he must be a great calculator indeed who succeeds. Simplify, simplify. Instead of three meals a day, if it be necessary eat but one; instead of a hundred dishes, five; and reduce other things in proportion. Our life is like a German Confederacy, made up of petty states, with its boundary forever fluctuating, so that even a German cannot tell you how it is bounded at any moment. The nation

▲ HENRY DAVID THOREAU

Part journal, part social commentary, and part sermon, this work summarizes and enlarges upon Thoreau's experiences at Walden Pond, near Concord, Massachusetts, where he built a cabin and lived in solitude for two years.

As you read this passage, look for Thoreau's criticisms of American society, his call for personal freedom, and what he says we must do to live in society.

▲ **WALDEN POND**

itself, with all its so-called internal improvements, which, by the way, are all grown establishment, cluttered with furniture and tripped up by its own traps, ruined by luxury and heedless expense, by want of calculation and a worthy aim, as the million house-holds in the land; and the only cure for it, as for them, is in a rigid economy, a stern and more than Spartan simplicity of life and elevation of purpose. It lives too fast. Men think that it is essential that the *Nation* have commerce, and export ice, and talk through a telegraph, and ride thirty miles an hour, without a doubt, whether *they* do or not; but whether we should live like baboons or like men, is a little uncertain. . . .

Interpreting Literature

1. What motivated Thoreau to go and live alone in the wilderness?

2. What is Thoreau's assessment of life at mid-century? To what does he compare life?

Seeing Relationships

3. What trends and tendencies of the period go hand in hand with the ideals Thoreau expresses?

CHAPTER 12 ★ REVIEW

Using Vocabulary

Context clues help a reader determine the meaning of an unfamiliar word. A clue might take the form of a definition, an explanation, a synonym or antonym, or further details that make the meaning clear. Write a sentence for each of the terms below. Include context clues so that the meaning of the words are clear to a reader unfamiliar with them.

lyceum   socialism
abolitionist   Underground Railroad

Reviewing Facts

1. **Summarize** advances in American education in the early 1800s.

2. **Describe** how Garrison, Douglass, and Clay influenced the abolitionist movement.

3. **Specify** the goals and achievements of the woman's rights movement during this period.

4. **Identify** the major religious groups and movements that emerged during the 1800s.

Understanding Concepts

Reform

1. Which of the nineteenth-century reform movements were hampered by opposition from groups concerned about their own economic interests? Explain.

Values and Beliefs

2. The Underground Railroad was run by decent people who broke the law. Under the law these people were technically stealing property. What values did they consider to be above the law? Do you think breaking the law is ever justified under certain circumstances? Explain.

Critical Thinking

1. **Making Global Comparisons** Slavery was abolished in Great Britain, France, and Latin America before it was abolished in the United States. What economic and political differences probably account for this?

2. **Comparing Fine Art** Compare this painting by James Hamilton, entitled *Scene on the Hudson,* with the painting *Among the Sierra Nevada Mountains* on page 348. Do the artists differ in the way they painted their scenes? How does the environment in Hamilton's painting differ from that in Bierstadt's work?

▲ *SCENE ON THE HUDSON* BY JAMES HAMILTON

Writing About History

Examples

Imagine you are the editor of a prominent newspaper in 1830. Write an editorial pointing out injustices that exist even as democratic changes are sweeping the country. Give examples of failure to provide freedom and equal opportunity for all people in the United States.

Cooperative Learning

Working in pairs, research the life of one American writer or poet of the 1800s, and review one of the writer's works. Have one partner write a biography and a description of the writer's contribution to American culture. Have the other partner write a review of the writer's work. Bind them into one booklet with the writer's name as a title. Display the booklets for other students to read.

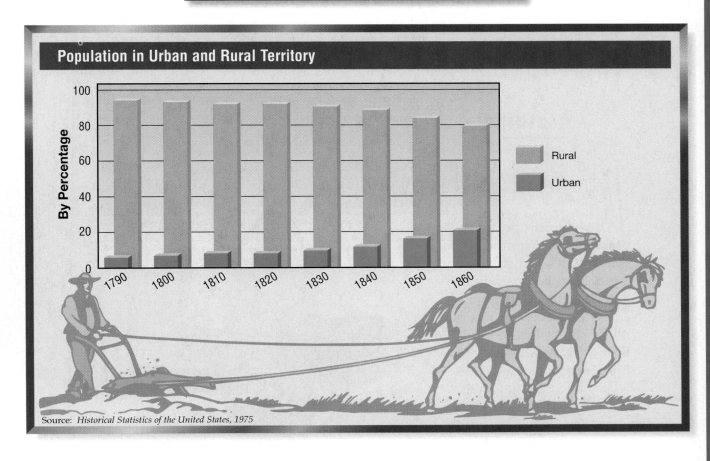

Population in Urban and Rural Territory

By Percentage

100
80
60
40
20
0

1790 1800 1810 1820 1830 1840 1850 1860

Rural
Urban

Source: *Historical Statistics of the United States, 1975*

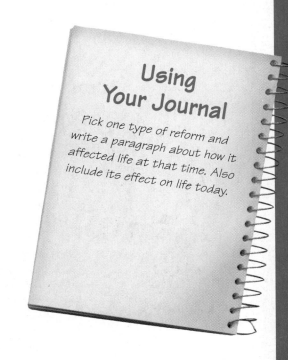

Social Studies Skills

Reading a Bar Graph

A bar graph is used to show relationships. A bar graph can be used to show how something changes over time. For example, the bar graph on this page shows how urban and rural populations changed during a certain time period.

Practicing the Skill

Use the bar graph and your understanding of Chapter 12 content to answer the following questions.

1. What time period is covered in the graph?

2. What do the vertical bars of the graph represent?

3. Throughout the time period covered, is the majority of the population urban or rural?

4. How is the population changing during the time period covered?

5. How might the trend shown in the bar graph affect the reforms discussed in the chapter?

Using Your Journal

Pick one type of reform and write a paragraph about how it affected life at that time. Also include its effect on life today.

Cultural Kaleidoscope

Clothing

High Fashion

The first European immigrants tried to reproduce in the Americas what they had left behind. Even after they gained independence and called themselves Americans, many still followed Europe's lead in matters of fashion. At the same time, Americans were forced to adjust their lifestyles to a new environment. The development of a unique American style in clothing and fashions was beginning.

▲ Nineteenth-century slippers and perfume

Hatboxes came in a variety of shapes and sizes. The well-dressed woman often wore an oversized hat or bonnet.
▼

▲
A variety of styles is shown in *The Sailor's Wedding*. During the 1830s and 1840s, more and more women wore full-skirted gowns with petticoats. One interesting fashion note is that for nearly 200 years moustaches and beards were almost never worn. Only in the 1850s did American men in large numbers begin to let their facial hair grow.

▲ Jewelry box

▶
A well-dressed man of the period often wore a top hat and a cape.

▶
Into the early 1800s, children, at least those in families wealthy enough to have portraits painted, wore the same kind of clothing their parents wore.

Chapter 10

Sectionalism

The Industrial Revolution brought changes to all sections of the United States. In the Northeast, the textile industry expanded rapidly. Other manufacturing and shipping industries also grew in importance. As a result, goods became cheaper and more widely available. Craft workers organized trade societies, and unskilled workers formed labor unions to improve their lives.

In the South the cotton gin and Britain's increased demand for cotton boosted the economy. Cotton became the major export not only of the South but of the nation. As a result, many Southerners' disapproval of slavery faded away.

In the Northwest, pioneers streamed over the Appalachian Mountains to settle the region. Soon towns became cities, and in these cities manufacturing sprang up. By 1820 more than one-fourth of the people in the United States lived west of the Appalachian Plateau.

Each section of the country had its own wants and needs. Often people in different sections quarreled over whether the national government should support a particular issue. These quarrels threatened American unity.

Henry Clay's "American System" was designed to benefit the economies of all sections, but this compromise brought unity for only a while. In the presidential election of 1824, four National Republicans, representing different sections, sought the office. In a close election, the House of Representatives decided on John Quincy Adams, much to the disgust of Andrew Jackson, who had received the most popular votes.

Chapter 11

Age of Jackson

By the election of 1828, sectional interests had strengthened, and the population was shifting from the Northeast to the South and the Northwest.

The new President, Andrew Jackson, was a man of the people, and his supporters became known as Democrats. During his administration, the power of the presidency increased, the American definition of democracy broadened, and the people began to expect more from their political system.

However, the new democracy did not extend to Native Americans and African Americans. The government forced Native Americans to move from their lands. African Americans remained enslaved in the South; they were second-class citizens in the North.

Meanwhile, tariffs, banking, and internal improvements still triggered sectional disputes. During debates on the issues of nullification and high tariffs, many feared that the Southern states might secede. Jackson's stand against the second Bank of the United States helped him win the 1832 election but, in the end, led to the Panic of 1837.

In the election of 1840, the Whig party captured the presidency for its candidate, William Henry Harrison, by trying to overcome sectionalism. However, Harrison died after only a month in office, and Vice President John Tyler became President. Unfortunately, Tyler disagreed with the Whigs on many issues, especially states' rights.

Chapter 12

The Spirit of Reform

Between 1820 and 1854, many Americans focused on social needs rather than political issues. Reformers wanted to better their world.

Thanks in part to Horace Mann, many states were providing free elementary education by 1850. State universities began to spring up, and some of the first schools for the academic education of women were founded. Programs for adult education and free public libraries became widespread.

Other reformers championed the causes of prisoners and the disabled. Many states opened insane asylums to care for the mentally ill, who formerly lived in jails.

Women began to organize for their rights. They failed to gain universal suffrage or general acceptance into professions, but for the first time many states allowed women to retain and to manage their property.

The dominant reform effort of the time was the abolitionist movement. Meanwhile, the Underground Railroad quietly smuggled enslaved African Americans out of the South.

American culture reflected the social changes going on. Poets, artists, and novelists described the American scene. Part of the scene was a religious renewal, a "Second Great Awakening." Among the new religious organizations were several utopian communities, such as the Shakers.

Understanding Unit Themes

1. **American Democracy**   What important democratic changes began to develop during the period of the Industrial Revolution?

2. **Economic Development**   How did the Industrial Revolution lead to changes in the American economy, its lifestyle, and its values?

3. **Humanities and Religion**   How did changes in religious philosophy relate to the growing leadership of religious groups in social reform?

4. **Conflict and Cooperation**   How did sectional interests over economic issues develop into conflicts and division within the United States?

UNIT FIVE
DIVISION AND REUNION
1825–1877

★★★

▲ BRASS CANDLESTICK, 1850S

 History AND ART

The Banjo Lesson
by Henry Tanner, 1893

American artist Henry Ossawa Tanner produced a number of realistic studies of American life. After he moved to Europe in the early 1900s, he found another source of inspiration—the Bible.

Setting the Scene

The slavery issue dominated American life during the first half of the nineteenth century. Compromise had worked in the past, but a growing antislavery movement would not let the moral shame of slavery die.

▲ UNION SOLDIER

Themes

- Civil Rights and Liberties
- Conflict and Cooperation
- Cultural Diversity
- U.S. Role in World Affairs

Key Events

- Monroe Doctrine
- Treaty of Guadalupe Hidalgo
- Compromise of 1850
- Confederate States formed
- Battles of Gettysburg and Vicksburg
- Surrender of General Lee
- Assassination of Lincoln
- Radical Reconstruction
- Compromise of 1877

Major Issues

- A belief in Manifest Destiny results in war with Mexico.
- The breakdown of the political party system with the death of the Whigs produces an inability to compromise over slavery.
- During the Civil War, the nation's welfare versus individual rights leads to a suspension of civil liberties.
- Although harsh, reconstruction of the Southern states gradually leads to a renewed Union.

▲ HONORARY BANNER, 1860

▲ CONFEDERATE BUGLE

Portfolio Project

Research one of the Latin American countries formed from the United Provinces of Central America. Create a time line of important events in the history of that country, from its inception to current time.

Global Perspectives

★★★★★ ★★

The World

	1825	1845	
Asia and Oceania			**1853** *Commodore Matthew Perry arrives in Japan*
Europe			◀ **1848** *Nationalist revolutions occur throughout Europe*
Africa			
South America			**1850** *Slave trade, but not slavery, ends in Brazil*
North and Central America			

The United States

	1825	1845	
Pacific and Northwest	**1830** *Fur traders open the Oregon Trail*	**1848** *Gold discovered in California*	
Southeast	▶ **1831** *Cyrus McCormick invents the reaper*		
Midwest			
Southwest	◀ **1836** *Texas Revolution, Battle of the Alamo fought*	**1848** *United States acquires Mexican Cession*	
Atlantic Northeast	**1825** *Erie Canal completed*	**1852** *Uncle Tom's Cabin published*	

Linking Across TIME

African Americans have made major contributions to our country's cultural life, especially in the area of music. Gospel, an exuberant and joyous celebration of faith through music, grew out of the religious services held by enslaved people. Blues, which grew out of their work songs and chants, had an indelible impact on the pioneers of rock 'n roll. Jazz, which some people consider the only new art form to be developed in the twentieth century, was influenced by both gospel and the blues.

1865

1885

▶ **1869** *Suez Canal opens*

▲ **1861** *Benito Juárez becomes President of Mexico*

1867 *Dominion of Canada is formed*

1867 *Alaska purchased from Russia*

1877 *Nez Percé War fought*

1872 *Yellowstone National Park created*

1875 *Black Hills opens to gold seekers*

▲ **1861** *Civil War begins*

1865

1885

CHAPTER 13

★★

Manifest Destiny
1825–1854

▼ MINIATURE BOOKS OF THE 1830s

Setting the Scene

Focus

The drive to expand the boundaries of the United States across North America became a single-minded goal for many Americans in the 1830s and 1840s. Through war with Mexico and diplomatic negotiations with Great Britain, the United States acquired Texas, Oregon, California, Utah, and the remainder of the Southwest. By 1850 thousands of settlers had crossed the Great Plains for new homes.

Concepts to Understand

★ Why geographic expansion to the Pacific became a national mission

★ How westward migration shaped the political development of Oregon and California

Read to Discover . . .

★ what made Americans determined to expand the size of the country.

★ the causes and results of the Mexican War.

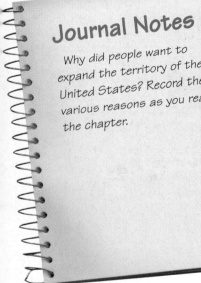

Journal Notes

Why did people want to expand the territory of the United States? Record the various reasons as you read the chapter.

CULTURAL

● **1839** *Charles Goodyear develops vulcanized rubber*

● **1844** *First telegraph message sent*

1835	1840

● **1836** *Battle of the Alamo fought*
● **1836** *Texas wins independence*

● **1842** *Webster-Ashburton Treaty ratified*

POLITICAL

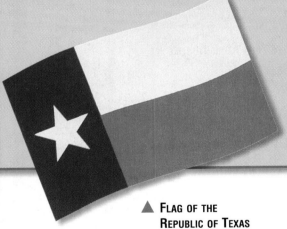

▲ FLAG OF THE REPUBLIC OF TEXAS

- **1847** *Brigham Young leads Mormons to the Great Salt Lake valley*

1845

- **1846** *United States and Britain set Oregon boundary*
- **1846** *Mexican War begins*

- **1853** *Stephen Foster pens "My Old Kentucky Home"*

1850

- **1853** *United States makes Gadsden Purchase*

★★

The Thirst for New Lands

Setting the Scene

Section Focus

The idea that the United States was bound to extend its borders from the Atlantic Ocean to the Pacific Ocean became known as "Manifest Destiny." Americans had begun moving to Texas in the 1820s. By the 1830s and 1840s, they were making their way to Oregon, California, and Utah. What began as a trickle of immigrants swelled to a flood; these American settlements, in turn, gave weight to arguments in favor of expansion and annexation.

Objectives

After studying this section, you should be able to
★ give reasons Americans wanted to expand their territory to the Pacific.
★ describe negotiations with Britain over disputed lands.
★ describe the overland migrations to Oregon and Utah.
★ explain why Texans wanted independence from Mexico and how Texas became part of the United States.

Key Terms

dark horse, joint resolution

◀ THE PRAIRIE HUNTER

---

*S*everal factors combined to produce the expansionist movement known as Manifest Destiny. Chief among these was the seemingly habitual ambition, nurtured by the restlessness of the American pioneer spirit, to move on to new land.

■ Westward to the Pacific

Expanding the United States to the Pacific involved risks, for it meant taking land claimed or settled by other peoples. The United States, with limited military power, had to weigh carefully the possibility of hostilities with Native Americans on the plains, with Mexico in Texas, and with Britain.

Rivals for the Land

The first area where the advance of American settlement caused serious friction with Britain was in the Northeast. Because of confusing language in the Treaty of Paris after the Revolution, the northern and eastern boundaries of Maine had been uncertain. As long as the region was unoccupied, this was not a serious matter.

In 1838, however, the British decided to construct an overland road to connect St. John on the Bay of Fundy with Montreal and Quebec. In February 1839, settlers from Maine, pushing into the fertile Aroostook (uh•ROOS•tuhk) Valley, clashed with British workers who were felling trees for the road project. The struggle, fought mostly with fists, is known as the Aroostook War. It nearly led to something more serious when Maine and New Brunswick called out their militias, and Congress authorized President Van Buren to call for 50,000 soldiers in case of war.

■ The Webster-Ashburton Treaty

In spite of friction and ill feeling, there were practical reasons for pursuing peace. The most important reason was that the United States and Great Britain each profited from the other's trade.

The negotiators—Daniel Webster, the American secretary of state, and Lord Ashburton, the husband of an American heiress—decided that it was impossible to fix the correct boundary of Maine. Instead, the 1842 treaty divided the disputed territory as fairly as they could. Great Britain got what it wanted most: enough land to make possible a direct land route from the St. Lawrence River to New Brunswick. The United States received what it wanted—the Aroostook Valley—along with other concessions on the northern boundaries of New Hampshire, Vermont, and New York.

■ Settlers Move West

The Oregon Territory extended from the Pacific Ocean to the Rocky Mountains, bordering Russian Alaska to the north and California to the south. Oregon was originally claimed by four countries—the United

▲ *Spirit of the Frontier* by John Gast, 1872 Driven by a sense of Manifest Destiny, Americans moved west. By 1848 the United States stretched unchallenged from sea to sea. *Over what area did the United States-British confrontation take place in the late 1830s?*

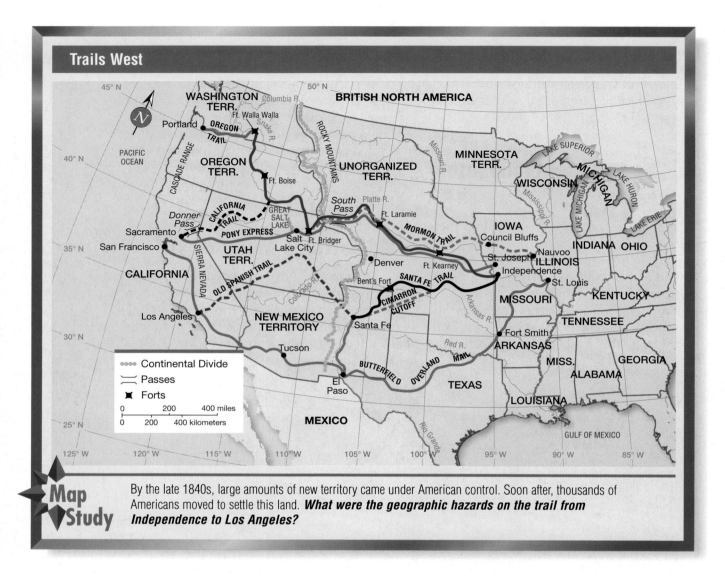

Trails West

By the late 1840s, large amounts of new territory came under American control. Soon after, thousands of Americans moved to settle this land. **What were the geographic hazards on the trail from Independence to Los Angeles?**

States, Great Britain, Spain, and Russia. By 1824, however, only the Americans and the British were left to compete for control of Oregon.

To Oregon

Until shortly before 1840 the joint occupation of Oregon was almost entirely a British affair. In the mid-1830s, however, American churches sent missionaries to Christianize the Native Americans. When the missionaries began to farm, they sent back glowing reports of the fertility of the soil.

In 1838 a party of American pioneers arrived by ship in the valley of the Willamette River; most newcomers, however, came by covered wagon over the Oregon

Trail. By 1842 there were perhaps 500 Americans in Oregon, and in the next year a single party of immigrants numbered 900.

By 1843 so many Americans had arrived in Oregon that they set up a government of their own. Like the Pilgrims and the Mayflower Compact, they drew up their own constitution. Its preamble, similar to the United States Constitution Preamble, read:

> **We the people of Oregon Territory, for the purpose of mutual protection and to secure peace and prosperity among ourselves, agree to adopt the following laws and regulations until such time as the United States of America extend their jurisdiction over us.**

The last phrase shows that the settlers were determined that the United States and not Britain should rule Oregon. By 1845, 5,000 Americans were living south of the Columbia River and demanding that their government take possession of the Oregon Territory.

To Utah

Another group of settlers moved west, not to expand United States territory but to escape from it. The Mormon Church and its founder Joseph Smith were forced to move several times to escape persecution. Many people resented the new religion because of its communal organization and Smith's teachings that a man could have more than one wife. The Mormons moved first to Ohio, then to Missouri, and then to Illinois. At Nauvoo, Illinois, they built a thriving community of 20,000 people. In 1844, however, Joseph Smith was jailed for ordering the destruction of a printing press that belonged to people who disagreed with him. An angry mob then killed Smith and his brother. Brigham Young, the new leader, believing that no safe refuge could be found in the United States, sought an isolated haven in territory that belonged to Mexico.

The move took place in 1847. The Mormons soon established flourishing settlements near the Great Salt Lake in Utah. They developed an advanced system for controlling the water supply in the semiarid regions of the Far West. Around Salt Lake City, irrigation transformed the desert into a garden spot.

■ Texas Independence

Texas—a vast, ill-defined area extending southwest from Louisiana to the Rio Grande and west to the foothills of the Rocky Mountains—belonged to Mexico. The original Spanish settlements in Texas were limited to a few hundred people and a dozen missions.

Visualizing History

▲ MORMONS MOVE WEST The Mormons ventured west across the Missouri River to the valley of the Great Salt Lake. Some poorer Mormons traveled to Utah in handcarts. *Who led the Mormons to Utah?*

Mountain Men

In the early nineteenth century, fashionable Europeans wore felt hats made of beaver fur. At one time milliners obtained their furs from Russia, but hunters exhausted the supply of beaver there. The next source was the woodlands of eastern North America until the beaver was hunted out there too. Then beaver were discovered in the Rocky Mountains.

Fur companies hired freelance trappers who over time became known as mountain men. As year-round wilderness residents, they learned to live independently. They also knew everything about capturing beavers.

A mountain man called the bait he used to lure the beaver "medicine." Actually it was a musky liquid that came from the glands of other beavers. The mountain man spread the liquid on a branch suspended above the trap.

Since beavers are water animals, a mountain man set his trap under water to mask smell. An animal caught in the underwater trap drowned quickly, and so the trapper did not have to worry about struggling with his catch and possibly getting hurt or damaging the pelt of the animal.

American Settlement of Texas

When Mexico broke away from Spain in 1821, its government sought migrants to come and develop Texas. In 1822 Stephen Austin, an American settler, took over a grant of land that the Spanish government had given his father. Mexican officials agreed that Austin could bring American settlers into Texas, provided that they became Roman Catholics and obeyed Mexican law.

Austin's settlement proved so successful that by 1830 Texas had attracted almost 30,000 Americans. In that year Mexico passed a law restricting further immigration because it was concerned about developments in Texas. Americans, knowing that Mexico's law against slavery was not strictly enforced in Texas, had brought thousands of enslaved people. In addition, they had failed to become Catholics, and the flood of settlers now outnumbered local Mexicans 10 to 1.

The Lone Star Republic

In 1833 Mexico elected General Antonio Santa Anna as president. When the new president abolished local rights, rebellion broke out in Texas. Late in 1835 Santa Anna marched his army north to subdue the rebels. In February 1836, with more than 2,000 troops, Santa Anna besieged 188 Texans in the Alamo, a mission station in San Antonio. After two weeks of resistance, the defenders of the Alamo were defeated.

The Mexican army pursued Sam Houston, the military leader of the Texans, and his troops toward the United States border. Then at San Jacinto (SAN juh•SIHN•tuh) Creek, Houston's forces turned and attacked. Crying "Remember the Alamo!" they surprised and defeated the Mexican troops and captured Santa Anna. Under pressure, Santa Anna signed a treaty accepting the independence of Texas. As soon as he was free, however, Santa Anna refused to be bound by the terms.

Texas Statehood

In 1836 Texas declared itself the Lone Star Republic and immediately voted to seek admission to the United States. Although there was strong Southern support to extend the area of cotton-growing by annexing Texas, Northern abolitionists charged that the whole history of Texas was a slaveholders' plot to enlarge their power.

Statehood Denied

Although Presidents Jackson and Van Buren refused to recommend annexation, the issue arose again in 1843. President John Tyler feared that Texas would ally itself with Great Britain. The British were interested in Texas as a new source of cotton—and as a market for their manufactured goods. Moreover, British antislavery societies hoped that the new country might be persuaded to free its enslaved workers.

The threat of Texas as a competing source of cotton and a possible haven for runaways alarmed Southerners. Secretary of State John C. Calhoun presented an annexation treaty to the Senate, but a 35–16 vote did not meet the two-thirds majority needed. The rejection of annexation sprang from Northern opposition to adding more slave territory to the Union and from fears that admission of Texas would bring on a war with Mexico.

Election of 1844

As the presidential election of 1844 approached, the issue of territorial expansion took center stage. Former President Van Buren, a Democrat, and Henry Clay, a Whig, were expected to be the rival candidates. Then the unexpected happened: Van Buren failed to receive the Democratic nomination.

▲ GENERAL SAM HOUSTON

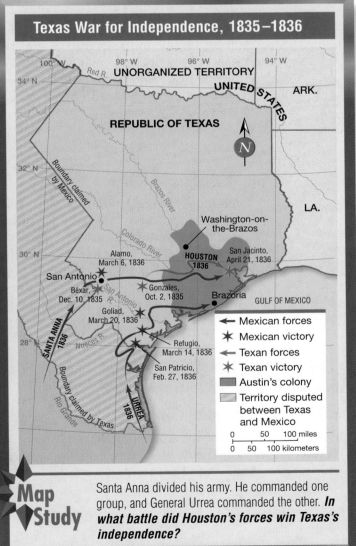

Texas War for Independence, 1835–1836

UNORGANIZED TERRITORY

UNITED STATES

ARK.

REPUBLIC OF TEXAS

LA.

Washington-on-the-Brazos

Alamo, March 6, 1836

HOUSTON 1836

San Jacinto, April 21, 1836

San Antonio

Béxar, Dec. 10, 1835

Gonzales, Oct. 2, 1835

Brazoria

GULF OF MEXICO

Goliad, March 20, 1836

SANTA ANNA 1836

Refugio, March 14, 1836

San Patricio, Feb. 27, 1836

URREA 1836

Boundary claimed by Texas

Rio Grande

Boundary claimed by Mexico

Red R.

Brazos River

Colorado River

San Antonio R.

Nueces R.

← Mexican forces
✳ Mexican victory
← Texan forces
✳ Texan victory
■ Austin's colony
▨ Territory disputed between Texas and Mexico

0   50   100 miles
0   50   100 kilometers

Map Study

Santa Anna divided his army. He commanded one group, and General Urrea commanded the other. *In what battle did Houston's forces win Texas's independence?*

A coalition of Westerners who wanted Oregon and Southerners who wanted Texas nominated the first **dark horse,** or unexpected candidate, in the history of the presidency—James K. Polk of Tennessee.

The Democrats dodged the slavery issue by linking the demands for Texas and Oregon. They placed their main emphasis on taking all of Oregon, where slavery would certainly never be established. This was dramatized by the campaign slogan "Fifty-four forty or fight!" (The parallel 54°40′ was the southern boundary of Alaska.)

Manifest Destiny became the principal issue of the campaign. To counter this unexpected challenge, the Whigs had only Henry Clay's great personal popularity and the slogan, "Who is James K. Polk?" which called attention to the obscurity of Clay's opponent.

Although Clay had earlier opposed admitting Texas into the Union, he issued a cautious statement that he would be glad to see the region annexed if the American people so desired and if war with Mexico could be avoided. Clay's hedging did not work, and Polk won the election by a slim margin.

Texas Becomes a State

Even though the election had been close, President Tyler, who was still in office, asserted that Polk's victory was a mandate for the admission of Texas to the Union. He asked Congress to admit Texas by a **joint resolution** that would require only a simple majority, instead of a treaty that required a vote of two-thirds of the Senate.

On Tyler's initiative in February 1845, both houses of Congress, by very narrow majorities, passed the joint resolution. In December 1845, the Lone Star Republic became the twenty-eighth state. The boundary between Mexico and Texas remained undetermined, and the Mexican government threatened war.

■ Division of Oregon

The risk of war with Mexico put pressure on the United States to settle the Oregon question. It was one thing to shout, "Fifty-four forty or fight!" in an election campaign. It was quite another to take on Great Britain, the greatest sea power in the world, and prepare to fight Mexico.

Great Britain also had reasons to settle the Oregon question peacefully. By 1846 the number of American settlers in Oregon had risen to 10,000 and United States expansionists were calling for "thirty thousand rifles" in Oregon to protect American interests. Rather than losing all of the territory, the British government was willing to relinquish the southern half.

The Hudson's Bay Company had trapped the beavers from the region there and had moved its principal base from the Columbia River to Vancouver Island. In 1846 Polk submitted to the Senate a British proposal to divide Oregon along the 49th parallel. In spite of the objections of Westerners, who accused the President of backing down on his demand for all of Oregon, the Senate approved the treaty, which was signed on June 15, 1846.

Section 1 ★ Review

Checking for Understanding

1. **Identify** Manifest Destiny, Aroostook War, Webster-Ashburton Treaty, Mormons, Brigham Young, Santa Anna, Sam Houston.

2. **Define** dark horse, joint resolution.

3. **List** the three rivals to American settlers for Western lands.

4. **Cite** two reasons why James K. Polk won the 1844 election.

Critical Thinking

5. **Identifying Assumptions** What assumptions did the idea of Manifest Destiny make about the rights of Native Americans and others to this land?

American Missionaries

The Spanish were the first Europeans to establish missions in the Americas. In sparsely populated regions of New Spain, the Spanish missionaries set up small communities that usually included a village, farmland, a fort, and a church.

In the 1800s, Americans called for missionaries to move beyond the frontier. Lyman Beecher, Congregationalist pastor and seminary president, in his *Plea for the West* (1832), argued that the future of the nation depended on Christianizing the West. Protestant and Catholic missionaries heeded Beecher's call. Organizations were founded to send missionaries and Bibles to remote Western settlements. Along with the strong challenge to repent and accept Christian beliefs, missionaries taught people to read and write.

A few Protestant missionaries also began to work among Native Americans in the West—a calling that Franciscans and Jesuits had felt since the early days of exploration. A pioneer Methodist missionary effort began in the Oregon Territory when Marcus and Narcissa Whitman helped establish a string of mission stations along the Columbia River in the 1830s.

The reports from the missionaries and poor economic conditions in the East drew more and more farmers west. Attracted by land, high prices, favorable markets, and rivers for transportation, Americans in large numbers became infected with "Oregon fever." In the 1840s and 1850s, thousands of settlers moved to Oregon to start a new life. Most people settled in the Willamette Valley.

Missionaries often tried to secure special protection for Native Americans, but they found it difficult to serve the needs of both the Native Americans and the advancing settlers. Missionaries also at times imposed their own values and traditions, which often led to few converts and deep resentment among Native Americans.

▲ MISSION IN THE SOUTHWEST, 1820S

Making the Religion Connection

1. Why did Lyman Beecher call for missionary work in the West?

2. Why might missionaries have found it difficult to serve the needs of Native Americans and settlers?

Linking Past and Present

3. How might missionary activity today differ from that of the 1800s? Describe what you think the primary responsibilities of missionaries are.

★★★★★★★★★★★★★★★★★★★★★★★★★★★★★★★★

War With Mexico

Setting the Scene

Section Focus

James K. Polk had been chosen as a presidential candidate because of his clear commitment to territorial expansion. He was determined to fulfill the pledges he made to his party during the campaign. In undertaking a war with Mexico, however, he would face stiff resistance from Northerners and Whigs in Congress.

Objectives

After studying this section, you should be able to

★ contrast the United States's short-term and long-range goals in the war with Mexico.

★ list the terms of the treaty of Guadalupe Hidalgo.

Key Term

consul

◀ OIL LAMP, 1840S

James K. Polk was a man who knew what he wanted. On his first day in office, he told a member of his cabinet that he had four great purposes: settle the Oregon question, lower the tariff, reestablish the independent treasury system abolished by the Whigs in 1842, and annex California. By his third year in office, Polk's strong will and hard work had accomplished his first three goals. Annexing California was more difficult.

■ Polk Attempts to Purchase California

New Englanders had traded with California for cattle hides and tallow for 50 years and had described the region as "the richest, the most beautiful, the healthiest country in the world." In the 1840s, it seemed that control of the region might soon change hands. The native population had staged four rebellions against the Mexican government, which was too distant and too disorganized to govern the region effectively. American officials feared that Great Britain, or even France, might annex California to acquire the great harbor of San Francisco.

In his annual message to Congress in December 1845, Polk cautioned Great Britain and France by repeating the "no colonization" principle of the Monroe Doctrine. He also urged the United States **consul,** or official representative, in Monterey, California, to "arouse in the bosoms of the Californians that love of liberty so natural to the American continent"—in other words, to stir up a revolution. Late in 1845 he sent John Slidell as envoy to Mexico to discuss the Texas question and to offer up to $25 million for California. So great was

Mexican anger at the loss of Texas that any Mexican official who dared to talk with the American diplomat could have lost his position and possibly his life. Slidell's visit, however, inspired a successful revolt against the Mexican government by those who opposed any negotiations with the United States. The new leaders were determined to go to war to win back Texas, and President Mariano Paredes refused to see Slidell. Because he could not present his case, Slidell returned to Washington, D.C. The Mexican government broke off diplomatic relations when the United States annexed Texas, making further negotiations impossible.

The failure of Slidell's mission did not end attempts by the United States to annex California. Mexico's leaders, already angry with the United States, might easily be provoked into war.

■ Outbreak of War

The spark that ignited the war between Mexico and the United States resulted from a dispute over the southern boundary of Texas. Mexico claimed it was the Nueces (nu•AY•suhs) River, while the United States said it was the Rio Grande 130 miles to the south. On hearing of the failure of Slidell's mission to Mexico City, Polk ordered General Zachary Taylor to move his troops south to the Rio Grande. Taylor's troops were, in effect, sent looking for trouble, waiting for an incident justifying retaliation.

War Begins

Late in April 1846, Mexican soldiers crossed the Rio Grande and attacked a small detachment of United States cavalry, which was in Mexican territory according to the Mexican point of view. When news of this attack on Taylor's force reached Washington, D.C., the President hastily revised a war message that he had been preparing in response to Slidell's rejection in Mexico City. Pointing out that his effort to negotiate peaceably with Mexico had failed, Polk argued that war had been begun "by the act

of Mexico herself." On May 13, 1846, Congress declared war by overwhelming majorities in both houses.

Many Americans refused to support a war of aggression against a weaker neighbor. It was, wrote the New England author James Russell Lowell, simply a Southern scheme to steal "bigger pens to cram in slaves." Whig members of Congress, including Abraham Lincoln, then a representative from Illinois, challenged Polk's statement that American blood had been spilled on American soil. Lincoln invited Polk to point out the spot where this had occurred.

Even American soldiers had their doubts about the legitimacy of the war. In 1846 Colonel Ethan Allen Hitchcock wrote:

> **❝** *I have said from the first that the United States are the aggressors. . . . We have not one particle of right to be here. It looks as if the government sent a small force on purpose to bring on a war, so as to have a pretext for taking California and as much of this country as it chooses, for, whatever becomes of this army, there is no doubt of a war between the United States and Mexico. . . . My heart is not in this business. . . but, as a military man, I am bound to execute orders.* **❞**

◀ **JAMES KNOX POLK**

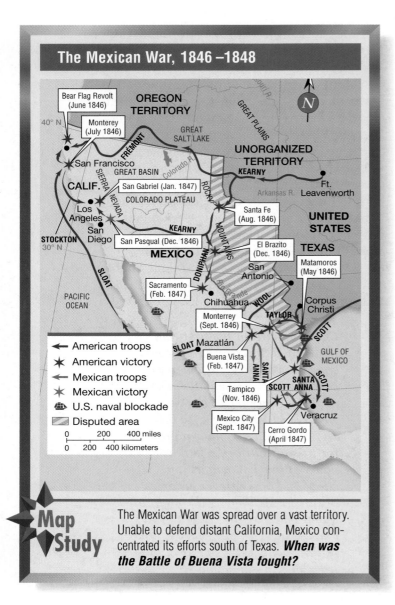

The Mexican War, 1846–1848

Bear Flag Revolt (June 1846)

OREGON TERRITORY

Monterey (July 1846)

GREAT SALT LAKE

GREAT PLAINS

FRÉMONT

San Francisco

GREAT BASIN

CALIF.

KEARNY

Ft. Leavenworth

Arkansas R.

San Gabriel (Jan. 1847)

COLORADO PLATEAU

SIERRA NEVADA

Colorado R.

UNORGANIZED TERRITORY

Los Angeles

San Diego

KEARNY

Santa Fe (Aug. 1846)

UNITED STATES

STOCKTON

San Pasqual (Dec. 1846)

MEXICO

El Brazito (Dec. 1846)

TEXAS

SLOAT

DONIPHAN

ROCKY MOUNTAINS

San Antonio

Matamoros (May 1846)

Sacramento (Feb. 1847)

Rio Grande

WOOL

Corpus Christi

PACIFIC OCEAN

Chihuahua

Monterrey (Sept. 1846)

TAYLOR

SCOTT

SLOAT

Mazatlán

Buena Vista (Feb. 1847)

SANTA ANNA

GULF OF MEXICO

Tampico (Nov. 1846)

SANTA ANNA

SCOTT ANNA

SCOTT

Mexico City (Sept. 1847)

Veracruz

Cerro Gordo (April 1847)

← American troops
✳ American victory
← Mexican troops
✳ Mexican victory
⛴ U.S. naval blockade
▨ Disputed area

0   200   400 miles
0   200   400 kilometers

Map Study

The Mexican War was spread over a vast territory. Unable to defend distant California, Mexico concentrated its efforts south of Texas. **When was the Battle of Buena Vista fought?**

Although attacking Polk for starting the war, the Whigs in Congress supported it by voting for supplies and troops. This action was not as illogical as it may seem, because it is not certain that war could have been prevented. Several months before Polk's message to Congress, the Mexican government had declared itself in favor of "a necessary and glorious war." Aware of the dismal failure of American efforts to invade Canada in the War of 1812, the Mexicans expected victory.

Polk's War Strategy

President Polk planned the military campaigns of the Mexican War as a three-part strategy. First, General Taylor and his troops invaded northern Mexico. In May they pushed the Mexican army across the Rio Grande and by September had taken the city of Monterrey. Taylor and his men then penetrated nearly 300 miles into Mexico and won the Battle of Buena Vista in February 1847.

As the second part of the war strategy, General Stephen Kearny headed west from Missouri with a small force of young recruits in July 1846. In August they took Santa Fe with hardly a shot fired in its defense. Kearny and his troops marched on to California, where they helped the Pacific Squadron defeat the Mexicans in Los Angeles in January 1847. A local revolt in northern California, with the assistance of a handful of American troops and a small fleet, had already shaken off Mexican authority. Thus California came under United States control, and fighting in the West ended.

When Mexico still refused to make peace, Polk launched the third part of his war strategy, sending General Winfield Scott to conquer Mexico City. With a force of 10,000, Scott sailed south and landed at Veracruz. In September 1847, after six months of difficult fighting, he occupied the capital.

Working to the Americans' advantage was the disorganization of the Mexican government. One group after another seized power in Mexico, so that sometimes it was difficult to know who headed the government; once three different men claimed to be president. Alfonso Toro, a Mexican historian, wrote of his country's hapless condition:

> **Although Mexico had an enormous war budget, she really lacked an army; for hardly worthy of the name was the assemblage of drafted men, badly armed, and . . . without confidence in their leaders. The soldiers, who were almost never paid but were maltreated and exploited by their chiefs, deserted whenever they could and even rebelled with arms in their hands when they were ordered to march. . . .**

Treaty of Guadalupe Hidalgo

After the capture of Mexico City, some months passed before a Mexican government could be organized to sign a peace treaty. Meanwhile, advocates of Manifest Destiny, including two members of Polk's cabinet, urged that the United States annex all of Mexico.

Trist in Mexico

President Polk, anticipating Scott's victory in Mexico City, sent Nicholas P. Trist, a clerk in the state department, to Mexico with instructions to offer the same terms that Slidell had offered earlier. After a long delay, Polk's patience with Trist gave out, and the President ordered him back to Washington, D.C. Trist, knowing that he was on the verge of a successful treaty, ignored the orders and stayed on to complete the negotiations.

In February 1848, before the movement for total annexation had proceeded very far, a peace treaty was signed at Guadalupe Hidalgo, outside Mexico City. While President Polk denounced the "exceptional conduct" of Nicholas Trist, he saw no alternative to submitting this treaty to the Senate. After a round of expansionist arguments by those who favored annexing all of Mexico, the Senate finally voted 38 to 14 in favor of the treaty.

Terms of the Treaty

The United States gained full title to Texas (with the Rio Grande as a boundary). It also gained California and the New Mexico territory (including present-day Arizona, Utah, Nevada, and parts of Colorado). The United

▲ ENTERING MEXICO CITY After six months of difficult fighting, General Winfield Scott forced his way into Mexico City. Scott's troops included young military officers Ulysses S. Grant and Robert E. Lee. *Why did some of the troops oppose the war?*

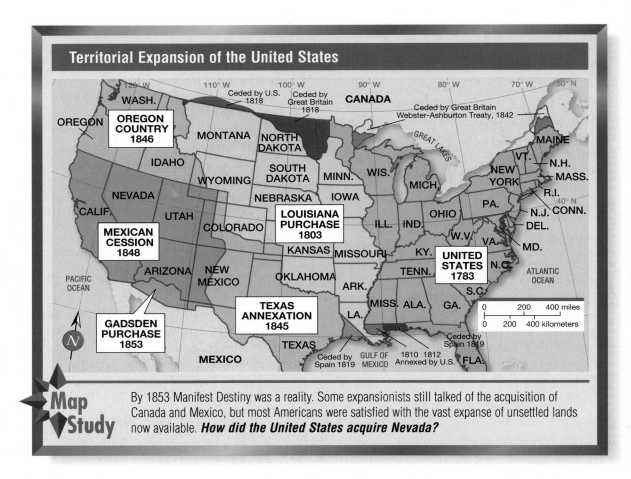

Territorial Expansion of the United States

Ceded by U.S. 1818
Ceded by Great Britain 1818
CANADA
Ceded by Great Britain
Webster-Ashburton Treaty, 1842

WASH.
OREGON
OREGON COUNTRY 1846
MONTANA
NORTH DAKOTA
GREAT LAKES
MAINE
IDAHO
SOUTH DAKOTA
MINN.
WIS.
MICH.
NEW YORK
VT.
N.H.
MASS.
R.I.
WYOMING
NEBRASKA
IOWA
NEVADA
CALIF.
UTAH
COLORADO
LOUISIANA PURCHASE 1803
ILL.
IND.
OHIO
PA.
N.J.
CONN.
DEL.
W.V.
VA.
MD.
MEXICAN CESSION 1848
KANSAS
MISSOURI
KY.
UNITED STATES 1783
N.C.
PACIFIC OCEAN
ARIZONA
NEW MEXICO
OKLAHOMA
TENN.
S.C.
ATLANTIC OCEAN
ARK.
GADSDEN PURCHASE 1853
TEXAS ANNEXATION 1845
MISS.
ALA.
GA.
LA.
MEXICO
TEXAS
Ceded by Spain 1819
GULF OF MEXICO
1810 1812 Annexed by U.S.
Ceded by Spain 1819
FLA.

0   200   400 miles
0   200   400 kilometers

Map Study By 1853 Manifest Destiny was a reality. Some expansionists still talked of the acquisition of Canada and Mexico, but most Americans were satisfied with the vast expanse of unsettled lands now available. *How did the United States acquire Nevada?*

States paid $15 million outright for California and New Mexico and also agreed to pay Mexican government debts amounting to $3,250,000. In 1853 the nation acquired the southern portion of New Mexico for $10 million as part of the Gadsden Purchase. In the Mexican Cession, Mexico lost only 1 percent of its population but half of its territory.

With the Gadsden Purchase, the United States completed its expansion across the continent. As a result, the nation stretched from the Atlantic Ocean to the Pacific Ocean. This land provided a route where the Rocky Mountains were low enough to build a railroad across the southern part of the country to California. Once the United States gained control of large areas of the West, Americans began moving into these regions in greater and greater numbers.

Section 2 ★ Review

Checking for Understanding

1. **Identify** John Slidell, Zachary Taylor, Winfield Scott, Treaty of Guadalupe Hidalgo.
2. **Define** consul.
3. **List** two reasons for the war between Mexico and the United States.
4. **Summarize** the provisions of the Treaty of Guadalupe Hidalgo.

Critical Thinking

5. **Evaluating an Action** Imagine you are a newspaper editor in the mid-1840s. Write your opinion on whether the United States's actions to wage war against Mexico were justified. Include your conclusion on what part Manifest Destiny played in the United States's decision to take these actions.

Interpreting Primary Sources

Migration

Shortly after California became United States territory, the gold rush began. Among the thousands of people who made the long and dangerous trek west was Alvin Coffey, an enslaved man. His holder took away all the money that Coffey made in the mines and later sold him to another man. Coffey eventually earned freedom for himself and his family. His account of the trip to California suggests some of the dangers and hardships faced by many of the forty-niners.

from *Reminiscences* by Alvin Coffey:

I started from St. Louis, Missouri, on the 2nd of April in 1849. There was quite a crowd of neighbors who drove through the mud and rain to St. Joe to see us off. About the first of May we organized the train . . . We crossed the Missouri River at Savanna Landing. . . . At six in the morning, there were three more went to relieve those on guard. One of the three that came in had cholera so bad that he was in lots of misery. Dr. Bassett, the captain of the train, did all he could for him, but he died at 10 o'clock and we buried him. . . . We got news every day that people were dying by the hundreds in St. Joe and St. Louis. It was alarming. When we hitched up and got ready to move, [the] Dr. said, "Boys, we will have to drive day and night." . . . We drove night and day and got out of reach of the cholera. . . . We got across the plains to Fort Lar[a]mie, the 16th of June and the ignorant driver broke down a good many oxen on the trains. There were a good many ahead of us, who had doubled up their trains and left tons upon tons of bacon and other provisions. . . . We crossed the South Pass on the Fourth of July. The ice next morning was as thick as a dinner-plate. On the morning of the 15th, we went to dry-digging mining. We dug and dug to the first of November, at night it commenced raining, and rained and snowed pretty much all the winter. We had a tent but it barely

▲ GOLD MINING IN CALIFORNIA, 1850S

kept us all dry. There were from eight to twelve in one camp. We cut down pine trees for stakes to make a cabin. It was a whole week before we had a cabin to keep us dry.

The wagon train went through Honey Lake to Deer Creek in Sacramento Valley and then to Redding Springs on October 13, 1849.

Examining the Primary Source

1. What danger did travelers face in St. Louis and St. Joseph?

2. What does the description of ice on the Fourth of July reveal about South Pass?

Critical Thinking

3. **Drawing Conclusions** Do you think that people in 1850 were more willing to take risks than they are today? Explain.

★★★★★★★★★★★★★★★★★★★★★★★★★★★★★★

Global Interests

Setting the Scene

Section Focus

Victory in the Mexican War and the acquisition of Oregon gave the United States vast new territories but also raised new issues. How would the United States connect its Pacific settlements with the East? Would expansion continue southward? Would Manifest Destiny continue to move American interests beyond North America?

Objectives

After studying this section, you should be able to

★ explain the events that brought about the Clayton-Bulwer Treaty.

★ compare the motivations for American interest in Cuba, Central America, China, and Japan in the mid-1800s.

Key Term

extraterritoriality

▲ CHINESE FAN

The acquisition of territory from Mexico and the division of Oregon completed United States expansion across the continent. The spirit of Manifest Destiny subsided in the North but not in the South.

■ The Caribbean and Central America

Whether dictated by law or by geography, the portion of the United States open to slavery was far smaller than the area closed to slavery. Many Southerners thought the only way to maintain the sectional balance was to expand southward. In 1848 a writer for *De Bow's Review*, a New Orleans financial journal, declared, "We have New Mexico and California. We *will* have old Mexico and Cuba!"

Cuba

Lying so close to Florida, Cuba offered tempting benefits—rich sugar plantations worked by thousands of enslaved people and a strategic location at the mouth of the Caribbean. So strong was the desire for Cuba among Southerners and some Northern investors that in 1848 the United States offered to buy Cuba from Spain for $100 million. The Spanish foreign minister refused, saying that he would rather see the island sink than sell it.

When negotiations failed, determined expansionists supported armed adventurers called "filibusterers," who set off to gain territory that might later be annexed to the United States. One of the best-known filibusterers was Narciso López. With the aid of prominent Southerners, López attempted three armed landings in Cuba with small bands of Americans. His goal was to start a revolt against Spanish rule, but he was captured swiftly and executed on his third try in 1851.

Interest in expansion to the south did not die with López, however. Prominent Northern Democrats such as President Franklin Pierce sought southern expansion. He raised America's offering price for Cuba to $130 million. When Spain still refused, Secretary of State William Marcy instructed United States ministers to Spain, Britain, and France to meet and decide how to obtain Cuba. The three diplomats drew up a statement known as the Ostend Manifesto, which declared that if Spain would not sell the island, the United States should take it by force. In part it said:

> " *After we shall have offered Spain a price for Cuba far beyond its present value, and this shall have been refused, it will then be time to consider the question, does Cuba, in the possession of Spain, seriously endanger our internal peace. . . ? Should this question be answered in the affirmative, then, by every law, human and divine, we shall be justified in wresting it from Spain. . . .* "

Published in 1854, this infamous document caused such protest that the secretary of state repudiated it, and the effort to buy Cuba was abandoned. Future attempts to expand slave territory were doomed because of Northern opposition.

Desire for a Canal Across Central America

American ambitions turned from expansion to development of the newly acquired territories. Hundreds made the long journey overland across the plains and the Rocky Mountains, but the longest route, by sea around Cape Horn, South America, was the safest. In January 1848, gold was discovered in California at Sutter's mill near Sacramento. Stories of instant riches led to a gold rush from the eastern United States and Europe. Many fortune seekers who took the ocean route saved time by crossing the narrow isthmus at Panama to board one of the few ships that would carry them to California. The gold rush aroused interest in the construction of a canal across Central America to connect the Atlantic and Pacific oceans. In 1846 the United States signed a treaty with

Narcisco López
1798?–1851

★★★★★ A MERICAN PORTRAITS ★★★★★★★

Narcisco López, a Venezuelan, fought for Spain against Simón Bolívar's South American independence forces, rising to the rank of general in the Spanish Army. Later he took up residence in Cuba, married, and became devoted to the interests of the Cuban people.

In 1848 he planned a revolt against Spanish rule, hoping for help from American supporters and for annexation of the island to the United States. When the revolt failed, he fled to America. López visited New Orleans where, in 1850, he asked for volunteers to join an expedition to win the island from Spain. His force of 600 landed in Cuba but found few Cubans willing to risk revolution. On a later expedition López was captured by the Spanish and executed.

In 1902 an independent Cuba raised its flag—one originally designed by López in red, white, and blue.

Visualizing History ▲ PERRY IN JAPAN This work of art painted on three separate panels shows Commodore Perry, accompanied by his color-bearer, delivering gifts to the emperor of Japan. *What favor did Perry seek?*

New Granada (later Colombia) by which it gained the right to preserve "free transit" across the Isthmus of Panama.

The British were also interested in controlling canal routes and in extending their influence along the entire Atlantic coast of Central America. Rival ambitions caused such tension that in 1850 Great Britain sent a special agent, Sir Henry Bulwer, to Washington, D.C., to confer with Secretary of State John M. Clayton. In the resulting Clayton-Bulwer Treaty, the United States and Britain agreed to jointly support the building of a canal through either Nicaragua or Panama. The cost and risks of such a venture delayed action by either country until after 1900.

■ The Opening of China and Japan

The acquisition of California gave the United States valuable ports from which to launch its Pacific trade. For centuries the prospect of trade with China had stirred people's imaginations because China produced valuable commodities and its potential 300 million customers were the largest untapped market in the world. United States trade with China had grown since the late eighteenth century, but until the 1840s this trade was limited to the port of Canton. As the oldest civilization in the world, the Chinese did not think they had much to gain from the outside world.

Trade with China

A weakened Chinese government could not long resist foreign trade, however. Through most of the early 1800s, British merchants found a way to break China's trade barriers and make enormous profits. In exchange for Chinese tea, silk, and porcelain, the merchants smuggled into China a drug called opium, which they acquired from Turkey and India. In 1839 Chinese forces tried to halt the smuggling. When the British resisted, war broke out. From 1839 to 1842, the British fought the First Opium War with China. When Great Britain won, it acquired the port of Hong Kong and various privileges for its merchants and missionaries.

Among these was the right of **extraterritoriality,** or the right of a foreigner accused of a crime to be tried under his or her own law rather than under Chinese law by Chinese courts. Later the British, aided by other European nations, forced China to grant special privileges to Christian missionaries, to set aside 16 "treaty ports" run by Westerners, and to allow European gunboats to patrol Chinese rivers.

The United States also secured privileges in China. In 1844 President Tyler sent Caleb Cushing, a diplomat, to China with four warships. Cushing persuaded the Chinese to grant generous trade arrangements. Because the United States was not interested in annexing parts of China, the Chinese were friendlier to Americans than to others. By 1850 American clipper ships carried most of the Chinese tea exported to Europe. American missionaries followed the traders; 88 of the 150 Protestant missionaries in China in 1851 were American.

Japan as a Port of Call

American ships sailing to China needed ports to take on fuel and supplies. Japan's location made it ideal for such ports of call. European traders had first come to the island country in the 1500s. Like the Chinese, the Japanese were uninterested in European goods, and they cut off almost all trade with Europe in the early 1600s. At the time, a military leader called a shogun ruled Japan. Although Japan also had an emperor, he held no real power.

Japan, however, had shut itself off from contact with most of the outside world for hundreds of years. The Japanese distrusted foreigners so intensely that sailors from shipwrecked whaling vessels had no guarantee of protection if they washed up on Japanese shores.

Japan did not trade again with the outside world until 1853 when a small United States fleet under Commodore Matthew C. Perry sailed into Tokyo harbor. Perry stayed only 10 days but left a message for the Mikado, or emperor, of Japan from President Millard Fillmore, who wrote:

66 *These are the only objects for which I have sent Commodore Perry, with a powerful squadron, to pay a visit to your imperial majesty's renowned city of Yedo: Friendship, commerce, a supply of coal and provisions, and protection for our shipwrecked people. . . .* 99

Perry returned the next year with more warships, all guns prepared for action. Perry also brought elaborate presents for the ruler of Japan, including a miniature telegraph and steam railroad. By this mixture of courtesy and threat, the Japanese were persuaded to open relations with the rest of the world.

Within five years after Perry's arrival, the shogun signed treaties with several nations, including Britain, Russia, Holland, and France as well as with the United States. Soon, Japanese leaders were convinced that they should adopt the industrial technology of Western nations, and Japan moved quickly to catch up with the West. Within one century Japanese influence rivaled American influence in the Pacific.

Section 3 ★ Review

Checking for Understanding

1. **Identify** Narcisco López, Franklin Pierce, Ostend Manifesto, Clayton-Bulwer Treaty, Matthew Perry.

2. **Define** extraterritoriality.

3. **Explain** how the Ostend Manifesto raised controversy.

4. **List** two reasons the United States government expressed an interest in China and Japan in the mid-1800s.

Critical Thinking

5. **Evaluating Foreign Policy** Evaluate Commodore Perry's strategy in Japan. What was the underlying message of Perry's visit?

Using Vocabulary

Imagine that you are an American diplomat in the 1840s. You have been assigned to negotiate trade agreements with the leaders of China and Japan. Explain the challenges and duties of your job, using the terms *consul* and *extraterritoriality*.

Reviewing Facts

1. **Specify** both agrarian and commercial reasons that promoted Manifest Destiny.
2. **Explain** the reasons for the war between the United States and Mexico.
3. **Name** two important events in the Texas independence movement.
4. **Summarize** why the United States was not able to acquire Cuba.
5. **Cite** two reasons why the nations of China and Japan were forced to initiate trade with Western countries.

Understanding Concepts

Expansion

1. Geography often plays a role in defining the borders of a nation. Explain the role of geography in supporting the belief that it was "natural" for the United States to expand to the Pacific Ocean.

Migration

2. The westward migration of pioneers in Conestoga wagons is a cherished part of American folklore. What factors made this migration such an adventure? Why do you think Americans continue to be fascinated by stories about these travels?

Critical Thinking

1. **Assessing Causes** Was war with Mexico inevitable? Explain the causes that made negotiations between the United States and Mexico nearly impossible, including the Mexican viewpoint.
2. **Analyzing Fine Art** Study the painting on this page entitled *October, 1867* by John Whetton Ehninger and answer the questions that follow.
   a. What does the painting tell you about these individuals and their time?
   b. What is your emotional reaction to the painting?

Writing About History

Definition

Write four separate definitions of the concept of Manifest Destiny as each of these four people might have defined it: James K. Polk, Santa Anna, a Native American of the plains, and a mountain man.

Cooperative Learning

Was President Polk a shrewd and visionary leader who expanded the power and borders of the United States, or was he a bully who took what he wanted

▲ *OCTOBER, 1867* BY JOHN WHETTON EHNINGER

without regard for other people's rights? You and a partner will evaluate Polk's presidency to answer this question. One of you will be a Polk supporter and the other an opponent. First, work together to compile a list of Polk's achievements. Then work separately and write an evaluation of each action according to your role of supporter or opponent. When you have finished writing, exchange and discuss each other's evaluations. Then present your findings to the class.

Social Studies Skills

Preparing Notecards for a Research Report

An important step to writing a research paper is preparing notecards from your research before writing your first draft. The following guidelines will help you prepare notecards with the critical information you will need to write your report well. Included is an example of what might appear on your notecard if your topic is "Pioneer Life."

Practicing the Skill

- On the first card, write the name of the author of the resource, the title, location, publisher, copyright date, and page number, according to the bibliographic style approved by your teacher. Later, you will use this same card when preparing your bibliography.

- Start the next card with the author's last name (and first name, if more than one author has the same last name). Include the title, too, if you are using more than one resource from this author. Also include the page number.

- Underneath the author's name and page number, take notes of one main idea only. Start by writing a sentence that summarizes the main idea—a generalization. Then list supporting statements.

- After you have taken notes from all your resources using a separate card for each main idea, sort through your cards, placing them in the order you will use to address the main ideas as you write. Now you are ready to write a rough draft of your report.

For further practice, research and prepare notecards for a report on the history of one of the Western states.

Weaver, page 439

Main Idea: The pioneers could not buy soap, so they had to make their own.

Supporting Statements:

1. The pioneers saved wood ashes in a barrel and fats and grease from cooking and butchering.
2. In the spring the pioneers poured water over the ashes in the barrel and allowed it to trickle out through a hole near the bottom.
3. This brown liquid called lye was collected and boiled in a kettle with fats and grease until it thickened to form a soft, jellylike, yellow soap.

Weaver, Robert B. "Pioneer Life." *World Book Encyclopedia.* Vol. 14. Chicago: Field Enterprises, 1991, pages 428–442.

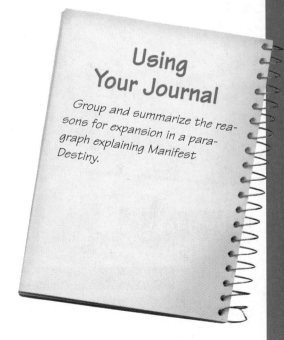

Using Your Journal

Group and summarize the reasons for expansion in a paragraph explaining Manifest Destiny.

CHAPTER 14

★★

Compromise and Conflict
1848–1861

Setting the Scene

▶ **LINCOLN CAMPAIGN TORCH**

Focus

Even though the nation as a whole was prosperous, deep political and social divisions could no longer be ignored. By the late 1840s, Southerners were defending slavery as a "positive good," while antislavery feelings in the North and West intensified. Political compromise worked in 1850, but by 1860 compromise was no longer possible. The election of Lincoln convinced Southerners that slavery would not be protected within the Union. Secession, they felt, was the only option left.

Concepts to Understand

★ How economic diversity led to differing views on slavery

★ How political conflict over slavery and the nature of the Union led to secession

Read to Discover . . .

★ the major differences between the North and the South.

★ the events that led seven Southern states to secede from the Union.

Journal Notes

What contributed to division of the Union? As you read the chapter, record the events, decisions, acts, and other activities that answer the question.

CULTURAL

● **1846** *Elias Howe patents sewing machine*

● **1851** *Herman Melville publishes* Moby Dick

1845

1850

● **1848** *First presidential election to be held on the same day in all states*

● **1850** *Compromise of 1850 passed*

POLITICAL

◄ DIARIST MARY CHESNUT OF SOUTH CAROLINA

• **1857** *National Teacher's Association organized*

• **1860** *Repeating rifle introduced*

1855	1860

• **1854** *Kansas-Nebraska Act passed*
• **1857** *Supreme Court rules Missouri Compromise unconstitutional*

• **1860** *South Carolina secedes from the Union*

A Union in Danger

Setting the Scene

Section Focus

The acquisition of New Mexico and California brought into the open the slavery issue. It became clear that some decision had to be made regarding the legality of slavery in these new areas. During this period there was remarkable national prosperity. Every major economic interest—cotton planting, wheat farming, manufacturing, and transportation—was booming. The huge gold strike in California paid for imports; the flood of gold expanded United States currency. Also, increasing numbers of immigrants began arriving.

Objectives

After studying this section, you should be able to

★ evaluate the impact of the issue of slavery on the 1848 presidential election.

★ explain why California's application for admission to the Union incited heated debates on the question of slavery and how the Compromise of 1850 temporarily reunited the nation.

★ explain how inventions and increased immigration affected the economic growth of the United States.

Key Term

popular sovereignty

◀ KEG USED ON THE ERIE CANAL

*E*ven before the war with Mexico had ended, growing antislavery sentiment in the North led the House of Representatives, with its Northern majority, to pass the Wilmot Proviso. This bill provided that all territory acquired from Mexico should be closed to slavery.

The Wilmot Proviso was defeated in the Senate, where the North and South were equally represented. Many Southern senators argued that Congress had no constitutional power to forbid slavery in the territories. If the representatives did outlaw slavery there, they would be denying slaveholders their rights as citizens.

■ The Election of 1848

There seemed to be no way of reconciling these opposing views on the issue of slavery in the new territories. When the Polk administration ended in 1849, no steps had been taken to provide for civil government in New Mexico and California.

Democrats and Whigs

In the presidential election of 1848, both Northerners and Southerners took precautions to play down discussion of slavery. The Democrats, although controlled by their

Southern wing, nominated a Northern senator, Lewis Cass of Michigan. Cass supported a compromise solution known as **popular sovereignty,** whereby voters within the territories would decide whether slavery would be permitted inside their borders. The Whigs, whose principal stronghold was in the North, nominated Zachary Taylor from Louisiana, a slaveholder himself. The Whig platform avoided the issue of slavery by focusing on Taylor's military accomplishments in the Mexican War.

The Free-Soil Party

Efforts to keep slavery out of the campaign failed, however. A third party emerged when a group of antislavery Northern Democrats and "conscience Whigs" united with the former Liberty party to form the Free-Soil party. This party, whose motto was "Free soil, free speech, free labor, and free men," nominated former President Martin Van Buren. Although the Free-Soil party gained no electoral votes, it received more popular votes than the Democrats had in New York, Vermont, and Massachusetts. In New York the Free-Soilers received enough Democratic votes to deprive Cass of that state's 36 electoral votes, which gave the election to Taylor with 163 electoral votes—exactly 36 more than Cass had.

■ The California Question

The issue of slavery in the new territories intensified after gold was discovered in California in 1848. By the end of 1849, an estimated 95,000 "forty-niners" from all over the world had settled in northern California.

Application for Statehood

With this tremendous growth in population came an urgent need for government. Crime and violence had become common in mining camps and towns, and military authorities could not control it. At the suggestion of President Taylor, a convention met in Monterey, California, in the fall of 1849 and adopted a constitution that, in part, provided a structure for the new government and outlined state boundaries. It also prohibited slavery. The newly created government immediately applied for admission to the Union as a free state in which slavery was forbidden. California's application for statehood touched off a long and bitter debate. Admission of California would tip the balance of power in the Senate in favor of the free states, already in the majority in the House. If California were admitted as a free state, Southern leaders warned, their states would leave the Union.

Compromise of 1850

To deal with this alarming situation, Henry Clay, who had been in retirement since his defeat in the presidential election of 1844, successfully ran for reelection as senator. The Whig senator from Kentucky, a master of negotiation, proceeded to arrange his last great intersectional compromise.

Visualizing History ▲ TOWARD COMPROMISE The intense debate in the Senate sparked by the California question led to yet another important political compromise. *Who arranged this last great intersectional agreement?*

Forty-Niners

Skeletons of horses and oxen marked the toll of death from exhaustion or starvation. The hardships, according to John Lloyd Stephens who described his own struggle, ". . . are beyond conception. Care and suspense, pained anxiety, fear of losing animals and leaving one to foot it and pack his 'duds' on his back, begging provisions, fear of being left in the mountains to starve and freeze to death . . . are things of which I may write and you may read, but they are nothing to the reality."

President Polk referred to the rich gold discovery in California in his annual message to Congress in December 1848. The secret was out. Within a year the gold fever attracted some 95,000 people to California. The three principal routes were across the Isthmus of Panama, around Cape Horn, or overland. Half of the forty-niners crossed the plains and mountains. Along the California Trail inexperienced travelers died by the hundreds. Those who survived the trail found life in California nearly as demanding.

THE EMIGRANTS' GUIDE TO CALIFORNIA,

CONTAINING EVERY POINT OF INFORMATION FOR THE EMIGRANT—INCLUDING ROUTES, DISTANCES, WATER, GRASS, TIMBER, CROSSING OF RIVERS, PASSES, ALTITUDES, WITH A LARGE MAP OF ROUTES, AND PROFILE OF COUNTRY, &C.,— WITH FULL DIRECTIONS FOR TESTING AND ASSAYING GOLD AND OTHER ORES.

BY JOSEPH E. WARE.

PUBLISHED BY J. HALSALL, No. 124 MAIN STREET, ST. LOUIS, MO.

Clay's compromise was a series of measures intended to satisfy Northern and Southern demands. The principal provisions favoring the North were that California be admitted as a free state and that the slave trade—but not slavery—be forbidden in the District of Columbia. The South, in turn, would gain a stronger Fugitive Slave Law, designed to suppress the Underground Railroad. In addition, the Mexican Cession, gained at the end of the Mexican War, would be divided into two territories, Utah and New Mexico, with the question of slavery to be decided by popular sovereignty when the territories were organized with territorial legislatures.

At first, Clay's proposals failed to receive sufficient support to pass. President Taylor opposed Clay and offered proposals of his own. However, Taylor died suddenly in the summer of 1850. His successor, Vice President Millard Fillmore, favored the compromise. The young Illinois senator Stephen A. Douglas, a Democrat, skillfully put through the compromise as five separate bills, which Fillmore duly signed. The Compromise of 1850 averted immediate disaster but, unhappily, turned out to be just a temporary truce.

■ Inventions and Industry

During the 20 years from 1840 to 1860, rapid growth became the dominant characteristic of the nation's economy. Among the reasons for this growth were new inventions, sufficient capital with which to build new factories, a class of businesspeople willing to start new enterprises, an increase in agricultural productivity, a growing labor supply, and a transportation system that connected farms to factories.

In 1850 two-thirds of the nation's people were engaged in agriculture. Industry was growing, though, partly because of a flood of new inventions. By 1861 the telegraph had made possible rapid communication throughout the continent and across the Atlantic. The rotary press allowed newspapers to publish far larger editions than ever before. Some inventions, however, had their greatest impact on Northern industries. For example, the sewing machine, invented by Elias Howe in 1846, revolutionized shirt-making by reducing the time it took to make one shirt from more than 14 hours to little more than an hour; when the technique was adapted for shoemaking, it made possible the mass production of shoes. Charles Goodyear's invention of vulcanized rubber in 1839 was widely used in industry and in the manufacture of waterproof garments.

Textile factories, powered by more efficient steam engines, increased in size as several operations were combined under a single roof. The techniques invented by Eli Whitney and Simeon North for making interchangeable parts and breaking down manufacturing into simple operations now

found applications in the mass production of clocks, watches, farm machinery, and sewing machines.

■ Developments in Agriculture

Inventions, innovations, and government policies allowed agricultural productivity to keep pace with the nation's fast-growing industries.

The Middle West, with its fertile plains, attracted farmers from the rocky and hilly lands of the Northeast as well as immigrants from Europe. Public lands could be purchased for as little as 25 cents an acre, and the Pre-emption Act of 1841 allowed squatters the opportunity to buy their land before someone else did.

The first great need was for plows that could cut through tree roots in recently cleared forestland and turn the tough sod of the prairies. In 1825 Jethro Wood began the

▲ COMMUNICATIONS AND TRANSPORTATION Westward expansion during the years 1820 through 1860 created an urgent need for better connections between locations. A canal boom was ushered in with the completion of the Erie Canal. *What innovations helped improve communications?*

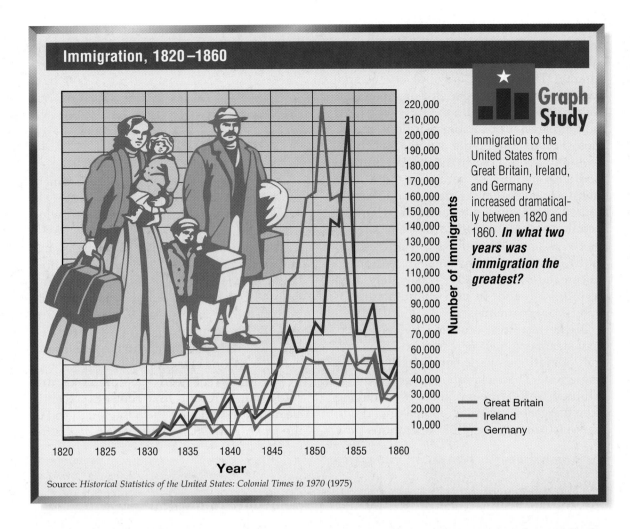

Immigration, 1820–1860

Number of Immigrants

220,000
210,000
200,000
190,000
180,000
170,000
160,000
150,000
140,000
130,000
120,000
110,000
100,000
90,000
80,000
70,000
60,000
50,000
40,000
30,000
20,000
10,000

1820 1825 1830 1835 1840 1845 1850 1855 1860

Year

— Great Britain
— Ireland
— Germany

Source: *Historical Statistics of the United States: Colonial Times to 1970* (1975)

Graph Study

Immigration to the United States from Great Britain, Ireland, and Germany increased dramatically between 1820 and 1860. *In what two years was immigration the greatest?*

manufacture of an iron plow with replaceable parts. John Deere of Moline, Illinois, soon developed a much-improved version made of steel instead of iron; by 1850 the Deere factories were turning out as many as 10,000 plows per year. The new plows enabled farmers to plant more land than they could harvest. To solve this problem, Cyrus McCormick, a Virginia blacksmith, took out a patent in 1834 on a mechanical "reaper," or grain harvester. By 1860 more than 100,000 of McCormick's reapers were in use. These inventions were accompanied by still others: a mechanical drill to plant grain, the threshing machine, and the horse-drawn hay rake.

Although the West benefited more from these inventions than did the South, which still depended on slave labor, the Southern economy also improved. Increased demand for raw cotton by an efficient British textile industry brought prosperity to the Deep South. In the 1850s, cotton production broke all previous records. By 1860 seven-eighths of the world's supply of cotton came from the United States, and raw cotton comprised three-fifths of the nation's exports.

■ Increased Immigration Fuels Factories

A necessity for sustained industrial growth is a sizable labor supply. Until about 1800, immigrants came to the United States at a rate of about 8,000 per year.

Coming to America

During the second quarter of the nineteenth century, however, a great migration from Europe to America began. Between 1840 and 1860, an average of more than

200,000 immigrants reached American shores every year. The reasons for this were both political and economic. Thousands of immigrants made the often perilous voyage to escape poverty.

Many English craftworkers, made jobless by the Industrial Revolution, sailed to America. The Scandinavians and the Dutch, whose native soil could not support rapidly growing populations, also came. So did the Irish, after a failure of their potato crop resulted in economic hardship and the starvation of thousands. Others, like the Germans, came to avoid political persecution. By 1860 one out of every eight Americans was foreign-born.

Hardships and Resentment

The move to America was difficult and dangerous. Immigrants, packed into overcrowded ships, often faced terrible conditions. Many times they suffered from malnutrition and disease, which resulted in the death of an estimated 10 percent of the passengers. Unfortunately, the problems of the immigrants continued even after they had found jobs and places to live—immigrants were forced to confront the bigotry of some established Americans who resented their different languages, religions, and customs.

Such resentment, along with the fear that immigrants would bring new and radical political ideas into the United States, led to the formation of secret societies. One of these was a nationwide secret political society called The Order of the Star-Spangled Banner, founded in 1849. Nicknamed "Know-Nothings" because members replied "I know nothing" when asked about their organization, they tried to keep recent immigrants from political office. They also demanded that immigration be restricted and that the naturalization period be extended to 21 years.

In spite of such hardships and prejudice, immigrants continued to flock to the United States. Although some migrated West to its rich farmlands, many immigrants remained in the North, often in such port cities as New York and Boston, where their ships had docked. One reason for this was that they had little money to continue their journeys. Also, the South already had a source of cheap labor—enslaved African Americans. The result was that immigrants supplied the North's growing industries with a steady stream of low-paid workers.

■ Transportation Ties North and West

With rapidly expanding markets came great advances in transportation. In the 1850s the United States built the largest merchant marine fleet in the world, inland navigation reached its peak, and railroad track mileage was increased.

▲ "KNOW-NOTHING" SONG SHEET COVER

Clipper Ships

In 1849 Great Britain repealed the Navigation Laws that had given special protection to British ships trading within its empire. The United States, however, continued to allow only its own ships to carry cargo between American ports. These advantages helped United States ships increase their total tonnage from 943,000 tons in 1846 to 2,226,000 tons in 1857.

The greatest triumph at sea for the United States was the clipper ship, which made its mark between 1845 and 1860. Characterized by very sharp bows, an immense spread of sail, and masts 200 feet high, clippers soon became the fastest oceangoing sailing vessels ever built. The clipper *Lightning* once logged over 500 miles in a 24-hour period.

Inland Waterways

During this decade inland navigation also reached its peak. The Erie Canal carried so much traffic that it had to be widened and deepened. The Great Lakes gained such importance as a water route that 6,000 ships sailed from Chicago in a single year. This was also the great period of steamboats on the Mississippi River. Mark Twain's *Life on the Mississippi* and *Huckleberry Finn* bear witness to the importance of the great river as a route for trade and commerce.

The days of great river traffic were numbered, however. As inventor Oliver Evans predicted in 1813:

> " *The time will come when people will travel in stages moved by steam engines, from one city to another, almost as fast as birds fly, fifteen or twenty miles an hour.* "

Railroads

Railroads were able to reach places that riverboats could not. By 1860 railroads tied the agricultural areas of the Northwest to the cities and ports of the Northeast. The first successful use of the steam locomotive in the United States occurred on the Charleston and Hamburg railroad line in South Carolina in 1831. Other lines began operation almost simultaneously.

Early railroads, however, were extremely expensive to build and maintain. Whereas state governments had funded the building of canals, private enterprise provided the money for the railroads. The new railroads cost what were then colossal sums. The Erie Railroad cost about $23 million to build, which is more than the United States paid for New Mexico and California.

By 1850 an era of great expansion began. By this time 9,000 miles of track had been laid; 10 years later the number of miles had increased to over 30,000, and railroads connecting the Atlantic seaboard to the Mississippi River crisscrossed the East. What continued to set the South apart from the North, however, was its "peculiar institution," slavery.

Section 1 ★ Review

Checking for Understanding

1. **Identify** Wilmot Proviso, Lewis Cass, Zachary Taylor, Free-Soil party, Stephen A. Douglas, Compromise of 1850, Elias Howe, John Deere, Cyrus McCormick, "Know-Nothings," clipper ship.

2. **Define** popular sovereignty.

3. **List** four provisions of the Compromise of 1850.

4. **Identify** two differences between the economic systems of the North and the South.

Critical Thinking

5. **Evaluating Policies**   Explain why acceptance of the idea of popular sovereignty would have been unacceptable to abolitionists.

Industrial Innovation

"What is the North," asked a Southerner in the 1850s, "but a conglomeration of greasy mechanics, filthy operatives, small-fisted farmers, and moonstruck theorists?" Southerners may have looked scornfully at manufacturing in the North, but Europeans were fascinated by "Yankee Notions" like machine-made clocks and buckets, canned food, and handguns with revolving chambers. These products were the result of Yankee ingenuity and the machine-tool industry, which mass-produced interchangeable parts.

The British called this industry "the American system of manufacturing," but "the Northeastern American system" would have been more accurate. More than half of America's 140,000 factories were concentrated between New York and Massachusetts, and they were the country's largest and most productive. The South had 20,000 factories, but they were small and concentrated on processing local products like cotton or tobacco rather than manufacturing.

In 1820 most manufacturing was done in homes or small shops. After 1820, however, the factory system began to take over. In factories the total process of manufacturing took place at one location. The need for a single location was due to the new sources of power—water and steam. The first factories used waterpower and were built in rural areas along rivers and streams.

Improved transportation and communication increased the importance of Northern cities as centers of trade. As city merchants grew wealthier, they sought investments that would further

▲ CRYSTAL PALACE, INDUSTRIAL EXHIBITION IN LONDON, 1851

increase their business. Much of their capital, or investment money, went into new manufacturing industries.

Connecticut inventor Eli Whitney started the use of interchangeable parts. These were identical machine parts that could be quickly put together to make a complete product. Because all the parts were alike, they could be manufactured with less skilled labor, and they made machine repair easier.

Making the Technology Connection

1. How might the level of industrialization affect the ability of the North and the South to wage war?

Linking Past and Present

2. Hypothesize why the South in the 1990s is not among the top few manufacturing centers.

★★

Dispute Over Slavery

Setting the Scene

Section Focus

The 1850s found the South feeling increasingly isolated—isolated from the industrial boom of the North and from the new technologies that were redefining agriculture in the West, and isolated by its support of the slave system. Was the Union doomed to be torn apart by the vast political and economic differences that separated the North and South?

Objectives

After studying this section, you should be able to

★ discuss how the majority of Southerners viewed and defended the institution of slavery.

★ explain the significance of the Kansas-Nebraska Act.

★ examine the reactions of both the North and the South to the Supreme Court's *Dred Scott* decision.

Key Term

obiter dictum

◀ COTTON CARDING PADDLES

---

*S*outhern legislatures made it increasingly difficult for slaveholders to emancipate their enslaved men and women. Some states decreed that free African Americans must either go somewhere else or be sold back into slavery. All African Americans, enslaved or free, had to carry identification passes when away from their homes. At night, patrols equipped with dogs and guns watched for runaways.

■ The South and Slavery

Although slavery was common in the South, the majority of people were not slaveholders. In addition, the bondage of African Americans assumed many different forms.

Forms of Slavery

Between house servants and their masters and mistresses, there was often a sense of trust and affection. Some enslaved people, especially in the cities, were hired out to other employers and thus were afforded some freedom of movement. The workforce of the successful Tredegar Iron Works in Richmond, Virginia, was African American.

Most African Americans, however, worked on plantations and lived lives marked by hard labor, cruel discipline, and isolation. Marriages between enslaved persons were not legally recognized. Families could be broken up by sale. It was against the law to teach enslaved persons to read, although some white Southerners broke that law.

In Defense of Slavery

To support the system, many Southerners developed an elaborate defense of slavery. Southerners argued that slavery was necessary to provide an adequate labor supply and was "a positive good" because all the enslaved person's material needs were provided. Finally, defenders of slavery tried to use arguments from science and the Bible to show that slavery was acceptable.

■ The Rift Widens

For a few years it looked as though the Compromise of 1850 might provide a permanent solution to the slavery controversy. In the North, however, opposition to the stringent Fugitive Slave Law included in the Compromise of 1850 increased. Under this law, the word of a slaveholder, or even one who claimed to be, was taken as conclusive proof of identity of the runaway. A suspected runaway (who might in fact be a free person) had no right to testify on his or her own behalf. Any citizen might be required to join in pursuit of a runaway.

To fight this injustice, most free state legislatures passed personal liberty laws that nullified the Fugitive Slave Law by forbidding

▲ HARRIET BEECHER STOWE'S *UNCLE TOM'S CABIN*

state officials to assist in the capture of runaways. Antislavery feeling in the North was also stimulated by Harriet Beecher Stowe's *Uncle Tom's Cabin,* a novel portraying slavery at its worst. The book sold 300,000 copies in 1852, its first year of publication.

Harriet Tubman
1820–1913

★★★★ AMERICAN PORTRAITS

Born to enslaved parents in Maryland, Harriet Tubman worked as a plantation field hand until she was nearly 30 years old. Then she made her break for freedom, escaping to the North with the help of the Underground Railroad.

Knowing full well the risks of being captured, Tubman nonetheless made 19 trips back into the South during the 1850s to help other enslaved people escape. Altogether she assisted more than 300 African Americans—including her aged parents—to escape bondage. While not the founder of the Underground Railroad, she certainly became its most famous and successful conductor. Known as the "Moses" of her people, Tubman maintained iron discipline among the escapees, and—despite huge rewards offered in the South for her capture and arrest—she always managed to elude her enemies.

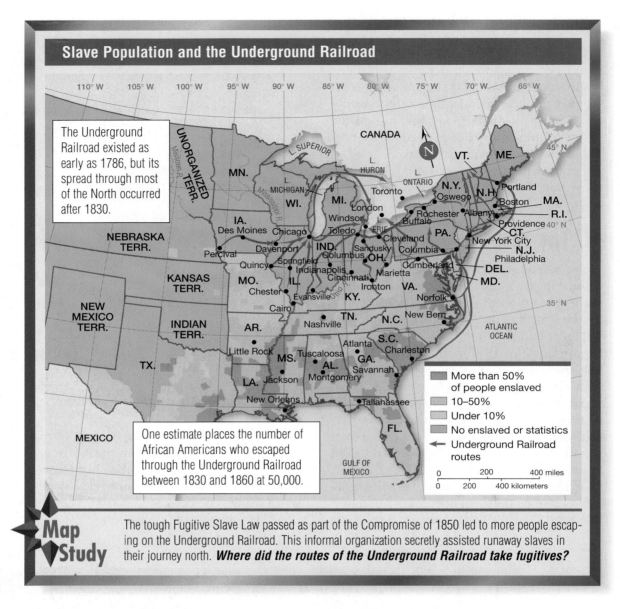

Slave Population and the Underground Railroad

The Underground Railroad existed as early as 1786, but its spread through most of the North occurred after 1830.

One estimate places the number of African Americans who escaped through the Underground Railroad between 1830 and 1860 at 50,000.

More than 50% of people enslaved
10–50%
Under 10%
No enslaved or statistics
Underground Railroad routes

0   200   400 miles
0   200   400 kilometers

Map Study The tough Fugitive Slave Law passed as part of the Compromise of 1850 led to more people escaping on the Underground Railroad. This informal organization secretly assisted runaway slaves in their journey north. *Where did the routes of the Underground Railroad take fugitives?*

Bloodshed on Free Soil

In 1854 the political truce over slavery ended with the passage of the Kansas-Nebraska Act. Senator Stephen A. Douglas of Illinois proposed the Kansas-Nebraska Act to encourage the rapid settlement of the trans-Missouri region and the building of a transcontinental railroad with terminals at St. Louis and Chicago. However, the act reopened intersectional controversy. It provided that the region be divided into two new territories, Nebraska and Kansas. The question of whether or not slavery would exist in the new territories was to be decided by popular sovereignty. This part of the act negated the Missouri Compromise, because

both territories lay above latitude 36° 30′. A clause specifically repealing the Missouri ban on slavery north of that line was added.

The Kansas-Nebraska Act was criticized. The repeal of the Missouri Compromise was denounced in the North. The South continued to demand that the North recognize the rights of slaveholders in the territories of the United States.

Bleeding Kansas

Settlers started at once to move into the Kansas Territory. Because the slavery issue was to be decided by popular vote, a race developed to see whether the majority of settlers would come from slave or free states.

A bloody struggle between the proslavery and antislavery factions assumed the proportions of a civil war. The violence in "bleeding Kansas" reached its peak on the eve of the presidential election of 1856.

Election of 1856

In the two years since the passage of the Kansas-Nebraska Act, the Whig party had broken up over the slavery issue. To fill the void, two new parties—the Americans and the Republicans—appeared. The American party, composed of Know-Nothings and some ex-Whigs, tried to divert people's minds from the slavery issue by whipping up feeling against immigrants. Its candidate in 1856 was former President Fillmore. The basic principle of the Republicans (who took their name from the party of Thomas Jefferson) based its platform on "free soil," or keeping slavery out of the territories. Strongly organized in every free state, the Republican party nominated General John C. Frémont.

Meanwhile, the Democrats dodged the slavery issue. To balance Southerners' dominance of the party, they nominated a Northerner, James Buchanan of Pennsylvania. With only a minority of the popular vote, Buchanan won the election with 174 electoral votes against 114 for Frémont and 8 for

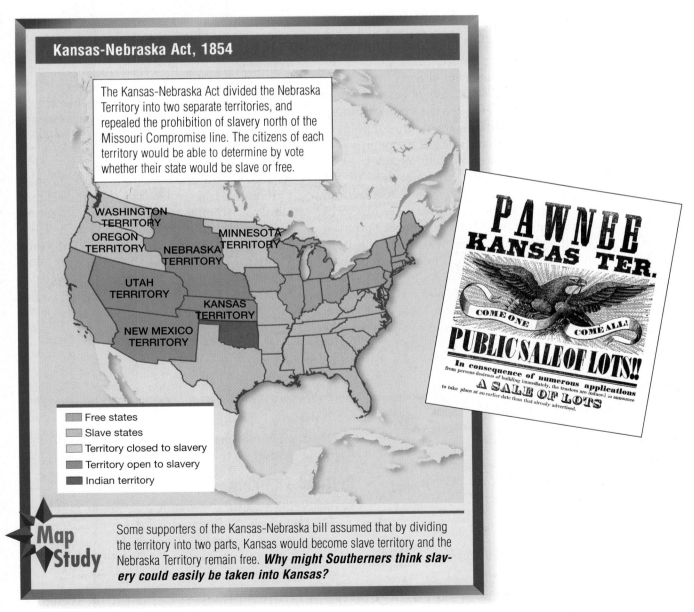

Kansas-Nebraska Act, 1854

The Kansas-Nebraska Act divided the Nebraska Territory into two separate territories, and repealed the prohibition of slavery north of the Missouri Compromise line. The citizens of each territory would be able to determine by vote whether their state would be slave or free.

WASHINGTON TERRITORY
OREGON TERRITORY
MINNESOTA TERRITORY
NEBRASKA TERRITORY
UTAH TERRITORY
KANSAS TERRITORY
NEW MEXICO TERRITORY

- Free states
- Slave states
- Territory closed to slavery
- Territory open to slavery
- Indian territory

PAWNEE KANSAS TER.
COME ONE COME ALL!
PUBLIC SALE OF LOTS!!
In consequence of numerous applications from persons desirous of building immediately, the trustees are induced to announce
A SALE OF LOTS
to take place at an earlier date than that already advertised.

Map Study Some supporters of the Kansas-Nebraska bill assumed that by dividing the territory into two parts, Kansas would become slave territory and the Nebraska Territory remain free. *Why might Southerners think slavery could easily be taken into Kansas?*

Fillmore. The Democrats swept the South and gained enough votes to win, while the Republican Frémont won two-thirds of the electoral votes of the free states.

■ The Dred Scott Decision

In his Inaugural Address in March 1857, President Buchanan suggested that the controversy over slavery in the territories be left to the Supreme Court, which had recently heard a case on this question and was expected to render a decision soon.

Dred Scott was an enslaved man taken by a former master from the state of Missouri into territory closed to slavery by the Missouri Compromise and then brought back to Missouri again. For more than 10 years, Scott sued for freedom on the grounds that residence in a free territory released him from slavery.

On March 6, 1857, Chief Justice Roger Taney (TAW•nee) delivered an opinion upholding completely the Southern point of view that Scott had no right to sue in a federal court. Taney ruled against Scott because, he claimed, the founders of the United States did not intend for African Americans to be citizens. The Missouri Compromise ban on slavery north of the 36° 30′ line, the Court said, was unconstitutional because Congress had no right to prohibit slavery in the territories.

Instead of settling the slavery dispute, the *Dred Scott* decision made it more bitter. If the decision stood, the Republican party might

Visualizing History ▲ DRED SCOTT The Supreme Court ruled that Dred Scott had no right to sue for his freedom in the federal courts because he was not a citizen. *Did the Dred Scott decision settle the slavery dispute?*

as well go out of existence, because its basic principle—free soil—had been declared unconstitutional. Republicans therefore claimed that the decision was not binding but was an *obiter dictum* (OH•buh•tuhr DIHK•tuhm), an incidental opinion not called for by the circumstances of the case. Southerners, on the other hand, called on the North to obey the decision as the price of the South's remaining in the Union.

Section 2 ★ Review

Checking for Understanding

1. **Identify** Harriet Beecher Stowe, James Buchanan, Dred Scott, *Uncle Tom's Cabin*, Republican party.

2. **Define** *obiter dictum.*

3. **State** three reasons Southerners used to defend slavery.

4. **Distinguish** Northern and Southern reactions to the passage of the Kansas-Nebraska Act.

Critical Thinking

5. **Analyzing a Ruling** Chief Justice Roger Taney ruled that Dred Scott could not sue for his freedom because he was not a citizen. Do you think Taney correctly interpreted the Constitution? Write two sentences to support your opinion.

Map and Graph Skills

Classifying Information

Look at a map of the United States. As you read the names of the states, various thoughts float through your mind. Perhaps you picture the places you would someday like to visit, or maybe you remember locations that have been in the news lately. As you scan the map, you organize the information in your mind by sorting the data into a pattern. In other words, you classify the map's information.

Classifying is a process of separating and arranging information into related groups or categories. Before you begin the process, you need to set up a classification system. You do this by defining the categories. When you evaluate a map in terms of the places you would like to visit, you classify the information into two categories: places you like to see and places you would not care to see. Frequently, a map legend defines the map's classification system and categories.

One of the many sources of information about history is maps. This map of the Compromise of 1850, for example, will be helpful in understanding the results of the compromise.

Compromise of 1850

ORE. TERR.

IOWA 1846 • WIS. 1848

MICH. 1837

UNORGANIZED TERR.

MINN. TERR.

UTAH TERR.

N.M. TERR.

CA. 1850

TEXAS 1845

MEXICO

- Free states
- Slave states
- Territory closed to slavery
- Territory open to slavery
- Indian territory

After examining the data on the map, follow these guidelines to help classify its information. Then complete the practice.

- **Determine** what information you need to classify.
- **Decide** on the major categories by looking closely at how the information can be broken down into parts.
- **Write** the data that fits in each category or, if you are making a chart, place the appropriate information in columns under each category.
- **Determine** what conclusions you can make after studying the information in each category.

Practicing the Skill

1. How many categories does the legend define for this map?

2. How does the map convey each distinct classification?

3. Keep the same classifications as shown on the legend. Make a chart, placing the appropriate information in columns under each category.

4. Based on the map and your prior knowledge of the subject, what conclusions could you draw about the Compromise of 1850?

5. Define another classification system and legend for the Compromise of 1850 map. Does your system provide more or less information than that shown on the existing map?

6. Study the map on page 399 that shows the results of the Kansas-Nebraska Act. Make a chart, using the map legend's classification system. Compare the chart and map with those of the Compromise of 1850. What conclusions can you draw?

★★★

Drifting Toward War

Setting the Scene

Section Focus

Both the North and the South watched with dread as events surrounding the election of 1860 led toward the dissolution of the Union. For Southerners, the election of Abraham Lincoln as President signaled that slavery could not be extended.

◀ CANNED FOODS AND MEDICINE, MID-1800S

Objectives

After studying this section, you should be able to

★ evaluate the importance of the Lincoln-Douglas debates.

★ identify the purpose of John Brown's raid at Harpers Ferry and reactions to it.

★ list the political events that led to the secession of seven Southern states.

Key Term

secession

The question of slavery in the territories left the nation in a state of almost hopeless confusion. The *Dred Scott* decision, supported in the South, was flatly opposed by the Republicans, dominant in the North.

■ Lincoln and Douglas

What effect did the *Dred Scott* decision have on the principle of popular sovereignty? Did the decision forbid the people of a territory to decide whether or not they wanted slavery?

Stephen A. Douglas and Abraham Lincoln were rival candidates in the election for senator from Illinois in 1858. Douglas—a short, thickset man nicknamed "The Little Giant" for his size and political influence—served in the Senate for 12 years and had a national reputation for his commitment to

popular sovereignty. The most prominent Democrat in Congress, he hoped to be elected President in 1860.

Abraham Lincoln was a man whose tall, angular frame inspired ridicule. Lincoln had served only a single undistinguished term in the House of Representatives. He defended the Compromise of 1850—even to the point of enforcing the Fugitive Slave Law. Although Lincoln was not an abolitionist, he believed that if slavery were confined to its existing area, Southerners themselves might eventually abolish it. As a former Whig who had only recently joined the Republican party, Lincoln enjoyed a local reputation as a clever lawyer and keen debater.

Debates

During the campaign Lincoln and Douglas traveled to seven Illinois towns to debate critical issues. Douglas attempted to show that Republicans in general—and Lincoln in particular—were abolitionists in disguise, bent on destroying the Union. During their debate at Freeport, Illinois, Lincoln put Douglas in a difficult position by asking the question, "Can the people of a territory in any lawful way . . . exclude slavery from their limits prior to the formation of a State Constitution?" Douglas was trapped. If he answered "Yes," he would appear to support popular sovereignty, thereby opposing the *Dred Scott* decision. A "yes" answer would improve his chances for reelection as senator, but cost him Southern support for the 1860 presidency. A "no" answer would make it seem as if he had abandoned popular sovereignty, on which he had based his political career. This answer would be welcomed by the South but could cost him the senatorial election.

Freeport Doctrine

To solve this dilemma, Douglas formulated the so-called Freeport Doctrine. Douglas said he accepted the *Dred Scott* decision that forbade Congress to bar slavery from the territories. However, he pointed out, a territorial legislature might effectively discourage slavery if it failed to pass laws to keep enslaved persons under control. Said Douglas, "Slavery cannot exist a day, or an hour, anywhere, unless it is supported by local police regulations." By admitting that a territorial legislature could practically nullify the *Dred Scott* decision, Douglas won a narrow victory in the election but lost Southern support for the presidency in 1860. Lincoln lost the election but gained a national reputation.

■ John Brown's Raid

John Brown, a fiery abolitionist, regarded himself as a heaven-sent agent whose mission was to liberate enslaved people and punish slaveholders. Brown had participated in the armed struggle against proslavery forces in Kansas. On October 16, 1859, with 21 followers, he seized the federal arsenal at Harpers Ferry, Virginia, intending to free and arm the enslaved men and women of the surrounding countryside. The siege ended with the capture of Brown by Colonel Robert E. Lee and the death of 10 of his men. At his Virginia trial for treason and murder, Brown expressed no remorse.

Found guilty, John Brown was hanged on December 2. Many Northerners regarded Brown as a martyr to the cause of freedom. The New England poet Ralph Waldo Emerson said that Brown had "made the gallows glorious like the cross." Southerners regarded Brown's punishment as just. They feared nothing so much as a slave revolt.

■ The Election of 1860

As the election of 1860 approached, Democrats split over the issue of slavery in the territories. A Northern wing of the party nominated Douglas for the presidency and backed popular sovereignty; a Southern wing nominated John C. Breckinridge of Kentucky and supported the *Dred Scott* decision. The Constitutional Union party, a third group composed mostly of former Southern Whigs, nominated

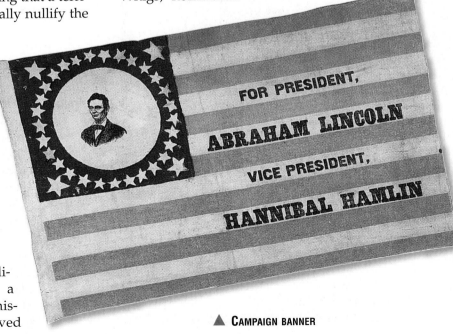

▲ CAMPAIGN BANNER

John Bell of Tennessee and attempted to avoid the slavery issue.

With such division among their opponents, the door to the presidency stood open for the Republicans. Their platform, designed to attract votes from many quarters, was that slavery should be left undisturbed where it existed, but that it should be excluded from the territories. They denounced John Brown's raid and also called for a protective tariff, free homesteads for settlers, and federal funds for internal improvements, including a railroad to the Pacific. In an attempt to attract recent immigrants, they were harshly critical of Know-Nothing attempts to make naturalization more difficult.

The Republicans nominated Abraham Lincoln as their candidate. Lincoln, the only one of the candidates to make no speeches, stayed quietly at his home in Springfield, Illinois.

The election was a clear victory for the Republicans. Lincoln gained a majority in the electoral college, winning more votes than all three of his opponents combined. Not even listed on the ballot in some Southern states, he carried every free state except New Jersey, where the vote was split between Lincoln and Douglas. Breckinridge carried the Deep South, and Bell and Douglas divided the border states.

■ The South Secedes

The Republican victory caused great alarm in the Deep South. Many Southerners felt that they had no other recourse but to leave the Union. Leadership there passed to the secessionists, some of whom had long been threatening to leave the Union. They looked on Lincoln as "a daring and reckless leader of the abolitionists." They predicted his election meant abolition and rebellion by those who were enslaved. Mississippi Senator Albert Gallatin Brown told a Southern audience:

66 *The North is accumulating power, and it means to use that power [for emancipation]. . . . When that is done, no pen can describe, no tongue can depict, no pencil can paint the horrors that will overspread this country. . . . Disunion is a fearful thing, but emancipation is worse.* 99

The Confederacy

During the four-month interval between Lincoln's election in November 1860 and his inauguration in March 1861, the seven states of the Deep South (South Carolina, Mississippi, Florida, Alabama, Georgia, Louisiana, and Texas) voted for **secession**—withdrawal from the Union.

These states based their right to secede on the theory of states' rights: the Constitution, they argued, was a contract among sovereign states. The free states had broken that contract by refusing to enforce the Fugitive Slave Law and by denying the Southern states their equal rights in the territories. Together the seven states drafted a

The Election of 1860

	Popular vote: 4,689,568	Electoral vote: 303
Lincoln	1,865,593	180
Breckinridge	848,536	72
Bell	592,906	39
Douglas	1,382,713	12

0   200   400 miles
0 200 400 kilometers

Map Study

The presidential election of 1860 split along sectional lines. Lincoln did not win in any states south of Pennsylvania and the Ohio River. *How many states did Douglas carry?*

constitution for their new alliance—the Confederate States of America—and called on the other slave states to join them.

Uneasy Truce

Government leaders made last-minute attempts at compromise. The most promising was a proposal by Senator John J. Crittenden of Kentucky. The keystone of the Crittenden Compromise was reestablishment of the 36°30' line, dividing the territories into slave and nonslave regions. Lincoln refused to agree to this proposal.

When Lincoln reached Washington, D.C., in late February 1861, eight slave states remained in the Union. Although the North generally agreed with Buchanan's view that states did not have the right to leave the Union, no one wished to fight to force them back in. General Winfield Scott expressed widespread public sentiment when he said, "Wayward sisters, depart in peace."

Lincoln's Position

Lincoln disagreed. In his first Inaugural Address, he said that "no state upon its own mere motion can lawfully get out of the Union." He argued that secession was a blow to the basic democratic principle that the will of the majority should prevail. Yet, like Buchanan before him, Lincoln suggested no active measures to force the Confederate states back into the Union. He proposed only to hold military posts not yet taken by the Confederates, to enforce federal laws where federal agents were not "obnoxious" to the

local population, and to deliver the mail "unless repelled." Although Lincoln still refused to make any concession regarding slavery in the territories, his address did not explicitly object to a constitutional amendment forbidding federal interference with slavery in the Southern states. Finally, he pleaded that the North and South be "not enemies, but friends" and said that "there need be no bloodshed or violence." Sadly, these hopes were soon dashed.

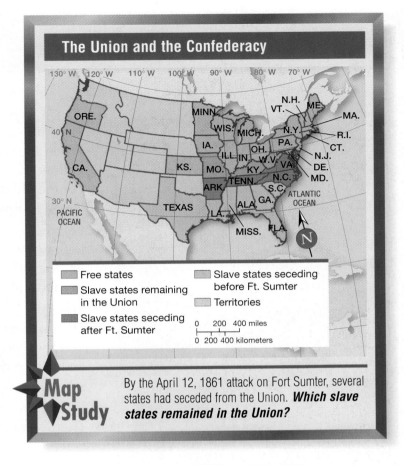

The Union and the Confederacy

Legend:
- Free states
- Slave states remaining in the Union
- Slave states seceding after Ft. Sumter
- Slave states seceding before Ft. Sumter
- Territories

Map Study By the April 12, 1861 attack on Fort Sumter, several states had seceded from the Union. *Which slave states remained in the Union?*

Section 3 ★ Review

Checking for Understanding

1. **Identify** Abraham Lincoln, John Brown, Crittenden Compromise, Confederate States of America.

2. **Define** secession.

3. **Identify** the opposing viewpoints demonstrated during the Lincoln-Douglas debates.

4. **List** three issues the Republicans used to their advantage in the election of 1860.

Critical Thinking

5. **Analyzing Choices**   Compile a list of events, other than the election of Lincoln, that might have led the seven Southern states to secede from the Union.

Follow the Drinking Gourd

When the sun comes back and the first quail calls,
Follow the drinking gourd,
For the old man is a-waiting for to carry you to freedom
If you follow the drinking gourd.

Follow the drinking gourd,
Follow the drinking gourd,
For the old man is a-waiting for to carry you to freedom
If you follow the drinking gourd.

The river bank will make a very good road,
The dead trees show you the way,
Left foot, peg foot traveling on
Follow the drinking gourd,

The river ends between two hills
Follow the drinking gourd,
There's another river on the other side,
Follow the drinking gourd,

Where the little river meets the great big river,
Follow the drinking gourd,
For the old man is a-waiting for to carry you to freedom
If you follow the drinking gourd.

▲ MOTHER AND CHILD

The struggles that tore the nation apart at mid-century were reflected in much of the period's writing. Spirituals—songs of salvation—provided the African Americans who wrote and chanted them not only with a measure of solace in bleak times but with a means for communicating secretly among themselves under their masters' watchful eye.

▲ MUSIC ON THE PLANTATION

Go Down, Moses

When Israel was in Egypt land,
Let my people go!
Oppressed so hard they could not stand,
Let my people go!

CHORUS
Go down, Moses,
Way down in Egypt land
Tell ole Pharaoh,
Let my people go!

Thus say the Lord, bold Moses said,
Let my people go!
If not I'll smite your first-born dead,
Let my people go!

No more shall they in bondage toil,
Let my people go!
Let them come out with Egypt's spoil,
Let my people go!

▲ *RIDE FOR LIBERTY*, BY EASTMAN JOHNSON, 1862

Swing Low, Sweet Chariot

Swing low, sweet chariot,
Coming for to carry me home,
Swing low, sweet chariot,
Coming to carry me home.

I looked over Jordan and what did I see
Coming for to carry me home,
A band of angels coming after me,
Coming to carry me home.

If you get there before I do,
Coming for to carry me home,
Tell all my friends I'm coming too,
Coming to carry me home.

Swing low, sweet chariot,
Coming for to carry me home,
Swing low, sweet chariot,
Coming to carry me home.

Interpreting Literature

1. What is the message from one enslaved person to another in "Follow the Drinking Gourd"?

2. Which spiritual equates the plight of the African Americans with that of another group? Which group?

Making Evaluations

3. Describe the mood of the spirituals.

Using Vocabulary

Each of the following terms can be considered a "cause" and an "effect." Define the terms below by writing two sentences for each. Write one sentence that explains the term as a cause and another sentence using the term as an effect. Here is an example: "*Secession* by Southern states was one cause of the Civil War." "One effect of the election of Abraham Lincoln was the Southern states' *secession*."

popular sovereignty   platform

Reviewing Facts

1. **Explain** how the slavery issue affected the presidential election of 1848.

2. **Classify** the provisions of the Compromise of 1850 into those that appealed to Southern states and those that appealed to Northern states.

3. **List** five inventions that hastened economic development between 1830 and 1860.

4. **State** three reasons why large numbers of immigrants came to the United States between 1830 and 1860.

5. **Explain** why the Kansas-Nebraska Act resulted in renewed fighting between slavery and anti-slavery forces.

6. **Summarize** the *Dred Scott* decision.

7. **Relate** the issue of popular sovereignty to the Lincoln-Douglas debates.

8. **Correlate** Brown's raid at Harpers Ferry to Southern attitudes about the North.

Understanding Concepts

Economic Diversity

1. Explain how economic diversity might have affected Northern and Southern views on slavery. Include in your answer differences between the Northern and Southern economies.

2. What role did improved transportation play in the expanding United States economy?

Political Conflict

3. How did the Southern states explain their right to secede from the Union?

4. Evaluate the impact of John Brown's attack at Harpers Ferry on Southern attitudes toward compromise with abolitionists.

Critical Thinking

1. **Linking Past and Present** The issues of slavery and popular sovereignty divided Americans in the 1850s. What are some issues today that divide Americans? What distinguishes a divisive issue from one that can be resolved through compromise?

2. **Analyzing Fine Art** Study the painting of John Brown and answer the questions that follow.

   a. Do you think the painting is realistic or idealized? Explain.

   b. Can you tell from the painting how the artist feels about John Brown? Explain.

▲ JOHN BROWN

Writing About History

Classification

Compile a list of changes that took place in the years between 1840 and 1860. Divide these changes into three categories: political, technological, and social. Next, create a subcategory that enumerates all the items that created conflict and tension between the North and South. Use these classifications to write an essay entitled "Factors That Divided North and South."

Cooperative Learning

You will work with two others in a group to conduct a mock trial to determine whether or not John Brown should be found guilty. Each member in your group will assume one of the following roles: defending attorney, prosecuting attorney, and judge. The defense and prosecution attorneys must prepare their cases to present before the judge. The judge must prepare at least two questions to ask each attorney. Present your trial to the class and poll them to determine John Brown's innocence or guilt.

Social Studies Skills

Making Inferences

You make an inference when you use facts to draw a conclusion that is not stated directly. Good inferences are based on sound reasoning and careful analysis of information.

Practicing the Skill

The following steps will help you make inferences from information presented in this passage about Southern slaveholders.

• Read the information carefully.

Slaveholders, called planters, were actually a very small percentage of the southern population. To be considered a planter, a person had to hold at least 20 slaves. Only about 4 percent of slaveholders had this many slaves. An extremely small percentage of slaveholders had more than 100 slaves. Jefferson Davis, who became the future President of the Confederacy, held as many as 3,000 slaves. The majority of slaveholders, however, were farmers who kept about 5 slaves.

About three-fourths of the Southerners had no slaves at all. These Southerners owned small farms on which they grew their own food and perhaps a cash crop such as tobacco or cotton. About 10 percent of this non-slaveholding southern population were poor whites. They supported themselves by hunting and fishing.

• Summarize the information:

The majority of the people in the South did not hold slaves. Those who did had very few. Only a few planters had large numbers of slaves.

• Decide what inferences or conclusions can be made based on what was read or heard but was not stated directly. Read the following inference based on the summary.

Slavery directly benefited economically only a few Southerners.

Use the three steps and what you have learned in this chapter to determine which of the following inferences seems reasonable.

1. Before the Civil War, the prosperity of the South depended on slave labor.

2. The absence of slavery in the North meant that Northerners were not prejudiced.

3. The Southern economy grew because of advances in farming equipment such as Deere's steel plow and McCormick's grain harvester.

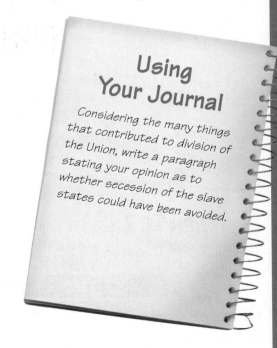

Using Your Journal

Considering the many things that contributed to division of the Union, write a paragraph stating your opinion as to whether secession of the slave states could have been avoided.

CHAPTER 15

★★★

The Civil War
1861–1865

► **CONFEDERATE CANNON**

Setting the Scene

Focus

The Civil War was a major turning point for the American people. It was the "last of the old wars and the first of the new." Still prominent were muzzle-loading rifles, horse cavalry, and chivalrous respect for the enemy. New were the use of railroads, the telegraph, ironclad ships, observation balloons, conscription, and the concept of "total war." When the fighting ended, 600,000 Americans had lost their lives, slavery had been abolished, and much of the South lay in ruins.

Concepts to Understand

★ Why it became necessary to curtail civil rights and freedoms during the Civil War

★ How military conflict led to total war between the North and South

Read to Discover . . .

★ the advantages of the Union and the Confederacy in the war.

★ how Lincoln's choice of Grant as commander of the Union armies helped the Union war effort.

Journal Notes

What was life like during the Civil War? Note details about it as you read the chapter.

CULTURAL	• The Pony Express links Missouri with California	• First transcontinental telegraph message is sent	• Julia Ward Howe's "Battle Hymn of the Republic" is published
	1860	**1861**	**1862**
POLITICAL	• Buchanan sends relief supplies to Ft. Sumter	• Seceding states form the Confederate States of America	• Emancipation Proclamation issued

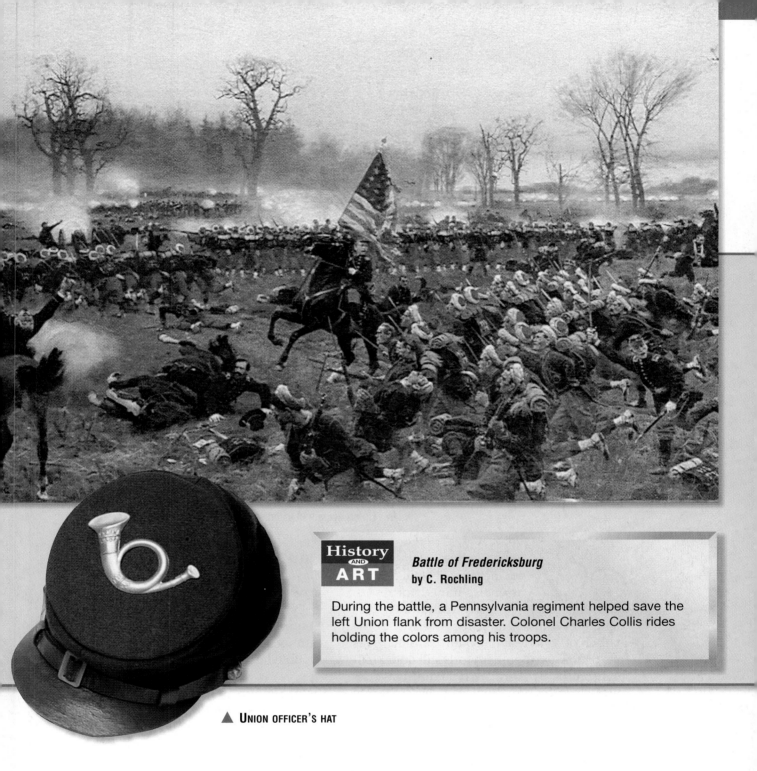

Battle of Fredericksburg
by C. Rochling

During the battle, a Pennsylvania regiment helped save the left Union flank from disaster. Colonel Charles Collis rides holding the colors among his troops.

▲ UNION OFFICER'S HAT

- First national currency goes into circulation

- Quakers found Swarthmore College in Pennsylvania

- Mark Twain publishes "The Celebrated Jumping Frog of Calaveras County"

1863	1864	1865

- Union victories at Gettysburg and Vicksburg

- Lincoln reelected

- Lincoln assassinated
- Lee surrenders to Grant
- Andrew Johnson becomes President

★★★

The Outbreak of War

Setting the Scene

Section Focus

The new President of the United States and his counterpart in the Confederacy each faced a formidable task. With the attack on Fort Sumter, war became the solution to the long-standing differences between the North and South. The war aims of both sides were simple. The goal of the South was to defend its independence. The goal of the North was to restore the Union by force. Each leader was determined to do what was necessary to win a quick victory. Neither could predict the terrible cost of the long war that was to come.

Objectives

After studying this section, you should be able to

★ explain the strategies of the North and South.

★ discuss the role of wartime diplomacy.

Key Terms

martial law, blockade

▶ UNION RECRUITMENT POSTER, 1861

As the Southern states seceded, they seized United States arsenals, mints, fortresses, and other public property within their borders. Fort Sumter, on a rocky island in the harbor of Charleston, South Carolina, was one of only two Southern forts still under federal control. By April 1861, the fort was running short of provisions because a supply ship sent by President Buchanan in January had been turned back by artillery fire from shore. Lincoln decided to resupply Fort Sumter, and he told South Carolina authorities of his decision.

Lincoln's decision placed Jefferson Davis, president of the Confederacy, in a difficult position. How long could the Confederates tolerate the fort of a "foreign" nation in the harbor of their major Atlantic port? If Davis allowed the fort to be resupplied, he would appear to be giving in to Lincoln. If he ordered that Fort Sumter or

the relief ships be fired upon, he risked war. Davis chose to take the fort before the ships arrived.

On April 12, 1861, shore batteries of the South Carolina militia opened fire on Fort Sumter. From inside the fort, Captain Abner Doubleday described the attack:

> ❝ *Showers of balls ... and shells ... poured into the fort in one incessant stream, causing great flakes of masonry to fall in all directions. When the immense mortar shells, after sailing high in the air, came down in a vertical direction, and buried themselves in the parade ground, their explosion shook the fort like an earthquake.* ❞

After 34 hours of bombardment, but no loss of life, Fort Sumter surrendered.

■ Preparing to Fight

News of the attack on Fort Sumter stirred nationalism in the North. When Lincoln requested 75,000 volunteers for 90 days to suppress the rebellion, more responded than could be equipped or trained. "I never knew what popular excitement could be," wrote a Bostonian to a friend in England. "The whole population, men, women, and children, seem to be in the streets with Union flags. . . . Nobody holds back." A similar wave of nationalism swept the South, as Jefferson Davis called for 100,000 volunteers. A visitor to the South found "revolutionary fervor in full sway. . . . Young men are dying to fight."

More Southern States Secede

Lincoln knew that conflicting forces existed in the eight slaveholding states that had not yet seceded. Nationalism worked for the Union, while the strongest argument for secession was slavery. He considered Delaware to be safe for the Union. But to remind the others that the war was to preserve the nation, and not to end slavery, the President declared:

> ❝ *The central idea pervading this struggle is the necessity of proving that popular government is not an absurdity. We must settle this question now, whether, in a free government, the minority have the right to break up the government whenever they choose.* ❞

Faced with the prospect of fighting their neighbors, however, four more states—Virginia, Arkansas, North Carolina, and Tennessee—abandoned the Union. Virginia's secession put Washington, D.C., in danger. To its west was Virginia. To the east was Maryland, where many people owned

▲ *SUNSET AT FORT SUMTER* by Conrad Wise Chapman, 1864 Chapman produced some of the most brilliant paintings associated with the Civil War. This work displays the artist's use of strong light and shade contrasts. Chapman, an enlisted soldier, was 22 years old when he painted this scene. *When did the bombardment begin?*

▲ THE IRONCLADS In the first battle of ironclad ships, the Union's Monitor defeated the South's Merrimac off Virginia in March 1862. The Union's blockade was saved, but the era of wooden warships was over. **Why was the blockade important?**

slaves and supported the Confederacy. If Maryland seceded, the Union capital would be in enemy territory. Lincoln determined to hold Maryland at all costs.

Riots in Baltimore

Only a week after Fort Sumter, as Union troops passed through Baltimore on their way to Washington, D.C., they were attacked by a mob aroused by pro-Confederate newspapers. The President responded by placing Baltimore under **martial law,** a form of military rule that includes suspending Bill of Rights guarantees. Persons who advocated secession or otherwise openly supported the Confederacy were arrested and held without trials. Although tensions in Maryland remained high throughout the war, Lincoln's action kept this strategically important state in the Union.

"I hope to have God on my side," Lincoln said, "but I must have Kentucky." The President's native state and Missouri were important because they controlled the Mississippi and Ohio rivers. Although Kentucky had a pro-Union government, Lincoln eventually put the state under martial law to stabilize it. In Missouri,

where slaveholders controlled the state, he supported rebellion against the pro-Confederate elected state government.

■ Strategies and Advantages

The Civil War was fought across the continent from southern Pennsylvania in the Northeast to New Mexico in the Southwest. Almost 3 million soldiers wore the uniforms of the Union or the Confederacy. Countless other men and women supported these troops—on the farms, in the factories, on the battlefields, and behind the lines.

The South's Leaders

The South had the better army, especially during the early years of the war. Because of a strong military tradition in the South, many Confederate officers had attended the United States Military Academy at West Point in New York. Most of the top officers in the United States Army resigned their commissions to fight for the Confederacy, among them Robert E. Lee. After his native Virginia seceded, Lee decided that he could not "raise my hand against my relatives, my children, my home." He rejected Lincoln's offer to lead the Union armies and took command of Confederate forces in Virginia.

The Union's Three-Pronged Strategy

The Union's military strategy was simple: **blockade,** or close off, Confederate ports and ruin its economy; invade the South and split it into thirds at the Mississippi River and through Tennessee and Georgia; and capture the Confederate capital at Richmond, Virginia. Southern strategy was even simpler. Southerners would be fighting for their independence on familiar terrain. To win, the South did not have to do anything except hold out against enemy attacks.

The South, formerly a region within a nation, became a "nation in arms." Men from 17 to 50 were drafted into the army and farmers were told what to plant. Women bore a large part of the burden of supplying clothing and medical supplies for the troops. Southerners felt they were fighting to preserve the cotton economy and the plantation culture. Because Europe was the major market for their cotton, they counted on European nations to provide war materials and other supplies.

Differences in Resources

The South would need Europe's help because the North was superior in nearly every type of resource. The Union had more than 80 percent of the manufacturing plants and most of America's merchant ships, railroad track, banks, minerals, grain crops, and meat. The Confederacy had less than one-half as many people as the North, and more than one-third of these were enslaved persons. The Confederacy was open to attack all along its border with the Union and along its extensive coastline. In short, the South was ill-equipped to wage war, even in its own defense.

The Confederacy also suffered from the very political theories that had created it. The Confederate constitution limited the authority of the central government and emphasized states' rights, a framework of government that was contrary to what was needed in wartime. As the war progressed, some state governments resisted the Confederacy's efforts to raise troops. Not until 1863 was the central government able to levy taxes to finance the war. It was forced to borrow and to issue worthless paper money to pay its bills. State governments also printed paper money and added to the economic chaos, which encouraged hoarding and damaged morale.

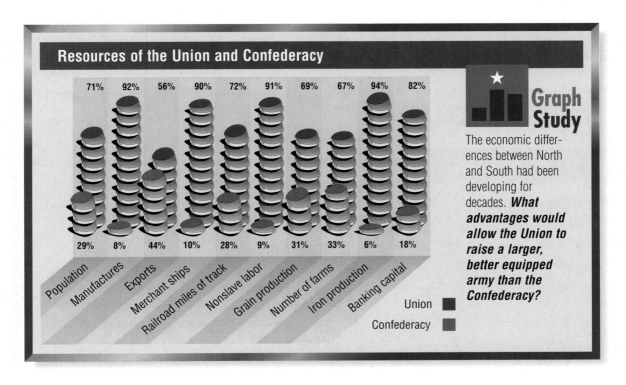

Resources of the Union and Confederacy

71% 92% 56% 90% 72% 91% 69% 67% 94% 82%

29% 8% 44% 10% 28% 9% 31% 33% 6% 18%

Population Manufactures Exports Merchant ships Railroad miles of track Nonslave labor Grain production Number of farms Iron production Banking capital

Union
Confederacy

Graph Study

The economic differences between North and South had been developing for decades. *What advantages would allow the Union to raise a larger, better equipped army than the Confederacy?*

▲ BLOCKADE RUNNERS

■ Wartime Diplomacy

The principal task of Union diplomacy during the Civil War was to prevent European nations from supporting the Confederacy. Europe's ruling classes continued to be concerned about maintaining their power and status at home, and they were not upset by the disintegration of the world's largest democracy. The British and French governments, in particular, were openly sympathetic to the Confederacy.

The South and Great Britain

The South expected Britain's aid because British textile mills used Southern cotton. Lincoln reminded the British that they needed Union wheat as much as Confederate cotton. To prevent Great Britain and the South from developing closer commercial ties, the President struck his first blow against the South.

The Blockade Begins

Six days after Fort Sumter fell, Lincoln announced a blockade of Southern ports. At the time, the action seemed foolish and impossible to enforce. To patrol a Confederate coastline 3,500 miles long, the United States Navy had just 42 wooden ships and fewer than 9,000 sailors, so at first the blockade was selective. But as the Union navy grew to 626 ships and about 59,000 sailors, the blockade reduced Confederate imports and exports to what could be carried in by "blockade runners"—small, fast vessels designed to sneak through openings in the sandbars that lined much of the Southern coast. Blockade runners could not begin to replace regular commerce, however, and Southern trade eventually shrank to a fraction of what it had been before the war, depriving Confederate armies of vital supplies.

Unable to break the blockade militarily, Southern leaders hoped to accomplish it diplomatically. If Britain recognized Confederate independence, its powerful navy could keep Southern cotton flowing to British textile mills. Southern diplomats arranged for British shipyards to build and outfit Confederate warships to prey on Northern shipping. These vessels, however, could not break the Union blockade, nor could Britain's need for cotton. Increased cotton production by Britain's colonies in Egypt and India replaced the loss of Southern cotton and eliminated the Confederacy's best hope for European intervention in the Civil War.

Section 1 ★ Review

Checking for Understanding

1. **Identify** Confederacy, Fort Sumter, Jefferson Davis, Robert E. Lee, three-pronged strategy.

2. **Define** martial law, blockade.

3. **List** three consequences of the attack on Fort Sumter.

4. **Summarize** the advantages of the North and South.

5. **Describe** the effects of the Union blockade and the Southern response to it.

Critical Thinking

6. **Analyzing Causes** The attack on Fort Sumter aroused intense patriotic feelings in the North. Comment on two aspects of this attack that you think contributed to Northerners' outburst of patriotism.

★★

The War on the Battlefield

Setting the Scene

Section Focus

The fighting began with two armies of immigrants, farm boys, schoolteachers, and store clerks. At first there was a curious, almost eager anticipation of battle. Yet when blood began to spill and young men on both sides fell wounded and dying, both the North and South began to confront the grim reality of a long and bitter war.

Objectives

After studying this section, you should be able to

★ identify the major battles of the war.

★ explain the significance of the battles of Antietam, Gettysburg, and Vicksburg.

Key Term

proclamation

▲ UNION SOLDIER'S GLOVE AND REVOLVER

There were two major areas of land warfare. The eastern theater, east of the Appalachians, centered on the region surrounding the two capitals, Washington, D.C., and Richmond, Virginia. Because the two cities were less than 100 miles apart, many battles occurred in this area.

The western theater centered around the Mississippi River and its tributaries. In many ways, the West was critical to victory. If Union armies gained control of the Mississippi River, the Confederacy would lose its western food supplies.

■ The War in Virginia

On July 21, 1861, with Lincoln's 90-day volunteers nearing the end of their enlistments, the Union army invaded Virginia to capture Richmond. About 30 miles from Washington, D.C., 30,000 Northern troops met a smaller Confederate force near a stream called Bull Run. Expecting victory and a quick end to the war, members of Congress and Washington civilians came along to picnic and watch the battle. What they saw was a confusing clash of two untrained armies. Union troops fought well at first, but the Confederates proved better organized. Using the railroad and telegraph, Confederate officers were able to quickly supply reinforcements. The Union army's retreat was reported for the London Times by a correspondent on the scene:

66 *I perceived several wagons coming from the direction of the battlefield; . . . a thick cloud of dust rose behind them, and running by the side of the wagons were a number of men in uniform. . . . Every moment the crowd increased, drivers and men cried out with the most vehement gestures, 'Turn back! Turn back! We are whipped!'* 99

Together, panic-stricken soldiers and civilians fled back to Washington. Indeed, Yankee predictions of a quick war could have come true. "Give me 10,000 fresh troops, and I will be in Washington tomorrow," Confederate General Thomas "Stonewall" Jackson said after Bull Run. Jefferson Davis, however, insisted on a defensive war, and the Union was saved.

After the disaster at Bull Run, Lincoln replaced General Irvin McDowell with General George McClellan, who trained and reorganized the Union army. But in 1862 the Confederates turned back McClellan at the Seven Days' Battle, General John Pope at the Second Battle of Bull Run, and General Ambrose Burnside at Fredericksburg. In May 1863, at Chancellorsville, Virginia, Lee smashed General Joe Hooker, who lost 17,000 men to an army half the size of his. "My God, my God," Lincoln cried when he learned of Hooker's terrible defeat, "What will the country say!"

■ Antietam and Gettysburg

Confederate military success in the eastern theater did not extend onto Northern soil. General Robert E. Lee's victory over bungling Union generals at the Second Battle of Bull Run in August 1862 encouraged him to invade the Union. His plan was to surprise Washington, D.C., from the north and destroy Northern morale. In September 1862, his 45,000 troops slipped into Maryland and disappeared into the mountains, where he split his army and sent "Stonewall" Jackson to seize the federal arsenal at Harpers Ferry. McClellan, who was to protect Washington by keeping between Lee and the capital, frantically chased after his enemy.

Antietam

At this point, incredible good luck befell McClellan. On a Maryland road, a Union

Visualizing History

▲ ROBERT E. LEE While Lincoln searched desperately for a general who could win in the east, the Confederates remained under the able command of General Robert E. Lee (on the white horse). But Lee's brilliant strategist, General Thomas "Stonewall" Jackson, was mortally wounded at Chancellorsville, and Lee mourned the loss of "my right arm." ***Which Union generals did Lee defeat in Virginia?***

patrol found 3 cigars wrapped in a copy of Lee's plans. McClellan realized that the Confederate forces were divided and that he could destroy Lee's army. On September 17, 1862, McClellan attacked Lee at Antietam (An•TEE•tuhm) Creek near Sharpsburg, Maryland. In the bloodiest single day of the war, McClellan forced Lee to retreat back into Virginia. The Confederates suffered more than 11,000 casualties. McClellan lost even more, and his army was too damaged to pursue Lee and finish him.

When news of Antietam was telegraphed to Lincoln, he called his cabinet together and told them:

> ... several weeks ago, I read to you an Order I had prepared. ... I think the time has come now. I wish it were a better time. ... The action of the army against the Rebels has not been quite what I should have best liked. But they have been driven out of Maryland.

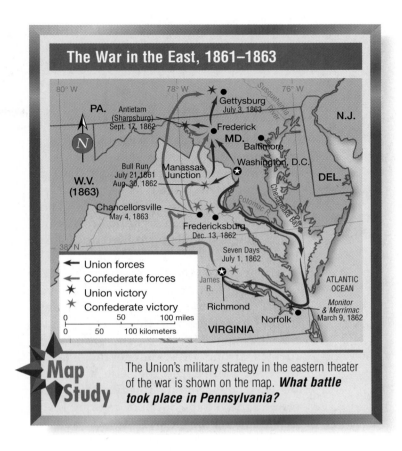

The War in the East, 1861–1863

Union forces
Confederate forces
Union victory
Confederate victory

0   50   100 miles
0   50   100 kilometers

Map Study

The Union's military strategy in the eastern theater of the war is shown on the map. *What battle took place in Pennsylvania?*

The Emancipation Proclamation

The order was in the form of a **proclamation,** or official public announcement, and known as the Emancipation Proclamation. Lincoln's order, issued on September 22, 1862, to free the slaves of the Confederacy made this conflict a war against slavery.

Encouraged by almost destroying Hooker's army of 130,000 at Chancellorsville, Lee crossed the Potomac again in June 1863, and moved into southern Pennsylvania. He was shadowed, however, by a Union army under General George G. Meade. An accidental clash between small units at Gettysburg developed into a bloody battle that marked the turning point of the war.

Gettysburg

As both armies gathered to do battle, Union troops took up positions on the crest of a low ridge. It became the Confederates' task to dislodge them from this high ground. Desperate Confederate attacks—

concluding on July 3 in a gallant but suicidal charge across an open field by General George Pickett's 15,000 troops—were all repulsed. After 3 days of fighting, Union casualties were more than 23,000. More than 28,000 Confederates were killed or wounded, about 7,000 of them in Pickett's charge. "Do not let the enemy escape," Lincoln wired the victorious Meade.

On July 4, Lee retreated into Virginia. Once again, the Union army failed to pursue him. "Our army held the war in the hollow of its hand," cried a frustrated Lincoln. "We had only to stretch forth our hands and they were ours. And nothing I could say or do could make the army move."

The Gettysburg Address

Although both sides suffered heavy casualties at Gettysburg, it was a devastating loss of life from which the sparsely populated South could not recover. On November 19, 1863, President Lincoln visited Gettysburg to dedicate the battlefield cemetery and to honor the soldiers buried there. In this Gettysburg address, the President promised that "these dead shall not have died in vain" (see Appendix).

■ War in the West

In 1861 the war in the west was a struggle for control of the border states. In Missouri the pro-Union state government that Lincoln supported waged its own civil war against Confederate sympathizers. Thousands were killed in fighting in Missouri before the first shots were fired at Bull Run in the east.

The western counties of Virginia, where pro-Union sentiment ran strong, were detached from the state after it seceded, and in 1863 they were admitted to the Union as the new state of West Virginia. Despite Kentucky's strong pro-Confederate leanings, the Union army held the state throughout the war. Thus, Union strategy in the border states deprived the South of a strong line of defense along the Ohio River.

In the following year, the Confederacy was squeezed from both north and south, as opposing forces battled for control of the Mississippi River. The Union advance began when General Ulysses S. Grant attacked two Confederate forts on the Kentucky-Tennessee border. First taking Fort Henry, on the Tennessee River, Grant surrounded Fort Donelson, on the Cumberland River, in February 1862. When the Confederate commander at Fort Donelson tried to negotiate, Grant's reply created his reputation as a tough, no-nonsense soldier: "No terms except unconditional and immediate surrender can be accepted."

The fall of Fort Donelson, with about 13,000 Confederate prisoners, opened the way for a Union advance south toward a railroad center at Corinth, Mississippi. From there Grant planned to move west along the railroad to capture Memphis, Tennessee, on the Mississippi River.

The Slaughter at Shiloh

The Union advance was slowed in April 1862 by the bloody, two-day battle of Shiloh on the Tennessee-Mississippi border. Grant's army was surprised near Corinth by the Confederates under General Albert Sidney Johnston. Union forces escaped disaster when reinforcements arrived and Johnston was killed.

Grant lost 13,000 of his 63,000 troops, and Confederate casualties numbered 11,000 of 40,000. Impressed by the determination of his enemy, Grant later wrote that after Shiloh, "I gave up all idea of saving the Union except by complete conquest."

The Union Takes New Orleans

Meanwhile, Flag Officer David Farragut was ordered to capture New Orleans. To reach the city, his warships had to move upriver from the Gulf of Mexico past 2 Confederate forts. After failing to destroy the forts, Farragut decided to pass under cover of darkness. As the maneuver began, the moon rose and the forts opened fire, hitting the first ship 42 times. After a 90-minute battle, 20 of the 24 Union ships made it past the forts, and New Orleans surrendered without firing a shot.

By the end of 1862, Union armies occupied all of western Tennessee and were probing south into Mississippi. Other armies were advancing north from New Orleans. Only the strongly fortified city of Vicksburg, Mississippi, blocked Union control of the river and success of the Union's western strategy.

■ Vicksburg and Chattanooga

As 1863 began, Union victory on the Mississippi River depended on taking the city of Vicksburg, and in late 1862 and early 1863, Grant made five attempts to capture the city. Finally, in May 1863, he began one of his most daring campaigns. After marching his army down the west bank of the Mississippi, below Vicksburg, he started inland. The Confederate commander at Vicksburg, thinking Grant was trying to trick him into the field, stayed behind his fortifications.

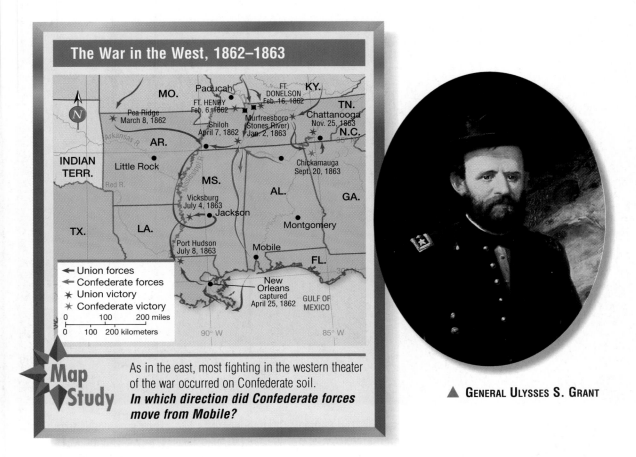

The War in the West, 1862–1863

MO.
Paducah
FT. HENRY
Feb. 6, 1862
FT. DONELSON
Feb. 16, 1862
KY.
Pea Ridge
March 8, 1862
Shiloh
April 7, 1862
Murfreesboro
(Stones River)
Jan. 2, 1863
Chattanooga
Nov. 25, 1863
TN.
N.C.
AR.
Chickamauga
Sept. 20, 1863
INDIAN TERR.
Little Rock
MS.
AL.
GA.
Vicksburg
July 4, 1863
Jackson
Montgomery
TX.
LA.
Port Hudson
July 8, 1863
Mobile
FL.
New Orleans
captured
April 25, 1862
GULF OF MEXICO

← Union forces
← Confederate forces
★ Union victory
✦ Confederate victory

0   100   200 miles
0   100   200 kilometers

Map Study

As in the east, most fighting in the western theater of the war occurred on Confederate soil.
In which direction did Confederate forces move from Mobile?

▲ GENERAL ULYSSES S. GRANT

Vicksburg Under Siege

Moving quickly, Union forces reached Jackson, the capital of Mississippi, almost without opposition. Then Grant turned and fought his way back west to the outskirts of Vicksburg. In 17 days his troops marched 180 miles and won 5 battles against larger forces. Then he laid siege to Vicksburg. It was a terrifying time for the population. Starving residents ate horses, mules, and dogs. As Union artillery bombarded the city, a woman wrote in her diary:

❝ *We are utterly cut off from the world, surrounded by a circle of fire. . . . The fiery shower of shells goes on day and night. . . . A shell came tearing through the roof, burst upstairs, tore up that room; . . . the pieces coming through both floors down into the cellar. . . .* ❞

On July 4, 1863, the same day that Lee began his retreat from Gettysburg, the starving city of Vicksburg surrendered. Five days later Port Hudson, the last Confederate port on the Mississippi River, also fell. Texas and Arkansas, the South's leading food producers, were now cut off from the rest of the Confederacy.

Battle for Chattanooga

Union forces now attempted to cut the Confederacy again—through eastern Tennessee and Georgia. The key was Chattanooga, a rail center on the Tennessee-Georgia border. In September 1863, a Union army under General William Rosecrans was badly defeated by Confederate General Braxton Bragg at the Battle of Chickamauga, in northwest Georgia. A Union officer described his army's retreat:

❝ *The march was a melancholy one. All along the road for miles, wounded men were lying. They had crawled or hobbled slowly away from the fury of the battle, become exhausted, and lain down by the roadside to die.* ❞

Visualizing History

▲ OVERLOOKING CHATTANOOGA The Battle of Chattanooga was one of the few battles in which Confederate forces outnumbered Union troops, 70,000 to 56,000. At first, Confederate troops forced their foes to retreat to the city. *What was the significance of the Battle of Chattanooga?*

Rosecrans retreated to Chattanooga, where the Confederates laid siege to his army and cut off its supplies. The Union forces were saved when Grant arrived with fresh supplies and reinforcements in late October and drove Confederate forces from the heights around the city. By the end of November, the Union forces had driven Bragg into

Georgia and Tennesee was in Union hands. By the end of 1863, only four states—Georgia, South Carolina, North Carolina, and Virginia—remained to be subdued. In early 1864, Lincoln gave General William T. Sherman command in the west and summoned Grant to accomplish what none of his other generals could do—crush Robert E. Lee.

Section 2 ★ Review

Checking for Understanding

1. **Identify** Bull Run, George McClellan, Antietam, Emancipation Proclamation, Gettysburg, Ulysses S. Grant, Vicksburg.
2. **List** early Confederate victories and when they occurred.
3. **Explain** Lincoln's timing in issuing the Emancipation Proclamation.

4. **State** why the Battle of Gettysburg was so significant.

Critical Thinking

5. **Making Inferences** Bull Run changed people's perception of the war. From this reaction, what can you infer about the way people on both sides viewed the war before Bull Run?

The Battle of Vicksburg

Control of the Mississippi River was critical to success for both the Union and Confederacy. As long as the South held Vicksburg, it controlled the 150 miles of river between that city and Baton Rouge. Vital supplies from western states flowed into the Confederacy across this stretch.

Unable to track Grant's army, Vicksburg's defenders were taken by surprise when he attacked from the south and east. Pinned against the river and swamp, the Confederates surrendered after a six-week siege.

▲ **PRESENT-DAY VICKSBURG**

◄ *FIRST AT VICKSBURG* by H. Charles McBarron The first battalion of the 13th U.S. Infantry fighting its way to the top of the Confederate lines at Vicksburg, Mississippi, May 19, 1863.

Before Grant could seize Vicksburg, however, he had to deal with a greater enemy—the wicked geography of the delta. Heavily fortified, Vicksburg was perched on a high bluff on the east side of a sharp bend in the Mississippi. North of Vicksburg lay the Yazoo Delta, a vast area of flat, swampy land half under water.

Grant descended the river from Memphis, where he sought unsuccessfully to approach the city through the delta. Grant then boldly crossed the Mississippi to the west bank, slipped south, and recrossed below Vicksburg. Contrary to established military strategy, and against the unanimous advice of his staff, Grant cut his supply lines, allowing only what food they could carry or get along the way.

Making the Geography Connection

1. What hazards might Grant have encountered in the delta?

2. Why was control of the Mississippi River important for the Union?

3. What tactic did Grant use to lay siege to Vicksburg?

Linking Past and Present

4. What places do you know of today where geography would pose problems for American troops?

★★★★★★★★★★★★★★★★★★★★★★★★★★★★★★★★

Behind the Lines

Section Focus

Financial, agricultural, and industrial resources played a major role in determining which side would win the war. But people were the most important resource. The war provided opportunities for African Americans and women to make additional contributions to their nation's vital interests.

Objectives

After studying this section, you should be able to

★ discuss behind-the-lines activity in the North and South.

★ explain the wartime roles played by women, African Americans, and Native Americans.

Key Terms

habeas corpus, conscription, bounty, greenback

◀ POWDER HORN

The Civil War was the largest war ever fought on the North American continent. Of the 1.5 million Southern white males of fighting age, about 900,000 served in the Confederate armies. Of 4 million such males in the North, about half fought in the war. In addition, more than 200,000 African Americans fought and served in the Union military, and thousands more performed manual labor for Confederate armies.

More Americans were killed in this war than in any other conflict in the history of the United States. Even in the early battles, the losses were shockingly high. As the war dragged on, the Union suffered terrible casualties but grew stronger. Confederate losses, however, gradually weakened the South's will to fight.

■ Wartime Government Power

Opposition to the war existed from the very beginning in both North and South. To carry on the war, President Lincoln and President Davis each exerted so much power that both were accused of acting like dictators. The Confederate government seized mules, wagons, food, and slaves for its armies. The Union government took over and operated private telegraph lines and railroads near war zones. Both Presidents suppressed opposition to the war by abusing the civil rights of citizens. Davis declared martial law in parts of the Confederacy, and he suspended the right of **habeas corpus,** which requires that persons who are arrested be brought to court to show why they should be held.

Discontent Grows

The North was a hotbed of discontent about the war. Abolitionists were irate over Lincoln's accommodating attitude toward slavery and about his refusal to make the end of slavery a goal of the war. They were joined by members of Lincoln's own party in Congress, a faction called the Radical Republicans, who opposed Lincoln's view that the war was only to preserve the Union.

The Copperheads

At the other extreme were the "Copperheads," mainly Democrats, who called for ending the war at any price, even if that meant welcoming the South and slavery back into the Union, or letting the slave states leave in peace. Some Copperheads encouraged Northerners to resist the war and others openly supported the South.

The Issue of Rights

Many of the measures Lincoln used to quiet opposition to the war violated constitutional guarantees of free speech, press, and assembly. He prevented a state legislature from meeting. He denied some opposition newspapers use of the mails and used the army to shut others down. And he ordered hundreds of suspected Confederate sympathizers jailed without the right of habeas corpus.

President Lincoln agonized over his decisions to deny American citizens their civil rights. He believed, though, that the survival of the nation during an emergency overrode the Constitution. In May 1863, Clement Vallandigham, a former Ohio congressman, made a speech in which he blamed the President for prolonging the war. He was arrested and sentenced to prison for the remainder of the war by a military court in Cincinnati. Vallandigham appealed to the Supreme Court for his release. But in 1864, in *Ex parte Vallandigham,* the Court refused to challenge the President and ruled that its authority did not extend to military courts.

■ Effects of the Emancipation Proclamation

When the Civil War began, there was not universal support in the North for a war to free enslaved persons. In many areas of the North there was open hostility to African Americans and laws that limited their rights. Slavery still existed in Washington, D.C., and in five states that remained in the Union.

Lincoln's Position

Lincoln, himself, was not an abolitionist. He regarded slavery as a moral wrong and a disaster for both blacks and whites, but he recognized the constitutional guarantees for slavery. He assured the South that he had "no purpose, directly or indirectly, to interfere with the institution of slavery where it now exists" but that he only opposed its extension into the territories. Again and again Lincoln declared that his goal was "to save the Union . . . not either to save or destroy slavery." If he acted any other way, he feared that the border states might join the Confederacy.

▲ PRESIDENT ABRAHAM LINCOLN

Pressure Mounts

As time passed, however, Lincoln came under increasing pressure to turn the war into a crusade against slavery. The abolitionists and the Radical Republicans demanded that Southern slaveholders be punished for the war by loss of their property. As the number of battlefield casualties grew, Northerners increasingly began to feel that such bloodshed was justified only if it destroyed an institution that violated human principles of freedom and dignity. In addition, Great Britain talked of mediating a settlement of the war. Lincoln realized that public opinion in Europe—and in Britain especially—was strongly opposed to slavery, and that no European government would defend the South in a war to abolish slavery.

The Proclamation Renews Spirit

After Lee's defeat at Antietam in 1862, Lincoln announced that he would free enslaved people in the Confederate states on January 1, 1863. But the Emancipation Proclamation did not immediately free anyone, because it applied only to the areas held by the enemy. The Proclamation, however, turned the war into a moral crusade and aroused a renewed spirit in the North. The number of African American volunteers for the army increased dramatically. As news of the Proclamation spread through the Confederacy, whenever Northern armies occupied Southern territory, thousands of African Americans poured into Union lines. The Emancipation Proclamation is "the greatest event of our nation's history, if not the greatest event of the century," said abolitionist editor Frederick Douglass.

Slavery in areas where the Emancipation Proclamation did not apply remained a problem, however. There were 800,000 enslaved persons in the border states and many more in areas of the South that the Union armies already had conquered. For these areas Lincoln recommended a policy of compensated emancipation—setting the enslaved free, but paying their owners for them. Congress, however, adopted this idea only for the District of Columbia, where there were just 3,000 enslaved people. Elsewhere, slavery was abolished by the Thirteenth Amendment to the Constitution, ratified in 1865.

■ Raising the Armies

At first, both North and South relied on volunteers and Lincoln's original 90-day volunteers were replaced by 3-year enlistments. But mounting casualties reduced enthusiasm for the war, and enlistments decreased.

Desertions

As the South's economy collapsed, and the scarcity of clothing and medicine was matched by shortages of food and shelter, Confederate desertions increased. "I am so tired for I never get any rest night or day, and I don't think I will last much longer," wrote a Georgia woman in despair. When Confederate soldiers received such letters, many saw no disgrace in going home to aid their suffering families.

The Draft

Both North and South were forced to resort to **conscription,** or the drafting of men for military service. In April 1862, the South, with less than one-half the population of the North, began drafting men aged 18 to 35. Later, as the need to maintain its armies increased, the Confederate congress raised the upper age limit to 50. In March 1863, the United States Congress created a military draft in the North.

The draft laws were incomplete and discriminatory. A draftee could avoid service by hiring a substitute, and a Union draftee could buy his way out by paying the government $300. Such provisions aroused criticism that it was "a rich man's war and a poor man's fight."

In the South, some state governors helped their citizens evade the draft. In the North, opposition to conscription led to riots in New York City in July 1863. A resident reported that for four days:

★★★★★★★★★★ ★★★★★★★★★★★★★★★★★★★★★★★★★★★★★★

Mess Call

One of the more unpleasant features of life in the Civil War armies was the food. Neither the Confederacy nor the Union enlisted men as cooks and no

▼ HARDTACK

training was available to those who received this assignment.

When in quarters, a company would receive a government issue of flour, pork, beans, potatoes, coffee, and the like. Initially, six or eight recruits would form a mess team and take turns cooking. If any of them actually knew anything about preparing meals, the group was fortunate. Later, the commanding officer assigned men to the cook tent, as often as not, to get them out of the ranks.

On the march, rations typically consisted of dried salt pork, hardtack (a saltless hard biscuit made from flour), and coffee. Southern soldiers usually went without coffee, and cornmeal was

substituted for hardtack. Veteran soldiers found fresh hardtack palatable enough.

With age, however, it might become infested with weevils. Some thought it better to eat it in the dark. Soldiers from both armies frequently supplemented meager rations by stealing crops and livestock from nearby farms.

★★★★★★★★★★★★★★★★★★★★★★★★★★

▲ SOLDIER'S CANTEEN

❝ . . . there were dreadful scenes enacted in the city. The police were successfully opposed; many were killed, many houses were gutted and burned: the . . . asylum was burned and all the furniture was carried off by women . . . . ❞

To those who enlisted, the North paid a **bounty,** or lump sum of money, of as much as $1,500 for a single 3-year enlistment. This led to the practice of "bounty jumping," whereby a man would enlist, collect his bounty and then desert, only to reenlist somewhere else.

African Americans Fight for the Union

▲ UNION SOLDIER PHOTOGRAPHED BY MATHEW BRADY

President Lincoln at first resisted appeals to enlist African Americans in the Union armies because he feared that such a policy would be resented in the border states. After the Emancipation Proclamation, the policy was changed. Nearly 200,000 African Americans enlisted for military service and an additional 150,000 served in the quartermaster and engineering corps. Black soldiers were commanded by white officers, were paid less, and were segregated from white troops, who often resented them. Many African American regiments distinguished themselves in combat, however, and 23 soldiers won the Congressional Medal of Honor during the war.

Until the very end of the war, the South refused to accept African Americans for military service. Confederate armies often used enslaved persons to dig fortifications, cook, drive wagons, and perform other labor, but there was widespread opposition to arming them for combat.

AMERICAN PORTRAITS

Clara Barton
1821–1912

Clara Barton grew up loving sports and intended to make teaching her career. After 18 years in education, however, she went to work for the U.S. Patent Office. She was in the nation's capital when the guns of the Civil War started blazing.

Though lacking medical training, Clara Barton left her desk job to care for sick and wounded Union soldiers. Traveling to the sites of some of the worst carnage of the war, she even ventured deep into the Confederacy to assist federal forces laying siege to Charleston. She regularly risked her life by passing through the front lines to deliver supplies and nurse the wounded.

After the war—before she founded the American Red Cross in 1877—Clara Barton worked to identify thousands of soldiers who had perished at the Andersonville prison camp in Georgia.

Native Americans and the War

The Civil War also dramatically affected Native Americans. The South acted quickly to gain support, sending commissioners to the Indian Territory to sign peace treaties. The Cherokee even fought on the Confederate side.

In 1864 the Union sent troops to restore its authority over the Native Americans. Federal victories over forces in Arkansas and in the Indian Territory showed the Native Americans the weakness of their Confederate allies.

The North then renegotiated treaties with their nations and took land away from those who had fought for the Confederacy.

■ Women Behind the Lines

The demands the war placed on civilian populations created new roles for women. Southern women were required to run plantations. On smaller farms, women plowed the fields and handled other chores. Southern households became miniature factories, with spinning wheels and looms turning out clothing for the Confederacy.

Changing Roles

The war forced many Southerners to abandon their romantic view of women as "belles" to be protected from rough work. Many women worked as government clerks and factory workers—including dangerous work in munitions factories, making weapons and ammunition for the troops. Some women accompanied the armies in the field, cooking, sewing, and washing.

On Farms and in Factories

Although most Northern women did not suffer from invading armies, they also were deeply affected by the war. In the North, the mechanical reaper and the sulky plow—where the operator rode on top of the plow itself rather than pushed it from behind—allowed women to take the place of husbands and sons. Industry's need for labor opened other opportunities in Northern factories. Many women needed such work to support their families.

On the Battlefield

Nurses were exposed to the worst horrors of the war. Dorothea Dix became superintendent of female nurses in the Union army and in this position fought corruption and prejudice against her sex. Even more effective in widening the role of women in hospitals was Clara Barton, who founded the American Red Cross.

Women also played a large part in America's first great private relief organization—the United States Sanitary Commission. This organization collected millions of dollars for projects to improve the living conditions of Union soldiers. It is little wonder that after the Civil War there was a renewed demand for woman suffrage.

■ Supplying the Armies

In a long war fought on a vast scale, victors are decided as much behind the lines as on the battlefield. The Confederacy was defeated largely because of its inability to produce industrial goods. Through war contracts, the Confederate government helped to stimulate industry in the South. It encouraged factories to supply its troops with arms and ammunition, but it lacked the industrial capacity to provide other necessities.

Graft and Corruption

The efforts of the Union government to supply its armies were hindered by overcharging and corruption. Army contractors sometimes supplied shoddy clothing, rotten meat, and defective shoes. The productivity of Northern factories was so great, though, that in spite of the graft, Union armies were better equipped than their enemy.

Financing the War

The Confederacy also was less able to finance the war than was the North. The South had intended to obtain money by selling cotton to Europe, but the Union blockade prevented this. To raise money, the Confederacy enacted an income tax and demanded 10 percent of all crops produced. The most important way that the Confederacy and its state governments raised money was simply by printing more of it. The Confederate government was able to operate only by forcing its citizens to accept its worthless currency in exchange for supplies.

The North was far more successful in financing the war. About one-fourth of the $4 billion needed came from taxation, and the rest from borrowing and issuing paper money.

During the war the federal government issued more than $2.5 billion worth of bonds. Like the Confederacy, the Union government also inflated its currency, but not to the point where it became worthless. The federal government issued $400 million worth of **greenbacks,** paper money that was not backed by gold or silver, but whose value rose and fell with the success of Union armies in the field.

Section 3 ★ Review

Checking for Understanding

1. **Identify** Clara Barton, Radical Republicans, Copperheads, Ex parte Vallandigham, Dorothea Dix.

2. **Define** habeas corpus, conscription, bounty, greenback.

3. **State** what factors caused Lincoln to change his war goals to include freeing the enslaved persons.

4. **List** the contributions made by African Americans to the war effort on both sides.

5. **Explain** how women supported the war effort behind the lines.

Critical Thinking

6. **Assessing Cause and Effect**   The war provided women opportunities that were not open to them before. What effect do you think this had on their views about their status in society?

Study and Writing Skills

▲ COMPANY E, 4TH U.S. INFANTRY at Fort Lincoln, District of Columbia, 1865

Analyzing Illustrations

The photographs and illustrations that appear throughout this book contain special information. They aid in your understanding of each chapter. The pictures identify the focus of the material, and they make the book more interesting.

Look carefully at each picture to analyze its content. The steps you can take to analyze the picture are simple.

1. **Look** at the picture to get a general sense of what the subject is about. The picture could give useful evidence about aspects of daily life.

2. **Read** the caption that goes with each picture or group of pictures.

3. **Decide** if the picture is a drawing, a painting, or a photograph. (There will be no photographs before the middle of the 1800s when photography was developed.)

4. **Decide,** if possible, whether a drawing or a painting was done by someone who lived at the time or someone who lived at a later time.

5. **Decide** whether a drawing is a posed portrait or an unposed photograph.

6. **Consider** the main theme and the general message of the picture.

7. **Identify** the main focus of the picture.

8. **Consider** how the figures in the picture support the main theme.

9. **Consider** how the use of color or lack of color supports the theme of the picture.

10. **Decide** why you think the picture is used at its location in the book.

Practicing the Skill

Using such a list can make understanding pictures easier. As an example, use the list to analyze the picture on this page. As you study the picture, consider the following questions.

1. All of the figures in the picture are African American soldiers. What does this tell you about the makeup of the Union army?

2. Study the expressions of the soldiers. What information does this give you?

As you look at the other pictures in this book, develop your own list of questions.

★★★★★★★★★★★★★★★★★★★★★★★★★★★★

Ending the War

Setting the Scene

Section Focus

In March 1864, it became Ulysses S. Grant's turn to face the brilliant Confederate general, Robert E. Lee. Lincoln brought Grant east and gave him command of all Union forces. At last the President found a commander who could win the war. The President, however, would not live to see the war's end.

Objectives

After studying this section, you should be able to

★ explain the changes in Union military strategy after Grant took command.

★ discuss the issues in the election of 1864.

Key Term

forage

◀ **CONFEDERATE HAT**

General Grant determined that to win the war he would utilize the Union's biggest advantages over the South—its overwhelming superiority in population and in production capacity. To end the South's ability to fight, he would not only defeat Confederate armies, but would destroy them. To end the South's will to fight, he would engage in "total war"—war against civilians and resources as well as against armies.

■ Grant in the East

Moving south into Virginia, in May and June 1864, Grant's force of 120,000 engaged the Confederate army of 60,000 almost continuously. At the Battle of the Wilderness, Lee stopped Grant in a forest where the fighting was so heavy that the woods caught fire, trapping the wounded in the flames and burning them to death. But instead of retreating after a defeat, as previous Union commanders had done, Grant kept advancing. He attacked Lee at Spotsylvania in a bloody battle that one soldier called "the most terrible twenty-four hours of our service in the war." In early June, Grant attacked Lee again, at Cold Harbor, where he ordered suicidal charges against fortified Confederate positions.

In less than a month, Union forces had suffered casualties greater in number than Lee's entire army. A Union officer protested that "our men have, in many instances, been foolishly and wantonly sacrificed." Grant knew that he could replace his losses while his enemy could not, and he promised "to fight it out along this line if it takes all summer."

In mid-June Lee retreated to Petersburg, south of Richmond, where Grant surrounded the Confederates and their capital and laid siege to the city. In July Lee attempted to break the siege by instructing General Jubal Early to move through Virginia's Shenandoah River valley to threaten Washington, D.C. Grant dispatched the Union cavalry under General Philip Sheridan to drive the Confederates from the area and told him "nothing should be left to invite the enemy to return." He ordered Sheridan to make the valley "a barren waste." By March 1865, Sheridan had carried out his orders so well, he reported to Grant, that a crow flying across the valley would have to carry its food. Meanwhile, Grant continued his siege of Richmond.

Sherman's March

In May 1864, as Grant invaded Virginia, he ordered General William T. Sherman and his 100,000 troops posted in Chattanooga, Tennessee, to engage and destroy the Confederate army in the west. The Confederates were forced to retreat toward Atlanta, Georgia, which Sherman captured in September and occupied until November, when he ordered the city evacuated and destroyed. City officials begged that Atlanta be spared, but Sherman replied:

❝ *You might as well appeal against the thunderstorm as against these terrible hardships of war. They are inevitable, and the only way the people of Atlanta can hope once more to live in peace and quiet at home, is to stop the war . . . .* ❞

As the Northern army abandoned the city, a Union officer described its destruction:

❝ *The heaven is one expanse of lurid fire; the air is filled with flying, burning cinders; buildings covering two hundred acres are in ruins or in flames; every instant there is the sharp detonation or the smothered booming sound of exploding shells and powder . . . .* ❞

To divide the South a second time, Sherman adopted Grant's tactics before Vicksburg—strike into enemy territory and **forage,** or

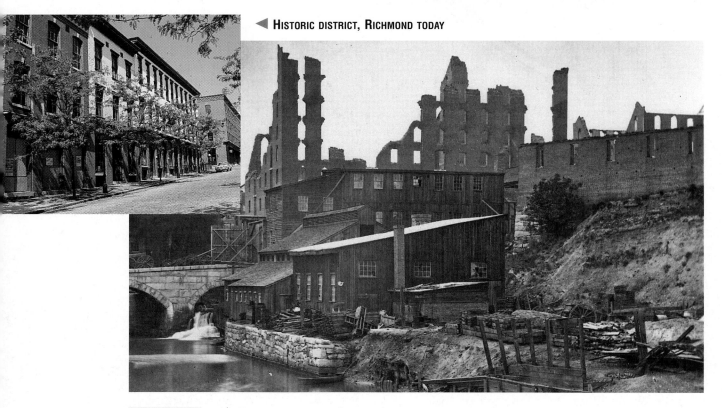

◀ HISTORIC DISTRICT, RICHMOND TODAY

Visualizing History

▲ DESTRUCTION IN THE SOUTH By April 1865 many major cities of the Confederacy, including Atlanta and the capital city of Richmond (above), had felt the full force of war. *Why did Sherman burn Atlanta?*

live off the land. His army marched southeast and for a month carved a path of destruction 60 miles wide through one of the richest agricultural regions of the South. Sherman reached the Atlantic coast at Savannah, Georgia, and reported to Grant that he had destroyed $100 million of property in Georgia—$20 million in military damage and "the remainder is simply waste and destruction."

As he entered Savannah on December 20, 1864, Sherman learned that five days before, outside Nashville, Tennessee, General George Thomas had destroyed the Confederates' western army. The war in the west was over. In February 1865, Sherman left Savannah and marched north through the Carolinas, destroying everything in his path and planning to link up with Grant at Richmond.

The Election of 1864

Throughout the war, federal, state, and city elections continued to be held in the North, but the war divided both major parties into War Democrats and Peace Democrats, Radical Republicans and Conservative Republicans. In the presidential election of 1864, the Republican party temporarily changed its name to the Union party to attract Democrats who supported the war.

Lincoln Runs for Reelection

The Unionists renominated Lincoln for President and chose a War Democrat for Vice President, Andrew Johnson, military governor of Tennessee. The Democrats nominated George McClellan, the popular general whom Lincoln had twice removed from command. But the Democrats drew up a peace platform that branded the war a failure and called for the immediate restoration of the Union.

Lincoln's chances for victory largely depended on the fortunes of the Union armies in the field. In mid-1864 the war was going badly, and Lincoln was certain that he would be defeated. But Sherman's capture of Atlanta in September, coupled with McClellan's refusal to support his party's platform,

Visualizing History ▲ **SHERMAN** Union General William T. Sherman brought the horror of war to the civilian population of Georgia and the Carolinas. *How did Sherman affect the outcome of the election of 1864?*

gave Lincoln the victory. The voters had decided that "it was not best to swap horses while crossing the river," Lincoln said.

"With Malice Toward None"

In his second Inaugural Address in March 1865, Lincoln reviewed the causes of the war and hoped for a peace without bitterness. Both sides "read the same Bible and pray to the same God," he noted, so "let us judge not that we be not judged." It may be, Lincoln said, that the war was divine vengeance on both North and South for two centuries of wrong to African American people.

Lincoln concluded his short address by extending charity to the defeated South. He directed his generals to offer the Confederate armies the most liberal terms of surrender and asked Northerners:

> 66 *With malice toward none, with charity for all . . . let us strive on to finish the work we are in, to bind up the nation's wounds, . . . to do all which may achieve and cherish a just and lasting peace among ourselves and with all nations.* 99

In the four years since the untried prairie lawyer delivered his first Inaugural Address, his stock had risen. In spite of violent attacks in Congress and in the press, Lincoln inspired affection and trust, as shown by the nicknames "Uncle Abe" and "Father Abraham." Many people had begun to appreciate the ability and strength of character hidden behind Lincoln's homely exterior. One of these was the novelist Nathaniel Hawthorne, who wrote about the President:

❝ *There is no describing the lengthy awkwardness nor the uncouthness of his movement; and yet it seemed as if I had been in the habit of seeing him daily, and had shaken hands with him a thousand times in some village street.... If put to guess his calling and livelihood, I should have taken him for a country schoolmaster as soon as anything else . . . [Yet, I like his appearance] . . . and, for my small share in the matter, would as [soon] have Uncle Abe for a ruler as any man whom it would have been practicable to put in his place.* ❞

■ The Final Days

While Lincoln was delivering his second Inaugural Address in March 1865, Grant was pressing in on Richmond and Sherman was marching through the Carolinas. Aware that the situation was hopeless, General Lee advised President Davis that he could no longer defend Richmond. The Confederate government fled south, and Lee's army finally evacuated the city. By April 4, 1865, President Lincoln was able to walk through the streets of the former Confederate capital.

▲ LEE (RIGHT) SURRENDERS TO GRANT AT APPOMATTOX COURT HOUSE Grant ordered Union troops not to celebrate. "The war is over," he said, "the rebels are our countrymen again." *How did Grant's surrender terms compare with Lincoln's attitude toward the South?*

Lee Surrenders

Just days later, Grant's forces cut off Lee's troops as they attempted to unite with other Confederate armies. Grant urged Lee to surrender in order to prevent "further effusion of blood." On April 9, 1865, the two men met at Appomattox Court House in central Virginia. Grant offered Lee generous terms: Southern soldiers could go home if they pledged not to fight again. The officers would keep their pistols and the men their horses.

When Lee's army came to lay down their arms, Union troops saluted each division as it appeared. As the Confederate forces marched before them, the Union troops watched silently, with "not a cheer, nor a word, nor whisper of vainglory," one Union officer described it, "but an awed stillness rather, a breath-holding, as if it were the passing of the dead."

Defying orders from President Davis, by June, all other Confederate generals also surrendered. The long, bitter struggle that split the nation finally came to an end.

Lincoln is Assassinated

President Lincoln did not live to see the end of the war, however. On April 14, 1865, just five days after Lee's surrender, Lincoln was assassinated by John Wilkes Booth, a fanatical Confederate sympathizer. Booth's deed was a tragedy for both North and South, for it removed the one person best equipped to "bind up the nation's wounds."

A Richmond newspaper called Lincoln's death "the heaviest blow which has ever fallen upon the people of the South." A young Southern woman confided to her diary, "The most terrible part of the war is now to come."

▶ JOHN WILKES BOOTH (BELOW) AND WANTED POSTER

Visualizing History ▲ President Lincoln was shot and killed while attending a play at Ford's Theater in Washington, D.C. An eyewitness later recalled that the theater was filled with "the shouts, groans, curses, smashing of seats, screams, and cries of terror." The items shown below the wanted poster and Booth's photo are the contents of Lincoln's pockets the day he died. *Why did many Southerners as well as Northerners mourn the loss of the President?*

Section 4 ★ Review

Checking for Understanding

1. **Identify** William T. Sherman, Andrew Johnson, Appomattox, John Wilkes Booth.
2. **Define** forage.
3. **Explain** the strategy that Grant adopted to defeat the Confederacy.
4. **Examine** how the tactics used by Union generals Philip Sheridan and William Sherman broadened the scope of the war beyond purely military engagements.

Critical Thinking

5. **Analyzing a Quotation**   To explain his reelection, Lincoln stated, "it was not best to swap horses while crossing the river." Explain the meaning of Lincoln's quotation and how it applied to him.

Using Vocabulary

For the first time, photography was used extensively to record history during the American Civil War. Regard each of the terms below as captions for a pictorial history of the Civil War. After each term, describe a photograph that would explain the concept or identify the term.

martial law
greenbacks
bounty
conscription
habeas corpus

Reviewing Facts

1. **List** two Southern military advantages and two Northern military advantages.

2. **State** the Union army's three principal goals.

3. **Explain** how technology played a role in determining the victor at Bull Run. Describe the results of Antietam and Gettysburg for the Southern army.

4. **Summarize** the effects the Emancipation Proclamation had on the war.

5. **State** two methods the North used to raise troops.

6. **State** two reasons Lincoln was reelected.

Understanding Concepts

Rights and Freedom

1. How did Lincoln violate constitutional rights during the war and for what reasons?

2. Why would African Americans be eager to fight for the Union army? Why was Lincoln initially reluctant to use African American soldiers?

Conflict

3. Why did Union victory come only after its generals decided to fight a ruthless war?

4. How did attitudes about the kind and extent of the war change after Bull Run?

Critical Thinking

1. **Evaluating Causes** List five factors that affected the military ability of both the Northern and Southern armies. Rank the items according to their importance in determining the outcome of the Civil War.

2. **Evaluating an Action** Grant's campaign against Vicksburg was a calculated risk. List the pros and cons of Grant's strategy. If he had failed, what likely consequences would he have faced?

3. **Analyzing Artifacts** Supporters for Lincoln expressed their support during the 1860 presidential election campaign with posters such as this one. Why did the creators of the poster choose those particular symbols to represent Lincoln? What other symbols can you suggest?

Writing About History

Argumentation

The Civil War resulted in enormous loss of life. Do you believe this loss was justified? Write an essay stating whether you believe the war was worth the cost. Write your argument from the perspective of a disabled Union or Confederate soldier or a Union or Confederate wife whose husband died fighting in the war.

Cooperative Learning

Each member in your group takes one of these roles: Union soldier, Confederate soldier, and British journalist. The journalist would like to get both viewpoints on the war. Each group member must prepare one question to be asked by the journalist. If you are the Union soldier, write a question for the journalist to ask the Confederate soldier and vice versa. If you are the journalist, write one question that you will ask each soldier. Conduct the interview in front of your classmates.

Social Studies Skills

Drawing Conclusions Drawing conclusions—that is, making judgments or decisions after deliberation—can help you in your studies. After reviewing what you know, ask yourself such questions as:

- Do I have all the information I need to make a valid conclusion?

- Have I weighed all the information fairly?

- How and why might new information cause me to change or modify my conclusion?

The map on this page shows the final campaigns of the Civil War. Like the early battles, the final struggles between the Union and the Confederacy took place in the eastern theater. From this information, you could conclude that it might have been unwise for the Confederacy to move their capital to Richmond, which appears to be a poor strategic location.

Practicing the Skill

Study the map, and then draw further conclusions by answering the questions that follow.

1. What conclusions can you make about what life must have been like for people living in Virginia during the final months of the war?

2. What conclusions can you make about whether or not the Confederates were fighting offensive or defensive battles?

3. **Analyzing Choices** What conclusions do you think led General Lee to finally surrender?

The Final Campaigns, 1864–1865

OHIO

PA.

N.J.

MD.

DEL.

W.V.

Fredericksburg

Washington, D.C.

The Wilderness
May 6, 1864

Spotsylvania
May 12, 1864

Richmond

Cold Harbor
June 3, 1864

ATLANTIC OCEAN

Lynchburg

Norfolk

KY.

Appomattox
Court House

VA.

Petersburg
siege
June 20, 1864–April 2, 1865

Union Naval
Blockade

Lee surrenders
April 9, 1865

TENN.

Raleigh

35° N

N.C.

Atlanta
occupied
Sept. 2, 1864

S.C.

Wilmington

Macon

Charleston

GA.

Savannah

80° W

← Union forces
← Confederate forces
★ Union victory
★ Confederate victory
✳ Indecisive battle

0   100   200 miles
0   100   200 kilometers

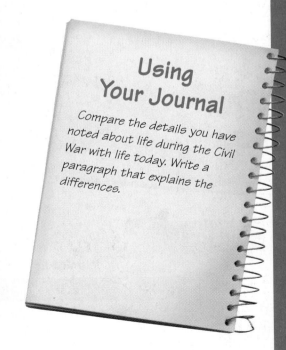

Using Your Journal

Compare the details you have noted about life during the Civil War with life today. Write a paragraph that explains the differences.

CHAPTER 16

★★★★★★★★★★★★★★★★★★★★★★★★★★★★★★★★★★★★★★

Reconstruction
1865–1877

► **ELECTION CAMPAIGN RIBBON, 1868**

Setting the Scene

Focus

Confederate war veterans who returned home after the war found their land devastated. African Americans quickly discovered that freedom did not mean equality. The first order of business for the federal government, however, was to readmit the Southern states to the Union. This proved difficult because white Southerners were bitter and Radical Republicans in Congress worked to keep their party in power.

Concepts to Understand

★ Why adaptation to new social conditions was necessary for newly freed men and women and white planters

★ How Radical Republicans sought to exercise power and authority over the Reconstruction process

Read to Discover . . .

★ why Reconstruction policies differed.

★ what the Compromise of 1877 established.

Journal Notes

As you read the chapter, note how racial equality was inhibited during Reconstruction. Write your findings in your journal.

CULTURAL

• **1866** *Fisk School, later Fisk University, founded in Nashville, Tennessee*

• **1871** *P. T. Barnum opens circus in Brooklyn, New York*

1865

1869

POLITICAL

• **1868** *President Johnson impeached by House; Senate fails to convict him*

• **1869** *Federal government completes Great Western Survey*

◀ TOY WHEELED HORSE, LATE 1800s

● **1876** *Alexander Graham Bell transmits message on telephone*

● **1879** *The Church of Christ, Scientist, chartered*

1873	1877

● **1873** *New York Stock Exchange closes for 10 days after economic panic begins*

● **1877** *Compromise of 1877 completed*
● **1881** *Kansas passes a prohibition law*

★★★★★★★★★★★★★★★★★★★★★★★

After Slavery

Setting the Scene

Section Focus

The Civil War saved the Union but shook the nation to its roots. The fall of the Confederacy toppled the planter aristocracy that had ruled the South. Also gone was slavery, the labor system that was the basis of Southern society. The end of slavery, however, did not solve the problems that the newly freed African Americans were to face.

Objectives

After studying this section, you should be able to

★ explain the changes in Southern society that occurred after the Civil War.

★ discuss the changes that freedom brought to African American families.

Key Terms

tenant farmer, sharecropper

◀ **BADGE NO LONGER WORN BY FREED AFRICAN AMERICANS**

When Confederate veterans—tired, ragged, and hungry—went home at the end of the Civil War, they returned to a ravaged land. Large areas of land had been systematically laid to waste by the armies of Sherman and Sheridan. One Mississippi woman remembered her father's homecoming after the war:

" *He had come home to a house stripped of every article of furniture. The plantation was stripped of the means of cultivating any but a small portion of it. A few mules and one cow made up the stock. . . . He owned nothing that could be turned into money without great sacrifice but five bales of cotton.* "

The wreckage stretched from South Carolina's Atlantic coast in the east to Tennessee in the west and from Virginia's Shenandoah Valley in the north through Georgia in the south. It was not only the land that was in ruin, however. Economically, politically, and socially, the South was in total disarray. Confederate money was worthless, and Southern banks were ruined. Government at every level had all but disappeared. There were no courts, no judges, no sheriffs, and no police— no law or authority except when groups of people took matters into their own hands. The war also left the South's transportation system in complete disorder. Roads were impassable, bridges had been destroyed or had washed away, and railroad tracks had been rendered unusable. For planters, the greatest economic blow was the loss of their enslaved workers, an investment worth more than $2 billion. When the workers were freed, the plantation system collapsed.

■ New Ways of Life

The devastation of war affected all levels of Southern society. For landowners it meant that their old way of life had been swept away.

The Plight of the Landowners

After his regiment surrendered at Appomattox, the planter Harry Hammond said he had "a pipe, some tobacco, and literally nothing else." Although Hammond owned a large plantation, he could find no one who could afford to buy his land when he put it up for sale. Hammond was saved from total ruin when most of the 300 African Americans on the plantation agreed to stay and work the land. In return for their labor, Hammond provided his formerly enslaved workers with housing, firewood, weekly food allotments, every other Saturday off, and $15 a year in cash after the crops were harvested. Hammond also agreed to provide the loan of a mule and a plow so that the workers could grow their own crops.

Not every planter was so fortunate. Southerners who had invested heavily in Confederate currency and bonds were wiped out financially when Confederate funds became worthless after the war. Many lost their land because of taxes or other debts they could not pay. Some sold their acres to anyone who could pay the outrageously low prices for which Southern farms and plantations were advertised in Northern newspapers. On other plantations and on small farms throughout the South, war widows struggled to hold on to their property and keep it producing.

The Plight of Workers

Poor African Americans and whites realized that social and economic status in the South was tied to the land, but few had money to buy land, even at such low prices. So some became **tenant farmers,** farming land that they rented. But even this was beyond the means of many poor Southerners, and more often they became **sharecroppers,** persons who worked the owner's land—sometimes using the owner's tools, animals, and seed—and received a share of the crops in return.

Although these arrangements seemed a solution that would provide a living for both workers and landowners, the system contained serious defects. For example, debt-ridden landowners wanted to get the highest possible return, so they pressured tenants to grow only cotton or tobacco, cash crops that paid the most. To prevent depletion of the soil, however, tenants should have planted a variety of crops, including food crops.

Tenants, black and white alike, usually had to buy seed, fertilizer, work animals, and food on credit, at interest rates as high as 40 percent. Thus, no matter how hard they worked, many tenants fell deeply into debt and remained trapped on the land until they paid those debts—no freer to leave than enslaved workers had been. As late as 1907,

▲ *THE WAY THEY LIVE* by Thomas Pollock Anshutz, 1879 Painter and teacher Thomas Anshutz concentrated on everyday scenes in the lives of rural and city workers. ***How did tenant farmers make a living?***

Frederick Douglass
1817–1895

Born enslaved, Frederick Douglass escaped (after one failed attempt) in 1838 and quickly emerged as a leading abolitionist. During the Civil War, he prodded President Lincoln to free African Americans, and he helped organize them to fight for freedom.

After Lincoln was assassinated, Douglass opposed the Reconstruction program of President Johnson. Instead he backed the Radical Republican plan. He used his oratorical ability to insist on full equality for African Americans in all parts of the nation, and he was a vigorous backer of the Fourteenth Amendment. He was particularly outspoken in support of the Fifteenth Amendment, guaranteeing African American men the right to vote. To Douglass, being able to vote meant that African Americans would not only be full citizens but would also have a weapon to protect their rights.

a federal investigator estimated that one-third of the farms in the Cotton Belt depended on the labor of tenants tied to the land by their debts. Years later a former enslaved person recalled the frustration that many African Americans felt about the system:

> *Lincoln got praise for freeing us, but did he do it? He gave us freedom without giving us any chance to live to ourselves and we still had to depend on the southern white man for work, food, clothing, and he held us through our necessity and want in a state of servitude but little better than slavery.*

From Slavery to Freedom

Even before the end of the war, some slaveholders noticed a change in the attitude of African Americans as they sensed freedom close at hand. Other planters were stunned, however, when enslaved workers they thought were content left without a word to try to reach the Union lines.

Freedom strengthened African American family ties. Families that had been separated were now reunited. Newspapers carried advertisements from African Americans seeking information about missing relatives:

> *$200 reward. During the year 1849, Thomas Sample carried away from this city, as his slaves, our daughter Polly, and son, Geo. Washington, to the State of Mississippi, and subsequently to Texas. . . . We will give $100 each for them, to any person who assist them, or either of them, to get to Nashville, or get word to us of their whereabouts, if they are alive.*

Freed men and women, many of whom had only first names, now went about choosing family names. Some chose the name of an ancestor or the name of a hero, like Lincoln. Some adopted their former slaveholder's family name, but many African Americans rejected such an idea. "That's my old rebel master's title," said one young man, "and I don't see any use in being called for him."

Newly freed workers who remained on the plantations as paid laborers usually refused to live in their old quarters. They objected to the common areas for cooking and washing and sought the privacy of separate cabins. For others, freedom meant leaving the plantation and their former masters and starting a new life. Some settled on the Great Plains and farmed land of their own. Others headed for large cities, hoping to find jobs there.

■ The Freedmen's Bureau

At the close of the war, Congress had created within the War Department a Bureau of Refugees, Freedmen, and Abandoned Lands, which became popularly known as the Freedmen's Bureau. Led by General O. Howard, the Bureau at first gave food and clothing to all families in the war-ravaged South. Its primary mission, however, was to help African Americans adjust to their new freedom. In addition, the Bureau provided medical help and founded 45 hospitals in 14 states.

Education

Sponsored by the Freedmen's Bureau and the American Missionary Association, hundreds of Northern school teachers went South after the war. Many were young women who had been active in the anti-slavery and women's rights movements, who now dedicated themselves to educating the newly freed African Americans. The teachers frequently found their students just as dedicated to getting an education. One African American teacher from Philadelphia who taught school in Georgia noted that many of her students worked in the fields in the morning and came to class "after their hard toil in the hot sun, as bright and as anxious to learn as ever." At the end of the day, these same classrooms were filled with adults, equally hungry for the education that had been denied to them. The Freedmen's Bureau also worked to establish colleges to train African American teachers, contributing to the founding of Howard University, Hampton Institute, Fisk University, and other colleges for African Americans.

Jobs

In addition, the Freedmen's Bureau tried to find jobs for formerly enslaved workers. It encouraged them to sign labor contracts

Visualizing History

▲ **FREEDMEN'S BUREAU SCHOOL** The Freedmen's Bureau set up hundreds of schools in the South for African American children and adults. *In what other ways did the Bureau help African Americans adjust to a new life?*

with planters to provide work in return for wages or a share of the crops. Because most formerly enslaved men and women could neither read nor write, Bureau agents tried to prevent them from being cheated in these contracts, but the Bureau never had enough agents to do this job fully.

Land

The dream of most freed men and women was to own land. During the war Union troops had seized large amounts of land from Southern planters, and Congress decided to distribute some of this land to formerly enslaved workers. On the Sea Islands of South Carolina, the Freedmen's Bureau was permitted to sell or lease confiscated land in parcels of up to 40 acres. Many newly freed African American families hoped that 40 acres and a mule would help them start their lives anew. However, when President Andrew Johnson decided to pardon Confederates, he restored their property rights. If their land had been distributed to African Americans, it was returned to its former owners.

General Howard went to the Sea Islands to tell African American farmers that their land was being returned to pardoned Confederates. He urged them to sign labor contracts to work on the land they briefly had owned. Most of the farmers refused to sign contracts, and a large number refused to give up their land. They were evicted against their will—some at bayonet point—by Union troops.

▲ *UPLAND COTTON* by Winslow Homer, 1879 Winslow Homer was one of the leaders in naturalism, painting realistic scenes of everyday life. Compare Homer's work with *The Way They Live* on page 441. **In what way are the paintings similar?**

Section 1 ★ Review

Checking for Understanding

1. **Identify** Freedmen's Bureau.

2. **Define** tenant farmer, sharecropper.

3. **List** three drawbacks to tenant farming.

4. **Describe** three changes in family life for African Americans after the war.

Critical Thinking

5. **Assessing Outcomes** Imagine that you are a newly freed worker living in the South. Write a short account of how freedom affects your life. Include ideas about the Freedmen's Bureau, segregation, former masters, and your chances to own land.

★★

Reconstructing the South

Setting the Scene

Section Focus

Northern leaders varied in their opinions of the best way to deal with the defeated South. President Lincoln had contended that the task was to restore the nation quickly and without bitterness. Others, however, felt that the South should be punished.

Objectives

After studying this section, you should be able to

★ compare the Lincoln and Johnson plans for Reconstruction with the plans of the Radical Republicans.

★ explain how the black codes and the return of former Confederates to power affected Reconstruction.

Key Terms

amnesty, mandate, disenfranchise, impeach

U.S. SENATE
Impeachment of the President
ADMIT THE BEARER
MARCH 13. 1868
Philip & Solomons, Wash. D.C.
Geo. T. Brown
Sergeant-at-Arms.

◀ TICKET TO IMPEACHMENT TRIAL

*R*econstruction did involve much more than merely rebuilding and repairing the war damage inflicted on the South. It also meant restructuring Southern society by granting rights to formerly enslaved persons and restoring the nation by readmitting Southern states to the Union.

■ Presidential Reconstruction

Before the end of the war, Congress and President Lincoln struggled with, and frequently clashed over, Reconstruction policies and programs.

Some believed that the South should be punished. President Lincoln argued that the task before the country was to restore the Union.

Lincoln's Plan

Before the war ended, Lincoln began to plan for the peace that would follow the war. Because his primary goal was to restore the Union as quickly as possible, the President favored a generous policy. Except for a few high-ranking Confederate officials, he offered **amnesty,** or pardon, to all Southerners who pledged an oath of loyalty to the United States. Lincoln proposed that when 10 percent of a state's voters in the 1860 presidential election had taken this oath, Congress would readmit the state to the Union.

Lincoln's plan did not address the plight of the newly freed African Americans. Although Lincoln strongly supported the Thirteenth Amendment, for a long time he personally had favored colonization of free African Americans in Africa and the Caribbean. He was willing, though, to let the

South handle the matter. The President urged, however, that African Americans who could read and write and those who had served in the Union army be allowed to vote.

The Radical Republicans' Plan

Resistance to Lincoln's plan surfaced at once from his Radical Republican opponents in Congress. The Radicals' alternative to Lincoln's plan came in the Wade-Davis Bill of 1864. This legislation proposed putting the South under military rule and required a majority of a state's electorate to take the loyalty oath as a condition for the state's readmission. Lincoln killed this bill with a pocket veto—he let the session of Congress expire without signing the legislation. However, when the states of Arkansas, Tennessee, and Louisiana met the conditions of Lincoln's plan, Congress refused to readmit them to the Union. The President then realized that a peace based on "malice toward none and charity for all" was not possible, and he began to negotiate with Radical congressional leaders. At this critical point, Lincoln was assassinated.

Johnson's Program

Andrew Johnson, who succeeded to the presidency, attempted to carry out Lincoln's Reconstruction policies. He was hampered in this effort because, as an unelected President, he had little popular following. In addition, as a former Democrat, he could not command the support of the Republican majority in Congress, and as a Tennessean and former slaveholder, he offended the Radicals. If these handicaps were not enough, he was viewed by his critics as being self-righteous, hot-tempered, stubborn, and crude.

In the summer of 1865, with Congress in recess, Johnson began to implement his Reconstruction program. His conditions for readmission were that each Southern state abolish slavery, repeal its ordinance of secession, and repudiate its war debts. When Congress returned in December, every state except Texas had followed Johnson's formula and asked to return to the Union. The Radicals, however, expressed alarm because the leniency of Johnson's plan allowed the return of traditional leadership in each of

▼ CARPETBAG

Visualizing History

▲ CONGRESSIONAL ACTION Controlled by the Radical Republicans, the Joint Committee on Reconstruction maintained the authority of Congress over Reconstruction. *What was the goal of the Civil Rights Bill of 1866?*

Life of the Times

Southern Pride

Soon after General Lee's surrender, the occupying Union army issued certain ordinances that were aimed at erasing all loyalty to the Confederacy. Many of these laws added insult to the

▼ MILITARY BUTTONS

injury of the defeated South. Ingenious Southerners, however, often found ways to circumvent these rules and keep their pride intact.

A "Button Order," for example, prohibited the wearing of Confederate military buttons. Because buttons of any type were scarce, Southerners resorted to using thorns from thornbushes as fastenings. Because replacement buttons were difficult to find, a clause permitted the "covering of formerly used buttons with cloth." Ingenious women draped Confederate buttons with black cloth. Thus, in obeying the Button Order, Southerners found a way that they could publicly display mourning for the Confederacy.

Another ordinance stated that the courts of Virginia could not issue any marriage license unless both parties took the oath of allegiance to the United States. More than one former Confederate prospective groom bristled at such an idea. Under much pressure, the Union general who issued the ordinance delayed its effective date for three days. During this interval, many hastily planned weddings took place.

---

these states, and Southern voters elected former Confederate officials to power. As a result, Congress refused to seat members from the Southern states.

White Men and Black Codes

The Radicals were also concerned about the status of African Americans in the South. Like Lincoln, President Johnson believed that this was a state matter and that federal jurisdiction stopped with the abolition of slavery. Consequently, the new Southern state governments endorsed the principle stated by the governor of Mississippi, "Ours is and ever shall be a government of white men."

The new Southern state legislatures passed a series of laws known as "black codes" that severely limited the rights of African Americans and made it plain that African Americans were still to have a subordinate status in the South. State

governments made few provisions for African Americans' schools.

In no Southern state were African Americans permitted to vote, testify against whites, handle weapons, or serve on juries. In some states, all African Americans were required by law to have steady work. Those who did not were arrested as vagrants and their labor sold to the highest bidder. Some states permitted African Americans to work only as farmers and servants and denied them many of the rights enjoyed by whites.

The North Responds

Northerners were outraged by the black codes, and even Johnson's supporters were alarmed by the actions of the Southern states. Their fears proved well founded. Events in the South increasingly led moderate Northerners to support the Radicals in Congress against the President.

In 1865, House and Senate leaders created a Joint Committee on Reconstruction to set congressional policy for restoring the Union. The Joint Committee proposed bills providing economic aid for African Americans and protection of their civil rights. Congress passed these bills, but President Johnson vetoed each one. Finally, in April 1866, Congress passed the Civil Rights Bill, which granted citizenship to African Americans and gave the federal government the power to intervene to protect the rights of freed men and women. When Johnson also vetoed this bill, Congress overrode his veto.

The Fourteenth Amendment

Fearing that the Civil Rights Act might be overturned in court, however, Congress passed the Fourteenth Amendment to the Constitution in June 1866. The amendment defined citizenship to include African Americans and required that no state deny any person "the equal protection of the laws." In addition, the amendment barred many Confederate political leaders from holding public office and prohibited any state from paying Confederate war debts.

President Johnson attacked the Fourteenth Amendment and campaigned against its ratification. As the 1866 congressional elections neared, it was clear that they would reveal whether the President or Congress would control the direction of Reconstruction.

The November election provided an overwhelming victory for the Radicals, who gained control of both the House and Senate. They now had the strength to override any presidential veto and could claim that they had been given a **mandate,** or command, from the public to enact their own Reconstruction program.

■ Radical Reconstruction

Now firmly in control, the Radical Republicans began implementing their policies for Reconstruction.

One goal was to sweep away the new state governments in the South and to replace them with military rule. Other goals were to ensure that former Confederate leaders would have no role in governing the South and that the freed African Americans' right to vote was protected.

Reconstruction Plans

Radical plans were inspired by self-interest as well as by concern for the freed African Americans and a desire to punish the South. The Radicals expected that African Americans would express their gratitude for freedom by voting Republican. Radical plans also were supported by Northern business leaders, who feared that a Congress controlled by Democrats might lower tariffs or destroy the newly established national banking system.

Many Radicals genuinely cared about the plight of the freed men and women, of course. They had been abolitionists and had pushed Lincoln into making emancipation a goal of the war. They believed in a right to equality and that government must rest on the consent of the governed. Senator Henry Wilson of Massachusetts summarized their position by saying:

> 66 *[Congress] must see to it that the man made free by the Constitution is a freeman indeed; that he can go where he pleases, work when and for whom he pleases . . . go into the schools and educate himself and his children; that the rights and guarantees of the common law are his, and that he walks the earth proud and erect in the conscious dignity of a free man.* 99

Reconstruction Legislation

In March 1867, Congress passed a Reconstruction Act that abolished the South's new state governments and put them under military rule. Except for Tennessee, the former Confederacy was divided into five military districts, each under command of a Union general. To be restored to the Union, each of the states was required to hold a

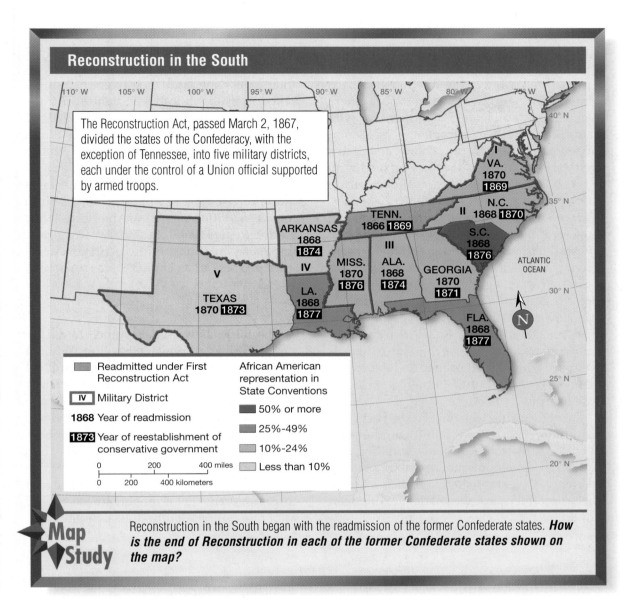

Reconstruction in the South

The Reconstruction Act, passed March 2, 1867, divided the states of the Confederacy, with the exception of Tennessee, into five military districts, each under the control of a Union official supported by armed troops.

I
VA.
1870
1869

N.C. 1868 1870

TENN.
1866 1869

II

S.C.
1868
1876

ARKANSAS
1868
1874

III

ATLANTIC OCEAN

IV

MISS.
1870
1876

ALA.
1868
1874

GEORGIA
1870
1871

V

TEXAS
1870 1873

LA.
1868
1877

FLA.
1868
1877

Legend:

Readmitted under First Reconstruction Act

IV   Military District

1868 Year of readmission

1873 Year of reestablishment of conservative government

0   200   400 miles
0 200   400 kilometers

African American representation in State Conventions

50% or more

25%–49%

10%–24%

Less than 10%

Map Study

Reconstruction in the South began with the readmission of the former Confederate states. *How is the end of Reconstruction in each of the former Confederate states shown on the map?*

constitutional convention with delegates elected by all adult males and to frame a state constitution that gave African Americans the right to vote. If the voters ratified the constitution, a state government could be elected. Finally, if Congress approved the constitution, if the state legislature ratified the Fourteenth Amendment, and if the amendment became a part of the Constitution, then the state would be readmitted to the Union. By 1868 Louisiana, Alabama, Arkansas, Florida, North Carolina, and South Carolina had met these requirements and regained statehood.

In 1869 Congress protected African American suffrage by passing the Fifteenth Amendment to the Constitution, providing that the right to vote "shall not be denied . . . on account of race, color, or previous condition of servitude." Congress required that states not yet complying with the Reconstruction Act—Virginia, Georgia, Mississippi, and Texas—ratify the Fifteenth Amendment as a further condition for readmission to the Union.

■ Carpetbag Government

By 1870 each of the 10 states under military rule had been readmitted to the Union. However, Radical Reconstruction had **disenfranchised**—or taken the right to vote from—many former Confederates. In addition, many other Southern white men boycotted elections. As a result, government in the Southern states was left to two small groups. One was a group of white Southern Union sympathizers whom Southerners nicknamed "scalawags." Northerners who came South—called "carpetbaggers"—comprised the other group. They gained this derogatory name because they arrived with all their belongings in cheap suitcases made of carpet fabric.

Some carpetbaggers were respectable, honest, and sincerely devoted to the public interest. However, enough of them were greedy and self-seeking so as to give the phrase "carpetbag governments" a reputation for graft, fraud, and waste. One carpetbag governor admitted to accepting more than $40,000 in bribes. Railroad franchises, public lands, and government contracts went to white Northerners and Northern businesses. As a result, Southern state debts rose sharply.

Carpetbag rule was not without achievement, however. Most public funds were spent honestly to encourage rebuilding and industrial development. Carpetbag governments also established public schools, including facilities for African American children.

Many Southern whites despised carpetbag governments. African American voters, however, saw the carpetbag governments as their best hope, and they overwhelmingly voted for Republican candidates. At the height of Radical Reconstruction, 700,000 African Americans could vote in the South compared to 625,000 whites. Even so, no African Americans were elected governors, and only in South Carolina did a state legislature have a majority of African American members. Fifteen African Americans were elected to the House of Representatives during Reconstruction, and two African American men served as United States senators.

The Radicals in Power

The Radicals were determined to reduce the presidential power that Lincoln had assumed during the Civil War and to remove Johnson as an obstacle to their plans. In March 1867, Congress passed the Army Appropriation Act, which severely limited the President's power as commander in chief. Accompanying this legislation was the Tenure of Office Act, which required Senate approval for the President to remove any government official whose appointment had required its consent.

▲ MEMBERS OF CONGRESS The first African American members of Congress are shown in this Currier and Ives print. The first African American senator, Hiram R. Revels, is at the far left. *What were the major achievements of Southern governments during this period?*

Challenging the Tenure Law

The Radicals knew that President Johnson wanted to remove Edwin Stanton, Lincoln's secretary of war, who remained in Johnson's cabinet but who openly sided with the Radicals. Characteristically, Johnson ignored these warnings. He continued trying to block Radical Reconstruction. Johnson also removed commanders in the Southern military districts who supported the Radicals and, while Congress was in recess, he fired Stanton.

To replace Stanton, Johnson appointed General Grant, but when the Senate reconvened it rejected Grant's nomination, and Grant resigned in favor of Stanton. Outraged, Johnson fired Stanton again—on February 21, 1868—this time replacing him with General Lorenzo Thomas. In answer, Stanton barricaded himself inside his office and refused to leave.

Johnson Impeached

The Radicals came to Stanton's support. Three days later, the House of Representatives voted to **impeach,** or charge, Johnson with "high crimes and misdemeanors" in office. As provided in the Constitution, the President was tried by the Senate. A two-thirds majority vote was needed for a conviction.

For more than two months amid intense public excitement, the Senate debated the President's fate. Radical members of the House, led by Thaddeus Stevens, presented the case against Johnson. Johnson's lawyers argued that Lincoln, not Johnson, had appointed Stanton to the Cabinet and, therefore, that the Tenure of Office Act did not apply.

On May 16, 1868, the Senate voted 35 to 19 to find Johnson guilty, just 1 vote short of conviction. Seven Republican senators were not able to find honest evidence that Johnson was guilty. Under tremendous political pressure, they refused to give in to partisan politics. Although Johnson remained in office for the last few months of his term, he was powerless to challenge the Radicals' policies.

The 1868 Election

The Radical Republicans sought a candidate in the 1868 presidential election who could sweep the country and keep them in power. They chose General Grant. The Democrats nominated Horatio Seymour, former governor of New York, and their platform condemned Radical Republican actions.

Although Grant won easily, by a vote of 214 to 80 in the electoral college, a small shift in the popular vote in key states would have given Seymour the election. Grant won because he was supported by the carpetbag governments of the South and because three Southern states had not yet been readmitted.

Section 2 ★ Review

Checking for Understanding

1. **Identify** Radical Republicans, Andrew Johnson, Fourteenth Amendment, Fifteenth Amendment, Tenure of Office Act.

2. **Define** amnesty, mandate, disenfranchise, impeach.

3. **List** two objections the Radicals had to Lincoln's Reconstruction plans.

4. **Explain** the purpose of the black codes.

Critical Thinking

5. **Determining Cause and Effect** The 1866 congressional elections served as a contest between President Andrew Johnson and the Radical Republicans for control of Reconstruction. What happened in the 1866 election? How do congressional elections during a President's term of office act as a barometer of presidential policies and popularity? Give specific examples.

Critical Thinking Skills

Making Predictions

A *prediction* is a foretelling of something before it happens. When you predict something, you are stating what you believe will happen in the future. Good predictions are based on present conditions as well as what has happened in the past.

Asking the questions that follow can help you predict the possible results of any historical event:

a. What related conditions existed prior to the event being studied?

b. What caused these conditions?

c. What was the event supposed to accomplish?

d. Based on the answers to these questions, what is your prediction about what will happen as a result of the event?

Note how the questions have been applied in predicting the results of the passage of the Fourteenth Amendment:

a. What conditions existed prior to the passing of the Fourteenth Amendment?

- African Americans were considered by many to be inferior to whites.
- African Americans were denied rights guaranteed to whites.
- Many people spoke out against the institution of slavery.

b. What caused these conditions?

- the belief of many people that African Americans were inferior
- the belief by many that African Americans should be considered equal

c. What was the amendment supposed to accomplish?

- All persons born and naturalized in the United States would have all the rights due them under the Constitution.

▲ FREED AFRICAN AMERICANS CAST THEIR FIRST BALLOTS

d. Predict what will happen as a result of the passage of the Fourteenth Amendment.

- Passage will cause conflict, unrest, and confusion.
- Equality for African Americans will have to come gradually.

Practicing the Skill

For practice in making predictions, apply these questions and make a prediction about the success of Lincoln's plan for Reconstruction had he lived to carry out his program.

★★

Restoring Southern Power

Setting the Scene

Section Focus

Reconstruction allowed the South to begin rebuilding its economy but proved to be of only temporary help to African American Southerners. As political and civil rights were restored to former Confederates, they were increasingly denied to African Americans.

Objectives

After studying this section, you should be able to

★ describe Southern resistance to Reconstruction.

★ discuss political and economic change in the South after Reconstruction.

Key Term

segregation

◀ **PLOW USED BY SHARECROPPER, 1860S**

Unable to strike openly at the federal government, opponents of Reconstruction organized secret resistance societies. The largest of these groups was the Ku Klux Klan. Started in Tennessee in 1866, the Klan spread throughout the former Confederacy. Hooded, white-robed Klan members rode in bands at night and threatened carpetbaggers, teachers in African American schools, and African Americans themselves. Using beatings, murder, and other violence to back up their threats, Klansmen broke up Republican meetings, tried to drive Freedmen's Bureau officials out of their communities, and tried to keep freed African Americans from voting.

Although by 1872 it had been greatly suppressed by federal troops, the Klan and similar organizations contributed to the establishment of Southern governments opposed to the Radicals. Democrats, often called "Redeemers," gained control of one Southern state after another, until by 1876 only South Carolina, Florida, and Louisiana did not have governments controlled by white Democrats, many of whom were former Confederates.

One reason for these Democratic successes in the South was that Northerners were becoming weary of Radical Reconstruction. In 1872 a group called the Liberal Republicans, including several prominent Republican leaders, opposed the Radicals and refused to support Grant for reelection because they considered him unfit for the presidency. The Liberal Republicans joined with the Democrats to nominate newspaper publisher Horace Greeley for President. Although Grant won reelection, the Radicals' power was weakened, and Grant's administration loosened its controls over the South. As fewer troops were sent to protect African American voters during Southern elections, white political power was restored.

▲ THE KU KLUX KLAN Members of the Ku Klux Klan used threats, beatings, and murder to keep African Americans and Republicans from voting. *Who were the Redeemers?*

■ The Compromise of 1877

The presidential election of 1876 brought the end of Radical Reconstruction. In the campaign the Republicans "waved the bloody shirt," or attempted to stir up bitter memories of the war. Democrats countered by attacking the excesses of Radical Reconstruction and the corruption they claimed was rampant in the Grant administration.

On Election Day, Democratic candidate Samuel J. Tilden, governor of New York, polled 250,000 more popular votes than the Republican Rutherford B. Hayes, Ohio's governor. Tilden was a vote short of a majority in the electoral college, but 20 electoral votes were disputed. One of these electoral votes was from Oregon, and it was challenged on a technicality. The other 19 involved disputed results from the 3 Southern states still under carpetbag rule—Florida, South Carolina, and Louisiana—where charges of massive voting fraud flew.

Electoral Commission

Republicans complained that Democrats had prevented African Americans from voting, and Democrats accused Republicans of using federal troops to raise its vote totals. These 3 states each filed 2 sets of election returns, 1 for Tilden and another for Hayes.

Because the Constitution did not provide for settling such a dispute, Congress appointed a commission of 5 members each from the House, the Senate, and the Supreme Court to settle the matter. Tilden needed only 1 of the disputed electoral votes to become President, but Hayes needed all of them. Voting strictly along party lines, the commission awarded all 20 disputed electoral votes to Hayes. Congress accepted the verdict on March 2, 1877, 2 days before the inauguration.

Reaching an Agreement

The Democrats were outraged at the commission's decisions, and they were determined not to be defrauded. There were threats of civil war and talk of blocking Hayes's inauguration. The Republicans were just as determined to keep control of the presidency, and they began to talk about a compromise. After negotiations between party leaders, the Democrats agreed to accept the election results and the Republicans agreed to several demands. Democrats were assured that a Southerner would become postmaster general, an important position because of the many federal jobs it controlled. Republicans also promised federal funds for internal improvements in the South. Most important, Republicans agreed to withdraw the remaining federal troops from the South. Without soldiers to protect them, the three remaining carpetbag governments collapsed and Reconstruction officially came to an end.

■ After Reconstruction

In many ways, the South after Reconstruction was similar to the South before the Civil War. As white Southern Democrats returned to power, African Americans lost many of their civil rights.

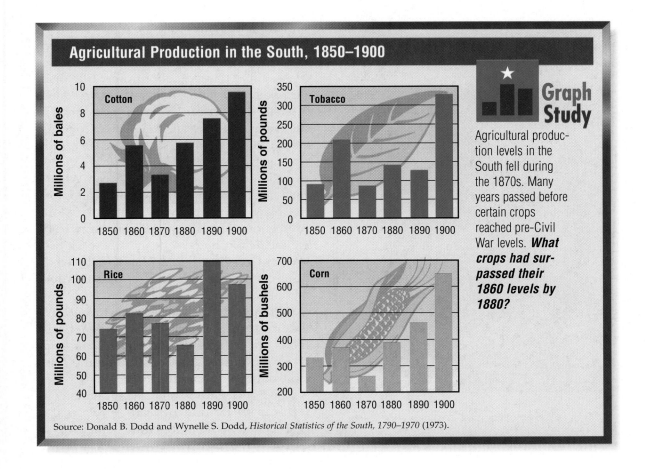

Agricultural Production in the South, 1850–1900

Cotton (Millions of bales): 1850, 1860, 1870, 1880, 1890, 1900

Tobacco (Millions of pounds): 1850, 1860, 1870, 1880, 1890, 1900

Rice (Millions of pounds): 1850, 1860, 1870, 1880, 1890, 1900

Corn (Millions of bushels): 1850, 1860, 1870, 1880, 1890, 1900

Graph Study

Agricultural production levels in the South fell during the 1870s. Many years passed before certain crops reached pre-Civil War levels. *What crops had surpassed their 1860 levels by 1880?*

Source: Donald B. Dodd and Wynelle S. Dodd, *Historical Statistics of the South, 1790–1970* (1973).

Segregation

For years, in the North as well as the South, **segregation,** or the practice of separating people on the basis of race, had been an accepted way of life. Even before the Civil War, custom in the North had separated African American and white travelers on railroads, coaches, and steamboats and in hotels. Such segregation also existed in Northern schools, churches, hospitals, and cemeteries. After Reconstruction, however, the South began to pass "Jim Crow" laws, which legally segregated blacks from whites in daily life.

Where possible, African Americans protested segregation. These protests helped to integrate the streetcar lines of Washington, D.C.; Richmond, Virginia; and Charleston, South Carolina. In 1875 Congress passed a Civil Rights Act requiring that all people have equal access to public places and transportation facilities. In 1883, however, the Supreme Court ruled that the act was unconstitutional, and by the 1890s Jim Crow laws were common throughout the South.

The "New South"

Despite the South's return to white supremacy, by the late 1870s there was increasing talk of a "New South." An alliance between powerful white Southerners and Northern financiers brought about the economic rebuilding of the South. Northern capital helped to build railroads, and by 1890 the South had twice the railroad mileage that it had had in 1860.

Better transportation encouraged the industrialization of the South. A growing iron and steel industry developed around Birmingham, Alabama, and in North Carolina tobacco processing became big business. Cotton mills appeared in countless small towns throughout the South. Nevertheless, far from populous Northern markets and paying high freight rates, Southern industries faced serious problems. To compete, Southern factory owners generally paid lower wages than did factories in the North.

With these developments in transportation and industry and with the spread of

ISAAC and ROSA, Emancipated Slave Children, From the Free Schools of Louisiana, Photographed by KIMBALL, 477 Broadway. N.Y. Entered according to Act of Congress, in the year 1863 by GEO. H. HANKS. in the Clerk's Office of the U. S. for the Sou. Dist. of N.Y.

▲ AFRICAN AMERICAN CHILDREN ATTENDING FREE SCHOOL

sharecropping in agriculture, the South's economy gradually revived. By 1900 Southern industrial production was four times what it had been in 1860.

Few Gains for African Americans

In many ways, Reconstruction aided the South. However, it also caused much bitterness in that region, helping to create the "Solid South"—a voting bloc dominated by the Democrats that did not break up for a century. Reconstruction also provided only limited and temporary help to Southern African Americans, whose rights it professed to defend.

As time passed, abolitionist idealism declined, and many Radicals proved more interested in African American votes than in the welfare of African Americans. Congress closed the Freedmen's Bureau after only five years, and it made no long-range plans to provide what the freed African Americans needed most—land and education. As the black codes revealed, without federal protection, for many African Americans emancipation merely meant a new kind of slavery—continued attachment to the white power structure as sharecroppers and tenant farmers.

Although immediate efforts to improve the lives of Southern African Americans failed, the Fourteenth and Fifteenth amendments wrote into the Constitution the principle of equality for all people.

The Fourteenth Amendment defined citizenship to include African Americans. It also said that no state could take away a citizen's life, liberty, or property without due process of law, and that every citizen was entitled to equal protection of the laws. The Fifteenth Amendment stated that the right to vote "shall not be denied . . . on account of race, color, or previous condition of servitude."

For many years these amendments remained almost a dead letter, but in the 1900s they provided the legal basis and, in part, the inspiration for movements to obtain for African Americans their full rights as citizens.

Section 3 ★ Review

Checking for Understanding

1. **Identify** Ku Klux Klan, Compromise of 1877, "Solid South."

2. **Define** segregation.

3. **Describe** the strategies and tactics used by the Ku Klux Klan. Discuss the reaction of African Americans to that organization.

4. **Explain** two important concessions that were made in the Compromise of 1877.

Critical Thinking

5. **Distinguishing Fact from Opinion** Describe the images of the South created by motion pictures and novels. What facts from the era refute these images?

▲ FOUNDRY, BIRMINGHAM, ALABAMA, 1887

► SEWING MACHINE, MID-1800S

Growth of Southern Manufacturing

Many factors pushed the postwar South toward industrialization. Most important, however, was the surplus labor supply. Widows, orphans, and displaced formerly enslaved workers needed work, and agriculture could not employ them all. This meant there was a large pool of cheap labor. In addition, Northerners and Europeans invested capital in fledgling Southern industries, as did a number of Southerners themselves.

Two industries that made spectacular advances in the postwar South were textiles and tobacco processing. Cotton mills sprang up in the major cotton-growing areas of the South. By 1900 there were 400 mills in operation. The postwar demand for a new product—cigarettes—and the invention of the cigarette-rolling machine in 1880 were the catalysts that fueled the development of the tobacco-processing industry.

Other industries based on agriculture or minerals also developed, such as steel manufacturing and making cottonseed oil. Still, despite gains in industrialization, the South remained primarily rural and agricultural until the industrial advances of the mid-twentieth century.

Making the Economics Connection

1. What factors led to the development of industry in the postwar South?

2. What Southern cities of the 1900s are noted as industrial centers?

Linking Past and Present

3. Why was the region's economy primarily agricultural until the mid-1900s?

Using Vocabulary

Create a classification system that demonstrates how these words below are related. First, write *Reconstruction* as your main heading. Under the main heading create several smaller categories. Challenge yourself to see how many different classifications you can devise.

tenant farmer	sharecropper
segregation	black codes
amnesty	carpetbagger
mandate	concession
impeach	

Reviewing Facts

1. **Cite** two reasons why tenant farming and sharecropping were used in the South.
2. **List** three services provided by the Freedmen's Bureau.
3. **Specify** two differences between the Reconstruction plans of Presidents Lincoln and Johnson and those of the Radical Republicans.
4. **List** the long-term successes and failures of Reconstruction for Southern African Americans.

Understanding Concepts

Adaptation

1. Explain how tenant farming and sharecropping were a means for Southern landowners to adjust to new conditions after the Civil War.

Power and Authority

2. What are the significant reasons that explain how the power of the Radical Republicans first grew and later diminished?

Critical Thinking

1. **Identifying Central Issues** The 1860s were a time of radical change. Summarize the string of events that caused so much political and social turbulence during the 1860s.

2. **Analyzing Fine Art** Study the painting on this page, entitled *A Visit from the Old Mistress* by Winslow Homer, and answer the questions that follow.

   a. Identify the two main figures.
   b. How does the artist contrast these figures?
   c. What idea do you think the artist is expressing?

Writing About History

Comparison

Imagine that you are a newly freed African American living in the South during Reconstruction. You have learned to read and write at a Freedmen's Bureau school. You write a letter to a long-lost relative living in the North describing the changes in your life. In your letter compare your life before the Civil War to life during Reconstruction. Include information about your work, your way of life, and your relations with whites.

Cooperative Learning

You belong to a group analyzing Reconstruction policies. Each member of your group will assume one of these roles: a Southern landowner, a Northern carpetbagger, and an African American sharecropper. Your goal is to write two Reconstruction

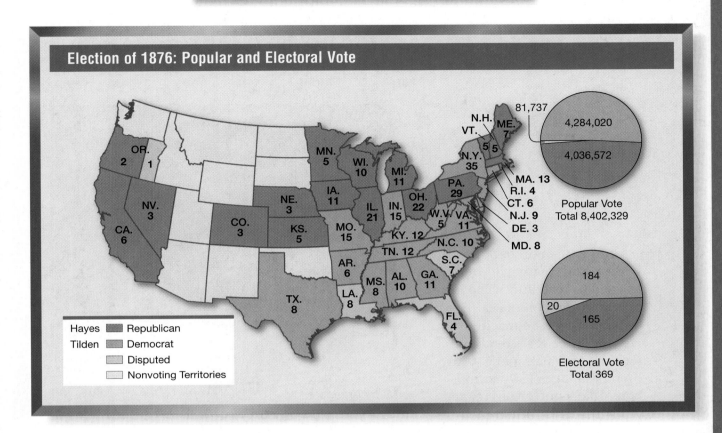

Election of 1876: Popular and Electoral Vote

OR. 2 | 1
NV. 3
CA. 6
CO. 3
KS. 5
NE. 3
MN. 5
WI. 10
IA. 11
MO. 15
AR. 6
TX. 8
LA. 8
MS. 8
AL. 10
GA. 11
S.C. 7
FL. 4
TN. 12
KY. 12
IL. 21
IN. 15
OH. 22
MI. 11
W.V. 5
VA. 11
N.C. 10
PA. 29
N.Y. 35
81,737
N.H.
VT. 5 | 5
ME. 7
MA. 13
R.I. 4
CT. 6
N.J. 9
DE. 3
MD. 8

Popular Vote
4,284,020
4,036,572
Popular Vote
Total 8,402,329

Electoral Vote
184
20
165
Electoral Vote
Total 369

Hayes — Republican
Tilden — Democrat
— Disputed
— Nonvoting Territories

laws that are acceptable to all. Write one law on voting rights for African Americans and a second law on the treatment of former Confederate soldiers.

Social Studies Skills

Interpreting an Election Map

Election maps let you see at a glance how different states voted. They also show trends in voting. For example, the election map on this page shows that people in the Far West voted primarily for Hayes.

Practicing the Skills

Use the election map and the information in the chapter to answer the following questions.

1. What do the numbers on the map indicate?

2. Is there a geographical trend in the way the states voted? If so, what is it?

3. Why is it helpful to include the two circle graphs along with the map?

4. On the basis of the popular vote, who should have won the election?

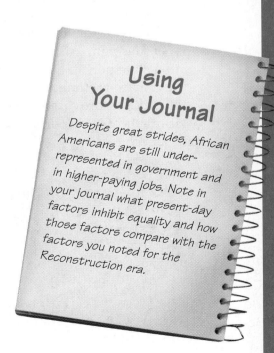

Using Your Journal

Despite great strides, African Americans are still underrepresented in government and in higher-paying jobs. Note in your journal what present-day factors inhibit equality and how those factors compare with the factors you noted for the Reconstruction era.

Cultural Kaleidoscope

Education

The One-Room Schoolhouse

Until education became widespread, many children learned to read and write in one-room schoolhouses. The backbone of the curriculum was the three R's—reading, writing, and arithmetic. Children of all ages learned mostly by rote—one group recited while the rest studied their lessons. Students today might view the one-room schoolhouse as primitive. Chalkboards and maps were rare, and students, lacking even paper and pen, used a slate and a slate pencil. Despite its drawbacks, the one-room schoolhouse provided many with their only opportunity for an education.

▲ Many American leaders saw in public schools a means of promoting national spirit.

▶ Many students received their learning from church schools, proprietary institutions, private tutors, or members of their own families.

PRUDENCE CRANDALL, PRINCIPAL OF THE CANTERBURY, (CONN.) FEMALE BOARDING SCHOOL.

RETURNS her most sincere thanks to those who have patronized her School, and would give information that on the first Monday of April next, her School will be opened for the reception of young Ladies and little Misses of color. The branches taught are as follows:—Reading, Writing, Arithmetic, English Grammar, Geography, History, Natural and Moral Philosophy, Chemistry, Astronomy, Drawing and Painting, Music on the Piano, together with the French language.

☞The terms, including board, washing, and tuition, are $25 per quarter, one half paid in advance.

☞Books and Stationary will be furnished on the most reasonable terms.

For information respecting the School, reference may be made to the following gentlemen, viz.—

ARTHUR TAPPAN, Esq.
Rev. PETER WILLIAMS,
Rev. THEODORE RAYMOND
Rev. THEODORE WRIGHT, } N. YORK CITY.
Rev. SAMUEL C. CORNISH,
Rev. GEORGE BOURNE,
Rev. Mr HAYBORN,
Mr JAMES FORTEN, } PHILADELPHIA.
Mr JOSEPH CASSEY,
Rev. S. J. MAY,—BROOKLYN, CT.
Rev. Mr BEMAN,—MIDDLETOWN, CT.
Rev. S. S. JOCELYN,—NEW-HAVEN, CT.
Wm. LLOYD GARRISON } BOSTON, MASS.
ARNOLD BUFFUM,
GEORGE BENSON,—PROVIDENCE, R. I.

Canterbury, Ct. Feb. 25, 1833.

◀ The hornbook for learning the alphabet was still in use during the 1800s in many schoolhouses.

The drive for public education had several causes. Americans fervently believed that the United States should be a land of equal opportunity, a land where people "start from a humble origin and can attain to the most elevated positions." To deny a child education was to close the door of opportunity.

Eventually adopted in 37 states, the McGuffey's Readers gave thousands of schoolchildren a shared background of popular culture and helped to mold the literary tastes of the reading public.

More and more schools provided desks in the 1800s. Earlier, students sat on backless wooden benches. The teacher's desk was often on a raised platform.

"And as for teachers—can't any young lawyer or preacher teach the boys and girls all they need to know?" With widespread acceptance of such views, it is not surprising that in the early nineteenth century most secondary education was supplied not by public, but by private schools.

Chapter 13

Manifest Destiny

Several factors influenced the American drive to the Pacific, including the desire to move onto new land, the belief that the plains were unsuitable for farming, commercial interests, and patriotism.

In Texas, disputes between American settlers and the Mexican government led to several conflicts. In 1836 Texas became independent, and in 1846 the United States and Mexico clashed over the southern boundary of Texas. The Mexican War ended with the Treaty of Guadalupe Hidalgo, which granted the United States full title to Texas, California, and what was then New Mexico territory.

Americans also sought to acquire Cuba but abandoned their efforts after several unsuccessful attempts. Americans did, however, succeed in laying the groundwork for a canal across the Isthmus of Panama. In East Asia, Americans opened up China and Japan for trade.

Chapter 14

Compromise and Conflict

Once the United States acquired New Mexico and California, the question arose concerning slavery in the new territories. The issue became more acute after the discovery of gold in California led to California's application for statehood as a free state. The solution, the Compromise of 1850, temporarily staved off further problems.

By 1850 the United States was booming economically, but many of the new developments benefited only the North. The South's feelings of isolation were intensified by its reliance on slavery, which created further tension. The rush among settlers from both slave and free states to populate the Kansas Territory culminated in bloodshed. The nation was further torn apart by the Dred Scott decision.

In the election of 1860, slavery was the key issue, with the Republican candidate, Lincoln, who was viewed as an abolitionist, victorious. In response, most of the Southern states seceded from the Union.

Chapter 15

The Civil War

The fall of Fort Sumter kindled patriotism in both North and South and started their preparation for war. The North drew upon advantages in manufacturing, population, transportation, and wealth, whereas the South relied on superior generals.

At first, Southern armies outmaneuvered Union forces in the east, awakening the nation to the reality that it would be a long and costly war. Southern invasions of the North were unsuccessful, however. In the western theater, Union armies gained control of border states. Grant's victory at Vicksburg segmented the South, while Sherman's march subdivided it again.

As the war dragged on, both sides were forced to conscript soldiers. Lincoln reversed an earlier decision and allowed African Americans to enlist. The character of the war also changed when Lincoln issued the Emancipation Proclamation, thereby making the end to slavery a reason for the conflict. Shortly after Lincoln was reelected, Lee surrendered. But chances for a peaceful reconciliation were weakened by Lincoln's assassination just five days later.

Chapter 16

Reconstruction

The Civil War had left the South in disarray, with the land, government, and transportation system in ruin. African Americans and whites set out to rebuild the South. Economically and politically, however, African Americans were thwarted by segregation and black codes.

The Radical Republicans' version of Reconstruction, advocating voting rights for African Americans and harsh treatment of former Confederates, was set in motion when the Radical Republicans gained control of Congress. Reconstruction governments were often handicapped by corruption. Eventually, white Southerners regained control of Southern state governments. Although Reconstruction was only partially effective for African Americans, a degree of cooperation was achieved between the North and the South.

Understanding Unit Themes

1. **United States Role in World Affairs** How did the spirit of Manifest Destiny affect the role of the United States in world affairs?

2. **Cultural Diversity** How were cultural differences between Northerners and Southerners a factor that caused the Civil War?

3. **Conflict and Compromise** Was a compromise on the slavery issue ever a feasible tactic? Why or why not?

4. **Civil Rights and Liberties** Compare the legal and social status of African Americans before and after the Civil War.

UNIT SIX
NEW HORIZONS
1860–1900

★★★

| CHAPTER **17** Into the West 1860–1900 | CHAPTER **18** The Rise of Industry 1860–1900 | CHAPTER **19** An Urban Society 1860–1900 | CHAPTER **20** The Gilded Age 1865–1900 | CHAPTER **21** Politics and Protest 1865–1900 |

History AND ART

Miners in the Sierra
by Charles Nahl and Frederick August
Wenderoth, 1851–1852

An abundance and variety of natural resources
were utilized for industrial production.

▲ HORATIO ALGER COVER

464

This was an age of optimism, coupled with a belief in the certainty of human progress. As pioneers continued to spread across the continent and immigrants flocked to industrial centers, Americans adapted to the rapidly changing environment in which they found themselves.

Themes

- Geography and Environment
- Conflict and Cooperation
- Influence of Technology
- Cultural Diversity

Key Events

- First transcontinental railroad
- Interstate Commerce Act
- Civil Service reform
- American Federation of Labor formed
- Sherman Antitrust Act
- Battle at Wounded Knee
- Populist party formed
- Pullman strike

Major Issues

- Transcontinental railroads allow the rapid settlement of the Great Plains.
- A wealth of natural resources and abundant labor makes the United States a major industrial power.
- The swift growth of industry creates a demand for new labor unions.
- The alliance between government and big business leads to widespread political corruption.
- Agrarian unrest promotes new political movements that seek to regulate commerce.

▲ SIOUX SHIELD

▲ EARLY PHONOGRAPH

▼ RIDING PLOW, C. 1880S

Portfolio Project

Design a political cartoon that shows the contrasting sides of one of the divisive issues of this era: for example, Native American and settler, labor and big business, or political machine and reformer.

Global Perspectives

★★★★★ ★★

The World

		1860	1875
Asia and Oceania			
Europe			**1870** *Germany unifies under Bismarck* ◀
Africa		**1867** *Diamond fields discovered in South Africa*	
South America		**1861** *Gabriel Moreno becomes president of Ecuador*	
North and Central America			

The United States

		1860	1875
Pacific and Northwest		**1869** *First transcontinental rail route is completed*	▲ **1876** *Sioux nation defeats Custer at Little Bighorn*
Southeast		**1870** *H. R. Revels of Mississippi becomes the first African American in Congress*	
Midwest			
Southwest		**1860** *The Pony Express is established*	
Atlantic Northeast		1860	◀ **1878** *First electric light company is established* 1875

Linking Across TIME

There has been a Jewish presence in North America for hundreds of years. Jews tended to gravitate to areas where they met little prejudice—Rhode Island, Pennsylvania, and South Carolina, for example. By the mid-1700s the largest concentration of Jews was found in South Carolina's major city, Charleston. The Jewish population in the United States remained relatively small until the late 1800s, when there was an influx of Jews from central and eastern Europe. Today, the United States has the largest Jewish population in the world.

1890

1882 *Germany, Austria, and Italy form the Triple Alliance*

▼ **1894** *Sino-Japanese War begins*

1900 *Boxer rebellion begins*

1905

▼ **1899** *Boer War starts*

1895 *Cubans revolt against Spanish rule*

▲ **1884** *First steel-skeleton construction is begun, making it possible to build skyscrapers*

▲ **1892** *Ellis Island becomes a receiving station for immigrants*

1890

1905

CHAPTER 17

★★★

Into the West
1860–1900

▲ **LANTERN, LATE 1800S**

Setting the Scene

Focus

The settlement of the Far West frontier was filled with hardships and tragedy as well as adventure. For Native Americans, the slaughter of the buffalo and gradual expansion of white settlement meant the end of their way of life. For miners, ranchers, and farmers, life on the Great Plains meant long hours of work, a harsh climate, and isolation.

Concepts to Understand

★ Why national expansion developed in the Great Plains region

★ How conflict between the Plains peoples and settlers led to the destruction of Native American society

Read to Discover . . .

★ the role of the railroads in the settlement of the Great Plains.

★ how life on the Great Plains measured up to settlers' expectations.

Journal Notes

What geographic and environmental features created hardships for those who settled and farmed the West? Make notes in your journal as you read the chapter.

CULTURAL

● **1866** *First major "long drive" moves Texas longhorns to Missouri*

● **1872** *Yellowstone National Park is created in Wyoming Territory*

| 1860 | 1870 |

● **1862** *Homestead Act passes*

● **1869** *First transcontinental railroad is constructed*

POLITICAL

▲ SIOUX WAR CLUB

History AND ART

The Last of the Buffalo
by Albert Bierstadt, 1889

Bierstadt sat on the banks of the Republican River in north central Kansas and worked out his idea for *The Last of the Buffalo.*

• **1883** *"Buffalo Bill" Cody opens his first wild west show*

• **1895** The Red Badge of Courage *published*

1880

1890

• **1884** *United States government prohibits Native American Sun Dance*

• **1890** *Census Department declares the frontier closed*

★★★★★★★★★★★★★★★★★★★★★★★★★★★★★★★★★★★

People of the Plains

Setting the Scene

Section Focus

The steady push of settlement across North America skipped over a thousand miles of treeless expanse before resuming again at the Pacific Coast. For a few years the United States government reserved most of the vast interior of the country to Native Americans because it believed these "Great Plains" to be too dry for farming. When settlers began to infringe on these territories, they met determined resistance from the Plains peoples.

Objectives

After studying this section, you should be able to

★ describe the Plains peoples' way of life.

★ give three reasons the Plains peoples' way of life came to an end.

Key Term

nomadic

► PLAINS WOOLEN JACKET AND LEGGINGS

The United States government had assigned Major Stephen H. Long the exploration of the region beyond the Mississippi River in 1820. In his report, Long used the term "Great American Desert" to describe the territory—a term that soon appeared on all the maps of the West. Believing the land to be completely desolate, many who ventured to California and Oregon completely avoided it, choosing to travel by clipper ship around Cape Horn at the tip of South America.

■ A Nomadic Life

The territory that early European explorers believed to be a desert was home to countless species of wildlife. Hundreds of millions of jackrabbits and prairie dogs, millions of wolves and coyotes, and an estimated 12 to 15 million American bison—usually called buffalo—roamed the Great Plains.

The region was also home to many different Native American nations. Some, like the Omaha and the Osage nations, lived in communities as farmers and hunters. Most of the Native Americans, however, including the Sioux [SOO], the Comanche [kuh•MAN•chee], and the Blackfeet, were **nomadic** peoples. They roamed vast distances, following their main source of food: the great herds of buffalo that lived on the plains.

For generations the nomadic peoples of the plains had only dogs to haul their possessions as they traveled from one hunting area to another. In the 1600s, horses, either traded or stolen from Spanish settlers in the Southwest, changed the Plains peoples' way of life. By the mid-1750s, almost every Plains people rode on horseback. Horses became a vital part of their social, economic, and political life. The Comanche were perhaps the best riders, but the Sioux, Cheyenne [shy•AN], Pawnee, Blackfoot, and Crow nations were nearly as skilled. In the deserts of the region that are the present-day states of Arizona and New Mexico, the Apache [uh•PA•chee] and Navajo [NAH•vuh•hoh] captured horses to sell to northern peoples.

The horse made the Plains people much more effective hunters than they had been on foot. It became easier to follow the buffalo, which provided the main source of food, skins for clothing and shelter, and bones for tools. The buffalo hunt not only yielded life's necessities, it also provided sport, ritual, worship, and training for war. Fighting from horseback, Native American warriors were better able to resist the encroachments of settlers and railroads.

■ Railroads Open the West

A Dakota newspaper editor wrote, "Without the railroad it would have required a century to accomplish what has been done in five years." What was "accomplished" was the killing of nearly all the buffalo and other prairie life, obstruction of the Plains peoples' way of life, and removal of any surviving peoples to reservations.

First Transcontinental Railroad

Railroad building in the West began at a furious pace during the Civil War. The most dramatic achievement was the completion of the first transcontinental line in 1869. Discussion of this project started when gold was discovered in California in 1848.

During the 1850s at least 10 routes were surveyed, and the Gadsden Purchase was acquired from Mexico principally because the Gila River valley provided the easiest route across the western plateau. Congress wanted to finance this gigantic project, but

▼ APACHE LEADER

▲ PLAINS LIFE Native Americans faced many hardships on the plains. *How did the extinction of the buffalo affect the Plains peoples' way of life?*

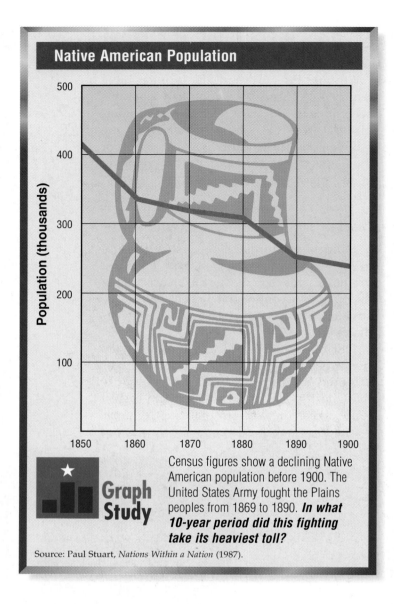

Native American Population

Population (thousands)

500
400
300
200
100

1850　1860　1870　1880　1890　1900

Graph Study

Census figures show a declining Native American population before 1900. The United States Army fought the Plains peoples from 1869 to 1890. *In what 10-year period did this fighting take its heaviest toll?*

Source: Paul Stuart, *Nations Within a Nation* (1987).

Construction proceeded rapidly as the 2 lines raced to get more government money and land. At the height of the competition, the Union Pacific builders employed 10,000 workers. Irish immigrant crews working for the Union Pacific and Chinese immigrants working for the Central Pacific sometimes laid as much as 10 miles of track a day—a remarkable feat because the digging and grading were done by hand. The Central Pacific had a difficult time in the Sierra Nevada ranges with snow that sometimes collected in drifts 60 feet deep. Its heavy equipment was carried from the East 19,000 miles around Cape Horn to California by a fleet of 30 ships.

On May 10, 1869, the "wedding of the rails" took place at Promontory Point, Utah. The whole country celebrated as a transcontinental telegraph reported the blow of a silver sledgehammer driving a golden spike to complete the railroad. A magnetic ball dropped from a pole on the top of the Capitol in Washington, D.C.; in Chicago a seven-mile procession paraded through the streets; in small towns citizens rang church bells.

Other Railroads

The first transcontinental line was soon followed by others—the Northern Pacific; the Atchison, Topeka, and Santa Fe; the Southern Pacific; and the Great Northern. Like other big businesses, the railroads needed people of ability, imagination, and drive. The greatest of the Western builders was James J. Hill, a small, short-tempered, red-bearded man of enthusiasm and energy. Beginning in 1879, Hill built the Great Northern, connecting the state of Minnesota and the Washington Territory, without government help. By encouraging settlement as soon as the rails were laid, Hill ensured that his line would have customers. He offered free transportation from Eastern ports, credit, farm machinery, and even free advice on how to improve crops. Hill's careful construction of the Great Northern kept maintenance costs down and enabled him to charge lower rates. As a result, his railroad became the leading carrier in the Northwest.

sectional rivalry caused delays. The South preferred that the eastern terminal be located at New Orleans; the North argued for St. Louis or Chicago. In 1862, with Southern representation temporarily withdrawn from Congress, the government passed an act to encourage the building of a Pacific Railroad.

The Union Pacific Company was to build west from Omaha, while the Central Pacific Company was to run lines east from Sacramento. The federal government loaned money to both companies at the rate of $16,000, $32,000, or $48,000 per mile, according to the terrain. Each company also received land grants along the right-of-way averaging 640 acres per mile.

Believing passionately in the life of the farmers on the plains, Hill wanted to promote maximum settlement. He expressed the idea that

> *Population without the Prairie is a mob, and the Prairie without Population is a desert.*

Killing of Buffalo

The railroads played a major role in the extermination of the buffalo. Though buffalo had formerly ranged eastward as far as Pennsylvania and the Carolinas, their natural habitat was the Great Plains, where they migrated north and south with the seasons. The Union Pacific Railroad effectively cut the huge herds in half. At first buffalo hunting supplied meat for railroad workers, but later it became "sport" for city vacationers to shoot the animals from train windows. In 1871 it was discovered that buffalo leather could be sold at a profit. Professional hunters killed millions for their hides. Trainloads of bones were shipped east to make fertilizer or charcoal. By 1886 only a few hundred buffalo were left, deep in the Canadian woods.

■ Plains Wars

To protect their lands and to stop the waste of the buffalo, Plains people had to fight. For two and one-half centuries they had maintained their way of life against Spanish, English, French, and American invaders. The last battles against overwhelming forces proved futile. The military effort to remove Native Americans from the plains was relentless, with the United States spending an estimated million dollars for each adult male Native American killed.

Taking of Native American Land

The first concentrated fighting broke out in Colorado just after the Civil War started in the East. Government officials tried to

Life of the Times

Native American Schools

In the 1870s and 1880s, the federal government passed legislation and instituted policies designed to assimilate Native Americans into white society.

Most of the 106 day and boarding schools operated by the federal government in 1881 were on or adjacent to reservation land. However, white educators believed that Native American children would learn more and be assimilated more quickly if they attended non-reservation boarding schools.

Many Native American parents showed reluctance when whites came to recruit their children for boarding school. For example, parents were particularly reluctant to send their daughters away from home. They understood that it would change the children's values. One mother of an especially bright 10-year-old girl refused to let her daughter go off to an industrial training school without her. Education and civilization, the mother explained, would make the child regard her mother as a savage. In the end, this mother was allowed to accompany her child to school.

▲ **PINE RIDGE, SOUTH DAKOTA, SCHOOL**

▲ *BLANKET SIGNAL* by Frederic Remington Artist Frederic Remington captured dramatic and compelling images of the vanishing Western frontier. *Why did the Dawes Act fail?*

the territorial government's plans to build a road through their sacred lands. Led by Red Cloud, they successfully resisted for several years. In the end, however, the Sioux lost their land to miners searching for gold in the Black Hills.

Efforts Toward Peace

After the bloody war with the Sioux, humanitarians in the East called for a change of government policies. The United States divided responsibility for the Native Americans between the Department of the Interior and the War Department. The Department of the Interior first was to placate Native Americans with gifts and to establish reservations; the War Department was to make war on those who resisted.

In 1867 the federal government sent a peace commission to meet with representatives of several nations, including the Comanche, Kiowa [KY•uh•WAW], Cheyenne, and Arapaho. This effort to end the constant warfare produced agreements that stipulated that the Native Americans were to live on two major reservations on the Great Plains, one in Oklahoma and one in the Dakota Territory. Not all nations were involved, however, so conflicts between Native Americans and the army continued.

Hostilities Resume

With the discovery of gold in the Dakota Territory in 1874, miners flooded into Sioux and Cheyenne lands. Two years later the Sioux, led by Chiefs Sitting Bull and Crazy Horse, attacked the miners and settlers. The conflict came to a climax in June 1876 at the Little Bighorn River, where a large group of Cheyenne and Sioux were camped. General George Custer attacked, but the Native Americans killed Custer and all of his troops at the Battle of the Little Bighorn. The Sioux victory meant only a brief reprieve. In 1881 they surrendered for a final time to the United States Army.

force the Arapaho and Cheyenne from an area that had been granted to them "forever" 10 years earlier. Warfare continued for 3 years until Black Kettle, the Cheyenne chief, was trapped at Sand Creek in eastern Colorado by Colonel John Chivington. The militia ignored Black Kettle's repeated attempts to surrender and killed men, women, and children.

In 1862 the Santee Sioux of Minnesota attacked a group of settlers who had moved into their hunting lands. After the militia defeated them, the Sioux were forced to move to reservations in the Dakota Territory. A short time later, the Oglala [oh•GLA•lah] Sioux became enraged at

▶ **NATIVE AMERICAN CRADLE**

The final clash occurred at Wounded Knee, South Dakota, in December of 1890, where more than 190 unarmed Native Americans were killed. With this tragic encounter, the wars came to an end.

Although Plains nations fought hundreds of battles from 1860 to 1890, their cause was doomed because they were dependent on the buffalo for food, clothing, fuel, and shelter. When the herds were wiped out, resistance became impossible. In spite of some victories and heroic deeds, such as the 1,500-mile march of the Nez Percé (NEHZ PUHRS) under Chief Joseph in 1877 to avoid capture, the result was inevitable. Chief Joseph's speech at his surrender summarized the hopelessness of the cause:

> *Our chiefs are killed. . . . The little children are freezing to death. My people . . . have no blankets, no food. . . . Hear me, my chiefs; I am tired; my heart is sick and sad. From where the sun now stands, I will fight no more forever.*

The Dawes Act

In 1887, three years before Wounded Knee, Congress passed the Dawes Act, which broke up Native American nations, even on the reservations. The Dawes Act gave each family 160 acres to cultivate. After a probation period of 25 years, Native Americans would be granted ownership of the land and United States citizenship.

The Dawes Act was the result of humanitarian opposition to the United States Army's extermination policy. In 1881 Helen Hunt Jackson had written *A Century of Dishonor,* a book that criticized the government policy toward Native Americans. Unfortunately, the new legislation did more harm than good. Plains peoples were nomads whose way of life was based on the buffalo hunt. They did not understand legal technicalities of land ownership, knew little about farming, and were demoralized by reservation life. Between 1887 and 1943, Native Americans lost to real estate speculators and dishonest government agents an estimated 86 million acres of the 138 million acres that had been set aside for them.

▲ GHOST DANCE SHIRT

Section 1 ★ Review

Checking for Understanding

1. **Identify** Sioux, Promontory Point, James J. Hill, Sitting Bull, Little Bighorn, Wounded Knee.

2. **Define** nomadic.

3. **Explain** how the expansion of the railroads benefited some people at the expense of others.

4. **Enumerate** the events that eventually brought an end to the Plains peoples' way of life.

Critical Thinking

5. **Formulating Hypotheses** Why did the United States government fight wars against Plains peoples in spite of the human costs?

Map and Graph Skills

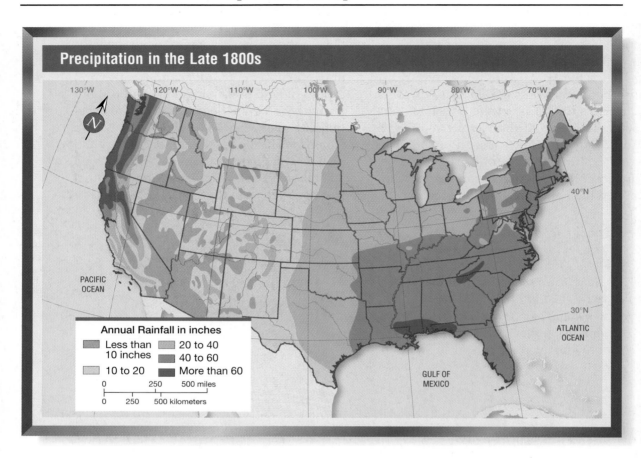

Precipitation in the Late 1800s

Annual Rainfall in inches
- Less than 10 inches
- 10 to 20
- 20 to 40
- 40 to 60
- More than 60

0   250   500 miles
0   250   500 kilometers

PACIFIC OCEAN

ATLANTIC OCEAN

GULF OF MEXICO

Analyzing Map Data

One way to tell the state of agriculture in a region is to study the amount of rainfall it receives. Studying data on rainfall helps you judge whether a region's agricultural potential is good, fair, or poor. The plains farmers had no way of doing this because accurate records of rainfall did not then exist.

Analysis is the process of separating data into its various parts and seeing how they relate to one another. Once you have analyzed data, you can then make better judgments based on it. For example, instruments exist today that collect data about rainfall. This data can be separated and organized so that it provides a comparison of different amounts and different geographic areas. This gives a basis by which to judge the agricultural potential of different areas.

Practicing the Skill

Analyze the data on the climate map of the United States by answering the following questions:

1. What data is shown on the map?
2. How is the data separated?
3. How is the data related?
4. What judgments can you make?

For further practice in analyzing map data, answer the same questions while studying the map on page 478.

★★

Ranching and Mining

Setting the Scene

Section Focus

The "Old West" that inspired romantic tales for over a century is based on the realities of cattle ranching and mining. Removal of buffalo and Native Americans from the plains and the opening of Eastern markets by the railroad introduced the great days of the cattle ranchers. Discoveries of more gold and silver in mountains of the West lured thousands of fortune seekers to the mining towns.

◀ NAT LOVE

Objectives

After studying this section, you should be able to

★ explain the role of the environment in the rise and fall of the long drive.

★ identify the realities behind the myths of the Old West.

Key Terms

maverick, long drive, vigilance committee, vaudeville, "Western"

---

he open-range cattle industry started in Spanish Texas. The Spanish brought the techniques of herding on horseback, roping, and the roundup to the Americas. From the Spanish, too, came the distinctive dress and equipment of the cowhand. The cattle in Texas were mainly Spanish in origin, although some were brought by American and French settlers to Texas when it was part of Mexico. The Great Plains, with its vast open grasslands, was well suited for raising cattle. Faced with such an opportunity, ranchers rapidly moved into the last frontier.

■ The Cattle Kingdom

After the Texas Revolution in 1836, **mavericks,** or unbranded cattle, multiplied on the open range. An estimated 330,000 head of cattle in 1850 grew to between 3 and 4 million head by 1860. There were so many that they could be bought for as little as $3 or $4 a head in Texas.

Cattle Drives

After the Civil War, opportunity developed for great profit in the cattle industry as growing cities of the North provided huge markets for meat. There were, however, no direct railroad lines from Texas to the North. The result was the **long drive.** As the spring of 1866 turned the grasslands green, cowhands drove herds of steers to railroad shipping centers in Missouri and Kansas. The routes of the long drives became known as trails—such as the Chisholm Trail from near San Antonio to Abilene, a station on the Kansas Pacific Railroad.

A single herd might number 2,500 and be attended by 8 to 10 cowhands, a trail boss, and wranglers to care for the horses. The life of a cowhand on the trail demanded discipline, endurance, and courage, but it paid well to those who survived. More than 30,000 cowhands may have ridden the trails

to deliver cattle from Texas to the North. Several thousand of these were African Americans, free to earn their first wages after the Civil War.

Life in the cattle towns was exciting, but many cowhands told exaggerated tales of daring that multiplied as dime novels—books of stories that sold for a dime—spread the myths of the "Wild West" in Eastern towns and cities. A typical tale was *The Life and Adventures of Nat Love: Better Known in the Cattle Country as "Deadwood Dick"—By Himself.* Love was an authentic African American cowboy whose story became part of the romance of the West.

For the investor, the profits obtained from a successful cattle drive were enormous.

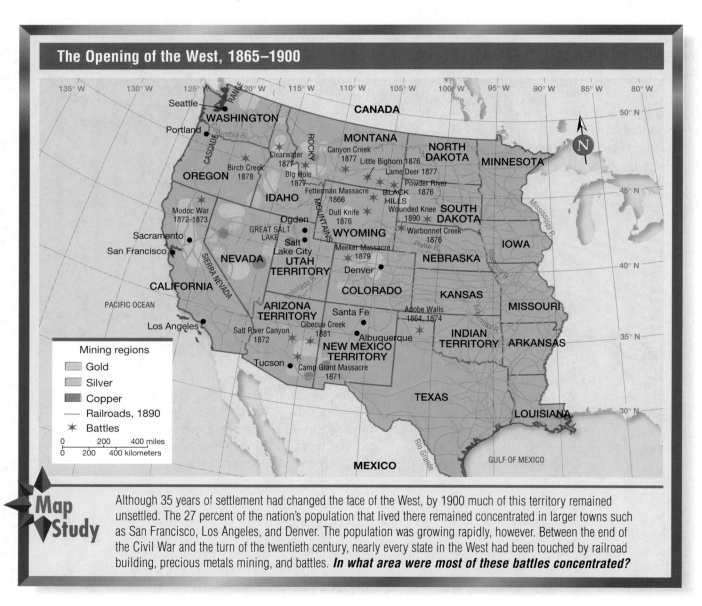

The Opening of the West, 1865–1900

Mining regions
- Gold
- Silver
- Copper
- — Railroads, 1890
- ✳ Battles

Map Study

Although 35 years of settlement had changed the face of the West, by 1900 much of this territory remained unsettled. The 27 percent of the nation's population that lived there remained concentrated in larger towns such as San Francisco, Los Angeles, and Denver. The population was growing rapidly, however. Between the end of the Civil War and the turn of the twentieth century, nearly every state in the West had been touched by railroad building, precious metals mining, and battles. *In what area were most of these battles concentrated?*

As the buffalo were cleared from the plains, the Cattle Kingdom expanded northward until, by 1885, it covered an area half as large as Europe, extending from Texas to Montana. From the East, even from Great Britain and France, people with cash to invest and a taste for adventure put their money in cattle.

Decline of the Cattle Industry

Although offering vast profits, the industry was beset by difficulties. Steers could go blind from drought, drown in flash floods, die in stampedes, or get infected by the dreaded Texas fever. They might be stolen by rustlers or shot by angry homesteaders trying to protect their crops. The open-range cattle industry collapsed even more rapidly than it had risen. Too many animals were put on the ranges, and overgrazing resulted. Overproduction drove prices down. Sheepherders and homesteaders competed with the cattle ranchers for land.

Nature helped to end the long drives. The cold winter of 1885 and 1886 was followed by a summer so dry that the grass withered and streams disappeared. In the winter of 1886–1887, terrible blizzards covered the ground with snow so deep that the cattle could not paw down to grass. Next came an unprecedented cold spell, with temperatures ranging as low as −60°F. "When spring finally came," wrote historian Ray Allen Billington,

> *. . . cattlemen saw a sight they spent the rest of their lives trying to forget. Carcass piled upon carcass in every ravine, gaunt skeletons staggering about on frozen feet, trees stripped bare of their bark. . . .*

The cattle industry survived this terrible blow, but the day of the open range was over. From then on herds were raised on fenced-in ranches, English Herefords replaced longhorns, and the cowhand became a ranch hand.

■ The Mining Frontier

The discovery of gold in California was just the beginning of prospecting in the West. Inspired fortune seekers moved to California.

Mining and Mining Towns

From California the fortune seekers spread east into the Great Basin and Rocky Mountain regions. A gold strike in Colorado in 1858 set off a stampede to the region the next year.

> *The first breath of spring started the hordes westward. Steamboats crowded to the rails poured throngs of immigrants ashore at every Missouri River town. . . . All through April, May, and June they left the jumping-off places in a regular parade of Conestoga wagons, hand carts, men on horseback, men on foot—each with "Pikes Peak or Bust" crudely pinned on their packs and wagon canvas. . . . By the end of June more than 100,000 "fifty-niners" were in the Pikes Peak country.*

The Colorado strike was followed by many other finds: gold in the Black Hills of South Dakota, copper in Montana, and silver in many places. The Comstock Lode at Virginia City, Nevada, yielded about $300 million worth of silver ore between 1859 and 1877. These discoveries attracted swarms of fortune seekers, and new mining towns appeared overnight.

The discovery of precious metals brought thousands of miners into a single area, giving rise first to makeshift camps and later to towns and cities. People from a variety of backgrounds mingled in these places. A study of one Western camp revealed that the population consisted of 37 from China, 35 from Great Britain, 29 from Mexico, 24 from other nations, and 81 from other parts of the United States. In addition, other newcomers, including a substantial number of women, set up businesses to serve the miners.

Despite differences in background, all of the miners shared one goal: an unbending desire to mine that lucky strike that would bring them wealth. After the minerals in one area were exhausted, miners would leave town, and a once-lively center of trade and commerce would become a deserted ghost town almost overnight. While the wealth lasted, however, mining communities could be spirited—as well as dangerous—places. One observer described one such mining town in this way:

66 *This human hive, numbering at least 10,000 people, was the product of 90 days. Into it were crowded all the elements of a rough and active civilization. . . . [F]illed with gambling tables and gamblers, and the miner who was bold enough to enter one of them with his day's earnings in his pocket seldom left until thoroughly fleeced. . . . Not a day or night passed which did not yield its full fruition of fights, quarrels, wounds or murders. . . . Street fights were frequent . . . and everyone was on his guard against a random shot.* 99

Human life was cheap in these communities of tents and crude dwellings, with their rows of saloons and gambling houses. There was a vital need for law enforcement agencies to settle disputes over mining claims and to punish or prevent crime. Self-appointed volunteers called **vigilance committees** sometimes provided law and order. Other times mass meetings drew up their own rules and elected their own officials. Soon the different communities of a region such as Colorado or Nevada would band together and demand territorial status or statehood. Usually the actual grant of statehood came after the arrival of homesteaders and miners, because cattle raisers were too nomadic to provide stable government.

The "Wild West"

The "Wild West" captured the imagination of Americans immediately. Dime novels and popular ballads spread the adventures of Wild Bill Hickok, Billy the Kid, and Jesse James. A Wild West Show became part of Barnum and Bailey's circus; and Annie Oakley, the sharpshooter, appeared on **vaudeville,** or live variety show, stages everywhere. The Wild West period lasted little more than 30 years, yet

CHAS. M. RUSSELL

"THE COWBOY ARTIST."

Charles M. Russell
1864–1926

AMERICAN PORTRAITS

Born in St. Louis, Charles Russell much preferred to watch the fur traders and men who worked along the Mississippi River than to attend school.

In 1880, at the age of 16, Russell set out for Montana to work as a cowhand and to observe Native American life. He began to paint life as he saw it, creating realistic scenes of the untamed West. Among Russell's favorite subjects were cowhands riding bucking broncos, Native Americans hunting buffalo, and outlaws holding up stagecoaches.

Little realizing the value of his paintings, he often gave them away. By the early 1890s, however, Russell was able to stop cowpunching and devote himself solely to art. By 1920 Russell's portrayals of "cowboys and Indians" commanded high prices, and he was recognized as one of the finest artists of the American West.

▲ MINING TOWNS The discovery of gold in Colorado and silver in Nevada started a rush to the West. Thousands flocked into "boom towns" like Creede, Colorado, to strike it rich. *How many "fifty-niners" went to Pikes Peak country?*

its fascination has continued in storybooks and comics, Western songs and costumes, and **"Westerns"**—movies produced by Hollywood and shown at movie theaters or on television.

The romance of the Wild West conceals some of the truth. The conquest of the plains and the Rockies by the invading cattle ranchers, miners, and homesteaders destroyed natural resources, wildlife, and human beings. Charles Marion Russell, a frontier artist, gave this sobering message in a speech to "forward-looking citizens" in Helena, Montana:

" *I have been called a pioneer. . . . a pioneer is a man who comes to a virgin country, traps off all the fur, kills off all the wild meat, cuts down all the trees, grazes off all the grass, plows the roots up, and strings ten million miles of wire. A pioneer destroys things and calls it civilization. I wish to God this country was just like it was when I first saw it and that none of you folks were here at all.* "

Section 2 ★ Review

Checking for Understanding

1. **Identify** Chisholm Trail, Nat Love, Cattle Kingdom, Comstock Lode, Annie Oakley.

2. **Define** maverick, long drive, vigilance committee, vaudeville, "Western."

3. **Summarize** the rise and fall of the open-range cattle industry.

4. **Examine** the realities of life that inspired the romanticized myths of the "Old West."

Critical Thinking

5. **Predicting Outcomes** Had the open-range system continued, what conflicts could have developed as the farmers settled the plains?

The Civil War shattered the illusions of many Americans, including writers. They had little use for the idealism of antebellum books. This postwar generation of writers depicted events and characters in the hard, cold light of reality. One master of the new realism was Mark Twain. In the following selection, Twain applies a light touch to his account of a journey to Carson City with two miners. As you read, determine what Twain is implying about human nature.

Roughing It (excerpts)

The snow lay so deep on the ground that there was no sign of a road perceptible, and the snowfall was so thick that we could not see more than a hundred yards ahead, else we could have guided our course by the mountain ranges. The case looked dubious, but Ollendorff said his instinct was as sensitive as any compass, and that he could "strike a beeline" for Carson City and never diverge from it. . . . For half an hour we poked along warily enough, but at the end of that time we came upon a fresh trail, and Ollendorff shouted proudly:

"I knew I was as dead certain as a compass, boys! Here we are, right in somebody's tracks that will hunt the way for us without any trouble. Let's hurry up and join company with the party."

So we put the horses into as much of a trot as the deep snow would allow, and before long it was evident that we were gaining on our predecessors, for the tracks grew more distinct. We hurried along and at the end of an hour the tracks looked still newer and fresher—but what surprised us was, that the *number* of travelers in advance of us seemed to steadily increase. We wondered how so large a party came to be traveling at such a time and in such a solitude. . . . Presently [Ballou] stopped his horse and said:

"Boys, these are our own tracks, and we've actually been circussing round and round in a circle for more than two hours, out here in the blind desert! By George this is perfectly hydraulic!". . .

All agreed that a campfire was what would come nearest to saving us, now, and so we set about building it. We could find no matches. . . . This was distressing, but it paled before a greater horror—the horses were gone! I had been appointed to hold the bridles, but in my absorbing anxiety . . . I had unconsciously dropped them and the released animals had walked off in the storm. . . .

▲ **COLORADO GHOST TOWN**

We were miserable enough, before; we felt still more forlorn, now. . . . At this critical moment Mr. Ballou fished four matches from the rubbish of an over-looked pocket. . . . when Mr. Ballou prepared to light the first match, there was an amount of interest centered upon him that pages of writing could not describe. The match burned hopefully a moment, and then went out. It could not have carried more regret with it if it had been a human life. The next match simply flashed and died. The wind puffed the third one out just as it was on the imminent verge of success. We gathered together closer than ever, and developed a solicitude that was rapt and painful, as Mr. Ballou scratched our last hope on his leg. It lit, burned blue and sickly, and then budded into a robust flame. Shading it with his hands, the old gentleman bent gradually down and every heart went with him. . . . The flame touched the sticks at last, took gradual hold upon them—hesitated—took a stronger hold—hesitated again—held its breath five heart-breaking seconds, then gave a sort of human gasp and went out.

Nobody said a word for several minutes. It was a solemn sort of silence; even the wind put on a stealthy, sinister quiet, and made no more noise than the falling flakes of snow. . . .

Then [next morning] came a white upheaval at my side, and a voice said, with bitterness: "Will some gentleman be so good as to kick me behind?" It was Ballou—at least it was a tousled snow image in a sitting posture, with Ballou's voice.

I rose up, and there in the gray dawn, not fifteen steps from us, were the frame buildings of a stage station and under a shed stood our still saddled and bridled horses!

▲ **PANNING FOR GOLD IN THE DAKOTA TERRITORY**

Interpreting Literature

1. Were the men in *Roughing It* experienced Western travelers? Explain.

2. Why does the narrator find the group's situation humiliating?

Analyzing Material

3. How does Twain's tone in this selection contribute to its humor?

★★★

Farming Moves West

Setting the Scene

Section Focus

For years the Great Plains resisted settlement. The main reason for farmers' unwillingness to venture into the plains was the totally new environment. Three forces worked to overcome the farmers' hesitation: new agricultural technology, westward expansion of the railroads, and European immigration.

Objectives

After studying this section, you should be able to

★ list three factors that made farming the plains possible.

★ summarize the problems faced by plains farmers.

Key Terms

meridian, commodity

◀ McCormick HARVESTING MACHINE

*I*n 1862 Congress passed the Homestead Act, enabling a head of a family to acquire a 160-acre farm for $10. To ensure that the land went to actual settlers, the act required that the owner must reside on or cultivate the land for 5 years. The act was passed as a result of nearly half a century of agitation by Western farmers and Eastern laborers.

■ Farming the Great Plains

The Homestead Act did not work out as planned. Through fraud, speculators rather than actual settlers gained possession of much land. The law required that a would-be homesteader put up a home and cultivate the land. Speculators paid relatives or employees to lay down a few logs as a "foundation" and scatter a few grains of corn. After five years they collected title to a large tract. A more important reason for the ineffectiveness of the Homestead Act was that much of the most desirable land near the railroad lines was usually controlled by the railroad companies themselves.

Technology

Before the plains could be settled, farmers had to be convinced that they could overcome the disadvantages of the dry environment. In the East a farmer could get water from a stream or by digging a well 10 to 20 feet deep. In the plains few streams ran year-round, and underground water was 30 to 300 feet down. The American farmer had always depended on trees for fuel, buildings, and fences. On the plains, trees were found only in the bottomlands near rivers.

Some of the difficulties of farming the plains were overcome by technology from the Industrial Revolution. Cheap iron and steel made possible the iron-encased, drilled well and the cast-iron windmill. Joseph Glidden sold his first barbed wire in 1874, making up for the lack of wooden fence rails.

Improved agricultural machinery cut the cost of raising crops. The reaper, in general use by 1865, was followed by the mechanical binder, which tied the grain into sheaves as fast as it was cut. By the 1880s 2 people and a team of horses could harvest and bind 20 acres of wheat a day. The steam-driven threshing machine also came into general use. In addition to solving technical problems, the Industrial Revolution created a vast new urban population and expanded the market for food, both in America and Europe.

Railroads

The ineffectiveness of the Homestead Act provided Westerners with a grievance but did not interfere with settlement. Although railroads sometimes discouraged the acquisition of free land, they actively promoted the sale of their own. They did not charge high prices because they wanted settlers to get the land into production. In fact, the most important factor in promoting settlement was the railroad.

Land-grant railroads had "Bureaus of Immigration" to persuade farmers to settle along their lines. They maintained offices in the principal European cities and agents in Eastern seaports to meet immigrants as they left the boat. Steamship companies and Western states advertised the region as so healthy that it cured all known diseases. The industrious person could expect to become wealthy; an $8,000 investment, it was claimed, might soon result in a steady income of $11,000 per year—an enormous sum considering that a 160-acre farm was homesteaded for $10. The West was pictured as a place where unmarried women would easily find husbands. "When a daughter of the East is once beyond the Missouri," said one railroad advertisement, "she rarely recrosses it except on a bridal tour."

To offset the myth of the "Great American Desert," a new myth was created. Some "experts" said that rainfall on the Great Plains would increase with the planting of

 ▲ SOD HOUSES Lack of trees on the Great Plains forced homesteaders to build homes from materials other than wood. One of the most common was sod cut from the grassy turf. *What were the environmental realities that farmers on the plains faced?*

trees or with simple cultivation; a Nebraska promoter summed it up in the catchy epigram, "Rain follows the plow."

As the plains were opened, the production of wheat—centering in Minnesota, the Dakotas, Kansas, and Nebraska—quadrupled. Wisconsin, too far from the market to send fresh dairy products, used its surplus milk for cheese production. Near every great city, truck gardens provided supplies of fresh vegetables.

■ Sod House Reality

The life of a Great Plains farmer seldom approached the railroad agents' glowing prophecies. The realities of the weather and economic conditions combined to make life on the plains hard.

Weather

The climate that was supposed to cure all known diseases turned out to be severe. In the summer the temperature might go over 100°F for days at a time. In winter there were periods of extreme cold, and terrible blizzards drove the snow through every chink in doors and windows. Families could be stranded in sod houses for many days.

Prairie fires were a constant danger in the spring and fall. Sometimes grasshoppers appeared in huge numbers and destroyed the crops.

Worst of all disasters was drought. The normal rainfall of the Plains region was markedly less than that of the wooded East, dropping from about 30 to 40 inches per year along the 98th **meridian,** or line of longitude, to 10 inches just east of the Rockies.

The greatest push westward into the Great Plains took place in the early 1880s, during a cycle of wet years that offered false promises of abundant crops. In the late 1880s, drought returned to drive thousands back east in despair.

In spite of all the difficulties, most settlers managed to adjust to their physical environment. Water from deep wells enabled them to plant gardens and trees around their homes. Railroads brought lumber and brick for houses to replace sod huts and coal to replace cornstalks or hay as fuel.

▲ BARBED WIRE The introduction of barbed wire, perfected in 1874, was a blessing for farmers. Previously farmers had made do with earth embankments and hedges to keep cattle out of their crops. *What equipment and materials were needed to farm on the plains?*

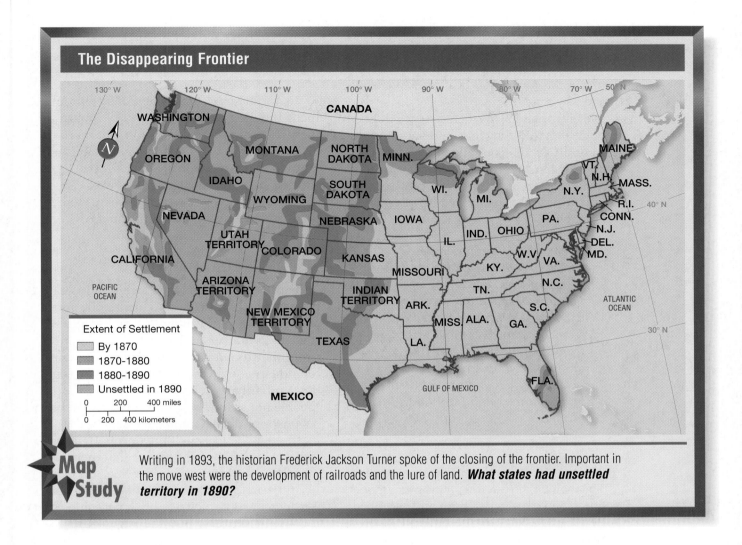

The Disappearing Frontier

WASHINGTON
OREGON
MONTANA
NORTH DAKOTA
MINN.
CANADA
IDAHO
WYOMING
SOUTH DAKOTA
WI.
MI.
MAINE
VT.
N.H.
MASS.
N.Y.
R.I.
CONN.
NEVADA
NEBRASKA
IOWA
IL.
IND.
OHIO
PA.
N.J.
DEL.
MD.
UTAH TERRITORY
COLORADO
KANSAS
MISSOURI
KY.
W.V
VA.
CALIFORNIA
ARIZONA TERRITORY
NEW MEXICO TERRITORY
INDIAN TERRITORY
ARK.
TN.
N.C.
S.C.
PACIFIC OCEAN
TEXAS
MISS.
ALA.
GA.
ATLANTIC OCEAN
LA.
FLA.
MEXICO
GULF OF MEXICO

Extent of Settlement
By 1870
1870-1880
1880-1890
Unsettled in 1890

0   200   400 miles
0 200 400 kilometers

Map Study

Writing in 1893, the historian Frederick Jackson Turner spoke of the closing of the frontier. Important in the move west were the development of railroads and the lure of land. *What states had unsettled territory in 1890?*

Economics

Plains farmers faced a second problem at least as frustrating as the weather. They were in the grip of economic forces beyond their control. Formerly, out of necessity as subsistence farmers, they had produced almost everything they needed. The independent farmer was admired in literature and melodramas, especially when contrasted with unhappy factory hands, the idle rich, or "city slickers." With the opening of great urban markets, however, farmers tended to specialize. Some farmers grew a single cash crop, such as wheat or corn; others might specialize in dairy production or cattle raising. Their incomes went up, but so did their expenses. Large-scale farming required a great deal of agricultural machinery. The need to buy clothing and food made farmers less independent.

A farmer's prosperity, perhaps even the ownership of the farm, might depend on the unpredictable price of grain in an international market. Farmers also became dependent on the railroad, which carried their crops to market, on the commission merchant who marketed it, and on the owners of grain elevators who stored it. Farmers who raised hogs or beef cattle were in a similar situation; they had little bargaining power and were forced to take whatever the meat packers paid.

Farming on the plains demanded large investments of money to drill wells, put up windmills, enclose fields in barbed wire, and buy machinery. Because few farmers could pay with cash, they had to borrow by mortgaging their land. Then, to pay interest on the mortgages, they were forced to concentrate more than ever on raising cash crops. If prices dropped or a lean year came, they could not meet their payments and lost their land. By 1900 about one-third of the farms in the corn and wheat areas were cultivated by tenants.

Not surprisingly, farmers protested. Even though they fed the cities and supplied the **commodities,** or economic goods, that paid for European investments, the wealth they created seemed to be siphoned off to others. Their attitude was expressed by a Nebraska newspaper:

> *There are three great crops raised in Nebraska. One is a crop of corn, one a crop of freight rates, and one a crop of interest. One is produced by farmers, who sweat and toil, from the land. The other two are produced by men who sit in their offices and behind their bank counters and farm the farmers.*

The Plains Women

For women, life on the plains often meant solitude and drudgery. "Born and scrubbed, suffered and died," is the epitaph given a woman in one of Hamlin Garland's poems. Yet the settlement of the West owed much to the endless toil of frontier women.

Women have written some of the best accounts of plains life, such as *Cimarron* by Edna Ferber and *My Antonia* by Willa Cather. While not minimizing the sufferings of pioneering, these novels reveal how much easier life became after the sod house days were past.

In *My Antonia* Cather mentioned a prominent building in Black Hawk, Nebraska, a new brick high school. As soon as farm communities had the funds, they established churches and schools. The Morrill Act helped states to establish universities. These were open to women as well as men; women had gained a new position of equality.

Declining Status of Farmers

Farmers, however, were losing status. For years they had been held up as the most admirable and the happiest of people. By the 1880s power and prestige had shifted from the rural areas to the cities. "Captains of industry" won the admiration of the public, and urban America regarded country people not as the backbone of the nation but as unsophisticated and backward.

In 1890 the Census Bureau reported that settlement had been so rapid "that there can hardly be said to be a frontier line." In reality, much land was still unoccupied, and new settlement continued at a brisk pace into the twentieth century, but the news that the frontier was closing encouraged prophets of doom, who saw the end of an era. They believed that the existence of unoccupied land at the frontier had provided a "safety-valve of social discontent," the idea that Americans could always make a fresh start.

Section 3 ★ Review

Checking for Understanding

1. **Identify** the Homestead Act, the Morrill Act, Willa Cather, Hamlin Garland.
2. **Define** meridian, commodity.
3. **Describe** the changes that made the West profitable for farmers.
4. **List** the problems the environment created for farmers on the plains.

Critical Thinking

5. **Analyzing Transfer of Risk**   In the 1800s farmers began to sell "futures," or to contract months in advance to sell a crop to a grain merchant for a certain price. What are the advantages and disadvantages to the farmer of selling crops this way? What are the problems to the grain merchant?

The Great American Desert

To Americans accustomed to well-watered, timbered lands east of the Mississippi River, the Great Plains seemed a vast and forbidding desert. The 100th meridian marked the line west of which annual rainfall was less than 20 inches. Farther west the annual rainfall was even less. Aquifers—strata of water-bearing rock—lay much farther below the surface than they did in the East, making hand-dug wells impractical.

The general aridity of the Great Plains region had caused explorers to label the area a desert. Major Stephen Long, leading an army expedition to explore the Great Plains in 1820, stated that ". . . it is almost wholly unfit for cultivation. . . . The scarcity of wood and water, almost uniformly prevalent, will prove an insuperable obstacle in the way of settling the country." Long prepared a map, labeled the region the Great American Desert, and influenced Americans' perception of the plains for decades. Almost every map published between 1820 and 1860 used Long's label. Americans' misconception about the plains delayed settlement until new technology—drilling machines and the windmill—tapped deep aquifers. Until the water runs out, technology has conquered geography.

▲ HOMESTEADERS, COBURG, NEBRASKA, 1887

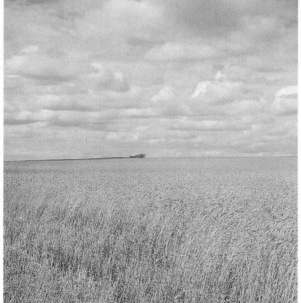

▲ NEBRASKA WHEAT FIELD

Making the Geography Connection

1. The absence of which resources led people to think of the Great Plains as a desert?

2. How could settlers adapt to the environment?

Linking Past and Present

3. How might the "mining" of aquifers affect people on the Great Plains today?

Using Vocabulary

Explain why each of these terms is used in a chapter about opening the West.

nomadic	maverick
long drive	vigilance committees
"Western"	meridian
commodity	vaudeville

Reviewing Facts

1. **Describe** the lives of the nomadic Plains peoples.

2. **Give** reasons why the Plains peoples' way of life came to an end.

3. **List** the factors that drew settlers to the West.

4. **Contrast** the open-range cattle industry with the system that replaced it.

5. **Specify** the changes that made farming attractive on the Great Plains.

6. **Discuss** the hardships faced in settling the Old West.

Understanding Concepts

Expansion

1. During the 1700s and early 1800s, most expansion took place east of the Mississippi. What changes and developments accelerated expansion west of the Mississippi?

2. What part did railroads play in the westward expansion?

Conflict

3. Explain the conflicts between Native Americans and settlers. What groups today might oppose unrestrained development and fencing of wilderness areas?

4. Conflict on the plains was not confined to wars with Native Americans. Open-range cattle ranchers often came into conflict with sheepherders and homesteaders. How might the interests of an open-range cattle industry conflict with those of other settlers?

Critical Thinking

1. **Recognizing Effects**   How did the railroads benefit from encouraging farmers and immigrants to settle near their rail lines?

2. **Analyzing Art**   Study the rendering on this page by a Cheyenne artist. It depicts a Ghost Dance, which was performed as a ritual that was believed would bring back the buffalo and restore the Native American way of life. In December 1890, United States soldiers tried to break up a large band of Ghost Dancers gathered at Wounded Knee Creek on the Pine Ridge Reservation in South Dakota. In the resulting massacre, many Native Americans were killed.

   a. Which part of the picture seems to be the most important? How does the artist draw your attention to it?

   b. What is unusual about the artist's portrayal of the Native Americans?

▲ CHEYENNE PICTOGRAPH HIDE, LATE 1800S

Writing About History

Narration

Write a day's entry in the diary of a 17-year-old traveling west by rail in 1870. Include details about the geographic features, the hardships, and the traveler's reactions.

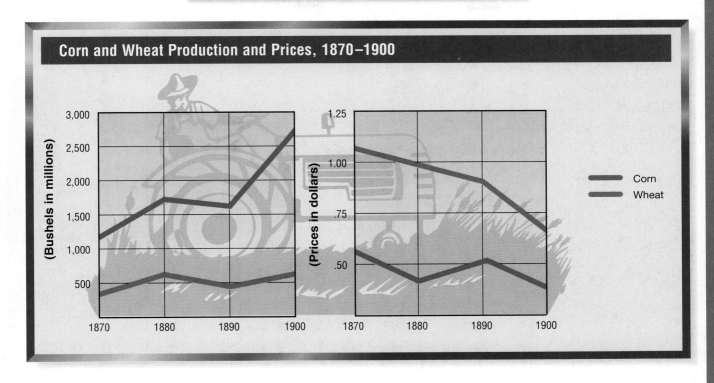

Corn and Wheat Production and Prices, 1870–1900

Cooperative Learning

Your group will research either the details of life during the days of the open-range cattle industry or the same details as depicted in "Westerns." Divide the research assignments so that each group member is responsible for a different aspect of real life or life in a "Western."

Social Studies Skills

Reading a Line Graph

Like a bar graph, a line graph is used to show a relationship between two variables. Study the graph on this page, then answer the questions.

Practicing the Skill

1. What is the time period in the graphs?
2. What is the independent variable in both graphs?
3. What are the dependent variables in the graphs?
4. What does each graph show?
5. What is the overall trend in the production of corn and wheat?

6. According to the chapter, what factors contributed to this trend?
7. What appears to be the trend in prices of corn and wheat between 1870 and 1900?

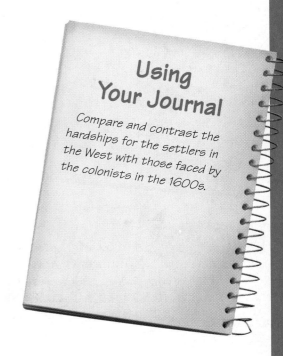

Using Your Journal

Compare and contrast the hardships for the settlers in the West with those faced by the colonists in the 1600s.

CHAPTER 18

★★★

The Rise of Industry
1860–1900

Setting the Scene

Focus

The United States developed into a great industrial power in the latter decades of the nineteenth century. By the year 1900, United States industrial production was the strongest in the world. This remarkable growth was the result of many different factors—cheap labor, abundant raw materials, new technology—but also of new forms of business organization.

▲ SPINDLETOP OIL FIELD, BEAUMONT, TEXAS

Concepts to Understand

★ Why business leaders believed that individual initiative benefited all of society

★ How lack of restrictions helped large companies but hurt small ones

Read to Discover . . .

★ what factors caused American industry to grow so rapidly.

★ how Andrew Carnegie and John D. Rockefeller were able to become industrial giants.

Journal Notes

When you read about Rockefeller and Carnegie, look for instances when they gave away some of their wealth. Note these instances in your journal.

CULTURAL	●**1869** *Mark Twain publishes* Innocents Abroad		●**1879** *Thomas Edison invents the first practical electric light*
	1860	**1870**	
POLITICAL	●**1865** *Civil War ends*	●**1873** *Panic of 1873 strikes*	

Factory Chimneys
by Maximillian Luce, 1896

Mass production—production of large quantities of goods at low cost—was the heart of the new industrial system.

◀ INVENTOR THOMAS ALVA EDISON

- **1882** *Standard Oil Trust formed*
- **1893** *First successful gasoline-powered car operated*

1880	1890

- **1884** *Congress establishes the Federal Bureau of Labor*
- **1893** *Colorado grants women the right to vote*

★★★

Industrialization Takes Hold

Setting the Scene

Section Focus

The tremendous industrial growth that occurred in the United States after the Civil War resulted from foundations that had been laid over the previous half-century. Agriculture flourished in the South and Midwest, and manufacturing increased in the Northeast. A transportation network spread people, products, and information across the nation. Yet greater growth was ahead.

Objectives

After studying this section, you should be able to

★ identify and explain the factors that encouraged industrial growth.

★ discuss the railroad's role in the growth of industry.

Key Terms

entrepreneur, economies of scale

◀ CASH REGISTER, 1878

nlike the South, the North emerged virtually undamaged by the Civil War, its railroads and factories intact. Furthermore, the war and Reconstruction eliminated Southern planters as rivals to Northern industrialists for political power, allowing industrial growth to proceed at an even greater pace. Although interrupted by depressions from 1873 to 1878, 1882 to 1884, and 1893 to 1896, America's industrial production doubled every 12 to 14 years. By the 1880s the United States had overtaken Great Britain as the world's industrial leader.

■ Resources

The change from a primarily agricultural society to an industrial one was possible because the United States had the means necessary for a changing and growing economy.

Among these were an abundance and variety of natural resources and large numbers of workers to turn raw materials into goods.

A Wealth of Natural Resources

Before the war, natural resources such as coal, iron ore, and petroleum had scarcely been touched. By the 1860s, however, methods for extracting and utilizing these resources were well developed.

As a result, the amount of coal mined in the United States more than doubled in every decade between 1840 and 1890. By the 1870s, vast deposits throughout the Appalachians from Pennsylvania to Alabama were being mined. Completion of the Soo Canal between Lake Superior and Lake Huron in 1855 allowed ships to move iron ore mined in Michigan and Wisconsin to iron and steel mills on the lower Great Lakes.

The American oil industry got its start in 1859 in western Pennsylvania when the first successful well was drilled. By 1900 oil fields extended as far west as Texas. Production had risen from 2,000 barrels per year in 1859 to 64 million barrels per year in 1900.

A Growing Labor Force

The human resources available to American industry were as important as the mineral resources. European capitalists sometimes had difficulty recruiting labor for new industries. Children of working-class families often were raised to follow traditional occupations, and in the European countryside peasants frequently were reluctant to leave their home villages. In the United States, however, labor was more mobile. Workers came to new jobs in cities the way pioneers moved to new lands.

Between 1860 and 1890, America's population more than doubled, rising from 31 million to nearly 75 million. The flood of immigration that had begun in the 1840s continued, contributing to this growth. Pulled by opportunities in America—and pushed out by the lack of them at home—14 million immigrants arrived between 1860 and 1900, more than twice the number of the previous 40 years. Many of these immigrants were adult males eager to find employment. These newcomers enlarged the labor pools that accumulated wherever jobs were available, and that helped keep industrial wages low.

■ Public Policies and Private Investment

American industry developed within a free enterprise system. Americans embraced a philosophy of laissez-faire, which comes from the French phrase meaning "let alone." As a result, American industries developed with few government restraints. In fact, some government policies actually encouraged industrialization. **Entrepreneurs,** or business organizers, sought and received special favors from Congress. Liberal immigration

laws ensured a steady supply of cheap labor. High protective tariffs encouraged American industries and raised manufacturers' profits by keeping out foreign goods. The federal government sold public lands containing vast mineral resources for a small proportion of their true value and assumed about one-third of the cost of building Western railroads. It gave railroads grants of money totaling more than $700 million and gave them public lands throughout the West equaling the size of Texas.

While European entrepreneurs often retired when they acquired enough money to buy their way into the upper class, Americans regarded moneymaking itself as a worthwhile goal. "Such opportunities for making money," wrote Thomas Mellon, a Pittsburgh judge who later became a banker, "never existed before in all my former experience."

The money to be made in American manufacturing and transportation attracted private investors. The savings of New Englanders—accumulated from the West Indies and China trade, from clippers and whalers, from textile mills and shoe manufactures—helped build hundreds of factories and thousands of miles of railroad track. An equally important source of private capital was Europe, especially Great Britain. By 1900 British investors owned

◄ OFFICE SECRETARY IN THE LATE 1800s

$2.5 billion in American railroad securities—more than twice the national debt of the United States.

■ Science and Technology

A flood of important inventions helped increase America's productive capacity and improved the network of transportation and communications that was vital to the nation's industrial growth. As American universities extended their activities beyond teaching, they became important centers of scientific research.

The Typewriter and the Telephone

The American public knew little of the university professors who extended the boundaries of science. People were greatly impressed, however, with inventors such as C. Latham Sholes, a Wisconsin printer whose idea for a typewriter in 1868 revolutionized business communications.

Equally inventive was Alexander Graham Bell, an immigrant from Scotland. Bell's profession was teaching deaf children to speak. He applied his speech training to developing the principles upon which the telephone is based. In 1876 he sent the first telephone communication to his laboratory assistant in the next room: "Mr. Watson, come here; I want you."

A year later he demonstrated the commercial value of his invention by sitting in Boston and talking with Watson in New York City—and the Bell Telephone Company was founded. By 1886 more than 250,000 phones were in use, mostly in businesses. This rapid growth created jobs for thousands of women as switchboard operators. By 1900 telephone rates had been lowered, and telephones increasingly began to appear in American homes.

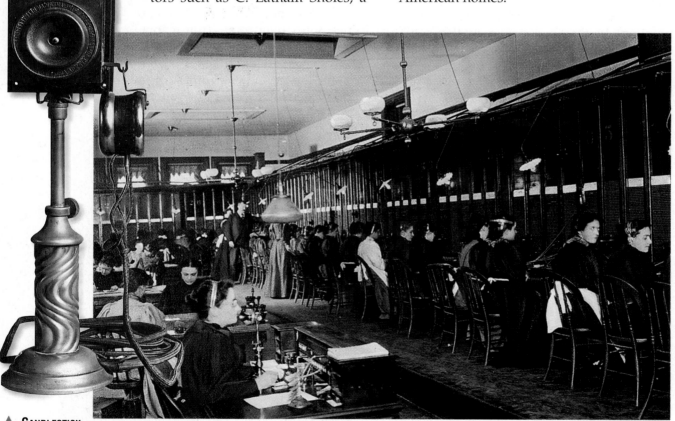

▲ CANDLESTICK TELEPHONE, 1890s

Visualizing History

▲ THE INFLUENCE OF THE TELEPHONE The telephone made business communications quick and personal. The job of the telephone operator was the first American occupation considered to be strictly "women's work." *Which person in this photograph is probably the manager? Why do you think this is so?*

Working-class Tenements

Working-class incomes varied greatly during the late nineteenth century. For example, in 1889 a carpenter earned $686 annually; a laborer, $384; and a young woman in a silk mill, only $130. Most working-class people lived crowded together in tenements designed to house as many families as possible.

Living conditions in tenements were primitive. Beds often consisted of boxes filled with straw. Few buildings had indoor plumbing, and in those that did, several families shared a bathroom. Living areas were cramped.

Rags, bones, and other garbage piled up outside, freezing in winter and reeking in summer. Disease festered because of the pervasive dirt and vermin.

Working-class men and women developed a community life as vibrant as their physical surroundings were bleak. Frequently this life was based on ethnic ties. Irish Americans gathered in taverns and parish churches. Jewish Americans organized Hebrew schools and Yiddish-speaking literary groups. Most immigrant groups and African Americans developed social clubs, storefront churches, and mutual-aid societies.

▲ **WORKING-CLASS FAMILY**

◄ **THE EVICTION**

Edison's Contributions

Perhaps even more famous than Bell was Thomas Alva Edison, who has been erroneously credited with inventing the electric light and moving pictures. Edison actually made few original discoveries. Instead, he was a great innovator who put the inventions of others to practical use. For example, Edison's redesign of Sholes's typewriter permitted people to type faster than they could write. His improvement of Bell's telephone allowed voices to be transmitted longer distances. His work on improving the telegraph led to one of his few actual inventions, the phonograph.

The incandescent electric light had been demonstrated in Britain in 1840. But it was Edison who, in 1879, developed cheap methods of supplying power and wire, as well as filaments that lasted more than just a few minutes. The incandescent bulb lighted America's cities and made industrial production possible 24 hours a day.

The Canning Industry

During the Civil War, soldiers in the Union army had received some rations in cans, an innovation that demonstrated the value of canned food. After the war the canning industry improved its methods, and by 1900 machines had been designed to make, fill, and seal cans. A large variety of canned foods began to appear on the shelves of the nation's stores.

Textiles, Clothing, and Shoes

America's textile industry had long depended on machines to turn fibers into cloth. In 1893 the invention of the Northrup automatic loom led to the manufacture of cloth at an even faster rate. Bobbins, which had previously been changed by hand while the loom was stopped, were now changed automatically without stopping the loom.

Great changes also occurred in the clothing industry. Standard sizes, developed

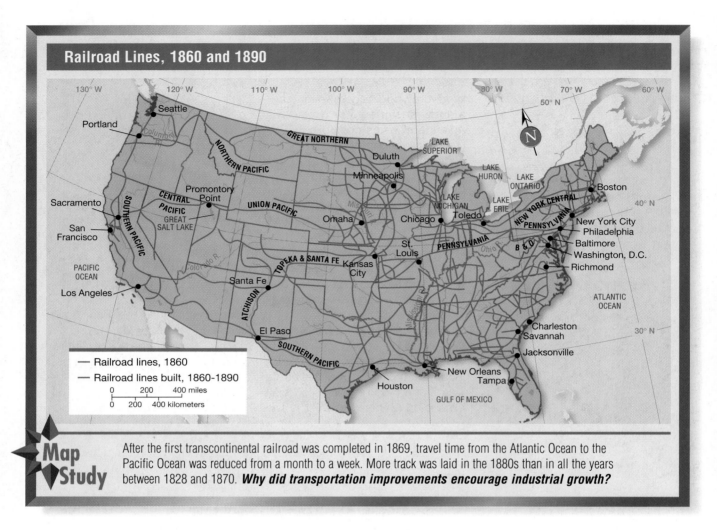

Railroad Lines, 1860 and 1890

Railroad lines, 1860
Railroad lines built, 1860-1890

0   200   400 miles
0   200   400 kilometers

Map Study

After the first transcontinental railroad was completed in 1869, travel time from the Atlantic Ocean to the Pacific Ocean was reduced from a month to a week. More track was laid in the 1880s than in all the years between 1828 and 1870. *Why did transportation improvements encourage industrial growth?*

---

from measurements taken of Union soldiers during the Civil War, were used in the manufacture of ready-made clothes. The use of power-driven sewing machines and cloth cutters moved the clothing business from small tailor shops to large factories.

Similar changes took place in shoe making. New processes and inventions made **economies of scale** possible. In other words, large factories could mass-produce shoes more cheaply and efficiently than smaller companies. These factories could also pass these savings on to their customers in the form of lower prices. By the turn of the century, local cobblers had nearly disappeared.

Steel, Oil, and Trains

Industrial growth was tied to advances in specific industries. The Bessemer process revolutionized American steelmaking in the 1870s. As steel was increasingly used for

products such as machines, rails, and building beams, industry in general began to expand. The boom in the oil industry, along with the development of oil-lubricated machine tools—metal lathes, punches, and drill presses used to make other machines—brought tremendous growth in industrial capability.

New technology also stimulated the growth of the railroad industry. The Bessemer process was a factor in the expansion of railroad operations. This process allowed the railroad companies to replace iron rails with steel, which held up better and was able to carry heavier loads.

Another innovation was the Westinghouse air brake. The brake allowed the cars and locomotives to stop simultaneously—another factor making longer trains and heavier loads possible. Kerosene lamps, and later electric lights, provided better headlights for nighttime travel.

Railroad Building

Perhaps no other single factor was more responsible for the growth of American industry than the expansion of the nation's railroads. At the end of the Civil War, there were 35,000 miles of railroad track in the United States, all of various gauges, or widths between the two rails.

Standardization and Consolidation

By the mid-1870s the amount of track had doubled, and by 1890 it had more than doubled again. In 1900 passenger and freight trains steamed along almost 200,000 miles of rails. By then track also was laid according to a standard gauge—4 feet, 8½ inches wide—so that freight could move from line to line without having to be unloaded from one car and reloaded onto another. This standardized railroad network bound all sections of the country into one market and one nation. Trains could carry bulky products long distances quickly and cheaply, making it possible for businesses to sell their goods across the continent. In 1860 railroads carried less than half as much freight as inland waterways. By 1890 railroads carried five times as much.

Railroads were not only the biggest shippers of industrial products; they were also American industry's best customers. In the mid-1880s, for example, rails were the single most important product of American steel companies. In addition, construction and operation of railroads required huge amounts of coal to power locomotives, lumber for ties and cars, iron for bridges, and petroleum products to lubricate moving parts.

Consolidating of smaller lines in the Midwest, East, and South was as important to development as the building of railroads spanning the West. Railroad building in the East was intended to promote specific cities or to serve local needs. As a result, hundreds of unconnected small lines, with tracks of varying gauges, were in use. The South had more than 400 railroads averaging less than 40 miles each. The challenge facing Eastern capitalists was to create a single rail system from this maze of small companies.

▲ *Across the Continent* by Currier and Ives, 1868 Currier and Ives produced America's most popular and successful prints of the 1800s. *Why did rail transport surpass water transport in the late 1800s?*

Railroad consolidation proceeded rapidly from the end of the Civil War to the turn of the century. By 1890 the Pennsylvania Railroad was a consolidation of 73 smaller companies with more than 5,000 miles of track. The Southern Pacific Railway had pieced together companies with 8,500 miles of lines. Eventually most rail traffic was controlled by 7 giant systems with terminals in major cities and scores of branches reaching into the countryside.

Getting a "Share of the Business"

In gaining and using such power, many railroad builders became tough, ruthless, and unethical competitors who amassed fortunes in the course of their activities. Railroad consolidator Jay Gould sold small lines that he owned to large railroads that he controlled at prices far above the small railroads' actual worth. When railroad builder Collis Huntington remarked, "It takes money to fix things," he meant bribing government officials, not repairing equipment! In describing his industry, railroad executive Charles Francis Adams, Jr., observed:

> *Honesty and good faith are scarcely regarded. Certainly they are not tolerated at all if they interfere with a man's getting his "share of the business." Gradually this demoralizing spirit of low cunning has pervaded the entire system. Its moral tone is deplorably low. . . .*

Cornelius Vanderbilt

One of the most successful railroad consolidators was Cornelius Vanderbilt, who built the New York Central system. By the mid-1850s, he had built the largest steamboat fleet in America. Yet Vanderbilt saw that the future of transportation was in railroads. So at age 73 he merged 3 short New York railroads he had purchased to form the New York Central, which ran from New York City to Buffalo. Within 4 years Vanderbilt extended his control over lines all the way to Chicago. In addition to bringing many lines under one management, Vanderbilt made great improvements in service. He was one of the first to use the Westinghouse air brake and the very first to lay a four-track main line—two tracks for freight and two for passenger traffic.

Vanderbilt, like other railroad tycoons, was a combination of shrewd speculator, ruthless competitor, and visionary. Yet Vanderbilt and other railroad entrepreneurs provided great benefits, too. Standard-gauge track was universally accepted, and standard time zones were established to simplify scheduling. The big systems were able to improve equipment, to shift cars from one section of the country to another according to seasonal needs, and to speed long-distance transportation. They made railroad operation so much more efficient that the average rate per mile for a ton of freight dropped from 2 cents in 1860 to less than 1 cent in 1900. The railroad executives also showed entrepreneurs how to operate large companies across great distances.

Section 1 ★ Review

Checking for Understanding

1. **Identify** Alexander Graham Bell, Thomas Alva Edison, Cornelius Vanderbilt.

2. **Define** entrepreneur, economies of scale.

3. **List** reasons for the growth of industry.

4. **Describe** how specific technology accelerated the growth of industry.

Critical Thinking

5. **Applying Ideas**   One writer noted that, "This standardized railroad network bound all sections of the country into one market and one nation." Explain what the writer meant by this statement and why this was so. Then name some standardizing influences that exist in the United States today.

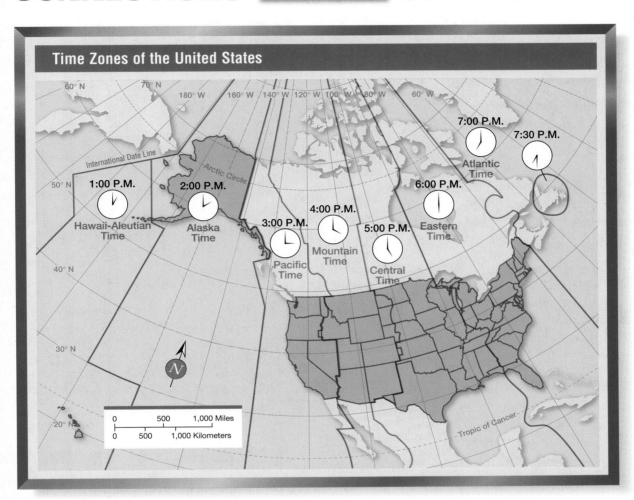

Time Zones of the United States

Standard Time Zones

Throughout most of the nineteenth century, few Americans could agree on the time of day because every community determined its own time by the position of the sun. When it was noon in New York City, for example, it was 11:55 A.M. in Philadelphia and 11:47 A.M. in Washington, D.C. Railways, however, required a single standard of time for scheduling and routing. In 1883 American and Canadian railroads established standardized time zones.

In 1884 delegates from 27 nations met in Washington, D.C., and divided the earth into 24 time zones. The base time zone was established with the Prime Meridian (0° longitude) as its midpoint. This zone extended about 7½ degrees on either side of the Prime Meridian. Since the Prime Meridian ran through Greenwich in Britain, the time in the base zone became known as Greenwich time.

Making the Geography Connection

1. Why did standardized time zones become necessary in the 1800s?

Linking Past and Present

2. If time zones were being set up today, do you think the base zone would be in Britain? Why or why not?

★★★

Growth of Big Business

Setting the Scene

Section Focus

As railroads gave industrialists access to raw materials and markets, great opportunities developed for business expansion. The result was "Big Business." By 1900 gigantic companies owned scores of plants, sold products nationwide, and had hundreds of millions of dollars in capital and credit behind them.

◄ COVER OF HORATIO ALGER NOVEL

Objectives

After studying this section, you should be able to

★ discuss the methods big business used to become successful.

★ explain why incorporation encouraged business growth.

Key Terms

corporation, holding company, trust, horizontal integration, vertical integration

---

The railroads were America's first "Big Business." Founding a major railroad consumed larger sums of money than any previous American enterprise. The investment required was so great that no one individual could make it. Instead, a large railroad line was organized as a **corporation**—a company formed by a group of investors who each receive a share of ownership in proportion to the amount they invested. Investors also enjoyed the protection of limited liability: they risked only the amount of their investment, even if the corporation went bankrupt and could not pay its bills.

The expansion of the railroads, along with other improvements in transportation and communication, created the mass market. No longer were manufacturers limited to local or regional sales. The mass market made mass production practical.

■ Benefits of Big Business

Corporate structure allowed entrepreneurs in many industries to raise the money they needed to launch or expand companies as opportunities arose. Big business enjoyed many advantages.

Efficiency in Production and Labor

Large companies could manufacture enough products to meet the demands of a national market. They produced better products at lower cost than their smaller competitors through the economies of scale that resulted from using the newest processes and combining operations formerly performed by separate companies. High salaries were offered in order to get expert managers. At the same time, they increased efficiency by establishing separate departments for specialized functions such as purchasing, production, research, distribution, and sales.

In conducting their operations, big companies organized work to gain maximum production from their employees. A steel company engineer, Frederick W. Taylor, developed a system to study and time workers and to make changes so their jobs could be performed more efficiently. Such studies even included counting the steps a worker took in moving from one place to another on the job and determining what size shovels were best for shoveling coal, rice, and iron ore!

The Big Business of Meatpacking

The advantages of big business were shown dramatically by the development of large meatpacking companies. In the past, fresh meat had been slaughtered locally, and every town had at least one slaughterhouse. When the refrigerated railroad car made it possible to ship fresh meat over long distances, huge companies such as Swift and Armour appeared, selling their products throughout the country. The big packers were so highly organized and efficient that they could sell meat at a loss and make their profit from the rest of the carcass. Chicago humorist Finley Peter Dunne, writing under the name of the fictional Irish saloon keeper

"Mr. Dooley," hardly exaggerated about Armour when he noted:

> *A cow goes lowin' softly into Armour's an' comes out glue, gelatin, fertylizer, celooloid, joolry, sofy cushions, hair restorer, washin' sody, soap, lithrachoor an' bed springs so quick that while aft she's still cow, for'ard she may be anything fr'm buttons to pannyma hats.*

Big Business Tactics

Because of their efficiency, organization, and size, large businesses were frequently in a position to take advantage of their competitors and sometimes of the public. Big companies could demand volume discounts from shippers. They could sell their products in an area at a loss until local competitors were forced to shut down or sell out. If a large company succeeded in getting a monopoly in its industry, it could raise consumer prices and pay less to suppliers of raw materials.

Big business in the late nineteenth century resulted from the vision of people who

AMERICAN PORTRAITS

Gustavus Swift
1839–1903

At the age of 16, Gustavus Swift borrowed $25, bought a cow, slaughtered it, and sold the beef at a $10 profit. From that point on, Swift devoted his life to making money from meat.

Swift first opened several butcher shops. With a talent for buying only the best cattle, he next moved to Chicago—capital of the cattle market—and went into business shipping livestock by rail to Eastern cities. He soon realized, however, that he could

make more money butchering the cattle in Chicago and shipping the meat.

At first, to prevent spoilage, Swift could ship only during winter months. But then he hired an engineer who developed a refrigerated railroad car that made it possible to ship year-round. As hungry workers swelled the size of Eastern cities, Swift & Co. made great profits by shipping huge quantities of meat to feed them.

▲ MARKETING GOODS Mass production of consumer goods, such as hats, combined with transportation improvements inspired entrepreneurs to print merchandise catalogs and open mail-order stores. *Why were big businesses able to sell for less than local companies?*

recognized great opportunities for wealth and were willing to take risks to get it. The companies they organized—American Tobacco, General Electric, and United Fruit, among them—came to dominate their industries and sold products not just nationwide but to the entire world.

Business Tactics

In attaining success, however, many entrepreneurs showed few scruples in driving competitors out of business. Their tactics included evading the law, bribing officials, destroying labor unions, and devastating the environment. Some entrepreneurs commonly sold products at below their cost until local businesses were forced to close down or sell out.

Mixed Feelings Toward Big Business

The American public, therefore, had mixed feelings about big business and its leaders. Americans worried about the corrupting influence of wealth and power. Yet others admitted that they benefited from big business's efficiency, its lower prices, and

the jobs it created. Historian Vernon L. Parrington said of the entrepreneurs:

> *These new Americans were primitive souls, ruthless, predatory, capable, single-minded men; rogues and rascals often, but never feeble, never hindered by petty scruples, never given to puling [whimpering] or whining. . . . Analyze the most talked-of men of the age and one is likely to find a splendid audacity coupled with immense wastefulness. A note of tough-mindedness marks them. . . . They fought their way encased in rhinoceros hides.*

Rags to Riches

Success in business became a best-selling theme in popular fiction. Horatio Alger became wealthy himself when he wrote novels like *Mark the Match Boy, Tattered Tom,* and more than 100 others—all "rags-to-riches" stories of young men who became successful in business because of hard work and lucky breaks.

The Role of Corporations

American law allowed the formation of business corporations, and conditions in the United States encouraged their existence. As a business form, the corporation offered a number of advantages over a partnership or a sole proprietorship. The corporation had a permanence that lasted beyond the lives of its owners or stockholders. That meant company managers could confidently plan far into the future.

Kinds of Companies

By selling stocks and bonds, a corporation could raise the capital, or investment money, for its operations. Small amounts of capital from many individual investors could be pooled into the huge sums needed to start or expand a large company. In that way no one investor would have to take a big financial risk. To reduce risk even more, investors could spread it out by purchasing stock in several corporations. One specialized form of corporation, the **holding company,** became very popular. Holding companies manufactured no products and had no customers. They existed only to own stock in other corporations. Through holding companies, wealthy capitalists could own controlling interests in many businesses.

Other companies were organized into trusts. **A trust** was formed when several companies gave control of their operations to a single board of trustees. The shareholders of each individual company continued to own it and keep its profits, but management of all companies in the trust was in the same hands. Through holding companies and trusts, entrepreneurs formed the huge business combinations that dominated the late nineteenth century. Some combinations were able to restrict or prevent competition among their members.

Ways to Combine Companies

Business consolidation—combining companies into one unit—took various forms. Sometimes companies were consolidated by **horizontal integration,** in which several firms engaged in the same kind of business were joined together. If a horizontal combination became large enough, it could achieve a monopoly of that industry.

Companies also were consolidated by **vertical integration,** which joined businesses engaged in different but related activities. A vertical combination, for example, might include under the same ownership individual companies that provided raw materials, transported those raw materials to factories, manufactured a product from those raw materials, and distributed and sold the finished product.

A horizontal combination, once established, was able to expand vertically because of the control its size gave it over both suppliers and distributors. Similarly, a vertical combination could become so efficient that it expanded horizontally by buying its competitors, forcing them into trusts, or driving them out of business.

Section 2 ★ Review

Checking for Understanding

1. **Identify** Frederick W. Taylor, Horatio Alger.

2. **Define** corporation, holding company, trust, horizontal integration, vertical integration.

3. **Describe** the practices that made big business successful, but at the same time open to criticism from many Americans.

4. **List** the various ways businesses can be organized.

Critical Thinking

5. **Evaluating Change** How might the shift to the prevalence of big business work to the advantage or disadvantage of a consumer? A worker? An owner of a small business?

★★

Captains of Industry

Setting the Scene

Section Focus

The oil and steel industries were each dominated by a man as ruthless as he was efficient. Rising from poverty to attain great wealth and power, John D. Rockefeller and Andrew Carnegie represented to many the American Dream.

Objectives

After studying this section, you should be able to

★ compare the methods used by Carnegie and Rockefeller to achieve success.

★ explain social Darwinism.

Key Terms

rebate, social Darwinism, philanthropy

◀ COVER OF *McCLURE'S MAGAZINE*

*A*lthough giant combinations arose to control the beef, flour, whiskey, tobacco, lead, and sugar industries, as well as many others, by 1900 the American economy ran on oil, and its backbone was steel. No industrialists exemplified the principles of doing "big business" in late-nineteenth-century America more than the entrepreneurs who dominated these two basic industries—John D. Rockefeller in oil and Andrew Carnegie in steel.

■ Rockefeller and the Standard Oil Trust

The most successful example of horizontal consolidation was the Standard Oil Trust, which gained a near monopoly of oil refineries and pipelines. The guiding genius behind Standard Oil was John D. Rockefeller, who during his 98 years, from 1839 to 1937, amassed what was at the time the world's largest fortune—almost $1 billion.

The Early Years

Rockefeller went to work at age 16 as a bookkeeper in a wholesale commission and produce company in Cleveland, Ohio. Dominated by the idea that he was "bound to be rich," he saved $800 in 3 years on a salary of $15 per week. At 19 he left his job and opened his own commission house. In only 4 years he increased his capital to about $100,000. Then in 1862, at age 23, he put all his money into a new and growing industry—petroleum refining.

Until the 1850s, petroleum, then called "rock oil," had been used only as a patent medicine. In 1855 scientists discovered that petroleum, when refined into kerosene, gave better light than whale oil in lamps and made a much better lubricant than animal fat.

The first oil well, drilled in 1859, set off a stampede to western Pennsylvania much like the California gold rush of 1849. Land values jumped from a few dollars an acre to hundreds of dollars a square foot, new towns appeared overnight, and the demand for kerosene spread worldwide. In spite of the Civil War, the petroleum industry grew so fast that by 1865 oil products had risen to fourth place among American exports.

Drilling for oil was always a big gamble, and Rockefeller realized oil refining was a safer investment. The entire oil business was highly disorganized, however. Fortunes were made and lost overnight as the price of oil fluctuated wildly. Rockefeller believed such unstable conditions resulted from competition among thousands of small producers and hundreds of small refiners.

Standard Oil Becomes a Giant

By 1870 Rockefeller's firm, the Standard Oil Company of Ohio, was the largest of 26 refineries in Cleveland, processing 2 or 3 percent of the crude oil produced in the United States. Over the next 9 years, Rockefeller gained control of more than 90 percent of the nation's refining business and brought order to a chaotic industry. But to achieve stability and efficiency in the oil business, Rockefeller used methods so shrewdly brutal that when they were revealed he became one of the most hated men in America.

One of Standard Oil's major weapons was the **rebate,** or discount, on freight charges. In 1872 the company offered to give certain railroads all its shipping business if those railroads secretly agreed to charge Standard Oil 25 to 50 percent less than they charged its competitors. In return for its business, these railroads also promised to tell Rockefeller the destinations of all his competitors' shipments. This information gave him valuable insights into his rivals' business dealings. These secret arrangements gave Standard Oil such an advantage over other Cleveland refineries that within 3 months all but 5 were forced

to sell out to Rockefeller. Once it controlled oil refining in Cleveland, Standard Oil moved rapidly toward a nationwide monopoly by allying with the strongest companies throughout the industry. In 1880 a committee of the New York legislature reported on the extent of Standard Oil's domination of the oil business:

❝ *It owns and controls the pipe lines of the producing regions that connect with the railroads. It controls both ends of these roads. It ships 95 percent of all oil. . . . It dictates terms and rates to the railroads. It has bought out and frozen out refiners all over the country. By means of the superior facilities for transportation which it thus possessed, it could overbid [its competitors for crude oil] in the producing regions and undersell [its competitors] in the markets of the world.* ❞

Visualizing **History** ▲ JOHN D. ROCKEFELLER Although he was ruthless in business dealings, John D. Rockefeller always carried dimes in his pockets to give to small children he encountered on the street. *What changes did Rockefeller bring to the oil industry?*

▲ IDA TARBELL Ida Tarbell was one of several American writers who played a major part in exposing social problems. ***What company did Tarbell target in her series of articles for* McClure's Magazine?**

By a secret agreement that became known as the Standard Oil Trust, Rockefeller moved in 1882 to consolidate his control of the oil industry further by combining 40 companies under a single management. Once in control of most of the refining and transportation of oil in the United States, Standard Oil expanded vertically. It gained control of oil fields to have an independent supply source, and it marketed natural gas. At the other end of the production process, Standard Oil moved into the distribution of petroleum products, both in the United States and overseas. Eventually Standard Oil controlled a fleet of oceangoing tankers and door-to-door delivery wagons in Europe. It even manufactured and sold cooking stoves to increase the demand for kerosene!

Following Standard Oil's Lead

Standard Oil's spectacular success led others to establish horizontal combinations of companies in industries as varied as whiskey, bituminous coal, and rope. The purpose of these combinations was mainly to prevent overproduction and to keep prices up. Yet it was difficult to control an entire industry and to keep new firms out of the market. Such efforts to obtain monopolies were greatly resented by small business people and consumers. Vertical combinations, on the other hand, were not monopolistic. The savings that resulted from the economies they brought to production were passed on to consumers in lower prices. Vertical combination thus became a common form of business organization.

Business Tactics Exposed

Although Rockefeller's rivals in the oil industry were painfully aware of his ruthless methods, it was an investigative journalist who exposed them to the public. This courageous woman was Ida Tarbell.

In 1903, in a series of brilliant articles in *McClure's Magazine,* Tarbell revealed Rockefeller's secret deals and his high-pressure tactics. She explained how companies controlled by Standard Oil continued to do business under their former names. She documented how, to conceal his control of these companies, Rockefeller appointed "dummy directors," who were sometimes employees such as errand-runners or secretaries.

Rockefeller, a devout churchgoer and Sunday school teacher, did not think that his actions were wrong. He pointed out that what he had done to destroy his competitors had not been illegal when he first did it. Rebates, for example, were granted by railroads to big shippers in many other industries. When buying out his competitors, Rockefeller offered to pay them in either cash or Standard Oil stock, advising them to take the stock. Those who took his advice became rich.

Much of Rockefeller's advantage over competitors came from his passion for efficiency and his hatred of waste. Standard Oil continuously improved its product. The company had few labor troubles because it paid its workers well. It tried to protect their jobs in times of depression and was one of the first companies to pay old-age pensions.

Andrew Carnegie, Master of Steel

The most remarkable example of the creation of a vertical combination was the giant steel corporation built by Andrew Carnegie.

Coming to Pittsburgh from Scotland at the age of 13, Carnegie went to work in a cotton factory where he earned $1.20 for working a 72-hour week. He saw an opportunity to grow with the railroad, however, and in 1853 he went to work as a clerk and telegraph operator for the Pennsylvania Railroad. His ability, energy, and ambition were so great that at age 23 he became superintendent of the railroad's western division.

Looking to the Future

While working for the railroad, Carnegie wisely invested his earnings in iron companies. As the railroads grew, Carnegie foresaw his opportunity for personal success in the increasing demand for rails, bridges, and locomotives. By age 30, when he left the railroad to manage an iron bridge company, his investments were producing an annual income of nearly $50,000.

After seven years making iron bridges, Carnegie again looked at the future and saw it was in steel. In 1873 he formed a group of investors to build the largest and most modern steel mill in the world near Pittsburgh. Carnegie was the first person in the United States to use two new ways of making steel—the Bessemer process and the open-hearth process. These processes enabled him to produce steel so cheaply that it could now be used for rails and construction girders, as well as for cutlery and precision machines.

Another Giant Is Born

Almost overnight Carnegie changed the character of the industry. Previously iron and steel had been manufactured at hundreds of small furnaces all over the country. But Bessemer converters and open-hearth furnaces required heavy investments of capital and huge amounts of coke and ore to keep them going. Small companies were soon forced out of business by big ones.

In less than 20 years, Carnegie was the greatest steelmaker in the world. One reason for his phenomenal success was that he took the guesswork out of making steel by getting the best technical and scientific experts he could find. Carnegie liked to boast that he "was smart enough to surround himself with men far cleverer than himself." For example, his managers were able to determine almost to the penny what it cost to produce a ton of steel. With this knowledge, Carnegie could set prices below his competitors and still make a profit. His chemists found uses for by-products previously considered to be industrial waste, and they discovered how to use low-grade ores.

▲ *THE STEEL MILL* by Maximillian Luce, 1895
Although the growth of the oil industry after the Civil War was phenomenal, the steel industry achieved even greater growth. ***What benefits did the success of these industries bring to the nation?***

In his constant effort to be more efficient, Carnegie combined all of the processes required for making steel into one great vertical combination. In addition to blast furnaces and steel mills, the Carnegie Steel Company controlled rich iron ore deposits near Lake Superior, fleets of ships to carry the ore over the Great Lakes, a railroad to carry the ore from the Lake Erie region to Pittsburgh, coal mines in Pennsylvania to fire the blast furnaces, and factories for producing finished steel products such as wire.

Crushing Labor and Gobbling the Competition

Seeking out the ablest people in the industry, Carnegie bought their loyalty by making them partners. Equally alert for ability inside his companies, he rapidly promoted exceptional employees. Common laborers in his mills fared less well, however, as he drove wages down and hours up. In 1892, with his partner, Henry C. Frick, he crushed the steelworkers' union, so that the 12-hour day remained standard for many years.

During the three major depressions of the late 1800s, while other steel companies closed down, Carnegie expanded. He rebuilt his factories to be even more efficient and acquired his weakened competitors.

■ Social Darwinism and the Industrialists

Andrew Carnegie was making $25 million a year at a time when there was no income tax. His workers, on the other hand, earned $8 or $9 a week. He made steel so cheaply and competed so mercilessly that remaining steel companies faced bankruptcy. Carnegie and most other great industrialists found justification for these actions and their consequences in a philosophy known as **social Darwinism,** which applied the biological theories of naturalist Charles Darwin to human society.

Darwin believed that in nature a competition exists in which only the fittest—the strongest, most clever, most efficient—

plants and animals survive. The weak individuals die out, and each species thereby remains strong and healthy. Philosophers such as Yale professor William Graham Sumner argued that this competition also operated in human society, and that industrialists like Rockefeller and Carnegie had succeeded because of their rare talents. "The millionaires are a product of natural selection," Sumner wrote. "They get high wages and live in luxury, but the bargain is a good one for society." Not surprisingly, Andrew Carnegie and John D. Rockefeller both believed wholeheartedly in the philosophy of social Darwinism. Carnegie called it a method better than elections for selecting leaders. "By a process of pitiless testing we discover who are the strong and who are the weak," he wrote. "To the strong we give power in the form of the autocratic control of industry and of wealth." Rockefeller told his Sunday school class that his business practices merely demonstrated "the survival of the fittest . . . a law of nature and a law of God."

Visualizing **History** ▲ **ANDREW CARNEGIE** If any entrepreneur symbolized the rags-to-riches legend, it was Andrew Carnegie. The son of poor immigrants, Carnegie built a company that by 1900 was making one-fourth of the nation's steel and serving a world market. *What caused Carnegie to believe the future was in iron and steel?*

▲ *The Hatch Family* by Jonathan Eastman Johnson, 1871 The artist portrays a family in fine clothing enjoying a comfortable afternoon at home. Note that parents, children, and grandchildren live in the household—a typical arrangement for the times among the rich as well as the poor. **What is philanthropy?**

But for Carnegie the achievement of great power and wealth was not enough. He looked beyond success to question whether those who profited from society owed anything to it in return.

Writing in the *North American Review* in 1889, Carnegie maintained that a wealthy person should:

> 66 . . . *[c]onsider all surplus revenues which come to him simply as trust funds, which he is called upon to administer . . . in a manner which, in his judgment, is best calculated to produce the most beneficial results for the community . . . becoming the mere agent and trustee for his poorer brethren, bringing to their service his superior wisdom, experience, and ability to administer, doing for them better than they would or could do for themselves.* 99

Carnegie practiced what he preached. In 1901 he sold his steel properties to the newly formed United States Steel Corporation for $250 million and withdrew from business to devote the rest of his life to **philanthropy,** or actions benefiting society. By the time he died in 1919, he had donated $350 million—mostly to building public libraries, improving education, and promoting research. Rockefeller also returned much of his fortune to society in gifts that totaled more than $500 million.

Sherman Antitrust Act

In 1881 *The Atlantic Monthly* published an article entitled "The Story of a Great Monopoly," by Henry Demarest Lloyd, telling how the Standard Oil Company had monopolized the oil-refining business. The article caused such a sensation that the magazine had to print three times as many copies as usual. Throughout the next decade, as it was revealed that many industries were in danger of being monopolized, demands for federal regulation came from many groups—small businesses, farmers, consumers, laborers, and even some big businesses.

Even officials of the great corporations began to have concerns about growing public cries for reform. Henry O. Havemeyer, head of the American Sugar Refining Company, which controlled a trust producing more than 90 percent of the nation's sugar, urged that manufacturers of products in general use should submit to some federal regulation.

In the election of 1888, both the Democratic and the Republican political parties promised action. Then in 1890, with only one dissenting vote, Congress passed the Sherman Antitrust Act. The Sherman Act wrote into federal law a traditional principle of English common law. This is the idea that private monopolies and artificial restrictions on trade were wrong. In the words of the act:

66 *Every contract, combination, in the form of trust or otherwise, or conspiracy, in restraint of trade or commerce among the several states or with foreign nations, is hereby declared to be illegal."* 99

The Sherman Act had little effect on preventing business consolidation. It was not strictly enforced and was so loosely worded that its meaning was doubtful. Did the law mean, for example, that all mergers were unlawful, that all business transactions must be open and public, that any contract that permitted one company to take business from another was illegal?

Under the Constitution, the answers to such questions are left to the federal courts, which in the 1890s were probably more favorable to business interests than at any other time in American history. In *United States* v. *E. C. Knight Company*, the Supreme Court in 1895 agreed that the American Sugar Refining Company was a trust and that it enjoyed a near monopoly in the manufacture of sugar. But the Court ruled that the company's activities did not violate the Sherman Act because manufacturing was not interstate commerce.

The Supreme Court's decision in the *Knight* case was followed by one of the greatest periods of business consolidation in American history. In 1890 there had been 24 trusts worth a total of $436 million. In 1900 there were 183 huge combinations with a total worth of more than $3 billion. At the same time, big business simply turned away from trusts and toward holding companies in creating combinations.

In spite of its early failures, the Sherman Act was an important law. It signaled to large corporations to be more aware of how their activities looked to the public. As a result, corporate image and public relations became important business concerns. Later regulation of big business and industry would depend on additional legislation, on the interpretations of future courts, and on attitudes in the executive branch about enforcement.

Section 3 ★ Review

Checking for Understanding

1. **Identify** John D. Rockefeller, Standard Oil, Ida Tarbell, Andrew Carnegie, Sherman Antitrust Act.

2. **Define** rebate, social Darwinism, philanthropy.

3. **Compare** the methods used by Rockefeller and Carnegie to build their industrial empires.

4. **Explain** why the Sherman Antitrust Act failed to control big business.

Critical Thinking

5. **Judging Actions** Would the United States have been better off with or without industrial giants such as John D. Rockefeller and Andrew Carnegie? Explain.

Social Studies Skills

Map and Graph Skills

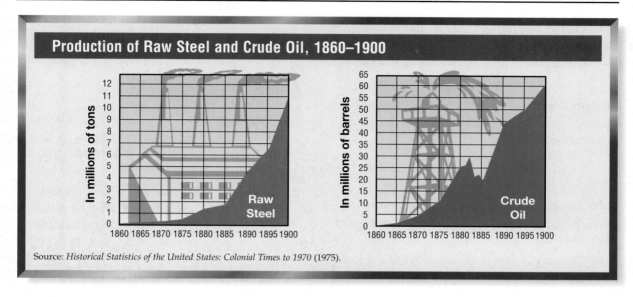

Production of Raw Steel and Crude Oil, 1860–1900

Source: *Historical Statistics of the United States: Colonial Times to 1970* (1975).

Reading a Line Graph

When historical information involves numbers and statistics, it often is presented on a graph. Graphic data can be presented in the form of circle graphs, bar graphs, or line graphs.

A line graph charts information about two variables. Line graphs typically show how one variable, depicted on the vertical axis, changes over time. Time, the second variable—whether minutes, hours, days, or years—is recorded on the horizontal axis. To maximize the information you obtain from a line graph, follow this procedure:

- **Read** the title to get a general idea of what the graph shows.
- **Examine** the labels. Labels define the two variables and explain what the lines and/or points on the graph represent. Labels also specify the units of measurement.
- **Analyze** the graph. Look for increases, decreases, and sudden shifts. Analyze the *amount* and the *rate* of change.
- **Draw** conclusions or generalizations from the statistics presented on the graph. What trends or patterns appear?

Practicing the Skill

1. Apply the steps on reading a line graph to analyze the two graphs on this page.

   a. What time period is under study in the graph?

   b. How many units are represented by each point on the vertical axis of each of the graphs? How much time is represented by each point on the horizontal axis of each graph?

   c. Approximately how much did steel and oil production increase between 1885 and 1890? During what 5-year period did the largest dip in oil production occur?

   d. What generalization can be made about steel and oil production between 1860 and 1875?

2. Explain why the statistics are shown on two different graphs.

Using Vocabulary

Use the listed vocabulary words to complete the sentences that follow. You will use all but one of the words. Write an original sentence using the remaining word.

entrepreneurs	horizontal integration
rebate	vertical integration
corporations	

1. Businesses organized as _____ can raise capital from a number of investors.
2. When governments practice laissez-faire policies, _____ can run businesses with very little government regulation.
3. Carnegie and Rockefeller consolidated a number of businesses using both _____ and _____ .

Reviewing Facts

1. **Enumerate** the factors that boosted industrial growth in the United States.
2. **State** the roles played by the railroad in the growth of American industry.
3. **Identify** the strategies that big business used to become successful.
4. **Summarize** the common elements in the strategies of Rockefeller, Carnegie, and Vanderbilt.
5. **Describe** the provisions of the Sherman Antitrust Act and its effects.

Understanding Concepts

Individual Initiative

1. Cite examples of individuals and how they used their initiative to shape industrial growth.
2. In what ways did Vanderbilt's individual initiative benefit others?

Government Restriction

3. Would a social Darwinist support or oppose laissez-faire government policies? Explain why.

4. Lack of government restriction benefited some businesses and hurt others. Which types of businesses benefited, and which might have been more successful with some protection?

Critical Thinking

1. **Judging Effects** Discuss how a big company manufacturing products high in both quantity and quality benefits the consumer and the company.
2. **Analyzing Political Cartoons** Study the cartoon on this page entitled "The Monster Monopoly," and answer the questions that follow.

   a. What figures are shown?

   b. Who or what does the monster symbolize?

   c. What does the cartoon suggest about big business?

▲ THE MONSTER MONOPOLY, 1884

Writing About History

Cause and Effect

Imagine you are a nineteenth-century writer who hopes to publish a collection of true rags-to-riches stories. Write a brief biography of a nineteenth-century captain of industry who began with little and built an industrial empire. Choose an entrepreneur from this chapter, or conduct research about another from the same period.

Focus on what you believe to be the causes of your subject's success. Write about the traits and experiences that influenced this person's growth. What decisions were the key to success? What risks did the entrepreneur take, and what were the results of those risks? Were there mistakes and failures along the road to success?

Cooperative Learning

Work with a partner to research the history of the Bell telephone system from the parent company's formation to its breakup into smaller companies. Then discuss between yourselves what the company's contributions to the nation were and why the system was broken up by the government. Present your findings to the class, with one partner explaining Bell's contributions and the other explaining why it was broken up. Compare your findings with those presented by other class pairs.

Social Studies Skills

Making Comparisons

To *compare* means to examine data in order to identify similarities and/or differences. You can compare things that are very different or that are very much alike. To make a comparison accurate, however, you must note at least one similarity and one difference.

Practicing the Skill

The graph on this page shows the production of bituminous coal from 1860 to 1900. Compare this graph with the graphs of raw steel and crude oil production found on page 513.

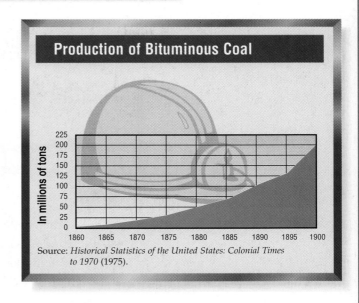

Production of Bituminous Coal

In millions of tons

225
200
175
150
125
100
75
50
25
0

1860 1865 1870 1875 1880 1885 1890 1895 1900

Source: *Historical Statistics of the United States: Colonial Times to 1970* (1975).

1. What three subjects can you compare by using these graphs?

2. Why is it easier to compare the production of coal and raw steel than that of coal and oil?

3. For the production of raw steel, what trend does the graph show? How does this trend compare with the production trends in the other two graphs?

Using Your Journal

Read over your notes about Rockefeller and Carnegie. Do you think that people who make enormous amounts of money have an obligation to donate some of it to society? Can you think of any modern-day "Rockefellers" and "Carnegies"? Organize your thoughts into a paragraph in your journal.

CHAPTER 19

★★★

An Urban Society
1860–1900

► UNION SYMBOL

Setting the Scene

Focus

One factor supporting industrialization in the late nineteenth century was the abundant labor supply. For workers, poor pay and working conditions led to a renewed interest in labor unions. Efforts by unions such as the Knights of Labor to improve conditions, however, were only modestly successful. The union movement was also influenced by the influx of millions of immigrants. These new arrivals crowded into America's cities and brought with them the cultural heritage of their old world.

Concepts to Understand

★ How unity among workers led to the growth of unions
★ How conflict between workers and employees resulted in unrest

Read to Discover . . .

★ the difficulties experienced by labor unions in the late 1800s.
★ the major factors behind the migration to American cities.

Journal Notes

What were some of the major obstacles facing immigrants coming to the United States in the late 1800s? Note examples as you read the chapter.

CULTURAL

● **1868** *Immigration drops to 130,000*

● **1876** *Central Park opens in New York City*

1860	1870

● **1867** *Great Western Surveys begin*

● **1872** *Victoria Claflin Woodhull, first woman presidential candidate, is nominated*

POLITICAL

◀ FAMILY AT ELLIS ISLAND, EARLY 1900S

History AND ART

Hester Street
by George Luks, 1905

Hester Street in New York City—part of a Jewish immigrant neighborhood—was filled with vitality and color.

- **1883** *Brooklyn Bridge in New York City is completed*

1880

- **1886** *Haymarket Square riot takes place in Chicago*

- **1893** *Columbian Exposition opens in Chicago*

1890

- **1892** *Steelworkers' strike put down at the Homestead mill*
- **1894** *Pullman strike ends*

★★★

The Workers' Plight

Setting the Scene

Section Focus

The new industrial age brought many problems for workers, who toiled long hours for low wages. In an attempt to improve working conditions, workers began to organize. In spite of rapid growth after the Civil War, unions encountered many difficulties.

Objectives

After studying this section, you should be able to

★ describe the conditions under which people worked during the late 1800s.

★ explain the obstacles faced by labor unions during this period.

Key Terms

real wages, company town, scrip, business cycle, blacklist, lockout, scab, collective bargaining

▲ COAL MINER'S HELMET

With the growth of industry, the number of factory workers rose from about 900,000 in 1860 to more than 3.2 million in 1890. Industrialization affected various aspects of workers' lives—where they worked and lived, the size of the workforce, and the nature of work itself. Many workers were forced to make the transition from skilled to semiskilled or unskilled labor. The experience and skill of such artisans as carpenters, silversmiths, and furniture makers no longer gave them any advantage over the unskilled. It took little training to tend a machine.

■ Problems

With machines taking the place of human skills, work became monotonous. Workers concentrated on highly specific, repetitive tasks and could take little pride in the fruits of their labor. As factories increased the efficiency of production, more and more people worked for fewer and fewer employers. The workers began to feel like "cogs in a wheel." Machines were designed to work at a given pace, and the workers were forced to try and keep up.

Unfair Conditions of Employment

Low wages and long hours posed additional burdens for industrial workers. Workdays of 10 to 14 hours were common. Although **real wages**—wages adjusted for inflation—rose more than 10 percent between 1870 and 1900, the average income remained inadequate. Most industrial workers earned between $400 and $500 a year during the 1890s; $600 was the minimum annual income needed to maintain a decent standard of living.

ELEMENTARY SCHOOL, EARLY 1900s

Visualizing
History

▲ CHILD LABOR Children were often employed in small, makeshift factories in which workers were hired on a piecework basis. *How were state labor laws evaded?*

In some industries workers were required to live in **company towns,** built and run by the companies. The best known was the town of Pullman, Illinois, where every citizen worked for the Pullman Palace Car Company. The usual practice was for companies to deduct money from the workers' pay for rent and advances to the company store as well as medical and fuel fees. Some companies paid their workers in **scrip,** or company money, that could be redeemed only at the company store. This store usually charged higher prices than did stores in other towns, and many workers remained in constant debt.

Health and Safety Hazards

Factory work was unhealthful as well as dangerous. Miners breathed coal dust all day. Factory workers breathed sawdust, stone dust, cotton dust, or toxic fumes. Heavy machines, grouped together on shop and mill floors for the sake of efficiency, caused an appallingly high injury rate among workers. An 1884 government report described working conditions for women in a small factory in Boston:

❝ *The work is dangerous . . . [they] are liable to get their fingers jammed under the bench, or caught in the die when it comes down to press the parts of the buttons together. A man (although not a surgeon) is provided to dress wounds three times for each individual without charge; afterwards, the person injured must pay all expenses. There are 35 machines in use, and accidents are of very frequent occurrence.* ❞

Child Labor

Children, some as young as six, were regularly employed as factory workers. Throughout the 1800s there were some efforts to restrict child labor, but state laws were usually worded in such a way that they could be easily evaded both by employers and by parents who needed the income. In 1885 in New Jersey, there were 340,000 children of school age. About 90,000 of them did not attend school; most worked full-time jobs. Industrial work was neither less difficult nor less dangerous for children than it was for adults. As a Pennsylvania newspaper, the *Luzerne Union,* reported in January 1876:

> ❝ *During the past week, nearly one boy a day has been killed, and the public has become so familiar with these calamities that no attention is given them after the first announcement through a newspaper or friend.* ❞

Job Insecurity

Always looming was the threat of pay cuts or layoffs. Workers were vulnerable to the **business cycle**—a recurring sequence of change in business activity. Beginning with a period of prosperity, business activity declines until a low point, or depression, is reached. A period of recovery follows when business conditions become more active. A period of prosperity is again reached. The cycle is then repeated.

In the late 1800s, business went through many such cycles. During slack periods employers kept their costs down by reducing wages or laying off workers. Millions of people lost their jobs or had their wages slashed during the depressions of 1873, 1882, and 1893. Workers looked to labor unions for protection.

■ The Revival of Labor Unions

The growth of labor unions during the early 1800s had been halting and sporadic, but conditions during the Civil War spurred the revival of unionism. With hundreds of thousands of workers not available while serving in the army, unions were in a strong position to demand better pay. During the war the number of local unions rose dramatically. To strengthen local unions, labor also began to organize on a national scale.

Problems With Organizing

Labor unions faced serious difficulties in organizing because of the mobility and diversity of the American labor force. Workers who did not "stay hitched," but moved from job to job were difficult to organize.

▲ ORGANIZING THE WORKERS Union leaders hoped to improve conditions for workers, such as these immigrants working at home. *What were the difficulties that unions encountered in organizing immigrants?*

▲ RAILWAY STRIKE The railway strike of 1877 resulted in one of the most violent upheavals in the history of American labor. ***How did the strike start?***

The constant influx of large numbers of immigrants—averaging more than one-third of a million a year between 1870 and 1900—also presented a problem. Differences in language, religion, and customs among the immigrants made it hard to unite them into an effective union.

Another problem was that different labor leaders had different goals. Some leaders envisioned uniting all workers into one large union in order to promote widespread reforms. Others believed that unions should be organized by particular crafts or industries and work only for short-term benefits.

Unions also faced strong opposition from employers. Workers were often required to take oaths swearing they would not join a union. If found to have been involved in union activity, a worker would be fired and often could not get another job because of **blacklists,** or records kept by employers of "troublemakers." Once blacklisted a laborer could get a job only by changing residence, trade, or even name. Another way employers retaliated against union organizing in a workplace was the **lockout**—whereby the factory was shut down—or by firing union members and hiring **scabs,** or replacement

workers. In any lockout or strike, the odds favored employers. Few unions had enough money to support their members through the long period of unemployment caused by a strike.

Problems With Public Image

Labor unions also had to fight public opinion. Many Americans viewed fixing wages and hours by **collective bargaining**—negotiation between an employer and a labor union—as violating the right of an individual to deal personally with the employer. Only infrequently did public opinion condemn employers when labor disputes resulted in violence. This happened during the Homestead lockout in 1892 when the Carnegie Steel Company hired a private army of 300 Pinkerton detectives armed with repeating rifles. Generally, however, labor unions were held responsible when disorder occurred.

Another problem for unions was that law enforcement agencies usually sided with the employers. Employers suffered no penalties for lockouts and blacklists. Union strikes and boycotts, on the other hand, were judged to be "conspiracies in restraint of trade" for which labor leaders might be jailed or fined. Contracts between employers and unions were not usually enforceable by law. When violence occurred, or was even threatened, the police—and sometimes armed troops—were sent to the aid of employers.

■ Railroad Strike of 1877

Despite these obstacles labor unions survived—sometimes just barely. Membership in the union fluctuated according to business conditions. Following the depression of 1873, 5,000 businesses closed, causing widespread unemployment and homelessness.

Union membership dropped from more than 300,000 to 50,000. Three million workers were unemployed. At this time there were no unemployment or relief benefits available from either the state or federal government. Tramps and hobos roamed the countryside; workers' rallies to demand relief were stopped or suppressed by mounted police.

Labor Responds to Wage Cuts

The hard times of the 1870s reached a climax in the railroad strike of 1877, which shook the nation as no labor conflict in its history had done before. It began when four Eastern railroads cut workers' wages. To protest the cuts, the workers went on strike. As other railroads cut wages, the strike spread to Chicago and beyond.

In city after city, strikers seized and sometimes destroyed railroad property. In Pittsburgh alone the Pennsylvania Railroad lost 2,000 cars, 25 locomotives, 2 roundhouses, and a railroad station. At the height of the strike, more than one-half of the freight on the nation's 76,000 miles of track had stopped running. Troops and workers clashed in the streets of Martinsburg, West Virginia, as well as Pittsburgh and Baltimore. Although the clashes were usually spontaneous, newspapers viewed them collectively as

> **"** *. . . an insurrection, a revolution, an attempt of Communists and vagabonds to coerce society and endeavor to undermine American institutions.* **"**

Management Gains a Costly Victory

In several cities order was restored only after President Rutherford B. Hayes had sent in federal troops. Hayes himself, however, was troubled. He felt railroad officials had brought on the crisis by their own ruthless actions. The President confided in his diary, "Shall the railroads govern the country or shall the people govern the railroads?"

When the railroad strike was over, more than 100 persons were dead, 1,000 had been jailed, and 100,000 workers had gone on strike. In addition there was such fear of violent revolution that state militia were reorganized. National Guard armories were built in many large cities as fortresses, where troops could hold out against strikers if necessary. Union leaders learned from the strike that they were not united or strong enough to defeat the powerful combination of business and government.

Section 1 ★ Review

Checking for Understanding

1. **Identify** 1877 railroad strike.

2. **Define** real wages, company town, scrip, business cycle, blacklist, lockout, scab, collective bargaining.

3. **Discuss** the hardships facing industrial workers during the late 1800s.

4. **Give** examples of problems unions faced once they were organized.

Critical Thinking

5. **Weighing Options** Imagine that you are an industrial worker in 1870. List the advantages and disadvantages of joining a union.

Study and Writing Skills

Summarizing

Imagine that you have received an expensive camera for your birthday. The instructions are complicated with at least 12 pages describing how to adjust the camera for certain shots. The more you read, the more confused you become. Finally, you discover a *summary* of the main steps, and your confusion disappears.

Summarizing is the process of recapping main ideas by bringing together the major points and excluding the minor ones. Knowing how to summarize is a useful skill for students who have to answer essay questions, take notes, and write research papers.

Read the following material carefully. Then answer the questions that follow.

▲ MOVING ASSEMBLY LINE, HIGHLAND PARK, MICHIGAN

During the late 1800s, the United States, like other modernized nations, was experiencing societal changes brought on by the shift from an agriculture-based economy to one based on industrial production. American life up to this time had been based on a rugged self-determinism, a belief that one should take care of one's self and family. This was largely done through owning and farming land.

To encourage settlement in the frontier, Congress passed laws that provided land to settlers who would cultivate it and pay a fee. Farmers moved west in greater and greater numbers. More land was occupied and improved in the closing years of the 1800s than had been occupied and improved during the first 250 years of American history.

The growth of industry lured many people to the cities and into jobs that required a new set of values. In new industrial centers, such as Pittsburgh and Chicago, there was work available for thousands. People in the industrial labor force faced profound changes in their lives. Often a man did not so much work for his family as he did for his boss. Further, working conditions and pay were often a source of discontent.

Long hours were another burden to workers. During the late 1800s, 65- and 70-hour workweeks were common. Labor unions began to organize, and although their intent was to lend support to exploited employees, it often made workers feel they were helpless to take care of themselves.

Practicing the Skill

1. Locate and list in order of appearance the main ideas expressed in the material.

2. Summarize the text by rewriting the main ideas in your own words.

3. For further practice in this skill, read the material under the subhead "Urbanization" in Section 4 of this chapter. Then, following the guidelines suggested in the example, list the main ideas of the material and write a short summary of the material presented.

★★

The Rise of New Unions

Setting the Scene

Section Focus

Individually, workers were powerless to change hazardous working conditions, low pay, and long hours. When little was done to improve their lot, workers in growing numbers came to accept the idea of forming new, better-organized unions.

Objectives

After studying this section, you should be able to

★ identify two of the strongest labor unions of the late 1800s.

★ evaluate the gains labor unions achieved during this period.

Key Terms

arbitration, industrial union, injunction

▲ JUDGE'S GAVEL

As industrialization was an urban phenomenon, so too were unions. Those states with the highest percentage of workers in industry had the greatest urban populations. It was in these industrial areas of the North and the Midwest that a score of new labor organizations were established in the late 1860s.

■ The Knights of Labor and the AFL Unions

By far the most influential labor organization was the Noble Order of the Knights of Labor. Founded in 1869 the Knights of Labor attempted to bring all laboring people—skilled and unskilled, black and white, men and women, white-collar and blue-collar—into one big union.

The Desire for Widespread Reform

Terence V. Powderly, an immigrant and a former railway switchtender, led the Knights of Labor after 1879. An eloquent speaker and a tireless organizer, Powderly believed a single, powerful union was the best means of gaining concessions from employers for better working conditions.

Powderly persuaded the Knights to support equal pay for women, temperance, abolition of child labor and, above all, establishment of cooperatively owned industrial plants. A man of peace, he opposed strikes and wished to submit labor disputes to **arbitration**—a process whereby an impartial third party helps workers and management reach an agreement.

Membership in the Knights grew rapidly in the early 1880s—especially after the striking Knights won the dispute against Jay Gould's Wabash Railway. Membership in the Knights soared from 100,000 in 1885 to 700,000 in less than a year. Some newspapers feared that Powderly would become stronger than the President.

The Knights of Labor, however, were soon swamped with troubles. The union had wasted its funds in unsuccessful attempts to set up cooperative businesses. Moreover, the effort to unite different kinds of labor into one big union had failed. Workers in different crafts and industries often had little in common with one another and little interest in working for the same goals.

Haymarket Square Riot

The decline of the Knights was hastened by the Haymarket Square riot in Chicago on May 4, 1886. This event followed a peaceful meeting of some 3,000 workers who gathered together to protest the shooting of striking McCormick Harvester Company workers by the police. As the meeting was breaking up, someone threw a bomb into a group of police officers. Seven persons were killed and more than 60 were injured. Although the identity of the bomb-thrower was never established, 8 anarchist leaders were arrested and found guilty of taking part in the crime. Four were later executed for murder. Although the Knights of Labor could in no way be held responsible for the Haymarket affair, it became identified with radicals and violence. From then on the Knights of Labor declined rapidly.

Foundation of the AFL

In 1886, the year the Knights began to decline, the American Federation of Labor (AFL) was organized. In its principles as well as its structure, the AFL differed greatly from the Knights. While the Knights had accepted a large number of unskilled workers, the AFL accepted only skilled workers. This policy indicated the reluctance of the

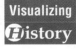
Visualizing History

▲ **TROUBLE AT THE HAYMARKET** On the night of May 4, 1886, a crowd gathered in Chicago's Haymarket Square to protest police violence. As the meeting was breaking up, a bomb was thrown into a group of police and the police fired into the crowd. ***What effect did the Haymarket affair have on the labor movement?***

AFL to accept women, African Americans, and immigrants—the majority of whom were unskilled—into their union. Also, the AFL organized workers into separate unions, each covering a particular craft.

Each union managed its own affairs with only occasional help from the national organization. The AFL's fees were relatively high, in order to restrict membership, build up strike funds, and provide benefits to members and their families in cases of sickness, unemployment, or death.

The AFL might never have enjoyed the success it did were it not for Samuel Gompers, its president for 37 years. Born in London, Gompers adapted some ideas of British trade unions, the best established in the world. Gompers, who prided himself on being practical, was interested only in day-to-day gains of AFL members—higher wages, shorter hours, and benefits for disabled workers.

So effective was the organization and leadership of the AFL that when hard times hit again in 1893, its member unions not only survived but thrived. Between 1890 and 1900, when other labor organizations lost members, AFL membership rose from 190,000 to 500,000.

■ The Pullman Strike

To address the needs of unskilled and semiskilled labor—and yet avoid the "one big union" approach—a new type of labor organization developed. This was the **industrial union,** in which all classes of workers in a single industry are joined together. Among those who saw the advantages of an industrial union was Eugene V. Debs, an officer of the Brotherhood of Locomotive Firemen, one of several railway unions. He felt that the separation of railway workers into different unions weakened their power. Conductors and engineers, the "aristocracy of labor," looked down on less skilled and lower paid workers, and the unskilled had no organization at all. Debs, therefore, started a new organization in 1893—the American Railway Union. This union included all types of railroad

workers—from conductors, firemen, and engineers to telegraph operators and station clerks. By 1894 the American Railway Union was powerful enough to force James J. Hill, the owner of the Great Northern Railway, to restore wage cuts.

Protest Leads to Walkout

Hardly had the Great Northern strike ended than the Pullman strike began in Pullman, Illinois, the company town built by George M. Pullman for his workers. Losing profit because of a reduced demand for its railroad cars, the Pullman Palace Car Company laid off two-thirds of its employees and cut the wages of the rest. It did not, however, reduce either the dividends it paid to stockholders or the rents charged to workers in the town. When a delegation of workers met with Pullman to protest the pay cuts, they were fired. At noon the following day, 10,000 Pullman workers walked off the job.

The American Railway Union took up the Pullman workers' cause. Debs's first move was to propose that the dispute be referred to arbitration. Pullman, however, replied, "There is nothing to arbitrate." Realizing that negotiating with Pullman was futile, the union called for members to refuse to work on any train that included a Pullman car. Railway workers answered

▲ PULLMAN AD

▲ THE PULLMAN STRIKE An economic depression gripped the nation in the 1890s. Layoffs and pay cuts made workers desperate. In the company town of Pullman, Illinois, a strike began that led to a tie-up of the nation's railroad system. *How was the strike broken?*

the union's call. Within 5 days 100,000 railroad workers had walked off the job. Railway traffic west of Chicago was almost paralyzed. Debs warned his followers not to interfere with the mail and appealed to them to be "orderly and law-abiding." A few mail trains were delayed, but there were few disturbances.

Federal Intervention Turns the Tide

Quickly, President Grover Cleveland stepped in. Over protests by the mayor of Chicago and the governor of Illinois, President Cleveland sent federal troops to guard mail trains. Immediately, rioting broke out as angry mobs, sympathetic to the strikers, taunted the soldiers. Members of the American Railway Union kept out of trouble but nevertheless received the blame. Even before the troops had arrived, the federal government obtained an **injunction,** or court order, forbidding the union to continue the strike. Debs refused to obey the injunction and was imprisoned.

Without Debs's leadership, the Pullman strike collapsed and with it the American Railway Union. From that point on, employers used the injunction as a means of breaking up strikes.

Although labor unions lost more disputes than they won, and most workers remained unorganized (only 4 percent of American workers belonged to unions in 1900), workers made some gains in the late 1800s. Federal and state legislation reflected the growing political influence of labor. Wages began to increase slowly, and the workday was shortened. Moreover, nearly every state passed laws regulating working conditions and requiring minimum standards of health and safety.

Section 2 ★ Review

Checking for Understanding

1. **Identify** Knights of Labor, American Federation of Labor, Terence V. Powderly, Samuel Gompers, Eugene Debs.

2. **Define** arbitration, industrial union, injunction.

3. **Summarize** the difficulties faced by the Knights of Labor and the American Railway Union.

4. **Examine** the achievements of labor unions during the late 1800s.

Critical Thinking

5. **Supporting an Opinion** Do you agree with Debs that an industrial union was more powerful than separate unions of craft workers? Why or why not?

★★★

Patterns of Immigration

Setting the Scene

Section Focus

Between 1860 and 1900 almost 14 million people came to America. Another 14.5 million came between 1900 and 1915. Even more significant than the increase in numbers was the changing character of immigration during these years. The vast majority no longer came from northern and western Europe but from southern and eastern Europe.

Objectives

After studying this section, you should be able to

★ identify the reasons that immigrants came to the United States.

★ distinguish between the "old" and the "new" immigration.

Key Term

pogrom, anarchism

◀ IMMIGRANT MOTHER AND DAUGHTERS, C. 1900

The thirteen colonies had been settled mainly by English settlers. Other settlers from Holland, Sweden, France, Scotland, Ireland, and Germany came later. After 1815, however, increasing numbers of immigrants started to arrive from Ireland. During these early years, a total of only about 400,000 immigrants had come to America. Beginning in the 1850s and continuing after the Civil War, immigration rose sharply.

■ The "Old Immigration"

During the period of "Old Immigration," which started in the 1830s and reached a high point in the 1840s, there was a great wave of immigration to America's shores. Between 1840 and 1850, an additional 1.5 million newcomers journeyed to the United States. Nearly one-half were from Ireland,

which was suffering from a potato famine. Between 1846 and 1860, about 1.5 million Irish immigrated to America, settling in New York and Boston, which functioned as ports of entry into the United States.

In the 1840s large numbers of Germans also began to come to America. Some left their homeland because of crop failures. Others came to escape political persecution after the failure of the Revolution of 1848. Still others were German Jews seeking religious freedom. Large numbers of German immigrants settled on farms and in cities in the Midwest—areas that were rapidly growing and had job opportunities. The Germans gave a distinctive flavor to such cities as Cincinnati, Milwaukee, and St. Louis. Then, in the 1850s, after the Gold Rush, Chinese immigrants began to come to the Pacific Coast. Many were hired to help build the railroads. About 100,000 Chinese had settled in the West by the mid-1870s.

During the colonial period, most immigrants were readily accepted. Workers were badly needed in all the colonies.

European agents of railroad companies and steamship lines described America as a land where riches could be had almost for the asking. Perhaps the most persuasive arguments for others to come to this country were the "America letters" written by recent immigrants to their family and friends. "If you wish to be happy and independent, then come here," wrote a German farmer from his new home in Missouri. In the 1840s and 1850s, however, some native-born Americans began to resent the newcomers, especially the Irish immigrants. Some Americans resented them because they dressed and sounded "different" and because they were Catholics.

■ The "New Immigration"

Until the 1880s most newcomers had come from the nations of northern and western Europe. After 1885, however, large numbers came from nations of southern and eastern Europe. The new immigrants were from Italy, Russia, and Poland as well as from the nations of the Austro-Hungarian Empire.

Italians were one of the largest groups of new immigrants. Many came from Sicily and the southern part of Italy. People in this region faced economic misfortune. Unemployment and overpopulation made existence perilous. As a result, millions of Italian Catholics chose to go to America.

Eastern European Jews were another sizable group of new immigrants. Although scattered throughout many countries, the

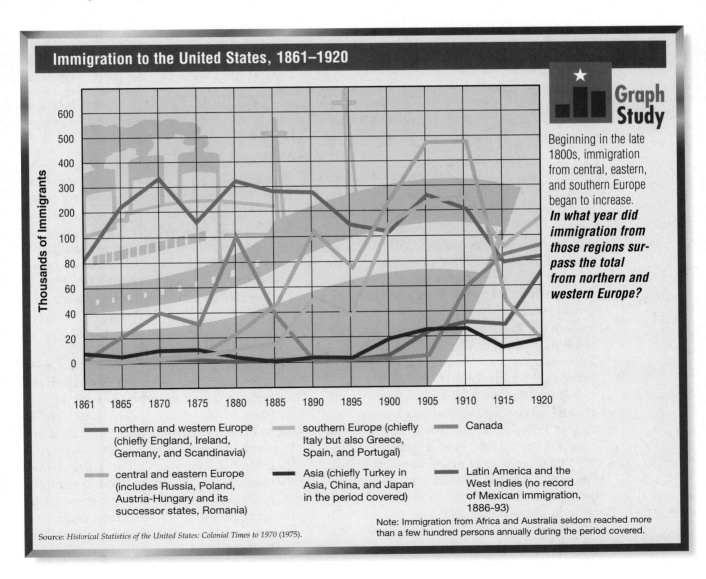

Immigration to the United States, 1861–1920

Graph Study

Beginning in the late 1800s, immigration from central, eastern, and southern Europe began to increase.

In what year did immigration from those regions surpass the total from northern and western Europe?

(y-axis) Thousands of Immigrants: 0, 20, 40, 60, 80, 100, 200, 300, 400, 500, 600

(x-axis) 1861, 1865, 1870, 1875, 1880, 1885, 1890, 1895, 1900, 1905, 1910, 1915, 1920

— northern and western Europe (chiefly England, Ireland, Germany, and Scandinavia)

— southern Europe (chiefly Italy but also Greece, Spain, and Portugal)

— Canada

— central and eastern Europe (includes Russia, Poland, Austria-Hungary and its successor states, Romania)

— Asia (chiefly Turkey in Asia, China, and Japan in the period covered)

— Latin America and the West Indies (no record of Mexican immigration, 1886-93)

Note: Immigration from Africa and Australia seldom reached more than a few hundred persons annually during the period covered.

Source: *Historical Statistics of the United States: Colonial Times to 1970* (1975).

Italian Cuisine

Between 1890 and 1910 about 2.7 million southern Italians immigrated to the United States. Coming from farms in Italy, they settled primarily in the cities on America's East Coast. By 1920 New York City had become home to more Italians than there were living in Venice, Genoa, and Florence combined. Italian Americans adjusted to many changes in their adopted country, and they adapted their cooking to substitute some more readily available ingredients.

Italian dishes became a lasting contribution to American culture. Pasta was enjoyed by everyone, sometimes several times a week. Macaroni, manicotti, spaghetti, and lasagna were first introduced to Americans by the little shops nestled among the blocks of tenements.

Italian bakery ovens produced the first pizzas, which had been a strictly Neapolitan item back in Italy. Opening in 1905, "G Lombardi" on Spring Street in New York's Little Italy became the first known pizzeria in the United States. Deep-dish, Chicago-style pizza, cooked in a black skillet, did not come along until 1943, when it was created by Ike Sewell and Ric Riccardo at Pizzeria Uno in Chicago. After World War II, the pizza industry boomed in the United States.

Jews of eastern Europe were confronted with many common problems wherever they lived. For one thing they were often the victims of religious discrimination. In many regions Jews were not allowed to own land, work in certain trades, or move out of areas that had been set aside for them.

These limitations on Jews created widespread poverty. In addition eastern European Jews lived in danger of **pogroms,** or organized massacres. Jewish immigrants seeking personal safety, religious freedom, and economic opportunity came to America.

Slavs made up a third group of new immigrants. "Slavs" is a broad label given to a people, generally from eastern Europe, who have similar languages and customs. In the late 1800s, large numbers of Slavs left Russia, Poland, and other countries to escape economic woes. Many Slavs also came in search of political freedom.

These newcomers were, for the most part, poor. They hoped to find a better life in America. In part it was their labor that made the rapid industrialization of the United States possible. For many people, immigrating to the United States was the only way for them to escape persecution in their homeland. One Jewish immigrant noted that "the only hope for the Jews in Russia is to become Jews out of Russia."

Ethnic Neighborhoods

The new immigrants flocked to the cities. There they lived together in ethnically homogeneous neighborhoods such as "Little Italy" or the Jewish "Lower East Side" in New York City. There they practiced the ways of life they were used to and spoke their native languages. The communities they established revolved around a number of traditional institutions. They re-created the churches, synagogues, clubs, and newspapers of their homeland and adapted them to their new environment.

Public Resentment

This huge influx of immigrants created special social problems. Because immigrants lived in their own neighborhoods, practiced their own customs, and spoke their own languages, many Americans wondered if they could ever be assimilated into American life. Some people, especially workers, blamed them for low wages. Others resented that many immigrants were Catholics or Jews.

The railroad strike of 1877 and the Haymarket Square riot of 1886 resulted in many people's fear of immigrants who, it was thought, believed in socialism or even **anarchism,** a belief in no direct government authority over society. A few politicians, notably Senator Henry Cabot Lodge of Massachusetts, were strongly reactionary in their response to the issue of immigration. They wanted immigration from southern and eastern Europe to be stopped completely. In 1896 Lodge argued for a bill that would exclude all prospective immigrants who could not read or write 25 words of the United States Constitution in some language. Lodge concluded that such a test would

❝ *. . . bear most heavily upon the Italians, Russians, Poles, Hungarians, Greeks, and Asiatics . . . races most affected by the test are those who[m] emigration has . . . swelled rapidly . . . and who are most alien to the great body of the United States.* **❞**

In the late 1800s, hostility grew toward many of the new racial and ethnic groups coming into the new country. The differences in customs, dress, and language of the new arrivals created a basic distrust of the foreign born by many native-born Americans. Some historians believe that this reaction was a response to the rapid changes occurring in America because of industrialization. For those native-born Americans who were uncertain and disturbed by social change, immigrants became easy targets of hostility.

Organized Opposition

Some Americans formed groups to counter what they considered the immigrant threat. One of these groups, the American Protective Association, was founded in

Visualizing History

▲ THE NEW IMMIGRANTS During the late 1800s, new immigrants poured into the United States, braving the long and difficult journey to start a new life. *Why did many people view these newcomers as a threat?*

1887 to protest the large number of Catholic immigrants. In some parts of the country, local laws were passed that prohibited immigrants from holding certain kinds of jobs and denied them other rights. Jewish immigrants, for example, were denied admission to some universities. In addition the immigrants faced actual physical attacks.

The anti-immigration movement was not limited to groups such as the American Protective Association. Some well-known scholars of the time were susceptible to these feelings as well. Historian and future President Woodrow Wilson and frontier historian Frederick Jackson Turner lamented the lessening flow of immigration from northern Europe and the rise in numbers of "inferior stocks" coming to America. One writer considered the new immigration a plot by European governments to "unload the sweepings of their jails and asylums."

Anti-Chinese Sentiment

Public resentment was not limited to newcomers from Europe, however. The Chinese, too, suffered discrimination on the Pacific Coast. The discovery of gold in 1849 and the subsequent demand for cheap labor first brought the Chinese to California. Many found work in the gold fields or on the construction of the Central Pacific Railroad. By 1852 there were some 25,000 Chinese men, women, and children living on the Pacific Coast and thereafter they came at the rate of 4,000 a year. By the end

of the 1870s, there were almost 75,000 Chinese in California alone. Their willingness to work for low wages prompted a violent anti-Chinese movement among the white workers of California. Such feelings intensified during hard economic times. During the depression that followed the Panic of 1873, unemployed workers in California attacked the Chinese. Some Americans began to demand that Chinese immigrants be excluded from the United States.

In 1879 Congress forbade the importing of foreign workers under contract—a law aimed primarily at the Chinese. Then, in 1882, Congress, responding to pressure from the western states, suspended nearly all immigration from China for 10 years.

▼ CHINESE AMERICAN CHILDREN

Section 3 ★ Review

Checking for Understanding

1. **Identify** Henry Cabot Lodge.
2. **Define** pogrom, anarchism.
3. **Explain** why people migrated from Europe to the United States.
4. **Differentiate** the "Old Immigration" from the "New Immigration."

Critical Thinking

5. **Understanding Bias** Throughout history people suffering hardship have found "scapegoats" on whom to blame their troubles. Explain why immigrants were chosen as scapegoats by native-born residents during the 1800s.

★★

City Life and Problems

Section Focus

With the rise of industrialism, the landscape of the nation changed. Railroads crisscrossed the continent. Where farms once stood, factories spewed forth black smoke. Thousands of Americans left the nation's farms hoping to make their fortunes in the city. Millions of immigrants came to better their lives and share in the benefits of the new industrial age.

Objectives

After studying this section, you should be able to

★ identify the factors that led to the growth of cities during the late 1800s.

★ list the problems resulting from an increase in the urban population.

Key Term

merchandising

◀ **BOOK ON URBAN LIFE BY JACOB RIIS**

*A*ll over the nation—but especially in the Northeast—cities were growing rapidly. This urban growth was a result of industrialization. In 1840, 1 out of every 12 Americans lived in a city with a population of more than 8,000. By 1900, however, 1 out of every 3 Americans lived in a large city.

Why were so many people attracted to the cities? One reason was that rising new industries held out the promise of jobs and opportunity. Where else could immigrants—or other Americans, for that matter—fulfill the "rags to riches" dream of making a fortune overnight? The cities of the 1890s held the promise of excitement and activity, in contrast to the isolation of rural farm life. There was running water, modern plumbing, museums, libraries, theaters, shops, convenient transportation, and countless things to see and do.

■ Urbanization

Between 1860 and 1900 American urban areas grew twice as fast as the total population. Chicago, which in the 1830s had been a frontier town with a few hundred residents, became a vast metropolis of almost 2 million people. New York became the second-largest city in the world. During the same span of years, Philadelphia grew from less than 600,000 people to about 1.3 million. Both Boston's and Baltimore's populations increased from about 200,000 to more than one-half million.

Industrial cities were essentially the product of mines, factories, steamships, and railroads. New cities appeared, or old ones mushroomed, near coal and iron deposits (Birmingham, Alabama, and Pittsburgh), sources of water power (Lowell and Lawrence, Massachusetts), shipping centers

Jane Addams
1860–1935

By the time the guns of World War I began blazing in 1914, Jane Addams was already famous as the founder of Hull House—the settlement house that served Chicago's immigrants and urban poor. By then peace had become her passion.

In 1915 Addams urged European leaders to find a way to end the mounting carnage. When the United States entered the war, she was labeled unpatriotic for holding true to her pacifist ideals. After the war ended in 1918, Addams worked to ensure no repetition of the "war to end all wars."

Addams was elected president of the Women's International League for Peace and Freedom in 1915 and held that office until 1929. Her devotion to world peace was recognized in 1931 when she was named corecipient, with educator Nicholas Murray Butler, of the Nobel Peace Prize.

(Baltimore and New York City), and at railroad centers (Omaha and Chicago). Industrial cities, especially in the Northeast, had the greatest growth, but cities in all regions experienced rapid growth. Between 1860 and 1900, Nashville grew from 16,000 to more than 80,000, Minneapolis from 2,500 to more than 200,000, and Los Angeles from 4,000 to more than 100,000.

Once established, cities seemed to generate their own growth. To serve industry such facilities as banks, insurance companies, docks, and warehouses developed. These, in turn, attracted more industry and workers. Immigrants could often find employment only in urban industrialized areas. Yet an even greater number of new workers came from rural areas of the United States.

■ Problems of City Life

The modern industrial city confronted many people with an unfamiliar and often unattractive environment. The new cities were built with less concern for the comforts of the inhabitants than for the profits of builders and real-estate speculators. People poured into the cities faster than housing could be built to accommodate them. Many had no choice but to live in tenements, poorly constructed and cramped five- or six-story buildings, which housed many families. Many of the rooms and tenements had no windows and were often dark, narrow, and airless.

As more and more people were crowded together and the buildings began to deteriorate, city slums developed. Lacking proper sanitation, tenements became foul-smelling and vermin-infested. Typhoid and other diseases often spread rapidly.

Lack of Social Services

Besides inadequate housing, there was a shortage of police and firefighters. City water was impure and sewers were often clogged. Garbage collection was sporadic. In addition there were no attempts at city planning. Little was done to provide for open spaces, parks, and playgrounds or to take advantage of rivers and other natural features. The few open spaces were often used as garbage dumps or left vacant with a scanty growth of grass and weeds competing with cinders and tin cans.

Rivers and harbors were polluted by sewage and factory wastes, and the air was fouled by smoke from thousands of chimneys. The new environment cut off people from sun, air, and natural beauty.

New Concerns Arise

The growth of cities created a demand for new sources of water because wells and brooks provided too scanty a supply and were often polluted. New York City, the first of the major cities to meet this problem head-on, built the Croton Aqueduct 25 miles outside the city limits.

Cities also had to come up with more efficient means of intercity transportation. This was accomplished by the horse car and later by the elevated railway, the trolley car, and the subway. The demand for space in preferred localities such as Wall Street in New York or the Loop in Chicago resulted in the creation of huge skyscrapers, which, in turn, added a vertical dimension to transportation—in the form of the elevator.

Rise in Crime

An unexpected problem of urban life, however, was the increase in crime. There had always been occasional violence and theft, but never on a scale demanding an organized police force. There had been nothing resembling modern police until the formation of the Metropolitan Police of London, known as "bobbies," around 1830.

Because the problems experienced by growing urban centers were new, old solutions could not be relied upon. It seemed as if the answers were as varied as the problems. Some people looked back to an earlier morality and sought to enforce the Puritan Sabbath as a means of regenerating the city. As a result restaurants and amusement places were closed. There were even efforts to forbid the running of trains and streetcars.

Public Awareness Spurs Legislation

One who faced the realities of life in factories, shops, and slums was Jacob A. Riis (REES), a Danish-American police reporter for New York newspapers. In the course of his work, Riis had seen again and again the connection between slums and human degradation. In 1890 he focused public attention on the problem in a best-selling book, *How the Other Half Lives*. By appealing to public conscience, Riis secured legislation that reduced the worst slum conditions, along with other measures that improved

Visualizing History

▲ **URBAN PROBLEMS** Poverty and overcrowding brought on many social problems in large cities throughout the United States. *What problems did residents of tenements in the nation's larger cities face?*

▲ A NATION OF CITIES As the United States became a nation of cities, public services expanded to serve the needs of the people. Paved roads, electric street lights, and streetcars improved transportation. *What did critics say about the appearance of cities?*

the lives of city dwellers, such as playgrounds for schools. Among his close friends was a rising young Republican politician, Theodore Roosevelt, whom he "educated" by taking him into tenements, sweatshops, and jails.

Settlement Houses Assist Communities

The year before *How the Other Half Lives* was published, Jane Addams founded, in a Chicago slum, the most famous settlement house in the United States, Hull House. About this neighborhood, Addams wrote:

    66 *[T]he streets were inexpressibly dirty . . . the street lighting bad. . . . Many houses have no water save the faucet in the back yard; there are no fire escapes. . . .* 99

Addams, a deeply religious woman, was inspired by a passionate desire to put her faith to work. Modeling her endeavor on Toynbee Hall, a settlement house in England,

Jane Addams was determined to improve the life of the "other half." Hull House soon had activities as varied as an art gallery and a gymnasium as well as hot lunches for factory workers and classes in English. Above all Addams was interested in helping children, believing that "a fence at the top of a precipice is better than an ambulance at the bottom." Addams surrounded herself with young people who were glad to enlist in a war against human suffering.

Similar convictions were the motivating forces behind the founding of other settlement houses, including the Henry Street Settlement in New York City, the Santa Maria Institute in Cincinnati, and the South End House in Boston. In addition to providing immediate services to neighborhood people, settlement houses were schools where hundreds of men and women learned social responsibility.

Many of these people later helped to promote reform legislation, either as political lobbyists or officeholders. "Graduates" of Hull House, for example, were instrumental in securing the first playgrounds in Chicago, better garbage collection, and the first Illinois factory inspection law. Frances Perkins, trained in a New York settlement house, embarked on a political career that led to her appointment as secretary of labor, the first woman to serve on a presidential cabinet.

■ Beautifying the City

Among the indictments against sprawling industrial cities were their ugliness and their lack of provision for rest and recreation. Architects and landscape designers were among those who sought remedies.

Public Buildings and Open Spaces

In 1876 New York City opened Central Park, designed by Frederick L. Olmsted and Calvert Vaux, as "a great breathing space for the toiling masses." Olmsted was the first person to use the term *landscape architect* as the name of this kind of work. Olmsted also designed Prospect Park in Brooklyn. Many other cities followed New York's example. In 1892 and 1893 Chicago hosted a World's Fair on fairgrounds designed by Olmsted, with buildings in the classical style surrounded by lagoons and landscaped grassy areas.

The Chicago World's Fair revealed that American architecture was dynamic and original. The best architects now thoroughly understood European styles and adapted them for modern use. The firm of McKim, Mead, and White used the Italian Renaissance style in their design for the Boston Public Library. Henry Richardson adapted Romanesque style in his design for churches, libraries, warehouses, and even department stores.

New Functional Architecture

The Transportation Building at the Chicago Fair, designed by Louis Sullivan, however, was based on a new concept: form follows function. Sullivan believed an architect should create designs that reveal a building's purpose and method of construction. He was one of the first architects to design skyscrapers. His influence, both directly and later through the work of his pupil Frank Lloyd Wright, reached worldwide.

The finest example of a structure in which form expressed function was the Brooklyn Bridge. Completed in 1883, 16 years after it was begun, it was the largest suspension bridge in the world at that time. Hung from great steel cables with a span half again as long as that of any previous bridge, it was designed and constructed by two German Americans, John Roebling and his son Washington Roebling. During the project, John was killed on the job. His son continued directing the work until he himself was injured. The work was then taken over by John's wife who, with her son's direction, completed the project.

Public Libraries

For those who wished to continue their education, American cities provided opportunities that had never existed before. In 1876 the American Library Association was founded to encourage "the best reading for the largest number at the least expense." By 1900 the public libraries, which receive support from taxes, revenues, and private donations, came to be recognized as "no less important than the schoolhouse in the system of popular education."

Downtown Shopping Districts

New means of **merchandising,** or the buying and selling of goods, were created to meet the growing needs of urban populations. One striking example was the department store. Stores such as A. T. Stewart and John Wanamaker were retail centers where nearly all kinds of goods were sold in one location. These stores had an enormous appeal to people of all classes. As a

▶ **FLATIRON BUILDING, NEW YORK CITY**

result the downtown areas of cities became centers where people came to shop. Merchants who wanted this new business were active in making sure that the areas were kept clean and attractive. New streets, sidewalks, and buildings were constructed.

Despite some setbacks, citizens made progress solving some of the problems facing the major cities. The availability of electricity enabled shops and factories to remain open after dark and thus stimulated urban nightlife as well.

Efforts by Municipal Governments

Throughout the late 1800s, city governments turned their efforts toward providing the services needed for their citizens. Steps were taken by city leaders to reduce crime, to improve recreational opportunities and living conditions, and to solve some of the public health problems that accompanied the rapid growth of the cities. Methods of identifying criminals, such as the use of photographs, were improved. Electric streetlights added a large measure of safety on city streets.

Many parks were built, usually toward the edges of already congested cities. Public utilities provided electricity, clean water, and sewage services for many urban areas. By 1898 approximately 350 communities had built publicly owned electric light companies, and by 1900 more than 3,500 public waterworks had been constructed nationwide.

The need for better communication spurred the use of a new innovation, the telephone. Within a few years after the telephone was invented in 1876, telephone exchanges were established in more than 80 cities. Within 20 years nearly 800,000 telephones were in use throughout the United States, twice as many as were in use in Europe. The impact of the telephone upon American life was enormous, linking many of the urban and rural areas of the nation almost instantly.

Despite these changes for the better, many social reformers felt that this was only a start. They contended that it was essential to find solutions for problems before the problems ever occurred. More and more reformers urged government to deal with the causes of social and economic problems. Jacqueline Shaw Lowell, the founder of the New York Charity Organization Society, expressed this attitude about the city's problems when she noted:

> *[There are] five hundred thousand wage earners in this city, 200,000 of them women, and 75,000 of those working under dreadful conditions. . . . If the working people had all they ought to have, we should not have the paupers and the criminals. . . . It is better to save them before they go under than to spend your life . . . taking care of them afterwards.*

Section 4 ★ Review

Checking for Understanding

1. **Identify** Jacob A. Riis, Jane Addams, Louis Sullivan.

2. **Define** merchandising.

3. **List** the factors that led to the growth of cities during the late 1800s and summarize the problems that developed as the population grew.

4. **Describe** the efforts made to improve life and conditions in the cities.

Critical Thinking

5. **Understanding Analogies** How does Jane Addams's theory that "a fence at the top of a precipice is better than an ambulance at the bottom" explain her focus on children?

Urban Pollution and Public Health

Citizens who complain about air pollution, poor water quality, and inadequate garbage disposal in modern cities might feel at home if transported to the New York City of 1866. A report on the sanitary conditions of the city in that year identified the following problems: (1) filthy streets; (2) neglected garbage and domestic refuse; (3) obstructed and faulty sewers and drains; (4) neglected privies and stables; (5) cattle pens and large stables in the more populous districts; (6) neglected and filthy markets; (7) slaughterhouses and hide and fat depots in close proximity to populous streets; (8) droves of cattle and swine in crowded streets; (9) swill-milk stables; . . . (10) bone boiling, fat melting . . . within the city limits; (11) . . . offensive exhalations . . . in gas manufacture; . . . (12) . . . dumping grounds and manure yards in vicinity of populous streets; (13) . . . management of refuse and junk materials; . . . (14) overcrowding of . . . public conveyances; . . . (15) neglect of dead animals in the streets and gutters of the city.

Such urban problems were not new. Examples can be found even in ancient times. Many cities, having become centers for trade, government, and religion, were large and crowded. Some historians place Rome's population at more than 1 million by the start of the first century A.D. Within 100 years overcrowding resulted in many of Rome's citizens living in apartment houses. Some apartments were 5 or 6 stories high and sheltered about 200 people each. Many of the city's residential structures were flimsy and poorly constructed, and living conditions paralleled those in the impoverished sections of nineteenth-century New York.

The living conditions of the urban poor left a great deal to be desired. Life in the crowded tenements was hazardous at best. Fires were an ever-present threat. In the late 1800s, the amount of damage from urban fires was on the rise.

▲ CITY STOREFRONT, C. 1910

Much of Chicago's downtown area burned in 1871, and two years later Boston experienced a devastating fire.

Another threat was illness. One reason for this was poor diet. Another was unsanitary conditions. Most tenement houses had neither indoor plumbing nor good ventilation.

Making the Environment Connection

1. Categorize the pollution problems under air, soil, and water.

2. Why do you think the speed of urban growth contributes to environmental problems?

Linking Past and Present

3. Which of these problems are unlikely to occur in modern cities?

Using Vocabulary

Use the following terms in sentences or short paragraphs. Relate them by using two or more of the terms in each sentence or paragraph.

real wages	company town
business cycle	blacklist
lockout	collective bargaining
arbitration	industrial union
injunction	tenement

Reviewing Facts

1. **Discuss** the hardships and problems that plagued industrial workers in the late 1800s and early 1900s.

2. **Report** on the problems facing labor unions in the late 1800s.

3. **Summarize** the achievements of labor unions during the late 1800s.

4. **List** the reasons why people immigrated to the United States.

5. **Cite** reasons for the growth of cities during the late 1800s.

6. **Identify** the problems created by growth in urban populations.

7. **Describe** efforts to improve nineteenth-century city life.

Understanding Concepts

Unity

1. How did Terence Powderly envision the Knights of Labor as being capable of confronting big business? How did his methods and goals differ from other union leaders'?

Conflict

2. With what groups did labor unions have conflict once they were organized? What were some of the reasons for the conflict? Explain how the conflict was resolved.

Critical Thinking

1. **Understanding Stereotypes** What stereotypes of labor unions were created because of the actions of a few union members or nonunion strikers? How did they work against the efforts of organized labor?

2. **Analyzing Photographs** Study the photograph on this page of an alley playground taken in the early 1900s and answer the questions that follow.

   a. What are the individuals in the photograph doing?

   b. What evidence do you see that conveys economic conditions?

   c. What title would you give this photograph?

Writing About History

Description

Imagine you are a reporter assigned to cover the railroad strike of 1877. Write an article describing the scene of the strike as you arrive. Include enough sensory details so that your readers can share your experience and sense the mood and emotions of the strikers and onlookers.

▲ TENEMENT ALLEY PLAYGROUND, C. 1910

Cooperative Learning

Work with a partner to research a major strike that occurred in the United States within the last five years. Find information on the workers' grievances. In addition find information on the company's position in the strike. Use this information to take turns as a union representative and a company representative questioning one another during an arbitration meeting.

Social Studies Skills

Reading a Cartogram

At first glance you may not have recognized the image on this page as a map of the United States; in fact, you may not have thought it was a map at all. Nevertheless, it is a striking indication of the vast differences in population among the various regions of the United States in 1900.

A cartogram is a type of map that purposely distorts physical space in order to highlight one aspect of physical, cultural, or human geography. Most maps, by contrast, try to minimize or disguise any sort of distortion.

Cartograms can show just about anything: population, income, highways, nuclear power, natural disasters, or food consumption. What is critical is that the size of individual areas reflects importance solely in relation to the information that the mapmaker wishes to emphasize. These maps have very specific uses.

Cartograms of today's population in the United States, based perhaps on age or gender, would be useful to someone in politics or marketing who needs to identify demographic trends.

Practicing the Skill

Use the cartogram on this page and your knowledge from the chapter to answer the questions below.

1. What fact about the United States population in 1900 is most evident from a quick glance at the cartogram?

2. In what ways might the information on the cartogram enhance your understanding of the text?

3. Which state was larger in 1900—Georgia or Maryland? How many people lived in each of these states?

4. Who might find a cartogram of natural disasters useful? Of food consumption? Explain your reasoning for each example you provide.

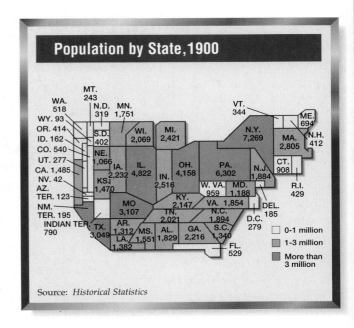

Population by State, 1900

WA. 518
MT. 243
N.D. 319
MN. 1,751
VT. 344
ME. 694
WY. 93
OR. 414
ID. 162
CO. 540
UT. 277
CA. 1,485
NV. 42
AZ. TER. 123
NM. TER. 195
INDIAN TER. 790
S.D. 402
NE. 1,066
KS. 1,470
WI. 2,069
MI. 2,421
N.Y. 7,269
N.H. 412
MA. 2,805
CT. 908
R.I. 429
IA. 2,232
IL. 4,822
IN. 2,516
OH. 4,158
PA. 6,302
N.J. 1,884
W. VA. 959
MD. 1,188
DEL. 185
D.C. 279
MO 3,107
KY. 2,147
VA. 1,854
TN. 2,021
N.C. 1,894
TX. 3,049
AR. 1,312
LA. 1,382
MS. 1,551
AL. 1,829
GA. 2,216
S.C. 1,340
FL. 529

☐ 0-1 million
☐ 1-3 million
■ More than 3 million

Source: *Historical Statistics*

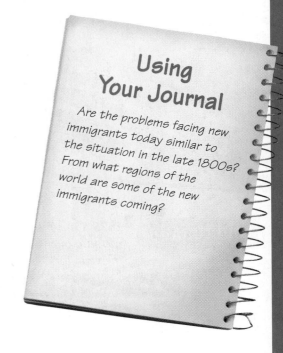

Using Your Journal

Are the problems facing new immigrants today similar to the situation in the late 1800s? From what regions of the world are some of the new immigrants coming?

CHAPTER 20

★★

The Gilded Age
1865–1900

▶ TIFFANY LAMP

Setting the Scene

Focus

American political life reached a low point between 1865 and 1900. Corruption in the form of graft and bribery became almost routine in local, state, and national governments. Both the Democratic and Republican parties came under the influence of lobbyists and other special interests. Neither party was ready for change, although the assassination of President Garfield prompted civil service reform.

Concepts to Understand

★ How the spoils system and lobbyists fostered corruption in government

★ How public protest by a free press worked to end political corruption

Read to Discover . . .

★ the major forms of political corruption.

★ new forms of leisure pastimes and amusements that attracted the interest of Americans before 1900.

Journal Notes

As you read the chapter, note the types of corruption and questionable ethics in government during the Gilded Age.

CULTURAL

● **1873** *One of the first schools of nursing opens at Bellevue Hospital in New York*

● **1876** *National Baseball League formed*
● **1883** *Joseph Pulitzer buys the* New York World

1865	1875

● **1872** *Crédit Mobilier scheme uncovered*

POLITICAL

● **1883** *Pendleton Act passes*
● **1884** *Cleveland elected President*

◀ CROQUET DRESS, LATE 1800s

- **1890** *Reporter Nelly Bly circles globe by train and steamship in 72 days*

- **1895** *William Randolph Hearst purchases the New York* Morning Journal

1885

1895

- **1890** *McKinley Tariff passes*

- **1896** *McKinley elected President*

★★★★★★★★★★★★★★★★★★★★★★★★★★★★★★★★★★★

A Tarnished Image

Setting the Scene

Section Focus

In the late 1800s, there were scandals at all levels of government. In the eyes of many critics, politics reached a low point. Although that low point was not maintained, it dealt a lasting blow to the image of politicians.

Objectives

After studying this section, you should be able to

★ identify the major causes of increased political corruption.

★ give examples of corruption at local, state, and national levels.

Key Terms

graft, political machine, kickback, ward, lobbyist, township

▲ *The Brains*, by Thomas Nast, 1871

The Gilded Age was a phrase coined by two authors of the period—Mark Twain and Charles Dudley Warner—in a novel about the corruption of the Grant administration. In the years following the Civil War, the quality of American government left much to be desired. Politicians were irresponsible, loyalties were shallow, and money was tainted.

In this post-Civil War period, the most ambitious and talented people were no longer attracted to politics but to business. Indeed, politics itself became something of a business. The goal of political entrepreneurs was to achieve power and position through political office. Often politicians were able to line their pockets with money. Corruption seemed to flourish at every level of government. At first the corruption was not apparent. Material progress had produced a society that appeared to be bright and attractive. Society and government were not what they appeared to be on the surface, however.

■ Political Machines

Some of the most outrageous examples of **graft,** or thievery in office, were those at the grassroots level of city government. A factor that contributed to corrupt city government was the rapid growth of cities.

Growth of Cities

In 1840 there were only 131 cities in the United States; by 1880 there were 939. In addition cities often doubled, tripled, or even quadrupled in size within a decade. Services for these large populations had to be expanded at a rate never experienced before. Providing increased police and fire protection, water supplies, and sewage disposal was a daunting task for what often were untrained and ill-paid city officials. At the same time, businesses were eager to get lucrative contracts for paving streets and building new schools. An alliance between business and politics that fostered corruption resulted.

Maintaining Control

The usual democratic restraints on abuses of power did not work well in the cities of this era. Large portions of the population of cities were immigrants who had little or no experience with urban living or with democratic government. Many were accustomed to corruption in government. Both poor immigrants and native-born residents had little time to worry about abstract notions of government. They worked from dawn to dusk just to keep food on the table. Those more well-off, who might have gone into politics, were busy making money in business and real estate. As a result, almost every major city was dominated by a **political machine**—a party-linked political organization that maintained power by controlling votes, controlling the courts, and controlling the police as well.

The strength of a political machine came from the bottom up, not from the top down. Local politicians took care of the needs of their voters. They often provided groceries to families who were needy, organized free celebrations on important national holidays, attended ethnic religious and social events, and even helped get people out of jail. In this way politicians earned the loyalty of their neighborhood citizens. When election time came around, the votes were always there, keeping the helpful politicians in power.

The "Tweed Ring"

The most notorious city machine was the "Tweed Ring" in New York City. In 1868 "Boss" William M. Tweed gained control of New York's Democratic machine, known locally by the name of its central meeting place—Tammany Hall. For the next 3 years, he and his underlings managed to steal millions of dollars of city funds. The usual way this was done involved a process known as the "kickback." A **kickback** was an arrangement whereby contractors would pad, or increase, the amount of their bills for city work and pay or "kick back" a percentage of that amount to politicians in the ring. In one

 Visualizing History

▲ THE TRUSTS Powerful trusts dominate the United States Senate in this 1889 cartoon by Joseph Keppler. The people's entrance to the Senate chambers (upper left) is shown bolted shut. *How did the trusts influence senators?*

example a county courthouse that should have cost taxpayers $250,000 actually cost $11 million. One plastering contractor was paid almost $3 million for 9 months' work.

In 1871 *The New York Times* published evidence of Tweed's rampant greed. At the same time, Thomas Nast, a brilliant political cartoonist, ridiculed Tweed in his cartoons for *Harper's Weekly.* Nast's cartoons found their mark and were devastating. Tweed was driven to complain: "I don't care a straw for your newspaper articles: my people don't know how to read, but they can't help seeing them . . . pictures." Tweed and his cronies were convicted of criminal conduct and driven from office.

In spite of Tweed's removal, Tammany Hall continued to be an active influence in New York politics. This was true because local machine leaders drew their power from the local neighborhoods that they served 24 hours a day. A good deal of the graft, however, was used to help needy residents of the neighborhood **wards,** small administrative divisions of a city.

Occasionally city graft became so flagrant that voters were driven to "throw the rascals out" and put in a reform administration. Such movements often failed. Reform candidates focused on economy and honest administration but failed to understand the reasons why the political machines commandeered so much loyalty and met with such success.

■ Widespread Corruption

Corruption was not limited to local governments. It also occurred at the state and federal levels. In addition to the corruption, government in the late 1800s was affected by a marked lack of leadership. Neither Congress nor the President provided the direction the nation needed.

▲ NAST AND TWEED Thomas Nast (left) entertained Americans with biting political cartoons in the late 1800s. The most well-known political machine was run by "Boss" William M. Tweed (right). *Why did corruption in the federal government spread during the Grant administration?*

In State Government

Politics at the state level was nearly as corrupt as in the cities. In many states big business stood to gain or lose large amounts of money as a result of legislative votes on various matters, such as tax rates and internal improvements. Thus, companies spent large sums to influence votes.

In pre-Civil War times, businesspeople influenced politicians by writing letters and inviting them to expensive dinners. After the war the demands on government increased to the point that the amount of money spent by state governments was huge, and the stakes for those seeking state contracts were high. Businesses now began to employ **lobbyists**—people paid to represent a company or a special interest group. Sometimes they tried to influence votes by offering money in the form of campaign contributions. If it was unclear who would win a race, contributions were given to both parties. Such payments were regarded by legislators and lobbyists alike as "insurance" against unfavorable legislation.

At other times money was offered in the form of outright bribes. When Jay Gould controlled the Erie Railroad, he was reported to have spent $500,000 in bribes during a single session of the New York state legislature. Of the relations between the Standard Oil Company and the government of Pennsylvania, one observer wrote, "The Standard has done everything with the Pennsylvania legislature except to refine it."

In Federal Government

In general there was more corruption in state and local politics than in national politics. By far the worst misconduct in the federal government occurred when Grant was President.

Grant had been a great general, but he was a poor President. Although he was personally honest, he seemed unable to distinguish decent people from the dishonest. Dazzled by wealth, he fell under the sway of the financial speculators James J. Fisk and Jay Gould, who reaped millions of dollars from their relationship with the President. Members of Grant's family, personal staff,

▲ **MR. DOOLEY** Humorist Finley Peter Dunne is dwarfed by his creation, Mr. Dooley. Like Nast, Dunne was a shrewd observer of political events at the turn of the century. *Which political party were new immigrants likely to join?*

and cabinet peddled influence and jobs in return for cash. At one time Grant's brother managed to hold four jobs by farming out the duties to other men.

Crédit Mobilier

In 1872 the scandals spread to Congress as well. A New York newspaper revealed that officers of the Union Pacific Railroad had formed their own construction company called the Crédit Mobilier. The contracts this company received enabled the railroad officers to reap enormous personal profits. To forestall investigation, the company distributed shares of stock "where it would do the most good." Grant's Vice President and several prominent members of Congress turned out to have accepted these thinly disguised bribes.

When the graft in his administration was uncovered, Grant declared that he would "let no guilty man escape." However, he protected many accused of wrongdoing from both investigation and punishment.

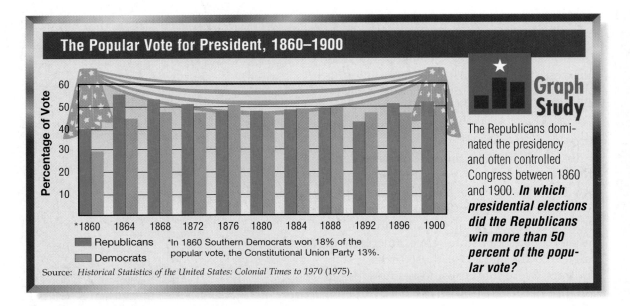

The Popular Vote for President, 1860–1900

Percentage of Vote

*1860 1864 1868 1872 1876 1880 1884 1888 1892 1896 1900

■ Republicans
■ Democrats

*In 1860 Southern Democrats won 18% of the popular vote, the Constitutional Union Party 13%.

Source: *Historical Statistics of the United States: Colonial Times to 1970* (1975).

Graph Study

The Republicans dominated the presidency and often controlled Congress between 1860 and 1900. *In which presidential elections did the Republicans win more than 50 percent of the popular vote?*

■ Postwar Political Parties

Even political analysts often found it difficult to explain the positions Democrats and Republicans took on major issues such as the tariff and railroad regulation. English writer James Bryce wrote:

❝ *Neither party has, as a party, anything to say on these issues, neither party has any clean-cut principles. . . . All has been lost except office or the hope of it.* ❞

Issues Split Parties

One reason that parties seemed so similar was that they both reflected sectional differences so accurately. At every level, from wards to **townships,** or smaller divisions of a county broken up into local government districts, political parties were popular, and democratic participation was high. They did not avoid any of the issues; rather they were split internally on most of them. In the Northeast, for example, with its strong banking system, both parties favored the gold standard. In the Midwest both parties favored increasing the amount of money in circulation. Republicans in the developing Midwest were protariff, while Southern Democrats were antitariff. Both

parties in the Northeast were divided on the tariff issue.

The humorist "Mr. Dooley," created by Finley Peter Dunne, described a hypothetical candidate for President as someone who was pulled in different directions by varied interests and needed to be all things to all people.

❝ *Wanted: a good, active Dimmy-crat, sthrong iv lung an' limb; must be . . . a sympathizer with th' crushed an' down throdden people but not be anny means hostile to vested inthrests; must advocate sthrikes, gover'mint be injunction, free silver, sound money, greenbacks, a single tax, a tariff f'r rivinoo . . . at home in Wall sthreet an' th' stock yards, in th' parlors iv th' r-rich an' th' kitchens iv th' poor.* ❞

Although fairly evenly matched in strength, the two parties were hardly identical. Though both parties received support from people in every walk of life, each had a distinctive base of support.

Republicans

The Republicans were supported by Western farmers and merchants, who benefited from Republicans' internal improvements and liberal land policies, and Eastern businesspeople, who benefited from high tariffs and national banks. The Republicans tended to be old-immigrant Protestants—Presbyterians, Methodists, Congregationalists, or Baptists. The Republicans' problem was to keep together its Eastern and Western wings, which differed on such issues as greenbacks, free silver, tariffs, and banking.

The Republicans' "patron saint" was Abraham Lincoln, whose birthday they honored with banquets and oratory. As the party that had led during the Civil War, they had great prestige in the North and the West. "The party that saved the nation must rule it," they proclaimed.

While critics attacked the Republicans for keeping alive war hatreds by "waving the bloody shirt," appeals to the memory of the Civil War were much more than that. Republican strength came from genuine devotion to the idea of the United States as a nation rather than as a federation of states. Many Republicans continued to be inspired by the party's early idealism. They felt that government existed to advance the public good.

Democrats

Democrats, too, looked back to the Civil War. From the end of Radical Reconstruction until well into the twentieth century, Southern states formed the "Solid South," never wavering in its allegiance to the Democrats.

The Democrats could not have remained a national party with only Southern support, however. The party depended on an alliance between white Southerners and Northern city machines. Democrats tended to get the support of recent immigrants, many of whom were Catholics or liturgical Protestants, such as Lutherans or Episcopalians. Their religious and cultural background was quite different from that of evangelical Protestants, such as Methodists and Baptists, who formed the core of the Republican party. The Democrats had allies among Western farmers, especially when crop prices were low, and among certain groups of businesspeople and owners of import companies who favored a lower tariff.

The Democratic party had two "patron saints"—Thomas Jefferson and Andrew Jackson. Like these leaders the Democrats claimed to represent the interests of ordinary Americans. The Democrats took issue with the Republican view of the United States as a nation. "This is no nation," said one Democrat. "We are free and independent states." In contrast to the Republicans' view that the federal government should take an active role in helping the needy and shaping national growth, the Democrats wanted to keep the federal government on a skimpy allowance and a short leash. "That government governs best which governs least" remained their motto.

During the entire period from 1865 to 1900, Democrats held the presidency for only two terms. Although they usually lost the White House, the Democrats were seldom far out of the running. Democratic candidates often got almost as many popular votes as their victorious opponents, and it was rare that the Republicans did not have to deal with Democrats in control of at least one house of Congress.

Section 1 ★ Review

Checking for Understanding

1. **Identify** William M. Tweed, Thomas Nast, Finley Peter Dunne.

2. **Define** graft, political machine, kickback, ward, lobbyist, township.

3. **Cite** examples of corruption that occurred in government.

4. **State** how Republicans and Democrats viewed the role of the federal government.

Critical Thinking

5. **Interpreting Satire** In his description of the ideal campaign candidate on page 548, what was Mr. Dooley expressing about politicians?

Interpreting Primary Sources

Political Corruption

None of William "Boss" Tweed's critics leveled more scathing attacks at his notorious Tammany Hall machine than did Thomas Nast, a cartoonist for *Harper's Weekly. Harper's* magazine pioneered the use of illustrations and cartoons to comment on significant political issues of the day. Under Nast's pen, Tweed and his cronies were depicted as vultures, jailed criminals, and smiling deceivers.

Tweed was well aware of the political damage that Nast's cartoons could do to him and the Tammany Hall political machine. He ordered his men to stop Nast from drawing his cartoons. Tweed cared little what the papers wrote about him because most of his constituents could not read. However, they could see and understand the message of the cartoons.

In this cartoon, "Who Stole the People's Money?" the answer is "'Twas Him." Tweed appears as the heavyset man in the left foreground of the cartoon.

On Tweed's right a man holds a hat labeled "chairs," a reference to the $179,000 New York City paid for 40 chairs and 3 tables. Other contractors and cheats—their names on their coats—complete the circle.

Articles and cartoons published in *Harper's Weekly* and *The New York Times* led to the downfall of the Tweed Ring. Citizens worked to remove Tweed and his accomplices from political office. Several members of the ring left the country, and Tweed himself was arrested in 1871. His first trial resulted in a hung jury, but a second trial brought a conviction. He died in jail in 1878.

▲ **WHO STOLE THE PEOPLE'S MONEY? 'TWAS HIM**

Thomas Nast was born in Germany but was brought to the United States as a child and spent most of his life there. Nast worked as a news illustrator for a number of national magazines, gaining a national reputation for his cartoons during the Civil War. Nast is also credited with creating the elephant and donkey symbols of the Republican and Democratic parties.

Examining the Primary Source

1. What label identifies the group in the circle?

2. What does clothing show in this cartoon?

3. How does the cartoon visually answer the question posed in its title, "Who Stole the People's Money?"

Critical Thinking

4. **Analyzing Information** What statement does Nast make in his cartoon about the extent of political corruption in New York City?

★★★

Calls for Good Government

Setting the Scene

Section Focus

During the 1870s and the 1880s, social reformers like Henry George tried to raise the alarm that official corruption threatened democracy in the United States. If reformers wanted rebellion, they were disappointed, but through their efforts, a slow and steady movement away from the abuses of the Grant administration began. The first hopeful sign was the election of Rutherford B. Hayes in 1876.

Objectives

After studying this section, you should be able to

★ identify the reforms made during the 1870s and the 1880s.

★ describe the tariff controversy.

Key Terms

patronage, rider, free-trader, protectionist

◀ **DEMOCRATIC BANNER, 1888**

*B*efore the administration of Rutherford B. Hayes, one of the common practices had been **patronage**—the assumed right of elected officials to control political appointments to unelected positions. Patronage employees made the federal government the epitome of apathy and astonishingly idle.

■ Civil Service Reforms

With the election of Hayes, the tone of national politics began to change. Hayes made some steps toward rescuing the presidency from congressional domination.

Hayes Begins Reforms

After his inauguration in 1877, Hayes named Carl Schurz, owner of a German-language newspaper in St. Louis, Missouri, and United States Senator from Missouri, to take charge of the Department of the Interior, which had previously been the scene of some of the worst examples of patronage. This practice was soon curbed. Hayes also forbade the practice of "shaking down" federal workers—forcing them to make political campaign contributions.

Hayes also defied congressional leaders by blocking important appointments favored by individual members of Congress. In addition he refused to sign otherwise acceptable legislation if Congress had attached **riders**—irrelevant amendments—of which he disapproved. He vetoed several appropriations bills with riders attached and finally won a clear-cut victory. Through his actions Hayes not only cut down on corruption but began to restore the balance of power between Congress and the President.

Election of 1880

Hayes's reforms brought him enemies among the Stalwarts, a group of Republican machine politicians who strongly opposed civil service reform. After Hayes declined to run for a second term, the party became divided between the Stalwarts, who wanted to nominate Grant for a third term, and the "Halfbreeds," who opposed Grant. After a prolonged deadlock at the national convention, the Republicans nominated dark horse James A. Garfield, a former Union general.

To blunt the old charge of disloyalty in wartime, the Democrats nominated General Winfield S. Hancock, a Union hero of the Battle of Gettysburg. The intellectual level of the ensuing campaign may be judged by the following excerpt from the speech of a Republican orator:

> " *I belong to a party that believes in good crops; that is glad when a fellow finds a gold mine; that rejoices when there are forty bushels of wheat to the acre. . . . [T]he Democratic party is a party of famine; it is a good friend of an early frost; it believes in the Colorado beetle and in the weevil.* "

Despite such inflammatory rhetoric, Garfield narrowly won the election.

The Pendleton Act

Under Hayes and Garfield, government was cleaner than it had been during the Grant administration, but the spoils system remained a constant source of inefficiency and graft. Disputes over patronage poisoned the relationship between the President and Congress. There was little momentum for reform.

In July 1881, however, as President Garfield entered the Washington, D.C., railroad station, he was shot by a disappointed office seeker. The unbalanced man cried, "I am a Stalwart and Arthur is President now." Garfield clung to life for two months, but in September Vice President Chester A. Arthur, a New York Stalwart, succeeded to the presidency.

Garfield's assassination excited public opinion against the spoils system. In 1883 Congress passed the Pendleton Act, which has been called (with some exaggeration) "the Magna Carta of civil service reform." This law allowed the President to decree which federal jobs would be filled according to rules laid down by a bipartisan Civil Service Commission. Candidates competed for

Visualizing History

▲ **ASSASSINATION OF THE PRESIDENT** President Garfield was shot only four months after his inauguration by a frustrated patronage seeker, Charles J. Guiteau. In this engraving, Guiteau flees while James G. Blaine, secretary of state, supports Garfield. ***After Garfield's death, who became President?***

AMERICAN PORTRAITS

Susan B. Anthony
1820–1906

From her Quaker upbringing, Susan B. Anthony learned that men and women were equal before God. She spent most of her 86 years trying to convince others of that equality.

After teaching school for several years, Anthony returned home to help run the family farm. While living in her father's house, she began to focus on the great reform movements of the day. Anthony first joined a temperance group and experienced gender discrimination firsthand when she was refused permission to speak at a temperance rally. Realizing that as long as women were propertyless and voteless they would also remain powerless, Anthony began devoting her considerable energies to securing equal rights for women. Throughout the four decades from the end of the Civil War to her death, she was the nation's foremost crusader for a woman's right to vote.

these jobs through examinations. Appointments could be made only from the list of those who took the exams. A civil service official could not be removed for political reasons.

Although President Arthur was a veteran of machine politics, he supported the Pendleton Act, placing 14,000 jobs (about one-tenth of the total) under the control of the civil service. The federal government had finally begun a shift away from the spoils system.

■ Cleveland in Office

The reform movement begun by Hayes and continued by Garfield and Arthur did not stop. Thus, the major theme of the presidential election of 1884 was honesty in politics.

Election of 1884

The Republican nominee, Representative James G. Blaine, was a man of great ability and personal charm. However, his reputation was clouded by charges that he had taken money for helping a railroad. As a result some independent reformers in the Republican party, called "Mugwumps," did not support him. The Democrats won Mugwump support by nominating Grover Cleveland, who earned a reputation for integrity as mayor of Buffalo and governor of New York.

The campaign of 1884 was a negative one, focusing less on issues and more on character assassination. Blaine was portrayed as a "tattooed man" with railroad stocks and bonds indelibly engraved on his skin. Cleveland was attacked on the grounds that he had hired a substitute to fight for him in the Civil War and that he had fathered an illegitimate child. Republicans chanted:

Ma! Ma! Where's my pa?
Gone to the White House,
Ha! Ha! Ha!

To which the Democrats countered:

Blaine, Blaine, James G. Blaine,
The continental liar from the
State of Maine.

Cleveland won the election by a narrow margin, becoming the first Democratic President elected since 1856. Balloting in New York was close. Had 600 voters switched to Blaine, he would have won the state—and the presidency. The Republicans retained control of the Senate, but the Democrats gained a majority in the House of Representatives.

▲ GROVER CLEVELAND

Visualizing History

▲ BLAINE This cartoon portrays James G. Blaine as a protector of tariffs. The person in the kilt is industrialist Andrew Carnegie. *In what ways was the campaign of 1884 a negative campaign?*

Reforms Continue

Unskillful in political maneuvering, Cleveland often met defeat in his dealings with Congress. Nevertheless, his devotion to the public good did much to restore the prestige of the presidency. Cleveland's first problem was to deal with the Democratic office seekers who swarmed to Washington seeking the fruits of his victory. If he were to make appointments on merit alone, he would split his party wide open. If he were to give in to the spoils system, he would lose the support of the Mugwumps and other reformers who had played a decisive part in electing him. As a compromise Cleveland appointed many "deserving Democrats" to office. He also made every effort to see that the new appointees were qualified.

Cleveland entered office with a weak understanding of most national issues but worked intensely at the job. Few Presidents have put in more study to determine what course of action to follow. His Republican predecessors, for example, had signed hundreds of private bills giving pensions to veterans unable to qualify under regular laws. Examining such bills with care, Cleveland found many of them fraudulent. One veteran, for example, asked for a pension for an injury suffered while *intending* to enlist. Cleveland disapproved of so many pension bills that his vetoes totaled more than those of all previous Presidents.

Cleveland worked to improve government efficiency and integrity. He supported the Presidential Succession Act, which established a line of succession to the presidency in the event of the death of the Vice President. He also won repeal of the Tenure of Office Act, which strengthened presidential independence. Interested in preserving public lands, Cleveland reclaimed land from private companies that had not lived up to the terms of their land grants.

■ Tariffs and the Election of 1888

The public question that Cleveland studied most seriously was the tariff. During the Civil War, duties had been raised from an average of 19 percent in 1861 to more than 40 percent in 1865.

Different Views on Tariffs

High tariff rates, which benefited manufacturers, were constantly attacked by farmers, consumers, shippers, and importers. These **free-traders** argued that a protective tariff was unfair government interference with the normal laws of supply and demand. Tariffs, they said, were subsidies paid to manufacturers out of the pockets of consumers.

Protectionists, on the other hand, defended the tariff as a means of nurturing fledgling industries in the United States. They argued that tariffs kept wages high by shielding them from competition with cheap foreign labor. Previous bills to lower the tariff had been defeated.

Shortly after Cleveland took office, Carl Schurz asked him about his views on the tariff issue. "You know I really don't know anything about it," replied the President. "In my political career as sherriff of Buffalo County, mayor of Buffalo, and governor of New York, it has, of course, not been an issue." Cleveland investigated the problem thoroughly. His studies convinced him that the existing tariff was responsible for the treasury's large surplus. Cleveland argued that the surplus was a sign of overtaxation. He proposed a reduction of the tariff—not because he was a free-trader, but because he was in favor of limited government. Excess money in the treasury, he said, was not good for the economy; it was a temptation to Congress, which was apt to spend it wastefully. The President's dramatic effort to lower the tariff was blocked by House Republicans.

Harrison Elected President

The tariff became the major issue in the presidential election of 1888. Openly avowing protection for the first time, the Republicans collected a record-breaking campaign fund. "Put all the manufacturers of Pennsylvania under the fire," said a Republican campaign manager, "and fry that fat out of them." The Republicans revived Henry Clay's name for the protective tariff, calling their economic program the "American system." Renominating Cleveland, the Democrats campaigned against unnecessary taxation. As in 1880 and 1884, the result was extremely close.

Although he got fewer popular votes than Cleveland, the Republican candidate, Benjamin Harrison, won a majority in the electoral college.

The new President was a quiet, reserved man, whom one observer called a "human iceberg." Harrison was too reserved to make a good Gilded Age politician. Still, he had an able legal mind and a distinguished career as an attorney in Indiana. He had been elected to the Senate in 1881.

Harrison had fought under Sherman at Atlanta and was not shy about "waving the bloody shirt" for votes. An ardent protectionist, he was conservative in fiscal policy and liberal when it came to veterans' pensions.

Treasury Surplus and the Tariffs

Once in office the Republicans promptly disposed of the treasury surplus by spending it, and it was the last time in history that the government held a surplus. Within two years the "Billion-Dollar Congress" had

▲ **PRESIDENT HARRISON** Unlike Cleveland before him, President Benjamin Harrison favored attempts to freely spend the mounting treasury surplus. *How long did it take the "Billion-Dollar Congress" to convert the surplus into a deficit?*

created a deficit, mostly through handouts to special-interest groups. The number of Civil War pensioners increased by more than half—many of them the same ones whom Cleveland had turned down.

Moving on to the election-winning tariff issue, the Republicans passed the McKinley Tariff of 1890, which was the highest in the country's history. It dried up revenue by levying rates so high that some foreign products were kept entirely out of the country.

Nearly every foreign product that competed with American-made products was heavily taxed, including such items as food, clothing, furniture, and tools. Western silver states supported the tariff in exchange for the passage of the Sherman Silver Purchase Act, which authorized the federal government to buy up 4.5 million ounces of silver a month.

Millions of dollars were spent on the improvement of harbors and waterways, coastal defenses, federal buildings, and naval expansion. Congress also passed the Sherman Antitrust Act and provided for admission to the Union of North and South Dakota, Montana, Washington, Idaho, and Wyoming.

Several Issues Hurt Republicans

The Republicans' position on protective tariffs, which had helped them win the presidency in 1888, hurt them two years later. Because there was little competition in the market, prices generally were falling; thus, debts were harder to repay.

Republicans also were hurt nationally by local Republicans in such states as Wisconsin and Massachusetts, who supported compulsory public school attendance where instruction was in English. Many Catholic and Lutheran immigrant families residing in these states wanted public funding for their parochial schools, in which students were taught in their first language. Republicans also pushed Prohibition at the grassroots level.

Democrats used these issues, together with that of a backfiring tariff, to attack the Republicans. The congressional elections of 1890 resulted in a Democratic landslide.

By 1892 the Republicans' position was even worse. Dispiritedly, they renominated Harrison, and the Democrats nominated Grover Cleveland again. Popular discontent with the Republicans was so high that for the first time since before the Civil War Democrats won not only the White House but both houses of Congress.

This time, however, Cleveland won by more than 350,000 popular votes and an electoral majority of 277 to 145. Cleveland became the only President in American history to serve two nonconsecutive terms.

Of larger importance than Cleveland's margin of victory was the support given to a third-party candidate, James B. Weaver. Weaver, who had been the candidate for the Greenback party in 1880, ran in 1892 under the banner of the new People's party, better known as the Populist party. By this time, a large part of the American electorate was already responding to the Populist philosophy.

Section 2 ★ Review

Checking for Understanding

1. **Identify** Rutherford B. Hayes, James Garfield, Chester Arthur, Grover Cleveland.

2. **Define** patronage, rider, free-trader, protectionist.

3. **Describe** political reforms made during the 1870s and the 1880s.

4. **Explain** the controversy over raising or lowering the tariff.

Critical Thinking

5. **Evaluating Reforms**   How could the civil service system limit the patronage system and cut down on corruption?

★★★★★★★★★★★★★★★★★★★★★★★

Cultural Life

Section Focus

The Civil War was also a turning point in cultural life. The period after the war was a time of rapid change. Some satirized the values of post-Civil War society, as in Twain and Warner's description of a poorly maintained Washington Monument. Others celebrated the country's emergence as an industrial giant.

◄ *THE BATH* BY MARY CASSATT

Objectives

After studying this section, you should be able to

★ discuss developments in literature, art, and higher education.

★ describe how various leisure activities expanded.

Key Terms

antebellum, realism, expatriate, yellow journalism

The United States was quickly becoming an urban, industrialized society. It needed citizens who could understand complex political and economic questions, and it needed literate workers and managers who could staff its offices, shops, and factories.

■ Education

In the late nineteenth century, the nation reformed its educational system. Public education and higher education benefited from the reforms.

Public Education

By 1900 many states had or were working toward compulsory school attendance. In cities, graded schools replaced one-room schoolhouses. The school year, which had traditionally been squeezed in between fall harvest and spring planting, was lengthened. Many cities also introduced free secondary education, and the number of public high schools increased from a few hundred in 1860 to more than 2,500 in 1890. Yet there remained much room for improvement. In 1900 the average child received only 5 years of schooling.

Private Colleges and Universities

The most far-reaching development in education during the late 1800s was the expansion of higher education. At mid-century most colleges and universities in the United States had poor equipment, scanty libraries, and ill-trained, overworked faculties. Fixed curricula that emphasized ancient Greek and Roman thought included little training in modern languages, history, or science. There were no first-rate graduate schools in law, medicine, or the liberal arts. No American scientific school compared well with the best in Europe.

By 1900 these weaknesses had been vigorously attacked. Responding to the need for more practical education, colleges in the United States reformed their fields of study. Courses in the social and natural sciences were made available, and the elective system, first introduced at Harvard, made it possible for students to choose an individual course of study.

Young scholars from the United States who were trained in the world's best universities—in Germany—brought back higher standards of scholarship and scientific research. Existing private universities were greatly expanded, and new ones were founded—most with the aid of wealthy businesspeople who supported the trend toward making education more useful. More than two dozen new schools were devoted specifically to technical training. The Massachusetts Institute of Technology and others like it supplied industry with highly trained engineers, metallurgists, and chemists. Also during this period the first graduate schools of business, such as the Wharton School of Finance, were established.

State Universities

Along with the growth of privately endowed universities and technical schools came an expansion of state universities. Such institutions owed a great deal to the Morrill Act of 1862, which gave public lands to each state as a grant to finance the endowment of colleges. While the main goal of these schools was to extend knowledge of "agriculture and mechanic arts," they were funded to teach science and classical studies as well. The University of California, Texas A&M, and most of the large state universities of the Midwest began as land-grant colleges.

Universities in the Midwest also played an important role in opening higher education to women for the first time. In the pre-Civil War era, women had been admitted to Oberlin and Antioch colleges in Ohio. After the war, coeducation became common west of the Appalachians. In the more conservative East, women founded private colleges of their own, such as Mount Holyoke, Vassar, Smith, Radcliffe, and Bryn Mawr. These colleges shared the same educational goals as all-male institutions.

The adult public also cried out for more learning. Beginning in 1874 as a summer program to train Sunday school teachers,

 History AND ART

▲ *SNAP THE WHIP* by Winslow Homer, 1872 Winslow Homer's painting captures the joy of a school recess. Homer is known for his vivid use of color and attention to detail. *What European artistic styles did he reject?*

Personal Hygiene

For polite society in the late nineteenth century, a virtual wall of silence surrounded the bathroom and related subjects. Such modesty would have been unthinkable in colonial America, or even on the farm, where privacy was rare. The invention of indoor plumbing—and with it the flush toilet—exemplified a revolution in personal hygiene and habits that transpired during the Gilded Age.

The word *toilet* reflected this change. Americans borrowed it from the French word *toilette*, which referred to grooming, as a euphemism for the British water closet, or simply, W.C.

Only when privy facilities were moved indoors did it become possible to treat this most human of topics with delicacy. The first bathroom in a household was installed in the New York residence of George Vanderbilt in 1855. Other wealthy families soon followed suit, although early plumbing systems were far from sanitary.

With the mass production of enamel-coated fixtures around the turn of the century, indoor plumbing in private homes became more commonplace. After cities acquired water and sewage systems, piping was run first to the kitchen. Next connected were washbasins and, finally, the bathtub and toilet. The bathroom thus became a room of genuine privacy.

▲ BATHROOM, c. 1880

---

the Chautauqua (shuh•TAW•kwuh) Institute in western New York sparked a movement that provided the masses with instruction in such subjects as literature, economics, science, and government through summer school instruction and correspondence school.

■ Literature

United States writers responded to the post-Civil War era in different ways. One popular school of postwar writers looked backward, striving to capture the romance of vanishing rural traditions. A center of such "local-color" writing was the South. Civil War and Reconstruction had swept away an entire way of life, leaving poverty and destruction in its wake. In the 1870s and the 1880s, Southern local colorists wrote nostalgically about **antebellum**—or pre-Civil War—manners, customs, and institutions.

Local colorists also wrote of vanishing ways of life in the small towns and fishing villages of New England, on the farms of the Midwest, on the ranches of the plains, and in the mining camps and boomtowns of the Wild West.

One of America's greatest writers was a local colorist named Samuel Clemens who wrote under the name Mark Twain. Twain wrote vivid and hilarious stories about his travels in the West. His most enduring works—*The Adventures of Tom Sawyer* and *The Adventures of Huckleberry Finn*—are tales of his boyhood home on the Mississippi River. Twain's books were not only acclaimed by critics but loved by the public. He combined shrewd observation and irreverent wit.

Twain's writing bridged the gap between popular and highbrow literature, between ordinary local-color writing and **realism,** a European-influenced movement that strove for accurate representation.

Realist writers wanted to get away from the emotional preoccupations of the romantic movement and the pretty, sentimental themes of popular literature. Realist writers took a close look at real people's lives and problems. William Dean Howells declared that novels should "speak the dialect, the language, that most Americans know." In *The Rise of Silas Lapham,* Howells depicted a crude but likable bumpkin—the new American millionaire. In *The Red Badge of Courage,* Stephen Crane depicted a Union soldier's fear and cowardice under fire. Other realists exposed the seamy underside of urban life. Critics of realism argued that realistic fiction was not uplifting, that its subject matter was often ordinary or even ugly, and that its characters' misdeeds were not always suitably punished.

▲ *THE LITTLE WHITE GIRL* by James Abbott McNeill Whistler, 1864 James Whistler adapted the concepts of Japanese color prints to his own style. ***What subjects did realist artists seek to portray?***

■ Art and Architecture

Realism was also an important force in American painting during the Gilded Age. Rejecting the classicism and romanticism of the first half of the century, realist painters portrayed ordinary people in everyday activities. Winslow Homer moved from painting Civil War scenes to subjects such as a schoolyard full of boys playing a rowdy game, a hunter and his dogs, or sailors at sea. Of another great realist painter, Walt Whitman said:

❝ *I never knew of but one artist, and that's Tom Eakins, who could resist the temptation to see what they thought ought to be rather than what is.* ❞

Some of America's greatest painters, however, became **expatriates**—people who choose to live outside their native country. John Singer Sargent, a portraitist of Europe's upper classes, lived in England. James Abbott McNeill Whistler and Mary Cassatt also lived in Europe. Cassatt was influenced by a style of painting called impressionism. Impressionists tried to capture the play of light, color, and pattern as they made immediate impressions on the senses.

The architecture of the Gilded Age was heavy and ornate. It is often called "Victorian," after Queen Victoria of Great Britain who reigned from 1837 to 1901. On the outside, Victorian houses had turrets, towers, porches, and gables. The development of better woodworking machines made it possible to add elaborate "gingerbread" decorations to roofs and porches of houses. The interior decor was similarly ornamented. Rooms were crowded with dark, thickly carved furniture, plush carpeting, heavy curtains, and countless knickknacks on ornate shelves.

Some dismissed the Victorian style as vulgar—a symbol of greed that characterized the Gilded Age. Others have celebrated the gaudiness as a symbol of the period's vitality and exuberance.

The Yellow Press and the Dime Novel

The Industrial Revolution brought some Americans unaccustomed leisure time. As machines took over the work of more and more hands, the time required to produce a shirt, a bucket, a pin, or a table was reduced to a fraction of what it had been. Hours of work, although still long by the standards of the twentieth century, were gradually reduced. As leisure time increased, new forms of entertainment developed.

Penny Newspapers

Journalism took new forms. In the late 1800s, improvements in papermaking and printing made it possible to produce newspapers more cheaply than before. At the same time, newspapers could make their profits entirely from advertisers. Copies were sold below cost to attract the greatest number of readers. These penny newspapers strove to amuse readers as much as to inform them. Their intended audience was not the educated middle and upper classes but clerks, laborers, and homemakers.

The pioneer among the penny newspapers was the *New York World,* purchased by Joseph Pulitzer in 1883. In 15 years its circulation rose from 15,000 to more than 1 million. Pulitzer, dedicating his paper "to the cause of the people rather than the purse-proud potentates," attacked unfair employers and grafting politicians with vigor. The real source of Pulitzer's success, however, was not politics but sensationalism. He was one of the first to use "scare headlines" like "Baptized in Blood" and "Death Rides the Rails." He also introduced the colorized Sunday supplement and the serialized comic strip. From the yellow ink he used in his comics came the term **"yellow journalism,"** which critics applied to the subject matter and style of the *World* and all its imitators. If he could not find news, Pulitzer made it. Once he sent a young reporter, Nelly Bly, to travel around the globe in less time than it took the hero of Jules Verne's popular novel, *Around the World in Eighty Days.*

▲ THE "YELLOW KID" COMIC STRIP, 1896

Dime Novels

Another form of reading matter produced for a mass market was the dime novel, which was designed especially to interest boys. These were adventure stories where heroes such as Mustang Sam and Deadwood Dick fought cattle rustlers and outlaws. Dime novels also portrayed the worlds of business and crime. Moralists suspected that these early paperbacks would corrupt the young. Defenders pointed out, however, that because dime novels were not the work of realists, no bad deed ever went unpunished; no good boy went without his just reward.

Sports and Entertainment

As work became less strenuous, many looked for leisure activities that involved physical exercise. Golf, croquet, and lawn tennis from Great Britain were popular sports with the middle and upper classes. College students brought in other British sports, including rowing, track, and rugby (from which American football was derived).

Baseball, however, was a truly American invention—its earliest form was played before the Civil War. College and club teams sprang up all over the country in the late 1800s. The first professional team was the Cincinnati Red Stockings in 1869; in 1876 the National League was organized. Professional baseball found a ready audience and loyal fans in crowded urban areas where working-class people had little money for entertainment.

The enthusiasm for baseball had started during the Civil War, and it appeared that everyone was playing ball. A writer for a Nevada Territory newspaper noted:

> *The rage for ball playing is very apparent. Old fellows whose hair and teeth are going and gone and young ones who have just got their first breeches and boots on are knocking and tossing and catching ball on the plaza and the streets from daybreak to dark.*

Towns that had no baseball called for teams. In an article in the Walla Walla *Statesman,* one writer explained why a team was needed.

> *There is scarce a one-horse town . . . that has not one or more ball clubs. The practice of these clubs affords healthful exercise— something required by young men too closely confined to* workshops and stores. In view of this advantage, cannot we have a baseball club at Walla Walla? In these dull times an organization of the kind would serve to drive away the blues.

After the modern safety bicycle was substituted for the dangerous "high wheeler," bicycling became a craze. There were hundreds of bicycle clubs; special trains carried cyclists into the country on Sundays, and special bicycle paths were built in parks and suburbs. A transcontinental bicycle route was wanted.

Cities became centers of cultural life. In a day when the motion picture had not yet been invented, theater and vaudeville shows enjoyed great popularity. Large cities boasted opera companies and symphony orchestras, theaters, and museums of fine art.

In 1891 Peter Tchaikovsky, the Russian composer, came to America and conducted one of his own works at the new Carnegie Music Hall in New York City. He wrote home that everything went wonderfully, and that he was received with even greater enthusiasm than he had been in his native land.

► **CAP ANSON OF THE CHICAGO WHITE SOX**

Section 3 ★ Review

Checking for Understanding

1. **Identify** Mark Twain, Stephen Crane, James Abbott McNeill Whistler, Joseph Pulitzer, Thomas Eakins.

2. **Define** antebellum, realism, expatriate, yellow journalism.

3. **Characterize** the local-color and realist styles of literature.

4. **Give** examples of how Americans entertained themselves.

Critical Thinking

5. **Supporting Opinions** Argue for or against compulsory education in a democratic society. Support your opinion with facts or arguments that show how your position supports democratic goals.

Improvements in Printing

During the late 1800s, improvements in printing led to the inexpensive mass production of newspapers, magazines, and books. In 1863 American inventor William A. Bullock produced the first web-fed press. This press printed on huge rolls of paper rather than single sheets. Printer Richard March Hoe perfected the continuous-roll press in 1871. This device made it possible to produce up to 12,000 full newspapers an hour.

In 1886 linotype typesetting machines cut the time required to set type to a fraction of that required to set it by hand. The linotype operator sat at a keyboard. When the operator touched a letter on the keyboard, a lead mold was placed in line with other letters. Each complete line of type was molded onto a single slug, and the slugs were made into printing plates. The linotype allowed text to be assembled much faster into columns and pages.

Improved printing technology led to rapid growth of the publishing industry. It also led to increased competition among newspaper publishers to get out the "latest edition."

Improvements in printing also aided the magazine industry. For nearly 20 years after the Civil War, the magazine industry was limited by technology. For the most part, magazines were monthlies or weeklies that reached a small readership. The leaders in the field included the *Atlantic Monthly* and *Harper's Magazine.*

Improvements in the printing process, however, led to a new form of magazine in the 1880s. Such popular magazines as the *Ladies' Home Journal* and the *Saturday Evening Post* reached larger audiences.

Another development leading directly from improvements in printing concerned the Sunday edition. Throughout the country major city newspapers created Sunday papers of 50 or more pages. Comic strips, which began as Sunday features, were moved into separate colored supplements. By 1900 the formula of the American newspaper—daily and Sunday—was in place. In addition the new techniques helped magazines such as *McClure's* and the *Saturday Evening Post* achieve mass circulation.

▲ NEWSBOY IN THE EARLY 1900S

Making the Technology Connection

1. What is a linotype machine?
2. How did improved methods of printing and typesetting affect the publishing industry?

Linking Past and Present

3. How is most publishing done today?

Using Vocabulary

Each term below has one of the following connotations: *political, economic,* or *cultural.* Classify each term under its respective connotation. Write a sentence that explains the connection between the term and its connotation.

antebellum   political machine
expatriate   protectionist
free-trader   realism
graft   rider
kickback   yellow journalism

Reviewing Facts

1. **Explain** the increase in political corruption following the Civil War.
2. **Describe** types of corruption that took place in government.
3. **Name** the Presidents who introduced reform or resisted corruption in government.
4. **List** some political reforms made during the 1870s and the 1880s.
5. **Point out** why some were in favor of higher tariffs and others were opposed.
6. **List** changes in higher education.

Understanding Concepts

Corruption

1. How might patronage and the spoils system have allowed for more corruption in government?

Public Protest

2. What events described in this chapter suggest that a free press can inspire public protest of corruption in government?

Critical Thinking

1. **Linking Past and Present** What businesses today depend on people having leisure time? Would all these businesses exist if work hours had not been shortened? Explain.

2. **Analyzing Illustrations** Study the advertisement on this page and answer the questions that follow.
   a. What is the product that is featured in the advertisement?
   b. This advertisement appeared in 1885. In what ways would a modern advertisement differ from this example? In what ways would the ads be similar?

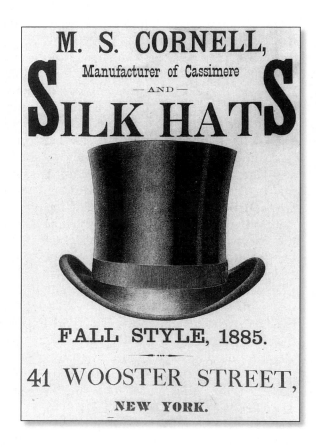

M. S. CORNELL,
Manufacturer of Cassimere
— AND —
SILK HATS
FALL STYLE, 1885.
41 WOOSTER STREET,
NEW YORK.

Writing About History

Definition

Imagine that you are an art critic attending the first showing of a group of American realist painters. Write a definition of realism that would be appropriate to include in an art review. To help your readers understand realism, use examples and comments about how this style contrasts with other schools of painting.

Cooperative Learning

Work with a partner to act out an interview between a newspaper reporter and a local political boss or a machine politician. Decide which role each of you will assume. The reporter should review information on corrupt government practices as were presented in the chapter. The politician should review information on party machines. The reporter should prepare a list of questions to ask the politician. The politician should prepare a list of answers to questions that he or she feels may be asked. After the interview, both of you should list what were the most pertinent points brought out in the interview. Compare your findings with those of other groups.

Social Studies Skills

Reading and Interpreting Political Cartoons

A political cartoon is meant to entertain as well as make a point about a current issue. Such cartoons often use caricatures, symbols, and/or analogies. Understanding a political cartoon involves understanding these caricatures, symbols, and analogies and determining the point of the cartoon.

Practicing the Skill

Use the following questions to help you interpret this political cartoon, "The Ladder of Fortune."

1. From the title, the words on the ladder, and the ladder's placement, what do the ladder and tree represent?

2. What are the keys to fortune?

3. What activities do not lead to success?

4. What are the rewards of climbing the ladder of fortune?

5. What people climb the ladder of fortune?

6. Why do you think the tree and the people in the foreground are in bright colors, whereas the people in the background are in black and white or dull colors?

7. Summarize in a sentence or two the point being made by this cartoon.

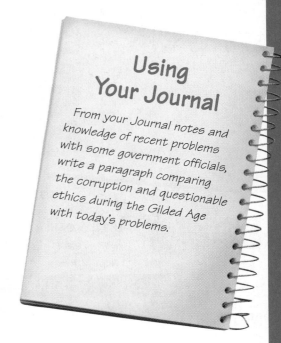

Using Your Journal

From your Journal notes and knowledge of recent problems with some government officials, write a paragraph comparing the corruption and questionable ethics during the Gilded Age with today's problems.

CHAPTER 21

★★

Politics and Protest
1865–1900

▶ **POLITICAL CAMPAIGN BUTTONS**

Setting the Scene

Focus

In the late nineteenth century, most Americans continued to live on the farm. By the 1880s, however, agriculture was in crisis. Farmers blamed their difficulties on abuses by the railroads, greedy bankers, and eastern industrialists. Farmers began to band together to fight these problems, which in turn led to the creation of a new political party, the Populists. Populism shared some goals with a larger movement aimed at redistributing the wealth and political power in the United States.

Concepts to Understand

★ Why economic inequity developed between farmers and urban workers

★ Why many reformers believed that social change would result in a more just and equitable society

Read to Discover . . .

★ some of the problems that American farmers faced in the 1880s.

★ what were the major goals of the Populist party.

Journal Notes

As you read the chapter, note in your journal the answers to these questions: Why was the Democratic party divided in 1896? What effect did this division have on the presidential election?

CULTURAL

● **1874** *National Woman's Christian Temperance Union formed in Cleveland*

● **1881** *Clara Barton founds the American Red Cross*

1865	1875

● **1871** *Civil Service Reform Act passed*

● **1877** Munn *v.* Illinois
● **1878** *Bland-Allison Act passes*

POLITICAL

I PLEAD FOR ALL. I RULE FOR ALL. I FIGHT FOR ALL. I PREACH FOR ALL.

I CARRY FOR ALL. I SAIL FOR ALL.

I FEED YOU ALL!

I BULL & BEAR FOR ALL. I FLEECE YOU ALL. I PHYSIC YOU ALL. I BUY & SELL FOR ALL.

History AND ART

I Feed You All
Lithograph, American Oleograph Company, 1875

During the mid- and late 1800s, the lithograph, made by printing from designs on stone or other surfaces, was a popular art form.

▲ RAILROAD CONDUCTOR'S BADGE

- **1891** *Hamlin Garland publishes* Main-Travelled Roads

- **1896** *Henry Ford builds his first* automobile

1885

1895

- **1892** *Populist national convention held in Omaha*

- **1896** *William J. Bryan delivers "Cross of Gold" speech*

★★★★★★★★★★★★★★★★★★★★★★★★★★★★★★★

Agrarian Unrest

Setting the Scene

Section Focus

In the late 1800s, most people in the United States still lived in rural areas, but the balance was rapidly shifting. The country's attention was on the future—on booming industry and bustling cities. While much of America prospered, farmers were struggling. As conditions grew worse, they organized to protest their exclusion from the table of plenty.

Objectives

After studying this section, you should be able to

★ identify the problems farmers faced during the late 1800s.

★ discuss the rise and fall of the Grange.

★ analyze the impact of the Interstate Commerce Act.

Key Terms

pooling, cooperative

◀ MOWER ADVERTISEMENT, C. 1868

There appeared, as if from nowhere, a plague of grasshoppers that destroyed not only the wheat but the morale of farmers on the Great Plains. The Norwegian American writer, Ole Rölvaag, described the coming of the grasshoppers in his novel *Giants in the Earth:*

> *They actually hurt me as they flew against my face and hands. The wagon . . . was literally filled with them. The road was seething. . . . I saw Father standing almost in despair. So thick were the grasshoppers in the cornfield of which both of us had been so proud, that not a spot of green was left to be seen. And within two hours . . . not a leaf was left. . . .*

The grasshoppers ate anything green, choked wells to the brim, broke the branches off fruit trees by their weight, and even devoured harnesses and tool handles. They came in clouds that darkened the sky and covered the ground.

■ The Plight of the Farmers

Even clouds of grasshoppers were only one of the hazards of life on the plains. There was always the threat of prairie fires, dust storms, and, worst of all, drought, which combined with hot winds and temperatures over 100°F to bake crops in the ground and to cake farmers' faces with the salt of their sweat.

Farm prices began to decline in the 1880s; the price of wheat fell from 91 cents a bushel in 1883 to 69 cents in 1886. This decline was largely the result of overproduction of crops. New inventions, such as steam-powered harvesting and threshing machines, had improved crop yields, and more efficient techniques greatly increased farm production. As prices declined farmers had to borrow more and more money. Costs of the new farm machinery that assisted with large harvests were high. Often farmers could afford such equipment only on a mortgage. High, too, were the costs of shipping crops to market. The more farm prices fell, the harder it became for farmers to pay back their loans.

Even farmers who were not investing in mechanized equipment frequently had to borrow money. They had to live for a full year on the payments they received for their crops in the fall. If the money did not last, they were forced to borrow. This meant they were at the mercy of interest rates. It also meant that farmers were pretty much forced to sell their crops as soon as they came in. At that time, of course, because of the large supply, prices were always low. This is why farmer organizations, most notably the Southern Alliance, began to look for other ways to finance and market crops. Many farmers also began to call for railroad regulations for a variety of reasons.

■ Railroad Abuses

Railroads opened vast stretches of the West to settlement, making it possible for farmers to get their crops to markets and to get manufactured goods from the East. Huge sums of money were required to finance the building of a railway system. The promise of quick profits made the railroad an attractive investment for shrewd business leaders. Millions of dollars were raised through the sale of stock to private investors, both American and European.

Because a railroad promised growth and prosperity for those along its path, state and local governments offered loans and land grants in order to obtain railroad connections. Not all the dealings were legal, however.

Unethical Business Practices

Some railroad companies spent millions of dollars in bribes to state legislators and other public officials in exchange for special favors, such as land grants, cash subsidies, pro-railroad laws, and tax exemptions. But they often evaded laws designed to make them provide services in return for the benefits they were granted.

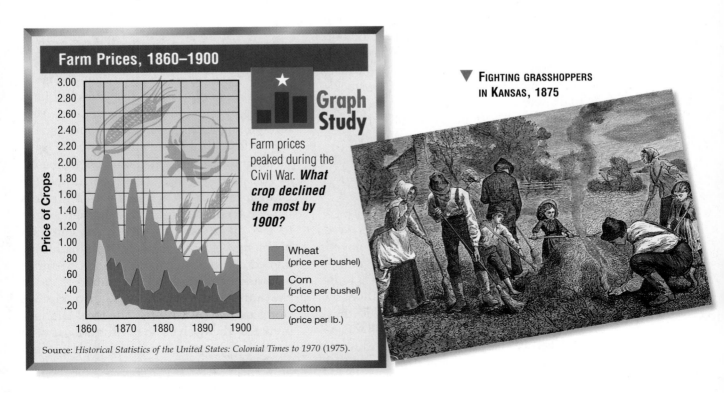

Farm Prices, 1860–1900

Graph Study

Farm prices peaked during the Civil War. *What crop declined the most by 1900?*

Wheat (price per bushel)
Corn (price per bushel)
Cotton (price per lb.)

Price of Crops

3.00 2.80 2.60 2.40 2.20 2.00 1.80 1.60 1.40 1.20 1.00 .80 .60 .40 .20

1860 1870 1880 1890 1900

Source: *Historical Statistics of the United States: Colonial Times to 1970* (1975).

▼ **FIGHTING GRASSHOPPERS IN KANSAS, 1875**

▲ Sears and Roebuck catalog, early 1900s

Another abuse was called "stock watering," the practice of increasing the number of shares of a company without adding to the company's assets. For example, when Jay Gould and James J. Fisk gained control of the Erie Railroad in 1868, they issued $71 million of stock on property worth $20 million. They made money by selling this "watered stock" to the public who did not know of the stock's actual lower value. Such action cheated all the stockholders. It also hurt the public because the railroads had to keep their rates high to pay dividends.

Unfair Pricing

In a day when trucks and highways were not yet dreamed of, railroads often enjoyed a natural monopoly; that is, in certain places there was no competition for services. Railroads took advantage of this situation by charging more for short hauls where they had a monopoly than for long hauls where they faced competition from other railroad lines. Thus, it cost shippers more to send goods from Poughkeepsie, New York, to New York City than to send goods from Chicago to New York City.

Sometimes competing railroad lines divided up traffic serving the same route, a practice known as **pooling.** Railroads pooled to make sure each line had enough traffic to pay costs and debts.

■ The Grange

Feelings against railroad abuses ran high all over the country but were especially strong in the West where there was almost no competition from other forms of transportation. This was because railroads had been favored by huge government subsidies in the form of land. Business owners and workers in the cities as well as farmers resented the railroads.

It was a nationwide farm organization, however, that began a movement against the unfair practices of the railroads. This organization tried to end railroad abuses with laws passed by state legislatures.

From Social Support to Political Action

The Patrons of Husbandry, commonly called the Grange, was an early national farm organization. It was founded in 1867 by Oliver Hudson Kelley. At first the main purpose of the Grange was to relieve the isolation and loneliness in the lives of farm families by providing social activities. Also, recognizing the importance of women on the farm, the Grange was the first fraternal organization to admit women on an equal basis.

The panic of 1873, however, turned the Grange into a reform lobby. As crop prices fell and credit became scarce, farmers began to talk about how to solve their common problems. Local Grange organizations pooled farmers' resources to set up mills, factories, banks, insurance companies, grain elevators, and **cooperatives,** or nonprofit stores owned by farmers. The local Granges involved themselves in local and national politics and pressed for state laws to help farmers.

By 1874 the Grange had 1.5 million members in states throughout the Midwest, the South, and the West. Its solidarity met with such success that several states passed "Granger laws" that fixed maximum freight and passenger rates, forbade railroads to discriminate between places or shippers, and attempted to regulate monopolies of such farmer necessities as grain elevators and warehouses.

Granger Laws Versus Business Interests

Private businesses protested loudly against the Granger laws. Their main argument was that government should not interfere with private enterprise. Railroad lawyers argued that Granger laws were unconstitutional because the Fourteenth Amendment forbade a state to "deprive any person of life, liberty, or property, without due process of law." They viewed a railroad corporation as a legal "person" that should not be deprived of its property by being forced to lower its rates.

Defenders of the Granger laws said railroads that had accepted generous aid from government should not claim to be devotees of laissez-faire capitalism. Further, they argued that laissez-faire rules did not apply to natural monopolies because there was no competition to keep prices down. The Grangers maintained that government must regulate railroads and other such monopolies in order to protect the public.

Supreme Court Decisions

In 1877 the Supreme Court decided in favor of the Granger laws in the case of *Munn* v. *Illinois.* The Court stated that common carriers, such as railroads, and public utilities, such as grain elevators, "stand in the very gateway of commerce" and "take toll of all who pass." Therefore these carriers must "submit to being controlled by the public for the common good."

In spite of such Court decisions, the Granger laws were unsuccessful. The railroads fought the laws by cutting services or threatening to lay no more track until the acts were repealed. Moreover, in the late 1870s, membership in the Grange declined and so did its political activity. The main cause of the Grange's collapse was its venture into business activities. The Grange set up plow and reaper factories, grain elevators, packing plants, and banks. Bitterly opposed by private companies and often not well run, these

★★★★ **AMERICAN PORTRAITS**

Willa Cather
1873–1947

Life on the prairie was a memorable experience for a young girl in the 1880s and the 1890s. The beauty of the land and the hardy determination of the pioneers lasted long in the memory of Willa Cather.

Born in Virginia in 1873, Willa moved with her family to a farm near Red Cloud, Nebraska, at the age of nine. The next eight years would provide the reflections for several novels, written years later.

Cather tried her hand at writing while teaching school in Pittsburgh in 1901 and then became an editor for *McClure's Magazine.* However, her real success did not begin until she started writing about life on the plains. Many of her famous novels, such as *O Pioneers!* (1913), tell of the tough, yet sensitive, nature of the immigrants who matched their determination against the demanding and lonely life on a plains farm.

Granger businesses usually failed. Their collapse discredited the Grange, and by 1880 its membership was less than one-fourth of what it had been in 1874. This effort of the Grangers to undercut the marketers had one favorable long-term result, however: the development of mail-order department stores, selling directly to the consumer. Montgomery Ward & Co., of Chicago, was founded in 1872 especially "to meet the wants of the Patrons of Husbandry."

The remaining Granger laws were dealt a mortal blow in 1886. In the Wabash Railway decision, the Supreme Court held that the states could control railroad traffic only within each state's own borders. They did not have the power to regulate railroad traffic that crossed state borders. Because most railroad traffic crossed state boundaries, the Court's decision effectively wiped out states' regulation of railroad rates.

The fall of the Grangers did not stop other organizations from taking its place. In the late 1800s, farmers' alliances, first formed locally, called for reform. One especially important local group was started in Texas in the mid-1870s. This group, guided by Dr. C. W. Macune, soon joined with similar groups in Arkansas and Louisiana to form a national alliance. It was called the National Farmers' Alliance and Industrial Union and was referred to as the Southern Alliance.

■ Interstate Commerce Act

The Supreme Court's ruling in the Wabash decision made it clear that regulation would have to come at the national level. In 1887 Congress passed the first federal law to regulate interstate commerce. The Interstate Commerce Act declared that the rates that railroads charged must be "reasonable and just"; it forbade pooling, rebates, and higher rates for short rather than long hauls.

The railroad companies were required to publish rates, give advance notice of all rate changes, and make annual financial reports available to the federal government. Violations of these provisions were punishable by fines of up to $5,000 for each offense. Enforcement of the law was placed under the Interstate Commerce Commission (ICC), a five-member panel appointed by the President.

As far as its immediate purpose was concerned, the Interstate Commerce Act was a failure. The ICC, lacking power to set rates, could only make recommendations or bring suits in the federal courts. Of 16 such cases that reached the Supreme Court, the Court held for the railroads in 15.

In 1892 Richard Olney, a corporate lawyer who later served as attorney general and secretary of state, wrote to a railroad official urging him not to advocate repeal of the Interstate Commerce Act. "It satisfies popular clamor for government supervision of the railroads," observed Olney, "at the same time that such supervision is almost entirely nominal."

In retrospect, though, the Interstate Commerce Act was a very important law. It established the precedent that the federal government might control large-scale private enterprise if the public good seemed to require it. It also provided a model for the regulatory commissions of today.

Section 1 ★ Review

Checking for Understanding

1. **Identify** the Grange, Interstate Commerce Act.
2. **Define** pooling, cooperative.
3. **Explain** why farmers failed to share in the economy's prosperity.
4. **Describe** the purposes of the Grange.

Critical Thinking

5. **Applying Principles** Some farmers believed their prosperity depended on producing more crops. State in your own words the law of supply and demand. Then explain how the law worked against farmers.

★★★

Rise and Fall of Populism

Setting the Scene

Section Focus

After the collapse of the Granger movement, farmers in the South and West began to form new organizations. In the 1890s these farmers' alliances grew into a new national political party. American farmers prepared to do battle to maintain their political power against the growing influence of industry.

Objectives

After studying this section, you should be able to

★ explain the motivations of the groups that supported greenbacks and free silver.

★ describe the campaign and results of the election of 1896.

★ discuss the Populist movement.

Key Terms

inflation, deflation, gold standard, third party

◀ GRANGE FARMER

"In God we trusted, in Kansas we busted," and "Going home to Mother"—so read signs on the wagons of "busted" farm families returning east during the hard times of the 1880s. Discontent grew to new heights in rural areas. Farm prices continued to fall, money was in short supply, and more and more people were losing their land to creditors.

Many blamed their problems not only on the drought but on human forces as well: greedy bankers, industrialists, and railroad companies that were accused of controlling government policies and bleeding rural areas dry. Like the Grangers, these men and women turned to politics to solve the problems caused by rapid economic change. The farmers' alliances, which spawned the Populist party, succeeded beyond the dreams of the Grangers.

■ Greenbacks and Free Silver

If there was anything that farmers in the late nineteenth century demanded more strongly than the regulation of natural monopolies or the reduction of the marketers' profits, it was "cheap money." The value of money, like that of any other commodity, changes according to the supply. If the number of dollars in circulation increases while there is no increase in the amount of goods and services for sale, the dollar buys *less*, and prices go up. This situation is called **inflation.** On the other hand, if the number of dollars in circulation decreases while there is no decrease in the amount of goods and services for sale, the dollar buys *more*, and prices go down. This situation is called **deflation.** In the three decades after the Civil War, the production of agricultural staples, such as wheat and cotton, nearly quadrupled while the supply of money increased very little. Thus, the prices received by farmers dropped by nearly two-thirds.

The Gold Standard

In 1865, with the value of currency inflated by the wartime issuance of United States notes, or greenbacks, there was $10.60 in circulation for every person in the country. By 1895 per capita circulation had sunk to $4.50. This was partly the result of a movement toward adoption of the **gold standard** in many nations. A country that adopted the

▲ *A PRAYER FOR RAIN* by A. B. Frost, 1894 On the Great Plains, farming had its agonies. Bumper crops brought low prices, and drought brought no crops. ***What was the goal of the Populist party?***

gold standard made all its currency convertible into gold. Formerly, most countries had been on a bimetallic standard of both gold and silver.

The difficulty with the gold standard in the late nineteenth century was that world production of gold did not increase as fast as world production of goods. This restricted the currency supply and drove prices down. Deflation was hard on farmers, who borrowed money more heavily than ever before. This resulted in thousands of farm owners losing their land.

As soon as greenbacks began to be called in during the late 1860s and prices began to drop, farmers started to demand inflation. They protested that bankers and bondholders had lent "50-cent dollars" during the war; they now wanted to be repaid in 100-cent dollars. In the midterm election of 1878, a Greenback party polled more than 1 million votes, electing 15 members to Congress.

The Demand for Free Silver

The Greenback movement declined after the mid-1870s as inflationists turned to free silver. Ever since the gold rush of 1849 had lowered the price of gold, silver miners had sold their silver commercially rather than selling it to the Treasury. In 1873 Congress, unaware of the potential of new silver mines, decided to stop coining silver money and adopted the gold standard. Six years later, after building up a gold reserve, the federal government resumed specie, or coin, payments. These events caused a howl of protest from Western silver miners because new mines, especially the famous Comstock Lode, produced a flood of silver that would no longer be coined. Denouncing what they called "the Crime of '73," silver miners demanded a policy of free silver, meaning that the government should coin all silver brought to the mint. They were joined by farmers of the West and the South who expected that free silver would mean a cheaper dollar and higher prices.

The strength of the silver movement was shown by the Bland-Allison Act of 1878, which was passed over President Hayes's veto. This law required that the treasury buy from $2 million to $4 million worth of silver a month and issue currency against it. Although adding to the money supply, the Bland-Allison Act did not halt deflation.

■ The Populist Movement

The election of 1892 was notable because for the first time since 1860, a **third party,** a minor political party, won electoral votes. The new organization, the People's, or Populist party, was principally an expression of farmers' grievances.

Government Policies

Ever since the Civil War, federal policies had favored industry over agriculture and the city over the country. In spite of the clamor for a cheaper dollar, the United States remained on the gold standard—to the advantage of creditors—and farm prices went steadily down—to the advantage of urban consumers. The protective tariff raised the price of the goods farmers bought, to the advantage of manufacturers, but American agricultural staples were sold overseas in an unprotected market. Legislation that favored agrarian, or farming, interests proved ineffective. State and federal regulation of railroads had been frustrated by adverse judicial decisions. When drought hit the Great Plains region in the late 1880s, the farmers were in a rebellious mood. In the West in general, economic distress was widespread; after the depression of 1893, feelings became so bitter that many citizens feared a revolution.

Forming a Party

The Populist party originated from two great farmers' organizations, which were formed after the decline of the Grange—the Southern Alliance, which covered the cotton and tobacco belt, and the Northern Alliance, especially strong in the Plains region. Although the two alliances failed to merge, they made similar demands—free silver, more paper money, cheaper credit, government ownership of railroads, and the restoration of railroad bounty lands to the federal government. After several congressional election successes and conferences in Cincinnati in 1891 and St. Louis in February 1892, a new political party was formed. The People's party held a national convention in Omaha in July 1892. Although mostly from farm organizations, delegates also represented the Knights of Labor and the followers of social reformers Henry George and Edward Bellamy.

Following the custom of the time, the convention nominated for President a Civil War veteran, James B. Weaver. There was nothing customary, however, about the Populist party's platform.

▲ **POPULIST LEADER MARY ELLEN LEASE**

The Omaha Platform

The preamble of the Omaha platform expressed indignation at the existing political and economic conditions. It condemned the political corruption, the newspapers dominated by business interests, the mortgage burden, and the condition of labor. The influence of social reformers was seen in the statements that "the land is concentrating in the hands of the capitalists" and that governmental injustice breeds "two great classes—tramps and millionaires." Turning to money and banking, the Populists characterized worldwide adoption of the gold standard as "a vast conspiracy against mankind . . . organized on two continents."

The following was perhaps the most zealously radical statement in the preamble of the Omaha platform:

> ❝ *We believe that the powers of government—in other words, of the people—should be expanded . . . as rapidly and as far as the good sense of an intelligent people and the teachings of experience shall justify.* ❞

The Omaha platform revealed that it was the agriculturalists—not organized labor—who dominated the Populist party.

The demands of organized labor were given a subordinate position. Excluded from the platform proper, labor's demands were placed among a miscellaneous list of resolutions that were given the title "Expression of Sentiments."

The Omaha platform seems less radical now than it did at that time. The Populists proposed not to overthrow the capitalist system but simply to change the rules. They aimed to achieve their ends not through revolution but through the orderly process of free elections. The Populist platform reveals an important function of third parties in the United States—to bring to public attention measures that the major parties later adopt as their own.

Election of 1892

The Populists' enthusiasm as they entered the campaign of 1892 had a religious tone. They adapted revival meeting hymns as party songs. Huge rallies were addressed not only by men but also by "women with skins tanned to parchment by the hot winds, with bony hands of toil, and clad in faded calico." The balloting revealed the distinct character of various regions in the People's party. All of its 22 electoral votes came from states lying west of the Mississippi River. In the South sympathy with Populist aims was widespread, but there was fear that the new party might divide the Democratic vote and

▲ BRYAN AND SILVER The British humor magazine *Puck* shows candidate William Jennings Bryan as a puppet being controlled by the silver-mine owners. ***Besides the mine owners, who supported free silver?***

let the Republican party back into power. Southern Democrats with Populist principles—"Popocrats"—nonetheless helped elect their own party's candidate, Grover Cleveland.

■ Cleveland's Second Term

Cleveland's second term proved difficult. Inheriting a treasury deficit from the Harrison administration, he had scarcely taken office when the panic of 1893 burst upon the country. Although Cleveland could not have prevented this disaster, he was blamed for it. Furthermore, he managed to antagonize almost every element in his party. For example, he angered "machine" politicians by putting 120,000 civil service jobs on the merit system. Cleveland also infuriated workers by using troops in the 1894 Pullman strike.

Cleveland Loses Democratic Support

Above all, Cleveland antagonized farmers by defending the gold standard. Fearful that the Sherman Silver Purchase Act would flood the United States Treasury with so much silver that it could not be redeemed in gold, he called a special session of Congress in 1893 and forced repeal of the law. Because most Western and Southern Democrats opposed him, he was able to do this only with Republican support. Even after federal buying of silver ceased, the gold standard was endangered because it was difficult for the government to keep an adequate gold reserve in the treasury. To obtain the precious metal, the Treasury Department sold United States bonds.

In one transaction J. Pierpont Morgan, the most powerful banker on Wall Street, obtained federal bonds so far below their market value that he and the bankers associated with him made $1.5 million. Western fury at the Morgan bond transaction was unbounded. The gold standard was bad enough, but to pay bankers to preserve it seemed to them almost treasonable.

▲ PRESIDENT GROVER CLEVELAND

The President's hope of lowering the prohibitive duties of the McKinley Tariff faded when a few Democratic senators joined the Republicans in tacking 633 amendments on a new tariff bill, thereby keeping rates almost at former levels. Cleveland let the resulting Wilson-Gorman Tariff of 1894 become a law without his signature, but he denounced the action of the rebellious senators as "a piece of party perfidy and dishonor."

Republicans Nominate McKinley

Meanwhile the Republicans had become, more than ever, identified with business interests. A dominant figure in the party was Mark Hanna, an Ohio businessman-politician. Big, bluff, and low-browed, Hanna became, perhaps unjustly, a symbol of the alliance between corporate wealth and politics. Anti-Republican cartoons habitually portrayed him in a suit covered with dollar signs. In 1896 Hanna used his great organizing talents to secure the Republican nomination for his friend William McKinley on a platform pledging high tariffs and maintenance of the gold standard.

Democrats Nominate Bryan

The Democratic national convention opened with such a bitter fight between Gold Democrats and Silver Democrats that it was almost impossible to keep a semblance of order. Then, with dramatic suddenness, the party found a leader in a rather obscure presidential candidate, William Jennings Bryan of Nebraska. Bryan combined a romantic devotion to free silver with a personality, voice, and presence that made him literally a spellbinder:

> **Burn down your cities and leave our farms, and your cities will spring up again as if by magic; but destroy our farms, and the grass will grow in the streets of every city in the country.**

Speaking at the convention, Bryan used images that seemed to identify the gold standard with evil itself:

> **You shall not press down upon the brow of labor this crown of thorns—you shall not crucify mankind upon a cross of gold!**

This speech contained hardly a single fact-based argument for a bimetallic standard. It was so charged with emotion that it made free silver a crusade—with Bryan as its standard bearer. Although only 36 years old, he received the Democratic nomination. Most Populists also agreed to support Bryan.

The Campaign for the Presidency

Breaking with tradition, which held that political campaigning was beneath the dignity of one who aspired to the presidency, Bryan traveled the country in search of support. In spite of all his efforts, though, Bryan's cause was doomed. Most large Democratic newspapers abandoned him; the Gold Democrats deserted the Democratic party and ran a separate candidate. Collecting an immense campaign fund, Hanna hired speakers and issued pamphlets aimed at countering the free silver arguments. McKinley was helped by the fact that prices of grain and cotton rose.

The most serious weakness in Bryan's campaign was that free silver was a poor issue on which to base an entire campaign. No one knew what the result of free coinage of silver would be; it would not have ended fluctuation in the value of money, and it might have caused a business panic.

McKinley Wins

The Republicans won the election of 1896 by a decisive margin, carrying all the thickly populated states of the Northeast and Midwest. It was a victory for industry over agriculture, city over country, North and East over West and South.

After their defeat in the election of 1896, the Populists ceased to be a force in politics. Though many at the time felt that all their efforts had failed, those who lived long enough saw most of the planks of their party's platform signed into law.

Section 2 ★ Review

Checking for Understanding

1. **Identify** Populist party, Mark Hanna, William McKinley, William Jennings Bryan.

2. **Define** inflation, deflation, gold standard, third party.

3. **Analyze** the causes of more rapid price declines on farm crops than on many other goods and services.

4. **List** two of the important objectives for the Populist party.

Critical Thinking

5. **Recognizing Common Goals** The alliance between laborers and farmers was hampered by each group's different interests. What did the two groups have in common that encouraged such an alliance?

CONNECTIONS

History AND MUSIC

CONNECTIONS

Folk Songs of Protest

Songs of protest are threaded throughout American History. In 1777 Americans marched to battle at Saratoga singing "Yankee Doodle." During the 1960s protesters marched for civil rights singing "We Shall Overcome." In the 1890s, too, Populists sang a protest song against bankers called "The Kansas Fool."

THE KANSAS FOOL

We have the land to raise the wheat
And everything that's good to eat;
And when we had no bonds or debt,
We were a jolly, happy set.
With abundant crops raised everywhere,
'Tis a mystery, I do declare,
Why farmers all should fume and fret,
And why we are so deep in debt.

The bankers followed us out west,
And did in mortgages invest;
They looked ahead and shrewdly planned,
and soon they'll have our Kansas land.

CHORUS

Oh Kansas fools! Poor Kansas Fools!
The banker makes of you a tool;
I look across the fertile plain,
Big crops—made so by gentle rain;
But twelve-cent corn gives me alarm,
And makes me want to sell my farm.

Other works expressed a tone that was partly serious and partly humorous.

STARVING TO DEATH
ON MY GOVERNMENT CLAIM

My name is Tom Hight,
An old bach'lor I am;
You'll find me out west
    in the county of fame,
You'll find me out west
    on an elegant plain,
Starving to death
    on my government claim.

Hurrah for Green County!
    the land of the free;
The land of the bedbug,
    grasshopper, and flea;
I'll sing of its praises,
    I'll tell of its fame,
While starving to death
    on my government claim.

Making the Music Connection

1. What complaints do farmers make in the first song?

2. How do these protest songs reflect the fears and concerns of farmers that organized interests were acting against them?

Linking Past and Present

3. Describe the complaints found in a current protest song.

★★★

Other Forces for Reform

Section Focus

Though the Gilded Age is often thought of as a period of greed, corruption, and self-centered individualism, it was also a period of reform. Like the Populists, whose strength lay mainly in the West, reformers in other areas were trying to call attention to problems.

Objectives

After studying this section, you should be able to

★ trace women's involvement in the temperance and suffrage movements.

★ discuss the political ideas of Karl Marx and Henry George.

Key Term

conspicuous consumption

◀ CARRIE NATION, FIGHTER FOR PROHIBITION

Reforms of the Civil War and Reconstruction periods encouraged people in the United States to look to government as the agent of social change. In the years of its unquestioned dominance, the Republican party had freed slaves, imposed a new way of life on the South, and opened the West to settlement. After the war, reformers who were dissatisfied with various aspects of life in the Gilded Age also looked to the government for action.

■ Temperance and Women's Rights

The period after the Civil War was not just a time of industrial progress, urban growth, and agrarian and labor discontent. Like the Jacksonian period, it also produced reforms designed to cure the ills of the new industrial society of the United States.

The Temperance Movement

Several reform movements that had begun earlier continued to reach toward their goals. Supporters of Prohibition, for example, formed a national political party in 1869; in 1872 they ran a presidential candidate. The temperance movement had never been more active.

Most effective were two national organizations that waged a ceaseless campaign against the evils of liquor and the saloon: the Anti-Saloon League and the Woman's Christian Temperance Union (WCTU). The WCTU revealed that women were learning the techniques of large-scale organization. Frances Willard, the head of the WCTU, made her group an effective force for causes other than temperance, such as prison reform and protective labor laws. Because women were far more likely than men to favor temperance, temperance advocates usually favored woman suffrage.

Woman Suffrage

Woman suffrage had its beginnings in the antebellum period; its first leaders were female abolitionists like Elizabeth Cady Stanton, who decided to put the antislavery cause ahead of their own. After the war woman suffrage was championed with renewed vigor.

In 1878 Susan B. Anthony of the National Woman Suffrage Association (NWSA) persuaded a sympathetic senator to propose the first woman suffrage amendment to the Constitution. It was voted down many times in the next 40 years. These defeats reflected the opinion of the majority of the people at the time, both male and female.

At the state level, suffragists had better success. By 1900 about half the states allowed women to vote on school issues, where their special knowledge of children was presumed to be a benefit. On the frontier, where women shared the hardships and dangers equally with men, support for woman suffrage was more widespread. By 1900, four states—Colorado, Wyoming, Utah, and Idaho—had granted women the right to vote.

▼ **ELIZABETH CADY STANTON**

Women and Unions

Women workers especially suffered exploitation during the new industrial age. By 1900 almost 5 million women were employed in the United States. It was not uncommon for women to work in "sweat shops" for 10 to 14 hours a day, often for less than $4 a week. Most unions, however, refused to accept women as members. One exception, the International Ladies' Garment Workers Union, had women leaders as well as women members. In 1903 a group of women formed the National Women's Trade Union League to campaign for better working conditions.

■ Socialism

Wherever industrialism appeared, there were people driven toward extreme solutions for the problems it created. Something seemed wrong with a system that produced

 Visualizing History   ▲ **WOMEN AND THE VOTE** The West led the way in granting woman suffrage. These women voted in Cheyenne, Wyoming, in 1888. *What other reform movement was reaching toward its goals before 1900?*

both the idle rich, who lived in mansions, and the unemployed poor, who lived in slums. Some were impelled toward socialism.

Experiments in Socialism

Socialists in the early 1800s did not attempt to change the economic system by gaining control of the government. Instead they tried to effect change by experimenting with cooperative communities. Robert Owen brought his idea of cooperative control of industry from England to New Harmony, Indiana, in 1825. Such socialist communities reached their peak in America in the 1840s.

Karl Marx and Socialism

Socialists of the late nineteenth century were dedicated to changing the entire social and political system, partly because of the influence of Karl Marx. Marx had been a student at the University of Berlin during the emergence of a new philosophical and literary movement that questioned established values. Searching for meaning in history, Marx finally wrote his economic philosophy in *The Communist Manifesto* in 1847 and in *Das Kapital,* the first volume of which was published in 1867. Marx predicted that capitalism was doomed. Fewer and fewer capitalists, he said, would control all wealth,

while the mass of the people would be pushed into the ranks of the proletariat (people without property). Eventually the proletarians would rise and overthrow their masters. History, said Marx, had seen continual class struggles, but the conflict between industrial workers and capitalists would be the last. When the workers eventually took control of society, Marx believed they would establish a classless society.

Marxist socialism appealed to many workers in the industrial countries of Europe. In the United States, however, it gained only a small following.

The American Socialist Party

Eugene V. Debs became a lifelong convert to socialism because of unjust treatment after his imprisonment in an Illinois jail during the Pullman strike. Declaring that in a democracy workers could gain control of the government and use it to change the free enterprise system, he organized the American Socialist party.

■ Dissenting Voices

Socialism was not the only remedy proposed at the time. Other solutions to fix society's ills included a single tax on land and a classless society.

▲ **AT THE OFFICE** In the early 1900s, professional careers were largely reserved for men, while secretarial jobs were thought to be women's work. ***How many women were employed by 1900?***

Boardinghouses

Beginning in the 1830s, farm girls moved to Lowell, Massachusetts, to work in the textile mills there. The mill owners set up boardinghouses with strict curfews and comfortable if sparse accommodations for the women.

The practice of boarding offended the sensibilities of some middle-class reformers. They complained that boarding weakened the family unit and helped spread disease. But many immigrants had a different point of view. They knew that all boardinghouses differed. In some tenements as many as 10 immigrants slept in a room.

But other boardinghouses were like the establishment of one immigrant woman who thought she would own her own home in America. Having difficulty just making ends meet shortly after she arrived in the United States, she cooked for four boarders. Initially she resented having to share her home, prepare meals, and attend to the needs of people she did not even know. However, the woman's attitude changed. She began to enjoy providing a home for new immigrants who otherwise would have no place to stay.

▼ RIDGE STREET, NEW YORK CITY

Henry George and the Single Tax

Another writer with a proposal for remaking society was Henry George, whose major work *Progress and Poverty* was published in 1879. George attacked the central problem posed by the socialists: Why should the advance of the industrial revolution, with more and more machinery for producing wealth, apparently result in more poverty? George said the problem was that ownership of land—the source of all wealth—was being concentrated in the hands of speculators. These speculators did not put the land to use. They merely waited for it to increase in value, meanwhile charging high rents that drove down wages and business profits. George criticized the growing gap between rich and poor:

❝ *We need not look far from the palace to find the hovel. When people can charter special steamboats to take them to watering places . . . build marble stables for their horses and give dinner parties which cost . . . a thousand dollars a head, we may know that there are poor girls on the street . . . [facing] starvation.* ❞

George did not propose socialism as a remedy. Instead he urged what he called the "single tax" on land values. The rate of the single tax would be based not on existing value but on *potential* value if the land were used efficiently. Thus there would be no profit in keeping land out of use and waiting for it to increase in worth; owners would either have to develop it themselves or sell it to someone else who would do so. George argued that this would cause prosperity by promoting maximum productivity and by plowing the profits of the land monopoly back into society. Although George's ideas had great appeal, the single-tax idea was too radical a change to be accepted completely. However, it did influence methods of taxation both in this country and abroad.

Thorstein Veblen and "Conspicuous Consumption"

Another widely read book, *The Theory of the Leisure Class,* was published in 1899 by Thorstein Veblen. The son of Norwegian immigrants, Veblen had been influenced by Populism in his early days in Wisconsin. Attending Yale and Johns Hopkins University, he became interested in the social sciences, especially economics. His appreciation for science led him to write with the cool detachment of an observer, not a fiery revolutionary.

Influenced by Darwin's theory of evolution, Veblen believed in the process of natural selection. He contended that the "leisure class," which was made up of those people who had great wealth, was *not* an example of the most fit. In fact Veblen argued that the leisure class hindered progress and evolution. Veblen believed that, like the dinosaur, the leisure class would eventually disappear.

Veblen used the phrase **conspicuous consumption** to describe the life of the upper class. Veblen described conspicuous consumption as the use of vast resources just for show. The phrase had deep meaning because the contrast between wealth and poverty was not hidden in the United States. The mansions that lined the streets of cities like New York and Chicago were within a few blocks of immigrant ghettos. However, Veblen's vision of a community of equals governed by an elite group of social planners was judged impractical by most Americans of his time.

Limited Support for Radical Changes

Probably the reason why radical formulas for altering society did not gain wide support was that many Americans did not want change. Even those at the bottom rung of the economic ladder often felt they had bettered their position from an earlier time.

A New England farm boy might find drawing wages of a dollar a day for a 60-hour week in a factory preferable to working from dawn to dark trying to make a living from a rocky farm. An immigrant might be living with her family in a single room and working in a windowless sweatshop, but for the first time in her life she was wearing shoes.

Even the poorest workers believed that in time they would also be able to "get ahead" and become property owners. They fervently believed in the "rags-to-riches" story and felt, like the heroes of the Horatio Alger series, that they could by work, perseverance, and luck rise to a higher station in life. If property rights were destroyed, what would happen to the American dream?

Working Through the Political Process

Also, the United States was so large and had so many different interests that no one idea attained universal appeal. Its citizens, wanting to improve their economic situation, worked through the political party process. These parties tried to appeal to as many groups as possible.

Section 3 ★ Review

Checking for Understanding

1. **Identify** Susan B. Anthony, Eugene V. Debs.
2. **Define** conspicuous consumption.
3. **Describe** the movements to gain voting rights for women.
4. **Compare** the solutions proposed by Karl Marx, Henry George, and Thorstein Veblen.

Critical Thinking

5. **Arguing an Opinion**   Women fought for the right to vote but had had success in only four states by 1900. Why did many states refuse them the right to vote? What arguments would you propose to justify women's right to vote in the late 1800s?

Critical Thinking Skills

Recognizing Ideologies

Identifying the motives or belief system behind a particular political position may help you form an opinion. One effective way to identify motives and beliefs is to analyze the benefits and costs associated with the issue. Ask questions, such as:

- Which people benefit if the issue passes? How do they benefit?
- Which people benefit if the issue fails? How do they benefit?
- Which people pay or suffer if the issue passes? How do they pay or suffer?
- Which people pay or suffer if the issue fails? How do they pay or suffer?

Throughout United States history, numerous minor political parties have initiated social or political reform. The goals of the minor party often centered on a single issue, and as popular support grew for that issue and public opinion changed, the "cause" was adopted by either the Democratic or Republican party. The minor party thus faded out as its goals were achieved.

The Populist party had an impact far beyond its showing in national elections. Several Populist proposals are in use today. The federal income tax, adopted as part of the Sixteenth Amendment in 1913, accounts for one-half of the monies collected at all levels of government. The Seventeenth Amendment placed into law the direct election of United States senators. The secret ballot, first used in the late 1890s, became standard practice in all elections. Primary elections are used to settle virtually all contests for majority-party nominations for state and congressional offices and for many local offices. Hundreds of cities and many states permit citizens to use the initiative and referendum, used in South Dakota in the late 1890s, to introduce legislation and vote on proposed laws.

▲ 1891 POLITICAL CARTOON, PARTY OF PATCHES

Practicing the Skill

Use the guidelines on recognizing ideologies mentioned in this skill and information from the chapter to analyze the proposals.

1. What benefits are associated with the use of a secret ballot? Who might oppose its use? Why?

2. In what way is the proposal for a secret ballot consistent with Populist goals?

3. Who benefits from the initiative and referendum proposal? Explain how these systems work.

4. Does the proposal for a federal income tax seem like a Populist idea? Explain.

Using Vocabulary

Use each of the following terms in a statement that might have been made by each of the following people:

Railroad owner: pooling
Farmer: cooperatives
Banker: inflation

Reviewing Facts

1. **Summarize** the factors that created financial hardships for farmers in the late 1800s.

2. **List** three purposes of the Granger laws.

3. **Specify** what the Interstate Commerce Act required of the railroads.

4. **Explain** why deflation hurt the farmers.

5. **Describe** the gold standard and its effect on the money supply.

6. **State** the reforms the Populists demanded in their platform.

7. **Compare** Karl Marx's solution to poverty with Henry George's.

Understanding Concepts

Economic Inequity

1. In the farmers' view, what groups enriched themselves at the farmers' expense?

Social Change

2. Which groups of people might be expected to support extreme solutions for social problems? What groups would likely oppose such solutions? Why did most Americans vote for more moderate candidates in the late 1900s?

3. What did the Populist party, the Grange, and the followers of Marx, George, and Veblen have in common?

Critical Thinking

1. **Understanding Cause and Effect** Explain how new agricultural technology helped the farmers. How did it financially hurt some farmers?

2. **Linking Past and Present** Today banks and lending institutions offer variable-rate loans with an interest rate that varies as prices rise and fall. What problem is this intended to solve?

3. **Proposing Strategy** Assume you are William Jennings Bryan's campaign manager in the 1896 election. Draw up a plan of recommendations to improve Bryan's chances of success.

4. **Contrasting Ideas** How did the Marxist theory of reform contrast with the methods used or envisioned by the other reform proposals discussed in this chapter?

5. **Comparing Fine Art** Study the two paintings on this page by artist John Singer Sargent. Then answer the questions.

   a. What is the mood in each of these works?

   b. What adjectives would you use to describe these paintings?

   c. Compare the use of color and light in these paintings.

   d. Which painting do you prefer? Explain.

Writing About History

Comparison

Assume you are a European tourist attending a rally at which the Populists describe their platform. Write a letter to a Marxist friend in Europe, comparing and contrasting the Populist approach to reform with the Marxist formula. You may wish to research additional details about Marx's theory.

Cooperative Learning

You will be part of a discussion between four people meeting in a Great Plains town in the year 1886. Divide the following roles among yourselves: a farmer, a banker, a railroad owner, and a politician. The purpose of this meeting is to discuss the problems of the farmer. Review Section 1 to gain background information on your role. The farmer will begin the meeting by stating his or her main concerns. The other members should discuss ways to answer the farmer's problems, although each individual should be prepared to argue why he or she cannot agree to a recommended change. End the meeting by having all members agree on two recommendations for helping the farmer.

Social Studies Skills

Reviewing Map Basics

Maps can be used to show many different kinds of information. For example, political maps show countries, states, and cities. Transportation maps show means of transportation such as train or plane routes; physical maps show geographical features such as mountains and lakes. In addition, there are military maps, weather maps, and building maps—and this is just a partial list.

Practicing the Skill

Look at the map on this page and answer the following questions.

1. What kind of map is shown?
2. What does the legend tell you?
3. How would you interpret voting in the states of California and Kentucky?

The Election of 1896

	Popular vote	Electoral vote
McKinley	7,102,246	271
Bryan	6,492,559	176

4. Could this map also be a political map? Why or why not?
5. How is this map different from the map on page 459? List at least four differences.

Using Your Journal

Reread your journal notes about the election of 1896. Think of another election in which one party was so divided that the candidate of the opposition party was able to win. Describe the circumstances in your journal.

Cultural Kaleidoscope

Life in the West

ON THE RANGE

The West and life on the range have always had a special mystique. Television, books, and the movies have kept alive the legend of the Western hero, but the reality of life on the range is overlooked. The work was hard, sometimes boring, and often dangerous. Determination, bravery, and endurance were required to tend great herds of restless and stubborn cattle or to prod a herd great distances on the long drive. Life on the range seems romantic in retrospect, but to the cowhands it was hard and often hazardous.

▶

The rope, or lariat, was an important tool in the hands of a skilled roper. Cowhands used the lariat to rope cattle, pull cattle out of mud, and haul wood to the campfire.

▼

The cowhand's clothing served a useful purpose. Chaps protected the legs during the long hours in the saddle.

◀

The cowhand took special care of the tack, equipment, and grooming tools for the horse. One important piece, the bridle, is used to control the movements of the horse by straps and metal pieces placed on the head and in the mouth of the animal.

Cattle owners kept track of who owned an animal by branding. Each ranch had its own easily recognizable brand.

Few cowhands owned their own horses. The cowhand chose his horse from the *remuda*, the herd of available horses.

A cowhand wore boots with tapered high heels to make sure his feet did not slip through the stirrups when riding.

589

Chapter 17

Into the West

In the early 1860s, many Native American nations lived on the Great Plains with the vast buffalo herds. Then, beginning in 1869, transcontinental railway lines opened the West. The Homestead Act made land easy to obtain, and the railroads actively promoted settlement. Pioneer farmers poured onto the plains by the thousands. The discovery of gold and other minerals and the promise of wealth from cattle also lured many people.

Native Americans fought this intrusion, but their cause was doomed. White hunters slaughtered the buffalo almost to extinction, and farmers, miners, and ranchers took much of their land. In 1890 at Wounded Knee, their resistance came to an end.

Chapter 18

The Rise of Industry

The United States had all the necessary ingredients for industry to grow—abundant natural and human resources, investment money, free enterprise economic system, and new inventions and technology.

By 1900 huge companies dominated the economy. Their efficiency resulted in cheaper production, higher quality, and lower prices that drove smaller competitors out of business. Corporations, monopolies, and trusts became the norm. Industrial leaders used social Darwinism to justify their actions. The Sherman Antitrust Act, passed in 1890, did little to control business practices.

Chapter 19

An Urban Society

With industrialization the work force grew and the workers' lives changed. Machines took over many traditional tasks of the worker. Hours were long, wages were low, and work places were hazardous. Unable to improve their lot individually, workers turned to labor unions.

Opposed by the big corporations, management and, to a certain extent, the government, labor unions resorted to strikes. However, even major strikes like the 1894 Pullman strike failed to win significant gains.

An important influence on labor were the large numbers of immigrants who provided unskilled labor for urban industries. They were primarily southern and eastern European and Chinese immigrants who flocked to the cities, where they created their own ethnic communities. Their unfamiliar languages and customs aroused anti-immigration sentiment.

Along with the influx of immigrants, rural Americans came to the rapidly growing cities. In this urban environment that was faced with daunting human and technical problems, a new way of life evolved.

Chapter 20

The Gilded Age

With industrialization and urbanization came political corruption. Scandals arose at every level of government. Political machines dominated almost all major cities.

Government in general lacked leadership, and reform efforts met with limited success. Civil service reform finally came in 1883 with passage of the Pendleton Act.

The society and culture changed as well. Education expanded and improved. Local-color writers like Mark Twain described their locales with realism and detail. Sporting events became a favorite leisure-time activity, as did vaudeville, penny newspapers, and dime novels.

Chapter 21

Politics and Protest

The prosperity of the Gilded Age did not extend to farmers, who were burdened with high costs, low incomes, and heavy debts. They organized into groups such as Granges and farmers' alliances. Ultimately these groups turned to politics.

The farmers joined with labor and other reform groups to form a new national political party—the Populist party. The Omaha platform of the Populist party in 1892 clearly reflected the interests of the farmer. The Populist party had some successes, but the movement died soon after William Jennings Bryan lost the 1896 presidential election.

Farmers were not the only ones seeking reform. The temperance movement had never been more active, and woman suffrage became a popularly debated issue across the country. At the same time, writers such as Karl Marx proposed socialism as an economic remedy while Henry George favored a "single tax" on land values. However, Americans on the whole were not interested in instituting radical change.

Understanding Unit Themes

1. **Geography and Environment**   Compare the American landscape and the environment in 1860 and 1900.

2. **Conflict and Cooperation**   How did the settlement of the West affect Native Americans? The nation as a whole? How might cooperation have resolved many conflicts?

3. **Influence of Technology**   In what ways did technology influence American life and society between 1860 and 1900?

4. **Cultural Diversity**   What ethnic groups played a role in the settlement of the West and in industrialization?

UNIT 7
ENTERING A NEW CENTURY
1867–1920

★★★

▲ BANJO, LATE 1800S

History AND ART

Cliff Dwellers
by George Wesley Bellows, 1913

Bellows's works often show elements of humor and adventure. His favorite themes, which include landscapes and athletic events, mark him as a uniquely American painter.

Setting the Scene

In an age of optimism, United States foreign policy shifted away from isolationism, and the nation became a major power in international affairs. Americans also took a look at their political institutions and concluded that change was necessary. Progressive-minded reformers sought a more democratic government while working to end a host of social ills.

Themes

- American Democracy
- Economic Development
- The Individual and Family Life
- U.S. Role in World Affairs

Key Events

- Purchase of Alaska and annexation of Hawaii
- Spanish-American War
- Building of the Panama Canal
- States institute direct primary, initiative, and referendum
- Formation of the National Association for the Advancement of Colored People
- Income taxes enacted
- "Bull Moose" party formed
- Federal Reserve System created
- Federal Trade Commission established

Major Issues

- Commercial interests and war with Spain lead to the acquisition of a colonial empire.
- Muckraking literature inspires a new generation of reformers who seek to correct social inequities.
- Reform-minded Presidents extend democracy and protect Americans from big business.

▲ TRAVEL TRUNK

▲ EARLY AIRPLANE

◀ CHILD'S TOY, EARLY 1900S

Portfolio Project

Read the amendments that passed during the time between 1867 and 1920. Choose one and rewrite it in your own words, making clear what the amendment is expected to accomplish.

Global Perspectives

The World

		1875		1890	
Asia and Oceania					**1894** Sino-Japanese War begins
Europe					◄ **1893** New Zealand becomes first nation to grant woman suffrage
Africa					
South America				► **1889** Brazil becomes a republic	
North and Central America					

ONE MILLION WOMEN OF THIS STATE WANT THE VOTE WE KNOW BECAUSE WE HAVE CANVASSED THEM A MILLION WOMEN IS A BIG MAJORITY VOTE YES NOV. 2

The United States

		1875		1890	
Pacific and Northwest					**1894** Hawaii becomes a republic
Southeast			◄ **1881** Booker T. Washington founds Tuskegee Institute		
Midwest					
Southwest					
Atlantic Northeast				▲ **1886** Statue of Liberty dedicated	

Linking Across TIME

A trip to the grocery store gives an indication of the Italian influence on American life. Foods like pizza, spaghetti, macaroni, minestrone, parmesan cheese, broccoli, and zucchini are all part of the American diet. However, they were all introduced by the Italian immigrants who came to the United States around the turn of the century.

► **1904** *Russo-Japanese War begins*

1905

1920

◄ **1908** *Belgium establishes control over the Congo*

1898 *Battleship* Maine *explodes; Spanish-American War begins*

▲ **1914** *Panama Canal opens*

1898 *Gold discovered at Nome*

▼ **1903** *Wright brothers' first flight*

► **1908** *Model T Ford produced*

1912 *New Mexico and Arizona become states*

1905

1920

CHAPTER 22

★★★

Imperialism
1867–1908

▼ RED LEATHER BOOTS
AND BUTTON HOOK

Setting the Scene

Focus

Foreign policy before the late nineteenth century had been dominated by two ideas. The first was President Washington's isolationist warning against entering into "entangling alliances." The second was President Monroe's warning to Europe against interference in the Americas. War with Spain, however, resulted in a more aggressive foreign policy and the acquisition of overseas colonies. Suddenly, the United States had become a major world power.

Concepts to Understand

★ How increased United States economic and political power led to the acquisition of an overseas empire

★ How confrontation with Spain resulted in war over Cuba

Read to Discover . . .

★ why Americans moved away from a policy of isolationism.

★ the problems and responsibilities that victory in the Spanish-American War brought the United States.

Journal Notes

Why did the United States become involved in the affairs of other countries? Record each country and the reasons for each as you read this chapter.

CULTURAL	● **1880** *"General" William Booth organizes the Salvation Army*	● **1891** *University of Chicago founded* ● **1893** *World's Columbian Exposition is held in Chicago*
	1875	**1885**
POLITICAL	● **1882** *Chinese Exclusion Act is passed*	● **1893** *Queen Liliuokalani of Hawaii is overthrown*

The Return of the Conquerors
by Edward Moran, 1898

Edward Moran painted this work to commemorate the American victory over Spain in the Spanish-American War. In the foreground is Admiral Dewey's flagship *Olympia*.

◀ EUROPEAN STEAMSHIP TICKET

• **1903** The Great Train Robbery *motion picture produced; first to have a fully developed plot*

• **1910** *Women make up 21 percent of the workforce*

1895

1905

• **1898** *Spanish-American War begins*
• **1899** *Hay initiates Open Door policy*
• **1900** *Boxer Rebellion in China*
• **1904** *Roosevelt Corollary announced*

• **1905** *Roosevelt arbitrates Russo-Japanese War*

★★

America Looks Abroad

Setting the Scene

Section Focus

Beginning in the 1500s, European nations built vast colonial empires. By the mid-1800s, many of these colonies had become independent. The Industrial Revolution caused new empire building. Germany, France, Belgium, Portugal, and Japan joined the race for colonies. The United States had grown entirely by expansion. Would the race for empire tempt a once-colonial people to seek colonies?

Objectives

After studying this section, you should be able to

★ discuss the emergence of the United States from isolationism.

★ cite two examples of arbitration averting war.

Key Terms

imperialism, isolationism, reciprocity, arbitration

◀ QUEEN LILIUOKALANI OF HAWAII

European colonialism was motivated by trade and adventure, power and profit, idealism and national patriotism. These nations also believed they had a "civilizing mission" toward nonwhite populations. The Industrial Revolution generated a need for markets for manufactured goods and new sources of raw materials. **Imperialism**—the policy of establishing colonies and building empires—answered these needs.

Isolationism, or separation from the political affairs of other countries, was a policy established by George Washington. In his farewell address, he warned against entangling alliances. Later the Monroe Doctrine emphasized the United States's desire to keep the Americas separate from Europe. Another factor affecting American foreign policy was the Declaration of Independence—the idea that people had the right to govern themselves.

■ Securing an American Continent

European control of parts of North America by France and Russia ended in the 1860s. The United States challenged a French expansion effort in 1861 and bought Russian territory in 1867.

End of French Expansion

Mexico's reform government under Benito Juárez (HWAHR•uhs) stopped payment of its foreign debts. French, Spanish, and British troops entered the country to force payment. The debts were collected and Spain and Britain left, but the French remained. Ignoring the Monroe Doctrine and taking advantage of the American Civil War, the French emperor Napoleon III overthrew the Republic of Mexico. In 1864

Napoleon III installed Austrian prince Maximilian as Mexico's emperor.

The United States protested and, after the Civil War, sent nearly 50,000 troops to the border at the Rio Grande. Napoleon's forces withdrew. The Mexicans promptly defeated Maximilian's army and executed Maximilian. The United States proved its willingness to back the Monroe Doctrine with force.

Acquisition of Alaska

Secretary of State William H. Seward believed in Manifest Destiny. He envisioned a United States empire and wanted to annex Canada, Hawaii, and several Caribbean islands.

Seward's only major achievement along this line was the purchase of Alaska in 1867. The undeveloped territory of Alaska, twice the size of Texas, was held by Russia, but the czar saw little value in the territory.

In 1867, when the Russian minister to the United States informed Seward that the czar wanted to sell Alaska, the secretary of state jumped at the chance. In a few hours, Seward arranged a treaty in which the United States would buy Alaska for $7.2 million—less than two cents an acre. After four months of selling the idea to Congress, the transaction was completed.

■ Economic Empire Building

At one time the United States had little need to look beyond its own borders for growth. Raw materials were abundant, and the home market was immense. By the 1890s, the country had developed into a great industrial nation, able to compete with European producers.

Reciprocity

James G. Blaine, secretary of state under Presidents Garfield and Harrison, wanted to open up new markets not by taking on

Visualizing History

▲ MINING GOLD IN THE YUKON Many settlers and prospectors came to Alaska after gold was discovered in the region in the late 1800s. *Why did Russia decide to sell Alaska to the United States?*

Visualizing **(H)istory** ▲ **ALASKA** The wealth of resources found in this scenic state proved Alaska's worth, even though its purchase was originally called Seward's Folly. *Why did some Americans call for the annexation of Hawaii?*

colonies, but by increasing American trade through **reciprocity**—the mutual lowering of tariff barriers. He tried, without much success, to include reciprocity provisions in the McKinley Tariff of 1890. He was able to chair a Pan-American Congress in Washington, D.C., in 1889. The goal of the group, which later became the Pan-American Union, was to promote economic cooperation and trade among the Americas. Success was limited, however, because the United States intervened, often forcibly, in Latin American affairs.

Should Hawaii Be Annexed?

American missionaries and traders first ventured to Hawaii in the early 1800s. American sugar growers followed. By the 1890s Hawaii was closely connected to the United States through commerce and the many Americans living there.

While many nationalities lived in Hawaii, native Hawaiian rulers were controlled by the American business community until the Hawaiian Queen Liliuokalani (lih•LEE•uh•woh•kuh•LAH•nee) came into power in 1891. She was determined to return control to her own people. In response, some American business leaders, with the help of marines from the cruiser *Boston,* took over the government.

The American minister to Hawaii wrote the Department of State that Hawaii was

ready to annex. President Cleveland disagreed. He decided that the use of American troops to overthrow the Hawaiian government was a violation of "national honesty." Despite criticism, Cleveland withdrew American soldiers from Hawaii. He also tried, but failed, to oust the revolutionary provisional government and put Liliuokalani back on her throne.

■ Challenging Great Britain

After the Civil War, the United States appeared ready to take a position among the powers of the world. Twice the United States forced Britain to submit to **arbitration,** or the settlement of a dispute by an impartial group.

Civil War Damages

In 1868 Charles Sumner, head of the Senate Foreign Relations Committee, claimed that Great Britain owed the United States more than $2 billion in damages for allowing Confederate ships to use British ports during the Civil War. If the British would not pay, Senator Sumner declared, the United States should take British-controlled Canada.

In 1871 Secretary of State Hamilton Fish arranged for arbitration. Britain did not want to risk war in Canada and feared that a hostile United States might supply Britain's enemies with warships. The United States backed down on its demand for "indirect" damages. In the Treaty of Washington, the United States was awarded $15.5 million, which Britain paid.

Venezuela Border Dispute

President Cleveland requested that the British put a long-standing Venezuela–British Guiana boundary dispute to arbitration. In July 1895 Secretary of State Richard Olney wrote the British government that their refusal to arbitrate violated the Monroe Doctrine. He warned:

> 66 *The United States is practically sovereign on this continent and its fiat is law upon the subjects to which it confines its interposition.* 99

Britain answered that the Monroe Doctrine had no standing in international law and did not apply to the situation.

Aware of the possibility of war, Cleveland asked Congress for authorization to appoint a commission to determine the boundary without consulting Britain. Americans responded with excitement, but Britain thought it "monstrous and insulting." For a few days, war seemed a strong possibility.

Fortunately, the British government backed down. Early in January 1896, Britain's attention was diverted from Venezuela by a dispute with Germany involving South Africa. Seeking to improve relations with the United States, Britain agreed to arbitration.

The boundary settlement turned out in Britain's favor and a new era of Anglo-American understanding emerged.

■ Strengthening the Navy

The Venezuelan crisis called attention to the fact that the United States had only three modern battleships. The crisis also popularized the writings of an American naval officer, Captain Alfred T. Mahan. Mahan believed that as America developed its industrial strength, the nation should look outward. Great nations of the past had built up foreign markets, expanded their merchant fleets, constructed navies to protect their commerce, and planted colonies in distant territories. Mahan argued that a modern nation needed sea power in order to become great.

At first Mahan had more influence abroad. Kaiser (Emperor) Wilhelm II of Germany studied his books and instructed German naval officers to read them. In Great Britain Mahan was showered with honors. Mahan influenced rising American leaders such as Senator Henry Cabot Lodge and Theodore Roosevelt and helped to shape United States naval policy.

Congress established a Naval Advisory Board in 1881 that pressed for larger naval appropriations. In 1883 Congress authorized construction of 1 more cruiser and 3 battleships. By adding 3 heavier and more powerful ships in 1890 and by voting for 13 new ships in 1895, Congress made it clear that it intended to have a navy capable of matching any enemy on the high seas.

Section 1 ★ Review

Checking for Understanding

1. **Identify** Maximilian, William Seward, Queen Liliuokalani, Charles Sumner.
2. **Define** imperialism, isolationism, reciprocity, arbitration.
3. **Show** how the French challenged the Monroe Doctrine in 1861.

4. **Describe** two instances of confrontation with Great Britain that were settled by arbitration.

Critical Thinking

5. **Understanding Cause and Effect** How did the writings of Captain Alfred T. Mahan lead to expanding the American navy?

Coaling Stations and Colonies

By the end of the 1800s, Americans began to think in terms of a different and broader Manifest Destiny. The original concept was changed to include overseas as well as westward expansion. The idea that it was the fate of the United States to extend its boundaries beyond the seas has been called the new Manifest Destiny.

The change in attitude toward foreign affairs was due to certain ideas and developments that occurred in the late 1800s. One such development was imperialism. Nations began to establish empires around the globe to build important new sources of raw materials and provide new avenues for investment.

More justification for imperialism was provided by Captain Alfred Thayer Mahan. Mahan believed that for a country to become a major sea power, its ships needed remote sources of supplies that could not be carried for an entire voyage. While commercial shipping required these supply stations, an armed navy needed them even more. The supplies, according to Mahan, were "first, fuel; second, ammunition; last of all, food."

Fuel became essential to shipping as nations switched from sail to steam power at the turn of the century. No ship could steam away from its home port for any great distance without refueling. A fleet that wanted to trade or fight very far beyond its home waters needed coaling stations in distant lands.

Mahan did not favor unchecked expansionism. Too many supply and fueling bases in foreign lands, he warned, could drain the resources

▲ U.S.S. *Iowa*, c. 1900

of the parent country and could become "a source of weakness, multiplying exposed points, and entailing division of force."

The United States had made some strides earlier in the century. One of these was the development of ironclad ships during the Civil War. However, after the war, the United States allowed its navy to deteriorate.

Mahan's ideas provided a real impetus for change. Influenced by Mahan's concepts, Congress passed the Naval Act of 1890, which appropriated additional money for battleships. By 1900 the United States had the naval power it needed to back up an expanded role in foreign affairs.

Making the Technology Connection

1. What supplies did coaling stations provide?

2. How did new technology influence American foreign policy?

Linking Past and Present

3. In what areas of the world does the United States have refueling stations today?

★★★

The Spanish-American War

Setting the Scene

Section Focus

Struggling for freedom under Spanish rule for years, Cubans had gained only greater repression. When a new revolution took place in 1895, Americans were moved by two impulses to intervene. Many urged American support for the repressed Cuban people, while others saw the revolt as an opportunity to expand the American empire.

Objectives

After studying this section, you should be able to

★ list the events that led to the United States's involvement in the Spanish-American War.

★ explain the reason for the involvement of the Philippines in the war.

Key Term

neutrality

◀ TIN TRAY WITH LIKENESS OF THEODORE ROOSEVELT

Americans were outraged when they found that the Spanish Governor-General Valeriano Weyler had ordered Cuban men, women, and children into "reconcentration camps." Weyler, unable to tell civilians from rebels, had set up the camps where 200,000 Cubans, an estimated one-eighth of the population, died of illness and starvation. Some leaders of the Cuban independence movement were naturalized American citizens who had returned to work in Cuba. When captured by Spanish authorities, they demanded protection by the United States.

Not all sentiment supported the Cubans, however. American business interests had invested more than $30 million in Cuba—mostly in sugar plantations—and wanted the revolt to end. Some plantation owners, doubting the capacity of the Cubans for self-government, favored the restoration of Spanish rule. The force of public opinion, however, caused many in the business community to change their minds.

Drawn Into War

Although President Cleveland preserved strict **neutrality,** or the refusal to take sides, in the Cuban struggle, he warned that if "the useless sacrifice of human life" went on, the United States might have to abandon the policy of "patient waiting." President McKinley, who came into office in the middle of the conflict, was also committed to neutrality. He even offered to buy Cuba, but was rejected. A peaceful solution seemed possible when Spain recalled General Weyler and offered Cuba a measure of local self-government. Assistant Secretary of the Navy Theodore Roosevelt was impatient

▲ THE *MAINE* Coverage of sinking of the *Maine* raised American anger against Spain. **Who was responsible for sinking the ship?**

with McKinley's negotiation with Spain and described the President as having "no more backbone than a chocolate eclair." William Randolph Hearst's *New York Journal* and Joseph Pulitzer's *New York World* fanned public anger with exaggerated and sometimes fabricated stories of Spanish atrocities in Cuba. This "yellow journalism" helped sell papers and encouraged war:

> ❝ *How long are the Spaniards to drench Cuba with the blood and tears of her people? . . . How long shall old men and women and children be murdered by the score, the innocent victims of Spanish rage against the patriot armies they cannot conquer? . . . How long shall the United States sit idle and indifferent?* ❞

"Remember the *Maine!*"

Public sentiment in favor of war was growing when, on February 9, 1898, the *Journal* printed a private letter written by Enrique Dupuy de Lôme, the Spanish ambassador to the United States, in which he called McKinley "weak and a bidder for the admiration of the crowd. . . . " This comment was a national insult. The ambassador resigned, but the damage to United States–Spanish relations was done.

Six days later the United States battleship *Maine,* anchored off the Cuban capital, Havana, exploded, killing 260 crew members. United States naval experts declared that the explosion came from outside the ship. Spanish experts replied that there were no mines.

The "yellow press" in 1898 expressed no indecision. Papers promptly blamed Spain and even printed diagrams showing just how the deed was done. "Remember the *Maine!*" became the battle cry throughout the United States.

Preparing for War

Congress responded to a torrent of public indignation against Spain by allocating $50 million for war preparations. McKinley, meanwhile, demanded that Spain give Cuba independence. Although at the last moment Spain claimed it was trying to comply, McKinley nevertheless delivered a warlike message to Congress. Congress demanded that Spain evacuate the island. When no reply to this ultimatum was received, Congress declared war on April 25.

While expansionists were excited about the prospects of gaining Cuba, humanitarian forces in Congress attached the Teller Amendment to the declaration of war. In it Congress pledged "to leave the government and control of the Island to the people" as soon as peace was established there.

■ "A Splendid Little War"

While the army prepared to invade Cuba, the conflict, called by Secretary of State John Hay a "splendid little war," began in the Pacific. Although the McKinley administration had no thought of expanding the territories of the United States, some officials believed that this was a prime opportunity to do so. One such person was Theodore Roosevelt.

The Philippine Connection

When John D. Long, secretary of the navy, was out of his Washington office, Roosevelt took charge. On February 25, 1898, he ordered on his own authority a Pacific squadron stationed in Hong Kong to sail for the Philippine Islands, a Spanish colony for 300 years, if war broke out. Commodore George Dewey, commander of the United States fleet, would try to prevent a Spanish fleet in Manila Bay from going to sea. As soon as war was declared, Dewey's fleet set sail; it penetrated Manila Bay on May 1 and rapidly destroyed the weaker Spanish fleet. The quick victory surprised the President, and an army of occupation was hastily organized to sail from San Francisco to the Philippines.

A native Filipino, Emilio Aguinaldo (AH•gee•NAHL•doh), had led an uprising against Spanish rule of the Philippines in 1896. Aguinaldo was exiled in Hong Kong, where Dewey met him and provided supplies so he could lead a revolt against the Spanish forces that remained in the islands. By the time the American army arrived in the

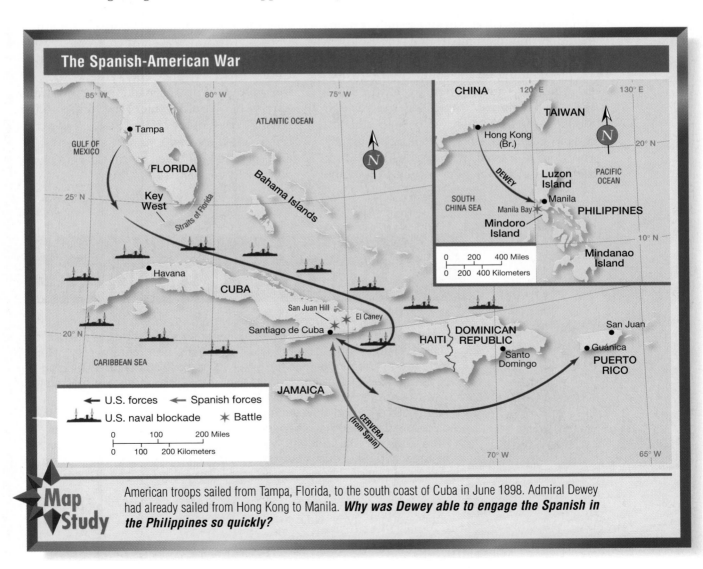

The Spanish-American War

← U.S. forces ← Spanish forces
U.S. naval blockade ✳ Battle

Map Study American troops sailed from Tampa, Florida, to the south coast of Cuba in June 1898. Admiral Dewey had already sailed from Hong Kong to Manila. *Why was Dewey able to engage the Spanish in the Philippines so quickly?*

Philippines, Aguinaldo's forces controlled all the territory except the city of Manila. When the Spanish surrendered and turned the Philippines over to the United States Army, it left unanswered the question of who would rule the islands after the war.

Fighting in Cuba

When war was first declared, McKinley had called for 200,000 volunteers to supplement the regular army, which numbered only 28,000. The War Department was inefficient. Nevertheless, 17,000 troops were declared ready to sail from Tampa, Florida, to Cuba by the middle of June. To fight a war in the tropics, they were issued heavy woolen uniforms left over from the western wars against the Plains peoples. Their ammunition was out-of-date; there were almost no medical supplies; and rations included inedible meat that the soldiers nicknamed "embalmed beef."

After landing on the south coast of Cuba, the Americans advanced on the city of Santiago. One regiment was called the "Rough Riders"—an assortment of college athletes, cowboys, miners, and law officers—led by Theodore Roosevelt, who had resigned from the Navy Department in order to join the fight. On foot because their horses were still in Florida, they charged up San Juan Hill. By securing the heights overlooking Santiago, they helped capture the city.

The Rough Riders were not alone in this attack. Among the other regiments was the all-black 10th Cavalry Regiment. Many African Americans had responded to the call for soldiers both because they identified with the Cubans' struggle for freedom and because they hoped it would improve their own lot. At least four of these African American soldiers were awarded the Congressional Medal of Honor.

Naval Encounters

At the outbreak of hostilities, an American squadron of new battleships under Admiral William T. Sampson was given the task of intercepting a Spanish squadron under Admiral Pascual Cervera (pahs•KWAHL suhr•VEHR•uh). Knowing that Cervera had left the Cape Verde Islands off the west coast of Africa in April, Americans feared he would attack the undefended Atlantic coast of the United States. They canceled hotel reservations at seaside resorts and prepared for defense, but Cervera headed directly for Santiago harbor.

Joseph Pulitzer
1847–1911

★ ★ ★ ★ ★ ★ ★ ★ ★
AMERICAN PORTRAITS

After emigrating from Hungary, Joseph Pulitzer made publishing history—and a personal fortune—by creating a new form of newspaper journalism.

As a soldier during the Civil War, Pulitzer noted how Americans loved to read newspapers. After the war, he bought and merged two St. Louis newspapers. Circulation soared as he filled his paper with scandals and attacks on big business. He later bought two New York papers, bringing to them the same successful recipe—sensationalism and controversy. He won a mass audience by running comic strips and covering fashions and sports.

After retiring, he saw his papers engage in "yellow journalism" to compete with William Randolph Hearst's flag-waving newspapers. Pulitzer took back control and returned his newspapers to their flamboyant investigative style.

▲ **MANILA BAY** United States naval ships in the Pacific, under Commodore George Dewey, sailed into Manila Bay on May 1, 1898. *When did Spain and the United States agree to an armistice?*

Sampson's superior force found the Spanish fleet at Santiago and blockaded the harbor. Once the American army took the heights overlooking Santiago, Cervera could surrender or try to break the blockade. On July 3, with little hope of victory, Cervera ordered his ships out of Santiago harbor. In the ensuing battle, all Spanish vessels were sunk. Only one American was killed and one was wounded. Effective Spanish resistance in Cuba ceased with the surrender of Santiago two weeks later. American troops went on to occupy another Spanish possession, the island of Puerto Rico. On August 12 Spain and the United States agreed to an armistice.

The "splendid little war" cost 5,000 American lives, mostly due to disease and food poisoning. The flag of the United States, an emerging world power, flew over distant islands. Had American isolationism ended?

Section 2 ★ Review

Checking for Understanding

1. **Identify** William Randolph Hearst, Joseph Pulitzer, Enrique Dupuy de Lôme, the *Maine,* Theodore Roosevelt, Rough Riders.

2. **Define** neutrality.

3. **List** the key events leading to war with Spain over Cuba.

4. **State** the importance of the naval battle between Admiral William T. Sampson and Admiral Pascual Cervera.

Critical Thinking

5. **Making Judgments** How did the United States justify going to war with Spain given a previous policy of noninvolvement?

SECTION 3

★★★

Becoming a World Power

Setting the Scene

Section Focus

After the Spanish-American War the United States was confronted by a host of questions and responsibilities. Congress debated what to do about the Philippine Islands. Commercial and industrial interests argued for annexation, but how could colonialism be reconciled with the principles of the Declaration of Independence?

Objectives

After studying this section, you should be able to

★ explain why the Philippine Islands were difficult to govern.

★ discuss the constitutional difficulties involved in colonization.

Key Term

protectorate

◀ **Army recruitment poster**

The Spanish-American War and the prospect of expanding in the Pacific brought a change of policy toward the Hawaiian Islands. Cleveland had resisted a move to annex them in 1893, and in 1897 the Senate had turned down an annexation treaty presented by McKinley. Hawaii, the halfway point between California and the Philippines, would be valuable as a naval base, however. In July 1898, before the war ended, the Hawaiian Islands were annexed by a joint resolution of Congress.

■ The Philippines

The armistice left Americans in control of the Spanish-owned Philippine Islands. The debate over whether to acquire and annex the Philippines was a stormy one.

Arguments For and Against Annexing the Philippines

Before entering the Spanish-American War, most Americans had no idea of annexing territory, particularly a territory 6,000 miles from the Pacific coast. McKinley confessed that before Dewey's victory he could not have come within 2,000 miles of placing the Philippine Islands on a map. Once he said, "If old Dewey had just sailed away when he smashed that Spanish fleet, what a lot of strong feelings he would have saved us."

Strong feelings developed against acquiring the islands. Several leading Democrats, including former President Grover Cleveland, were opposed. Many influential private citizens agreed with them. Prominent Republicans such as Speaker of the House Thomas B. Reed and several senators fought annexation as a violation of American tradition.

Senator Henry Cabot Lodge spoke for those who wanted a larger American role in world affairs. Business interests thought of new markets and fields of investment. Public opinion was excited by the prospect of acquiring an empire. Patriotism merged with belief in social Darwinism, or the belief in the "survival of the fittest." If the United States was the most fit to govern the Philippines, why should it haul down the Stars and Stripes and allow Japan or Germany or some other power to step in and take them?

For others, like Reverend Josiah Strong, there was a sense of mission based on racial and religious bias. Strong, in his book *Our Country,* blended social Darwinism with his interest in spreading Christianity. He felt the nationality groups were in a competition from which Anglo-Saxons were destined to emerge victorious.

Settlement with Spain

McKinley, a deeply religious man, wrestled with the problem, then reported that through prayer he had decided to:

>   . . . [E]ducate the Filipinos, and uplift and civilize and Christianize them, and by God's grace, do the very best we could by them, as our fellow men for whom Christ died.

Actually, Catholic missions had been started in the Philippines in the 1500s. McKinley instructed his peace commissioners to ask for all of the Philippine Islands. When Spain resisted, the United States offered to pay $20 million for them. In the treaty, signed December 10, 1898, Spain gave up control over Cuba and surrendered Puerto Rico, the Pacific island of Guam, and the Philippine Islands. Anti-imperialist feeling in the Senate was so strong that the treaty was ratified by only a two-vote margin. A Senate resolution promising eventual independence to the Filipino people was defeated only by the tie-breaking vote of the Vice President.

The United States encountered problems in trying to govern the Philippines. The

▲ THE BIG STICK To many people around the world, the United States in the late 1800s and early 1900s used its power to spread its influence. ***Why did the United States encounter difficult problems in trying to govern the Philippines?***

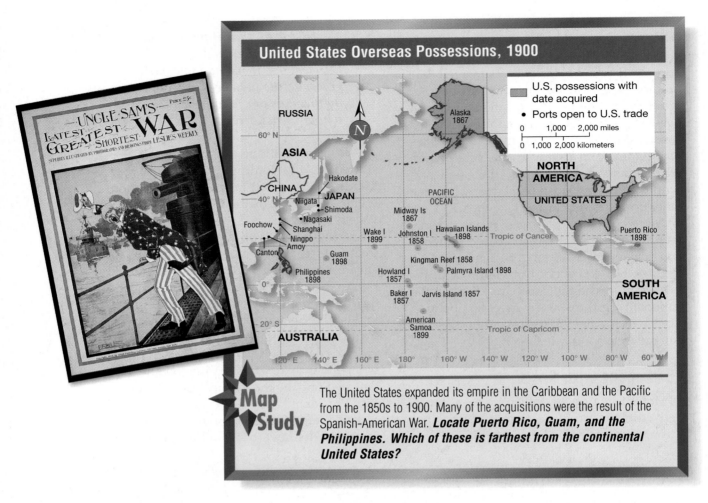

United States Overseas Possessions, 1900

U.S. possessions with date acquired

• Ports open to U.S. trade

Map Study

The United States expanded its empire in the Caribbean and the Pacific from the 1850s to 1900. Many of the acquisitions were the result of the Spanish-American War. *Locate Puerto Rico, Guam, and the Philippines. Which of these is farthest from the continental United States?*

7,100 islands had 7.5 million people, who were divided into 43 ethnic groups speaking 87 different languages and dialects. The Filipinos ranged from people living in the forests to highly literate city dwellers.

Filipino Resistance

Filipino patriots had helped the American forces capture the islands. Once it became clear that the United States intended to annex the Philippines, however, a new uprising broke out—this time against the Americans. Feeling that they had been cheated out of their independence, Filipino soldiers took to the hills. A revolutionary government was set up under Emilio Aguinaldo. Its leaders adopted a republican constitution. Aguinaldo and the other Filipino leaders knew that if the republic were to succeed, they must gain the loyalty of the people and set up diplomatic relations with other countries.

Fighting between Filipino and United States forces broke out in February 1899. Within two months, the Filipinos had been driven from their capital city, and the government fled. Aguinaldo continued to carry on guerrilla operations that produced some success. Aguinaldo's capture in March 1901, however, for all practical purposes ended the Filipinos' military efforts. More than 60,000 troops—four times the number sent to Cuba—and three years of fighting were required to suppress the Filipino patriots and put down the revolt.

At the conclusion of the fighting, Andrew Carnegie commented to a friend in the government:

66 *You seem to have finished your work of civilizing the Filipinos; it is thought about 8,000 of them have been completely civilized and sent to heaven. I hope you like it.* 99

Many Americans were distressed to find their country at war with an independence movement. Mark Twain suggested that Old Glory should have its white stripes painted black and its stars replaced with skull and crossbones.

Even before the Filipino uprising was put down, President McKinley declared that American policy toward the islands would be for the good of the Filipinos. The President stated,

> 66 *The Philippines are ours, not to exploit but to develop, to civilize, to educate, to train in the science of self-government.* 99

President McKinley sent two commissions to investigate the conditions in the Philippines and set up a civil government.

There were several changes during the first years of United States rule in the Philippines. The English language replaced Spanish as the language of general usage. The number of American business enterprises grew quickly, largely because Americans were permitted to sell their goods tariff-free in the Philippines. Street names were Americanized.

Resentment against American rule in the Philippines was moderately relieved in 1901 when President Theodore Roosevelt appointed William Howard Taft as the first civilian governor. Genuinely devoted to the interests of the island people, Taft started a program to prepare the Filipinos for self-government, and public schools were established. The United States bought out large foreign landowners and passed laws to keep property in the hands of the Filipinos.

Taft did not believe that the Philippines would be ready for independence for many years, though. In 1907 an elective legislature was set up, and in 1916 the United States promised that the Philippines would have independence eventually. That independence was finally granted in 1946.

Life of the Times

★★★★★★★★★★★★★★★★★★★★★★★★★★★★★★★★★★★★

Imperial Fruits

Tropical fruits, such as lemons and oranges, first came to North America in the 1500s by way of the Spanish explorers and missionaries in Florida. More exotic tropical fruits were unavailable to the average person until the late nineteenth century.

Tropical fruits such as bananas, coconuts, and pineapples appeared on the breakfast tables of ordinary Americans for the first time when steamships reduced travel time from the tropics. Foods such as bananas, which easily rotted, could be transported expeditiously by steamship from the Caribbean islands to the United States. The imperialistic impulse that brought the United States distant colonies also inspired business entrepreneurs to build plantations. In 1899 Lorenzo Dow Baker and Minor Keith founded the United Fruit Company; their goal was to own and operate banana plantations in Central America. Baker and Keith realized enormous profits and indirectly helped coin the term "banana republics" for Costa Rica, Guatemala, and Nicaragua—where American corporations often influenced United States policy.

★★★

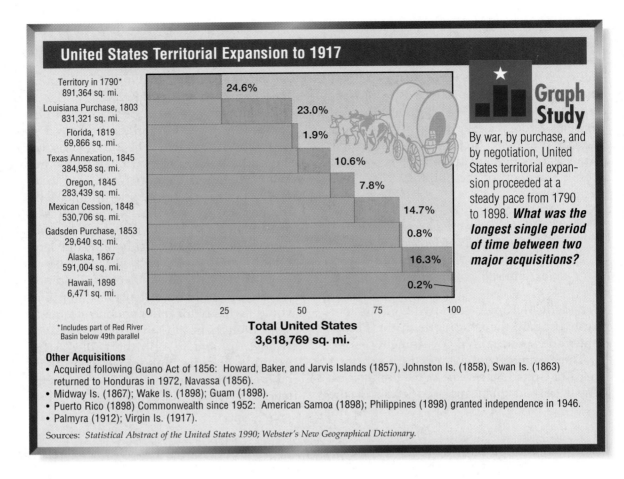

United States Territorial Expansion to 1917

Territory in 1790*
891,364 sq. mi. — 24.6%

Louisiana Purchase, 1803
831,321 sq. mi. — 23.0%

Florida, 1819
69,866 sq. mi. — 1.9%

Texas Annexation, 1845
384,958 sq. mi. — 10.6%

Oregon, 1845
283,439 sq. mi. — 7.8%

Mexican Cession, 1848
530,706 sq. mi. — 14.7%

Gadsden Purchase, 1853
29,640 sq. mi. — 0.8%

Alaska, 1867
591,004 sq. mi. — 16.3%

Hawaii, 1898
6,471 sq. mi. — 0.2%

**Total United States
3,618,769 sq. mi.**

*Includes part of Red River
Basin below 49th parallel

Graph Study

By war, by purchase, and by negotiation, United States territorial expansion proceeded at a steady pace from 1790 to 1898. *What was the longest single period of time between two major acquisitions?*

Other Acquisitions
• Acquired following Guano Act of 1856: Howard, Baker, and Jarvis Islands (1857), Johnston Is. (1858), Swan Is. (1863) returned to Honduras in 1972, Navassa (1856).
• Midway Is. (1867); Wake Is. (1898); Guam (1898).
• Puerto Rico (1898) Commonwealth since 1952: American Samoa (1898); Philippines (1898) granted independence in 1946.
• Palmyra (1912); Virgin Is. (1917).

Sources: *Statistical Abstract of the United States 1990; Webster's New Geographical Dictionary.*

■ Problems of an Overseas Empire

The new possessions posed constitutional problems summarized in the question, "Does the Constitution follow the flag?" Congress, according to the Constitution, may not set tariff duties on goods carried from one part of the United States to another. Did this mean that no duties would be laid on goods from American colonies? The Constitution guarantees to all American citizens certain civil rights. Did constitutional guarantees of civil rights extend to the people of the new colonies who knew nothing of American justice?

The Supreme Court decided that the Constitution did not cover overseas possessions. Puerto Rico, the Court ruled, was a dependency; therefore Congress could set tariffs on its products. Other decisions determined that inhabitants of dependencies enjoyed full civil rights only if granted them by congressional legislation.

Cuba

According to the Teller Amendment, the United States pledged to withdraw from Cuba when order was restored. After three years of civil war, however, the island was in terrible condition. The United States Army remained in Cuba to set up a republican government, oversee Cuban finances, and establish public health and sanitation programs.

In 1901, to protect its interests in Cuba, the United States Congress added the Platt Amendment to an army bill. This amendment, which governed the relations between Cuba and the United States for 33 years, provided that: (1) Cuba should not make any treaty with another nation that weakened its independence; (2) Cuba should allow the United States the right to buy or lease naval stations; (3) Cuba's public debt should not exceed its capacity to pay; and (4) the United States should have the right to intervene to protect Cuban independence and keep order. These conditions, written into Cuba's constitution and into a treaty with the United States, made Cuba an American **protectorate**—a nation or region controlled by a stronger state. The attitude that Cuba was part of "the white man's burden" was reflected in an editorial by William Allen White in Kansas's *Emporia Gazette:*

> " *Only Anglo-Saxons can govern themselves. The Cubans will need despotic government for many years to restrain anarchy until Cuba is filled with Yankees.* "

For almost four years, Cuba was under military rule directed by General Leonard Wood. The greatest achievement of Wood's administration was the suppression of yellow fever. An American medical team under Dr. Walter Reed proved the theory of a Cuban physician, Carlos J. Finlay: that yellow fever is transmitted by the stegomyia mosquito. American doctors and volunteers allowed themselves to be bitten by mosquitoes, and some of them died as martyrs to medical progress. Major William C. Gorgas, an Army doctor, carried on a campaign to eliminate mosquitoes from Havana. By 1901, for the first time in centuries, there was no yellow fever in the Cuban capital.

Puerto Rico

The United States had made no prior commitment to withdraw from Puerto Rico as it had done in Cuba. That island's cultural ties

Visualizing **History**

▲ AN OVERSEAS EMPIRE As in most wars, the civilians suffered many hardships. Thousands of Filipinos perished from sickness, starvation, and other indirect effects of war. The Philippines gained independence in 1946. *When was Puerto Rico granted territorial status?*

with Spain and Latin America through the Roman Catholic Church, the Spanish language, and other traditions had existed for nearly 300 years. Yet, the United States chose to keep the island as its territory.

After a brief period of military rule, Congress gradually allowed Puerto Rico a degree of self-government. The Puerto Rican people demanded either independence or complete self-rule under the American flag. In 1917 they were granted territorial status and made citizens of the United States.

Section 3 ★ Review

Checking for Understanding

1. **Identify** William Gorgas, Walter Reed, "white man's burden," Platt Amendment.

2. **Define** protectorate.

3. **Explain** ways in which the President and Congress resolved the annexation difficulties in the Philippines.

4. **Describe** how problems with Cuba and Puerto Rico were resolved.

Critical Thinking

5. **Making Decisions** Analyze the reasoning of the Supreme Court on constitutional guarantees for overseas possessions. Do you agree with their conclusions? Explain.

Interpreting Primary Sources

Anti-Imperialist Politics

As the Democratic presidential candidate in 1900, William Jennings Bryan became a leader of the anti-imperialist cause. The following passage illustrates the cause's major arguments.

From William Jennings Bryan's speech to the Democratic National Convention, 1900—

The principal arguments . . . advanced by those who enter upon a defense of imperialism are:

First—That we must improve the present opportunity to become a world power and enter into international politics.

Second—That our commercial interests in the Philippine Islands and in the Orient make it necessary for us to hold the islands permanently.

Third—That the spread of the Christian religion will be facilitated by a colonial policy.

Fourth—That there is no honorable retreat from the position which the nation has taken. . . .

It is sufficient answer to the first argument to say that for more than a century this nation has been a world power. . . .

It is not necessary to own people in order to trade with them. . . .

We do not own Japan or China, but we trade with their people. . . .

The religious argument varies . . . from a passive belief that Providence delivered the Filipinos into our hands, for their good and our glory, to the exultation of the minister who said that we ought to "thrash the natives (Filipinos) until they understand who we are," and that "every bullet sent, every cannon shot and every flag waved means righteousness."

▲ McKINLEY TAILORS AN EXPANDING UNCLE SAM

. . . If true Christianity consists in carrying out in our daily lives the teachings of Christ, who will say that we are commanded to civilize with dynamite and proselyte with the sword?

Examining the Primary Source

1. Identify the sentences that introduce Bryan's answers to the four arguments he cites.

2. What evidence does Bryan give to refute the argument that commercial interests necessitate control of the Philippines?

Critical Thinking

3. **Making Comparisons** Analyze Bryan's description of the imperialists' attitude toward the Filipinos. Then compare that attitude with the attitude of those who embraced the idea of Manifest Destiny toward Native Americans.

★★★★★★★★★★★★★★★★★★★★★★★★★★★

A New Arena

Setting the Scene

Section Focus

Americans expected President Roosevelt to adopt an aggressive foreign policy. Roosevelt was resolved that the United States should be a great power. In the Western Hemisphere, he enlarged the scope of the Monroe Doctrine and secured United States domination of the Caribbean. In the Pacific and East Asia, he attempted to keep a balance of power and restrain first Russian, then Japanese, ambitions.

Objectives

After studying this section, you should be able to

★ give examples of Roosevelt's "Big Stick" diplomacy.

★ discuss the goals and results of the "Open Door" policy in China.

★ discuss America's concerns over the Russo-Japanese War.

Key Terms

anarchist, corollary, partitioned, sphere of influence, indemnity

◀ **THEODORE ROOSEVELT, BRONZE RELIEF**

*I*n the Western Hemisphere, the acquisition of Puerto Rico and the establishment of a protectorate over Cuba gave the United States a new interest in this region. American expansion into the Pacific brought closer contact with East Asian nations, particularly China. Several European countries, along with Japan, were fiercely competing for trading rights in China. The United States entered a new and complex arena of international politics.

■ The Election of 1900

In 1900 William Jennings Bryan, again the Democratic candidate, attempted to make imperialism the paramount issue of the presidential campaign. The Republicans again nominated McKinley for President. Theodore Roosevelt, who had become governor of New York, received the nomination for Vice President. As much as possible, the Republicans avoided discussion of imperialism because they were divided. The result was an even greater Republican victory than that in 1896.

Six months after his second inauguration, McKinley spoke of the United States's new position in the world. Previously a strong supporter of isolationism, he announced a change of heart, saying:

❝ *Isolation is no longer possible or desirable. God and man have linked the nations together. No nation can longer be indifferent to any other....* ❞

He explained that America's diversity of products and its efficiency in producing them had so increased that there was an urgent need for more markets. He proposed reciprocity treaties with foreign nations, providing for mutual lowering of tariffs.

McKinley did not live to put his new policy into effect. The day after delivering his speech he was shot by an **anarchist,** one who opposes all forms of government. Just short of 43 years old, Roosevelt became the youngest President.

■ The Big Stick

Theodore Roosevelt had a genius for the dramatic gesture. He told young men, "Don't flinch, don't foul, hit the line hard." Roosevelt's actions were sometimes impulsive, sometimes unwise, but he firmly believed that power imposed responsibility. One of Roosevelt's mottoes in foreign policy was a West African saying, "Speak softly and carry a big stick."

The Panama Canal

The "Big Stick" was most in evidence in the Caribbean. Roosevelt and others believed that in addition to saving time for commercial shipping, a canal would answer the strategic need to shuttle warships between the Atlantic and the Pacific oceans.

This was clearly demonstrated during the Spanish-American War. The battleship *Oregon,* ordered from Puget Sound to Cuba, was forced to steam 14,000 miles around Cape Horn—3 times as far as if there had been a canal.

In the 1800s a French company had made a vain and costly effort to cut through Panama. Early in the 1890s, an American company started to dig a canal through Nicaragua but soon abandoned the attempt. In 1901 Britain, which also had an interest in the canal, agreed that the United States could build, control, and fortify a canal, provided that ships of all nations were charged equal toll.

Immediately, Secretary of State John Hay offered Colombia, which controlled Panama, $10 million and a yearly rent of $250,000 for the right to construct a canal through Panama and control a narrow strip of land on either side. However, feeling that the price was too low and fearful of losing control of Panama, the Colombian senate unanimously refused to ratify the agreement.

Roosevelt was furious. He let it be known privately that he would not mind if Panama revolted. On November 3, 1903, a revolution broke out, and an independent Republic of Panama was proclaimed. On November 6 the United States recognized Panama's independence. Less than two weeks later the United States and Panama signed a treaty for the canal.

Roosevelt defended his Big Stick diplomacy in Panama on the ground that he advanced "the needs of collective civilization" by speeding up the building of an inter-ocean canal. His action was widely condemned in the United States as unjustifiable aggression. In Latin America it aroused dislike and distrust of the United States.

The engineering difficulties involved in cutting through the Isthmus of Panama were enormous and were compounded by the tremendous health problems encountered in the tropics. In 1885 an English writer wrote of Panama:

> 66 *In all the world there is not perhaps now concentrated in any so much foul disease. . . . The Isthmus is a damp, tropical jungle, intensely hot, swarming with mosquitoes . . . the home, even as Nature made it, of yellow fever, typhus, and dysentery.* 99

George W. Goethals, a colonel in the Corps of Engineers, directed the engineering feat that completed the canal in 1914. Dr. William C. Gorgas, who had cleaned up Havana, reduced the health threats in Panama.

Venezuela

Roosevelt, like Cleveland, defended Venezuela from possible European aggression, strengthening the Monroe Doctrine. By 1902 Venezuela owed money to citizens of several European countries. Cipriano Castro, the Venezuelan dictator-president, refused either to pay the debts or submit them to arbitration. Roosevelt said the Monroe Doctrine did not protect Latin American nations against punishment for misbehavior.

After consultation with the American State Department, Great Britain and Germany, Venezuela's two principal creditors, blockaded Venezuelan ports to force payment. The blockade was very unpopular in the United States because it was perceived as a violation of the Monroe Doctrine. Feeling was intensified when Venezuelan gunboats were sunk and Venezuelan ports bombarded. Public anger moved Roosevelt to press for an end of the blockade and the submission of the dispute to arbitration. Although both parties agreed to arbitration, Great Britain was quicker to respond than Germany was. This added to Roosevelt's distrust of the rising German empire.

Roosevelt Corollary

In 1903 Argentine foreign minister Luis Drago urged that forcibly collecting debts from bankrupt countries be made a violation of international law. If the United States opposed Drago and allowed foreign nations to block the coasts and bombard the cities of defaulting Latin American nations, the door was left open to further aggression. If, however, the United States outlawed forcible collection of debts, it might be pushed into defending financial dishonesty. The President's reply to the Drago Doctrine became known as the Roosevelt **Corollary,** or addition, to the Monroe Doctrine. Whenever an American republic was guilty of "chronic wrongdoing," said Roosevelt, the United States might have to intervene itself.

Dominican Republic

The Roosevelt Corollary was first applied in the Dominican Republic. In 1905 the United States assumed the responsibility of collecting Dominican customs. The United States Marine Corps collected the duties and divided them to support the Dominican government and to pay that nation's debts to European countries.

Roosevelt's successor, President William Howard Taft, continued Roosevelt's policies but with a shift of emphasis. Taft's secretary of state, Philander C. Knox, promoted American business interests abroad with the slogan, "Every diplomat a salesman." In Latin America this "dollar diplomacy" resulted in increased sales of United States goods—including warships—and in efforts to increase American investments there.

Although Taft described his brand of diplomacy as "substituting dollars for bullets," sometimes he used both. In 1912 he sent marines to Nicaragua to install a more friendly government and to force acceptance of a loan from New York bankers. Such policies increased the unpopularity of the United States in Latin America.

■ The Balance of Power in East Asia

Roosevelt realized that the position of the United States in East Asia was weak. He called the Philippines the "Achilles' heel" of

 THE PANAMA CANAL Work on the Panama Canal began in 1904 and lasted 10 years. *What difficulties were encountered?*

▲ SPHERES OF INFLUENCE Cities in China grew into centers of trade. Major international powers divided China into spheres of influence. ***What clash of interest led to the Russo-Japanese War?***

American defense; they were easily vulnerable to attack by Japan. China and Russia also posed problems.

China and the Open Door

At the close of the nineteenth century, it looked as though China, like Africa, would be **partitioned,** or divided, among stronger powers. In 1898 and 1899, Russia, Germany, France, and Great Britain forced China to lease its ports, some of them for 99 years. Each "leasehold" was expected to become the center of a **sphere of influence**—an area where a European nation controlled economic development.

The United States and Great Britain, in order to ensure open avenues of trade with China, decided to oppose the parceling out of Chinese territory. Early in 1898 the British government proposed a joint declaration with the United States in favor of the "Open Door"—with the goal of preserving equal trading opportunities in China for all foreign nations. At that time the United States was

cool to the idea, but its annexation of the Philippines changed the American attitude.

John Hay, secretary of state, thought that the days of American isolationism must end. Having defended the acquisition of an overseas empire, he agreed with Great Britain on the policy of an Open Door in China. In September 1899, Hay sent notes to countries with leaseholds in China asking that they keep the ports open to vessels of all nations on equal terms.

Boxer Rebellion

While foreign countries debated control of China, Chinese secret societies were organizing to oust foreign control. One of these was called "the Boxers" by Westerners because of the physical exercises they practiced.

When a falsified story was printed in America suggesting that Westerners were negotiating the dismantling of a Chinese monument, the Boxer Rebellion broke out. With secret aid from the Chinese government, the Boxers intended to wipe out "foreign devils" and their Christian converts. They killed more than 200 foreigners, mostly missionaries and their families. For 7 weeks the Boxers laid siege to foreign embassies in Beijing.

During this crisis Hay worked to prevent full-scale retaliation and war against China and to persuade the leaseholding powers not to use the Boxer Rebellion as an excuse to partition the country. In July 1900, he sent a second set of Open Door notes. This time he declared that the policy of the United States was to seek ways to "preserve Chinese territorial and administrative entity."

The United States lacked sufficient military power to enforce Hay's Open Door notes of 1899 and 1900. Equal trading opportunities in China and the preservation of China's territorial integrity lay in maintaining a "balance of power" among the nations with ambitions in East Asia.

Russo-Japanese War

China's two closest neighbors, Japan and Russia, were especially threatening. In 1893 Japan established a protectorate over the independent kingdom of Korea and obtained Formosa and other islands off China's northeast coast. Japan had designs on the resource-rich Chinese province of Manchuria, in which Russia was already established. The Russians hoped to move into Korea. This clash of interests led to the Russo-Japanese War in 1904.

Japan won victories over Russia on both land and sea. By the summer of 1905, both countries were ready to make peace. The Japanese secretly asked Roosevelt if he would serve as go-between. After consulting the czar, Roosevelt formally offered to help make peace. Both nations accepted the President's proposals and sent diplomats to a peace conference in Portsmouth, New Hampshire, in August 1905.

Treaty of Portsmouth

The President induced Japan to give up claims for a money **indemnity,** or payment for damages, and Russia to give up the southern half of the island of Sakhalin (SA•kuh•LEEN). Japan also took over Russian interests in southern Manchuria.

The war altered the balance of power in East Asia. Now it was no longer Russian expansion that was most to be feared, but Japanese. Roosevelt himself believed that there was potential danger of war.

Roosevelt arranged a compromise in 1907 and 1908, known as the Gentlemen's Agreement. In a complicated series of maneuvers, he soothed Japanese anger and showed the Japanese that he was not afraid of them. To check Japanese expansion toward the Philippines, Roosevelt recognized Japan as dominant in Korea and Manchuria.

The resolution of the Russo-Japanese War was an example of Roosevelt's efforts to use arbitration rather than war to settle controversies. Although he upgraded America's military power, he believed that the United States had an obligation as a leader of an interdependent world to act responsibly.

Section 4 ★ Review

Checking for Understanding

1. **Identify** Big Stick diplomacy, John Hay, Drago Doctrine, Roosevelt Corollary, Open Door, Boxer Rebellion, Russo-Japanese War.

2. **Define** anarchist, corollary, partitioned, sphere of influence, indemnity.

3. **State** instances where Theodore Roosevelt used Big Stick diplomacy.

4. **Indicate** how President Theodore Roosevelt acted as peacemaker in the Russo-Japanese War.

Critical Thinking

5. **Understanding Cause and Effect** Explain how Roosevelt's Big Stick diplomacy led to ill feeling against the United States throughout Latin America.

Using Vocabulary

Assume that you are a reporter for an antiadministration newspaper covering the Latin American situation in 1903. Write a feature article describing Theodore Roosevelt's policies using the following vocabulary terms.

imperialism   protectorate
isolationism   sphere of influence
reciprocity   corollary

Reviewing Facts

1. **State** three reasons why the United States abandoned isolationist policies after the Civil War.

2. **Explain** how confrontation with Great Britain in 1895–1896 led to strengthening the American navy.

3. **Describe** the position of the President and press regarding war with Spain over Cuba. Why did McKinley change his mind?

4. **List** three reasons America went to war over Cuba. Which was most important?

5. **Discuss** why Hawaii had fewer difficulties accepting its position as a United States possession than did Puerto Rico or the Philippines.

6. **Show** why Americans favored an Open Door policy in China.

7. **Indicate** why the United States needed to build the Panama Canal.

Understanding Concepts

Economic and Political Power

1. How did the use of the Big Stick in Latin America increase American wealth and political power?

2. How did a show of force with Great Britain and Germany enhance the American position in Latin America?

3. Why was the United States unable to avoid military confrontation in Cuba?

Critical Thinking

1. **Recognizing Stereotypes** How did adherence to social Darwinism cause the United States to stereotype people who lived in countries under their possession? In what ways did stereotyped thinking influence political and economic policies toward these territories?

2. **Analyzing Fine Art** The painting on this page by Frederic Remington depicts the bravado of the Rough Riders. Analyze the painting and answer the questions that follow.

   a. What is happening in the painting?

   b. What details do you see in this scene?

   c. Do you think Remington has captured the reality of battle? Why or why not?

▲ *CHARGE OF SAN JUAN HILL* BY FREDERIC REMINGTON

Writing About History

Argumentation

Write a headline and article for a Hearst newspaper urging war with Spain over Cuba. Remember, the article is designed to stir up public opinion in favor of conflict. Take into account national honor; persecuted people wanting freedom; business interests in Cuba; the superior economy and government of the United States; and the strategic position of Cuba.

Cooperative Learning

Work in a group of five to research and organize responses to the following questions. Select a note taker to record your group's answers and a spokesperson to share your answers with the rest of the class.

- Do you think the United States was justified in the actions it took to secure rights to build the Panama Canal?

- What should be the chief objectives of American foreign policy?

- Is it desirable for the United States to have an empire? Why or why not?

- Was the United States right to intervene in the Cuban revolution? Why or why not?

Social Studies Skills

Reading a Special-Purpose Map

There are many kinds of maps, such as physical, political, and land-use maps. However, some maps do not fit any of these categories. They are called special-purpose maps. They are drawn to show a specific feature, area, or situation. For example, this map shows the Panama Canal.

Because special-purpose maps are unique, each must be analyzed on its own. Each map will have a unique legend, scale, grid, and style. Depending on what a map shows, it may have elements you have not encountered before.

Practicing the Skill

Use the map and what you have read in the chapter to answer the following questions.

1. In what country is the Panama Canal located?

2. What is the land on both sides of the canal called?

3. What are the approximate geographical coordinates of the canal?

4. How many sets of locks are part of the canal?

5. About 22 miles of the canal is situated on what lake?

6. To go from the Atlantic Ocean to the Pacific Ocean, what general direction would a ship travel?

7. About how long is the Panama Canal according to the map?

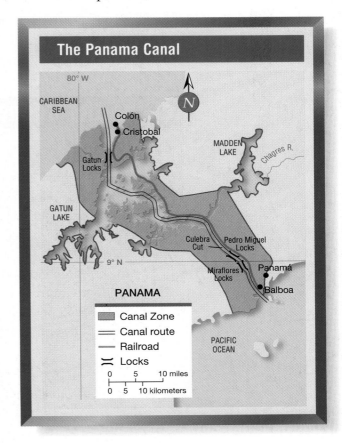

The Panama Canal

- Canal Zone
- Canal route
- Railroad
- Locks

0   5   10 miles
0   5   10 kilometers

Using Your Journal

Write a paragraph grouping and summarizing the reasons for becoming involved in the affairs of other countries. What was the major reason?

CHAPTER 23

★★

The Progressive Era
1893–1920

▲ WOOD AND LEATHER ROCKING HORSE

Setting the Scene

Focus

In the late 1800s, the Grangers and Populists had sought to resist corrupt government and unfair business practices. By 1900 their stalled efforts were given fresh life by a new group of reformers—the progressives. These optimistic, largely urban, middle-class reformers were confident in their ability to improve government and the quality of life. Their reforms were based not only on traditional democratic values but also on the new philosophy of pragmatism and study of the social sciences.

Concepts to Understand

★ How values and beliefs shaped the program of the Progressive Era

★ Why reform efforts were successful in correcting the worst abuses of big business and government

Read to Discover . . .

★ the types of reform that progressive leaders advocated.

★ the limitations of progressivism.

Journal Notes

Note in your journal, as you read the chapter, how women continued to push for the right to vote.

CULTURAL

● **1890** *Census shows population of the United States at 63 million*

● **1897** *The first subway system is completed in Boston*

1890	1900

● **1890** *Sherman Silver Purchase Act passes*

● **1902** *Oregon adopts the initiative and referendum*

POLITICAL

◀ FRANKLIN SAVINGS BANK

History AND ART

The Lone Tenement
by George Wesley Bellows, 1909

This urban scene displays the artist's vigorous and sponta-neous style. Bellows is also remembered for his sports paint-ings, particularly prizefights.

• **1909** *National Association for the Advancement of Colored People (NAACP) is formed*

• **1920** *Sinclair Lewis's* Main Street *is bestseller*

1910

1920

• **1917** *United States declares war on Germany*

• **1920** *Ratification of woman suffrage*

★★

Sources of Progressivism

Setting the Scene

Section Focus

The 1900s saw many challenges and opportunities for change. As city populations exploded with immigrants and rural Americans attracted by jobs, squalid slums and worker discontent also grew. In the face of threats of radical change, a variety of moderate reformers worked to protect, preserve, and improve American society.

◀ LABOR UNION POSTER

Objectives

After studying this section, you should be able to

★ discuss the role of the muckrakers in identifying social ills and promoting social change.

★ explain how methods and strategies used in business and education influenced social reform.

Key Terms

social gospel, pragmatism

Despite widespread social, political, and economic change in the late 1800s, the Gilded Age produced no broad effort to improve society. Populism was a large movement, but it was farm based and did not attract urban workers to its goals. The labor movement was also large, but it involved itself primarily with issues related to workers' jobs, wages, and working conditions.

Alternating periods of prosperity and depression accompanied industrialization in the late nineteenth century. Economic contractions shook the United States in the mid-1870s and well into the mid-1880s. The depression that followed the Panic of 1893, however, was the worst the nation had yet seen. As the split between rich and poor became too wide to ignore, Americans of all classes began to ask hard questions about the nation's political and economic systems, and they saw much that alarmed them.

■ Inequality in America

Not until the 1890s did Americans begin to show widespread concern about the direction in which their society was moving. Increasing poverty was one area of concern.

The Gap Between the Rich and Poor

Millions of American laborers worked long hours for low wages in the late 1800s. Wages of industrial workers averaged $10 to $12 for a 60- to 80-hour week. One of every 5 women worked, frequently for as little as

$6 to $8 a week, and children received even less. If workers were injured in industrial accidents, were laid off when business slowed, or became unemployed for any reason at all, their income completely stopped. At the other end of the scale were the immensely rich, the people who owned huge yachts, palatial estates, private railroad cars, and summer retreats covering thousands of acres. In 1900, when Andrew Carnegie earned $25 million from his steel company, the average worker made $500.

While 20 percent of the nation's families lived in comfort, 80 percent barely subsisted. A 1904 study estimated that 10 million Americans—12 percent of the nation's population—were "underfed, underclothed, and poorly housed." Relief for the poor was of little help because it was local, unsystematic, and largely dependent on private charity for funds.

It was not just the disparity of wealth that was alarming but also the distribution of political power. Not only did wealthy industrialists seem beyond the reach of government, they even appeared to dominate it. With such vast wealth and power at the top of society and such grinding poverty at the bottom, many Americans feared revolution.

Socialist Solutions

Some Americans turned to socialism as the answer. Edward Bellamy's 1887 novel *Looking Backward 2000–1887* made socialism seem an attractive alternative to the existing industrial society. His book tells the story of a nineteenth-century person in the United States who awakens from a prolonged hypnotic trance to find himself alive in a socialist paradise in the year 2000. All business has been merged into one big trust run by the people themselves; there is work and leisure for all without a trace of poverty or crime. Bellamy's vision of a socialist utopia made such an impact that his book sold 1 million copies, and numerous Nationalist Clubs were founded to advance his ideas.

Bellamy had no real program for action, however, and his followers eventually drifted toward other reform movements. Bellamy's influence, though, was reinforced by other socialist writers. Socialist ideas were widely circulated by popular authors such as Jack London and Upton Sinclair.

Popular labor leader Eugene V. Debs also lost faith in capitalism after being jailed during the Pullman strike of 1894. Declaring that in a democracy workers could gain control of the government and use it to change the free enterprise system, he organized the American Socialist party.

Opposed to Debs and other moderates were radical socialists such as Daniel De Leon, who preached that democratic reform was useless. "We Socialists are not reformers; we are Revolutionists," he

Weekly Wages in the Woolen Industry

Occupation and Location	Men 1890	Men 1900	Women 1890	Women 1900
New England Bobbin hands, doffers, and filling and roving	Median weekly rates in dollars			
carriers.............................	4.50	5.00	3.00	4.00
Dresser tenders and beamers....................	12.00	8.00	6.00	6.50
General hands, helpers, and laborers....................	6.50	7.00	5.00	5.50
Loom fixers.....................	12.50	13.50	—	—
Overseers and foreman..	19.50	19.50	—	—
Spinners..........................	7.50	9.50	5.50	6.00
Weavers..........................	7.50	9.00	6.50	7.50
All Occupations..............	7.50	8.00	6.50	6.50
Middle States All Occupations..............	7.50	9.00	5.00	5.00
Southern States All Occupations..............	6.50	6.50	3.50	3.50
Central States All Occupations..............	8.50	8.00	4.00	4.00
Pacific States All Occupations..............	9.50	9.50	5.00	5.00
All Sections All Occupations for workers under 16......	3.00	3.50	3.00	3.50

Source: Twelfth Census of the United States, 1900 *Special Reports: Employees and Wages (1903)*.

Chart Study Note the differences in pay rates for skilled and unskilled labor for men and women, the regional variations in pay, and the lower wages for children. *Why are no rates shown for female supervisors?*

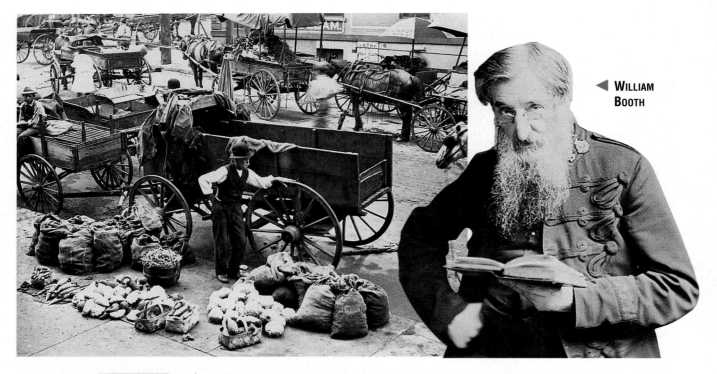

WILLIAM BOOTH

▲ THE SOCIAL GOSPEL The Salvation Army, after being established in England by General William Booth, was organized in the United States in 1880. It helped provide food, lodging, and hope for the urban needy. *What else did the Salvation Army provide?*

declared. "We care nothing for forms. We want a change of the inside of the mechanism of society. . . ." De Leon argued that even labor unions were traitors to the working class because they compromised with the industrialists. He proposed to organize all workers into new industrial unions that would eventually take over American business.

The Wobblies

Debs and De Leon briefly cooperated in 1905 in founding such a labor union, the Industrial Workers of the World, or "Wobblies." Debs soon withdrew, however, and the IWW rejected De Leon in favor of more radical leaders who preached murder and sabotage. The preamble of the IWW's constitution declared, "The working class and the employing class have nothing in common. There can be no peace so long as hunger and want are found among millions of working people. . . ."

Wherever the IWW existed, there were confrontations, strikes, sabotage, and often violence. The IWW remained strong, however, until after World War I, when Americans rejected radical politics.

More Moderate Voices

Most socialists were more moderate than the Wobblies, however, and the socialist movement gained strength throughout the early 1900s. At its height in 1912, Debs polled nearly 1 million votes as the Socialist party candidate for President. Although this was less than 10 percent of the total votes cast, the socialist movement had an importance greater than its numbers indicated. Other more moderate reformers called "progressives" owed much of their success to a growing public feeling that the only way to save the capitalist system was to improve it.

■ Progressive Leadership

The Progressive Era occupied the first 15 years of the twentieth century. Although the reforms of this period are sometimes called the Progressive movement, that label can be misleading. Unlike the Populists, the progressives were not a political party.

Who the Progressives Were

Although a Progressive party was formed in 1912, progressives also were found in both major parties. Nor were progressives united by a geographic section or by an occupation. Instead, they were a broad and largely unorganized group of reformers who often worked independently, each seeking solutions to a specific problem. Some were local reformers, while others worked for change at state or national levels. The reforms progressives advocated sometimes even conflicted.

Also unlike the Populists, the progressives were generally not the victims of existing conditions. They were mostly urban middle-class professionals who worked as journalists, social workers, educators, and clergy. Although they themselves were not suffering, they sympathized with those who were.

The Social Gospel

Progressives among Catholic priests, Jewish rabbis, and Protestant ministers began to preach a new **social gospel:** that religious organizations should work to improve society as well as to meet the spiritual needs of their congregations. Leaders such as Washington Gladden, Josiah Strong, and Walter Rauschenbush were concerned about social problems. Rauschenbush explained his view:

> ❝ *Our business is to make over an antiquated and immoral economic system. . . . Our inherited Christian faith dealt with individuals; our present task deals with society.* ❞

In 1908 the National Council of the Churches of Christ was founded to support social reform. In every large city the Salvation Army—a religious group devoted to helping the needy—provided food, lodging, and hope for the despairing and poor. Like the settlement houses of the late 1800s, urban churches began to consider the whole person by providing recreational facilities, adult-education classes, nurseries, and counseling.

Women Reformers

Women also became a driving force for progressive reform. That women figured so largely in the Progressive movement was an indication that their status was improving.

Ida Tarbell
1857–1944

AMERICAN PORTRAITS

After teaching school briefly, Ida Tarbell made her career as a writer and editor. She wrote hundreds of articles and many books, but her reputation as a "muckraker" rests on one book, *The History of the Standard Oil Company*, initially published as articles in *McClure's Magazine.*

Her interest in Standard Oil was deeply personal. Her father claimed that the company had forced him out of the oil tank business and had caused his partner to commit suicide. *McClure's* asked her to write about Standard Oil because of her knowledge of the oil business and because of her flair for writing.

For two years she researched Standard Oil's practices. Her revelations created such a popular furor that Standard Oil was investigated and eventually broken up by the Supreme Court for violating federal antitrust laws.

By 1900 women's colleges in the North and East had been turning out well-trained graduates for two generations. These women were aware of and interested in the various issues of the day. National women's clubs devoted to the study of such issues were common. By 1910 these clubs had nearly 1 million members.

Furthermore, the rights of women were expanding. By 1900 every state recognized the right of women to make a will. Most states recognized the right of women to dispose of their own wages, and some states had given them the right to equal guardianship of children. More importantly, five Western states had adopted woman suffrage.

The settlement-house movement, which women continued to lead, expanded into broader areas of reform such as slum clearance and legislation to limit working hours and outlaw child labor. Florence Kelley left Jane Addams and Hull House in Chicago and founded the National Consumers League, where she organized boycotts of goods produced by children or by workers in unsafe or unhealthful conditions. Another former Hull House social worker, Julia Lathrop, became the first head of the federal Children's Bureau, created in the Department of Labor in 1912 and now part of Health and Human Services. Other female progressives included Carrie Chapman Catt, widely known for her work in the woman's suffrage movement. Elizabeth Platt Decker headed the General Federation of Women's Clubs, which attracted nearly 1 million women in the early 1900s to promote the arts, education, and community health.

Striving for Big-Business Efficiency

Ironically, progressive reformers owed a great debt to the big businesses that so many of them detested. Unlike Populists, who believed that common people could solve society's problems, progressives put their faith in experts. Although critical of the methods and power of business leaders, progressives admired their ability to run large companies smoothly and efficiently. Progressives were confident that just like the trained managers, scientists, and effi-

ciency experts who solved business problems, expert reformers could analyze and solve problems that kept society from running smoothly.

■ Educators and Investigators

In the mid-1800s, most American colleges were small, church-supported institutions less concerned with knowledge than with shaping the character of their students. Graduates who wanted to pursue further studies often went to Germany, where universities awarded an advanced degree, the Ph.D. These students brought back to America a learning style that emphasized questioning and research instead of memorizing facts. They pioneered changes in American colleges.

The Influence of Pragmatism

Coupled with educational reform was a new way of thinking known as **pragmatism,** an approach to problem solving that was popularized by Harvard philosopher William James. Pragmatists questioned the absolute truth of science. They believed that scientific laws stated only what was *probably* true and that ideas must be tested to see if they worked.

By the late 1800s many American colleges offered courses in social work, economics, political science, and sociology and granted advanced degrees. Professors such as social scientist Richard Ely at the University of Wisconsin taught students to solve problems pragmatically. At Johns Hopkins University, historian Henry Adams taught students how to do research and told them, "By the instrumentality of scholars great improvement of society is to be made." American colleges thus provided a core of reformers to study society and change it.

Pragmatist John Dewey, who taught at the University of Chicago, argued that the value of government actions should be measured by the good they do. Harvard Law School professor Oliver Wendell Holmes, Jr., was a pragmatist. In his book *The Common*

Law, he wrote that law should not be an absolute set of principles but a tool to meet the needs of society. When Holmes was appointed to the Supreme Court in 1902, his ideas began to influence its decisions.

The Muckrakers

Other, more popular, writers played a major role in investigating and exposing a variety of social problems. President Theodore Roosevelt compared these writers to a character in John Bunyan's book, *Pilgrim's Progress,* who constantly looked downward and raked filth, and he labeled them "muckrakers."

Most muckrakers were journalists who wrote for popular magazines like *McClure's Magazine, Cosmopolitan,* and *Collier's.* Although similar to the "yellow journalism" of the period, these articles were not written to boost sales but to expose conditions the writers had found deeply disturbing. For example, in 1902 Lincoln Steffens wrote a series of articles for *McClure's Magazine* that described shocking graft and corruption in city governments across the nation. He was followed in the same magazine by Ida Tarbell's exposé of the corrupt business practices of the Standard Oil Company. In 1906 David Phillips shocked the nation with a series in *Cosmopolitan* about links between big business and 75 United States senators.

Other muckrakers revealed the results of their investigations in books. In 1906 John Spargo's *The Bitter Cry of the Children* wrote about abuses of child labor, and two years

Visualizing History

▲ THE MUCKRAKERS The investigative reporting of journalists such as Ida Tarbell, Ray Stannard Baker, and Lincoln Steffens (above) made them frequent contributors. *Why did President Roosevelt call such reporters "muckrakers"?*

later, Ray Stannard Baker's *Following the Color Line* revealed the long pattern of discrimination against African Americans in both the North and the South. Still other muckrakers were novelists who used fiction to criticize existing social conditions. In *The Octopus,* Frank Norris told how railroads dominated wheat farmers in a rich Western valley. Despite their revelations of society's ills, most muckrakers were not activists. They merely identified problems and argued for reform but counted on others to accomplish it.

Section 1 ★ Review

Checking for Understanding

1. **Identify** *Looking Backward,* Wobblies, Ida Tarbell, John Dewey, Oliver Wendell Holmes, muckrakers.

2. **Define** social gospel, pragmatism.

3. **Describe** the inequities in society in the late 1800s.

4. **List** five social problems exposed by the muckrakers.

Critical Thinking

5. **Understanding Cause and Effect** What relationship do the ideas of philosophy professor William James have to progressive reform?

▲ THEODORE DREISER

A major literary development in the late nineteenth century was naturalism, which developed out of realist fiction. Naturalist writers carried the vivid detail of realism a step further by depicting environmental factors. In his first novel, *Sister Carrie*, published in 1900, Theodore Dreiser describes the compelling attraction as well as the cold indifference of life in growing cities.

Sister Carrie (excerpts)

To Carrie, the sound of the little bells upon the horse-cars, as they tinkled in and out of hearing, was as pleasing as it was novel. She gazed into the lighted street when Minnie brought her into the front room, and wondered at the sounds, the movement, the murmur of the vast city which stretched for miles and miles in every direction.

Mrs. Hanson, after the first greetings were over, gave Carrie the baby and proceeded to get supper. Her husband asked a few questions and sat down to read the evening paper. He was a silent man, American born, of a Swede father, and now employed as a cleaner of refrigerator cars at the stock-yards. To him the presence or absence of his wife's sister was a matter of indifference. Her personal appearance did not affect him one way or the other. His one observation to the point was concerning the chances of work in Chicago.

"It's a big place," he said. "You can get in somewhere in a few days. Everybody does."

It had been tacitly understood beforehand that she was to get work and pay her board. He was of a clean, saving disposition, and had already paid a number of monthly installments on two lots far out on the West Side. His ambition was some day to build a house on them. . . .

"You'll want to see the city first, won't you?" said Minnie, when they were eating. "Well, we'll go out Sunday and see Lincoln Park."

Carrie noticed that Hanson had said nothing to this. He seemed to be thinking of something else.

"Well," she said, "I think I'll look around tomorrow. I've got Friday and Saturday, and it won't be any trouble. Which way is the business part?"

Minnie began to explain, but her husband took this part of the conversation to himself.

"It's that way," he said, pointing east. "That's east." Then he went off into the longest speech he had yet indulged in, concerning the lay of Chicago. "You'd better look in those big manufacturing houses along

Franklin Street and just the other side of the river," he concluded. "Lots of girls work there. You could get home easy, too. It isn't very far." . . .

In 1889 Chicago had the peculiar qualifications of growth which made such adventuresome pilgrimages even on the part of young girls plausible. . . . It was a city of over 500,000, with the ambition, the daring, the activity of a metropolis of a million. Its streets and houses were already scattered over an area of seventy-five square miles. Its population was not so much thriving upon established commerce as upon the industries which prepared for the arrival of others. The sound of the hammer engaged upon the erection of new structures was everywhere heard. . . .

The entire metropolitan center possessed a high and mighty air calculated to overawe and abash the common applicant, and to make the gulf between poverty and success seem both wide and deep.

Into this important commercial region the timid Carrie went. She walked east along Van Buren Street through a region of lessening importance, until it deteriorated into a mass of shanties and coalyards, and finally verged upon the river. She walked bravely forward, led by an honest desire to find employment and delayed at every step by the interest of the unfolding scene, and a sense of helplessness amid so much evidence of power and force which she did not understand. . . .

Through the open windows she could see the figures of men and women in working aprons, moving busily about. The great streets were wall-lined mysteries to her. . . .

▲ WORKER IN SHOE FACTORY, 1895

Interpreting Literature

1. Why do you think Carrie came to live with her sister?

2. What kind of attitude about life in the city at this time does Mr. Hanson exemplify?

3. Do large cities today hold the attraction that they held for Carrie and other ambitious men and women at the turn of the century? Why or why not?

★★★

Progressive Reforms

Setting the Scene

Section Focus

Progressive reforms affected government, consumer's rights, and education. People began to speak out against children working in mines, mills, and factories and to back temperance and woman suffrage. Although early accomplishments were mainly local changes, later reforms occurred at state and national levels.

Objectives

After studying this section, you should be able to

★ explain how reforms strengthened democracy.

★ describe the advances made by social reformers and government in protecting adult and child workers.

Key Terms

direct primary, initiative, referendum, recall

WOMEN VOTE FOR PRESIDENT

And for All Other Officers in All Elections on the Same Terms as Men in

Wyoming, Colorado, Utah and Idaho

WHY NOT IN NEBRASKA?

◀ WOMAN SUFFRAGE POSTER

*I*t is fitting that the earliest evidence of progressive activism dealt with cities. Being primarily city residents, progressives were viewed as representative of the increasing importance of the nation's urban centers. What is perceived as the initial progressive reform came even before the muckrakers began to write. This reform was inspired not by a book or a magazine article but by a natural disaster.

■ Reforms in Government

In 1900 a hurricane roared in from the Gulf of Mexico and devastated the coastal city of Galveston, Texas. When the political machine that controlled city government proved incapable of responding to the disaster, local reformers and business leaders convinced the state legislature to allow them to take control. In April 1901, the mayor and city council were replaced by five commissioners chosen in a nonpartisan election. Four of the commissioners were local business leaders who applied their management experience to running the city, and it quickly recovered. Reformers in other cities were impressed. Galveston's experience demonstrated the benefits of running a city like a business.

Changes in City Government

From the commission plan developed another progressive reform—the city-manager plan. In this reform an elected city council hired a professional manager to run city government, much as the directors of a business would hire a superintendent to run a factory.

Early city managers often were engineers, because much of the business of running a modern city—such as sewage disposal, water supply, and paving streets—was technical. By 1915 more than 400 cities had adopted commission or city-manager plans.

Even in cities where progressives could not reshape government, reform mayors fought powerful combinations of political bosses, unethical business leaders, and corrupt city officials. Reform mayors such as Tom Johnson in Cleveland, Samuel "Golden Rule" Jones in Toledo, and Hazen Pingree in Detroit gained national attention. All three left successful businesses to battle corruption in city government and to force streetcar lines, electric companies, and other utilities to behave in the public interest.

Voting Reforms

At the state level, political reform was first achieved in Wisconsin. Robert La Follette, after twice failing to become Republican

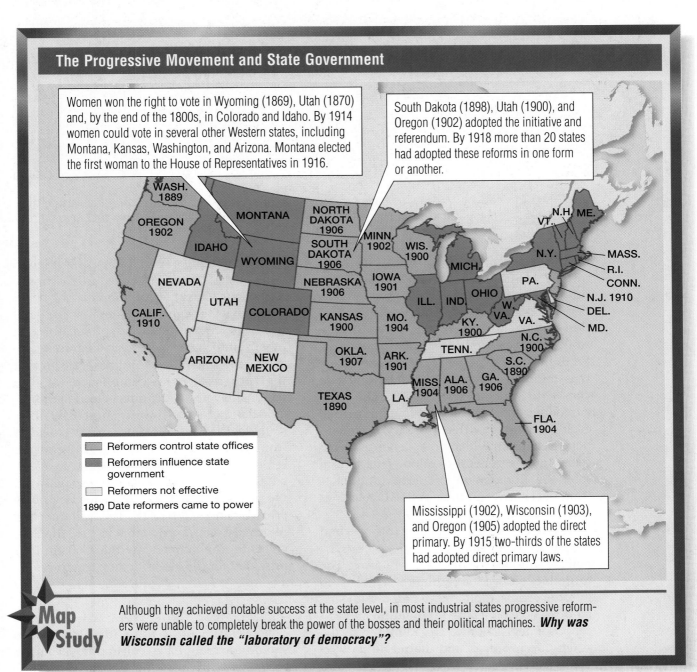

The Progressive Movement and State Government

Women won the right to vote in Wyoming (1869), Utah (1870) and, by the end of the 1800s, in Colorado and Idaho. By 1914 women could vote in several other Western states, including Montana, Kansas, Washington, and Arizona. Montana elected the first woman to the House of Representatives in 1916.

South Dakota (1898), Utah (1900), and Oregon (1902) adopted the initiative and referendum. By 1918 more than 20 states had adopted these reforms in one form or another.

Mississippi (1902), Wisconsin (1903), and Oregon (1905) adopted the direct primary. By 1915 two-thirds of the states had adopted direct primary laws.

- ■ Reformers control state offices
- ■ Reformers influence state government
- ■ Reformers not effective
- **1890** Date reformers came to power

WASH. 1889
OREGON 1902
MONTANA
NORTH DAKOTA 1906
IDAHO
WYOMING
SOUTH DAKOTA 1906
MINN. 1902
WIS. 1900
MICH.
N.H. ME.
VT.
N.Y.
MASS.
R.I.
CONN.
NEVADA
NEBRASKA 1906
IOWA 1901
PA.
N.J. 1910
DEL.
UTAH
COLORADO
ILL.
IND.
OHIO
W. VA.
VA.
MD.
CALIF. 1910
KANSAS 1900
MO. 1904
KY. 1900
ARIZONA
NEW MEXICO
OKLA. 1907
ARK. 1901
TENN.
N.C. 1900
S.C. 1890
MISS. 1904
ALA. 1906
GA. 1906
TEXAS 1890
LA.
FLA. 1904

Map Study Although they achieved notable success at the state level, in most industrial states progressive reformers were unable to completely break the power of the bosses and their political machines. *Why was Wisconsin called the "laboratory of democracy"?*

▲ **THE RIGHT TO VOTE** Women parade for the right to vote in New York. Suffragists (left) are forced to eat during a hunger strike. *Which region of the nation was first to grant woman suffrage?*

candidate for governor, finally was elected in 1900. He used his office to attack the tradition of party nominating conventions. Because party bosses controlled the selection of convention delegates, they also controlled the selection of election candidates. From his own experience, La Follette knew that reformers had little chance of being chosen to run for office. In 1903 he pressured the state legislature to require that each party hold a **direct primary,** a preliminary election in which voters choose candidates for the general election. This reform took the nomination of party candidates from the bosses and their political machines and gave it to the people.

To reduce the control that big business and the party bosses had over state legislators, La Follette introduced three other reforms. The **initiative** allowed a group of citizens to introduce legislation and required the legislature to vote on it. The **referendum** allowed proposed legislation to be submitted to the voters for approval, and the **recall** allowed voters to remove an elected official from

office by holding a special election. Although none of these ideas originated in Wisconsin, La Follette's great success in enacting them there gave the state a reputation as "the laboratory of democracy," and progressives in other states copied Wisconsin's reforms.

The most significant political reform that the progressives accomplished at the national level was the direct election of senators. Because they were chosen by their state legislatures, senators were shielded from direct public pressure. Progressive reformers felt that if its members were elected, the Senate would be more responsive to the public will and less influenced by powerful business interests. The call for this reform became so great that in 1913 the Seventeenth Amendment to the Constitution provided for direct election of senators.

Slow Progress for Women

It was difficult to argue that the people should have a greater voice in government affairs without including women, especially because they were increasingly holding jobs in factories, business offices, and schools, as well as taking prominent roles in reform movements. In addition, some progressives believed that if women gained the right to vote, their influence would help push through other reforms. By 1914, 11 Western states had granted women full suffrage. In the East, women promoted their cause by holding parades and circulating petitions. Many women believed, however, that a constitutional amendment would be needed to gain the vote nationwide.

■ Consumer Protection

A basic principle that American business inherited from Great Britain was *caveat emptor,* Latin for "let the buyer beware." This meant that people who purchased worthless life insurance, bread made with sawdust, or colored water labeled as medicine had only themselves to blame for not being more careful. Progressives argued that consumers had no way of knowing when meat was prepared under unsanitary conditions, children's cough syrup was dosed with opium, or other products were similarly misrepresented.

Regulating the Insurance Industry

In 1905 Charles Evans Hughes, a lawyer who worked for the New York legislature, investigated the insurance industry. He uncovered bribery of elected officials and huge salaries insurance executives paid to themselves and to family members they hired. Consequently, New York—and later other states—passed laws to regulate insurance companies and to protect the interests of policyholders.

Making Buildings Safer

At the local level, protection for consumers often came in the form of city zoning laws. The laws regulated how land and buildings could be used. Building codes prohibited some of the worst features of tenements by setting minimum requirements for light and air, fire escapes, room size, and sanitation.

Ensuring the Safety of Food and Medicine

Passage of pure food and drug laws demonstrated the effectiveness of the muckrakers in influencing consumer protection. Articles in *Collier's* about harmful medicines in 1906 convinced the chief chemist of the Department of Agriculture to perform experiments on himself and then to call for regulation. Even more sensational was the publication in 1906 of Upton Sinclair's bestselling book, *The Jungle,* a fact-based novel that portrayed horribly unsanitary conditions in slaughterhouses:

> **66** *There would be meat that had tumbled out on the floor, in the dirt and sawdust, where workers had tramped and spit uncounted billions of [tuberculosis] germs. There would be meat stored in great piles in rooms; and the water from leaky roofs would drip over it, and thousands of rats would race about on it.* **99**

An outraged President Theodore Roosevelt demanded reform, and Congress responded with legislation. The Pure Food and Drug Act established a government agency, the Food and Drug Administration, to protect consumers from unsafe medicines and foods. The Meat Inspection Act was passed on the same day in 1906. These laws regulated the content and inspection of food, prohibited the use of addictive drugs in nonprescription medicines, and required accurate labels on food and drug products. State governments followed with similar legislation to regulate food and drugs that did not cross state lines.

■ Protecting Workers

"I aimed at the public's heart," Upton Sinclair complained, "and by accident I hit it in the stomach." Sinclair did not intend *The Jungle* to focus public attention on impure food. Instead he wanted to expose

▲ CHILD LABOR One concern for reformers was protecting children, such as these workers in a Pennsylvania coal mine. Because canaries are very sensitive to poisonous gases, they were used to detect such gases in coal mines. *How was child labor reform achieved?*

the terrible working conditions in slaughterhouses. One of the grim realities of industrialization was the frequency of industrial accidents.

Workers' Compensation

Workers who suffered industrial accidents had little protection. Employers argued that industrial accidents were not caused by unsafe conditions but by carelessness, and they often fired employees who were seriously disabled. Progressives joined labor union leaders to pressure state legislatures for workers' compensation laws. These laws established insurance funds into which employers made payments. Workers who were injured by industrial accidents were paid from the fund. In 1902 Maryland was first to pass such legislation, and by 1911 10 of the states had workers' compensation laws on the books. Workers' compensation laws not only

helped injured workers, they improved working conditions for all workers because employers with low accident rates paid lower insurance premiums. Related progressive legislation established state agencies to inspect factories, limited workers' hours, and attempted to end crowded, unsanitary work environments.

Protecting Women: *Muller* v. *Oregon*

Many progressives were especially interested in improving working conditions for women. By 1900 about 20 percent of all workers were women, and progressive reformers believed women workers needed special protection. In 1903 Oregon passed a law limiting female factory workers to a 10-hour day. Employers challenged the law as violating a woman's civil right to work as long as she chose, and in 1908 the case was appealed to the Supreme Court.

To defend the law in *Muller* v. *Oregon*, progressive attorney Louis D. Brandeis presented research that convinced the Court that long working hours damaged women's health, and the Oregon law was upheld. After the *Muller* decision, several other states quickly passed similar laws.

Muller v. *Oregon* was a revolutionary legal decision. For the first time, the Court looked beyond legal principles and precedents and applied pragmatism to the law. The Court began to weigh what was best for society when it decided cases. In so doing, it took the first step toward becoming an instrument of social reform.

Protecting Children

Probably the most emotional progressive labor reform was the campaign against child labor. Although children had always worked on family farms, urban children found factory work dangerously monotonous and conditions often unhealthy or unsafe. Reformers established a National Child Labor Committee in 1904 to campaign for the abolition of child labor.

Muckraker John Spargo's 1906 book, *The Bitter Cry of the Children*, presented detailed evidence of the conditions of child labor in America. He told of anthracite coal mines, where thousands of "breaker boys" were hired at age 9 or 10 to pick slag out of coal and were paid 60 cents for a 10-hour day. He described how the work permanently bent their backs and often crippled their hands. He revealed that in textile mills more than one-eighth of the employees were less than 16 years old and that some children entered cotton factories at age 7 or 8. Public opinion was so stirred by such information that by 1914 all but one state set a minimum age for employment and many established other limits on child labor as well. At the federal level, the newly established Children's Bureau had few powers, but it investigated and published information that helped the campaign to improve the well-being of child workers.

Life of the Times

Boy Scouts

While many progressive reformers focused on social issues, others concentrated on keeping the nation's youth under control.

Organizations such as the Boy Scouts of America (BSA) arose to provide supervised activities that stressed old-fashioned values and sheltered adolescents from the lures of the city. Scouts hiked in the school year, camped in the summer, and attended weekly meetings packed with instruction, drills, and games. Scouting channeled adolescent energy into the wholesome pursuit of specialized merit badges acquired by passing tests on woodcraft, reconnaissance, and citizenship skills.

The Boy Scouts of America was designed, in part, to reinforce what were perceived at the time to be traditional American male values. BSA executives and scoutmasters strongly opposed girl scouting and were reluctant to involve the Boy Scouts in service projects on which Boy and Girl Scouts worked as equals.

"BE PREPARED"

"DO A GOOD TURN DAILY"
COPYRIGHTED BY BOY SCOUTS OF AMERICA. 1916.

■ Varieties of Reform

In addition to reforming labor practices, many progressives insisted that business be regulated in ways to protect the public interest. Because of their great influence and power, large corporations commonly gained tax breaks from state legislatures.

Robert La Follette, the governor of Wisconsin, determined that railroads paid less than half the property taxes of other businesses. He obtained reform laws to tax railroads on a more equal basis. La Follette also established a commission to regulate the railroads in the state. Other states followed Wisconsin's lead.

On the federal level, Congress began to tax corporate profits in 1909. Although the Supreme Court in 1895 had declared an income tax unconstitutional, in 1913 the Sixteenth Amendment empowered the federal government to levy such a tax.

Public Utilities

The Progressive Era also was a time when reformers called for regulation of public utilities such as streetcar lines, waterworks, and electric-light companies. Many states set up public service commissions with the power to control the rates charged by public utilities. Some city reformers, doubtful that regulation could force utility companies to act in the public interest, called for city governments to buy them out and run the utilities directly. By 1915, for example, all but 1 of the 36 largest cities owned or operated their own waterworks.

Health, Recreation, and Education

Progressive reform was also felt in other areas. It resulted in playgrounds and dental clinics for children. Private charities multiplied and broadened their social usefulness. The Rockefeller Foundation, for example, led a campaign to eradicate hookworm, which was causing serious health problems in rural areas of the South. Juvenile courts and reform schools were set up to care for young lawbreakers. Progressives began to show concern about America's natural resources. State and federal governments passed conservation laws and set aside public recreation areas.

The reform impulse also resulted in great progress in education. Many states passed laws requiring children to attend school, and the number of high schools more than doubled between 1900 and 1920. The school year was lengthened and the curriculum enriched by courses in music, art, home economics, and industrial arts.

The Fight Against Alcohol Use

Long at the forefront of the temperance movement was the Woman's Christian Temperance Union (WCTU), founded in 1874. By 1890, it already had 150,000 members.

Like so many progressive reforms, temperance was first accomplished at the local level. By 1914 nearly half the people of the United States lived in areas where the sale of alcohol was illegal, and 12 states had passed statewide Prohibition laws. In 1919 Prohibition became nationwide when the Eighteenth Amendment was added to the Constitution.

Section 2 ★ Review

Checking for Understanding

1. **Identify** Galveston, Seventeenth Amendment, Charles Evans Hughes, Upton Sinclair, *Muller* v. *Oregon*, John Spargo, WCTU.

2. **Define** direct primary, initiative, referendum, recall.

3. **Describe** the commission plan as a form of city government.

4. **Discuss** three reforms that came out of the Progressive movement that promoted stronger and more direct involvement by citizens in government.

Critical Thinking

5. **Understanding Cause and Effect** Explain why progressive reforms strengthened the cause of woman's suffrage.

Reform Judaism

By 1880 about 250,000 Jews lived in America; most were of German ancestry. Many practiced Reform Judaism, a form of Judaism that arose in the 1800s in answer to the changing conditions of emancipated Jews in Germany.

Isaac Mayer Wise organized Reform Judaism in the United States in the mid-1800s. Wise initiated reforms in worship that became important elements of this form of Judaism. These reforms included family pews, baring of the head, and abolishing non-Biblical festival days. In comparison to Orthodox Judaism, Reform Judaism maintains only those traditional ceremonies considered meaningful to the modern Jew.

Influenced by liberal Protestantism and the social gospel of reformers, many Jews began to adapt their religious customs and rituals to the American way of life. For example, they adopted a congregation structure similar to that of American Christians. Like their liberal Christian counterparts, Reform Jews supported such progressive social reforms as child labor laws and collective bargaining. Attorney and later Supreme Court Justice Louis D. Brandeis, for example, was an ardent champion of progressive causes.

After 1880 Jewish immigrants flooded into America, many escaping persecution in Russia. Reform Jews helped these newcomers make their way in the United States. The help was given partly because of their belief in social reform and partly because they feared that these poor, old-fashioned, Yiddish-speaking Jews would create an anti-Jewish reaction among American Christians. The Russian Jews were Orthodox—observing traditional Jewish beliefs and rituals. In turn, Orthodox Jews reintroduced the Reform Jews to a number of customs and rituals that had been discarded by their parents.

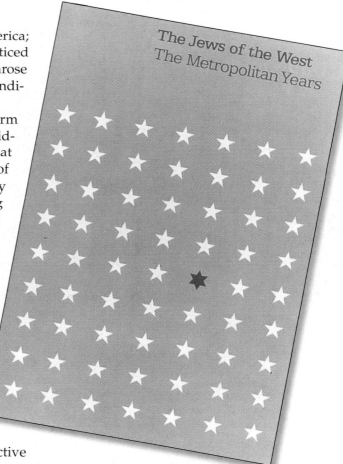

The Jews of the West
The Metropolitan Years

▲ A POSTER CELEBRATING JEWISH CONTRIBUTIONS TO AMERICA

Making the Religion Connection

1. In what ways were Reform Jews influenced by the American way of life?

2. For what reasons did Reform Jews help Russian Jewish immigrants?

Linking Past and Present

3. How have American Jews helped Russian Jewish immigrants in recent times?

★★★

Limits of Progressivism

Setting the Scene

Section Focus

While progressivism resulted in many last-ing changes, reform had its limits. Much pro-gressive reform was based on traditional American attitudes about race, sex, and nationalism. As a result, not all Americans shared equal-ly in the ben-efits of reform.

Objectives

After studying this section, you should be able to

★ describe progressive attitudes about immi-grants and racial minorities.

★ explain why African American leadership changed.

Key Term

literacy test

◀ WOODEN ICE SKATES, EARLY 1900S

The achievements of progres-sive reform at the national level were less far-reaching than its successes at local and state levels. It was more difficult to create nationwide demands for reform than to organize effec-tive campaigns on a smaller scale. The fed-eral government also was more difficult to prod into action. The Senate, chosen by boss-dominated state legislatures until 1913, was a highly conservative body. In the House of Representatives, powerful figures such as committee heads and the speaker usually resisted change.

The Supreme Court became somewhat less conservative than it had been in the 1890s, as progressives Oliver Wendell Holmes (1902), Charles Evans Hughes (1910), and Louis D. Brandeis (1916) were appointed to the Court. Yet the majority of justices seldom were will-ing to extend federal power into new areas.

Partly because of the attitude of the courts, many of the evils described by the muck-rakers were considered outside the constitu-tional sphere of the federal government's powers, making national reform nearly impossible.

The benefits of progressivism were spread unevenly in other ways, too. Many middle-class progressives feared labor unions almost as much as they did trusts. So although progressives worked with labor leaders to improve working condi-tions, few objected when businesses orga-nized effectively to prevent unions in their plants—often with cooperation from local courts and police. Therefore, wage gains during the Progressive Era went only to skilled workers. The earning power of unskilled workers actually dropped because prices increased more rapidly than their rates of pay.

Reformers and Immigrants

Among the many factors that held down the wages of unskilled workers was the continuing flood of immigrants to the United States, averaging one million a year during the Progressive Era—largely from southern and eastern Europe. This "New Immigration" caused widespread alarm, as immigrant men and women competed for unskilled jobs in American mines, mills, and factories.

In addition, the newcomers seemed to have more difficulty fitting in to established American culture than the "old immigrants" from northern and western Europe. Pressure from labor-union leaders and such organizations as the Immigration Restriction League persuaded Congress in 1897, 1913, and 1915 to enact laws requiring all immigrants to pass **literacy tests,** tests to show they could read English. All three laws were vetoed, but such a law passed over President Woodrow Wilson's veto in 1917.

Reform and Immigrant Cultures

Many progressives feared the socialist ideas that immigrants brought from Europe. As middle-class reformers, progressives wanted to change capitalism, not abolish it. Many also worried about preserving existing values and culture. Therefore, many progressive reforms were aimed at weakening the political strength of immigrant numbers and instilled in newcomers what reformers thought were proper American values.

In calling for reform of city government, one writer complained about:

> *[t]he mass of ignorant voters, who now help the vicious bosses to govern our cities. . . . A colony of Italians, Scandinavians, Germans, or Irish, preserving their national language and their national ideas, and living as foreigners among us is very difficult to reach, but their votes count just as much as the votes of the most highly educated men among us.*

Visualizing History

▲ **ADULT CLASSES** Many businesses organized English classes for their employees. The classes were held in the plant so that workers could attend at the end of their shift. *Why would employers consider learning English important?*

▲ STRIVING FOR JUSTICE Booker T. Washington (right) and W.E.B. Du Bois were among the most important African American leaders of the period. Both men had the same goals, but they took different approaches to those goals. *What organization did Du Bois help form?*

When progressives reformed government by defeating political bosses and machines, they also destroyed the system that provided immigrant groups with a political voice, political jobs, and political power.

Education and Resistance

As reformers obtained child labor laws and school attendance laws, they forced immigrant children out of factories and into classrooms. Many states made the study of American history a required course in public schools during the Progressive Era. Educator John Dewey advised that it was essential to teach students to be good citizens.

With the great increase in immigration in the late 1800s, other functions were thrust upon the schools. Besides teaching intellectual skills and citizenship, the schools taught patriotism and gave Americans a sense of unity. In this way, schools assisted in the work of assimilating newcomers into American culture by teaching the English language and stressing American values.

In the late 1800s American education was rapidly becoming free, public, and almost universal. In fact, by 1900 most states had compulsory education laws. These laws required that children attend school for a certain part of each year.

As a result, enrollment increased. In 1870 less than 60 percent of all children ages 5 to 17 were enrolled in elementary and secondary schools. By 1900 the figure was over 72 percent. The number of public high schools increased from about 150 in 1870 to nearly 6,000 by 1900. The greatest growth occurred in the Northeast and the Midwest.

The benefits of public school education, however, were not shared by everyone. Most pupils were middle- and upper-class children who chose to go to a public school rather than to be privately educated. Many immigrant children did not complete their schooling. Many poor immigrants needed their children to work to add to the family income. Forced to work at an early age, they sometimes did not even finish elementary school.

■ Progressives and Race

The most conspicuous limit to progressivism was its attitude about race. Like most white Americans at that time, most progressives believed that nonwhite races were inferior. Therefore, reformers did not object to the segregation of Japanese Americans in San Francisco schools in 1906, nor did they oppose sharp cuts in Japanese immigration that began in 1907.

Ignoring the Problems of African Americans

In addition, progressives accepted widespread discrimination against African Americans. Although many progressives sympathized with their plight, most reformers agreed with Theodore Roosevelt, who stated that Africans "as a race and in the mass are altogether inferior to whites."

Few progressives objected to the Jim Crow laws that Southern states had passed after Reconstruction to restore segregation. In 1896, when the Supreme Court ruled in *Plessy* v. *Ferguson* that segregation was constitutional as long as separate facilities were equal, no progressive campaign was launched for reform. While Southern whites were lynching African Americans and barring them from voting or holding public office, progressives were crusading for primary elections, direct election of senators, and other reforms to spread democracy. Like most whites, progressives generally accepted the South's Jim Crow system, partly because of indifference and partly because African Americans in the North also were restricted to low-paying jobs, segregation, and inferior social status.

The Struggle for Equality Continues

These circumstances help explain a shift in African American leadership during the Progressive Era. At the turn of the century the most influential African American leader was Booker T. Washington. Formerly enslaved, Washington founded Alabama's Tuskegee Institute in 1881 to train African Americans in 30 trades. Washington argued that equality would be achieved not through campaigns for reform but when African Americans gained the education and skills to become valuable members of their communities. In 1895 he spelled out this view:

❝ . . . *[T]he agitation of questions of social equality is the extremist folly. . . . [P]rogress in the enjoyment of all privileges that will come to us must be the result of severe and constant struggle rather than of artificial forcing. No race that has anything to contribute to the market of the world is long in any degree ostracized.* **❞**

Yet as the great changes in society that accompanied progressive reform largely bypassed African Americans, a new leadership arose that rejected Washington's approach to achieving equality. The most prominent new African American leader was W.E.B. Du Bois, a Harvard-educated history professor at Atlanta University. Du Bois argued that suffrage was the way to end white supremacy, stop the lynching of

Visualizing History

▲ **EDUCATION** Progressives believed in compulsory public education to keep children out of factories and to provide them with proper values. *Why did many states require high school students to study American history?*

▲ IN THE CITIES The rapid growth of cities led to a push for building codes and zoning laws. Other areas of progressive reform included child labor and foods. *In what other areas did progressives help change American society?*

African Americans, and gain better schools. In 1905 Du Bois and 28 other leaders convened at Niagara Falls to demand full political rights and responsibilities for African Americans as well as an end to racial discrimination.

This call eventually resulted in the founding of the National Association for the Advancement of Colored People (NAACP) in 1909. "The power of the ballot we need in sheer self-defense," Du Bois said, "else what shall save us from a second slavery?" Du Bois became the editor of the NAACP's magazine, *The Crisis*. In fiery editorials he called for African Americans to fight openly against injustice and discrimination.

The End of the Progressive Era

Despite the failure of most progressives to be concerned about such questions, progressive reform helped change American society in many ways. Although they excluded large groups from their efforts, the progressives expanded democracy, reformed education, and improved the quality of life for millions of men, women, and children. Except for the two amendments to the Constitution in 1919 and 1920, progressivism in America ended as the United States entered World War I. Americans turned from reforming their own society to a crusade to "make the world safe for democracy."

Section 3 ★ Review

Checking for Understanding

1. **Identify** Booker T. Washington, W.E.B. Du Bois, *Plessy* v. *Ferguson*.

2. **Define** literacy test.

3. **Describe** how some progressive reforms worked to limit the political power of immigrants.

4. **Discuss** the status of African Americans during the Progressive Era.

Critical Thinking

5. **Making Comparisons**   Compare the methods of Booker T. Washington and W.E.B. Du Bois for increasing African Americans' participation in society.

Critical Thinking Skills

▲ **A** GROUP OF IMMIGRANT WOMEN AT WORK

Recognizing Fallacies in a Line of Reasoning

A fallacy in a line of reasoning is an error in thinking something out. The fallacy may be an unsupported argument or a mistaken conclusion.

To determine whether there is a fallacy in a line of reasoning, ask the following questions:

- Is there any connection between the facts and the conclusion? If not, the statement contains a fallacy. If there is a connection, go on to the next question.

- Is there only a loose connection between the facts and the conclusion? If there is, go on to the next question.

- Are there enough facts given to reach the conclusion, or is additional information needed? If more facts are needed, the statement contains a fallacy.

The following example contains a statement of fact and a conclusion. Read the statement and note how the three steps have been applied:

In the early 1900s, the managers of women workers were almost always men. This was because women lacked the ability to direct others. (There is a loose connection between the fact that men were managers and the conclusion that women did not have the ability. But more facts are needed to support that inability was the reason. What roles did lack of educational opportunities for women and biases of male bosses play? The conclusion that women did not have management ability is not supported. The reasoning contains a fallacy.)

Practicing the Skill

For further practice in this skill, read the following sentences, and determine if a fallacy exists. If so, explain why a fallacy is present.

1. The Constitution did not contain provisions against child labor, so the government was powerless to do anything about it.

2. The muckrakers published many books and articles, so the entire public became more aware of social injustices.

3. It was difficult to operate a democratic government and not allow women to vote, so many Western states granted women full suffrage by 1914.

Using Vocabulary

Imagine that you are a muckraker who is investigating the need for urban reform. Use the following words to write an article summarizing the corruption and stating your recommendations.

social gospel   referendum

recall   pragmatism

direct primary   initiative

Reviewing Facts

1. **Discuss** the role of the muckrakers in promoting social change.

2. **Describe** the inequalities that existed between the upper and lower classes of society.

3. **List** the improvements in city government achieved through progressive reform efforts.

4. **Explain** why reform was more successful at state and local levels than at the national level.

5. **State** the connection between progressive reform and big business management methods.

6. **Identify** reforms that improved the lives of industrial workers.

7. **Indicate** the importance of the socialist movement in early twentieth-century reform.

8. **Discuss** why progressives were not considered to be radical reformers.

Understanding Concepts

Reform

1. To what extent did reform in government extend democracy in the Progressive Era?

2. What changes did labor reforms bring to other areas of society in the early 1900s?

Values and Beliefs

3. Describe the values of the people who preached the social gospel and pioneered social programs.

4. How did progressives' beliefs about immigrant cultures influence their reform activities?

Critical Thinking

1. **Understanding Cause and Effect** To what extent were progressive reformers inspired by the Populists? Consider the membership, goals, and approach to problem solving of each reform group.

2. **Analyzing Artifacts** Study the picture on this page from *Harper's Weekly* and answer the questions that follow.

   a. What is the purpose of this picture?

   b. What is the central focus of the picture?

   c. Do you think this picture is effective? Explain your answer.

Writing About History

Classification

Classification is the writing method that organizes information about a complex whole into smaller, more useful categories.

Use classification to organize all the progressive reforms discussed in this chapter and to write an essay on how progressive reform changed society. Your teacher will give you specific instructions on the essay's length and the assignment's due date.

Cooperative Learning

Working in a group of three, organize a debate among candidates for governor during the early 1900s. Select one student to be a socialist follower of Eugene Debs, another to be a socialist follower of Daniel De Leon, and the third student to be a progressive reform candidate. Candidates should prepare statements expressing their views regarding reform, what they will do once elected, and why voters should support them. After completing their statements, students should exchange them with the other group members so that each candidate can prepare a rebuttal statement to the other candidates' positions.

Social Studies Skills

Understanding History Through Political Cartoons

In a single picture, a political cartoon from the past can provide special insight into the issues that concerned the public. When you look at a political cartoon, study all the details—the setting, the faces, the clothing, the potential action—and they will help you understand history when it was current news.

Practicing the Skill

Analyze the political cartoon on this page, then answer the questions that follow.

1. What is the setting for the cartoon?

2. How does it tell you who the "good guys" and the "bad guys" are?

3. On each of the giants is printed a different name: J.J. Hill, Morgan, Gould, Oxnard, and Rockefeller. Do you know who these "giants" are? Would your answer be different if you were in high school in 1904? Explain.

4. What does the cartoon tell you about what was happening at the time?

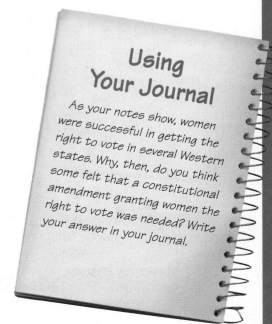

Using Your Journal

As your notes show, women were successful in getting the right to vote in several Western states. Why, then, do you think some felt that a constitutional amendment granting women the right to vote was needed? Write your answer in your journal.

CHAPTER 24

★★★

White House Reformers
1900–1914

► **EARLY TELETYPEWRITER**

Setting the Scene

Focus

After the turn of the century, progressive reforms at the national level were aided by three strong-minded Presidents: Theodore Roosevelt, William Howard Taft, and Woodrow Wilson. These Presidents had different political philosophies, styles, and temperaments. Yet each worked to control big business, gain protection for workers, and protect the American people from social ills.

Concepts to Understand

★ How interests and positions of the progressives were translated into federal legislation

★ How business practices worked to limit economic competition

Read to Discover . . .

★ in what ways Roosevelt was successful or disappointing as a progressive leader.

★ what progressive reforms were achieved by Wilson as President.

Journal Notes

Note instances in your reading where Presidents appealed directly to the nation in order to gain support for new or controversial programs.

CULTURAL
- **1902** *First Rose Bowl game played*
- **1903** *Orville Wright flies first heavier-than-air airplane*
- **1906** *San Francisco earthquake causes extensive damage*
- **1907** *Electric washing machine invented*

1900

1904

POLITICAL
- **1901** *Theodore Roosevelt becomes President*
- **1906** *Pure Food and Drug Act passed*

The Grand Canyon of the Yellowstone
by Thomas Moran, 1872

On a government expedition to the West, Moran made sketches for a series of paintings. His work prompted Congress to designate Yellowstone a national park.

◀ BASEBALL CAP, EARLY 1900S

● **1908** *First Model T Ford automobile produced*

● **1913** *Congress designates Mother's Day as the second Sunday in May*

1908

1912

● **1908** *William Howard Taft elected President*

● **1912** *Woodrow Wilson elected President*
● **1912** *Progressive party is formed*
● **1913** *Federal Reserve System created*

★★★★★★★★★★★★★★★★★★★★★★★★★★★★★★★★

The Square Deal

Setting the Scene

Section Focus

When Theodore Roosevelt succeeded William McKinley as President, leaders of industry feared that he would use the power of his office to break up existing trusts. With Roosevelt's first speeches, their worst fears were realized. The President made it clear that he intended to carry out his "Square Deal," based on the idea that every individual is "entitled to no more and to receive no less."

Objectives

After studying this section, you should be able to

★ explain why Theodore Roosevelt became known as a "trustbuster."

★ identify the series of events that led to settlement of the 1902 coal strike.

★ examine Roosevelt's efforts for conservation of wilderness areas.

★ discuss Roosevelt's legacy to the United States.

Key Term

conservation

◀ **INDUSTRIAL FLATIRON**

W hen Theodore Roosevelt received the Republican vice-presidential nomination in 1900, the powerful Republican leader Mark Hanna warned that there would be only one life between "that cowboy" and the White House. When the election resulted in a Republican victory, Hanna turned to McKinley and said, "Now it is up to you to live." However, after McKinley's assassination in 1901, Theodore Roosevelt—the "cowboy," the reformer, the progressive—did indeed become President of the United States.

■ The Trustbuster

Roosevelt described his approach to social problems as the "Square Deal," a belief that all people should have an equal opportunity to succeed through strong personal ethics, a sense of fairness, and adherence to the spirit of the law. Roosevelt also promised America that he would continue McKinley's policies unbroken. Not having become President by election, Roosevelt felt he did not have the authority to push a general program of reform through Congress. During this time, however, industries were merging at an all-time high rate. This rash of mergers prompted Roosevelt to urge Congress to pass legislation regulating big business.

Popular Support for Regulation

When Congress did not respond, Roosevelt turned to the American people to garner support for his program. The response was overwhelming. Government leaders responded with a series of moves designed to limit the trusts. First, the attorney general took the Northern Securities Company to court. In 1904 the Supreme Court overturned previous court decisions and ruled that Northern Securities, which had tried to attain a monopoly of northwestern railroads, had violated the Sherman Act.

Legislation to Assist Antitrust Suits

Roosevelt was not opposed to all trusts. He believed the government should leave honest corporations alone. Only the trusts that damaged the public or worked outside the law should be regulated or broken up. In his own words, "We draw the line against misconduct, not against wealth."

Roosevelt also understood that trust-busting suits could not prevent monopolies. Well-considered cases brought to court at the appropriate time, however, could force even the most powerful trust to obey the law. Roosevelt's reputation as a trustbuster grew.

Eventually, Congress followed Roosevelt's lead and, in 1903, passed the Expedition Act, which gave federal antitrust suits precedence on the dockets of circuit courts. An act of Congress also established the Department of Commerce and Labor, empowered to investigate interstate commerce. In addition, the Department of Justice started more trust-busting suits against corporations than they had at any time during the three previous administrations.

■ The Coal Strike of 1902

One of the most prolonged strikes in United States history started in May 1902, when nearly 150,000 workers walked out of the anthracite mines of eastern Pennsylvania. Terrible conditions precipitated this strike: low wages, frequent layoffs, and the requirement to live in cheaply built company towns. The strikers drew widespread public support.

Visualizing History

▲ ON STRIKE The major weapon for men and women workers against management was the strike. Coal miners at Shenandoah, Pennsylvania, demonstrate to win better pay and working conditions during the 1902 coal strike. *How was the strike settled?*

▲ FACTORY WORKERS ON STRIKE

Management and Labor in a Deadlock

John Mitchell, who represented the United Mine Workers, asked mine operators to consider allowing an independent party to determine whether miners' wages were adequate. But George F. Baer, principal spokesperson for the mine employers, refused Mitchell's suggestion, saying that "anthracite mining is a business and not a religious, sentimental, or academic proposition." Baer further alienated a public already sympathetic to the workers when he refused to listen to the miners' complaints, to submit to arbitration, or to recognize the United Mine Workers as the true representative of the mine workers. This attitude and the strong conviction behind the miners' position caused the strike to drag on, with no prospect of settlement. Appeals for action poured in to the President.

Presidential Action Helps Resolve the Strike

Roosevelt had no power to force an agreement, yet he resolved to use whatever influence he had to end the strike. Early in October, Roosevelt invited representatives of the operators to meet union representative Mitchell at the White House. Nothing was accomplished in a stormy session, but public opinion soured even more toward the employers.

Faced with this deadlock, Roosevelt considered a legally questionable seizure of the mines by federal troops, but after a conference between Elihu Root, the President's representative, and J. Pierpont Morgan, whose banking firm indirectly controlled most of the anthracite mines, Morgan was able to put enough pressure on the operators to force them to back down. Morgan's action was apparently prompted by concern that United States businesses would suffer if the strike continued. Roosevelt's action in using the prestige of his office and his personal influence to settle the strike was recognized in this country and abroad as an important precedent. The London *Times* commented:

> 66 *The President has done a very big and entirely new thing. We are witnessing not merely the end of the coal strike, but the definite entry of a powerful government on a novel sphere of operation.* 99

■ Efforts at Conservation

Even before Theodore Roosevelt became President, the nation was adopting a policy of **conservation**, the planned management of natural resources to prevent destruction or neglect. In 1872 an act of Congress created Yellowstone National Park, and the 1890s saw the establishment of four more national parks. In 1891 Congress enacted the Forest Reserve Act, empowering Presidents to set aside land for national forests and withdraw forest lands from the public domain. In this way, land could be set aside for preservation rather than left available for private claim or purchase.

Action Based on Personal Commitment

Roosevelt's efforts to preserve the nation's natural resources stemmed from a deep love for America's wilderness. His beliefs made conservation popular. He stimulated public interest in the subject by writing, by taking publicized holiday trips to the West, and by constantly pushing for better conservation laws. Roosevelt also used the power and prestige of the presidential office to promote the cause.

Laws to Preserve Our Natural Legacy

The Newlands Act of 1902, supported by Roosevelt, provided federal aid to irrigation projects in arid states. He also enforced laws against the illegal occupation of public lands. Using the Forest Reserve Act, Roosevelt more than tripled the amount of land previously set aside for national forests.

Roosevelt also enlisted states' aid in the conservation effort. In May 1908 he called a national conference on conservation that resulted in the creation of more than 40 state conservation commissions and a National Conservation Commission, which began an inventory of the nation's natural resources.

Wisconsin senator Robert La Follette, though often critical of Roosevelt, predicted that future historians would conclude that Roosevelt's greatest achievement was not the Square Deal, but the preservation of the nation's natural resources for the benefit of all.

■ Further Regulation

As the presidential election of 1904 approached, the "Old Guard" of the Republican party was unhappy at the prospect of four more years of the Rough Rider in the White House. The New York *Sun* accused Roosevelt of "bringing wealth to its knees" and "putting labor unions above the law." It seemed possible that Mark Hanna might try to block Roosevelt's nomination, but Hanna died in February 1904. Roosevelt had popular opinion behind him and was, as even his enemies admitted, the ablest politician of the day. He received the unanimous nomination from the Republican national convention.

After being elected to a full term in 1904, Roosevelt felt confident enough to respond to the growing public clamor for stricter regulation of the railroads. The Interstate Commerce Commission had only limited success in controlling the unfair practices and political influence of these powerful businesses. Newspaper editor William Allen White spoke for many when he wrote:

> " *The railroads cannot name senators, pack state conventions, run legislatures, and boss politics generally . . . and then successfully maintain that they are private carriers doing a private business.* "

▲ CONSERVATION Theodore Roosevelt was an avid supporter of the conservation movement. Roosevelt worked to protect wildlife and scenic areas. *What was the purpose of the Newlands Act?*

Some leaders proposed that the railroads be owned and operated by the government. Thinking such a step would lead to far-reaching disaster, Roosevelt urged tighter regulation as an alternative. As a result of popular support, clever politics, and willingness to compromise, Roosevelt was able to push the Hepburn Bill through the Senate 18 months after he urged Congress to act.

The Hepburn Act of 1906 strengthened the Interstate Commerce Act of 1887 in several ways. It abolished the "free pass" that railroads granted to politicians and other influential people such as newspaper editors. It widened the jurisdiction of the Interstate Commerce Commission to include express companies, pipelines, ferries, and sleeping-car companies. Railroad corporations were restrained from operating other businesses.

Most important of all, the Interstate Commerce Commission was granted power to fix rates, although its decisions could be appealed to the courts. Complaints to the commission soon multiplied 40 times, and a great many rates were lowered.

Roosevelt also urged legislation to address abuses in the food and meatpacking industries. The Meat Inspection Act of 1906 gave government the right to inspect meats sold in interstate commerce and the right to enforce cleaner conditions in meatpacking plants.

■ Assessing Roosevelt's Progressive Policies

In spite of Roosevelt's many accomplishments, Congress offered much resistance to his ideas. His legislative achievement was so unimpressive that some critics accused Roosevelt of producing "more noise than accomplishment."

Roosevelt and Politics

Roosevelt failed to effect a revision of the tariff, regarding the issue as "political dynamite." He did use the issue to his advantage, however, occasionally threatening to bring it up unless congressional leaders supported other legislative measures. Roosevelt also never seriously supported long-overdue efforts to make the banking system more stable and the currency system more flexible.

One reason for the failure to produce much reform legislation was Roosevelt's feeling that politics was "the art of the possible." His philosophy of reform was one of gradualism: he was willing to accept half a loaf if he could not get the whole. Furthermore, the Republican leaders in Congress, carryovers from the McKinley-Hanna period, were unsympathetic to progressive legislation.

Roosevelt and History

Although Roosevelt accomplished less than he seemed to promise, he restored the people's faith in the power of the federal government to serve their interests. Through his Square Deal philosophy, he promoted the idea that the cure for the evils of unrestrained individualism was not socialism but moderate reform. Above all he created a demand for reform. According to one historian, "Roosevelt was the best publicity man progressivism ever had."

Section 1 ★ Review

Checking for Understanding

1. **Identify** J. Pierpont Morgan, Expedition Act, Forest Reserve Act, Hepburn Act, Square Deal.

2. **Define** conservation.

3. **Explain** why Roosevelt preferred regulation to trust-busting.

4. State how Roosevelt influenced the solution of the 1902 coal strike.

Critical Thinking

5. **Understanding Cause and Effect** Analyze how Roosevelt's conservation policies grew out of his love for the American wilderness.

The Conservation Movement

By the beginning of the twentieth century it was becoming clear that the natural resources Americans had long taken for granted were—in fact—in danger of being used up. Theodore Roosevelt, a champion of conservation, made an effective case for the wise and scientific use of natural resources by people of all ages.

To the Society of American Foresters in 1903, Roosevelt said, "First and foremost, you can never afford to forget for one moment what is the object of forest policy. . . . Your attention should be directed not to the preservation of the forests as an end in itself, but as the means for preserving and increasing the prosperity of the nation."

Roosevelt's 1907 Arbor Day message to schoolchildren said in part, "Within your lifetime the nation's need for trees will become serious. . . . You will want what nature once so bountifully supplied and man so thoughtlessly destroyed; and because of that want you will reproach us, not for what we have used, but for what we have wasted. . . ."

Roosevelt abhorred the way the country's national resources were being exploited. For example, irreplaceable resources such as natural gas were wasted, and fires and floods, caused by poor management of land and water services, were common. Roosevelt wanted not only to protect wildlife and scenic areas, but also to ensure efficient use of soil, minerals, and forests.

The National Reclamation Act, also known as the Newlands Act of 1902, was the first major conservation law passed under Roosevelt. It provided for replacing natural services and set aside funds from public land sales for irrigation projects in the West.

During Roosevelt's terms, the size of the national forests were increased from about 40 million acres to more than 190 million acres. Roosevelt also worked to preserve other valuable lands as well. At his direction, the Department of the Interior set aside 80 million acres of coal lands.

▼ ARAPAHO NATIONAL FOREST, COLORADO

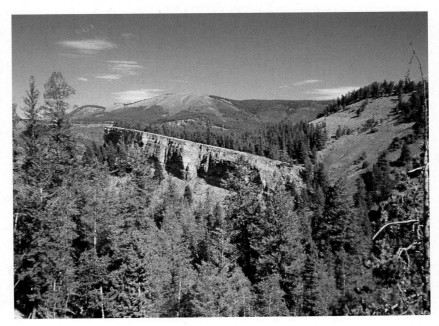

Making the Environment Connection

1. What did Roosevelt suggest was the object of forest policy?

2. How did Roosevelt's conservation program relate to the Square Deal?

Linking Past and Present

3. Why has forest conservation received renewed emphasis in recent years?

The Taft Presidency

Setting the Scene

Section Focus

In 1908 Theodore Roosevelt declined to run for reelection, accepting the custom that limited Presidents to two terms. Although his successor, William Howard Taft, was a supporter of Roosevelt's progressive policies, Taft's presidency led not only to a split between Taft and Roosevelt but also to a division of the Republican party itself.

Objectives

After studying this section, you should be able to

★ explain the impact of the Payne-Aldrich Tariff.

★ examine the public reaction to the Ballinger-Pinchot controversy.

★ describe the reactions of Roosevelt and the public to Taft's leadership.

Key Term

income tax

◀ ROOSEVELT AND TAFT IN CONFLICT

Although a distinguished public servant, having served as a judge, as governor of the Philippines, and as Roosevelt's secretary of war, Taft was a reluctant President. His true ambition lay in the judicial, not the executive, branch of government. Remarking on the snow, sleet, and rain that pelted the people coming to his Inaugural Address, Taft said, "Even the elements do protest."

■ Taft in Difficulty

Taft began his term as President by addressing the tariff issue, largely ignored during Roosevelt's eight-year term. Since passage of the Dingley Tariff of 1897, prices had advanced more rapidly than wages, and many blamed the resulting high cost of living on unduly high tariff rates. Some, including Taft, also believed that high rates encouraged monopoly.

Subversion of Tariff Reform

Congress met in March 1909, and within less than a month the House of Representatives passed a measure, introduced by Sereno Payne of New York, that provided for substantial reductions in the tariff without abandoning the principle of protection. Under the leadership of conservative Senator Nelson W. Aldrich of Rhode Island, however, more than 800 amendments were tacked onto the House bill. Many of these amendments were designed to conceal higher rates, such as changing a duty on certain small articles from so much "per hundredweight" to so much "per hundred."

When Aldrich attempted to railroad the amended bill through the Senate, he was met with resistance in his own party. Several Republican senators, nicknamed "the Insurgents," used their privilege of unlimited debate to reveal the way Aldrich and his allies were carrying out the demands of high-tariff lobbyists instead of the people. Too late, Taft attempted to persuade the Old Guard leaders to reduce the rates, but they made only slight concessions before the bill received Senate approval.

By the time the bill reached Taft's desk, the Payne-Aldrich Tariff contained high duties on iron ore, coal, and hides and increases on other materials. The bill, however, allowed for a corporation tax, established a tariff commission to make a scientific study of rates, and provided for some flexibility in rates at the discretion of the President. For these reasons, and because he feared a split between the Old Guard and the Insurgents in his own party, Taft signed the bill despite its weaknesses.

The public saw Taft's action as a betrayal of his campaign promise. On a speaking tour in the Midwest, Taft argued that the bill fulfilled the Republican platform, adding:

> *If the country . . . wishes the manufacturers all over the country to go out of business, and to have cheaper prices at the expense of the sacrifice of many of our manufacturing interests, then it ought to . . . put the Democratic party in power. . . .*

Despite his efforts, there continued to be widespread dissatisfaction with the tariff and with Taft for supporting it.

Controversy Over an Administrative Dispute

Another blow was dealt to Taft's popularity when a conflict developed between Taft's secretary of the interior, Richard A. Ballinger, and the chief forester, Gifford Pinchot. Ballinger reopened for private purchase certain lands in Montana, Wyoming, and Alaska that had been withdrawn while Roosevelt was President. Pinchot, a well-known conservationist, protested these actions and publicly accused Ballinger of fraud. Taft, convinced of Ballinger's innocence—later confirmed by a congressional investigating committee—dismissed Pinchot for insubordination. But the public viewed Taft's action as a move against the conservation effort begun by Roosevelt, and Taft's popularity plummeted. Even though Ballinger was exonerated of the charges, he eventually resigned his post.

Unpopular Alignment with the Old Guard

Immediately following the Ballinger-Pinchot controversy came an outbreak of Insurgent Republicanism in the House of Representatives, which took the form of an attack on the Old Guard Speaker of the House, Joseph G. "Uncle Joe" Cannon. The speaker had come to enjoy a power over legislation greater in some ways than that of the President. He appointed all committees, he decided what bills should be referred to which committees, and by almost absolute control over debate he could push some measures through without discussion and see that others never reached the floor.

▲ ROOSEVELT AND TAFT In this cartoon, a smiling Roosevelt celebrates with Taft, his chosen successor. Soon, however, Roosevelt and Taft found themselves at odds. ***Why did Taft dismiss Gifford Pinchot?***

Life of the Times

The Elderly in Greenwich Village

Although Progressive leaders used the power of government to improve society, not all Americans benefited from reform efforts. Growing old for many Americans in the early 1900s meant a life of poverty, or near poverty, and dependence for many Americans.

The aged poor showed imagination in making ends meet. For example, a survey of elderly residents of New York's Greenwich Village in 1914 showed 74-year-old Mrs. S. working as a janitor in exchange for free rooms and 75-year-old Miss F. subletting one of her three rooms to cover $10 of her $16 monthly rent. Seventy-year-old Mrs. N. took in sewing and washing.

Even when entirely dependent on charity, many aged people managed to create opportunities for recreation. Miss M., financially supported by her church, lived "in proud isolation, scorning her neighbors," and repeated poetry that she had learned as a child in Canada. "I used to go to lectures at [the public] school," she said, "but the only lectures they have now are economical, and I have enough of that at home, and I don't like it!"

The conservative Cannon used the powers of this office to hold up progressive legislation. He also cooperated with Aldrich during the tariff debacle in 1909. Furthermore, Cannon had long been an opponent of conservation. With the motto "Not one cent for scenery," he had stalled the creation of national parks and forests.

Finally, in March 1910, a coalition of Democrats and Republican Insurgents forced a change in the rules of the House that stripped the speaker of much of his power. This attack on Cannon hurt Taft, who in order to keep party harmony aligned himself with the speaker. Thus, by signing the Payne-Aldrich Tariff, by supporting Ballinger against Pinchot, and by backing Cannon, Taft gave the impression that he had "sold the Square Deal down the river." An Insurgent senator described Taft as "a large good-natured body entirely surrounded by people who know exactly what they want." Popular indignation was so great that the congressional elections of 1910 resulted in a sweeping Democratic victory, with Democrats taking the majority in the House and Democrats and Republican Insurgents wresting control of the Senate from the Old Guard.

■ Roosevelt Proclaims "New Nationalism"

During his retirement Roosevelt tried hard to maintain faith in the man he had chosen as his successor, but he found public opinion toward Taft had worsened. In spite of Roosevelt's intention to remain out of politics, Taft's disappointing performance as President soon drew Roosevelt back into the political arena.

Roosevelt aligned himself with the Insurgents in the Republican party, who had started to call themselves "Progressive Republicans," or simply "Progressives." In a speech at Osawatomie, Kansas, during the congressional election of 1910, Roosevelt spoke of a new set of policies that he called the "New Nationalism." In words that recalled the Populist platform of the 1890s and foreshadowed the New Deal of the 1930s, Roosevelt said:

> We are face to face with new conceptions of the relations of property to human welfare. . . . The man who wrongly holds that every human right is secondary to his profit must now give way to the advocate of human welfare, who rightly maintains that every man holds his property subject to the general right of the community to regulate its use to whatever degree the public welfare may require it.

In his New Nationalism speech, Roosevelt outlined a much more radical program of action than he had ever proposed while in the presidency. He favored both state and federal legislation to actively promote human welfare, including laws to protect women and children in the labor force and workers' compensation for those injured on the job.

Attacking the courts for declaring certain progressive legislation unconstitutional, Roosevelt suggested that state judges be subject to recall and that Supreme Court decisions be reversible by popular vote. By taking such stands, Roosevelt established his position as the natural leader of the Progressive Republicans.

■ Taft's Successes

Despite Taft's political problems, his administration experienced several successes. Although it was Roosevelt who was nicknamed the "trustbuster," Taft actually prosecuted twice as many antitrust cases in four years as his predecessor had in seven. Taft established the Tariff Board to investigate tariff rates, and under his leadership a federal budget began to take shape. Taft also supported the Sixteenth Amendment, giving Congress power to collect **income taxes,** or taxes on the income of individuals and companies, and the Seventeenth Amendment, calling for direct election of United States senators. In addition, during his administration two new states—New Mexico and Arizona—were admitted to the United States.

Taft genuinely supported Roosevelt's Square Deal policies, but unlike Roosevelt, who claimed an executive right to do anything not forbidden, Taft's judicial background allowed him to use "only those powers expressly authorized by law." Taft also lacked his predecessor's gift for dramatizing issues and enlisting public support. To some degree, Taft brought his political troubles on himself. He had a very different temperament from other politicians, and he had a hard time keeping up with the incessant work of the office. He did not really want to be President; his greatest ambition—later fulfilled—was to sit on the Supreme Court. In addition, he did not enjoy politics, and it is not surprising that he was not a success as a politician. In the end, Taft's administration would be remembered for its failures rather than its achievements.

Section 2 ★ Review

Checking for Understanding

1. **Identify** Payne-Aldrich Tariff, Richard Ballinger, Joseph Cannon, New Nationalism, "the Insurgents."

2. **Define** income tax.

3. **List** the reasons the public thought Taft was destroying the Square Deal.

4. **Explain** Theodore Roosevelt's return to national politics with the New Nationalism program.

Critical Thinking

5. **Making Judgments** Analyze how Taft's leadership led to increasing the power and authority of the federal government.

★★

The Election of 1912

Setting the Scene

Section Focus

With his New Nationalism speech, Theodore Roosevelt returned to the political arena. As the election of 1912 approached, he remained convinced that Taft was unfit for another term as President, and it was not in Roosevelt's nature to sit on the sidelines. Thus the great question in American politics as the campaign began was whether Roosevelt would run again for the presidency.

Objectives

After studying this section, you should be able to

★ relate the events that led to the formation of the Progressive party.

★ explain how a split in the Republican party helped lead to Woodrow Wilson's election in 1912.

Key Term

inheritance tax

◀ POLITICAL CARTOON, 1912 PRESIDENTIAL ELECTION

Senator Robert La Follette, a man of great ability and a leader of the recently formed National Progressive Republican League, had the support of many Progressive Republicans for the 1912 presidential nomination. When La Follette suffered a temporary nervous collapse, however, the Progressives turned to Roosevelt. Explaining that his no-third-term pledge referred to a third consecutive term, Roosevelt declared himself a candidate against Taft for the Republican nomination.

■ Roosevelt Challenges Taft

The heated, emotional struggle for control of the Republican party reached its climax at the national convention in June. Conservatives rallied behind Taft, as did many former supporters of the Square Deal who thought Roosevelt too radical or who disliked his running for a third term. Except for some devoted followers of La Follette, the Progressive Republicans lined up for Roosevelt. In states where convention delegates were chosen in primary elections, Roosevelt was generally the choice of the voters.

The Taft forces, however, had the immense advantage of controlling the party machinery. The convention chairperson Elihu Root kept such a tight hold on proceedings that he was accused of driving a steam roller over the Roosevelt forces. The convention's Credentials Committee gave 235 of 254 convention seats to Taft. When Taft received the nomination on the first ballot, Roosevelt charged the Republican party leaders with stealing the nomination. He stood ready, he said, to carry on the battle for progressive principles outside the party.

■ Formation of Progressive Party

In August a convention met in Chicago to found a new political party—the Progressive party. The delegates were a curious mixture—college professors, social workers, newspaper editors, former Rough Riders, wealthy people motivated by social conscience, and some professional politicians.

Senator Albert J. Beveridge, who had followed Roosevelt out of the Republican party, called on the new party to work for a nobler America. The Progressives, said Beveridge, stood for "social brotherhood" as opposed to "savage individualism," for a "representative government that represents the people," as opposed to invisible government controlled by corrupt bosses and the "robber interest."

The Progressive platform demanded reforms such as a more direct democracy through such means as the initiative and referendum, for conservation of natural resources for the general welfare, for woman suffrage, and for labor reforms such as the prohibition of child labor.

In addition, Progressives called for revision of the currency system and the introduction of an **inheritance tax,** which would be a percentage of the value of an inheritance, levied on the privilege of an heir to receive this property.

The party nominated Theodore Roosevelt for the presidency and immediately acquired a party symbol when the former President announced that he felt "as strong as a bull moose." The Progressive party had a strong enthusiasm and one of the most popular individuals in public life. It also had abundant campaign funds, supplied by wealthy business people who believed that capitalism could survive only if it was reformed.

The Bull Moose crusade was a forlorn hope, however. Most of the Progressives were amateurs with little or no knowledge of practical politics. Party machinery could not be set up in thousands of election districts overnight. All that Roosevelt accomplished by bolting from the Republican party was to give control of the Republican party to the Old Guard, and to ensure the election of a Democratic President.

"Look up, not down—
Look out, not in—
Look forward, not backward—
And lend a hand."

Founders' Day
October 27, 1912

THE
Progressive
Party

Visualizing **History**

▲ ROOSEVELT THE CAMPAIGNER
Theodore Roosevelt was a vigorous and effective campaigner. The Progressive party platform included a minimum-wage law for women, workers' compensation laws, and strong regulation of child labor. *Who were the Republican and Democratic candidates in the 1912 election?*

■ Woodrow Wilson and the New Freedom

When the Democratic convention met at Baltimore in June 1912, there was discord between the progressive wing, to which William Jennings Bryan belonged, and the conservative wing, whose delegates represented city political machines. Although

Visualizing History

▲ TAFT AND SONS Theodore Roosevelt once said, "Taft has the most lovable personality I have ever come in contact with." Their friendship was wrecked, however, on the realities of politics and ambition. ***On what ballot was Taft nominated in 1912?***

disclaiming any desire for another nomination, Bryan was influential in seeing that the Democratic platform was as progressive as that of the Bull Moose party itself. After a protracted struggle, Woodrow Wilson, who had won national fame as a reform governor of New Jersey, received the nomination on the 46th ballot, partly through the help of Bryan.

Two Progressive Platforms

In the ensuing campaign Taft was not active, privately expressing the opinion that Wilson was sure to win. The real battle took place between Roosevelt and Wilson. Both men supported progressivism, although under different labels. Wilson countered Roosevelt's New Nationalism with what he called the "New Freedom."

Although there appeared to be little distinction between the philosophies of the two candidates, they did in fact differ. Roosevelt's New Nationalism accepted big business as a fact of life and proposed a more powerful

federal government and a strong executive to keep it under control. Wilson's New Freedom viewed monopolies as absolute evils, the antithesis of free competition. He also advocated the use of federal power to ensure more equality of opportunity.

Two Contrasting Candidates

The differences between Wilson and Roosevelt were striking. Roosevelt had long been the best-known political figure in the United States. Wilson, a former university president and college professor, had been active on the American political scene for only three years. Roosevelt, the former Rough Rider, was thought of by the public as a strong fighter in a war on privilege. While Roosevelt enjoyed mixing with all sorts of people, Wilson was aloof.

One writer likened Roosevelt to a great national spectacle, like Niagara Falls. People jammed the halls when he spoke, but it is not certain that they came so much to listen as to gape.

On the campaign platform Wilson's tall, angular figure displayed an ease of manner and his homely face exhibited a warmth he often lacked in personal relations. From his early teens, he had often dreamed of persuading people by using his power of eloquence. Even his strongest enemies had to admit that he could be very persuasive. Although Wilson lacked the magnetism of his rival Roosevelt, he knew how to touch people's conscience and appeal to their sense of reason.

An attempt to assassinate Roosevelt gave him an opportunity to demonstrate his courage and self-possession. On his way to deliver a speech in Milwaukee he was shot in the chest. Pausing only long enough to make sure that his assailant received protection of the police, Roosevelt insisted on delivering his speech before receiving medical attention. Not seriously wounded, he was later able to resume his campaign at full speed.

Results of the Election

The results of the election fulfilled Taft's prediction of victory for Wilson. Although he won the presidency, Wilson actually had fewer popular votes than Roosevelt and Taft combined. Because of the split in the Republican vote, however—and also a surprisingly strong Socialist party vote—Wilson carried 40 of the 48 states, with a total of 435 electoral votes; his opponents together received only 96 electoral votes. So, for the first time since Grover Cleveland's election in 1892, a Democrat became President of the United States.

Wilson's Previous Career

Woodrow Wilson had gained national prominence as a foe of privilege and as an individual with strong powers of leadership. During eight years as president of Princeton University, he not only raised standards and improved teaching, but also fought social privilege as represented by social clubs. As governor of New Jersey he successfully fought political bosses who represented special interests, not the interests of the people as a whole. Under his leadership, the New Jersey legislature enacted an elaborate program of progressive measures.

The extraordinary successes gained by the "scholar in politics" can be explained partly by the fact that from childhood he had been ambitious to hold high office. Not only had he trained himself in public speaking, but he had also devoted much of his life to studying the techniques of effective political leadership. A long-time admirer of the British government, he developed the theory that the President, like the British prime minister, should take the initiative in guiding and promoting legislation. The President alone, in his opinion, stood for the interests of the entire nation.

In addition to books on government, Wilson had written a history of the United States and many articles, mostly on political topics. He was well informed on domestic issues, especially the tariff. A Southerner who had lived his adult life in the North, a Democrat who admired Alexander Hamilton as well as Thomas Jefferson, a scholar who knew the past as well as the present, Wilson was able to see public questions in perspective.

Section 3 ★ Review

Checking for Understanding

1. **Identify** Bull Moose party, New Freedom.

2. **Define** inheritance tax.

3. **Explain** why Roosevelt left the Republicans and helped form the Progressive party.

4. **Describe** the Progressive party platform.

Critical Thinking

5. **Recognizing Stereotypes** Analyze whether supporters of the Progressive party were radical reformers or dreamers.

Critical Thinking Skills

Supporting Generalizations

A generalization is a statement that offers a general characteristic rather than a specific one. Sometimes when making a point or offering an interpretation, an author may make a generalization and then give supporting statements. At other times, however, you may be given only a generalization without supporting statements, or supporting statements without a generalization. In such cases you will need to use your understanding of the content and thought processes to supply what's missing—either the generalization or the supporting statement.

As a historian, it is important to back up generalizations with supporting statements or evidence. Here are guidelines for making supporting statements.

- They must relate directly to the generalization.
- They must be logical.
- They must be based on fact.

Study the map of the election of 1912, noting how the two guidelines have been applied to the following generalizations:

- The Southern states had a great influence on the election of the Democratic candidate, Woodrow Wilson.

Supporting statement:

The election map shows that all electoral votes from the Southern states went to Woodrow Wilson. (This statement relates directly to the generalization, is logical, and is based on fact.)

- The citizens who voted preferred Woodrow Wilson.

Supporting statement:

Woodrow Wilson won the election of 1912. (This statement relates directly to the generalization and is logical, but it is not based on fact. The majority of citizens who voted did not vote for Wilson.)

The Election of 1912

	Popular vote:	Electoral vote:
Wilson	6,296,547	435
Roosevelt	4,118,571	88
Taft	3,486,720	8

0 200 mi.
0 200 km

- The Western states did not support any one candidate.

Supporting statement:

California, Nevada, and Utah each gave their electoral votes to a different candidate. (This statement relates directly to the generalization, is logical, and is supported by fact.)

Practicing the Skill

For practice in supporting generalizations, write a supporting statement for the following generalizations. Use information you have learned from this chapter.

1. Theodore Roosevelt, although popular with the public, had difficulty getting "Square Deal" measures through Congress.

2. William Howard Taft continued Roosevelt's reform program, but the public lost confidence in his presidential leadership.

★★

Wilson's Progressivism

Setting the Scene

Section Focus

Before becoming President, Woodrow Wilson had held only one political office, governor of New Jersey from 1910 to 1912. In those two years, he had successfully worked for an elaborate program of progressive laws. Wilson began his first presidential term determined to obtain major social reform at the federal level.

Objectives

After studying this section, you should be able to

★ explain why Wilson had congressional support for his programs.

★ list the accomplishments of Wilson's domestic program, including legislation on tariffs and on trusts.

Key Terms

rediscount, price-cutting, interlocking directorate

◀ NUTCRACKER IN LIKENESS OF WOODROW WILSON

The new President entered office with several handicaps. He was a minority President, chosen by only 42 percent of the voters. With no experience in national politics, he knew few Democratic party leaders. In addition, the Democratic party at the time comprised a loose alliance of local interests not expected to work well together. Long out of office, the Democrats lacked people with experience in government at the federal level.

■ Wilson and Congress

Although inexperienced in national politics, Wilson enjoyed certain advantages upon entering office. The 1912 election results sent Congress a clear message that most Americans demanded progressive legislation. If the Democrats did not support the President in the creation of this legislation, warned a member of Congress, they would be "turned into the wilderness for 40 years more." No prominent Democratic leaders opposed Wilson, as Republicans Cannon and Aldrich had thwarted Taft. On the contrary, Wilson enjoyed the loyal support of most Democrats—including Bryan, the most influential man in the party, whom Wilson appointed secretary of state.

Wilson's first Inaugural Address was one of the shortest and most eloquent ever delivered. He began by asking the meaning of the Democratic triumph at the polls. His answer was that it meant little "except when the Nation is using that party for a large and definite purpose." To Wilson, the purpose was to do away with the evils that, along with many blessings, industrialism had brought. The President described these evils as the "inexcusable waste" of natural resources, the "human cost" of unrestrained individualism, and the use of government "for private and selfish purposes." Wilson

▲ **INAUGURATION OF A NEW PRESIDENT** The shortcomings of industrial America were widely recognized when Woodrow Wilson became President in March 1913, so it was no surprise that his brief Inaugural Address was devoted to domestic reform. *What goals did Wilson set forth in his Inaugural Address?*

also stated his goals—not, he said, Democratic or Republican goals but goals for all the nation. After calling for reform of tariffs and banking, equality of business opportunity, improvements in agriculture, and conservation of natural resources, he concluded:

❝ *This is not a day of triumph. It is a day of dedication. Here muster not the forces of party, but the forces of humanity. . . . I summon all honest men, all patriotic, all forward-looking men to my side. God helping me, I will not fail them, if they will but counsel and sustain me!* ❞

■ The Underwood Tariff

The President lost no time in embarking on his program of reform. Like Taft, Wilson at once called Congress into special session. Appearing in person before Congress—the first President to do so in 100 years—he

delivered a special message on the tariff. This short speech made headlines nationwide and illustrated Wilson's long-standing belief that the President's greatest power lay in focusing public attention on important issues.

Wilson's message charged that high tariffs had:

❝ *. . . built up a set of privileges and exemptions from competition behind which it was easy . . . to organize monopoly; until . . . nothing is obliged to stand the tests of efficiency and economy. . . .* ❞

Lower rates, he claimed, would help businesses by putting them under "constant necessity to be efficient, economical, and enterprising. . . ." Opening the American market to foreign products would at the same time open foreign markets to American goods. Wilson warned, however, against undue haste, making it clear that he did not favor removing protective duties entirely.

The House of Representatives soon passed a bill, sponsored by Alabama Representative Oscar W. Underwood, embodying the President's recommendations. The real fight occurred in the Senate, where previous attempts to lower the tariff had foundered, and where the Democrats had only a six-vote majority. Lobbyists swarmed to Washington, pressuring senators to alter the bill. But before senatorial opposition could crystallize, Wilson again appealed to the people. He denounced the "insidious" lobbyists and asked an aroused public to insist that Congress put an end to "this unbearable situation." The President then held personal conferences with Democratic senators and wrote letters to those threatening to oppose him. Under such varied and unrelenting pressure from the executive office, the Senate voted to accept the House bill with little change.

The Underwood Tariff Act represented the first substantial drop in import duties since 1857. It attempted to fix duties at a level where costs of production in the United States and abroad would be equalized, thus lowering the duty paid on almost 1,000 articles. It removed protection entirely from industries that already competed successfully with foreign producers.

A most important section of the Underwood Tariff Act was the provision for levying an income tax, now legalized by the Sixteenth Amendment. Originally introduced merely to make up for losses in revenue created by lower tariffs, the income tax became the federal government's chief source of revenue in a very short time.

■ The Federal Reserve Act

As the tariff debate reached a crescendo, Wilson appeared before Congress to introduce the second major item in his reform program: a revision of the banking and currency system. The purpose of the revision was to provide businesses with cheaper and more available credit. Like the tariff message, Wilson's speech was so brief that many influential newspapers published the entire text.

Flaws in the Banking System

In 1907 a sharp panic had revealed serious weaknesses in the American banking and currency system. There were runs on banks, many of which closed or stopped lending as a result. In 1908 Congress set up the National Monetary Commission, headed

◀ FEDERAL RESERVE SYMBOL

Visualizing History

▲ STRUCTURE OF THE FEDERAL RESERVE By 1994 the United States had more than 11,000 commercial banks. Nearly 40 percent of these were member banks that belonged to the Federal Reserve System. *What flaws in the banking system was the Federal Reserve System set up to correct?*

by conservative Senator Aldrich, to investigate the situation and propose change. After four years of study, the Aldrich Commission reported that the financial organization of the United States was flawed in four respects.

First, American banking lacked stability in times of crisis. Banks did not keep enough money on reserve to cover sudden withdrawals, and there was not enough cooperation between banks.

Second, America's currency was inflexible. The amount of money in circulation was based on the amount of gold and silver in the treasury, plus the bonds held by the national banks. The present system provided no way to increase or decrease the supply of money according to the investment needs of the country.

Third, there was no central control of banking practices. In other modern industrialized countries, central banks, such as the Bank of England and the Bank of France, directed banking policy. Nothing similar had existed in this nation since Andrew Jackson had destroyed the second Bank.

Finally, the commission found that too much bank capital was concentrated in New York City and on Wall Street. Meanwhile, other parts of the country, especially isolated rural districts, often suffered from a lack of adequate banking facilities and credit.

Although few questioned the list of ills in the banking and currency system, government leaders disputed the cure. Bankers favored a great central bank, privately controlled, like the first and second Banks of the United States. Many progressives, especially Bryan, called for strict federal control of banking and credit. It was Wilson's difficult task to select a plan that would work and at the same time win support from both bankers and Bryan's followers.

Central Banking Authority

The plan Wilson finally chose was called the Federal Reserve Act. Again, under constant pressure from the President, Congress finally passed the law in December 1913. The Federal Reserve Act promptly became one of the most important and useful pieces of legislation in United States history.

The new system provided for 12 Federal Reserve Banks situated throughout the country. All national banks were required to join them, and other banks could join if they wished. The Federal Reserve did not deal directly with individuals but instead serviced member banks. These "banks for bankers" concentrated reserves, so they could provide support to individual banks in times of temporary difficulty such as a "run." They also provided for local investment needs and made it easier to move funds from one part of the country to another.

The Federal Reserve Act provided a compromise between private and public control. The Federal Reserve Banks themselves were privately owned, a majority of their directors being elected by the member banks. Overall control of the Federal Reserve Banks, however, remained in the hands of a Federal Reserve Board, whose 7 members were appointed by the President, subject to approval by the Senate, for 14-year terms. Thus the center of the nation's financial power moved from Wall Street in New York City to Washington, D.C.

Flexible Money Supply

Before passage of the Federal Reserve Act, local banks frequently lacked funds to make sound loans to businesspeople and farmers. For want of adequate funds, stores and factories closed, and crops rotted. The Federal Reserve Act greatly improved this situation by providing for a new form of "flexible" currency known as Federal Reserve notes. The new money went into circulation when local banks needing cash brought businesspeople's promissory notes to Federal Reserve Banks. In return, the Federal Reserve Bank issued Federal Reserve notes, assessing the member bank a small fee called a **rediscount.**

When a Federal Reserve Bank bought promissory notes, it could print and issue more paper money, using those notes as part of the security, or collateral, thereby protecting the value of the currency. Then, when the notes were paid and the money came back to the Bank, the currency was retired.

The Federal Reserve Banks also controlled the amount of money in circulation by raising or lowering the rediscount rate, or the rate at which they charged for rediscounting. Raising the rate discouraged banks from lending and so "contracted" the currency; lowering the rate encouraged lending and "expanded" the currency. Thus currency and credit in any Federal Reserve District expanded or contracted according to the economic needs of that region.

On the whole, the Federal Reserve Act made the banking system responsive to the needs of a great industrial nation. It succeeded in its first great test, during World War I, when it assisted industrial expansion and helped finance the war effort.

■ Wilson Regulates Trusts

Shortly after signing the Federal Reserve Act, Wilson asked Congress to pass an antitrust law more effective than the Sherman Antitrust Act. Denying any desire to interfere with legitimate business activities, his message to Congress proposed various methods of preventing the "indefensible and intolerable" abuses of private monopoly.

Federal Trade Commission

Late in 1914, Congress responded to Wilson's requests by passing two laws. The first, the Federal Trade Commission Act, established a Federal Trade Commission to

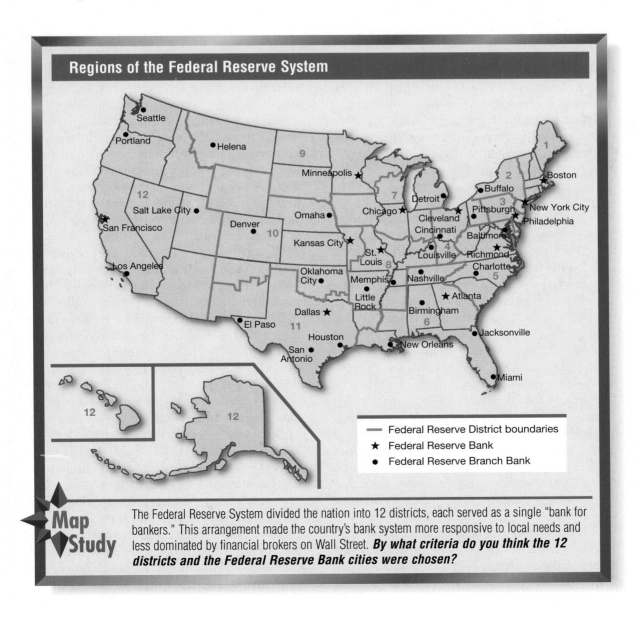

Regions of the Federal Reserve System

— Federal Reserve District boundaries
★ Federal Reserve Bank
● Federal Reserve Branch Bank

Map Study The Federal Reserve System divided the nation into 12 districts, each served as a single "bank for bankers." This arrangement made the country's bank system more responsive to local needs and less dominated by financial brokers on Wall Street. *By what criteria do you think the 12 districts and the Federal Reserve Bank cities were chosen?*

AMERICAN PORTRAITS

W.E.B. Du Bois
1868–1963

The first African American to receive a Harvard Ph.D., W.E.B. Du Bois was a distinguished educator who refused to accept racial inequality. Du Bois initiated the Niagara Movement in 1905 to fight racial discrimination against African Americans in the United States.

For 24 years, Du Bois served as editor of the NAACP's journal, *The Crisis*, using it as a tool to assert demands for racial justice and equality. Between 1910 and 1930, his influence shaped not only the NAACP but a generation of African American intellectuals and activists.

In 1919 he organized the first Pan-African Congress, which promoted the idea that all people of African descent throughout the world should work together to combat the effects of discrimination. *Pan-Africanism* is still strong today among nations in Africa, where Du Bois moved in 1961.

---

investigate and regulate business practices. The commission had power to order companies to "cease and desist" from unfair conduct. In actual practice, though, Wilson's appointees to the commission failed to take strong actions against trusts.

Clayton Antitrust Act

In October 1914, less than a month after passage of the Federal Trade Commission Act, Congress passed the Clayton Antitrust Act. This act forbade several practices that destroyed competition or prevented new businesses from being developed. These practices included ruinous **price-cutting,** whereby a large company deliberately sold goods at a loss to drive weaker competitors out of business; "tying" of contracts, whereby a purchaser of goods from a particular company had to agree not to trade with its competitors; and intercorporate investment, whereby a company bought part ownership in a rival concern. The act also outlawed **"interlocking" directorates** between large corporations and banks, whereby the same people acted as directors in many different companies.

The Clayton Act also contained two sections favorable to trade unions. As noted earlier, the Sherman Act, by forbidding conspiracies, had proven more effective against labor unions than against business monopolies. In the Danbury Hatters' case, fought out in the federal courts from 1903 to 1915, a union had been ruined financially by being forced to pay triple damages to a business concern whose product had been boycotted. To discourage such use of antitrust laws, the Clayton Act stated that "nothing in the antitrust laws shall be construed to forbid the existence and operation of labor . . . organizations."

In addition, ever since the jailing of Eugene V. Debs for contempt of court in the 1894 Pullman strike, labor unions had protested the use of court injunctions forbidding strikes and boycotts. In answer to their protests, the Clayton Act forbade federal courts to issue injunctions against peaceful strikes, picketing, boycotts, or union meetings.

The Clayton Antitrust Act lost most of its effectiveness because of loose wording and unfavorable interpretations by the federal courts. The protection of labor unions from suits under the Sherman Act was limited to unions pursuing their "legitimate" purposes—and it was the courts that defined the word *legitimate.* Injunctions might still be issued when "necessary to prevent irreparable damage to property or to a property right," which again left a large loophole for conservative judges.

Wilson's Other Accomplishments

The Clayton Act completed the legislative program that Wilson had originally promoted. Wilson, however, did not stop there, turning his attention to other domestic issues.

Domestic Legislation

Additional legislation passed during his first term included the establishment of 12 regional Federal Farm Loan Banks, endowed with public funds in order to provide loans for agriculture. A Federal Highways Act, designed to help farmers get their produce to market, allotted federal funds to states for road construction and development. Wilson also supported the Keating-Owen Child Labor Act, which prohibited the employment of children under age 14 in factories producing goods for interstate commerce. The Adamson Act, passed under threat of a nationwide tie-up in transportation, established an 8-hour day for railroad workers.

Under Wilson's directed eye, much constructive legislation had been passed quickly. Wilson supplied a skillful and dynamic leadership, sometimes keeping Congress in session throughout the hot summer months. Chauncey Depew, a noted conservative Republican, said that for a man regarded as a mere theorist, Wilson had accomplished "the most astonishing practical results."

Segregation in the Capital

The reforms Wilson achieved did not have "practical results" for African Americans, however, as the President brought Jim Crow to Washington. The nation's capital had been desegregated since Reconstruction, but Wilson, a native Virginian, strongly believed in separating the races. Therefore, his administration segregated drinking fountains, rest rooms, and lunch counters in government office buildings and assigned jobs according to race.

A number of prominent African American leaders like W.E.B. Du Bois, who had supported Wilson in 1912, turned against him. African American newspaper editor William Monroe Trotter blamed Wilson's New Freedom for a "new slavery for your Afro-American fellow citizens." Yet the President exemplified the racial prejudice of many other progressive reformers.

Wilson also opposed woman suffrage at first. Later, however, he modified his position. During this second term, the Nineteenth Amendment gave women the right to vote.

Wilson's efforts during the beginning of his first term focused almost exclusively on domestic matters. In fact, foreign affairs did not even receive mention in his first Inaugural Address. But by the end of his term, world events overshadowed these domestic achievements, and soon Wilson's role as architect and promoter of progressive legislation was all but forgotten. It was obscured by growing tensions in foreign affairs that resulted in tragedy for him and for the world.

Section 4 ★ Review

Checking for Understanding

1. **Identify** Underwood Tariff, Federal Reserve Board, Federal Trade Commission, Clayton Antitrust Act.

2. **Define** rediscount, price-cutting, interlocking directorate.

3. **Explain** how the Federal Reserve System works.

4. **Describe** the provisions of the Clayton Antitrust Act that limited the power of monopolies.

Critical Thinking

5. **Making Judgments** Evaluate the effect of Wilson's antitrust legislation and the creation of the Federal Reserve System on the economy of the nation.

Using Vocabulary

Write a paragraph describing Wilson's New Freedom program. Use the following terms:

progressivism   labor
antitrust   monopoly
free competition   income tax

Reviewing Facts

1. **Describe** the progressive beliefs of Theodore Roosevelt.

2. **Identify** the sources of support for Roosevelt's Square Deal and New Nationalism.

3. **Cite** two important achievements of William Howard Taft's administration.

4. **Compare** the progressivism of Woodrow Wilson and Theodore Roosevelt based on their respective programs.

Understanding Concepts

Interests and Positions

1. Show how Taft's policies seemed to go against Roosevelt's Square Deal.

Economic Competition

2. In what way did big-business practices and tactics in the early 1900s slow or inhibit economic competition?

Critical Thinking

1. **Linking Past and Present** Compare Theodore Roosevelt's approach to conservation of natural resources with those of Presidents during the 1980s and 1990s.

2. **Analyzing Political Cartoons** Study the cartoon on this page showing President Woodrow Wilson, then answer the questions that follow.

   a. Do you think the cartoonist has a favorable or unfavorable view of Wilson? Explain.

   b. What point is the cartoonist making?

   c. What symbols did the cartoonist use to get his message across to the viewer?

Writing About History

Argumentation

Imagine you are a campaign manager for Theodore Roosevelt, William Howard Taft, and Woodrow Wilson during the election of 1912. Write a campaign speech with slogans for Roosevelt, Taft, and Wilson that reflects the views of each candidate and his party.

Cooperative Learning

Organize the class into three debate groups. Each group will then choose one of the following three topics:

1. The Ballinger/Pinchot controversy over protecting wilderness areas

2. The Payne/Aldrich debate over protective tariffs

Imports and Tariff Duties

Year	VALUE OF IMPORTS (Millions of dollars) Total	Free	Dutiable	DUTIES COLLECTED (Millions of dollars)	DUTIES COLLECTED (Percent of total value of imports)
1880	$ 628	$ 208	$ 420	$ 183	29.1%
1885	$ 579	$ 192	$ 387	$ 178	30.8%
1890	$ 766	$ 258	$ 508	$ 227	29.6%
1895	$ 731	$ 377	$ 354	$ 149	20.4%
1900	$ 831	$ 367	$ 464	$ 229	27.6%
1905	$1,087	$ 517	$ 570	$ 258	23.8%
1910	$1,547	$ 761	$ 786	$ 327	21.1%
1915	$1,648	$1,033	$ 616	$ 206	12.5%
1920	$5,102	$3,116	$1,986	$ 326	6.4%

Source: *Historical Statistics of the United States: Colonial Times to 1970* (1975).

3. The mine workers/mine owners dispute in the coal strike of 1902

You will work within your group to research and prepare arguments on both sides of the issue. Conduct the class debates when each group has completed its preparation.

Social Studies Skills

Analyzing Trends

A table presents statistics in an easily analyzed format. Tables group information into horizontal rows and vertical columns. The table format facilitates quick comparisons, thus helping you recognize and analyze trends. Use the table on this page to help you practice analyzing trends.

Practicing the Skill

1. What years are covered by the table? How many years separate each row of data?

2. Explain the trend in the total value of imports represented on this table.

3. Explain the trend in total duties collected in the time period covered by the table.

4. Explain the trend in percent of total value of imports between 1880 and 1910.

5. Study the columns on the value of imports in the table. Explain the trend in percent of total value of imports between 1910 and 1920.

6. What congressional action affected the collection of duties after 1910? Explain.

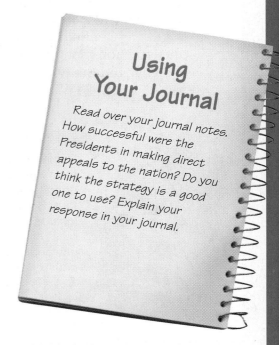

Using Your Journal

Read over your journal notes. How successful were the Presidents in making direct appeals to the nation? Do you think the strategy is a good one to use? Explain your response in your journal.

Cultural Kaleidoscope

Transportation

Moving Into The Fast Lanes

As America evolved into a world power at the turn of the twentieth century, it also began to look differently at itself. The frontier was nearly gone and in its place, from 1880 to 1914, booming industrial expansion became a hallmark of American culture. No symbol better expresses this period than the automobile. Although the auto was invented in the nineteenth century, it is truly a twentieth-century phenomenon that touched and changed the way Americans lived.

▶ Beginning in 1908, the Ford Model T reached unparalleled sales, justifying its nickname of the car that put the world on wheels.

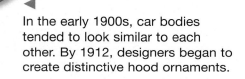

◀ In the early 1900s, car bodies tended to look similar to each other. By 1912, designers began to create distinctive hood ornaments.

◀ Some automakers outfitted their vehicles with horns operated by hand or by foot. Some luxury cars included two horns—a quiet one for use in the city and a louder one fcr country driving.

▲ There had been only a handful of automobiles on American highways by 1895. By 1920 there were nearly 5 million, and the automobile was beginning to remake American life.

▶ No better proof of the impact of the automobile exists than in the popular songs of the day.

▲ Headlights were then called headlamps and were typically constructed of brass.

▼ Modern cars still have four wheels and run on gasoline. Yet they look very different from cars of 80 years ago. Shown is the front compartment of the 1914 Mercer Raceabout.

Chapter 22

Imperialism

In the last decades of the nineteenth century, Americans reassessed and abandoned their traditional isolationist policy. Because of growing industrial power, trade and contacts with Latin America increased. In the Pacific, American interest in Hawaii led to its annexation in 1898.

In 1898 the United States went to war with Spain. Americans sympathized with an independence movement in Cuba seeking to overthrow Spanish control. The Spanish-American War was over in six months.

As a result of the war, the United States gained a colonial empire and with it the challenge of governing overseas territories—Puerto Rico, Guam, and the Philippines. Questions soon arose over whether native people living in colonial possessions were entitled to the same civil rights as American citizens. Eventually the Supreme Court of the United States ruled that the Constitution did not cover overseas possessions.

As the United States expanded into the Pacific, Americans were anxious to renew trade opportunities with the Chinese. To protect any potential trade between the two countries, Secretary of State John Hay asked the Chinese in 1899 to grant an "Open Door" trade policy.

President Theodore Roosevelt strengthened American involvement in world affairs. He defended Venezuela from possible European aggression and he issued the Roosevelt Corollary, a statement that attempted to justify United States intervention in Latin America. In addition, Roosevelt negotiated an end to the Russo-Japanese War. Perhaps most important, Roosevelt prevented Colombia from putting down an insurrection in Panama City. This action allowed Panamanians to establish the Republic of Panama. Roosevelt quickly negotiated a treaty for the rights to build a canal across Panama.

Chapter 23

The Progressive Era

Beginning about 1900 a large, loosely organized group of urban, middle-class professionals—including journalists, social workers, educators, ministers, and socially conscious politicians—became concerned about the need for social change in the United States. These reformers—called "progressives"—were the first to thoroughly investigate social problems that they felt were unjust and undemocratic. Progressives were concerned that if society's problems were not solved, democracy and capitalism might be threatened.

The goal of progressives was an efficient, smoothly functioning nation where each social problem could be managed by experts trained in that area. The many areas in which the progressives focused their efforts included the following: reform of the political system, business regulation, consumer protection, limits on immigration, tax reform, protection of working women and children, labor and education reform, and temperance. Journalists called "muckrakers" brought many of these problem areas to public attention, and most Americans supported calls for change. Reform occurred first at local and state levels.

Although progressives had the nation's best interests at heart, some reforms came at the expense of immigrants and racial minorities. Reformers tried to extinguish immigrant cultures, and they neglected African Americans almost completely.

Chapter 24

White House Reformers

Theodore Roosevelt, William H. Taft, and Woodrow Wilson were reform Presidents. They sought to improve the welfare of the average American citizen, regulate big-business practices, and conserve the nation's natural resources.

Roosevelt supported the progressive movement with his domestic goal to give everyone a "Square Deal." He soon became known as a "trustbuster." Roosevelt also helped settle the coal strike of 1902. Roosevelt's greatest achievement lay in the area of conservation.

During Taft's administration the Constitution was strengthened with the Sixteenth Amendment's passage (providing for an income tax) and the Seventeenth Amendment (allowing direct election of senators). Taft also created the Tariff Board to investigate duties.

One of Wilson's first acts as President was to help pass the Underwood Tariff Act, which lowered import duties and introduced a federal income tax. Wilson achieved a progressive legislative program. He implemented a reform of banking and currency practices, secured passage of a labor reform bill, and engineered legislation regulating trusts.

Understanding Unit Themes

1. **American Democracy**   In what ways did reforms in government help the middle class and hinder African Americans?

2. **Economic Development**   How did the opening of new markets in East Asia and the acquisition of territories create economic growth in the United States?

3. **The Individual and Family Life**   In what ways did social and political reforms improve the quality of life for many?

4. **U.S. Role in World Affairs**   How did American foreign policy change around 1900? Give examples of this change.

5. **U.S. Role in World Affairs**   How did Roosevelt's role in resolving the Russo-Japanese War show that the United States had become a world leader?

UNIT EIGHT
CRUSADE AND DISILLUSION
1914–1932

★★

CHAPTER **25**	CHAPTER **26**	CHAPTER **27**
World War I Era 1914–1920	The Decade of Normalcy 1920–1928	The Depression Begins 1928–1932

▼ **WALL TELEPHONE**

▲ **DUSTER COAT**

History AND ART

Third Avenue
by Charles Goeller, 1933–1934

Scenes of city life during the Great Depression were important themes for many artists.

Setting the Scene

The spirit of progressive reform dwindled as the United States drifted toward the conflict of World War I. Once the war ended, the national mood was no longer progress and optimism but "normalcy" and isolation. During the 1920s, Americans elected conservative Republican leaders.

Themes

- Conflict and Cooperation
- Influence of Technology
- The Individual and Family Life
- United States Role in World Affairs

Key Events

- World War I begins in Europe
- Germany resumes unrestricted submarine warfare
- Congress declares war on Germany
- The Senate rejects the Treaty of Versailles and the League of Nations
- Teapot Dome oil scandal
- Stock market crash
- Bonus Army marches on Washington

Major Issues

- Violation of neutral rights leads the United States to declare war on Germany.
- Despite Wilson's leadership, an isolationist mood defeats the Treaty of Versailles and the League of Nations.
- Prosperity of the 1920s fails to reach African Americans and farmers.
- Widespread depression and human misery after the crash prompts the federal government to provide direct relief.

BLOOD or BREAD
Others are giving their blood
You will shorten the war—
save life if you eat only what
you need and waste nothing.
UNITED STATES FOOD ADMINISTRATION

▲ GOVERNMENT POSTER, WORLD WAR I

◄ GERMAN HELMET, EARLY 1900s

Portfolio Project

Create a map of Latin America indicating the affairs that involved the United States in the region from 1914 to 1932.

Global Perspectives

The World

		1910		1920	
Asia and Oceania					
Europe		**1914** *World War I begins*	**1919** *Treaty of Versailles signed* **1917** *Russian Revolution begins*	▲ **1922** *Mussolini and his Fascists march on Rome*	
Africa				◄ **1922** *Egypt becomes independent*	
South America					
North and Central America		**1912** *U.S. Marines land in Nicaragua*	**1916** *U.S. Marines land in Dominican Republic; Mexico warns U.S. not to invade*		

The United States

SPIRIT *of* 1917

JOIN THE
UNITED STATES MARINES
AND BE
FIRST IN DEFENSE ON LAND OR SEA
APPLY AT
24 East 23rd Street · · · · New York, N.Y.

		1910		1920	
Pacific and Northwest					
Southeast					
Midwest				◄ **1920** *Prohibition begins nationwide*	
Southwest					
Atlantic Northeast			◄ **1917** *U.S. declares war on Germany and Austria-Hungary*		

Linking Across TIME

While the great migration of Eastern Europeans to the United States came at the end of the 1800s, the first Eastern European immigrants arrived nearly 200 years before. John Smith, the leader of Jamestown, wanted to exploit the colony's pine trees for pitch and turpentine. So he sent to Poland, where the manufacturing of naval stores was well established, for skilled workers. The first Polish artisans arrived in 1608, probably as indentured servants. Colony records listed them as free members of the community some 11 years later.

1930 **1940**

▼ **1928** *Chiang Kai-shek and his Kuomintang army win control of China*

1930 *London Naval Agreement signed*

1935 *Pope Pius XI condemns Nazi atrocities*

1930 *Uruguay wins soccer's first World Cup*

1935 *Bolivia and Paraguay end three-year war*

1923 *Teapot Dome oil scandal erupts*

1925 *Scopes "Monkey" trial captures national attention*

1935 *Malcolm Campbell sets new land speed record of 301 mph*

1936 *Centennial of Texas Independence celebrated*

1929 *Stock market crashes, triggering the Great Depression*

▲ **1931** *Empire State Building opens*

1930 **1940**

CHAPTER 25

★★

World War I Era
1914–1920

▶ CONGRESSIONAL
MEDAL OF HONOR

Setting the Scene

Focus

When Europe went to war in 1914, the United States sought to stay out of the conflict. Both sides disregarded American neutrality. Germany's use of unrestricted submarine warfare and economic ties to Great Britain eventually led the United States into the bloody struggle. Mobilization called for many sacrifices by the American people. The Senate, however, rejected Wilson's proposed peace settlement, and wartime fervor led to intolerance.

Concepts to Understand

★ How conflict became evident in American society during and after World War I

★ How Wilson's idealism and American economic interests led to controversy over foreign policy

Read to Discover . . .

★ why the United States declared war on the German Empire in 1917.

★ why the United States did not join the League of Nations.

Journal Notes

What was the general attitude of the American people during World War I? Record your observations as you read the chapter.

CULTURAL

● **1915** *First transcontinental telephone is hooked up*

● **1917** *Temperance movement leads to prohibition laws in 29 states*

1914

1916

● **1914** *World War I begins when Austria-Hungary declares war on Serbia*

● **1916** *Germany agrees to restrict submarine warfare*
● **1917** *United States declares war on Germany*

POLITICAL

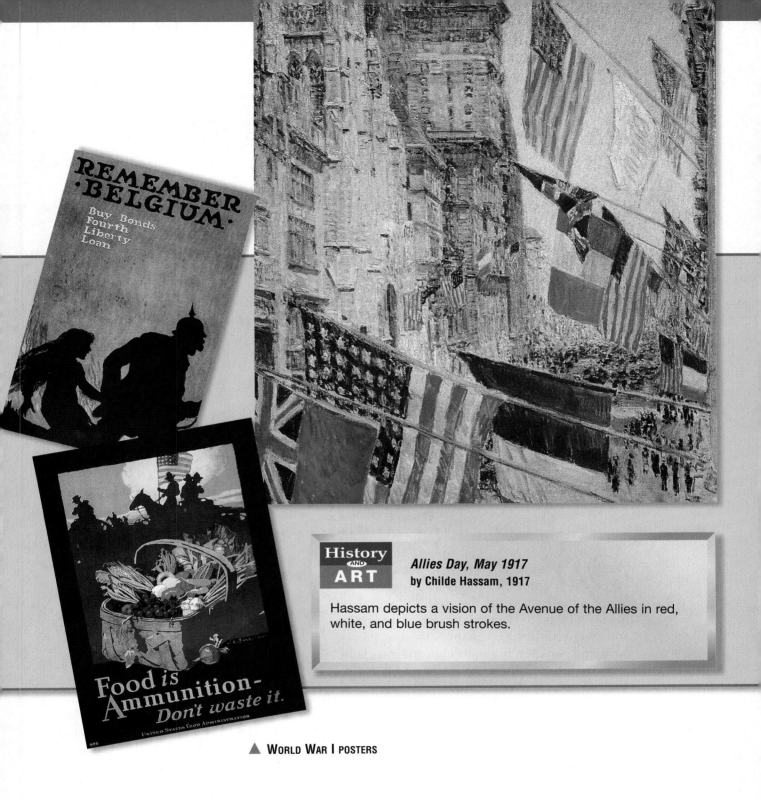

▲ WORLD WAR I POSTERS

• **1918** *Daylight saving time is first adopted*

1918

• **1918** *Wilson proclaims his Fourteen Points*

• **1919** *Sherwood Anderson publishes* Winesburg, Ohio

1920

• **1919** *Versailles peace conference is held*
• **1920** *Nineteenth Amendment is ratified*

★★★★★★★★★★★★★★★★★★★★★★★★★★★★★★

Prelude to War

Section Focus

On the day he took office, President Woodrow Wilson remarked to a friend that it would be an irony of fate if his administration had to deal mainly with foreign affairs. But Wilson's administration soon was confronted with difficult and complex foreign problems that involved the fate of the world.

Objectives

After studying this section, you should be able to

★ describe Wilson's foreign policy toward Latin American nations.

★ identify the causes of World War I.

★ explain why the United States had difficulty remaining neutral during the war.

Key Term

contraband

◄ *REVOLUTION* BY JOSÉ CLEMENTE OROZCO, 1920

President Wilson's focus on domestic issues was demonstrated in his first Inaugural Address in 1913. He was comfortable with and well-informed on matters such as the tariff and banking. But in foreign affairs neither Wilson nor those he counted on for advice were experienced.

■ Wilson's Moral Diplomacy

As President, Wilson resolved to "strike a new note in international affairs" and to see that "sheer honesty and even unselfishness . . . should prevail over nationalistic self-seeking in American foreign policy." However, other forces at work at home and abroad frustrated his hope to lead the world by moral example.

Political Unrest in Mexico

For nearly 30 years, Mexico had been ruled by a dictator, Porfirio Díaz (pawr•FEE•rih•oh DEE•AHS). He brought stability and encouraged foreign investment in Mexico's economic development. When Díaz was overthrown in 1911, Mexico entered a period of political chaos.

Francisco Madero (frahn•SEES•koh muh•DEHR•oh) came to power. Investors in Mexico feared that the new president would confiscate all property owned by foreigners. Businesspeople and foreign diplomats plotted with units of the Mexican army to overthrow Madero. Before Wilson took office, General Victoriano Huerta (veek•toh•ree•AH•noh WEHR•tuh) seized power, and Madero was murdered—presumably on Huerta's orders.

American capitalists supported Huerta in the belief that he would support business interests. Other countries with large Mexican investments recognized the new ruler. Repulsed by Huerta's brutality, Wilson refused to recognize the new government. He was convinced that without United States support "the unspeakable Huerta" would be overthrown.

Wilson Intervenes

Because Huerta remained in power, Wilson looked for a reason to intervene. In April 1914, American sailors on shore in the city of Tampico (tam•PEE•koh) clashed with Mexican authorities. Seeing a chance to overthrow Huerta, Wilson sent marines to seize the Mexican port of Veracruz (VEHR•uh•KROOZ). Although Wilson expected the Mexican people to welcome his action, anti-American riots broke out in Mexico and throughout Latin America. The President's intervention also was condemned in the European press.

Shocked by world reaction, Wilson accepted an offer from the ABC powers (Argentina, Brazil, and Chile) to mediate the dispute. The ABC powers supported Wilson by recommending that Huerta go into exile.

Venustiano Carranza (vay•noos•TYAH•noh kuh•RAN•zuh) was installed as Mexico's president.

Yet trouble continued between the United States and Mexico. Mexican forces opposed to Carranza conducted raids into the United States. Led by Pancho Villa (PAHN•choh VEE•yuh), guerrillas burned the town of Columbus, New Mexico, and killed 18 Americans. Wilson sent 6,000 troops under General John J. Pershing across the border to find and capture Villa. A year-long expedition failed to capture the guerrillas and resulted in a clash with the Mexican army. Tensions eased in January 1917 when Wilson's growing concern over the war in Europe caused him to recall the troops.

In the Caribbean

Wilson followed Roosevelt's example by ordering marines in Nicaragua, Haiti, and the Dominican Republic to preserve order and set up governments viewed by Americans as more stable than those in control. In 1917 the United States expanded its naval power in the Caribbean by purchasing Denmark's strategically valuable Virgin Islands.

Visualizing History

▲ **MARINES IN VERACRUZ** In April 1914 President Woodrow Wilson ordered American forces into Mexico to seize the port of Veracruz. *How did Latin American nations respond to American intervention?*

■ War in Europe

While Wilson was dealing with problems in Mexico and the Caribbean, Europe began one of the bloodiest wars in its history. After almost 50 years of general peace, tensions built up.

Setting the Stage for War

In the late 1800s, as Europe became industrialized and nations sought to establish empires, tensions arose among colonizing nations. Within Europe itself, nationalism also heightened rivalries and tension. Much of central and eastern Europe was ruled by empires that included several nationality groups, each with its own language. Many of these groups wanted to form independent nations by joining with similar groups in other nations. In Austria-Hungary, for example, Slavic groups resented being ruled by the Germans and Magyars (Hungarians). They wanted to join other Slavic peoples to form a South Slav, or Yugoslav, nation in the Balkans.

The Balkans were an area of Slavic peoples in southeastern Europe that for decades had been fought over by three major powers—Russia, Austria-Hungary, and the Ottoman Empire (Turkey and its provinces). In 1908 Austria-Hungary annexed two Balkan territories once ruled by the Turks, Bosnia and Herzegovina (HEHRT•suh•goh•VEE•nuh). Serbia, a Balkan nation on Austria-Hungary's border, called on Russia, its historic protector, for help. The Russians, weakened from their defeat by Japan in 1905 and wanting the Balkans for themselves, did nothing.

This instability and the complex rivalries led to an arms race as each country sought to defend itself. The arms race generated more mistrust and helped military leaders achieve more power and influence in European governments.

Formation of Alliances

The European nations made alliances with one another for mutual self-defense. The Triple Alliance drew together Germany, Austria-Hungary, and Italy. Fearing isolation

Visualizing History ▲ **PANCHO VILLA** Many Americans viewed Pancho Villa as nothing more than a bandit. To Mexico's poor, however, he was a democratic savior. *What action did Wilson take against Villa?*

in Europe, France and Russia agreed to help each other if either became involved in war with Germany or Austria-Hungary. France arranged a separate partnership with Great Britain known as the Entente Cordiale (AHN•TAHNT KAWR•DYAHL), meaning "cordial understanding." After Russia's defeat in 1905 reduced Britain's fear of Russian power, all three nations came together to form the Triple Entente.

War Begins

Tensions were high in June 1914, when Archduke Franz Ferdinand, heir to the throne of Austria-Hungary, visited Bosnia. His assassination by Slavic nationalist Gavrilo Princip provided the incident that ignited Europe into war. Austria-Hungary declared war on Serbia on July 28, 1914.

One month after the assassination, war exploded in Europe. To protect its status as a European power, Russia felt it had to defend Serbia. Believing that Germany would aid Austria-Hungary, Russian armies mobilized along the borders of both nations. Germany demanded that Russia halt its threatening acts and that France pledge neutrality in the event of a war between Russia and Germany. Both Russia and France rejected Germany's demands. On August 1 Germany declared war on Russia;

on August 3 it declared war on France. The German army crossed neutral Belgium on its way to invade France.

Responding to the invasion of Belgium, Great Britain declared war on Germany. Europe was divided into two camps. Those fighting for the Triple Entente were called the Allies. Italy (which switched sides in 1915) France, Russia, and Great Britain formed the backbone of the Allies. What remained of the Triple Alliance—Germany and Austria-Hungary—joined with the Ottoman Empire and Bulgaria to form the Central Powers.

■ United States Neutrality

As war consumed Europe, Americans hoped the vast Atlantic Ocean would keep them out of the conflict. President Wilson stated that this was "a war with which we had nothing to do."

Taking of Sides

Despite a neutral stance, America could not help but take sides. Immigrants of European nationality groups gave many Americans roots that influenced their opinions. Many of the 8 million German Americans were sympathetic to their homeland. Many Irish Americans, seething from British domination of Ireland, also hoped for a German victory. In general, however, the common heritage shared by the United States and Britain, and America's historic links with France, put American public opinion on the side of the Allies.

Both Sides Strain Neutrality

America's neutrality did not protect it from either the Allies or the Central Powers. The British imposed a blockade on the Central Powers. They planted mines in the North Sea, forced neutral ships into port for inspection, opened American mail, and redefined **contraband,** or prohibited materials, so that not even food could be shipped to Germany. Trade between the United States and the Central Powers shrank.

At the same time, exports from the United States to the Allies nearly quadrupled, as war materials and food from America helped the Allies. Ties between the United States and the Allies became closer when the United States government lent the Allies $2 billion. The American public purchased another $2 billion in British and French war bonds.

To retaliate against the British blockade, cut off Britain's war supplies, and starve Britain into submission, the Germans relied on a new weapon—the submarine. The "U-boat" broke long-established rules of warfare by sinking unarmed ships. International law required that unarmed ships not be sunk without providing for the safety of passengers and crews.

Visualizing History

▲ ASSASSINATION IN SARAJEVO The assassination of Archduke Ferdinand and his wife proved to be a fateful event. Within a month, the continent of Europe was ablaze with war. *How did the United States react to the start of war?*

▲ **WAR ON THE SEAS** United States neutrality was put to a test when German submarines attacked American vessels in the Atlantic. *Why were submarine attacks considered a barbaric act of war?*

In 1915 the British passenger liner *Lusitania* was sunk. Nearly 1,200 passengers drowned—including 128 Americans. Some Americans felt that this act was grounds for war. But others thought that people who traveled on ships of warring nations did so at their own risk, especially when Germany had taken out newspaper ads warning Americans not to travel on the *Lusitania.*

The Sussex Pledge

Wilson steered a middle course on the issue of the U-boats. He refused to take extreme measures against Germany. However, he sent several messages to Germany insisting that its government safeguard the lives of noncombatants in the war zones.

Late in March 1916, Wilson's policy was tested when a U-boat torpedoed the French passenger ship *Sussex,* injuring several Americans on board. Although Wilson's advisers favored breaking off relations with Germany, the President chose to issue a final warning. He demanded that the German government abandon submarine warfare or risk war with the United States. Germany did not want to strengthen the Allies by drawing the United States into the war. So it offered to compensate Americans injured on the *Sussex* and promised with certain conditions to sink no more merchant ships without warning. The Sussex Pledge, as it was called, met the foreign-policy goals of both Germany and the President by keeping the United States out of war a little longer.

Section 1 ★ Review

Checking for Understanding

1. **Identify** Victoriano Huerta, Pancho Villa, Austria-Hungary, Serbia, Triple Alliance, Triple Entente, *Lusitania,* U-boat.

2. **Define** contraband.

3. **Cite** two causes of World War I.

4. **Describe** two trends that made American neutrality difficult.

Critical Thinking

5. **Evaluating Tactics**   Can German U-boat attacks on the *Lusitania* and *Sussex* be justified? Explain your position.

Map and Graph Skills

Interpreting a Political Map

The ability to read and understand a map is a skill that may be applied in many areas and is useful in the study of history. There are many kinds of maps in use today. In this text, you have studied several different types: historical, physical, thematic, and political.

Historical maps show places and events from the past. Physical maps show natural features such as mountains, valleys, plains, and bodies of water. Thematic maps deal with specialized information, often on a single topic such as population density, land use, languages, and natural resources.

A political map shows the political boundaries or borders of a state, country, and/or region. Political maps change whenever political borders change. A political map of the world today looks very different from one only 10 years old.

Follow these procedures when you evaluate a political map:

- **Determine** the time period covered by the map. This may be given in the title, although some political maps supply the date in the copyright.
- **Read** the map title and scale.
- **Examine** the legend. What information, other than political boundaries, is provided by the map?
- **Analyze** the lines of latitude and longitude. These lines are constant—they do not change. Use them when you compare change in boundaries over time. Boundaries are usually represented by a solid dark line.

Practicing the Skill

Apply the information from the chapter and the guidelines shown as you analyze the map of Europe in 1914.

1. What countries shown on this map maintained neutrality during World War I?

2. How might location have influenced neutrality?

3. Explain this statement: In 1914 the borders of the United Kingdom were determined by geography, not just politics.

4. Compare the map on this page with the map of Europe on page 702. What became of Austria-Hungary?

5. Compare the two maps. What happened to Serbia?

6. Compare the two maps. Before World War I, Finland was part of what nation?

7. Compare the two maps. What became of the Baltic Provinces?

Europe in 1914

Allies
Central Powers
Neutral nations

0   250   500 miles
0 250 500 kilometers

★★

America Enters the War

Setting the Scene

Section Focus

In the presidential election of 1916, the Democrats again chose Woodrow Wilson as their candidate. This time the campaign focused on Wilson's diplomatic skills, using the slogan "He kept us out of the war." Americans, however, gave his policies a less-than-ringing endorsement. When the election votes were counted, Wilson won, but it was a very close race.

Objectives

After studying this section, you should be able to

★ identify the events that led the United States to enter World War I.

★ describe the role of the United States in helping the Allies to achieve victory over the Central Powers.

Key Term

armistice

◄ DISTINGUISHED SERVICE CROSS

*I*n 1916 Wilson ran for reelection on a peace ticket under the slogan "He kept us out of the war." Although Wilson never used the slogan himself, he emphasized that he had kept "peace with honor."

Wilson defeated the Republican candidate Charles Evans Hughes in a close election. Following his reelection, Wilson devoted his energies to finding a peaceful solution to the war. The President realized the only sure way to keep Americans out of the European conflict was to end this terrible war altogether.

A quick victory eluded both sides, as defensive weapons proved superior to offensive tactics. The war was especially gruesome. The use of poison gas and such other new weapons as the tank and the machine gun, along with enormous casualty lists, ended the optimism that had pervaded western Europe before the war.

■ "Peace Without Victory"

On December 18, 1916, Wilson asked the warring nations to state their peace terms. As a neutral party, he hoped to negotiate a settlement, but both sides responded with terms that their opponents would not accept. In spite of these replies, Wilson addressed the Senate on January 22, 1917, calling for "peace without victory." "A victor's peace," he argued, "would leave a sting, a resentment, a bitter memory upon which terms of peace would rest only as upon quicksand. Only a peace between equals can last."

Submarine Warfare Resumes

The Germans soon dashed Wilson's hope of mediating an end to the war. German losses on the battlefield and the shortages caused by the British blockade forced Germany to resume unrestricted submarine warfare. German naval commanders claimed they could starve Britain into submission in five months if the German government gave U-boats permission to sink ships on sight. The Germans felt that even if this violation of their Sussex Pledge drew the United States into the war, the Americans could not raise an army and transport it to Europe in time to prevent the Allies from collapsing. Therefore, Germany decided to risk American involvement and, on January 31, 1917, announced that all vessels in waters near Great Britain, France, and Italy would be sunk without warning.

On February 3, 1917, Wilson responded to this threat by breaking off diplomatic relations with Germany. When goods piled up in American ports because ships feared to sail, he asked Congress for the power to arm merchant ships. This measure passed the House of Representatives easily, but an 11-person filibuster blocked the bill on the Senate floor. The President refused to be stopped by the effort of this "little group of willful men." Finding the authority in a 1797 law, Wilson armed the merchant ships.

Drawn Into War

Meanwhile, other events caused the nation's antagonism toward Germany to mount. The British government revealed that it had intercepted a cable from the German foreign minister, Arthur Zimmermann, to the German ambassador in Mexico. Zimmermann instructed the ambassador to arrange an alliance between Mexico and Germany in the event that the United States entered the war. To encourage Mexico's cooperation, Germany promised that Mexico would regain Texas, Arizona, and New Mexico upon a German victory. American newspapers published the Zimmermann Note, outraging the public. Then, between March 12 and March 19, four American merchant ships were sunk without warning. Two days later Wilson called a special session of Congress to consider "grave questions of national policy."

On April 2, 1917, Wilson appeared before Congress with a heavy heart. In one of the most eloquent speeches ever delivered in the Capitol, the President asked the members of Congress to declare war on Germany:

▲ **PREPARING FOR WAR** Americans register for the draft. The World War I era produced this classic recruitment poster, which has been used ever since. *What events drew the United States into the war?*

▲ JOHN J. PERSHING

Visualizing History ▲ AMERICANS IN FRANCE General John J. Pershing (center), arriving in France at Boulogne in June 1917, commanded the American forces. ***What was the status of the conflict when the United States entered the war?***

" *It is a fearful thing to lead this great, peaceful people into war, into the most terrible and disastrous of all wars, civilization itself seeming to be in the balance. But the right is more precious than peace, and we shall fight for the things which we have always carried nearest our hearts—for democracy, for the right of . . . free peoples as shall bring peace and safety to all nations and make the world itself at last free. To such a task we dedicate our lives and our fortunes, everything we have. . . . [T]he day has come when America is privileged to spend her blood and her might for the principles that gave her birth and happiness and the peace which she has treasured. God helping her, she can do no other.* "

In his war message, the President insisted that the United States's quarrel was only with the "military masters" of Germany, and he expressed friendship for the German people. Maintaining that the United States had "no selfish ends to serve," Wilson stated that the people of the United States would be fighting to make the world "safe for democracy" and to promote "peace and safety to all nations." Four days after Wilson's message, Congress, after a spirited debate, declared war on Germany by the overwhelming margins of 82 votes to 6 in the Senate and 273 to 50 in the House.

■ Status of the Allies

When the United States entered the war, the Allies seemed in danger of defeat. U-boats were sinking ships at a rate that threatened to wipe out the entire merchant tonnage of the world; the British Isles had only a two-month supply of food with no relief in sight. Late in 1917 the Italians suffered a severe defeat at the village of Caporetto. Russia's military effort slackened and then ceased after the overthrow of the czar and the Bolshevik, or communist, revolution. In March 1918, Russia signed the Treaty of Brest-Litovsk, surrendering to Germany immense areas of land including Ukraine.

With one of the richest grain-growing areas in the world now in its possession, Germany hoped to relieve severe food shortages. Russia's withdrawal from the conflict also freed German armies to fight on the Western Front—the area along the French-German border where the war had been stalemated for nearly four years.

The World at War: World War I

Allies
Central Powers
Neutral nations
← **Allied offensive**
← **Central Powers offensive**
✶ **Sites of conflict**
✶ **Allied victory**
✶ **Central Powers victory**
✶ **Indecisive battles**

The Western Front

The Eastern Front

Map Study

Although most action in World War I occurred in Europe, it was truly a world conflict. Note the battles outside Europe, the intercontinental alliances, and Europe's division of Africa. **Why were so many battles fought in the Middle East?**

Doughboys

After Congress declared war, hundreds of thousands of Americans followed urgings such as "DON'T READ AMERICAN HISTORY, MAKE IT!" which appeared on a recruitment poster designed by James Montgomery Flagg, the leading poster artist of the war. Volunteers gave different reasons for joining the armed services. "Because girls like soldiers"

▶ SOLDIER, 1917

was a popular response; "to see the world" was another. Allied troops welcomed the Americans whose shipshape appearance—prior to entering the trenches—inspired the unique nickname "doughboys."

The war was more than the odor of the trenches; the agony of poison gas; and the trauma of violent tremors, which indicated battle shock. To relieve the monotony, soldiers organized musicals and variety shows, betting pools, and holiday celebrations.

Inter-Allied boxing matches and baseball provided additional diversion. Military experience proved a turning point in the lives and attitudes of many young men. For some, the war was the greatest adventure of their lives.

▼ THE ROCK OF THE MARNE BY MAL THOMPSON

Among the doughboys who never lost touch with his wartime friends was Harry Truman, who chose several buddies from Battery D to advise him when he became President in 1945.

■ Raising an Army

The Allies did not expect the United States to participate in combat because in the spring of 1917 American forces numbered only 200,000. In addition, the army possessed only 1,500 machine guns, 55 obsolete airplanes, and no heavy artillery.

The Draft

Although these numbers looked discouraging, the United States mobilized rapidly. On May 18, 1917, Congress passed the Selective Service Act, requiring all men between the ages of 21 and 30 to register for military service. In June nearly 10 million young men signed up. The draft eventually extended to all men between 18 and 45 and resulted in the induction of 2.8 million men into the armed forces. Another 2 million men and women volunteered for military service.

Twelve weeks after war had been declared, the first United States soldiers landed in France. On July 4, symbolically recalling the American-French partnership during the American Revolution, Colonel Charles E. Stanton stood at the tomb of France's great war hero, Marquis de Lafayette, and said, "Lafayette, we are here." More than 2 million American soldiers comprising 42 infantry divisions reached France before the war ended. This vast new reservoir of military strength was an important factor in the Allied victory.

African Americans

Among those drafted to serve in the war were some 370,000 African Americans; of these, 200,000 served overseas. African American soldiers encountered rampant discrimination and prejudice in the army, where their units were completely segregated from white units. In addition, African Americans were not allowed to serve in the Marine Corps, and the 10,000 in the navy were restricted to the lower ranks.

Still, in the bitter battles along the Western Front, African American soldiers fought valiantly, winning praise from both the French commander, Marshal Henri Pétain (ahn•REE pay•TAN), and the United States commander, General John Pershing. African American soldiers in one infantry regiment won 21 American Distinguished Service Crosses and 68 French military decorations. The entire 369th Infantry won the highly prized French decoration, the Croix de Guerre (KRWAH dih GEHR), for gallantry.

Victory on Land and Sea

In the spring and early summer of 1918, Germany made a last desperate effort to win the war and nearly succeeded. Starting in March, the Germans almost penetrated the British lines; a second drive in June threatened Paris. United States troops helped to stop the advance, distinguishing themselves in a counterattack at Château-Thierry (SHA•TOH TYEH•REE), a town less than 50 miles from Paris.

The tide turned in mid-July as Marshal Ferdinand Foch (FAWSH), supreme commander of the Allied armies, ordered a great counteroffensive along the Western Front close to the German border. Pershing requested that American troops be assigned a section of the front for themselves—an area near Verdun. In mid-September 550,000 "doughboys"—the nickname given American soldiers—won an overwhelming victory at St.-Mihiel (san mee•yehl). Then an even larger force drove toward the key city of Sedan, breaking through well-defended portions of the German lines.

By early November, the Allies were poised to advance onto German soil. Realizing the war was lost, the Germans signed an **armistice,** or temporary stop to the fighting, on November 11, 1918.

American naval forces joined the British in waging war against Germany's deadly U-boats. The invention of the depth charge, an underwater explosive, provided the Allies with a new weapon, but its effective use demanded hundreds of patrol vessels to watch for U-boats and protect Allied ships by convoying, or escorting, them out of dangerous areas. So, in addition to 79 destroyers, the United States supplied more than 100 small "sub-chasers" plus a variety of former yachts, tugs, and fishing boats—"almost any craft which could carry a wireless, a gun, and depth charges was boldly sent to sea." By the end of 1917, the number of U-boat casualties was slashed in half. In 1918 the United States Navy took the principal role in laying mines across the North Sea, which prevented U-boats from reaching the Atlantic Ocean and isolated those already at sea from ports and supplies.

◀ WORLD WAR I SHELL

Section 2 ★ Review

Checking for Understanding

1. **Identify** Zimmermann Note, Selective Service Act, John Pershing, doughboys.

2. **Define** armistice.

3. **Explain** the meaning of the phrases "peace without victory" and "Lafayette, we are here."

4. **Summarize** the events that brought the United States into the war.

Critical Thinking

5. **Assessing Outcomes** Would Germany have won if the United States had not entered the war? Explain your position.

★★★

War on the Home Front

Setting the Scene

Section Focus

In order to raise and equip vast armies, increase the size of the navy elevenfold, and keep munitions and food flowing to the Allies, massive reorganization of American business, industry, and agriculture was needed. Victory in World War I was due, in large part, to the great efforts and sacrifices made on the home front.

Objectives

After studying this section, you should be able to

★ explain how the war was financed.

★ describe how public opinion was shaped by the government.

★ discuss the goals of Wilson's Fourteen Points.

Key Term

victory garden

Save a loaf a week - - Help win the war

▲ **WORLD WAR I POSTER, 1918**

---

he United States found itself ill-equipped for battle when it entered World War I. The most immediate domestic concern that Congress faced was to keep the United States and Allied armies supplied by gearing United States industry to the war machine. In addition, the federal government needed to raise money to pay for the war and to mobilize the American people to support the war effort.

■ Mobilizing the Economy

To accomplish these goals, Wilson and Congress applied the Progressive Era's ideals of efficiency, control, and conformity in society to the war effort at home. "It is not an army that we must shape and train for war," said the President, "it is a nation."

Organizing Industries

The government's solution to the problem of supplying the troops was to place most industries under the control of federal agencies. The most important of these—the War Industries Board—handled purchasing for both the Allies and the United States. Under the leadership of Bernard Baruch, a Wall Street stockbroker, the War Industries Board attempted "to operate the whole United States as a single factory dominated by one management." Enlisting the most able businesspeople in America to direct the war effort, the government received the cooperation of business to convert factories to war production. Federal officials determined how raw materials would be allocated and what prices should be fixed.

The Fuel Administration was in charge of boosting coal and oil production, while encouraging people to conserve. The agency introduced such conservation methods as daylight savings time and shortened workweeks for nonwar-related factories. The Railroad Administration took charge of the railroads and ran them as a single system. The War Labor Board worked to prevent labor disputes.

Labor unions generally supported the war effort, hoping that cooperation would result in goodwill from the government and big business. Union leaders saw in the war opportunities for higher pay, better working conditions, and the right to organize and bargain collectively. Membership in unions doubled, and unions won concessions, such as the eight-hour day that industries had long opposed.

Involvement of Women

Wartime also meant increased opportunities for American women. Millions of jobs given up by men who volunteered or were drafted were filled by women. For the first time, women were welcomed in many occupations. Female workers became an essential part of the nation's war effort in war industries and defense plants.

Despite the progress toward social and economic equality the war offered them, many women wondered how the United States could be fighting to save democracy and still deny them the vote at home. Activists for woman suffrage continued to work during the war.

Involvement of African Americans

African Americans might well have asked similar questions because Southern states continued to deny them the right to vote. Also, African American soldiers fighting in Europe encountered far less discrimination from Europeans than they had experienced in their own country.

Nevertheless, the war offered new opportunities for African Americans at home. Job opportunities and high wages during the

▲ AT HOME During the war more and more women became a vital part of the labor force. In addition, women volunteered for noncombat duty on the war front or for a military Home Guard in the United States. *What happened to the suffrage movement during the war?*

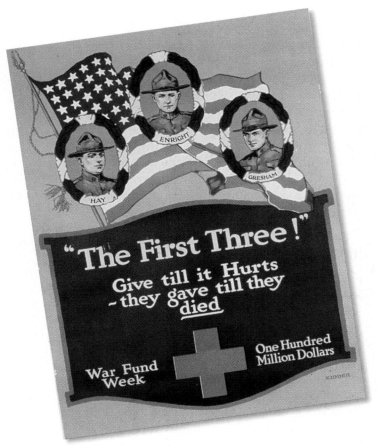

▲ **POSTER SUPPORTING BONDS**

Impact of War on Civilians

The war had a great impact on the lives of all American civilians. Using the slogan "Food Will Win the War—Don't Waste It," the Food Administration, directed by Herbert Hoover, supervised efforts to reduce food consumption. Families were encouraged to "Hooverize" by "serving just enough" and by having Wheatless Mondays and Meatless Tuesdays.

Citizens were also encouraged to plant **victory gardens,** gardens for raising their own vegetables. To increase wheat production, the federally financed Grain Corporation guaranteed farmers first $2.00, then $2.26 per bushel. In 1918 it bought the entire American wheat crop. The combined efforts of the Food Administration and the American public were tremendously successful.

The Cost of War

World War I was costly. By its end the United States was spending about $44 million a day, or a total of about $33 billion. Of that amount, $10 billion went to the Allies as loans. The government raised about one-third of the money to finance the war through taxation. Income taxes were increased, although only wealthier families paid income taxes at that time. Corporations also paid higher taxes, including an "excess profits" tax, designed to return war profits to the government. The government also levied excise duties on items as varied as theater tickets, chewing gum, and phonograph records.

The government borrowed the rest of the money—more than $20 billion—from the American people by selling four issues of Liberty Bonds and a postwar issue of Victory Bonds. Posters, rallies, and "Liberty Loan sermons" encouraged people to buy the bonds.

Purchasing bonds became an act of patriotism. Even children were urged to use their pennies to buy War Savings Stamps. Boy Scouts sold the stamps under the slogan "Every Scout to Save a Soldier." Twenty-one million people—more than one-fifth of the nation's population—subscribed to the Fourth Liberty Loan.

war pulled 500,000 African Americans from Southern farms to munitions-producing Northern factories. Most were offered only unskilled or semiskilled jobs, but by war's end, more than 100,000 African Americans held jobs as skilled workers or factory supervisors.

Although discrimination against African American workers led to race riots in 26 Northern cities in 1919, African Americans in the North made significant economic gains during the war. As a result, migration northward continued after the war ended. One African American wrote a letter to a Chicago newspaper explaining this "great migration." African Americans, he said, were:

> ❝ . . . compelled to go where there is better wages and sociable conditions, believe me . . . many places here in [Alabama] the only thing that a black man gets is a peck of meal and from 3 to 4 lbs. of bacon per week, and he is treated as a slave. ❞

Controlling Public Opinion

Success of the war effort depended heavily on voluntary civilian cooperation. Therefore, the government wanted to make sure that Americans understood and supported the nation's war aims.

Selling the War to Americans

The Committee on Public Information under the leadership of journalist and author George Creel was established to "sell" the war to America. Creel described his job as "the world's greatest adventure in advertising." He recruited advertising people, commercial artists, authors, songwriters, entertainers, public speakers, and motion-picture companies to help him.

Millions of pamphlets were distributed explaining the causes and aims of the war. Thousands of "four-minute men" spoke at movie theaters and public halls and gatherings in support of the war effort. Although this flood of propaganda reinforced the President's image of the war as a moral crusade, it also helped promote widespread intolerance.

Control of War Protesters

To prevent spying and resistance to the war effort, Congress passed the Espionage and Sedition acts. Severe penalties imposed by these laws silenced most war opposition. Loyalty Leagues, organized by Creel, encouraged Americans to spy on their neighbors and to report those who might be "disloyal." In addition, the postmaster general was given authority to ban certain newspapers, magazines, and pamphlets from the mail. Thousands of people were imprisoned, sometimes for opinions expressed in private conversations. People were arrested for criticizing the President, for questioning the American form of government, for criticizing the army or even military uniforms. Socialist leader Eugene Debs was arrested and sentenced to 10 years in prison for merely telling an audience to "resist militarism, wherever found." People were even jailed for criticizing the Red Cross and the YMCA.

War fever was responsible for the vigorous enforcement of these laws, and the courts generally upheld the principle behind them. About 3,000 cases involving convictions under the Espionage and Sedition acts were heard on appeal in federal courts. After the war some of these cases

George M. Cohan
1878–1942

★★★★★★★★★★★★ AMERICAN PORTRAITS

By the time he wrote "Over There"—the most popular song of World War I—George M. Cohan was already one of America's biggest stars. At the age of 14, he was creating songs and skits for his family's vaudeville act. By his early 20s, he was writing, producing, and starring in hit Broadway shows.

Claiming that he had been born on the 4th of July (actually July 3), Cohan discovered early in his career that he could excite crowds with such patriotic appeals as his "I'm a Yankee Doodle Dandy."

When American troops left for France in 1917, he quickly penned "Over There," touching the chord of nationalistic fervor sweeping the country. His song became America's war anthem. In 1940 Congress awarded Cohan a Medal of Honor for "Over There" and "You're a Grand Old Flag," another patriotic song.

reached the Supreme Court. In the land-mark case *Schenck* v. *United States* (1919), Justice Oliver Wendell Holmes, writing for a unanimous Court, stated:

> **When a nation is at war, many things that might be said in time of peace are such a hindrance to its efforts that their utterance will not be endured so long as [soldiers] fight and that no Court could regard them as protected by any constitutional right. . . .**

The Court refused, however, to support punishment when no "clear and present danger" of hurting the United States existed or when the accused was jailed for unpopular political beliefs.

Persecution of Germans

War fever was also to blame for the mistreatment and persecution of German Americans. Despite Wilson's insistence that Americans were "the sincere friends of the German people," anti-German sentiment ran high. Many school systems banned the teaching of the German language, and orchestras stopped performing the music of Beethoven, Schubert, and Wagner.

■ Wilson's Fourteen Points

While the war was foremost in the President's mind, Wilson never ceased to think ahead to peace. In January 1918, Wilson went before Congress to present his goals

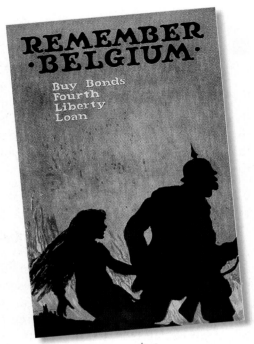

▲ **LIBERTY LOAN POSTER**

for a lasting peace. With his Fourteen Points (see Appendix), the President hoped to establish a new world order.

The Fourteen Points were based on "the principle of justice to all peoples." The President proposed to eliminate the general causes of war through disarmament, freedom of the seas, and open diplomacy instead of secret agreements. Wilson also addressed the right of peoples to live under a government of their own choosing. Finally, he proposed an international peacekeeping organization.

Although Wilson's words appealed to a world weary of war, other Allied leaders did not support him. They wanted German territory and to punish Germany. A formidable challenge lay ahead for the President if he were to see his dream of peace realized.

Section 3 ★ Review

Checking for Understanding

1. **Identify** Bernard Baruch, George Creel, War Industries Board, Liberty Bonds, Espionage and Sedition acts, Fourteen Points.

2. **Define** victory garden.

3. **Describe** three ways that Americans at home supported the war effort.

4. **List** the two ways the government raised money for the war.

Critical Thinking

5. **Defending an Opinion** Was government action to suppress opposition to the war justified? Formulate your own opinion and use facts to defend it.

★★★★★★★★★★★★★★★★★★★★★★★★★★★★

After the War

Setting the Scene

Section Focus

As Kaiser Wilhelm abdicated the German throne and fled, Germany signed an armistice. Now the Allies faced the task of constructing a framework for peace. Wilson still had support at home and enjoyed great popularity abroad. The opportunity to carry out his peace plan seemed at hand. However, his political blunders and the demands of Allied leaders doomed his chances.

Objectives

After studying this section, you should be able to

★ describe the outcome of the Versailles peace conference.

★ explain why the Senate rejected the Treaty of Versailles.

★ identify domestic problems that arose after the war.

Key Terms

covenant, deported

◀ **WORLD WAR I** HELMET

Midterm elections in the United States in November 1918 showed a changing attitude toward Wilson and his policies. Realizing that Democrats faced heavy losses in the elections, the President appealed to voters to show support for his peace program by returning Democrats to Congress. Instead, voters elected Republican majorities in both houses.

■ The Peace Plan Opposed

Shortly after the election, Wilson announced his intention to head the American delegation to the peace conference. His decision was not received well by those who thought that as President his place was at home. Wilson faltered again when he failed to include any prominent Republicans in the American delegation to the conference.

Peace Conference

The peace conference opened at the palace of Versailles in January 1919, but most of the sessions took place in Paris. Delegates from 27 nations attended. The proceedings, however, were dominated by the leaders of the three most powerful nations—the United States's President Wilson, Britain's Prime Minister David Lloyd George, and France's Premier Georges Clemenceau (KLEH•muhn•SOH). With Vittorio Orlando, the Italian premier, these men became known as "the Big Four." Because their meetings were held in secret, Wilson was robbed of an effective weapon—direct appeal to public opinion. Secrecy also seemed to violate the Fourteen Points, which pledged "open covenants openly arrived at." Nevertheless, the President scored an immediate triumph by forcing plans for a League of Nations into the

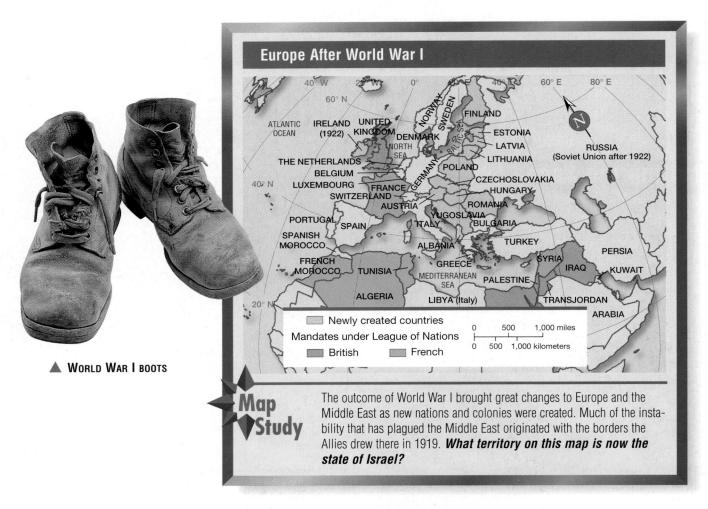

Europe After World War I

Newly created countries
Mandates under League of Nations
British
French

0   500   1,000 miles
0   500   1,000 kilometers

Map Study

The outcome of World War I brought great changes to Europe and the Middle East as new nations and colonies were created. Much of the instability that has plagued the Middle East originated with the borders the Allies drew there in 1919. ***What territory on this map is now the state of Israel?***

▲ **WORLD WAR I BOOTS**

peace treaty. In mid-February the **covenant,** or charter, of the League, written by Wilson himself, was accepted by the conference.

Opposition Grows

During Wilson's absence his political influence in the United States weakened alarmingly. The likelihood that Wilson's peace program would fail became evident when 39 Republican senators and senators-elect—far more than enough to prevent ratification of a treaty—signed a statement opposing the League of Nations. Instead of trying to repair the rift, however, Wilson publicly denounced the "narrow, selfish, provincial purposes" of his opponents and insisted that the League be part of the peace treaty. At the peace table, he tried to appease his critics at home by calling for changes designed to protect American interests. To accept such changes, the Allies required Wilson to make further concessions in their favor.

Treaty of Versailles

Despite Wilson's hopes, it was a victor's peace. In the Middle East, the Ottoman Empire lost territory. In Europe, Austria-Hungary was split up. The greatest humiliation was reserved for the Germans, however. Germany lost territory and was stripped of its colonies. In addition, Germany was required to pay for damage it had done in Europe and to repay the Allies for the cost of the war. Although many of the Fourteen Points were ignored, Wilson trusted the League of Nations to right injustices after the desire for revenge subsided.

Difficulty at Home

The peace settlement complete, in July 1919 President Wilson came home to face his foes. Although he hoped Americans would support the treaty, they criticized it from all sides. In Congress a small group of senators branded the League a "treacherous and treasonable scheme," while a much larger group wanted the Senate to ratify the treaty but with amendments that would preserve the nation's freedom to act independently.

Instead of compromising, Wilson insisted that the Senate ratify the treaty without changes. Convinced that he could defeat his opposition by appealing to public opinion, Wilson went directly to the people. Starting in Ohio in September, he traveled 8,000 miles and made 37 major speeches in less than a month on behalf of the treaty. Almost everywhere his reception was warm; he seemed to be regaining popular support. Had his strength held out, he might have won the battle, but the physical strain proved too great for the President. He collapsed in Colorado on September 25 and was forced to abandon his speaking tour. Shortly after returning to the White House, Wilson suffered a stroke that paralyzed one side of his body and impaired his speech. He was bedridden for months, isolated from even his closest advisers.

With the President silenced, in November 1919, and again in March 1920, the Senate refused to ratify the Versailles treaty. Instead, the United States negotiated a separate peace treaty with each of the Central Powers in 1921.

■ America's Postwar Problems

The fate of the treaty was only one of the problems the United States faced after World War I. Demobilizing the armed forces, returning to a peacetime economy, and coping with fears of espionage presented the country with serious challenges.

Demobilization

The United States began to demobilize as soon as the hostilities ended. Within a short time, the army was reduced to less than 500,000, and economic controls were lifted. The businesspeople left Washington, D.C.,

and industry converted to peacetime production. With Wilson preoccupied with the peace treaty and later incapacitated, the nation received little overall direction. Industry enjoyed a brief postwar boom, resulting from the increased demand for consumer goods that had been scarce during the war. Unfortunately, government spending during the war brought inflation that nearly doubled the cost of living by 1919, and prices rose to a point where many consumers could not afford to pay for new items. Consequently, after 1920 business activity slowed. Farmers were especially hard-hit. Slackening demands for food and the end of government price guarantees caused agricultural prices to plummet. Many farmers who took advantage of high wartime crop prices and went into debt to expand their farms now faced bankruptcy.

▲ *SIGNING OF THE TREATY OF VERSAILLES* by John Johansen, 1919 The greatest obstacle at the peace conference was that many countries were interested chiefly in gaining territory and inflicting punishment on Germany. *Who played major roles in treaty negotiations?*

Visualizing
History

▲ ANTI-IMMIGRANT SENTIMENT A 1920 cartoon shows immigrants taking jobs from Americans. *How did many Americans view labor leaders?*

Labor Unrest

High prices also contributed to labor unrest after the war, and when the War Labor Board disbanded, the truce between employers and organized labor ended. A record number—3,600—strikes occurred in 1919, most meeting with little success. Four of them—the Seattle general strike, the Boston police strike, the steel strike, and the coal strike—were highly disruptive and had effects that lasted well into the 1920s.

In January 1919, only 2 months after the armistice, 35,000 shipyard workers from Seattle, Washington, went on strike to gain an increase in their wages. The next month union workers in all Seattle industries walked off their jobs in support of the shipyard strikers. Many city residents viewed the strike as revolutionary. They responded by hoarding food and fuel and by purchasing guns. Seattle's mayor blamed the situation on dangerous radicals and after 5 days used the state militia to break the strike.

In September 1919, another major city was hit by labor unrest as Boston's police force went on strike for better wages and working conditions. Looters soon were in the streets, smashing windows and stealing goods. When the mayor was unable to restore order, Massachusetts governor Calvin Coolidge

called out the state guard. A new police force was hired, and Coolidge received national acclaim for his view that "There is no right to strike against the public safety by anybody, anywhere, anytime."

Later that month more than 350,000 steelworkers went on strike across the nation, demanding better wages, an 8-hour rather than a 12-hour day, and the right to join a union. Two-thirds of the strikers were immigrants. Most of the office workers and supervisors who refused to join the strike were American-born. The companies blamed the strike on radicals who told "these foreigners . . . that if they would join the union they would get Americans' jobs." When the companies hired replacement workers, violence broke out, and federal troops were called in to protect them. After 4 months, the strikers gave up with no gains.

While the steel strike was underway, 450,000 coal miners walked off their jobs nationwide. Overworked and underpaid, the strikers demanded a 60 percent pay increase and a 30-hour week. Since at the time coal was the nation's major energy source, the government responded quickly. Obtaining a court order, it forced the strikers back to work. Eventually, however, coal miners won a large pay increase to an average of $7.50 a day.

Red Scare

Many Americans had long suspected a link between labor unrest and political radicalism. The strikes of 1919 helped fuel a larger "Red Scare" than the United States experienced after the war. When the Bolsheviks seized power in Russia in 1917, they called on workers everywhere to revolt. In 1919 communism seemed to have great appeal among the poverty-stricken peoples of war-torn Europe. Although the overwhelming majority of American labor leaders were not allied with the Communists, nevertheless, many Americans suspected them of planning revolution.

The same laws used to quiet opposition and suppress civil liberties during the war were now turned against radicals. Immigrants—especially those with Russian names—came under suspicion. Attorney General A. Mitchell Palmer rounded up 6,000 immigrants that the government suspected of being Communists and **deported**—expelled from the country—nearly 600 of them. Some of the immigrants deported had become American citizens, and some were deported without trials.

Racial Tension

Accompanying the Red Scare was a wave of racism. Racial tensions rose as white soldiers returning from Europe found themselves competing for jobs and housing with African Americans who had come north during the war. During the summer of 1919, race riots broke out in many Northern cities. The worst was in Chicago, where nearly 40 people were killed and more than 500 injured. One journalist described the scene:

“ *During this wild week mobs of whites pursued and beat and killed [African Americans]. Other mobs of [African Americans] pursued and beat and killed whites. . . . Armed bands in motor trucks dashed wildly up and down the streets, firing into houses. . . .* ”

Few cities in the United States escaped racial violence in the early 1920s. Even after the Red Scare died down, racial intolerance lived on in organizations such as the Ku Klux Klan, which spread from the South to become a powerful national force.

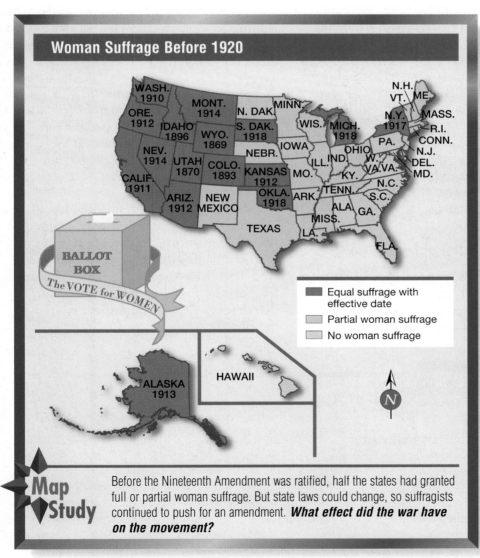

Woman Suffrage Before 1920

Equal suffrage with effective date
Partial woman suffrage
No woman suffrage

Map Study

Before the Nineteenth Amendment was ratified, half the states had granted full or partial woman suffrage. But state laws could change, so suffragists continued to push for an amendment. *What effect did the war have on the movement?*

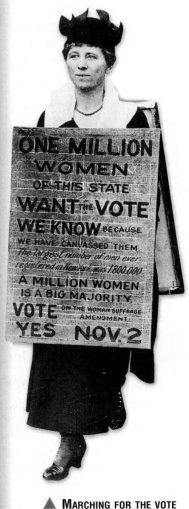

▲ MARCHING FOR THE VOTE

■ Wilson's Legacy

Despite a lack of presidential leadership as Wilson's second term drew to a close, Congress and the states implemented important laws. However, Congress would not approve joining the League of Nations.

In 1920 Congress passed the Esch-Cummins Act, which turned the operation of railroads back to their owners. This statute gave the Interstate Commerce Commission almost complete power to fix rates as well as to regulate railroad financing, but the commission was now less concerned with restraining railroad companies than it was with helping them.

Prohibition

World War I helped to add two amendments to the Constitution—both the culmination of century-old reform movements. Prohibition, which had made great gains before the war began, made even greater advances during the war. "Hooverizing" put American citizens in the mood to sacrifice, and war needs compelled the federal government to forbid the use of grain to manufacture liquor. By January 1919, two-thirds of the states had ratified the Eighteenth Amendment, which prohibited "the manufacture, sale, or transportation" of intoxicating beverages.

The Nineteenth Amendment

The war also advanced the cause of woman's rights. It was difficult to deny demands that women be allowed to vote after they had performed traditionally male jobs in factories and fields and served with courage and devotion behind the lines in Europe. On the eve of the 1920 presidential election, after decades of struggle, women gained suffrage when the Nineteenth Amendment was ratified.

A Warning

Wilson's final year and a half in office left the country virtually leaderless. The President had recovered sufficiently to transact routine business, but his energies still were focused on getting the United States into the League of Nations. Retaining a belief that the American people would not retreat from world leadership, he urged that the election of 1920 be a "great and solemn referendum" on the League issue.

The 1920 election saw Wilson's party and the League repudiated at the polls. The country wanted to turn its back to world responsibilities. In 1923, shortly before he died, Wilson warned:

> ❝ *I can predict with absolute certainty that within another generation there will be another world war if the nations of the world do not concert the method by which to prevent it.* ❞

Few people listened to Wilson's warning, however. Most Americans wanted to put their memories of war, suffering, and sacrifice behind them. The war to end all wars was over. The United States had done its part in making the world "safe for democracy." It was time to start enjoying the peace.

Section 4 ★ Review

Checking for Understanding

1. **Identify** Treaty of Versailles, League of Nations, Eighteenth Amendment, Nineteenth Amendment.

2. **Define** covenant, deported.

3. **List** the provisions of the Versailles treaty.

4. **Describe** the economic problems of the United States after the war.

Critical Thinking

5. **Analyzing Motives** Explain why "peace without victory" was so difficult to achieve at Versailles.

Changing the Map of Europe

Part of President Wilson's peace program following World War I called for self-determination of nations. Before the war Europe was a complex mosaic, or pattern, of distinct ethnic groups. Many of these groups lived within the borders of nations dominated by other ethnic groups. Wilson believed that national boundaries should be drawn to give each ethnic population its own nation.

Other powers at the Versailles peace conference, however, had their own plans. Allied leaders wanted to weaken the Central Powers by dividing their land. Some Allies also wanted their enemies' territory for themselves.

Germany's land area was greatly reduced. Germany's colonies were given over to the Allies as mandates, territories ruled by the Allies with the approval of the League of Nations. Alsace and Lorraine were returned to France. The French also received control of the coal-rich Saar Basin for 15 years.

The Allies signed individual peace treaties with other nations, most of them centering on territorial topics that focused on partitioning the Austro-Hungarian Empire. With the end of the Hapsburg dynasty, Hungary became independent, and Austria was left a small, economically weak country.

From the ashes of the old Russian and Austro-Hungarian empires, new nations emerged in eastern Europe. Among these countries were Finland, Estonia, Lithuania, Latvia, Poland, Czechoslovakia, and Yugoslavia.

▲ THE BIG FOUR, DECEMBER 1918

Wilson's secretary of state, Robert Lansing, noted that the boundaries created after the war were artificial and did not follow ethnic population patterns. Lansing stated that they would last only as long as dissatisfied nations were too weak to change them. He believed that when one nation became confident of its strength and began to seek to remedy these boundaries, a new war would take place. Twenty years later that became the case.

Making the Geography Connection

1. How did Wilson think national boundaries should be determined in Europe after World War I?

Linking Past and Present

2. How did the desire for autonomy among ethnic groups affect the Soviet Union in the 1990s?

Using Vocabulary

Imagine that you have kept a diary of events of World War I. Write headlines of three diary entries using each of the following terms in a headline.

covenant   deported

contraband   victory garden

armistice

Reviewing Facts

1. **Discuss** Wilson's foreign-policy views and how they related to his actions in Latin America.

2. **State** how nationalism and alliances created the conditions that led to World War I.

3. **Identify** two reasons the United States declared war on Germany.

4. **Cite** changes in economic and political policies that were imposed in the United States during World War I.

5. **List** two actions taken by the American military that helped win the war.

6. **Describe** the terms of the Versailles treaty.

7. **Explain** why Wilson was frustrated with Congress after the war.

8. **Summarize** the social difficulties confronting the United States after the war.

Understanding Concepts

Conflict

1. Identify the two types of nationalism that existed in Europe and explain why each was a factor in causing World War I.

2. Explain how Wilson's ideals influenced his actions and made compromise difficult.

Interests

3. Explain how economic and political interests in the United States were factors in its inability to remain neutral in World War I.

4. Analyze how competing interests made the adoption of Wilson's Fourteen Points difficult.

Critical Thinking

1. **Evaluating Foreign Policy** Consider the United States's neutrality policy before entering the war. Evaluate the feasibility of this policy. Consider the events that forced the United States to abandon neutrality and enter the war.

2. **Expressing Viewpoints** During World War I the government worked to control public attitudes about the war. In your opinion, was it necessary for the government to take such actions? Explain your viewpoint.

3. **Analyzing Fine Art** Study the mural by José Clemente Orozco entitled *Revolutionists* on this page, then answer the questions that follow.

   a. What themes are illustrated?

   b. What was happening in Mexico in the early 1900s that may have inspired this work?

   c. Why would a wall mural be a good way to spread a message?

Writing About History

Comparison

Write an essay to compare Woodrow Wilson's ideals with the realities he faced in the world of politics. Before you begin writing, make two lists. In one, list Wilson's foreign-policy goals. In the other, enumerate his actions. Use these lists to help you plan and write your essay.

Cooperative Learning

Work with a partner to write two newspaper editorials on the United States government's methods of controlling public opinion during World War I—one supporting the government's policies and the other opposing them. Before writing, collaborate on a list of pros and cons about the government's activities, including the Espionage and Sedition acts and the Committee on Public Information. Then each of you should take opposite positions and write an editorial. When you have finished, exchange your editorials. After reading your partner's work, write a "letter to the editor" as a rebuttal to his or her position.

Social Studies Skills

Analyzing Graphic Data

To successfully analyze complex information, you must first break it into smaller parts that you can examine more easily. By analyzing the information presented in the bar graph on this page, you can obtain a clearer understanding of American military support for its Allies in Europe.

The graph provides information about the United States Army between April 1917 and November 1918. In analyzing its detail you can see that one set of bars shows the growth in total size of the American army from the time the United States entered the war until the armistice was signed. The other set of bars shows how many of those troops were sent to fight in Europe.

Practicing the Skill

Use your analysis of the graph in answering the following questions to better understand American involvement in the war:

1. When the United States declared war, fewer than 250,000 soldiers were ready to fight. When was the first month that the United States had 1 million troops in the army? By what month were there 1 million American soldiers in Europe?

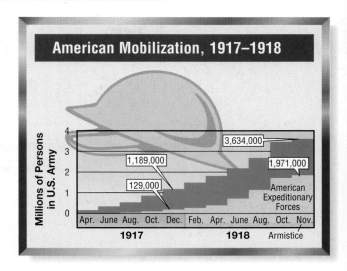

American Mobilization, 1917–1918

Millions of Persons in U.S. Army

3,634,000
1,189,000
1,971,000
129,000
American Expeditionary Forces

Apr. June Aug. Oct. Dec. Feb. Apr. June Aug. Oct. Nov.
1917 **1918** Armistice

2. Between what months was there the greatest increase in the size of the American army?

3. About what percentage of the United States Army was in Europe by the end of 1917? By the armistice a year later?

4. After reading about America's mobilization to fight the war in the chapter, what information does this graph provide about the efficiency of that effort?

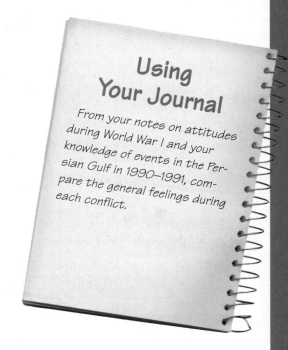

Using Your Journal

From your notes on attitudes during World War I and your knowledge of events in the Persian Gulf in 1990–1991, compare the general feelings during each conflict.

CHAPTER 26

★★

The Decade of Normalcy
1920–1928

▶ THE CLOCHE, POPULAR WOMAN'S HAT OF THE 1920S

Setting the Scene

Focus

The decade that followed World War I differed considerably from the Progressive years that came before it. Voters turned to conservative leaders who promised to turn the country away from European affairs and inward to "normalcy." For many Americans this shift meant preserving the values of rural America and enjoying prosperity. For others it meant a fascination with a dazzling new assortment of consumer goods, entertainment, and changing fashions.

Concepts to Understand

★ Why shifts in government policies and increased production resulted in economic change

★ How social change affected the arts, the role of women, and minorities

Read to Discover . . .

★ ways United States involvement in international relations changed following World War I.

★ what signs of social tension were evident in the 1920s.

Journal Notes

What was the Harlem Renaissance? Jot down details about it as you read the chapter.

CULTURAL	
● **1920** *First commercial radio broadcast is aired*	● **1925** *John Scopes trial over teaching evolution in Dayton, Tennessee, occurs*
● **1922** *Lincoln Memorial is dedicated*	

1920	**1923**

POLITICAL	
● **1920** *Warren Harding is elected*	● **1923** *Calvin Coolidge becomes President after Harding's death*
● **1921** *Washington Conference is held*	

▲ TROMBONE USED IN JAZZ GROUP, 1920S

• **1927** *First "talking" motion picture,*
The Jazz Singer, is released

• **1929** *Chicago mobsters murder seven*
rival gang members in the St. Valentine's
Day Massacre

1926	1929

• **1926** *United States intervenes in*
Nicaragua
• **1928** *Kellogg-Briand Pact is negotiated*

• **1929** *Herbert Hoover becomes President*

★★

The Harding Years

Section Focus

The internationalism of Woodrow Wilson was reversed under the administrations of the next three Presidents—all Republicans. The party's slogan "America First" hailed the country's unparalleled prosperity, characterized by remarkable achievements in the field of business.

◀ 1920 REPUBLICAN CAMPAIGN PIN

Objectives

After studying this section, you should be able to

★ describe the accomplishments of the Washington Conference.

★ explain the provisions of the National Origins Act.

★ describe the scandals in the Harding administration.

Key Terms

reparation, technological unemployment, open shop, welfare capitalism

The end of the war created new problems for the United States. After the dismantling of the War Industries Board, business lost the profitable military contracts of the war years. Four million recently demobilized service men and women needed work. In 1920 and 1921, unemployment soared, as did prices. Labor unrest was reflected in the United States Steel strike and the Boston police strike of 1919.

■ The Election of 1920

Several prominent men sought the Republican nomination in 1920, the prize going to a dark horse, Ohio senator Warren G. Harding. Harding's running mate was Massachusetts governor Calvin Coolidge. To oppose Harding, the Democrats chose Ohio governor James M. Cox, a loyal Wilson supporter. Cox's running mate was Franklin D. Roosevelt, who, like his distant cousin, Theodore, had served as assistant secretary of the navy. The strategy chosen by Cox was as Wilson desired—to campaign for the League of Nations.

The Republicans were divided on the issue. Harding said he favored "a society of free nations" to keep peace. Most prominent Republicans took this to mean that Harding supported their decision to join the League, but anti-League Republicans seemed certain that Harding opposed it. Thus, as journalist Walter Lippmann pointed out, Harding received support from "men and women who thought a Republican victory would kill the League, plus those who thought it was the most practical way to procure the League."

The election was an overwhelming Republican victory. Harding carried every Northern and Western state and even broke the Democratic Solid South by carrying Tennessee. A key to the election results may be found in the President's reassuring slogan—"a return to normalcy"— coined by Harding during his campaign. It suggested a return to "the good old days," to the conditions that prevailed before the shocks of World War I.

■ Postwar Foreign Policy

After his election, Harding announced that his administration would not lead the United States into the League of Nations "by the side door, back door, or cellar door." The United States was too powerful, too economically interconnected, and too widely involved in world affairs to retreat into isolationism, however, and participated actively in many League conferences.

War Debt

One international problem that demanded a solution was $10.3 billion in Allied war debts owed to the United States for food and war materials. The debtor nations had difficulty meeting their payments. They argued that high American tariffs had closed the United States market to their imports and slowed their economic recovery. Furthermore, debtor nations argued, because the United States had lost fewer people in the war than the other Allies, it should be willing to pay more of the financial cost. The United States government, however, took the position that the Allies had gained territory and **reparations,** or payments for damages, as a result of the victory while the United States had claimed no reward, and that to cancel these debts would destroy faith in international agreements.

Eventually the United States made agreements with 17 of the 20 debtor nations, reducing the debts by 30 to 80 percent. Most of the money the Allies paid actually came from Germany. To pay its reparations, Germany obtained private bank loans from other countries—especially the United States.

The Washington Conference

At the time of the Harding administration, the United States, Great Britain, and Japan were experiencing costly and competitive naval buildups that originated during the war. There was also friction in East Asia, caused mainly by conflicts over commercial rights in China and by Western suspicion of Japan's recent territorial gains. After World War I, Japan had acquired all of Germany's Pacific islands north of the equator as well as the Chinese port of Kiaochow (jee•OW•JOH). Japan also treated the rest of the Chinese province of Shantung as its own.

In the hope of resolving these problems, the administration hosted an eight-nation conference in Washington, D.C. The negotiations, which lasted from November 1921 to February 1922, led to three important treaties.

The Four-Power Treaty

The Four-Power Treaty, signed by the United States, Great Britain, France, and Japan, was an agreement among the four

 ▲ NOT ROOM FOR BOTH By showing the League of Nations agreement trying to replace the Constitution in ruling the nation, this artist expressed concern that joining the League would deprive the United States of the freedom to set its own policies. *What role did the 1920 election play in resolving this issue?*

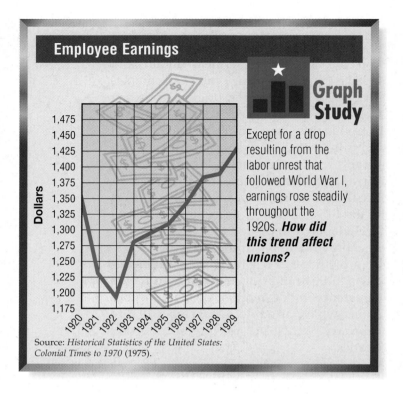

Employee Earnings

Graph Study

Except for a drop resulting from the labor unrest that followed World War I, earnings rose steadily throughout the 1920s. *How did this trend affect unions?*

Source: *Historical Statistics of the United States: Colonial Times to 1970* (1975).

---

policies of John Hay into a treaty. The signers agreed to preserve equal commercial rights in China and to refrain from "taking advantage of conditions in China to seek special rights or privileges." Following this policy, Japan soon withdrew from the province of Shantung.

Although the immediate results of the Washington Conference were encouraging, the conference failed to reach an agreement limiting military forces on land. Moreover, the treaties had notable shortcomings. Under the Five-Power Treaty, naval powers could still build unlimited numbers of smaller combat vessels, such as submarines and destroyers. In addition the Four-Power Treaty did not commit the signers to active military defense of their allies; indeed, such a commitment might have been unacceptable to the United States. The Nine-Power Treaty made no provision for enforcement of the Open Door policy.

great powers to respect one another's Pacific holdings. In case of disagreements or a threat from another nation, the signers also agreed to confer "fully and frankly."

The Five-Power Treaty

Under the Five-Power Treaty, the 5 naval powers of the United States, Great Britain, Japan, France, and Italy agreed to freeze their navies at 1921 levels and thus avoid the financial strain of further naval buildups. The signers further agreed to halt the building of large warships for 10 years; some ships under construction would even be scrapped. The treaty also included an agreement by the United States and Great Britain not to build new fortifications or naval bases in the western Pacific. This provision gave Japan control of nearby waters in exchange for agreeing to remain at inferior naval strength.

The Nine-Power Treaty

The Nine-Power Treaty—signed by the United States, France, Great Britain, Japan, Italy, Belgium, China, the Netherlands, and Portugal—put the "Open Door" China

■ Business Normalcy

From the start Harding's handling of domestic problems made it apparent that normalcy meant a general retreat from government regulation of business. Although the federal government actively aided businesses by levying protective tariffs, promoting foreign trade, and breaking strikes, its policy in other matters was laissez-faire. There was little effort to enforce the antitrust laws that regulated business mergers. Reflecting the dominant feeling of the time, regulatory agencies such as the Interstate Commerce Commission and the Federal Trade Commission were largely unsympathetic to policies restricting private enterprise.

The Fordney-McCumber Act

The new trend was immediately seen in the tariff laws. In 1922 Congress passed the Fordney-McCumber Act, raising import duties to high levels. This protected agriculture as well as certain young industries, such as rayon, china, and the optical-glass and chemical products for which the United States seized patents from Germany during the war. Because the Fordney-McCumber Act authorized the President to raise or lower duties by as much as 50 percent, rates often went still higher.

Creating the Bureau of the Budget

Because World War I had raised the national debt from less than $10 per person to over $200, the Harding and Coolidge administrations attempted to lower this burden by making the government more fiscally responsible. In 1921 Congress created the Bureau of the Budget in the Treasury Department.

The efforts of the Bureau of the Budget to introduce savings were especially supported by Coolidge, who felt so strongly about curbing the nation's expenditures that he devoted serious attention to routine federal purchases such as lead pencils and typewriter ribbons. After the Washington Conference, there was no threat of war on the horizon, and even military expenditures were greatly lowered.

Changes in Taxation

Andrew Mellon, secretary of the treasury from 1921 to 1932 and a wealthy man, believed that heavy taxes on excess profits "penalized success" and discouraged investment in productive enterprise. At Mellon's insistence, Congress abolished the wartime excise and excess profits taxes and reduced tax rates on incomes by nearly two-thirds. Even with these cuts, the nation's prosperity produced enough tax revenue to reduce the national debt by $8 billion between 1921 and 1929.

■ Labor and Labor Unions

Between 1921 and 1928, the average annual wage for workers rose from $1,227 to $1,384. However, new manufacturing caused **technological unemployment**—jobs lost when occupations become obsolete. Although people replaced by machines usually found jobs elsewhere, the transition was sometimes difficult. Not only were they often forced to leave home to find employment, but they also frequently lost the benefit of long years spent learning a particular skill.

The introduction of jukeboxes and sound films, to cite an extreme example, caused widespread unemployment among musicians. Although the assembly line lowered the costs of production, many laborers could not stand the monotony and nervous tension caused by working at a speed set by the machine.

Union Decline

The "prosperity decade" saw labor unions decline in strength. Even the American Federation of Labor, one of the largest organizations, had difficulty holding its members in the face of antiunion activities. Employers joined to promote the **open shop**—a shop where workers do not have to

▲ **KKK** Members of the Ku Klux Klan parade down Pennsylvania Avenue in Washington, D.C., in September 1926. The KKK spread from the South to gain national power in the 1920s. *How did the Klan as well as many other Americans react to increased immigration after World War I?*

join a union. Labeled the "American Plan," in practice the open shop meant a shop closed to union members. To further reduce the power of unions, companies promoted **welfare capitalism,** a system to make employees feel more a part of the business by enabling them to buy shares of stock, by instituting profit sharing, and by providing such fringe benefits as medical care, retirement pensions, and recreational facilities. Moreover, wages and conditions improved somewhat during the 1920s. With some improvement in their standards of living and the relative weakness of unions, striking seemed pointless to many workers.

Strikebreaking

Although Herbert Hoover, secretary of commerce, persuaded President Harding to make a successful personal appeal to the leaders of the steel industry to abandon the 12-hour day, the federal government was usually on the side of the employers. Thus Attorney General Harry M. Daugherty helped to break railroad and coal strikes in 1922 by obtaining injunctions that prohibited every conceivable union activity, including picketing, making public statements to the press, and jeering at strikebreakers. In 1919 the Indiana State Guard—and eventually federal troops—protected strikebreakers at United States Steel. In addition the Supreme Court continually whittled away at the protections that unions thought they had secured by the Clayton Act of 1914. Once again, injunctions were freely used to stop strikes and boycotts.

■ Restricting Immigration

In the decade before World War I, approximately 1 million persons a year came to live in the United States, over two-thirds of these from countries in southern and eastern Europe. To slow down this tide of immigration, Congress passed in 1917 an act requiring a literacy test, designed to exclude large numbers of immigrants.

The act, however, had little effect. New immigrants congregated in such cities as New York and Chicago, where opportunities for employment were greatest. Established immigrants resented the new immigrants' increasing political power. Even more, they

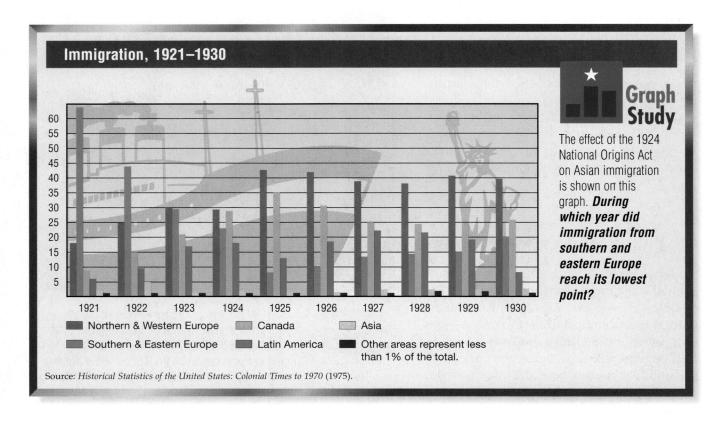

Immigration, 1921–1930

Graph Study

The effect of the 1924 National Origins Act on Asian immigration is shown on this graph. *During which year did immigration from southern and eastern Europe reach its lowest point?*

- Northern & Western Europe
- Southern & Eastern Europe
- Canada
- Latin America
- Asia
- Other areas represent less than 1% of the total.

Source: *Historical Statistics of the United States: Colonial Times to 1970* (1975).

feared that the newcomers, most of whom were Catholic, would overthrow traditional Protestant values. Conservative labor unions were angered by the willingness of poor immigrants to work for very low wages. Employers, who had previously favored unrestricted immigration as a means of hiring cheap labor, now came to fear that the new immigrants were radicals who would fight for a communist revolution.

The National Origins Act

During and after World War I, feeling against "hyphenated-Americans" was stimulated by anti-German hysteria, by the Red Scare, and by the Ku Klux Klan. When immigrants came to the United States, fleeing their war-torn countries in the hopes of finding wealth and opportunity, Congress took quick action. In 1921 Harding signed the Emergency Quota Act, which cut the number of people admitted to the United States. According to this act, only 3 percent of the total number of people in any national group already living in the United States in 1910 would be admitted during a single year.

Three years later the National Origins Act made restriction a permanent policy. This 1924 law temporarily reduced the quota still further. It also provided that after 1927 a total of only 150,000 immigrants would be admitted to the United States per year, their nationalities apportioned on the basis of the 1920 census. This meant that more than 85 percent of the new immigrants would be from Europe—mainly from Great Britain, Ireland, Germany, and Scandinavia.

The intention of the National Origins Act was clearly to discriminate against certain nationalities and races. This became even more apparent when immigrants from Asia and Africa were either assigned very small quotas or barred entirely. Japanese immigration was completely excluded. The Japanese regarded the law as a national insult, and the day it went into effect was declared a day of public mourning and national humiliation in Japan. The incident discredited moderate Japanese politicians who sought to cooperate with the United States and advanced the cause of reactionary militarists in Japan.

 History AND ART

▲ THE PASSION OF SACCO AND VANZETTI by Ben Shahn, 1932 Many Americans rallied to the defense of Nicola Sacco and Bartolomeo Vanzetti. **Why did this case arouse controversy?**

Sacco and Vanzetti

An event that for many came to symbolize mistrust of immigrants in the United States was the trial of Nicola Sacco and Bartolomeo Vanzetti. These two Italian immigrants and anarchists were accused in 1921 of killing two men during a robbery in Massachusetts. They were convicted, but many thought they never received a fair trial. It was believed that the trial judge was prejudiced against the defendants because of their ethnic backgrounds and political beliefs. For years attempts were made to obtain a retrial, but in 1927 Sacco and Vanzetti were executed. In his final statement in court, Vanzetti continued to maintain his innocence of the crime, saying:

> 66 . . . [M]y conviction is that I have suffered for things that I am guilty of. I am suffering because I am a radical and indeed I am a radical; I have suffered because I was an Italian and indeed I am an Italian. . . . 99

The question of the guilt or innocence of Sacco and Vanzetti has never been answered with certainty. Their trial made many people think critically about the American justice system, however.

■ Scandals Among Harding's Advisers

Although President Harding was personally honest, there was more corruption in his administration than in any previous one. Harding's poker-playing friends, known as "the Ohio Gang," used their ties to the President and the attorney general to sell government appointments, pardons, and immunity from prosecution.

Less than 18 months after Harding took office, his administration was racked by scandal. It was discovered that Charles R. Forbes, the director of the Veterans Bureau and a close friend of Harding, had made illegal deals that had netted him hundreds of thousands of dollars in commissions. When this fact became public, the attorney for the Bureau, who was also involved, shot himself. His suicide was closely followed by that of Jesse Smith, a close friend of Attorney General Harry M. Daugherty, who himself was later accused of corruption while in office.

The worst scandal involved Harding's secretary of the interior, Albert B. Fall, who secretly leased to private interests some oil lands, which had been set aside for the navy at Teapot Dome, Wyoming, and Elk Hills, California. In return Fall received bribes totaling more than $300,000. Eventually the Senate investigated the Teapot Dome scandal, and Secretary Fall went to prison.

When Harding learned what was going on, he complained privately that he had been betrayed. He said that he had no troubles with his enemies, but his friends—they were a different story. In the summer of 1923, Harding traveled to Alaska, deeply concerned and depressed over the scandals in his administration. On his return he became severely ill. He died on August 2, shortly before news of the scandals broke to the public.

Section 1 ★ Review

Checking for Understanding

1. **Identify** Fordney-McCumber Tariff, Washington Conference, National Origins Act.

2. **Define** reparation, technological unemployment, open shop, welfare capitalism.

3. **Cite** two foreign-policy problems the United States faced after the war.

4. **Summarize** the treaties negotiated at the Washington Conference.

Critical Thinking

5. **Analyzing Changes** Explain why the election of Harding fit America's mood and why this mood had changed since 1917.

Household Technology

". . . [T]he wise woman," proclaimed a 1920s electric company ad, "delegates to electricity all that electricity can do." Inventions such as electric irons, vacuum cleaners, and washing machines changed the lives of urban middle-class housewives in the decade of the 1920s. But these devices changed only the way women spent their time, not how much time they spent.

One study revealed that upper middle-class homemakers employed only half as many full-time servants as their mothers had. These women did work their mothers had hired others to do. Although some women found that laborsaving devices gave them more leisure time, others said that the dirt and soot caused by automobile traffic and nearby factories made their homes dirtier than those of the previous generation. Most of the women surveyed said they spent less time on housework than their mothers, but parenting and other demands had increased. "So many things our mothers didn't know about, we feel that we ought to do for our children," said one woman.

The technological innovations were developed by such creative individuals as Charles Steinmetz. Steinmetz gained recognition in electrical science, and General Electric offered him a job with an excellent salary and superb research facilities.

Known as the "Electrical Genius of GE, " Steinmetz made contributions to science and science engineering that sped the nation into an age of electricity. More than 200 patents flowed from his work, which included the study, explanation, and harnessing of alternating current. Before Steinmetz, it had been impossible to transmit electricity more than 3 miles without using multiple generators.

▲ VACUUM CLEANER ADVERTISEMENT, 1920S

Making the Technology Connection

1. What laborsaving devices aided American housewives during the 1920s?

2. How did laborsaving devices and innovations of the period affect American homemakers?

Linking Past and Present

3. What technologies of today have changed the way people spend their time?

★★★★★★★★★★★★★★★★★★★★★★★★★★★★★★★

The Coolidge Era

Section Focus

When awakened to hear that Harding had died, Vice President Coolidge was at his boyhood home in Vermont. His father, a justice of the peace, administered the oath of office in the flickering light of a kerosene lamp. This homey scene typified the small-town values that the new President held—values which many Americans still shared and cherished.

Objectives

After studying this section, you should be able to

★ discuss the changes to industry Henry Ford introduced.

★ outline the problems of farmers and the government's response.

★ describe the background and details of the Kellogg-Briand Pact.

Key Term

domestic market

◀ AUTOMOBILE ADVERTISEMENT, 1920S

Coolidge had traits often associated with small-town America. He was conservative, cautious, and given to few words. In public speeches and magazine articles, he preached the old-fashioned virtues of honesty, thrift, and hard work. His philosophy of government was simple: economy and laissez-faire. To take as little action as possible was with Coolidge almost a principle of life; he once said, "Four-fifths of all our troubles in this life would disappear if we would only sit down and keep still."

■ The Election of 1924

By 1924 the scandals of the Harding administration had surfaced, hurting the Republican party. This presented the Democratic party with a ready-made issue for the presidential campaign.

The Democrats Are Divided

The Democrats threw away their chances for victory at their national convention, however. The party was deeply divided over two issues: Prohibition—which the rural regions favored and the cities opposed—and more importantly, the Ku Klux Klan.

This secret society, which took its name and ritual from the Southern organization of Reconstruction times, was designed to intimidate African Americans, Catholics, Jews, immigrants, and "foreign ideas," such as the League of Nations. By the mid-1920s the Klan had become a force in American politics, despite its willingness to use terror and violence.

At the 1924 Democratic convention, the rivals for the nomination were William G. McAdoo of California and Governor Alfred E. Smith of New York. McAdoo favored Prohibition and received most of his support from the western and southern regions of the United States. Governor Smith was a Roman Catholic and opponent of Prohibition. His strongest backing came mostly from urban areas of the Northeast. Smith's supporters wanted an outright condemnation of the Ku Klux Klan, a move that Southern and Western delegates blocked.

The two candidates were deadlocked for so long that the cowboy-humorist Will Rogers suggested that the eventual nominee might be born at the convention. By the time a compromise candidate—John W. Davis of West Virginia—was nominated on the one-hundred-and-third ballot, the Democrats had lost all chance of winning the election.

The Republicans Win

The Republicans campaigned on the slogan "Keep Cool with Coolidge"; the way to keep business thriving, they said, was not to "rock the boat" but to keep in power the party that favored business. This strategy was successful. In an election that attracted only half the eligible voters to the polls, Coolidge won easily.

■ Business

During the 1920s many Americans went almost dizzy with prosperity. As business boomed and wages rose, former luxuries became necessities. A combination of increased leisure time for both men and women, new gadgets, new amusements, and more money to spend resulted in something approaching glorification of wealth and of the material comforts that went with it.

The Impact of the Automobile

The outstanding symbol of the new age was the automobile. In the early twentieth century, when the manufacture of automobiles in the United States was just beginning, driving cars was a sport for the wealthy. It was Henry Ford who almost single-handedly changed the automobile from a toy of the wealthy to a necessity for all. Ford's famous "Model T"—affectionately known as the "Tin Lizzie"—was so cheap that most families could afford it. Ford applied many of the familiar techniques of successful industrialists, such as the use of standardized parts and the formation of a vertical organization to combine different

★★★★**A**★★★★★★ **MERICAN PORTRAITS**

Will Rogers
1879–1935

Part Native American, Will Rogers grew up in the West and became a cowboy while in his teens. He landed jobs with Wild West shows, where he would mix in a few jokes while doing his rope-twirling act. Aiming good-natured barbs at famous people, he became known as the "cowboy philosopher."

By 1920 Will Rogers was a star of both stage and screen. Starting in 1926, his daily newspaper column spread his humorous views of life and politics throughout the nation. Claiming "I don't make jokes—I just watch the government and report the facts," he always poked fun in a lighthearted way and was never hostile; one of his favorite sayings was "I never met a man I didn't like."

By the late 1920s audiences were listening to his commentary on radio. To Americans, Rogers had become a national treasure.

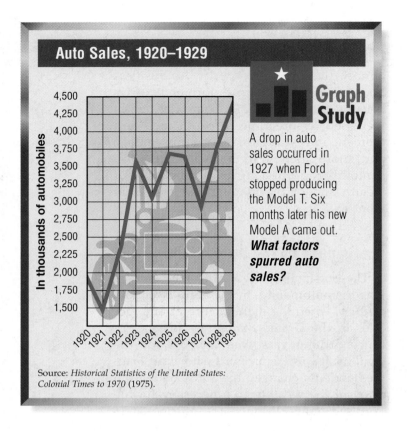

Auto Sales, 1920–1929

Graph Study

A drop in auto sales occurred in 1927 when Ford stopped producing the Model T. Six months later his new Model A came out.

What factors spurred auto sales?

In thousands of automobiles

4,500
4,250
4,000
3,750
3,500
3,250
3,000
2,750
2,500
2,225
2,000
1,750
1,500

1920 1921 1922 1923 1924 1925 1926 1927 1928 1929

Source: *Historical Statistics of the United States: Colonial Times to 1970* (1975).

operations. But Ford's greatest achievement was the assembly line, which divided operations into such simple tasks that most of the work could be done by unskilled labor. Furthermore, by bringing the parts to the workers, assembly lines sped up production so fast that Ford could boast that:

> 66 . . . *[R]aw iron ore at the docks at 8:00 Monday morning could be marketed as a complete Ford car on Wednesday noon, allowing 15 hours for shipment.* 99

Ford's economies so reduced costs that an American automobile, which sold for an average price of $2,123 in 1907, could be bought for as little as $290 in 1924. While reducing costs, he staved off unionization by nearly doubling wages in 1914 to $5 a day. Other employers resented Ford because his pay scale was so high that it caused discontent among their own workers. It was Ford's belief that mass-production methods and low prices would produce an immense market for goods. This turned out to be correct,

and the simplicity of the formula spawned imitators. By the mid-1920s other great trusts, notably General Motors and Chrysler, were competing successfully with Ford.

The impact of the automobile on life in the United States was revolutionary. Although small businesses generally continued to decline, new fields for small enterprises— garages, gas stations, diners, and tourist homes—appeared. Draft animals disappeared from farms as tractors took their places. The isolation of rural areas lessened, as cars put towns within easy reach of many farmers, and put the country within reach of city dwellers.

The Growth of Big Business

It seemed that Americans had discovered a magic formula for producing wealth and fulfilling human wants on a scale never before thought possible. Its ingredients were mass production, standardized products, and a nationwide market. This formula tended to favor big businesses over small because only big businesses could set up assembly lines, do the research necessary for constant development of new products, and afford nationwide advertising. It was natural then that the 1920s should see much concentration of industry. Mergers and holding companies helped to concentrate industry by reducing competition. The chain store soon became a familiar sight on Main Street, capturing one-fourth of the grocery business by 1929.

Whereas many Americans had formerly regarded big business as an enemy, they now relied on it both to supply cheap products and to create new opportunities for wealth. The stock market provided striking evidence of this when, for the first time in history, some members of the general public began to buy securities. The prices of shares of stock, especially those connected with new industries, mounted to dizzying heights. More and more purchasers "invested in the future."

With wealthier Americans speculating in the stock market, money to run business came from more and more diverse sources. Business, on the other hand, was becoming more and more concentrated. One device used by businesspeople to concentrate financial power was the "pyramiding" of holding companies, whereby it was possible—with a relatively small outlay of capital—for businesspeople to gain control of immense industrial properties.

The Plight of Agriculture

Farmers were the one great economic group that did not share in the Coolidge prosperity. The average income for farmers in 1929 was less than one-third of the average income for the rest of the country.

Falling Prices and Shrinking Markets

Technological advances led to greater production, which caused a slump in farm prices even while farmers' costs mounted. As one account puts it:

66 *Freight rates, wages, taxes, farm implements, and the like, all of which went into the farmers'* *cost of production, remained high or came down via the stairway, while farm prices took the elevator.* 99

Farm prices took disastrous slides in 1920 and 1921 and did not recover. Wheat went from almost $2.50 a bushel to less than $1.50. The foreign market dwindled because the United States had changed from a debtor to a creditor nation. Before World War I, foreign investments in the United States exceeded American investment abroad; the principal means of making up this unfavorable credit balance was for the United States to export agricultural staples, such as wheat and cotton. During the war the balance shifted the other way, principally because of United States loans to the Allies. With the return of peace, countries owing the United States money preferred not to buy its products. Great Britain, for example, often bought wheat from Argentina or Canada, especially after the Fordney-McCumber Tariff reduced the American market for British goods.

The **domestic market,** the market composed of buyers and sellers within the country, also diminished. New fabrics such as rayon lessened the demand for cotton; the

Visualizing History ▲ ON THE ASSEMBLY LINE Finishing touches are put on a Model A at a Ford plant in Dearborn, Michigan. *What effect did assembly-line production have on the price of automobiles?*

History AND ART

▲ *WHEAT* by Thomas Hart Benton, 1967 During his later career, Thomas Hart Benton chronicled America's past. *Why did the domestic market for agricultural products diminish during the 1920s?*

substitution of tractors and trucks for draft animals reduced the need for fodder. Faced with decreasing demands for the traditional staples, farmers might have been expected to shift to other products—but that was easier said than done. A Southern tenant farmer usually had no skill at anything but raising cotton. A Dakota wheat farmer usually lacked the capital and the knowledge to change, say, to dairy farming, which in any case was not well suited to that region. Moreover, many farmers had borrowed heavily during the war to buy new land at inflated prices. The only obvious way to pay off the debt was to raise more crops. But more crops meant unsalable surpluses; unsalable surpluses meant low prices. Low prices made the debt burden even heavier.

The Influence of the Farm Bloc

Early in Harding's administration, members of Congress from the Midwest and Plains states formed the Farm Bloc. It included about 25 senators and 100 representatives from both parties. Strong enough to hold a balance of power in Congress, the Farm Bloc forced through several laws favoring farmers. The Capper-Volstead Act of 1922 made farm cooperatives free of antitrust laws; the Intermediate Credits Act of 1923 set up federal banks to make loans to aid farm cooperatives.

None of the laws, however, dealt with the farmers' major problem: surpluses they could not sell. If wheat farmers were to benefit from the 42-cent-a-bushel protective tariff, which eliminated foreign competition, they somehow had to limit the amount of wheat put on that market.

The Farm Bloc supported the McNary-Haugen Bill. This bill proposed that the federal government buy crop surpluses and sell them abroad, while protecting the United States market with a high tariff. This would immediately raise the domestic price. Whatever losses the government suffered would be covered by an equalization fee—a tax

▲ FARM LANTERN, 1920s

charged against producers. Supporters of the bill claimed that it would help farmers as the tariff helped manufacturers.

Twice the bill passed Congress, but both times President Coolidge vetoed it. The idea would not work, he insisted, and furthermore, a "healthy economic condition is best maintained through a free play of competition." Thus, farmers failed to obtain protections similar to those many businesses received at the time.

■ Foreign Affairs

During the 1920s both Republican Presidents worked to promote world peace through individual agreements. During Coolidge's administration, France and the United States took the lead in promoting a treaty that attempted to "outlaw war."

Called the Kellogg-Briand Pact after the American secretary of state and the French foreign minister who proposed it, the treaty was eventually ratified by 64 nations, each agreeing to abandon war "as an instrument of national policy" and to settle disputes by peaceful means. The treaty was hailed as a great victory for peace. The pact, often called the Pact of Paris, was signed by most nations only under certain conditions. The primary condition of most was to retain the right to defend themselves against acts of aggression. The United States also stated that the pact did not overrule the principles of the Monroe Doctrine.

A serious weakness of the pact was that it had no means of enforcement. No provisions were set down in the event there were acts of aggression among signer nations.

Although the United States generally participated in talks and treaties with European and Asian nations during this period, its manner toward Latin America remained protective. The Harding and Coolidge administrations—following the Roosevelt Corollary to the Monroe Doctrine—occasionally sent troops to "preserve order" in Caribbean countries. They became increasingly aware, however, that the Latin American people acutely resented such intervention. Although not willing to give up the right to intervene, Secretary of State Charles Evans Hughes believed troops should be sent to Latin America only to promote political stability, not to assist American investors. Accordingly, in the mid-1920s, United States Marines withdrew from the Dominican Republic and Nicaragua, where they had been sent in the previous decade to maintain order.

Section 2 ★ Review

Checking for Understanding

1. **Identify** Henry Ford, assembly line, McNary-Haugen Bill, Farm Bloc.

2. **Define** domestic market.

3. **List** three ways that the automobile changed American life.

4. **Summarize** the farmers' situation in the 1920s and how government reacted.

Critical Thinking

5. **Supporting an Opinion** Would you agree that Coolidge did not regard farming in the same way he viewed big business? Explain.

▲ EDNA ST. VINCENT MILLAY

After World War I, divergent movements in American literature grew up in New York's Harlem and Greenwich Village and in the nation's heartland. Two poets who typify these movements are Edna St. Vincent Millay and Langston Hughes.

In the first of the following selections, Millay captures the tireless energy of youth. In the selection by Hughes, the poet uses rhythms of the jazz age to reflect his African American pride.

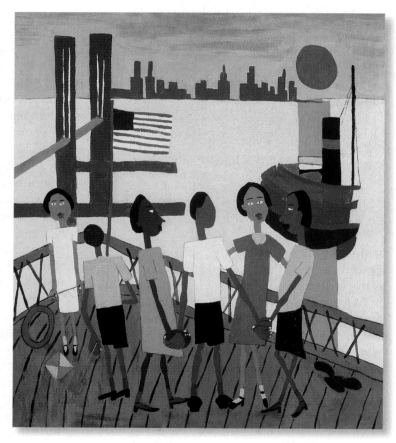

▲ *FERRY BOAT TRIP* BY WILLIAM H. JOHNSON, 1934

Recuerdo by Edna St. Vincent Millay

We were very tired, we were very merry—
We had gone back and forth all night on the ferry.
It was bare and bright, and smelled like a stable-
But we looked into a fire, we leaned across a table,
We lay on a hill-top underneath the moon;
And the whistles kept blowing, and the dawn
    came soon.
We were very tired, we were very merry—
We had gone back and forth all night on the ferry;
And you ate an apple, and I ate a pear,
From a dozen of each we had bought somewhere;
And the sky went wan, and the wind came cold,
And the sun rose dripping, a bucketful of gold.
We were very tired, we were very merry,
We had gone back and forth all night on the ferry.

We hailed, "Good-morrow, mother!" to a
    shawl-covered head,
And bought a morning paper, which neither
    of us read;
And she wept, "God bless you!" for the
    apples and the pears,
And we gave her all our money but our
    subway fares.

Dream Boogie

by Langston Hughes

Ain't you heard
The boogie-woogie rumble
Of a dream deferred?
Listen closely:
You'll hear their feet
Beating out and beating out a—
You think
It's a happy beat?
Listen to it closely:
Ain't you heard
something underneath
like a—
What did I say?
Sure,
I'm happy!
Take it away!
Hey, pop!
Re-bop!
Mop!
Y-e-a-h!

▲ *Li'l Sis* by William H. Johnson, 1944

▲ Langston Hughes

Interpreting Literature

1. What period of time is covered in the three stanzas of "Recuerdo"?

2. How many speakers are there in "Dream Boogie"? What device is used to set them apart?

3. What differences and similarities in voice can you find between the authors of these selections?

Identifying Viewpoints

4. What views of American life in the 1920s do Millay and Hughes embody?

★★

The "Roaring Twenties"

Section Focus

The 1920s saw striking changes in American society. Radio and film became immensely popular. The arts flowered. "Coolidge prosperity" provided more leisure time and more spending money for new gadgets. The availability of credit helped many to buy more than they could afford. Women adopted new standards of behavior. To many, however, these changes suggested a loss of important traditional values.

Objectives

After studying this section, you should be able to

★ describe changes in women's lives during the 1920s.

★ outline developments in the arts and education during this period.

Key Term

postwar disillusionment

◀ COOLIDGE CAMPAIGN POSTER, 1924

From a Long Island airfield on May 20, 1927, a small plane called the *Spirit of St. Louis* took off for France. Twenty-five-year-old Charles Lindbergh set off to make the first nonstop solo flight across the Atlantic. Thirty-three and one-half hours later, Lindbergh landed near Paris. Huge crowds greeted him. An American naval vessel brought him home, and even greater crowds welcomed him back to the United States. "Lucky Lindy," as he was called, became a hero of the age.

President Coolidge called him "a boy representing the best traditions of his country." In an era when the ideals and heroes of history were questioned, when politics was riddled with graft, and when machines seemed to be replacing people, Lindbergh helped people restore some confidence in themselves. He proved that Americans were still capable of pioneering, even in the machine age. Quiet, courageous, and self-reliant, Lindbergh showed that not all the old values of life had disappeared, despite the changing priorities of modern society.

■ New Directions in Society

The rapid changes caused by the progress of technology in the 1920s brought with them some serious problems. Automobiles, though they offered an exciting new freedom of movement, also killed as many Americans in 1928 and 1929 as had lost their lives in battle during World War I. Cities lost some of their attractiveness as automobiles enabled people and businesses to move to the suburbs. The easily available "canned

▲ **LINDBERGH'S HISTORIC FLIGHT** Because a huge fuel tank blocked his plane's windshield on his transatlantic flight, Lindbergh used a periscope to see. Lindbergh's heroics inspired other pilots like Amelia Earhart (right). *In what way was Lindbergh a symbol of the 1920s?*

entertainment" provided by radio and motion pictures seemed to discourage Americans from creating their own amusements.

Prohibition

Unfortunately, during the 1920s crime became big business. Gangsters such as Al Capone and Dutch Schultz consolidated the illegal liquor trade on many of the same principles used to consolidate the automobile and steel industries. The Prohibition Bureau, set up to enforce the law against the distilling and sale of liquor, was understaffed, underpaid, graft-ridden, and ineffective. Although liquor consumption dropped substantially during Prohibition, illegal

drinking by millions created an illegitimate billion-dollar industry. The entrepreneurs in this illegal business became wealthy enough to buy beautiful homes in Florida, steel-plated limousines, and fabulous jewels, such as Capone's 11.5-carat diamond ring. Some gangsters became powerful enough to corrupt local governments.

Rural America, with its traditional values and churchgoing ways, tended to support Prohibition, but the cities generally opposed it. The customary diets of several urban ethnic groups included liquor, and many city dwellers resisted Prohibition as the work of religious crusaders. Regardless, Prohibition was never fully enforced. Many people supported Prohibition publicly while privately continuing to drink.

▲ AL CAPONE

Despite the success of the illegal liquor trade, Prohibition actually gained in popularity during the 1920s. In 1928 voters elected more supporters of Prohibition to Congress than ever before, as well as a "dry" President, Herbert Hoover. The popularity of Prohibition was a sign of continuing faith in the possibility of achieving a better life, of a longing for the ideals that had eroded in the horrors of World War I.

▼ MOVIE POSTER, 1920S

Traditional standards of behavior were changing as Americans left the villages for the cities and the farms for the factories. Prohibition seemed a way to halt this change in values.

Women in the 1920s

The 1920s saw women express greater personal freedom. A dramatic new woman of the 1920s—the "flapper"—demanded the same freedom enjoyed by men. She sometimes smoked cigarettes and drank liquor and dressed in a way her mother and grandmother would not have believed possible. While most women in the 1920s were not flappers, these new women demonstrated how modern behavior was changing.

American family life was also changing. Couples had fewer children because of increased knowledge about family planning, divorce rates increased, and more women than ever before sought employment outside the home.

Women in the Workplace

Having achieved the right to vote, women sought financial independence as well. Many young single women became salesclerks in department stores, secretaries, or telephone operators, for example. In 1920, 25 percent of female workers were in clerical and sales work. Eventually the employees in those particular jobs became almost exclusively female. Graduates of women's colleges began to seek jobs in business rather than in more traditional jobs such as teaching. But many women, especially married women who had to work to support families, were confined to jobs with long hours, poor conditions, and low wages. Women who worked outside the home suffered severe discrimination, often receiving only 50 to 60 percent of a man's wages for the same work. Further, women continued to meet with difficulty when trying to enter prestigious professions such as science and law.

Individual women made great contributions in many fields—often under difficult circumstances. Amelia Earhart learned to fly

Radio

The 1920s ushered in a host of technologies still heavily used today. Among the most significant breakthroughs was commercial radio. In November 1920, radio station KDKA in Pittsburgh broadcast news of Harding's landslide victory, in one of the first commercial broadcasts in history. Within the next two years, almost 600 radio stations began operation. One million Americans tuned in daily to hear their favorite radio programs.

Radio, from its earliest days, was financed through the sale of advertising time and offered a wide variety of information, advice, and entertainment. Farm families particularly appreciated the Department of Agriculture broadcasts of farm market prices. Weather reports were universally popular. Dramas, adventures, and comedies, each with a cast of actors and a sound effects technician, were performed live in the radio studio as the broadcast aired. Sports reached new heights in popularity. News, music, advice, and quiz shows were other early radio programs.

Radio, like so many technologies that emerged in the post–World War I period, served to shrink the world, bringing immediate contact and communication, and a common experience to people in all parts of the world.

▲ ADVERTISEMENT, 1929

◀ RADIO RECEIVER, 1929

planes and became the first woman to complete a solo flight across the Atlantic. Dorothy Thompson became a famous journalist. Mary McLeod Bethune—an African American woman born into poverty—founded her own college, founded the National Council of Negro Women, and served as a government consultant.

Women in the Home

Most Americans—both men and women—continued to believe that a married woman's place was in the home. Thus, in spite of a spirit of independence, most women continued to be bound by the belief that their role was different from that of men, that they were to be mothers and homemakers. With new electric technology, the nature of being a homemaker changed. New household appliances, such as refrigerators and vacuum cleaners, commercial laundries, and canned food made hard, time-consuming domestic duties much easier. Many who stayed at home and became mothers, particularly in middle-class families, managed motherhood by listening to child-rearing experts who promoted regularly scheduled feedings for children and regimented routines for such children's extracurricular activities as music lessons and clubs.

■ Cultural Achievements

American culture thrived in the 1920s. Literature, architecture, music, painting, movies, radio—all flourished during this time.

American Literature

Some writers of the period, such as novelist Willa Cather and poet Robert Frost, tried to recapture the spirit and traditions

▲ **WORKING FOR JUSTICE** Activists like Mary McLeod Bethune fought to pass a federal law against lynching. *What attitudes might explain why lynching and other such incidents increased in the 1920s?*

Postwar disillusionment, disappointment or dissatisfaction with the way things were after the war, was often manifested as criticism of American life. Henry Ford said that "history is bunk," and a school of "debunking" historians reexamined the past and reevaluated more accurately the facts behind the myths of many American heroes. Many American writers did the same. In his novels *Main Street* and *Babbitt,* Sinclair Lewis depicted the absurdities of life in small-town America. H. L. Mencken mocked the "vast . . . herd of good-natured animals" who made up most of the machine-age society. Mencken saw no hope for improvement. "If I am convinced of anything," he wrote, "it is that Doing Good is in bad taste."

The Arts

Achievements in American literature were matched in the arts. New city skyscrapers and suburban homes expanded the opportunities of architects like Frank Lloyd Wright, who achieved worldwide fame for his bold use of new materials and for architectural designs free of traditional influence.

◄ **SINGER AND ACTRESS ETHEL WATERS**

of rural America; others, such as poet Carl Sandburg, examined what was happening in America's cities. In Eugene O'Neill, the United States produced its finest playwright. O'Neill found material in many aspects of American life—from the rage of a worker in the hold of a steamship in *The Hairy Ape,* to family tension in a decaying New England town in *Desire Under the Elms.* Ernest Hemingway, who had driven an ambulance on the Italian front during World War I, wrote about the meaningless violence of war in *A Farewell to Arms.* His fiction created a new literary style characterized by direct, simple, spare prose. The poet T. S. Eliot saw a world filled with "hollow men" and, in *The Wasteland,* one that would end "not with a bang but a whimper."

In jazz, which started with African American Dixieland bands in New Orleans, America produced a new form of music. At first seen as corrupting the morals of young people, jazz was soon accepted as an important art form. In the fine arts, the American scene was brilliantly portrayed by such painters as Reginald Marsh, Thomas Hart Benton, George Bellows, and Edward Hopper. In photography, Alfred Stieglitz achieved an international reputation.

Also during this period, the young motion-picture industry mushroomed. The first feature-length film appeared in 1915. By 1929 there were about 100 million paid admissions to movie theaters every week—proof that moviegoing had gained respectability. During the 1920s the motion-picture industry moved from New York to southern California. Mary Pickford, Charlie Chaplin, Douglas Fairbanks, Gloria Swanson, and Clara Bow were among the first stars of the silent screen. In 1927 Warner Brothers introduced "talking" pictures, which made the movies more popular than ever.

■ Changes and Challenges in Education

A significant amount of the new wealth of the 1920s went into education, both through taxes for new public schools and through private donations to colleges and universities. The introduction of the school bus made possible the gradual replacement of bare, one-room country schoolhouses with large, well-equipped central schools. High school was no longer the privilege of the well-off but was also attended by the children of farmers and workers—although graduation from high school remained the exception rather than the rule. Both high school and college enrollment increased steadily.

Visualizing History

▲ THE SCOPES TRIAL Opposing attorneys Clarence Darrow (left) and William Jennings Bryan pose during the Scopes trial. Scopes was later freed on appeal, but the trial proved too much for Bryan, who died a week after it ended. *What basic clash of values in 1920s society did the trial illustrate?*

A philosophy of education, long championed by John Dewey, emphasized learning through direct experience and experiment rather than through memorization. Greater emphasis was placed on science, which Dewey viewed as a way of using both thought and activity to investigate nature.

Some religious groups found these new educational theories threatening and were able to gain laws in some states to prevent the teaching of evolution in public schools. This set the stage for a battle between science and religion. It came in 1925, at the trial of John T. Scopes, a teacher in Dayton, Tennessee, who was willing to be arrested for teaching evolution to his high-school class. The American Civil Liberties Union (ACLU) had raised money to test the new antievolution law in Tennessee and had asked Scopes if he would volunteer for the cause. The famous attorney Clarence Darrow defended Scopes, while William Jennings Bryan aided the prosecution for the antievolution forces. After a sensational trial, Scopes was convicted, but Bryan, who took the witness stand as an expert on the Bible, was made to look foolish through Darrow's penetrating questioning. The Scopes case symbolized the tensions of the

1920s, as some Americans tried to resist the tide of social change and to preserve older values and beliefs.

■ The Harlem Renaissance

World War I had been a liberating experience for many African Americans. This was especially true of those who went abroad. For the first time they were freed from the second-class citizenship they suffered in the United States. But the prejudice and discrimination that awaited them at home helped to create a spirit of pride and protest, forging a new unity and a new African American:

> ❝ . . . *who had pride in heritage and self and who, through poetry, music, dance, and the theater, was able to create works of beauty out of travail and sufferings, as well as out of the more humorous facts of life.* ❞

A striking outcome of this new spirit among African Americans was the "Harlem Renaissance." In New York City, the intellectual capital of the United States, a number of highly talented African Americans rose to fame. Some were in the performing arts, including actors Charles Gilpin and Richard B. Harrison, singers Roland Hayes and Ethel Waters, dancer Bill Robinson, and singer-actor Paul Robeson. Others were scholars, including sociologist E. Franklin

▲ WRITER COUNTEE CULLEN

Frazier and economist Abram L. Harris. Still others were writers, such as poets Countee Cullen and Langston Hughes and novelists Jessie H. Fauset, Zora Neale Hurston, and Walter White.

More influential than the intellectuals and artists among African Americans themselves was a dynamic leader from Jamaica, Marcus Garvey. A spokesman for "Negro Nationalism," which exalted African American culture and traditions, Garvey formed the Universal Negro Improvement Association, which soon boasted a million members. Garvey told his followers they would never find justice in America and proposed to lead them to Africa. People were not interested, but Garvey stimulated the pride of African Americans in their history and heritage.

Section 3 ★ Review

Checking for Understanding

1. **Identify** Amelia Earhart, Mary McLeod Bethune, John T. Scopes.

2. **Define** postwar disillusionment.

3. **Cite** the factors that resulted in increased crime in the 1920s.

4. **Summarize** changes in women's personal and economic status during the 1920s.

Critical Thinking

5. **Evaluating Achievements** How are the advances made by women in the 1920s significant to the lives of American women today?

Interpreting Primary Sources

The Harlem Renaissance and Visual Arts

Although the outpouring of literature, art, and music known as the Harlem Renaissance involved only a handful of artists and writers, the power of their work brought international attention and acclaim to Harlem in the 1920s and the 1930s. The visual artists associated with the Harlem Renaissance were a diverse group of people. Some, such as Edwin A. Harleston and Laura Wheeler Waring, painted in a style that was virtually indistinguishable from that of their white European and American peers. Others, such as Lois Mailou Jones and Aaron Douglas, used African design motifs to shape a distinctively African American art.

Aaron Douglas, the best-known visual artist of the Harlem Renaissance, was perhaps also the one most influenced by African design. He developed his style of geometric symbolism as a painter of murals on public buildings. The painting shown here, *The Creation*, shows several elements characteristic of Douglas's style: a figure that represents not a particular person but all humankind; subtle, barely differentiated shades of purple and gray; and shapes such as circles, arches, and waves. Douglas believed that art can be a bridge between different cultures and peoples. He asserted this belief through his paintings, which describe human experience in a streamlined visual language that people of different times, places, genders, and races can easily understand.

Douglas inspired the Harlem Renaissance by actively searching out and training other artists. His efforts were rewarded in 1928 when the first all-African American art show in the United States was held in New York City. Many of the exhibitors became eminent in American art. Their efforts spread the spirit of the Harlem Renaissance well beyond New York.

▲ *THE CREATION* BY AARON DOUGLAS

Examining the Primary Source

1. Identify one shape, besides the circle, in the painting. What might it stand for?

2. Suggest what the circles represent.

3. What might the hand and figure symbolize?

Critical Thinking

4. **Making Inferences** What emotions might the figure in the painting be experiencing? Explain your viewpoint.

5. **Drawing Conclusions** What foods, clothes, or celebrations reflect the origins of several groups of Americans?

Using Vocabulary

Imagine that you are the chairperson of a large industrial company in the 1920s. Write a letter to the President using the terms below.

welfare   open shop
capitalism

Reviewing Facts

1. **State** two reasons Harding was elected President in 1920.

2. **Summarize** foreign-policy actions of Harding and Coolidge.

3. **List** three ways that Harding and Coolidge helped stimulate business in America.

4. **Explain** why Congress enacted the Emergency Quota Act and the National Origins Act.

5. **Discuss** how Henry Ford's innovations contributed to the growth of the economy.

6. **Describe** ways farmers were affected by tariffs and improved technology.

7. **Cite** evidence that the 1920s changed the arts and the lives of women and African Americans.

Understanding Concepts

Economic Change

1. Explain why urban dwellers of all economic levels would support the economic changes of the 1920s.

Social Change

2. Art, literature, and music thrived in the 1920s. What changes in society do you think inspired artists, writers, and musicians?

Critical Thinking

1. **Drawing Conclusions**   Explain how changes in business and manufacturing during the 1920s sparked a revolution in social customs, arts, and entertainment.

2. **Analyzing Fine Art**   Study the painting of singer and actor Paul Robeson on this page by artist Betsy Graves Reyneau, then answer the questions that follow.

   a. What does the painting tell you about the artist's view of Robeson?

   b. What title would you give this painting?

▲ PAUL ROBESON IN THE ROLE OF OTHELLO

Writing About History

Narration

Choose a topic from Chapter 26 and write an imaginary news report that could be narrated over radio. When you have finished writing, reread your narrative and imagine you are the listener. Rewrite any parts that are unclear or do not adequately convey the sights, sounds, and feelings of the topic.

Cooperative Learning

Work in groups of four to evaluate the changes that took place in the 1920s. One member of each group should assume one of the following roles: business owner, farmer, African American, flapper. The goal of your group is to write four paragraphs

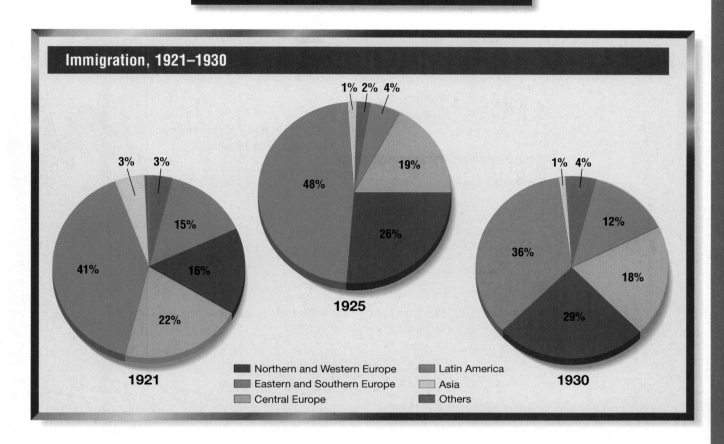

Immigration, 1921–1930

1921
3%
3%
15%
41%
16%
22%

1925
1% 2% 4%
48%
19%
26%

1930
1% 4%
36%
12%
18%
29%

Northern and Western Europe
Eastern and Southern Europe
Central Europe
Latin America
Asia
Others

that discuss the changes from these four perspectives. Have each group member read the paragraph describing the changes that affected him or her.

Social Studies Skills

Interpreting Graphic Data

When historical information involves numbers and statistics, it is often presented as a graph. Graphs frequently have an advantage over printed text because they make organizing and comparing detailed or complex information much easier.

Practicing the Skill

The circle graphs above provide immigration data. Use the guidelines and information from the chapter to interpret the data shown on them.

1. What is the purpose of these graphs?

2. How do the data in the graphs relate to information in the chapter?

3. What does each part of the graphs represent?

4. What significant changes or other relationships do the graphs show?

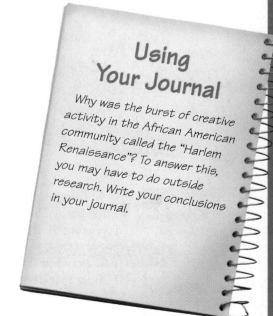

Using Your Journal

Why was the burst of creative activity in the African American community called the "Harlem Renaissance"? To answer this, you may have to do outside research. Write your conclusions in your journal.

CHAPTER 27

★★

The Depression Begins
1928–1932

▶ **APPLE VENDOR DURING THE DEPRESSION**

Setting the Scene

Focus

Most Americans believed that the election of Herbert Hoover as President in 1928 would continue a decade of prosperity. This optimism quickly disappeared. A prolonged slump in agriculture, industrial overproduction, high tariffs, and the stock market crash all contributed to the worst economic depression in the nation's history. By 1932 millions of Americans were out of work. When Hoover's best efforts to revive the economy proved unsuccessful, the nation turned to a new President.

Concepts to Understand

★ Why economic change from prosperity to depression was triggered by the stock market crash

★ How political policy changed as a result of the Depression

Read to Discover . . .

★ how President Hoover tried to lift the country out of the Depression.

★ why Hoover's political leadership was not more successful.

Journal Notes

As you read the chapter, record in your Journal how the American people conflicted with the government during the Depression.

CULTURAL			
• First color motion pictures are demonstrated by George Eastman	• Ernest Hemingway publishes A Farewell to Arms	• Sinclair Lewis is the first American to win Nobel Prize for Literature
1928	**1929**	**1930**
• Hoover is elected	• Stock market crashes	• Hawley-Smoot Tariff is passed
POLITICAL			

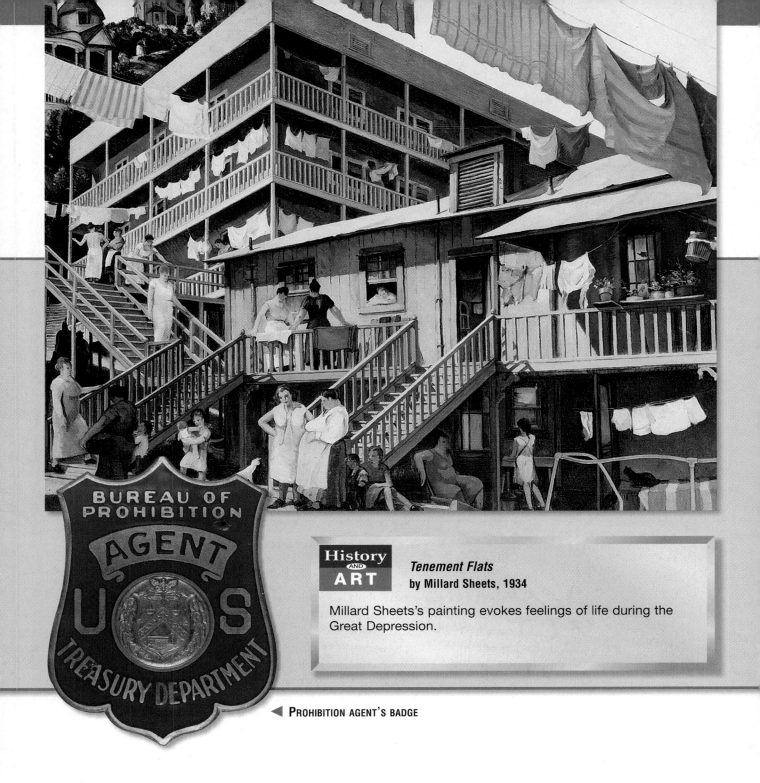

History AND ART

Tenement Flats
by Millard Sheets, 1934

Millard Sheets's painting evokes feelings of life during the Great Depression.

◀ **PROHIBITION AGENT'S BADGE**

- *"The Star-Spangled Banner" becomes official U.S. national anthem*

- *Amelia Earhart is first woman to fly solo across the Atlantic*

- *San Francisco Ballet founded*

1931

1932

1933

- *Hoover vetoes Veteran Bonus*

- *RFC is established*
- *Bonus Army marches on Washington, D.C.*

- *Franklin D. Roosevelt becomes President*

★★★

The Stock Market Crashes

Section Focus

When Calvin Coolidge declared, "I do not choose to run in 1928," he cleared the way for Herbert Hoover to head the Republican ticket. Many people believed that electing Hoover President would help continue the prosperity. With the great stock market crash of 1929, however, and the chain of economic problems that followed, this optimism disappeared.

Objectives

After studying this section, you should be able to

★ explain how Hoover's philosophy affected his economic policy.

★ explain the major causes of the Great Depression.

Key Terms

armory, securities, speculation, on margin, installment buying

◄ HOOVER CAMPAIGN BUTTON, 1928

erbert Hoover easily won the Republican nomination in 1928. A successful geologist, he had spent eight years as secretary of commerce in the Harding and Coolidge administrations. The Democrats chose Alfred E. Smith, four-time governor of New York. Their race for the presidency was marked by the influence of a new invention—the radio.

■ The Election of 1928

The most visible issue in the election campaign was Prohibition. Both candidates vowed to continue enforcing Prohibition. The Prohibition issue, however, masked other important differences between the candidates. Hoover represented rural, agrarian

interests; Smith represented urban, industrial interests.

Religion was at the core of a smear campaign against Smith's Catholicism. Wild tales circulated alleging that Catholics had turned certain Washington church sites into **armories,** or storehouses for guns. Some believed that the White House under Smith would become a branch of the Vatican. Hoover was embarrassed by these accusations and tried to quash them.

Late in the campaign, Hoover made a speech to offer his ideas on the proper relationship of government to business. Government, Hoover claimed, should be "an umpire instead of a player in the economic game." Government had a part to play—conservation of natural resources, scientific research, and flood control were places where Hoover believed government could make useful contributions. To him, personal liberty depended on economic freedom. He reminded his listeners that:

> " *Our experiment in human welfare has yielded a degree of well-being unparalleled in the world. . . . We are nearer to the ideal of abolition of poverty and fear from the lives of men and women than ever before in any land.* "

Prosperity was the campaign issue that proved most damaging to the Democrats. The almost uninterrupted prosperity the country had enjoyed during the 1920s was associated in the minds of many voters with the Republican party. Republican campaign slogans such as "two cars in every garage" gave the Democrats no chance of winning the election.

Hoover won an impressive victory in the Electoral College with a vote of 444 to 87, taking 58 percent of the popular vote and carrying all but 8 states. His appeal to rural Protestant voters even broke the Democrats' traditional hold on the Solid South, resulting in a Republican win in 5 Southern states. Although Smith lost the election, he won nearly twice as many votes as had the Democratic candidate in 1924. Of greater significance, Hoover became the first presidential winner to lose in the nation's 12 largest cities. A shift in the rural-urban balance of political power in America was in the wind.

■ Hoover in the White House

When he took office in March 1929, Herbert Hoover still radiated optimism. In his Inaugural Address, he predicted that the

▲ **CRIME FIGHTER ELIOT NESS**

▲ *PROHIBITION RAID* by Thomas Hart Benton, 1929 An unwanted result of Prohibition was the stimulus it gave to illegal activity. Thomas Hart Benton's *Prohibition Raid* is symbolic of the time. *What did the Wickersham Commission recommend?*

United States would soon be "in sight of the day when poverty will be banished from this nation."

Prohibition

Hoover did not believe that government should let economic events run their course but rather that it should help people to help themselves. He appointed commissions to investigate problems such as housing, retirement pensions, unemployment insurance, child welfare, and conservation. One commission, headed by former Attorney General George W. Wickersham, devoted 2 years to investigating Prohibition. The 11 members of the commission disagreed among themselves on whether Prohibition should continue. Most felt that the "noble experiment" was ineffective and promoted crime, yet the commission as a whole recommended that Prohibition be continued.

Farmers' Problems

The plight of farmers was an issue that demanded more immediate action. In April 1929, Hoover called Congress into special session to pass farming legislation. Members of Congress from farm states demanded that the federal government buy surplus farm products and sell them abroad. Hoover opposed this on the grounds that "no government agency should engage in buying and selling and price-fixing of products." Instead the President proposed that the federal government help farmers use their own organizations to market produce more efficiently and adjust supply to demand.

Following this recommendation, Congress passed the Agricultural Marketing Act of 1929, which created a Federal Farm Board with $500 million at its disposal to help existing farm organizations and to form new ones. The Farm Board established national cooperatives—such as the National Livestock Marketing Association and the American Cotton Cooperative Association—and then loaned these organizations money to help keep prices stable. It was too little, too late. Farmers were soon worse off than ever.

■ The Crash of 1929

The market value of **securities,** or stocks and bonds, on the New York Stock Exchange more than tripled between 1925 and 1929—from $27 billion to $87 billion. In the summer of 1929, for example, a share of General Motors rose from $268 to $391 and by September 2 rose even higher—to $452 per share.

Visualizing History ▲ EFFECTS OF THE CRASH One day after the stock market crash, Walter Thornton advertised his car for sale. Panic hit the stock market as people frantically tried to sell. *What effect did speculation have on the stock market in 1929?*

Speculation

As prices rose, more and more people began speculating. **Speculation** is engaging in a risky business venture on the chance that a quick or sizable profit can be made. People bought shares they thought would rise in price quickly, and after prices went up they would sell the stocks for a profit.

To maximize the potential profits on their investments, speculators commonly bought stock **on margin.** To buy stock in this way one made a small cash down payment and borrowed the rest from a stockbroker. For example, for $2,000 a person could buy 100 shares on margin rather than pay cash for 10 shares of stock at $200 per share. The purchaser simply put down 10 percent of the price (or $20 per share) and borrowed the other $18,000 from a broker, who would then hold the shares of stock as collateral for the loan. So long as prices continued to rise, investors could sell the stock later, repay the loan, and reap the profit.

Stock Market Begins to Decline

Some bankers, brokers, and economists were concerned, however, because they knew the stocks for many companies were greatly overpriced in comparison to the earnings and profits the companies were making. Yet most investors were swept along on the tide of the day's optimism. Meanwhile, the market continued its dizzying climb. By the end of 1929, brokers' loans to those who had bought on margin exceeded $7 billion. The Federal Reserve Board tried to restore stability to the market by advising banks not to loan money for buying stocks on margin, but few banks listened.

In September 1929, the market started to waver as some professional speculators sensed danger and began to pull out, and prices slipped. Late in October real disaster struck. On Thursday, October 24, almost 13 million shares of stocks were frantically traded. As stocks' values dropped below the amounts borrowed to purchase them, brokers demanded that investors repay their loans. If they could not, the brokers offered the stock for sale.

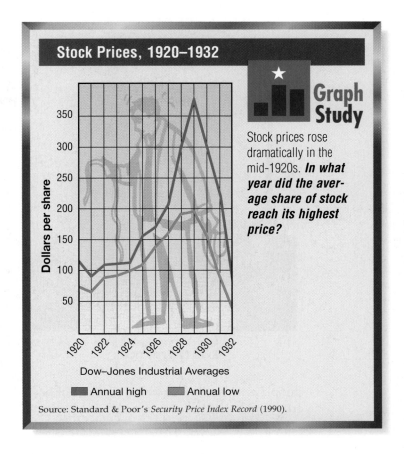

Stock Prices, 1920–1932

Graph Study

Stock prices rose dramatically in the mid-1920s. *In what year did the average share of stock reach its highest price?*

Dollars per share

Dow–Jones Industrial Averages

■ Annual high   ■ Annual low

Source: Standard & Poor's *Security Price Index Record* (1990).

Black Tuesday

Recognizing what was going on, investment bankers tried to shore up market prices by purchasing as many shares as they could. The effort was not enough to stabilize an overvalued market. On October 29—Black Tuesday—the bottom fell out. Some 16 million shares were sold, causing such a collapse that by mid-November the average price of securities had been cut nearly in half. This cost investors about $30 billion, a sum that represented almost one-third of the value of all goods and services produced in the United States in 1929. The loss was equal to the total wages of all Americans that year.

About 1.5 million Americans had been involved in purchasing stock. Many investors lost their entire life savings.

It was the failure of banks that hit people the hardest. Banks loaned money to brokerage houses, which in turn bought stock themselves or loaned money to investors for speculative stock purchases. When loan payments were not forthcoming, many banks went bankrupt. In the aftermath, millions of

▲ TELEGRAPHIC TICKER

people who had never bought stock but had trustingly kept their money in savings accounts lost everything as the banks closed.

■ Causes of the Great Depression

The collapse of the stock market was only a prelude to a catastrophic economic decline from which the United States did not recover for 12 years. The causes of the Great Depression were so complex that economists have debated the issue ever since.

Overproduction and Underconsumption

One cause of the Depression was overproduction. Laborsaving machinery had increased the production capacity of the nation's industries so much that far more goods were produced than the American population could consume. For a time, consumer purchasing power was bolstered by **installment buying**—an agreement whereby a purchaser made a down payment and paid the rest of the cost in periodic regular installments to which an interest charge was added. By the late 1920s, most consumers

who could afford high-cost items such as refrigerators, cars, or stoves had bought them on an installment plan. Consumer spending began to decrease. From January to September 1929, for example, the number of automobile purchases dropped by one-third.

Another cause of the Depression was underconsumption. In the 1920s the rich got richer much faster than the rest of the people. Some 30,000 families at the top of the economic pyramid had as much income as did the 11 million families at the bottom. Though production increased, employment stood still and workers' wages went up very slowly. In 1929 more than two-thirds of the nation's families were earning less than $2,500 per year, a sum said to be the minimum income for a decent quality of life. About one-fifth of the nation lived in dire poverty. Thus there was insufficient purchasing power to support the nation's mass-production industries.

Agricultural Slump and Surpluses

A prolonged slump in agriculture, which affected the economic life of the entire country, was another factor. Farmers were heavily indebted to banks, which held mortgages on farmlands throughout the nation. The declining value of farms made it harder for farmers to get credit. Banks that had invested heavily in farm mortgages were in danger of failing.

In addition, huge farm surpluses produced a drop in farm prices so great that farmers often spent more money growing and marketing their products than they received in selling them. The resulting loss in farmers' purchasing power further reduced the consumption of manufactured goods—a condition that only added to the problem of underconsumption.

Tariffs and Taxes

The Great Depression was not solely a result of economic practices. Many of the economic policies of the Harding and Coolidge administrations during the 1920s set the stage for problems by the end of the decade. Policies such as the high Fordney-McCumber tariff, combined with an insistence on collecting war debts, interfered with world trade and destroyed foreign markets for American products, especially in agriculture. The Mellon tax policies, which aided the upper class, contributed to the uneven distribution of wealth. Failure to curb or discourage the stock market's early boom made the ultimate crash more severe.

Once started, the Great Depression took on a momentum of its own. Individuals with mortgages on their homes, who had bought cars and other goods on credit and who had purchased stocks on margin, "lost their shirts." They stopped buying, for example, luxuries like radios, causing radio manufacturers to close down plants or run them only part-time. Thousands of workers were laid off as orders were canceled for copper, wood cabinets, and glass radio tubes. Montana copper miners, Minnesota lumberjacks, and Ohio glassworkers in turn lost their jobs.

Because these jobless workers could not meet mortgage payments or repay loans, they lost their property. Banks that had lent them money failed, wiping out the savings of their depositors. Such chain reactions closed down more and more factories, drove more and more firms into bankruptcy, and put more and more Americans out of work.

Russell Hunter, a brass worker in the Naugatuck Valley region of Connecticut, known as the "Brass Valley," describes what the early years of the Depression were like:

❝ During Hoover's time, we went on short time. After a while, when things really were bad, in 1932, we were working sometimes five hours a week, one day a week. That was tough, trying to raise a family. Nobody lost their jobs completely. They shared [the work] to give everybody something to do. Still, you had to go on welfare. People got by going on the welfare. At that time, people were losing their homes, automobiles. . . . ❞

The mood of the country was changing. Feelings of optimism were giving way to feelings of fear.

GNP, Stock Values, and Unemployment

Year	Gross National Product (in billions)	Stock Values, New York Stock Exchange (in billions)	Unemployment (Percent)
1920	$140.0	$5.5	5.2
1921	127.8	4.7	11.7
1922	148.0	5.7	6.7
1923	165.9	5.9	2.4
1924	165.5	5.9	5.0
1925	179.4	7.6	3.2
1926	190.0	8.6	1.8
1927	189.8	10.5	3.3
1928	190.9	13.7	4.2
1929	203.6	17.9	3.2
1930	183.5	14.4	8.7
1931	169.3	7.5	15.9
1932	144.2	3.8	23.6

Chart Study Study each column heading, noting the years that show the greatest change. *What was the worst year of the Great Depression for both business and labor?*

Section 1 ★ Review

Checking for Understanding

1. **Identify** Wickersham Commission, Agricultural Marketing Act.

2. **Define** armory, securities, speculation, on margin, installment buying.

3. **Explain** how speculation caused the stock market to rise.

4. **List** four causes of the Great Depression.

Critical Thinking

5. **Synthesizing Ideas** Who was to blame for stock market speculation and the problems it caused—stockbrokers, banks, speculators, or the government? Explain your answer.

The Stock Market

"Sooner or later," said economist Roger Babson on September 5, 1929, "a crash is coming . . . factories will be shut down . . . men will be thrown out of work . . . the result will be a serious business depression." However, most analysts assured Americans that the stock market was healthy and thriving.

A stock exchange is an organized system for buying and selling shares, or blocks of investments, in corporations. In the late 1920s, the value of stocks on the New York Stock Exchange climbed to dizzying heights. To take advantage of the boom, investors borrowed money to buy stocks, a practice known as buying on margin.

In other words, speculators were using their own money to make a relatively small down payment on the stock and borrowing the remainder of the purchase price from a stockbroker. The broker in turn borrowed the money lent to the speculator from a bank. The brokers' loans were call loans—loans that could be called in at any time by the borrower or lender.

The 1920s seemed to be a period of never-ending prosperity. The values of common stock had been increasing steadily year after year. In 1926 more than 450 million shares of stock were traded on the New York Stock Exchange. In 1927 the total rose to more than 570 million. Speculators believed they could make a quick profit in the market. Bankers knew they could make money by lending to brokers. Brokers knew they could come out ahead by lending to customers. Everyone, it seemed, was trying to get rich quickly.

The boom could last only as long as investors added money to the pool. By 1929 everyone with money to invest had bought into the market, and it ran out of new customers. Prices stopped rising. People sold shares to pay the interest on their loans. As shares were sold,

prices fell. Panicked investors tried to minimize their losses.

On October 29, less than two months after Babson's prediction, the market crashed. The crash was a symptom, not a cause, of the Great Depression.

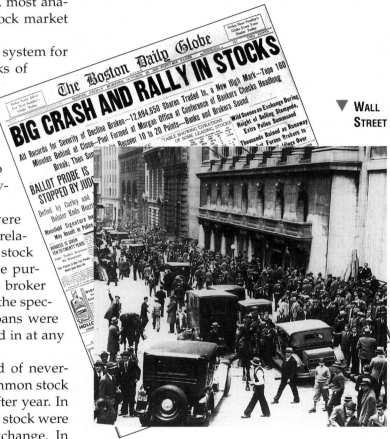

▼ WALL STREET

Making the Economics Connection

1. What series of events occur when the stock market crashes?

2. Why did people begin selling shares of stock in the fall of 1929?

Linking Past and Present

3. Compare the 1929 stock market crash with the savings and loan crisis of the 1980s.

★★

Hoover's Policies

Section Focus

Before 1929 the federal government had responded to economic depressions by considering different monetary or tariff policies. During the Great Depression, however, the government was forced to seek more vigorous remedies for the nation's vast economic problems. Failing to succeed in domestic policies, President Herbert Hoover made peace the cornerstone of his administration.

Objectives

After studying this section, you should be able to

★ list the ways in which Hoover tried to end the Depression.

★ describe the change in policy toward Latin America under Hoover.

★ describe the Hoover-Stimson Doctrine and evaluate its effectiveness.

Key Term

moratorium

▲ **UNION LABEL SYMBOL**

No sooner had the stock market collapsed than President Hoover asked leaders of industry, finance, and labor to come to the White House. The President asked labor leaders to abandon or postpone wage demands, industry leaders to keep employment high, and bankers to continue lending.

Hoover and other leaders tried to restore public confidence by issuing optimistic statements. Their rosy predictions were contradicted by worsening conditions, however, and the phrase "prosperity is just around the corner" became a joke. The Republican campaign slogan "Two cars in every garage" had become "Two families in every garage." The President's position was made all the more difficult because he was blamed for the Depression.

■ Domestic Economic Concerns Loom

In dealing with Congress and the public, Hoover was limited by his inflexible views. A man of great ability and possessing a sincere desire to serve the nation, he lacked the practical political experience that comes from being a legislator or state executive. Even with such skills, his position would have been difficult. Republican party leaders never gave him their whole-hearted support, and members of the Farm Bloc were in open revolt. As a result of the midterm elections of 1930, the Democrats made gains in the Senate and won control of the House of Representatives. This shift in power led to a Congress that was hostile to Hoover's policies during the last two years of his administration.

Tariffs

Like President Taft in 1909, Hoover was unable to control Congress on the tariff issue. The Hawley-Smoot Tariff started in the House as a protection for farmers, but by the time it passed the Senate, it had turned into the highest protective tariff in peacetime history. It raised the average duty on raw agricultural materials and other items above the Fordney-McCumber Act levels.

By the time the Hawley-Smoot bill reached the President's desk in 1930, more than 1,000 leading economists had signed a letter urging him to veto it. They argued that it would help inefficient producers, raise consumer prices, reduce foreign markets, and cause ill will toward the United States in other countries. This opinion was voiced by many newspapers, bankers, and even by a number of manufacturers. Now Hoover faced a dilemma. If he used his veto power, he would isolate himself politically by breaking with the Republican values he held so strongly. Furthermore, he would abandon the one feature of the bill he had fought so hard for—a revised Tariff Commission with the authority to raise and lower rates. He therefore signed the bill in spite of the warnings.

Within a year, 25 nations retaliated with laws to restrict purchases of American goods, causing foreign trade with the United States to drop rapidly. Some American corporations managed to avoid international barriers by establishing factories overseas. Ironically, an act designed to promote American economic recovery instead created employment overseas.

Farmers

American farmers, beleaguered throughout the 1920s, were hit even harder. Farmers' income was cut by more than half between 1929 and 1932; their burden of debt became unbearable. During this crisis the Farm Board tried to maintain the price of wheat and cotton by buying up the surplus of these crops. The Farm Board also attempted—without success—to persuade farmers to plant less, in order to reduce the amount of farm produce grown and thus to prevent further surplus crops. The immense quantities of wheat and cotton held by the government actually drove prices down, however, because buyers feared that the government would sell these surpluses as soon as prices rose. Finally, in 1931 the Farm Board acknowledged defeat and stopped its purchases. Immediately prices dropped even lower. By 1932 farmers were receiving only 38 cents a bushel for wheat that in 1929 had sold at $1.04. Even Hoover's relatives in Iowa suffered from the depressed farm economy. Harry Terrell, a farmer who lived in the same neighborhood as President Hoover in Iowa, described conditions in the following way:

> **" *I was born across the road from the farm of Herbert Hoover's uncle. I knew the Hoover family, distant cousins of the President. Even people like them, they had times just like the rest of us. . . . Corn was going for eight cents a bushel. One county insisted on burning corn to heat the courthouse, 'cause it was cheaper than coal."* "

■ Hoover's Strong Resolve

Hoover was deeply affected by all the misery and poverty around him, but as a staunch believer in private enterprise, he feared direct government handouts would destroy personal initiative. Hoover therefore offered government help to banks and businesses in the hope that restored financial health at the top of the economic pyramid would eventually trickle down to relieve unemployment at the bottom. Keeping his attitude positive and his resolve strong, Hoover sought to inspire confidence in a people ravaged by hopelessness and despair: "Ninety percent of our difficulty in depression is caused by fear."

History AND ART

▲ *DROUGHT-STRICKEN AREA* by Alexander Hogue, 1934 The collapse of farm prices was compounded by a terrible drought in 1930. *How did President Hoover feel about providing direct relief to the unemployed?*

In 1932, after Hoover's initial resistance, Congress established the Reconstruction Finance Corporation (RFC). With $2 billion in resources, the RFC made loans to hard-pressed railroads, insurance companies, banks, and even state and local governments—but not to individuals. The RFC favored projects that were "self-liquidating"; that is, projects designed to pay their way so the government would eventually get back its money. Thus projects such as toll bridges and dams that would produce electric power were favored over those that could have been socially useful but brought in no revenue, such as playgrounds, schools, and city halls.

There was a point beyond which Hoover refused to use the power of the federal government. He feared that too much reliance on federal action would result in the "paternalism" and "state socialism" he had warned against in 1928. He opposed direct federal relief for the unemployed because he believed it would weaken the self-respect of those who received it, undercut the efforts of private charity, and that it would destroy the tradition of local responsibility for the unfortunate. Hoover, therefore, vetoed the Garner-Wagner bill in 1932, which would have given direct aid to the unemployed. He also vetoed the Norris bill, which would have put the government in the business of producing and selling electricity in the Tennessee Valley—thus setting up direct competition with private companies.

■ Efforts for Peace

The desire for world peace was strong during these hard times, partly because preparation for war was costly, and partly because few had forgotten the horrors of World War I.

As a Quaker and a pacifist, Herbert Hoover believed that war was morally wrong; as administrator of Belgian relief between 1914 and 1917, he saw firsthand the devastation of World War I. Hoover was committed to world peace. As he stated in 1928:

> *I think I may say that I have witnessed as much of the horror and suffering of war as any other American. From it I have derived a deep passion for peace. Our foreign policy has one primary objective, and that is peace.*

Hoover's peace efforts were aided by his many years spent overseas. The most widely traveled man ever to occupy the White House, he had visited every continent and knew many foreign leaders personally.

Latin America

As secretary of commerce, Hoover had come to understand Latin America's distrust of the United States. Before his inauguration in March 1929, he made goodwill tours of 10 Latin American countries. Hoover stressed that the United States wished to be a friend to its neighbors in Latin America. Many expressed doubts about how effective Hoover's efforts would be. Hoover's Latin American policies reflected a sincere desire to improve relations. In addition to successfully arbitrating a long-standing boundary dispute between Chile and Peru, Hoover abandoned military intervention in Latin American countries.

The Clark Memorandum, written by Undersecretary of State J. Reuben Clark, argued the position that the Roosevelt Corollary to the Monroe Doctrine had no historical basis. Clark wrote, "The Monroe Doctrine states a case of the United States v. Europe, not of the United States v. Latin America." In other words, the Monroe Doctrine could no longer be used to justify American intervention in Latin America.

In accordance with this principle, Hoover withdrew troops from Nicaragua and refused to intervene in the affairs of Latin American states that, because of political chaos, had repudiated their debts to the United States. While this nonintervention policy helped to convince many Latin Americans that the United States had no aggressive intentions, it won Hoover little goodwill. The Hawley-Smoot Tariff had hurt Latin America's economy, and the region's resentment of the power of the United States did not disappear.

▲ **SOUP KITCHEN** People line up at a 1930s Chicago soup kitchen, operated by gangster Al Capone. Government made few efforts to help citizens fight the effects of the Depression. *What was the Garner-Wagner bill intended to provide?*

Disarmament

Hoover strongly favored disarmament, not only because of his personal beliefs but also because military spending and increased taxes depleted valuable resources. Shortly after taking office, Hoover made arrangements for a new conference in London on naval disarmament. Its goal would be to extend the limits on battleships that had been set in the Five-Power Treaty signed in 1921–1922.

After four months of talks, the London Naval Conference of 1930 produced a treaty fixing ratios for the submarines, cruisers, and destroyers of the United States, British, and Japanese navies. Italy refused to sign. France, fearing aggression by Germany and Italy, said that it favored disarmament only if other powers would agree to give France assurance of protection. In the end, France chose not to sign.

Ever since 1927 a disarmament conference hosted by the League of Nations had been meeting at Geneva. Its work was hampered by the activities of lobbyists for arms manufacturers and by mutual mistrust among the delegates. For five years it had gotten nowhere, focusing on such trivial issues as the influence of fog on war. In 1932 President Hoover proposed to the Geneva Conference that the nations of the world either entirely abandon aggressive weapons or cut existing arms by one-third. No action resulted. With Adolf Hitler's rise to power in Germany, however, and Japanese invasions into China, disarmament now seemed like an invitation to aggression. Hoover's proposal could have succeeded only if the United States had been willing to join an alliance of nations committed to "collective security," whereby members would all agree to come to the aid of any member nation who was threatened with aggression.

War Reparations

By 1931 Germany was in the throes of a serious depression. Germans could not continue paying war reparations to the Allies without defaulting on their debts to American private investors. Hoover, like

▲ JAPAN AND MANCHURIA An American cartoon condemns Japan's 1931 seizure of Manchuria. *What was the American response to the Japanese invasion?*

Harding and Coolidge before him, believed that reparations were "a European problem." But heavy war debts and rising unemployment caused great discontent among the German people and led directly to the rapid growth of two antidemocratic parties—the Communist party and the Nazi party.

Moratorium

The Allies were unlikely to cancel German reparation payments, which they used to pay off their own war debts to the United States. To address the problem, in 1931 Hoover proposed an international **moratorium,** or suspension, for one year of all war-debt payments to the United States. Hoover's aim was to protect United States investments in Germany and to save the German Republic from collapse, as well as to stimulate international trade. Secretary of State Henry L. Stimson urged that war debts and reparations be canceled completely, but Hoover refused. To do so would have been a highly unpopular measure and would have worsened Hoover's already poor relations with Congress.

The Hoover-Stimson Doctrine

The Hoover administration encountered problems in the Far East. In September 1931, Japan seized China's rich province of Manchuria. Taking advantage of the civil war in China and the weak condition of the Western nations, Japanese armies speedily overran Manchuria. This action was in direct violation of the Nine-Power Treaty of 1922, which guaranteed China's sovereignty, and the Kellogg-Briand Pact, which outlawed wars of aggression. It also breached the Charter of the League of Nations, to which both China and Japan belonged.

The Intent of the Doctrine

China appealed to the League of Nations, which turned to the United States for help. President Hoover, however, refused to consider either economic or military action. Instead, he sent an army officer to serve on a League commission to investigate Japanese actions in Manchuria. Secretary Stimson proclaimed in 1932 that the United States would refuse to recognize the legality of any territorial arrangement that violated the Kellogg-Briand Pact. The Hoover-Stimson Doctrine, designed to enlist world opinion against aggressor nations, did nothing to aid China and served only to irritate the Japanese.

Although the nonrecognition policy had been worked out by Hoover and Stimson together, it meant different things to each of them. Stimson wanted the policy to act as a warning, which later might be backed up by economic or military aid. According to Hoover, the statement itself was enough. The United States, he said, did not exist to police the world. Economic sanctions might lead to war, he said, and Japanese aggression in Asia did not "imperil the freedom of the American people." Hoover then said that should the United States be obliged to

> **❝ . . . arm and train Chinese, [we would] find ourselves involved in China in a fashion that would excite the suspicions of the whole world. ❞**

Nor were the British and French governments willing to apply sanctions. The failure of Western nations to take action only encouraged Japanese expansion into China and Southeast Asia.

Public Opinion

The American public was not prepared to support any interventionist effort that could potentially involve the United States in war once again. This feeling was evident in 1931 when Congress overwhelmingly overrode Hoover's veto and voted to give independence to the Philippines within 10 years. This measure pleased Filipino leaders; it also pleased the United States business community, who wanted to keep Filipino products out of America. However, a major reason for passage of the bill was that the American people no longer wanted to defend the islands, upholding the American anti-imperialist past.

Section 2 ★ Review

Checking for Understanding

1. **Identify** Hawley-Smoot Tariff, Reconstruction Finance Corporation, Clark Memorandum, Hoover-Stimson Doctrine.

2. **Define** moratorium.

3. **Summarize** why Hoover disapproved of relief programs and direct involvement in business.

4. **List** three actions Hoover took to promote ties with Latin America.

Critical Thinking

5. **Predicting Consequences** What message did the United States and its allies send to leaders such as Adolf Hitler by not taking action against Japan?

Study and Writing Skills

Writing a Persuasive Argument

A persuasive argument is one in which the reader or listener is urged to do something or believe in the same thing as does the writer or speaker.

The following guidelines will help you organize and write a persuasive argument:

a. Before writing, research the topic. What are the facts, and how do people feel about it?

b. Tailor your argument to your audience.

c. Support your argument with solid facts and examples.

d. Save the most persuasive arguments for last, then end your paper by summarizing.

▲ PRESIDENT HERBERT HOOVER

Imagine that the following is a paper that you wrote as Herbert Hoover defending his war debt moratorium. Note how the guidelines were applied:

I am writing to you, the people of France, as you continue to heal the wounds inflicted by the Great War. My heart and thoughts are with you. There is depression, unemployment, and debt. Germany, for all its past offenses, is teetering on the brink of collapse. Europe, like America, is fighting the effects of this demoralizing depression. The time has come to close the gap between how we feel about that Great War. Let us consider our children's future, and not so much our temporary feelings of outrage for a war that is over. Abide with me in my decision to place a one-year, international moratorium on all war debts. It is time to let go of the past and resurrect the quality of life that has been obscured by this spectre of debt.

After reading this, it should be clear to Hoover's audience that:

a. Hoover researched the topic.

b. Hoover tailored this paper for the French people.

c. His remark about America's suffering made the point that all countries were linked by common interests.

d. He mentioned the future of the world's children as perhaps the most persuasive argument, making the reader realize that feelings of revenge could affect the world for years to come. Then he summarized the argument with an appeal to let go of the past and to restore the quality of life that had been lost.

Practicing the Skill

For practice in this skill, write a persuasive argument against the Hawley-Smoot Tariff. Determine your audience before you begin writing.

★★★

The Depression Worsens

Setting the Scene

Section Focus

Between Election Day in November 1932 and Inauguration Day in March 1933, the nation's economy hit rock bottom. National income had dropped from $81 billion to $41 billion. Over 25 percent of the nation's workers were unemployed, and many others worked only part-time. Thousands of businesses were bankrupt, thousands of banks had closed, and farmers were in revolt.

Objectives

After studying this section, you should be able to

★ compare the condition of workers and farmers in the early 1930s.

★ discuss the mood of the country as the election of 1932 approached.

Key Term

lame duck

▶ DEPRESSION SCRIP, EMERGENCY MONEY

The Depression was uneven in its impact. While many people lost their jobs, the majority of Americans did not. Instead many found their hours reduced. The few who kept their jobs and did not have their hours or wages cut actually were better off because prices declined. Even so, for most Americans the mood was gloomy—and for good reason. In 1932 over 30,000 companies closed. In just 2 months in 1931 over 800 banks failed, wiping out the life savings of thousands of depositors.

All over the United States, families not able to pay their rent or mortgages were evicted from their homes. Some ended up in communities of makeshift shacks on the outskirts of cities.

■ Want in the Land of Plenty

As the Depression deepened, fear and despair replaced the buoyant optimism of the 1920s. "I'm afraid, every man is afraid," steel industrialist Charles M. Schwab admitted. "I don't know, we don't know, whether the values we have are going to be real next month or not."

Fear

Loss of confidence affected all sorts of people. Some who lost their jobs suffered such emotional effects that they became unemployable. "My father spent two years painting his father's house," one man later remembered. "He painted it twice. It gave him something to do."

Business leaders hesitated to build new factories or to bring out new products. Frightened bankers became unwilling to lend money, even to borrowers with good character and ample collateral. On the stock market, security prices dropped dramatically. Stock in Radio Corporation of America (RCA) dropped from $101 per share in 1929 to $2.50 in 1932.

Starvation

One of the great ironies of the Depression was that starvation existed in the midst of plenty. The productive capacity of farmers did not slacken. On the contrary, farmers' problems resulted, in part, from their ability to grow more food than they were able to sell. Already in a depression throughout most of the 1920s, the collapse of the farm economy after 1929 wreaked havoc on rural America. Despite Hoover's programs, grain prices dropped so low that farmers heated their homes by shoveling their crops into their furnaces. They protested low agricultural prices by declaring "farmers' holidays" and tried to prevent food shipments to cities. In Iowa farmers blockaded highways and dumped milk trucks in an attempt to make milk scarce and raise its price. In Oregon they slaughtered sheep because mutton prices were lower than what it cost to ship the animals to market. Meanwhile, in America's cities people picked through garbage looking for scraps of meat.

Virginia Durr, an Alabama activist for tenant farmers' rights, described the suffering when she said, "Have you ever seen a child with rickets shaking, as with palsy? No proteins, no milk. And the companies pouring milk into the gutters. . . . People with nothing to eat and they killed the pigs."

▶ APPLE SELLER, NEW YORK CITY, 1932

Visualizing History

▲ "HOOVERVILLES" Many families lost their homes during the Great Depression because they were unable to meet mortgage payments or pay rent. Some of the homeless found living quarters in shacks constructed of tin and old crates. Villages of these makeshift shacks, such as this one in Seattle, Washington, sprouted up throughout the nation. *How did the rate of unemployment change between 1930 and 1933?*

★★

Depression Needy

Counting the families of the unemployed and the underemployed—those who could find only part-time work—34 million Americans were living without enough money to buy adequate food or to pay rent and mortgages.

The tragedies of the Depression became so commonplace that children played games with names like "Eviction" and "Relief." Yet even play was a luxury for some children who, foraging for food, had to fight grown men and women for the garbage in city dumps. Other people survived by eating weeds or dog biscuits that they stole from the local pound. The severe needs of people during the Depression resulted in an increase in health problems. Poor or inadequate nutrition made Americans vulnerable to disease, and the incidence of typhoid, dysentery, tuberculosis, and heart and stomach disorders increased.

The problems of families became acute when they could not pay their rent, and they were evicted from their homes. Homeless people often devised ingenious makeshift shelters. Some built shacks from packing boxes, and others camped in sewer pipes.

ORK-IS-WHAT-I
ANT-AND-NOT-CHARITY
HO-WILL-HELP-ME-
ET-A-JOB-7-YEARS-
V-DETROIT. NO-MONEY
NT-AWAY-FURNISH-
ST-OF-REFERENCES
HONE RANDOLPH 8381 Room

★★

▲ *DUST BOWL* BY ALEXANDER HOGUE

■ The Human Cost of the Depression

Although business leaders promised Hoover that they would not cut wages of remaining workers, as the Depression deepened, their situation changed.

Wage Cuts and Unemployment

In October 1931, United States Steel Corporation cut salaries and wages by 10 percent, and employers in other industries soon followed. By 1933 salaries had decreased 40 percent and hourly wages by 60 percent. The average family's income fell from $2,300 in 1929 to $1,600 in 1932. More layoffs followed the wage cuts. In 1930, 4 million workers were unemployed; by 1933 the number of jobless Americans more than tripled.

In cities throughout the country breadlines and soup kitchens appeared on sidewalks as local governments and private charities struggled to feed the poor. In some cases the lines stretched for blocks as people waited for their only good meal each day.

As unemployment grew, Hoover's Reconstruction Finance Corporation began to loan money to state governments for relief, but these and other relief funds proved woefully inadequate. Toledo, Ohio, for example, could only spend 2 cents for each relief meal it served. New York City provided only $2.39 per week to each family on relief. In many other cities, after private charity was exhausted, there was nothing.

Hoovervilles

Throughout the nation, families who could not pay their rent or make their mortgage payments were evicted from their homes. Some moved in with relatives if they could. The less fortunate ended up in makeshift communities dubbed "Hoovervilles" on the outskirts of cities. One woman later remembered Oklahoma City's Hooverville:

> *Here were all these people living in rusted-out car bodies. I mean that was their home. There were people living in shacks made of orange crates. One family with a whole lot of kids were living in a piano box. This wasn't just a little section, this was maybe ten miles wide and ten miles long. People living in what ever they could junk together.*

People who were even less fortunate slept in doorways or on park benches. Desperate men grubbed in garbage cans to feed their families. Nearly every street corner had its apple seller. So many apples were available because of a surplus of the fruit in the Pacific Northwest. To reduce the surplus, the International Apple Shippers Association set up a system for unemployed people to sell the apples. A person could get a credit for $1.75 for a crate of 100 to 120 apples, then turn around and sell the apples for 5 cents each, making a small profit. However, as more and more people tried to make money this way, apple vendors reacted by raising the price to $2.25 a crate. Unless a person sold more than half a crate, he or she made no profit.

Other jobless Americans banded together in hunger riots, smashing into grocery stores and grabbing whatever food they could carry. Begging increased dramatically, and the song "Brother, Can You Spare a Dime?" became a bitter testimony to veterans who remembered fighting a war to protect American values and to make the world safe for democracy.

■ The Bonus Army

In May 1932, some 1,500 unemployed army veterans and their families marched on Washington, D.C., to demand early payment of the bonus Congress had promised to pay them in 1945. Within sight of the White House, some set up a Hooverville in an area across the Potomac River known as Anacostia Flats. Others occupied abandoned buildings in the area. As they demonstrated daily in front of the White House and the Capitol, their numbers increased to more than 20,000.

The government tried to keep the protesters peaceful. President Hoover supported their right to express their views and even provided them with army tents, cots, and field kitchens. When Congress

★★★★**A**★★★★★★ **MERICAN PORTRAITS**

Dorothea Lange
1895–1965

By the time she finished high school, Dorothea Lange had chosen her career. She wanted to be a photographer—even though she had never used a camera.

After taking a photography course, Lange journeyed from New York to San Francisco, where she ran a portrait business for 10 years. Then the Depression struck. Lange became a documentary photographer, her compassion showing clearly in her photos. By the mid-1930s she was documenting the life of California's migrant laborers, work that earned her a position with the Farm Security Administration (FSA). Her FSA photos revealed poverty's brutal effects on rural Americans. Lange later traveled through the dust bowl states, capturing people's suffering in a book called *An American Exodus, A Record of Human Erosion.*

rejected their demands, most of the veterans left Washington. About 2,000 refused to leave, however. After a clash between the veterans and the local police, Hoover called in the army. General Douglas MacArthur, commander of the troops, carried out the President's orders to clear the veterans from federal buildings. Using tanks, machine guns, and tear gas, his troops drove the veterans out of Washington and burned their camp. Historian Frederick Lewis Allen described the sudden chaos that resulted:

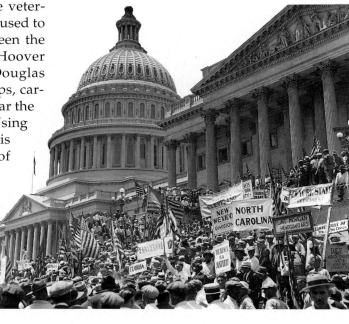

“ *Cavalrymen were riding into the crowd, infantrymen were throwing tear-gas bombs, women and children were being trampled and choking from the gas; . . . [People] were running wildly, pell-mell across uneven ground, screaming as they stumbled and fell. The troops moved slowly on, scattering before them veterans and homegoing government clerks alike. . . . That evening, the Washington sky glowed with fire. Even after midnight the troops were still on their way with bayonets and tear-gas bombs.* ”

Visualizing History

▲ **THE BONUS ARMY** Veterans of World War I converged on Washington, D.C., in 1932. They hoped to persuade Congress to grant them immediate payments of a bonus, not due until 1945. *How did the federal government react to the bonus marchers?*

Many Americans blamed Hoover for the use of brutal and excessive force against the veterans. He seemed more than ever an inflexible leader.

■ Fear of Revolution

During this time of bewilderment and despair, fear of revolution started to spread. Lloyds of London, a British insurance company, began to write policies for riot insurance in the United States. Looking for scapegoats, Americans blamed the Depression on the very people they had admired and willingly followed a few years earlier—industrialists and bankers. Public outrage increased when a Senate investigation charged that some of the nation's wealthiest were trying to get away without paying taxes on their huge incomes. Others were accused of using unscrupulous business practices to increase their wealth in the midst of such widespread poverty and suffering.

Radical Alternatives

The unrest in society offered hope to both Socialists and Communists, who preached that the Depression marked the end of capitalism, which would soon be replaced by a system that distributed goods more fairly. Both groups proposed that government control the means of production and distribution. Both promised that a planned economy would result in greater abundance for all. "Folks are restless," observed Mississippi Governor Theodore Bilbo, "communism is gaining a foothold. . . . In fact, I'm getting a little pink myself."

Such radical alternatives were weakened because Socialists and Communists bitterly opposed each other and destroyed each other's credibility. The Socialists proposed to gain their power by persuasion and the ballot box. The Communist party, however, held that capitalism could not be overthrown without violent revolution—what Earl Browder, the general secretary of the party, called the "omelet theory." Just as it was impossible to make an omelet without breaking eggs, Browder explained, it was impossible to make a revolution without breaking heads.

Using the Forces of Democracy

Fears of a revolution in the United States proved to be unfounded, however. Although many Americans were suffering, were angry, and wanted a change, protest movements tended to be splintered. No single leader emerged to galvanize them or act as a unifying force. Most Americans clung to their democratic traditions and expressed their anger at the ballot box.

■ The Election of 1932

As the presidential election of 1932 approached, the Democrats sensed victory for the first time since 1916.

The Candidates

The Democratic national convention rejected Al Smith's bid for renomination and instead chose New York Governor Franklin D. Roosevelt as their candidate. The former secretary of the navy had run as the Democratic candidate for Vice President in 1920. In 1928, while Smith was losing the presidential election to Hoover, Roosevelt

▲ *HOME RELIEF STATION* by Louis Ribak, 1935–1936 The painting expresses the frustration felt by the American people during the Depression years. *What did the election of 1932 reveal about American public opinion concerning the Hoover administration and its response during the most difficult years of the Depression?*

had won New York's race for governor and in the process proved himself to be a remarkable vote-getter. In 1930 he had been reelected by a huge majority.

The Democratic Platform

The Democratic platform of 1932—the briefest in United States political history—urged the repeal of Prohibition and made general proposals for reform and recovery. The Democrats' most effective asset, however, was Roosevelt himself. Setting the tone for what became a whirlwind campaign, he flew by plane to the Democratic convention to become the first candidate to accept a presidential nomination in person.

In his acceptance address, he pledged "a new deal for the American people." In later speeches, however, he was vague and described the "New Deal" in broad terms only. It remained clear that Roosevelt intended to take action that would help "the forgotten man at the bottom of the economic pyramid." He summed up the history of the Hoover administration in four sentences:

> 66 *First, it encouraged speculation and overproduction through its false economic policies. Second, it attempted to minimize the crash and misled the people as to its gravity. Third, it erroneously charged the cause to other nations of the world. And finally, it refused to recognize and correct the evils at home which it had brought forth; it delayed reform, it forgot reform.* 99

The Republicans Nominate Hoover

The Republicans, meanwhile, gloomily renominated Hoover, who suffered the problem of having to defend his policies in the midst of a terrible Depression. He maintained that hard times were the result of economic collapse abroad—for which his administration could not be held responsible. Hoover flatly rejected Roosevelt's position that government had "a positive duty to see that no citizen shall starve." "You cannot," warned Hoover, "extend the mastery of government over the daily life of a people without somewhere making it master of people's souls and thoughts."

Democrats Victorious

On Election Day, the Republican victories of the 1920s were completely reversed as Roosevelt carried 42 of the 48 states. This landslide revealed not only a widespread willingness to blame the Republicans for the Depression but also a desire to use government as an agency for human welfare.

Yet even at the bottom of the worst depression in history, few Americans favored the overthrow of capitalism, either by violent or peaceful means. The election results revealed that the Socialists polled 900,000 votes and

▲ INAUGURATION DAY During the ride to Roosevelt's inauguration, Hoover seemed glum while Roosevelt appeared confident. *What happened to the American economy between Election Day 1932 and Inauguration Day 1933?*

the Communists only 100,000. This meant that their combined share was a little more than 2 percent of all of the votes cast.

■ Banking Panic

In the time between Roosevelt's election in November and his inauguration in March, the Twentieth Amendment was added to the Constitution, changing the date of the presidential inauguration from March 4 to January 20. Had this amendment gone into effect sooner, it would have been better for the country. For four months Hoover as President was a **lame duck,** an officeholder with little influence, because his term was about to end. During this time the nation was virtually leaderless. The new President—Franklin D. Roosevelt—was without power to act.

Withdrawing Funds

During this short time, the entire banking system disintegrated, and the economy ground almost to a standstill. Although thousands of smaller banks had already failed, most of the larger banks seemed to be able to hold firm during this time. Despite Roosevelt's promise that upon becoming President he would take action to rescue the nation from the Depression, in early 1933 the entire country was seized by a banking panic. Having lost faith in the nation's economy, thousands of depositors withdrew their money from banks and hoarded cash and gold. Given such a situation, even the most stable banks were bound to stop payments eventually because there was not enough gold in circulation to cover all deposits.

Visualizing History

▲ DEPRESSION LIFE These three children, ages 5, 12, and 7, were discovered living in an abandoned house. Many Americans demanded action to escape such economic woes. *What candidate won the 1932 election?*

Bank Closings

As the situation deteriorated, state governors issued proclamations closing the banks of their states until confidence could be restored. By March 4—the day Roosevelt would take the oath of office—almost every private bank in the country was closed or placed under restriction by state regulation. From 1930 to the eve of the inauguration, more than 5,400 banks had shut down. The people of the nation waited anxiously to see what the new President would do.

Section 3 ★ Review

Checking for Understanding

1. **Identify** bonus army, General Douglas MacArthur.

2. **Define** lame duck.

3. **Describe** the mood of the country as the Depression worsened.

4. **Explain** why farmers destroyed crops and livestock even though people were hungry.

Critical Thinking

5. **Identifying Problems**   What part did the public's lack of confidence in government play in the banking crisis?

Using Vocabulary

Imagine that you must write a handbook on tips for investing in the stock market. Write an entry about speculation that explains the pros and cons. Use these terms:

speculation   on margin

securities   installment buying

Reviewing Facts

1. **Explain** how overproduction or underconsumption was one cause of the Great Depression.

2. **Describe** the effects of the Hawley-Smoot Tariff.

3. **Summarize** Hoover's actions to combat the Depression and the philosophy behind the actions.

4. **List** two defeats Hoover had in foreign policy.

5. **Cite** reasons for the rise of communism and socialism during the Depression.

6. **State** three reasons Franklin D. Roosevelt won the election of 1932.

7. **Discuss** the banking crisis of 1933 and relate it to the overall mood of Americans.

Understanding Concepts

Economic Change

1. Was America's appetite for money and consumer goods a cause of the Great Depression? Explain how activities such as stock market speculation and installment buying contributed to the crisis.

2. How did economic changes affect American faith and beliefs about the United States? Why do you think some Americans feared a revolution? Explain the increased activity among the Socialists and Communists in America.

Political Policy

3. Explain why Hoover's political beliefs were popular while the economy was doing well but increasingly unpopular during the Depression.

4. Do you think Roosevelt, using the platform he proposed in 1932, would have won the 1928 presidential election? Explain your answer.

Critical Thinking

1. **Contrasting Ideas** Explain the difference between laissez-faire economics and Hoover's beliefs about government in the economy.

2. **Analyzing Fine Art** Study the painting on this page entitled *The Bowery*, by Reginald Marsh, then answer the questions that follow.

   a. Who are the people in the painting?

   b. Would you consider this work a realistic work? Explain.

Writing About History

Cause and Effect

Write an essay on how the Great Depression might have affected a young person your age. Before you begin writing, make a list of the worries, fears, and hardships the Depression caused. Use this list to write an essay on the effect these factors might have had on an individual your age. Include how the Great Depression would have affected your ideas about careers and school, your self-esteem and way of life, and your hopes for the future.

Cooperative Learning

Work in groups of three to analyze the causes of the Great Depression. Assign each group member two of the causes listed on pages 743–745 of your text. Have each group member make a list of economic and social effects that might have resulted from his or her cause. For example, if your subject is underconsumption, explain how this factor affected store owners, manufacturers, and consumers. When you have finished your individual lists, create a master list entitled "How the Great Depression Changed America."

Social Studies Skills

Reading a Line Graph

A line graph is used to show a relationship between two variables. The independent variable goes on the x-axis, and the dependent variable goes on the y-axis.

By using different colors or different types of lines, a line graph can have two or more curves. Thus, two or more items can be graphed on the same grid.

The three curves shown here are used to show how something changes over time. To interpret the data in a line graph, do the following.

- Read the title of the graph.
- Determine what the x-axis and y-axis represent.
- Determine what each of the three curves represents.
- Determine the changes or other relationships the graph shows.

Practicing the Skill

Use the graph and your understanding of Chapter 27 to answer the following questions.

1. What is the time period in the graph?
2. What is the independent variable in the graph?
3. What is the dependent variable in the graph?
4. What does each curve show?
5. When were wheat and corn prices the highest? The lowest?
6. What is the overall trend in the prices of wheat, corn, and cotton?
7. How did this trend affect farmers during the Great Depression?

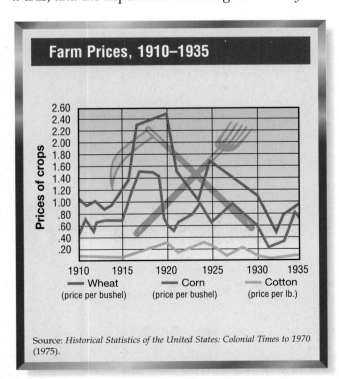

Farm Prices, 1910–1935

Prices of crops

2.60 2.40 2.20 2.00 1.80 1.60 1.40 1.20 1.00 .80 .60 .40 .20

1910 1915 1920 1925 1930 1935

—— Wheat (price per bushel) —— Corn (price per bushel) —— Cotton (price per lb.)

Source: *Historical Statistics of the United States: Colonial Times to 1970* (1975).

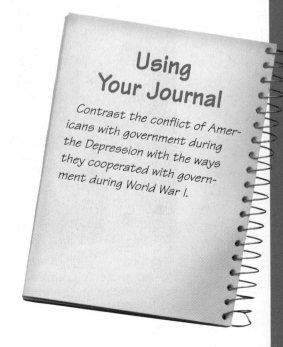

Using Your Journal

Contrast the conflict of Americans with government during the Depression with the ways they cooperated with government during World War I.

Cultural Kaleidoscope

The 1920s

Fashions in the 1920s

During the 1920s, postwar America rebelled against many of the social values that were in place at the turn of the century. Nowhere was this revolution more evident than in the fashions of the period. The flapper, embodying independence and social rebellion, became the model for the new woman.

During the 1920s straight, unfitted dresses were in vogue. Skirts seemed to rise and fall with the stock market. When Wall Street boomed during the 1920s, skirt lengths rose above the knee.

The straw hat, or boater, was the common head-wear for men.

Poised and chic couples set a sophisticated style of dress in the 1920s.

Many women adopted a new kind of hat style, a drooping, bell-shaped hat called a cloche.

◄ Bow tie

▼ Artist John Held, Jr., helped create the image of youth in the 1920s. His art often appeared on the cover of popular magazines.

► Woman's earring

"ALL WET"

► The changes in society gave women a greater measure of intellectual and economic independence.

Chapter 25

World War I Era

Wilson, an idealist who believed in fair play, wanted the United States to stop using military force and economic pressure as a tool of foreign policy. However, he ended up imitating his Republican predecessors by sending American troops into the Caribbean. Latin Americans came to resent his "moral imperialism" as much as Theodore Roosevelt's "Big Stick."

When war erupted in Europe in 1914, the United States declared neutrality. But British and French propaganda, American business interests, and German submarine warfare persuaded Americans to side with the Allies.

An apparent conspiracy between Mexico and Germany against the United States and the sinking of four American merchant ships ended American neutrality. Congress declared war on Germany in April 1917.

Unprepared for war, Americans mobilized with incredible speed. The production of armaments became a top priority, and government agencies such as the War Industries Board reorganized the economy to supply them. The draft was reinstated and propaganda was produced to influence public opinion. The government raised money for the war effort through taxes and selling bonds.

When the balance of the war tipped in favor of the Allies, an armistice was signed in November 1918. The Allies rejected most of Wilson's peace plan. After the war the United States experienced economic and social unrest, punctuated by strikes and race riots.

Chapter 26

The Decade of Normalcy

By the 1920s Americans wanted to get on with their lives, forget about public affairs, and stay out of wars. Warren G. Harding understood this when he promised "normalcy," a return to the values and practices of the past. The United States was now too enmeshed in world affairs to return to isolationism and continued to be involved in foreign diplomacy.

President Harding and his Republican successor Calvin Coolidge eased restrictions on business and looked after business interests. These policies seemed to work as the growth of new, urban industries fueled an economic boom during the 1920s. The growing prosperity was a key factor in the decline of labor unions' strength.

Major social changes and cultural achievements took place during the 1920s. Prohibition brought on a crime wave. The success of radio advertising increased the demand for consumer goods. The automobile affected more than the economy; it seemed to change the American way of life. Along with their newly won suffrage, American women demanded economic opportunity. In the "Harlem Renaissance," African Americans reflected a new spirit of pride and protest.

After World War I, however, feelings against immigrants led Congress to seriously restrict all immigration into the United States.

Chapter 27

The Depression Begins

Herbert Hoover slid into the presidency in 1928 full of optimism. In foreign policy Hoover practiced a "Good Neighbor" policy with Latin American republics. In domestic policy he assured Americans that as long as business thrived, the country would prosper.

▲ **Bonus Army skirmish, 1932**

Farmers, however, were already experiencing a depression, and government relief proved ineffective. On Black Tuesday, October 29, 1929, the stock market crashed, losing much of its value. This touched off a business and economic decline from which the country did not recover for more than a decade. The Great Depression was caused not only by stock market speculation but also by the effects of World War I, the depressed condition of agriculture, and unwise government policies.

By the end of the 1920s, thousands of Americans were jobless, and many farmers lost their land. Hoover offered to help banks and businesses but opposed direct federal relief to the unemployed because he feared that government handouts would destroy Americans' drive to work.

The American economy had hit rock bottom by the 1932 presidential election. Signs of instability and rebellion appeared everywhere. In the election, Democrat Franklin D. Roosevelt won the presidency by a wide margin.

Understanding Unit Themes

1. **Conflict and Cooperation**   Explain why Americans felt so willing to cooperate with their government during World War I but felt in conflict with it during the Depression. What accounted for these changes in attitude toward the government? Give examples of ways people cooperated with the government and ways they engaged in conflict.

2. **Influence of Technology**   How did technological innovation alter the lives of Americans in both war and peace? What was one important technology that revolutionized both?

3. **The Individual and Family Life**   Trace the social changes covered in the unit from war to peace, from prosperity to depression. Think about other social changes during the era. How do you think all these changes affected families—for better and for worse?

UNIT NINE
TIMES OF CRISIS
1932–1960

★★★

CHAPTER **28**	CHAPTER **29**	CHAPTER **30**	CHAPTER **31**
The New Deal 1932–1939	World War II 1933–1945	The Cold War 1945–1952	Search for Stability 1952–1960

▲ WPA PLAY POSTER, 1936

▲ M-1 RIFLE, FIRST USED DURING WORLD WAR II

History AND ART

B-17 Base in England
by Peter Hurd, 1943

Less than 25 years after World War I, the United States found itself at war again. This war, however, was far different. It was a fight for survival, and before it was over, it involved almost every nation in the world.

768

Setting the Scene

Several major crises deeply affected the United States between 1930 and 1960. A great depression endangered the nation's economic system, and foreign military power threatened its national security. Americans committed themselves to economic recovery and to fighting—first, the Axis Powers in World War II, and later, the spread of communism.

Themes

- American Democracy
- Civil Rights and Liberties
- Conflict and Cooperation
- U.S. Role in World Affairs

Key Events

- New Deal legislation
- Dust Bowl
- Japanese attack Pearl Harbor
- Surrender of Germany and Japan
- United Nations Charter
- Cold War
- Truman Doctrine
- North Atlantic Treaty Organization
- Korean War
- Polio vaccine
- Suez Crisis
- Castro controls Cuba

Major Issues

- New Deal programs attempt to relieve economic hardships and pull the United States out of the Great Depression.
- Aid to the Allies and the Japanese attack on Pearl Harbor pulls the United States into World War II.
- The desire to contain communism leads the United States to assume a more active role in world affairs.

▼ WORLD WAR II POSTER

Together We WIN

▲ FLYING GRUMMAN WILDCAT FIGHTER, 1942

Portfolio Project

Identify something you consider a symbol of the era and describe the ideas and emotions connected with it. Try to include visual materials.

Global Perspectives

The World

	1930		**1940**
Asia and Oceania			
Europe		◄ **1934** *Hitler becomes Der Führer of Germany*	**1939** *World War II begins in Europe*
Africa			
South America		**1938** *Venezuela becomes the third-largest oil-producing nation in the world*	
North and Central America			

The United States

Pacific and Northwest			◄ **1941** *Japanese surprise attack on Pearl Harbor brings the United States into World War II*
Southeast			
Midwest			
Southwest		**1937** *Parts of the Southwest and the Great Plains become a dust bowl*	
Atlantic Northeast	**1930**	◄ **1933** *Newly inaugurated President Franklin D. Roosevelt launches New Deal*	**1940**

Linking Across TIME

The Chinese and Japanese have played a major role in American life, especially in California and Hawaii, since the mid-1800s. They may have set foot on the North American continent hundreds of years before. Some scholars believe that Hui Shen, a Chinese missionary, explored the Pacific coast of North America as early as the 400s! There is solid evidence to suggest that Chinese sailors regularly visited California in the mid-1500s. Before the closing of Japan in the 1600s, Japanese sailors, too, probably ventured as far as California.

▼ **1945** *Atomic bombs devastate Hiroshima and Nagasaki*

1950

1960

◀ **1956** *Revolts in Poland and Hungary*

1956 *Suez Crisis*

1959 *Fidel Castro takes over Cuba*

1958 *First successful launch of a U.S. satellite*

1955 *AFL-CIO merge to form one union*

▲ **1946** *United Nations headquarters is established in New York*

1950

1953 *McCarthyism stirs national interest*

1960

CHAPTER 28

★★

The New Deal
1932–1939

▶ SHOVEL, CIVILIAN
CONSERVATION CORPS

Setting the Scene

Focus

When Franklin D. Roosevelt took the oath of office, Congress and the American people were eager to follow the President's leadership. Within months, laws were passed to provide relief, recovery, and reform of the economic system. Two years later, however, millions of Americans were still unemployed, and the New Deal came under increasing criticism. Throughout Roosevelt's second term, many programs were reshaped to permanently change the way government relates to its citizens.

Concepts to Understand

★ Why the political leadership of Roosevelt was effective at bringing about New Deal reforms

★ How New Deal economic reform differed from previous policies

Read to Discover . . .

★ how New Deal legislation attempted to end the Depression.

★ what long-term effects the New Deal programs had on American society.

Journal Notes

What role did women play in the Roosevelt administration? Note the details in your journal.

CULTURAL
- **1932** *American speed skaters and bobsledders earn medals in the Winter Olympics*

- **1934** *Severe drought in the Great Plains creates a dust bowl*
- **1935** Middletown *is published*

| 1932 | 1934 |

POLITICAL
- **1933** *Repeal of Prohibition*
- **1933** *"Hundred Days" begins after Roosevelt's inauguration*

- **1934** *Securities and Exchange Commission is established*
- **1935** *Social Security Act is passed*

We Demand
by Joe Jones, 1934

Depression painter Joe Jones emphasized working people in his art. In *We Demand,* he concentrated on the efforts of workers to organize the protest to improve their wages and conditions of employment.

 ▲ NEW DEAL POSTERS

• **1936** *Tornadoes kill more than 400 Southerners in 5 states*

• **1938** *Thornton Wilder's play* Our Town *wins Pulitzer Prize*

1936

1938

• **1936** *Roosevelt is reelected*
• **1937** *Roosevelt attempts to pack the Supreme Court*

• **1938** *Fair Labor Standards Act passes*

★★★

Roosevelt Takes Charge

Setting the Scene

Section Focus

President Roosevelt's Inaugural Address attempted to lift the gloom and fear that had blanketed the country. At last, a new President promised action against the Depression. Congress and the American public—some in eager anticipation and others out of desperation—were ready to follow the President's lead.

Objectives

After studying this section, you should be able to

★ identify the traits that made Franklin Roosevelt an effective leader.

★ describe how Roosevelt garnered ideas and support for his New Deal.

Key Term

fireside chat

▲ PERSONAL BANK CHECKS

W ithin his Inaugural Address Franklin D. Roosevelt made the same promises about the nation's recovery that Herbert Hoover and his advisers had been making since 1929. Roosevelt promised that the nation "will endure as it has endured, will revive and will prosper." Unlike Hoover, however, the new President reflected the popular mood of the nation by blaming bankers, "the unscrupulous moneychangers," for allowing starvation in the midst of plenty. The nation was in a kind of war, he said, and strong presidential leadership was needed. Sketching the need for various relief and reform measures, the new President called for immediate legislation. If Congress failed to act quickly, Roosevelt promised to ask for executive authority "as great as the power that would be given to me if we were in fact invaded by a foreign foe."

■ A Strong Leader

Before taking office, Roosevelt displayed little evidence of the leadership he would offer in his 12 years in the White House. One writer described him as "an amiable man . . . who without any important qualifications for the office, would very much like to be President." His outstanding attribute was his name, which his cousin Theodore Roosevelt had made well known in American politics.

Early Life

The only son of wealthy parents, FDR, as his friends called him, attended the best schools. At the time of his election, Roosevelt had been in politics for more than 20 years, yet his views on many issues were unknown. Nor did many Americans realize that he had overcome a serious physical handicap.

In 1921, at age 39, Roosevelt was stricken with polio. Fighting back against the crippling disease, he regained the use of his hands and arms, but he remained paralyzed from the waist down. His painful recovery toughened him and, at the same time, gave him genuine sympathy for the less fortunate. Playwright Robert Sherwood, a close associate, described his toughness and compassion:

> ❝ *I tried continually to study him, to try to look beyond his charming and amusing and warmly affectionate surface into his heavily forested interior. But I never understood what was going on in there. . . . He could be a ruthless politician, but he was the champion of friends and associates who for him were political liabilities . . . and of causes which apparently competent observers assured him would be political suicide.* ❞

A Master Politician

Both friends and foes agreed that, despite his complexity, Roosevelt was master of the art of politics. Few Presidents had such varied political training—at local, state, and federal levels—in elected and appointed offices. Elected to the New York legislature in 1910, at the height of the Progressive Era, Roosevelt learned about local government. As assistant secretary of the navy during World War I, he had an insider's view as the Wilson administration organized the federal government to wage war. As governor of New York when the stock market crashed, FDR dealt with many of the same problems he would face as President.

Perhaps Roosevelt's greatest strength as a politician was his warm and understanding approach to people. Where Hoover had withdrawn to the isolation of the White House as the Depression settled in, Roosevelt reached out by radio to the American people in a series of **fireside chats.** These were informal talks in which the President calmly but confidently explained in simple

Visualizing History

▲ A MANDATE FOR CHANGE Farmers in debt, workers without jobs, and bankrupt business owners wanted the government to take bolder action. Americans responded enthusiastically to Franklin D. Roosevelt's call for action to fight the Great Depression. *What personal qualities did Roosevelt bring to the presidency?*

terms the nation's problems and how the New Deal planned to defeat the Depression. Millions of radio listeners felt that the President was talking directly to them. After a fireside chat, Roosevelt sometimes received as many as 50,000 letters a day.

Roosevelt also knew how to use the press better than his predecessor. Hoover had avoided reporters and refused to answer questions unless they were written out in advance. In contrast, FDR allowed reporters to barrage him with questions during frequent press conferences. This approach made him popular with the press—important shapers of public opinion—and focused public attention on Washington, D.C., and his New Deal programs. "Gone is the fortress that was the White House," wrote one reporter after Roosevelt took office.

Getting Things Done

A product of the Progressive Era, FDR retained the progressives' approach to solving society's problems. As President he was a pragmatist and an experimenter. He sometimes asked three or four people with conflicting opinions to do the same job and compared the results. FDR compared himself to a quarterback on a football team who called a play, and if it did not work, tried another. Action, he felt, was better than inaction. Most Americans, desperate for relief from the effects of the Depression, agreed with him.

The "Brain Trust"

Roosevelt also had trust in the ability of experts to plan for society. Even before receiving the Democratic nomination for President, he gathered a group of professors from Columbia University to advise him. This group of economists, political scientists, and attorneys was nicknamed the "brain trust" by the press. After Roosevelt became President, the brain trust stayed on to help him plan New Deal recovery programs. In selecting his cabinet, FDR named people who presented a variety of viewpoints and ideas—Northerners and Southerners, liberals and conservatives. He

named Republican Harold Ickes as secretary of the interior, and for secretary of agriculture he chose Henry A. Wallace, whose father had the job under Harding. For secretary of labor Roosevelt named the first woman cabinet officer, former child labor reformer Frances Perkins. Other women held important positions in almost every New Deal agency. Like Secretary Perkins, many of these women had been social workers. Now the President was calling upon them to administer the federal government's social and relief programs.

Eleanor Roosevelt as Adviser

Outside the brain trust, the adviser that Roosevelt relied on most was his wife, Eleanor. Because of his paralysis, FDR moved with difficulty in a wheelchair or with heavy braces on his legs. As a result, he asked Eleanor to assume a significant role in his administration. The President called her his "eyes and ears" outside the White House. During the first year of the New Deal, she traveled extensively to attend political rallies, tour factories, visit coal mines, and contact many people that FDR might not otherwise have

Visualizing History ▲ SECRETARY OF LABOR Frances Perkins was appointed secretary of labor by Roosevelt. A long-time advocate of minimum wage and maximum hour laws, child-labor restrictions, and other progressive reforms, she was one of only two cabinet members to serve throughout Roosevelt's four terms. *What was unique about her appointment?*

Eleanor Roosevelt
1884–1962

Eleanor Roosevelt did not herself hold public office until she was a 61-year-old widow. But as First Lady she fought tenaciously for social justice and added a sense of compassion to the New Deal.

Although painfully shy as a young girl, Eleanor Roosevelt emerged as a vibrant public personality during the 1920s when her husband, FDR, was recovering from polio. She did all she could to keep his name in the public mind. After Roosevelt's election, she spoke for people who otherwise would have been ignored—women, the poor and the underprivileged, and African Americans.

Sensitive to racial injustice, she spoke up so strongly for civil rights that she won African American support for the New Deal. A lecturer and columnist, Eleanor Roosevelt later worked for global human rights in the United Nations.

---

met. At cabinet meetings, the President would report, "My missus says that people are working for wages well below the minimum . . . in the town she visited last week." Eleanor Roosevelt shared Franklin's concern for the victims of the Depression—close friends thought that her concern was even deeper than his—and the belief that decisive government action was needed to conquer society's ills.

■ The First New Deal

President Roosevelt fulfilled his promise to provide "action now." Americans waited to see what he would do.

Restoring Faith in Banks

On Sunday, March 5, 1933, the day after his inauguration, Roosevelt called a special session of Congress. On Monday he used an old law still on the books to suspend the nation's banking activity. Many Americans had lost faith in banks after the crash, withdrew their money, and kept it at home. Banks needed depositors' funds to make loans that would help recovery, but, in many areas, the loss of deposits was so great that banks had to close their doors. After a week

in office, the President went on the radio with his first fireside chat. He explained that only healthy banks would be allowed to reopen. He assured Americans that it would be "safer to keep money in a reopened bank than under the mattress." The next day most banks began to do business again, and in a few days deposits exceeded withdrawals. As the President's calm assurances restored public confidence in the nation's financial system, the bank crisis ended.

The Hundred Days

That first week was just the beginning of feverish activity. In the "Hundred Days" between March 9 and June 16, 1933, Congress passed 15 major bills, more than had ever been enacted in such a short time. Most were bills that the President submitted and that Congress passed with little debate. Seldom had a President enjoyed such overwhelming support.

Meeting "Each Day's Troubles"

Roosevelt took office with no clear idea of how to solve the nation's economic crisis. "There's nothing to do," he said, "but meet each day's troubles as they come." The New

▲ **BANK CLOSINGS** Afraid for the safety of their savings, panicked depositors line up outside a bank. Such "runs"—when all depositors tried to withdraw their money at the same time—usually caused those banks to fail, making their depositors' fears come true. *How did Roosevelt handle the bank crisis?*

Deal, therefore, was not a carefully worked out reform plan. Instead, it was a series of measures quickly drawn up to attack the Depression in many ways at once. Some laws were in response to special demands from specific groups in society. Some were even passed against the President's wishes, but he signed them to head off something that he might like even less, or to avoid holding up other legislation. However, New Deal programs had three general purposes: recovery from the Depression, relief for its victims, and reform of the economic system. Much legislation reflected all three goals.

From 1933 to early 1935, the dominating goals of the Roosevelt administration were recovery and relief. During the "First New Deal," as this phase was called, the President and his advisers thought that a series of temporary measures could get the economy moving again. From this beginning, recovery would come on its own momentum. Therefore, little additional legislation followed the Hundred Days of the First New Deal. The administration merely implemented the laws that the Senate and the House had created and waited for recovery to occur.

Section 1 ★ Review

Checking for Understanding

1. **Identify** FDR, brain trust, Frances Perkins, the Hundred Days.

2. **Define** fireside chat.

3. **Cite** the political experience that prepared Roosevelt to lead the nation out of the Depression.

4. **Explain** Roosevelt's approach to solving problems.

Critical Thinking

5. **Making Comparisons** Compare Roosevelt's style in managing the crisis to Hoover's. Why did the public support Roosevelt?

★★★

Reform, Relief, and Recovery

Setting the Scene

Section Focus

Many of the laws passed during the Hundred Days were popularly known by their initials—AAA, NRA, TVA, and CCC. People jokingly called them the New Deal's "alphabet soup," yet the programs gave the American people a sense of hope. Many were intended as stopgap measures, but their effects are still felt today.

◀ **WPA POSTER, LATE 1930S**

Objectives

After studying this section, you should be able to

★ give examples of how Roosevelt's policies helped and hurt the rural poor.

★ compare the effectiveness of measures aimed at farmers and city workers.

Key Terms

deficit spending, pump priming, dole, foreclosure

---

oth Hoover and Roosevelt believed that prosperity would return with a little help to spark the economy. So, like Hoover, FDR sought the help of the business community and spoke of an alliance of "business and banking, agriculture and industry, and labor and capital." But he differed from Hoover in the amount and variety of legislation he proposed and in his willingness to call on the full powers of the federal government to solve national problems.

■ Financial Reform

In June 1933 Congress passed the Glass-Steagall Act. This law prohibited banks from investing in the stock market and created a Federal Deposit Insurance Corporation (FDIC) to insure depositors' savings. Although the program was opposed by the American Bankers' Association as "unscientific, unjust, and dangerous," federal insurance made people feel that their money would be safe in banks.

Congress also responded to the demand that the government prevent stock market fraud. The Federal Securities Act of 1933 required companies that issued or marketed stocks and bonds to provide complete and truthful information to purchasers. Congress followed this act in 1934 with the Securities and Exchange Commission (SEC) to regulate the stock market.

When Roosevelt took office, he faced strong pressure to inflate the currency. A number of senators and representatives wanted to stimulate recovery by putting into circulation billions of dollars in new paper money. Roosevelt, however, rejected inflation and took a conservative approach in his early efforts to achieve recovery. Still, he realized that to keep relief agencies from

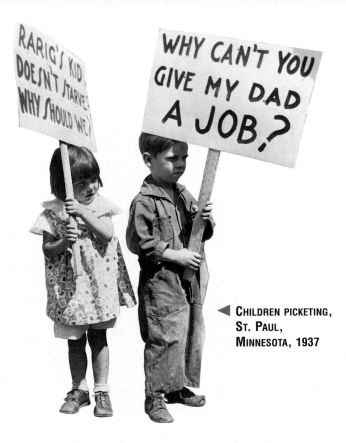

Children picketing, St. Paul, Minnesota, 1937

The Federal Government Steps In

In May 1933 Congress established a Federal Emergency Relief Administration (FERA). FERA made outright grants to states and municipalities to distribute as they chose. They generally provided a **dole**—direct gifts of money, food, and clothing. Although the dole was the cheapest and quickest form of relief, its critics were concerned that people who received handouts would lose their self-respect and job skills, making them even more unemployable. So once the federal government had met the need for emergency relief, New Dealers searched for alternatives to the dole.

The Public Works Administration (PWA), created in June 1933, offered jobs instead of handouts. Under the direction of Secretary of the Interior Harold Ickes, the program provided jobs on construction projects—improving highways and building dams, sewer systems, waterworks, schools, and other government buildings. The PWA generally worked through private contractors, and Ickes broke down long-standing racial barriers in the construction trades by insisting that contractors hire African Americans.

In the autumn of 1933, Harry Hopkins, head of the FERA, won approval for a Civil Works Administration (CWA) to hire jobless persons. During the winter of 1933–1934, the CWA employed 4 million people—300,000 of them women. The CWA built or improved 1,000 airports, 500,000 miles of roads, 40,000 school buildings, and 3,500 parks, playgrounds, and playing fields. But the cost of all this was tremendous—$1 billion in just five months. In the spring of 1934, Roosevelt gave in to fierce criticism from conservatives and cancelled the program.

The TVA

One early New Deal program combined emergency relief and pump priming with long-term economic and social planning. In May 1933, after Roosevelt's prodding, Congress established the Tennessee Valley Authority (TVA), designed to promote the development of a seven-state region.

Before the TVA, the natural resources of the Tennessee Valley had long been exploited.

closing and millions of Americans from starving, **deficit spending** was necessary. In other words, the federal government's annual spending would have to exceed its income.

■ Help for the Jobless

From deficit spending, the New Deal moved to **pump priming**—pouring government money into the economy through loans and federal spending in the hope of stimulating recovery. Roosevelt called for government to give money directly to people who would spend it. Increased spending would increase demand for consumer goods, New Dealers claimed, which would stimulate production and create jobs.

By 1933, 12 million to 15 million Americans—1 of every 4 workers—was unemployed, and many were on the verge of starvation. At first Roosevelt, like Hoover, thought that local agencies should handle relief until industry and agriculture recovered enough to provide jobs. It soon became clear, however, that states, cities, and local charities had exhausted their resources.

Forests were leveled, and heavy rainfalls caused erosion and disastrous floods. Poor farmers attempted to work worn-out land, and many people were on relief.

Employing as many as 40,000 workers at a time, the TVA built 20 dams for flood control and improved 5 others. The TVA also moved farmers from marginal lands, reforested millions of acres, built power plants and fertilizer factories, and even started new towns. But the most notable change was the immense amount of cheap electricity that the TVA produced. Its increased availability allowed farmers to install refrigerators, milking machines, and other equipment. Cheap power also attracted industry.

Despite its obvious benefits, the TVA had its critics. Some charged that funds for the TVA should be used to support programs nationwide. Above all, the TVA was attacked by the power companies. One goal of the TVA was to provide a basis to determine fair electricity rates all over the country. But private power companies argued that to use the TVA for this purpose was unfair because the government charged large parts of the cost of electricity production to the cost of flood control and navigation. For the federal government to take over the production of private power, they argued, was unfair and communistic. Although the power companies were powerful enough to prevent any more regional authorities like the TVA, the New Deal did build other power plants, the most famous of which was the Grand Coulee Dam in Washington state.

The CCC

The most generally admired New Deal relief agency was the Civilian Conservation Corps (CCC), established in March 1933. It offered outdoor work to unemployed single men, 18 to 25 years old, at $30 per month, $22 of which went back to their families. By midsummer the CCC had established 1,500 camps. During its existence, the CCC helped conserve the nation's natural resources by putting 3 million young men to work planting trees, fighting forest fires, building reservoirs, and stopping soil erosion.

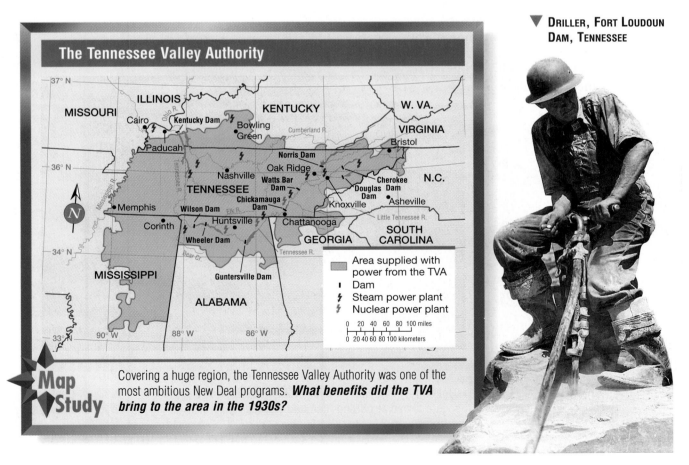

▼ DRILLER, FORT LOUDOUN DAM, TENNESSEE

The Tennessee Valley Authority

Area supplied with power from the TVA
I Dam
⚡ Steam power plant
⚡ Nuclear power plant

0 20 40 60 80 100 miles
0 20 40 60 80 100 kilometers

Map Study Covering a huge region, the Tennessee Valley Authority was one of the most ambitious New Deal programs. *What benefits did the TVA bring to the area in the 1930s?*

■ Relief for Agriculture

The impoverished condition of farmers in the Tennessee Valley was by no means unique in 1933. Since 1929 banks had foreclosed on the property of 10 percent of the nation's farmers. In **foreclosure** actions, when a borrower cannot make loan payments, the bank seizes the property that was put up as security for the loan. Farmers threatened to stop producing food unless their debt burden and agricultural prices improved. The New Deal provided relief for heavily indebted farmers by placing a five-year moratorium, or freeze, on mortgage foreclosures. But New Dealers recognized that the root of the farmers' plight was low agricultural prices, and that this situation was related to a problem that had plagued farmers since the end of World War I —overproduction.

The Agricultural Adjustment Act

Roosevelt proposed an unusual approach: stop agricultural surpluses by paying farmers to *not* produce crops. In May 1933, Congress passed the Agricultural Adjustment Act (AAA), under which the government paid farmers who reduced production of basic crops like cotton, wheat, tobacco, hogs, and corn. Funds for these payments came from a tax levied on flour mills,

slaughterhouses, and other businesses that processed food.

In 1933 cotton farmers plowed under a quarter of their acreage, and hog producers killed 6 million piglets instead of fattening them for market. In 1934 and 1935, farmers withdrew 10 million acres from production and received more than $1 billion in benefit payments. Surpluses were greatly reduced by 1936, and total farm income rose by more than 50 percent.

Large commercial farmers, who concentrated on one crop, benefited more than smaller farmers who raised several. The crop reduction program actually hurt some people. In the West and Southwest, Mexican migrant workers suffered when growers raised less produce and so hired fewer pickers. Tenant farmers and sharecroppers were forced off the land they worked as owners took it out of production. About 150,000 white tenants and almost 195,000 African American tenants left farming during the 1930s. To stop this trend, the New Deal created the Farm Security Administration to give loans to help tenants purchase land.

▲ **JOBS** Unemployment was a major problem during the Depression. Many New Deal programs were aimed at putting men and women back to work. *Why were jobs important to economic recovery?*

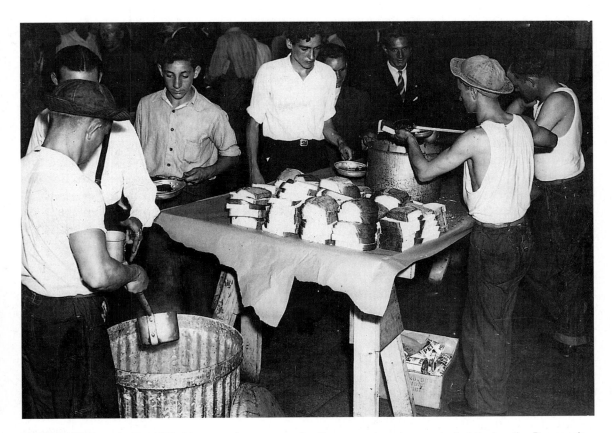

▲ THE CCC Many work programs for the unemployed were started during the Roosevelt administration. The CCC offered outdoor work to unemployed single men. *What work did the CCC do?*

But only 3,400 African American farmers received any of this money. Landless farmers joined other urban and rural migrants who wandered the country in search of jobs.

The Dust Bowl

In 1934 and 1935 a terrible disaster struck the Great Plains and added to the number of farmers on the move. The origins of the disaster arose during World War I, when high crop prices tempted farmers to grow wheat and cotton on what traditionally had been grazing lands. Plows broke up the deep, tough sod that had prevented erosion and conserved moisture in this semiarid region. When the years from 1933 to 1935 were unusually dry, the area began to turn to desert. Dust storms carried away so much topsoil that a haze obscured the sun, sometimes as far away as the Atlantic coast. Between 1934 and 1939, nearly 350,000 farm families left the dust bowl.

To take care of immediate distress, Congress provided the farmers in the dust bowl with funds for new seed and livestock. For long-term solutions, the Department of Agriculture helped farmers plant millions of trees in shelter belts to cut wind velocity and help retain moisture. The government also encouraged farmers to return the land to grazing. Yet there was much criticism of New Deal farm policies. Many farmers did not like being told what to raise or how much to plant. To others, decreasing food supplies when people were hungry seemed immoral. However, the New Deal provided more direct assistance to farmers than to any other group, and saved thousands of farm families from poverty and despair.

Native Americans and the New Deal

The New Deal worked to change long-standing government policies affecting Native Americans, including a reversal of the gradual loss of land and tribal authority. Earlier, the federal government had opted for a number of different policies with widely divergent goals.

With the end of the frontier wars in the late 1800s, the federal government had at long last abandoned a policy that could fairly be summarized as expulsion and extermination. The General Allotment Act in 1887 provided for the division of reservation land into plots to be granted to individual Native Americans. This arrangement was based on the idea that the best thing for Native Americans was to make them as much like other Americans as possible.

The education system reinforced this idea: children were taken from home at an early age, crowded into boarding schools, and given some "book learning" before being sent back to the reservation. They acquired little knowledge of the culture of their ancestors. Meanwhile, older people received just enough food to sustain them.

However well-meaning, this policy was scarcely better than the old policy. By 1934 Native Americans held only 48 million of the 133 million acres they had possessed in 1887. Although Native Americans were citizens of the United States, state laws often discriminated against them, and the federal government generally ran their affairs for them.

Some improvement began during the Coolidge administration with a reorganization of health services for Native Americans. Later, President Hoover appointed two dedicated individuals as commissioner and deputy commissioner of Indian Affairs. They began a reform of the workings of the department.

The Indian Reorganization Act

More action on Native American affairs was taken during the New Deal years. The Roosevelt administration promoted a new approach that was made law in the Indian Reorganization Act in 1934. This act repealed the allotment policy and returned to tribal ownership Native American lands previously open to sale.

According to John Collier, commissioner of Indian Affairs, the act had a worthwhile purpose. It would enable Native Americans "to earn a decent livelihood and lead self-respecting, organized lives in harmony with their own aims and ideals."

Instead of promoting individual ownership, the federal government now encouraged Native Americans to revert to their own traditions. Instead of being weakened, tribal organization was strengthened. Native Americans were encouraged to become members of the federal Indian Service. Children were now taught the traditions of their own people in school. Ceremonies, art forms, and handicrafts were revived.

New Benefits

The new arrangements brought benefits that could be seen in the reversal of two disturbing trends: Native American landholdings increased after 1934, and the Native American population once again began to increase. Since then Native Americans, now a rapidly growing minority group, have continued to fight in the courts and legislatures for religious freedom, water rights, and land claims.

■ Industrial Relief

Roosevelt's advisers believed that industry, like agriculture, suffered from overproduction. In June 1933 the New Deal tried to help industry with the National Industrial Recovery Act (NIRA).

The NIRA

To control production, the NIRA provided that representatives of labor and of management from competing companies draw up "codes of fair competition" in each industry. These codes set the prices of products to eliminate discount selling. They shortened workers' hours in order to create more jobs, and they established minimum-wage levels. To spread production among as many firms as possible, factories were limited to two shifts a day. To direct this complex program, the act created the National Recovery Administration (NRA).

Power to enforce the codes was very limited, so the NRA used the power of public opinion to enlist the cooperation of business. Those that signed code agreements were given signs with blue eagles and the words "We Do Our Part." Consumers were encouraged to purchase goods only from businesses that displayed the signs. The NIRA, however, never worked out as planned. Prices rose faster than wages. Businesses complained that large companies wrote the codes to favor themselves and to put small competitors out of business.

Workers Turn to Unions

Probably no group suffered more than people who worked for hourly wages. By 1933 one-third of these workers were unemployed. The earnings of the rest had shrunk as their rates or hours were cut. The idea spread that the best way to restore workers' wages and purchasing power was to strengthen labor unions. Under Section 7a of the NIRA, every NRA code guaranteed workers the right to organize unions and to bargain collectively with their employers. As a result, between May and October 1933, American Federation of Labor (AFL) membership jumped by about a million workers.

In 1934 a wave of strikes swept the nation as workers demanded the right to organize for improved wages and job security. Many of these strikes became violent, and most resulted in defeat for the workers, as police generally sided with employers. Although sympathetic to organized labor, the only

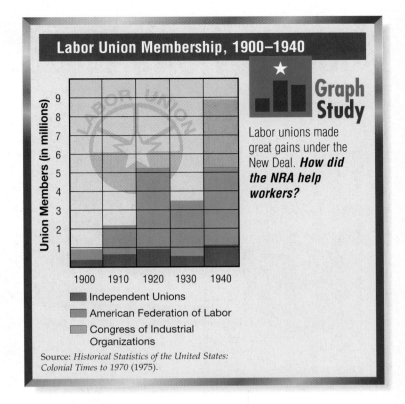

Labor Union Membership, 1900–1940

Union Members (in millions)

Graph Study

Labor unions made great gains under the New Deal. *How did the NRA help workers?*

■ Independent Unions
■ American Federation of Labor
■ Congress of Industrial Organizations

Source: *Historical Statistics of the United States: Colonial Times to 1970* (1975).

way the NRA could punish a company was to take away its Blue Eagle symbol. Workers began to demand stronger labor laws.

New Solutions Needed

As the nation entered 1935, American spirits sagged. Despite the New Deal, farm prices and industrial wages were well below 1929 levels, and workers remained unemployed and poor. To many Americans, the New Deal was taking too long and accomplishing too little. FDR clearly saw that he must find other means to restore prosperity.

Section 2 ★ Review

Checking for Understanding

1. **Identify** FDIC, FERA, PWA, CCC, AAA, NRA, Section 7a.

2. **Define** deficit spending, pump priming, dole, foreclosure.

3. **List** three programs designed to create jobs by employing workers on projects to benefit the nation.

4. **Explain** Roosevelt's theory that giving money directly to people would stimulate economic recovery.

Critical Thinking

5. **Making Judgments** During widespread unemployment, is government money better used as a dole or for more expensive work-relief programs? Why?

▲ **FARM IN THE DUST BOWL**

The Dust Bowl

As the entire nation struggled to cope with the Depression, farmers in Kansas, Oklahoma, and Texas suffered from the scourges of drought and dust. From the 1890s to the 1920s, grasslands in this part of the Great Plains were put to the plow, and when rain fell, they were bountiful. But in the 1930s, the rains failed. As crops withered, leaving bare dirt exposed, the region's high winds lifted the fine topsoil to create dust storms called "dusters."

Large-scale mechanized farming on the plains after 1900 exposed huge areas of soil. Farmers eager to maximize yields overtilled the soil and burned wheat stubble to kill weeds. These poor soil-conservation practices and the long drought created a dust bowl on the plains throughout most of the 1930s, as millions of tons of airborne powdery topsoil buried crops and killed livestock.

The dust bowl took its toll on people too. People sat helpless while their farms blew away. They sometimes lost their way and died in the thick storms while only yards from their houses. Thousands of families abandoned their land to seek work in the fields and orchards of California, Oregon, and Washington. Many migrants, however, could not find work even after they reached their destination. Those who stayed on their land were encouraged to plant crops that conserved the soil.

Making the Environment Connection

1. How did humans change the natural environment of the Great Plains in the early twentieth century?

2. How was a dust bowl created in this region?

Linking Past and Present

3. What soil-conservation practices are used today?

★★★

The Second New Deal

Setting the Scene

Section Focus

Some of Roosevelt's critics planted seeds of dissatisfaction with the New Deal by appealing to the jobless, the displaced, the underpaid, and the elderly. These victims of the Depression were fertile ground for the radical ideas floating about in 1935. FDR recognized that the New Deal must be reassessed and redirected. Yet even after strong voter support in the 1936 presidential election, Roosevelt faced continued opposition.

◀ UNION CARDS

Objectives

After studying this section, you should be able to

★ list the special interest groups that challenged Roosevelt.

★ outline the steps the Second New Deal took to achieve reform.

★ identify the events that led to the end of the New Deal.

Key Terms

coalition, craft union, industrial union, recession

For the 10 million unemployed Americans in 1935, Senator Huey Long's slogan, "Every Man a King," was an appealing fantasy but a far cry from their reality. They received just enough relief to keep themselves and their families alive. Their miserable dole seemed hardly worth the humiliation it caused. Millions of elderly Americans faced a similar stark reality, without savings, without adequate medical care, and without hope.

■ Attacks on the New Deal

The radical critics of the New Deal posed a strong threat to the Roosevelt administration. As time passed, the ranks of New Deal critics grew. Some wanted a more active government. Others felt that the government was interfering too much in American life.

Three Prominent Attackers

Every week Father Charles E. Coughlin, the "Radio Priest" whose broadcasts reached 40 million listeners, bitterly attacked Roosevelt. Originally a New Deal supporter, Coughlin accused the President of turning the New Deal into a "raw deal." His political organization, the National Union for Social Justice, called for such socialistic measures as heavy taxes on the wealthy and a guaranteed income for everyone. Gradually, Coughlin began expressing anti-Semitic, or anti-Jewish, views. In 1942 Catholic leaders ordered him to stop broadcasting.

An even more dangerous rival to Roosevelt was Huey Long, senator from Louisiana. With the backing of the rural poor, he became extremely powerful in his home state and used it as a base on which to build national popularity. With his folksy, humorous manner, Long knew how to win

▲ NEW DEAL CRITICS Father Charles Coughlin (left) reached millions of listeners before the Catholic Church made him stop his radio broadcasts. Until his assassination, Senator Huey Long (right) was equally popular. *What idea did these leaders share?*

audiences. He proposed confiscating the property of the rich and giving every family a home, $2,000 a year, and a free college education for their children. His followers organized hundreds of "Share-Our-Wealth" clubs.

Less colorful than Father Coughlin or Senator Long, but just as threatening, was Dr. Francis Townsend. A former public health official, Townsend was shocked by the plight of older Americans who were no longer able to compete for jobs. He proposed a plan that he claimed would provide relief for the elderly and at the same time stimulate economic recovery, calling for the federal government to pay all Americans over age 60 a pension of $200 per month. Recipients would be required to spend their entire pension check within 30 days. Townsend claimed that not only would this plan end the suffering of older Americans, but the money they pumped into the economy would increase consumption and create jobs. The pensions could be financed by a national sales tax on consumer goods, Townsend argued. His innovative plan attracted millions of devoted advocates.

Fighting Back

Roosevelt's annual address to Congress in January 1935 answered his attackers. He admitted that "we have not weeded out the overprivileged and we have not effectively lifted up the underprivileged." The President announced a "Second New Deal" to put recovery on a new course. This new phase showed greater concern for the less fortunate and abandoned efforts to enlist the support of business.

The political groups supporting the New Deal also changed. Roosevelt had played down partisanship to gain the support of moderate and progressive Republicans. Now he devoted his energies to achieving his goals through the Democratic party alone. To strengthen it, he attempted to form a **coalition,** or combination, of separate groups whose members could be counted on to vote for Democrats. To the traditional source of Democratic political power—the South and Northern urban political machines—Roosevelt attempted to add labor unions, farmers, and African Americans. Many of the Second New Deal's programs were intended to appeal to these groups.

Work Relief and Social Security

The most immediate result of the New Deal's shift in attitude was the President's demand for large-scale work relief. Responding to Roosevelt's request, Congress appropriated funds in April 1935 for "work relief and to increase employment by providing useful projects." An immense new agency, the Works Progress Administration (WPA) was set up under the direction of Harry Hopkins to provide a chance for all people to use their skills to earn an income.

The WPA employed writers, teachers, librarians, actors, musicians, and artists. A "junior WPA," the National Youth Administration (NYA) helped high school and college students stay in school by giving them part-time work, such as typing and library cataloguing. Existing work-relief programs were expanded. The Reconstruction Finance Corporation lent large sums to businesses and to local governments. The Civilian Conservation Corps increased the number it employed. The Public Works Administration finally rolled into high gear and provided hundreds of thousands of jobs.

The unemployable needed help during the Depression as much as the unemployed. Persons with no source of support and no ability to earn an income had no place to go. To remedy this problem, Congress in 1935 passed the Social Security Act. Under this program, the federal government financed state unemployment insurance plans through payroll taxes paid by employers. Federal grants to states provided care for dependent mothers and children. The core of the program was retirement benefits, paid for by taxes on workers and employers, that people could collect when they stopped working at age 65.

The Social Security Act had flaws. For example, the act did not protect some groups who needed it most, such as farm workers and domestic help. Since 65 percent of all African American employees in the 1930s fell into these two categories, the act neglected this group the most. Yet the Social Security Act was a landmark in reforming society. It set the policy that an industrial society was responsible for those who, through no fault of their own, are unable to work.

Business and Labor

Several pieces of legislation demonstrated Roosevelt's efforts to appeal to the political coalition he was forming. Early in the New Deal, taxes remained at levels set in the 1920s. Now Congress passed tax increases on the incomes of wealthy Americans, inheritance taxes on the property of deceased persons, and higher taxes on corporations. Although the law was attacked as communistic, Roosevelt was more interested, some felt, in heading off the various "share-the-wealth" schemes than he was in actually redistributing the nation's wealth.

Visualizing **History**

▲ **ATTACK ON THE NEW DEAL** Some Americans thought the New Deal was too restrictive to free enterprise. This cartoonist shows Uncle Sam tied down by New Deal agencies and laws, much as Gulliver was bound by the Lilliputians in the book *Gulliver's Travels.* **Why might critics have thought this way?**

▲ *CONCERT AT THE LINCOLN MEMORIAL* by Mitchell Jamieson WPA artists painted murals in many government offices. Mitchell Jamieson's mural of African American opera singer Marian Anderson's famous concert before an integrated audience of 73,000 at the Lincoln Memorial is in the offices of the United States Department of the Interior in Washington, D.C. *What political favor did Roosevelt want from African Americans?*

The Wagner Act

Next to the Social Security Act, the most important and lasting legislation of the Second New Deal was the National Labor Relations Act, also called the Wagner Act, passed in July 1935 after the Supreme Court declared the National Industrial Recovery Act unconstitutional. The Wagner Act set up a National Labor Relations Board (NLRB), which could hold secret elections in factories to find out whether workers wanted to unionize. The board could arbitrate grievances, reinstate workers fired for supporting unions, and order employers to stop antiunion activities.

The Wagner Act stimulated a burst of labor union activity. But the AFL was ill-equipped in both philosophy and structure to organize workers in mass-production industries such as radio, steel, automobiles, and textiles. The AFL was a federation of **craft unions**—unions where all members had the same skill. In mass-production industries, however, workers from many crafts or skills often worked in a single plant. To have several unions undermined unity. So some labor leaders proposed that factory workers be organized in an **industrial union**—a union to which all workers in a single industry belong, regardless of the job they perform. When the AFL rejected this approach, these leaders abandoned it to form the Congress of Industrial Organizations (CIO).

The CIO

"If I went to work in a factory, the first thing I'd do would be to JOIN A UNION," read the slogan signed by President Roosevelt on union recruiting posters, as the CIO moved into industries that the AFL had long neglected. By 1936 the CIO had signed up enough steelworkers to threaten a nationwide strike. Instead, in March 1937 the nation's largest steel producer, the United States Steel Corporation, recognized the union as bargaining agent for its workers, established a 40-hour workweek, and increased wages. Just beginning to recover from the Depression, the company was not willing to risk a major strike. The smaller producers did not follow this lead, however, and bloody strikes broke out around the country. But by 1941, the steelworkers' union had contracts with the entire industry.

Meanwhile, the CIO moved into the automobile industry, where management discouraged worker unity by exploiting racial and religious tensions among African Americans, Southern whites, and Catholic ethnic groups. Although hourly wages in the industry were high, seasonal layoffs reduced the average worker's annual earnings to less than $1,000. Workers also resented the "speed-ups" that occurred when management increased the rate at which cars moved along the assembly line.

The Autoworkers Strike

The CIO did not want to challenge the auto industry until the struggle with the steel companies had ended. But autoworkers were impatient for change and took matters into their own hands, using a strike strategy called the sit-down strike. Rather than walking off their jobs, strikers remained in the factory. The company could not hire new workers to continue production, nor could it remove the strikers by force without risking violence to the factory. One striker later remembered:

> 66 *We were nervous. We didn't know we could do it. Those machines had been kept going as long as we could remember. When we finally pulled the switch and there was some quiet, I finally remembered something. . . . that I was a human being, that I could stop those machines. . . .* 99

The sit-down strike was not originated by the autoworkers, nor was it unique to them. The radical International Workers of the World first used the technique against General Electric in 1906. But in the late 1930s factory workers, taxi drivers, maids, secretaries, and salesclerks sat down at their jobs to protest their pay and working conditions.

Union success in the auto, steel, and other industries swelled the ranks of organized labor during the Second New Deal. The CIO grew especially rapidly because it was willing to organize women workers, whom the AFL had ignored. From less than 3 million in 1933, union membership more than tripled by 1939. Organized labor showed its

appreciation for the Wagner Act and other New Deal programs by giving political support to the Democrats.

■ The 1936 Election

The Democrats renominated Roosevelt for President in 1936, and they enthusiastically endorsed the New Deal. The business community, however, contributed to his 1936 campaign only about one-fifth as much as it contributed in 1932, and many newspapers turned against FDR. The Republican nominee, Kansas governor Alfred M. Landon, denounced Roosevelt for endangering the "American system of free enterprise." He labeled Social Security as "unjust, unworkable, stupidly drafted, and wastefully financed," and attacked many other New Deal programs.

Four years of New Deal programs, however, had forged a new political coalition for the Democrats. Farmers, labor unions, retirees, and many ethnic groups supported Roosevelt and his programs. African American voters abandoned an allegiance to the Republican party that dated back to Reconstruction to support the party of Roosevelt. FDR's New Deal had not offered special programs for African Americans, but it had not tried to exclude them either. African American workers, who often were the first fired when hard times hit, owed much to New Deal relief programs, and they showed their gratitude at the polls. On Election Day, Roosevelt won in a landslide, and Democrats elected huge majorities to the House and Senate.

■ The New Deal and the Supreme Court

Before he could continue the New Deal in his second term, Roosevelt believed he had to eliminate opposition on the Supreme Court. During 1935 and 1936 the Court struck down New Deal programs, including the NIRA and AAA. Never before had the Court declared so much legislation unconstitutional. Roosevelt and his supporters

★★★

Sit-down Strikes

Passage of the Wagner Act boosted workers' morale and inspired imaginative techniques to bring reluctant managers to the negotiating table. Chief among their strategies was the sit-down strike. On December 30, 1936, the UAW members of General Motors' Fisher Body plant in Flint, Michigan, sat down at their work stations. Meanwhile, workers at other General Motors plants followed suit or struck in more traditional ways: picketing factories, seizing plants by force, and jeering at scabs—workers sent to take their places.

General Motors strike veteran Bob Stinson described how workers managed to get food and keep in touch with their families during the sit-down: "The soup kitchen was outside the plant. The women handled all the cooking, outside of one chef who came from New York. He had anywhere from 10 to 20 women washing dishes and peeling potatoes in the strike kitchen. Mostly stews, pretty good meals. They were put in containers and hoisted up through the window. . . .

"We had a ladies' auxiliary. They'd visit the homes of the guys that was in the plant.

They would find out if there was any shortage of coal or food. Then they'd maneuver around amongst themselves until they found some place to get a ton of coal."

Since the strikers were not going to starve, GM decided to freeze them out. It turned off the heat in the plant. But after six weeks, when the strikers still refused to give in, General Motors signed a contract with the UAW.

▼ FLINT, MICHIGAN, PLANT STRIKE

★★★★★★★★★★★★★★★★★★★★★★★★★★★★★★★★★

believed that "9 old men" on the Court, 7 of whom had been appointed by Republican Presidents, were interfering with the New Deal's attempts at recovery. Laws that helped millions of people, passed by large majorities in Congress, were being rejected by the Court, often by margins of 5 to 4.

Roosevelt considered his landslide reelection to be a mandate to curb the Supreme Court. In February 1937 the President presented legislation allowing him to appoint an additional justice to the Supreme Court for each justice over 70 years of age. Although the Court's size would increase from 9 to 15, Roosevelt argued that it needed "an infusion of younger blood." The "court-packing" bill caused a furor even in the President's own party. Many Americans were alarmed by the threat it posed to the system of checks and balances. Enough Democrats joined the Republicans in Congress to defeat Roosevelt's proposal. Although he suffered a major setback and lost many supporters, the President claimed that he had "lost the battle but won the war." While debate on the

"court-packing" bill raged in Congress, in two 5-to-4 decisions, the Court upheld the constitutionality of the two major laws of the Second New Deal—the Social Security Act and the Wagner Act.

■ Later New Deal Measures

By 1937 the economy had recovered nearly to 1929 levels, although widespread unemployment still remained. Roosevelt's financial advisers urged a cutback in spending and a balanced federal budget. Federal Reserve banks tightened credit, and the WPA cut the number of its employees in half.

Difficult Times Continue

The economy quickly slumped into a **recession,** a mild downturn in the business cycle, that critics called a "Roosevelt Depression." Huge crop surpluses collapsed agricultural prices, and industrial production dropped by one-third, almost to 1932 levels. The President blamed the slump on businesses that, he claimed, failed to reinvest profits in production and on monopolies that kept prices artificially high. To meet the economic crisis, the President again expanded the work-relief programs of the WPA and stepped up military spending. People went back to work and prices rose. But the recession proved that hard times were not yet over.

In 1938 Congress passed a number of New Deal measures that carried out earlier policies. A Fair Labor Standards Act abolished child labor and placed a ceiling on hours and a floor under wages, at least for workers in businesses classified as "interstate commerce." A new Farm Security Administration promoted the well-being of impoverished farmers. A new AAA attempted to cope with surpluses by paying farmers not only to produce less but also to improve the soil and to control erosion. In addition, a food-stamp plan helped to distribute farm surplus among those on relief.

The Opposition Succeeds

These were some of the last New Deal programs. In the fall of 1937, when Roosevelt called a special session of Congress, not one of his proposals was enacted. Both in 1937 and in 1938 Congress rejected the President's request to reorganize the executive branch. These defeats were largely the result of a coalition of Republicans and conservative Southern Democrats who increasingly opposed the President in Congress. Roosevelt tried to weaken this coalition by

Visualizing History

▲ **PACKING THE COURT** Although Roosevelt was overwhelmingly reelected in 1936, most people reacted negatively in 1937 to his attempt to pack the Supreme Court. *In this cartoon, what does the donkey's reaction symbolize?*

supporting liberal Democrats against incumbents in the 1938 primary.

Roosevelt's attempted "purge" of his own party ended in defeat. In most cases, the conservative Democrats won. In the November election the Republicans staged a modest comeback, picking up seats in both houses of Congress. The coalition of Republicans and Southern Democrats was growing powerful and could block further extension of the New Deal.

Roosevelt accepted the judgment of the voters in the 1938 election. In January 1939 he announced that he would propose no further New Deal programs. Instead, he turned his attention to the growing threat of war in Europe.

Section 3 ★ Review

Checking for Understanding

1. **Identify** Father Coughlin, Huey Long, WPA, NLRB, CIO, court-packing.

2. **Define** coalition, craft union, industrial union, recession.

3. **Explain** the steps in Dr. Townsend's recovery plan.

4. **Describe** steps the New Deal took toward reform after 1935.

Critical Thinking

5. **Contrasting Ideas** How did the second New Deal differ from the first in its objectives, support base, program focus, and success? Which was more successful?

Critical Thinking Skills

Predicting Consequences

Consequences are the effects and repercussions that result from a decision or action. Sometimes the consequences of an action take you by surprise. More often, with a little forethought you can anticipate possible consequences. To help predict consequences you can:

- **Restate** the action or decision under consideration.
- **Link** the action with relevant prior circumstances.
- **Map** out all possible outcomes or consequences.
- **Analyze** the possibilities. Are some consequences more likely to occur than others?

Read the information that follows. Then complete the Practicing the Skill to help you predict consequences.

Much of the government activity of the 1930s revolved around improving economic conditions and employment opportunities. The American labor movement worked toward these goals long before Roosevelt's New Deal. But the progress of the labor movement was impacted, either negatively or positively, by the actions and decisions of employers, Congress, and the courts. Based on your historical understanding, predict the effect of these actions on the labor movement.

- Court interpretation of the Sherman Antitrust Act of 1890 finds that union strikes are "in restraint of trade or commerce."
- Clayton Act of 1914 holds that the courts cannot stop peaceful strikes, pickets, or boycotts.

- Fair Labor Standards Act of 1938 outlaws child labor and limits maximum workday hours.
- Taft-Hartley Act of 1947 halts strikes that might endanger national health and safety.

Practicing the Skill

1. Predict the effect of the Clayton Act on the power of American labor unions.

2. Was the Fair Labor Standards Act a victory for labor or for business? Explain.

3. Predict the effect of the Taft-Hartley Act on police and firefighters.

4. Today the quest for improved worker rights focuses on issues such as sexual harassment, equal opportunity for the disabled, and access to health-care benefits. Why have these issues replaced earlier ones?

★★

The Impact of the New Deal

Setting the Scene

Section Focus

Just as Roosevelt's fireside chats over the radio reached the American people, his New Deal programs touched their lives. From relief for the poor, to wages and working conditions, to regulation of the nation's economy and financial markets, programs affected society at every level. The New Deal involved the federal government in American life to an extent unprecedented in the nation's history.

Objectives

After studying this section, you should be able to

★ identify changes that the New Deal caused in American society.

★ evaluate the effects of the New Deal on life today.

Key Term

ethnic group

▶ **WPA POSTER, 1940**

JOBS FOR GIRLS & WOMEN
GOOD PAY
GOOD MEALS
GOOD SURROUNDINGS
GOOD WORKING CONDITIONS
IF YOU WANT A GOOD JOB in
HOUSEHOLD EMPLOYMENT
APPLY AT-OR-WRITE TO
ILLINOIS STATE EMPLOYMENT SERVICE

*S*ociologists Robert and Helen Lynd in 1929 published a study of values, behaviors, and everyday life in the 1920s in a typical American city that they called "Middletown." (It was actually Muncie, Indiana.) In 1935 they returned to "Middletown" for a follow-up study and found that the Depression and the New Deal had profoundly affected the families living in that community.

■ The New Deal and Society

The Depression affected every part of society. Its impact was felt at home and at work. The New Deal brought relief for some, but problems remained. In 1937 President Roosevelt said, "I see one-third of a nation ill-housed, ill-clad, ill-nourished."

Adapting to the Depression at Home

During the Depression, both births and divorces decreased as people could not afford either event. Older people moved in with working relatives. Many families rented rooms to boarders or moved to smaller and less expensive homes. Housewives took in laundry and sewing to help support their families. Sales of prepared food declined, and many people canned foods at home.

Changes at Work

Competition among adults for jobs resulted in stronger child labor laws, and the number of working children declined during the 1930s. Consequently, the number of high school and college students rose.

In Middletown, the Lynds noted that when a man lost his job and could not find

▲ A. Philip Randolph As a young man, A. Philip Randolph quickly became aware of the discrimination African Americans faced in employment. He became a leader in the labor movement. *What civil rights measures were enacted during the New Deal?*

another, traditional family roles often were reversed, "with the woman taking a job for whatever money she could earn and the man caring for the household." Still, women were accused of taking men's jobs, and businesses often refused to hire married women.

Most women who worked outside the home, with the exception of farm and domestic workers, benefited from the New Deal. Women's wages rose and working conditions improved. The greatest direct assistance to women came from the Women's Division of the WPA. It employed between 300,000 and 400,000 women, some in traditionally female white-collar jobs such as teacher, nurse, and librarian. But most worked on canning and sewing projects. Their pay was low, but it often made the difference between food and famine.

■ Minorities

African Americans did not fare well under the New Deal. In addition, the government failed to enact any major civil rights measures during this period.

African Americans Get Mainly the Same Old Deal

As the poorest of the poor, African Americans often fell through the cracks of broad legislation such as the AAA and the Social Security Act. For example, although the AAA gave money to rural landowners, in the South 80 percent of all African American farmers owned no land. In addition, Roosevelt offered no civil rights program and did little to challenge the segregation that continued to exist throughout the nation, and he tolerated job discrimination. Even some government agencies refused to hire African Americans. Those that did, such as the CCC and armed forces, segregated African Americans and whites. In addition, African Americans received lower wages than white workers and were not assigned to certain jobs.

Nevertheless, Roosevelt appointed more African Americans to government posts than any President before him. Although most African American officials filled secondary posts, they influenced the President as an unofficial "black cabinet." Heading the cabinet was Mary McLeod Bethune, director of the Negro Affairs Division of the National Youth Administration. A personal friend of Eleanor Roosevelt, she often expressed the cabinet's concerns to the First Lady, who then carried them to FDR.

One concern of African Americans during the Depression was an increase in lynching and other acts of mob violence against them. Roosevelt supported a 1934 federal antilynching bill that held local sheriffs accountable for the frequent lynchings of African Americans in the South. But he never made the bill a legislative priority, and it finally died in the Senate in 1938.

One reason New Deal programs for African Americans were so limited was the opposition of powerful congressional committee heads who were from the South. As a result Roosevelt accepted NRA codes, for example, that permitted a lower minimum wage in the South than in the rest of the nation. FDR felt that if he pushed these Southern legislators too strongly, he would lose their support.

White Ethnic Groups Do Well

In general, the federal government responded more favorably to white **ethnic groups,** groups of people who shared the same culture, religion, and customs. During the 1930s the federal Office of Education sponsored a radio series called "Americans All . . . Immigrants All." The show celebrated the cultural vitality of a democracy made up of people from many lands. It also indicated the Democrats' awareness of the political power that ethnic groups could exercise if they were organized. Immigrants and their children made up 40 percent of the white population at that time. They tended to vote in groups and could swing elections, especially in large urban areas. Americans of Irish, Italian, and Polish descent became major partners in the New Deal coalition.

■ Popular Culture

The 1930s were somber years compared to the fads and frivolity of the 1920s. Literature and the arts generally turned to more realistic themes about poverty and human suffering.

Literature

Grim times provided powerful themes for American authors such as John Dos Passos, whose trilogy of novels called *U.S.A.* focused on fictional characters who lost their ideals and became hardened by society. Perhaps the most powerful novel of the era was John Steinbeck's *Grapes of Wrath,* the story of a family who left their Oklahoma farm in the dust bowl and headed to the migrant labor camps of California.

There was also much escapism in popular culture, as people turned to entertainment when things became grim. The best-selling book of the decade was Margaret Mitchell's *Gone with the Wind.* Although set in the South during the Civil War and Reconstruction, it offered a hopeful account of Scarlett

Visualizing History

▲ AT THE MOVIES The decade of the 1930s was a golden era for motion pictures. Popular fare included the Fred Astaire and Ginger Rogers musicals and Disney favorites such as *Snow White and the Seven Dwarfs.* **How many Americans attended the movies every week?**

▲ MASS ENTERTAINMENT Clark Gable and Vivien Leigh starred in the movie of the 1930s best-selling novel, *Gone With the Wind.* The film was a big hit because people got nearly 4 hours of entertainment for just 10 to 25 cents. *What other mass entertainment medium was popular in the 1930s?*

O'Hara's efforts to rebuild her life and had much meaning for readers who had gone through the 1929 crash and the Depression.

Entertainment

As "talkies"—films with sound—became common during the 1930s, about 85 million people escaped the realities of the Depression for a few hours each week at the movie theater. There they watched movies that were often about the lives of happy and successful people. Continued improvements in sound technology ushered in the era of musicals, and audiences delighted at the dance routines of Fred Astaire and Ginger Rogers. Cartoon characters, such as Mickey Mouse, made audiences laugh, and as color-film technology spread, full-length animated features like Walt Disney's *Snow White and the Seven Dwarfs* provided more fantasy and escape.

At home families could listen to network radio programs broadcast coast-to-coast. Daytime radio offered "soap operas," where characters suffered through daily crises. At night comedy, adventure, and musical variety programs dominated the airwaves. And the performances of Arturo Toscanini conducting the NBC Symphony of the Air brought classical music for the first time to millions of radio listeners.

The Automobile

Just as books, movies, and the radio provided Americans with an emotional outlet from the realities of the Depression, the automobile made them feel that they could physically escape their problems. Americans' love affair with cars, which began during the prosperity of the 1920s, continued throughout the poverty-stricken 1930s. The number of automobiles increased from 26 million in 1933 to 32 million by 1940. During the depths of the Depression, almost half the families in the United States owned a car, even though many could not afford to buy gasoline.

Yet despite the expense, many Americans continued to drive their cars during the 1930s. By late in the decade, thanks to government work projects, a maze of paved highways crisscrossed the nation. Large numbers of people took off down these two-lane roads, some searching for employment and others pioneering what became an American institution—the family vacation by car.

The Influence of the New Deal

In the arts, as in so many other areas of society, the New Deal played a role. The WPA helped unemployed actors, artists, writers, and musicians. The Federal Theatre Project sponsored performances of Shakespeare as well as children's plays. Some 6,500 writers put together state and regional guidebooks and recorded life stories of formerly enslaved people, immigrants, and Native Americans.

The Federal Arts Project had artists paint murals and sculptors create statues, many of which still can be viewed today. The artistic works of William Gropper, Peter Blume, and Jack Levine reflected social concerns. Photographers like Dorothea Lange and artists like Ben Shahn documented people's lives during the Depression. Arts projects were among the most controversial New Deal programs, however. Critics called them socialistic. In 1939 Congress cut off funds for the theater project, and the other arts programs were discontinued as employment rose during World War II.

To many people who lived through it, the New Deal seemed to have changed American society. Yet it was not the revolutionary assault on capitalism that some of its critics charged. The New Deal changed the lives of

▲ COMIC STRIP HERO LITTLE ORPHAN ANNIE

farmers through crop subsidies and rural electrification. It changed the lives of industrial workers by strengthening labor unions and expanding collective bargaining. It provided Social Security and welfare programs for the aged, the unemployed, and dependent children. In so doing, it turned a government that previously had responded more to business groups into a government open to labor, farmers, and other interests.

Yet the New Deal did not adopt national planning of the economy, as some of Roosevelt's advisers had expected. Rather than government owning industry, the New Deal emphasized federal regulation of private enterprise. Rather than overturning capitalism, New Dealers believed that they had helped to save it.

Section 4 ★ Review

Checking for Understanding

1. **Identify** black cabinet, John Steinbeck, Margaret Mitchell, soap operas, Federal Arts Project.

2. **Define** ethnic group.

3. **Summarize** the impact of the New Deal on African Americans.

4. **Discuss** popular forms of entertainment in the 1930s.

Critical Thinking

5. **Seeing Relationships** Analyze how the Depression influenced themes in American art and literature during the 1930s.

▲ JOHN STEINBECK

In *The Grapes of Wrath*, John Steinbeck chronicles the hardships of the Joads, an Oklahoma farm family whose plight resembles that of the downtrodden everywhere. As you read the excerpt from Steinbeck's novel, look for statements that reveal the beliefs, concerns, and attitudes of tenant farmers during the 1930s.

The Grapes of Wrath (excerpts)

The owners of the land came onto the land, or more often a spokesman for the owners came. They came in closed cars, and they felt the dry earth with their fingers, and sometimes they drove big earth augers into the ground for soil tests. The tenants, from their sun-beaten dooryards, watched uneasily when the closed cars drove along the fields. And at last the owner men drove into the dooryards and sat in their cars to talk out of the windows. . . .

If a bank or a finance company owned the land, the owner man said, The Bank—or the Company—needs-wants-insists-must have-as though the Bank or the Company were a monster, with thought and feeling, which had ensnared them. . . . The owner men sat in the cars and explained. You know the land is poor. You've scrabbled at it long enough, God knows.

The squatting tenant men nodded and wondered and drew figures in the dust, and yes, they knew, God knows. If the dust only wouldn't fly. If the top would only stay on the soil, it might not be so bad.

The owner men went on leading to their point: You know the land's getting poorer. You know what cotton does to the land; robs it, sucks all the blood out of it.

The squatters nodded—they knew, God knew. If they could only rotate the crops they might pump blood back into the land. Well, it's too late. And the owner men explained the workings and the thinkings of the monster that was stronger than they were. . . .

The squatting men raised their eyes to understand. Can't we just hang on? Maybe the next year will be a good year. God knows how much cotton next year. And with all the wars—God knows what price cotton will bring. Don't they make explosives out of cotton? And uniforms? Get enough wars and cotton'll hit the ceiling. Next year, maybe. They looked up questioningly.

We can't depend on it. The bank—the monster has to have profits all the time. It can't wait. It'll die. . . .

The squatting men looked down again. What do you want us to do? We can't take less share of the crop—we're half starved now. The kids are hungry all the time. We got no clothes, torn an' ragged. If all the neighbors weren't the same, we'd be ashamed to go to meeting.

And at last the owner men came to the point. The tenant system won't work any more. One man on a tractor can take the place of twelve or fourteen families. Pay him a wage and take all the crop. We have to do it. We don't like to do it. But the monster's sick. Something's happened to the monster.

But you'll kill the land with cotton. We know. We've got to take cotton quick before the land dies. Then we'll sell the land. Lots of families in the East would like to own a piece of land.

The tenant men looked up alarmed. But what'll happen to us? How'll we eat?

You'll have to get off the land. The plows'll go through the dooryard.

And now the squatting men stood up angrily. Grampa took up the land, and he had to kill the Indians and drive them away. An Pa was born here, and he killed weeds and snakes. Then a bad year came and he had to borrow a little money. An' we was born here. There in the door—our children born here. And Pa had to borrow money. The bank owned the land then, but we stayed and we got a little bit of what we raised.

We know the—all that. It's not us, it's the bank. A bank isn't like a man. Or an owner with fifty thousand acres, he isn't like a man either. That's the monster.

▲ COVER OF *THE GRAPES OF WRATH*

▶ DESTITUTE FAMILY, OZARKS

Interpreting Literature

1. Locate passages where the tenant men are beseeching or protesting.

2. What is the "monster"? Do you think this is an apt metaphor? Why or why not?

Evaluating Viewpoints

3. Steinbeck clearly sides with the tenant farmers. What arguments could be made for the banks and the owners? Which viewpoint do you favor?

Using Vocabulary

Write sentences about Roosevelt's New Deal using these vocabulary words.

deficit spending	**foreclosure**
dole	**recession**
pump priming	

Reviewing Facts

1. **Explain** the purpose of the bank holiday in the first Hundred Days.

2. **Compare** the purposes of New Deal legislation before and after 1935.

3. **Cite** the means Roosevelt used to advocate, promote, and gain public support for his New Deal programs.

4. **Identify** specific New Deal programs that provided help to various types of needy people in society.

5. **Describe** Roosevelt's attempts to help farmers.

6. **Discuss** developments and achievements within organized labor movements during the 1930s and the role that the New Deal played in these developments.

7. **Specify** groups that did not fully share in the benefits of the New Deal.

8. **List** ways the New Deal supported the arts during the Depression.

Understanding Concepts

Economic Reform

1. Which New Deal programs would you classify as achieving lasting economic reform? Explain your reasons for your choices.

Political Leadership

2. Much of the success of the New Deal relied on the charismatic personality and leadership of Franklin Roosevelt. Explain how he used these assets to gain support for his controversial and complicated New Deal policies.

Critical Thinking

1. **Finding Explanations** Though farmers received substantial assistance during the New Deal and have since, many farmers have continued to suffer economically. What problems inherent in farming could possibly account for this recurring difficulty?

2. **Analyzing Fine Art** Study the detail from the painting *City Life* that is on this page, then answer the questions that follow.

   a. What is going on in the painting?

   b. How does the artist give depth to the painting?

   c. Has Arnautoff created a mood in the work? Explain.

   d. If you were to rename this work, what would you entitle it? Explain your choice.

▲ *CITY LIFE* BY VICTOR ARNAUTOFF, 1934

CHAPTER 28 ★ REVIEW

Writing About History

Argumentation

Assume the nation has entered a depression in the 1990s. As a member of Congress devoted to economic reform, write an argument proposing and supporting deficit spending to stimulate the economy and to finance expanded government assistance programs. Think about what reasons an economist might have to favor such programs. Also think carefully about the reasons why some of your constituents would favor such policies and why others would oppose them.

Cooperative Learning

Working in a group of three, assume roles of government officials during Roosevelt's term. One member should assume the role of a Roosevelt supporter in Congress and present an argument to Congress for enlarging the Supreme Court. The second member should assume the role of an anti-Roosevelt senator and address Congress, refuting the need to enlarge the Court. The third member will listen to both arguments and decide which is the more effective. All group members should then be prepared to argue either position before the class if called upon by the teacher.

Social Studies Skills

Reading a Table

Tables are a useful way to organize information that you want to compare. Use the table on this page and information from the chapter to answer the following questions.

Practicing the Skill

1. How many years does the information presented in the table cover?

2. What is the subject of the table?

3. Which column shows how much money each person in the country would owe if the federal debt were divided equally among all the people?

4. What year was the federal deficit at its highest level? What was happening in the United States at that time?

The Federal Budget and Deficit

	Federal Receipts (in billions of dollars)	Federal Deficit (in billions of dollars)	Gross Federal Debt (in billions of dollars)	Per Capita Federal Debt (total dollar amt.)
1940	6.9	−2.7	43.0	325
1939	6.6	−2.9	40.4	309
1938	7.0	−.1	37.2	286
1937	5.6	−2.8	36.4	283
1936	4.2	−3.5	33.8	264
1935	3.8	−2.4	28.7	226
1934	3.1	−3.3	27.1	214
1933	2.1	−2.6	22.5	179
1932	2.0	−2.7	19.5	156

Source: *Historical Statistics of the United States: Colonial Times to 1970* (1975).

5. During the time period shown, did the federal government ever spend less money than it received?

6. If the federal deficit decreased in 1940, why didn't the federal debt also decrease?

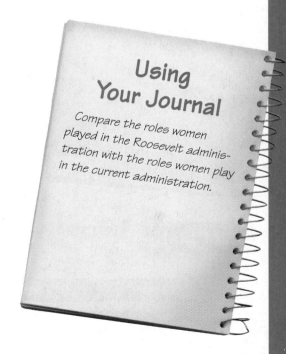

Using Your Journal

Compare the roles women played in the Roosevelt administration with the roles women play in the current administration.

CHAPTER 29

★★

World War II
1933–1945

► SILVER STAR, AWARDED
FOR GALLANTRY IN ACTION

Setting the Scene

Focus

The Depression of the 1930s was worldwide. When a new war engulfed Europe, Roosevelt sought to aid the British. After Japan attacked Pearl Harbor in 1941, America entered the war directly. Initially, Allied prospects were bleak, but by 1944 the tide had turned. Victory in the Pacific, however, came only after the use of nuclear weapons.

Concepts to Understand

★ Why international alliances were formed between Germany, Italy, and Japan

★ How the Allies prevented Germany and Italy from winning the military conflict in Europe

Read to Discover . . .

★ what events led the American people to abandon isolationism and neutrality.

★ why Roosevelt was more successful than Wilson in helping to form a world peacekeeping body.

Journal Notes

Consider the interests, fears, and concerns of the nations involved in World War II. Record examples in your journal as you read the chapter.

CULTURAL

● **1931** *Pearl Buck publishes* The Good Earth

● **1936** *Babe Ruth and Ty Cobb named to baseball's Hall of Fame*

1930   **1935**

● **1933** *United States recognizes the government of the Soviet Union*

● **1939** *Germany attacks Poland; war in Europe begins*

POLITICAL

Tank boots, 1943

History AND ART

Follow Me!
by Charles McBarron, Jr.

United States forces take the key central Philippine island of Leyte in October 1944.

- **1940** *Color television is demonstrated by the Columbia Broadcasting System*
- **1942** *Sugar and gasoline are rationed*

1940

- **1940** *Selective Service Act passed*
- **1941** *Japanese attack Pearl Harbor*

- **1945** *Tennessee Williams's play* The Glass Menagerie *opens in New York*

1945

- **1944** *Allies invade Normandy*
- **1945** *Nuclear weapons first used*

★★★

World Affairs, 1933–1939

Setting the Scene

Section Focus

Like President Woodrow Wilson, for whom he had worked during World War I, Franklin D. Roosevelt was greatly interested in world affairs. But when he entered the White House in 1933, recovery from the Depression kept most of his energy and attention focused on the United States. As Europe again moved toward war, however, the President experienced growing concern with events overseas.

Objectives

After studying this section, you should be able to

★ discuss how the Depression influenced American foreign policy.

★ explain the reasons for Japan's aggression in Asia.

Key Terms

fascism, totalitarian, appeasement

◄ **MILITARY ALUMINUM CANTEEN**

Like his distant cousin Theodore, Franklin D. Roosevelt was acquainted with the world beyond the shores of the United States. He had made more than a dozen trips to Europe, and he had first-hand knowledge of the Caribbean area. Through family connections with the China trade, he had acquired an interest in Asia. He resembled Theodore Roosevelt, too, in realizing that as a world power the United States had a commitment to help preserve the peace of the world. As a former associate of Woodrow Wilson, he believed in world organization to promote international cooperation and to solve disputes.

For most of his first two terms, however, Franklin D. Roosevelt focused on domestic affairs. Events in Europe and Asia seemed distant when compared to the crisis of the Depression. In addition, the President rec-

ognized that Americans, pressed by hard times at home, cared little about the world at large. So although Roosevelt believed that German expansion posed a threat to the United States, he was cautious in his efforts to alert the nation to this danger. Only when dealing with affairs in the Western Hemisphere did Roosevelt act with his typical bold political style.

■ New Deal Foreign Policy

At his first inaugural in 1933, President Roosevelt pledged that the United States would be a "good neighbor" in the family of nations. He pledged to respect the sovereign rights of all nations in the Western Hemisphere. A few weeks later, he applied the phrase "Good Neighbor" specifically to the administration's Latin American policy.

Peaceful Intentions in Latin America

President Roosevelt and Secretary of State Cordell Hull worked to improve relations with the United States's southern neighbors. Later that year, at the Pan-American Conference at Montevideo, Uruguay, the United States agreed to a resolution that "no state has the right to intervene in the internal affairs of another." Roosevelt demonstrated his commitment to the Good Neighbor policy by recalling American troops from Haiti and Nicaragua, where they had been protecting American property since the 1920s. When Cuba erupted in revolution in 1933, Roosevelt used diplomacy, not troops, to help restore order. When Mexico seized American-owned oil companies in 1938, Roosevelt resisted demands for military action and sought a peaceful settlement.

Domestic Recovery Determines Foreign Decisions

During Roosevelt's first years in office, the United States seemed less inclined to cooperate with Europe. The New Deal adopted a policy of economic isolation, and its recovery programs included attempts to solve agricultural and industrial production problems without considering the rest of the world. In 1933 delegates from more than 60 nations met in London to bring about cooperation in confronting world depression. Roosevelt wrecked the conference by rejecting proposals to peg the value of the dollar to any other currency. He feared that such a move would hurt his efforts to raise American farm prices.

Only when the United States had achieved some recovery from the Depression was the President willing to consider economic cooperation with other nations. Secretary of State Hull believed world prosperity and goodwill could be gained by reducing tariffs. At Hull's urging, Congress passed the Reciprocal Trade Agreements Act of 1934, allowing the State Department to make treaties with other countries to mutually lower import duties. Within six years, the United States had reached such agreements with more than a dozen nations.

Recognition of the Soviet Union

Another change in foreign policy took place when the United States recognized the government of the Soviet Union. Since the Bolshevik Revolution of 1917, the United States had refused to recognize the communist government. After their revolution, the Soviets tried to encourage communism throughout the world. By 1933, however, the USSR was beset by serious economic problems at home and seemed less of a threat. Much more threatening was the rising power of Japan, the Soviets' rival in Asia. The President hoped that a strong Soviet Union could slow Japanese expansion. In addition, Roosevelt saw the Soviets' need for food and industrial equipment as a market for American farmers and manufacturers. "The United States would probably

 Visualizing History ▲ JAPANESE EXPANSION Japanese forces first moved into Manchuria in 1931. Japan established the puppet state of Manchukuo a year later. *How did Roosevelt hope to slow Japan's aggression in Asia?*

▲ **MUSSOLINI** Italy's dictator Benito Mussolini gives the Fascist salute during an address. After Italy surrendered to Allied forces, Mussolini was captured and executed by the Italian people. *What plans did Mussolini have in common with Adolf Hitler?*

recognize the Devil," Will Rogers joked, "if it could sell him pitchforks." Recognition of the Soviet Union helped improve relations but did little to increase trade or to check Japanese militarism.

■ Aggression and Appeasement

American hopes to concentrate on domestic affairs, relatively isolated from foreign concerns, were quickly dashed. Events in the world began to send off alarms of trouble ahead.

Japanese Expansion in the Pacific

Between 1872 and 1925, Japan's population nearly doubled, causing severe problems for that small island nation. To sustain industrial growth Japan needed larger markets for its products and more raw materials for its factories. To meet these needs and to ease overcrowding in the home islands, Japan pursued a policy of expansion in the Pacific.

During World War I, Japan supported the Allies but used the war to increase its influence in China. After the war Japan was bitter toward the West. The Washington Conference of 1921 cost Japan most of its gains in China and limited Japan's naval power. When the United States joined other Western nations in 1924 in banning immigrants from Japan, its leaders looked to military solutions for their nation's problems.

In September 1931, Japanese troops invaded and occupied mineral-rich Manchuria in northeastern China. When the League of Nations demanded that Manchuria be returned to China, Japan ignored the order.

Threats From Germany and Italy

On March 5, 1933, the day after Roosevelt took office, the German parliament voted Adolf Hitler, the National Socialist (Nazi) leader, the power he needed to begin a program of conquest in central and eastern Europe. In Italy, dictator Benito Mussolini made similar plans to control the Mediterranean and to expand Italy's empire in Africa.

Mussolini and Hitler followed a new political doctrine known as **fascism** (FASH•ihz•uhm), a form of government in which a dictator and supporters cooperate to seek more power for their nation, usually at the expense of rights for individuals. Each ruler established a **totalitarian** state—a nation that totally controls the life of its people. The Fascists in Italy and the Nazis in Germany set up all-powerful official parties. Both whipped up support with huge patriotic rallies, parades, music, and appeals to national pride and racial hatred, and both used force to silence all opposition.

Each dictator blamed his country's problems after World War I on undesirables in society. Mussolini accused Italy's Communists of causing strikes and social unrest.

The Nazis blamed Germany's economic chaos on its Jewish population. They restricted Jews, boycotted Jewish-owned stores, and destroyed synagogues. Both Hitler and Mussolini hinted that another war might be necessary to right the wrongs they felt had been done to their countries by the Treaty of Versailles.

The glorification of war by Italy, Germany, and Japan was not idle talk. In 1935 Mussolini attacked and took control of Ethiopia in Africa. In 1937 Japanese armies invaded the rest of China. In March 1938 Hitler marched into Austria. In 1936 General Francisco Franco rebelled against the republican government of Spain, and German and Italian tanks, bombers, and troops helped Franco win a bitter civil war that lasted until 1939.

Bargaining for Peace

The response of Great Britain and France was **appeasement,** a policy of giving aggressor nations what they wanted in order to avoid war. Like the Americans, the British and French were disillusioned by World War I and wanted peace. Much as they disliked Italian, German, or Japanese expansion, they disliked the thought of war

Visualizing History   GERMANY UNDER HITLER   In 1935 Adolf Hitler announced that he intended to ignore the Versailles treaty and began to rearm Germany. In 1936 his army reoccupied the Rhineland on Germany's border with France. *How did Great Britain and France respond when Hitler began to act aggressively in Europe?*

even more. Pacifism reached new heights: a majority of the students in the debating union at Britain's Oxford University voted that on no account would they go to war for king or country. Appeasement reached its peak at the Munich Conference of September 1938 when British and French leaders allowed Hitler to annex part of Czechoslovakia in return for his promise to make no further territorial demands. British Prime Minister Neville Chamberlain returned from Germany to tell a jittery world that the Munich Pact meant "peace for our time." Winston Churchill, however, who soon would replace Chamberlain as prime minister, observed that "Britain and France had to choose between war and dishonor. They chose dishonor. They will have war."

Neutrality

The American people were also determined to avoid war. World War I had left the United States with a huge domestic debt and billions of dollars in foreign debts that could not be collected. Americans also wanted to avoid war for a number of other reasons. A congressional investigation of the munitions industry revealed that American manufacturers had made large profits by supplying arms and credit to the Allies during the years 1914–1917. This led to the notion that American participation in World War I had been arranged by "merchants of death," assisted by British propagandists. There was increasing feeling that William Jennings Bryan had been correct in 1914 in urging that the United States supply no arms to the belligerents, make them no loans, and abandon defense of neutral rights on the high seas. To prevent being drawn into war again, Congress passed Neutrality Acts in 1935, 1936, and 1937. These laws barred the transportation or sale of arms to warring nations and banned loans to nations at war outside the Western Hemisphere.

The restrictions of the Neutrality Acts did not please Roosevelt who believed they would "drag us into the war instead of keeping us out." He had wanted legislation that would allow him more discretion—for example, to embargo supplies on one side but not to the other. On October 5, 1937, he warned the American people that war was contagious:

> **" Innocent people are being cruelly sacrificed to a greed for power and supremacy. . . . Let no one imagine that America will escape. . . . War is contagion, whether it be declared or not. "**

Roosevelt signed the Neutrality Acts without protest. However, he would have preferred some freedom to distinguish between aggressors and victims. The President believed that Germany, Italy, and Japan were "bad neighbors" who were bent on war. In a speech in October 1937, Roosevelt called for the abandonment of isolation, but American public opinion forced him to drop any idea of collective action against aggressor nations. "It's a terrible thing," Roosevelt remarked, "to look over your shoulder when you're trying to lead—and find no one there."

Section 1 ★ Review

Checking for Understanding

1. **Identify** Benito Mussolini, Munich Conference, Neutrality Acts.

2. **Define** fascism, totalitarian, appeasement.

3. **Describe** what influence the Depression had in shaping American foreign policy.

4. **Examine** Japan's objectives in its aggressive expansion in Asia.

Critical Thinking

5. **Evaluating Policy** Should one country intervene militarily in the affairs of another to protect property owned by its citizens? Explain.

★★★

Moving Closer to War

Setting the Scene

Section Focus

As war in Europe became a certainty, a great debate took place among Americans over what role the United States should play. Isolationists opposed any American involvement in European affairs and wanted the United States to act independently in the world. On the other side of the debate, internationalists believed that America's own security was linked to the success of Europe's struggle against Hitler.

Objectives

After studying this section, you should be able to

★ discuss Germany's military conquest of Europe during the late 1930s and early 1940s.

★ list the steps by which the Roosevelt administration increased American support to the Allies and the effects these steps had.

Key Terms

blitzkrieg, lend-lease

◀ **BRONZE STAR, AWARDED FOR HEROISM**

The most outspoken isolationists in Congress were progressive Republicans mainly from the Midwest and the West. Their primary support came from a number of newspapers, most notably those in the William Randolph Hearst chain. On the radio Roosevelt's New Deal critic, Father Charles Coughlin, also lined up with the isolationists. An America First Committee sponsored rallies around the country against the war. A frequent speaker was the popular pilot Charles Lindbergh who warned that "the only way our American life and ideals can be preserved is by staying out of this war." The internationalists were strongest in the Democratic party and generally represented states in the South and the Northeast. They looked to President Roosevelt for leadership.

■ Europe at War Again

As Churchill had predicted, the Munich agreement failed to appease Hitler, who in March 1939 swallowed up the rest of Czechoslovakia and demanded territory in Poland. Britain and France pledged to defend Poland from Hitler, and they asked the Soviet Union to join in an alliance to contain Germany. In August 1939, however, Soviet dictator Joseph Stalin signed a nonaggression pact with Germany. By removing the threat of war on two fronts, the pact cleared the way for Hitler to invade Poland. Hitler still doubted that Britain and France would resist him, however.

▲ **PURPLE HEART**

▲ THE FALL OF POLAND Nazi troops march through the streets of Warsaw after the fall of Poland. The conquest of Poland had taken little more than a month. *What point does the cartoon express?*

Outbreak of War

Before dawn on September 1, 1939, German forces crossed into Poland in an attack so fast and brutal that a new word was coined—**blitzkrieg,** meaning "lightning war." This time Britain and France decided to fight, and on September 3 they declared war on Germany.

President Roosevelt declared that the United States would remain neutral, but he added, "Even a neutral cannot be asked to close his mind or his conscience." Within weeks he asked Congress to lift the Neutrality Acts' arms embargo that prevented Britain and France from buying American weapons. Although Congress was flooded with telegrams urging it to "keep America out of the blood business," after weeks of debate, it agreed to sell arms to the Allies if they paid cash and carried the goods in their own ships.

Near Disaster at Dunkirk

After a lull in the fighting over the winter of 1939–1940, Hitler launched an invasion of Norway and Denmark. Next, the German armies swept into the Netherlands and Belgium, where for the first time they met resistance from British and French troops. In May 1940, German forces defeated the Allied army and drove it to the sea at the French town of Dunkirk on the Belgian border. Cut off from retreat by land, the army was saved when 300,000 British and French troops were evacuated across the English Channel in a heroic nine-day rescue effort aided by 600 private boats.

Battle of Britain

In June 1940, Italy invaded France and declared war on Great Britain. In response, President Roosevelt announced that, although the United States would not enter the war, it would extend as much aid as possible to the democracies. On June 22 France surrendered, and Britain faced the threat alone.

As the German air force bombed British airfields, factories, and cities to prepare the way for German armies to cross the English Channel, Britain found leadership in its new prime minister, Winston Churchill. Offering only "blood, toil, tears, and sweat," he pledged:

66 *. . . we shall defend our island, whatever the cost may be. We shall fight on the beaches. We shall fight on the landing grounds. We shall fight on the fields and in the streets. We shall fight in the hills. We shall never surrender. . . . until, in God's good time, the New World, with all its power and might, steps forth to the rescue and liberation of the Old.* 99

America Abandons Neutrality

Prime Minister Churchill asked the United States for a loan of 50 destroyers to protect British shipping from German submarines. Recognizing that the isolationists in Congress would block approval of the loan, Roosevelt decided to act on his own. In September 1940, by executive order, he transferred 50 old World War I destroyers to Britain in return for the use of bases in Newfoundland and the Caribbean.

Meanwhile, for months London suffered bombing day and night by hundreds of German planes. The fighter pilots of the Royal

▶ WATCHING THE GERMAN ARMY ENTER PARIS

Visualizing History

▲ DUNKIRK As the trapped British and French armies awaited evacuation at Dunkirk, they were bombarded by German planes and artillery. The largest retreat in military history was accomplished by the British navy and private boats ranging from yachts to tugboats, all protected by the Royal Air Force. Huge amounts of equipment were left behind, but Britain's army was saved from total destruction. ***What effect did the fall of France have on American foreign policy?***

▲ **ARRESTING OPPONENTS** Hitler's secret police, the Gestapo, arrested Jews and other opponents of the government by the thousands. Many were sent to large prisons called concentration camps. Resistance by the imprisoned against Nazi atrocities took many forms, including trying to escape and rebelling against their captors. *How did Americans react to the fall of France and the threat to Britain?*

Air Force, however, kept the Germans from gaining control of the skies over Britain and forced Hitler to abandon his invasion plans. "Never in the field of human conflict," said Churchill, "was so much owed by so many to so few."

America Realizes Its Peril

The fall of France and the threat to Britain shook many Americans out of their belief that events outside the Western Hemisphere were none of their business. The possibility that Hitler and Mussolini might add the British and French fleets to their own made the Atlantic Ocean suddenly seem narrower, and Congress began to heed Roosevelt's warnings. It appropriated billions of dollars for defense and passed a Selective Service Act in September 1940, the first peacetime draft in American history, adding 800,000 men to the armed forces.

Roosevelt's Leadership Endorsed

In the presidential election of 1940, the debate between internationalists and isolationists was carried on in both major parties. The Republicans nominated a newcomer to politics—Wendell Willkie, a Wall Street lawyer and utility company executive, best known for his criticism of the New Deal. For Democrats the question was whether Roosevelt would seek a third term, breaking the precedent set by George Washington. With the United States facing war in Europe and Asia, Roosevelt felt his experience was needed. He kept silent until the Democratic convention, then announced that he would accept the nomination.

At first, both candidates agreed on foreign-policy issues. But when Willkie slipped in the polls, he began to warn that Roosevelt's reelection would mean war. Roosevelt's promise to keep American troops out of war, Willkie said, was no better than his promise to balance the budget. In November 1940, Roosevelt won reelection. With the world in crisis, most American voters did not want to gamble on a change in leadership.

Aid to a Desperate Britain

The British government was running out of money to pay for weapons, so the President proposed that the United States abandon its "cash and carry" policy. But not wanting to revive the old war-debts controversy, Roosevelt suggested a **lend-lease** policy, wherein the United States would merely lend goods to Britain, which the British could return or replace after the war. Lend-lease again stirred debate, but public opinion was shifting in Roosevelt's favor. A poll in January 1941 showed that 60 percent of Americans believed that it was more important to help Britain than to keep out of war. In March 1941, large majorities in both houses of Congress passed lend-lease, authorizing the President to send American supplies and weapons to other nations on any terms he thought would protect the security of the United States.

Battle for the Atlantic

It was one thing to enact lend-lease, however, and another to get supplies across the Atlantic in time to help. When Hitler attacked Yugoslavia and Greece in the spring of 1941, the Nazis overran those countries before lend-lease aid could reach them. When Hitler's bombers failed to knock out Britain, he ordered his submarine fleet to starve that nation into submission.

In trying to make sure that lend-lease supplies reached their destination, the United States was drawn step-by-step into the critical battle of the Atlantic. As German U-boats sank British and American supply ships almost daily, Roosevelt ordered the United States Navy to protect merchant shipping. By the fall of 1941, American and German warships were exchanging fire, and in October a German U-boat sank an American destroyer, killing more than 90 members of its crew. Congress responded by revising the Neutrality Acts to allow merchant ships to be armed.

Germany Turns on a Former Ally

While German-American tensions were escalating in the Atlantic, in June 1941 Hitler, wanting Russia's vast wheat and oil supplies, suddenly attacked the Soviet Union. As German armies quickly advanced into the USSR, Stalin signed an alliance with Great Britain, and the United States offered lend-lease aid. American isolationists were outraged that Roosevelt would aid the Soviets. But Churchill knew that American aid to the Soviet Union would reduce German pressure on Britain. In supporting Roosevelt's decision, he remarked:

> ❝ *I have only one purpose, the destruction of Hitler. . . . If Hitler invaded Hell I would at least make a favorable reference to the Devil in the House of Commons.* ❞

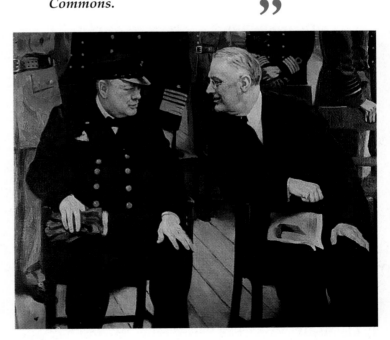

Visualizing History ▲ STRATEGY SESSION Before the United States entered the war, Roosevelt and Churchill met to coordinate Allied strategy and to make peacetime plans. Out of this meeting off the North American coast in August 1941, plans emerged for the United Nations. *How did Churchill feel about helping Stalin?*

By the end of November 1941, very few Americans were preaching isolation. Most agreed with Roosevelt that the United States must be an "arsenal of democracy" to supply Great Britain and the Soviet Union against Hitler. In fact, about 15,000 Americans were already at war, most in British or Canadian uniforms.

■ Aggression in the Pacific

While the American public's attention was fixed on the Atlantic and Europe, events were taking place in the Pacific and Asia that would eventually plunge the United States into war. Already in China, Japan moved against European colonies in Southeast Asia. This vast region contained the rice, rubber, tin, zinc, and oil needed for Japan's expanding industries. With France defeated, Britain on its knees, and the Soviets retreating in front of German armies, the United States was the only remaining obstacle to Japanese ambitions in the Pacific.

Embargo

In September 1940, Japan allied with the Axis Powers, Germany and Italy, and the United States responded by cutting off exports of scrap metal to Japan. As Japan continued its aggression in Asia, Roosevelt extended the embargo to include other products with possible military uses. In July 1941, he told the Japanese that the United States would help them find raw materials if they abandoned their policy of conquest. When Japan rejected his proposal, the President halted all trade with Japan and ordered American forces in the Pacific to prepare for war.

Appeal for Peace

On October 18, 1941, the Japanese prime minister, Prince Fumimaro Konoye, resigned. Konoye had been willing to negotiate with the United States because he did not believe Japan could defeat America in a war. The new prime minister, General Hideki Tojo, did not share Konoye's views. He favored war to eliminate American and British influence in Asia.

By late November, as the United States continued to insist that Japan honor the Open Door policy, Japanese leaders decided that if the dispute did not quickly come to a favorable conclusion, they would attack. Nonetheless, on November 20, negotiations were opened in Washington, D.C. Representing the United States was Secretary of State Cordell Hull. Ambassador Admiral Kichisaburo Nomura and special envoy Saburo Kurusu represented Japan.

The Talks Stall

As negotiations deadlocked, Roosevelt realized that war was inevitable. On December 6, the President appealed for peace directly to Japan's Emperor Hirohito. American officials did not know that, on November 26, a Japanese fleet had put to sea, headed for the United States's main naval base in the Pacific—Pearl Harbor in Hawaii.

Section 2 ★ Review

Checking for Understanding

1. **Identify** Winston Churchill, Selective Service Act, Pearl Harbor.

2. **Define** blitzkrieg, lend-lease.

3. **Describe** why hostilities developed between the United States and Japan.

4. **Explain** the importance of the election of 1940.

Critical Thinking

5. **Citing Evidence**   What actions and policies demonstrated that Congress and Roosevelt recognized the possibility that the United States would be drawn into war?

★★★

The United States at War

Setting the Scene

Section Focus

Three days after Congress declared war on Japan, Germany and Italy declared war on the United States. Americans now faced war in both Europe and Asia. Japan's unprovoked attack had ended the public debate over foreign policy. The American people were now united in their determination to win the war.

Objectives

After studying this section, you should be able to

★ discuss the course of the war in Europe and in Asia.

★ describe the Atlantic Charter and the agreements the Allies reached at the Yalta Conference.

Key Term

Holocaust

◀ UNITED STATES POSTER AFTER BOMBING OF PEARL HARBOR

With little warning, Japanese bombers attacked the American fleet based at Pearl Harbor. Shortly after noon on Sunday, December 7, 1941, President Roosevelt had just finished lunch when he received an urgent telephone call from Frank Knox, the secretary of the navy. The secretary had just received a wire from Hawaii: "Air Raid on Pearl Harbor. This is no Drill."

In 2 hours, Japanese planes sank many vessels, including 5 battleships and 3 destroyers, and heavily damaged many others. The attack also destroyed about 250 airplanes, and about 4,500 people were killed or wounded. Only the fleet's aircraft carriers, out of the harbor on maneuvers, escaped the devastation.

■ The World at War

However determined the American people were to defeat the Axis Powers—Germany, Italy, and Japan—the immediate outlook was bleak.

Japanese Victories in the Pacific

The destruction of the American fleet removed Japan's only obstacle in the Pacific. For six months the Japanese won victory after victory, capturing American bases at Guam and Wake Island, conquering Britain's colonies at Hong Kong and Singapore, and occupying the independent kingdom of Thailand. In April 1942, American forces on the peninsula of Bataan in the

Philippines finally surrendered. Meanwhile, the Japanese forces conquered Burma and the East Indies.

German Success in Europe

Axis forces occupied nearly all of Europe, and Britain was besieged. In North Africa, German General Erwin Rommel, "the Desert Fox," led an Italian-German force toward the Suez Canal, pushing the British back to the borders of Egypt. By summer 1942 the Germans had pushed deep into the Soviet Union, capturing the rich farmland of Ukraine and threatening the cities of Stalingrad, Leningrad, and Moscow. Success or failure of the war in Europe depended on whether the Soviet Union could hold out until the United States and Britain could launch an offensive on the western front.

Even before Japan attacked Pearl Harbor, American strategists had decided that in the event of war, United States forces would concentrate on defeating Hitler before dealing with Japan. Not only did the United States have closer ties with the countries occupied by Germany, but Germany seemed a greater threat to the Western Hemisphere, where Nazi sympathies were strong in several Latin American nations. Churchill agreed with this plan, observing that

> " . . . [T]he defeat of Germany. . . will leave Japan exposed to an overwhelming force, whereas the defeat of Japan would by no means bring the World War to an end. "

Turning Point of the War

Meanwhile, German troops launched a second attack on the Soviets in 1942. In the spring they moved toward the oil fields near the Caspian Sea, and by midsummer

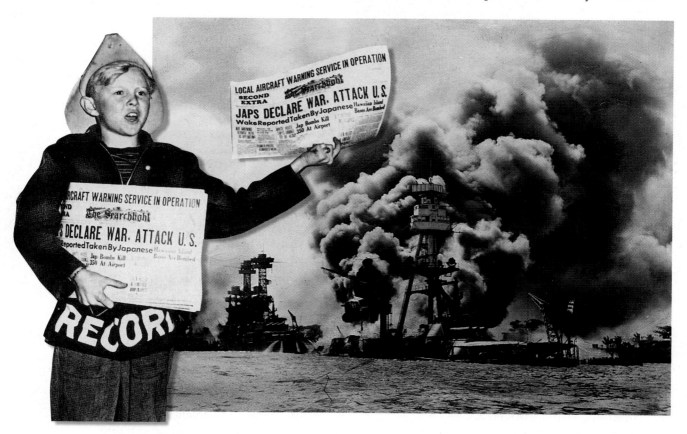

▲ PEARL HARBOR Japan's surprise attack on Pearl Harbor severely damaged the United States Pacific Fleet. In addition, about 250 warplanes were destroyed and more than 2,400 Americans were killed. *How did the attack affect American public opinion about isolationism?*

World War II in Europe and Africa

Legend:
- Major Axis Powers
- Greatest extent of Axis control
- Allied or Ally-controlled
- → Allied forces
- ◄ Supply lines

0   500   1,000 miles
0   500   1,000 kilometers

SUPPLY LINES FROM U.S.

D-DAY June 6, 1944

Nov. 8, 1942

Aug. 15, 1944

July 10, 1943

Oct. 23, 1942

FINAL SOVIET DRIVE July-August, 1944

SUPPLY LINE TO SOVIET UNION

Map Study Churchill and Roosevelt delayed an attack in Europe to first fight in the Mediterranean. Some historians believe this was a plan to weaken Soviet power in postwar Europe. **What reasoning might support such a theory?**

they were more than halfway to their goal. Stalin pleaded with the Allied leaders Roosevelt and Churchill for an invasion of western Europe that would take some pressure off the Soviet Union. Churchill told him that such a second front in Europe was a year away. Soviet troops were left to face the Germans alone.

In September 1942, the Red Army made a desperate and heroic stand at Stalingrad. For four months, Soviet and German troops battled house-to-house for control of the city. Although the German invasion was halted, Stalingrad was reduced to rubble and the Soviets suffered more casualties defending it than the United States did in the entire war. Stalin never forgave Roosevelt and Churchill for allowing this to happen.

In November the Soviet army counterattacked. Taking advantage of the Russian winter, the Red Army surrounded Hitler's freezing forces. In February 1943, the tattered remains of the invading German army, only one-third of its 330,000 men still alive, surrendered.

German Weak Point Exposed

In North Africa, American and British forces, working first separately and then together, pushed Rommel and his Afrika Korps into Tunisia. Under the command first of Major General Lloyd R. Fredendall and then of Major General George S. Patton, American forces checked Rommel's drive at Kasserine Pass and took El Guettar and Bizerte. Under General Bernard L. Montgomery, the British took Tripoli and Tunis. By May, Rommel had fled, nearly 250,000 Axis troops had surrendered, and the campaign in North Africa was over.

Allied victories in North Africa cleared the way for an attack on what Churchill called "the soft underbelly" of Europe. In August 1943, British and American forces took Sicily, and in September they invaded the Italian mainland. After his defeat in Sicily, Mussolini was overthrown, and the new Italian government quickly surrendered. German troops still occupied Italy, however, and put up fierce resistance in the mountainous terrain. Not until June 1944 did the Allies enter Rome. Axis forces remained in control of northern Italy.

■ Victory in Europe

American and British air forces had already begun round-the-clock bombing of German industrial and transportation centers. But Hitler's armies had to be defeated on the ground.

Normandy Invasion

On June 6, 1944, the greatest amphibious force in history—176,000 troops carried in 5,000 vessels—crossed the English Channel to land along a 60-mile stretch of coastline in France. Planning for the "D-Day" invasion at Normandy had been under way for more than two years.

▲ **D-DAY** American troops, under heavy fire from German defenders, stormed the coast of France from Coast Guard landing barges. British, Canadian, and free French forces also participated in the invasion. *How did the Normandy invasion take pressure off Soviet forces?*

Under the command of American General Dwight D. Eisenhower, a million Allied forces were in France within a month after D-Day. On July 25 the Americans broke through the German line. By early August, General George Patton and his forces were racing across northern France through open countryside. In August American and British troops broke out of Normandy and struck rapidly eastward, entering Paris on August 25, 1944. In September they crossed the western border of Germany.

Rapid Soviet Advance from the East

At the same time, the Soviets closed in from the east. In January 1944, the Red Army freed Leningrad from an 890-day German siege, during which 800,000 residents died. By spring Soviet troops had freed Ukraine, and in July they entered Poland. In August Romania and Bulgaria surrendered, opening the Balkans to the Soviets. In December they entered Hungary. By the end of 1944, most of eastern Europe was in Soviet hands.

Germany Surrenders

In December 1944, Hitler ordered a counterattack in Belgium. Although Allied lines "bulged," the Germans could not break through. The Battle of the Bulge was the last German offensive. In March 1945, the Allies crossed the Rhine River and moved into the heart of Germany. Meanwhile, the Soviets pushed from the east, taking Berlin in April 1945. In April, Hitler committed suicide in his underground shelter in Berlin, and on May 7, 1945, German leaders agreed to an unconditional surrender. Franklin D. Roosevelt, who led the nation through the Depression and the war, however, did not witness this event. Only days before Hitler's suicide, the President died of a massive cerebral hemorrhage.

Crimes Against Humanity

As they entered Germany, Allied armies discovered evidence of one of the most terrible acts of the war—the Nazi **Holocaust,**

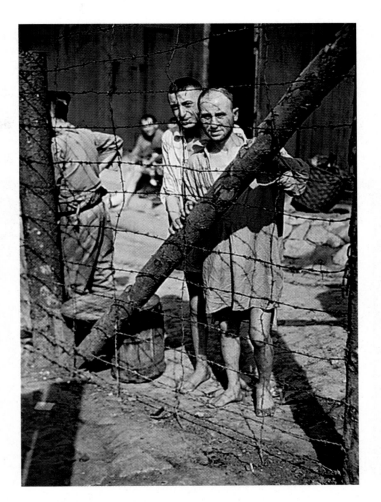

Visualizing History ▲ CONCENTRATION CAMPS The condition of survivors in Nazi death camps such as Belsen, Auschwitz, and Buchenwald horrified the world. *Why were the death camps created?*

or deliberate extermination of millions of European Jews and other civilians. As early as 1942, the United States government had received reports that Hitler had ordered the murder of all Jews in German-occupied territories. Only in 1944 did Roosevelt respond to criticism within his own administration that the United States was passively accepting the murder of Jews. He created a War Refugee Board, but for 6 out of 10 Jews in Europe, action came too late. Not until Allied troops reached the Nazi death camps—at Auschwitz, Dachau, Buchenwald, and elsewhere—and found the survivors and the gas chambers in which so many had died was the horrible truth fully realized. The Nazis had killed 12 million people, of whom 6 million were Jews.

■ War in the Pacific

In May 1942, American warships defeated a Japanese fleet in the Battle of the Coral Sea. In June Japanese forces tried to take the Midway Islands, an atoll in the central Pacific about 1,200 miles (1,920 kilometers) northwest of Hawaii. The naval and air

Battle of Midway that ensued was a great victory for the Allies, resulting in the first major defeat of the Japanese navy. It slowed the Japanese advance across the central Pacific, brought an end to the threat to Hawaii, and ended Japanese naval superiority in the Pacific. Japan still held many heavily fortified Pacific islands. So the Allies

World War II in the Pacific

Japanese Empire, 1936
Extent of Japanese control, 1942
Allies
Neutral nations
Allied troop movements
Major battles
Atomic bomb explosions

Map Study

While a joint British-American force freed Southeast Asia from Japanese occupation, American forces recaptured strategic islands as the forces moved northward toward the Philippines and Japan itself. *What strategic importance does the map show for Iwo Jima and Okinawa?*

adopted a military strategy called "island hopping"—to cut Japanese supply lines by capturing key islands and to use them as bases to attack other Japanese strongholds, especially the Philippines and eventually Japan itself.

Guadalcanal

In August 1942, Americans took the first step in the long and bloody road to Tokyo when marines landed on Guadalcanal in the Solomon Islands. The struggle for Guadalcanal was fought on the ground, at sea, and in the air, lasting six months. Not until 1943 did Japan's resistance there come to an end.

In attacking the United States, Japan had failed to realize the industrial power of America and its ability to mobilize that power rapidly. Of the 19 ships sunk at Pearl Harbor, 17 were returned to duty by December 1942, and new ships were constantly added. The navy worked out new ways of fueling and repairing ships at sea, allowing fleets to stay at sea for long periods of time.

During 1943 and 1944, American forces "island-hopped" toward the Philippines and Japan. In October 1944, Allied forces under the leadership of American General Douglas MacArthur landed in the Philippines. MacArthur's advance was matched by amphibious operations directed by Admiral Chester Nimitz against Japanese-held islands in the central Pacific.

Iwo Jima and Okinawa

In 1945 the last of Japan's island outposts fell with the taking of Iwo Jima (EE•woh JEE•muh) in March and Okinawa (oh•kuh•NAH•wuh) in June. Though Iwo Jima measures only a few square miles, American marines suffered more than 20,000 casualties in capturing it. Japan now began to use kamikazes (KAH•mih•KAH•zeez), suicide pilots who flew bomb-laden planes into American ships. During the invasion of Okinawa, kamikazes scored 279 hits on United States vessels.

By the summer of 1945, after Germany was defeated, all Allied power was turned against Japan. The Soviet Union agreed to declare war on Japan and confront Japan's forces in Manchuria. But the conquest of the Japanese islands was left to the United States. America's long-range B-29 bombers had been bombing Japan from bases on recaptured Pacific islands since June 1944. In one raid alone in March 1945, more than 83,000 Tokyo civilians were incinerated by American incendiary bombs. But despite such heavy casualties, Japan's military leaders rejected calls for unconditional surrender. American commanders worried that an invasion of Japan would meet heavy resistance and might cost a million lives.

Hiroshima and Nagasaki

Since early in the war, American scientists had secretly been developing an atomic bomb. First tested in New Mexico in July 1945, it gave Harry Truman, who became President after Roosevelt's death, another choice, and Soviet leader Stalin told Truman to "make good use of it."

After the Japanese government rejected Truman's final warning to surrender or risk "utter destruction," on August 6 an atomic bomb destroyed 60 percent of Hiroshima, a major Japanese industrial city. When Japan still refused to surrender, a second bomb was dropped on the city of Nagasaki on August 9, causing almost as much destruction as the first. The two attacks took about 150,000 Japanese lives. When reports of the death and devastation reached Tokyo, the stunned emperor, telling his people that "the unendurable must be endured," asked for peace. The final surrender took place on September 2, 1945, on the battleship *Missouri* anchored in Tokyo Bay.

◀ **AMERICAN MILITARY HELMET NICKNAMED THE "STEEL POT"**

▲ **MEETING AT YALTA** Looking tired and drawn, Roosevelt (center) poses with Stalin (right) and Churchill during a break in their meetings at Yalta. Two months later, Roosevelt was dead. *What agreements were reached at Yalta?*

■ Wartime Diplomacy

The first planning for peace took place in August 1941 when Roosevelt and Churchill met on a ship off the coast of Newfoundland. At that meeting they issued the Atlantic Charter, a statement of principles on which depended "hopes for a better future for the world." Much like Wilson's Fourteen Points, the Atlantic Charter looked forward to a world where people would have the right to choose their form of government.

After Pearl Harbor, Roosevelt turned his attention to forming an alliance among the nations fighting against Hitler. On January 1, 1942, representatives of the 26 countries at war with the Axis Powers agreed to support the principles of the Atlantic Charter. They promised full economic and military support in the war, and they agreed not to make a separate peace.

In holding the great alliance together, Roosevelt and Churchill kept constantly in touch. Although they often did not agree on strategy, neither wavered in admiration for the other. Working closely with the other major Allies was more difficult. Japanese troops had pushed China's government

deep into the interior, and Chinese leaders were unhappy that the war in Europe was the top priority. General Charles de Gaulle (dih•GOHL), leader of the French government in exile, disapproved of the United States's recognizing a government in south France that was friendly to the Nazis.

Cooperation with the Soviet Union proved the most difficult problem. Stalin had almost never been outside of his country and was suspicious of capitalist nations. Even so, the alliance between the United States and Great Britain and the Soviet Union lasted until the end of the war. Germany could not be defeated without Soviet aid, and the Soviets depended on supplies from Britain and the United States.

Planning for War and Peace

Cooperation in plans for war and peace was worked out in a series of international conferences. At Casablanca, Morocco, in January 1943, Roosevelt and Churchill agreed to demand "unconditional surrender" from the Axis Powers, assuring the Soviet Union that its allies would not sign a separate peace treaty with Germany.

At Cairo, Egypt, in November 1943, Roosevelt and Churchill met Chinese leader Chiang Kai-shek (jee•AHNG ky•SHEHK) and agreed that Japan should be stripped of its Pacific empire and Korea given independence. From Cairo, Roosevelt and Churchill flew to Tehran, capital of Iran, to meet with Stalin. There they promised that the D-Day invasion of France would be launched the next year. In return Stalin agreed to begin a new offensive against Germany at the same time from the east.

The Yalta Conference

In February 1945, Roosevelt, Churchill, and Stalin met for the last time at Yalta, in the Soviet Union. They agreed publicly that the United States, Britain, and the Soviet Union, along with France, should occupy Germany after the war, but they promised to encourage some form of representative government for the other peoples of Europe. They also agreed on a conference to be held at San Francisco in April 1945 to establish a world peace organization.

Secret agreements at Yalta covered the terms on which the Soviet Union could enter the war against Japan after Germany was defeated. The Soviets were promised Japanese territories, and that they could keep Outer Mongolia, in China, and obtain an ice-free naval port. In return, Stalin agreed to support the Nationalist government of Chiang Kai-shek instead of the Chinese Communists who were challenging Chiang for power.

Although the Yalta agreements later were attacked as a "sellout," at the time it seemed vital to keep the Soviet Union from making a separate peace with Germany when American and British forces were still fighting in the west. Even more important, the United States wanted Soviet support in the war against Japan.

Roosevelt's Death

When he reported to Congress on his Yalta trip, Roosevelt looked tired and pale. Two months later, on April 12, 1945, the President died suddenly at Warm Springs, Georgia. The nation he led for more than 12 years was shocked, and newspapers that printed daily lists of soldiers and sailors who had died in action added the name: "Roosevelt, Franklin D., Commander in Chief."

The United Nations

Two weeks after Roosevelt's death, representatives of 50 nations met at San Francisco to make plans for a new world organization. But the talks at San Francisco were made more difficult by rising suspicions among the Allies. The Soviet Union was keeping a firm hand on Poland and seemed to be breaking its Yalta promises. Still, the meeting at San Francisco produced a charter for the United Nations (UN). The preamble of the UN Charter pledged all the countries signing it to "faith in fundamental human rights," to "justice and respect" for the terms of peace treaties, and to the goal of living together. In July 1945, when the Senate ratified the Charter by a vote of 89 to 2, the United States became the first nation to join the UN.

Section 3 ★ Review

Checking for Understanding

1. **Identify** D-Day, Dwight Eisenhower, Harry Truman, Atlantic Charter, Yalta Conference.

2. **Define** Holocaust.

3. **Summarize** the progression of the war in Asia, Europe, Africa, and the Pacific.

4. **List** the meetings held among Allied leaders between 1941 and 1945.

Critical Thinking

5. **Anticipating Consequences** In a wartime alliance, what risk is carried by each nation that agrees not to make a separate peace?

The Atomic Bomb

"We must not be the most hated and feared people in the world," a physicist wrote, urging President Truman not to use the atomic bombs that would kill some 150,000 mostly civilian Japanese.

Rumors that the Nazis might develop an atomic bomb spurred American and British efforts to build one. Scientist Albert Einstein wrote President Roosevelt urging that a major research program begin at once so that the nation would be the first with the bomb.

The secret project, later called the Manhattan Project, was carried out primarily at facilities in Oak Ridge, Tennessee, and, later, at Los Alamos, New Mexico. American physicist J. Robert Oppenheimer was the director, and he persuaded many top physicists to join the project. On July 16, 1945, the bomb was tested atop a steel tower in a lonely desert track at Alamogordo, New Mexico, called *Jorada del Muerto*, Journey of Death.

President Truman did not know the bomb existed until a few weeks before his decision to use it. Truman, who had taken office after President Roosevelt's death on April 12, received word of the test results in Potsdam, Germany, where he was in conference with Churchill, Stalin, and their top advisors. Roosevelt had told Churchill about the bomb. Although some historians disagree about why atomic bombs were dropped on Japan and about the ethical issues involved, President Truman believed the bombing was justified: "The dropping of the bombs stopped the war, saved millions of lives."

▲ THE DEVASTATION AT HIROSHIMA

Making the Science Connection

1. Why did the United States start the Manhattan Project?

Linking Past and Present

2. Given the present concerns about the dangers of nuclear war, do you think the United States was right to develop nuclear weapons? Why or why not?

★★

War on the Home Front

Setting the Scene

Section Focus

To fight the Axis Powers, the United States had to mobilize people and resources more quickly than ever before. By 1944 more than 11 million men and women were in uniform. As the number of industrial workers also rose to new heights, the war accomplished what the New Deal had never been able to—it ended the Depression's unemployment.

Objectives

After studying this section, you should be able to

★ discuss efforts to mobilize the economy for war production.

★ explain the war's impact on women, African Americans, and Japanese Americans.

Key Term

wildcat strike

◀ ROSIE THE RIVETER, SYMBOL OF WOMEN WORKERS DURING WORLD WAR II

Americans were amazed at the speed with which industry turned to making war materials. When in May 1940 President Roosevelt talked of producing 50,000 airplanes a year, some thought he was asking the impossible. Yet, by 1944 the number of planes produced annually had risen to about 100,000. Mass production was so effective in the ship industry that the average time for building a freighter dropped from a year to less than 2 months. In 4 years American shipyards put to sea tonnage equal to the entire merchant fleet of all the other countries of the world.

■ The Production Battle

As in World War I, federal agencies took on the direction of private companies doing war work. After a Senate investigation revealed corruption and mismanagement among companies involved in war production, in January 1942 Roosevelt gave a War Production Board strong regulatory power. Its head, Donald Nelson, could seize vital materials, order industrial plants to convert to war production, and prohibit manufacture of products he considered unessential to the war effort.

Rapid Conversion to War Production

Within weeks of Pearl Harbor, production of bicycles, beer cans, refrigerators, toothpaste tubes, and more than 300 other items was cut back or banned. Automobile manufacturers were ordered to convert production to tanks and other war supplies. Entire new industries were created. Synthetic rubber, for example, became important when Japan's conquest of Southeast Asia cut off America's supply of natural rubber. By the end of 1942, nearly 33 percent of American production went to war materials, and by 1944 nearly 50 percent. Production of all goods nearly doubled, and America's production of war materials matched the total output of Germany, Italy, and Japan combined.

In May 1941, Roosevelt set up the Office of Scientific Research and Development to mobilize science and technology for the war effort. Among the many inventions that came from this agency were DDT, which controlled insects and made jungle fighting more tolerable; the bazooka, a weapon that enabled an infantry soldier to destroy a tank; and radar, which determined the position and speed of airplanes and ships.

Financing the War

To raise funds for the war effort, the federal government increased taxes and sold war bonds in amounts ranging from $25 to $10,000. In 1942 the government extended the income tax for the first time to include middle- and lower-income people. To make collection easier, the government in 1943 began to require that employers deduct taxes from workers' paychecks before they received them.

The war increased employment, and workers' earnings rose as war production brought longer workweeks and overtime. As people had more money to spend, and as the shift to war materials made consumer goods scarce, prices rose. To combat inflation, in 1942 Congress created the Office of Price Administration, which set price ceilings on consumer products and began to ration goods that were in short supply. By war's end 20 items—including sugar, meat, butter, coffee, gasoline, fuel oil, and shoes—required government-issued rationing coupons to be presented at the time of purchase. Despite attempts to hold down prices, however, the cost of living rose 29 percent during the war, leading to demands for higher wages.

Life of the Times

★★★★★★★★★★★★★★★★

The Home Front

Fan magazines reflected the changing role of women during the war. Magazines such as *Modern Screen* and *Photoplay-Movie-Mirror* used the lives of the stars to encourage patriotism, discourage extravagance, and sell products designed with the working woman in mind. In the 1920s and 1930s, fan magazines had emphasized movie stars' extravagant lifestyles, often depicting the stars as carefree, excessive consumers who felt little responsibility for the rest of society. Now *Photoplay* told readers that actress Ann Sheridan used her grocery money to buy Victory Bonds. An advertisement in the same magazine portrayed the use of lipstick as a woman's patriotic duty. Lipstick, the advertisement said, raised wartime morale, enhanced self-confidence, and proved that women could do "men's" work without sacrificing their femininity.

▲ Actress Ann Sheridan

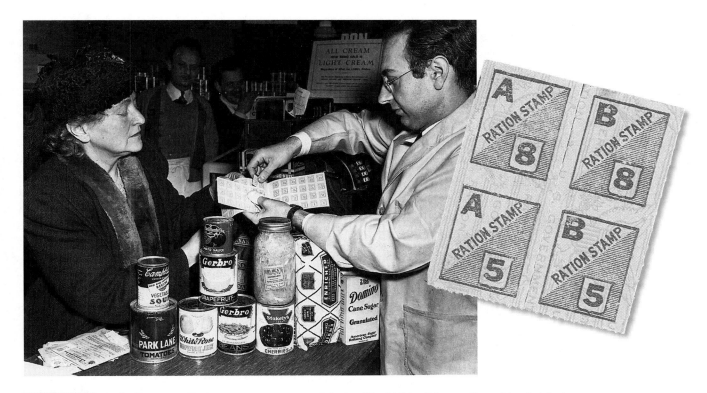

▲ RATIONING Ration stamps were used during World War II in an attempt to distribute essential goods fairly. Meat, butter, sugar, and gasoline were among the items that were rationed. *How did the cost of living change during the war years?*

To help prevent strikes, a National War Labor Board was established to settle labor disputes by mediation. Although this task was made easier by the no-strike pledges that both the AFL and the CIO made after Pearl Harbor, there were many small **wildcat strikes**—work stoppages without union approval—and a short national strike by 500,000 coal miners. Even though most labor unions kept their no-strike pledge, an act passed in 1947 outlawed strikes against war industries.

■ The War and Social Change

The need for defense workers altered traditional patterns of American society. As millions of men joined the armed services, more women than ever before entered the labor force. "If you can drive a car, you can run a machine" became an advertising slogan for industries.

Women Assume Nontraditional Roles

The government, newspapers, radio, and newsreels encouraged women to take factory jobs as a patriotic duty, and 5 million American women entered the workforce during the war. "Rosie the Riveter," who first appeared in overalls in a Lockheed Aircraft poster, became a national symbol of the vital contribution women were making to the war effort.

More than ever before, women filled jobs that were not traditional for females. They worked on production lines, in steel mills, on the docks, and in other jobs that required heavy manual labor. Outside war industries, women also took over such traditionally male jobs as driving buses and trucks and working as train conductors, lumberjacks, and barbers. Most of these new workers were married and had children. Yet women still encountered resistance from male workers. As one female aircraft worker described it:

> *The men really resented the women very much. . . . [A]fter a while they realized that it was essential that the women worked there, 'cause there wasn't enough men, and the women were doing a good job.* "

To encourage women to work, the government offered job-training courses, and Congress appropriated funds for child-care centers, but even this was not enough to meet the need. Federal and state governments suspended laws that limited the hours women could work, and women's wages rose as the concept of equal pay for equal work spread. Although at first most women considered their new employment to be temporary, by war's end 80 percent said they wanted to keep their jobs.

Opportunities for African Americans

The need for workers also speeded the shift of African Americans from farming to manufacturing. Many African Americans left the South and moved to cities in the Northeast, the Midwest, and California to work in war industries. Some companies hired few African Americans before the war, but by 1945 thousands of African Americans had jobs in defense plants.

Resentment Toward Social Change

Between 1941 and 1945, one of every five Americans relocated to another part of the country. The movement of so many Americans to fill jobs in war industries created housing shortages, crowded schools, and heightened social tensions. Old-timers resented the newcomers, regardless of their race. In California there were prejudices against "Okies," white migrants from Oklahoma and Texas who arrived in the 1930s to look for work after losing their farms in the Dust Bowl. In many cities prejudices arose against newly arrived African Americans. The police were needed to help African American families move into public housing in Detroit, when angry mobs tried to block them. It took federal troops to break a strike of streetcar operators in Philadelphia, who protested against the promotion of African American workers.

The federal government's response to racial discrimination during the war was uneven. In 1941 African American labor leader

Visualizing History

▲ NEW OPPORTUNITIES World War II offered increased job opportunities for women and for African Americans. Although women's wages rose, they still averaged 60 percent less than men's wages. *How did the government encourage women to work?*

Charles Drew
1904–1950

Born and raised in the segregated city of Washington, D.C., Charles Drew refused to let racial prejudice bar him from professional success. After graduating from Amherst College in Massachusetts, he earned his M.D. degree at Canada's McGill University.

In the 1930s Drew conducted pioneering research on blood plasma, and he established a model blood plasma bank. When the United States entered World War II, Drew was asked to head the military's blood plasma program. By collecting, storing, transporting, and transfusing donated blood plasma, this program saved the lives of countless wounded soldiers. But in 1942 Drew resigned when the military refused to accept blood donations from African Americans unless their blood was segregated from the blood of white donors and was given only to black soldiers.

A. Philip Randolph threatened to lead 100,000 protesters on Washington, D.C., to demand an end to discrimination in defense jobs and the armed forces. In order to stop the march, Roosevelt established the Fair Employment Practices Commission to promote minority hiring in government offices and in companies that had war contracts. But while it opposed discrimination, the commission did not reject segregation. Even the military remained segregated, and although hundreds of thousands of African Americans served in uniform in every capacity from cooks to fighter pilots, most served in all-black units.

Detention of Japanese Americans

The most significant racial discrimination of the war involved the removal of Japanese Americans from the West Coast. About 90 percent of all Japanese Americans, outside Hawaii, lived in California and the Pacific Northwest. Because of immigration restrictions after 1924, two-thirds had been born in the United States and were citizens by birth. Yet government officials were suspicious of their loyalty. When war broke out, residents of California, Oregon, and Washington feared that with the Pacific fleet at Pearl Harbor severely damaged, they were vulnerable to invasion at any time. Californians, in particular, were concerned that their neighbors of Japanese descent might engage in sabotage. Army General John DeWitt investigated and reported that:

66 *The Japanese race is an enemy race and while many second and third generation Japanese born on United States soil have become 'Americanized,' the racial strains are undiluted. . . . It, therefore, follows that along the vital Pacific Coast over 112,000 potential enemies of Japanese extraction are at large today.* 99

Based on such reports, beginning in February 1942, the government moved 110,000 Japanese Americans to detention centers surrounded by barbed wire and patrolled by soldiers and confined them there for the duration of the war.

The order to evacuate Japanese Americans from the West Coast came quickly. Detainees had as little as 48 hours to make arrangements for their homes, businesses, and

▲ INTERNMENT OF JAPANESE AMERICANS During World War II, persons of Japanese descent were sent to internment camps. More than 70,000 were Nisei, or American-born. *How did the Supreme Court rule on the detainees' appeal to protect their rights?*

farms. Many had to sell their property at a loss or abandon it. Bargain hunters descended on them, taking advantage of their plight.

Arriving at one of 10 detention camps in isolated areas of Utah, Wyoming, Arizona, and other sparsely settled Western states, they were put to work at menial, low-paying jobs. Their military guards searched their quarters for "weapons," sometimes confiscating kitchen knives, scissors, and even knitting needles. Entire families lived out the war in a single room in army-style barracks furnished with cots and bare light bulbs. Since the authorities had no plans for running the camps, the detainees established their own camp governments, schools, and newspapers.

Almost immediately detainees appealed to the courts to protect their rights. When the issue came before the Supreme Court in December 1944, in *Korematsu* v. *United States*, the justices upheld the government's policy as necessary for national security.

Despite their unhappy experience, most Japanese Americans remained loyal to the United States. Thousands served in segregated military units. A Japanese American army unit recruited from detention camps fought in the Italian campaign and was the army's most decorated unit in American military history. However, the government's policy toward Japanese Americans at home became a blot on the nation's war record.

Section 4 ★ Review

Checking for Understanding

1. **Identify** War Production Board.

2. **Define** wildcat strike.

3. **Explain** how the productive capacity of the industries of the United States aided the Allies' war effort.

4. **Contrast** the war's effects on African Americans and on Japanese Americans.

Critical Thinking

5. **Formulating Hypotheses** Why were Japanese Americans detained during the war while Americans of German or Italian descent were not?

Interpreting Primary Sources

Who Is an American?

Peter Ota was 15 when he was interned, or sent to a detention camp for Japanese Americans, in 1942. When he reached draft age, Ota was required to register for military service. He served in an armored division of the United States Army. In the following passage, Ota reflects on the effects of his internment on himself and his children.

From Studs Terkel, "The Good War, An Oral History of World War Two":

We came back to Los Angeles at the end of the war, believing that there was no other way but to be American. We were discouraged with our Japanese culture. My feeling at the time was, I had to prove myself. I don't know why I had to prove myself. Here I am, an ex-GI, born and raised here. Why do I have to prove myself? We all had this feeling. We had to prove that we were Americans, okay?

. . . We moved to a white community near Los Angeles. It was typical American suburb living. We became more American than Americans, very conservative. . . .

My children were denied a lot of the history of what happened. If you think of all those forty years of silence, I think this stems from another Japanese characteristic: when shame is put on you, you try to hide it. We were put into camp, we became victims, it was our fault. We hide it.

My oldest daughter, Cathy, in her senior year at college, wanted to write a thesis about the camp experience. She asked if we knew people she might interview. Strange thing is, many people, even now, didn't want to talk about it. Some of the people she did talk to broke down. Because this was the first time they had told this story.

▲ **JAPANESE AMERICAN CHILDREN AT INTERNMENT CAMP**

Examining the Primary Source

1. What effect did Peter Ota's experiences during World War II have on his feelings and opinions concerning Japanese culture?

2. How does Ota explain the long silence of Japanese Americans on the internment camps? Do you agree or disagree with Ota's explanation?

Critical Thinking

3. **Drawing Conclusions**   What, in your opinion, may have prompted Ota's daughter to write about the camp experience?

Using Vocabulary

Use each of the following words in a statement about the aggressor nations in World War II, the kind of warfare they conducted, and world response.

appeasement   Holocaust
fascism   totalitarian

Reviewing Facts

1. **List** reasons for isolationist policies in the United States and appeasement in Europe.

2. **State** the reasons for Japan's territorial ambitions in Asia.

3. **Chronicle** the steps by which the United States progressed from neutrality to war.

4. **Discuss** the priorities and sequence of the Allies' military campaigns in World War II.

5. **Explain** the difficulties Roosevelt and Churchill faced in dealing with Chiang Kai-shek, de Gaulle, and Stalin.

6. **Describe** how World War II affected women and minorities in the United States.

Understanding Concepts

International Alliances

1. How did World War II underscore the importance of an international organization such as the United Nations?

2. Explain the importance of Germany's 1939 nonaggression treaty with the Soviet Union to Hitler. Why do you suppose the Soviet Union signed it?

Military Conflict

3. Analyze Hitler's strategy for war. After his early victories, where did he go wrong?

4. Why did kamikaze missions pose such a deadly threat to American forces? What does this strategy suggest about the values and patriotism of the Japanese?

Critical Thinking

1. **Evaluating Policy** Economic problems at home was one reason that the United States initially avoided involvement in World War II. What subsequent developments suggest that this policy may have been self-defeating?

2. **Analyzing Fine Art** Study the painting of V-J Day on this page, then answer the questions.

   a. Does the painting have a central focus?

   b. Could you understand the meaning of this painting if it did not have a caption?

▲ *V-J Day—Crowds cheering at Times Square* by Edward Dancig, 1947

Writing About History

Description

Write an extended definition of neutrality. Begin with a formal definition, followed by examples of neutrality as demonstrated by the Neutrality Acts. Use comparison and contrast to expand on the definition by showing how later foreign policy began to depart from neutrality as defined.

Cooperative Learning

As a class, create a courtroom with students role-playing a panel of judges, a three-member prosecution team, three defense attorneys, a jury, three defendants, and an audience. Put the following people on trial for crimes against humanity: Adolf Hitler—for beginning World War II and establishing the Nazi death camps; a German military officer—for carrying out orders to execute Jews in a death camp; General Hideki Tojo—for ordering kamikaze attacks against Allied forces.

Social Studies Skills

Seeing Relationships on a Line Graph

Line graphs are commonly used to plot change over time. Frequency or quantity is charted on the y, or vertical, axis, while time is recorded on the x, or horizontal, axis. A line graph may help you see the relationship between a particular date and the frequency of a particular event.

To search for possible relationships, follow these procedures:

   a. Read the title and labels on the graph.

   b. Note any shifts in frequency or quantity at particular time points.

   c. Relate these changes to your knowledge of historical events.

Practicing the Skill

Use the line graph on this page to answer the following questions.

1. Which decade depicted on the graph shows the smallest increase in the number of women joining the labor force?

2. Which decade shows the largest increase in the number of women joining the labor force?

3. World War I was fought during which decade? World War II?

4. Summarize the apparent relationship between each war and the employment of women.

5. Many women moved from higher-paying industrial jobs into clerical ones after World War II. Is this information represented on the graph? Explain.

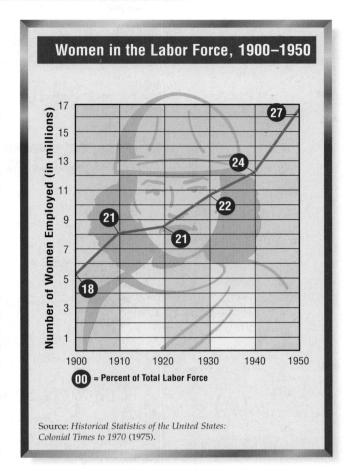

Women in the Labor Force, 1900–1950

Number of Women Employed (in millions)

00 = Percent of Total Labor Force

Source: *Historical Statistics of the United States: Colonial Times to 1970* (1975).

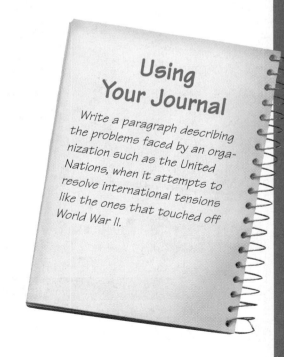

Using Your Journal

Write a paragraph describing the problems faced by an organization such as the United Nations, when it attempts to resolve international tensions like the ones that touched off World War II.

CHAPTER 30

★★

The Cold War
1945–1952

▼ REBUILDING BERLIN, THE
MARSHALL PLAN AT WORK

Setting the Scene

Focus

Within months after the end of World War II, the United States and the Soviet Union entered into a period of intense confrontation and rivalry. American leaders sought to maintain workable links with the Soviets while trying to check communism in Europe. Later this containment policy was applied to China, but it could not prevent the outbreak of war in Korea. At home, Americans sought to adjust to a peacetime economy.

Concepts to Understand

★ Why the political and economic power of the United States and the Soviet Union were set against each other

★ How effective presidential leadership resulted in aggressive foreign and domestic policies

Read to Discover . . .

★ ways the United States sought to contain the Soviet Union.

★ the effect the cold war had on Americans at home.

Journal Notes

How did the fear of communism become a serious threat to American democracy during the Truman administration? Record relevant points as you read the chapter.

CULTURAL

● **1945** Harvey *by Mary Chase wins Pulitzer Prize for plays*

● **1947** *Jackie Robinson first plays for Brooklyn Dodgers*

1944   **1946**

POLITICAL

● **1945** *Harry S Truman becomes President on death of Franklin D. Roosevelt*

● **1946** *Winston Churchill makes "iron curtain" speech*
● **1947** *Truman Doctrine announced*

▲ PRESIDENT HARRY S TRUMAN AND
GENERAL DOUGLAS MACARTHUR

• **1948** *Largest telescope in the world is dedicated at Mount Palomar Observatory*

• **1950** *National Council of Churches of Christ is formed, representing 30 denominations*

1948

1950

• **1948** *Berlin airlift*
• **1948** *Communist forces take China*
• **1949** *NATO created*

• **1950** *North Korea invades South Korea*

★★

The Start of the Cold War

Setting the Scene

Section Focus

The Allies' goal of establishing democratic governments throughout Europe after World War II proved to be elusive. To Churchill and Truman, democracy meant political and economic systems like those in Great Britain and the United States. Western democracy was unacceptable to Stalin, who began to establish Soviet-style communism in Eastern Europe. To implement a policy of containment, the Truman administration provided massive economic aid to war-torn Western Europe, joining with these countries in the first peacetime alliance in United States history.

Objectives

After studying this section, you should be able to

★ describe the changes in Eastern Europe and the factors that made communism strong after World War II.

★ outline the foreign policy goals of the Truman administration.

★ explain how the United States became a world power after World War II.

Key Terms

communism, satellite nation, purge, buffer, guerrilla, containment, collective security

◀ **UN** FLAG

*P*resident Truman's policies from the beginning of his administration showed his determination and the high degree to which he was personally involved in handling both domestic and international affairs. On his desk he kept a sign: "The buck stops here." In times of great crisis, Truman showed an extraordinary capacity for quick, effective, yet restrained action.

■ East-West Suspicions

In 1945, during the first months of his administration, President Truman concentrated his attention on winning the war against Germany and Japan. Like Roosevelt, he supported the creation of the United

Nations as a world peacekeeping organization. But Truman was much more suspicious than Roosevelt had been of the Soviet Union and its dictator, Joseph Stalin.

Soviet Control of Eastern Europe

When the war ended, the alliance between the United States, Great Britain, and the Soviet Union unraveled. While there was a common enemy, Western democracies and Soviet leaders had overlooked their political, economic, and social differences. After the war, suspicions returned. Soviet expansion into Eastern Europe heightened American fears of **communism,** a system in which society as a whole, represented by the Communist party, owns and controls property and the means of production.

As fighting ended, Soviet troops occupied much of Eastern Europe. The Soviet leaders, who had promised free elections in these nations, did not follow through. In Hungary, where free elections were held in November 1945, communist candidates received only 17 percent of the vote. Unwilling to lose control, Stalin later suppressed elections in Hungary and in the other nations of Eastern Europe. Then, under elections supervised by Soviet troops, voters gave 90 percent of the vote to communist candidates in Poland. This pattern was repeated in all Soviet-occupied areas, helping to establish communist governments throughout Eastern Europe. Nations that were held under Soviet domination came to be called **satellite nations.**

To restore the devastated Soviet economy, the Soviets removed whole factories, transportation equipment, and machinery from the satellite nations. Stalin also ordered **purges,** or forced removals, of leaders of satellite nations who were deemed disloyal.

The Iron Curtain

The leaders of Western Europe and the United States watched with grave concern as the Soviet Union crushed all opposition in the nations of Eastern Europe after 1945. Former Prime Minister Winston Churchill identified the new threat in a speech in March 1946 at Fulton, Missouri. With President Truman on the platform, Churchill warned:

> ❝ . . . [F]rom Stettin on the Baltic to Trieste on the Adriatic, an iron curtain has descended across the continent. Behind that line lie all the capitals of the ancient states of central and eastern Europe. ❞

The phrase "iron curtain" would be used to describe Soviet policy in Europe from 1945 to 1989. The West, said Churchill, must meet this challenge with force, if needed, because the Communists had no respect for weakness. Truman and his advisers agreed that a "get tough" policy was their only choice.

▲ AN IRON CURTAIN Former Prime Minister Winston Churchill and President Truman appear together during Churchill's speech at Fulton, Missouri. *What message did Churchill give to the American people?*

The Strength of Communism

Following World War II, the United States began to withdraw troops from Europe, leaving the Soviet army as the most powerful military force in Europe. As a result of the German invasion, the Soviet Union had lost 20 million people and suffered devastation of land, property, and industry. Feeling threatened by Western powers, the Soviet Union wanted to create a **buffer,** or safety zone, on its western border. Soviet troops stationed there ensured that the nations of Eastern Europe would remain its allies.

Communism's Promises

The Communists promised to abolish poverty, privilege, and private property. They guaranteed productive work, shelter, education, health care, and a classless society in the new "people's democracies" of war-torn Eastern Europe.

The Communists saw the world as divided between forces of progress and forces of oppression. Soviet rhetoric incited revolts in other impoverished nations, as people living in poverty listened eagerly to the Communists' plans. Communists began to organize resistance to governments they considered to be reactionary and imperialist. Sometimes they organized groups of **guerrilla** forces— armed bands that were not a part of a regular military unit—to foment civil war.

Containment

President Truman responded with a policy of **containment**—preventing the further spread of communism. This policy was based on the belief that foreign policy goals of Soviet leaders included conquering other nations—not simply the securing of their own borders. Containment, however, did not win universal support.

Some who opposed the policy believed that it was too soft. Angry with the advance of communism, they called for a quick and decisive victory over the Soviet Union. Another view was expressed by Walter Lippmann, a newspaper columnist. Lippmann argued that Soviet troops remained in Eastern Europe to protect the Soviets' western border. He warned that the United States could not contain the Soviet Union everywhere. Such a policy, he said, would require the United States to defend all anticommunist governments—no matter how repressive or unpopular they might be.

Lippmann published his newspaper columns on containment in a book called *The Cold War*. The title, a term coined by Lippmann to refer to a state of war that did not involve actual bloodshed, came to be used by everyone, including the President, to describe the icy rivalry that existed between the United States and the Soviet Union.

Aid to Europe

The cold war was like no other struggle that had ever engaged the United States. It required a constant state of military preparedness; it called for military support for countries believed to be in danger of a communist takeover. It had other economic costs, as both the United States and the Soviet Union tried to "buy" allies with gifts ranging from food to steel mills.

The Truman Doctrine

The policy of containment began in Europe. Great Britain, in financial trouble, was forced to notify United States officials early in 1947 that it would withdraw its soldiers from Greece and end aid to Turkey. United States diplomats in Greece warned that this could lead to a communist takeover. Already, they said, Soviet-supported guerrillas were controlling much of the country. It was feared that if Greece fell to the Communists, Turkey would be next.

President Truman decided that the United States must act. In March 1947 he told Congress that if the United States was not willing to give aid to Greece and Turkey to contain communism, democratic governments everywhere would be threatened. Truman's warning that the nation faced a crisis was clear:

> *" I believe that it must be the policy of the United States to support free peoples who are resisting attempted subjugation by armed minorities or outside pressures. . . . If we falter in our leadership, we may endanger the peace of the world—and we shall surely endanger the welfare of our own nation. "*

Truman's policy, known as the Truman Doctrine, proposed that the United States provide military and economic aid to Greece and Turkey. Immediately approved by Congress, the Truman Doctrine superseded the Monroe Doctrine, shifting the United States away from peacetime isolationism.

The Marshall Plan

Soon after the Truman Doctrine went into effect, the administration proposed a plan for economic aid to Europe. The situation in Europe was desperate in 1947. There were shortages of food, fuel, and raw materials, and European nations needed money to rebuild industries and transportation systems.

The Truman administration realized that economic woes in France, Italy, and other Western European countries might lead to the election of communist governments. The nation's leaders were also concerned that Europe's faltering economy would affect United States markets.

In June 1947, Secretary of State George C. Marshall went beyond the Truman

Europe After World War II

Legend:
- ▨ British
- ▨ French
- ▨ American
- ▨ Russian
- — Air corridors
- — Iron Curtain
- ◎ Jointly occupied cities

Map Study

After being invaded twice in less than 30 years, the Soviets especially feared future German power. Thus, after World War II, the Allies agreed to divide and occupy Germany. ***What other nation was divided after the war?***

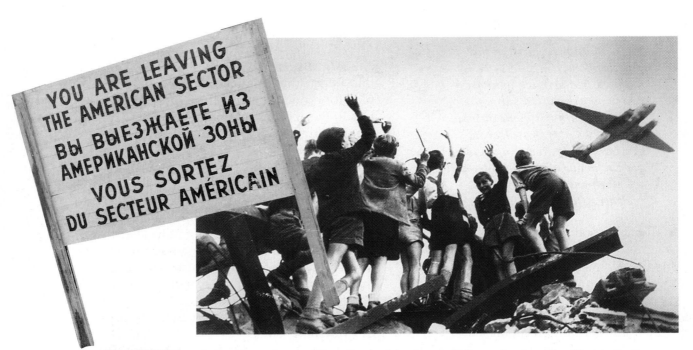

▲ THE BERLIN AIRLIFT When the Soviets closed off the routes from the West to Berlin, American and British cargo planes carried on an around-the-clock airlift. Berlin children, standing in the rubble of their shattered city, watch an American bomber fly in with supplies. *What effect did the airlift have on the Soviet blockade?*

Doctrine to propose a massive recovery plan for European nations. Under the Marshall Plan, American aid in the form of money, supplies, and machinery would help to end Europe's "hunger, poverty, desperation, and chaos." The United States offered the Marshall Plan to all nations in Europe—including the Soviet Union. Believing that the plan would promote the interests of United States capitalism, the Soviet Union and Eastern European communist nations turned it down.

The nations of Western Europe, on the other hand, welcomed the Truman administration's offer. Drawing up detailed plans for restoring production and controlling inflation, they also agreed to change trade laws—tariffs and quotas that blocked the flow of commerce.

The Marshall Plan was an enormous success. During the Truman years, the United States gave more than $13 billion in loans and grants to the nations of Western Europe. To administer aid effectively, the 16 Western European nations formed the Organization for European Economic Cooperation, the first step toward European economic unity.

■ The Berlin Airlift

At the end of the war, the Allies had decided on a joint occupation of Germany. The United States, Great Britain, France, and the Soviet Union each controlled a zone, or section, of Germany. They also each controlled a section of the capital, Berlin, in the Soviet-controlled zone.

Failing to reach agreement with the Soviet Union, the Western powers in May 1948 announced plans to join their 3 sections of Germany to form an independent nation. The Soviet Union responded by closing off all traffic from West Germany to Berlin. They thought that this move would force the West to back down from its control of West Berlin. President Truman saw this action as a test of Western determination. Instead of sending troops through the land corridor to Berlin and risking war, Truman ordered a massive airlift to supply Berlin's 2 million people. Night and day for more than 10 months, British and United States cargo planes carried food, medicine, clothing, raw materials, and even coal to Berlin. In May 1949, the Soviet Union finally lifted its blockade. Truman said:

> *When we refused to be forced out of Berlin, we demonstrated to the people of Europe that with their cooperation we would act, and act resolutely, when their freedom was threatened.* ""

■ North Atlantic Treaty Organization

Believing that rebuilding their economies without rebuilding their military strength might invite Soviet aggression, five Western European states formed an alliance in March 1948. They invited the United States, the world's only atomic power, to join their alliance. With Senate approval, Truman began talks to create a North Atlantic Treaty Organization (NATO), which formed in April 1949.

NATO linked into a military alliance the United States, Great Britain, Canada, Belgium, Italy, France, the Netherlands, Luxembourg, Iceland, Denmark, Norway, and Portugal. Greece, Turkey, and West Germany joined later. NATO was based on **collective security,** an agreement by which "an armed attack against one or more of them in Europe or North America shall be considered an attack against all of them." General Dwight D. Eisenhower, commander of NATO's forces, exercised sole authority over the atomic weapons that the United States committed to the defense of NATO.

Then, in September 1949, the Soviet Union exploded its first atomic bomb. Much sooner than military experts had expected, the United States had lost its nuclear monopoly. Faced with this new threat, Congress quickly passed the NATO appropriations bill. In 1955 the Soviet Union and its satellites countered NATO by establishing their own military alliance—the Warsaw Pact. The arms race was well underway.

Within a few years, both the United States and the Soviet Union developed a new and more powerful weapon—the hydrogen bomb. Later, other nations, including Great Britain, France, and China, also built nuclear weapons.

▲ GENERAL DWIGHT D. EISENHOWER

Section 1 ★ Review

Checking for Understanding

1. **Identify** cold war, Truman Doctrine, Marshall Plan, NATO, Berlin airlift.

2. **Define** communism, satellite nation, purge, buffer, guerrilla, containment, collective security.

3. **Explain** how the Soviet Union controlled its satellite nations.

4. **Summarize** the Truman administration's major foreign policy goals.

Critical Thinking

5. **Analyzing Policies** How did exercising the Truman Doctrine in Greece nullify the Monroe Doctrine of 1823?

Critical Thinking Skills

Hypothesizing

Hypothesizing is the process of forming a tentative explanation based on available evidence. A hypothesis offers a possible answer to a problem, or an explanation for why a situation or condition exists.

The Occupation of Berlin

Allied Sectors in Berlin
- British
- American
- French
- Russian
- ✈ Airports

A hypothesis cannot be judged right or wrong until it is confirmed or disproved by additional evidence. The following guidelines will help you form hypotheses from historical maps:

a. **Determine** the situation that the map is showing and write it as a statement.

b. **Form** some possible hypotheses that may explain the statement you have written.

c. **Gather** additional evidence about the situation and test each hypothesis.

d. **Accept** or reject each hypothesis as an explanation for the situation.

Look at the historical map on this page showing the Allied occupation of Berlin. Note how the guidelines on forming hypotheses have been applied.

a. Berlin was divided and occupied by the Allies. The Soviets occupied East Berlin. West Berlin was divided into French, British, and American sectors.

b. *Hypothesis:* Berlin was divided because the Allies wanted to keep the city for themselves.

Hypothesis: Berlin was divided among the Allies because the Western nations did not want the Soviets to have control of it.

Hypothesis: Berlin was divided so that its citizens would have self-government.

Hypothesis: Berlin was divided because the Western Allies feared Soviet intentions in Europe.

c. Gather additional evidence to test these hypotheses. Historians use many sources of information to understand an event. Written primary sources are often the most reliable record of what happened. Diaries, documents, eyewitness accounts, journals, and letters are primary sources. Research additional information in this chapter, other textbooks, encyclopedias, and other sources.

d. Accept or reject each hypothesis based on the evidence gathered. The information provided from reading Chapter 30 and from doing additional research might indicate that the second hypothesis best explains the statement of the situation.

Practicing the Skill

For further practice in hypothesizing, apply the guidelines to the map of the election of 1948 on page 854.

★★

The Cold War in Asia

Setting the Scene

Section Focus

In Asia the end of World War II brought peace only to the people of Japan. Under the United States's occupation, the Japanese renounced militarism, disbanded their army, democratized their society, and embarked on a program of economic development that brought them unprecedented prosperity. In contrast, the rest of Asia was caught up in the cold war. As tensions grew, the cold war escalated into a hot war.

Objectives

After studying this section, you should be able to

★ cite the outcome of the United States's occupation of Japan.

★ explain the political situation in China after the war.

★ explain why the United Nations waged a limited war in Korea.

Key Term

defense perimeter

◀ CHINESE COMMUNIST LEADER MAO ZEDONG

At the close of World War II, the aims of the United States in Asia were to restore peace, help Asian peoples to resist foreign rule, and restore Asian trade with the world. The United States felt it had a special commitment to the Philippines, Japan, and China.

On July 4, 1946, the United States carried out its promise of independence for the Philippines. In return for special business rights and the lease of military bases, the United States gave the Philippine nation tariff concessions in American markets and $600 million to repair war damage. Later, when communist-led guerrilla groups revolted against the government, the United States sent money and weapons to put down the rebellion. Despite difficult economic and political problems, the Philippines became an independent, democratic nation.

■ The Occupation of Japan

In July 1945, shortly before the United States dropped atomic bombs on Hiroshima and Nagasaki, the leaders of Great Britain, the United States, and the Soviet Union met in Potsdam, near Berlin. They discussed how they would deal with Germany and Japan after the war.

The agreement regarding Japan provided that Japanese militarists be punished and Japan disarmed, Japanese rule be restricted to their home islands, and the Japanese be reeducated so that a democratic Japanese nation could be formed. American troops would occupy Japan until these aims were accomplished. To carry out this Potsdam Declaration, General Douglas MacArthur was named Supreme Commander of the Allied Powers.

Under MacArthur's leadership, Japan's military was dismantled. A few militarists were tried and convicted of war crimes and hanged. Under American direction, a new constitution provided for elected representative government and woman suffrage. Most other aspects of Japanese culture remained intact. The emperor remained as a symbol of Japan's unity, but he was no longer to be looked upon as a god.

MacArthur encouraged economic opportunity and trade unionism, and he attempted to redistribute large rural tracts to landless Japanese. A reorganized school system taught democratic values. The Allies had planned to make Japan pay reparations for war damages, but MacArthur realized that the Japanese lacked the resources to pay such compensation. Instead, Japan received nearly $2 billion in aid. The Japanese people accepted the reforms. In a treaty signed in San Francisco in 1951, the country gained back its independence. Japan achieved a remarkable recovery, eventually establishing itself as the leading economy of Asia.

■ Communist Triumph in China

Japan's surrender left China a divided nation. The Communists under Mao Zedong [MOW dzuh•DUNG] controlled the north, the Nationalists led by Chiang Kai-shek held the southwest, and Japanese armies occupied the center. The United States helped the Nationalist armies take the land the Japanese had held. In planning for peace, President Roosevelt had insisted to Churchill and Stalin that China be treated as a power. As a result, China gained a permanent seat on the UN Security Council.

Civil War

Since the early 1930s, a civil war between the nationalist government and the Communists had ravaged China. During World War II, both sides stopped fighting one another and fought the Japanese. In the war against Japan, Mao's Communists grew to

Douglas MacArthur
1880–1964

★★★★★★★★★ AMERICAN PORTRAITS

Douglas MacArthur was born into a military family. His father won the Congressional Medal of Honor during the Civil War and later became the army's top-ranking general. Following in his father's footsteps, MacArthur saw action during World War I and was twice wounded. By 1918 he had risen to the rank of general. When Japan attacked Pearl Harbor, MacArthur was stationed in the Philippines, where he led its defense.

Ordered to retreat in 1942, he pledged: "I shall return." He kept his promise in 1944 by leading the liberation of the islands. After the war, as commander of U.S. occupation forces in Japan, he wrote its constitution. From July 1950 until President Truman fired him in April 1951, MacArthur commanded UN forces in Korea. Some Republican leaders urged MacArthur to run for President, but he declined and retired.

Visualizing
History

▲ **AMERICANS IN KOREA** President Truman ordered American forces to the Korean peninsula in June 1950 after North Korean troops invaded South Korea. In the conflict with North Korea, the United States was directly fighting a communist nation for the first time. *What was the outcome of the conflict?*

be a strong guerrilla force. Through his promise of land reform, as well as military and political pressure, Mao's forces were able to extend their control over much of mainland China. The civil war of the 1930s had greatly weakened the Nationalists.

After Japan surrendered, the conflict between the Communists and the Nationalists again flared. To prevent the extension of communist power, Truman sent General George C. Marshall to China. Marshall was unsuccessful. As the Communists gained strength, Chiang asked Truman to send military aid. Marshall, now secretary of state, advised that it was more important to spend the limited foreign-aid resources of the United States on saving Western Europe from Stalin rather than on saving China from Mao. In addition, a fact finder Truman sent to China reported no attempt to save it from the Communists could succeed because:

> **❝** *The only basis on which national Chinese resistance to Soviet aims can be revitalized is through the presently corrupt, reactionary and inefficient Chinese National government.* **❞**

Having already given Chiang's forces $2 billion in aid, the State Department judged that further help would not save the Nationalists from their own internal weaknesses. By the end of 1949 Mao Zedong's forces had forced Chiang's army off the mainland to Taiwan and a few other small islands.

Aftermath of Communist Victory

Truman's China policy came under bitter political attack. Nationalist supporters accused Truman of "writing off" Chiang and losing China to the Communists. Truman believed, however, that most Americans would not support the massive military intervention needed to save Chiang's government.

The United States recognized the nationalist government in Taiwan as the government of all of China and blocked attempts by Mao's government to gain a seat in the United Nations. To protest the exclusion of the Chinese communist government, the Soviet Union walked out of the United Nations Security Council and boycotted its proceedings.

The Korean War

June 25–November 25, 1950

- North Korea
- South Korea
- Area held by UN forces, September, 1950
- ← Communist advance
- ← UN counteroffensive
- — UN front line, November 25, 1950

0   50   100 miles
0   50   100 kilometers

CHINA

Yalu River

Pyongyang, Oct. 19

38th Parallel

SEA OF JAPAN

N

UN LANDING, SEPT. 15

Inchon

Seoul, Sept. 28

YELLOW SEA

Pusan

November 26, 1950–July 27, 1953

- ← Chinese (Communist) counteroffensive
- — Line of Jan. 24, 1951
- ← UN advance
- - - - Armistice Line, July 27, 1953

0   50   100 miles
0   50   100 kilometers

Tumen R.

USSR

CHINA

Yalu River

NORTH KOREA

Pyongyang

38th Parallel

SEA OF JAPAN

N

Panmunjom

Inchon

Seoul

SOUTH KOREA

Taegu

YELLOW SEA

Pusan

Map Study The Korean War began in June 1950 when North Korean forces invaded South Korea. For three years UN troops and communist forces battled up and down the Korean peninsula. *When did UN forces land at Inchon?*

War in Korea

The Allied nations had promised Korea "independence" at the Cairo conference in 1943. That did not occur. When the Japanese surrendered, Soviet Union troops occupied Korea north of the 38th parallel. Aided by Korean Communists, they set up a communist government. As with other Soviet satellite states, North Korea sealed itself off from other countries of the world. A 1948 UN fact-finding commission was not allowed to travel north of the 38th parallel.

In the south the United States supported the government of Syngman Rhee, who was chosen in UN-supervised elections. In 1948 the UN recognized the South Korean Republic as the government of all Korea.

United States military and diplomatic experts advised that Korea should be viewed as outside the **defense perimeter,** or area that could be protected, of the United States because of the great cost of defending it. The next year the United States withdrew most of its troops from Korea.

Fighting Begins

On June 25, 1950, North Korean troops invaded South Korea. Poorly armed, the South Koreans were no match for the North. The Truman administration was not sure whether North Korea was acting by itself or as the agent of the Soviet Union or China. The invasion, however, became a vital test for the UN. Calling an emergency meeting of the Security Council, the United States won a 9-to-0 vote to order North Korea to withdraw its troops. Because of its boycott, the Soviet Union was not present for the vote. On June 27, 1950, as the invasion continued, the Security Council called on all UN members to aid South Korea.

MacArthur in Command

President Truman quickly appointed General MacArthur to command all UN troops in Korea and instructed him to limit the fighting to South Korean territory below the 38th parallel. Truman also ordered United States military forces to Korea without asking Congress to declare war, claiming he was acting under his authority as commander in chief and under the United Nations Charter.

During the summer of 1950, North Korean troops pressed UN forces down the Korean peninsula until they had their backs to the water at Pusan (POO•SAHN), a major port in South Korea. In the fall, however, General MacArthur planned a surprise landing midway up the peninsula at the South Korean port of Inchon.

This landing gave the UN troops the offensive, and MacArthur was given authority by the UN Security Council to liberate North Korea and unite it with the South. By November, UN troops were as far north as the Yalu River valley, bordering communist China, when 200,000 Chinese troops crossed the border to aid the North Koreans. MacArthur's troops were once again pushed back.

Truman Fires MacArthur

A major disagreement soon developed between MacArthur and Truman over the conduct of the war. MacArthur wanted the United States to bomb China and to help Chiang Kai-shek invade China from Taiwan. Truman, however, did not want to risk war with China. In April 1951, Joseph Martin, Republican leader of the House of Representatives, released a letter he had received in which MacArthur criticized the President. MacArthur's letter was a deliberate challenge to the principle that the civilian power of the President must be superior to that of the military. Truman felt he had no choice but to remove MacArthur from command. He explained, "I could do nothing else and still be President of the United States."

The Senate Foreign Relations and Armed Services Committee opened hearings to determine the circumstances of MacArthur's dismissal. Two months of hearings dispelled much of the controversy. Truman's decision emerged as acceptable to the country.

The Conflict Ends

Years of fighting had produced a stalemate in Korea. Presidential candidate Dwight Eisenhower in 1952 pledged to "go to Korea," to settle hostilities. The war continued until 1953, when a cease-fire was declared. Korea was left a divided country, much as it had been before the war began. The Korean struggle was costly for the United States, which lost more than 54,000 troops. But as a result, many neutral nations drew closer to the United States, and noncommunist ones began to arm for their own defense.

Section 2 ★ Review

Checking for Understanding

1. **Identify** Chiang Kai-shek, Mao Zedong, Douglas MacArthur.

2. **Define** defense perimeter.

3. **Explain** why the United States's China policy failed.

4. **Summarize** the important events that led to the Korean War.

Critical Thinking

5. **Choosing a Position**   Explain the two positions represented by Truman and MacArthur on Korea. Which position would you have chosen?

★★

Cold War America

Setting the Scene

Section Focus

Life in cold war America was marked by a search for security. African Americans and women sought to keep the gains they had made during the war, and many Americans struggled to maintain their standard of living in the face of postwar inflation. For some, security meant exposing the subversives they suspected were operating in society and at high levels of their government. In the face of mounting opposition, Truman attempted to pursue policies that addressed these concerns.

Objectives

After studying this section, you should be able to

★ explain changes in the American labor force after the war.

★ describe the condition of African Americans during the 1940s.

★ evaluate the Truman presidency.

Key Terms

jurisdictional strike, featherbedding, subversive

◀ SENATOR ROBERT TAFT

World War II brought great changes to the nation's economy. War industries solved the unemployment problem of the Depression. In fact, with 16 million people in the United States armed services, there was actually a shortage of workers in industry. The number of African American workers in defense industries more than tripled. Six million women joined the labor force, a rise of nearly 60 percent.

■ Prosperity Continues

When the war ended in 1945, people were fearful of depression. In the past, when government spending for war materials stopped and soldiers returned home to look for jobs, unemployment spread. Even if the factories kept running, some newly hired African American and women workers now feared that they would be replaced by returning soldiers.

Fears of a depression proved groundless. After a slight drop in business activity, the number of Americans with jobs actually increased. Several factors contributed to the continuing prosperity. As the United States kept feeding not only its own people but millions of people overseas, farm income remained high. During the war Americans, due to rationing and scarcity of consumer goods, had saved $30 billion. Now they spent their savings for postponed purchases. In addition Congress stimulated postwar business by cutting wartime taxes nearly $6 billion. Instead of depression, consumer demand stimulated a sharp rise in prices, or inflation. Defense spending, which had dropped to $15 billion by 1949, escalated to $50 billion by 1953, pouring even more money into the economy. In addition the Marshall Plan restored markets in Europe for American goods.

In some ways the cold war economy of the 1950s resembled the wartime economy of the 1940s. The government's military spending continued to stimulate industrial production, while a portion of the labor force continued in military service.

Women

Immediately following World War II, soldiers returning from service took the places of many women who were employed in factories. In the automobile plants the proportion of women on assembly lines dropped from 25 percent in 1944 to 7.5 percent in 1946. The head of the Women's Bureau, a federal agency set up to protect women's interests, stated that "women ought to be delighted to give up any job and return to their proper sphere in the kitchen." Federal and state aid to child-care centers in factories was stopped.

Yet continued prosperity created new job opportunities. By 1952 more than 2 million more women were employed than in 1946. The kinds of work available to women were changing. This change was dramatically reflected in the experience of African American women. Between 1940 and 1950 the percentage of African American women employed as domestic servants dropped from 72 to 48 percent. The number of those working as farm laborers fell from 20 percent to 7 percent. At the same time, the percentage hired by factories rose from 7 percent to 18 percent. The rise in female employment did not mean that women had gained economic equality, however. Women in industries earned less than two-thirds as much as men.

■ Gains for African Americans

As a group, African Americans benefited from the postwar economic boom. Many made the transition from farming to manufacturing, from rural areas to cities, from the South to other regions of the country. The number of African American workers in white-collar, skilled, and supervisory jobs nearly tripled, increasing from about 300,000 to nearly 900,000. As opportunities for African Americans opened up fields such as law, nursing, and professional sports, average income—even adjusted for inflation—almost doubled.

▼ 1953 PACKARD CONVERTIBLE

▲ PURCHASING POWER The United States enjoyed an economic boom in the early postwar years. Increasing consumer demand for necessities as well as luxury items fueled inflation, however. *How did job opportunities change for women during the early 1950s?*

Changing social attitudes helped these advances. The war against Germany and the cold war both played a part. The horrifying racism of the Nazis helped to make some Americans more sensitive to racism in their own country. They began to realize that not only African Americans, but also Asian Americans, Hispanic Americans, and other minorities had been treated unfairly and denied social and economic opportunities.

During this period, African Americans worked hard to gain civil rights. During the war, the membership of the National Association for the Advancement of Colored People (NAACP) rose from 100,000 to 351,000. The NAACP hired teams of able lawyers to bring a series of lawsuits to the federal courts to end violations of the constitutional rights of African American citizens. Like women, however, African Americans fell short of gaining full equality in the 1940s.

In the North, African Americans often lived in crowded inner-city areas. Wages averaged about 60 percent of those paid to white workers. African American workers were still likely to be "last hired, first fired." In the South old patterns of segregation and racism remained. African American Southerners resented that their children had to attend separate schools that were often ill-equipped and understaffed. They objected to Jim Crow laws that forced them to use segregated facilities. Even worse, most African American Southerners were denied the vote, either by custom or by law. Almost none held political office.

■ Inflation in the Postwar Years

Government spending on wartime military programs and for postwar domestic programs brought prosperity and inflation. During periods of inflation the amount of money in circulation increases and prices rise sharply as the demand for goods exceeds the supply.

Because increased taxes were not sufficient to pay the costs of war, the federal government ran a large deficit during World

War II. The national debt rose from $50 million to nearly $270 billion. The government borrowed much of this money from Federal Reserve Banks. Using the federal bonds that the government gave as security, the banks issued new money. As a result, there was four times as much money in circulation in 1945 as there was in 1938.

As inflation drove prices up, the purchasing power of paychecks decreased. When consumers could not buy as much, factories slowed production, returning to a 40-hour week, and employers stopped paying overtime. Workers, losing purchasing power, demanded pay raises and often went on strike. In 1946 there were nearly 5,000 strikes, in which nearly 4.6 million workers took part—a record that is unlikely to be surpassed. Some strikes hit industries basic to the national economy such as steel, transportation, and coal. When railroad workers went on strike, President Truman asked Congress for power to draft them into the army. Fortunately, however, the strike ended before this measure was necessary.

■ The Taft-Hartley Act

Union activities were a major issue in the congressional elections of 1946. The anxiety caused by the strikes in basic industries helped conservative, antilabor candidates. The Republicans showed new vigor as they ran on the slogan, "Had enough?" For the first time in 18 years, they gained control of both the Senate and the House.

An immediate result of this swing toward conservatism was the Taft-Hartley Act, passed over President Truman's veto in 1947. Intended to keep unions from abusing their power, the act outlawed practices such as the closed shop, which forced business owners to hire only union members; **jurisdictional strikes,** which forced businesses to recognize one union instead of another; **featherbedding,** which limited workers' output in order to create more jobs; and high fees charged to workers for joining a union. In addition, unions were forbidden to use their money to support political campaigns.

Veterans Return

After World War II, thousands of military personnel came home. They poured off the troop ships and into the arms of families, wives, and girlfriends. When the celebrating was over, however, these former soldiers faced the task of rebuilding their lives and returning to their jobs or education.

As the nation adjusted to a peacetime economy, there was turmoil in the job market. Thousands of veterans hunted for jobs while wartime industries changed to peacetime production.

Many veterans decided to take advantage of the Servicemen's Readjustment Act of 1944. More popularly known as the G.I. Bill of Rights, this legislation assisted veterans in finding employment, education, and medical care. Many who went to college on G.I. Bill assistance were married men with young children. At most colleges and universities, housing was not sufficient for this increased enrollment. For some veterans the answer was a small mobile home or house trailer.

▲ **MEMORIAL OF JAPANESE SURRENDER**

During the late 1940s and the early 1950s, many campuses included large trailer parks where "GIs" and their families lived. Lasting relationships developed from the strong sense of community in these parks, which helped veterans adjust to civilian life.

◀ **SOLDIERS RETURNING HOME AFTER WORLD WAR II**

The Taft-Hartley Act was a very controversial measure. Its supporters claimed the law held irresponsible unions in check the way the Wagner Act of 1935 restrained antiunion activities of employers. Labor leaders called the act a "slave labor" law. They claimed it erased many of the gains that unions had made since 1933. In addition, they deeply resented that union leaders had to swear they were not members of the Communist party.

■ Election of 1948

As the presidential election of 1948 drew near, the Democratic party was divided. Southern Democrats objected to Truman's civil-rights program, which included proposals to end racial, religious, and ethnic discrimination, to abolish immigration quotas, and to integrate the armed forces.

The Candidates

Many white Southerners left the Democratic party to form the "Dixiecrat" party, which nominated South Carolina Governor Strom Thurmond for President. Other Democrats thought Truman was taking too hard a line against the Soviet Union. They supported the Progressive party ticket led by former Vice President Henry Wallace. Truman appeared certain to lose the election; he had lost the support of both the right wing and the left wing of his party. The Democrats renominated Truman only after party leaders failed to persuade General Eisenhower to accept the nomination.

The Republicans united behind their candidate for President, Governor Thomas E. Dewey of New York. Dewey was so confident that he would win that he avoided discussing issues and simply called on Americans to join him in building unity.

The Campaign

Far behind in the public-opinion polls, President Truman pursued an aggressive campaign from the beginning. First, he called the Republican Congress back into special session and asked them to carry out the promises of the Republican party platform by passing civil rights and other progressive legislation. When they failed to act, Truman had his campaign theme: The "do-nothing, good for nothing" Republican 80th Congress. Setting out on a "whistle stop" tour of the country by train, Truman covered 30,000 miles, giving some 350 speeches along the way.

Right up to Election Day, the pollsters predicted a Republican victory. But Truman won 2 million more votes than Dewey and piled up a 303-to-189 margin in the Electoral College. Truman had held together the New Deal coalition. He won labor support for his veto of the Taft-Hartley Act. He won support from African American voters for his civil-rights proposals. He won the farmers' vote for his support of high farm price supports. Not only did Truman defeat Dewey, but the Democrats regained their majority in Congress.

The Fair Deal

In his Inaugural Address in January 1949, Truman called for a Fair Deal, a return to and expansion of Roosevelt's New Deal policies. President Truman asked for slum clearance, federal subsidies for public schools, government-backed medical insurance, aid to farmers, and higher minimum wages. Although the Democrats held a majority, the new Congress was still influenced by an alliance of Republicans and conservative Southern Democrats. Together they blocked most of Truman's proposals to Congress.

In 1949 postwar prosperity slipped into a recession. Unemployment reached 7 percent of the labor force. The recession lasted only a few months, however. A tax cut passed in 1948 took effect, making more money available. The New Deal's built-in stabilizers such as price supports for agriculture and social security benefits helped to lessen the effect of the economic downturn. Beginning in 1950, the Korean War changed the economic picture sharply. Rearmament now competed with the demand for consumer goods. The war also fueled anticommunist sentiment at home.

▲ TRUMAN DISPLAYS HEADLINE THAT WRONGLY PROJECTED DEWEY AS THE WINNER

The Election of 1948

	Popular vote:	Electoral vote:
Truman	24,105,812	303
Dewey	21,970,065	189
Thurmond	1,169,063	39

Map Study The Democratic party split in 1948. *From which region did Thurmond receive his strongest support?*

■ Fear of Communists

The cold war and the Korean War heightened fear of communism in the United States. A communist spy ring, which had been sending atomic secrets to the Soviet Union, was uncovered in Canada. To Americans, this explained the Soviets' success in developing an atomic bomb so early. Americans began to suspect that there might be other communist sympathizers and spies in the government, universities, press, and the arts—all working to undermine American democracy. In a period of international tensions, national insecurity led to a search for scapegoats.

Constitutional Rights

The question arose: Should the rights of Communists be protected by the Constitution? In 1949, 11 members of the Communist party in the United States were convicted of conspiracy. The courts held that since the Communist party was organized to overthrow the United States government by force, its members were not entitled to protection by the free speech rights of the First Amendment. Although there were relatively very few Communist party members in the United States, the suspected communist conspiracy led to extensive precautions. Many people were forced to take loyalty oaths before being hired for jobs. Government officials were subjected to security checks.

Loyalty Oaths

During the postwar period, a tendency grew among many Americans to mistake criticism of American institutions for disloyalty. As Judge Harold Medina told the jury that convicted the 11 Communists of conspiracy, taking away the right to criticize does not make a country stronger. Instead, allowing abuses of rights to go unchecked makes it weaker. In several rulings during this period, however, the Supreme Court found state loyalty oaths to be constitutional. The Court noted that the states had a constitutional right to assurance that an employee was not engaged in subversive activity.

 ▲ CHARGES OF SUBVERSION In the early 1950s, Senator Joseph R. McCarthy (left) claimed that Communists had infiltrated educational institutions and high levels of government. *What cold war events stirred McCarthy and others?*

Subversives

The "loss" of China to the Communists and the stalemated Korean War helped to create this mood in the United States that was much like the Red Scare in the years following World War I. Critics of Truman accused the President of having lost China, alleging that his close advisers were Communists or communist tools. Senator Robert A. Taft, Republican leader in the Senate, claimed that the State Department was "riddled" with **subversives,** or individuals attempting to overthrow the government. Taft said that State Department officials had:

 . . . surrendered to every demand of the Soviet Union and promoted, at every opportunity, the communist cause in China.

In 1948 the House Committee on Un-American Activities heard testimony from Whittaker Chambers, a magazine editor. Chambers admitted that he had been a communist spy in the 1930s and said that he had received secret documents from Alger Hiss, then a high-ranking State Department official. At first, few people believed Chambers's story. However, Richard M. Nixon, a young representative from California, pressed the case forward. Finally, Chambers produced several rolls of microfilm of secret documents he claimed to have received from Hiss. Hiss denied these charges. Though not convicted of spying, Hiss was found guilty of lying under oath.

McCarthyism

Increased fears of communist subversion were fertile ground for more reckless voices. At a Lincoln's Day speech in February 1950, Senator Joseph R. McCarthy of Wisconsin accused the Democratic party of "twenty years of treason." McCarthy charged that Roosevelt had deliberately sacrificed the navy at Pearl Harbor and had "sold out" to the Soviet Union at Yalta. In addition, McCarthy claimed to have a list of "card-carrying Communists" in the State Department.

While McCarthy never produced the list, nor a shred of evidence to support his charges, he ruined the careers of many government officials. A growing atmosphere of hysteria inspired other "witch-hunts." Private groups used the communist label to drive liberal professors out of colleges. They made sure books they believed to be subversive were removed from schools. They had many broadcasters, writers, and entertainers barred from television and kept many actors from working on the stage and in films.

Years later a Senate committee determined that McCarthy's accusations and investigations had been groundless. The use of indiscriminate, unfounded political accusations to destroy or assassinate the character of one's opponent came, in time, to be known as McCarthyism.

■ Truman's Legacy

In 1952 President Truman announced that he would not run for reelection. By the time Truman left office, he had become unpopular. The successful Soviet atomic bomb explosion, the defeat of the Nationalists in China, and the problems with carrying out the war in Korea, all contributed to charges that Truman was "soft on communism." Other Americans thought his loyalty program had hurt innocent people.

Instances of corruption in high places were also discovered—some of the President's closest aides had received valuable gifts in return for political favors. Although Truman was not personally involved, the "Truman scandals" gave the Republicans a ready-made issue for the 1952 elections.

The problems Truman faced were new and complex. Congress was often suspicious or hostile, yet Truman got many of his programs enacted. Americans were tired of foreign involvements, yet he managed to keep the nation from retreating into isolationism. Truman's reputation as leader rose after he left the White House. Most of the Fair Deal measures he called for eventually became law. His policy of "containment" was continued by other Presidents. He set the United States on a course that included aid for those in need and an unwavering defense of democracy everywhere.

Section 3 ★ Review

Checking for Understanding

1. **Identify** Taft-Hartley Act, Alger Hiss, Joseph McCarthy.

2. **Define** jurisdictional strike, featherbedding, subversive.

3. **List** reasons why economic growth continued after World War II.

4. **Compare** gains made by African Americans in their struggle for equality with the limitations on their achievements.

Critical Thinking

5. **Drawing Conclusions** Why was Senator McCarthy, with groundless accusations, able to generate mass hysteria about communism?

▲ FLORIDA FAMILY MOVING NORTH

African American Migration

African American migration from the rural South to Northern and Western cities between 1910 and 1950 was one of the largest migrations in American history. African Americans migrated in search of greater economic opportunity and a better life than the drought, boll weevils, racism, and poverty they were accustomed to in the South. Much of the African American migration took place during the two world wars.

During World War I, industrial agents traveled the South promising jobs with high wages and free transportation to the North. Soon the African American population of cities such as Chicago, Cleveland, and Detroit swelled. Detroit alone saw an increase of over 600 percent.

In the 1940s rural Southern African Americans streamed into Northern and Western cities for two main reasons. First, around 1940 cotton farming became mechanized. Far fewer workers

were needed, and many African Americans became jobless. Second, many saw great opportunity in wartime industries.

Although social and economic gains in the cities were limited by racial prejudice, African Americans acquired a political voice. Their migration forever changed the face of American politics and society.

Making the Geography Connection

1. Where did African Americans migrate to from 1910 to 1950?

2. Why did they migrate from the rural South?

Linking Past and Present

3. Where did many people migrate to in the 1970s and 1980s?

Using Vocabulary

Using the following vocabulary, write a paragraph describing the Soviet establishment of an iron curtain and the development of the cold war.

communism   satellite nation
containment   subversive
purge   buffer

Reviewing Facts

1. **Discuss** how and why the Soviets created a buffer of satellite states.

2. **Explain** why communism appealed to people in certain parts of the world.

3. **Summarize** arguments for and against containment and the Truman Doctrine.

4. **Cite** actions taken in the Philippines and Japan after World War II that led to successful economic recovery.

5. **Examine** the reasons for the charge that Truman was soft on communism.

6. **Detail** events leading to war in Korea.

7. **List** the advances made by African Americans.

8. **Explain** how the Truman agenda for prosperity at home and abroad enabled him to win in 1948.

Understanding Concepts

Political and Economic Power

1. How did the United States use its position as the strongest and wealthiest nation in the world to shape economic recovery in Europe?

Leadership

2. Analyze the qualities that made President Truman an effective leader.

Critical Thinking

1. **Applying Ideas**   What does the term "cold war" mean and how does it apply to this era?

2. **Applying Principles**   How was the Truman Doctrine applied in assisting Greece, by the Marshall Plan, and in creating NATO?

3. **Testing Conclusions**   According to some experts, the United States failed to save China because of its loyalty to the Nationalists and its ignorance of China's true situation. Test this theory using information from the text.

4. **Analyzing Political Cartoons**   Study the political cartoon on this page and answer the questions that follow.

   a. Whom do the individuals in the cartoon represent?

   b. What is the cartoonist saying about Truman's power?

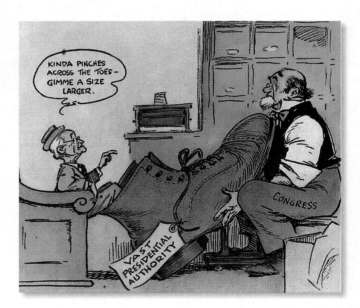

Writing About History

Comparison

Write an essay comparing the purposes and provisions of the Monroe Doctrine and the Truman Doctrine. Address such questions as: What were the foreign policy objectives that the United States tried to accomplish in each case? What commitment of resources was required to support each doctrine? Explain what the differences indicate about fundamental changes in foreign policy between 1823 and 1947.

Cooperative Learning

Working in groups of three, conduct a debate about the possible alternatives of United States foreign policy in Europe after World War II. One member should propose and support pulling troops out of Europe to lessen the Soviets' perceived need for a buffer of satellites. Another should support the contention that the Soviets wanted to conquer other nations as well as secure their own borders, and only a heavy military presence in Europe would contain them. The third member should decide which position was best supported and write an opinion that examines the best points of each argument. All members should be prepared to argue either position in front of the class if called on by the teacher.

Social Studies Skills

Reading and Interpreting Bar Graphs

As in the two bar graphs on this page, a bar graph can take more than one form. Many bar graphs are like the smaller one—vertical bars. The larger bar graph is different in that the bars are horizontal and there are no *x*-axis gradations. However, it still organizes data for easy comparison and analysis.

To interpret the data in a bar graph, do the following:

a. Read the title of the graph.

b. Determine what the bars represent by studying the *x*- and *y*-axes.

c. Determine the changes or other relationships the graph shows.

Practicing the Skill

Use the bar graphs that appear on this page and your understanding of chapter content to answer the following questions.

1. Using the three steps above, explain what is shown in the larger bar graph.

2. How much aid did Norway receive under this plan?

3. Using the three steps above, explain what is shown in the smaller bar graph.

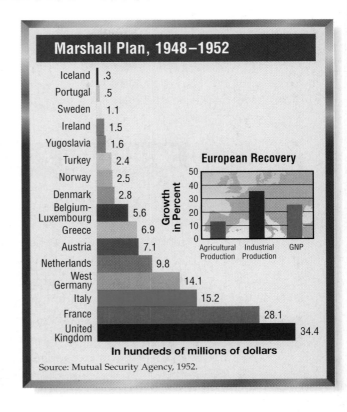

Marshall Plan, 1948–1952

Country	Amount
Iceland	.3
Portugal	.5
Sweden	1.1
Ireland	1.5
Yugoslavia	1.6
Turkey	2.4
Norway	2.5
Denmark	2.8
Belgium-Luxembourg	5.6
Greece	6.9
Austria	7.1
Netherlands	9.8
West Germany	14.1
Italy	15.2
France	28.1
United Kingdom	34.4

In hundreds of millions of dollars

Source: Mutual Security Agency, 1952.

European Recovery (Growth in Percent — Agricultural Production, Industrial Production, GNP)

4. Why do you suppose the United Kingdom and France received the largest amounts of aid?

5. What do you think is the relationship between the two bar graphs?

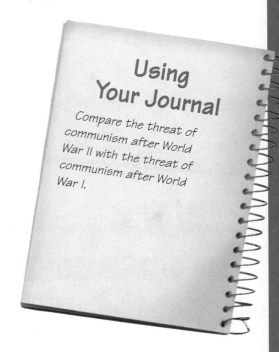

Using Your Journal

Compare the threat of communism after World War II with the threat of communism after World War I.

CHAPTER 31

★★★

Search for Stability
1952–1960

▼ **1957 CHEVROLET**

Setting the Scene

Focus

A war hero, Dwight D. Eisenhower became one of the most popular Presidents of modern times. His domestic and foreign policies were stable and consistent. At home, the nation was generally prosperous. In foreign policy he continued Truman's efforts at containment. The cold war expanded into the Middle East, Africa, and Latin America. Covert operations increased, and American troops were sent into Lebanon.

Concepts to Understand

★ Why the United States's international leadership led to the use of covert operations in other countries

★ How economic growth stimulated the economy during the 1950s

Read to Discover . . .

★ how President Eisenhower viewed his role as President.

★ how the lives of most Americans improved following World War II.

CULTURAL

● **1952** *Ralph Ellison publishes* Invisible Man

● **1955** *Jonas Salk develops vaccine to prevent polio*

1950	1953

● **1950** *McCarthy charges communist influence in government*
● **1952** *Eisenhower elected President*

● **1953** *Truce in the Korean War reached*
● **1954** *Geneva Conference divides Vietnam*

POLITICAL

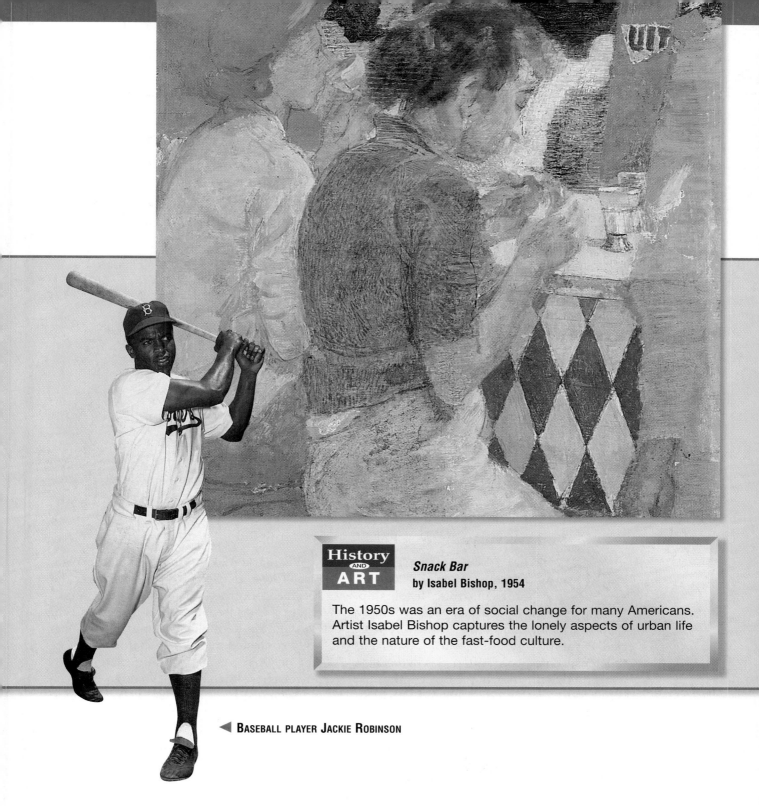

Snack Bar
by Isabel Bishop, 1954

The 1950s was an era of social change for many Americans. Artist Isabel Bishop captures the lonely aspects of urban life and the nature of the fast-food culture.

◀ BASEBALL PLAYER JACKIE ROBINSON

• **1957** *The musical* West Side Story *premieres in New York*

1956

• **1955** *Formation of the AFL-CIO*
• **1956** *Suez crisis erupts*

• **1960** *There are more than 45 million television sets in American homes*

1959

• **1959** *Castro comes to power in Cuba*
• **1960** *Soviets shoot down a United States U-2 surveillance plane*

★★

The Eisenhower Years

Setting the Scene

Section Focus

As the Truman presidency ended, the fear of communism preoccupied the nation. In Asia the United States was engaged in a long and frustrating war with the Communists. In other parts of the world, a dangerous cold war between communism and American interests intensified. The nation was ready for new leadership to guide it through these troubling times.

Objectives

After studying this section, you should be able to

★ describe President Eisenhower's style of leadership.

★ explain how Senator Joseph McCarthy's influence came to an end.

Key Term

presidential succession

◄ EISENHOWER CAMPAIGN BUTTON

After 7 years of the Truman administration and 20 years of Democratic leadership, the Republicans hoped that 1952 would be their year. They knew Americans were worried about the continuing war in Korea and the tense cold war. Americans were also concerned with the charges of communist infiltration in the government. President Truman's reputation was damaged by news reports that some of his officials had accepted bribes. These issues gave the Republicans their rallying cry for the election. They ran against "Korea, communism, and corruption."

■ The Election of 1952

As their candidate, the Republicans picked one of the most popular war heroes, Dwight D. Eisenhower.

When asked to run for President in 1948, Eisenhower refused. By 1952, however, he became concerned that isolationists might regain the White House and agreed to run. He won the Republican nomination after a hotly contested race with Senator Robert A. Taft of Ohio. As his running mate, Eisenhower chose Richard M. Nixon, a 39-year-old senator from California who had made his reputation pursuing alleged Communists in government.

"I Like Ike"

The Republicans adopted the slogan "It's time for a change!" Eisenhower, known as "Ike," promised to end the war in Korea and took a hard line against corruption. "I like Ike" became the Republican rallying cry.

Eisenhower's promise to keep his administration clean was soon regarded with skepticism. Charges were disclosed that Richard

Nixon had received gifts from California businesspeople totaling $18,000 while he was a senator. For a while, it looked as though Nixon might be dropped from the ticket. But in a nationwide speech broadcast on radio and television, he insisted the funds had been used for legitimate political purposes. He did admit that his family had kept one gift, a cocker spaniel puppy named "Checkers." The "Checkers speech" saved Nixon, who remained on the Republican ticket.

Eisenhower Defeats Stevenson

The Democrats nominated Adlai Stevenson, governor of Illinois. Stevenson was a thoughtful and eloquent liberal, but his campaign was burdened by the need to defend the actions of the Truman administration.

It is doubtful that Stevenson ever had a chance to win against the popular Eisenhower. If he did, he lost it two weeks before Election Day, when Eisenhower promised to make a trip to Korea if elected. The election was a landslide for Eisenhower. He received in excess of 6 million popular votes more than Stevenson and carried the Electoral College by 442 to 89 votes. The Republicans also gained an eight-seat majority in the House. The Senate was evenly divided between Democrats and Republicans.

■ A New Style of Leadership

Although Eisenhower was a career soldier, he did not run the White House like an officer commanding an army. Instead, he acted as the chief administrator or leader of the White House team.

Hidden-Hand Presidency

Under Eisenhower the cabinet assumed new importance and acted as a genuine advisory board. For the first time in history, the cabinet had a full-time secretary, an agenda, and regularly kept minutes. Eisenhower made Sherman Adams, former governor of

Visualizing History ▲ Eisenhower becomes President Dwight D. Eisenhower proved to be a popular campaigner and was the first Republican to be elected President since 1928. *How great was his margin of victory over Stevenson in 1952?*

▲ **LYNDON JOHNSON** Senate Majority leader Lyndon Johnson (right), shown here meeting with Prime Minister Harold Macmillan of Great Britain, took an active role in domestic and foreign policy issues. *What congressional coalition supported President Eisenhower?*

New Hampshire, his chief of staff. Adams wielded great power by controlling access to the President.

The advantages of Eisenhower's kind of administration were clear. If, for some reason, the President was unable to lead, the government would not come to a standstill. Cabinet members could easily take over day-to-day operations. Indeed, Eisenhower suffered serious illnesses three times during his presidency, and each time the White House staff carried on with little difficulty. Critics claimed that the President was abdicating his responsibilities. At crucial times he seemed unaware of decisions made by his aides. Historians later described Eisenhower's management style as a "hidden-hand presidency."

The Bricker Amendment

Eisenhower hoped to establish good working relations with Congress, but members of his own party sometimes made this difficult. Still angry over the secret agreements that President Roosevelt had made with Stalin and Churchill at Yalta, Republican Senator John Bricker of Ohio introduced a bill to limit presidential power. The Bricker Amendment required Senate ratification of all agreements made by the President with other nations. It also prohibited the President from making a treaty that conflicted with the laws of any state.

Eisenhower believed that the Bricker Amendment would limit the President's power to deal effectively with other nations. It would also allow any state to disrupt United States foreign policy. Although most Republicans in Congress supported the Bricker Amendment, the Eisenhower administration fought hard against it. In February 1954, the bill was defeated by a single vote. Wearily, the President commented:

❝ *If it is true that when you die the things that bothered you most are engraved on your skull, I am sure I'll have there the mud and dirt of France during the invasion and the name of Senator Bricker.* ❞

■ McCarthy's Influence Ends

Some Americans believed that a Republican President would put an end to Senator Joseph McCarthy's charges that the government was filled with Communists. But McCarthy continued his crusade and subjected many government officials to humiliating investigations.

For a time McCarthy succeeded in giving the impression that he was saving the country from communism. A public opinion poll taken in 1954 reported that 50 percent of the people favored him and 29 percent opposed him. Senators wary of McCarthy's influence with the voters were reluctant to oppose him.

Although the President privately disapproved of McCarthy and his methods, Eisenhower refused to attack him publicly. The President believed that if he fought

McCarthy, he would only give him more publicity. This tactic, however, deprived McCarthy's opponents in Congress of Eisenhower's leadership.

McCarthy's underhanded tactics were finally exposed to the public in 1954. In televised hearings regarding possible communist subversion in the army, Americans observed McCarthy's callous disregard of law and fairness. After the hearings ended, the Senate passed a resolution condemning McCarthy for his conduct.

Presidential Disability

In September 1955, President Eisenhower suffered a heart attack. Although the President recovered rapidly, the nation's confidence was shaken. The stock market dropped more sharply than it had since 1929. Then, within the next two years, Eisenhower suffered two major illnesses.

The President's health focused attention on the question of **presidential succession,** the order in which others fill the office of President. Although Eisenhower had kept the government running smoothly during his illnesses, Americans wondered what would happen if the President remained ill. The Constitution provides that the Vice President becomes President if the President is unable to handle the duties of office. However, it does not say who is to decide whether the President is, or is not, able to serve.

The matter was addressed in 1967 after ratification of the Twenty-fifth Amendment, which outlines procedures when the President is disabled. Moreover, it deals with the situation when a President feels capable of continuing in office but is thought by others to be incapable.

The Election of 1956

In 1956 the Republicans renominated Eisenhower. The Republicans claimed that the Eisenhower administration had brought peace and prosperity to the nation. Eisenhower had ended the war in Korea and avoided other world conflicts. The Democrats, nominating Adlai Stevenson for a second time, capitalized on fear about the President's health. They played upon the public's concern that Vice President Nixon might become President.

Eisenhower won by a greater margin than in 1952. The President's popularity did not rub off on his party, however. Democrats won control of both the House of Representatives and the Senate.

In his second term, Eisenhower was more independent of his party than any other President in the twentieth century. Many conservative Republicans regarded Eisenhower as too liberal in domestic affairs and too interventionist in foreign affairs. However, "modern Republicans" and some Democrats supported the President. His policies won support from the two Democratic leaders in Congress, House Speaker Sam Rayburn and Senate Majority Leader Lyndon Johnson. On domestic issues, an alliance developed between "modern Republicans" and moderate-to-liberal Democrats.

Section 1 ★ Review

Checking for Understanding

1. **Identify** Adlai Stevenson, Richard Nixon, "Checkers speech," Bricker Amendment.

2. **Define** presidential succession.

3. **Explain** the need for an amendment concerning presidential succession.

4. **State** reasons for Eisenhower's appeal to moderate Democrats.

Critical Thinking

5. **Evaluating Performance**   Describe Eisenhower's leadership style and discuss its advantages and disadvantages.

Critical Thinking Skills

Discovering Symbolism in History

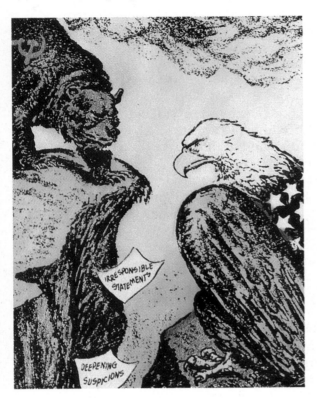

▲ COLD WAR CARTOON

Neil Armstrong was the first person to walk on the moon. This accomplishment had a powerful impact on people all over the world. One reason this event had such an impact was that people saw his walking on the moon as a symbol, and they attached extra meaning to it.

A *symbol* is something used to represent or stand for something else—often an abstract idea, concept, or feeling. Symbols are all around us, even though we often do not recognize them as such. All words, for example, are symbols for objects or ideas.

A familiar symbol is the American flag, which stands for the United States and patriotic pride. Other familiar symbols include the color purple, which stands for royalty; lions, which stand for courage; and the skull and crossbones, which symbolizes death.

Armstrong's moon walk symbolizes human progress, the power of modern technology, and our never-ending curiosity about the universe. The following guidelines will help you discover symbolism in history:

- Think about the event or condition being studied. What is the main activity in it?
- What overall condition led to this main activity?
- Who or what situation could be affected by this activity?
- What consequences could there be for those who are affected?
- What statement could be made that would demonstrate the symbolism, or meaning, of this event?

For example, possible statements of the symbolism in McCarthyism include:

  a. McCarthyism symbolized a callous disregard for law and fairness.

  b. McCarthyism symbolized cold war mistrust between two superpowers.

  c. McCarthyism symbolized a pervasive fear of communism.

  d. McCarthyism symbolized America's desire to safeguard its values and ideologies.

  e. McCarthyism symbolized fanaticism.

Practicing the Skill

1. Analyze the political cartoon on this page. What do the two figures symbolize?
2. Read Section 3 of this chapter. Reread the guidelines that are listed above. Then, use the guidelines to list examples of the symbolism you found in the Eisenhower Doctrine.

★★★

"The Straight Road"

Setting the Scene

Section Focus

Democratic administrations had leaned toward the interests of labor. When Eisenhower accepted the presidential nomination, he promised that in economic matters he would "travel the straight road down the middle." As a result, the nation enjoyed an unprecedented period of prosperity and witnessed the rapid development of big business and agribusiness.

OHIO AFL-CIO
UNITED IN PURPOSE

◀ **LABOR UNION SYMBOL**

Objectives

After studying this section, you should be able to

★ explain the Eisenhower administration's economic policies.

★ discuss the plight of the small farmer in the 1950s.

Key Term

agribusiness

---

*T*hroughout both of his administrations, Eisenhower steered a course between conservatism and liberalism. Ike's middle course pleased most Americans. At the beginning of his administration it looked as though he might try to undo the New Deal. Like Hoover, Eisenhower believed that the role of government should be limited. Eisenhower advocated cutting the budget, reducing taxes, and ending government regulation of business. He condemned the Tennessee Valley Authority as "creeping socialism" and tried unsuccessfully to arrange for private industry to build new power plants in Tennessee, Alabama, and Kentucky.

Eisenhower and the New Deal

Despite this conservative agenda, Eisenhower recognized that New Deal programs were strongly supported by most Americans. He wrote in a private letter:

" *Should any political party attempt to abolish Social Security, unemployment insurance, and eliminate labor laws and farm programs, you would not hear of that party again in our political history.* **"**

The debate during Eisenhower's presidency was not over ending such New Deal programs as Social Security or the minimum wage, but over how much larger to allow them to become. With President Eisenhower's encouragement, Congress extended Social Security to 7 million more people and increased benefits. Congress also extended unemployment compensation to 4 million more people. Eisenhower tried to persuade Congress to enact a health insurance program partly funded by the federal government, but Congress rejected the legislation.

■ Business and Labor

Big business also had an ally in the White House. During the 1950s, 3,000 companies merged with the 500 largest corporations without any antitrust challenges by the government. The nation's 100 largest companies controlled more than 30 percent of all industrial production. Some corporations, such as General Motors and American Telephone and Telegraph, had annual budgets that were larger than those of many countries.

The American labor movement grew more slowly than big business, but it continued to gain strength. In 1955 the American Federation of Labor (AFL) and the Congress of Industrial Organizations (CIO) merged, forming the AFL-CIO. The merger increased the strength of organized labor and made it easier for workers to form local unions.

Organized labor tried hard to win pay increases. During the 1950s, take-home pay and buying power rose sharply. Workers also enjoyed longer paid vacations. Walter Reuther, United Auto Workers president, observed that the movement was developing a "whole new middle class."

Organized labor was not very successful in its efforts to organize the lowest-paid factory workers and office workers. Often, these workers were women or minorities. The growth in AFL-CIO membership actually slowed by 1957.

Union growth was also adversely affected by congressional investigations into corrupt union practices. The investigations revealed that strong-arm tactics were used by some unions to force employers into accepting the unions. The Teamsters' Union, accused of misappropriating funds, was expelled from the AFL-CIO. These revelations began to turn public opinion against unions.

■ Farm Problems

Despite the prosperity of the 1950s, it was a difficult time for many of the nation's farmers. Between 1948 and 1956, the farmers' share of the national income dropped from 9 to 4 percent. While the average American enjoyed a per capita income of $1,629, the farm population averaged $632 a year.

Visualizing History ▲ LABOR UNIONS MERGE George Meany (left), president of the AFL, and Walter Reuther (right), president of the CIO, shake hands on the merger of the two unions. *How did the joining of these unions help organized labor?*

Betty Friedan (free•DAN) was one of the first to analyze the lives of women. When she began her analysis, most women were homemakers or worked in low-paying jobs.

In 1957 she began a year-long study of her Smith College classmates. She discovered that many of these well-educated women were leading unhappy lives. With additional research it became clear to Friedan that American women were failing to find fulfillment in life. Instead, they were succumbing to "the feminine mystique"—a belief that they were supposed to ignore their talents and interests and live only for the achievements of their family.

In 1963 Friedan published *The Feminine Mystique*, a book that sparked the modern women's liberation movement. In 1966 she helped found the National Organization for Women (NOW) to lead the fight for equal rights.

Betty Friedan
1921–

Question of Price Supports

Eisenhower was reluctant to have the government continue to guarantee farmers set prices for their products. The heart of the issue, according to the administration, was

> 66 [W]hether our farms are to continue to be operated by freemen. Or . . . to offset some very real and obvious problems that farmers now face, will government go in the opposite direction and subsidize agriculture in such a manner that it also takes control? 99

But without strong price supports from the government, the small family farmer faced economic ruin. Overproduction from better seeds, fertilizers, and mechanization kept farm prices low. Legislation reduced but did not end price supports or the farm surplus.

Many small farm families gave up and sold out to large farm owners who raised only a single crop and used the latest machinery and agricultural methods. Because of their efficiency, the large farm owners could cut their costs and still make a profit. More small farmers were unable to compete with the **agribusinesses,** or modern large-scale farms that covered 1,000 acres or more. By 1959 half of the nation's farmland belonged to 4 percent of the farmers.

Seasonal Workers

There were other problems associated with America's changing agricultural patterns. Large farm owners hired seasonal workers to cultivate and harvest their crops. Many of the workers were Mexican Americans from California and the Southwest, but as many as 400,000 workers were Mexicans allowed into the United States on short-term visas. Unprotected by the National Labor Relations Act or federal minimum wage laws, these migrant workers labored long hours for little pay and endured terrible living conditions. Their children grew up with little, if any, education.

■ Prosperity and Recession

Much of the economic growth of the 1950s was due to a tremendous increase in consumer credit. Effective advertising enticed Americans to borrow more and more money to buy houses, cars, and consumer goods. This growing demand, in turn, encouraged industries to produce more goods and hire more people.

Economic Slump

President Eisenhower worried that this rapid growth of the economy would lead to inflation, or rapidly rising prices. Because of this he tried to hold down government spending, both for domestic and military projects. But in 1957 and 1958, his attempts to balance the budget set off a recession. Sales dropped and manufacturers laid off workers. Unemployment rose to 7.6 percent of the workforce. Eisenhower resisted congressional pressure for a tax cut to stimulate the economy. Finally, late in 1958, boom times returned again.

Mounting Criticism

Although President Eisenhower remained a popular leader during the late 1950s, he was sharply blamed by some critics for not moving quickly enough. Some detractors charged that the President ignored important national issues such as civil rights and the protection of natural resources.

Scandals

At the same time, the administration also had to deal with a number of scandals. The most publicized scandal revolved around Sherman Adams, the President's closest adviser. In the spring of 1958, congressional hearings disclosed that Adams had received gifts from a wealthy Boston industrialist who was under investigation by the government. Adams was forced to resign. The recession and the scandals hurt the Republican cause during the 1958 elections, and the Democrats strengthened their control of both houses, winning 15 additional seats in the Senate and 48 seats in the House.

Accomplishments

Despite these difficulties, Eisenhower received praise for some of his efforts. In foreign policy, he sought to ease world tensions. During his last year in office, the President visited an unprecedented number of nations on a goodwill tour. He affirmed that

> **Our basic aspiration is to search out methods by which peace in the world can be assured with justice for everybody.**

At home, he backed government grants to help in the building of more schools for the nation's expanding school-age population. Eisenhower also supported the National Defense Education Act of 1958. This law provided a $295-million fund to provide loans to college students for their education.

In 1959 two new states were added to the union. On January 3 Eisenhower issued a proclamation making Alaska the 49th state—the first new state since Arizona and New Mexico joined the Union in 1912. On August 21, Hawaii became the 50th state.

Section 2 ★ Review

Checking for Understanding

1. **Identify** creeping socialism, AFL-CIO, migrant workers.

2. **Define** agribusiness.

3. **Characterize** the economic philosophy and practice of Eisenhower.

4. List two problems connected with farming in the 1950s.

Critical Thinking

5. **Comparing Trends**   Compare developments in business and agriculture during the 1950s, including the impact on workers.

★★

An Affluent Society

Setting the Scene

Section Focus

The economic growth of the 1950s brought great changes to the nation. For the first time, most Americans enjoyed a life of abundance. This prosperity greatly changed the way people lived. Advances in technology and medicine coupled with economic prosperity gave Americans great confidence in the future.

Objectives

After studying this section, you should be able to

★ describe the effect of affluence on American life.

★ give examples of advances in medical technology.

★ explain the pressures of conformity in the 1950s.

Key Term

automation

◀ THE TELEVISION GENERATION

After World War II, Americans were ready to settle down and enjoy a period of peace and prosperity. Industry responded to the demands of Americans by turning out huge quantities of new goods. New communities and housing developments were built as people moved from the cities to the suburbs. Americans were on the move, and they relied heavily on the automobile for this new mobility. People anxiously awaited each year's new car models with their added gadgets and longer "tail fins." Highways stretched across the country carrying more and more traffic. A new suburban lifestyle evolved among middle-class Americans.

New technology and continuing prosperity allowed many Americans to enjoy more leisure time. At the same time, the number of available leisure activities increased.

■ An Economy of Abundance

In 1958 economist John Kenneth Galbraith published *The Affluent Society*, in which he claimed that America's postwar prosperity was a new phenomenon. In the past, Galbraith said, all societies were based on an "economy of scarcity," in which the productivity of the economy was limited by a lack of resources and overpopulation.

In the 1950s, however, the United States and a few other highly industrialized nations were experiencing what Galbraith called an "economy of abundance." Up-to-date technology enabled these nations to produce an endless variety and amount of goods and services for their people. The citizens of these countries were enjoying a standard of living never before thought possible. Poverty was disappearing, except

▲ COMPUTERS COME OF AGE Early computers, such as the UNIVAC, occupied entire rooms and used vacuum tubes rather than microchips to process information. ***How did businesses first use computers?***

within such groups as the unskilled, uneducated, and new immigrant population.

Some critics accused Galbraith of overstating the situation, but the facts and figures seemed to support it. Americans produced more than they could use, and this new wealth was being distributed throughout the population. During the 1920s the wealthiest 5 percent of the population received 35 percent of the country's income, but by 1960 this group received only 18 percent.

Life for most Americans was easier than ever before. They earned more money than they needed for such necessities as food and housing. With their surplus income, they purchased automobiles, household appliances, and other luxury items. The number of Americans owning their own homes went up from 40 percent to 60 percent between 1940 and 1960. Americans also had more free time as working hours were reduced and they were given holidays with pay. Not only were Americans better off, but they were more secure. Unemployment insurance and social security now covered the majority of jobholders.

■ Technological and Scientific Progress

The United States made spectacular leaps in the field of science. With more money to spend, an increase in the number of university-trained scientists, and a growing commitment to the future, the United States led the world in new technological developments. America's factories and industries began to use **automation,** the technique of operating a production system using mechanical or electronic devices. With automated production methods, goods could be produced more efficiently and quickly than with human workers.

During the 1950s the use of computers began to revolutionize American industry. Businesses used computers for many purposes. Computers took over bookkeeping functions such as billing and inventory control. They were also used for such things as making hotel reservations, sorting bank checks, guiding satellites, predicting election results, forecasting weather conditions, identifying fingerprints, and setting type for printing.

Automation and computers in the workplace caused many workers to lose their jobs. In the long run, however, computers and automation created more jobs than they eliminated. And the new jobs usually demanded a higher level of education.

Breakthroughs in medicine during the 1950s were also impressive. In April 1955, Americans learned of one of the most important discoveries in the history of medicine. After many years of research, United States scientist Dr. Jonas Salk had developed a vaccine for preventing the dreaded childhood disease known as polio. The Salk vaccine was proven effective after a huge test run on 1,830,000 schoolchildren. Within a few years, cases of polio nearly disappeared.

By 1960 other major illnesses, including pneumonia, tuberculosis, and diphtheria, were nearly wiped out. Life expectancy in the United States increased. While cancer and heart disease continued to be serious threats to the lives of Americans, researchers made important advances in diagnosing and treating these diseases.

From Cities to Suburbs

In the 1950s the automobile changed the face of America. No longer did people have to live near their places of work. Those who lived and worked in the city could move to less-crowded places. This migration of city residents caused rapid growth of suburbs. In the years after World War II, cities became ringed by seemingly endless housing developments carved out of the less densely settled country land. Shopping centers with vast parking lots were built to serve the new suburban population. Businesses and factories also began relocating from the cities to the suburbs, where their workers now lived. The Highway Act of 1956 contributed to the growth of the suburbs by adding 41,000 miles to the interstate highway system.

Meanwhile, cities began to experience serious problems. To handle the flood of automobile traffic, new highways had to be built, often destroying whole urban neighborhoods. Those who were left behind to live in the cities often included poor people and the members of minority groups. With a declining population, cities faced growing financial problems. Taxes could no longer keep up with the demands for such services as public transportation, police protection, housing, and education.

Pressures to Conform

In the affluent 1950s, a new house in the suburbs, a larger television in the living room, and the newest model automobile in the garage represented the fulfillment of the

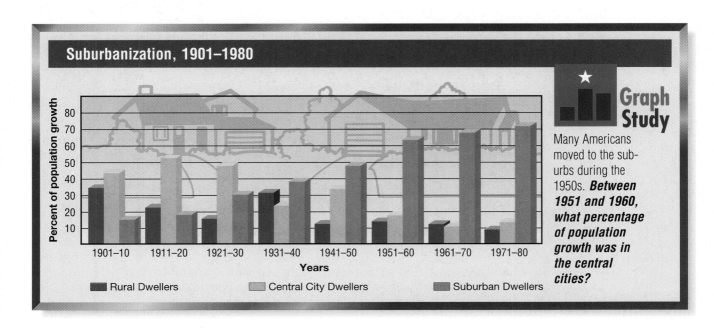

Suburbanization, 1901–1980

Percent of population growth

Years

■ Rural Dwellers   ■ Central City Dwellers   ■ Suburban Dwellers

Graph Study

Many Americans moved to the suburbs during the 1950s. *Between 1951 and 1960, what percentage of population growth was in the central cities?*

"American Dream." For many young couples, the suburbs offered comfort, security, and a pleasant place to raise their children. Yet it soon became clear that this new lifestyle had problems of its own.

Critics noted that a strong pressure to conform characterized American suburban life. Suburban neighborhoods were usually filled with people who were very much alike. They were generally typified as being young, with comfortable incomes, and having jobs in the service industries. Often this conformity led to discrimination or ostracism of those who seemed "different." For example, in many suburbs racial and religious minorities were unable to buy homes. To some extent, the high cost of homes in the suburbs was the reason, but prejudice was an even more important factor. Often suburban residents refused to sell homes to minority families. If minority families did move to the suburbs, others in the community made them feel unwelcome.

Many writers criticized the trend toward conformity in American life in the 1950s. Nonfiction works, such as David Reisman's *The Lonely Crowd* (1950) and William H. Whyte's *The Organization Man* (1956), and novels such as Sloan Wilson's *The Man in the Gray Flannel Suit* (1956) tried to explain the pressure to conform. Sometimes, as represented in *The Man in the Gray Flannel Suit,* these pressures were so subtly pervasive as to make people feel they had little control over their own lives:

> **" ** *[I]t seemed as though all I could see was a lot of bright young men in gray flannel suits rushing around New York in a frantic parade to go nowhere. They seemed to be pursuing neither ideals nor happiness— they were pursuing a routine. . . . I thought I was on the sidelines watching that parade. . . . It was quite a shock to glance down and see that I too was wearing a gray flannel suit.* **"**

The pressures to conform in business were especially great. Employees who wanted to advance to better positions took care to adhere to the company's rules. This often meant being loyal to the corporation and being "one of the team." Outside work

▲ **SUBURBAN LIFE** During the postwar years, many Americans moved from the farms and cities to the suburbs—and many young people discovered a new cast of heroes such as Davy Crockett. *What advantages did suburban living offer?*

Child Rearing by Spock

Millions of women, voluntarily and involuntarily, left their wartime jobs to make room

▼ **DR. BENJAMIN SPOCK**

for returning soldiers. Just as women had received training for the skilled positions they held during the war, they looked to experts for training in their new positions as mothers. Dr. Benjamin Spock obliged them by publishing *Baby and Child Care* in 1946.

Spock urged flexibility in child care, but he also advised mothers to give undivided attention to their infants. "For [a baby's] spirit to grow naturally," Spock admonished, "he needs someone to dote on him. . . ." One mother, a homemaker and career woman, wrote Spock describing her anxiety because she might not be giving her son enough affection. She wondered whether she or her child needed more help.

▲ **BEST-SELLING CHILD CARE BOOK**

Some experts on childhood asserted that Spock's permissive methods led to a generation of young people in the next decade who were used to getting their own way.

it meant having the "right" type of family life and belonging to the "right" clubs and religious groups. Social critics complained that Americans were in danger of losing their individuality.

■ Changes in Family Life

During the 1950s there were renewed social pressures on women to remain at home. Women's magazines ran articles such as "Should I Stop Work When We Marry?" and "The Business of Running a Home." The immensely popular *Pocket Book of Baby and Child Care* by Dr. Benjamin Spock said that raising children was more important and rewarding than the extra money or satisfaction that a woman might get from a job. Many women who had gone to college or had careers traded their aspirations and jobs for marriage and motherhood. The number of women who worked

continued to rise, but women lost ground in the workplace. They were still paid less than men for doing the same work. They were also shut out of better jobs with higher salaries.

After World War II, more women dropped out of school and married at an early age. The nation's birthrate increased so rapidly that people refer to the period between 1945 and 1961 as the "baby boom." During the baby boom, more than 65 million children were born in the United States.

Parents in the prosperous 1950s wanted their children to have all the things that they had not been able to have during the Depression and war years. They gave their children an increasing amount of material goods and emphasized the benefits of living the "good life." Parents also allowed their children greater freedom than they themselves had known as youngsters. Critics pointed to this new "permissiveness" as the major cause of the rise in juvenile delinquency.

▲ WATCHING TELEVISION The most popular of the 1950s television shows were comedies, variety shows, and "Westerns" starring Roy Rogers (above), Hopalong Cassidy, and other stars. **Why were some people worried about the effects of watching television?**

■ The Impact of Television

One of the symbols of the prosperity of the 1950s was the television set. In 1945 fewer than 1 in every 20,000 people had a television. But within a few years, televisions were everywhere, and they were almost as common as telephones.

Beginning with the election of 1952, television brought national politics into American living rooms. There were televised broadcasts of political party conventions in which not only the public speeches but the goings-on in committee meetings were recorded. During the campaign, both the Republican party and the Democratic party spent millions on television advertising and broadcasts. Although television stirred greater interest in voting, it also posed disturbing questions. Would television give an unfair advantage to the candidate who used television most effectively and who could afford to buy the most airtime?

Some critics also worried that television would have a negative effect on American culture. In the early 1950s, George Gallup, one of the country's first pollsters, voiced concern that:

❝ *[O]ne of the real threats to America's future place in the world is a citizenry which daily elects to be entertained and not informed.* ❞

Supported by advertisers trying to reach the widest possible audience, television programs often appealed to the lowest common denominator of public taste. In order to avoid offending potential customers, advertisers would not buy time on programs that dealt with controversial issues. As a result, television furnished entertainment that was intended "to fix the attention but not engage the mind."

Yet the 1950s has often been called the "Golden Age of Television." Many of the country's most talented writers, comedians, musicians, and actors flocked to the new medium. There they could reach an audience of millions.

Section 3 ★ Review

Checking for Understanding

1. **Identify** John Kenneth Galbraith, Jonas Salk, Benjamin Spock, baby boom.

2. **Define** automation.

3. **Discuss** changes that occurred in American life as a result of abundance, affluence, and the growth of technology.

4. **Report** how minority groups were adversely affected by pressures to conform.

Critical Thinking

5. **Analyzing Results** Examine the ways the television and the automobile changed the American lifestyle during the 1950s. How would your life be different without them?

▲ CHUCK BERRY

◀ ELVIS PRESLEY, ROCK-AND-ROLL STAR OF THE 1950s

Origins of Rock and Roll

During the Eisenhower years, many teenagers rebelled against the pressure to conform by rejecting the mellow pop music favored by their parents. Teens of the 1950s preferred the heavily accented beats and repetitious lyrics of rock and roll.

Rock and roll developed in the mid-1950s. It was a derivation of the rhythm and blues that African American musicians had created for black audiences years before. It also often had some elements of country music. In rock and roll, the tempo was quicker, the accented beats were moved, and electrically amplified instruments—mostly guitars—were used.

Because rock and roll was such a departure from the sentimental love songs of the past, it shocked and dismayed many parents. Teenagers, however, were sold. One of the first rock hits, recorded in 1955, was Bill Haley and the Comets'

Rock Around the Clock, which sold 17 million copies. In 1956 Elvis Presley came on the rock scene. In his performances he moved to the beat of the music. Presley set the musical style for a decade. The lyrics of most rock-and-roll music remained about love, although some writers and performers, most notably Chuck Berry, treated the subject with wit and humor.

Making the Music Connection

1. How did rock-and-roll music evolve?
2. Why did rock and roll shock and dismay parents?

Linking Past and Present

3. What conflicts exist in rock and roll today?

★★★★★★★★★★★★★★★★★★★★★★★★★★★

Foreign Policy

Setting the Scene

Section Focus

In the 1950s affluence at home contrasted sharply with political upheaval abroad. Forces were changing the international landscape. The Eisenhower administration aggressively waged a campaign against communism. Fully aware of the consequences of nuclear war, Eisenhower attempted to manage international conflict through cooperative alliances.

LIFE — John Glenn's Personal Album — MAKING OF A BRAVE MAN — ASTRONAUT JOHN GLENN — FEBRUARY 2, 1962

◀ ASTRONAUT JOHN GLENN

Objectives

After studying this section, you should be able to

★ discuss Eisenhower's approach to foreign policy and the Eisenhower Doctrine.

★ describe how the fear of nuclear war affected the cold war.

★ discuss why American relations with Latin America were poor in the 1950s.

Key Term

covert

During the 1950s the Eisenhower administration labored to contain communism, particularly in newly independent nations in Asia and Africa. Eisenhower used diplomacy, military power, and covert activities to achieve these goals.

President Eisenhower and Secretary of State John Foster Dulles (DUH•luhs) expanded the nation's network of alliances in order to contain communism. In Western Europe, the United States took a leading role in NATO. In Southeast Asia, the United States helped to create the Southeast Asian Treaty Organization (SEATO). In the Middle East, the United States counted on the cooperation of the Central Treaty Organization (CENTO), and in Latin America, the United States promoted the Organization of American States (OAS). These alliances created a formidable counterbalance to the influence of the Soviet Union.

■ The Influence of Dulles

President Eisenhower's foreign policy was greatly influenced by Dulles. After serving in the United States Senate in the late 1940s, Dulles had years of experience in high-level diplomacy, particularly with Asian nations. Secretary Dulles favored a vigorous foreign policy, denouncing Truman's "containment" policy as inadequate. Instead, he advocated "liberation" of Eastern European nations that were under Soviet domination:

❝ *If our policy is to stay where we are, we will be driven back. It is only by keeping alive the hope of liberation, by taking advantage of that wherever opportunity arises, that we will end this terrible peril which dominates the world. . . .* **❞**

Dulles threatened "massive retaliation" against communist aggression. "If you are scared to go to the brink [of nuclear war], you are lost," he said. Accordingly, the Department of Defense reduced the size of the regular army and increased its nuclear arsenal.

Eisenhower tempered Dulles's tough stance and took a more cautious approach. He insisted that "there is no alternative to peace." A nuclear war might well mean the end of civilization. Therefore, the Eisenhower administration continued Truman's policy of containment.

■ War and Peace in Asia

Containing communism became a global challenge for Eisenhower. In Asia the end of one conflict was followed by the start of another one.

End of the Korean War

Carrying out his campaign promise, Eisenhower went to Korea in December 1952. Peace negotiations to end the Korean War, however, seemed to go nowhere. Exasperated, Eisenhower threatened the Communists with possible use of nuclear weapons. Finally in July 1953, after long and bloody fighting, the United Nations Command and the North Koreans reached a settlement. Korea was divided along a line close to the 38th parallel.

Southeast Asia

The United States then was faced with a new problem in Southeast Asia. After Japan surrendered Indochina in 1945, France tried to regain control of its colonies. The people, however, wanted to rule themselves. Ho Chi Minh, a Communist, headed an independence movement called the Vietminh to drive the French from Vietnam, one of the countries of Indochina. The United States stayed out of the fighting but supplied weapons and supplies to the French.

In 1954 the Vietminh surrounded French troops at Dien Bien Phu. The French asked the United States to bomb communist positions. Eisenhower believed that a French defeat might lead to communist domination of all of Southeast Asia.

Secretary Dulles favored giving military support to France. But when Eisenhower could get no support from the leaders of Congress or from other Western nations, he decided to stay out of the war. Dien Bien Phu fell in May 1954, and the French soon withdrew from Indochina.

Visualizing History ▲ EISENHOWER AND DULLES President Eisenhower delegated much of the conduct of foreign affairs to his secretary of state, John Foster Dulles (left). *What policy did Dulles favor to fight communist aggression?*

Visualizing History

▲ THE UNITED STATES AND IRAN Shah Mohammad Reza Pahlavi came to power in Iran in 1953 with the help of secret American funds. He was later overthrown during the Iranian revolution of 1979. *Why did Eisenhower involve the CIA in Iran?*

At a conference in Geneva, Switzerland, in 1954, Vietnam was divided along the 17th parallel. North of that line, Ho Chi Minh's communist forces took control. To the south, a United States-supported government under Ngo Dinh Diem was set up. Diem's regime was dictatorial, inefficient, and unpopular. Communist-supported guerrillas began to fight against Diem's government. The United States provided most of the money for South Vietnam's defense. President Eisenhower had avoided war in Vietnam, but he had tied American prestige to the survival of Diem's unpopular and dictatorial government.

■ The Eisenhower Approach

When it came to solving foreign problems, Eisenhower preferred using diplomacy and **covert,** or secret, activities carried out by the Central Intelligence Agency (CIA).

In Iran and Guatemala

In 1953 President Eisenhower became concerned when the Iranian prime minister seized control of the Anglo-American Oil Company. The President feared that Iran was aligning itself with the Soviet Union, which would endanger oil supplies to Western nations. Under Eisenhower's orders, the CIA secretly funded a successful revolt by the young shah of Iran. Later Iran signed an agreement allowing United States, British, and French companies to share in Iranian oil production.

In 1954 the CIA helped to remove another unfriendly government. The Guatemalan government of Colonel Jacobo Arbenz Guzman had seized property of the American-owned United Fruit Company. The United States learned that Guzman was getting weapons from communist nations. Concerned that Guatemala would become a communist foothold in Latin America, the Eisenhower administration funded a coup that overthrew the government.

In both Iran and Guatemala, the revolutions appeared to have been inspired from within the nation. Only later did people learn of the CIA's role.

Secretary Dulles believed the events in Vietnam, Iran, and Guatemala were evidence of the Soviet Union's intention to spread communism. He argued that newly emerging nations should choose sides in the worldwide struggle between communism and democracy.

"Third World" Neutrality

In 1955 representatives from 29 Asian and African states met and signed an agreement calling for racial equality and self-determination. Two thousand delegates, from countries containing more than half the world's population, saw themselves as the "Third World." They declared their intention to remain independent of both the "First World"—the West—and the "Second World"—the Soviet Union.

The policy of neutralism was hotly debated. Some observers compared neutralism to isolationism and defended it as necessary for new and comparatively weak nations. Others attacked neutralism. Secretary Dulles took the position that no nation had the right to remain neutral in a conflict between "tyranny and freedom."

■ Middle East Powder Keg

During the 1950s the United States was drawn into the affairs of the Middle East. Before World War II, American businesses had begun to exploit the area's rich oil supplies. After the war the United States became increasingly dependent on Mideast oil. Americans were anxious to protect this oil supply. Many Americans also were interested in the survival of Israel, established in 1948 as a Jewish homeland.

The Middle East was like a "powder keg ready to explode." Arab nations believed that Israel was on land belonging to the Palestinians. They threatened to destroy Israel. Also, deep divisions existed among the Arab nations. Poverty and discontent were widespread. Finally, Soviet expansion posed a threat to Western oil supplies.

The first explosion came in 1956 in Egypt. Egypt's President Gamal Abdel Nasser was anxious to gain military superiority over the Jewish state. To get weapons, Egypt signed a commercial treaty with the Soviet Union, exchanging cotton—Egypt's major cash crop—for tanks and guns. The United States had tried to forge friendly relations with Egypt by offering to loan the nation money to build a giant dam across the Nile River. But Nasser's overtures toward the People's Republic of China and the Soviet bloc forced Dulles to cancel the loan. Nasser responded by seizing the Suez Canal in July 1956.

The British, French, and Israelis decided to attack Egypt and reclaim the Suez Canal, which provided a vital trade link between Europe, the Middle East, and Asia. Acting independently of the United States, they invaded Egypt in October.

The world seemed on the verge of another major war. During a heated debate in the United Nations, the United States voted with the Soviet Union to condemn the actions of Israel, Great Britain, and France. This pressure forced the three nations to agree to withdraw from Egypt.

The Suez crisis greatly embarrassed the United States. Three of its strongest allies had acted alone. The affair might have shattered the Western alliance if Soviet action to crush the Hungarian revolution had not persuaded them to close ranks again.

▲ NASSER AND THE SUEZ CRISIS
Warfare in the Middle East was close at hand after Egyptian leader Nasser seized the Suez Canal. Then Egypt was invaded by Britain, France, and Israel. *What caused Britain, France, and Israel to withdraw?*

▲ CONFLICT IN HUNGARY The Hungarian revolt began when workers and students demonstrated for reform in 1956. Here, Hungarian citizens capture a Soviet tank in strife-torn Budapest. *How did the revolt end?*

The Eisenhower Doctrine

After the Suez crisis, the Soviets supported Egypt and offered to help build a new dam, the Aswan, across the Nile. President Eisenhower worried that the Soviets would gain new strength in the region. In January 1957, Eisenhower asked Congress to give him authority to use United States military forces to defend any Middle Eastern country that requested help against the forces of "international communism." Congress overwhelmingly approved the so-called Eisenhower Doctrine.

A year later the president of Lebanon asked Eisenhower to send troops to protect his government. He feared that Nasser and the Soviet Union might encourage a revolt in Lebanon.

In July 1958, American soldiers entered Lebanon. American troops remained in Lebanon until new elections established a stronger government. By taking this action, the United States showed that it intended to play a leading role in the Middle East. Yet the basic problems of the Middle East—poverty, rivalry and strife, and the threat of communist aggression—still defied solution.

The NATO Alliance

After President Eisenhower took office in 1953, he attempted to strengthen NATO under a unified command. But France was fearful of German resurgence and strongly opposed the plan. Western defenses were strengthened, however, when West Germany was allowed to rearm and join NATO.

The NATO alliance faced other difficulties. Europeans had mixed feelings about the United States. European Socialists and Communists regarded the United States as a materialistic nation where workers were exploited in order to increase the profits of a few great trusts. Conservatives believed Europe would be Americanized. In Britain and France, many people blamed the United States for their nation's loss of power in the world. But Soviet aggression persuaded Western Europe and the United States to maintain a common front.

Political uprisings in two of its satellites prompted the Soviet Union to reassert its control over Eastern Europe. In October 1956, anti-Soviet riots broke out in some Polish cities. The Soviet Union ultimately agreed to Polish demands for more freedoms. In Hungary, however, what began as peaceful protests ended with open fighting. When communist leaders tried to put down the unrest, the Hungarians turned against them. On October 30, 1956, after less than a week of fighting, Budapest radio told the Hungarians: "You have won!" For five days jubilant Hungarians tasted freedom. Then on November 4, Soviet tanks and troops rolled through Budapest and overwhelmed its defenders. In the United States there was sympathy for the Hungarians, but little could be done without risking war.

■ Trouble in Latin America

While the United States worried about communist gains in Europe, Asia, and Africa, it ignored Latin America. There, the great poverty of the majority of the people and the concentration of land and power in the hands of a few created a breeding ground for political instability.

Latin Americans had good cause to believe they were "forgotten neighbors." They saw the United States pouring billions of dollars into remaking Europe's economy and strengthening weak governments in Asia. Yet Latin America received little United States foreign aid.

In 1958 Vice President Nixon made a good-will visit to Latin America. In some of the countries he visited, Nixon faced hostile demonstrations. In Peru and Venezuela, mobs threw stones and beat sticks against Nixon's car. This shocking attack on the Vice President brought home to people of the United States their neglect of Latin America's problems.

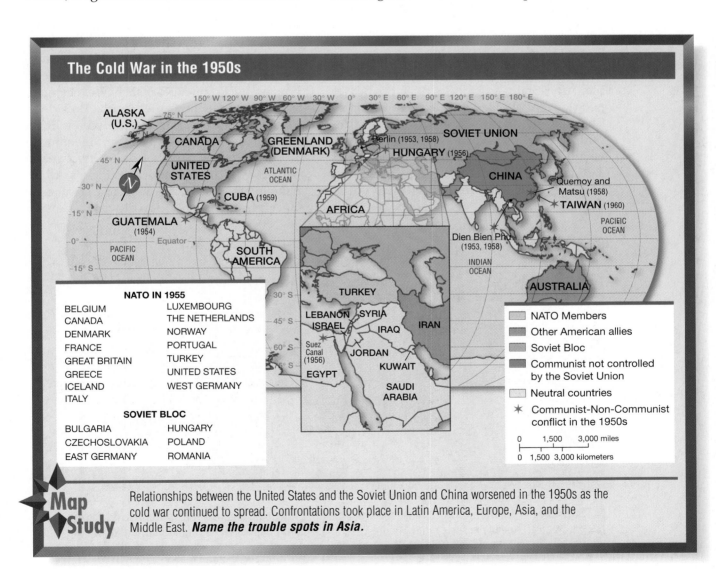

The Cold War in the 1950s

NATO IN 1955

BELGIUM	LUXEMBOURG
CANADA	THE NETHERLANDS
DENMARK	NORWAY
FRANCE	PORTUGAL
GREAT BRITAIN	TURKEY
GREECE	UNITED STATES
ICELAND	WEST GERMANY
ITALY	

SOVIET BLOC

BULGARIA	HUNGARY
CZECHOSLOVAKIA	POLAND
EAST GERMANY	ROMANIA

- NATO Members
- Other American allies
- Soviet Bloc
- Communist not controlled by the Soviet Union
- Neutral countries
- ★ Communist-Non-Communist conflict in the 1950s

0   1,500   3,000 miles
0 1,500 3,000 kilometers

Map Study

Relationships between the United States and the Soviet Union and China worsened in the 1950s as the cold war continued to spread. Confrontations took place in Latin America, Europe, Asia, and the Middle East. *Name the trouble spots in Asia.*

Events in Cuba further soured United States-Latin American relations. In 1959 a resistance movement headed by Fidel Castro forced the resignation of Cuba's corrupt dictator, Fulgencio Batista. Castro became a popular figure in the United States, and there was hope that the two nations would establish friendly relations. But American enthusiasm for Castro waned when he made friendly moves toward the Communists, denounced the United States, and seized private property. Castro also sought the military support of the Soviet Union. In response, President Eisenhower cut the quota of sugar the United States imported from Cuba and broke off relations with the Castro government.

■ Thaws in the Cold War

During the Eisenhower administration, the cold war spread to all continents. Yet there were signs that a "thaw" was possible. After Stalin's death in 1953, the Soviet people were allowed a little more freedom. The new premier, Nikita Khrushchev, denounced Stalin as a brutal tyrant. The Soviets now talked of peaceful coexistence and said that war in the atomic age would be so horrible that "the living will envy the dead."

In July 1955, Eisenhower met with the leaders of the Soviet Union, France, and Great Britain in Geneva, Switzerland. He made a strong plea for nuclear disarmament, saying that it would:

❝ *. . . ease the fears of war in the anxious hearts of people everywhere. . . . It would make [it] possible for every nation, great and small, developed and less developed, to advance the standards of living of its people. . . .* ❞

The summit, however, settled nothing. In 1958 tensions between the superpowers escalated once more, this time over the divided city of Berlin. The Soviets threatened to cut off Western access to Berlin unless the West recognized the East German government. When the crisis cooled down, both sides made new efforts to reduce world tensions. In 1959 Vice President Nixon and Premier Khrushchev exchanged visits. Khrushchev met with President Eisenhower at Camp David, where they made plans for a second summit meeting.

The new thaw was short-lived. Two weeks before the second summit meeting was to be held, in May 1960, an American U-2 surveillance plane was shot down over the Soviet

▲ **COLD WAR RELATIONS** During the era of the cold war, UN forces were sent to keep peace in Africa, the Middle East, and other hot spots. *What signs pointed toward a thaw in the cold war?*

Eisenhower's Farewell Address

The U-2 incident and the failure of East-West negotiations brought Eisenhower's years in office to a frustrating close. After the death of Secretary Dulles in 1959, Eisenhower took over more of the direction of foreign policy himself. He traveled widely in Europe, Asia, the Middle East, and Latin America to promote "peace and goodwill" and a "better understanding of America." But he was unable to lessen the tensions of the cold war and the threat of nuclear confrontation.

Still, Eisenhower remained a popular President, as near to a "father figure" as any President since George Washington. Like Washington, Eisenhower gave a farewell address. In it he warned against the overpowering influence of the military-industrial complex:

▲ U-2 PILOT GARY POWERS

Union. The CIA had sent it to spy on and photograph Soviet nuclear sites and missile bases. Khrushchev denounced Eisenhower as a prisoner of the "war mongers" and refused to take part in the meeting. Relations between East and West once again turned colder.

66 *We must never let the weight of this combination (of the military and industry) endanger our liberties or democratic processes. We should take nothing for granted. Only an alert and knowledgeable citizenry can compel the proper meshing of the huge industrial and military machinery of defense with our peaceful methods and goals, so that security and liberty may prosper together.* 99

The President's message was impressive because it came from a man who had spent most of his life as a soldier.

Section 4 ★ Review

Checking for Understanding

1. **Identify** John Foster Dulles, Ho Chi Minh, Gamal Abdel Nasser, SEATO, CENTO, OAS, Fulgencio Batista, Fidel Castro, U-2.

2. **Define** covert.

3. **Describe** the Eisenhower administration's foreign policy.

4. **State** reasons why European attitudes toward the United States changed in the 1950s.

Critical Thinking

5. **Locating Evidence** What event described in this section supports the idea that the containment policy might result in supporting unpopular or repressive regimes?

Using Vocabulary

Use these vocabulary words in a statement about the influence of technology on business and agriculture.

agribusiness   **automation**

Reviewing Facts

1. **State** reasons why Americans elected Ike by overwhelming majorities in 1952 and 1956.

2. **Explain** the Eisenhower administration's dilemma regarding the farm problem.

3. **Show** how Eisenhower policies toward health and welfare programs and big business reflected his middle-course economic policy.

4. **Identify** technological advances of the 1950s that contributed to the strength of the American economy.

5. **Describe** the effects of economic growth and affluence on American life.

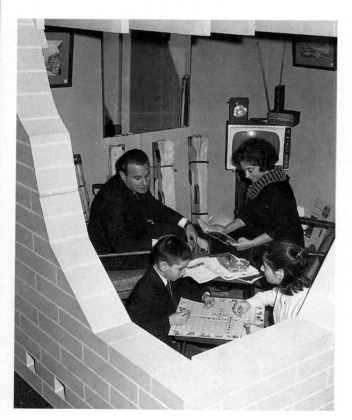

6. **Cite** the differences between Dulles's and Eisenhower's approaches to foreign policy.

7. **Discuss** how the following groups were affected by the pressure to conform: (1) middle-class families, (2) African Americans, (3) women.

8. **Speculate** about the effects of the nuclear threat on the conduct of the cold war.

Understanding Concepts

International Leadership

1. If you were to examine Eisenhower's leadership style as commander of NATO forces, how would you expect it to differ from his international leadership style as President? Why?

2. What is your opinion of Eisenhower's use of covert operations to remove unfriendly foreign governments? Explain.

Economic Growth

3. What factors stimulated economic growth in the 1950s?

4. How did the growth of the television industry both reflect and stimulate economic growth?

Critical Thinking

1. **Demonstrating Reasoned Judgment**   Find an example of Eisenhower's actions that supports both national security and global security. Did he take any steps in the interest of national security at the possible expense of global security? Support your answer.

2. **Locating Examples**   What lifestyle changes reflected the "economy of abundance" during the 1950s?

3. **Analyzing Photographs**   Study the photograph of the bomb shelter on this page, then answer the questions that follow.

   a. What do you think the photographer was trying to show with this picture?

   b. Do you think this photograph was part of an advertisement, a news story, or for another purpose? Explain.

Writing About History

Description

Imagine you are a journalist in 1961 just after Eisenhower left office. Write a profile of Eisenhower for a popular publication, focusing on his personal traits, his leadership style, or both. For details, refer to biographies and reference books covering the history of the 1950s.

Cooperative Learning

Working in a group of four, research life in the United States during the Eisenhower administration. Divide the research assignments so that different members are responsible for finding information about news events, movies, television shows, popular music, theater, art achievements, literary publications, advances in science and technology, sports events, and fashion trends for those years. Have members record their findings. Combine the reports to form a history of the Eisenhower years.

Social Studies Skills

Identifying Trends

Tables can draw attention to both the similarities and differences between groups. An analysis of a table may enable you to identify trends and patterns between groups.

To identify a trend, you must carefully compare a table's statistics. Look at each column's data. Look at each row. Are there similarities between columns? Between rows? Are any patterns apparent? What generalizations can you make?

Practicing the Skill

Use the table to answer these questions.

1. Compare income for white families between 1950 and 1960. What income is earned by the largest percent of white families in 1950? 1955? 1960?

2. Compare income distribution for nonwhite families between 1950 and 1960. What income is earned by the largest percent of nonwhite families in 1950? 1955? 1960?

3. Write a generalization that identifies the trend in distribution for minority and white families.

Income Distribution by Families

	1950		1955		1960	
More than $15,000			1.5	—	4.1	.6
$12,000–$14,999	3.5	.3	2.0	.3	4.6	1.6
$10,000–$11,999			3.2	.3	6.6	2.7
$7,000–$9,999	6.1	1.6	14.0	3.1	21.3	8.7
$5,000–$6,999	15.1	3.4	23.3	10.6	24.5	15.4
$3,000–$4,999	35.7	17.8	30.3	28.3	19.9	24.5
Less than $3,000	39.4	76.9	25.7	57.3	19.2	46.5

☐ Whites
☐ African Americans and Others

Source: *Historical Statistics of the United States: Colonial Times to 1970* (1975).

4. What percent of white families earned more than $15,000 in 1960? Nonwhite families?

5. How does income change for most families in the 1950s? State the trend.

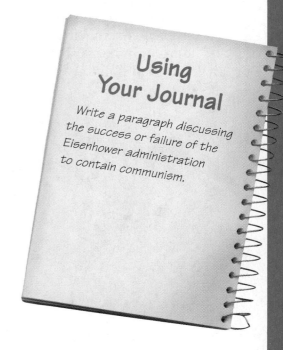

Using Your Journal

Write a paragraph discussing the success or failure of the Eisenhower administration to contain communism.

Cultural Kaleidoscope

A Changing Society

Innovations

From important discoveries and innovations like computers, penicillin, open heart surgery, and the polio vaccine to more mundane accomplishments like TV dinners, the period from the 1930s to the 1960s was a time of discovery and unbounded imagination. New technology transformed the nature of work and helped Americans enjoy more leisure time. At the same time, the number of available leisure activities increased. By the 1950s Americans were enjoying a standard of living far beyond any they had previously known.

Progress in electronics began to revolutionize home entertainment. Probably no form of entertainment has matched the effects of television. Developed in the 1930s, television went on the market in the late 1940s. Fewer than 1 million households had a set in 1949. Within four years, the number had soared to 20 million.

First used in America in the 1930s, credit cards grew in popularity during the 1950s when computers allowed for fast and accurate billing.

The electric iron, such as this 1936 model, became a necessary domestic appliance.

With new means of refrigeration widely available after World War II, Americans could store quantities of food for months on end. By 1956, 9 of 10 American families owned a refrigerator. Other symbols of the affluent society: by 1956, 3 of 4 families owned at least one auto, 3 out of 5 owned their own home. In 1945 only 9,000 private swimming pools were in use. In 1957 alone more than 50,000 pools were installed.

Refrigerator-Freezers!

THE FINAL FROST BARRIER!

IT'S HERE! A FROST-PROOF FOOD FREEZER! NO FROST! NO FROST-LOCKED FOODS! NO DEFROSTING!

You'll feel like a queen . . .
* Trim Upright Freezer with award-winning Sheer Look and embossed white-bright Lacework Styling.
* Takes so little floor space—only 32 inches wide—yet this 16 cu. ft. Frost-Proof Imperial Freezer sho...

* Serve family meals in minutes. Be always ready for gues...
* Shop once a week. Enjoy bulk buying that cuts fo...
* Cook and bake in quantity. Enjoy "free" da...
* Freeze leftovers, like stew, turkey, cake...
* Have fun freezing your own fruits a...

IN MIND!

SPAM A NEW HORMEL MEAT NET WEIGHT INCLUDING JUICES 12 OZ

Between the 1920s and the advent of the television age, millions of Americans learned about the important events of the day from radio. By the mid-1930s, two-thirds of American homes had at least one radio—less than half that many had telephones.

More and more Americans, it seems, were eating canned foods. Hormel's Spiced Ham, better known as Spam, quickly established a strong position. Part of the impetus came during World War II when Spam's price and shelf life made it a staple of the soldier's diet. In Korea, Spam is considered an imported luxury item.

UNIT NINE DIGEST

Chapter 28

The New Deal

Franklin D. Roosevelt's New Deal was a two-part program of emergency measures and long-range planning with three specific aims—recovery from the Depression, relief for victims of the Depression, and reform of the nation's economic system.

During Roosevelt's first days in office, Congress enacted an unprecedented number of new programs. The second phase of the New Deal emphasized social reform rather than short-term emergency measures. Out of these efforts came large-scale public works programs and a Social Security system.

Roosevelt won reelection in 1936 by a landslide. However, problems with the Supreme Court and other setbacks in Congress slowed the pace of the New Deal. But by then its programs already had altered the role of government in American life.

Chapter 29

World War II

During FDR's first and second administrations, the Good Neighbor policy committed the United States to a policy of nonintervention in Latin America. In Europe, FDR recognized the Soviet Union and sought to maintain neutral relations with other nations.

When war in Europe broke out in 1939, German victories prompted the United States to aid the Allied nations of Britain and France. In 1941, after Japanese planes bombed Pearl Harbor, the United States declared war on Japan and Germany. For the second time in 25 years, the American economy converted to war production and transformed the nation's way of life.

By the time an ailing Roosevelt was reelected to a fourth term, Germany and Japan had suffered major defeats on all fronts. Germany surrendered in May 1945. Japan surrendered after American planes dropped atomic bombs on Hiroshima and Nagasaki. Before the war ended, the United Nations formed in hopes of maintaining international peace and cooperation.

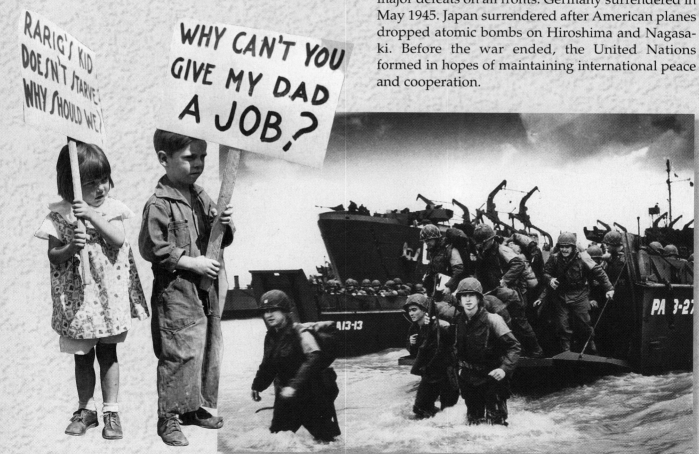

Chapter 30

The Cold War

After World War II, the Soviet Union drew an "iron curtain" between Eastern Europe and the rest of Europe. An intense war of words, rivalry, and confrontation soon developed between the West and the Soviet Union.

Western fear that communism would spread led to a policy of containment. The Marshall Plan also gave massive economic aid to war-torn Western Europe. The United States, Canada, and nations of Western Europe established the North Atlantic Treaty Organization (NATO); Eastern European communist countries responded with the Warsaw Pact.

Meanwhile, the cold war spread to Asia. In 1949 Mao Zedong established a communist government in China, despite American efforts to prevent it. In Korea, Americans fought a "hot war" to stop a communist takeover of the peninsula.

At home the Truman administration pushed for economic and social reform. Inflation was rising, and labor resorted to strikes to increase wages. Fear generated by the cold war led to a search for Communists in the federal government.

In the early 1950s, the country began a long period of economic prosperity. The growing economy created millions of new jobs. Encouraged by their new economic strength, African Americans began to lobby for their civil rights.

Chapter 31

Search for Stability

In 1953, Dwight D. Eisenhower brought a new style of leadership to the White House. Although friendly to corporations, Eisenhower also expanded New Deal programs. Despite inflation and a brief recession, businesses and working men and women prospered. Farmers, however, did not fare well.

For many Americans, affluence and a new confidence in the future came with economic growth. A new way of life evolved as families moved from the cities to the suburbs and wage earners commuted to work.

Under Eisenhower, America's cold war containment policy continued through diplomacy, aid, and covert operations. His efforts to lessen tensions and reduce the Soviet nuclear threat, however, failed.

Understanding Unit Themes

1. **American Democracy**   How did the role of government in American democracy change during the Depression and the New Deal? What changes persist to the present?

2. **Civil Rights and Liberties**   Throughout the 1930s and 1940s, women gained new employment opportunities and a recognized place in the workforce. How do you account for the ground they lost in the 1950s?

3. **Conflict and Cooperation**   How does the purpose of the United Nations differ from that of NATO, the Warsaw Pact, and the alliances of World War II?

4. **U.S. Role in World Affairs**   Describe United States efforts to contain the spread of communism worldwide from 1948–1960. What were the results of these efforts?

UNIT TEN
REDEFINING AMERICA
1954–PRESENT

★★

▲ VIETNAM VETERAN'S HAT

History AND ART

Mural on Building
Davenport, Iowa

Vivid images abound in this colorful mural commemorating American leaders and important events.

892

American society from the mid-1950s to the present has been described as a roller coaster. Americans were taken to new heights of optimism and confidence but lows of doubt and frustration as well. In addition, growing awareness of new technology redefined the way Americans lived and worked.

Themes

- Civil Rights and Liberties
- Conflict and Cooperation
- Cultural Diversity
- Role in World Affairs

Key Events

- Desegregation in public schools
- Kennedy's assassination
- War in Vietnam
- Watergate scandal
- Camp David Peace Accords
- Persian Gulf War
- Congress approves NAFTA

Major Issues

- The growing civil rights movement opens the political process for thousands of Americans.
- Involvement in Vietnam polarizes Americans at home and tarnishes the nation's image abroad.
- Illegal activities by high-level government officials result in the Watergate scandal.
- Democratic movements lead to the end of the Soviet Union.
- The United States and allies liberate Kuwait after Iraqi invasion.
- America seeks to redefine its role in the new world order and meet rising challenges at home.

▲ TALL SHIPS, PART OF BICENTENNIAL CELEBRATION

◀ POLITICAL CAMPAIGN BUTTONS

Portfolio Project

Make a poster for an imaginary benefit concert similar to the "Live Aid" concert. Select a topic from the leading challenges facing America in the late 1990s. Make sure to note this topic on the poster, along with the location of the concert and what artists will be performing.

Global Perspectives

★★★★★★★ ★★★

The World

		1950				1965	
Asia and Oceania			**1954** *French are defeated in Vietnam*				**1966** *China's Cultural Revolution begins*
Europe						**1961** *Berlin Wall built*	
Africa					◄ **1960** *"Year of Africa" —many countries become independent*		
South America							
North and Central America					**1959** *St. Lawrence Seaway opens*		

The United States

		1950				1965	
Pacific and Northwest				◄ **1959** *Alaska and Hawaii become states*			
Southeast			**1955** *Rosa Parks inspires Montgomery bus boycott*			**1965** *Freedom March from Selma to Montgomery*	
Midwest			**1954** Brown *v.* Board of Education *decision*				
Southwest						◄ **1966** *First artificial heart implanted*	
Atlantic Northeast		1950				1965	

Linking Across TIME

The United States has long been known as a nation of immigrants. Throughout its history, people from other countries came to its shores seeking a better way of life. In the late 1980s, the major sources of immigration to the United States were Asia, the Caribbean, and Latin America. Among the countries that sent the most immigrants were China, Colombia, the Dominican Republic, Ecuador, Guyana, Haiti, India, Jamaica, the Philippines, and South Korea. At the same time, however, immigrants came from another 150 countries. It is not surprising then that some people have called the United States the world in microcosm, or miniature.

1975 *American military evacuate Saigon*

1980

1995

1993 *Israel-PLO treaty signed*

◀ 1989 *Communism crumbles in Eastern Europe*

1994 *War continues between Bosnia and Serbia*

1993 *Apartheid ends in South Africa*

1974 *Isabel Perón becomes president in Argentina*

1982 *Argentina invades Falkland Islands*

◀ 1983 *American troops invade Grenada*

1994 *Haitian leader Aristide returns from exile*

▼ 1989 *Exxon Valdez oil spill in Alaska*

1994 *Northridge earthquake hits Southern California*

1980 *Michigan's unemployment rate is nation's highest*

1990 *Navajo nation elects its first president*

1974 *President Nixon resigns office of the presidency*

1987 *Worst Wall Street stock market plunge in history*

1980

1995

CHAPTER 32

★★

The Civil Rights Era
1954–1975

▶ **CELEBRATING KWANZAA,
HOLIDAY BASED ON TRADI-
TIONAL AFRICAN FESTIVAL**

Setting the Scene

Focus

During the 1950s, African Americans rebelled against their second-class status. The ranks of civil rights advocates swelled, and African Americans, joined by some white liberals, began following the nonviolent ideas of Dr. Martin Luther King, Jr. They fought for equality first in the South and eventually in the North. Met with violence at every turn, many African Americans abandoned King's ideas and developed new philosophies. Whatever their ideas, these civil rights activists inspired hope to other minorities.

Journal Notes

What was life like for civil rights activists during the 1950s and 1960s? Note details about it in your journal as you read the chapter.

Concepts to Understand

★ Why efforts to gain civil rights created an effective movement for change
★ How the civil rights movement led to social upheaval

Read to Discover . . .

★ legislation that addressed civil rights issues.
★ the kind of impact the civil rights movement had on other minorities.

CULTURAL	• **1959** *Jazz pioneer Ornette Coleman releases* The Shape of Jazz	• **1962** *Richard Wright pens* Another Country • **1964** *Dr. King wins Nobel Peace Prize*
	1954	**1960**
POLITICAL	• **1955** *Montgomery bus boycott begins* • **1957** *Congress passes the first civil rights legislation since Reconstruction*	• **1964** *Civil Rights Act is passed* • **1965** *"March for Freedom" begins* • **1965** *Voting Rights Act is passed*

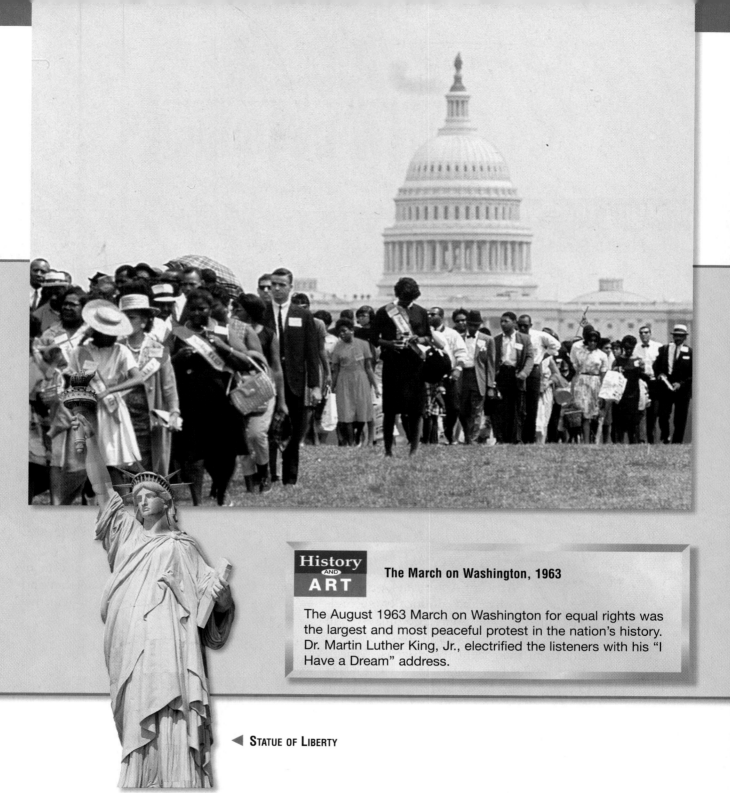

History AND ART

The March on Washington, 1963

The August 1963 March on Washington for equal rights was the largest and most peaceful protest in the nation's history. Dr. Martin Luther King, Jr., electrified the listeners with his "I Have a Dream" address.

◀ STATUE OF LIBERTY

- **1966** Soul on Ice *states Black Panther aims*

- **1967** *Carl Stokes is elected mayor of Cleveland, Ohio*
- **1968** *Martin Luther King, Jr., is assassinated*

1966

- **1972** *Joseph Walker publishes* The River Niger
- **1973** *Toni Morrison publishes* Sula

- **1972** *Congress approves Equal Rights Amendment*

1972

★★★★★★★★★★★★★★★★★★★★★★★★★★★★★★★★★★★★★★

A New Beginning

Setting the Scene

Section Focus

Almost a century after passage of the Fourteenth and Fifteenth amendments, African Americans were still victims of discrimination and segregation. In the South these attitudes were entrenched not only in custom but also in law. The battle to obtain equal rights for African Americans would have to be fought in the courts, in the news media, and in the consciences of the American people. For the civil rights movement, the 1950s marked a new beginning in the ongoing struggle for equality.

Objectives

After studying this chapter, you should be able to

★ discuss the effects of the *Brown* v. *Board of Education* decision.

★ describe major events in the early civil rights movement.

Key Terms

nonviolent resistance, federalized

▶ DR. MARTIN LUTHER KING, JR.

The end of Reconstruction left African Americans economically and politically second-class citizens. The sharecropping system and "Jim Crow" segregation laws worked to deny them their rights as citizens. African American leaders began to work toward restoring their full civil rights in the early decades of the twentieth century, but the movement did not come into full flower until almost 50 years later.

During the 1950s and the early 1960s, African Americans boldly rejected their second-class status and the humiliating practice of forced separation. They fought for equal opportunities in jobs, housing, and education. They fought against segregated schools, buses, and trains; they fought against separate facilities in restaurants, hotels, libraries, and hospitals. They won an important ally when the Supreme Court issued several decisions against racial discrimination. But the main force behind the civil rights movement came from citizens—African American and white—who banded together in an effective protest movement.

■ Brown v. Board of Education

One of the Supreme Court's most significant rulings of the 1950s came in May 1954. Three years earlier, Linda Brown's parents had sued the school board of Topeka, Kansas, for not allowing their daughter to attend an all-white school, miles closer to their home than the segregated elementary school she was assigned to attend.

The Supreme Court ruled in *Brown* v. *Board of Education of Topeka, Kansas* that it was unconstitutional to separate schoolchildren by race. The Brown decision reversed the

Court's decision in *Plessy* v. *Ferguson,* an 1896 ruling that had upheld the constitutionality of "separate but equal" public accommodations. *Plessy* had become the basis for Jim Crow laws and legal segregation in many states.

The Southern Manifesto

The Supreme Court's ruling in *Brown* v. *Board of Education* called for major changes in many states, especially those in the South. Some border states integrated their schools, but the South remained segregated. The governor of Virginia threatened to close the state's public schools and send white children to private schools. A group of 101 southern members of Congress signed a "Southern Manifesto," which called the Court's ruling "a clear abuse of judicial power" and pledged use of "all lawful means to bring about a reversal of this decision."

■ Boycotts and Demonstrations

The decisions of the Warren Court gave legal support to African Americans' struggle for civil rights. But most civil rights battles, particularly in the South, were fought by brave men and women who broke down barriers of segregation one by one.

Rosa Parks Takes a Stand

In December 1955, an African American seamstress from Montgomery, Alabama, became one of the first to take a stand. At the end of the workday, Parks boarded a segregated bus in which all the seats allotted for African Americans were filled; she took a seat in the front, which was reserved for white riders. Because Parks refused to give up her seat, she was arrested.

The arrest of Rosa Parks aroused anger in Montgomery's African American community. Many of its leaders believed that now was the time to challenge Alabama's segregation laws. At a meeting held at the Dexter Avenue Baptist Church, a boycott of the city's buses was called. The 26-year-old minister of the church, Dr. Martin Luther King, Jr., was asked to lead the boycott.

On the day of Rosa Parks's trial, almost all the African American riders who usually took the buses began a nearly year-long boycott. Because a majority of the regular bus riders were African American, the bus company lost much of its business.

▲ **ROSA PARKS** Rosa Parks refused to give up her seat to a white bus rider. She meets with her lawyer after she was charged with breaking the law. ***What actions did civil rights leaders take to protest Parks's arrest?***

School Desegregation

Melba Patillo Beals was one of the African American teenagers who integrated Little Rock's Central High School in the fall of 1957. Despite the danger, Beals felt proud to participate in what she saw even then as a historic happening.

In the following passage, Melba Beals recalls some of her experiences at the formerly all-white high school.

"I went in not through the side doors but up the front stairs, and there was a feeling of pride and hope that yes, this is the United States; yes, there is a reason I salute the flag. . . . The troops were wonderful. . . . [But] they couldn't be with us everywhere. . . . We'd be showering in gym and someone would turn your shower on to scalding. You'd be walking out to the volleyball court and someone would break a bottle and trip you on the bottle . . . first you're in pain, then you're angry, then you try to fight back, . . . And then you just mellow out and you realize that survival is day-to-day and you start to grasp the depth of the human spirit, you start to understand your own ability to cope no matter what. That is the greatest lesson I learned."

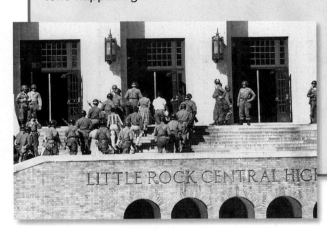

LITTLE ROCK CENTRAL HIGH

◀ **CENTRAL HIGH SCHOOL, LITTLE ROCK, ARKANSAS, 1957**

Rosa Parks was convicted and fined $10. Dr. King and other African American leaders were arrested for sponsoring an "illegal boycott." Then, in November 1956, the Supreme Court ruled that segregation in public transportation was illegal. The bus company ended its policy of segregation. The African American citizens of Montgomery, assured of equal treatment, resumed riding the buses. The Montgomery bus boycott galvanized the civil rights movement, and in Martin Luther King, Jr., that movement found an inspiring leader.

King Preaches Nonviolence

African American churches and their ministers took the lead in organizing the civil rights movement. Dr. King, a Baptist minister, drew from his own faith and also from techniques of the Indian leader Mohandas Gandhi. Like Gandhi, King encouraged the use of **nonviolent resistance,** or peaceful means to effect change. He told people to disobey unjust laws but asked them to love their oppressors and never fight with them even if provoked. He explained that public opinion, not violence, would force authorities to change unjust laws:

> ❝ *Injustice must be exposed, with all the tension its exposure creates, to the light of human conscience and the air of national opinion before it can be cured.* ❞

In 1957, to carry on this nonviolent struggle against discrimination in public places all over the South, King and other African American leaders founded the Southern Christian Leadership Conference (SCLC). In addition to the SCLC and its student branch—the Student Nonviolent Coordinating Committee—there were many other groups organized to promote civil rights.

Among them were such long-established African American organizations as the National Association for the Advancement of Colored People (NAACP), which fought discrimination in many legal cases, including *Brown* v. *Board of Education;* the National Urban League, which established community programs for minorities in cities; and the Congress of Racial Equality (CORE), which worked for economic and political opportunities for African Americans. Dr. King remained at the forefront of the movement as it continued to grow in the 1960s. In 1964 he received the Nobel Peace Prize for his nonviolent leadership.

■ Crisis in Little Rock

Not wanting to create controversy, the Eisenhower administration and Congress refused to pass civil rights legislation. As a result, civil rights groups turned to the courts for settlement of their grievances.

In 1953 Eisenhower appointed Earl Warren as Chief Justice of the United States Supreme Court. Warren began to move the Court toward a more liberal interpretation of the Constitution in decisions on individual rights. Also in 1953 the NAACP brought a number of civil rights cases before the Court. Thurgood Marshall, the NAACP's leading lawyer, wanted the Court to strike down state laws that required racial segregation in public schools. He argued that African American children were not getting the same quality of education as white children.

On May 17, 1954, the Court handed down a historic decision in *Brown* v. *Board of Education of Topeka*. It overturned the 1896 *Plessy* v. *Ferguson* decision that segregation was constitutional so long as equal facilities were provided for both races. The Court declared

❝ *We conclude that in the field of public education, the doctrine of "separate but equal" has no place. Separate educational facilities are inherently unequal.* **❞**

In *Brown* v. *Board of Education of Topeka,* the Supreme Court did not set a deadline for ending segregation. However, in May 1955, the Court called for the implementation of integration "with all deliberate speed."

Civil Rights Legislation

The ruling needed the active support of President Eisenhower, but the President believed that the federal government should remain neutral concerning controversial issues that affected state and local governments. He remarked, "I don't believe you can change the hearts of men with laws and decisions."

In 1957 Congress passed the first civil rights law since Reconstruction. The act created a civil rights division within the Department of Justice and gave the government the power to seek court injunctions against those who denied any citizen's constitutional rights.

Confrontation

In September 1957, the state of Arkansas tested the federal government's policies on civil rights. A federal court had ordered that

 ▲ CRISIS IN LITTLE ROCK Central High School in Little Rock, Arkansas, became the focus of court-ordered desegregation in 1957. After Governor Orval Faubus used the Arkansas National Guard to prevent nine African American students from attending, Eisenhower sent federal troops to Little Rock. *How was the crisis resolved?*

▲ PROTESTING FOR RIGHTS

under the jurisdiction of the federal government, 10,000 members of the Arkansas National Guard to surround the school so that the students could enter safely.

As Daisy Bates, then the president of the Arkansas NAACP, later remembered:

66 . . . the nine [African American] pupils marched solemnly through the doors of Central High School, surrounded by twenty-two soldiers. An Army helicopter circled overhead. Around the massive brick schoolhouse 350 paratroopers stood grimly at attention. . . . Within minutes a world that had been holding its breath learned that the nine pupils . . . had finally entered the 'never-never-land.' 99

nine African American students be admitted to the all-white Central High School in Little Rock, Arkansas. The state's governor, Orval Faubus, defied federal authority and sent National Guard troops to prevent the students from attending.

President Eisenhower tried to persuade Governor Faubus to obey the court order. The governor withdrew the troops, but without their presence the African American students were exposed to an angry mob that threatened them with physical harm. Forced to act to maintain order, Eisenhower sent in 1,000 paratroopers and **federalized,** or put

Troops remained in Little Rock for the rest of the year, however, and Central High School was closed for the 1958–1959 academic year.

As the Eisenhower administration drew to a close, the nation remained racially divided. Custom and years of intimidation kept many African Americans from voting. Between 1957 and 1960, the Justice Department brought only 10 suits to secure voting rights for African Americans. Only 25 percent of African American adults voted in states of the deep South, and only 5 percent in Mississippi. The movement for civil rights was just beginning.

Section 1 ★ Review

Checking for Understanding

1. **Identify** *Brown* v. *Board of Education*, Earl Warren, Southern Manifesto, Rosa Parks, Martin Luther King, Jr.

2. **Define** nonviolent resistance, federalized.

3. **Explain** Martin Luther King's philosophy of nonviolence.

4. **Describe** why Eisenhower sent federal troops into Little Rock.

Critical Thinking

5. **Analyzing a Viewpoint**   How would you evaluate Eisenhower's stand on civil rights? Explain why many African Americans in the South would not be content with this approach.

History AND RELIGION
CONNECTIONS CONNECTIONS

▲ THE BRADFORD SINGERS GOSPEL GROUP

◀ DR. MARTIN LUTHER KING, JR.

African American Churches and the Civil Rights Movement

African Americans in the South had long heard the message of the Christian scriptures that God is on the side of the oppressed. They concluded that if it was true in ancient Israel it could also be true in the American South. From the organization of the Montgomery bus boycott in 1955 until the March on Washington in 1963, African American churches played the central role in devising strategies and mobilizing volunteers for the civil rights movement. The message of the gospel became the message of the movement. The churches called for protest without retaliatory violence, confrontation without conflict.

Many leaders of the Southern Christian Leadership Conference and other organizations were ministers. In 1957 King, Bayard Rustin, and others had founded the SCLC in the wake of the Montgomery bus boycott to work toward full citizenship rights for African Americans and their integration in all aspects of society.

The SCLC took a leading role in the Freedom Rides challenging segregation on public transportation and other public accommodations.

Dr. King's first Southern Christian Leadership Conference drive in the North was launched in Chicago in July 1966 for open housing.

Some of them were arrested for taking part in demonstrations. Dr. Martin Luther King, Jr., himself was arrested repeatedly for demonstrating in Birmingham. In response to a group of Birmingham ministers who criticized King as an "outside agitator" he wrote from jail: ". . . just as the apostle Paul left his village of Tarsus and carried the gospel of Jesus Christ to the far corners of the Greco-Roman world, so am I compelled to carry the gospel of freedom beyond my own hometown."

Making the Religion Connection

1. How was the message of the gospel related to the civil rights movement?

2. Why were civil rights leaders sometimes jailed?

Linking Past and Present

3. How are African American churches involved in politics today?

★★★

Successes and Setbacks

Section Focus

During the Kennedy-Johnson years, there were successes and setbacks for the civil rights movement. Kennedy moved slowly at first. However, violent events soon forced his hand, and he used the federal courts as well as troops to enforce desegregation in the South. Lyndon Johnson continued the former President's policies and succeeded in getting them passed into law.

Objectives

After studying this section, you should be able to

★ describe advances made in civil rights during the Kennedy-Johnson administrations.

★ describe the setbacks and difficulties the civil rights activists faced during the 1960s.

Key Term

sit-in

◀ "IN A FREE GOVERNMENT . . . " BY JACOB LAWRENCE

As the 1960s began, leaders for the civil rights movement—both African Americans and liberal whites—stepped up the tactics of nonviolent resistance throughout the South. Although eventually many of these tactics resulted in great gains for the movement, they generally were met with violence. People were attacked and killed, and only the federal government was strong enough to do something about it.

■ Students Stage Sit-ins

During the winter of 1959 and 1960, civil rights groups held marches, demonstrations, and boycotts to end segregation in public places. They especially challenged the practice of not serving African Americans at many southern lunch counters. In February 1960 four African American students sat down at a segregated lunch counter in a local store in Greensboro, North Carolina. They refused to leave until they were served. Their action was known as a **sit-in**, and before long students were staging sit-ins all over the South. By September 1961, 70,000 students were using this tactic to produce social change.

By 1960 the crusade for civil rights had become a national movement. As a result, many Americans were now beginning to recognize the moral evil of racial discrimination. King wrote:

66 *The law cannot change the heart—but it can restrain the heartless. It will take education and religion to change bad internal attitudes—but legislation and court orders can control their external aspects.* 99

■ Kennedy and Civil Rights

In contrast to Eisenhower's cautious stand on civil rights, President Kennedy had promised vigorous support of the movement. Kennedy was aware of the support he needed from African American voters to win the 1960 election. Yet his slim victory over Nixon, coupled with the fear of losing southern Democratic support in Congress, made him act less forcefully than the words of his campaign had seemed to promise.

Kennedy's cautious attitude disappointed white liberals and African American leaders. He waited until 1962 to sign an executive order ending segregation in government-owned housing. And although Kennedy appointed African Americans to his administration as well as to federal judicial positions, he also appointed some judges who supported segregation. Events in the South, however, soon forced Kennedy to take a more active role in civil rights.

The Freedom Riders

In the spring of 1961, civil rights activists volunteered as "Freedom Riders" to ride buses into segregated terminals throughout the South. In May busloads of Freedom Riders were attacked by mobs in the Alabama cities of Anniston and Birmingham. A bus was fire-bombed and riders were beaten and clubbed. As more and more Freedom Riders poured into southern cities, local police were unable or unwilling to protect them from angry racists. The President was forced to use federal marshals to restore order. The Justice Department also pressured the Interstate Commerce Commission to bring lawsuits against those terminals that refused to comply with regulations on desegregation.

While Kennedy was in office, from 1961 to 1963, the Department of Justice brought 6 times as many lawsuits to protect African American voting rights as it did under Eisenhower, from 1958 to 1960. As a result, by 1964, the percentage of African American citizens registered to vote in the deep South had risen from 25 to 40 percent, largely as a result of the work of the Freedom Riders.

Violence in Birmingham

Violence that broke out in Birmingham was the last straw for Kennedy. From that point on, Kennedy wholeheartedly sided

▲ CHALLENGING SEGREGATION Civil rights groups challenged the practice of not serving African Americans at many southern diners. Here, two African Americans refuse to leave a segregated Raleigh, North Carolina, lunch counter until they are served. *What was their tactic called?*

▲ THE ROAD TO MONTGOMERY Dr. Martin Luther King, Jr., led a five-day march from Selma to Montgomery, Alabama, in March 1965. Marches were an effective way for African Americans to protest discrimination. *What demonstration did King lead in April 1963?*

with Martin Luther King and the civil rights activists. In April 1963, King led a demonstration in Birmingham, Alabama. On the orders of Police Commissioner Eugene "Bull" Connor, police used fire hoses, clubs, and snarling dogs on demonstrators, including women and children. National television carried the sight of this violence into millions of homes across America. Viewers were shocked and outraged. Kennedy sent 3,000 troops to restore peace in the city. In June he proposed a new civil rights bill that would outlaw segregation throughout the nation.

■ Trouble in Southern Universities

During Kennedy's administration the Department of Justice brought numerous suits for desegregation of schools. In September 1962, James Meredith, a 29-year-old African American Air Force veteran, sought entrance to the University of Mississippi. Although Meredith was backed by a court order, Governor Ross Barnett declared,

"Never! We will never surrender to the evil and illegal forces of tyranny." Kennedy immediately sent in federal marshals and eventually the Mississippi National Guard to enable Meredith to enter the university safely. Meredith was able to attend classes, but two people were killed in a mob action.

Another confrontation between state and federal powers took place in June 1963—this time in Alabama. Governor George Wallace symbolically stood in a doorway to prevent desegregation of the University of Alabama at Tuscaloosa. Kennedy immediately federalized the Alabama National Guard and ordered the troops to make sure African Americans were allowed to enter. As a result, Wallace backed down.

The violence of such confrontations convinced Kennedy that federal legislation against segregation and discrimination was needed. Kennedy quickly proposed laws that would forbid segregation in stores, restaurants, hotels, and theaters and that would prohibit discrimination in employment. But progress on school desegregation was slow. Most African American school children in the south continued to attend all-black schools.

The March on Washington

In August 1963, for the 100th anniversary of the Emancipation Proclamation, African American leaders planned to hold the largest civil rights demonstration in the nation's history. This "March on Washington for Jobs and Freedom" would press for the passage of Kennedy's proposed civil rights bill, which was being debated in Congress.

King's Dream of Freedom

More than 200,000 demonstrators, both African American and white, converged on the nation's capital. They sang hymns and spirituals as they gathered near the Lincoln Memorial. As one 15-year-old African American girl described it:

> ❝ *There was this sense of hope for the future—the belief that this march was the big step in the right direction. It could be heard in the voices of the people singing and seen in the way they walked. It poured out into smiles.* ❞

At the Lincoln Memorial the marchers heard eloquent speeches, especially from Dr. Martin Luther King, Jr., who, in a famous address, described his dream of freedom and equality for all people:

> ❝ *I have a dream that one day this nation will rise up and live out the true meaning of its creed: 'We hold these truths to be self-evident; that all men are created equal' . . . And when this happens, and when we allow freedom to ring, when we let it ring from every village and hamlet, from every state and every city, we will be able to speed up that day when all God's children . . . [will] join hands and sing in the words of the old . . . spiritual: 'Free at last, Free at last, Thank God Almighty, we're free at last.'* ❞

The leaders of the march then left for a meeting with President John F. Kennedy at the White House.

A New Civil Rights Act

The March on Washington was a historic event for the civil rights movement. It not only awakened millions to the plight of African Americans living in the South but also confirmed for Congress the widespread support for a civil rights bill.

Progress was slow. In 1963, 9 years after the *Brown* decision, only one-half of one percent of African American public school children in the 11 former Confederate states were attending desegregated schools. Some southern communities desegregated public facilities only after boycotts and sit-ins. Others refused, however, and some even used violence to intimidate nonviolent protestors.

After President Kennedy's assassination on November 22, 1963, President Johnson was determined to continue Kennedy's civil rights policies. So he accepted

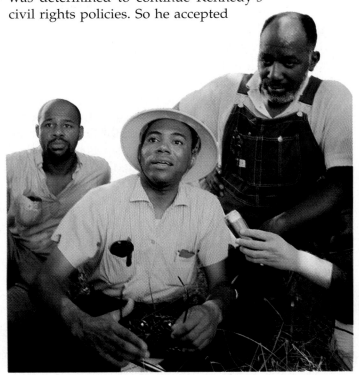

Visualizing History

▲ JAMES MEREDITH In 1962, against the wishes of the governor of Mississippi, the Supreme Court ordered that James Meredith (center) be allowed to enroll at the University of Mississippi. *What action did the federal government take to enable Meredith to enter the university safely?*

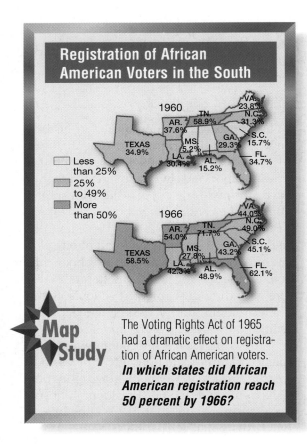

Registration of African American Voters in the South

1960

VA. 23.8%
N.C. 31.3%
TN. 58.9%
AR. 37.6%
S.C. 15.7%
TEXAS 34.9%
MS. 5.2%
GA. 29.3%
LA. 30.4%
AL. 15.2%
FL. 34.7%

Less than 25%
25% to 49%
More than 50%

1966

VA. 44.0%
N.C. 49.0%
AR. 54.0%
TN. 71.7%
S.C. 45.1%
TEXAS 58.5%
MS. 27.8%
GA. 43.2%
LA. 42.3%
AL. 48.9%
FL. 62.1%

Map Study

The Voting Rights Act of 1965 had a dramatic effect on registration of African American voters. *In which states did African American registration reach 50 percent by 1966?*

the challenge of getting Kennedy's proposed bill passed. It had passed the House of Representatives in February 1964 but was stalled in the Senate where southern segregationists intended to kill it. Even though Johnson himself was from the South, he had broken with the segregationists early in his career. Johnson was aided in his goal by national remorse over Kennedy's assassination. To take advantage of this, the President called for speedy action:

On July 2, the President signed into law the Civil Rights Act of 1964. The strongest civil rights act since Reconstruction stated that all citizens should have equal access to such public facilities as parks and libraries and to such private businesses serving the public as restaurants and theaters. It forbade discrimination in education and strengthened the right to vote. It also outlawed job discrimination because of race, sex, religion, or national origin. Passage of the Voting Rights Act of 1965 helped pave the way for more African Americans to vote. Activist John Lewis said:

" *These elections signal a new level of maturation in American politics. They demonstrate the willingness of white voters to set aside racial differences, and they reflect the fact that many minorities have gained the broad political experience and skills to make them solid candidates for major office.* "

The Voting Rights Act of 1965 also helped other minorities. It set aside a New York state law requiring voters to be able to read English, enabling such groups as Puerto Ricans and Mexican Americans to vote.

Section 2 ★ Review

Checking for Understanding

1. **Identify** Freedom Riders, Eugene "Bull" Connor, James Meredith, March on Washington.

2. **Define** sit-in.

3. **Summarize** the advances and setbacks of the civil rights movement during Kennedy's presidency.

4. **Describe** the effects of the Voting Rights Act of 1965 on African American political power.

Critical Thinking

5. **Evaluating Events** The March on Washington is seen as one of the major events of the civil rights movement. Why was the march so effective?

Critical Thinking Skills

▲ REGISTERING TO VOTE, BATESVILLE, MISSISSIPPI

Identifying Cause and Effect

Passage of the Civil Rights Act of 1964 did not bring an end to the civil rights movement. Though the act had addressed segregation, there was still a battle to fight over voting rights. Despite federal laws that already granted them the vote, many African Americans in the South were deprived of their rights by threats and violence or by unfair eligibility tests.

Dr. Martin Luther King, Jr., decided it was time to push for voting rights, and selected Selma, Alabama, as the starting place for his campaign. This was because in Selma most of the African Americans who applied to vote were turned down. Dr. King wanted to dramatize this injustice.

In January 1965, King organized a voter registration drive in Selma. However, the county sheriff deputized whites and attacked groups of African Americans with dogs and cattle prods as they tried to register.

On March 7, Dr. King organized a "march for freedom" from Selma, Alabama, to the state capitol in Montgomery, 50 miles away. More than 25,000 people from all over the country joined in. Police armed with billy clubs, bull-whips, and tear gas, urged on by angry mobs, met the marchers. Many marchers were injured in the clash that followed, and 2 white demonstrators were killed. The marchers reached Montgomery only after Johnson sent federal troops to provide protection.

National outrage over events in Selma helped speed the passage of the Voting Rights Act of 1965. It did away with literacy tests in many southern states and provided for federal assistance in registering African Americans. Steps were also taken to eliminate the poll tax, forbidden by the Twenty-fourth Amendment yet still used to keep the poor from voting. In a single year, more than 400,000 people, mostly African Americans who had not previously voted, were registered.

As a result, African American candidates began to win election as state legislators, mayors, and members of Congress. Within 25 years after the Voting Rights Act, the number of African American elected officials in the South rose from about 100 to 5,000. Southern politicians who had championed desegregation appealed to African American voters for support in their election campaigns.

Practicing the Skill

1. Why did Dr. Martin Luther King, Jr., select Selma, Alabama, as the starting place for the movement's voting rights campaign?

2. What effect did the events at Selma have on subsequent voting rights legislation?

★★★★★★★★★★★★★★★★★★★★★★★★★★★★★★

New Directions

Setting the Scene

Section Focus

As the civil rights movement progressed, African Americans found their situation unchanged in many ways. Laws had not altered prejudice, and improvement in their economic status had practically ceased. As many African Americans were stopped from exercising their rights, some began to change their ideas about how to go about gaining equality.

Objectives

After studying this section, you should be able to

★ list some of the factors responsible for discontent among some African Americans.

★ explain what new philosophies were developed by African Americans to deal with the discontent.

Key Terms

racism, black nationalism, black power, assimilation, busing

◀ MALCOLM X HAT

espite gains made at the national, state, and local levels through peaceful change in cooperation with whites, progress in civil rights was slow. It was especially slow in social and economic areas. Unemployment for African Americans, for example, was much higher than the national average. As a result, by the mid-1960s a growing number of African Americans adopted a new, more radical approach to the problem of **racism,** that is, racial prejudice or discrimination. They believed in taking immediate action not only to gain political and legal rights, but to end discrimination in housing, education, and employment. Instead of following King's philosophy of integration and nonviolence, radical groups began to put forward a new theory and expressed their willingness to use violence to protect themselves and to achieve just treatment.

■ New Leadership

Many whites reacted with alarm to the new direction in the civil rights movement. They were especially worried about groups that openly preached black revolution. These whites felt the new philosophies African Americans were developing threatened their way of life.

The Black Muslims

The Nation of Islam, known as the Black Muslims, was originally founded in the early 1930s, and was led by Elijah Muhammad. This group appealed to African Americans to embrace the Islamic faith and preached **black nationalism.** This philosophy stated that African Americans should completely separate themselves from whites and form their own self-governing communities—their own nation. They also advocated a program of self-defense. Their ideas—popularized by a talented speaker and minister known as Malcolm X—received national attention in the early 1960s. In his autobiography, Malcolm X talked about his views:

> ❝ ... I'm not for wanton violence, I'm for justice. ... I feel that when the law fails to protect [African Americans] from whites' attacks, then those [African Americans] should use arms, if necessary, to defend themselves. ... ❞

By 1964, however, Malcolm X came to favor an integrated society instead of separatism. Therefore, he broke with the Black Muslims. Apparently as a result of his public disagreements with them, he was shot and killed in February 1965. Although in the end Malcolm X came to favor integration, his earlier ideas continued to influence many young African Americans after his death. By the late 1960s, the Student Nonviolent Coordinating Committee (SNCC) and the Congress of Racial Equality (CORE), which had originally supported King's tactics, had become more radical.

Black Power

In May 1966, the head of SNCC, Stokely Carmichael, developed the idea of **black power** to further racial equality. This philosophy stated that blacks should "take back control of all aspects of their lives—social, political, and economic. As expounded by the black nationalists, it meant separation from white society, by violent means if necessary."

The philosophy of black power moved away from the idea of **assimilation**—the policy of incorporating different racial or cultural groups into the dominant society—and preached racial distinctiveness, pride, and leadership.

Many members and leaders of the civil rights movement had been white liberals. Now groups like SNCC and CORE moved whites out of leadership positions. African Americans began to reexamine their African heritage. Some took African names or wore "Afro" hairstyles and African-style clothing. They demanded that schools adopt programs in African-American studies.

Black power created a deep division among civil rights activists. This new idea was firmly rejected by such groups as the NAACP, which saw it as a threat to law and order. However, it would be black power that, from this point on, would more strongly influence the future development of the civil rights movement.

The Black Panthers

One of the most militant black-power groups was the Black Panthers. Founded in 1966 by Huey Newton, Bobby Seale, and Eldridge Cleaver, the Black Panthers urged African Americans to arm themselves and confront white society in order to force whites to grant them equal rights. Cleaver's *Soul on Ice* (1967) served as a statement of Black Panthers' aims:

 ▲ **NATION OF ISLAM** The Nation of Islam, founded in Detroit, Michigan, by Wali Farad, gained many converts during the 1950s and 1960s. *What were the goals and objectives of black nationalism?*

> *What the white man must be brought to understand is that the black man . . . does not intend to be tricked again into another hundred-year forfeit of freedom. Not for a single moment or for any price will the black men now rising up in America settle for anything less than their full . . . share . . . in the sovereignty of America.*

■ The Battle in the North

Although the major battles for civil rights were fought in the South, the movement's leaders recognized that segregation and prejudice also existed in the North. King shifted his demonstrations from the South to such northern cities as Chicago, where he protested housing discrimination, unemployment, and urban poverty. Northern African American populations tended to be concentrated in the inner cities, where poverty was widespread and discontent was high.

Discontent Leads to Riots

Frustration over urban conditions led to a series of riots in many cities. Often occurring in the heat of summer, these riots were sometimes triggered by an incident between police and African American citizens. When riots erupted, looting and burning also broke out.

The first major riot took place in the Harlem section of New York City in July 1964. Other riots broke out that year in Philadelphia and Chicago. In August 1965, a riot in the African American neighborhood of Watts in Los Angeles left 34 people dead, more than 3,000 arrested, and $20 million in property damage. The summer of 1966 brought new disruptions in New York, Atlanta, Cleveland, Detroit, Chicago, San Francisco, and Los Angeles. Federal troops and National Guardsmen entered Detroit in July 1967, after much of the city was in flames. When the riot was over, 40 people had been killed and hundreds more were injured. Thousands were left homeless, and many businesses were in ashes.

Most of the riots took place outside the South, in parts of the United States where African Americans supposedly enjoyed

★★★A★★★★★★★ AMERICAN PORTRAITS

Malcolm X
1925–1965

Born Malcolm Little in Omaha, Nebraska, this future religious leader and activist became a member of the Nation of Islam while serving a prison sentence for burglary. As was the custom in this religious sect, Malcolm dropped his "slave" name in favor of the letter X.

Malcolm X became a powerful and eloquent minister in the Nation of Islam. He taught the religious faith while advocating a position of independent African American political action, black power, pride, and self-defense. The Nation of Islam, sometimes referred to as the Black Muslim movement, stressed the need for African American unity, and advocated a position of separation in a time when most civil rights workers dedicated themselves to achieving racial and economic integration.

Malcolm X eventually broke with the Nation of Islam, moderated his separatist stance, and agreed to work with other civil rights activists to fight racism, discrimination, and injustice. However, Malcolm was assassinated shortly thereafter by rival members of the Nation of Islam.

▲ SUMMER OF 1965 Members of the National Guard patrol the streets of the Watts section of Los Angeles in August 1965. Watts was the site of one of many urban racial confrontations to erupt in the United States during the middle and late 1960s. *What event set off a wave of riots in April 1968?*

equal rights. Adam Clayton Powell, Jr., an African American member of Congress from New York City, offered an explanation. In the South, he said, what African Americans wanted was relatively easy for whites to give: the right to sit at a drugstore counter or in the front of a bus. In the North, African Americans had long been able to sit where they pleased. Now they wanted "a bigger piece of the pie"—better jobs, more money, better places to live. Some white jobholders and property owners felt threatened.

The Kerner Commission

In response to the violence spreading across America, President Johnson appointed a National Advisory Commission on Civil Disorders, known as the Kerner Commission, to look into the problem. The Kerner Commission laid responsibility for the ghettos at the feet of white society.

Although African Americans suffered greater loss of life and property, the riots tended to harden white prejudices. The urgently requested commission report was quietly received and produced little change.

The Death of Martin Luther King, Jr.

Despite the Kerner Commission report, violence continued to grow. Then in 1968 the violence reached a climax with the assassination of Dr. Martin Luther King, Jr. In April of that year, King was in Memphis, Tennessee, to support a strike of African American sanitation workers. He was planning a national poor people's campaign to promote economic gains for African Americans and all poor people.

There had been many threats against King's life over the years. Dr. King, however, had always dismissed them. Yet prophetically, King told a church meeting the night of April 3:

> ❝ . . . I've been to the mountain top, and I don't mind. . . . I've looked over and I've seen the Promised Land. I may not get there with you, but I want you to know tonight that we as a people will get to the Promised Land. ❞

◀ **STOKELY CARMICHAEL**

The next day, he was killed by a sniper. Ironically, the murder of the great teacher of nonviolence set off a week of rioting, arson, and looting in 125 American cities. It was as if King's death swept away the last bit of faith in a peaceful solution. "America," announced Stokely Carmichael, "must be burned down in order for us to survive." Rioting took place in Washington, D.C., just blocks from the White House. President Johnson ordered troops to enforce a curfew and protect government buildings.

■ The Civil Rights Movement After 1968

Between the *Brown* decision and King's death, the civil rights movement made great gains. After King died, however, the movement's leaders feared that they would begin to lose some of their hard-won victories. Richard Nixon, who won the presidency in 1968, had his own agenda. He wanted to make the Republicans so powerful that they would control both the White House and Congress in 1972. To do that, he needed to lure southern Democrats into the Republican ranks.

To this end, Nixon developed a "southern strategy." He appointed a southern justice to the Supreme Court. The President also reversed a Johnson administration policy that cut off federal funds to racially segregated school systems. Although federal policy had been affirmed in 1968 by the Supreme Court in *Green* v. *County School Board*, Nixon ignored the Court's ruling and instructed the Justice Department to support school boards that were seeking to delay desegregation.

Contrary to Nixon's hopes, his appointments to the Supreme Court did not guarantee a reversal of the *Green* decision. Instead, the Court affirmed integration by means of **busing**—transporting children to a school outside their residential area to achieve racial balance in that school. White Americans in the South and most other regions of the nation resisted busing, and Nixon denounced it. The Nixon administration's open opposition to busing for desegregation intensified public controversy over the issue.

Nixon's agenda moved many people and much of government policy to the right, away from the liberal policies of the Kennedy-Johnson years. Many civil rights gains were lost or delayed. However, despite the setback, the movement continued. It would make gains in the future and strongly influence other minorities.

Section 3 ★ Review

Checking for Understanding

1. **Identify** Malcolm X, Stokely Carmichael, Kerner Commission, Watts, "southern strategy."

2. **Define** racism, black nationalism, black power, assimilation, busing.

3. **Summarize** the goals of the black-power movement.

4. **Cite** two reasons for the summer riots during the 1960s.

Critical Thinking

5. **Making Comparisons** Explain how the views of Malcolm X on the problem of racism differed from those of Martin Luther King, Jr.

★★

The Impact of Civil Rights

Setting the Scene

Section Focus

All the efforts made by civil rights activists during the 1950s and 1960s had a far greater impact than just to help African Americans gain equality in America. Other disadvantaged groups—women, Hispanics, and Native Americans—found new hope in the African Americans' struggle and formed movements of their own. These movements found support because of the atmosphere in the nation as a whole. Because of the civil rights struggle and the Vietnam War, a great number of people had begun to question the status of American society and the policies of the government.

Objectives

After studying this section, you should be able to

★ describe the gains made by women and minorities.

★ explain why the Equal Rights Amendment was not ratified.

Key Terms

feminist, sexism, bilingualism

▶ SHIRLEY CHISHOLM

---

*D*uring the 1960s and 1970s, young Americans became leaders in promoting social justice. They were determined to close the gap between the realities of American life—discrimination, poverty, and social inequalities—and the nation's ideal of "liberty and justice for all."

■ The Women's Rights Movement

Women constituted more than 50 percent of the population in the United States in the 1970s. However, their political, economic, legal, and social status resembled that of a disadvantaged minority. Minority women faced a special problem in that they encountered sexual and racial discrimination at the same time.

Status of Women

In 1977 women held less than 5 percent of the elective offices in the United States. There had been few female senators or governors, no Supreme Court justices, and no mayors of major cities in the history of the republic. Of the 435 members of the House of Representatives, only 18 were women. In her autobiography *Unbought and Unbossed,* Shirley Chisholm, the first African American woman to serve in the House of Representatives, wrote:

❝ *When I decided to run for Congress, I knew I would encounter both anti-black and anti-feminist sentiments. What surprised me was the much greater virulence of the sex discrimination.* ❞

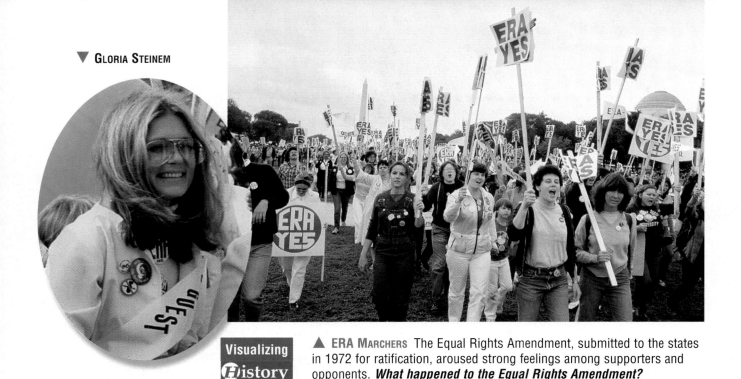

GLORIA STEINEM ▼

Visualizing History

▲ **ERA MARCHERS** The Equal Rights Amendment, submitted to the states in 1972 for ratification, aroused strong feelings among supporters and opponents. *What happened to the Equal Rights Amendment?*

Representative Chisholm was elected for a second term in 1970. In 1972 she ran against George McGovern for the Democratic nomination for President. She served in Congress for the next decade and continued to support equal rights for minorities and women. After serving in Congress, she then turned her talent to teaching on the college level. About her accomplishments, she noted:

❝ *I hope that my having made it, the hard way, can be some kind of inspiration, particularly to women.* ❞

In 1960 women made up one-third of the nation's workforce. Yet, most of their jobs offered less pay and prestige than those positions that men held. For every dollar on average that a man earned on a job in the 1960s, a woman with the same job earned only 59 cents. During the rest of the 1960s and into the next decade the economic situation of women improved slightly.

In 1976 the United States Department of Labor reported that full-time working men averaged 75 percent more pay than full-time working women. Dissatisfied with the slow progress, many women began calling for stronger action.

The publication in 1963 of *The Feminine Mystique* by Betty Friedan had inspired demands for change. Friedan rejected the notion that the destiny of women was only to be wives and mothers. She described how the media had created an image of women that was designed to imprison them in their households and bar serious consideration of them as competitors in the labor market.

National Organization for Women

In 1966 Betty Friedan joined with other **feminists,** or women activists, to establish the National Organization for Women (NOW). The organization's Statement of Purpose read:

❝ *. . . [To] take action to bring women into full participation in the mainstream of American society now, assuming all the privileges and responsibilities thereof in truly equal partnership with men.* ❞

Among its early successes, NOW helped end separate classified employment ads for men and women, and airline rules that required female flight attendants to retire at age 32. In the 1960s and 1970s, NOW and

▲ PHYLLIS SCHLAFLY

similar groups helped increasing numbers of women to enter professions. Banks, realtors, and department stores were forced to grant loans, mortgages, leases, and credit that they long had denied to female applicants.

The Equal Rights Amendment

Following intense lobbying by women's groups, in 1972 Congress voted to submit the Equal Rights Amendment (ERA) to the states for ratification. This amendment stated that "equality of rights under the law shall not be denied or abridged by the United States or by any state on account of sex."

Not all women supported ERA, however. Phyllis Schlafly, founder of STOP ERA, dismissed the women's rights movement as "a series of sharp-tongued, high-pitched, whining complaints by unmarried women." STOP ERA supporters contended that the ERA would force women to give up their traditional roles as wives and mothers, and that they would lose certain legal protections in the family and in the workplace. As a result of a vigorous campaign by STOP ERA and other groups, the Equal Rights Amendment failed to obtain the votes needed for ratification.

Women Make Progress

Despite the failure of the ERA, women continued to make progress. **Sexism**—treating people differently because of their gender—was recognized and outlawed in the workplace by 1971. Princeton, Yale, and other traditionally all-male colleges began to open their doors to females.

Women were also becoming increasingly important in the business world. By the mid-1970s, nearly half of all married women worked outside the home; almost all who had graduated from college worked.

Women also were becoming an important force in politics in the 1970s. By the 1980s, there were more women than ever in both the Senate and the House of Representatives, as well as on the Supreme Court, in the cabinet, and in state government offices. In 1984, Representative Geraldine Ferraro became the first female major-party candidate to run for Vice President.

■ Hispanic Activism

At this time, Hispanics also became active in campaigning for equal rights. By the 1970s Hispanic Americans had become the second-largest minority in the United States, next to African Americans. Spanish-speaking people made up almost 8 percent of the population and were the largest minority group in several states. New York City alone had about 2 million Spanish-speaking people. Part of Miami, Florida, became known as "Little Havana" because it was home to hundreds of thousands of Cuban immigrants.

Visualizing History

▲ HISPANIC AMERICANS By the 1970s Hispanic Americans were the second-largest minority in the United States. *What group made up the largest number of Hispanics?*

Mexican Americans made up the largest group of Hispanic peoples. For years, thousands of Mexican Americans labored as migrant farm workers, moving from place to place to harvest seasonal crops. They were not protected by federal minimum-wage laws, unemployment insurance, or social security.

In 1965 Cesar Chavez organized a nationwide coalition and asked Americans to boycott California grapes picked by nonunion labor. After enduring five years of such persistent protest, most California grape growers relented and agreed to sign a contract with Chavez's union, the United Farm Workers.

During the 1970s, Hispanic Americans began to organize. The League of United Latin American Citizens (LULAC) won suits in federal courts to guarantee Hispanic Americans the right to serve on juries, to send their children to unsegregated schools, and to be taught in Spanish as well as in English. The use of two languages is called **bilingualism.** As their political strength grew, more Hispanic Americans were elected to local and state offices as well as to Congress.

Native Americans Organize

Like the Hispanics, Native Americans organized during the 1960s and 1970s. Their plight captured national attention when a 1966 study revealed that Native Americans suffered from malnutrition and disease to such an extent that their life expectancy was only 46 years. They had less formal education than any other minority group, and their family income was less than one-half the national average.

Termination Policy

After World War II, the federal government tried to incorporate Native Americans into white society. A new policy called "termination" was established in 1953. This meant that the federal government stopped recognizing Native American nations as legal entities that were separate from state government. Now, the nations would be subject to the same local governments as whites. The government in Washington worked to make Native Americans give up their cultures and adapt to white society.

Native Americans were so angry that they began speaking out more forcibly. A group of younger Native Americans had breathed life into the National Congress of

► RUSSELL MEANS, AIM LEADER

▲ AMERICAN INDIAN MOVEMENT FLAG

American Indians (NCAI), set up in 1944. As a result of their activity, President Eisenhower put a stop to termination without consent. Later Presidents did not revive it during the 1960s. They made some efforts to provide tribes with government money.

Declaration of Indian Purpose

In 1961, more than 400 representatives of 67 Native American nations met in Chicago to draw up a bill of rights for Native Americans. They called it the Declaration of Indian Purpose, and in it they committed themselves to Indian nationalism and intertribal unity. The delegates also stated their belief in "red power," and demanded an end to federal control of Native American affairs. "We simply want to run our lives our own way," said one young leader.

As a result, in 1968, the Congress passed the Indian Civil Rights Act, which guaranteed Native American reservation dwellers some of the rights provided to other citizens under the Bill of Rights.

However, some Native Americans wanted to take more direct action. In the state of Washington, men from more than 50 Native American groups led a "fish-in." They deliberately broke game laws and risked imprisonment to protest the loss of their former fishing and hunting grounds.

In 1973 a more militant group, the American Indian Movement (AIM), seized the reservation at Wounded Knee, South Dakota. They demanded that lands taken from Native Americans in violation of federal treaties be returned. They also demanded

that development programs on reservations be managed by their own governments, and not the federal Bureau of Indian Affairs. The takeover ended after a standoff between federal agents and Native Americans, and federal policies toward Native Americans began to change.

The Pueblo of Taos, New Mexico, regained Blue Lake, a place sacred to their religious life. In 1975 a federal court declared that the Passamaquoddy and the Penobscot nations had a valid claim to more than half the state of Maine and to $25 billion in damages and unpaid rents.

Visualizing History

▲ NATIVE AMERICANS Native Americans fought in the nation's wars and honored those who gave their lives for freedom. Many pressed for economic and political equality and compensation for the loss of their land. *What action did Native Americans take at Wounded Knee in 1973?*

Section 4 ★ Review

Checking for Understanding

1. **Identify** Shirley Chisholm, Betty Friedan, NOW, ERA, Phyllis Schlafly, Cesar Chavez, LULAC, "red power," AIM.

2. **Define** feminist, sexism, bilingualism.

3. **List** three inequalities between men and women that existed in the 1970s.

4. **State** two demands that were made by Hispanics and Native Americans.

Critical Thinking

5. **Analyzing Point of View** Analyze the backlash to the women's rights movement in the 1970s. What stereotypes of women continue to exist today?

Using Vocabulary

Using the following vocabulary terms, write a paragraph describing the development of the civil rights movement.

nonviolent resistance	sit-in
federalized	racism
black nationalism	black power
assimilation	busing

Reviewing Facts

1. **List** two results of the Supreme Court's *Brown* v. *Board of Education* ruling.

2. **Cite** two results of the Montgomery bus boycott.

3. **Arrange** in chronological order significant events in the civil rights movement that occurred between 1953 and 1963.

4. **Describe** how Johnson followed through on Kennedy's policies regarding civil rights.

5. **List** two results of the black-power movement.

6. **Describe** the aims and objectives of the women's rights movement.

7. **Summarize** advances made by Native American peoples.

Understanding Concepts

Civil Rights

1. Explain the factors in American society that helped the civil rights movement grow.

2. Evaluate the importance of leadership to the civil rights movement in the 1950s and 1960s.

Social Upheaval

3. Compare the results of the late 1960s riots with the goals of the black-power movement. Use this information to formulate an opinion of the use of violence in demonstrations.

4. Why did the civil rights movement cause so much turmoil? Explain how the demands of African Americans affected other minorities and what the results were.

Critical Thinking

1. **Evaluating Tactics** Though Martin Luther King, Jr.'s, methods for change were nonviolent, they were not passive. What were some challenges faced by nonviolent civil rights demonstrators? Why was their nonviolence an effective tactic?

2. **Analyzing Fine Art** Study the mural that appears on this page. Then answer the questions that follow.

   a. Describe what the mural is showing.

   b. What can you tell about the artist by looking at the mural?

   c. What can you tell from the mural about the artist's feelings toward African American culture?

Writing About History

Description

Imagine that you are one of the first Freedom Riders on a bus traveling in the South during the spring of 1961. Write a two-page paper in which you describe your feelings and fears as you take part in this pioneering civil rights tactic. Describe various incidents that occur along the highway and at stops at segregated bus terminals. Describe the feelings of other African Americans and whites accompanying you on the Freedom Rides. Include at least one conversation you have with another rider.

Cooperative Learning

You will work in a group with two others to analyze three activist movements of the 1970s: the women's rights movement, the Hispanic movement, and the Native American movement. The goal of your group is to find as many similarities between these movements as you can. Each group member should choose one of these movements. First, work individually to make a list of the goals of each group and the methods used to attain them. Next, work with your partners to compile a master list of similarities between the three movements. Present your list to the class and discuss the findings.

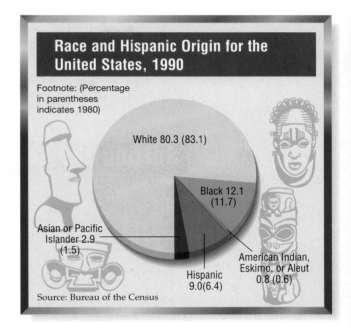

Race and Hispanic Origin for the United States, 1990

Footnote: (Percentage in parentheses indicates 1980)

White 80.3 (83.1)

Black 12.1 (11.7)

Asian or Pacific Islander 2.9 (1.5)

American Indian, Eskimo, or Aleut 0.8 (0.6)

Hispanic 9.0 (6.4)

Source: Bureau of the Census

Social Studies Skills

Interpreting Demographic Data

Demographics is the data used to show the characteristics of a human population in terms of size, growth, density distribution, and vital statistics. The information can be presented in a number of ways: in circle graphs, bar graphs, or line graphs. One application of demographic data in the study of history or political science is to understand the relative voting strength of different ethnic groups. Candidates for political office need demographic information about their region in order to identify and target voter groups and to devise strategies that will attract those voters.

Practicing the Skill

Study the circle graph on this page, which shows the racial background of United States citizens and the origins of Hispanics according to the 1990 census.

1. What does the circle graph suggest about the problems a small group such as Native Americans might have effecting change through the political process?

2. The Asian American population almost doubled between 1980 and 1990. Hypothesize reasons this rate of growth might be higher than that of other ethnic minorities.

3. Did the percentage of people of Hispanic origin increase or decrease between 1980 and 1990? Did the percentage of people of Asian or Pacific Islander background increase or decrease?

4. What do the numbers in parentheses represent? What changes does this information show?

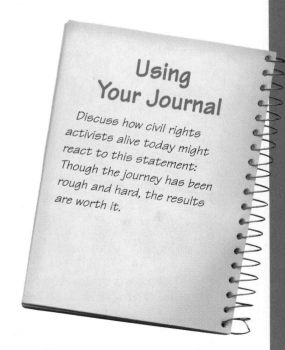

Using Your Journal

Discuss how civil rights activists alive today might react to this statement: Though the journey has been rough and hard, the results are worth it.

CHAPTER 33

★★★★★★★★★★★★★★★★★★★★★★★★★★★★★★★★★★★★★★

The Vietnam Era
1954–1975

► **SOLDIER STANDING GUARD**

Setting the Scene

Focus

President Kennedy's handling of foreign policy was tested strenuously as cold war challenges arose during the Vietnam Era. Kennedy faced a failed Cuban invasion, a missile crisis, quarrels over nuclear testing, and the beginnings of the war in Vietnam. During the Johnson years, this conflict became the focus of attention for the nation. More and more, the American people became divided over this issue.

Concepts to Understand

★ How social upheaval divided the nation and affected government policy during the Vietnam Era

★ Why public opinion was divided over the conduct of the war in Vietnam

Read to Discover . . .

★ lessons Kennedy learned from his handling of foreign policy.

★ what events set off political turmoil during this period.

Journal Notes

What do you think it would have been like to be President of the United States during the Vietnam War? Note details about it in your journal as you read the chapter.

CULTURAL	• **1955** *Ford offers seatbelts as optional equipment*	• **1964** *The Beatles appear on* The Ed Sullivan Show

1955	**1960**

POLITICAL	• **1959** *Castro takes power in Cuba*	• **1961** *Peace Corps is established* • **1962** *Cuban Missile Crisis*

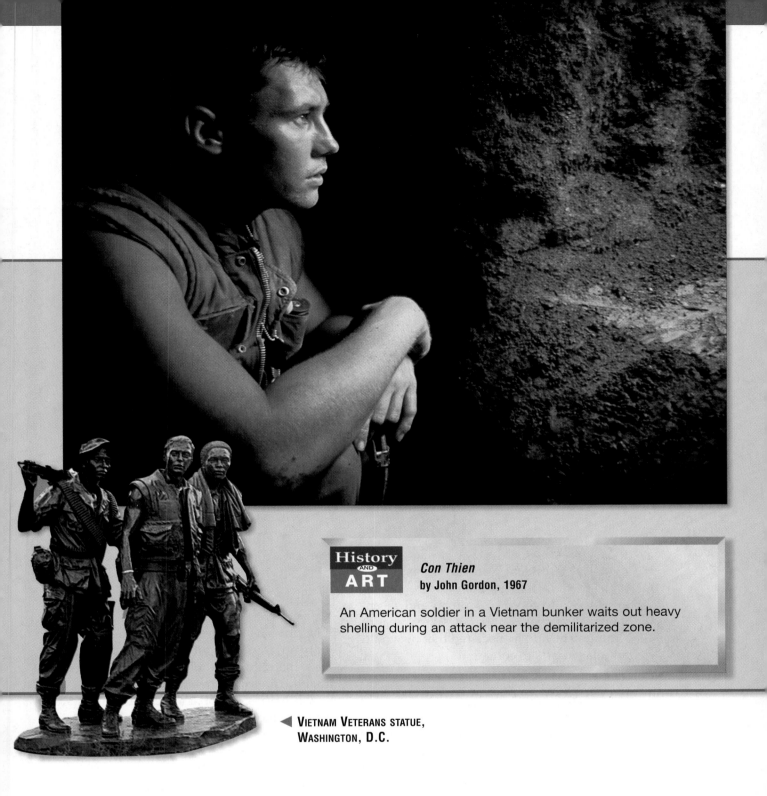

Con Thien
by John Gordon, 1967

An American soldier in a Vietnam bunker waits out heavy shelling during an attack near the demilitarized zone.

◀ VIETNAM VETERANS STATUE,
WASHINGTON, D.C.

●**1967** *Green Bay Packers win first Super Bowl, 35–10, over Kansas City Chiefs*

●**1970** *First Earth Day observed as millions protest pollution*

1965	1970

●**1968** *Peace talks to end Vietnam War begin in Paris*
●**1968** *Robert Kennedy is assassinated; Nixon becomes President*

●**1970** *Kent State University students riot*
●**1971** *Pentagon Papers are published*
●**1972** *President Nixon visits China*

★★

Cold War Challenges

Setting the Scene

Section Focus

President Kennedy entered office with little firsthand experience in international affairs. Yet he had to meet such challenges as the buildup of nuclear arms, anti-United States feeling in Latin America, and instability in economically developing nations in Africa and Asia. He achieved some triumphs, but in other cases his inexperience led him into mistakes.

Objectives

After studying this section, you should be able to

★ discuss Kennedy's responses to Soviet and international communism.

★ explain the purposes of the Alliance for Progress and the Peace Corps.

Key Terms

reactionary government, credibility gap

◀ **CUBAN LEADER FIDEL CASTRO**

President Kennedy's basic aims in foreign policy were similar to those of Truman and Eisenhower. His major concern was the threat of communism, and he declared that he would not relax efforts to contain it.

■ Crises in Cuba

In 1959 Fidel Castro had led a movement to overthrow Fulgencio Batista—the corrupt dictator then ruling Cuba—and had set up a new government. Castro soon established ties with the Soviet Union and began to adopt Marxist-influenced policies. As a result, the Eisenhower administration began to view Cuba as a threat to democracy in the Western Hemisphere. Eisenhower authorized the Central Intelligence Agency to train and arm Cuban exiles secretly for the overthrow of Castro.

The Bay of Pigs Invasion

The CIA believed that an invasion of Cuba by these exiles would touch off a popular uprising against Castro. Kennedy's military advisers approved the project. In office less than three months, Kennedy agreed that the invasion should proceed.

On April 17, 1961, a force of 1,400 Cuban exiles came ashore at the Bay of Pigs on the south coast of Cuba. From the start the invasion went poorly. There was no popular uprising by the Cuban people. Within hours Castro's forces had the invaders surrounded.

The failed invasion hurt the prestige of the new Kennedy administration and strengthened Castro's position in the world. It also allowed Soviet leader Nikita Khrushchev to pose as the defender of Latin America against United States imperialism.

The Alliance for Progress

The Castro movement, known as "Fidelismo," threatened to spread to other countries in Latin America. Promoted by Cuban agents, it often found support among the poverty-stricken and those seeking more political power. Kennedy announced a new economic program for Latin America—called the Alliance for Progress—that emphasized social reform and political freedom. Its purpose was to develop long-term economic growth among 19 Latin American nations, thus making it less likely that poverty would drive people in these countries to support communist-inspired revolutions. Over a 10-year period, the United States pledged $20 billion to help Latin American countries provide better schools, housing, and health care, as well as introduce fairer methods of taxation and redistribution of large landholdings to small farmers.

Even though United States aid to Latin America quadrupled, the results were uneven. In some countries—notably Chile, Colombia, Venezuela, and the Central American republics—the Alliance succeeded in promoting reform. In others, however, much of the money was diverted for the benefit of the military and the wealthy.

The Cuban Missile Crisis

On October 22, 1962, President Kennedy appeared on television and made a chilling announcement. U-2 spy planes from the United States had taken photographs proving that the Soviet Union had placed missiles on Cuba. The medium-range missiles were capable of reaching Atlanta and New Orleans; intermediate-range missiles were capable of reaching as far north as Pittsburgh and Detroit and as far west as Denver. Kennedy ordered a naval blockade to keep the Soviets from delivering anymore missiles, and he demanded that the Soviets dismantle all their missile sites in Cuba. As Soviet ships approached, war seemed imminent.

Secretly, the Soviet Union offered to remove the missiles if the United States promised never to invade Cuba. As negotiations continued, Khrushchev added another demand: that the United States remove its own missiles from the Soviet border of Turkey. President Kennedy rejected this demand because it would weaken the NATO alliance. The President's brother, Attorney General Robert Kennedy, suggested they ignore the new proposal and accept the Soviet Union's first offer.

After five agonizing days, when the world appeared on the brink of nuclear disaster, the Soviet ships turned back from the blockade. Soviet leaders also decided to withdraw their missiles from Cuba. President Kennedy won strong public support for his firm stand.

■ The Peace Corps

To help developing nations all over the world fight poverty and disease, Kennedy set up the Peace Corps in 1961. Like the Alliance for Progress, the Peace Corps was organized to help prevent the spread of communism.

Peace Corps Volunteers

The Corps was made up of volunteers from the United States who wanted to help people in developing nations. After a period of rigorous training, Peace Corps volunteers went to countries that had asked for their assistance. There they lived among the people and helped them solve local problems. They laid out sewage systems in Bolivia, trained medical technicians in Chad, and built a model town in Pakistan. A high proportion of volunteers taught English and practical skills. In return they received only a living wage and a small vacation allowance. By late 1963 there were 11,000 Peace Corps volunteers serving in 40 countries.

Peace Corps volunteers in economically developing nations of Africa, Asia, and Latin America witnessed firsthand the problems and potential of newly independent nations. Many countries often lacked the necessary institutions to make the transition from colonial status to political and economic independence.

▲ SUMMIT MEETING When Khrushchev and Kennedy met at Vienna in June 1961, the two leaders treated one another with wary politeness. ***What agreement did they reach on nuclear testing?***

Nationalism in Africa

By 1961, 27 newly independent nations had been formed from European colonies in Africa. When Europeans established boundary lines of the colonies in the 1800s and early 1900s, they failed to take into account the existing ethnic and cultural divisions. Even decades later, it was difficult to obtain loyalty to the new nation-states.

Since the beginning of colonial rule, nationalist groups in Africa had resisted European control, often violently. Following World War II, these relatively small efforts for freedom swelled into powerful mass movements.

In 1961 ethnic rivalries in the Congo, later renamed Zaire, broke out into civil war. When the mineral-rich province of Katanga attempted to secede because of tribal and regional differences, two Congolese leaders called for Soviet military aid. The United States, however, backed the efforts of the United Nations to arrange a cease-fire. In 1963, after intervention by U. N. troops, the Congo was reunited. Other attempts at superpower intervention were generally rebutted as most African nations developed a policy of nonalignment.

■ Challenges From the Soviet Union

Although holding to the containment policy, Kennedy sought means of relieving the tensions of the cold war. In his inaugural address he had said, "Let us never negotiate out of fear, but let us never fear to negotiate." In June 1961, he met with Khrushchev in the Austrian capital, Vienna. The two men treated each other with wary politeness, but they could find no area of agreement. Khrushchev may have thought that he could intimidate Kennedy, who had recently been embarrassed by the Bay of Pigs disaster. The Russian leader handed Kennedy a near-ultimatum on East Germany and Berlin. He insisted that the Western powers recognize the German puppet state and that the four-power postwar occupation of Berlin, which was completely surrounded by East Germany, come to an end. The President refused.

The Berlin Wall

The communist answer was to build a wall through Berlin, blocking free movement between their section of Berlin and the rest of the city. This weakened the economy of West Berlin, which had drawn much of its labor from the Russian sector. The wall also prevented the flight of refugees seeking to escape the oppression of East Germany. Those attempting to escape were shot down by East German police.

In June 1963, Kennedy visited West Berlin. A vast, cheering crowd gathered to hear him at the city hall. The President told them:

❝ *Freedom has many difficulties and democracy is not perfect, but we have never had to put up a wall to keep our people in. . . . All free men, wherever they may live, are citizens of Berlin, and therefore, as a free man I take pride in the words, 'Ich bin ein [I am a] Berliner.'* ❞

The Berlin Wall stood for nearly 30 years as a menacing symbol of the cold war division between East and West.

Quarrels Over Nuclear Testing

In 1961 the Soviet Union broke a three-year moratorium on testing nuclear weapons in the atmosphere. The Soviets exploded more than 40 bombs, one with 3,000 times the power of the bomb that destroyed Hiroshima. Kennedy attempted to persuade the Soviets to ban above-ground testing because nuclear fallout pollutes the atmosphere of the whole world. The Soviets would not agree to a method of inspection satisfactory to Americans. Not wanting the Soviet Union to gain nuclear superiority, the United States also resumed testing.

In August 1963, the United States, the Soviet Union, and Great Britain signed a test-ban treaty that prohibited atomic tests in the atmosphere, in outer space, and underwater. It did not, however, ban underground testing or reduce the total number of nuclear weapons. In September 1963, the Senate ratified the treaty by a vote of 80 to 19.

Dominican Intervention

Cold war tensions were again heightened when the United States intervened in the Dominican Republic. In April 1965, Lyndon Johnson, who was then in the White House,

▲ **BARRIER TO FREEDOM** The Berlin Wall dividing the East German and West German parts of the city was hastily constructed in August 1961. West Berliners decorated their side and questioned the wall's existence. *Why was the wall built?*

received word that rebels were trying to overthrow the rightist military government that controlled the island country. Fearing that the rebels were controlled by Communists, Johnson ordered 20,000 marines to the Dominican Republic. This was the first time the United States had openly sent troops to the Caribbean since 1926.

Many Latin Americans criticized this military action. They charged that fear of a communist takeover, similar to that of Cuba by Fidel Castro, was leading the United States to support **reactionary governments,** or extremely conservative governments with oppressive policies. Nonetheless, most members of Congress continued to support the President. By a margin of 312 to 52, the House of Representatives voted in support of sending American troops to prevent a communist takeover anywhere in Latin America. But the Dominican incident raised suspicions of a **credibility gap,** a lack of believability growing out of the difference between official statements and practices.

■ Israel and Korea

Two other incidents caused friction with the Soviet Union during the 1960s. One had to do with Israel. The other was the *Pueblo* incident in Korea.

Arab-Israeli War

Hostilities between Israel and the Arab nations in the Middle East were common and continuing. The United States, which had traditionally supported Israel since its founding in 1948, continued that support during the Arab-Israeli War of 1967. The Soviet Union, on the other hand, backed and armed Egypt, Syria, and Jordan, the three Arab nations involved. Being on opposite sides in this conflict heightened cold war tensions between the two superpowers. However, the speed of Israel's victory prevented an out-and-out clash between the two countries.

Later in 1967, President Johnson met with Soviet Premier Aleksey Kosygin at Glassboro, New Jersey, to try to smooth relations between the United States and the Soviet Union. Although they discussed their nations' views and goals, they came to no agreement.

The *Pueblo* Incident

In January 1968, the North Koreans seized a United States ship, the *Pueblo,* and its 83 crew members. The *Pueblo* was a spy vessel, which used electronic equipment to obtain information about communist North Korea. As long as the ship stayed in international waters at least 12 miles from shore, its activities were considered legal. North Korea, however, claimed that the *Pueblo* had illegally entered its waters.

American officials were stunned. Some people wanted to retaliate, but President Johnson could not afford a conflict with North Korea while the United States was involved in the Vietnam War. As a result, the crew members remained prisoners for nearly a year.

Section 1 ★ Review

Checking for Understanding

1. **Identify** Bay of Pigs, Nikita Khrushchev, Alliance for Progress, Peace Corps, Berlin Wall, *Pueblo.*

2. **Define** reactionary government, credibility gap.

3. **Explain** why the Bay of Pigs invasion failed.

4. **State** two possible reasons why Khrushchev sent missiles to Cuba.

Critical Thinking

5. **Making Inferences** Besides being an economic policy, the Alliance for Progress was an attempt to stop communism. Explain this aspect of the program.

Changing Nature of Warfare

Technology always affects the conduct of war. In fact, changes in the way wars are fought are often the result of changes in technology.

During the Revolutionary War, armies were outfitted with flintlock muskets—notoriously inaccurate. The soldier fired at the enemy when he saw "the whites of his eyes," a distance of less than 50 yards. With the Civil War and the introduction of a more accurate bullet, rifles were deadly up to 300 yards.

In some ways the Civil War was the first modern war. It was the first war in which railroad lines were vital, and the first in which telegraph lines, ironclad ships, and observation balloons were used as a matter of course. It foreshadowed World War I, since the armies often dug in, and sometimes fought from elaborate trenches. It also represented a step toward the concept of "total war," with less and less distinction between civilians and soldiers.

Over time, battles became increasingly impersonal, as soldiers killed and were killed by unseen enemies. Field telephones, first used in World War I, enabled soldiers to direct their fire thousands of feet behind enemy lines.

Airplanes were introduced, and pilots dropped bombs by hand from open cockpits. Bombing quickly became more sophisticated, and by World War II, bombers flying over enemy territory in Europe dropped hundreds of bombs in a single mission.

Modern-day warfare has become even more detached. Weapons systems are computer-controlled. Pilots use radar to direct heat-seeking missiles at enemies miles away.

During the Vietnam War, United States pilots flew huge B-52s on bombing raids over North Vietnam. Helicopters supplied food and ammunition to United States field forces, transported troops, and promptly evacuated the wounded.

▶ MARINE DURING GULF WAR

▲ WORLD WAR I SOLDIERS

Making the Technology Connection

1. How did technological advances affect battlefield tactics? Which advance do you think has had the greatest effect on modern warfare?

Linking Past and Present

2. How do today's radio and television influence the perception of war on the home front? Do you think the media has had too great an influence?

★★★★★★★★★★★★★★★★★★★★★★★★★★★★

War in Vietnam

Setting the Scene

Section Focus

Perhaps the biggest cold war challenge was the war in Vietnam. Kennedy increased the number of military advisers in South Vietnam, but his tragic death prevented him from finding a solution. Although Kennedy's intentions for the future were not clear, Johnson continued the established policy of containment and honored the commitments made by Eisenhower and Kennedy.

Objectives

After studying this section, you should be able to

★ explain how the Gulf of Tonkin incident led to the escalation of the war in Vietnam.

★ explain why the Tet offensive was the turning point of the Vietnam War.

Key Terms

war of national liberation, escalation, search-and-destroy strategy

◀ SOLDIER'S BOOTS, VIETNAM WAR

In setting United States policy in Vietnam, both Kennedy and Johnson were torn between a wish to limit American involvement in a country halfway around the world and fear of a communist victory that would swallow up all of Southeast Asia. Ultimately, however, involvement increased and, before long, American troops were engaged in combat.

■ Trouble in Southeast Asia

During the Kennedy years, the Soviet Union lent its support to **wars of national liberation.** These were wars to free a nation from the control of another country, and they took place in many economically developing nations.

War in Laos

When Kennedy took office in 1961, the Southeast Asian nation of Laos was in danger of falling to communist guerrilla forces. The CIA and the Joint Chiefs of Staff pressed for a strong defense of Laos. Kennedy, on the other hand, believed a diplomatic solution could be found. In the end Kennedy avoided war by striking a compromise with Khrushchev—first by agreeing to a cease-fire and then by establishing a neutral government. Fighting between the Laos government and the guerrilla forces soon resumed, however.

Kennedy and Vietnam

Another hot spot was Vietnam, a former French colony in Southeast Asia. It had been divided into North and South Vietnam in 1954. North Vietnam was controlled by the communist government of Ho Chi Minh. South Vietnam was controlled by a noncommunist government supported first by France and then by the United States. In the late 1950s the Vietcong—South Vietnamese communist guerrillas—began fighting to overthrow the United States-backed government of Ngo Dinh Diem and to reunite South Vietnam with the North. Both Eisenhower and Kennedy responded by sending military aid and advisers to South Vietnam. By late 1963 Kennedy had increased the number of advisers to 16,000.

Kennedy's Vietnam policy was complicated because Diem was a corrupt and unpopular dictator, a French-educated, upper-middle-class Catholic who ruled a largely Buddhist country. Middle- and lower-class Buddhists distrusted both Diem and the West. In his efforts to remain in power, Diem took increasingly harsh and undemocratic measures.

■ Johnson's Choices

During the 1964 campaign Johnson ran as the candidate of peace and restraint. "We seek no wider war," he repeatedly promised.

"We don't want our American boys to do the fighting for Asian boys." At the same time, the President did not want to appear weak or to leave the door open for a communist victory in Vietnam.

As the military situation in Vietnam continued to deteriorate, the war dominated the foreign policy of the administration. When President Johnson entered the White House, South Vietnamese President Ngo Dinh Diem had just been assassinated. Within three months, another revolution took place in South Vietnam. This was followed by a series of governments, as one military faction after another gained power in South Vietnam.

The President faced disagreeable choices. He could admit defeat and pull out. If the "domino theory" was correct, the rest of Southeast Asia would soon fall to the Communists. Another option was continuing limited support of South Vietnam's government, but the instability of that government would probably mean eventual defeat. Finally, he could actively enter the war and attack North Vietnam. This would mean the loss of lives and vast expense, and also the possibility of war with the People's Republic of China.

Visualizing History

▲ **ESCALATION** By the end of 1965, there were nearly 200,000 American troops in Vietnam. By the end of 1968, the total had increased to more than 500,000. *What was the Gulf of Tonkin Resolution?*

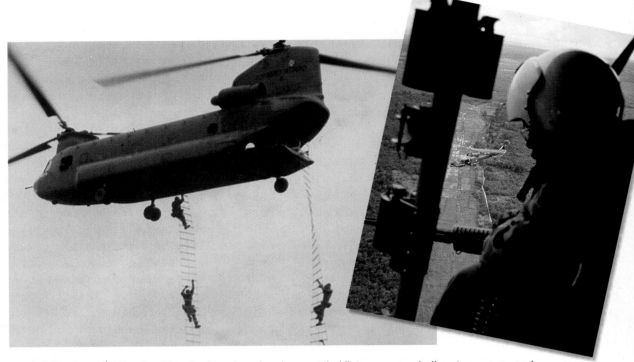

▲ **THE AIR WAR** As American involvement in Vietnam grew, helicopters were used extensively because they were effective at pinpointing enemy positions. ***What were the goals of search-and-destroy missions?***

By the summer of 1964 Johnson began to move cautiously toward the third alternative. In secrecy the United States began limited bombing of positions held by the Vietcong and supported limited commando raids on North Vietnam's coast.

■ Escalation

Johnson reported that North Vietnamese torpedo boats fired on two American destroyers in the Gulf of Tonkin on August 2 and 4, 1964. Calling these attacks unprovoked, he asked Congress for authorization to bomb North Vietnam.

Gulf of Tonkin Resolution

On August 7 the Senate and House quickly passed the Gulf of Tonkin Resolution, authorizing the President to "take all necessary steps, including the use of armed force" to prevent further aggression. In effect, Congress, with only two dissenting votes, handed its war powers over to the President.

Johnson, however, had kept important information from Congress. The two American destroyers had been assisting the South Vietnamese military in conducting electronic spying on North Vietnam. It was unclear whether the ships had been attacked. Furthermore, Johnson did not reveal that a draft of the resolution had been prepared three months before the attack, in case such an event occurred.

President Johnson regarded the Gulf of Tonkin Resolution as a blanket approval of the war effort from Congress. At the suggestion of his military advisers, he ordered the bombing of bases in North Vietnam.

Until August 1964, the fighting in South Vietnam had been between South Vietnamese government troops and the Vietcong. After the Gulf of Tonkin incident, however, North Vietnam began sending its own troops to fight in the South. As the United States expanded its role, the civil war grew into a major conflict between American and communist forces.

In February 1965, after the Vietcong attacked an American base in South Vietnam, Johnson ordered an **escalation,** or military expansion, of the war. He ordered American planes to begin bombing targets in North Vietnam, and, in April 1965, made the fateful decision that American ground forces should engage in combat.

In the Vietnam War the United States faced a far more difficult situation than it had in Korea. In Korea the United States fought as an agent of the United Nations, with widespread support from noncommunist countries. Now the United States stood almost alone in its military support of South Vietnam's government, and much of world opinion was hostile to American policy in Vietnam. The South Vietnamese communists had strong support in rural areas and military aid from North Vietnam. Most noncommunist South Vietnamese were indifferent or opposed to their government, no matter what group happened to be in power.

A Different Kind of War

Military operations turned into a "dirty, ruthless, wandering war" without a battlefront. The Vietcong guerrillas used hit-and-run tactics. Not as well equipped as the Americans, the Vietcong and North Vietnamese used ambushes, boobytraps, and small-scale attacks. They moved swiftly by night and by day hid in the jungles or in friendly villages. Using terrorism against civilians, the Vietcong controlled much of the countryside.

Search and Destroy

To counter such tactics, American troops adopted a **search-and-destroy strategy.** American forces tried to search out enemy troops, bomb their positions, destroy their supply lines, and force them out into the open for combat. By 1966 American planes had dropped nearly the same tonnage of bombs in Vietnam as had been dropped in the Pacific in World War II.

Napalm, a jellied gasoline that explodes, splatters, and clings to whatever it touches, was dropped from airplanes. In order to improve visibility, American planes sprayed chemical defoliants—Agent Orange, for example—that stripped leaves from trees and shrubs, turning farmland and forest into wasteland. American troops burned villages believed to be hiding communist supporters.

■ Resistance to Peace

The United States poured increasing numbers of troops into Vietnam. During the height of the conflict, more than 500,000 American soldiers were serving in Vietnam. The number of American dead continued to rise: from 5,008 in 1966 to 9,377 in 1967 and 14,489 in 1968.

Once the United States had escalated the fighting, there seemed to be no way of leaving without damaging its international prestige. North Vietnam's leader, Ho Chi Minh, kept his forces in battle despite the massive bombing of his country, believing that North Vietnam could simply outlast the United States in the war.

The Vietnam War

Map Study

Throughout the war United States troops and the government of South Vietnam controlled the major cities. *What strategy did the Vietcong use?*

Between 1965 and 1967, American officials estimated that some 2,000 attempts were made to open direct negotiations, all unsuccessful. Other nations, including Great Britain, Poland, and the Soviet Union, offered plans to negotiate between the two sides. None succeeded.

■ Tet and Retreat

At the end of 1967, General William Westmoreland, American commander in Vietnam, had assured the country that the end of the war was in sight. Vastly enlarged American forces expanded the "search-and-destroy" missions. American bombers destroyed North Vietnamese factories, roads, bridges, and cities. Secretary of State Dean Rusk said the enemy "was hurting very badly."

Vietcong Attack Turns the Tide

January 30, 1968, marked a turning point in the war. The supposedly exhausted communist guerrillas abruptly launched major offensive strikes. Early that morning a handful of Vietcong soldiers attacked the United States Embassy compound in Saigon—the very center of the American presence in South Vietnam. Together, the Vietcong and the North Vietnamese then launched massive attacks on all American bases in South Vietnam and on most of South Vietnam's major cities and provincial capitals. Taken by surprise by the assault during the celebration of Tet, the Vietnamese lunar New Year, Americans and South Vietnamese sustained heavy losses. After fierce fighting, they finally drove back the communist offensive.

Militarily, the communists were defeated. Politically, however, they scored a victory. The American people were shocked that the enemy that was supposedly on the verge of defeat could launch such a large-scale attack. Television coverage of the attack and the destruction that followed shook the nation's confidence. When General Westmoreland requested an additional 209,000 troops for Vietnam—in addition to the 500,000 already there—it seemed like another admission that the United States could not win the war.

Peace Talks Begin

Finally, on March 31, 1968, Johnson announced that he would halt nearly all bombing of North Vietnam. He offered to send special negotiators to hold peace talks with the North Vietnamese and the Vietcong. A few days later, on April 3, North Vietnam accepted Johnson's offer to begin peace negotiations. Diplomats from the United States and North Vietnam met in Paris in May 1968, but they could not agree on terms. Prospects for peace in Vietnam grew dim. After a lull, the war continued, and the number of American troops in Vietnam reached a new high. It would be five long years of continued bitter struggle, however, before the United States left the war in Vietnam behind.

Section 2 ★ Review

Checking for Understanding

1. **Identify** Vietcong, Gulf of Tonkin Resolution, General William Westmoreland.

2. **Define** wars of national liberation, escalation, search-and-destroy strategy.

3. **Explain** what mistake Johnson's military advisers made about the Vietcong and the North Vietnamese.

4. **Explain** why the Tet offensive was the turning point of the Vietnam War.

Critical Thinking

5. **Expressing Problems Clearly** Some political analysts called Vietnam a "quagmire." Write two statements that explain the difficult choices the United States faced in Vietnam.

Map and Graph Skills

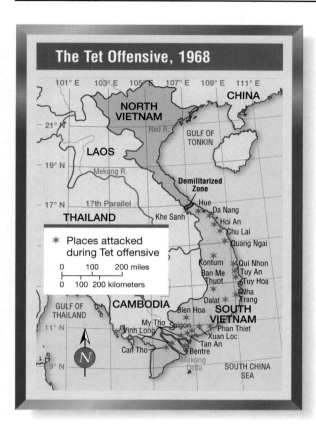

The Tet Offensive, 1968

* Places attacked during Tet offensive

0   100   200 miles

0   100 200 kilometers

Interpreting Military Maps

In your study of American history, you often use maps. Maps are especially helpful for studying the progression of war. A military map shows the area where battles occur, where victories have been won, and who controls various sites.

Military maps vary in the level of detail provided. Some military maps show only the major battles fought over the course of a war. Others may show detailed troop movements and defensive positions during a particular battle or over a specific period of time.

To interpret military maps, follow these guidelines:

a. Read the map title. This will indicate the location and time period covered on the map.

b. Read the items listed in the map key. This tells what the symbols on the map represent. For example, areas under the control of a particular nation or region may be represented by a color. Battle sites may be symbolized by crossed swords, a shell burst, or a star. Military movements and offensives may be illustrated with solid or broken lines and arrows.

c. Study the map itself. This will reveal the actual events or sequence of events that took place. Notice the geography of the area and try to determine how it would affect military strategy.

Practicing the Skill

Nearly 8,400 communist troops infiltrated South Vietnam's major cities and government installations during the Tet offensive. Overall, more than thirty cities were attacked, with the heaviest fighting in Saigon and Hue. Before the offensive was over, an estimated 33,000 communist soldiers died.

Look at the military map of Southeast Asia on this page. Then follow the above guidelines to answer these questions.

1. What time period is represented on the map?

2. From the map, can you tell the outcome of the attacks?

3. Where are the attack sites with respect to North Vietnam?

4. Important supply lines ran through the countries of Laos and Cambodia for communist troops and ammunition. Which side do you think Laos and Cambodia favored? Explain.

★★

Protest and Reaction

Setting the Scene

Section Focus

As casualties mounted, there was strong opposition to the war among a growing number of Americans. They lost confidence in their government. Soon, large numbers of disillusioned youths began demonstrating against United States involvement in Vietnam. In the middle of all the chaos, *Newsweek* reported that the United States was "divided and confused as never since the Great Depression."

Objectives

After studying this section, you should be able to

★ list reasons for opposition to the war.

★ describe the values and beliefs of the youth counterculture.

Key Terms

student deferment, conscientious objector, teach-in, commune, counterculture

◀ **ANTIWAR BUTTON**

After Tet, criticism of American involvement in Vietnam increased. One of the nation's most trusted news broadcasters, Walter Cronkite, reported:

> 66 *We have too often been disappointed by the optimism of the American leaders to have faith any longer in the silver linings. . . . To say that we are closer to victory today is to believe, in the face of evidence, the optimists who have been wrong in the past. To suggest we are on the edge of defeat is to yield to unreasonable pessimism. To say that we are mired in stalemate seems the only realistic, yet unsatisfactory conclusion.* 99

Hearing Cronkite's broadcast, President Johnson turned to his aides and said, "It's all over." He recognized that he had lost the battle for public opinion.

■ Growing Opposition to War

Gradually, as America moved deeper into the Vietnam War, opposition grew. The United States's reasons for fighting in Southeast Asia began to be questioned.

Senate Hearings on the War

Beginning in January 1966, the Senate Foreign Relations Committee held "educational" hearings on Vietnam. The televised hearings carried the senators' doubts about the war to millions of American homes.

Hawks and Doves

Before long, Americans became divided into two groups. Those who supported the war were called "hawks" and those who opposed "doves." For a long time, polls showed that most Americans sided with the "hawks." But doubts began to grow. By May 1967, even the Secretary of Defense Robert McNamara had begun to question America's role in the war.

■ Student Protests

Many of those opposed to the war were students who openly protested America's involvement in Vietnam. The antiwar movement was centered on college campuses, which had also been the source for activists in the civil rights movement.

Protests Against the Draft

A number of the antiwar protests focused on the draft. Many of those facing the draft did not understand why the war was being fought or why they should go. Students also protested against the government's unfair practices. A person with a limited education from a low-income family was far more likely to be sent to fight in Vietnam than someone with a good education from an upper-income family, and African American soldiers made up a disproportionately large number of American soldiers fighting overseas.

One policy that contributed to this inequity was the practice of giving **student deferments.** Young men were safe from the draft as long as they were enrolled in college. In 1966 alone, there were 1.8 million deferments. Some men who did not serve were **conscientious objectors.** They received this status by belonging to an organized religious body with pacifist views. About 500,000 young men simply refused to report when they were drafted. Some fled to other countries, such as Canada or Sweden. Around 3,000 young men went to prison rather than fight in a war they opposed. Some antiwar protesters used the tactics of civil disobedience and demonstrations that they had learned from the civil rights movement.

Visualizing History

▲ DEMONSTRATIONS AND CONFRONTATION Reacting against the antiwar demonstrations, many Americans began to counter with demonstrations in support of American troops. Many antiwar demonstrations were accompanied by violence. In May 1970 six students were killed during separate confrontations at Jackson State and Kent State (above right). *Why did many students protest the war?*

Letters From Vietnam

A soldier's life is charged with action and danger, but it also holds long periods of tiresome waiting and inactivity. Writing letters to family and friends back home is one way generations of soldiers have fought boredom and loneliness. United States soldiers in Vietnam were no different. They shared their lives, their fears, and their desires through their letters. Here First Lieutenant Robert Michael Murray writes to his fiancée.

6 July [1967]

My Darling Claudia,

It's raining outside. A damp smell in the air and the raindrops slamming onto the plasterboard roof. Sound of cricket and frog, and the rumble of distant bomb explosions shake the earth here many miles away. Lightning flashes bare the heavens for a brief glimpse at a troubled sky watching over a war-torn land. The area is flooded, and mud clings to boots with a slurp-sucking sound. Soaked uniform hanging on chair to dry and shriveling up into a wrinkled mass. A chilling air is coddled by two ceiling fans and swirled through my body. . . .

Sometimes you have to pretend you're not really lonely or else you'd find yourself going out of your mind. But when the day is done, and you're lying alone with your thoughts, then there's no more fooling and that's when it really hurts. The days seem to go by quickly, but the weeks seem forever. Today I have been in Vietnam 73 days, 10½ weeks, a little over 2½ months. The guys who are over here now tell me, looking back, that the time flew by. But right now it seems so very long.

I love you,

Michael

◀ COLLECTION OF VETERAN'S ITEMS

Some university students and teachers held **teach-ins** to study the history of the war and to protest against its expansion.

Violence on Campus

While most protests were peaceful, some turned violent. One occurred in April 1968 at Columbia University in New York City. It began when students seized college buildings and ended in a riot marked by both police brutality and student retaliation.

Two of the most tragic episodes of the antiwar movement took place in May 1970. After President Nixon announced the invasion of Cambodia, protests erupted on scores of campuses. At Kent State University in Ohio, rioting reached such an intensity that the National Guard was sent in. On May 4, a contingent of guardsmen, harassed by students, fired into the crowd, killing 4 students and wounding 10. On May 14, at Jackson State University in Mississippi, student protest was suppressed by the state police, who fired randomly into a dormitory. Two students were killed, 9 were wounded. These events precipitated a nationwide student strike. Hundreds of colleges and universities suspended classes or closed down completely.

The campus violence that erupted was not limited to the United States. During this time and before, there were student riots in Rio de Janeiro, London, Paris, Rome, Madrid, Warsaw, and Prague. In Prague, student protests triggered a rebellion that led to the overthrow of the communist regime that had ruled Czechoslovakia since 1948. However, after a few months 200,000 Soviet troops crushed the revolt and reestablished control.

New Beliefs and Values

Some young people rebelled against established values and searched for a new set of beliefs. They studied different religions and philosophies. In an attempt to achieve expanded awareness, some experimented with drugs that cause hallucinations. They proclaimed their freedom of expression and individuality by wearing long hair and unconventional clothing. Some even left family and comfortable homes to live in **communes**—communities in which living quarters, food, and work were shared.

In their rejection of their parents' values, the "hippies," or "flower children" as they were frequently called, were said to have established a **counterculture**—with values and practices that conflicted with those of established society. The counterculture was symbolized in an outdoor rock concert, the Woodstock festival held in New York in August 1969. More than 400,000 people attended what *TIME* called "history's biggest happening."

A Conservative Backlash

The actions and protests of the Woodstock generation caused a reaction among a growing number of conservative Americans who had become angry over the demonstrations, the riots, and a war that seemed to be going nowhere. The sight of long-haired draft protesters outraged many who did not hesitate to support their government in time of war. Many working-class Americans were offended by the actions of students they considered privileged. The deep anger these Americans felt soon developed into a backlash against the antiwar movement.

■ 1968: The Turning Point

By 1968, a kind of turning point had been reached in American society. With the Tet offensive and the protests, polls showed that the majority of Americans had turned against the President's handling of the war.

Johnson had become so unpopular that he seldom appeared in public for fear of hostile crowds. Even the President's own party was divided over the war.

The Race for President

By this time, Eugene McCarthy, a Democratic senator from Minnesota—and a dove—had announced that he was going to challenge Johnson for the Democratic Party's presidential nomination. Although Johnson won the first primary election in New Hampshire, his margin of victory was narrow. McCarthy received more than 40 percent of the votes. Then, four days after this primary, Democratic Senator Robert Kennedy, who also opposed the war, announced that he too would run for the nomination.

Johnson had always intended to run for reelection in 1968. When he realized just how little support he had, however, he made a decision that was surprising to many. The President decided to drop out of the race. On March 31, 1968, he stunned the nation by announcing, "I shall not seek, and I will not accept, the nomination of my party for another term as your President." With Johnson withdrawn, Vice President

Visualizing History

▲ ASSASSINATION During the 1968 Democratic primary, Robert F. Kennedy won a number of victories. On June 5, 1968, the night of his victory in the California primary, Kennedy was assassinated. ***What two Democratic candidates remained in the race?***

Hubert Humphrey became the administration candidate and the preferred choice for many longtime Democrats.

Soon it appeared that Kennedy was pulling in front of McCarthy and Humphrey. Kennedy's program and popularity seemed broad enough to rebuild the Democratic coalition shattered by Vietnam. Then on June 5, 1968, just after winning the Democratic primary in California, Kennedy was assassinated by an Arab nationalist, angry at Kennedy for his support of Israel.

In August the Democrats held their national convention in Chicago. Now that Kennedy was dead, Humphrey was expected to win the nomination. However, furious at the Vice President's support of the war, about 10,000 protesters gathered in Chicago. Reflecting the "silent majority's distaste for the protesters, Chicago Mayor Richard Daley, himself a Democrat, advised his police to get tough with the protesters. While violence reigned outside, the convention nominated Hubert Humphrey for President and Senator Edmund Muskie of Maine for Vice President.

The Candidates

The splintering of the Democratic party made the Republican candidate, Richard M. Nixon, the front-runner in the election of 1968. Although defeated in his campaign for President in 1960 and for governor of California in 1962, Nixon had remained active in national politics. For his vice-presidential running mate, Nixon chose Spiro T. Agnew, governor of Maryland.

In his campaign, Nixon promised to unify the nation, return dignity to the presidency, stabilize American foreign policy, and lead a war against crime in the streets. He said he had a plan for ending the war in Vietnam, but he did not provide details.

A third candidate, George Wallace, governor of Alabama, ran as an Independent in all 50 states. He selected General Curtis LeMay as his running mate. Wallace was against federally enforced civil rights, including desegregation and busing; black power; "pointy-headed intellectuals"; and social unrest. As a result of his civil rights stand, he attracted support in the South. Wallace also appealed to blue-collar workers in the North as well as the South. Leaders of organized labor, however, campaigned hard for Humphrey and moved much of the blue-collar vote back to the Democrats.

The Election of 1968

On Election Day, Nixon won, though the vote was very close. He received 31.8 million votes, while Humphrey had 31.3 million and Wallace, 9.9 million. In the electoral college, Nixon won 301 votes to 191 for Humphrey and 46 for Wallace. However, although the people had elected a Republican President, the Democrats kept their majorities in both houses of Congress.

Speaking to reporters after his election, Nixon recalled seeing a young girl carrying a sign at one of his rallies that said: "Bring Us Together." This, he promised, would be his chief effort as President.

Section 3 ★ Review

Checking for Understanding

1. **Identify** hawks, doves, Robert McNamara, Woodstock, Eugene McCarthy, Hubert Humphrey.

2. **Define** student deferment, conscientious objector, teach-in, commune, counterculture.

3. **List** two reasons why some Americans began to oppose United States involvement in Vietnam.

4. **Explain** how the conservative backlash developed.

Critical Thinking

5. **Synthesizing Ideas** How did the war in Vietnam and increasing violence at home affect Americans' confidence in President Johnson?

★★

Secrecy and Summitry

Setting the Scene

Section Focus

The foreign policy of the Nixon administration was one of secrecy and surprise. Also during his administration, Nixon secretly plotted the bombing of Cambodia and the expansion of the war in Indochina. As opposition to the war heated up, government documents came to light that indicated Nixon, along with Kennedy and Johnson, had deceived the public about what was really going on in the Vietnam War. Finally, Nixon gave in and began withdrawing American troops.

Objectives

After studying this section, you should be able to

★ explain why Nixon pursued détente in foreign policy.

★ list and describe the steps that President Nixon took to end American involvement in Vietnam.

Key Terms

détente, summit, shuttle diplomacy

◀ VIEW AT THE VIETNAM MEMORIAL

*S*urprising both his supporters and his critics, Richard Nixon as President shed his long-held image as a "cold warrior." He opened a dialogue with the communist leaders of China and entered into a series of agreements with the Soviet Union. Nixon recognized the legitimacy of the communist regimes of Eastern Europe.

■ A New Policy

Like Woodrow Wilson, President Nixon took almost sole charge of foreign policy. To help him handle foreign policy matters, Nixon appointed Henry A. Kissinger, a brilliant political scientist, as his national security adviser. Kissinger's job was to present the President with policy options in which the probable consequences of each policy were outlined. Kissinger also undertook secret missions abroad. In 1973 Nixon appointed Kissinger secretary of state.

Nixon, like Wilson, wanted to be remembered as a peacemaker. In his Inaugural Address he proclaimed:

❝ *After a period of confrontation, we are entering an era of negotiation. Let all nations know that during this administration our lines of communication will be open. We seek an open world—open to ideas, open to the exchange of goods and people. . . .* ❞

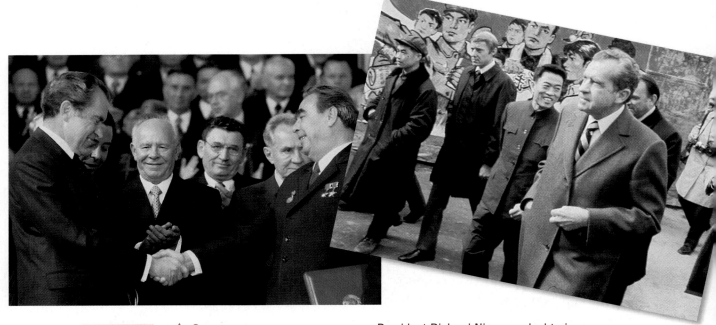

▲ OPENING THE LINES OF COMMUNICATION President Richard Nixon worked to improve relations with the communist superpowers. The thaw in relations was reflected in the President's visits to the Soviet Union (left) and China (right). *What is détente?*

Nixon Proclaims Détente

Nixon proclaimed a policy of **détente,** or relaxation of tensions between the United States and the communist bloc. He maintained that it would be a "safer world and a better world if we have a strong, healthy United States, Europe, China, Russia, and Japan, each balancing the other."

To achieve this balance Nixon proposed a meeting between the United States and the Soviet Union to discuss strategic arms limitations. The SALT negotiations, as they were called, began in Helsinki, Finland, in 1969. Before the conclusion of SALT I in 1972, the two sides had agreed to ban biological warfare and limit the growth of nuclear weapons.

SALT culminated in the May 1972 Moscow **summit,** or diplomatic meeting, between the superpowers. In addition to signing the SALT agreement, Nixon and the Soviet leader, Leonid Brezhnev, also agreed to increase trade, exchange scientific information, and cooperate in preventing pollution.

Nixon and China

President Nixon also sought improved relations with China. He began by lifting trade and travel restrictions. The President also withdrew the Seventh Fleet from

defending Taiwan, an island which China claimed as its own.

The Chinese responded to Nixon's initiatives in a variety of ways. More important, the Chinese accepted Henry Kissinger's proposal that he visit Beijing secretly to open discussions with Chinese leaders. During Kissinger's meeting with Chinese Premier Zhou En-lai (JOH EHN•lye), he arranged for President Nixon to visit China in February 1972. President Nixon's sensational announcement that he would visit Beijing foreshadowed the 1971 admission of the government of the People's Republic of China to the United Nations.

■ War in Vietnam

During the 1968 presidential campaign, Nixon declared that he had a plan for ending the Vietnam War. After his inauguration he resumed negotiations with the North Vietnamese, but they produced little.

The President faced a dilemma: if he continued United States involvement in the war, public opposition would increase. If he withdrew United States troops without a peace agreement, he would be the first President of the United States ever to lose a war.

The Pentagon Papers

To make matters worse, in June 1971, *The New York Times* published a secret Department of Defense study. *The Pentagon Papers*, as they were called, documented that for two decades, four Presidents had escalated the nation's involvement in Indochina.

The Pentagon Papers were evidence of the growing power of the executive branch. They contained details of decisions made by Presidents and their advisers without the consent of Congress. *The Pentagon Papers* also showed how the administrations acted to deceive Congress and the public about Vietnam.

President Nixon was outraged over the "leaking" of the secret documents. He ordered the Justice Department to go to court to stop further publication of the papers. Nixon hoped the court would affirm the government's right to restrain publication in matters of national security, but the Supreme Court decided that *The Pentagon Papers* were not vital to national security.

The federal government then brought charges against Daniel Ellsberg, one of the authors of *The Pentagon Papers*, for leaking the documents to the press. President Nixon also authorized a group of people who were called "the Plumbers" to break into the office of Ellsberg's psychiatrist to collect information about him. When their activities came to light, the charges against Daniel Ellsberg were dropped.

The United States in Vietnam, 1950–1975

1950 **May 8** President Truman sends U.S. aid and advisers to French forces in Indochina	**May 10** Paris Peace Talks begin between U.S. and N. Vietnam
1954 **May 7** French defeated by Communists at Dien Bien Phu	**1969** **January 25** First full session of Paris Peace Talks with Vietcong and S. Vietnam also represented
July 20–21 Geneva Conference provides cease-fire and divides Vietnam	**March 16** My Lai massacre (revealed in November 1969)
1957 Vietcong begin attacks in South Vietnam	**June 8** President Nixon announces the withdrawal of 25,000 U.S. troops from Vietnam
1960 **Dec. 20** Vietcong form National Front for the Liberation of South Vietnam	**Sept. 3** Death of Ho Chi Minh
1961 **Nov. 16** President Kennedy increases number of U.S. advisers in Vietnam	**Oct. 15** Vietnam Moratorium Day—nationwide antiwar demonstrations across the U.S.
1963 **Nov. 1** Ngo Dinh Diem assassinated	**1970** **Feb. 20** Presidential adviser Henry A. Kissinger opens secret peace negotiations in Paris
1964 **July 24** U.S. rejects French President de Gaulle's plan to neutralize all of Indochina	**April 29** U.S. troops invade Cambodia
Aug. 2–4 Gulf of Tonkin—N. Vietnam attacks a U.S. destroyer and U.S. retaliates	**May 4** Four antiwar students killed during demonstrations at Kent State University, Ohio
Aug. 7 Gulf of Tonkin Resolution—Congress grants President Johnson authority to use force against aggression	**July 24** Senate votes to repeal Gulf of Tonkin Resolution
1965 **Feb. 7–8** First U.S. bombing of North Vietnam	**1971** **Nov. 12** President Nixon limits U.S. ground forces in Vietnam to a defensive role
March 2 Rolling Thunder bombing campaign begins against North Vietnam	**1972** **April 15–20** Widespread antiwar demonstrations in U.S.
March 8–9 President Johnson sends 3,500 Marines (first combat troops) to join 23,500 U.S. advisers	**June 17–22** Watergate break-in and arrests
1966 **March 2** U.S. forces number 215,000	**Aug. 12** Last U.S. ground combat troops leave Vietnam
Dec. 31 U.S. forces number 389,000	**Dec. 18–30** Bombing of Hanoi and Haiphong resumed to break stalled peace negotiations
1967 **May 19** First U.S. air strike against central Hanoi	**1973** **Jan. 27** Cease-fire in Vietnam agreed upon
1968 **Jan. 30–Feb. 24** Tet offensive by Vietcong	**Feb. 12** N. Vietnam releases first U.S. prisoners of war
March 31 President Johnson announces cessation of bombing of N. Vietnam north of 20th parallel and that he will not seek reelection	**1974** **Aug. 9** President Nixon resigns
	1975 **April 29–30** North Vietnamese capture Saigon; American personnel evacuated; Vietnam War ends

Source: *The New York Times*, April 30, 1985; *An Encyclopedia of World History*, 5th ed. (1972); Gorton Carruth, *What Happened When* (1989); James S. Olson, *Dictionary of the Vietnam War* (1988)

Chart Study

American involvement in Vietnam grew rapidly after the first combat troops arrived in 1965. In 1975 troops from North Vietnam moved into South Vietnam, and it came under Communist control. **When did the Tet offensive take place?**

AMERICAN PORTRAITS

Maya Lin

1959–

Maya Lin was a 21-year-old architecture student at Yale University when her design for the Vietnam Veterans Memorial was selected in a national competition. Lin's simple but powerful and unique design joined two gleaming black granite walls inscribed with the names of the war's 58,000 dead and missing. While Maya's work was initially controversial, today the memorial is a symbol of national healing.

Maya was born and raised in Athens, Ohio. Her parents, both of whom had emigrated from China in the 1940s, were college professors. Maya was a good high school student, with a particular aptitude for mathematics.

In 1988, Maya Lin designed the Civil Rights Memorial in Montgomery, Alabama. Recently she completed a memorial at Yale University and designed the interior of the Museum of African Art in New York City.

President Nixon's response to the publication was a further sign that the credibility of his administration was eroding. Nixon himself, it was revealed, had ordered the secret bombing of North Vietnamese sanctuaries in Cambodia in 1969. In April 1970, Nixon, without consulting Congress, ordered an invasion of Cambodia to drive the North Vietnamese out of the country. Protests against the war now intensified.

Nixon Announces Vietnamization

To quiet opposition to the war, Nixon announced a policy of "Vietnamization." Vietnamization consisted of two steps: the phased withdrawal of United States troops, and their replacement by conscripts from Vietnam. Nixon hoped that Vietnamization, combined with saturation bombing of North Vietnam, would allow the United States to withdraw from the war "with honor."

By the end of the war, the total tonnage of bombs dropped by the United States on Vietnam was more than twice that dropped by the United States on all targets in both World War II and the Korean War.

Finally, on January 23, 1973, the United States, South Vietnam, North Vietnam, and the Vietcong signed a cease-fire agreement, ending the military presence of the United States in Vietnam. The war, however, did not end for the people of Vietnam. Although United States troops withdrew from South Vietnam, North Vietnamese troops did not.

The End of the War

In 1974 the weakened forces of South Vietnam abandoned distant outposts they could no longer defend, and North Vietnamese forces captured several provincial capitals. In January 1975, North Vietnam launched a major offensive. By late March they drove South Vietnamese troops from a region known as the Central Highlands, approximately 160 miles north of Saigon. While thousands of civilians retreated with the soldiers, many died in the gunfire or from starvation. The South Vietnamese army soon collapsed, and by early April, the North Vietnamese army had reached the outskirts of Saigon.

Hoping to stall the communist drive, President Gerald Ford, Nixon's successor, requested more than $700 million in military aid for South Vietnam. Congress, however, approved only $300 million, to be used chiefly to evacuate Americans from Saigon. On April 29, as North Vietnamese troops overtook Saigon, the United States carried out an emergency evacuation of all remaining Americans and many South Vietnamese refugees.

The war ended when the Saigon government surrendered on April 30, 1975. North and South Vietnam were formally united as the Socialist Republic of Vietnam on July 2, 1976.

■ War in the Middle East

On October 6, 1973, the Jewish holiday of Yom Kippur, Egyptian and Syrian troops launched surprise attacks against Israeli forces. Their objective was to recapture the territory Egypt and Syria had lost to Israel during the Six-Day War of 1967. Caught by surprise, the Israeli troops were pushed back, but they quickly regrouped and launched their own attack, pushing into Syria and across the Suez Canal into Egypt.

Israel appealed to the United States for help, and President Nixon responded with a massive airlift of $2 billion in military supplies. At the same time, the Soviet Union continued to supply Egypt and Syria. American aid to Israel angered the Arab countries, and quickly they retaliated by placing an embargo on the shipment of oil to the United States and other countries that supported Israel.

Even as the United States and the Soviet Union gave aid to the opposing sides, they worked through the United Nations Security Council to arrange a cease-fire. In late October, the nations of Israel, Egypt, and Syria agreed to terms. By the end of 1973, a UN peacekeeping force had been sent to the Middle East to police the region.

After the conflict, Secretary of State Henry Kissinger worked with Israel and Egypt to

Visualizing History

▲ THE FALL OF SAIGON On April 28, 1975, President Ford ordered the emergency helicopter evacuation of all Americans remaining in Vietnam. *When did the United States end its military involvement in Vietnam?*

reduce tensions in the Middle East. For the next two years, he engaged in **shuttle diplomacy,** flying back and forth between the capitals of the two nations in an effort to produce a lasting peace. Kissinger's efforts yielded two important results. Early in 1974 Golda Meir, the prime minister of Israel, and Anwar el-Sadat, the president of Egypt, agreed to establish diplomatic relations again between their countries. Then in September 1975, Israel and Egypt agreed to withdraw their forces from the cease-fire line. Although significant problems remained, a measure of peace had been achieved in the Middle East.

Section 4 ★ Review

Checking for Understanding

1. **Identify** Henry Kissinger, Leonid Brezhnev, SALT, Zhou En-lai, *The Pentagon Papers*, Daniel Ellsberg, Vietnamization.
2. **Define** détente, summit, shuttle diplomacy.
3. **List** three steps taken during Nixon's presidency to end United States involvement in Vietnam.

4. **Describe** how Henry Kissinger's shuttle diplomacy helped to end war in the Middle East.

Critical Thinking

5. **Evaluating Foreign Policy** Evaluate the pros and cons of Nixon's use of secrecy in China and Vietnam.

Using Vocabulary

Imagine you are a reporter who is covering the diplomatic meeting between the superpowers at Moscow in May 1972. Use the following vocabulary words to write an article describing the history of the United States's cold war struggle against communism.

reactionary government   **summit**
credibility gap   **escalation**
war of national liberation   **détente**
search-and-destroy strategy

Reviewing Facts

1. **Summarize** Kennedy's relations with Khrushchev.

2. **Explain** the many foreign policy challenges that Kennedy faced in Southeast Asia.

3. **State** two reasons why it was difficult for the United States to win the war in Vietnam.

Understanding Concepts

War

1. Explain how Americans' perceptions of communism influenced United States policy to support South Vietnam.

Social Upheaval

2. Evaluate the effectiveness of violent versus nonviolent demonstrations. What were the results of nonviolent demonstrations in the early 1960s?

Critical Thinking

1. **Inferring Results**   What lessons about military intervention do you think President Kennedy learned from the Bay of Pigs?

2. **Analyzing Art**   Study the photograph on this page of the Vietnam Veterans Memorial, then answer the questions that follow.

   a. Compare the Vietnam Memorial with other national monuments and memorials. In what way is the design of the Memorial unique?

b. The Vietnam Veterans Memorial is one of the most visited of our nation's monuments. Why do you think this is so?

Writing About History

Narration

Imagine that it is 1968 and you have just received a draft notice in the mail. Though you are legally obligated to join the military, many Americans at this time are refusing to be drafted. Write an essay explaining whether or not you will fight in the war.

Cooperative Learning

Work with two other group members to explore the options facing President Kennedy during the Cuban missile crisis. List two potential consequences of each option.

Social Studies Skills

Reading Terrain Maps

Two kinds of terrain maps are shown on page 947—a terrain model and a topographic map. The two maps show roughly the same area of Vietnam. The terrain model is a representation of the shape of the land, with hills and valleys shown. Although the actual model is only two-dimensional, the shading and shapes of the dark areas make the model appear three-dimensional.

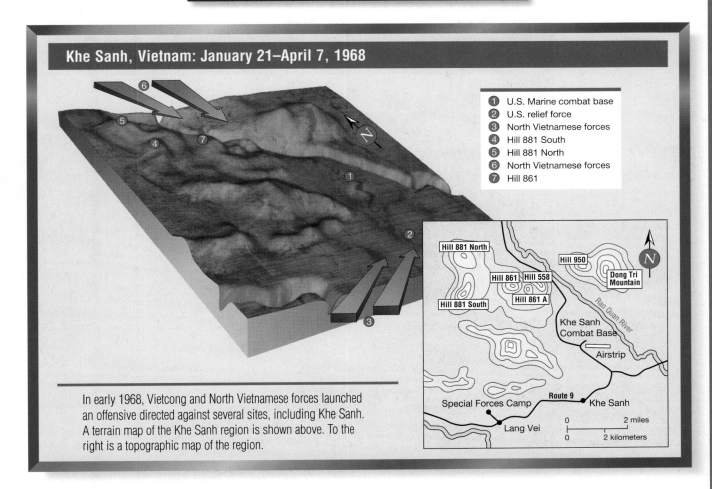

Khe Sanh, Vietnam: January 21–April 7, 1968

1. U.S. Marine combat base
2. U.S. relief force
3. North Vietnamese forces
4. Hill 881 South
5. Hill 881 North
6. North Vietnamese forces
7. Hill 861

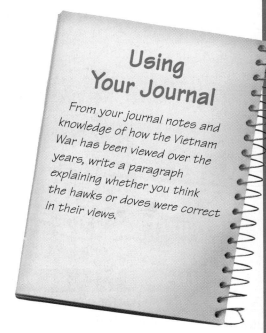

Hill 881 North
Hill 950
Hill 861   Hill 558
Dong Tri Mountain
Hill 881 South   Hill 861 A
Rao Quan River
Khe Sanh Combat Base
Airstrip
Special Forces Camp   Route 9   Khe Sanh
Lang Vei
0   2 miles
0   2 kilometers

In early 1968, Vietcong and North Vietnamese forces launched an offensive directed against several sites, including Khe Sanh. A terrain map of the Khe Sanh region is shown above. To the right is a topographic map of the region.

The topographic map is a two-dimensional map showing elevations using contour lines. A contour line represents points that are all at the same elevation. Each contour line represents a successively higher or lower elevation. The vertical distance between contour lines is the same for all lines in a particular topographic map.

Practicing the Skill

Use the two terrain maps to answer the following questions.

1. The 3-D terrain model shows the paths of North Vietnamese forces during one part of the Tet offensive. Over what land features did the North Vietnamese forces travel?

2. Why do you suppose there are no distance or elevation scales on the 3-D model?

3. Can elevation of the hills in either map be determined? Why or why not?

Using Your Journal

From your journal notes and knowledge of how the Vietnam War has been viewed over the years, write a paragraph explaining whether you think the hawks or doves were correct in their views.

CHAPTER 34

★★

Camelot to Watergate
1960–1976

▶ **HYDRANT DECORATED FOR NATION'S BICENTENNIAL**

Setting the Scene

Focus

During the brief administration of John F. Kennedy, his leadership and the American people were repeatedly tested by staggering challenges at home and abroad. During Johnson's administration federal spending for social programs, along with the cost of the war in Vietnam, strained the government's budget. The Nixon administration was troubled by questions about illegal activities that led to Nixon's resignation and left the nation with deep wounds.

Concepts to Understand

★ How election mandates affect a President's ability to govern
★ How presidential power is balanced by the other branches of federal government

Read to Discover . . .

★ how Kennedy's and Johnson's approaches to economic problems differed from Nixon's.
★ what developments caused Nixon to resign the presidency.

Journal Notes

In what ways has corruption affected politics in America? Note details in your journal as you read the chapter.

CULTURAL

● **1964** *The Beatles come to America*

● **1968** *Cost of mailing a letter increases to 6 cents*
● **1969** *Neil Armstrong walks on the moon*

| 1960 | 1965 |

● **1963** *Kennedy assassinated; Lyndon Johnson becomes President*

● **1968** *Nixon appoints Warren Burger head of Supreme Court*
● **1969** *Nixon announces new federalism*

POLITICAL

The Peace Corps in Ethiopia, 1966
by Norman Rockwell

Rockwell's painting depicts a young American volunteer giving instructions on the use of a plow. Peace Corps volunteers worked in many developing countries around the world.

◀ PRESIDENT JOHN F. KENNEDY

• **1971** *Amtrak passenger service begins*

• **1976** *Bicentennial celebration of the United States*

1970

1975

• **1973** *Vice President Agnew resigns*
• **1974** *Watergate scandal unfolds; Nixon resigns*

• **1975** *Several of Nixon's aides are convicted*

★★

Kennedy's New Frontier

Setting the Scene

Section Focus

By the late 1950s, many people in the United States felt it was time to attack the nation's problems vigorously. Despite the prosperity of the postwar years, poverty was still prevalent. Eisenhower, the first President to be legally limited to two terms, would soon be leaving office. The people looked to his still-unchosen successor to provide strong, active leadership.

Objectives

After studying this section, you should be able to

★ describe important legislation Kennedy proposed during his term of office.

★ describe the impact of Kennedy's death on the nation.

Key Terms

mandate, pragmatist, urban renewal

◀ **DECORATIVE FLAG, COMPUTER ART**

ashington, D.C., glittered during the Kennedy years. As never before, millions became familiar with the occupants of the White House. The public's enchantment with Kennedy was not shared by Congress, however. Many of Kennedy's most important legislative efforts would have to wait until after his death to become law.

■ The Election of 1960

In the 1960 presidential campaign, the Republicans chose Vice President Richard M. Nixon and the Democrats chose Senator John F. Kennedy of Massachusetts. As his vice-presidential running mate Nixon chose UN Ambassador Henry Cabot Lodge. To win Southern support, Kennedy chose Texas Senator Lyndon B. Johnson.

The backgrounds of the two presidential candidates presented striking contrasts. Kennedy was a Catholic and the second-oldest son of a wealthy family. Nixon, born in California, was from far more humble origins, and his Quaker mother had struggled to keep the family together.

There were also similarities between the two men. Both were young: Nixon was 47 years old, and Kennedy was 43. Nixon and Kennedy were experienced legislators, both having served in the House of Representatives or in the Senate. Nixon had also served eight years as Eisenhower's Vice President.

The Impact of Television

The political differences between the candidates were small. Both were considered "cold warriors" who believed that communism was the chief threat to the way of life in the United States. Senator Kennedy hoped to take advantage of Republican weaknesses and challenged Nixon to a series of televised debates. Nixon was the more skilled debater, and most who heard the debates on radio declared Nixon the winner. Yet, the millions more who watched on television thought a well-prepared, poised, and youthful Senator Kennedy won the debates. The debates were one of the earliest examples of the strong impact television would have on politics in the United States.

The Issue of Religion

Political observers wondered whether Kennedy's religion would be an obstacle to his election. No Catholic had ever been elected President, and some believed that a Catholic could not make official decisions independent from the Roman Catholic Church. Kennedy answered by stressing his belief in the separation of church and state. He declared he would resign, rather than violate either his conscience or the interests of the nation.

Kennedy won the election, finally laying to rest the idea that a Roman Catholic could not be elected President. Analyzing his victory, Kennedy concluded, "It was TV more than anything else that turned the tide." However, he carried the election by one of the narrowest margins in American history. He won the popular vote by 120,000 out of 68 million votes cast and the Electoral College by 303 to 219. In several states a difference of only a few thousand votes would have swung the electoral votes the other way. As a result, Kennedy did not enter office with a clear **mandate,** or endorsement, of his ideas from the American people. Nevertheless, though he was cautious at first, the new President moved ahead with his domestic program.

► KENNEDY-NIXON DEBATE

Visualizing History

▲ THE 1960 ELECTION At the start of the 1960 election campaign, polls showed Richard Nixon in the lead. Kennedy, who had been less in the public eye than Nixon, began to draw enthusiastic responses on the campaign trail and revealed that he was highly informed and poised under fire. *What impact did the televised debates have on voters?*

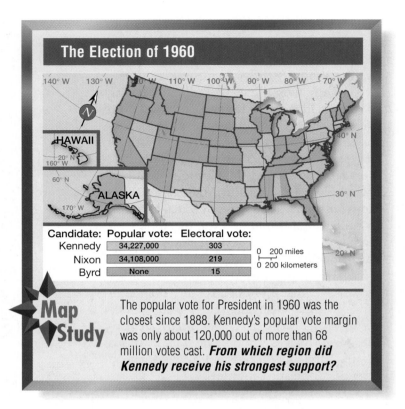

The Election of 1960

Candidate:	Popular vote:	Electoral vote:
Kennedy	34,227,000	303
Nixon	34,108,000	219
Byrd	None	15

0 200 miles
0 200 kilometers

Map Study

The popular vote for President in 1960 was the closest since 1888. Kennedy's popular vote margin was only about 120,000 out of more than 68 million votes cast. *From which region did Kennedy receive his strongest support?*

■ The New Frontier

Kennedy devoted his Inaugural Address to defining the role of the United States in a divided world. The torch, he said, had been "passed to a new generation," committed to the rights for which the United States had stood since the Revolution. He warned the communist world that the United States would remain strong, but he also urged both sides to renew the search for peace. He wanted both to join forces against the common enemies of "tyranny, poverty, disease, and war itself." In ringing tones, he declared:

> ❝ My fellow Americans, ask not what your country can do for you: Ask what you can do for your country. My fellow citizens of the world: Ask not what America can do for you, but what together we can do for the freedom of man. ❞

The Kennedy administration became known as the "New Frontier." For the first time, the future of the United States lay in the hands of those born in the twentieth century. The President and his closest advisers

were intelligent and tough-minded. They were sure of their ability to make the country and the world better places to live in.

In public the new President mixed idealism with realism and informality with dignity. Although he showed a great deal of idealism, Kennedy was also a **pragmatist**—one who searches for practical solutions to problems. Above all, Kennedy seemed to have the gift of leadership that inspired trust and devotion. Kennedy's qualities seemed to appeal not only to those in the United States but to people all over the world.

■ Kennedy's Economic Program

Essentially, Kennedy's New Frontier was a continuation of Roosevelt's New Deal and Truman's Fair Deal. Kennedy promised to stimulate the economy with tax cuts and increased federal spending.

Promoting Economic Growth

In 1960, though the country was still prosperous, the economy was slowing down. When Kennedy became President, the nation's rate of economic growth was only 3 percent a year. Kennedy looked for ways to increase growth and create more jobs. In stimulating the economy, he chose not to rely on federal spending, which tends to cause inflation. Instead, he sought to increase business production and efficiency. His administration also asked businesses to hold down prices and labor leaders to hold down requests for pay increases.

Conflicts With Steel Companies

Prodded by Secretary of Labor Arthur Goldberg, labor unions in the steel industry agreed to reduce their demands for higher wages. Despite this agreement, several steel companies raised prices sharply in 1962. Kennedy denounced the steel company executives and threatened to have the Department of Defense buy cheaper steel from foreign companies. He also instructed the Justice Department to investigate whether the steel industry was guilty of price-fixing. The steel companies backed down and cut their prices. To achieve this victory, however, Kennedy had strained his relations with the nation's business leaders. As a result of his actions to stimulate the economy, Kennedy achieved his aim of raising the growth rate, which doubled during his administration.

Legislative Victories

Kennedy was able to win some legislative victories in his domestic program. After getting a bill for federal aid to public schools passed, he tried to wipe out areas of poverty, notably in the Appalachian Mountain region, in much of the South, and in the nation's inner cities. Kennedy supported the Area Redevelopment Act, designed to encourage industries to move into economically depressed areas. His Housing Act of 1961 called for $5 billion for **urban renewal,** or programs to improve homes and neighborhoods in the inner cities.

Perhaps his most significant victory was increased funding for the National Aeronautics and Space Administration (NASA). Kennedy challenged the nation and NASA with the goal of putting an astronaut on the moon by 1970. There were those who objected to spending an estimated $20 billion for the space program, but Kennedy saw space exploration as a challenge to the nation's prestige and a symbol of cold war rivalry with the Soviet Union.

Conflict With Congress

Although Kennedy achieved some legislative victories, conflict with Congress prevented him from getting much of his domestic program passed. Despite the fact that the Democratic party enjoyed large majorities in both houses, a coalition of conservative Southern Democrats dominated Congress, rejecting many New Frontier measures.

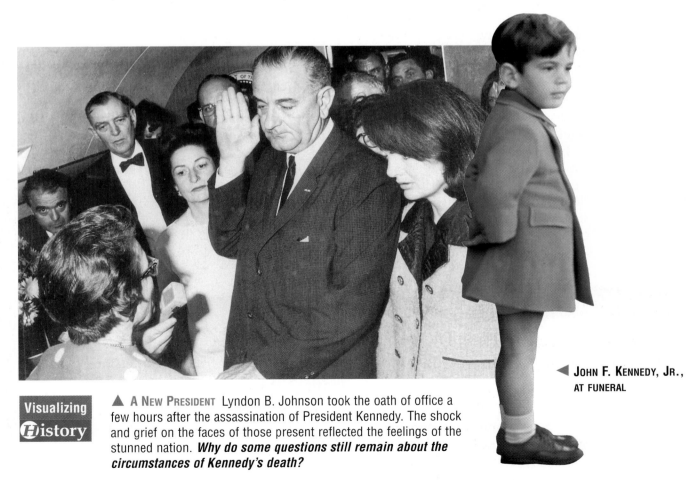

◀ JOHN F. KENNEDY, JR., AT FUNERAL

Visualizing History ▲ A NEW PRESIDENT Lyndon B. Johnson took the oath of office a few hours after the assassination of President Kennedy. The shock and grief on the faces of those present reflected the feelings of the stunned nation. *Why do some questions still remain about the circumstances of Kennedy's death?*

When Kennedy proposed that the government recognize the problems of cities by creating a new cabinet department for urban affairs, Congress voted down the proposal. Kennedy also asked for a national health insurance program, medicare, to help older citizens pay their medical bills. The Senate defeated this bill, which was opposed by many doctors. The President called the Senate's action a "serious defeat for every American family."

■ Tragedy in Dallas

Kennedy hoped to achieve a greater mandate for his domestic program in the election of 1964. To that end, he traveled to Dallas, Texas, to smooth party differences and gather support. In Dallas, on November 22, 1963, the President was assassinated.

The sense of tragedy and grief that many felt was caught by a conversation between the newspaper columnist Mary McGrory and Daniel Moynihan, a member of Kennedy's staff. In response to McGrory's remark that "we'll never laugh again," Moynihan replied, "Heavens, Mary, we'll laugh again. It's just that we'll never be young again." It was this feeling of youth snuffed out, of promise unfulfilled, that made Kennedy's death seem peculiarly tragic to many.

The country and the world were deeply shocked and saddened at this loss. Americans everywhere grieved over the President's death. In Italy, people brought flowers to the gates of the American embassy in Rome. In India, crowds wept in the streets of New Delhi. In Africa, President Sékou Touré of Guinea said, "I have lost my only true friend in the outside world."

The Warren Commission

Kennedy's alleged assassin, Lee Harvey Oswald, was himself shot to death only two days after the assassination. This event led to speculation that Oswald was killed to protect others who may have helped plan the crime. In 1964, a national commission headed by Chief Justice Warren concluded that Oswald was indeed the assassin and that he acted alone. The commission's report did leave important questions unanswered, though, and theories still persist that Oswald acted as part of a conspiracy. None of those theories has gained wide acceptance, however.

Johnson Takes Over

Kennedy was succeeded in office by Vice President Lyndon B. Johnson. Johnson took the oath of office on the plane that carried Kennedy's body from Dallas back to Washington, D.C. From Kennedy, Johnson inherited both unsolved problems and unfulfilled promises.

In domestic policy, Kennedy's New Frontier program was stalled in Congress. Yet, only two years after his death, most of these programs became law. The public reaction to the young President's tragic death, combined with the political skills of Lyndon Johnson, made possible sweeping social reform.

Section 1 ★ Review

Checking for Understanding

1. **Identify** New Frontier, Housing Act of 1961, NASA.

2. **Define** mandate, pragmatist, urban renewal.

3. **List** three economic programs undertaken by President Kennedy.

4. **Explain** why many of Kennedy's domestic programs were not passed.

Critical Thinking

5. **Analyzing Results** How did the lack of an election mandate affect Kennedy's ability to govern?

CONNECTIONS

CONNECTIONS

▲ ASTRONAUT IN SPACE

▼ PHOTOGRAPH OF EARTH FROM THE MOON

Space Race

Americans were stunned by the news that the Soviets had put a satellite—*Sputnik I*—into orbit around the earth in October 1957. Physicist Edward Teller called the launch a Soviet victory in "a battle more important and greater than Pearl Harbor." President Eisenhower told the panicked nation that only its pride, not its security, was damaged.

Americans, however, were threatened by what they considered Soviet technical superiority. In response, Congress passed the National Defense Education Act, which financed science and foreign-language programs in schools. In addition, the National Science Foundation's curriculum-development budget was dramatically increased. Congress also created the National Aeronautics and Space Administration (NASA) in 1958. Huge sums of money were allocated to develop space technology and compete with the Soviets in space.

In the spring of 1961, Alan Shepard, Jr., became the first American to make a space flight. On February 20, 1962, Lieutenant Colonel John Glenn became the first American to orbit the earth. Shortly after Shepard's flight, Kennedy challenged the nation to a great undertaking. He pledged America to landing an individual on the moon by 1970. In July 1969 Commander Neil A. Armstrong, Colonel Edwin E. Aldrin, Jr., and Lieutenant Colonel Michael Collins took off in Apollo.

When they reached the moon, Collins remained aboard the command spacecraft while Aldrin and Armstrong descended to the surface in a lunar module. Millions watched on television as Armstrong became the first human being to set foot on the surface of the moon.

Making the Science Connection

1. How did Americans feel about the success of *Sputnik?*

2. What actions were taken in response to *Sputnik?*

Linking Past and Present

3. Why do you think the United States space program today has less support than it did in the 1960s?

★★

The Great Society

Setting the Scene

Section Focus

Lyndon Johnson was a big man, with great energy and ambition. Sharing the same goals as Kennedy, Johnson carried into legislation the former President's war on poverty. As a former Senate leader, Johnson conceived and skillfully guided through Congress more significant domestic legislation than had been passed since the New Deal.

Objectives

After studying this section, you should be able to

★ explain how Johnson's belief in consensus helped him win the 1964 election.

★ discuss Johnson's efforts to fight poverty in the United States.

Key Term

consensus

◀ *SILENT SPRING* BY RACHEL CARSON

Aided by the Kennedy cabinet and relying on his long experience in government, Lyndon Johnson quickly made the transition from Vice President to President. On November 27, 1963, five days after John F. Kennedy's assassination, Johnson appeared before a joint session of Congress. His words assured the nation's representatives that he intended to carry out Kennedy's programs:

66 *. . . the ideas and ideals which [Kennedy] so nobly represented must and will be translated into effective action. John Kennedy's death commands what his life conveyed—that America must move forward.* 99

Elected to the House of Representatives in 1937 and the Senate in 1948, Johnson was at home in Congress. During the 1950s he was the powerful Democratic Majority Leader of the Senate. Although a Southerner, Johnson had taken a moderate position on most issues and had been a leader in passing the Civil Rights Act of 1957.

■ The Election of 1964

As President, Johnson continued an effective policy of working through **consensus,** or general agreement, that he had developed in Congress. With skilled bargaining, compromising, and even verbal arm-twisting, Johnson reinforced his favorite Biblical quotation, "Come let us reason together." He took over the responsibilities of the chief executive with firmness and strength, determined to pursue the Democratic party's goals of social justice.

In the election of 1964, Johnson used these goals to campaign for President. His campaign plan offered something for everyone: business and labor, rich and poor, young and old, African American and white. Known as "the Great Society," Johnson's domestic program was an effort to expand upon Kennedy's ideas as well as to make a contribution of his own. It was designed to fight poverty, discrimination, unemployment, pollution, and other social ills of America. At the same time, he pledged to provide major tax cuts for individuals and corporations.

To offer voters "a choice, not an echo," Republicans selected an outspoken conservative, Barry Goldwater, to run against Johnson and his liberal running mate, Hubert Humphrey. The Arizona senator ran a determined, uncompromising campaign. His opposition to the Civil Rights Act of 1964 turned away African American voters. His coolness to social security made older people fearful. His support of the open shop hurt him with organized labor. Above all, Goldwater's suggestion that military commanders should be allowed to decide for themselves whether to use nuclear weapons made many people nervous.

As predicted, Johnson's wide appeal won him more than 60 percent of the popular vote. Goldwater carried only his home state of Arizona and 5 Southern states, where former "Dixiecrats" switched to the Republican party. In addition, the Democrats increased their majorities in both houses of Congress. The Great Society had won an overwhelming mandate.

■ War on Poverty

In the mid-1960s the United States had the highest standard of living in the world. But behind the Great Society program was a new awareness that many Americans did not share in the general prosperity.

The Other America

Contributing to this awareness was a book by Michael Harrington entitled *The Other America*, published in 1962. In response to economist John Kenneth Galbraith, who wrote in *The Affluent Society* that only "pockets" of poverty remained, Harrington claimed that as many as 40 million Americans—one-fourth of the population —were poor. He charged:

▲ HELP FOR NEGLECTED AMERICANS The War on Poverty reached into Appalachia where poor soil and lack of education affected many lives. *Why did some writers and leaders call for the government to help the poor?*

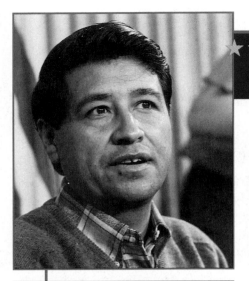

AMERICAN PORTRAITS

Cesar Chavez
1927–1993

Born to Mexican American migrant workers, Cesar Chavez picked crops in the Southwest as a child and young man. At age 25, he began organizing farm workers to win better pay and working conditions.

Early in the 1960s, Chavez founded a union for migrant farm workers and later merged it with another to form the first large-scale organization of farm workers. He then organized a strike against grape growers.

The strike drew national attention as Chavez borrowed tactics from the civil rights movement—marches and a 25-day fast.

Yet the grape growers would not settle. The tide began to turn in 1968 when Chavez asked the American people to boycott grapes. Growers' profits tumbled as consumers began to side with the workers. The strike lasted until 1970, when the growers finally agreed to settle.

> " *The United States contains an underdeveloped nation, a culture of poverty. Its inhabitants do not suffer the extreme poverty of the peasants of Asia . . . yet the mechanism of the misery is similar. They are beyond history, beyond progress, sunk in a paralyzing, maiming routine.* "

Most of the American people knew little of the great mass of human misery, said Harrington. The poor were hidden away in the slums of central cities, in rural areas—especially in Appalachia and the Deep South—and on Native American reservations. Many of the poor were elderly people leading "lives of quiet desperation" in secluded rooms.

It was not possible for these people to "pull themselves up by their bootstraps," Harrington believed. Automation had done away with the jobs of many workers, and small farmers could no longer compete with agribusiness. Then, too, displaced factory workers and farmers did not have the opportunity for the training and work experience needed for new jobs. Further, pensions and social security did not adequately cover medical expenses for older citizens.

Johnson Declares War

Johnson announced his strategy in his first State of the Union Address on January 8, 1964: "This administration . . . declares unconditional war on poverty in America." A new Office of Economic Opportunity (OEO) aimed its billion-dollar budget at illiteracy, unemployment, and disease. The OEO-sponsored VISTA (Volunteers in Service to America) sent workers to improve conditions in poor neighborhoods. Job Corps provided training for the unskilled, while Project Head Start helped poor children prepare for school. The Elementary and Secondary Education Act of 1965 gave direct massive federal aid to public and parochial schools. A similar act provided college scholarships for needy students.

The Great Society's War on Poverty extended federal influence into areas that had traditionally been handled by local governments, private enterprise, or religious groups. In some cases OEO was granted power to overrule local governments.

The emphasis was not simply on relief but on helping poor people help themselves. For example, community action programs taught people to organize protests and put pressure on landlords, employers, and even government agencies to effect change.

Medicare

After nearly 20 years of opposition by those who believed that the government should stay out of health care, Congress passed the Medicare Act. Medicare provided people over age 65 with hospital care. Medical centers were to be set up in areas where such facilities were lacking. The act provided funds for medical schools to increase enrollments and reduce the shortage of doctors.

■ Immigration Reform

To many thousands of immigrants, the United States already represented a "great society"—a land of newfound opportunity and freedom. The doors of this great society had opened wide to immigrants from northwestern Europe and nearly closed to others, because of a quota system that the United States established in 1924.

Out of 157,000 immigrants admitted each year, Great Britain and Ireland were allotted 83,000; India, with a population of 450 million, and Andorra, with a population of 6,400, each were allotted 100. Presidents Truman, Eisenhower, and Kennedy had been unable to persuade Congress to change this system.

Standing beneath the Statue of Liberty, which welcomed immigrants to the country, Johnson signed the Immigration Act of 1965. The law replaced national quotas with global quotas and favored those with special skills. As a result, immigration to the United States from Asia and Latin America increased sharply.

Under Johnson's leadership Congress passed a great number of other important laws in a few months. "We did reach consensus," he concluded. "I think we did convince the vast majority of Americans that the time for procrastinating had passed."

His programs were well-received in part because people saw benefits for themselves. Some businesspeople, for example, benefited from the War on Poverty because of the increased purchasing power of poor people. Johnson's program also included subsidies to farmers.

■ Rising Costs End Great Society

Great Society programs required large sums of money. Federal spending for social purposes rose from $54 billion in 1964 to $98 billion in 1968. Federal budget problems and national inflation made Great Society spending an issue for debate. The $20-billion-a-year cost of the Vietnam War made things worse.

Guns and Butter

At first, Johnson tried to finance the war with taxes, explaining that the nation could afford both guns and butter. New social programs and rising war costs made the federal deficit climb to $28 billion by 1968. The President realized that without additional taxes, either social or military programs would have to be cut. He asked Congress for a tax increase. Congress refused unless the President would cut the budget. Johnson chopped $6 billion out of proposed domestic spending, marking the end of the Great Society.

End of an Era

Lyndon Johnson left office in January 1969 a discouraged man. Unable to build a Great Society at home and wage a war at the same time, he had to waive his chance for another term. The American people had rejected Johnson's policies in Vietnam. Supporters of Nixon, he knew, were not sympathetic to the Great Society programs. The nation had become deeply divided.

The 1960s had begun as a time of youth, optimism, and confidence in the future and ended in war, riots, and violence. Three national heroes—President John F. Kennedy, Dr. Martin Luther King, Jr., and Senator Robert Kennedy—had been assassinated. Tens of thousands of young Americans had been killed or wounded in the most unpopular war the United States had ever fought. The New Frontier and the Great Society programs, designed to make life better for the poor and the needy, had also become casualties of the war.

▲ END OF THE GREAT SOCIETY
President Johnson felt increasing criticism because of the growing dissent over the war and increasing opposition within his own party. *What decision did the President make in 1968 regarding his political future?*

After the unhappy events of 1968, the year itself ended on an ironic note of hope and progress. Late in December 1968 the United States succeeded in sending the first astronauts into orbit around the moon. During one of the most difficult years in American history, the nation had scored a great technological achievement. The photographs sent back from space made planet Earth seem small, peaceful, and beautiful. It brought a new feeling to Americans that no matter how difficult, the problems they faced could be solved.

Growing Concern for the Environment

During the 1960s, greater emphasis was placed on the environment. Many conservation projects had been started during the Great Depression, mostly as a means of providing work for the unemployed. During the same period, the dust bowl demonstrated the need for soil conservation. As time went on, scientists discovered more about the effects of pollutants on the environment, and people became more concerned with environmental health.

The individual most responsible for launching the environmental movement and prompting new regulations was Rachel Carson. From her earliest days, Carson had two great loves: nature and books. At first, she planned to be a writer, but she switched majors from English to biology during her junior year of college. Carson was able to combine her twin loves by becoming a science author.

An aquatic biologist by training, Rachel Carson wrote about the sea with great insight. Her most important book, *Silent Spring* (1962), dealt with the environment. Long aware of the threat posed by careless use of toxic chemicals, she researched carefully and wrote movingly about how modern industry and agriculture were poisoning the planet. *Silent Spring* sparked a federal investigation that backed her conclusions and led to tougher laws regarding harmful chemicals. Rachel Carson died soon after publication of *Silent Spring,* unaware of the ecology movement that her work would inspire.

Section 2 ★ Review

Checking for Understanding

1. **Identify** Barry Goldwater, *The Other America*, Office of Economic Opportunity, Medicare Act.
2. **Define** consensus.
3. **Explain** the Great Society.
4. **List** four programs that were part of the War on Poverty.

Critical Thinking

5. **Classifying Information**   Do all Americans define poverty the same way? Think of what poverty means to you. Make a list of guidelines that you would use to classify Americans who live in poverty. Would your classification meet government standards?

Interpreting Primary Sources

Collage Art in the 1960s

The decade of the 1960s was a fresh period in American art when artists experimented with a variety of media, materials, techniques, and styles. Robert Rauschenberg mastered the technique of *collage,* a two-dimensional art form using a variety of images.

Rauschenberg came into prominence in the mid-1950s when he began to incorporate pieces of discarded cloth, wood, crumpled printed materials, and other manufactured objects, such as tin cans or bottles, onto his canvases. He referred to these works as "combine paintings."

The bold drips and splatters of Rauschenberg's brushwork, as well as his use of geometric shapes and colors, reflect his debt to abstract expressionism, an artistic movement that came into vogue after World War II. Yet his works also point to the emergence of pop art in the 1960s, an artistic style that used commonplace subject matter from popular culture.

Rauschenberg's kaleidoscope-like works often reflect an interesting interplay between reality and art, everyday life and technological achievement. His collages often draw on themes from history. In *Kite* Rauschenberg focuses attention on social unrest in the early 1960s. This is seen in the clash of troops and flags, and an army helicopter poised either to strike or bring assistance. Yet the images of the bald eagle and the military flag parade also stir feelings of patriotism and national pride.

When displayed in 1963, *Kite* may have reminded viewers of American troops in Little Rock or Birmingham, Korea or Vietnam. The eagle, perhaps stained with blood, is positioned at the top of the collage where vertical paint thrusts resemble rocket blasts. This suggests American global power or the will to dominate outer space. The pale blue sky and white areas of the collage are spattered by ominous black markings. *Kite* is thus a statement of discord, a view of America filled with aggression and torn by turmoil.

▼ *KITE* BY ROBERT RAUSCHENBERG, 1963

Examining the Primary Source

1. Which of the images in the collage were probably mass-produced? How can you tell?

2. Describe an image that appears twice in this collage. Why do you think the artist repeated this image?

Critical Thinking

3. **Analyzing Information** Interpret the meaning of Rauschenberg's title *Kite.*

4. **Drawing Conclusions** How does *Kite* capture the dynamic change of a nation?

★★★

An Imperial Presidency

Setting the Scene

Section Focus

Under Nixon the office of the President became more powerful, threatening the balance among the three branches of government. Although Nixon used presidential powers chiefly in foreign affairs, he also expanded them for his own purposes at home. Although he projected a new image during the campaign, the specter of the ruthless Richard Nixon of his early career haunted the White House. His time in office came to be known as the "imperial presidency."

Objectives

After studying this section, you should be able to

★ describe how Nixon tried to deal with the economic problems of the early 1970s.

★ explain how Nixon handled the war on crime and the energy crisis.

Key Terms

stagflation, balance of payments, new federalism, revenue sharing

◀ SEAL OF THE REPUBLICAN NATIONAL COMMITTEE

To Americans and foreigners alike, the United States in the late 1960s had lost its direction. Not only was it losing the war in Vietnam, but its industries were losing their competitive edge. A sense of defeat and decay became apparent. Deep social, political, and racial divisions were threatening to tear society apart. Richard Nixon claimed that he had a "plan to end the war in Vietnam" and "bring Americans together." His promise of peace in Vietnam and tranquility at home appealed to many.

■ Nixon's Political Career

Richard M. Nixon was the first President in modern times to be elected after having lost a previous bid for the presidency. After losing the 1962 California gubernatorial race, his political career seemed over. In the 1968 campaign, however, he changed his public image. The old Nixon had been intensely partisan and ruthless. When he had run for Congress from California in 1946 as a newly discharged naval officer, he charged that his opponent had strong ties to communist organizations. Political opponents called him opportunistic and self-serving.

The new Nixon, however, impressed observers as calm, broad-minded, and statesmanlike. He promised that his administration would be "open to new ideas, open to men and women of both parties, open to the critics as well as those who support us." Bringing the nation together proved difficult, however. With the Democrats in control of Congress, Nixon saw many of his domestic proposals rejected.

The War Against Crime

One of Nixon's domestic successes was his war against crime. During the 1968 campaign, Nixon spoke out against permissive attitudes toward the rights of those accused of crimes. Nixon criticized the record of the Supreme Court under Chief Justice Earl Warren. He denounced Supreme Court decisions that curtailed the powers of the police in the interrogation of suspects and that forbade the use of electronic "bugging" equipment for gathering evidence. Such decisions, Nixon maintained, violated "the first civil right of every American to be free of domestic violence." He promised to fill vacancies on the Supreme Court with judges who would not "weaken the peace forces as against the criminal forces."

Nixon eventually succeeded in his campaign to change the liberal thrust of the Court. When Chief Justice Warren resigned shortly after Nixon took office, the President nominated Warren Burger, a respected conservative judge, to take his place. He also placed three other conservative justices on the Court. The Burger Court, known to critics as the Nixon Court, did not abolish the protections of criminal suspects set up by the Warren Court. It did, however, whittle them down. Its harder line against criminals was dramatically revealed when it reversed the opinion of the Warren Court that capital punishment was a violation of the Bill of Rights.

Nixon's Economic Policies

Nixon inherited difficult economic problems. The combined costs of President Johnson's War on Poverty and the Vietnam War had produced a large federal budget deficit and mounting inflation. Between 1964 and 1969, the dollar lost one-fifth of its purchasing power.

Stagflation

The President tackled inflation by curtailing the supply of money. By the end of 1970, however, it was apparent that the plan was not working. Restricting the supply of money drove interest rates up, and higher

Visualizing History

▲ THE BURGER COURT The Supreme Court is generally referred to by the name of its chief justice. Thus, in 1969, when Warren E. Burger became chief justice, the Supreme Court became known as the Burger Court. *Why had President Nixon criticized the Warren Court?*

Shopping Malls

A 1973 report on New Jersey's Cherry Hill Mall observed that the shopping mall had become to the suburb what Main Street once was to the small town—the focus of community life. The period between 1971 and 1975 was a heyday of mall construction. Cities and suburbs across the United States became home to enclosed malls featuring, under one roof, a fairly predictable array of small specialty stores for books, gifts, and shoes.

Large malls typically included major department stores as dependable "anchors" for sales and customers, as well as several popular restaurants. Some malls also had portable boutique stands that sold everything from perfume to wicker.

Mall managers were enormously successful in not only attracting shoppers, but also walkers, joggers, and vast crowds of teenagers just "hanging out." Malls became such popular gathering places in the early 1970s that a

▲ MALL OF THE AMERICAS, BLOOMINGTON, MINNESOTA

high school in Bethesda, Maryland, held its senior prom at one.

Despite the carefully controlled environment that malls maintain through regulated climate, piped-in music, security personnel, and squeaky cleanliness, they did not escape the social upheaval of the 1970s. Several large malls became sites for Vietnam War protests.

interest rates discouraged investment. Unemployment increased, and the stock market declined. The slowdown in business activity reduced federal revenues, and inflation accelerated. This economic slowdown, coupled with inflation, was called **stagflation.**

To meet the problem of stagflation, Nixon turned to other, less conservative measures. In August 1971 he announced his New Economic Policy, which called for a 90-day freeze on wages, prices, and rents. This was followed by a system of wage and price controls in November. In January 1973 the President relaxed controls, and prices rose sharply. In response, a new freeze was imposed in June.

President Nixon also took steps to end the recession by stimulating the economy. He proposed tax cuts for both businesses and individuals, hoping that when the demand went up, production would rise and unemployment would fall. After making some revisions in the President's proposals, Congress enacted tax cuts in December 1971. The President also used deficit spending to fight recession.

These measures, however, failed to solve the problem of stagflation. Although the tax cuts and deficit spending helped to ease the recession, they added to inflation. On the other hand, while the controls slowed inflation for a time, they did little to help the economy grow or to lower unemployment.

A Balance of Payments Deficit

Inflation caused prices to rise not only on domestic goods, but on exports. So, fewer exports were purchased. This resulted in a balance of payments deficit. The **balance of payments** is the difference between the money paid to and received from other nations. In this case, the nation was spending more than it received. Between 1970 and 1971, the nation's balance of payments deficit jumped from $4 billion to $22 billion.

The deficit was evidence that the United States had lost its dominance in world markets. Between 1950 and 1970, for example, the United States's share of world automobile production dropped from 76 to 31 percent, and the same phenomenon was occurring in the textile, shoe, and electrical equipment industries.

A serious effect of the balance of payments deficit was that it weakened other nations' confidence in the value of the dollar. Because world trade depends on stable money and because the dollar was the major currency in the world, the dollar crisis threatened to disrupt trade.

Trying to improve the economic situation, Nixon acted decisively. To combat inflation, in August 1971 he announced, as noted earlier, a 90-day freeze on prices and wages. To discourage imports, he placed an additional duty of 10 percent on all goods purchased from abroad. He also allowed the dollar to decline in value in relation to foreign currencies, making it more expensive for Americans to buy goods from other countries. Therefore, goods made in the United States became cheaper than foreign-made goods, and that promoted exports.

Although Nixon's policies brought some relief, inflation, chronic unemployment, and the loss of foreign markets remained a problem throughout his presidency. The measures also caused ill will in nations that depended on American markets for their products.

The New Federalism

Nixon also announced his **new federalism,** which was intended to reduce the federal government's role in the economy and turn many of its tasks over to state and local governments. Following the President's lead, Congress passed a series of **revenue-sharing** bills that granted federal funds to local agencies to use as they saw fit.

■ The Energy Crisis

Another problem concerned energy. In the fall of 1973, Arab nations placed an embargo on crude oil shipments from the Middle East. The purpose of the embargo was to force the United States to stop supporting Israel in its struggle with the Arab states. Support for Israel did not change, but the embargo produced an energy crisis in America—and near panic. In some areas the price of petroleum shot up nearly 400 percent, and there were shortages of gasoline for cars and heating oil for homes, schools, and businesses.

Although the United States had about one-sixteenth of the world's population, Americans consumed about one-third of the world's energy. Most of this energy came from such nonrenewable resources as oil, gas, and coal. Coal reserves were abundant in America but supplied less than 20 percent of the nation's energy needs. By 1973, the United States was importing about 6 million barrels of oil each day, or about 36 percent of the oil needed to heat homes and to keep factories and automobiles running.

President Nixon announced a plan to make the country self-sufficient in energy by 1980. He called for higher taxes on imported oil and encouraged Americans to take conservation measures, such as lowering their thermostats at home and at work. Congress passed a law requiring states to lower the speed limit on highways to 55 miles per hour to save gasoline and approved the construction of a pipeline in Alaska for the shipment of newly discovered oil to refineries.

▼ SIGN OF THE TIMES

Temporarily... 10 GALLONS PER CUSTOMER We appreciate your business & cooperation.

▲ ENERGY CRISIS One of the nation's most important concerns during the Nixon administration was the energy crisis. Long lines of cars at gas stations were a sign of the times.
What actions did the administration take to conserve energy?

Congress provided some tax incentives to encourage energy research and put the nation on year-round daylight saving time for two years.

After the Arab nations lifted the oil embargo in March 1974, most Americans forgot about the energy crisis mentality. They began once again to use fuel in increasing quantities. However, fuel prices began a steep rise as the oil shortage continued. In the 1960s the major oil-exporting nations had formed the Organization of Petroleum Exporting Countries (OPEC). By 1970 OPEC had begun to raise prices, and over the next decade the cost of oil increased from less than $2 a barrel to more than $30 a barrel. The increases in the price of oil by the OPEC members contributed to the problems that plagued the American economy throughout the 1970s.

Section 3 ★ Review

Checking for Understanding

1. **Identify** Warren Burger.

2. **Define** stagflation, balance of payments, new federalism, revenue sharing.

3. **Point out** how Nixon affected the criminal justice system.

4. **Describe** two features of Nixon's economic policies.

Critical Thinking

5. **Evaluating Policy** Write an evaluation of the effectiveness of Nixon's policy for handling inflation.

★★★

The Watergate Scandal

Setting the Scene

Section Focus

The public disclosure of Richard Nixon's involvement in the Watergate scandal culminated in his resignation from office. It also led Congress and the Supreme Court to reassert their constitutional powers. Although confidence in the government was shaken by Watergate, the bicentennial, or the 200th anniversary of the American Revolution, was cause for celebration.

Objectives

After studying this section, you should be able to

★ explain how the constitutional process solved the Watergate crisis.

★ list the ways in which Congress sought to reassert its constitutional powers.

Key Terms

executive privilege, impound, deregulation

◀ STREET SIGN, WASHINGTON, D.C.

Not surprisingly, the Republican party nominated President Nixon as its candidate in the election of 1972. Nixon ran against Senator George McGovern of South Dakota, who won the Democratic nomination with the support of a coalition of activists—young people, African Americans, and women.

■ A Crisis in the Presidency

Almost from the beginning, however, the McGovern campaign derailed itself. McGovern's running mate, Senator Thomas Eagleton, was forced to withdraw when it was disclosed that he had been hospitalized for depression. In addition, Democratic party regulars and labor union leaders were cool, if not hostile, toward the liberal McGovern's candidacy.

In contrast, President Nixon conducted a perfect campaign. The almost-complete withdrawal of United States troops from Vietnam defused the war issue, and the summits in Beijing and Moscow signaled an easing of cold war tensions. Moreover, the President solidified his support among "middle Americans" by calling for law and order, by opposing busing, and by making continuous appeals to patriotism.

On Election Day the President received 61 percent of the popular vote and won every electoral vote except those of Massachusetts and the District of Columbia.

CREEP

It was later learned, however, that this tremendous victory was not won entirely fairly. During the campaign the President and his political advisers organized the Committee to Reelect the President (CREEP) and collected more than $50 million for Nixon's reelection campaign, some of which was illegally received. Some campaign contributions were used to finance "dirty tricks" against the Democrats.

The Watergate Break-in

A group of CREEP employees were caught "bugging" the offices of the Democratic National Committee in the Watergate building in Washington, D.C. Although the President's press secretary dismissed the break-in as a "third-rate burglary," this seemingly insignificant incident had serious consequences for the President.

Rumors began to circulate that the President himself had ordered the Watergate break-in. Stories were published in the *Washington Post* and other newspapers that linked key members of the White House staff and CREEP to the break-in. It was reported that key Nixon advisers had paid the Watergate burglars almost $1 million in "hush money" to plead guilty and say nothing else at their trials. To quiet the rumors, the President ordered his attorney general to appoint a special prosecutor, Harvard law professor Archibald Cox, to investigate the case.

The Investigation

At the same time, a special Senate committee began to hold televised hearings on the break-in and other abuses alleged to have been committed during the campaign of 1972. Starting in May 1973, millions of Americans watched in fascination as a parade of witnesses testified about illegal activities carried out by the White House staff and by CREEP. Perhaps the most startling discovery was that the President tape-recorded most of the conversations he had in the Oval Office.

The Trial

Following these revelations, federal grand juries indicted members of the Nixon administration for their illegal activities, including the unauthorized wiretapping, burglaries, illegal campaign contributions, and the bribing of witnesses. Eventually 25 people connected with the administration—including former Attorney General John Mitchell and two of Nixon's closest White House aides, H. R. Haldeman and John D. Erlichman—were convicted and served prison terms for Watergate-related crimes.

■ The President Answers

Month after month President Nixon continued to deny any involvement in Watergate. Claiming **executive privilege,** or the principle that the President does not have to give information to other branches of the government, Nixon refused to turn over the White House tapes to the special prosecutor. In October 1973, he offered to provide written summaries of the tapes.

The Saturday Night Massacre

When the special prosecutor insisted on having the tapes, Nixon ordered the attorney general to remove Cox. Both the attorney general and his top assistant resigned rather than carry out the President's order. Finally Nixon found a Justice Department official who was willing to fire Cox. The dismissal of the special prosecutor became known as the "Saturday Night Massacre," and it provoked a wave of public protest as well as the first serious calls for Nixon's impeachment.

Agnew Resigns

October 1973 proved to be a disastrous time for Richard Nixon for other reasons as well. His Vice President, Spiro Agnew, was forced to resign in disgrace. A grand jury found that Agnew, while governor of Maryland, had taken bribes from contractors who did business with the state. It was further revealed that Agnew continued to receive such payments while he was Vice President. Nixon nominated Gerald Ford, the Republican leader of the House of Representatives, as the new Vice President.

Nixon Proclaims Innocence

In an effort to quiet public outrage over the Saturday Night Massacre, Nixon appointed another special prosecutor in

November 1973. In April 1974, the President released written transcripts of 47 tape-recorded conversations. Even though the transcripts had been heavily edited, many believed the tapes indicated the President had indeed been involved in covering up the Watergate scandal. Nevertheless, the President still continued to proclaim his innocence:

66 *If read with an open and fair mind and read together with the record of actions I took, these transcripts will show that what I have stated since the beginning to be the truth . . . my actions were directed toward finding the facts and seeing that justice was done, fairly and according to the law.* 99

Tapes Reveal Cover-up

In July the Supreme Court ruled that the President had to turn over the tapes themselves, not just their transcripts. A month later Nixon complied and handed over the tapes. One tape provided direct evidence that on June 23, 1972, only six days after the Watergate break-in, the President had

arranged a cover-up. With this news, even the President's strongest supporters conceded that there was sufficient evidence to support impeachment. They advised Nixon that it seemed certain the House would impeach him and that the Senate would find him guilty. On August 8, 1974, Nixon announced on national television that he would resign. He also expressed hope that his departure would begin the process of healing the country.

■ Ford Becomes President

The next day Gerald Ford was sworn in as the thirty-eighth President. President Ford appointed Nelson Rockefeller, former governor of New York, as his Vice President, making them the first unelected presidential team in the nation's history.

At first, President Ford inspired public confidence. He assured a joint session of Congress that his administration would be free of "illegal tappings, eavesdropping, buggings, or break-ins." The new President seemed to be a decent, candid, and trustworthy man.

A month after entering office, however, Ford damaged his public image by granting Richard Nixon an unconditional pardon for

▲ WATERGATE The Watergate hearings led to criminal charges against several top White House aides, including H. R. Haldeman (left) and Jeb Stuart Magruder (speaking at hearing). President Nixon disavowed knowledge of the break-in. *What is executive privilege?*

▲ President Nixon leaves the White House

all crimes he committed or may have committed while in office. Ford insisted that he was acting not out of sympathy for Nixon, but in the public interest. He wanted to avoid the publicity and national division that a trial would create. Nevertheless, the pardon aroused fierce and widespread criticism of the new President.

Congress Reasserts Its Authority

When he took office, Gerald Ford promised to adopt a policy of "communication, conciliation, compromise, and cooperation" with Congress. He expected good relations with Congress, since he had served for 25 years as a representative and almost a decade as House Republican leader. However, the President and Congress were often at odds because Ford was a conservative, and liberal Democrats controlled both houses of Congress. In addition, the new President confronted a Congress that was determined to reassert its authority over what some critics called the "imperial presidency."

Congress Attacks Executive Privilege

To counter the trend toward greater presidential power and curb future abuses, Congress passed a series of laws. In the last year of the Nixon administration, as Watergate weakened the President, Congress attempted to regain some of its power. In November 1973, it passed the War Powers Act in spite of President Nixon's veto. This law required that the President report to Congress within 48 hours after sending combat troops abroad or after engaging in any military action. Unless Congress approved his action, the President had to withdraw all troops within 60 days. After the Watergate crisis, Congress passed the Congressional Budget and Impoundment Control Act of 1974, which allowed Congress to force the President to spend any appropriations that he attempted to **impound,** or withhold, unless he could justify his action to both houses.

Quarrels Over the Economy

One of the biggest problems facing President Ford and Congress was the economic recession. To Ford, inflation and the nation's dependence on foreign oil were the greatest threats to recovery. The Democratic Congress was more alarmed by the highest rates of unemployment and the lowest levels of productivity since the Great Depression of the 1930s.

Like Nixon, President Ford wanted to cut spending on social welfare programs and adopt an energy program. He favored **deregulation,** or removing price controls, of gas and oil. This would cause a rise in prices so people would use less. Increased profits would go toward helping companies find alternate forms of energy. Congress, however, did not cooperate. Ford, in turn, prevented the enactment of liberal Democratic legislation by the use of the veto power.

Ford's Foreign Policy

At first, Congress allowed the President greater leeway in foreign policy than it had to past officeholders. Ford met with leaders of NATO and the Warsaw Pact to sign the Helsinki Accords in August 1975. Under the terms of the accords, the parties recognized the borders of the countries of Eastern Europe and committed themselves to respect and protect the human rights of their citizens.

Soon, however, in foreign policy, as in domestic affairs, Ford came into conflict with the Democratic-controlled Congress. In 1975 Congress refused President Ford's request for additional funds to aid South Vietnam and Cambodia in their continuing civil wars. As a result, the Cambodian government surrendered to the repressive Khmer Rouge forces on April 17. Twelve days later the North Vietnamese and the Vietcong overran Saigon and forced the government of South Vietnam to surrender. Communist regimes were now in control everywhere in Indochina except Thailand, which remained an ally.

■ The Bicentennial

Despite difficulties with Congress, President Ford headed for Boston to participate in the opening ceremonies of the bicentennial, celebrating the nation's 200th birthday. As July 4, 1976 approached, most people in the United States caught the bicentennial spirit. Cities, towns, and villages held parades and concerts and displayed fireworks. A procession of Conestoga wagons traveled to Valley Forge, Pennsylvania, and eighteenth-century sailing ships from many countries majestically sailed into New York Harbor on the Fourth of July.

▲ **THE NATION'S BICENTENNIAL** In 1976 Americans were anxious to put the tragedy of the Vietnam War and the Watergate affair behind them. A bicentennial spirit swept the nation as millions participated in parades, fireworks displays, and other activities. *Who was the nation's President during this time?*

As the bicentennial ended, the nation felt a new sense of hopefulness. It knew that the constitutional system had curbed the abuses of the imperial presidency. The people of the United States were proud of achievements such as the space program, and they began to regain their sense of confidence.

Section 4 ★ Review

Checking for Understanding

1. **Identify** George McGovern, CREEP, Archibald Cox, Gerald Ford, War Powers Act, Helsinki Accords.

2. **Define** executive privilege, impound, deregulation.

3. **Explain** why Nixon resigned.

4. **Summarize** actions Congress took to reassert its authority.

Critical Thinking

5. **Interpreting Viewpoints** Explain why many Americans, although dismayed by the Watergate scandal, felt proud of the way their government functioned during the crisis.

Using Vocabulary

Each of the terms below has significance for the concept of presidential power. Use each of these terms in a sentence, describing how it is related to this concept.

mandate   executive privilege
pragmatist   impound
consensus

Reviewing Facts

1. **Describe** Kennedy's presidential style.
2. **State** two legislative victories and two legislative setbacks for Kennedy.
3. **Identify** four achievements of the Johnson administration.
4. **Describe** why there was a decrease in United States dominance of world markets.
5. **Explain** the significance of Nixon's new federalism.
6. **Chart** the sequence of events that led to Nixon's resignation.

Understanding Concepts

Mandates

1. Examine the Kennedy and Johnson presidencies and describe how an election mandate affected each man's ability to govern.
2. Explain the importance of political consensus to President Johnson.

Presidential Power

3. What function did secrecy serve in the Nixon presidency? Why did some Americans and members of Congress resent this tactic?
4. When President Nixon resigned over Watergate, some nations expressed astonishment that Americans would force their highest leader to step down over a "relatively small offense." Is it important for our nation to hold politicians accountable for their actions? Explain.

Critical Thinking

1. **Comparing and Contrasting** Explain how Kennedy and Johnson differed in their relationships with Congress.
2. **Drawing Conclusions** What are the lessons of the Watergate scandal? Would you agree that our system of government was vindicated by this affair? What long-term repercussions do you think Watergate had on Americans' views of government and politicians?
3. **Analyzing Fine Art** Study the painting that appears on this page, then answer the questions that follow.
   a. What do you think the artist is expressing in this painting?
   b. How does the artist lead your eye around the composition?
   c. Do you like this painting? Why or why not?

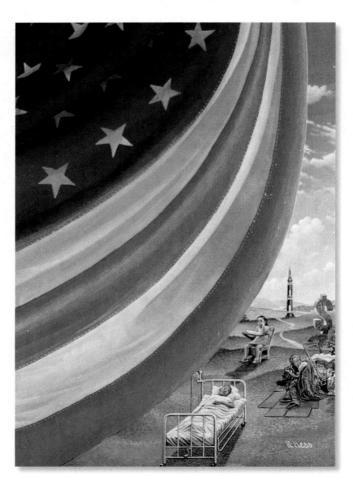

Writing About History

Cause and Effect

Imagine you are a reporter for the *Washington Post* and you have discovered evidence of the President's involvement in the Watergate break-in. You are aware of Nixon's tremendous power as well as his denial that he had anything to do with it. Write a follow-up article after the President has resigned, reviewing the importance of the media and its effect on the resignation.

Cooperative Learning

You will work in small groups to investigate testimony before the Senate subcommittee on Watergate. Each group member should select a different witness to research. Use the actual transcripts of the hearings to discover the process the committee really went through. Then meet together and discuss your findings with the class.

Social Studies Skills

Analyzing Political Maps

An election map is a type of political map. It shows how each state voted in an election. The legend indicates which candidate each color represents. Popular vote and electoral vote are sometimes shown on the map with each state.

Practicing the Skill

Use the election map on this page and the election map on page 952 to answer the following questions.

1. What election results does the map show?

2. Who were the candidates in the 1968 election?

3. Speculate on why Wallace won only Southern states.

4. Compare this election map with the election map on page 952. In both, the popular votes are relatively close, but the electoral votes are not so close. How can this be explained?

5. In comparing the two maps, where was Nixon consistently weak?

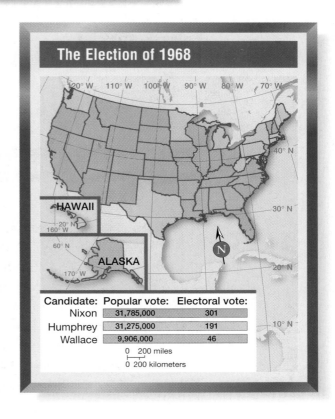

The Election of 1968

Candidate:	Popular vote:	Electoral vote:
Nixon	31,785,000	301
Humphrey	31,275,000	191
Wallace	9,906,000	46

0   200 miles
0 200 kilometers

Using Your Journal

Review your journal notes about corruption in the government as evidenced by the Watergate scandal. Write a paragraph describing how public awareness of that corruption affected people's views during later scandals in government. To answer, you may have to do extra research.

CHAPTER 35

★★

Search for Solutions
1976–1992

▶ **YELLOW RIBBON TREE TIE**

Setting the Scene

Focus

Despite success in foreign affairs, Jimmy Carter rapidly lost the people's confidence. In the next election, they turned to the conservative Ronald Reagan to restore their confidence. During his administration, the economy recovered and relations with the Soviet Union improved. But Reagan left a mixed legacy, and problems with the economy were passed on to his successor, George Bush, who also had to redefine America's role in world affairs.

Concepts to Understand

★ How the leadership of Carter, Reagan, and Bush shaped events and policies

★ How reform and change altered the world's political landscape

Read to Discover...

★ what important changes took place in the Soviet Union and Eastern Europe in the late 1980s and early 1990s.

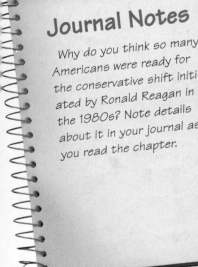

Journal Notes

Why do you think so many Americans were ready for the conservative shift initiated by Ronald Reagan in the 1980s? Note details about it in your journal as you read the chapter.

CULTURAL

● **1979** *Inflation reaches unprecedented rates*

● **1980** *United States boycotts Moscow Olympics*
● **1983** *Sally Ride is first American woman in space*

1975	1980

POLITICAL

● **1978** *Camp David Accords are signed*
● **1979** *Iran seizes 52 American hostages*

● **1981** *Sandra Day O'Connor is first woman named to Supreme Court*
● **1983** *Reagan announces Strategic Defense Initiative*

History AND ART

Three Flags
by Jasper Johns, 1958

The paintings of American artist Jasper Johns typically featured two-dimensional objects of everyday life as subjects. Johns, for example, painted pictures that consisted entirely of flags, maps, numbers, and letters of the alphabet.

◀ UNITED STATES SOLDIERS, ACTION DURING THE GULF WAR

- **1986** *Space shuttle* Challenger *explodes*
- **1989** *Bicentennial of the Constitution*

- **1990** *Detroit Pistons win National Basketball Association championship*

1985

1990

- **1986** *Iran-contra scandal*
- **1987** *Reagan and Gorbachev sign nuclear arms reduction treaty*

- **1991** *Persian Gulf War begins*
- **1991** *The Soviet Union collapses*

★★★

Crisis of Confidence

Setting the Scene

Focus

Americans felt a deep sense of pride and patriotism as they celebrated the Bicentennial in 1976. These feelings, however, could not erase the painful memories of two of the most disillusioning events in United States history—the Vietnam War and the Watergate scandal. Americans were ready for new leadership to bolster the national mood and solve the difficult problems that loomed ahead.

Objectives

After studying this section, you should be able to

★ state reasons for the American public's crisis of confidence.

★ explain how moral principles directed President Carter's domestic and foreign policy.

Key Terms

cartel, double-digit inflation, pork-barrel legislation

◀ HOSTAGE TERRY ANDERSON AFTER HIS RELEASE

At the time of its Bicentennial in 1976, the United States was faced with the grim prospect of diminishing vital natural resources. One result was that the nation was no longer self-sufficient in its production of energy. By then, the United States was importing more than half of its oil. Competition from Japan, Germany, and other countries threatened America's giant automobile and steel industries. With rising inflation and unemployment, the lifestyles of many Americans were critically affected.

There were equally serious problems in foreign affairs. Political turmoil in economically developing nations upset global stability. The Soviet Union pursued an increasingly aggressive foreign policy as the nuclear arms race continued. As the United States began its third century, the American people wondered if the government was capable of meeting these challenges.

Election of 1976

Soon after Gerald Ford became President in 1974, he began to campaign for his election in 1976. The public regarded Ford as a warm, easygoing man of high integrity, but had doubts about his intellectual capabilities and competence as a leader. As a result, conservatives in the Republican party rallied behind Ronald Reagan, the former governor of California. Ford survived the challenge and won the Republican nomination, but only by a few votes.

The Democratic presidential primaries were crowded with candidates including several who were nationally known. One, however, was a political outsider. James Earl "Jimmy" Carter, Jr., a former governor of Georgia, had no previous experience in the federal government. He toured the nation meeting voters face to face. Carter made a virtue of this inexperience:

To almost everyone's surprise, Carter won many of the primaries and secured the Democratic nomination for President. This was partly because his informal, down-home style appealed to Americans tired of the "imperial presidency."

During the presidential campaign, Jimmy Carter vowed to restore people's faith in the federal government by making it more open and efficient. He promised major new programs for energy development, tax reform, welfare reform, and national medical care. Conservatives liked him because he promised to balance the budget. Liberals supported him because he insisted he would not let unemployment rise as a means of lowering inflation.

Although the vote was close, Carter won the election. He took 51 percent of the popular vote and 297 electoral votes to Ford's 48 percent and 241 electoral votes. Carter achieved his victory by combining the support of the old Democratic coalition of the industrial Northeast and the Solid South (except for Virginia). For the first time since 1848, a candidate from the Deep South had been elected President. To a great extent, Carter owed his margin of victory to African American Southern voters.

■ Energy and Economic Shocks

President Carter believed that America's most serious domestic problem was its increasing dependence on oil as an energy source. Experts warned that world supplies of oil, a nonrenewable resource, would soon be exhausted. The oil-producing countries belonged to a **cartel,** an association of nations promoting its economic interests, the Organization of Petroleum Exporting Countries (OPEC). They set prices at ever-higher levels. Rising oil prices added substantially to the price of consumer goods.

Carter's Energy Program

To address the problem, Carter proposed a national energy program. He persuaded Congress to create a Department of Energy. In order to conserve oil, he promoted the

Visualizing History

▲ **AN INFORMAL PRESIDENCY** Both Jimmy Carter and his wife Rosalyn lived a relatively simple life. Both came from close-knit families that stressed hard work, dedication, and religion. *What electoral group helped Carter win the 1976 election?*

Gasoline Consumption and Prices

Year	Consumption (billions of gallons)	Cents per Gallon		
		Reg.	Prem.	No lead
1973	110.5	40	45	NA
1974	106.3	53	57	55
1975	109.0	57	61	60
1976	115.7	59	64	61
1977	119.6	62	67	66
1978	125.1	63	69	67
1979	122.1	86	92	90
1980	115.0	119	128	125

Source: Statistical Abstract of the United States, 1981

Chart Study Gasoline prices increased steadily beginning in 1973. *In what years did prices affect consumption?*

use of coal and such renewable energy sources as solar energy. The President wanted Americans to join together in a moral crusade against rising consumption:

> **[The nation's] decision about energy will test the character of the American people and the ability of the President and Congress to govern this nation. This difficult decision will be the 'moral equivalent of war'—except that we will be uniting our efforts to build and not to destroy.**

The President asked all Americans to make personal sacrifices to reduce their energy consumption. Because the sacrifices he asked people to make were voluntary, however, the public was confused about the seriousness of the crisis. When Carter later proposed stronger methods of restricting consumption, such as a 10 percent tax on all imported oil and emergency authority to impose gasoline rationing, Congress rejected them. Carter did, however, convince Congress to lift controls on domestic oil production and to impose a "windfall profits" tax on the oil companies' huge earnings.

Double-digit Inflation

Sharp rises in the price of oil and gasoline contributed to **double-digit inflation,** or a rise in the general level of prices of 10 percent or more. By 1980 it cost more than $200 to purchase the same goods that $100 would have bought only 10 years earlier. At the same time, the Federal Reserve Board raised interest rates to all-time highs in an effort to discourage borrowing and bring the economy under control. These policies helped reduce inflation but caused a severe business recession.

■ Governmental Disunity

Even though the Democrats held the presidency and had a majority in both houses of Congress, there was a lack of unity between the two branches of government. This was largely because Carter was unwilling to play politics. For example, in 1977 he announced that he would veto appropriation bills for a series of costly dams, canals, and other water projects. Passing such **pork-barrel legislation,** or bills that benefit only a small part of the country, was a common practice. Carter's move saved the nation millions of dollars, but it cost him valuable support.

Carter's inability to sell his political position on important issues puzzled many people. He followed a cautious middle course, promising to reduce government spending while endorsing expensive social programs. The President would not "choose up sides," as newspaper columnist James Reston observed. "Confronted with a series of ambiguous questions, he simply refused to give simple answers." As a result, the public became confused about Carter's goals. By 1979 his popular support had fallen dramatically.

■ Morality in Foreign Policy

In contrast to his leadership in domestic policy, President Carter's foreign policy was clearly defined. Carter denounced past

American foreign policy as "lacking moral principle." A man of strong religious beliefs, Carter argued that instead of relying on military and economic might, the United States must try to be "right and honest and truthful and decent" in its dealings with other nations.

The Panama Canal

Carter demonstrated his new policy over the Panama Canal, which the United States had controlled since 1903. In 1978 he won Senate ratification of the Panama Canal treaties, which transferred control of the canal from the United States to Panama by the end of the century. This action removed a major symbol of United States interventionist policy and signaled a new approach to Latin American relations.

Respect for Human Rights

In his dealings with other nations, Carter expressed a "clear-cut preference for those societies which share with us an abiding respect for human rights." His administration cut off military and economic support to several Latin American governments considered dictatorial and repressive. Carter also strongly condemned the Soviet Union for imprisoning people who protested government policies and for not allowing more of its Jewish citizens to emigrate.

Tension Over Afghanistan

Tension between the United States and the Soviet Union heightened when Soviet troops invaded Afghanistan late in 1979. In keeping with Carter's noninterventionist policy, the United States refrained from sending troops to the area. Instead, the President imposed an embargo on the sale of grain to the Soviet Union and called for a boycott of the 1980 Summer Olympic Games to be held in Moscow.

■ The Troubled Middle East

Carter's greatest foreign policy triumph and his greatest failure involved the Middle East. Since its early history, the region had been troubled by deep political and religious conflicts. Carter acknowledged that:

▲ **AGREEMENT AT CAMP DAVID** President Carter meets with Egyptian President Anwar el-Sadat (left) and Israeli Prime Minister Menachem Begin (right) to sign the Camp David Peace Accords. **What was the goal of the agreement?**

▲ HOSTAGE CRISIS In November 1979 Iranian radicals seized more than 50 Americans as hostages. President Carter condemned the action as "an act of terrorism outside the boundaries of international law." *What actions did Carter take to resolve the crisis?*

" *[The Middle East] has long been a textbook for pessimism, a demonstration that diplomatic ingenuity was no match for intractable human conflicts.* "

The Camp David Accords

Despite this view, President Carter made a bold move to negotiate a peace treaty between Egypt and Israel, nations that had been bitter enemies for 30 years. In 1978 Carter brought Egypt's President Anwar el-Sadat and Israel's Prime Minister Menachem Begin together at Camp David, the presidential retreat in Maryland. The leaders talked for 14 days. More than once the discussions broke down, but Carter persisted until the leaders reached an agreement on September 17, 1978. In front of a joint session of Congress, with Sadat and Begin in the gallery, Carter announced:

" *This is the first time that an Arab and an Israeli leader have signed a comprehensive framework for peace. It contains the seeds of a time when the Middle East, with all its vast potential,*

may be a land of human richness and fulfillment, rather than a land of bitterness and continued conflict. "

The Camp David Accords, which were formally signed in 1979, established peace between Egypt and Israel. Most of the other Arab nations expressed strong opposition to the treaty because they felt Egypt should not have acted alone. Also the issue of the Israeli-occupied territories inhabited by Palestinians was yet to be solved. Still, an important first step toward peace in the Middle East had been taken.

Crisis With Iran

This success, however, could not make up for Carter's inability to resolve the crisis with Iran in 1979. The United States had long supported the Shah of Iran. Iran served as a major supplier of oil and as a reliable buffer against Soviet expansion in the Middle East. Yet many Iranians had grown unhappy with the Shah's rule. The Shah had brought Western technology and reform to his people with immense revenues from oil, but these changes had only widened the gap between the wealthy and the extremely poor.

Some Islamic leaders objected to the Western social reforms and customs that had been introduced into Iran, claiming that they ran contrary to their religious traditions. Huge protests forced the Shah to flee in 1979, and an Islamic republic replaced the monarchy.

The new regime, headed by the religious leader Ayatollah Ruholla Khomeini (koh•MAY•nee), viewed the United States with deep distrust because of its ties with the Shah. Anti-American feelings were so strong that on November 4, 1979, militants stormed the American embassy in Tehran, the Iranian capital, and took hostage more than 50 Americans. The militants threatened to kill the hostages or try them as spies.

Negotiations for the freedom of the hostages were unsuccessful. As pressure mounted to secure their release, Carter felt he had no choice but to launch a military rescue. One morning in April 1980, Americans awoke to the shocking news that a mission to rescue the hostages had failed. Eight members of the rescue team had died in a helicopter crash in Iran. Despite this setback, Carter persisted in his diplomatic efforts to free the hostages.

■ Election of 1980

The hostage crisis became a key issue in Carter's bid for reelection. Carter fought off a strong challenge from Senator Edward Kennedy of Massachusetts for the Democratic nomination. As Election Day grew near, however, the American people became increasingly impatient with the situation in Iran.

The Republicans chose former California governor Ronald Reagan as their candidate. Reagan's chief opponents in the primaries were two moderate Republicans, former United Nations Ambassador George Bush and Illinois Representative John Anderson. After his nomination, Reagan picked Bush as his running mate. Anderson decided to run for President as an independent candidate, hoping to appeal to voters who were unhappy with Reagan and Carter.

The Republicans adopted a conservative platform calling for reductions in taxes and government spending in order to restore prosperity. The party did endorse, however, higher defense spending to strengthen the role of the United States in world affairs.

Throughout the campaign, Reagan hammered at Carter's lack of leadership and the nation's weak economy. He promised voters economic growth and development instead of the sacrifices and restraints that Carter advocated. Carter responded by picturing Reagan as unsympathetic to the needs of the poor and minority groups. On Election Day, Reagan claimed victory with 51 percent of the popular vote and 489 electoral votes. Carter won 41 percent, with 49 electoral votes. John Anderson and other candidates of minor parties split the rest of the vote. The conservative tide that elected Reagan resulted in a Republican Senate and reduced the Democratic House of Representatives.

President Carter's failure to obtain release of the hostages sealed his defeat. Only after Ronald Reagan was sworn in on January 20, 1981, did Iran release the Americans, ending their 444 days in captivity.

Section 1 ★ Review

Checking for Understanding

1. **Identify** OPEC, Anwar el-Sadat, Menachem Begin, Camp David Accords, Shah of Iran, Ayatollah Ruhollah Khomeini, John Anderson.

2. **Define** cartel, double-digit inflation, pork-barrel legislation.

3. **List** three features of Carter's energy program.

4. **Summarize** President Carter's successes and failures in negotiations with nations in the Middle East.

Critical Thinking

5. **Evaluating Leaders** Explain why Carter's unwillingness to play politics eroded his support in Congress.

★★★

A Conservative Shift

Setting the Scene

Section Focus

Despite the hope they had felt in 1976, Americans became increasingly dissatisfied with the government during Carter's administration. Angered over economic conditions, the energy crisis, and the President's inability to free the hostages, the people turned to a new leader to restore their confidence. The voters were not only reacting against Carter, however, but giving voice to a growing conservative movement that rejected the liberalism of the 1960s and demanded changes in the way the government met challenges at home and abroad.

Objectives

After studying this section, you should be able to

★ explain the conservative shift in Americans' political convictions in the late 1970s and early 1980s.

★ describe President Reagan's economic recovery plan, which included cutting taxes and reducing spending.

★ describe Reagan's foreign policy regarding the Soviet Union.

Key Terms

supply-side economics, federal deficit, glasnost, perestroika, privatized

◀ REPUBLICAN PARTY SYMBOL

Reagan's election indicated a significant conservative shift in Americans' political convictions. In addition to support from traditionally conservative groups such as fundamentalist Christians and antifeminists, many groups that had historically voted Democratic broke with their party and supported Reagan. These included former liberals, blue-collar workers, ethnic voters, and Southerners, who became known as "Reagan Democrats." The 69-year-old Reagan also attracted many older voters.

As a whole, the Reagan conservatives believed that the federal government should withdraw from most areas of domestic life.

They were against liberal social programs and government restrictions on business. In foreign policy, they favored a strong military to stand against communism.

■ Reagan's Economic Program

President Reagan acted quickly to limit the size of the federal government. His first act as President was to place a freeze on the hiring of federal employees. At the same time, he began to ease government controls on many business activities. He set up a task force headed by Vice President Bush to review federal regulations. As President, Reagan moved to fulfill his campaign promise to get the economy going again. In February 1981, he told Americans:

66 *Since 1960 our government has spent $5.1 trillion. Our debt has grown to $648 billion. Prices have exploded by 178 percent. . . . [We] know we must act and act now. We must not be timid. . . .* 99

To take care of the problem, Reagan proposed a new economic program, which came to be called "Reaganomics."

Cutting Taxes

The first part of the President's program was to make deep cuts in federal taxes. He predicted that income tax reductions would increase consumer spending and would also encourage investments, especially by the wealthy. Similarly, cuts in corporate taxes would allow companies to expand production and hire more workers. Reagan's beliefs were based on an economic theory called **supply-side economics,** which claimed that the economy could best be stimulated by increasing the supply of goods rather than the demand.

Reducing Government Spending

The second part of Reagan's program was to reduce government spending by ending federal job-training programs and cutting back the amount of federal money going into medicare, food stamps, and education. Critics predicted that Reagan's proposal would cause great suffering for the economically disadvantaged. Reagan denied this, claiming that there would always be a "safety net" of government aid for truly needy Americans.

■ Results of Reaganomics

Although the President faced opposition to his proposals, he had personal qualities that helped to promote his position: a great ability to communicate with his audience and a sense of humor. In March 1981, when he was shot and seriously wounded, the

Visualizing History

▲ **ASSASSINATION ATTEMPT** In March 1981 President Reagan survived an attempt on his life outside a Washington hotel. His press secretary, a police officer, and a Secret Service agent were also wounded. *What was Reagan's chief concern when he took office?*

▲ **A POPULAR PRESIDENT** Some observers noted that President Reagan's strong victories in the 1980 and 1984 elections were due to his personal appeal as well as to growing public support for his conservative policies. *Who were the Democratic candidates in 1984?*

President's aides visited him in the hospital. They assured him that the business of government was continuing as usual. "What makes you think I'd be happy about that?" Reagan quipped.

With his great popularity and shrewd handling of Congress, Reagan soon got much of his economic program passed. The final bill included $39 billion in tax cuts and a 25 percent cut in income taxes. The results of Reaganomics, however, were not quite what the President had hoped. Spending cuts, together with high interest rates, brought inflation down, but at first the cure was painful.

Recession

In 1982 a severe economic recession occurred. Business bankruptcies, factory closings, and farm foreclosures increased at alarming rates. By the end of the year, more than 11 million Americans—10 percent of the workforce—were jobless. Blaming President Reagan's economic programs for the recession, the Democrats won back many seats in the congressional elections.

Recovery

By 1983, however, the economy began to turn around. The Federal Reserve Board lowered interest rates, making it easier for businesses and individuals to borrow money. The inflation rate dropped just as the 25-percent cut in income taxes was putting more money into the hands of consumers. Feeling new confidence in the economy, Americans made purchases they had put off during the recession. Sales of every type of goods and service shot upward, and industries hired back workers who had been laid off during the recession. By the end of Reagan's second term in 1988, unemployment had dropped to 5.5 percent—the lowest in 14 years.

To hail the recovery, President Reagan went before Congress in 1984, saying:

❝ *. . . America is back—standing tall, looking to the '80s with courage, confidence, and hope. . . . Send away the hand-wringers and doubting Thomases.* ❞

The Federal Debt Increases

Although Reagan promised to balance the budget, the federal debt greatly increased during his first term. He cut taxes, which meant the government received less revenue. In addition, Congress, now controlled by the Democrats, refused to make the deeper cuts in social programs that Reagan requested. On top of that, Reagan himself increased government spending in certain areas, especially defense. The result was the most unbalanced budget in American history.

By 1984 the **federal deficit,** or the difference between the amount of money the government took in and what it spent, was nearly $200 billion a year. When the government spends more money than it collects, it has to borrow to make up the difference. The more the government borrows, the more interest it owes on its debts. In 1984 the interest alone on the federal debt amounted to $153.8 billion, an increase of more than $55 billion from Reagan's first year in office.

■ Election of 1984

Despite the federal deficit, Reagan was still popular, and the economy had made a healthy recovery. These factors made Reagan a formidable candidate for President in the 1984 election. To run against him, the Democrats nominated a traditional liberal, former Vice President Walter Mondale. Mondale created a precedent by choosing Representative Geraldine Ferraro of New York to run as his Vice President. She was the first woman candidate from a major party to run for this office.

Mondale claimed that Reagan's tax and budget cuts benefited only the wealthy. Reagan countered that his economic program had aided all Americans by sharply reducing inflation. To cut the deficit, Mondale proposed raising taxes, always an unpopular political step. Reagan, however, continued to oppose any increases and insisted that economic expansion and deeper cuts in government spending would reduce the deficit.

In November Americans gave the President an overwhelming vote of confidence. Winning 59 percent of the popular vote, he captured 49 states and took 525 electoral votes to Mondale's 13. Reagan won the biggest electoral margin in history.

■ A Conservative Court

With this tremendous mandate, Reagan began his second term confident in his policies. One of his priorities was to appoint conservative justices to the Supreme Court and the lower federal courts. In 1981, the President had appointed Sandra Day O'Connor, the first woman to serve on the Court. In 1986 Reagan selected Antonin Scalia, and a year later he chose Anthony M. Kennedy.

With Reagan's appointees in place, the Supreme Court began to hand down the kind of conservative rulings for which Reagan had hoped. For example, one decision cut back affirmative action programs that had benefited minorities.

■ Strengthening America's Defenses

President Reagan strongly supported America's space program, both as a means of restoring the nation's self-confidence and as a means of strengthening its defenses. Americans took pride in their successes in space exploration, and the launch of reusable space shuttles marked a new era in the space program.

Support for SDI

Reagan had a special interest in the military aspects of the space program. In 1983 he announced a new research project to create a shield that would intercept and destroy nuclear ballistic missiles. It was called the Strategic Defense Initiative (SDI), nicknamed "Star Wars." Opponents feared that SDI would stimulate an intensified nuclear competition between the United States and the Soviet Union. Reagan and the project's supporters, however, believed SDI would improve chances of nuclear disarmament.

Military Buildup

In addition to Star Wars, Reagan also promoted a military buildup, including new bombers, submarines, and missiles and better training for ground troops. Other aspects of his defense program included placing new nuclear missiles in Europe, basing intercontinental missiles in Western states, and developing expensive new B-2 "stealth" bombers. Stealth bombers are military aircraft designed so that radar cannot easily detect them.

The Cost of Defense

Aside from Star Wars, Reagan's military buildup cost $1 trillion. This caused a sharp rise in the federal deficit. As the deficit increased, a greater share of tax revenues went to pay the interest on the national debt. This left less money available for new programs in education, the environment, and public housing.

Congress responded in 1985 by passing the Gramm-Rudman Act, which put greater pressure on Congress and the President to reach agreement on reducing the budget. If they were unable to reduce the annual deficit to certain limits, this legislation set up automatic, across-the-board federal spending cuts.

Reagan, however, still refused to increase income taxes. He was able to maintain this position only because in 1986 a great drop in oil prices occurred. Fear of inflation lessened as interest rates dropped. Nevertheless, by 1988 the national debt had reached $2.3 trillion.

■ Improved Relations With the Soviet Union

Reagan's desire for a strong defense was based on his belief that the Soviet Union, which he called an "evil empire," was a serious threat to the United States. He aimed to contain and counter communism throughout the world, and he followed this policy until relations with the Soviet Union suddenly began to improve.

When Mikhail Gorbachev (GAWR•buh•CHAWF) became Soviet premier, his country's economy, which was highly centralized under the control of the Communist party, was on the verge of collapse. For decades,

Visualizing History

▲ THE CHALLENGER DISASTER On January 28, 1986, the space shuttle *Challenger* exploded in space, killing all seven astronauts on board. The tragedy temporarily halted the space program. *What innovation had the shuttle introduced?*

Physical Fitness

Men and women of early times got plenty of exercise—their lives revolved around the physical tasks involved in the procuring of food and shelter. Beginning with the industrial age and the invention of the steam engine, and continuing into the post-World War II technological age, adults and children became more and more sedentary.

In 1956, President Dwight D. Eisenhower established the President's Council on Youth Fitness. President John F. Kennedy enlarged the scope of the Council to include all age groups, and changed the name to the President's Council on Physical Fitness. In the following decades, interest in physical fitness bloomed.

Tracking individuals over many years, scientists studied the effect of exercise on the body. They concluded that physical inactivity is a significant risk factor for the development of several major illnesses including coronary heart disease. They have also found that regular exercise increases fitness and health. Health professionals of the 1970s and 1980s stressed the benefits of aerobic exercise. Jogging, aerobic dance, exercise bikes, rowing machines, and mini-trampolines were familiar fitness activities of the time. More recent studies have documented the health benefits of moderate, less intense workouts, and the popularity of bicycling and walking has grown.

---

the party had focused on building up the Soviet Union's position as a superpower and neglected the needs of the people. As a result, farms and factories underproduced and the standard of living was low. The centralized communist system of government was also showing serious strain. The people had no voice and had grown very apathetic in the face of total party control.

Gorbachev Sets New Policy

To save his country and party, Gorbachev set some new policies. First, he introduced **glasnost,** meaning "openness." This policy gave people the right to speak freely—and, Gorbachev hoped, in support of his reforms. Then Gorbachev began **perestroika,** a restructuring of the economy and the government. Instead of party officials deciding everything from Moscow, local farm and factory managers now had the power to make some decisions. The nation's businesses were **privatized,** or transferred from government to private ownership. To lessen the party's control of government, Gorbachev scheduled the first elections in 70 years in which the people had a real choice.

Gorbachev Makes an Astounding Offer

Gorbachev knew that if the arms race could be halted, it would free people and money to produce consumer goods in the Soviet Union. Peace would also allow him to concentrate all his energies on domestic reforms, and could lead to trade agreements and economic aid from the West. So, Gorbachev made the United States an astounding offer, announcing that the Soviet Union would reduce its nuclear weapons.

Reagan and Gorbachev Hold Summit Meeting

When Reagan and Gorbachev met at Reykjavík, Iceland, in 1986, the two leaders tried but could not come to an agreement on the issue of the Strategic Defense Initiative.

Reagan insisted on pursuing it, and Gorbachev opposed it. When they met again a year later at Washington, D.C., however, they signed a treaty calling for the removal of all intermediate-range nuclear weapons from Europe. This was the first agreement that eliminated an entire class of nuclear weapons. Unbelievably, the cold war was slowly coming to an end.

Along with agreeing to limit nuclear weapons, Gorbachev took other surprising steps that affected international relations. Admitting that the Soviet Union's intervention in Afghanistan had been "morally wrong," he withdrew Soviet troops. He also released political prisoners and allowed freer emigration of Soviet Jews.

■ A Hands-Off Presidency

Although Reagan was a strong leader when it came to establishing public policy, he adopted a "hands-off" attitude toward the day-to-day operations of the presidency. This attitude led to scandals that would tarnish Reagan's final years in office, though he remained popular.

A Master of Delegation

Reagan gave far greater responsibilities to his staff than any other recent President had. The President's detachment allowed his subordinates to function independently. Some acted for financial gain. Others made policy on their own.

The Iran-Contra Scandal

The worst fiasco to hit the Reagan administration was the Iran-contra scandal of 1986. Several of the President's national security aides, including John Poindexter, Robert McFarland, and Lieutenant Colonel Oliver North, had schemed to sell weapons to the Iranians to win the release of American hostages in the Middle East. Then they had diverted the profits from these arms sales to the contras, Nicaraguan guerrillas who were fighting to topple the Sandanista government ruling the nation. This was a violation of a congressional ban on such financing.

Critics charged that an undercover foreign policy was being carried out against the express will of Congress. Defenders maintained that the executive branch was forced to take these measures because of congressional interference with the President's authority to conduct foreign policy. A special commission was set up to study the Iran-contra case. Although the commission cleared the President of direct blame, it found fault with Reagan for allowing aides to make policy decisions without his knowledge.

The Iran-contra scandal helped the Democrats win back a Senate majority in 1986. The election produced a divided government—with the presidency held by the Republican party and control of Congress held by the Democrats. Democratic majorities in Congress acted as a brake on the Reagan administration.

Section 2 ★ Review

Checking for Understanding

1. **Identify** Reaganomics, Walter Mondale, Geraldine Ferraro, Sandra Day O'Connor, Gramm-Rudman Act, Strategic Defense Initiative (SDI), Mikhail Gorbachev, Lieutenant Colonel Oliver North, contras.

2. **Define** supply-side economics, federal deficit, glasnost, perestroika, privatized.

3. **List** three measures Reagan took to restore the economy.

4. **Describe** three controversial weapons proposals of the Reagan administration.

Critical Thinking

5. **Evaluating Policies** Evaluate whether technology such as the SDI will help prevent nuclear war.

Social Studies Skills

Map and Graph Skills

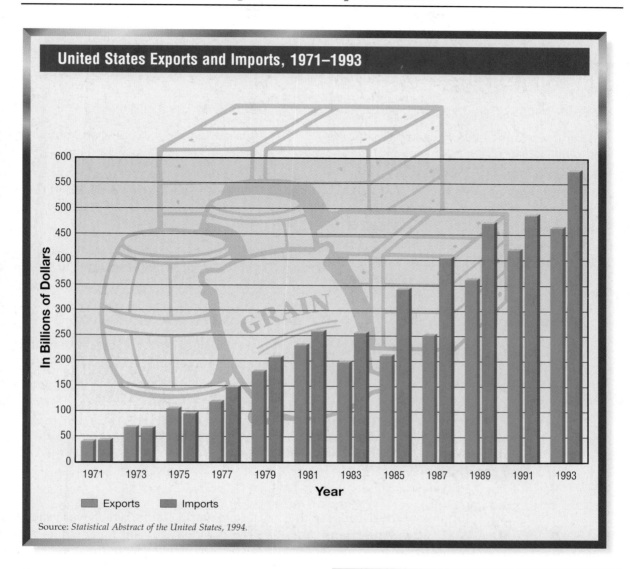

United States Exports and Imports, 1971–1993

In Billions of Dollars

Year

■ Exports ■ Imports

Source: *Statistical Abstract of the United States, 1994.*

Reading a Bar Graph

Exports are the merchandise and materials made or mined in one country and sold or traded to another. Imports are the goods and materials a country buys or trades for from other countries. A surplus balance of trade means that a country exports more than it imports: that is, a nation sells more goods than it purchases from other countries. A deficit balance of trade indicates a greater volume of imports than exports.

Practicing the Skill

Refer to the bar graph to answer these questions.

1. What is the graph's unit of measurement?

2. What year had the largest deficit balance of trade?

3. Analyze the growth trends of both exports and imports from 1971 to 1993.

★★★★★★★★★★★★★★★★★★★★★★★★★★★★★★★

A New Presidency

Setting the Scene

Section Focus

Despite his difficulties, Reagan was still popular when he left office. Promising to continue Reagan's policies, Vice President George Bush won a resounding victory in 1988. In foreign affairs, Bush acted decisively to meet the challenges of what he called "a new world order" and tried to forge a different path for America in the post-cold war world. Domestically, however, many felt his leadership lacked direction, and problems with the economy continued to plague society.

Objectives

After studying this section, you should be able to

★ explain how the spread of democracy led to the formation of a new world order.

★ describe America's role in the post-cold war world.

★ discuss the reasons for discord between the legislative and executive branches of government under Bush.

Key Terms

coup d'état, drawdown, user taxes, junk bonds, underemployed

◀ ROAD SIGN IN KUWAIT

*T*hroughout the decades of the cold war, Americans and Soviets had lived under the threat of nuclear war as each side built mighty arsenals and viewed almost all disputes around the world in terms of the East-West struggle. Then, with almost surprising suddenness, democratic movements erupted throughout the Soviet Union's Eastern European satellites. Popular demands for political, social, and economic reform toppled one communist government after another. Eventually, even the Soviet Union itself split into independent republics.

Without a Soviet adversary, the United States was the only superpower left. It faced the critical challenge of establishing a new role in world affairs, which was tested when Iraq invaded Kuwait. Meanwhile, America also faced challenges in the domestic arena. Troubled by severe economic problems, a divided government tried to work toward a solution.

■ Election of 1988

In the election of 1988, there was tough competition for both the Republican and Democratic presidential nominations. In the end, the Republicans selected Vice President George Bush. The final Democratic contenders were the Reverend Jesse Jackson and Massachusetts Governor Michael

Dukakis. Jackson, who appealed to a "rainbow coalition" of minorities and reformers, picked up support along the way and ran a much stronger race than expected. Dukakis, however, won the nomination.

Early in the race, Dukakis led Bush in the public polls. Then Bush's campaign team unleashed a string of negative television advertisements that portrayed the liberal Dukakis as unpatriotic and soft on criminals. Dukakis, however, failed to respond strongly to these charges. As a result, Dukakis lost his lead to Bush. Slick television commercials seemed to replace debating real issues.

Saying, "Read my lips," the Vice President pledged not to raise taxes. Bush also promised the nation that if elected he would follow Reagan's economic policies. On Election Day he won a resounding victory, taking 40 of the 50 states, with 49 million popular votes and 426 electoral votes. Dukakis had 42 million popular votes and 112 electoral votes.

■ A Tidal Wave of Change

George Bush came to the presidency with a great deal of experience in foreign policy. In addition to being Vice President, he had been Ambassador to the United Nations, Ambassador to China, and Director of the CIA. This training served Bush well, for he was immediately confronted with a tidal wave of change around the world.

Change in Eastern Europe

Gorbachev's new policies in the Soviet Union triggered demands for change in Eastern Europe. In 1989 the people of the satellite nations of Poland, Hungary, Czechoslovakia, Bulgaria, Romania, and East Germany overthrew their communist rulers and forced democratic elections. When the East German government fell, crowds tore down the Berlin Wall that had divided Germany and symbolized the "iron curtain" that separated Eastern Europe and Western Europe.

Visualizing History

▲ THE BARRIER FALLS In November 1989 the Berlin Wall, which had separated the two Germanys since 1961, was opened. On the first weekend after the wall was opened, 3 million visitors crossed from East Berlin to visit West Berlin. *What had the Berlin Wall symbolized?*

Born in a segregated city—Greenville, North Carolina—Jesse Jackson became involved in civil rights activities while a college student. He went on to join Dr. Martin Luther King, Jr.'s, protest marches in Selma, Alabama. Later, Jackson was selected to head Operation Breadbasket, a program designed to promote the hiring of more African Americans by major businesses. After Dr. King was killed, Jesse Jackson emerged as the best-known African American leader in America.

In 1971 Jackson launched his own organization: People United to Save Humanity (PUSH). Supported by a "rainbow coalition" he unsuccessfully sought the 1984 Democratic presidential nomination. When he ran again in 1988, he finished a strong second in the primaries, proving that an African American could be a serious presidential contender.

Jesse Jackson
1941–

The end of the cold war allowed some countries to renew and rethink relationships. In October 1990, East Germany and West Germany reunited. As Western European nations took steps toward political and economic union, Eastern Europe sought to forge new ties with them—especially economic ones. In July 1991, the Warsaw Pact between Eastern Europe and the Soviet Union was terminated. This left the future of NATO, which was also a military alliance, in doubt.

The Collapse of the Soviet Union

The loss of Eastern Europe was only the beginning. Despite Gorbachev's efforts to save his country, the Soviet Union itself collapsed. Glasnost and perestroika had unleashed two forces that would bring it down. One was the people's demand for democracy. The other was the desire of different ethnic groups for self-rule; the Soviet Union had been organized without regard for ethnic boundaries. As rumblings for independence began, Gorbachev even dispatched troops to preserve the Soviet Union.

The catalyst came in August 1991 when a group of hard-line Communists attempted a **coup d'état,** or a sudden revolt, and proclaimed an old-style communist government. The plotters arrested Gorbachev and ordered troops to Moscow. They failed, however, to take into account Boris Yeltsin, the recently elected president of the Russian Republic. Appearing before crowds gathered in front of the Russian parliament building, Yeltsin condemned the coup and called for the people's help. To protect him, tens of thousands of Moscow's citizens stood guard unarmed, ready to face down an expected attack. The soldiers refused to carry out orders, and the coup collapsed. Gorbachev was back in office, but Yeltsin now held the real power.

Both men knew that the Communist party had been behind the coup. Soon, Gorbachev stepped down as general secretary and abolished the party. Without communism holding the Soviet state together, the country itself shattered. Republic after republic declared its independence.

On December 25, 1991, Gorbachev formally resigned as Soviet president, saying, "We are living in a new world." His resignation marked the end of what was left of the Soviet Union. By this time, 11 of the 15 former republics had organized a loose union called the Commonwealth of Independent States (CIS).

Troubles in the New States

All the former Soviet and communist bloc states faced serious economic troubles. In trying to set up capitalist economies, the new governments began lifting state controls on economies already in decline. So production fell, prices rose, and unemployment spread. People suffered from shortages of fuel, food, medicine, and housing.

Another problem was ethnic rivalry. Without tight communist control there was a rise of nationalism, and old hatreds surfaced. These hatreds led to the outbreak of bloody civil wars in many states. The worst was in what was formerly Yugoslavia.

Although western nations, including the United States, quickly recognized the new countries, they were uncertain what kind of aid to send. Some people wanted to send cash to help support the new democracies. Others feared even a non-communist Russia might someday threaten world security and favored increasing trade and sending advisers, along with food and medicine. For the most part the United States government followed the latter course.

Part of the reason the United States was concerned about Russia was that it had most of the former Soviet Union's nuclear weapons. In 1992, Bush and Yeltsin met at Camp David and agreed to drastic reductions. Afterward, the President declared that the meeting marked "a new relationship based on trust, based on a commitment to economic and political freedom."

■ The Persian Gulf War

Meanwhile, the Persian Gulf War gave President Bush an opportunity to further define America's role in the post-cold war world. On August 2, 1990, Iraq's president, Saddam Hussein, sent invasion forces into Kuwait, its oil-rich neighbor. To punish this aggression, Bush froze $20 billion of Iraqi money in American banks and banned imports of Iraqi oil. The United Nations demanded that Saddam Hussein withdraw his forces and called for countries throughout the world to halt all trade with Iraq. But Iraqi troops remained in Kuwait.

Operation Desert Shield

Bush, with assistance from 25 nations around the world, assembled a huge military coalition he called "Operation Desert Shield." The United Nations then authorized military action to restore Kuwait's independence. The coalition waited for 6 months, however, hoping that diplomacy and the threat of force would prevent a war.

Operation Desert Storm

Finally, Bush initiated Operation Desert Storm. He ordered massive air strikes against Iraq on January 16, 1991, rejecting calls for further delay:

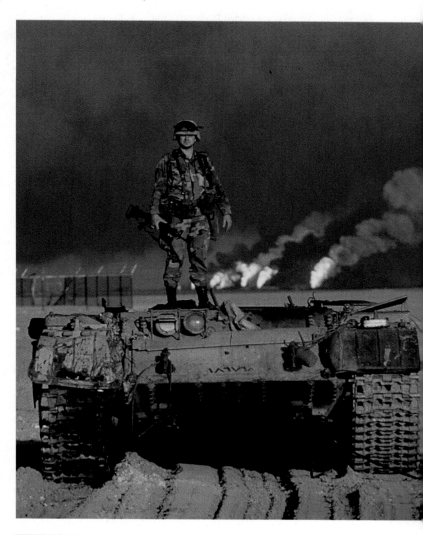

Visualizing History ▲ THE PERSIAN GULF WAR In January 1991 the United States launched a massive air and missile assault on Iraq after Iraq refused to withdraw from Kuwait. **Why had Iraq invaded Kuwait?**

▲ **COMING HOME** American military personnel return after taking part in Operation Desert Storm. Coalition forces took part in the military action after diplomatic efforts failed. **Who was the military leader of the operation?**

> ❝ *The world could wait no longer. . . . While the world waited, Saddam Hussein met every overture of peace with open contempt. While the world prayed for peace, Saddam Hussein prepared for war.* ❞

After a month of bombing, General Norman Schwarzkopf led a lightning-swift ground assault. Just 100 hours later, Allied forces had crushed the Iraqi army and freed the Kuwaiti people. "Kuwait is liberated," Bush announced. "America and the world have kept their word."

■ Rethinking America's Military Role

The Persian Gulf War caused people in the United States to begin rethinking America's military role in the world. Some leaders felt the United States should scale down its military. They pointed out that the source of a country's power in the new world order promised to be its economy rather than its military. Examples of just such a change were evident by the emergence of Germany and Japan. So, as the federal deficits skyrocketed, Bush called for cuts in defense spending, and Congress made even greater reductions. The Pentagon planned a **drawdown** that would bring troops home from overseas bases in Europe and Asia.

Other experts, however, warned that the United States should maintain a strong military—and that the cost would be worth it. They pointed out that Cuba, North Korea, Vietnam, and the People's Republic of China remained communist nations. Although China had shown some signs of change by instituting various free-market programs, its Communist party leaders had massacred prodemocracy demonstrators at Beijing's Tiananmen Square in 1989.

■ Divided Government

Whereas President Bush acted decisively in foreign affairs, he was accused of wavering leadership at home. Part of the problem was that the government was divided again, with the presidency held by one party and Congress controlled by the other. During the Bush administration, this hindered the process of government.

Bush and Congress in Gridlock

Congress ignored or drastically changed many of the President's proposals. The President, in turn, vetoed many bills, knowing that the Democrats generally lacked the two-thirds vote needed to override his vetoes. The executive and legislative branches of the government quickly became gridlocked over such issues as reforming campaign financing, improving public education, recharging the economy, reducing the federal deficit, and balancing the budget.

Taxation Issues

When the federal deficit rose to a record level of $300 billion, Bush realized he would have to increase revenues. To do so, however, he was forced to break his campaign pledge of "no new taxes." In 1992, after weeks of negotiations with Democratic congressional leaders, Bush agreed to raise some taxes. Among these were gasoline, tobacco, and other **user taxes,** or taxes on products used by consumers. The President also agreed to make deep cuts in medicare and military spending. Although this plan was defeated by conservative Republicans, the President and congressional leaders finally hammered out a compromise bill.

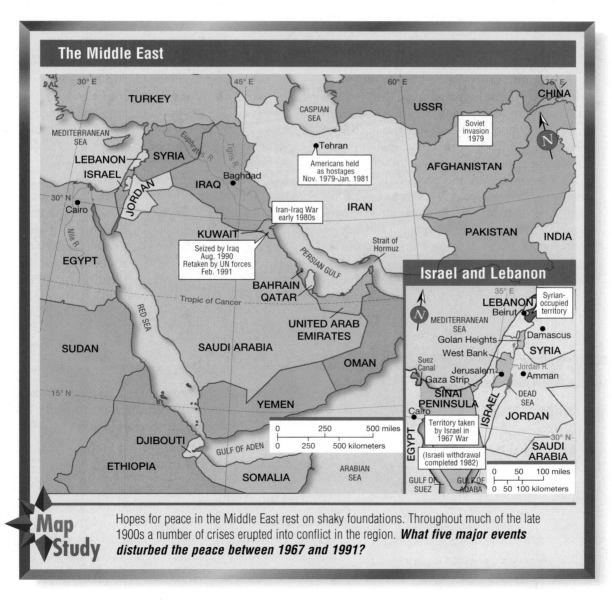

Map Study

Hopes for peace in the Middle East rest on shaky foundations. Throughout much of the late 1900s a number of crises erupted into conflict in the region. *What five major events disturbed the peace between 1967 and 1991?*

Economic Woes in the Early 1990s

During the Bush administration, the economy grew more slowly than at any time since the end of World War II. Among other factors, sharply rising oil prices following Iraq's invasion of Kuwait threw America into a recession that persisted longer than expected.

Consumer and Corporate Debt and Unemployment

The long recession was partly caused by consumer and corporate debts incurred during the Reagan era. Deregulation had allowed banks and savings and loans (S&Ls) to lend money more freely. Corporations funded mergers with **junk bonds,** or high-risk bonds that offer high yields.

Consumers ran up large debts on credit cards and home mortgages. The federal government, too, spent far more than it received. These debts limited the ability of consumers, corporations, and the government to spend and invest.

As a result, banks and S&Ls failed at rates unseen since the Great Depression. Airlines went out of business. Famous department stores filed for bankruptcy. Industries announced plant closings and layoffs of workers.

By mid-1992, almost 10 million Americans were unemployed. Another 6 million workers were **underemployed.** This means that these people held part-time jobs while looking for full-time work.

The Problem of Homelessness in America

As unemployment rose, people migrated from one state to another in search of jobs, and some found themselves homeless. Homeless people included battered women, runaway children, alcoholics, drug abusers, deinstitutionalized mental patients, and people lacking family support. Homelessness reflected rising rents, lower wages for unskilled workers, and the urgent need for low-cost housing. Estimates of the number of homeless people in America ranged as high as 3 million.

The Los Angeles Riots

The recession, poverty, and homelessness hit particularly hard at minorities living in inner cities. Racial tensions ignited after four white police officers in Los Angeles who were videotaped beating an African American man, Rodney King, were acquitted. The city erupted into days of arson, looting, and rioting that claimed more lives than had the 1965 riots in Watts. Conservatives blamed the Los Angeles riots on welfare programs that weakened the family and individual initiative. Liberals blamed the government's general neglect of inner cities during the Reagan-Bush years.

Section 3 ★ Review

Checking for Understanding

1. **Identify** George Bush, Jesse Jackson, Michael Dukakis, Boris Yeltsin, Commonwealth of Independent States (CIS), Saddam Hussein, Operation Desert Storm, General Norman Schwarzkopf, Tiananmen Square.

2. **Define** coup d'état, drawdown, user taxes, junk bonds, underemployed.

3. **Describe** changes in Eastern Europe that resulted from breaking free of the Soviet Union.

4. **Discuss** the reason why the United States resorted to force against Iraq.

Critical Thinking

5. **Identifying Alternatives** In your opinion, should Presidents concentrate more on domestic issues or on foreign policy? Explain your answer.

As the Brain Grows Older

Life expectancy in the United States increased dramatically in the twentieth century. In the early 1900s, most people died before the age of 50. By the year 2000, the average life expectancy will be 80 years for women and 76 for men. Even more significant is the fact that by 2000, 13 percent of all Americans will be 65 years of age or older. By 2025, one-fourth the population will be over age 65.

The aging population has prompted scientists to study the changes that occur in the brain with age. What these studies show is that the brain loses little functioning during most of the adult years. After age 65, deterioration in memory, spatial skills, and reasoning begins. What is most noticeable in the over-65 population, however, is the greater variation in brain function between individuals. That is, some people show only slight mental decline, while others show very noticeable losses. Alzheimer's disease, a

▲ SENIOR CITIZENS HIKING

condition that limits brain functioning, especially in memory, language, reasoning, and spatial abilities, afflicts millions of older adults in this country.

Research in the 1990s has centered on ways that older individuals can maintain or regain their intellectual strength. Just as diet and exercise have been shown to have a direct impact on physical fitness, researchers hope to identify educational, nutritional, and medical breakthroughs that can build mental fitness.

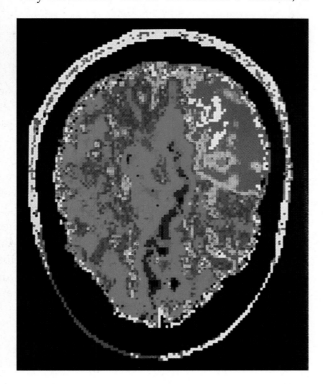

▲ BRAIN SCAN

Making the Science Connection

1. How does brain functioning change with age?

2. Describe two educational or nutritional factors that could be studied in relation to brain function.

Linking Past and Present

3. Why are declines in brain function, and diseases such as Alzheimer's, of particular significance at this time? Identify possible consequences if methods to slow intellectual decline are not identified.

Using Vocabulary

On a separate sheet of paper, write three headings: *Carter, Reagan, Bush.* Classify each of the following terms under the Presidents to which they are related. Some terms belong in more than one category.

double-digit
  inflation
supply-side
  economics
glasnost
coup d'état
user taxes

pork-barrel
  legislation
federal deficit
perestroika
drawdown
junk bond
underemployed

Reviewing Facts

1. **Explain** how Carter's election was partly a result of Watergate.

2. **Summarize** Carter's foreign policy philosophy.

3. **Describe** why Ronald Reagan appealed to the American people.

4. **Discuss** how Mikhail Gorbachev tried to save the Communist party and the Soviet Union.

5. **Describe** the problems faced by the former Soviet and communist bloc states.

6. **Explain** how the problems between Kuwait and Iraq helped define America's new role in world affairs.

7. **Discuss** the reason for Bush's decision to break his campaign promise and raise taxes.

Understanding Concepts

Leadership

1. Analyze how the image of the President may have affected popular support during the Carter and Reagan administrations.

Reform and Change

2. How does the role of the United States government in the economy during the 1980s and 1990s compare to its role during the early 1900s?

Critical Thinking

1. **Assessing Programs** The United States has had difficulty implementing an energy policy. Evaluate Carter's energy program. Explain why it was only partially successful.

2. **Analyzing Media** Television has exposed Americans to an unprecedented amount of news and information.

   a. In what ways does television benefit society?

   b. Do you think the overall effect of television is a positive one or a negative one? Explain.

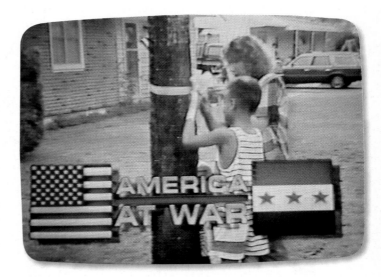

Writing About History

Classification

Write an essay on the changing relations between the United States and the Soviet Union during the Carter, Reagan, and Bush administrations. Before you begin writing, divide your information into two classifications: (1) events, policies, and actions that eased tensions between the United States and the Soviet Union, and (2) events, policies, and actions that kept the two nations apart.

Cooperative Learning

Organize into four groups to research and analyze the two ways to reduce the federal deficit. Two groups will research and present arguments for and

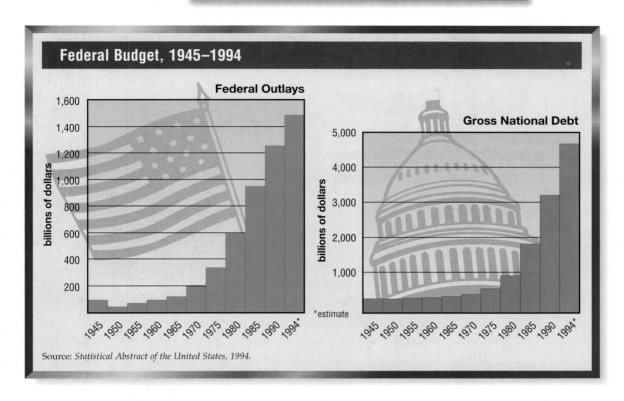

Federal Budget, 1945–1994

Federal Outlays

billions of dollars

1,600
1,400
1,200
1,000
800
600
400
200

1945 1950 1955 1960 1965 1970 1975 1980 1985 1990 1994*

Gross National Debt

billions of dollars

5,000
4,000
3,000
2,000
1,000

1945 1950 1955 1960 1965 1970 1975 1980 1985 1990 1994*

*estimate

Source: *Statistical Abstract of the United States, 1994.*

against raising taxes. The other two groups will research and present arguments for and against reduced government spending. You will have one class period to prepare. Select a representative from your group to report your arguments to the class. The members of the class should evaluate the arguments and decide which method would be best.

Social Studies Skills

Interpreting Economic Data

The graphs on this page show economic information for the United States from 1945 to 1994. The first graph shows total federal expenditures, or outlays. The second graph shows total gross national debt.

Practicing the Skill

Using the two graphs and your understanding of the chapter, answer the following questions.

1. Why do you suppose both outlays and federal gross debt declined between 1945 and 1950?

2. Describe the trend shown in each graph.

3. What do you think may have contributed to the large increase beginning in 1975?

4. How might the difference in the *y*-axis scales cause problems in interpreting the data in the two graphs?

5. How are the two graphs related?

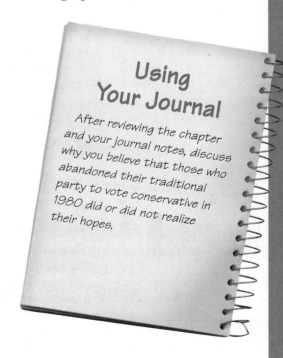

Using Your Journal

After reviewing the chapter and your journal notes, discuss why you believe that those who abandoned their traditional party to vote conservative in 1980 did or did not realize their hopes.

CHAPTER 36

★★

Toward a New Century
1992–Present

▶ **HAITIAN REFUGEE BOAT**

Setting the Scene

Focus

As the twentieth century came to an end, a new world order was emerging. Nations were becoming more integrated, and their leaders were acquiring a more global outlook. As the United States struggled to define its role in this new world, urgent concerns at home threatened changes in government. Despite attempts by political leaders to be more responsive to the needs of the American people, voter dissatisfaction continued to grow.

Concepts to Understand

★ What changes occurred in government as a result of Clinton's election

★ How Americans were dealing with the challenges they faced

Read to Discover ...

★ how Clinton's policies—both domestic and foreign—affected Americans.

★ what challenges face the American government and people in the future.

Journal Notes

What do you think it would be like to be an immigrant from another country coming to the United States during the 1990s? Note details about it in your journal as you read the chapter.

CULTURAL

• Eric Clapton's "Unplugged" wins Grammy award

• Projections show Hispanics as largest minority by 2010

• Scientists estimate 1 million Americans have HIV

1992	1993	1994

POLITICAL

• Bill Clinton is elected President
• Yugoslav Federation breaks up

• Israel and PLO negotiate peace with American help
• Congress approves NAFTA

• Israel and Jordan, assisted by United States, sign peace treaty

The 1996 Election

President Bill Clinton and Vice President Al Gore were reelected in 1996. Their successful campaign ran on the slogan of "Building a Bridge to the Twenty-first Century."

◀ **AIDS** RIBBON

- *Internet revolutionizes communications*

- *President Clinton signs historic welfare reform bill*

- *100th anniversary of the first Boston Marathon*

| **1995** | **1996** | **1997** |

- *President Clinton authorizes $20 billion in loans and loan guarantees to Mexico*

- *Yasir Arafat elected as Palestinian President*

- *President Clinton begins second term*
- *Hong Kong returned to China*

★★

Reinventing Government

Setting the Scene

Section Focus

The office of the presidency in the 1990s changed from the conservatism of the 1980s, as voters elected a Democrat President. President Clinton's reelection, in 1996, reflected an overall public approval of his first term. However, Republicans maintained control of Congress, forcing Democrats and Republicans to work together for the benefit of the country.

◀ MEMORIAL BUTTON, INAUGURATION DAY 1993

Objectives

After studying this section, you should be able to

★ explain why many Americans demanded a change in government in 1992.

★ explain how gridlock between Congress and the President affected the process of government.

★ discuss the campaign issues of the 1996 presidential election.

Key Terms

incumbent, filibuster, downsizing, line-item veto, appropriations bill

---

At the beginning of the twentieth century, progressives had worked to strengthen and enlarge the small federal government. Their objective was to equip government to handle the social and economic problems caused by industrialization. Toward the end of the century, government had grown so large that more Americans worked in local, state, and national government than in the manufacturing industries.

Many Americans believed government had grown too large and complex, that it taxed too heavily, and spent too much. Leaders from both major parties and a number of minor parties promised to renovate government and make it more responsive to the needs of the people.

■ Demands for Change

As the election of 1992 approached, many Americans expressed a need for change. Public opinion turned against Washington, D.C. "insiders" and **incumbents,** or those people currently holding office. Voters blamed incumbents for the recession, the federal deficit, and government gridlock.

Government Scandals

Scandals deepened Americans' anger toward incumbents. Revelations that some members of the House of Representatives had bounced checks repeatedly at the House bank outraged many citizens. They asked how these officials could manage the nation's economy when they bungled their own personal finances. Further angered when members of Congress voted to raise their own salaries, many political leaders and citizens took action. Ultimately, the movement led to the ratification in 1992 of the Twenty-seventh Amendment. This amendment prohibited any congressional pay raise from taking effect until after the following election, thus giving the voters a chance to react.

Another uproar followed President Bush's nomination of Clarence Thomas to the Supreme Court in 1991. One of Thomas's former coworkers, law professor Anita Hill, testified before the Senate Judiciary Committee that Thomas had sexually harassed her. Thomas strongly denied the charge.

The Senate narrowly confirmed Thomas to the Supreme Court, but many Americans were angry, noting the absence of any women on the Senate Judiciary Committee.

Three-Way Race for President

After victory in the Persian Gulf War, President Bush's reelection seemed assured. Several Democrats declined to run against him. The lengthening recession, however, raised new doubts about his leadership and encouraged challengers to enter the race.

Among the leading Democratic candidates for President was Governor Bill Clinton of Arkansas. Early in the campaign, the press raised questions about Clinton's character and his failure to serve in the armed forces during the Vietnam War. Yet, after victories in the primaries, Clinton won the nomination.

Texas billionaire H. Ross Perot fashioned a strong third-party challenge. Perot had promised to run if volunteers could collect enough petitions to place his name on all 50 state ballots. The outpouring of volunteers expressed demand for change as well as unhappiness with the two major parties.

Election of 1992

During the campaign, Clinton painted the recession as the President's most glaring failure. He made the economy his number-one issue.

In an election that saw the largest number of voters ever in American history, Clinton received 43 percent of the popular vote, while Bush captured 38 percent and Perot 19 percent. Clinton received less than a majority because of Perot's strong showing, the highest for any third-party candidate since 1912.

Although Republicans gained seats in the House of Representatives, Democrats retained control of both houses of Congress. Moreover, voters defeated a large number of incumbents and elected a record number of women and minority candidates. Twenty-four new women members were elected to the House, and four won Senate seats. Jay Kim was the first Korean American and Nydia Velazquez the first Puerto Rican woman in the House of Representatives. Carol Moseley Braun of Illinois was the first African American woman senator, while Ben Nighthorse Campbell was the first Native American in the Senate in more than 60 years.

A New Democrat

President Clinton identified himself as a "New Democrat" who put less faith in big government to solve all problems. Only 46 years old, Clinton was a complex person

Visualizing History ▲ **H. Ross Perot** A strong third-party challenge was given by Ross Perot in the 1992 presidential election. *What percentage of the popular vote did Perot receive?*

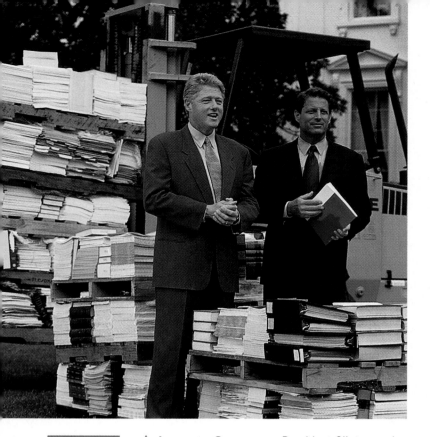

▲ INEFFICIENT GOVERNMENT President Clinton and Vice President Al Gore stand by piles of books which contain federal rules and regulations. *What program was started to make government more efficient?*

who, at times, presented different images to different people. He embraced middle-class values, playing rock music, jogging, and exhibiting a taste for fast foods.

Yet Clinton had graduated from such elite institutions as Georgetown University and the Yale Law School and had attended Oxford University as a Rhodes scholar. Reflecting a tension between these facets of his personality, Clinton changed positions on a number of issues. Critics complained that these shifts showed that Clinton was a pragmatic politician and compromiser rather than a committed leader.

Clinton's Programs

During the campaign, Clinton had promised a middle-class tax cut. But larger-than-expected budget deficits made Clinton conclude that reducing the deficit would better strengthen the economy. He abandoned plans for the tax cut and instead supported specific tax increases to raise more revenue.

Congress passed the deficit reduction plan, but then defeated the Clinton administration's $16 billion spending plan that had been intended to stimulate the economy. Opponents of the spending plan had successfully argued that increased spending while trying to cut the deficit sent a mixed message to Americans.

To deal with the problem of crime, President Clinton focused largely on prevention. His crime bill gave grants to cities and states to hire a total of 100,000 new police officers. The program also contained a "3 strikes and you're out" policy that mandated life imprisonment for those convicted of 3 major felonies. The crime bill banned many types of assault (military-style) weapons, and the Brady Law established a waiting period for the purchase of hand guns. This waiting period gave authorities a chance to determine whether the buyer had a criminal record.

President Clinton and Vice President Al Gore also planned ways to redesign the national government. They called for greater use of computer technology to sustain services with fewer workers, and they launched a National Performance Review to examine and evaluate the efficiency of each government agency. The purpose of the review was to eliminate outdated and unnecessary functions and to shrink the bureaucracy to create a government that "works better and costs less."

■ Gridlock Continues

With Democratic majorities in both houses of Congress, the President hoped at last to end government gridlock. After initial success, however, gridlock continued because Democrats had split into two camps on some issues. Conservative Democrats were uncomfortable with many of Clinton's proposals. They considered ways to cut back some social programs and many environmental and regulatory provisions.

By contrast, Republicans remained united in their opposition to most administration programs. In the Senate, Republicans used delaying tactics, such as the **filibuster,** to block passage of certain bills. To filibuster means to keep talking for hours until a majority of the Senate either abandons the bill or agrees to modify its most controversial provisions.

The Clinton Health Plan

A central goal for the administration was to set up a system of health care to provide for the 15 percent of Americans with no health insurance. The President named his spouse, Hillary Rodham Clinton, an experienced attorney, to lead a task force that would recommend changes in the health-care system.

The Clinton plan called for guaranteed health benefits for all Americans. The plan required employers to shoulder much of the burden for health insurance for their employees. As a result, the plan was opposed by small-business owners who feared that they could not afford it. The insurance industry, which stood to lose revenue, also opposed the plan.

Republicans challenged the Clinton health-care plan, deriding it as too big, complicated, and costly. Some Democrats also deserted the President's plan and proposed a variety of alternatives. No plan earned enough support to be passed, however.

Criticism Increases

Accusations against his personal morals and financial ethics also hurt the President. A key issue was the Whitewater scandal. Clinton had invested in Whitewater, an Arkansas land development project that had gone bankrupt. Congress investigated the business deal, and a special prosecutor was appointed.

Middle-class Americans who still felt economically insecure also criticized the President. Early in Clinton's term the economy improved as unemployment fell, inflation remained low, and the federal deficit declined. Yet many men over the age of 50 had lost their jobs because of cutbacks in the defense industry and through corporate **downsizing,** the process by which companies seek to achieve savings by reducing the number of midlevel employees.

The 1994 Congressional Elections

In 1994 mounting criticism of the Clinton administration led voters to turn control of Congress over to the Republicans for the first time in 40 years. Republicans added 52 House seats and 8 Senate seats. Every Republican incumbent running for reelection won,

Visualizing History

▲ HEALTH CARE REFORM First Lady Hillary Rodham Clinton led a task force that was to recommend changes in the health-care system. Here she speaks to a group of medical students about her proposals. *Why did small-business owners oppose the Clinton health plan?*

while prominent Democrats lost, including House Speaker Tom Foley.

A key to the Republican victories was their "Contract with America" that proposed lower taxes, stronger restrictions on immigration, tougher anti-crime laws, limits on congressional terms, a balanced budget, and the **line-item veto.** This kind of veto would allow the President to veto particular items in an **appropriations bill** without having to veto the entire bill. An appropriations bill sets aside money for a specific purpose. The new Republican Speaker of the House, Newt Gingrich of Georgia, blamed New Deal and Great Society programs for creating a culture of poverty and violence. Condemning the growth of large government, Gingrich vowed to "erase the slate and start over."

■ A Contract with America

Newt Gingrich and the voters' demand for change deserved much of the credit for the Republicans' upset victory in 1994. Seeking to end the Republicans' long years in the minority, Gingrich devised a plan to make the congressional campaigns a national election rather than many separate local elections. He arranged for Republican candidates to sign the "Contract with America," outlining the program they agreed to enact if they won the majority. After the election, House Republicans elected Gingrich Speaker. He articulated their policies, led them into legislative battle, and became the most visible congressional opponent to President Clinton. Republicans saw their victory as a mandate to dismantle the welfare state and to transfer power from the federal government back to the states.

Republican Agenda in Congress

As they promised, House Republicans passed most of the "Contract with America" within their first hundred days in the majority. While House rules allowed the majority to act quickly, however, the Senate offered the minority a greater voice. Public opposition to cutting Medicare and Social Security also restrained congressional eagerness.

Congress passed legislation to hold itself accountable to all of the employment laws and regulations it set for business. It restricted "unfunded mandates," laws that required states to take action without providing federal funds to pay for it. In addition, Congress gave the President a line-item veto to cancel particular items in

★★★★**A**★★★★★★★★
AMERICAN PORTRAITS

On August 10, 1993, Ruth Bader Ginsburg was sworn in as the 107th justice of the United States Supreme Court. The second woman ever to serve on the Court, Justice Ginsburg attended law school at a time when women often suffered discrimination. Ginsburg experienced discrimination firsthand when, in 1960, Supreme Court Justice Frankfurter refused to hire her as his law clerk because she was a woman. Having a keen sense of fairness, Ginsburg successfully argued against a number of laws that treated men and women differently, even when the laws gave women favorable treatment.

When Ginsburg became a judge on the United States Court of Appeals, she carefully thought out her decisions just as she had carefully prepared her cases when she was a lawyer. Largely because of those decisions, the Senate approved her appointment to the Supreme Court.

Ruth Bader Ginsburg

1933–

a spending bill without having to reject the entire bill. These measures aimed not only at reducing the deficit but at reducing the federal government's presence in everyday American life.

The Republican Congress seemed to be setting the government's agenda. The President responded with vetoes or threats of vetoes. Clinton forced Congress to restore funds for education, job training, child care, and the environment. He made protection of Social Security, Medicare, and Medicaid issues as well.

Government Shutdown

Late in 1995 congressional leaders reached a showdown with the White House over the federal budget. To reduce deficits, Republicans wanted to turn Medicaid— health care for the poor—over to the states. President Clinton said this plan would hurt poor children. Meeting with congressional leaders in his office, Clinton pointed to his desk and said: "If you want somebody to sign your budget, you're going to have to elect someone else to sit there because I'm not going to do it." Still, Speaker Gingrich believed that if Congress stood firm, the President would sign their budget rather than risk shutting down the government.

When neither side would back down, the federal government had to close for lack of operating funds. Government agencies sent their employees home and suspended some federal services. National parks and Smithsonian museums turned away visitors. The public blamed Congress for the government's shutdown, and President Clinton's approval rating rose.

Reaching a Compromise

Congress and the President finally acknowledged the need to compromise. They reached an agreement to balance the budget in 7 years. Indicating his willingness to work with the conservative Congress, President Clinton declared that "the era of big government is over."

Congress responded by increasing the minimum wage as the President had

Visualizing History ▲ NEWT GINGRICH Speaker of the House Newt Gingrich led House Republicans in their efforts to pass the "Contract with America." Most of the measures passed. Only term limits and the balanced-budget amendment stalled. *What is the line-item veto?*

requested. Congress also passed a health-care bill. Although smaller in scale than Clinton's original proposal, the new law made it easier for workers to keep their health insurance when they changed jobs. In addition, the President signed a welfare reform bill in August 1996. This law significantly revised the 60-year-old welfare system and fulfilled Clinton's promise to "end welfare as we know it."

By 1996, the combined effect of tax increases, spending cuts, an improved economy, and a halting of costly new government programs significantly reduced the annual federal deficit. The deficit fell from $300 billion a year in 1993 to $117 billion in 1996—the lowest since 1980. The federal debt represented a smaller proportion of the entire economy than in any other industrial nation. Despite this good news, economists still raised grave concerns. As more people neared retirement, Medicare and Social Security costs would increase faster than government revenues. Some reform would be necessary to save these popular programs.

The Election of 1996

During the 1996 elections, Democrats portrayed Speaker of the House Newt Gingrich and the Republican "Contract with America" as reckless and extreme. The more unpopular Gingrich became, the more Clinton's public standing improved. Democrats renominated President Clinton and Vice President Gore for a second term without opposition.

After considering a wide field, Republicans nominated the Senate majority leader, Kansas senator Bob Dole, as their candidate. A 35-year veteran of Congress, Dole had been more moderate than the zealous House Republicans. As his main issue, Dole promised an across-the-board tax cut of 15 percent. For his running mate, Dole chose former Representative Jack Kemp, an author of the federal tax cuts under President Ronald Reagan.

A wounded veteran of World War II, Senator Dole at 73 was a generation older than President Clinton. Dole described himself as a bridge to better times in the American past. "To those who say it was never so, that America has not been better, I say you're wrong, and I know because I was there," he said. President Clinton offered himself as a bridge to the future. His campaign emphasized improving the quality of life as Americans entered the twenty-first century.

The presidential debates helped define the candidates' positions on certain issues. Senator Dole talked about his plans to cut taxes and to get tough on crime. He also attacked the President's record on anti-drug enforcement. President Clinton stressed favorable economic news and spoke to voters' concerns about education, drugs, and the environment.

Character and values became issues late in the campaign. Dole asked why Americans did not feel greater outrage over the appearance of scandal and impropriety in the Clinton administration. However, rather than responding to charges against his personal ethics, Clinton argued that attacking one's opponent did nothing to solve the nation's problems. President Clinton promoted his own program of family values, especially the protection of children. He

▲ THE PRESIDENTIAL DEBATES President Clinton and former Senator Dole debated each other in Connecticut and California. In the second debate (above), citizens asked candidates questions about the economy, the environment, and foreign policy. *How did President Clinton propose to protect children?*

proposed regulation of cigarette advertisements to discourage children from smoking. In addition, he called for a "V-chip" to screen violence out of television programs and endorsed school uniforms. Clinton campaigned against the gun lobby, the tobacco lobby, and the Republican Congress. Clinton cited the Family Leave Act, which allowed employees unpaid time off for family emergencies, as a major accomplishment of his administration, while pointing out that Senator Dole had voted against the act. Such issues especially appealed to women voters, who supported Clinton by a wide margin.

Election Results

As Election Day approached, the candidates increased their efforts in states such as Ohio, Florida, and California where the race was closest. Bob Dole, knowing he needed a strong finish, campaigned day and night, sleeping only a few hours on the plane between stops. Once again, Ross Perot ran as an independent candidate. He bought blocks of network television time to appeal directly to voters across the nation, but far fewer people responded to his message. President Clinton tried to help congressional candidates by appearances in states where close races could determine the majority party in Congress.

The anger that voters had shown in the previous two elections had diminished. People felt more comfortable with the economy and optimistic about the future.

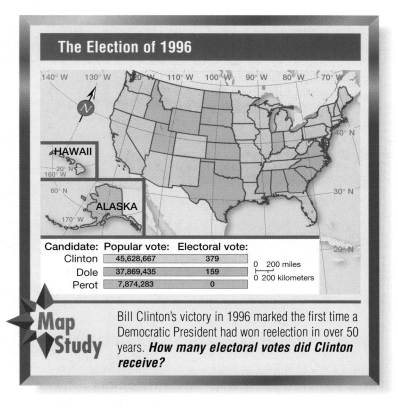

The Election of 1996

Candidate:	Popular vote:	Electoral vote:
Clinton	45,628,667	379
Dole	37,869,435	159
Perot	7,874,283	0

Map Study

Bill Clinton's victory in 1996 marked the first time a Democratic President had won reelection in over 50 years. *How many electoral votes did Clinton receive?*

However, voter turnout was one of the lowest in history for a presidential election. Fewer than half of the eligible voters in the country participated.

As the demand for change lessened, Clinton won reelection easily, receiving 49 percent of the popular vote. Dole received 41 percent of the vote, and Perot 8 percent. While reelecting a Democrat as President, the voters also returned Republican majorities to Congress. Both parties would have to seek common ground if they wanted to avoid further gridlock.

Section 1 ★ Review

Checking for Understanding

1. **Identify** Bill Clinton, H. Ross Perot, Hillary Rodham Clinton, Newt Gingrich, Contract with America, Bob Dole.

2. **Define** incumbent, filibuster, downsizing, line-item veto, appropriations bill.

3. **List** two reasons for the voters' demand for change during the early 1990s.

4. **Explain** why the majority of the federal government shut down in 1995.

Critical Thinking

5. **Making Comparisons** In your opinion, what factors could have contributed to the high voter turnout in 1992 and the low voter turnout in 1996?

★★

America in a Changing World

Setting the Scene

Focus

When the Soviet Union dissolved in 1991, the world changed, and America's role changed with it. United States foreign policy was no longer based on containing communism. President Clinton's administration sought to enlarge the global community of market-oriented democracies.

▶ TRAVEL PASSPORT

PASSPORT

United States of America

Objectives

After studying this section, you should be able to

★ describe President Clinton's foreign policies.

★ explain what role the United States played in settling conflicts around the world.

Key Terms

multinational state, genocide, ethnic cleansing, global economy, multinational corporation, trade deficit, creditor nation, debtor nation, globalized corporation

The struggle between communism and democracy was virtually over. Yet, throughout the world violent and bloody wars erupted over ethnic hatreds, political boundaries, and religious views.

■ Foreign Policy

President Clinton generally attempted to achieve his foreign policy goals through diplomacy or by using economic pressures. Whenever the prospect of using military force arose, however, the President tried to work cooperatively through the United Nations.

Civil War in Somalia

One of the first crises to confront the Clinton administration was civil war in the east African nation of Somalia. Beginning in the 1980s, different clans, groups of people with a common ancestry, battled for control of the government, while civilians died of hunger. When Clinton took office, 28,000 American troops were already protecting deliveries of food to the starving Somalians as part of a United Nations mission.

The longer American troops remained in Somalia, the more they were drawn into the conflict. Under fierce criticism for not providing adequate protection for American troops, President Clinton called for the withdrawal of all United States personnel. By 1995 United States forces had been withdrawn and rival factions had signed a peace agreement. However, continued fighting delayed the formation of a stable government.

Bloodshed in the Balkans

The United States and the world had to deal with mounting tensions in the Balkans, a peninsula in southeastern Europe. During the cold war, Yugoslavia had been a multinational state, or a republic with many different ethnic groups. Although its six republics each had a dominant ethnic group, their populations were mixed. Dividing the people were centuries-old differences of ethnicity, religion, and territorial claims.

In 1991 the republics of Slovenia, Croatia, Bosnia-Herzegovina, and Macedonia declared their independence. They did so after Serbia, the largest of the former republics, refused to allow the other republics greater autonomy. Under its leader Slobodan Milosevic (swoh•boh•dahn mee•LAH•soh•veech), Serbia began waging war against the breakaway states.

Violent fighting occurred in Bosnia-Herzegovina, where problems among Serbs, Croats, and Muslims steadily increased. In 1992 Bosnia's Croats and Muslims voted for independence, but Bosnian Serbs wanted to retain ties with Serbia. The creation of an independent Bosnia led to war among the Serbs, Croats, and Muslims. Bosnian Serb forces followed a policy of **genocide**—the systematic destruction of an ethnic, political, or cultural group—against the Muslims and Croats. The Serbs also engaged in what is known as **ethnic cleansing,** in this case, the expulsion of Bosnian Muslims and other non-Serbs from areas under Bosnian Serb control. As a result of the fighting, about 200,000 people died and nearly 3 million lost their homes.

A New Role for NATO

The United States and western Europe encouraged the UN to institute an arms embargo against all the former Yugoslav states, place trade sanctions on Serbia, and send a peacekeeping force into Bosnia.

In addition, the United States persuaded its NATO allies to stage air strikes against Bosnian Serb military sites—the first time that NATO had ever launched a military offensive. At that point, Bosnian Serb leader Radovan Karadzic (RAH•doh•vahn ka•RAH•dzihk) requested the diplomatic services of former United States President Jimmy Carter. Carter managed to arrange a shaky truce that turned increasingly fragile as warfare erupted again in early 1995.

Visualizing History

▲ SOMALIA American troops served to protect food deliveries to starving Somalians, while rival clans battled for power. *Why did President Clinton receive criticism over U.S. involvement in Somalia?*

The Dayton Peace Accords

The tide of the Balkan war turned in the spring of 1995. A Croatian offensive reclaimed lost territory, while driving many Serbs out of Croatia. NATO also increased its military strikes against Bosnian Serb positions. These events finally brought Bosnian Serbs, Muslims, and Croats to the peace table in Dayton, Ohio. The Dayton peace accords, reached in November 1995, established a Bosnian state divided into two separate Croat-Muslim and Serb regions. It also provided for arms control, free elections, and protection of human rights in Bosnia.

As part of the Dayton agreement, NATO furnished 60,000 troops—including 20,000 Americans—to maintain peace in Bosnia. The United States insisted that Bosnian Serb leader Radovan Karadzic remove himself from Bosnian politics and that he and others responsible for ethnic cleansing be prosecuted as war criminals. In September 1996, Bosnian Muslim leader Alija Itzetbegovic (ah•LEE•hah ee•zeht•BEH•goh•veech) was elected as chairman of a three-way presidency among Serbs, Croats, and Muslims.

Conflict in Chechnya

By the mid-1990s, tensions in the Russian Federation were rising as demands for self-rule grew. The north Caucasus republic of Chechnya attempted to secede from the Federation. Russian President Boris Yeltsin reacted by sending forces into Chechnya. The

Volunteers

Rain fell on America's Midwest in record levels from April to June 1993. The waters of the vast Mississippi and Missouri river systems flooded hundreds of low-lying cities and towns. At least 50

▼ ERECTING A BARRIER

people were killed, and millions of acres of prime farmland were covered by water. The Great Flood of 1993 caused damage in nine states at a cost of over $10 billion.

People of all ages volunteered to fill sandbags and raise the flood walls. Others transported personal belongings, livestock, and machinery to safety. Still others assisted at emergency shelters. Federal agencies, the National Guard, and private relief organizations all stepped in to help.

Many volunteers came from outside the flooded area. One man

from Ohio drove a truck loaded with bottled water to Des Moines, Iowa, at his own expense, after the city's water treatment plant had been knocked out by the flood. Several residents from Homestead, Florida, came to help as a way to pay back the help they had received after Hurricane Andrew devastated their city in 1992.

---

vastly outnumbered Chechen forces held off the Russian military. Fighting largely centered around the capital city of Grozny. More than 30,000 people died in the fighting.

Unrest in Haiti

Closer to home, unrest in the Caribbean nation of Haiti posed difficult challenges for the United States. In December 1990, a Roman Catholic priest, Jean-Bertrand Aristide (ah•ree•STEED), won the presidency of Haiti in the country's first fully democratic elections. In September 1991, however, the Haitian military, headed by Lieutenant General Raoul Cédras (SAY•drahs), overthrew Aristide, who sought refuge in the United States. These new rulers of Haiti used violence—even murder—to put down opposition, causing thousands of Haitians to flee to the United States.

Attempts to Restore Democracy

Seeking to topple the Haitian military government and restore democracy, the United Nations used economic pressure. The UN imposed an embargo on oil and arms in October 1993 and on all trade seven months later. In June 1994 President Clinton banned financial transactions between the United States

and Haiti. Despite this pressure, Haiti's rulers retained their tight grip on the country.

When economic pressure failed, the United Nations authorized the United States to lead an invasion to drive the military rulers out of Haiti and reinstate Aristide. On September 18, 1994, on the eve of the planned invasion, President Clinton sent former President Jimmy Carter to negotiate with Haiti's military rulers. The threat of an invasion persuaded the generals to step down peacefully. The next day, 2,000 American troops met no resistance when they landed in Haiti.

United Nations and American peacekeeping troops helped in the transition to democratic rule. Yet conflict among rival political groups threatened progress toward a stable government. In December 1995, however, a peaceful election brought Réne Preval to the presidency.

■ Moves Toward Peace in the Middle East

Although bloody wars seemed to be raging all over the post–cold war world, there were breakthroughs toward peace. The United States played an important role in several peace efforts in the Middle East.

Israeli-PLO Agreement

Of all the conflicts in the Middle East, the Arab-Israeli conflict had been the most enduring and difficult. When Israel was created from British-occupied Palestine in 1948, Palestinian Arabs had been forced to move to the West Bank of the Jordan River. This area soon came under the control of Jordan, however. With the support of Arab leaders, in 1964 some of these displaced people formed the Palestine Liberation Organization (PLO) to work toward the elimination of Israel and the creation of an independent Arab Palestine.

Fearing attack by its Arab neighbors, in 1967 Israel seized the Gaza Strip from Egypt and Jordanian territory west of the River Jordan, including Jordan's part of Jerusalem, the capital. For 20 years after the 1967 war, Arabs and Israelis could not agree on the future of the Israeli-occupied territories. Then in 1987 the Palestinians in both areas began an uprising. Finally, in October 1991 the United States helped start Israeli-Arab peace talks. Peace talks continued after President Clinton took office.

The peace talks proceeded erratically, until September 13, 1993, when Israeli Prime Minister Yitzhak Rabin (EE•tsahk rah•BEEN) and Palestine Liberation Organization leader Yasir Arafat (YAH•suhr AIR•uh•FAHT) reached an agreement. The PLO recognized Israel's right to exist, and Israel recognized the PLO as the representative of the Palestinians. In addition, both parties agreed on a framework for limited Palestinian self-rule in the Gaza Strip and the West Bank. In 1995, Israel and the PLO agreed on the removal of Israeli forces from other Palestinian areas and significant Palestinian self-rule by mid-1996. Moreover, Palestinians voting in 1996 elected Yasir Arafat as their first president.

Peace Between Israel and Jordan

President Clinton also helped to work out a peace agreement between Israel and Jordan. In July 1994, Israel's Prime Minister Rabin and Jordan's King Hussein signed a historic peace treaty officially ending the state of war that had existed between their countries for nearly half a century. The treaty also set up a framework for cooperation in environmental protection, tourism, and trade. The two former adversaries stated that they supported a "just, lasting, and comprehensive peace between Israel and its neighbors."

There was growing opposition to the peace plan. Palestinian leaders contended that growing Israeli settlements on the West Bank violated the spirit of the agreement.

Visualizing History

▲ ISRAEL AND THE PLO Prime Minister Benjamin Netanyahu (left) and PLO leader Yasir Arafat (right) have continued the peace process between Israelis and Palestinians.
To what office was Arafat elected in 1996?

Israelis feared that a fully independent Palestinian state would be a threat to their nation. Israeli leaders drew away from implementing the agreement when militant Palestinian groups attacked Israeli settlements.

In November 1995, an Israeli who opposed his government's policy with the Palestinians assassinated Prime Minister Rabin. A series of terrorist attacks further rocked Israel, and the 1996 election of a more conservative prime minister, Benjamin Netanyahu (neh•tahn•YAH•hoo), signaled a shift toward a harder line in negotiations with the Palestinians.

■ America in a Global Economy

In recent years, innovations in technology and economics have transformed national and regional economies into a **global economy**—an economic world with interdependence among countries. Developments in transportation and communications have made international trade an economic driving force in today's world. Part of this pattern is the growth of **multinational corporations,** companies that produce and market goods in different countries.

The United States has long based its economic prosperity on selling its goods abroad. By the 1970s, however, the United States was losing its economic dominance. America experienced **trade deficits,** purchasing more from foreign nations than it sold in foreign markets. By the early 1970s, the United States had changed from a **creditor nation,** or a lending nation, to a **debtor nation,** or a borrowing one.

The United States reacted to its declining economic position by competing harder in the global marketplace, streamlining industry, using new technology, and opening new markets. Many American companies have become **globalized corporations,** ones that operate throughout the world.

The government also pursued ways to strengthen America's economic position in the global marketplace. In 1992 the United States, Canada, and Mexico signed the North American Free Trade Agreement (NAFTA), which lifted all tariffs among the three nations, making North America the world's largest free trade area.

The agreement offered American companies a chance to open factories in Mexico, where wages were lower. Mexican and Canadian markets would also be more open to American products and services. Critics argued that American workers would be displaced by trade pacts that lowered trade barriers. However, the Senate approved the treaty after an almost year-long battle.

The American economic picture improved from 1990 to 1995, as exports rose 28 percent. The United States achieved a trading surplus with nearly every nation, but continued to carry an overall trade deficit. Yet for the first time since 1985, the World Economic Forum rated the United States economy as the most competitive in the world.

Section 2 ★ Review

Checking for Understanding

1. **Identify** Alija Itzetbegovic, Jean-Bertrand Aristide, Réne Preval, Raoul Cédras, Palestine Liberation Organization (PLO), Yitzhak Rabin, Yasir Arafat, Benjamin Netanyahu.

2. **Define** multinational state, genocide, ethnic cleansing, global economy, multinational corporation, trade deficit, creditor nation, debtor nation, globalized corporation.

3. **Describe** the methods used by the United States, NATO, and the UN to bring peace to the Balkans.

4. **Cite** two results of the peace talks between Israel and the PLO.

Critical Thinking

5. **Making Judgments** Describe the pros and cons of American companies' moving factories to foreign countries to take advantage of lower wages.

Map and Graph Skills

Interpreting Statistics

Often presented in graphs and tables, statistics, or numerical data, need to be carefully examined to determine their real significance. Use the following steps to interpret statistical information:

- **Scan** the graphs, reading the title and labels to get an idea of what is being shown.
- **Check** the graphs for unfamiliar terms. When you find one, look up the term in your book's glossary or in a dictionary.
- **Examine** the statistics, looking for increases and decreases, similarities and differences. Determine if the data are relevant to a particular topic.
- **Determine** the conclusions you can draw from the statistics.

Practicing the Skill

Use the guidelines above to help you interpret the statistics on the graphs on this page. Then answer these questions:

1. What subject do all these graphs deal with?

2. What do the graphs' keys tell you?

3. What do the labels on the horizontal axes tell you?

4. Which company has the greatest total assets?

5. Which company has the greatest foreign assets?

6. Which company has the highest percentage of foreign sales?

7. How are assets and sales related?

8. Which companies sell more of their products nationally than internationally?

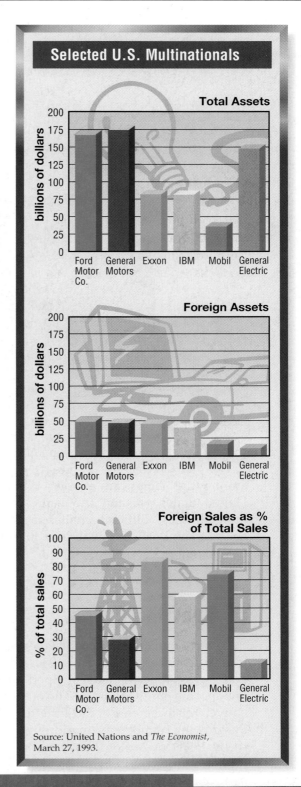

Source: United Nations and *The Economist,*
March 27, 1993.

★★★

Challenges and Opportunities

Setting the Scene

Section Focus

As the twentieth century came to a close, issues such as poverty and welfare, terrorism, threats to the environment, health risks, and increased immigration faced the United States. These complex issues left Americans seeking solutions for a better society.

Objectives

After studying this section, you should be able to

★ identify the challenges and opportunities facing the United States in the 1990s.

★ describe some of the proposed solutions to these challenges.

Key Terms

wetland, acid rain, illegal alien, multicultural society

◀ LAPTOP COMPUTER

*V*oters' demands for change in government during the 1990s reflected a great concern among the American people. While the United States was on the verge of new opportunities, difficult challenges threatened to diminish the quality of life in the United States.

■ Growing Poverty

Poverty remained a major challenge confronting Americans. Since the 1930s, the federal government had helped many low-income families who had no other alternative. Yet these efforts did little to reduce the growing number of Americans in poverty. By 1996 one out of every eight children was receiving Aid to Families with Dependent Children (AFDC).

For many Americans the troubling aspects of poverty include how poverty contributes to crime and violence, and how crime and violence affect the young. In many cities, gang activity rose.

The Income Gap

Not only did the number of poor people increase, but the income gap between the rich and poor grew wider than at any time since the 1930s. Partly responsible were changes in the American economy. In the past, the wide range of good jobs in industry had helped people with a high school education enter the middle class. In the latter part of the twentieth century, however, low-skill manufacturing declined and high-technology and service companies increased. A high school diploma was no longer enough to guarantee a good job. Workers who could take advantage of the technological revolution did better. Salaries of college graduates increased steadily, especially for those in high-technology and service companies. More people than ever entered professions such as education, law, and medicine.

Attempts at Welfare Reform

Both Democratic and Republican leaders called for reforming the welfare system, but for different reasons. Some sought reform because of welfare's great cost to America and the need to decrease the deficit. Others argued that the system had to change because it created a "culture of poverty" in which the poor were trapped by their dependence on welfare.

President Clinton's 1994 welfare reform plan offered increased education and training for welfare recipients to send them back to work. The plan also called for a crackdown on "deadbeat parents" by using the Internal Revenue Service to collect overdue child support. The Clinton plan, however, stalled in Congress.

Some members of Congress offered different ideas. Republican Speaker of the House Newt Gingrich argued for cutting public assistance and emphasized that it was up to the poor to find work. Gingrich also advocated relying on private charities, not the government, to rescue the most impoverished.

In 1996 the Republican Congress passed a welfare reform bill that ended Aid to Families with Dependent Children. The federal government would now offer states block grants of aid, rather than pay poor people directly. States would be able to take money formerly used for welfare and use it as incentives for businesses to hire people currently on welfare.

Students as a Resource

Seeking to help students who had left school early, some cities started volunteer programs to provide them with job skills and scholarship opportunities. In addition, President Clinton helped establish Ameri-Corps in 1993. This program employed

Visualizing History

▲ **WELFARE REFORM** President Clinton signed a historic welfare reform bill in 1996, which gave states more control over programs and limited the time people can receive benefits to five years. *How did President Clinton propose to use the Internal Revenue Service in his 1994 welfare reform plan?*

students to deal with issues such as improving low-income housing and cleaning up the environment. Students earned a salary and, after completing their service, a scholarship to continue their education.

■ The Cost of Terrorism

Escalating terrorism posed new dangers to Americans of all ages. In 1993 Islamic radicals bombed New York City's World Trade Center in an effort to force the United States to abandon its support for Israel and Egypt. In 1995 the bombing of a federal office building in Oklahoma City claimed the lives of 168 people, among them 15 children in the building's day care center. Two suspects arrested shortly after the bombing, and later tried, had ties to a private American militia group. Militia members often believed that the federal government and other powerful interests were conspiring to rob them of their freedom.

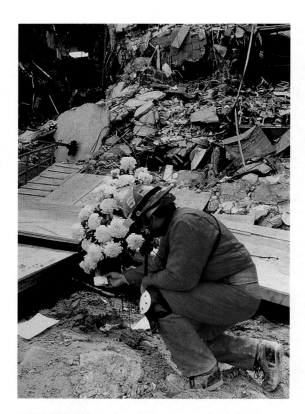

▲ TERRORISM A worker at the Oklahoma City bombing site leaves memorial flowers. *How did the government react to the increase in terrorism?*

To combat terrorism the government sought new powers, such as increased wiretapping. This raised the question of whether Americans would accept infringements of their civil liberties in order to suppress terrorist violence. After the Oklahoma City bombing, concrete barriers closed off Pennsylvania Avenue in front of the White House. These barriers served as a reminder of terrorism's cost.

■ The Environment

Threats to the environment troubled Americans at the end of the twentieth century. The battle continued between those who wanted to preserve natural wilderness and those who favored greater development of natural resources.

Clinton and the Environment

When President Clinton took office, he wanted to protect the environment, but he also promised to "grow the economy." The President often tried to placate both developers and environmentalists through a series of compromises. One compromise between loggers in the Pacific Northwest and environmentalists permitted both the logging industry and the habitat of endangered species, such as the spotted owl, to survive. President Clinton also took steps to stop further loss of America's **wetlands,** areas such as tidal flats and swamps that contain much soil moisture. Moreover, in 1996 the President protected Utah's southern red-rock cliffs and canyons from mining, by declaring them a national monument.

Acid Rain

One of the more controversial environmental issues concerned **acid rain,** precipitation contaminated by acidic gases given off when environmental pollutants such as oil, gas, or coal burn. Environmentalists calling for stricter regulations contended that acid rain kills fish, damages crops, and strips forests. Developers warned that more regulations meant higher costs for companies that burn fossil fuels, forcing them either to find other energy sources or to install pollution-control devices. Accepting either option, they argued, would increase production costs, sending fuel prices spiraling upward and leading to the loss of jobs.

Increasing Risks to Health

In the 1990s there were increasing risks to the health of the American people. Diseases such as AIDS (*acquired immunodeficiency syndrome*) killed thousands and devastated society in the United States and worldwide. Drug addiction continued to be a concern, which caused many to demand more government involvement to halt the problem.

The Spread of AIDS

During the 1980s and 1990s, AIDS spread rapidly throughout the United States and the world. By the mid-1990s, AIDS was the third-leading cause of death among Americans aged 25 to 44. From 1981 through 1996, more than 400,000 AIDS cases were diagnosed in the United States. During the early 1990s there were 20,000 AIDS-related deaths a year, and estimates placed the number of Americans infected with HIV, (human immunodeficiency virus) which often leads to AIDS, at 1 million.

Responding to these alarming statistics, the federal government launched programs to educate Americans about the dangers of AIDS. President Clinton appointed a federal AIDS policy coordinator. In addition, Congress increased funding for AIDS research and fully funded the Ryan White Care Act, providing $275 million to cities for AIDS treatment.

Drug Abuse

Drug abuse also continued to spread. Between 1991 and 1996, there was a significant increase in marijuana use among high school students. In addition, the use of cocaine and crack cocaine, a more potent form of the drug that is smokable, rose among men, women, and young people.

Moreover, women using cocaine while pregnant can cause their babies to be born addicted. These children, sometimes called cocaine babies, often suffer serious and lasting health problems.

The Issue of Immigration

Immigration became a pressing issue in the 1990s, when economic and political ills around the world brought a new tide of immigrants to the United States. Many of the new immigrants were refugees from the former Soviet Union, eastern Europe, Southeast Asia, Cuba, and Haiti, fleeing from political repression and economic hardships in their homelands. Some newcomers were **illegal aliens,** people who enter a country without a legal permit. Total legal immigration reached nearly 1 million a year during the late 1980s, yet declined by nearly 200,000 by 1995.

Illegal Aliens

Many Americans blamed increased immigration for the loss of jobs and higher taxes. Immigration took on an even more emotional tone in states with large concentrations of illegal immigrants such as Florida, Texas, and California. For example, California's governor Pete Wilson blamed much of his state's economic problems on the costs of providing state services for illegal immigrants. Wilson argued, "We can no longer allow compassion to overrule reason."

In November 1994 California voters approved Proposition 187, which banned illegal aliens from enrolling in public schools and using nonemergency medical care and other social services. Proposition 187 stirred anger among legal immigrants, who reacted strongly to what they considered ethnic prejudice.

The Treatment of Legal Immigrants

Congress also limited the rights of legal immigrants by limiting their access to welfare benefits. Although immigrants applied for welfare benefits less often than American citizens, the number of legal immigrants kept rising. This growth in population increased costs for the government.

As part of its welfare reform bill in 1996, Congress barred legal immigrants who were not yet citizens from receiving many benefits, including food stamps and Social Security. Family members who sponsored immigrants were expected to bear more of their financial burdens.

The Question of Diversity

Tying directly into the debate on immigration was the question of diversity. Some Americans believed that the different peoples who make up the United States should retain their individual cultural heritages. They saw the United States as a **multicultural society** in which everyone should respect each other's uniqueness. As Mayor Sharpe James of Newark, New Jersey, said, "Our diversity is our strength." Others believed, as many had in years past, that the United States should be a melting-pot society in which immigrants from around the world blend into one unique people.

■ The Struggle for Equal Rights

One group that sought equal rights during the 1990s were Americans with disabilities. In 1990 Congress passed the Americans with Disabilities Act. This law prohibited discrimination against the more than 40 million Americans who had physical, hearing, or visual impairments. Television news correspondent John Hockenberry, who himself uses a wheelchair, commented: "Our struggle for inclusion in this society is a test of whether American society truly wants diversity and freedom for all."

■ The Information Superhighway

As America faced the twenty-first century, creative new forms of communication became available via computer networks forming an "information superhighway." This superhighway carries vast amounts of digitized information across fiber-optic telecommunication circuits at rapid speeds.

The cold war gave rise to the original network, ARPANET, in 1969. ARPANET allowed the Department of Defense to communicate with contractors and universities working on defense projects.

By the 1990s millions of people had access to an international computer network, the Internet. The Internet offered easy access to information on a global scale and continued to grow rapidly. Users could browse library catalogs, view works of art, and converse electronically with others who shared similar interests.

The Internet also offered unprecedented freedom of expression around the world, as demonstrated on the sixth anniversary of the 1989 Tiananmen Square massacre. Chinese police prevented any public commemorations. Yet they could not stop the image of the Chinese Statue of Liberty from appearing on the Internet with the slogan: "It is painful to recall, but it is never to be forgotten."

Section 3 ★ Review

Checking for Understanding

1. **Identify** AmeriCorps, AIDS, Ryan White Care Act, Proposition 187, Internet.
2. **Define** wetland, acid rain, illegal alien, multicultural society.
3. **Describe** efforts to reform the welfare system in the United States.
4. **Cite** government attempts to deal with increased immigration.

Critical Thinking

5. **Evaluating Tactics** How do you think the government can most effectively solve the problem of poverty? Explain your answer.

Environmental Issues of the Twenty-first Century

The industrialized world has purchased prosperity at the expense of the environment. The conflict between economic growth and environmental protection may well become the central issue of the twenty-first century.

The disappearing ozone layer—part of the upper atmosphere—is linked to the widespread use of chlorofluorocarbons (CFCs), commonly found in such products as aerosols and foam packaging. Ozone depletion may cause an increase in skin cancer. Another concern is global warming caused by high levels of carbon dioxide and other gases that trap heat from the sun in the atmosphere and cause a greenhouse effect. The destruction of rain forests, which absorb carbon dioxide and release oxygen, compounds the problem. Many scientists believe that global warming could cause polar ice caps to melt, raising ocean levels and flooding coastal cities.

Disposal of wastes, especially toxic and nuclear materials, will also be a continuing issue. The United States alone produces 40 million tons of toxic wastes annually.

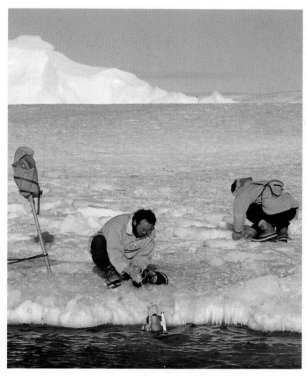

▲ SCIENTISTS TAKING WATER SAMPLES, ARCTIC RESEARCH PROJECT

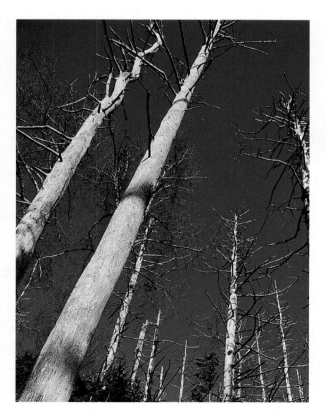

▲ EFFECTS OF ACID RAIN

Making the Environment Connection

1. What is the cause of global warming?

2. How do you think future technology will affect environmental problems?

Linking Past and Present

3. What can individuals do to slow down the destruction of the environment?

Hunger of Memory (excerpts)

▲ RICHARD RODRIGUEZ

Hispanic Americans cherish their heritage, and many speak only Spanish among their friends and family. However, most of their children's teachers speak only English. As a result, Hispanic students often find school confusing and humiliating. Richard Rodriguez describes his struggle to become "educated" in his auto-biography, *Hunger of Memory*. As you read this excerpt, notice how the author's attitude toward books changes.

From an early age I knew that my mother and father could read and write both Spanish and English. . . . For both my parents, however, reading was something done out of necessity and as quickly as possible. . . . Their reading consisted of work manuals, prayer books, newspapers, recipes. . . .

. . . I privately wondered: What was the connection between reading and learning? Did one learn something only by reading it? . . . [A sign said:] CONSIDER BOOKS YOUR BEST FRIENDS. Friends? Reading was, at best, only a chore. I needed to look up whole paragraphs of words in a dictionary. Lines of type were dizzying, the eye having to move slowly across the page, then down, and across. . . . What bothered me most, however, was the isolation reading required. To console myself for the loneliness I'd feel when I read, I tried reading in a very soft voice. Until: "Who is doing all that talking to his neighbor?" Shortly after, remedial reading classes were arranged for me with a very old nun.

At the end of each school day, for nearly six months, I would meet with her in the tiny room that served as the school's library. . . . Most of the time we took turns. I began with my elementary text. Sentences of astonishing simplicity seemed to me lifeless and drab: "The boys ran from the rain. . . . She wanted to sing. . . . The kite rose in the blue." Then the old nun would read from her favorite books, usually biographies of early American presidents. Playfully she ran through complex sentences, calling the words alive with her voice, making it seem that the author somehow was speaking directly to me. I smiled just to listen to her. I sat there and sensed for the very first time some possibility of fellowship between a reader and a writer, a communication. . . .

I entered high school having read hundreds of books. My habit of reading made me a confident speaker and writer of English. Reading also enabled me to sense something of the shape, the major concerns, of Western thought. . . . In these various ways books brought me academic success as I hoped that they would. But I was not a good reader. Merely bookish, I lacked a point of view when I read. Rather, I read in order to acquire a point of view. I vacuumed books for epigrams, scraps of information, ideas, themes—anything to fill the hollow within me and make me feel educated. . . .

. . . One day I came across a newspaper article about the retirement of an English professor at a nearby state college. The article was accompanied by a list of the "hundred most important books of Western Civilization." "More than anything else in my life," the professor told the reporter with finality, "These books have made me all that I am." . . . I clipped out the list and kept it for the several months it took me to read all of the titles. Most books, of course, I barely understood. While reading Plato's *Republic*, for instance, I needed to keep looking at the book's jacket comments to remind myself what the text was about. Nevertheless . . . I looked at every word of the text. And by the time I reached the last word, relieved, I convinced myself that I had read *The Republic*. In a ceremony of pride, I solemnly crossed Plato off my list.

THE LIBRARY BY JACOB LAWRENCE, 1960

Interpreting Literature

1. How did the writer's attitude toward reading change over time?

2. What benefits from reading do you think the writer especially appreciated because he was Hispanic American?

Making Comparisons

3. Why do you think Rodriguez's parents viewed books differently from his teachers?

Using Vocabulary

Assume that you are a magazine reporter covering the state of the economy during President Clinton's first term. Write an article detailing your findings using the following vocabulary words.

global economy
multinational corporation
trade deficit
creditor nation
debtor nation
globalized corporation

Reviewing Facts

1. **Discuss** why people turned against incumbents in the 1992 election.

2. **Explain** why Clinton charged that the economic recession was Bush's most glaring failure.

3. **Describe** Clinton's crime program, including its overall focus.

4. **Explain** why gridlock in Congress reappeared despite the fact that the Democrats controlled the Presidency and held majorities in both the House and the Senate.

5. **Summarize** the campaign issues for the 1996 presidential election for President Clinton and Bob Dole.

6. **Summarize** the United States's reaction to the war in the Balkans.

7. **Describe** the events that led to the overthrow of Jean-Bertrand Aristide in Haiti and the efforts of the United States to restore him to power.

8. **Describe** the positive breakthroughs in the Middle East in which the United States played a part.

Understanding Concepts

Change

1. How did President Clinton carry out the charge by Americans to "reinvent government" during his first term?

Challenge

2. What challenges do the American people face in the future, and what are some possible solutions to them?

Critical Thinking

1. **Synthesizing Information** Were any of the problems the United States faced in the last decade of the twentieth century truly new? Explain your answer.

2. **Analyzing Art** The personal computer has become a common tool in homes, schools, and offices. In addition, the computer has revolutionized graphic, illustrated, and animated art. Study the art on this page and answer the questions that follow.

   a. Does the computer extend the creative capacity of artists? Explain.

   b. What do you think the artist is trying to say in this work?

   c. What title would you give it?

CHAPTER 36 ★ REVIEW

Writing About History

Argumentation

Write an argument that supports or opposes Clinton's first-term health-care plan. State the controversy or problem clearly, and give your position or your solution to the problem. Gather relevant facts and statistics that support your position and logically disprove opposing positions.

Cooperative Learning

Form a study group and research news sources to determine recent happenings in Somalia, the Balkans, Haiti, and the Middle East. Evaluate the continuing major problems in each area, the key figures working out solutions, any additional breakthroughs that have occurred, and how these further developments could affect the United States. Present your findings to the class.

Social Studies Skills

Analyzing Trends

Equality in the workplace is an ideal goal for many Americans. Several groups of people have strived for equality for women and/or minority groups in the United States. Analyzing data in a table can help determine these groups' success.

To analyze a table and determine trends, you must carefully examine the title, all the heads, and the data in each row and column of the table. By comparing each row and each column you can determine any similarities and patterns.

Practicing the Skill

Use the table on this page to answer the following questions.

1. What are the three parts of the table?

2. In order for the percentage of women and minorities in the workforce to increase, what group's percentage must decrease? Is this happening?

3. Are minorities and women achieving equality of earnings in the workplace?

The Labor Force, 1983–1993

	1983	1985	1990	1993
Total workforce (in thousands)	70,976	77,002	85,082	85,211
Percentage of total workforce				
Male	59.6	59.2	57.6	56.8
Female	40.4	40.8	42.4	43.2
White	87.0	86.3	85.4	85.0
Black	10.4	10.9	11.3	11.4
of Hispanic origin	NA	NA	8.2	8.3
Ratio of weekly median earnings				
Females to Males	66.7	68.2	71.8	76.8
Blacks to Whites	81.8	78.0	77.0	77.4
Hispanics to Whites	NA	NA	71.9	70.0

Source: *Statistical Abstract of the United States*, 1994.

4. How do the percentages of minorities in the workforce compare with the percentages of those minorities in the population? (See the Chapter Review for Chapter 32.)

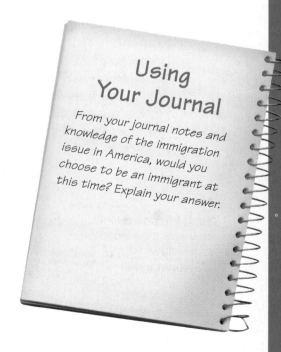

Using Your Journal

From your journal notes and knowledge of the immigration issue in America, would you choose to be an immigrant at this time? Explain your answer.

Cultural Kaleidoscope

The World of Music

ROCKING INTO THE FUTURE

Rock and roll music has been one of the most popular forms of musical expression in the twentieth century. It began as a mixture of styles, borrowing elements from rhythm and blues and country music as well as the popular ballads of the 1950s. Today's rock musicians show the willingness to explore new boundaries. In pushing for new sounds, they have made use of synthesizers and electronic sounds, classical instrumentation, and Latin and African phrasings and rhythms. Rock performers in the late 1900s have created one of the most popular and unique postwar arts.

▲

In the late 1970s and early 1980s, Janet Jackson was best known as the sister of Michael Jackson and for her appearances in televised situation comedies. Her musical albums *Rhythm Nation* and *Janet* pushed her to the top echelon of rock performers.

► Such keyboard instruments as the piano, organ, and synthesizer add to rock's eclectic appeal.

► Innovations ranging from the jukebox to the compact disc have helped the popular appeal of rock and roll.

▼ Whitney Houston's billowy soprano voice made "I Will Always Love You" one of the top-selling singles of the 1990s.

▼ The appeal of Seattle's Pearl Jam is based on the group's hard-rocking sound and the expressive vocals of lead singer Eddie Vedder.

Chapter 32

The Civil Rights Era

In the 1950s many African Americans renewed their fight for full equality and an end to segregation and discrimination. Their efforts were aided by the Supreme Court's decision in *Brown* v. *Board of Education* that stated separation by race was inherently unequal. A quiet pioneer of the civil rights movement was Rosa Parks, who in 1955 refused to give her seat on a Montgomery bus to a white man. Dr. Martin Luther King, Jr., emerged as a powerful and inspiring leader for nonviolent protest against unjust segregation laws. The efforts of the civil rights movement culminated in the March on Washington where hundreds of thousands of Americans gathered to demonstrate peacefully for racial harmony and justice.

Inspired by the energy of civil rights leaders, women and other minority groups began to work for change in their own right.

Chapter 33

The Vietnam Era

In setting United States policy in Vietnam, President Johnson was torn between his wish to limit American involvement and his fear of a communist victory. Passage of the Gulf of Tonkin Resolution gave Johnson the power to wage war on North Vietnam as he saw fit. American planes began bombing North Vietnam targets and in April 1965 the President decided to engage American troops in combat. Unable to end the war quickly, the

United States found itself increasingly drawn into the conflict.

In January 1968 North Vietnam staged the Tet offensive. Though it was turned back, Americans began to question whether or not the war could be won. When Johnson decided not to run for reelection, Republican Richard Nixon, campaigning on the promise to "bring the nation together," was elected President.

Nixon expanded the war into neighboring Cambodia and Laos to stop enemy lines of supply. This effort failed while antiwar protests increased. Finally, Nixon opted for "Vietnamization," the withdrawal of American troops and replacing them with Vietnamese soldiers.

Chapter 34

Camelot to Watergate

After narrowly winning the 1960 election, President Kennedy wanted to stimulate the economy and to improve life for the poor, but he moved cautiously on civil rights legislation. Kennedy was assassinated before many of his goals could be realized.

Vowing to continue the work of John Kennedy, President Johnson set out to implement his domestic program known as the Great Society—a blueprint for the elimination of poverty and discrimination in America. As the United States was drawn more into the Vietnam War, however, Johnson's attention focused on foreign affairs.

President Nixon came to the White House with the hope of bringing America together. A cornerstone of his domestic policy was a greater emphasis on local decision making and revenue sharing.

Nixon easily won reelection in 1972. However, throughout his second term, evidence surfaced linking high officials in his administration to a campaign of illegal activity. Finally, transcripts of secret White House tapes proved that Nixon had attempted a cover-up. Faced with impeachment, the President resigned and was succeeded by Gerald Ford.

Chapter 35

Search for Solutions

After Vietnam and Watergate, Americans wanted a change in leadership. Outsider Jimmy Carter barely defeated Gerald Ford in the 1976 election. Carter's domestic policy focused on the energy problem. Poor relations with Congress, however, caused his efforts to falter.

Carter displayed bold initiative in foreign policy. He won Senate ratification of a new Panama Canal treaty and took a tough stand against countries that violated human rights. His greatest triumph was negotiation of a peace treaty between Israel and Egypt. His greatest failure was his inability to secure the release of American hostages in Iran.

Republican Ronald Reagan soundly defeated Carter in the 1980 election. Reagan quickly began to lower taxes and reduce government spending on social programs. Reagan fought communism vigorously, especially in Latin America where he rallied support for contra rebels in Nicaragua. Reagan's overwhelming victory in his 1984 reelection bid demonstrated strong support for his policies.

Reagan began his second term intent on keeping the United States strong. The military buildup added to social spending sent the federal deficit soaring. In foreign affairs changing conditions in the Soviet Union eased strained relations with the United States.

The late 1980s and early 1990s were years of astonishing change. One communist government after another toppled, until even the Soviet Union split into independent republics. When Iraq invaded Kuwait in 1990, President Bush acted decisively. When Iraq refused to meet a deadline for withdrawal, United States-led forces launched a devastating series of attacks on Iraqi defenses.

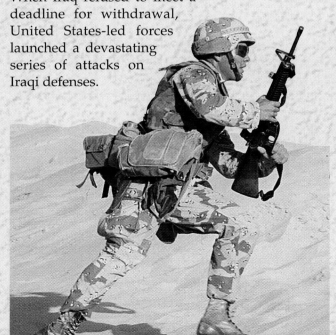

Chapter 36

Toward a New Century

In the 1992 election, President Bush faced challenges from within his own party as well as from Democratic and independent candidates. After 12 years of Republican rule, voters elected Democrat Bill Clinton President in 1992 and reelected him in 1996.

American society faced pressing problems at home and abroad. Environmentalists struggled with opponents who favored greater use of natural resources. Public health issues, such as the AIDS epidemic and drug abuse, continued to take their toll. Migration patterns to the United States changed. Immigration from Europe decreased, and immigration from Latin America and Asia increased.

The American people and government and business leaders pondered ways to deal with the federal deficit and other economic and social problems that troubled the nation.

Federal government attempts to address these problems produced few long-lasting solutions. Partisan politics played a role in the deadlock. The Clinton administration and Congress often were at odds and found it difficult to compromise.

Understanding Unit Themes

Civil Rights and Liberties

1. How have the goals of the civil rights movement evolved?

Conflict and Cooperation

2. What events since World War II helped create a spirit of cooperation between the United States and the Soviet Union? Which events represented low points in their relationship?

Cultural Diversity

3. How have immigration and increased global interdependence contributed to a more culturally diverse American society?

United States Role in World Affairs

4. Why has the United States's relationship with other countries become more interdependent since World War II?

Appendix Contents

Atlas Key

SYMBOL KEY			
◉ National capital	── International boundary	▢ Non-subject
★ State/province capital	▪▪▪▪ Disputed boundary	┴┴ Canal/waterway
● Major city	▪▪▪▪▪ Undefined boundary	⌇ Waterfall
○ Other city	── State/province/republic boundary	▲ Peak

THE WORLD PHYSICAL/POLITICAL

- ● World's most populous cities
- ─── International boundary
- ─ ─ ─ Disputed boundary
- ········· Undefined boundary

0	1000	2000 Miles
0	1000	2000 Kilometers

Projection: Robinson

CENTRAL AMERICA AND WEST INDIES

Projection: Bipolar Oblique Conic Conformal

0	250	500 Miles
0	250	500 Kilometers

ARCTIC OCEAN

BEAUFORT SEA

BAFFIN BAY

Point Barrow

ALASKA (U.S.)

Yukon R.

Mt. McKinley 20,320 ft. (6,194 m.)

Bering Strait

BERING SEA

GULF OF ALASKA

Great Bear Lake

Great Slave Lake

HUDSON BAY

Davis Strait

Cape Farvel

LABRADOR SEA

NORTH AMERICA

Mackenzie R.

ROCKY MOUNTAINS

Lake Winnipeg

Great Lakes

CANADA

Cape Mendocino

UNITED STATES

GREAT PLAINS

Missouri R.

Mississippi R.

Chicago

APPALACHIAN MTS.

New York

Cape Hatteras

ATLANTIC OCEAN

Los Angeles

International Date Line (Sunday)

Tropic of Cancer

HAWAIIAN IS. (U.S.)

MEXICO

BERMUDA (U.K.)

See inset below
GULF OF MEXICO

Mexico City

CARIBBEAN SEA

VENEZUELA

GUYANA

SURINAME

FRENCH GUIANA (FRANCE)

Equator

PACIFIC OCEAN

COLOMBIA

GALÁPAGOS IS. (ECUADOR)

ECUADOR

AMAZON BASIN

Amazon R.

Cape São Roque

Pariñas Point

PERU

SOUTH AMERICA

BRAZIL

ANDES MOUNTAINS

MATO GROSSO PLATEAU

WESTERN SAMOA

BOLIVIA

Rio de Janeiro

TONGA

Tropic of Capricorn

PARAGUAY

GRAN CHACO

Paraná R.

São Paulo

Mt. Aconcagua 22,834 ft. (6,960 m.)

URUGUAY

Buenos Aires

CHILE

ARGENTINA

West Longitude

FALKLAND IS. (U.K.)

Strait of Magellan

Cape Horn

SOUTH GEORGIA I. (U.K.)

Drake Passage

Antarctic Circle

THE BAHAMAS

GULF OF MEXICO

CUBA

Tropic of Cancer

TURKS AND CAICOS IS. (U.K.)

ATLANTIC OCEAN

HAITI

DOMINICAN REPUBLIC

VIRGIN ISLANDS (U.S. AND U.K.)

ANTIGUA AND BARBUDA

MEXICO

BELIZE

JAMAICA

PUERTO RICO (U.S.)

ST. KITTS AND NEVIS

GUADELOUPE (FRANCE)

DOMINICA

GUATEMALA

HONDURAS

MARTINIQUE (FRANCE)

ST. LUCIA

EL SALVADOR

CARIBBEAN SEA

ST. VINCENT AND THE GRENADINES

BARBADOS

PACIFIC OCEAN

NICARAGUA

N

NETHERLANDS ANTILLES (NETHERLANDS)

GRENADA

ARUBA (NETHERLANDS)

TRINIDAD AND TOBAGO

COSTA RICA

PANAMA

VENEZUELA

COLOMBIA

GUYANA

ARCTIC OCEAN

ALAALLIT NUNAAT
(GREENLAND)
(DENMARK)

GREENLAND
SEA

SVALBARD IS.
(NORWAY)

FRANZ JOSEF IS.
(RUSSIA)

Cape
Zelaniya

KARA SEA

LAPTEV SEA

EAST
SIBERIAN SEA

VERKHOYANSK
RANGE

Denmark Strait

ICELAND

FAROE IS.
(DENMARK)

JAN MAYEN
(NORWAY)

NORWEGIAN
SEA

North Cape

North Cape

BARENTS
SEA

URAL MOUNTAINS

SIBERIA

CENTRAL
SIBERIAN
PLATEAU

Lena R.

SEA OF
OKHOTSK

Cape
Lopatka

KURIL IS.
(RUSSIA)

Arctic Circle

See Inset below

NORTH
SEA

Lake Ladoga

EUROPEAN PLAIN

WEST
SIBERIAN
PLAIN

Ob R.

Yenisey R.

ASIA

Lake
Baikal

RUSSIA

EUROPE

ALPS

Danube

Volga R.

CASPIAN
DEPRESSION

KAZAKSTAN

ARAL
SEA

MONGOLIA

ALTAI MTNS.

VERKHOYANSK
RANGE

Changchun

NORTH
KOREA

SEA
OF
JAPAN

JAPAN

Cape Finisterre

BLACK SEA

Mt. Elbrus
18,510 ft.
(5,642 m.)

CASPIAN SEA

GEORGIA
ARMENIA

UZBEKISTAN

KYRGYZSTAN

TIANSHAN

GOBI

Shenyang

Beijing

Tianjin

Seoul

SOUTH
KOREA

Tokyo

AZORES IS.
(PORTUGAL)

ATLAS MOUNTAINS

MEDITERRANEAN SEA

TURKEY

LEBANON

SYRIA

TURKMENISTAN

TAJIKISTAN

TAKLIMAKAN

Mt. Everest
29,028 ft.
(8,848 m.)

HIMALAYAS

Chongqing

Wuhan

EAST
CHINA
SEA

Shanghai

Chang Jiang
(Yangtze R.)

Tropic of Cancer

International Date Line (Monday)

MOROCCO

TUNISIA

ISRAEL
JORDAN

IRAQ

AZERBAIJAN

AFGHANISTAN

PLATEAU
OF IRAN

IRAN

PAKISTAN

NEPAL

BHUTAN

CHINA

TAIWAN

CANARY IS.
(SPAIN)

ALGERIA

LIBYA

EGYPT

QATTARA
DEPRESSION

Cairo

KUWAIT

BAHRAIN

QATAR

UNITED
ARAB
EMIRATES

SAUDI
ARABIA

Delhi

Ganges

INDIA

Calcutta

BANGLADESH

MYANMAR

LAOS

HONG KONG

MACAO (PORTUGAL)

SOUTH
CHINA
SEA

Manila

MARSHALL ISLANDS

W. SAHARA
(MOROCCO)

Cape
Blanc

MAURITANIA

MALI

NIGER

CHAD

SUDAN

ERITREA

YEMEN

DJIBOUTI

OMAN

ARABIAN
SEA

Mumbai
(Bombay)

BAY OF
BENGAL

THAILAND

VIETNAM

PHILIPPINES

GUAM (U.S.)

FEDERATED STATES
OF MICRONESIA

CAPE
VERDE

SENEGAL

GAMBIA

GUINEA-
BISSAU

GUINEA

SIERRA LEONE

LIBERIA

BURKINA
FASO

GHANA

NIGERIA

BENIN

TOGO

CÔTE D'IVOIRE

AFRICA

CENTRAL
AFRICAN REP.

ETHIOPIA

ETHIOPIAN
HIGHLANDS

Cape Asir

SOMALIA

Cape Comorin

SRI
LANKA

MALDIVES

CAMBODIA

BRUNEI

MALAYSIA

SINGAPORE

PALAU

Equator

KIRIBATI

SÃO TOMÉ AND PRÍNCIPE

EQUATORIAL GUINEA

CAMEROON

GABON

CONGO

UGANDA

RWANDA

CONGO
(ZAIRE)
BASIN

Zaire

Lake
Victoria

KENYA

Kilimanjaro
19,340 ft.
(5,895 m.)

SEYCHELLES

INDIAN
OCEAN

Jakarta

INDONESIA

PAPUA
NEW
GUINEA

SOLOMON
ISLANDS

NAURU

TUVALU

ZAIRE

BURUNDI

TANZANIA

COMOROS

Cape
York

CORAL
SEA

VANUATU

FIJI

ANGOLA

ZAMBIA

MALAWI

MOZAMBIQUE

MADAGASCAR

MAURITIUS

RÉUNION
(FRANCE)

Tropic of Capricorn

GREAT DIVIDING RANGE

NEW
CALEDONIA
(FRANCE)

NAMIBIA

BOTSWANA

ZIMBABWE

Mozambique Channel

WESTERN
PLATEAU

AUSTRALIA

ATLANTIC
OCEAN

SOUTH
AFRICA

SWAZILAND

LESOTHO

Cape of
Good Hope

Mt. Kosciusko
7,310 ft.
(2,228 m.)

TASMAN
SEA

East
Longitude

Prime Meridian

KERGUELEN IS.
(FRANCE)

NEW
ZEALAND

N

Antarctic Circle

ANTARCTICA

FINLAND

NORWAY

SWEDEN

St. Petersburg

IRELAND

UNITED
KINGDOM

DENMARK

ESTONIA

LATVIA

Moscow

RUSSIA

London

NETHERLANDS

BELGIUM

GERMANY

POLAND

LITHUANIA

RUSSIA

BELARUS

N

ATLANTIC
OCEAN

Paris

LUXEMBOURG

CZECH
REPUBLIC

SLOVAKIA

UKRAINE

FRANCE

SWITZERLAND

AUSTRIA

HUNGARY

MOLDOVA

SLOVENIA

CROATIA

ROMANIA

PORTUGAL

SPAIN

ITALY

BOSNIA
HERZEGOVINA

SERBIA

YUGOSLAVIA

BULGARIA

GEORGIA

BLACK SEA

MONTENEGRO

ALBANIA

MACEDONIA

GIBRALTAR
(U.K.)

MEDITERRANEAN

GREECE

TURKEY

0   250   500 Miles

0   250   500 Kilometers

TUNISIA

MALTA

SEA

CYPRUS

SYRIA

LEBANON

UNITED STATES

- ⊛ National capital
- ★ State capital
- ● Major city
- ○ Other city
- —— International boundary
- —— State boundary

Scale: 0 — 150 — 300 Miles / 0 — 150 — 300 Kilometers

Projection: Albers Equal Area

CANADA

MAINE
Moosehead Lake
Bangor
Mt. Washington 6,288 ft. (1,905 m.) ★ Augusta
Lake Champlain Burlington
Montpelier ★ N.H. Lewiston
VT. Portland
Concord
Manchester
MASS.
Boston
Cape Cod
Worcester
Springfield
Hartford Providence
New Haven R.I.
CONN.

Lake of the Woods
Red Lake
Duluth
MINNESOTA
WISCONSIN
Minneapolis ★ St. Paul
Rochester
Green Bay
Appleton
Madison ★ Milwaukee
Racine
Dubuque
Rockford
IOWA
Cedar Rapids
Davenport
Des Moines
Sioux City
Omaha
Council Bluffs
Lincoln
Topeka ★
Lawrence
Kansas City
Independence
Jefferson City ★
Kansas City
Harry S. Truman Res.
MISSOURI
Springfield
OZARK PLATEAU
Tulsa
R.S. Kerr Res.
Lake Eufaula
ARKANSAS
Fort Smith
Little Rock ★ North Little Rock
Hot Springs
Pine Bluff
Lake Texoma
Greenville
Dallas
Shreveport
LOUISIANA
Toledo Bend Res.
Hattiesburg
MISSISSIPPI
Lake Pontchartrain
Baton Rouge ★
Biloxi
Houston
Lake Charles
Lafayette
New Orleans
Sam Rayburn Reservoir

MICHIGAN
Lake Superior
Lake Michigan
Lake Huron
Grand Rapids
Flint
Lansing
Detroit
Ann Arbor
Chicago
South Bend
Toledo
Fort Wayne
Aurora
Joliet
Gary
Hammond
ILLINOIS
Peoria
Springfield
Decatur
CENTRAL LOWLAND
INDIANA
Muncie
Indianapolis
Cincinnati
OHIO
Dayton
Columbus
Parkersburg
Evansville
Louisville
Frankfort
Lexington
KENTUCKY
Owensboro
Nashville
Knoxville
TENNESSEE
Chattanooga
Huntsville
Memphis
Tennessee River
Birmingham
Tuscaloosa
ALABAMA
Montgomery ★
Meridian
Jackson ★
Mobile
Pensacola
COASTAL PLAIN
Tallahassee ★
FLORIDA

Lake Erie
Cleveland
Akron
Canton
Youngstown
PENNSYLVANIA
Pittsburgh
Wheeling
WEST VIRGINIA
Charleston
Huntington
Harrisburg
Philadelphia
Camden
Trenton
Dover
DEL.
MD.
Baltimore
Annapolis ★
Washington ⊛
Arlington
D.C.
DELAWARE BAY
Wilmington
VIRGINIA
Richmond
Newport News
Norfolk
CHESAPEAKE BAY
Roanoke
Roanoke River
Greensboro
Durham
Raleigh
Winston-Salem
NORTH CAROLINA
Mt. Mitchell 6,684 ft. (2,037 m.)
Charlotte
Spartanburg
Greenville
Columbia ★
SOUTH CAROLINA
Charleston
GEORGIA
Augusta
Atlanta
Macon
Columbus
Albany
Savannah
Jacksonville
Orlando
Cape Canaveral
Tampa
St. Petersburg
Lake Okeechobee
Palm Beach
Miami Beach
Miami
Cape Sable
Key West
Straits of Florida

NEW YORK
Rochester
Niagara Falls
Buffalo
Binghamton
Erie
Utica
Syracuse
Albany ★
Susquehanna River
Newark
Yonkers
New York
N.J.
Allentown
Lake Ontario
ADIRONDACK MTNS.
Hudson River
St. Lawrence River
APPALACHIAN MOUNTAINS
CUMBERLAND PLATEAU
Cumberland River
Chattahoochee R.
Alabama R.
Mississippi River
Ohio River
Wabash R.
Tennessee River

ATLANTIC OCEAN

Cape Hatteras

GULF OF MEXICO

N

THE BAHAMAS

CUBA

95° 90° 85° 80° 75° 50° 70° 65°
45° 65° 40° 35° 70° 30° 25°
95° 90° 85° 80° 75°

OZARK PLATEAU

NORTH AMERICA

- ⊛ National capital
- ● Major city
- ○ Other city
- —— International boundary

Scale bar:
0 — 250 — 500 — 750 Miles
0 — 250 — 500 — 750 Kilometers

Projection: Azimuthal Equal Area

LATIN AMERICA

⊛ National capital
● Major city
○ Other city
— International boundary

| 0 | | 500 | 1000 Miles |
| 0 | 500 | 1000 Kilometers | |

Projection: Miller Cylindrical

EURASIA

- ⊛ National capital
- ● Major city
- ○ Other city
- — International boundary
- --- Disputed boundary
- ···· Undefined boundary

ALBAN.	—Albania
BAH.	—Bahrain
B.H.	—Bosnia and Herzegovina
CR.	—Croatia
ISR.	—Israel
KUW.	—Kuwait
LIECH.	—Liechtenstein
LITH.	—Lithuania
LUX.	—Luxembourg
MACE.	—Macedonia
MON.	—Monaco
MONT.	—Montenegro
S.M.	—San Marino
SL.	—Slovenia
SWITZ.	—Switzerland
U.A.E.	—United Arab Emirates

0   500   1000 Miles
0   500   1000 Kilometers

Projection: Robinson

N

MIDDLE EAST

- ⊛ National capital
- ● Major city
- ○ Other city
- ——— International boundary
- - - - - Disputed boundary
- ········· Undefined boundary

| 0 | 100 | 200 | 300 Miles |
| 0 | 100 | 200 | 300 Kilometers |

Projection: Azimuthal Equal Area

ASIA

Trabzon
Erzurum Mt. Ararat ▲
16,945 ft.
(5,165 m.)
Lake
Van
Malatya
Diyarbakir
Ardabil
Tabriz
Lake
Urmia
Mashhad
Gaziantep
Aleppo
Mosul
Urmia
Irbil
Rasht
ELBURZ
Qazvin   MTNS.
Hamah
Deir-ez-
Zor
Kirkuk
Tehran   ▲ Mt. Demavend
18,386 ft.
(5,604 m.)
SYRIA
Hims
IRAQ
Tigris
Hamadan
Qom
GREAT SALT DESERT
Damascus
Baghdad
Bakhtaran
Arak
ISRAELI-OCCUPIED
Karbala
Zarqa
JORDAN
Al Hillah
An Najaf
An Nasiriyah
Esfahan
IRAN
PLATEAU
OF
IRAN
Birjand
Amman
SYRIAN
DESERT
Ahvaz
Abadan
Al Basrah
KUWAIT
Hawalli
Kuwait
Al Ahmadi
Bushehr
Shiraz
Kerman
Zahedan
Tabuk
AN NAFUD
DESERT
Ha'il
Buraydah
Ad Dammam Manama
BAHRAIN
QATAR
Al Hufuf   Doha
PERSIAN
GULF
Bandar 'Abbas
Strait of Hormuz
Dubai
Abu
Dhabi
GULF OF OMAN
Tropic of Cancer
Cape Al Hadd
NAJD PLATEAU
Madinah
Yanbu al Bahr
Riyadh
UNITED ARAB
EMIRATES
Muscat
RED
SAUDI   ARABIA
TUWAYQ MTNS.
Jiddah
Makkah
At Ta'if
ARABIAN PENINSULA
RUB AL
KHALI
OMAN
Duqm
SEA
ASIR MOUNTAINS
Salalah
Lake
Tana
San'a ▲ Mt. Nabi Shu'ayb
12,336 ft.
(3,760 m.)
Al Hudaydah
Al Ghaydah
YEMEN
Al Mukalla
ARABIAN SEA
Ta'izz
Bab
el
Mandeb
Aden
GULF OF ADEN
Cape Asir
SOCOTRA
(YEMEN)

MESOPOTAMIA
EUPHRATES R.

See inset below

AFRICA

- ⊛ National capital
- ● Major city
- ○ Other city
- —— International boundary
- ---- Disputed boundary

Projection: Azimuthal Equal Area

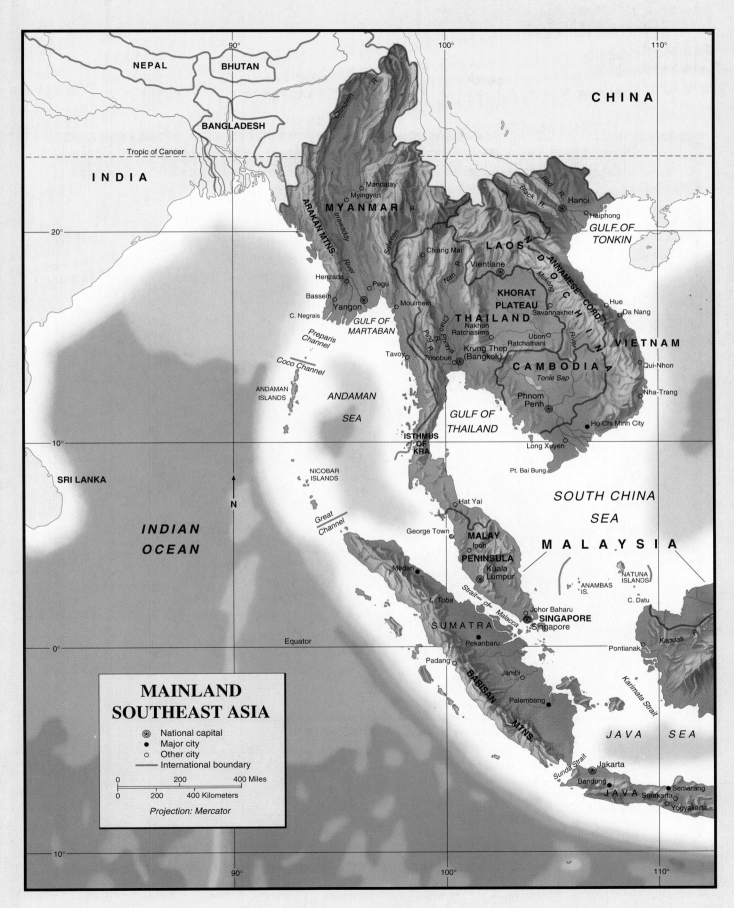

MAINLAND SOUTHEAST ASIA

⊛ National capital
● Major city
○ Other city
— International boundary

0 _____ 200 _____ 400 Miles
0 __ 200 __ 400 Kilometers

Projection: Mercator

NEPAL

BHUTAN

BANGLADESH

CHINA

Tropic of Cancer

INDIA

20°

Chindwin R.

Mandalay
Myingyan

MYANMAR

Irrawaddy R.

ARAKAN MTNS.

Salween

Chiang Mai

Nan R.

LAOS

Hanoi
Haiphong

Black R.

Red R.

GULF OF
TONKIN

INDOCHINA

ANNAMESE CORD.

River

Henzada

Pegu

KHORAT
PLATEAU

Vientiane

Mekong

Savannakhet

Hue
Da Nang

Bassein

Yangon

THAILAND

Nakhon
Ratchasima

VIETNAM

C. Negrais

GULF OF
MARTABAN

Moulmein

Ping R.

Chao Phraya

Ubon
Ratchathani

River

Qui-Nhon

Preparis
Channel

Tavoy

Thonburi

Krung Thep
(Bangkok)

CAMBODIA

Nha-Trang

Coco Channel

Tonle Sap

ANDAMAN
ISLANDS

ANDAMAN
SEA

Phnom
Penh

Ho Chi Minh City

10°

SRI LANKA

ISTHMUS
OF
KRA

GULF OF
THAILAND

Long Xuyen

Pt. Bai Bung

NICOBAR
ISLANDS

SOUTH CHINA
SEA

INDIAN
OCEAN

N

Great
Channel

Hat Yai

George Town

MALAY

Ipoh

MALAYSIA

NATUNA
ISLANDS

PENINSULA

Kuala
Lumpur

ANAMBAS
IS.

C. Datu

Medan

L. Toba

Strait of Malacca

Johor Baharu

SINGAPORE
Singapore

Equator

SUMATRA

Pekanbaru

Pontianak

Kapuas

Padang

BARISAN

Jambi

Karimata Strait

MTNS.

Palembang

JAVA
SEA

Sunda Strait

Jakarta

Bandung

JAVA

Surakarta

Semarang

Yogyakarta

90°

100°

110°

0°

10°

United States
Databank

★ ★

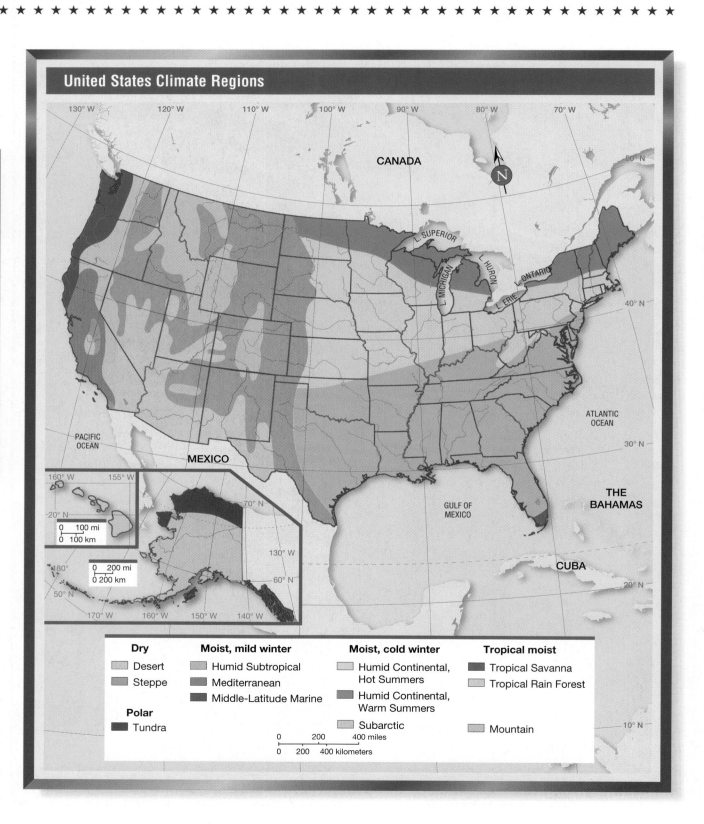

United States Climate Regions

Dry
- Desert
- Steppe

Polar
- Tundra

Moist, mild winter
- Humid Subtropical
- Mediterranean
- Middle-Latitude Marine

Moist, cold winter
- Humid Continental, Hot Summers
- Humid Continental, Warm Summers
- Subarctic

Tropical moist
- Tropical Savanna
- Tropical Rain Forest
- Mountain

Population of the United States

Year	Population			Year	Population		
1790	3,929,214	4.5	–	1900	76,212,168	21.5	21.0
1800	5,308,483	6.1	35.1	1910	92,228,496	26.0	21.0
1810	7,239,881	4.3	36.4	1920	106,021,537	29.9	15.0
1820	9,638,453	5.5	33.1	1930	123,202,624	34.7	16.2
1830	12,866,020	7.4	33.5	1940	132,164,569	37.2	7.3
1840	17,069,453	9.8	32.7	1950	151,325,798	42.6	14.5
1850	23,191,876	7.9	35.9	1960	179,323,175	50.6	18.5
1860	31,443,321	10.6	35.6	1970	203,302,031	57.5	13.4
1870	38,558,371	10.9	22.6	1980	226,542,203	64.0	11.4
1880	50,189,209	14.2	30.2	1990	248,709,873	70.3	9.8
1890	62,979,766	17.8	25.5				

Key:

☐ Population per square mile of land

☐ Percentage increase over preceding census

Source: U.S. Department of the Census; *Statistical Abstract of the United States*, 1994.

Population Distribution by Age

Source: *Statistical Abstract of the United States*, 1994.

Major Religions in the United States

Roman Catholic Church	58,267
Southern Baptist Convention	15,232
United Methodist Church	8,785
National Baptist Convention	3,500
Muslims	6,000
Jews	5,981
Evangelical Lutheran Church	5,245
Church of Jesus Christ of Latter-Day Saints (Mormon)	4,336
Church of God in Christ (Pentecostal)	3,710
Presbyterian Church (U.S.A.)	3,778
National Baptist Convention of America	3,500
Lutheran Church (Missouri Synod)	2,607
Episcopal Church	2,472
African Methodist Episcopal Church	3,500
Assemblies of God	2,235
Greek Orthodox Archdiocese of North and South America	1,950
United Church of Christ	1,584
Churches of Christ	1,690
American Baptist Churches in the U.S.A.	1,528
African Methodist Episcopal Zion Church	1,200
Christian Churches and Churches of Christ	1,071
Christian Church (Disciples of Christ)	1,023
Orthodox Church in America	1,030

In thousands

Source: *Statistical Abstract of the United States*, 1994; *Time* magazine (November 19, 1990).

Political Parties in Power

George Washington, 1789–1797

John Adams, 1797–1801
Thomas Jefferson, 1801–1809

James Madison, 1809–1817

James Monroe, 1817–1825

John Quincy Adams, 1825–1829
Andrew Jackson, 1829–1837

Martin Van Buren, 1837–1841
William H. Harrison/John Tyler, 1841–1845
James K. Polk, 1845–1849
Zachary Taylor/Millard Fillmore, 1849–1853
Franklin Pierce, 1853–1857
James Buchanan, 1857–1861
Abraham Lincoln, 1861–1865
Andrew Johnson, 1865–1869
Ulysses S. Grant, 1869–1877

Rutherford B. Hayes, 1877–1881
James A. Garfield/Chester A. Arthur, 1881–1885
Grover Cleveland, 1885–1889
Benjamin Harrison, 1889–1893
Grover Cleveland, 1893–1897
William McKinley, 1897–1901
Theodore Roosevelt, 1901–1909

William H. Taft, 1909–1913
Woodrow Wilson, 1913–1921

Warren G. Harding, 1921–1923
Calvin Coolidge, 1923–1929

Herbert C. Hoover, 1929–1933
Franklin D. Roosevelt, 1933–1945

Harry S Truman, 1945–1953

Dwight D. Eisenhower, 1953–1961

John F. Kennedy, 1961–1963
Lyndon B. Johnson, 1963–1969

Richard M. Nixon, 1969–1974
Gerald R. Ford, 1974–1977
James E. Carter, Jr., 1977–1981
Ronald W. Reagan, 1981–1989

George H. W. Bush, 1989–1993
William J. Clinton, 1993–

Federalist	Democratic
Democratic Republican	Whig
	Republican

Graduation Rates

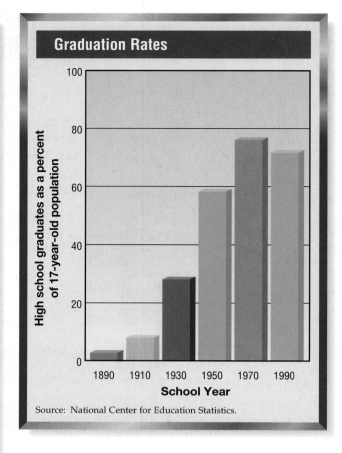

Source: National Center for Education Statistics.

Life Expectancy

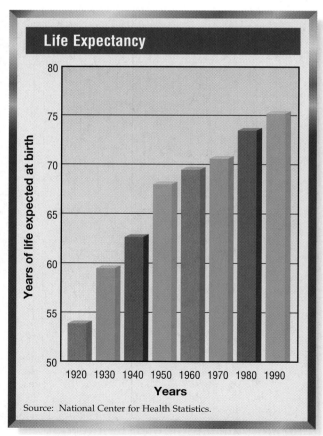

Source: National Center for Health Statistics.

The United States

STATE*	YEAR ADMITTED	POPULATION (1990)	LAND AREA (sq. mi.)	CAPITAL	LARGEST CITY	HOUSE REP. (1990)**
1. Delaware	1787	666,168	1,954	Dover	Wilmington	1
2. Pennsylvania	1787	11,881,643	44,819	Harrisburg	Philadelphia	21
3. New Jersey	1787	7,730,188	7,418	Trenton	Newark	13
4. Georgia	1788	6,478,216	57,918	Atlanta	Atlanta	11
5. Connecticut	1788	3,287,116	4,845	Hartford	Bridgeport	6
6. Massachusetts	1788	6,016,425	7,838	Boston	Boston	10
7. Maryland	1788	4,781,468	9,774	Annapolis	Baltimore	8
8. South Carolina	1788	3,486,703	30,111	Columbia	Columbia	6
9. New Hampshire	1788	1,109,252	8,969	Concord	Manchester	2
10. Virginia	1788	6,187,358	39,597	Richmond	Virginia Beach	11
11. New York	1788	17,990,455	47,223	Albany	New York	31
12. North Carolina	1789	6,628,637	48,718	Raleigh	Charlotte	12
13. Rhode Island	1790	1,003,464	1,045	Providence	Providence	2
14. Vermont	1791	562,758	9,249	Montpelier	Burlington	1
15. Kentucky	1792	3,685,296	39,732	Frankfort	Louisville	6
16. Tennessee	1796	4,877,185	41,219	Nashville	Memphis	9
17. Ohio	1803	10,847,115	40,952	Columbus	Columbus	19
18. Louisiana	1812	4,219,973	43,566	Baton Rouge	New Orleans	7
19. Indiana	1816	5,544,159	35,870	Indianapolis	Indianapolis	10
20. Mississippi	1817	2,573,216	46,913	Jackson	Jackson	5
21. Illinois	1818	11,430,602	55,593	Springfield	Chicago	20
22. Alabama	1819	4,040,587	50,750	Montgomery	Birmingham	7
23. Maine	1820	1,227,928	30,864	Augusta	Portland	2
24. Missouri	1821	5,117,073	68,898	Jefferson City	Kansas City	9
25. Arkansas	1836	2,350,725	52,075	Little Rock	Little Rock	4
26. Michigan	1837	9,295,297	56,809	Lansing	Detroit	16
27. Florida	1845	12,937,926	53,997	Tallahassee	Jacksonville	23
28. Texas	1845	16,986,510	261,194	Austin	Houston	30
29. Iowa	1846	2,776,755	55,874	Des Moines	Des Moines	5
30. Wisconsin	1848	4,891,769	54,313	Madison	Milwaukee	9
31. California	1850	29,760,021	155,973	Sacramento	Los Angeles	52
32. Minnesota	1858	4,375,099	79,616	St. Paul	Minneapolis	8
33. Oregon	1859	2,853,733	96,002	Salem	Portland	5
34. Kansas	1861	2,477,574	81,823	Topeka	Wichita	4
35. West Virginia	1863	1,793,477	24,086	Charleston	Charleston	3
36. Nevada	1864	1,201,833	109,805	Carson City	Las Vegas	2
37. Nebraska	1867	1,578,385	76,877	Lincoln	Omaha	3
38. Colorado	1876	3,294,394	103,729	Denver	Denver	6
39. North Dakota	1889	638,800	68,994	Bismarck	Fargo	1
40. South Dakota	1889	696,004	75,897	Pierre	Sioux Falls	1
41. Montana	1889	799,065	145,556	Helena	Billings	1
42. Washington	1889	4,887,941	66,581	Olympia	Seattle	9
43. Idaho	1890	1,006,749	82,750	Boise	Boise	2
44. Wyoming	1890	455,975	97,104	Cheyenne	Cheyenne	1
45. Utah	1896	1,727,784	82,168	Salt Lake City	Salt Lake City	3
46. Oklahoma	1907	3,145,585	68,678	Oklahoma City	Oklahoma City	6
47. New Mexico	1912	1,515,069	121,364	Sante Fe	Albuquerque	3
48. Arizona	1912	3,665,228	113,642	Phoenix	Phoenix	6
49. Alaska	1959	550,043	570,373	Juneau	Anchorage	1
50. Hawaii	1959	1,108,229	6,423	Honolulu	Honolulu	2
District of Columbia (Washington, D.C.)	–	606,900	61	–	–	–
United States of America	–	248,709,873	3,536,341	Washington, D.C.	New York	435

* Numbers denote the order in which states were admitted.
** Number of members in House of Representatives

Presidents of the United States

★ ★ ★ ★ ★ ★ ★ ★ ★ ★ ★ ★ ★ ★ ★ ★

** The Republican party during this period developed into today's Democratic party. Today's Republican party originated in 1854.

George Washington

1

1789–1797

Born: 1732
Died: 1799
Born in: Virginia
Elected from: Virginia
Age when elected: 56
Occupations: Planter, Soldier
Party: None
Vice President: John Adams

John Adams

2

1797–1801

Born: 1735
Died: 1826
Born in: Massachusetts
Elected from: Massachusetts
Age when elected: 61
Occupations: Teacher, Lawyer
Party: Federalist
Vice President: Thomas Jefferson

Thomas Jefferson

3

1801–1809

Born: 1743
Died: 1826
Born in: Virginia
Elected from: Virginia
Age when elected: 57
Occupations: Planter, Lawyer
Party: Republican**
Vice Presidents: Aaron Burr, George Clinton

James Madison

4

1809–1817

Born: 1751
Died: 1836
Born in: Virginia
Elected from: Virginia
Age when elected: 57
Occupation: Planter
Party: Republican**
Vice Presidents: George Clinton, Elbridge Gerry

James Monroe

5

1817–1825

Born: 1758
Died: 1831
Born in: Virginia
Elected from: Virginia
Age when elected: 58
Occupation: Lawyer
Party: Republican**
Vice President: Daniel D. Tompkins

Presidents

John Quincy Adams

6

1825–1829

Born: 1767
Died: 1848
Born in: Massachusetts
Elected from: Massachusetts
Age when elected: 57
Occupation: Lawyer
Party: Republican**
Vice President: John C. Calhoun

Andrew Jackson

7

1829–1837

Born: 1767
Died: 1845
Born in: South Carolina
Elected from: Tennessee
Age when elected: 61
Occupations: Lawyer, Soldier
Party: Democratic
Vice Presidents: John C.
Calhoun, Martin Van Buren

Martin Van Buren

8

1837–1841

Born: 1782
Died: 1862
Born in: New York
Elected from: New York
Age when elected: 54
Occupation: Lawyer
Party: Democratic
Vice President: Richard M.
Johnson

William H. Harrison

9

1841

Born: 1773
Died: 1841
Born in: Virginia
Elected from: Ohio
Age when elected: 67
Occupations: Soldier, Planter
Party: Whig
Vice President: John Tyler

John Tyler

10

1841–1845

Born: 1790
Died: 1862
Born in: Virginia
Elected as V.P. from: Virginia
Succeeded Harrison
Age when became President: 51
Occupation: Lawyer
Party: Whig
Vice President: None

James K. Polk

11

1845–1849

Born: 1795
Died: 1849
Born in: North Carolina
Elected from: Tennessee
Age when elected: 49
Occupation: Lawyer
Party: Democratic
Vice President: George M. Dallas

Zachary Taylor

12

1849–1850

Born: 1784
Died: 1850
Born in: Virginia
Elected from: Louisiana
Age when elected: 63
Occupation: Soldier
Party: Whig
Vice President: Millard Fillmore

Millard Fillmore

13

1850–1853

Born: 1800
Died: 1874
Born in: New York
Elected as V.P. from: New York
Succeeded Taylor
Age when became President: 50
Occupation: Lawyer
Party: Whig
Vice President: None

Franklin Pierce

14

1853–1857

Born: 1804
Died: 1869
Born in: New Hampshire
Elected from: New Hampshire
Age when elected: 47
Occupation: Lawyer
Party: Democratic
Vice President: William R. King

James Buchanan

15

1857–1861

Born: 1791
Died: 1868
Born in: Pennsylvania
Elected from: Pennsylvania
Age when elected: 65
Occupation: Lawyer
Party: Democratic
Vice President: John C. Breckinridge

Abraham Lincoln

16

1861–1865

Born: 1809
Died: 1865
Born in: Kentucky
Elected from: Illinois
Age when elected: 51
Occupation: Lawyer
Party: Republican
Vice Presidents: Hannibal Hamlin, Andrew Johnson

Andrew Johnson

17

1865–1869

Born: 1808
Died: 1875
Born in: North Carolina
Elected as V.P. from: Tennessee
Age when became President: 56
Succeeded Lincoln
Occupation: Tailor
Party: Republican
Vice President: None

Ulysses S. Grant

18

1869–1877

Born: 1822
Died: 1885
Born in: Ohio
Elected from: Illinois
Age when elected: 46
Occupations: Farmer, Soldier
Party: Republican
Vice Presidents: Schuyler Colfax, Henry Wilson

Rutherford B. Hayes

19

1877–1881

Born: 1822
Died: 1893
Born in: Ohio
Elected from: Ohio
Age when elected: 54
Occupation: Lawyer
Party: Republican
Vice President: William A. Wheeler

James A. Garfield

20

1881

Born: 1831
Died: 1881
Born in: Ohio
Elected from: Ohio
Age when elected: 49
Occupations: Laborer, Professor
Party: Republican
Vice President: Chester A. Arthur

Chester A. Arthur

21

1881–1885

Born: 1830
Died: 1886
Born in: Vermont
Elected as V.P. from: New York
Succeeded Garfield
Age when became President: 50
Occupations: Teacher, Lawyer
Party: Republican
Vice President: None

Grover Cleveland

22   **24**

1885–89, 1893–97

Born: 1837
Died: 1908
Born in: New Jersey
Elected from: New York
Age when elected: 47; 55
Occupation: Lawyer
Party: Democratic
Vice Presidents: Thomas A. Hendricks, Adlai E. Stevenson

Benjamin Harrison

23

1889–1893

Born: 1833
Died: 1901
Born in: Ohio
Elected from: Indiana
Age when elected: 55
Occupation: Lawyer
Party: Republican
Vice President: Levi P. Morton

Presidents

William McKinley

25

1897–1901

Born: 1843
Died: 1901
Born in: Ohio
Elected from: Ohio
Age when elected: 53
Occupations: Teacher, Lawyer
Party: Republican
Vice Presidents: Garret Hobart,
  Theodore Roosevelt

Theodore Roosevelt

26

1901–1909

Born: 1858
Died: 1919
Born in: New York
Elected as V.P. from: New York
Succeeded McKinley
Age when became President: 42
Occupations: Historian, Rancher
Party: Republican
Vice President: Charles W. Fairbanks

William H. Taft

27

1909–1913

Born: 1857
Died: 1930
Born in: Ohio
Elected from: Ohio
Age when elected: 51
Occupation: Lawyer
Party: Republican
Vice President: James S. Sherman

Woodrow Wilson

28

1913–1921

Born: 1856
Died: 1924
Born in: Virginia
Elected from: New Jersey
Age when elected: 55
Occupation: College Professor
Party: Democratic
Vice President: Thomas R.
  Marshall

Warren G. Harding

29

1921–1923

Born: 1865
Died: 1923
Born in: Ohio
Elected from: Ohio
Age when elected: 55
Occupations: Newspaper Editor,
  Publisher
Party: Republican
Vice President: Calvin Coolidge

Calvin Coolidge

30

1923–1929

Born: 1872
Died: 1933
Born in: Vermont
Elected as V.P. from: Massachusetts
Succeeded Harding
Age when became President: 51
Occupation: Lawyer
Party: Republican
Vice President: Charles G. Dawes

Herbert C. Hoover

31

1929–1933

Born: 1874
Died: 1964
Born in: Iowa
Elected from: California
Age when elected: 54
Occupation: Engineer
Party: Republican
Vice President: Charles Curtis

Franklin D. Roosevelt

32

1933–1945

Born: 1882
Died: 1945
Born in: New York
Elected from: New York
Age when elected: 50
Occupation: Lawyer
Party: Democratic
Vice Presidents: John N. Garner,
   Henry A. Wallace, Harry S Truman

Harry S Truman

33

1945–1953

Born: 1884
Died: 1972
Born in: Missouri
Elected as V.P. from: Missouri
Succeeded Roosevelt
Age when became President: 60
Occupations: Clerk, Farmer
Party: Democratic
Vice President: Alben W. Barkley

Dwight D. Eisenhower

34

1953–1961

Born: 1890
Died: 1969
Born in: Texas
Elected from: New York
Age when elected: 62
Occupation: Soldier
Party: Republican
Vice President: Richard M. Nixon

John F. Kennedy

35

1961–1963

Born: 1917
Died: 1963
Born in: Massachusetts
Elected from: Massachusetts
Age when elected: 43
Occupations: Author, Reporter
Party: Democratic
Vice President: Lyndon B. Johnson

Lyndon B. Johnson

36

1963–1969

Born: 1908
Died: 1973
Born in: Texas
Elected as V.P. from: Texas
Succeeded Kennedy
Age when became President: 55
Occupation: Teacher
Party: Democratic
Vice President: Hubert H. Humphrey

Presidents

Richard M. Nixon

37

1969–1974

Born: 1913
Died: 1994
Born in: California
Elected from: New York
Age when elected: 55
Occupation: Lawyer
Party: Republican
Vice Presidents: Spiro T. Agnew,
   Gerald R. Ford

Gerald R. Ford

38

1974–1977

Born: 1913
Born in: Nebraska
Appointed by Nixon as V.P. upon
Agnew's resignation; assumed
presidency upon Nixon's resignation
Age when became President: 61
Occupation: Lawyer
Party: Republican
Vice President: Nelson A. Rockefeller

James E. Carter, Jr.

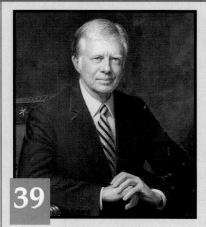

39

1977–1981

Born: 1924
Born in: Georgia
Elected from: Georgia
Age when elected: 52
Occupations: Business, Farmer
Party: Democratic
Vice President: Walter F. Mondale

Ronald W. Reagan

40

1981–1989

Born: 1911
Born in: Illinois
Elected from: California
Age when elected: 69
Occupations: Actor, Lecturer
Party: Republican
Vice President: George H.W. Bush

George H.W. Bush

41

1989–1993

Born: 1924
Born in: Massachusetts
Elected from: Texas
Age when elected: 64
Occupation: Business
Party: Republican
Vice President: J. Danforth Quayle

William J. Clinton

42

1993–

Born: 1946
Born in: Arkansas
Elected from: Arkansas
Age when elected: 46
Occupation: Lawyer
Party: Democratic
Vice President: Albert Gore, Jr.

Presidents

Documents of America's Heritage

★ ★

The Magna Carta

The Magna Carta, signed by King John in 1215, marked a decisive step forward in the development of constitutional government in England. Later, it became a model for colonists who carried the Magna Carta's guarantees of legal and political rights to America.

1. That the English church shall be free, and shall have her rights entire, and her liberties inviolate;. . .

2. We also have granted to all the freemen of our kingdom, for us and for our heirs forever, all the underwritten liberties, to be had and holden by them and their heirs, of us and our heirs forever. . . .

39. No freeman shall be taken or imprisoned, or diseased, or outlawed, or banished, or in any way destroyed, nor will we pass upon him, nor will we send upon him, unless by the lawful judgment of his peers, or by the law of the land.

40. We will sell to no man, we will not deny to any man, either justice or right.

41. All merchants shall have safe and secure conduct to go out of, and to come into, England, and to stay there and to pass as well by land as by water, for buying and selling by the ancient and allowed customs, without any unjust tolls, except in time of war, or when they are of any nation at war with us. . . .

42. It shall be lawful, for the time to come, for any one to go out of our kingdom and return safely and securely by land or by water, saving his allegiance to us (unless in time of war, by some short space, for the common benefit of the realm).

60. All the aforesaid customs and liberties, which we have granted to be holden in our kingdom, as much as it belongs to us, all people of our kingdom, as well clergy as laity, shall observe, as far as they are concerned, towards their dependents.

63. . . . It is also sworn, as well on our part as on the part of the barons, that all the things aforesaid shall be observed in good faith, and without evil duplicity. Given under our hand, in the presence of the witnesses above named, and many others, in the meadow called Runnymede, between Windsor and Staines, the 15th day of June, in the 17th year of our reign.

The Mayflower Compact

On November 21, 1620, 41 colonists aboard the Mayflower *drafted this agreement. The Mayflower Compact was the first plan of self-government ever put in force in the English colonies.*

In ye name of God Amen. We whose names are underwritten, the loyall subjects of our dread soveraigne Lord King James, by ye grace of God, of Great Britaine, Franc, & Ireland king, defender of ye faith, &c. Haveing undertaken, for ye glorie of God, and advancemente of ye Christian faith and honour of our king & countrie, a voyage to plant ye first colonie in ye Northerne parts of Virginia, doe by these presents solemnly & mutualy in ye presence of God, and one of another, covenant, & combine ourselves togeather into a Civill body politick; for our better ordering, & preservation & furtherance of ye ends aforesaid; and by vertue hereof to enacte, constitute, and frame such just & equall Lawes, ordinances, Acts, constitutions, & offices, from time to time, as shall be thought most meete & convenient for ye generall good of ye colonie: unto which we promise all due submission and obedience. In witnes whereof we have hereunder subscribed our names at Cap-Codd ye -11- of November, in ye year of ye raigne of our soveraigne Lord King James of England, France, & Ireland ye eighteenth, and of Scotland ye fiftie fourth. Ano Dom. 1620.

Virginia Statute of Religious Liberty

The concept of separation of church and state had been part of the American fabric since the 1600s. In 1777 Thomas Jefferson drafted a bill to establish religious freedom in Virginia. The bill was made law in 1786.

2. *Be it therefore enacted by the General Assembly,* That no man shall be compelled to frequent or support any religious worship, place of ministry whatsoever, nor shall be enforced, restrained, molested, or burthened in his body or goods, nor shall otherwise suffer on account of his religious opinions or belief; but that all men shall be free to profess, and by argument to maintain, their opinion in matters of religion, and that the same shall in no wise diminish, enlarge or affect their civil capacities.

3. And though we well know that this Assembly, elected by the people for the ordinary purposes of legislation only, have no power to restrain the acts of succeeding Assemblies, constituted with powers equal to our own, and that therefore to declare this act to be irrevocable would be of no effect in law, yet as we are free to declare, and do declare, that the rights hereby asserted are of the natural rights of mankind, and that if any act shall hereafter be passed to repeal the present or to narrow its operation, such act will be an infringement of natural right.

Washington's Farewell Address

At the end of his second term as President, George Washington spoke of the dangers facing the young nation. He warned against the dangers of political parties and sectionalism, and advised the nation against permanent alliances with other nations.

Citizens by birth or choice of a common country, that country has a right to concentrate your affections. The name of American, which belongs to you, in your national capacity, must always exalt the just pride of patriotism more than any appellation derived from local discriminations. With slight shades of difference, you have the same religion, manners, habits, and political principles. You have in a common cause fought and triumphed together. . . .

In contemplating the causes which may disturb our Union, it occurs as matter of serious concern that any ground should have been furnished for characterizing parties by geographical discriminations: Northern and Southern; Atlantic and Western. . . .

No alliances, however strict between the parts, can be an adequate substitute. They must inevitably experience the infractions and interruptions which all alliances in all times have experienced. . . .

The basis of our political systems is the right of the people to make and to alter their constitutions of government. But the constitution which at any time exists, till changed by an explicit and authentic act of the whole people, is sacredly obligatory upon all. . . .

The great rule of conduct for us, in regard to foreign nations, is in extending our commercial relations to have with them as little political connection as possible. So far as we have already formed engagements, let them be fulfilled with perfect good faith. . . .

Relying on its kindness in this as in other things, and actuated by that fervent love toward it which is so natural to a man who views in it the native soil of himself and his progenitors for several generations, I anticipate with pleasing expectations that retreat in which I promise myself to realize, without alloy, the sweet enjoyment of partaking, in the midst of my fellow citizens, the benign influence of good laws under a free government, the ever favorite object of my heart, and the happy reward, as I trust, of our mutual cares, labors, and dangers.

The Star-Spangled Banner

During the British bombardment of Fort McHenry during the War of 1812, a young Baltimore lawyer named Francis Scott Key was inspired to write the words to "The Star-Spangled Banner." Although it became popular immediately, it was not until 1931 that Congress officially declared "The Star-Spangled Banner" as our national anthem.

O! say can you see, by the dawn's early light,
What so proudly we hail'd at the twilight's last gleaming,
Whose broad stripes and bright stars through the perilous fight,
O'er the ramparts we watched, were so gallantly streaming?
And the Rockets' red glare, the Bombs bursting in air,
Gave proof through the night that our Flag was still there;
O! say, does that star-spangled banner yet wave
O'er the Land of the free and the home of the brave!

On the shore, dimly seen through the mists of the deep,
Where the foe's haughty host in dread silence reposes,
What is that, which the breeze o'er the towering steep,
As it fitfully blows, half conceals, half discloses?
Now it catches the gleam of the morning's first beam,
In full glory reflected, now shines on the stream.
'Tis the star-spangled banner; O! long may it wave
O'er the land of the free and the home of the brave.

The Monroe Doctrine

In an 1823 address to Congress, President James Monroe proclaimed what has become known as the Monroe Doctrine. The doctrine was designed to end European influence in the Western Hemisphere. In addition, it showed the world the American spirit of strength and unity, and became a cornerstone of United States foreign policy.

. . . The citizens of the United States cherish sentiments the most friendly in favor of the liberty and happiness of their fellowmen on that side of the Atlantic. In the wars of the European powers in matters relating to themselves we have never taken any part, nor does it comport with our policy so to do. It is only when our rights are invaded or seriously menaced that we resent injuries or make preparation for our defense.

With the movements in this hemisphere we are of necessity more immediately connected, and by causes which must be obvious to all enlightened and impartial observers. The political system of the allied powers is essentially different in this respect from that of America. This difference proceeds from that which exists in their respective governments; and to the defense of our own, which has been achieved by the loss of so much blood and treasure, and matured by the wisdom of their most enlightened citizens, and under which we have enjoyed unexampled felicity, this whole nation is devoted. We owe it, therefore, to candor and to the amicable relations existing between the United States and those powers to declare that we should consider any attempt on their part to extend their system to any portion of this hemisphere as dangerous to our peace and safety.

With the existing colonies or dependencies of any European power we have not interfered and shall not interfere. But with the governments who have declared their independence and maintained it, and whose independence we have, on great consideration and on just principles, acknowledged, we could not view any interposition for the purpose of oppressing them, or controlling in any other manner their destiny, by any European power in any other light than as the manifestation of any unfriendly disposition toward the United States. . . .

Our policy in regard to Europe, which was adopted at an early stage of the wars which have so long agitated that quarter of the globe, nevertheless remains the same, which is not to interfere in the internal concerns of any of its powers; to consider the government de facto as the legitimate government for us; to cultivate friendly relations with it, and to preserve those relations by a frank, firm, and manly policy, meeting in all instances the just claims of every power, submitting to injuries from none. . . .

Memorial and Protest of the Cherokee Nation

While Native Americans were being forced from their homeland, Cherokee leaders put their protest before the United States Senate. Their call for justice went unheard.

It cannot be concealed that the situation of the Cherokees is peculiarly distressing. In adverting to that situation it is not done to arouse, at this late day, a useless sympathy, but only as matter of history, and from necessity in giving a fair and impartial illustration of their difficulties. It is well known to those who have paid any attention to their history for the last five years, that they have been contending for the faithful execution of treaties between their nation and the United States, and that their distresses have not been mitigated; their efforts seem to have increased their difficulties. It remains for them to seek an adjustment by treaty, and an equitable acknowledgement of their rights and claims, so far as circumstances will permit.

For this purpose, this delegation has been deputed, as the proper organ of the Cherokee people, to settle, by treaty, their difficulties; and they wish, in sincerity, to have them settled, for the good, peace, and harmony of the whole nation.

The Seneca Falls Declaration

One of the first documents to express the desire for equal rights for women is the Declaration of Sentiments and Resolutions, issued in 1848 at the Seneca Falls Convention in New York. Led by Lucretia Mott and Elizabeth Cady Stanton, the delegates adopted a set of resolutions that called for woman suffrage and opportunities in employment and education. Excerpts from the Declaration follow.

When, in the course of human events, it becomes necessary for one portion of the family of man to assume among the people of the earth a position different from that which they have hitherto occupied, but one to which the laws of nature and of nature's God entitle them, a decent respect to the opinions of mankind requires that they should declare the causes that impel them to such a course.

We hold these truths to be self-evident: that all men and women are created equal; that they are endowed by their Creator with certain inalienable rights; that among these are life, liberty, and the pursuit of happiness; that to secure these rights governments are instituted, deriving their just powers from the consent of the governed. Whenever any form of government becomes destructive of these ends, it is the right of those who suffer from it to refuse allegiance to it, and to insist upon the institution of a new government, laying its foundation on such principles, and organizing its powers in such form, as to them shall seem most likely to effect their safety and happiness. Prudence, indeed, will dictate that governments long established should not be changed for light and transient causes; . . . But when a long train of abuses and usurpations, pursuing invariably the same object, evinces a design to reduce them under absolute despotism, it is their duty to throw off such government and to provide new guards for their future security. . . .

The history of mankind is a history of repeated injuries and usurpations on the part of man toward woman, having in direct object the establishment of an absolute tyranny over her. To prove this, let facts be submitted to a candid world. . . .

Now, in view of the entire disfranchisement of one-half the people of this country, their social and religious degradation, in view of the unjust laws above mentioned, and because women do feel themselves aggrieved, oppressed, and fraudulently deprived of their most sacred rights, we insist that they have immediate admission to all the rights and privileges which belong to them as citizens of the United States. . . .

The Emancipation Proclamation

On January 1, 1863, President Abraham Lincoln issued the Emancipation Proclamation, which freed all slaves in states under Confederate control. The Proclamation was a significant step toward the Thirteenth Amendment (1865) that ended slavery in all of the United States.

Whereas on the 22d day of September, A.D. 1862, a proclamation was issued by the President of the United States, containing among other things, the following, to wit: That on the 1st day of January, in the year of our Lord 1863, all persons held as slaves within any state or designated part of a state, the people whereof shall then be in rebellion against the United States, shall be then, thenceforward, and forever free; and the executive government of the United States, including the military and naval authority thereof, will recognize and maintain the freedom of such persons and will do no act or acts to repress such persons, or any of them, in any efforts they may make for their actual freedom.

That the executive will, on the 1st day of January aforesaid, by proclamation, designate the states and parts of states, if any, in which the people thereof, respectively, shall then be in rebellion against the United States; and the fact that any state or the people thereof shall on that day be in good faith represented in the Congress of the United States by members chosen thereto at elections wherein a majority of the qualified voters of such states shall have participated shall, in the absence of strong countervailing testimony, be deemed conclusive evidence that such state and the people thereof are not then in rebellion against the United States. . . .

And, by virtue of the power and for the purpose aforesaid, I do order and declare that all persons held as slaves within said designated states and parts of states are, and henceforward shall be, free; and that the executive government of the United States, including the military and naval authorities thereof, will recognize and maintain the freedom of said persons.

And I hereby enjoin upon the people so declared to be free to abstain from all violence, unless in necessary self-defense; and I recommend to them that, in all cases when allowed, they labor faithfully for reasonable wages.

And I further declare and make known that such persons of suitable condition will be received into the armed service of the United States to garrison forts, positions, stations, and other places, and to man vessels of all sorts in said service. . . .

Documents

The Gettysburg Address

On November 19, 1863, President Abraham Lincoln gave a short speech at the dedication of a national cemetery on the battlefield of Gettysburg. His simple yet eloquent words expressed his hopes for a nation divided by civil war.

Four score and seven years ago our fathers brought forth on this continent a new nation, conceived in liberty, and dedicated to the proposition that all men are created equal.

Now we are engaged in a great civil war, testing whether that nation or any nation so conceived and so dedicated can long endure. We are met on a great battlefield of that war. We have come to dedicate a portion of that field as a final resting place for those who here gave their lives that that nation might live. It is altogether fitting and proper that we should do this.

But, in a larger sense, we can not dedicate—we can not consecrate—we can not hallow—this ground. The brave men, living and dead, who struggled here have consecrated it far beyond our poor power to add or detract. The world will little note nor long remember what we say here, but it can never forget what they did here. It is for us, the living, rather, to be dedicated here to the unfinished work which they who fought here have thus far so nobly advanced.

It is rather for us to be here dedicated to the great task remaining before us—that from these honored dead we take increased devotion to that cause for which they gave the last full measure of devotion; that we here highly resolve that these dead shall not have died in vain; that this nation, under God, shall have a new birth of freedom; and that government of the people, by the people, and for the people, shall not perish from the earth.

I Will Fight No More

In 1877 the Nez Perce Indians fought the government's attempt to move them to a smaller reservation. After a remarkable attempt to escape to Canada, Chief Joseph realized that resistance was hopeless and advised his people to surrender.

Tell General Howard I know his heart. What he told me before I have in my heart. I am tired of fighting. Our chiefs are killed. Looking Glass is dead. It is the young men who say yes or no. He who led the young men is dead. It is cold and we have no blankets. The little children are freezing to death. My people, some of them have run away to the hills and have no blankets, no food; no one knows where they are—perhaps freezing to death. I want to have time to look for my children and see how many I can find. Maybe I shall find them among the dead. Hear me my chiefs. I am tired; my heart is sick and sad. From where the sun now stands, I will fight no more forever.

The Pledge of Allegiance

In 1892 the nation celebrated the 400th anniversary of Columbus's landing in America. In connection with this celebration, Francis Bellamy, a magazine editor, wrote and published the Pledge of Allegiance. The words "under God" were added by Congress in 1954 at the urging of President Dwight D. Eisenhower.

I pledge allegiance to the Flag of the United States of America and to the Republic for which it stands, one Nation under God, indivisible, with liberty and justice for all.

Documents

Douglass's Speech to the Congregational Church in Washington, D.C., 1883

Frederick Douglass marked the twentieth anniversary of the emancipation of the enslaved people of the District of Columbia with a speech that probed the relations between African Americans and white Americans.

The sky of the American Negro is dark, but not rayless; it is stormy, but not cheerless . . . As the war for the Union recedes into the misty shadows of the past, and the Negro is no longer needed to assault forts and stop rebel bullets, he is in some sense, of less importance. Peace with the old master class has been war to the Negro. As the one has risen, the other has fallen. The reaction has been sudden, marked, and violent. It has swept the Negro from all the legislative halls of the Southern States, and from those of the Congress of the United States. It has, in many cases, driven him from the ballot box and the jury box. The situation has much in it for serious thought, but nothing to cause despair . . .

Time and events which have done so much for us in the past, will, I trust, not do less for us in the future. The moral government of the universe is on our side, and cooperates, with all honest efforts, to lift up the down-trodden and oppressed in all lands, whether the oppressed be white or black . . .

What is to be the future of the colored people of this country? Some change in their condition seems to be looked for by thoughtful men everywhere; but what that change will be, no one yet has been able with certainty to predict . . .

In every great movement men are prepared by preceding events for those which are to come. We neither know the evil nor the good which may be in store for us. Twenty-five years ago the system of slavery seemed impregnable. Cotton was king, and the civilized world acknowledged his sway. Twenty-five years ago no man could have foreseen that in less than ten years from that time no master would wield a lash and no slave would clank a chain in the United States.

Who at that time dreamed that Negroes would ever be seen as we have seen them-to-day marching through the streets of this superb city, the Capital of this great Nation, with eagles on their buttons, muskets on their shoulders and swords by their sides, timing their high footsteps to the Star Spangled Banner and the Red, White and Blue? . . .

The Fourteen Points

On January 8, 1918, President Woodrow Wilson went before Congress to offer a statement of aims called the Fourteen Points. Wilson's plan called for freedom of the seas in peace and war, an end to secret alliances, and equal trading rights for all countries. The excerpt that follows is taken from the President's message.

. . . We entered this war because violations of right had occurred which touched us to the quick and made the life of our own people impossible unless they were corrected and the world secured once for all against their recurrence. What we demand in this war, therefore, is nothing peculiar to ourselves. It is that the world be made fit and safe to live in; and particularly that it be made safe for every peace-loving nation which, like our own, wishes to live its own life, determine its own institutions, be assured of justice and fair dealings by the other peoples of the world, as against force and selfish aggression. All the peoples of the world are in effect partners in this interest, and for our own part we see very clearly that unless justice be done to others it will not be done to us.

The program of the world's peace, therefore, is our program, and that program, the only possible program, as we see it, is this:

I. Open covenants of peace, openly arrived at, after which there shall be no private international understandings of any kind, but diplomacy shall proceed always frankly and in the public view.

II. Absolute freedom of navigation upon the seas, outside territorial waters, alike in peace and in war, except as the seas may be closed in whole or in part by international action for the enforcement of international covenants.

III. The removal, so far as possible, of all economic barriers and the establishment of an equality of trade conditions among all the nations consenting to the peace and associating themselves for its maintenance.

IV. Adequate guarantees given and taken that national armaments will be reduced to the lowest point consistent with domestic safety.

V. Free, open-minded, and absolutely impartial adjustment of all colonial claims, based upon a strict observance of the principle that in determining all such questions of sovereignty the interests of the population concerned must have equal weight with the equitable claims of the Government whose title is to be determined. . . .

XIV. A general association of nations must be formed under specific covenants for the purpose of affording mutual guarantees of political independence and territorial integrity to great and small states alike. . . .

Franklin D. Roosevelt's First Inaugural Address

The New Deal was launched March 4, 1933, the day that Franklin D. Roosevelt became President. At a time when the nation was in the depths of the Great Depression, the address showed a great sense of leadership and encouraged the American people.

I am certain that my fellow Americans expect that on my induction into the presidency I will address them with a candor and a decision which the present situation of our nation [impels]. This is preeminently the time to speak the truth, the whole truth, frankly and boldly. Nor need we shrink from honestly facing conditions in our country today. This great Nation will endure as it has endured, will revive and will prosper. So, first of all, let me assert my firm belief that the only thing we have to fear is fear itself—nameless, unreasoning, unjustified terror which paralyzes needed efforts to convert retreat into advance. In every dark hour of our national life a leadership of frankness and vigor has met with that understanding and support of the people themselves which is essential to victory. I am convinced that you will again give that support leadership in these critical days.

In such a spirit on my part and on yours we face our common difficulties. They concern, thank God, only material things. Values have shrunken to fantastic levels; taxes have risen; our ability to pay has fallen; government of all kinds is faced by serious curtailment of income; the means of exchange are frozen in the currents of trade; the withered leaves of industrial enterprise lie on every side; farmers find no markets for their produce; the savings of many years in thousands of families are gone.

More important, a host of unemployed citizens face the grim problem of existence, and an equally great number toil with little return. Only a foolish optimist can deny the dark realities of the moment.

Yet our distress comes from no failure of substance. We are stricken by no plague of locusts. Compared with the perils which our [ancestors] conquered because they believed and were not afraid, we have still much to be thankful for. Nature still offers her bounty, and human efforts have multiplied it. Plenty is at our doorstep, but a generous use of it languishes in the very sight of the supply. Primarily this is because the rulers of the exchange of mankind's goods have failed, through their own stubbornness and their own incompetence, . . .

Brown v. Board of Education

On May 17, 1954, the Supreme Court ruled in Brown *v.* Board of Education *that racial segregation in public schools was unconstitutional. This decision provided the legal basis for court challenges to segregation in every aspect of American life.*

The plaintiffs contend that segregated public schools are not "equal" and cannot be made "equal," and that hence they are deprived of the equal protection of the laws. Because of the obvious importance of the question presented, the Court took jurisdiction. . . .

Our decision . . . cannot turn on merely a comparison of these tangible factors in the Negro and white schools involved in each of the cases. We must look instead to the effect of segregation itself on public education.

In approaching this problem, we cannot turn the clock back to 1868 when the Amendment was adopted, or even to 1896 when *Plessy v. Ferguson* was written. We must consider public education in the light of its full development and its present place in American life throughout the nation. Only in this way can it be determined if segregation in public schools deprives these plaintiffs of the equal protection of the laws.

Today, education is perhaps the most important function of state and local governments. Compulsory school attendance laws and the great expenditures for education both demonstrate our recognition of the importance of education to our democratic society. . . . In these days, it is doubtful that any child may reasonably be expected to succeed in life if he is denied the opportunity of an education. Such an opportunity, where the state has undertaken to provide it, is a right which must be made available to all on equal terms.

We come then to the question presented: Does segregation of children in public schools solely on the basis of race, even though the physical facilities and other "tangible" factors may be equal, deprive the children of the minority group of equal educational opportunities? We believe that it does.

. . . .We conclude that in the field of public education the doctrine of "separate but equal" has no place. Separate educational facilities are inherently unequal. Therefore, we hold that the plaintiffs and others similarly situated for whom the actions have been brought are, by reason of the segregation complained of, deprived of the equal protection of the laws guaranteed by the Fourteenth Amendment. . . .

John F. Kennedy's Inaugural Address

President Kennedy's Inaugural Address on January 20, 1961, set the tone for his administration. In his address Kennedy stirred the nation by calling for "a grand and global alliance" to fight tyranny, poverty, disease, and war.

We observe today not a victory of party but a celebration of freedom—symbolizing an end as well as a beginning—signifying renewal as well as change. For I have sworn before you and Almighty God the same solemn oath our forebears prescribed nearly a century and three-quarters ago.

The world is very different now. For man holds in his mortal hands the power to abolish all forms of human poverty and all forms of human life. And yet the same revolutionary beliefs for which our forebears fought are still at issue around the globe—the belief that the rights of man come not from the generosity of the state but from the hand of God.

We dare not forget today that we are the heirs of that first revolution. Let the word go forth from this time and place, to friend and foe alike, that the torch has been passed to a new generation of Americans born in this century, tempered by war, disciplined by a hard and bitter peace, proud of our ancient heritage—and unwilling to witness or permit the slow undoing of those human rights to which this nation has always been committed, and to which we are committed today at home and around the world.

Let every nation know, whether it wishes us well or ill, that we shall pay any price, bear any burden, meet any hardship, support any friend, oppose any foe to assure the survival and the success of liberty.

This much we pledge—and more.

To those old allies whose cultural and spiritual origins we share, we pledge the loyalty of faithful friends. United, there is little we cannot do in a host of cooperative ventures. Divided, there is little we can do . . .

Let us never negotiate out of fear. But let us never fear to negotiate. . . . Let both sides explore what problems unite us instead of belaboring those problems which divide us. . . . Let both sides seek to invoke the wonders of science instead of its terrors. Together let us explore the stars, conquer the deserts, eradicate disease, tap the ocean depths, and encourage the arts and commerce. . . .

And so, my fellow Americans—ask not what your country can do for you—ask what you can do for your country.

My fellow citizens of the world—ask not what America will do for you but what together we can do for the freedom of man.

I Have a Dream

On August 28, 1963, while Congress debated wide-ranging civil rights legislation, Martin Luther King, Jr., led more than 200,000 people on a march on Washington, D.C. On the steps of the Lincoln Memorial he gave a stirring speech in which he eloquently spoke of his dreams for African Americans and for the United States. Excerpts of the speech follow.

. . . There are those who are asking the devotees of civil rights, "when will you be satisfied?"

We can never be satisfied as long as the Negro is the victim of the unspeakable horrors of police brutality. . . .We cannot be satisfied as long as the Negro's basic mobility is from a smaller ghetto to a larger one. We can never be satisfied as long as a Negro in Mississippi cannot vote and a Negro in New York believes he has nothing for which to vote. . . .

I say to you today, my friends, that in spite of the difficulties and frustrations of the moment I still have a dream. It is a dream deeply rooted in the American dream.

I have a dream that one day this nation will rise up and live out the true meaning of its creed, "We hold these truths to be self-evident, that all men are created equal."

I have a dream that one day on the red hills of Georgia the sons of former slaves and the sons of former slaveowners will be able to sit down together at the table of brotherhood.

I have a dream that one day even the state of Mississippi, a desert state sweltering with the heat of injustice and oppression, will be transformed into an oasis of freedom and justice.

I have a dream that my four little children will one day live in a nation where they will not be judged by the color of their skin, but by the content of their character. . . .

. . . When we let freedom ring, when we let it ring from every village and every hamlet, from every state and every city, we will be able to speed up that day when all of God's children, black men and white men, Jews and Gentiles, Protestants and Catholics, will be able to join hands and sing in the words of the old Negro spiritual: "Free at last! Free at last! Thank God Almighty, we are free at last!"

Peacemaking and Peace-Keeping for the Next Century

In 1945 the United States and other nations helped establish the United Nations to provide a forum for nations to settle their disputes by peaceful means. In March 1995, during the 50th anniversary year of the UN, Boutros Boutros-Ghali, the organization's Secretary General, spoke about the principal issues of international peace and security.

—Most of today's conflicts take place within states. They are fought not only by armies but also by irregular forces. Civilians are the main victims. Humanitarian emergencies are commonplace. State institutions often have collapsed.

—The demands go beyond traditional peace-keeping. Recent operations have demobilized troops; promoted national reconciliation; restored effective government; and organized and monitored elections.

—Civic operations are as important as military operations.

—Long term economic and social programmes may be needed to address the original causes of conflict.

United Nations peace efforts have become more expensive, more complex and more dangerous. . . .

In Somalia, the United Nations responded to a unique situation. All semblance of governmental authority had collapsed. Chaos endangered the lives of innocent people throughout the country. Massive refugee flows took place within and across borders. Infants starved to death before the cameras of the world media.

The aim of the United Nations Operations in Somalia (UNOSOM) was to provide basic security, services and administration to the people, while assisting in a negotiating process to restore legitimate and effective State authority. . . .

The United Nations can only facilitate, encourage and assist; it cannot impose a solution on the parties—even when the solution is one that the parties at one time seemed prepared to accept.

Thus we have learned a lesson: how and when to withdraw.

And perhaps we have taught a lesson as well: that when warring parties reject U.N. help and endanger the U.N. mission, they will find that the U.N.'s patience is not unlimited. They will find that they cannot expect to be supported yet continue to act irresponsibly. . . .

As a workable system of international and human security comes into being, the need for peace operations will decrease. The three pillars of such a system must be: consistent response, adequate human and financial resources, and sustained political resolve.

Responsibility for resolving disputes and conflicts lies with the parties themselves. But the international community, by selecting carefully among the instruments at its disposal, and mobilizing the necessary political and economic support, can play an indispensable role in supporting their efforts.

Gazetteer

★ ★

The gazetteer is a geographical dictionary that lists political divisions, natural features, and other places and locations. Following each entry is a description, its latitude and longitude, and a page reference that indicates where each entry may be found in this text.

A

Afghanistan country in south central Asia (33°N/63°E) 995

Africa continent of the Eastern Hemisphere south of the Mediterranean Sea and adjoining Asia on its northeastern border (10°N/22°E) 12

Alabama state in the southeastern United States; 22nd state to enter the Union (32°45'N/87°30'W) 213

Alaska state in the United States, located in northwestern North America; territory purchased from Russia in 1867 (64°N/150°W) 610

Albany capital of New York located in the Hudson Valley; site where Albany Congress proposed first formal plan to unite the 13 colonies (40°45'N/73°45'W) 59

Allegheny River river in western Pennsylvania uniting with the Monongahela River at Pittsburgh to form the Ohio River (40°N/82°W) 96

Andes Mountains mountain system extending along western coast of South America (13°S/75°W) 12

Antarctica continent located around the South Pole (80°15'S/127°E) 39

Antietam Civil War battle site in western Maryland (39°45'N/77°30'W) 419

Appalachian Mountains chief mountain system in eastern North America extending from Quebec and New Brunswick to central Alabama (37°N/82°W) 57

Appomattox Court House site in central Virginia where Confederate forces surrendered ending the Civil War (37°N/77°W) 437

Arctic Ocean ocean in the northernmost part of the world (85°N/170°E) 12

Arizona state in the southwestern United States; 48th state to enter the Union (34°N/113°W) 378

Arkansas state in the south central United States; acquired as part of Louisiana Purchase (34°45'N/93°45'W) 265

Aroostook Valley fertile farming region in Maine (47°N/68°W) 367

Asia continent of the Eastern Hemisphere forming a single landmass with Europe (50°N/100°E) 12

Atlanta capital of Georgia located in the northwest central part of the state (33°45'N/84°30'W) 398

Atlantic Ocean ocean separating North and South America from Europe and Africa (5°S/25°W) 12

Australia continent and country southeast of Asia (25°S/125°E) 12

B

Baltimore city on the Chesapeake Bay in central Maryland (39°15'N/76°45'W) 57

Barbary Coast north coast of Africa between Morocco and Tunisia (36°45'N/3°E) 255

Baton Rouge capital of Louisiana located on the Mississippi River in the southeastern part of the state (30°30'N/91°15'W) 275

Bay of Pigs site of 1961 invasion of Cuba by U.S.-trained Cuban exiles (22°N/79°W) 924

Beijing capital of China located in the northeastern part of the country (40°N/116°30'E) 619

Berlin city in east central Germany; former national capital divided into sectors after World War II; city reunited in 1989 (52°31'N/13°30'E) 819

Black Hills mountains in southwestern South Dakota; site of conflict between the Sioux and white settlers during 1870s (44°15'N/103°45'W) 478

Boston capital of Massachusetts located in the eastern part of the state; founded by English Puritans in 1630 (42°15'N/71°W) 57

Brazil country in eastern South America (9°S/53°W) 39

C

California state in the western United States; attracted thousands of miners during gold rush of 1849 (38°15'N/121°15'W) 12

Cambodia country in Southeast Asia bordering Gulf of Siam; official name Democratic Kampuchea (12°N/105°E) 933

Canada country in northern North America (50°N/100°W) 303

Charleston city in South Carolina on the Atlantic coast; original name Charles Town (32°45'N/80°W) 213

Château-Thierry World War I battle site in France (49°N/3°15'E) 693

Chautauqua Lake lake in western New York State (42°15'N/79°45'W) 559

Chesapeake Bay inlet of the Atlantic Ocean in Virginia and Maryland (37°N/76°W) 57

Chicago largest city in Illinois; located in northeastern part of the state along Lake Michigan (41°45'N/87°30'W) 265

China country in eastern Asia; mainland (People's Republic of China) under communist control since 1949 (36°45'N/93°E) 12

Chisholm Trail pioneer cattle trail from Texas to Kansas (34°N/98°W) 478

Cincinnati city in southern Ohio on the Ohio River; grew as result of increasing steamship traffic during the mid-1800s (39°15'N/84°30'W) 153

Cleveland city in northern Ohio on Lake Erie (41°30'N/81°45'W) 265

Colorado state in the western United States (39°30'N/107°W) 378

Columbia River river flowing through southwest Canada and northwestern United States into the Pacific Ocean (46°15'N/124°W) 150

Concord village northwest of Boston, Massachusetts; site of early battle of the American Revolution on April 19, 1775 (42°N/71°W) 113

Connecticut state in the northeastern United States; one of the original 13 states (41°45'N/73°15'W) 57

Cuba country in the West Indies, North America (22°N/79°W) 605

Czechoslovakia former country in central Europe; now two countries, the Czech Republic and Slovakia (49°30'N/16°E) 702

D

Delaware state in the northeastern United States; one of the original 13 states (38°45'N/75°30'W) 57

Detroit city in southeastern Michigan; site of significant battles during the French and Indian War and the War of 1812; center of automobile industry (42°15'N/82°15'W) 150

dust bowl area of the Great Plains where the drought of the 1930s turned the soil to wind-borne dust (37°N/98°W) 783

E

Egypt country in northeastern Africa (27°N/30°E) 693

England division of the United Kingdom of Great Britain and Northern Ireland (56°30'N/1°45'W) 12

Erie Canal waterway connecting the Hudson River with Lake Erie through New York State (43°N/76°W) 265

Erie, Lake one of the Great Lakes between Canada and the United States (42°15'N/81°30'W) 50

Europe continent of the northern part of the Eastern Hemisphere between Asia and the Atlantic Ocean (50°N/15°E) 12

F

Florida state in the southeastern United States (30°30'N/84°45'W) 95

Fort Duquesne French fort on the site of Pittsburgh, Pennsylvania (40°30'N/80°W) 96

Fort Sumter Union fort during the Civil War located on island near Charleston, South Carolina; site of first military engagement of Civil War (32°45'N/80°W) 412

France country in western Europe (49°45'N/0°45'E) 12

Fredericksburg city and Civil War battle site in northeast Virginia (38°15'N/77°30'W) 419

Freeport city in northern Illinois; site of 1858 Lincoln-Douglas debate (42°15'N/89°30'W) 403

G

Galveston city on the Gulf of Mexico coast in Texas; created nation's first commission form of city government (29°15'N/95°W) 632

Georgia state in the southeastern United States (32°45'N/83°45'W) 57

Germany country in central Europe; divided after World War II into East Germany and West Germany; unified in 1989 (50°N/10°E) 689

Gettysburg city and Civil War battle site in south central Pennsylvania; site where Lincoln delivered the Gettysburg Address (39°45'N/77°15'W) 419

Great Basin interior drainage area in Nevada (40°15'N/117°15'W) 376

Great Britain commonwealth comprising England, Scotland, and Wales (56°30'N/1°45'W) 92

Great Lakes chain of five lakes, Superior, Erie, Michigan, Ontario, and Huron, in central North America (45°N/87°W) 95

Great Plains flat grassland in the central United States (45°N/104°W) 376

Great Salt Lake lake in northern Utah with no outlet and strongly saline waters (41°15'N/112°45'W) 238

Greece country in southeastern Europe (39°N/21°30'E) 702

Guadalcanal island in the Solomons east of Australia (9°45'S/158°45'E) 882

Guam United States possession in the western Pacific Ocean (14°N/143°15'E) 610

H

Harlem northern section of Manhattan in New York City; cultural center of African Americans in the early and mid-1900s (40°45'N/74°W) 734

Harpers Ferry town in northern West Virginia on the Potomac River (39°15'N/77°45'W) 403

Hartford capital of Connecticut located on the Connecticut River in the central part of the state (41°45'N/72°45'W) 57

Hawaii state in the United States located in the Pacific Ocean (20°N/157°W) 610

Hiroshima city in southern Japan; site of first military use of atomic bomb, August 6, 1945 (34°15'N/132°30'E) 822

Hispaniola island in the West Indies in North America, where Haiti and the Dominican Republic are located (17°30'N/73°15'W) 50

Hong Kong British colony along the southern coast of China in Asia (21°45'N/115°E) 610

Hudson Bay large bay in northern Canada (60°N/86°W) 12

Hudson River river flowing through New York State into the Atlantic Ocean at New York City (52°45'N/74°W) 57

Hungary country in central Europe (47°N/20°E) 702

Huron, Lake one of the Great Lakes between the United States and Canada in North America (45°15'N/82°45'W) 50

I

Idaho state in the northwestern United States; ranks among top states in silver production (44°N/115°15'W) 478

Illinois state in the north central United States; one of the states formed in the Northwest Territory (40°30'N/90°45'W) 213

India country in southern Asia (23°N/77°30'E) 12

Indian Territory land reserved by the United States government for Native Americans, now the state of Oklahoma (36°N/98°15'W) 316

Indiana state in the north central United States; one of the states formed in the Northwest Territory (39°45'N/86°45'W) 213

Indochina region in Southeast Asia (17°15'N/105°15'E) 879

Iowa state in the north central United States acquired as part of the Louisiana Purchase (42°N/94°15'W) 12

Iran country of the Middle East in southwestern Asia (31°15'N/53°30'E) 702

Iraq country of the Middle East in southwestern Asia (32°N/42°30'E) 883

Israel country of the Middle East in southwestern Asia along the Mediterranean Sea (32°45'N/34°E) 883

Italy country in southern Europe along the Mediterranean Sea (44°N/11°15'E) 689

J

Jamestown first permanent English settlement in North America; located in southeastern Virginia (37°15'N/76°45'W) 57

Japan island country in eastern Asia (36°30'N/133°30'E) 610

K

Kansas state in the central United States; fighting over slavery issue in 1850s gave territory the name "Bleeding Kansas" (38°30'N/98°45'W) 378

Kentucky state in the south central United States; border state that sided with the Union during the Civil War (37°30'N/87°30'W) 212

Kings Mountain Revolutionary War battle site in northern South Carolina (35°15'N/81°15'W) 137

Korea peninsula in eastern Asia between China, Russia, and the Sea of Japan, on which are located the countries of North Korea and South Korea (38°15'N/127°30'E) 822

Kuwait country of the Middle East in southwestern Asia between Iraq and Saudi Arabia (29°N/47°45'E) 702

L

Lebanon country in southwest Asia along the Mediterranean Sea (34°N/34°E) 883

Lexington Revolutionary War battle site in eastern Massachusetts; site of first clash between colonists and British, April 19, 1775 (42°26'N/71°13'W) 113

Little Rock capital of Arkansas located in the center of the state; site of 1957 conflict over public school integration (34°45'N/92°15'W) 398

London capital of United Kingdom located in the southeastern part of England (51°30'N/0°15'W) 12

Los Angeles city along the Pacific coast in southern California; industrial, financial, and trade center of western United States (34°N/118°15'W) 376

Louisiana state in the south central United States (30°45'N/92°45'W) 213

Louisiana Territory region of west central United States between the Mississippi River and the Rocky Mountains purchased from France in 1803 (40°N/95°W) 95

M

Maine state in the northeastern United States; 23rd state to enter the Union (45°30'N/69°45'W) 57

Maryland state in the eastern United States; one of the original 13 states (39°15'N/76°30'W) 57

Massachusetts state in the northeastern United States; one of the original 13 states (42°15'N/72°30'W) 57

Mediterranean Sea sea between Europe and Africa (36°15'N/13°30'E) 33

Mexico country in North America south of the United States (23°45'N/104°W) 277

Mexico, Gulf of gulf south of the United States and east of Mexico in North America (25°15'N/93°45'W) 12

Michigan state in the north central United States; one of the states formed in the Northwest Territory (45°N/85°W) 265

Michigan, Lake one of the five Great Lakes located in the north central United States (43°15'N/87°15'W) 50

Midway Islands United States possession in the central Pacific Ocean; site of Battle of Midway, June 1942 (28°N/177°W) 610

Milwaukee city in eastern Wisconsin along Lake Michigan (43°N/88°W) 528

Minnesota state in the north central United States; fur trade, good soil, and lumber attracted early settlers (46°15'N/96°15'W) 398

Mississippi state in the southeastern United States; became English territory after French and Indian War (32°30'N/89°45'W) 213

Mississippi River river flowing through the United States from Minnesota to the Gulf of Mexico; explored by French in 1600s (29°N/89°W) 50

Missouri state in the south central United States; petition for statehood resulted in sectional conflict and the Missouri Compromise (40°45'N/93°W) 12

Missouri River river flowing through the United States from the Rocky Mountains to the Mississippi River near St. Louis (38°45'N/90°15'W) 50

Montana state in the northwestern United States; cattle industry grew during 1850s (47°15'N/111°45'W) 378

Montgomery capital of Alabama located in the central part of the state; site of 1955 bus boycott to protest segregation (32°30'N/86°15'W) 398

Montreal city on the St. Lawrence River in southern Quebec, Canada (45°30'N/73°30'W) 50

Moscow capital of former Soviet Union and capital of Russia (55°45'N/37°30'E) 818

N

Nashville capital of Tennessee located in the north central part of the state (36°15'N/86°45'W) 213

Natchez city in western Mississippi along the Mississippi River (31°30'N/91°15'W) 265

National Road road from Baltimore, Maryland, to Vandalia, Illinois (40°N/81°30'W) 265

Nebraska state in the central United States (41°45'N/101°30'W) 378

Netherlands country in northwestern Europe (53°N/4°E) 39

Nevada state in the western United States (39°30'N/117°W) 378

New Amsterdam town founded on Manhattan Island by Dutch settlers in 1625; renamed New York by British settlers (40°45'N/74°W) 57

New Hampshire state in the northeastern United States; one of the original 13 states (44°N/71°45'W) 57

New Jersey state in the northeastern United States; one of the original 13 states (40°30'N/74°45'W) 57

New Mexico state in the southwestern United States; ceded to the United States by Mexico in 1848 (34°30'N/107°15'W) 378

New Orleans city in southern Louisiana in the Mississippi Delta (30°N/90°W) 213

New York state in the northeastern United States; one of the original 13 states (42°45'N/78°W) 57

New York City city in southeastern New York State at the mouth of the Hudson River; largest city in the United States (40°45'N/74°W) 59

Nicaragua country in Central America (12°45'N/86°15'W) 616

Normandy region along French coast and site of D-Day invasion, June 6, 1944 (48°N/2°W) 820

North America continent in the northern part of the Western Hemisphere between the Atlantic and Pacific oceans (45°N/100°W) 39

North Carolina state in the southeastern United States; one of the original 13 states (35°45'N/81°30'W) 57

North Dakota state in the north central United States; Congress created Dakota Territory in 1861 (47°15'N/102°W) 378

Northwest Territory territorial division north of the Ohio River and east of the Mississippi River (47°30'N/87°30'W) 212

O

Oberlin college and town in northern Ohio (41°15'N/82°15'W) 558

Ohio state in the north central United States; first state in the Northwest Territory (40°30'N/83°15'W) 213

Ohio River river flowing from Allegheny and Monongahela rivers in western Pennsylvania into the Mississippi River (39°N/85°W) 50

Ohio Valley valley of the Ohio River, which flows from Pennsylvania to the Mississippi River at Cairo, Illinois (37°30'N/88°W) 11

Oklahoma state in the south central United States; Five Civilized Tribes moved to territory 1830–1842 (36°N/98°15'W) 378

Omaha city in eastern Nebraska on the Missouri River (41°15'N/96°W) 498

Ontario, Lake one of the five Great Lakes between Canada and the United States (43°30'N/79°W) 50

Oregon state in the northwestern United States; adopted woman suffrage in 1912 (43°45'N/123°45'W) 378

Oregon Trail pioneer trail from Independence, Missouri, to the Oregon Territory (42°30'N/110°W) 368

P

Pacific Ocean world's largest ocean located between Asia and the Americas (0°/175°W) 12

Panama country in the southern part of Central America, occupying the Isthmus of Panama (8°N/81°W) 621

Panama Canal canal built across the Isthmus of Panama through Panama to connect the Caribbean Sea and the Pacific Ocean (9°15'N/79°45'W) 621

Pearl Harbor naval base at Honolulu, Hawaii; site of 1941 Japanese attack, leading to United States entry into World War II (21°21'N/157°57'W) 822

Pennsylvania state in the northeastern United States (41°N/78°15'W) 57

Persian Gulf gulf in southwestern Asia between Iran and the Arabian Peninsula (27°45'N/50°30'E) 995

Philadelphia city in eastern Pennsylvania on the Delaware River; Declaration of Independence and the Constitution both adopted in city's Independence Hall (40°N/75°W) 57

Philippines island country in southeast Asia (14°30'N/125°E) 605

Pittsburgh city in western Pennsylvania; one of the great steelmaking centers of the world (40°30'N/80°W) 213

Plymouth town in eastern Massachusetts; first successful English colony in New England (42°N/70°45'W) 57

Portugal country in southwestern Europe (38°15'N/8°15'W) 39

Potomac River river flowing from West Virginia into Chesapeake Bay (38°N/77°W) 57

Promontory Point site in Utah where the first transcontinental railroad was completed (41°45'N/112°15'W) 498

Providence capital of Rhode Island; site of first English settlement in Rhode Island (41°45'N/71°30'W) 57

Puerto Rico United States possession in the West Indies (18°15'N/66°45'W) 50

Pullman company town south of Chicago; site of 1894 railroad strike (41°45'N/87°30'W) 519

Q

Quebec city in Canada, capital of Quebec Province, on the St. Lawrence River; first settlement in New France (46°45'N/71°15'W) 50

R

Raleigh capital of North Carolina located in the north central part of the state (35°45'N/78°45'W) 265

Rhode Island state in the northeastern United States; one of the original 13 states (41°30'N/71°45'W) 57

Richmond capital of Virginia located in the central part of the state; capital of the Confederacy during the Civil War (37°30'N/77°30'W) 137

Rio Grande river between the United States and Mexico in North America; forms the boundary between Texas and Mexico (26°N/97°30'W) 50

Roanoke island off the coast of present-day North Carolina that was site of early British colonizing efforts (35°N/75°39'W) 57

Rocky Mountains mountain range in western United States and Canada in North America (50°N/114°W) 303

Russia name of republic; former empire of eastern Europe and northern Asia coinciding with Soviet Union (60°30'N/64°E) 12

S

Sacramento capital of California located in the north central part of the state (38°30'N/121°30'W) 368

St. Augustine city in northeastern Florida on the Atlantic coast; oldest permanent existing European settlement in North America, founded in 1565 (30°N/81°15'W) 50

St. Lawrence River river flowing from Lake Ontario, between Canada and the United States, through Canada to the Atlantic Ocean (48°N/65°15'W) 57

St. Louis city in eastern Missouri on the Mississippi River (38°45'N/90°15'W) 153

St. Mihiel World War I battle site in France (49°N/5°30'E) 693

Salt Lake City capital of Utah located in the northern part of the state; founded by Mormons in 1847 (40°45'N/111°45'W) 368

San Antonio city in south central Texas (29°30'N/98°30'W) 371

San Francisco city in northern California on the Pacific coast (37°45'N/122°30'W) 368

Santa Fe capital of New Mexico located in the north central part of the state (35°45'N/106°W) 368

Saratoga Revolutionary War battle site in the Hudson Valley of eastern New York State (43°N/73°51'W) 131

Savannah city in eastern Georgia (32°N/81°W) 57

Sea Islands group of islands off the coast of Georgia and South Carolina (31°15'N/81°W) 444

Seneca Falls town in New York State; site of woman's rights convention in 1848 (43°N/77°W) 341

Sierra Nevada mountain range in eastern California (39°N/120°W) 478

South Africa country in southern Africa (28°S/24°45'E) 693

South America continent in the southern part of the Western Hemisphere lying between the Atlantic and Pacific oceans (15°S/60°W) 39

South Carolina state in the southeastern United States; one of the original 13 states (34°15'N/81°15'W) 57

South Dakota state in the north central United States; acquired through the Louisiana Purchase (44°15'N/102°W) 378

Soviet Union former country in northern Europe and Asia (60°30'N/64°E) 807

Spain country in southwestern Europe (40°15'N/4°30'W) 12

Stalingrad city in the former Soviet Union on the Volga River; present name Volgograd (48°45'N/42°15'E) 819

Suez Canal canal built between the Mediterranean Sea and the Red Sea through northeastern Egypt (31°N/32°15'E) 883

Superior, Lake one of the five Great Lakes between Canada and the United States in North America (47°45'N/89°15'W) 50

T

Tampa city in west central Florida (28°N/82°30'W) 498

Tennessee state in the south central United States; first state readmitted to the Union after the Civil War (35°45'N/88°W) 213

Tennessee Valley valley of the Tennessee River, which flows from the Appalachian Mountains to the Ohio River (35°30'N/88°15'W) 781

Tenochtitlán Aztec capital on the site of present-day Mexico City (19°30'N/99°15'W) 12

Texas state in the south central United States; Mexican colony that became an independent republic before joining the United States (31°N/101°W) 213

Tokyo capital of Japan located on the eastern coast of Honshu Island (35°45'N/139°45'E) 822

Toronto city in Canada on Lake Ontario; capital of the province of Ontario (43°45'N/79°30'W) 251

Trenton capital of New Jersey located on the Delaware River in the central part of the state; site of Revolutionary War battle in December 1776 (40°15'N/74°45'W) 131

U

Union of Soviet Socialist Republics *See* Soviet Union.

United Kingdom country in northwestern Europe made up of England, Scotland, Wales, and Northern Ireland (56°30'N/1°45'W) 689

United States country in central North America; fourth largest country in the world in both area and population (38°N/110°W) 146

Utah state in the western United States; settled by Mormons in 1840s (39°30'N/112°45'W) 378

V

Valley Forge Revolutionary War winter camp northwest of Philadelphia (40°N/75°30'W) 131

Veracruz city in eastern Mexico on the Gulf of Mexico coast (19°15'N/96°W) 376

Vermont state in the northeastern United States; 14th state to enter the Union (43°45'N/72°45'W) 146

Vicksburg city and Civil War battle site in western Mississippi on the Mississippi River (32°21'N/90°52'W) 421

Vietnam country in southeastern Asia (16°N/108°E) 935

Virginia state in the eastern United States; colony in which first permanent English settlement in the Americas was established (37°N/78°W) 57

W

Wall Street street in New York City at the center of the financial district (40°45'N/74°W) 535

Washington state in the northwestern United States; territory reached by Lewis and Clark in 1805 (47°30'N/121°15'W) 378

Washington, D.C. capital of the United States located on the Potomac River at its confluence with the Anacostia River, between Maryland and Virginia; coinciding with the District of Columbia (38°53'N/77°02'W) 213

West Virginia state in the east central United States (39°N/80°45'W) 378

Willamette River Valley valley of the Willamette River in western Oregon (45°N/123°W) 368

Wisconsin state in the north central United States; passed first state unemployment compensation act, 1932 (44°30'N/91°W) 265

Wounded Knee site of battle between settlers and Native Americans in southern South Dakota in 1890 and of Native American movement protest in 1973 (43°26'N/102°30'W) 478

Wyoming state in the western United States; territory provided women the right to vote, 1869 (42°45'N/108°30'W) 478

Y

Yorktown town in southeastern Virginia and site of final battle of Revolutionary War (37°15'N/76°30'W) 137

Z

Zaire country in central Africa (1°S/22°15'E) 926

Glossary

★ ★

A

abolitionist 1800s reformer who worked to end slavery (p. 342)

acid rain acid precipitation in the form of rain (p. 1016)

agribusiness large farming operation that includes the cultivation, processing, storage, and distribution of farm products (p. 869)

amendment alteration to the Constitution (p. 160)

amnesty act of a government by which pardon is granted to an individual or groups of persons (p. 445)

anarchism a belief in no direct government authority over society (p. 531)

anarchist one who opposes all forms of government (p. 616)

antebellum customs, manners, and institutions that existed before the Civil War (p. 559)

appeasement policy of compromising or giving in to demands in an attempt to avoid trouble and maintain peace (p. 809)

appropriations bill draft of a law setting aside funds for a specific use (p. 1007)

arbitration hearing and resolution of a disagreement between two parties through an impartial third party (pp. 524, 600)

armistice temporary suspension of hostilities between opponents (p. 695)

armory place or building where arms and military equipment are stored (p. 740)

artillery weapons for discharging missiles (p. 116)

assimilation process of one group or culture absorbing another (p. 911)

astrolabe instrument used to observe positions of celestial bodies (p. 27)

automation technique of operating a machine, manufacturing process, or system that will do a job formerly performed by humans (p. 872)

B

balance of payments difference between the value of a nation's imports and its exports; also known as balance of trade (p. 964)

bicameral political system based on two legislative chambers (p. 144)

bilingualism ability to speak two languages (p. 918)

blacklist record kept by companies of employees or former employees who are disapproved of or are to be punished or boycotted (p. 521)

black nationalism belief of militant blacks who advocate separatism from whites and forming self-governing black communities (p. 910)

black power mobilizing economic and political power of African Americans to improve their condition (p. 911)

blitzkrieg war conducted with great speed or force (p. 812)

blockade to close off something (p. 415)

bond certificate that earns interest and is redeemed for cash on a specific date (p. 209)

bounty money paid to recruit soldiers for military service; payment to encourage an action (p. 427)

boycott refusal to buy goods or have dealings with a country or other entity, usually to express disapproval or force acceptance of certain conditions (p. 100)

buffer area designed to separate and serve as a protective barrier; neutral area separating conflicting forces (p. 840)

business cycle sequence of economic activity, usually consisting of recession, recovery, growth, and decline (p. 520)

busing transportation of children to a school outside their residential area to establish racial integration in that school (p. 914)

C

cabinet a group of advisers to the President (p. 205)

capital money invested in a business (p. 26)

caravel small ship with a broad bow (p. 27)

carrack large merchant ship (p. 27)

charter formal document granting the right of self-rule (p. 17)

classical relating to ancient Greece or Rome (p. 17)

closed shop system where all workers in a particular industry are required to be union members or employer agrees to hire only union members (p. 291)

coalition alliance, combination, or union of parties, people, or states formed for a specific action or purpose (p. 789)

collective bargaining negotiation between organized workers and management to reach an agreement on wages, hours, and working conditions (p. 521)

collective security an agreement to provide for common defense (p. 843)

commodity economic good; product of agriculture; article of commerce (p. 488)

commonwealth self-governing political unit of independent states associated in a common allegiance (p. 65)

commune group of people living together with collective ownership and use of property, often having shared goals, philosophies, and ways of life; large cooperative farms (p. 939)

communism system of government in which the Communist party controls the political, economic, cultural, and social life of the people; economic system in which society as a whole, represented by the Communist party, owns all means of production, distribution, and exchange of goods (p. 838)

compact covenant, agreement, or contract between two or more parties (p. 321)

company town village built and run by a company where workers are required to live (p. 519)

compass device for determining direction by means of a magnetic needle (p. 27)

confederation nonbinding political alliance of independent countries, states, or groups (p. 13)

congregation body of church members; people meeting for worship and religious instruction (p. 65)

conquistador Spanish adventurer in sixteenth-century Americas (p. 42)

conscientious objector person who refuses to perform military service or to bear arms on the grounds of moral or religious principles or beliefs (p. 937)

conscription compulsory enrollment of people for military service (p. 426)

consensus general agreement; judgment arrived at by most of those concerned; group solidarity in sentiment and belief (p. 956)

conservation the planned management of natural resources to prevent destruction or neglect (p. 652)

conspicuous consumption lavish spending for show (p. 584)

constitution plan of government in America; basic principles and laws of a nation, state, or social group that determine the powers and duties of the government and guarantee certain rights to its people (p. 67)

consul official appointed by a government to reside in a foreign country to represent the interests of the citizens of the appointing country (p. 374)

containment policy of preventing the expansion of a hostile power; post-World War II foreign policy stating the United States would hold Soviet influence within its existing limits (p. 840)

Continental American paper money used as currency instead of British coins (p. 126)

contraband goods or merchandise whose importation, exportation, or possession is forbidden (p. 687)

cooperative enterprise or organization owned by and operated for the benefit of those using its services (p. 570)

corollary proposition added to another as a natural consequence or effect (p. 617)

corporation form of business consisting of a group of people authorized by law to act as a single person and having an identity that survives its incorporators (p. 502)

cotton gin a machine that cleans the seeds from cotton fibers (p. 294)

counterculture one with values and mores that run contrary to those of established society (p. 939)

covenant formal and binding agreement between two or more parties (p. 702)

covert secret or undercover; not openly shown or engaged in (p. 880)

crack cocaine purified cocaine in the form of small chips (p. 1019)

craft union labor union in which all members practice the same occupation or skill (p. 790)

credibility gap lack of trust stemming from difference between official government statements and practices (p. 928)

creditor nation a nation that lends money (p. 1013)

creole resident of the Spanish colonies born of Spanish parents (p. 44)

currency paper money that is in circulation as a means of exchange (p. 154)

D

dark horse political candidate unexpectedly nominated, usually as a compromise between groups (p. 372)

debtor nation a country that owes money (p. 1013)

defense perimeter boundary of military protection (p. 848)

deficit spending government practice of borrowing money in order to spend more money than is received from taxes (p. 780)

deflation economic condition in which the volume of available money or credit decreases, resulting in the decline of the price of goods and services (p. 574)

deported remove from a country an alien presence is unlawful (p. 705)

depression economic condition marked by an extended and severe decline in production and sales, and a severe increase in unemployment (p. 153)

deregulation act of removing restrictions and regulations (p. 970)

Glossary

détente relaxation of cold war tensions between the United States and the Soviet Union that began in the early 1970s (p. 942)

direct primary election in which nominations of candidates for office are made by voters (p. 634)

direct tax one paid directly to the government rather than being included in the price of goods; a tax collected directly from the person on whom the tax burden is expected to fall (p. 100)

disenfranchised having had the legal right to vote taken away (p. 449)

disestablished deprived of the status and privileges of an established position (p. 145)

dissenter protester; one who differs in opinion from the majority (p. 63)

dole money or goods given as charity; grant of government funds to the unemployed (p. 780)

domestic market market composed of buyers and sellers within a nation (p. 723)

downsizing to reduce operations or number of employees (p. 1007)

duty tax on imported goods (p. 92)

dynasty series of rulers from the same family; powerful family that holds its influence for a long time (p. 18)

E

economies of scale ability of large businesses to operate more cheaply and efficiently than smaller ones, resulting in lower per-unit costs for the products of large companies (p. 498)

effigy crude image or representation of a hated person (p. 104)

emancipation freeing of enslaved persons; act or process of freeing from restraint, control, or the power of another; freedom from bondage (p. 145)

emigration departure from one's place of residence or country to live in another (p. 289)

encomienda system of rewarding conquistadores with tracts of land, including the right to tax and demand labor from Native Americans who lived on the land (p. 44)

entrepreneur person who organizes, manages, and assumes the risks of a business or enterprise (p. 495)

enumerated commodity colonial product that Parliament said could be shipped only to Britain (p. 92)

enumerated powers those mentioned specifically one after another in the Constitution (p. 212)

envoy person delegated to represent one government in its dealings with another; a messenger, representative (p. 130)

escalation increase in extent, volume, number, amount, intensity, or scope (p. 932)

ethnic cleansing expulsion or extermination of a group from a country (p. 1009)

ethnic group groups of people who share the same culture, religion, and customs (p. 797)

excise tax one paid by a manufacturer and passed on to those who buy the product; a tax on the manufacture, sale, or consumption of a product within a country (p. 209)

executive privilege principle that the executive branch of government is exempt from disclosing information when such disclosure would adversely affect the functions and decision-making processes of the presidency or national security (p. 968)

expatriate person who leaves his or her native country to live elsewhere (p. 560)

expedition a journey with a specific purpose (p. 239)

extraterritoriality exemption from the application or jurisdiction of local law (p. 382)

F

fascism system of government that is strongly nationalistic and allows private ownership of property while controlling general economic policies; government characterized by racism and militarism; a repressive one-party dictatorship (p. 809)

favorite son presidential candidate supported by the delegates of the candidate's native state at a national political convention (p. 302)

featherbedding requiring of an employer under a union rule or safety statute to hire more employees than are needed (p. 852)

federalism system of government in which power is distributed between national and state governments (p. 159)

federalized brought under federal government jurisdiction (p. 902)

feminist person who acts on behalf of women's rights (p. 916)

feudalism a system in which powerful leaders gave land to nobles in return for pledges of loyalty and service (p. 15)

filibuster the use of delaying tactics to prevent action in a legislative assembly (p. 1006)

fireside chat the name used to describe how former President Franklin D. Roosevelt talked to people by radio (p. 775)

forage to live off the land (p. 432)

foreclosure legal procedure for reclaiming a piece of property when the owner is unable to keep up the mortgage payments (p. 782)

free-trader one that practices or advocates trade without taxes or tariffs (p. 555)

frigate medium-sized warship smaller than a destroyer; used for escort and patrol duties (p. 251)

G

genocide deliberate and systematic destruction of a group (p. 1009)

gentry the upper class of England (p. 73)

global economy economic interdependence among countries of the world (p. 1013)

globalized corporation firms that do business and have offices or factories in many countries (p. 1013)

gold standard monetary system in which a nation's currency is based on the value of gold (p. 574)

graft acquisition of money or power in dishonest or questionable ways while in public office (p. 544)

greenback paper money that was not backed by gold or silver; legal-tender notes issued by the United States government (p. 429)

grievance formal expression of a complaint (p. 116)

guerrilla soldier who barrages the enemy with surprise attacks, harassment, sabotage, and other nontraditional warfare (p. 840)

H

habeas corpus legal principle which requires that people who are arrested be brought to court to show why they should be held; writ inquiring into the lawfulness of retaining a person who is imprisoned or detained in custody (p. 424)

holding company one that gains control of other companies by buying their stock (p. 505)

Holocaust systematic mass murder of 12 million European civilians, especially Jews, by Nazis during World War II (p. 821)

horizontal integration joining together of businesses that are engaged in similar business activities or processes (p. 505)

humanism interest in classical Greek and Roman arts, literature, knowledge, and culture (p. 17)

I

illegal alien noncitizen who is in a country illegally (p. 1019)

impeach to bring charges of a crime against a federal or state public official with the intent of removing the official from office (p. 451)

imperialism act of creating an empire by dominating other nations (p. 598)

implied powers those suggested but not directly stated in the Constitution (p. 212)

impound to refuse to spend congressionally allocated funds; to seize and hold in the custody of the law (p. 970)

impressment form of military and naval conscription, usually by force, practiced by Britain and other European countries (p. 245)

income tax tax on the net income of an individual or business (p. 659)

incumbent current officeholder (p. 1002)

indemnity security or protection against hurt, loss, or damage; exemption from incurred penalties or liabilities (p. 619)

indentured servant person who agreed to work for an employer in colonial America for a specified time in exchange for passage to America (p. 58)

industrial union union that represents every worker in a single industry regardless of his or her job (pp. 526, 790)

inflation decline in money's value when more money is printed, resulting in increased prices of goods and services (p. 573)

inheritance tax tax on an inheritance that an heir must pay to receive the inheritance (p. 661)

initiative procedure enabling citizens to propose a bill by petitioning with a specific number of signatures from registered voters (p. 634)

injunction court order requiring an individual or company to do something or to prohibit a given action; used frequently to stop strikes (p. 527)

installment buying system of paying for goods at regular intervals, usually with interest added to the balance (p. 744)

interlocking directorate system under which the same people serve on the boards of directors of several firms within the same industry (p. 670)

internal improvements roads, canals, and other transportation needs inside a nation's boundaries (p. 259)

isolationism policy or belief that a nation should limit its alliances and involvement in international political and economic affairs (p. 598)

isthmus narrow piece of land connecting two larger land areas (p. 40)

J

joint resolution a resolution passed by both houses of Congress requiring only a simple majority vote (p. 372)

joint-stock company form of business organization; pooled funds of many investors or stockholders who can independently sell their shares of the company (p. 26)

judicial review Supreme Court's power to review all congressional acts and executive actions and reject those it considers unconstitutional (p. 234)

jurisdictional strike one resulting from a dispute between unions over which union should represent the workers in a company or industry (p. 852)

K

kickback payback of a sum received from increased fees because of a confidential agreement or act of coercion (p. 545)

L

laissez-faire government doctrine of noninterference in business practices and in the economic affairs of individuals; literally, "let do" (p. 233)

lame duck elected official who continues to hold office during the period between the election and the inauguration of a successor (p. 761)

land speculator person who purchases land to resell for profit; one who buys or sells land in expectation of profiting from future price changes (p. 99)

lend-lease transfer of goods and services to an ally (p. 815)

line-item veto power to veto a single part of a bill (p. 1007)

line of demarcation north-south line of longitude through the Atlantic Ocean dividing lands in the Americas claimed by Spain and Portugal (p. 38)

literacy test tests to show if immigrants could read (p. 641)

lobbyist person who promotes or secures the passage of legislation by influencing public officials (p. 547)

lock chambers with gates at each end used to raise or lower boats as they pass from a level of higher elevation to a level of lower elevation or the reverse on a river or canal (p. 263)

lockout closed factory or place of employment caused by a strike; withholding of employment by an employer (p. 521)

long drive cattle run in which a large herd is moved across great distances to a railhead, where they are shipped to market (p. 478)

Loyalist American colonist who supported the British government; one who is or remains loyal to a political cause, party, or government (p. 116)

lyceum voluntary organization providing public lectures, concerts, and entertainments to promote the improvement of its members and their useful knowledge (p. 337)

M

maize a large seeded grass cultivated by people in the central valley of Mexico which became the forerunner of corn (p. 8)

mandate clear expression of the wishes of voters, as shown in election results (pp. 448, 951)

manor large estate owned by a noble on which peasants lived and were protected in exchange for their services (p. 15)

martial law form of military rule that suspends Bill of Rights guarantees; law administered by the military in an emergency situation when civilian law-enforcement agencies are not able to maintain order (p. 414)

maverick unbranded range animal or cattle; a motherless calf (p. 477)

mechanics' lien law charge against a bankrupt employer, insuring that wages owed to workers be the first payments made (p. 292)

melting-pot society a place where ethnic, social, and cultural assimilation is going on (p. 1020)

mercantilism the theory that a state's power depended on its wealth (p. 48)

mercenary paid soldier hired for service in the army of a foreign country; one that serves merely for wages (p. 116)

merchandising buying and selling of goods in a business for a profit (p. 537)

meridian line of longitude; a great circle on the surface of the earth passing through the poles (p. 486)

mestizo person in the Spanish colonies born of Spanish and Native American parents (p. 44)

militia group of civilians declared by law to be called to military service and trained as soldiers to fight in emergencies (p. 94)

monopoly exclusive control of a product or service in a particular market by a single company (p. 106)

moratorium official authorization to suspend payments, as with a debt; officially authorized period of waiting (p. 751)

mudslinging making malicious often untrue charges against an opponent (p. 310)

mulatto person of Spanish and African or Native American and African ancestry (p. 44)

multicultural society society in which all people respect unique cultures (p. 1020)

multinational corporation a corporation that operates divisions in more than two countries (p. 1013)

multinational state nation with many different ethnic groups (p. 1009)

N

nationalism feeling of loyalty and devotion to one's country, honoring that nation above all others and promoting its culture and interests rather than those of other nations (p. 258)

naval store products of pine forests used in wooden shipbuilding and maintenance (p. 61)

neutrality refusal to take sides (p. 603)

new federalism Richard Nixon's policy of economic partnership between the federal and state governments whereby states and municipalities received less federal funding (p. 965)

nomadic frequent roaming from place to place without a fixed pattern of movement, usually following a food source (p. 470)

nonimportation agreement one between colonial merchants and planters not to import certain goods (p. 100)

nonpartisan free from party affiliation, bias, or designation (p. 222)

nonviolent resistance objection or demonstration to gain political ends without use of violence (p. 900)

northwest passage water route to Asia through North America sought by European explorers (p. 47)

nullification state declaration of a federal law to be invalid (pp. 225, 320)

O

obiter dictum incidental opinion that is issued by a judge or court but is not binding (p. 400)

on margin method of buying stock with a small cash down payment and the rest borrowed from a stockbroker. Stockbroker holds shares of stock as collateral for the loan; borrower repays broker from stock resale profits (p. 743)

open shop employment practice in which eligibility is not determined by union membership (p. 715)

P

parliament supreme legislative body in Britain made up of nobility, clergy, and commons (p. 16)

partitioned divided into two or more territorial units having separate political status (p. 618)

Patriot American colonist who favored separation before and during the Revolutionary War (p. 116)

patronage practice of elected officials to make appointments to unelected government positions for political advantage or repayment of favors (p. 551)

patroon landowner in the Dutch colonies who received rent, taxes, and labor from tenant farmers (p. 70)

peninsulares government and church officials in Spanish colonial America who had been born in Spain (p. 44)

philanthropy actions to promote human welfare and benefit society (p. 511)

piracy robbery on the high seas (p. 244)

platform declaration of the principles and policies adopted by a political party or candidate (p. 327)

pocket veto indirect rejection of a legislative bill by the President by retaining the bill unsigned until after Congress adjourns (p. 316)

pogrom organized massacres of unarmed people, especially Jews (p. 530)

political machine party organization in big cities that holds power by controlling votes, courts, and police (p. 545)

pooling illegal agreements among individual railroads to divide the total volume of freight among their lines and to keep rates high (p. 570)

popular sovereignty principle that the settlers within a federal territory have the power to decide the legality of slavery within that territory (p. 389)

post-war disillusionment period after a war in which the populace is disenchanted (p. 732)

pragmatism belief that government actions should meet the needs of society; practical approach to problems and affairs (p. 628)

preamble introductory part of a constitution or statute that states the reasons for and intent of the law; introduction to a document (p. 116)

presidential succession the order in which others fill the office of President (p. 865)

presidio Spanish fort in the Americas built to protect mission settlements (p. 45)

price-cutting reduction of prices to a level designed to cripple competition (p. 670)

privateer armed private ship commissioned by the government to attack ships of an enemy (p. 217)

proclamation official formal public announcement (p. 419)

proprietor individual who received legal and exclusive right to American colonial land from the king of England and who was expected to administer the land according to English laws (p. 60)

protectionist one who advocates government protection for domestic producers and manufacturers through restrictions on imports (p. 555)

protective tariff high tax on imports intended to protect domestic products from foreign competition rather than to yield revenue (p. 208)

protectorate country that is technically independent, but whose government and economy are controlled by a stronger power; the nation or region controlled by a stronger nation (p. 613)

public land land belonging to the national government and therefore to the people (p. 146)

pueblo apartment-like buildings of adobe and cut stone built by Native Americans (p. 11)

pump priming government money invested in the economy to stimulate a self-sustaining economic recovery (p. 780)

purge large-scale forced removal of officials who show signs of disloyalty to their superiors (p. 839)

Q

quadrant instrument used to measure altitudes (p. 27)

quorum number of officers or members of a body that must be present to legally transact business (p. 206)

R

racism belief that a particular race is superior to others (p. 910)

ratify to officially approve a proposal (p. 145)

reactionary government government characterized by ultraconservative policies (p. 928)

real wages income adjusted to compensate for reduced earning power due to inflation (p. 518)

realism European-influenced literary movement that strove for accurate representation of nature or real life without idealization (p. 559)

rebate discount in the form of a refund or part of a payment for a product or service (p. 507)

recall removal of an elected official by voters in a special election (p. 634)

recession downturn in the nation's economy marked by reduced economic activity (p. 792)

reciprocity mutual lowering by nations of tariff barriers; recognition by one of two countries of the validity of privileges granted by the other (p. 600)

redcoat derogatory term for British soldiers in the colonies, referring to their red uniforms (p. 101)

rediscount small fee charged to a member bank by the Federal Reserve Bank upon acceptance of a business's promissory note (p. 668)

referendum process by which people can vote directly on a proposed law (p. 634)

Renaissance revival of interest in the arts, literature, culture, and learning of ancient Greece and Rome, c. 1400–1600 (p. 17)

reparation payments made by nations defeated in war as a penalty for damages caused to other countries (p. 713)

revenue sharing plan to share or divide income (p. 965)

revenue tariff low tax on imports intended to provide income for the government rather than protection of domestic products from foreign competition (p. 208)

rider unrelated amendment attached to a bill under legislative consideration (p. 551)

right of deposit right to temporarily put goods ashore for transfer to other ships without paying import duties (p. 150)

right of self-determination right of people to choose their own government and be free from rule by a foreign country (p. 116)

S

saga prose narrative or heroic poem about legendary figures and events from the heroic age of Norway and Iceland (p. 36)

salutary neglect policy of noninterference by a governing nation in order to produce a beneficial effect (p. 93)

samurai member of the military class of feudal Japan (p. 23)

satellite nations East European nations politically and economically under Soviet domination; country dominated or controlled by another more powerful country (p. 839)

scab nonunion replacement workers during a strike or union members who refuse to strike and continue working (p. 521)

scrip money that can only be redeemed at a company store (p. 519)

scurvy sickness caused by lack of ascorbic acid (p. 29)

search-and-destroy strategy military tactic used to force enemy into open combat (p. 933)

seceding withdrawing from a large political body (p. 152)

secession formal withdrawal from an organization (p. 404)

securities stocks, bonds, and other financial instruments traded on a stock exchange (p. 742)

segregation enforced separation of racial groups in schooling, housing, and other public areas (p. 455)

serf peasant of the Middle Ages who was bound to the land (p. 15)

sexism prejudice or discrimination based on gender (p. 917)

sharecropper agricultural worker who cultivates part of another person's land, receives supplies and equipment from the landowner, and in return gives the landowner part of the harvest (p. 441)

shogun one of a line of military governors ruling Japan until the revolution of 1867–1868; Japanese commander in chief (p. 23)

shuttle diplomacy negotiations carried out by an intermediary who shuttles back and forth between the disputants (p. 945)

sit-in occupying seats or sitting on the floor of an establishment as a means of protest (p. 904)

social contract agreement among individuals forming an organized society that defines and limits the rights and duties of each (p. 116)

social Darwinism sociological theory that states only the fittest survive social competition and experience social advancement (p. 510)

social gospel application by religious organizations of Christian principles to social problems (p. 627)

socialism economic system in which government partly owns and controls production and distribution of goods produced (p. 349)

Spanish Armada large fleet of seemingly invincible ships dispatched by King Philip II of Spain to England in retaliation against English piracy (p. 48)

specie money in the form of gold and silver coin (p. 100)

speculation risky business venture involving buying or selling in the hope of making a large, quick profit (p. 743)

sphere of influence area in China during the late 1800s where trade was controlled by a foreign power (p. 618)

spoils system practice of dismissing government job holders affiliated with a defeated party and replacing them with supporters of the winning party (p. 315)

stagflation persistent inflation combined with static consumer demand and relatively high rate of unemployment (p. 964)

stock partial ownership interest in a company sold in the form of shares to raise operating capital (p. 26)

strait narrow passageway connecting two larger bodies of water (p. 40)

student deferment official postponement of military service (p. 937)

subsistence farming level of farming at which farmers produce only enough to feed and maintain their families (p. 61)

subversives people working secretly, attempting to overthrow or undermine a government or political system (p. 855)

suffrage right to vote (p. 214)

summit diplomatic meeting of the superpowers; conference of highest level government officials (p. 942)

T

tariff tax on imported goods (p. 208)

teach-in lecture, debate, and discussion on controversial topic (p. 938)

technological unemployment jobs lost as the result of machines doing the jobs formerly accomplished by humans (p. 715)

tenant farmer agricultural worker who rents and farms land from another person and pays the rent either in cash or with a portion of the crop (p. 441)

textile fabric, especially woven or knitted; cloth (p. 288)

third party minor political party operating in addition to two other major parties in a nation or state normally characterized by a two-party system (p. 575)

toll fee charged for a privilege such as the use of a means of transportation (p. 264)

totalitarian type of government controlled by a single person or party; suppressing freedom and controlling every aspect of life (p. 809)

township local unit of government within a county (p. 548)

trade deficit economic condition in which the value of a nation's imports is more than the value of its exports (p. 1013)

traitor one who commits treason (p. 136)

treason attempt to overthrow the government of the state to which the offender owes allegiance (p. 116)

tribute payment by one nation or ruler to another to acknowledge submission, or as the price of protection (p. 151)

trust combination of companies to gain control of an industry and reduce competition (p. 505)

turnpike road barricaded by spiked poles where travelers stop to pay a fee to use the road (p. 264)

U

ultimatum a demand that would have serious consequences if ignored (p. 272)

Underground Railroad a secret organization that had hiding places throughout the Northern states and Canada to bring enslaved people out of the South and to freedom (p. 343)

Glossary

unicameral legislature consisting of a single chamber (p. 147)

urban renewal construction program to replace or restore a city or urban area (p. 953)

V

vaudeville stage entertainment consisting of various acts (p. 480)

vertical integration joining together of businesses that are involved in different but related activities or processes (p. 505)

veto action by which an executive rejects a bill submitted by a legislature; to refuse to approve (p. 144)

viceroy person who rules a country or province as the representative of the monarch (p. 45)

victory gardens gardens for raising one's own vegetables, especially during wartime (p. 698)

vigilance committee organization of citizens who take the law into their own hands for their protection (p. 480)

W

ward division of a city for representative, electoral, or administrative purposes (p. 546)

war of national liberation conflict with goal of freeing one nation from the control of another (p. 930)

welfare capitalism system of benefit programs offered to workers by employers intended to reduce the appeal of unions (p. 716)

"Western" novel, story or Hollywood motion picture depicting life in the western United States during the latter half of the nineteenth century (p. 481)

wetland land or area containing much soil moisture (p. 1017)

wildcat strike work stoppage initiated by a group of workers without formal union approval or in violation of a contract (p. 829)

writ of assistance written order that allowed officials to conduct unrestricted searches for smuggled or illegal goods (p. 99)

writ of mandamus court order requiring specific action on the part of person or organization served (p. 234)

Y

yellow journalism type of newspaper reporting in the late 1890s that featured sensational headlines and stories (p. 561)

Index

D

E

F

H

I

J

K

L

Index

O

Index

Q

R

S

Index

T

U

V

W

X

Y

Z

Acknowledgments

★ ★

30 "Constitution of the Five Nations," from William N. Fenton, ed., *Parker on the Iroquois*, Copyright © 1868 by Syracuse University Press; used by permission. **31** "Navajo Song of the Rain Chant," from Nataline Curtis, ed., *The Indians' Book*, Harper and Brothers, 1907; used by permission. **110** From Thomas Paine, *American Crisis, Number 1*, reprinted in *The Annals of America*, vol. 2, Chicago: Encyclopaedia Britannica, 1968. **236** Southgate letter from James A. Henretta, et al, *America's History*, Chicago: Dorsey Press, 1987. **242** From James Fenimore Cooper, *The Prairie*, Albany: State University of New York Press, 1962. **362** From Henry David Thoreau, *Walden and Other Writings*. New York: Doubleday, 1970. **379** Coffey "Reminiscences" from *Eyewitness: The Negro in American History* by William L. Katz, rev. ed. New York: Pitman Publishing Corp., 1971. **482** From Mark Twain, *Roughing It*. Berkeley: University of California Press, 1972. **614** From *Official Proceedings of the Democratic National Convention. . . . 1890*, reprinted in *The Annals of America*, vol. 12. Chicago: Encyclopaedia Britannica, 1968. **630** From Theodore Dreiser, *Sister Carrie*. New York: W.W. Norton, Critical Ed., 1970. **726** "Recuerdo" by Edna St. Vincent Millay, From *Collected Poems*, Harper & Row, Copyright © 1922, 1950 by Edna St. Vincent Millay. Reprinted by permission of Elizabeth Barnett, Literary Executor. **727** "Dream Boogie," reprinted by permission of Harold Ober Associates, Inc. Copyright © 1932, 1951 by Langston Hughes, Copyright renewed 1979 by George Houston Bass. **800** From John Steinbeck, *The Grapes of Wrath*, Copyright © 1939, renewed © 1967 by John Steinbeck. Used by permission of Viking Penguin, a division of Penguin Books USA, Inc. **833** Ota excerpt from *"The Good War": An Oral History of World War Two* by Studs Terkel. Copyright © 1984. Reprint by permission of Pantheon Books, a division of Random House. **900** Beals excerpt from Henry Hampton and Steve Fayer, *Voices of Freedom*. New York: Bantam Books, 1990. **1022** From *Hunger of Memory* by Richard Rodriguez. Copyright © 1981 by Richard Rodriguez. Reprinted by permission of David R. Godine, Publisher. **1071** "I Have a Dream" copyright © 1963 by Martin Luther King, Jr. Used by permission, Joan Daves Agency.

Photo Credits

★ ★

COVER, Jim Barber Studio, (bkgd) Aaron Haupt; **x**, (l,br) The Granger Collection, (tr) R. Krubner/H. Armstrong Roberts; **xi**, (tl) Shelburne Museum, Shelburne VT (tr) Henry Ford Museum, (cl) The Granger Collection, (cr) file photo, (cb) Aaron Haupt, (bl) courtesy Hormel Foods, Aaron Haupt, (br) Reuters/Bettmann; **xii**, (tl) The Granger Collection, (tr) North Wind Picture Archives, (b) courtesy PHYSICS TODAY Magazine; **xiii**, (tl) The Granger Collection, (tr) Ted Wood/Black Star; **xiv**, (l) Stock Montage; **xv**, (tl,tc) The Granger Collection, (tr,cl) Brown Brothers, (cr) Bettmann Archive, (bl) UPI/Bettmann, (br) courtesy David Godine Publishers; **xvi**, (l) New York Historical Society, (r) The Time Museum; **xvii**, (tl) Reuters/Bettmann, (tr) Mark Burnett/Central Ohio Council of BSA, (bl) Aldo Tutino/Art Resource, (br) FPG Intl; **xviii**, (l) Bettmann Archive, (ct) courtesy Independence National Historic Park/Eastern National Park and Monument Association, (cb) Archive Photos, (r) American Antiquarian Society; **xix**, (tl) UPI/Bettmann, (tc) John Launois/Black Star, (tr) Richard Howard/Black Star, (bl,bc) Stock Montage, (br) The Granger Collection; **xx**, (t) Library of Congress, (b) National Museum of American Art, Washington, DC/Art Resource; **xxi**, (t) Library of Congress, (b) The Sonnabend Collection, NY; **xxii**, courtesy PHYSICS TODAY Magazine; **xxiv**, William J. Weber; **xxv**, (t) The Art Collection of the Boatman's National Bank of St. Louis, (b) Missouri Historical Society; **xxvi**, (t) Estate of Mrs. Edsel B. Ford, (b) Metropolitan Museum of Art; **xxvii**, (t) The Granger Collection, (b) H. Armstrong Roberts; **xxviii**, (t) file photo, (b) The Granger Collection; **xxix**, (t) The Granger Collection, (b) Reuters/Bettmann; **xxx**, General Electric Company; **xxxi**, (t) Andy Levin/Photo Researchers, (b) Joseph DiChello;

xxxii, (t) Architect of the Capitol, (b) Alex Maclean/Landslides; **xxxiii**, (t) The Granger Collection, (b) Lynn Stone; **xxxiv**, (t) Margot Granitsas/Photo Researchers, (b) The Granger Collection; **1**, (t) North Wind Picture Archives, (b) Joe Sohm/Photo Researchers; **2**, (t) Chuck O'Rear/H. Armstrong Roberts, (b) file photo; **3**, (tl,b) Scala/Art Resource, (tr) The Granger Collection; **4**, (t,c) Boltin Picture Library, (b) Larry Hamill; **5**, **6**, Boltin Picture Library; **7**, (t) Bettmann Archive, (b) courtesy of the School of American Research, Santa Fe; **8**, Bettmann Archive; **9**, George C. PageMuseum; **10**, Bettmann Archive; **11**, Werner Forman/Art Resource; **13**, George Hunter/H. Armstrong Roberts; **14**, (t) courtesy Museum of Natural History, Raleigh NC, (b) Mark Burnett; **15**, Erich Lessing/Art Resource; **16**, (t) The Granger Collection, (b) North Wind Picture Archives; **17**, The Granger Collection; **18**, Scala/Art Resource; **19**, **20**, British Museum; **21**, SEF/Art Resource; **22**, The Granger Collection; **23**, (l) Aldo Tutino/Art Resource, (r) British Museum; **24**, Metropolitan Museum of Art; **25**, Boltin Picture Library; **26**, H. Armstrong Roberts; **27**, (l) The Granger Collection, (r) Scala/Art Resource; **28**, Giraudon/Art Resource; **29**, The Granger Collection; **30**, (t) file photo, (b) Cranbrook Institute of Science; **31**, G.L. French/H. Armstrong Roberts; **32**, British Museum; **34**, Erich Lessing/Art Resource; **35**, (t) Bridgeman Art Library, London, (b) Werner Forman/Art Resource; **36**, **37**, The Granger Collection; **38**, Scala/Art Resource; **40**, Giraudon/Art Resource; **41**, Scala/Art Resource; **42**, Peabody Museum of Salem; **43**, **44**, The Granger Collection; **45**, North Wind Picture Archives; **46**, (t) file photo, (b) The Granger Collection; **47**, **48**, The Granger Collection; **49**, (l) National Archives of Canada, (r) The Granger Collection; **52**, The Granger Collection; **54**,

Boltin Picture Library; **55**, (t) Wadsworth Athenaeum, Hartford CT, (b) H. Armstrong Roberts; **56**, H. Armstrong Roberts; **58**, North Wind Picture Archives; **62**, The Granger Collection; **63**, courtesy The Pilgrim Society, Plymouth MA; **64**, Bettmann Archive; **65**, The Bettmann Archive; **67**, **68**, The Granger Collection; **69**, Chase Manhattan Bank; **70**, **71**, **72**, The Granger Collection; **73**, The Shelburne Museum, Shelburne, VT; **75**, Bettmann Archive; **76**, The Granger Collection; **77**, Bettmann Archive; **78**, (l,r) North Wind Picture Archives; **80**, (l) file photo, (r) Bettmann Archive; **82**, (t) The Granger Collection, (b) Boltin Picture Library; **82-83**, (b) David McGlynn/FPG Intl; **83**, (tl) Smithsonian Institution, American Museum of Natural History, (tr) Roger K. Burnard, (br) file photo; **84**, (l) E. Cooper/H. Armstrong Roberts, (r) Bettmann Archive; **85**, The Granger Collection; **86**, (l,c) The Granger Collection, (r) Folger Shakespeare Library, Washington DC; **87**, (l) Bettmann Archive, (r) The Granger Collection; **88**, (t) Boltin Picture Library, (bl) Joslyn Art Museum, (br) Laurie Platt Winfrey, Inc; **89**, (t) The Granger Collection, (bl) courtesy American Antiquarian Society, (br) courtesy Independence National Historic Park/Eastern National Park and Monument Association; **90**, The Granger Collection; **91**, (t) Red Hill - The Patrick Henry National Memorial, Brookneal VA, (b) North Wind Picture Archives; **92**, **93**, The Granger Collection; **94**, Stock Montage; **96**, Culver Pictures; **97**, The Art Gallery of Ontario; **98**, The Granger Collection; **100**, Culver Pictures; **101**, National Portrait Gallery, Washington DC/ArtResource; **102**, Bettmann Archive; **103**, Library of Congress; **104**, Old North Church, Boston; **105**, (l) Bettmann Archive, (r) The Granger Collection; **106**, Archive Photos; **107**, (l) Stock Montage, (r) Bettmann Archive; **108**, (l) The Granger

Park; **435,** (tl) file photo, (tr) L.L.T. Rhoades/ Devaney Stock Photos, (b) Library of Congress; **436,** Library of Congress; **438,** Bettmann Archive; **439,** (t) file photo, (b) Boltin Picture Library; **440,** The American Numismatic Society; **441,** The Granger Collection; **442,** National Portrait Gallery, Washington DC/Art Resource; **443, 444,** The Granger Collection; **445,** file photo; **446,** (l) collection of Nancy Gewirz, Antique Textile Resource, (r), North Wind Picture Archives; **447,** (all) Larry Sherer/ Time-Life Books; **450, 452,** Library of Congress; **453,** Smithsonian Institution; **454,** file photo; **456,** Library of Congress; **457,** (t) Collection of Picture Research Consultants, (b) Smithsonian Institution; **458,** National Museum of American Art, Washington DC/Art Resource; **460,** (t) F. Sieb/H. Armstrong Roberts, (c,bl) The Granger Collection; **461,** (tl) The Shelburne Museum, Shelburne VT, (tr,c,bl) The Granger Collection, (br) W. Talarowski/H. Armstrong Roberts; **462,** (l) Smithsonian Institution, (r) Library of Congress; **463,** (l) Bettmann Archive, (r) Larry Sherer/Time-Life Books; **464,** (t) National Museum of American Art/Art Resource, (b) file photo; **465,** (l) Smithsonian Institution photo #744404, (bl,r) The Granger Collection; **466,** (t,b) Culver Pictures, (c) Library of Congress; **467,** (t) Library of Congress, (cl) Chicago Historical Society, (cr) Culver Pictures, (b) National Park Service Collection; **468,** Anthracite Museum Complex; **469, 470,** (all), The Granger Collection; **471,** (l) National Museum of American Art, Washington DC/Art Resource, (r) Bettmann Archive; **473,** Stock Montage; **474, 475,** The Granger Collection; **477, 480,** Bettmann Archive; **481,** The Henry Ford Museum, The Edison Institute; **482,** (t) The Granger Collection, (b) Randy Trine; **483,** The Granger Collection; **484,** State Historical Society of Wisconsin **485,** Bettmann Archive; **486,** (l) The Granger Collection, (r) Bettmann Archive; **489,** (l) courtesy Sperry/ New Holland, (r) The Granger Collection; **490, 492,** The Granger Collection; **493,** (t) Giraudon/ Art Resource, (b) National Portrait Gallery, Smithsonian Institution, Washington DC/Art Resource; **494,** NCR Corporation; **495,** The Granger Collection; **496,** (l) courtesy AT&T, (r) The Granger Collection; **497,** (l) National Museum of American Art, Washington DC/ Art Resource, (r) Bettmann Archive; **499,** Scala/ Art Resource; **502,** The Granger Collection; **503,** Stock Montage; **504,** Culver Pictures; **506, 507, 508,** The Granger Collection; **509,** Giraudon/Art Resource; **510, 511, 514, 516,** The Granger Collection; **517,** (t) The Brooklyn Museum, Dick S. Ramsay Fund, (b) The Granger Collection; **518,** Anthracite Museum Complex; **519,** (l) The Granger Collection, (r) Bettmann Archive; **520, 521,** The Granger Collection; **523,** Bettmann Archive; **524,** Aaron Haupt; **525,** Bettmann Archive; **526, 527, 528,** The Granger Collection; **530,** (l) Bob Mullenix, (r) Arnoldo Mondadori Editore, Milano; **531- 536,** The Granger Collection; **537,** Archive Photos; **539,** Bettmann Archive; **540,** The Granger Collection; **542,** Art Resource; **543,** (t) The Granger Collection, (b) Collection of Picture Research Consultants Inc; **544-551,** The Granger Collection; **552,** (l) Archive Photos, (r) The Granger Collection; **553,** The Granger Collection; **554,** (l) Bettmann Archive, (r) The Granger Collection; **555,** The Granger Collection; **557,** Bettmann Archive; **558,** The Granger Collection; **559,** Bettmann Archive; **560,** Tate Gallery/Art Resource; **561, 562, 563,** The Granger Collection; **564,** Bettmann Archive; **565,** The Granger Collection; **566,** The Ralph E.

Becker Collection, Smithsonian Institution; **567,** (t) The Granger Collection, (b) B&O Railroad Museum, Baltimore; **568, 569,** The Granger Collection; **570,** Sears, Roebuck and Company; **571, 572,** TheGranger Collection; **573,** Library of Congress; **574, 575,** The Granger Collection; **576,** (l) The Granger Collection, (r) Bettmann Archive; **577,** The Granger Collection; **579,** From THE DEPRESSION YEARS AS PHOTOGRAPHED BY ARTHUR ROTHSTEIN, Dover Publications, Inc.; **580,** National Portrait Gallery, Smithsonian Institution/Art Resource; **581,** (l) National Portrait Gallery, Smithsonian Institution/Art Resource, (r) The Granger Collection; **582,** courtesy Metropolitan Life Insurance Company; **583,** Archive Photos; **585,** The Granger Collection; **588,** (t) Steve Smith/H. Armstrong Roberts, (r) The Granger Collection, (bl) M. Roessler/H. Armstrong Roberts, (br) file photo; **589,** (t) The Granger Collection, (bl) Bob Mullenix, (br) KS Studios; **590,** The Granger Collection; **591,** (tl) Collection of Picture Research Consultants Inc, (tr), Library of Congress, (bl) The Granger Collection; **592,** (l) David Diaz Guerrero/collection of Roddy Moore, (r) Los Angeles County Museum of Art, Los Angeles County Fund, CLIFF DWELLERS by George Bellows; **593,** (tl) Library of Congress, (tr) Mark Burnett, (b) Boltin Picture Library; **594,** (t) file photo, (bl) Brown Brothers, (br) David Austen/Stock Boston; **595,** (t) SEF/Art Resource, (cl) Giraudon/Art Resource, (cr) The Granger Collection, (bl) Bettmann Archive, (br) courtesy Ford Motor Company; **596,** Mark Sexton/ Peabody Essex Museum; **597,** (t) courtesy US Naval Academy Museum, (b) The Granger Collection; **598,** courtesy Hawaii Visitor's Bureau; **599,** The Granger Collection; **600,** (l) file photo, (r) Johnny Johnson; **602,** North Wind Picture Archives; **603,** Collection of David J. and Janice L. Frent; **604,** (l) The Granger Collection, (r) file photo; **606,** Brown Brothers; **607, 608,** The Granger Collection; **609,** National Archives; **610,** The Granger Collection; **611,** (l) file photo, (r) Mark Burnett; **613,** California Museum of Photography; **614,** Library of Congress; **615,** Smithsonian Institution; **617,** The Granger Collection; **618,** SuperStock; **620,** National Guard Bureau; **622,** Boltin Picture Library; **623,** (t) The Granger Collection, (b) Larry Hamill; **624,** courtesy Labor Archives and Research Center, San Francisco State Universtiy; **626,** (l) Charles Phelps Cushing/H. Armstrong Roberts, (r) The Granger Collection; **627,** Culver Pictures; **629, 630,** Brown Brothers; **631,** The Granger Collection; **632,** Nebraska State Historical Society; **634,** (l) SuperStock, (r) Schlesinger Library, Radcliffe College; **636,** (l) Library of Congress, (r) UPI/Bettmann; **637,** Mark Burnett/Central Ohio Council of BSA; **639,** courtesy American Jewish Historical Society, Waltham MA; **640,** Smithsonian Institution; **641,** (l) Chicago Historical Society, (r) Lewis Hine/International Museum of Photography at George Eastman House; **642,** (l) courtesy The NAACP, (r) Library of Congress; **643,** The Granger Collection; **644,** H. Armstrong Roberts; **645,** Library of Congress; **646,** North Wind Picture Archives; **647,** Theodore Roosevelt Collection, Harvard College Library, by permission of the Houghton Library, Harvard University; **648,** courtesy AT&T; **649,** (l) file photo, (b) National Baseball Library; **650,** Devaney Stock Photos; **651, 652,** Brown Brothers; **653,** (l) Craig Kramer, (r) Paul Nesbit; **655,** Lloyd Lemmermann; **656,** Theodore

Roosevelt Collection, Harvard College Library by permission of The Houghton Library, Harvard University; **657,** file photo; **658,** Library of Congress; **660,** Theodore Roosevelt Collection, Harvard College Library by per- mission of The Houghton Library, Harvard University; **661,** (t) file photo, (b) Library of Congress; **662,** Library of Congress; **665,** Smithsonian Institution; **666,** (l) The New York Historical Society, (r) Smithsonian Institution; **667,** (l) file photo, (r) Tim Courlas; **668,** Bettmann Archive; **670,** National Portrait Gallery, Smithsonian Institution/Art Resource; **672,** The Bettmann Archive; **674,** (t) H. Armstrong Roberts, (c) W.H. Clark/H. Armstrong Roberts, (bl) Henry Ford Museum, (br) The Granger Collection; **675,** (tl,b) H. Armstrong Roberts, (tr) The Granger Collection; **676,** The Granger Collection; **677,** (t) Lloyd Lemmermann, (b) Library of Congress; **678,** (l) file photo, (c) National Museum of American Art, Washington DC/Art Resource, (r) Collection of Picture Research Consultants Inc; **679,** (l) Collection of Colonel Stuart S. Corning, photo by Rob Huntley/Lightstream, (r) The National Archives; **680,** (t) SEF/Art Resource, (c) United Nations photo, (bl) Franklin D. Roosevelt Library, (br) Museum of the City of New York; **681,** (t) file photo, (b) H. Armstrong Roberts; **682,** Bettmann Archive; **683,** The Granger Collection; **684,** Bettmann Archive; **685,** UPI/Bettmann; **686,** Bettmann Archive; **687,** The Granger Collection; **688, 690,** Bettmann Archive; **691,** (l) UPI/Bettmann, (r) file photo; **692,** (l) The Granger Collection, (r) Bettmann Archive; **694,** (l) Culver Pictures, (r) The Granger Collection; **695,** Collection of Colonel Stuart S. Corning, photo by Rob Huntley/ Lightstream; **696,** The Granger Collection; **697,** (l,r) Bettmann Archive; **698,** American Red Cross, Washington DC; **699, 700,** The Granger Collection; **701, 702,** Collection of Colonel Stuart S. Corning, photo by Rob Huntley/ Lightstream; **703,** National Portrait Gallery, Smithsonian Institution/Art Resource; **704,** Bettmann Archive; **705,** file photo; **707,** The Granger Collection; **708,** Museo Nacional de Arte Moderno, Mexico City; **710,** Private col- lection, photo by Rob Huntley/Lightstream; **711,** (t) Thomas Hart Benton "City Activities with Dance Hall" from America Today, 1930. Distemper and egg tempera with oil glaze on gessoed linen. Size: 92x134" Collection, The Equitable Life Assurance Society of the United States. Photo 1988 by Dorothy Zeidman, (b) 1992 Jan White Brantley, courtesy Louisianna Jazz Club Collection, Louisianna State Museum; **712, 713, 715,** Bettmann Archive; **717,** (t) UPI/Bettmann, (b) Bettmann Archive; **718,** Collection of David J. and Janice L. Frent; **719, 720,** file photo; **721,** The Granger Collection; **723,** (l) Ford Motor Company, (r) Collection of Colonel Stuart S. Corning, photo by Rob Huntley/Lightstream; **724,** (l) National Museum of American Art, Smithsonian Institution, Washington DC/Art Resource, (r) Bettmann Archive; **725,** SuperStock; **726,** (l) Brown Brothers, (r) National Museum of American Art, Washington DC/Art Resource; **727,** (t) National Museum of American Art, Washington DC/Art Resource, (b) Bettmann Archive; **728,** Smithsonian Institution; **729,** (l) Bettmann Archive, (r) The Granger Collection; **730,** (t) Bettmann Archive, (b) The Granger Collection; **731,** The Granger Collection; **732, 733,** Bettmann Archive; **734,** The Granger Collection; **735,** The Howard University Gallery of Art, Washington D.C.; **736,** National